PROFESSIONAL HOTEL MANAGEMENT

Dr. JAGMOHAN NEGI
Ph.D., FHCIMA (London)
Advance Professional Course on Tourism (WTO, Switzerland)
Formerly Director
National Council for Hotel Management and Catering Technology, New Delhi

GAURAV M.J.

S. CHAND
PUBLISHING

S Chand And Company Limited
(ISO 9001 Certified Company)

S Chand And Company Limited

(ISO 9001 Certified Company)

Head Office: D-92, Sector–2, Noida – 201301, U.P. (India), Ph. 91-120-4682700

RegisteredOffice: A-27, 2nd Floor, Mohan Co-operative Industrial Estate, New Delhi – 110 044

Phone: 011-49731800

www.**schandpublishing.com**; e-mail: **info@schandpublishing.com**

Marketing Offices:

Chennai : Ph: 23632120; chennai@schandpublishing.com

Guwahati : Ph: 2738811, 2735640; guwahati@schandpublishing.com

Hyderabad : Ph: 40186018; hyderabad@schandpublishing.com

Jalandhar : Ph: 4645630; jalandhar@schandpublishing.com

Kolkata : Ph: 23357458, 23353914; kolkata@schandpublishing.com

Lucknow : Ph: 4003633; lucknow@schandpublishing.com

Mumbai : Ph: 25000297; mumbai@schandpublishing.com

Patna : Ph: 4011400; patna@schandpublishing.com

First Edition 1997
Second Edition 2002
Reprint 2008
Third Revised Edition 2014; ***Reprint 2025***
Reprint 2026

ISBN: 978-81-219-1518-2 **Product Code:** H8PHM64HTRM10ENAC14O

PRINTED IN INDIA

By Shri Shyamlal Printing Press Private Limited, Plot 20/4, Site-IV, Industrial Area Sahibabad, Ghaziabad – 201 010 and Published by S. Chand And Company Limited, A-27, 2nd Floor, Mohan Co-operative Industrial Estate, New Delhi – 110 044.

PREFACE TO THE THIRD EDITION

In these days of globalization many aspects need be taken into account for managing a hotel. In the hospitality industry, consumer satisfaction is the foremost and decisive factor in its success. The people at the helm of affairs in the hotel industry should know the multidimensional elements of the business. The staff of the hotel must be thoroughly aware of the food culture and the related aspects of a particular item. All the relevant things need be done from the management side for the traveller to feel at home in their hotel. Because the visitors, especially the foreigners, are the ambassadors of different cultures and civilizations, they spread and assimilate various cultures and lifestyles across the globe. Hence, the degree of hospitality should always be kept at the level of global standards.

Although relevant literature on this particular subject is available in abundance, yet one book covering all the significant and vital factors regarding the hotel industry in a well-coordinated shape has not, to the best of the knowledge, been produced so far. Maximum efforts have been done to fill this vacuum. Evidently, the readers will find this book interesting, benefiting and useful as well.

This book, an essential text for hospitality management students, examines the relevance and applications of general management theory and principles to hospitality organizations. Using contemporary material and case studies, the book indicates ways in which performance may be improved through better use of human resources. Rigorous academic theory is related to hospitality practice, based on the authors' great knowledge of the hospitality industry. The text takes a vocational basis and the illustration of the theory with the real-life examples of hospitality management in action provides a solid and stimulating introduction to the subject.

The book, definitely has the intrinsic potential to grasp the student's interest because of its relevance to hospitality. This edition helps readers develop the wide-ranging knowledge and analytical skills they need to succeed in today's burgeoning and dynamic hotel industry. This comprehensive volume encourages critical thinking by providing different points of view through contributions from leading industry professionals and academics. Within a coherent theoretical structure, this updated edition enables readers to formulate their own ideas and solutions.

This comprehensive text serves as a basic reader for students on introductory hospitality management programmes or non-specialist but related degrees such as tourism and business studies, both at undergraduate and postgraduate level. It provides students with a solid grounding in the industry, covering all sectors of the hospitality industry, both commercial and non-commercial, and sets it within the context of the tourism industry. Professional hotel management breaks away from tradition by looking at the wider industry. Written by experts in the hospitality field, this book combines an accessible reading style with current and relevant case studies on a variety of hospitality companies from across the globe.

This revised edition provides a practical, up-to-date and comprehensive approach to how professionals across the industry manage different departments within their operation. From the front office to finance, from marketing to housekeeping, this resource offers advanced theory played out in practical problems. Multidimensional case studies are a notable feature, with complex management problems portrayed from multiple viewpoints. Covering the latest issues affecting the industry, this text gives students and professionals an up-to-date, dynamic learning resource. The content of this book should enhance students' understanding of the dynamic nature of the tourism and hospitality industry. In addition, the text includes activities to deepen students' understanding and help them to apply theories and concepts. Furthermore, students should be able to develop enquiry, problem-solving and decision-making skills through these activities.

Readers seeking management careers in hospitality will enter a dynamic industry filled with opportunities. The rewards are many, but so are the challenges. Today's hospitality managers must deal with such complex factors as globalization, terrorism threats, ecotourism, internet commerce, new business and financial models, and rapidly changing consumer demands. The book gives readers the industry know-how and the management skills needed to thrive in all aspects of the field, from food service to lodging to tourism. It features both historical perspectives and discussions of new trends in a variety of sectors. This book has the most thorough coverage of the hospitality industry, covering food production, foodservice, lodging, housekeeping and, hospitality careers, and hospitality management. Upon successful completion of this text, readers will have a strong grasp of the many facets of the hospitality industry. It is vital for hospitality management students to understand key management concepts as part of the complex and intimate nature of the services industry. This work is suitable for hospitality students who need to be able to use management tools and techniques to become successful hospitality managers.

Hospitality management is a multidisciplinary field of study with the purpose of preparing people with the expertise, commitment, and skills for management, marketing, and operations positions in the expanding industry that provides food, accommodations, and tourism services to people away from home. As a field of study, hospitality management is interdisciplinary. It draws upon a wide range of basic disciplines to provide the fundamental knowledge and skills that are required to fulfil the diverse demands placed upon individuals in management positions within the hospitality industry. Recognizing that the individual educated for today is soon out of date, the academic emphasis of the programme is on principles, analytical tools, processes, and systems. These change relatively slowly. However, it is recognized that at least a minimal exposure to the skills and knowledge, which make up the present state of the art is necessary to understand the principles. Likewise, it is recognized that the students in the programme are composites of many talents, and that in hospitality and tourism, pure academic ability cannot predict professional success. Thus, the programme has as a basic objective of the presentation of an academic curriculum to develop management capability through interdisciplinary subject exposure, problem identification, basic concepts, decision-making, theory, and management application. Because technology is such a vital part of the business world, students are required to maintain an active knowledge of information technologies when accepted into the industry. In addition, students are encouraged to develop foreign language skills to better prepare for this increasingly international industry.

The hotel industry would be constantly changing. Globalization, industry wide focus on sustainability and corporate responsibility are just some of the forces converging and resulting in widespread change. The result is an industry that requires future leaders in hospitality and tourism to be well versed in past, current, and emerging management practices. To this end, this edition features both historical perspectives and discussions of new trends in a variety of sectors. Our goal, as it has been all along, is to provide educators and students with the most up-to-date content with the hope that the next generation of hospitality leaders will be fully prepared to great the challenges of this dynamic industry.

In our efforts to present the industry in an organized and responsible manner, we have divided the book into different primary sections encompassing every thing from students concerns about their role in the industry and operational issues to the function of management. The organization of the chapters should also help students understand the relationship among the various topics.

Teachers and research scholars will benefit from rich content of the book. We have provided a number of examples and updated photos that will reflect well students. Several sections of the book have been revised and /or expanded based upon teachers feedback, such as:

- Inclusion of new and emerging industry segments.
- More culinary examples including international culinary programmes.
- New trends in on-site food service including those related to vending.

- An expanded section on franchising along with considerations of the global marketplace.
- More examples of the use of technology in both food service and lodging.
- New focus on electronic resources in the management section.
- Addition of emerging perspectives on management and organization world of hospitality alive.
- The significance to the hospitality industry of the topics covered.
- Specific learning objectives at the beginning of each chapter will help students focus their efforts and alert them to the important concepts discussed. These are tied directly to the chapter headings, which facilitates learning assessments.
- Tables, figures, diagrams and photos take a closer look at specific trends or practices in the hospitality industry.
- Case studies support the chapter discussions by highlighting examples from today's hospitality organizations and associations.
- Notes on global hospitality practices continue to appear to give students more of an international perspective on their studies.
- The careers in hospitality icon appears throughout the book in the text to alert students to specific discussions of career opportunities in the hospitality industry.
- Inclusion of objective type quizzes such as multiple choice, matching type, fill in the blanks, true and false are incorporated in view of the requirement of students specially for the semester system.

Any comments and suggestions for the improvement of the book will be gratefully acknowledged.

Dr. JAGMOHAN NEGI

GAURAV M.J.

PREFACE TO THE FIRST EDITION

The increased competition and complexity of tourism and hotel industry as well as the sophisticated demands of tomorrow's travellers, mean that tourism and hotel employees will need to be better educated. Both are changing industries and have gone through drastic transformation. The emergence of several hotel chains-Indian Hotel Company, East India Hotels Ltd., India Tourism Development Corporation, Hotel Corporation of India, U.P Hotels and Restaurants Ltd., Sterling Holiday Resorts etc. have totally revolutionized the Indian Tourism and Hotel Industry. At government and industry's level, Hotel Management Institutes, Food Craft Institutes and Travel and Tourism Institutes have been established to improve the industry's expertise. Many universities, polytechnics and private education institutes have started hotel and tourism courses at certificate, diploma, degree, post-graduate and doctorate levels.

Now, hotel management has become a profession which young boys and girls are proud to join, and get trained for various level positions. The hotel management education has proliferated into a series of courses offering technical certificate courses of specialized nature, diploma, degree, post graduate and master degree programmes in hotel, catering and tourism.

A hotel combines production and sale, under one roof. It is in close and intimate contact with its customers, who consume hotel products at the point of sale. Basically, it is a capital intensive business, i.e. high capital to sales ratio. Being a service-oriented industry, it places strong emphasis on die management of people taking into account different nationalities, their cultural tastes and all personal values, including education, standard of living etc.

In the functioning and operational stage, the hotel and restaurants are required to maintain standards as per the requirement of the star classification or grading system. There is also a trend in the construction of low-budget hotels to cater the needs of the young, low-income, middle income group and budget tourists.

Professional Hotel Management is an attempt to give a general idea to students, teachers, practitioners, consultants and research scholars, describing the managing of a hotel business. The approach adopted is to provide a simple and reasonably comprehensive outline of various departments of a modern hotel. The whole book and each of its chapter is intended to provide a frame work, within which the hotel business may be studied in such depth as may be required for a specific purpose.

The book is primarily based on what the author learnt through practical training and observations in hotels of international repute during the last 33 years. Talks and discussions with the hoteliers, managers, and employees in the various levels of the hotel job, proved very interesting and fruitful. The book also attempts to provide a comprehensive in-depth treatment for the inter-related elements of tourism and hotel business. This book is designed to serve as a practical guide for managers, executives, trainees, investors, potential owners and planners as well as one needing to know how to structure a profit yielding operation.

Appendices covering technical terms, organisation charts, abbreviations, and comprehensive bibliography and index are of special interest. The treatment is profusely supported by illustrative figures, charts, diagrams, photographs etc.

I would appreciate constructive comments on any point and invite suggestions from readers for the improvement in the book.

JAGMOHAN NEGI

B-11, Institute of Hotel Management
Pusa, New Delhi-12
Tel. 5711502

Febraury, 1997

ACKNOWLEDGEMENTS

In our day-to-day work and activities, we got benefited from discussions with our colleagues at various Institutes of Hotel Management, Universities and Colleges, dealing with specialized area of teaching and research subjects, such as hotel management, administration and finance, food production, housekeeping, economics, human resource development, sales and marketing, engineering and maintenance, security services, store-keeping, documentation, communication business policy, tourism and economics, audio-visual aids and computers, etc.

Many faculty members from hospitality management programmes around the world have provided helpful information and feedback in the preparation of the manuscript. Many of our colleagues were quick to answer questions for us or to guide us to proper sources in their particular areas of expertise. Colleagues from the University of New Hampshire, Department of Hospitality Management, Department of Hotel Administration, Cornell University, and the Washington State University, School of Hospitality Business Management have provided us with numerous insights that have shaped this text in important ways. We are also grateful to the professors and industry professionals who reviewed the previous editions and early drafts of this edition. Their comments and suggestions have helped us immensely in the preparation of this book.

Many industry professionals assisted in the preparation of text by providing helpful input on particular sections or by providing us with supporting materials including photos. Again, we will mention a few here who helped us, at the risk of not mentioning all who helped. As always, the published research work forms an important part of the chapters of this book and, indeed, has influenced other portions of the text in important ways as well.

We must thank and acknowledge the many individuals who provided direct assistance in the preparation of this edition. First and foremost, we thank for their tireless efforts in changing or editing photos. Their perseverance and organizational skills are impressive. We would also like to acknowledge many people who have helped in shaping this book. Ms Suniti, and Rituska have been the source of many ideas found in this text. Their advice and critical observations have been vital to developing the text over the course of earlier editions. They also have made major contributions to the test bank developed for earlier editions.

The individuals and organizations that provided information and support are referred in citations throughout the text.

Finally, we are thankful to the management and the editorial team of S.Chand & Company Pvt. Ltd., New Delhi for all help ans support in publication of this book in a record time, and in such a fine format.

Dr. JAGMOHAN NEGI

GAURAV M.J.

CONTENTS

CHAPTER 1

Principles and Concepts

OBJECTIVES

After studying this chapter you should be able to:

1. *Define the term 'hotel industry' and 'a guest'*
2. *Understand the functions of hotel management in:*
   (i) *Planning*
   (ii) *Organisation*
   (iii) *Staffing*
   (iv) *Directing*
   (v) *Controlling.*
3. *Understand hotel management as an art as well as a science*
4. *Break-up of a hotel into different departments.*
5. *Understand business policies and strategies for hotel business.*
6. *Explain the Policy of:*
   (i) *Employment*
   (ii) *Rate structure*
   (iii) *Insurance*
   (iv) *Advertisement*
   (v) *Accounting*
   (vi) *Credit*
   (vii) *Catering*
   (viii) *Financial*
   (ix) *Operational*
   (x) *Post-operation control*
   (xi) *Other policies for hotel business.*
7. *Understand the techniques of management of hotel business*
8. *Know the practical use of increasing profitability; and*
9. *Specify the management by objectives, management by results and programme evaluation techniques.*
10. *Understand the various laws relating to hotel and*
11. *Understand hoteliering as a profession.*

INTRODUCTION

The profession of hotel management is one of the most challenging ones. Although there are many hotels operating in our country, least importance has been given to the diversified knowledge, the variety of skills, and the ingenuity demanded of the successful hotel manager. The hotel business is most satisfying because it brings employees into contact with other people, mostly in pleasant surroundings and the rewards are tremendous. Some of the works in these hotels are unpleasant and it is the responsibility of the management to help overcome a natural reluctance to perform these duties. The hotel management has more responsibilities than the hotel employees. The management has to try to inculcate harmony as well as maximum productivity, and earnings, for the establishment.

Management of people in hotels is probably the most complex and demanding job because a mix of cultures and nationalities are involved taking into account the nationalities, and tastes, values and individual likes and dislikes that must be adhered to. It requires dealing with the five M's, Men, Materials, Money, Machine and Methods. Management is the co-ordination of all resources through the process of planning, organising, directing and controlling, in order to meet the desired objectives. These objectives are to be clearly determined, understood and stated prior to initiating the management process.

Hoteliering is an art as well as a science. In fact, contemporary economic conditions have caused 'hoteliering' as an art concept to recede to the background. The emphasis now is on the protection of capital and maximising profit for the owner. Profit connected with the hotel business does not usually come as profit generated by the sale of food, beverages and lodging to the general public. Most of the finances in this business come as a result of acquiring as much real estate manipulation, as actual hoteliering.

Earnest Henderson Sr. of the Sheraton Hotel Corporation[1] has very aptly explained the changes taking place in the hotel industry. As recently as two or three decades ago, the stature of a hotelman was often measured by his personal charm, his popularity and his social standing. Today the priorities are shifting. May be we are sacrificing some of the industry's glamour on the altar of hard facts, know-how and a familiarity with the tools of scientific management. But it is the latter that pays off when the monthly statement or annual report is issued. Sometimes facts and knowledge pay bigger dividends. Modern competitive conditions in hotel, tourism and catering industry, demand a scientific approach for its successful operation.

The field of hotel management is inter-disciplinary. It draws ideas from tourism, travel, economics, psychology, accounting and finance, food technology, management, food chemistry, microbiology, physics, architecture, engineering, marketing, law etc., and from these disciplines are formulated approaches, systems, and analytical tools designed to make hoteliering a satisfying experience for people when they are away from home.

Managing a hotel is a complex activity involving the application of a wide range of skills and a broad spectrum of knowledge to many types of business problems. It essentially deals with employees, guests, suppliers and other trade men who have the prime human relationship through which the hotel functions.

The task of directing and co-ordinating the work of all departments demands considerable expertise on the part of the management. The conditions in which a hotel

1. Earnest Henderson of the Sheraton Hotel Coporation, USA.

functions constantly change. With increasing rapidity, – costs of operation are continuously rising, manpower is in short supply, finance is proving difficult to secure etc.

The scope of management in the hoteliering and catering industry demands expertise unlike that in most other industries, as being an integral part of the hotel industry it demands 24-hour service throughout the year and a full range of commercial activities occur under the same roof. The purchase of raw materials and their subsequent preparation and processing, are linked closely to the sale of finished goods/articles.

Hotel management, whether at a small, medium or large scale, must be concerned with ways to trim costs and expenses and beware of the amount of increase in prices. Basic hotel management optimizes the return on the resources of the enterprises and provides a healthy climate where hospitality can be extended. It is a science of knowledge based on certain basic principles.

PROFITABILITY AND CUSTOMERS' SATISFACTION

In this business, there are two main objectives: profitability and the customer. Profitability implies the ability to stay in the hotel business, maintaining and increasing the capital in use and generating sufficient funds to retain in the business. The profitability of the hotel is the ultimate objective whereas the provision of a satisfactory standard of accommodation facility and food and beverage service is the means by which an ultimate objective is achieved. Most of the hoteliers/hotel managers are concerned with the following questions :

1. How to increase room tariffs ?
2. How to increase the room/bed occupancy ?
3. How to utilise restaurant facilities in a better way ?
4. Are the bars full enough ?
5. Is the standard of hotel service good ?
6. Is the standard of food good ?
7. Are the food and liquor operations well controlled ?
8. Is every employee of the hotel fully employed ?
9. Are all the operating expenses well under control ?

Thus, professional management of hotels is a dynamic task of constantly balancing two main factors: profitability and customer satisfaction. A successful manager will be one who anticipates the thrust of change, who directs and opts for action. The success in this highly competitive and lucrative industry lies in the fact that you progress from limited skills and horizons of a specialists, to broader concepts and talents of a generalist manager. Hotel management is complex and requires professional skills. It requires purposive application of the techniques of planning, organising, integrating and measuring business efforts. Your ability to get work done through others can stem from competence, position, personality or character. Of all the attributes, character may well be the most essential.

Authority can be conferred, earned or achieved. The most rewarding authority is that which is deserved. Authority of knowledge combined with character, will make you a successful manager in this hospitable industry. As a good hotel manager, you should inculcate highly developed analytical skills to evaluate opportunities and to anticipate problems in order to establish objectives that set appropriate priorities and which are realistic in the light of the available human and material resources.

You require the catalytic action of leadership to galvanise the organisation into accomplishing what will encourage participaion and involvement. Get help in identifying or internalizing the goals of the manager and the organization. As an effective manager, you have to be loyal to your people, which will inspire loyalty in return. If you are enthusiastic your employee will do the work assigned to them with enthusiasm. If you are optimistic and charitable your employee will be cheerful and tolerant. As an effective leader, you will motivate your people by setting an example of a proper combination and reward, for a good performance and close supervision.

As an effective manager do not tell your experienced employee how to do the job. Neither should you fail to give the employee adequate guidance as to what he wants to do, when the job is to be completed, if and when progress reports are required, when they are to be observed, what is to be done when there are problems in the hotel. You should co-ordinate the work of your team, check the progress and re-establish goals if the situation makes this advisable.

You should never set yourself apart from the goals and inspirations of your employees. Work with them to help them develop their abilities and broaden their background. Dedicate yourself to create the kind of work atmo-sphere that encourages and enables employees to do their best. Recognise that you have the responsibility and take the blame when things go wrong instead of passing the buck. Give credit and praise to the staff when things go well.

The hotel industry is in the phase of applying sophisticated management techniques. As an aspirant to the professional hotel management, you need to understand and develop skills to manage effectively the inter-relationship of the wide variety of functions in a modern hotel.

THE MANAGMENT PROCESS

The way managers conduct themselves plays an important part in the vitality of the hotel. As already explained, the following are the main management processes as applied to hotel business :

1. Planning :

Planning may be defined as the analysis of relevant information from the present and past and assessment of probable future development so that the right course of action may be determined that will enable the organisation to meet its objectives. The plans must be objective, structural and flexible. The management first determines what must be done to bring about the desired objectives and then decides how to implement it. Planning occurs at all levels of organisation.

In a hotel, all management including supervisory management, carries out the same basic work, although the means of its implementation differ due to the peculiar characteristics of the business. Planning is the projected course of action. In this function, the hotel management attempts to include and control the speed and direction of change. It determines what must be done to bring about the desired objectives and then decides how to do it. Planning occurs at all levels of the hotel organisation. Hotel management at the higher level plans issuing of stock for company expansion. The supervisory hotel management plans for the work schedule for the following week. Large hotel companies have three, five, or even more levels of management. Good managers consult, advise and suggest as they plan and make decisions. The objective cannot be reached without integrated planning and support of several managers. For example,the top hotel management decides the food cost. This objective will be meaningless without the knowledge and support of the Chef, who plans and prices the menu. In order to assure the success to the plan, chef can re-order the menu combinations. The sales manager no longer discounts high food cost items as his major sales promotion technique. The steward begins a campaign to reduce waste and spoilage, and the hostess trai her dining room staff to sell high profit desserts and appetizers.

2. Origanisation :

Organisation may be defined as a process of arranging the parts of the organisation, *i.e.* work, people and the system. Having once set the objectives, management begins to organise how to achieve them. Organisation is the establishment of structure through which sub-divisions of the job are defined, arranged and coordinated. This process consists of delegation, decentralisation etc. in which time and staff are the essential factors.

Organisation is the establishment of a structure through which sub divisions of the job are defined, arranged and co-ordinated. The whole work is divided into different sections. Like planning, organisation is also carried out at all levels which is management's responsibility. In small hotels, interaction can take place on a personal level by communicating with each other. To organise in this context means, first, to identify and arrange systematically, i.e., department-wise, all the different types of jobs, that the various departments need so that they function in harmony attempting to co-ordinate. The total organisation is known as 'structure' which includes every level of management, every job and sub-division of each job. Such organisation may be presented in the form of charts and diagrams. In small hotels plans can easily be carried out informally through direct verbal instructions. In large hotel companies organisation is a management science and is a means for affecting all the objectives. In considering the hotel organisation structure the principle of departmentalisation and span of management are to be considered. The organisational analysis could be presented through organisational manuals and organisation charts. The process of organisation consists of delegation, decentralisation, etc.

3. Staffing :

Staffing involves recruiting, selecting, orienting, training and developing employees who are capable of carrying out their assignments. Staffing is handled by the Personnel Department.

Staffing involves recruiting, selecting, orienting, training and developing employees who are capable of carrying out their assignments. In large hotels, staffing is handled by Personnel Departments. There is a Personnel Department which recruits all employees for operational jobs, and some of the lower management jobs like assistant departmental heads. For senior management levels, the personnel department's role is finding and screening the most qualified applicants, with the final selection left to the concerned departmental heads. The management makes the final selection of departmental managers. Hotel Management in the collective sense identifies those who are charged with directing the affairs of the hotel business. It is a group of persons who get their authority and responsibility from ownership. The authority, responsibility and the other resources of the enterprise are utilised to provide efficient service to the clientele.From the sale of this service, hotel management earns its own compensation,the salaries of the employees and the dividend for the owners/ shareholders. Hotel management personnel carry the titles of managers or supervisors, like F & B Manager/supervisor, Front Office Manager, Catering Manager, Laundry Manager, Lobby Manager etc. There are jobs like hostess, bell captain and headwaiter etc., which lack management titles. The duties and responsibilities are the distinguishing characteristics of these hotel managerial positions.

In small hotels such as sole proprietorship, the owner is the sole member of the top management. In the case of medium sized hotels like partnership, firms/private companies, the departmental heads are next highest in responsibility and authority. There are also some Supervisors or Assistant Managers. In the case of large organisations like joint stock companies, top management includes only the limited number of important executives within any organisation.

4. Directing :

Directing initiates the employees to implement what is to be done. Following the right pattern of leadership, communication, motivating employees, supervision and personnel planning, are some of the things required to be carried out.

Directing is the technique of inducing employees to do their jobs effectively and efficiently. Unfortunately, many hotel managers fail to cultivate a rapport with their colleagues. An understanding of human relations is essential for the desired results,which includes :

1. Following the right pattern of leadership
2. The ability to communicate
3. Motivating employees
4. Proper supervision and
5. Personnel planning.

5. Controlling :

Controlling is the process by which management reviews and evaluates the results of other functions. Information geared from the review must be used to revise the plan, to re-order the organisation, to change the staff or to redirect the employees. Controlling may be defined as the interpretation of information so that correct action may be taken in order to achieve these objectives. It aims to check achievement against plans. It sets up standards, measures performance with standards and takes corrective actions or revision of standards. Information plays the most important part in controlling the budgetary and non-budgetary control measures which are the main measures of control.

Control is the process by which hotel management reviews and evaluates the results of its other functions. For dynamic hotel management, control is imperative.The management process is a continuous one. It is modified by the knowledge and experience. It is concerned with the immediate direction to his staff and its review. In large hotels higher level managers are sometimes prone to do more than controlling the lower level staff. There are several budgetary and non-budgetary control measures. Control, therefore, may be defined as the interpretation of information, so that correct action may be taken in order to achieve the objectives.

Standardisation in policy is not possible for efficient and successful running of the hotel business. Many factors, like central, and municipal, state, local laws and regulations, customs, trade unions, trade associations, availability of qualified personnel, environmental consideration etc. require constant modification and complete reversal of certain laid-down hotel policies. In a sole proprietorship or partnership organisation, the owners have the authority to establish the overall policy for its operation but it is delegated to the general manager. In large hotel companies, the control office formulates broad management policies and assigns home executives to see to it that they are properly implemented but the standard cannot always be followed; therefore, the ultimate decision is made by the general manager.

Duties involved in managing a hotel can be, broadly, summarized under the following headings :

1. Organising various departments
2. Staff management
3. Financial interpretations and control
4. Marketing and sales promotions, and
5. Personal contacts with and knowledge of the clients.

The term 'Management' has two meanings. It is used first to identify those who are charged with directing the affairs of the business enterprise. Management is that group of persons who get their authority and responsibility from ownership and who use these, along with other resources of the enterprise, to produce a product. From the sale of this product, management earns its own compensation, the employees' get their salaries and the dividends are paid to the owners. In the hospitality business, product is primarily 'service'. The other application of management as an art are the things that management does. Thus one distinguishes managing from consulting or managing from doing routine and operative tasks[2].

NEW HORIZON: 21ST CENTURY

In the past quarter century, hotels have widened their horizons to include 'marketing', 'sales', 'blitz', 'franchise' and 'FIT', one-number reservation systems, development of indoor courtyards, sauna, solar heating pools and female staff management. The hotel and catering industry is a rich field that is waiting to be harvested. A study sponsored by the American Hotel and Motel Association noted that the lodging industry is: an industry facing a market of tremendous potential, beset on every side by rising costs and declining service, operating in an era of truly dynamic change, that is hoping for, but not stimulating the technological and management breakthrough to solve the problems ahead.[3]

Successful future hotel managers will be those who anticipate change, who are willing to accept challenges, and are confident to succeed. The authority of the hotel manager stems from competence, position, personality and character. The aspirants to the hotel and catering industry need to understand and develop management skills, to cope with the versatile functions and competitiveness of today's hotel. In the past, education for the hotel manager was rough experience. Most managers did not have the advantage of college/institutional education. As the demand for the hotel industry grew there was a great need for trained managers and departmental heads. The bulk of future management requirements of the hotel industry had to be met from graduates from Hotel Management Institutes and Food Craft Institutes, who are educated and trained in the field of hotel management. The hotel industry's leaders would do well to mark the advice by an experienced hotelier, William Ash, once Managing Director of the 650-room International Hotel in Los Angeles : It is my opinion, that the so called professional management would do well to realise that there are many facts of business from which they might learn."[4]

Hotel management can be interpreted as management is what management does. It is dynamic. It is result oriented. The success of hotel lies in good management. Traditionally, all hotel managers spend their time in doing, instead of planning, organising, staffing, directing

2. Jerome, J. Vallen, James, R. Abhey and Dunnovan L. Sapienza, Page 14.
3. The American Hotel and Motel Association, USA, Operation Reakthrough, New York.

and controlling the actual tasks of management; they were involved with the routine jobs of production and service at the cost of other important managerial jobs. This tendency is still prevalent in some establishments, '*firstly*', due to the small size and expensive nature of introduction of sound management programmes and '*secondly*,'the concept of combining management and working positions. Another factor responsible for this state of affairs may be the traditional concept of entertaining that has long been associated with the independently owned hotels. Hotel managers in these establishments remain in touch with the needs of their guests which tempts management to participate in the minute details of service.

Men of outstanding technical competence sometimes fail when they assume the management of a department or business. A highly skilled cook may not be a capable 'Chef' de Cuisine'(Executive Chef) despite his outstanding culinary skill. Similarly, an outstanding Room Clerk may prove to be a failure as a house manager/resident manager despite his knowledge. Hotel management is a combination of professional and technical abilities. The starting point of hotel management is managerial principles. The large number of graduates from hotel and catering institutions entering directly into management jobs, indicate the growing need for professionals. Less technical skill is needed in this industry compared to some other professions but this does not mean that no technical competence at all is necessary. It is only technical competence that can assure the successful implementation of managerial principles. All the managerial functions which include planning, organising, staffing, directing and controlling, are applied to the hotel trade. The levels of management depend on the technical knowledge of the hotel staff.

ART OR SCIENCE ?

Managing the people is much easier to define than management as an art. The people who manage can be identified more clearly than the things they do. The things that management produces are not readily discernible. They are not products like club sandwiches or a clean rest-room. Yet the management is responsible for both. Although the average employees cannot see the things that management is doing, management does produce. It is the very productive nature of management that explains the success of one hotel and the failure of another. Traditionally, hotel managers have spent their time in doing instead of planning, organising, staffing, directing and controlling the real task of management. Hotel managers remain involved with routine jobs of production and service. In large establishments management cannot do every job. It must get the work done by others.

Is hotel management an art, science or both ?

Lucius Boomer of Waldrof Astoria Fame, publisized one of the very first texts on the principles and practices of hotel management in 1925. Even at that early stage he concluded his work with some comments on the question of Art Vs. Science. Mr. Boomer was so certain about the growth of scientific hotel management that he cautioned the readers not to lose sight of the Art of 'inn-keeping'. Currently the emphasis in hotel management is on the scientific management. Scientific management will optimise the physical and human aspect which management can work most successfully. The application of art and science in the field of hotel management will give benefit to management, labour, ownership and guests. The management techniques reached the surface of the industry quite recently, compared to the productive industries. Initially, the subject of professionalism in hotel management was

4. Mr. William Ash, former Managing Director of 650-room International Hotel in Los Angeles.

ignored by such arguments as you cannot run a hotel like a factory or restaurant management is an art and not a science. Some still argued that the management of hotel services and guests is an art. The weakness of this argument lies in the fact that it is solely an art and nothing can be learnt from hotel management that comes from the study of management, the science. As a science, management is thought to have a scientific body of knowledge, based on certain fundamental principles. The study of management, as it applies to hotel fields, is the starting place for whoever seeks a career in this world-wide industry. According to Webster, 'the hotel is a building or institution providing lodging, meals and services for the public.' [5]Every effort is made to give the readers an insight into behind the activities, the organisation, and the cooperation that is necessary in providing the services accepted by the public, with the hope that they will get a clear concept of this industry.

Hotels are found in every city. In our country, the hotel industry has been mainly managed by individuals. Most of the hotels are of average size and are financed by individuals. They keep the ownership and management united. Owing to expansion in the hotel sector, joint stock companies have come into existence and most of the deluxe hotels are managed by them.

The principal factor that determines the guest attitude towards a hotel is 'service' although other amenities such as rooms, food and beverage are tangible ones. The nature of hoteliering places strong emphasis on people. There are industries who have introduced mechanisation in their operation and functions, the business of hotels cannot follow this lead. The personalised service in hoteliering cannot be mechanised and automated. The human aspect is the determining element of the hotel business.

Hoteliering is unique in many ways. There are different business operations simultaneously under one roof which guarantee jobs that are challenging and diversified. Presence of human elements promotes interest in a hotel job and provides a challenge. Each client who enters the hotel offers an opportunity to learn about human nature. The industry offers the employees not only the responsibilities for its product but also the satisfaction of being instrumental in bringing customer's satisfaction and of personally receiving their approval.

The hotel offers a clean, safe, pleasant environment as far as working conditions are concerned. The hotel managers and departmental heads have worked their way up through the ranks. It is a variable trade, changes in national economy are quietly reflected in the hotel trade as well. The techniques, ideas and moods of operation of hoteliering undergo continuous alteration.

Another characteristic feature we find in the case of hoteliering is that practically every service offered, requires the efforts of minimum two departments. In all the high level hotels, the employees who sell or serve a product have no control over its preparation, production or quality. This requires co-operation among the various departments of the hotel. For example, Mr. Gaurav is an incoming guest in a hotel. He approaches the Lobby Manager and has to go to his room. It will involve the front office, the uniform department, and the housekeeping department. Co-operation of all of them is very essential for providing efficient service to the guests.

The majority of the jobs in the hotel trade are of a semi-skilled nature. A person of average intelligence can easily learn the skills and regular routine. One must be able to adjust

5. Webster Dictionary

rapidly to a variety of unexpected and unpredictable situations. One has to have to control one's emotions even when under tremendous pressure. One has to display leadership and analytical abilities. One must have wholehearted interest and dedication to this profession.

The hotel job is a twenty-four hours a day, seven days a week, business. Employees have to work while the others are relaxing or enjoying a holiday. One must adjust to the busy cycle of work. In our country the position of working in a hotel ranks from high to low on the social prestige scale, although a job in a hotel is considered quite prestigious now-a-days. For those in this trade, sincere advice is, once the hotel work really gets into your blood, the love for this business will come through experience and your motto must be 'Life is Service'.

Pix 1.1 : Hotel Management Training Session

Case Study 1.1

A Day in the Life of Mr. Amar: an Entrepreneur

Very few young people consciously choose to become entrepreneurs. But, somewhere along the way, a few may decide that they want to work for themselves and run their own show. Others will be drawn to occupations that will almost force them to start their own businesses. That's what hap- penned to Amar. Twenty, years ago, he fell in love with the restaurant business. Today, he owns and operate a 150-room hotel and resort in the Garhwal Mountains in Himalayas. He never planned to become part of the travel and tourism industry. Now he can't imagine working in any other field.

The first job he ever had was in the restaurant business. He started part-time as a dining room attendant in a large, bustling restaurant while he was still in high school. For ₹ 5 an hour plus tips, he set and cleared tables and made sure that each customer always had a fall glass of water. Within months, he was angling to become a cook. The prospect of mastering an impressive array of skills drew him to the kitchen. The work was challenging, demanding, and fast paced. He head his calling.

His first big break came just after he graduated from college with a degree in business. A small restaurant near his hometown suddenly came up for sale. The place had been limping along for years, but he'd always believed that it had great potential. While he had already been accepted at restaurant school, his intuition told him that this was a once-in-a-lifetime opportunity. Four months later, his partner and he was the proud and slightly terrified owners of a restaurant. They knew they were taking a big risk, but they believed that it was a well-calculated risk. As much as they wanted the restaurant, he had agreed not to buy it unless they thought they had a pretty good chance of succeeding. He knew the area. Between them, they had 15 years of experience in the business. The sellers agreed to hold the mortgage for the first five years. They hired the best people they could find and paid them top money to review the books and inspect the physical plant. They also drew up a detailed agreement outlining the steps they would follow in case either of them wanted to terminate the partnership. They were both totally committed to the venture, and they were both sure that they were taking a big gamble, but they tried to plan for every eventuality.

The first four years were difficult. They worked long hours and took very little money out of the business. They exploited every opportunity to build the business. They squared our, shoulders and pushed on whenever they encountered a setback. They were lucky in that business conditions were generally good, but they made a lot of luck for ourselves by working hard. And they never deluded ourselves about the difficulties they faced.

They took another major calculated gamble at the end of our fourth year and decided to sell. They turned a good profit and decided to buy a small inn. This time, they agreed from the outset that they would sell after four years if they could get a fair profit. They followed the same principles that had made the restaurant successful. They watched our costs and made sure that our services were realistically priced. They never missed an opportunity to promote the business. They delivered what they promised. They went out of our way to hire and keep good employees. They did our homework. They sought the best professional advice but always made their own decisions. They recognized that risk taking was part of their job.

They sold the inn for the price they wanted, on schedule. He then bought his current establishment in the Garhwal. His partner decided to go back into the restaurant business. They're still good friends and often discuss working together again in the future. Nobody is born with the skills necessary to be a successful entrepreneur. That kind of talent has to be developed. Drive, ambition, and commitment are musts. After that, the ability to make and exploit your own luck conies into play. Being your own boss is a tremendous amount of work. But he wouldn't have it any other way.

HOTEL ORGANISATION AND OPERATION

The ideal factors for hotel operations are dependent upon planning, staffing and capabilities of the individuals who establish this basic criteria. It is not possible to have a model hotel organisation. The plan for each particular hotel depends on the location, the type of service offered, the structural layout of the hotel, the background and training of the manager and the type of ownership.

The staffing requirements depend upon a number of factors such as :

1. Size of the property
2. Type of the property
3. The degree of luxury as reflected in the extent of personal service
4. Rate of occupancy
5. The basic design of the hotel in facilitating operations and housekeeping
6. The extent to which laundry, maintenance and other functions are contracted out
7. The use of labour saving devices, machines and computers.

The typical staff : room relationship are produced in Table 1.1.

Table 1.1 : Typical Staff-room Ratios

S.No.	Type of Property	Staff-room Ratios
1.	Supplementary Accommodation units such as apartments, condominiums	0.10 : 1 to 0.05 : 1
2.	Budget Hotels etc. (economy class hotels, one-star and two-star hotels)	0.35 : 1 to 0.10 : 1

3.	Medium Grade Hotels such as middle class hotels, three-star hotels etc.	0.8 : 1
4.	Luxury Hotels (Four-star, Five-star Deluxe Hotels)	2 : 1
5.	Resort Hotels (Medium Grade)	0.6 : 1
6.	Convention Hotels (Superior Grade)	1.0 : 1

The basic function of all the hotels is the same. An effort is made here to give an explanation of the functions performed by each department and the role played by each position within a department. This will give a good grasp of the variety of duties performed and of the importance of these duties to the hotel operation. The variation is mostly in case of specific methods, procedures and forms used.

Fig. 1.1, and 1.2 indicate the departmental structure of a hotel and Fig. 1.3 and 1.4, the departments in a large hotel.

Departmental Structure of a Hotel

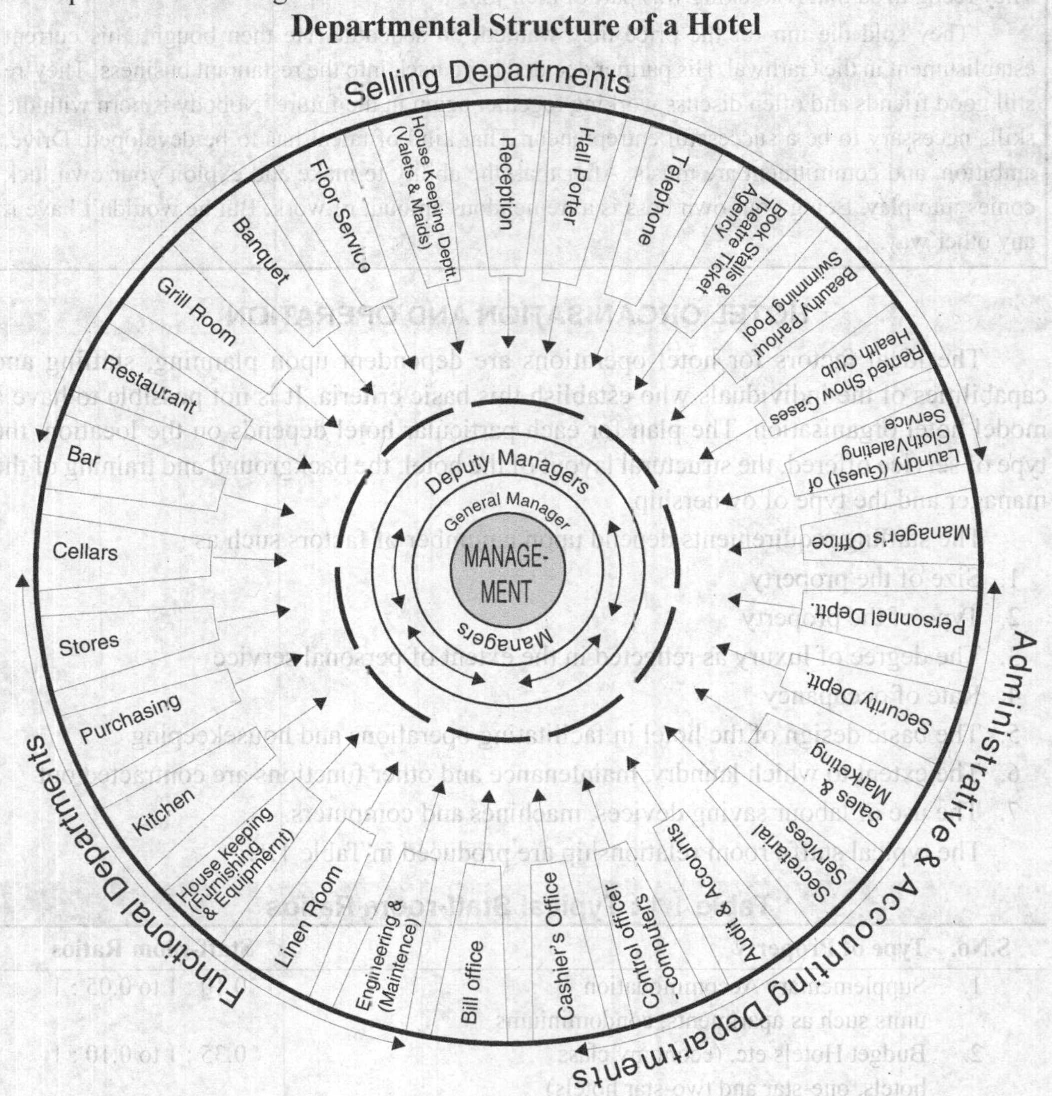

Fig. 1.1 : Typical Departmental Structure of a Hotel.

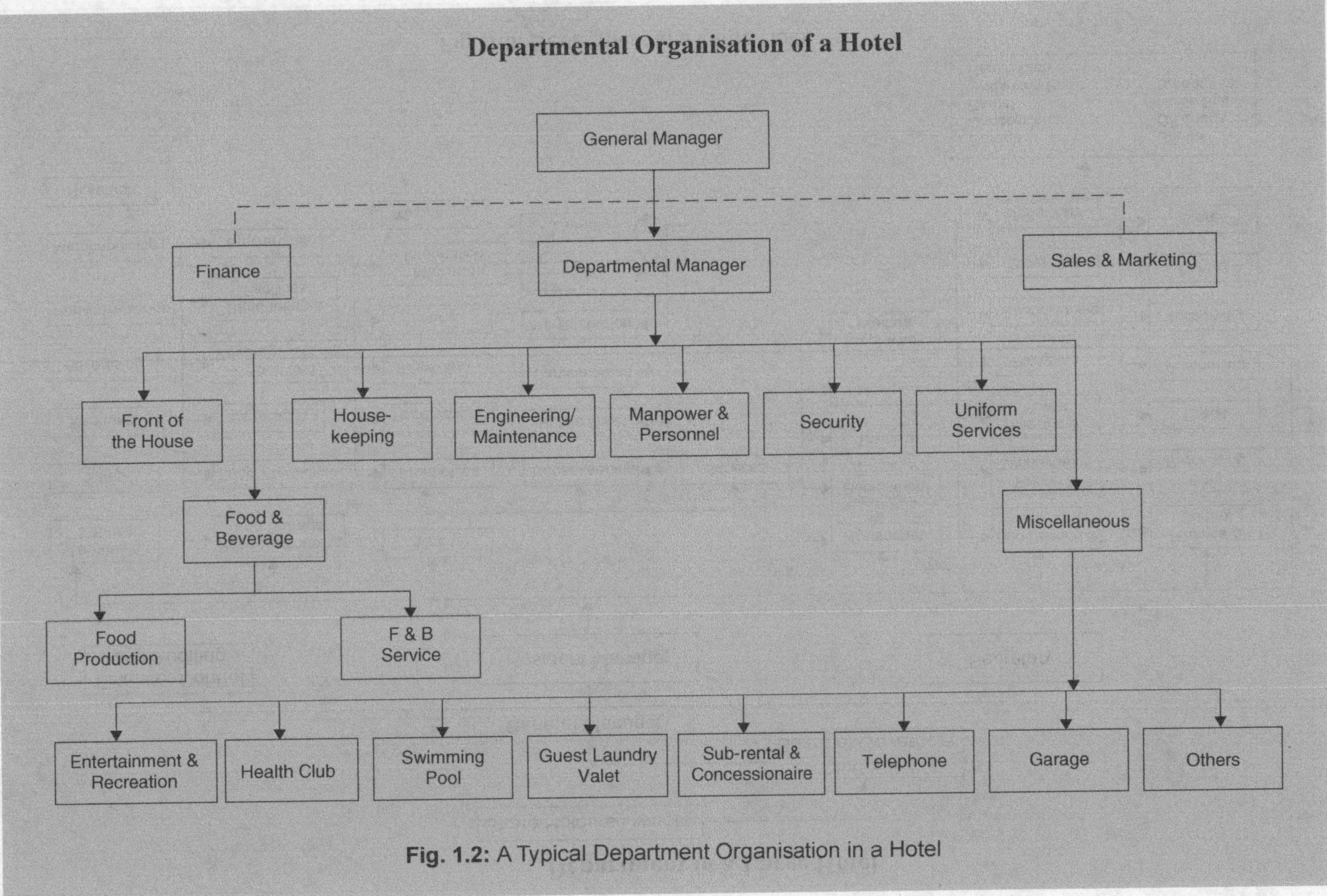

Fig. 1.2: A Typical Department Organisation in a Hotel

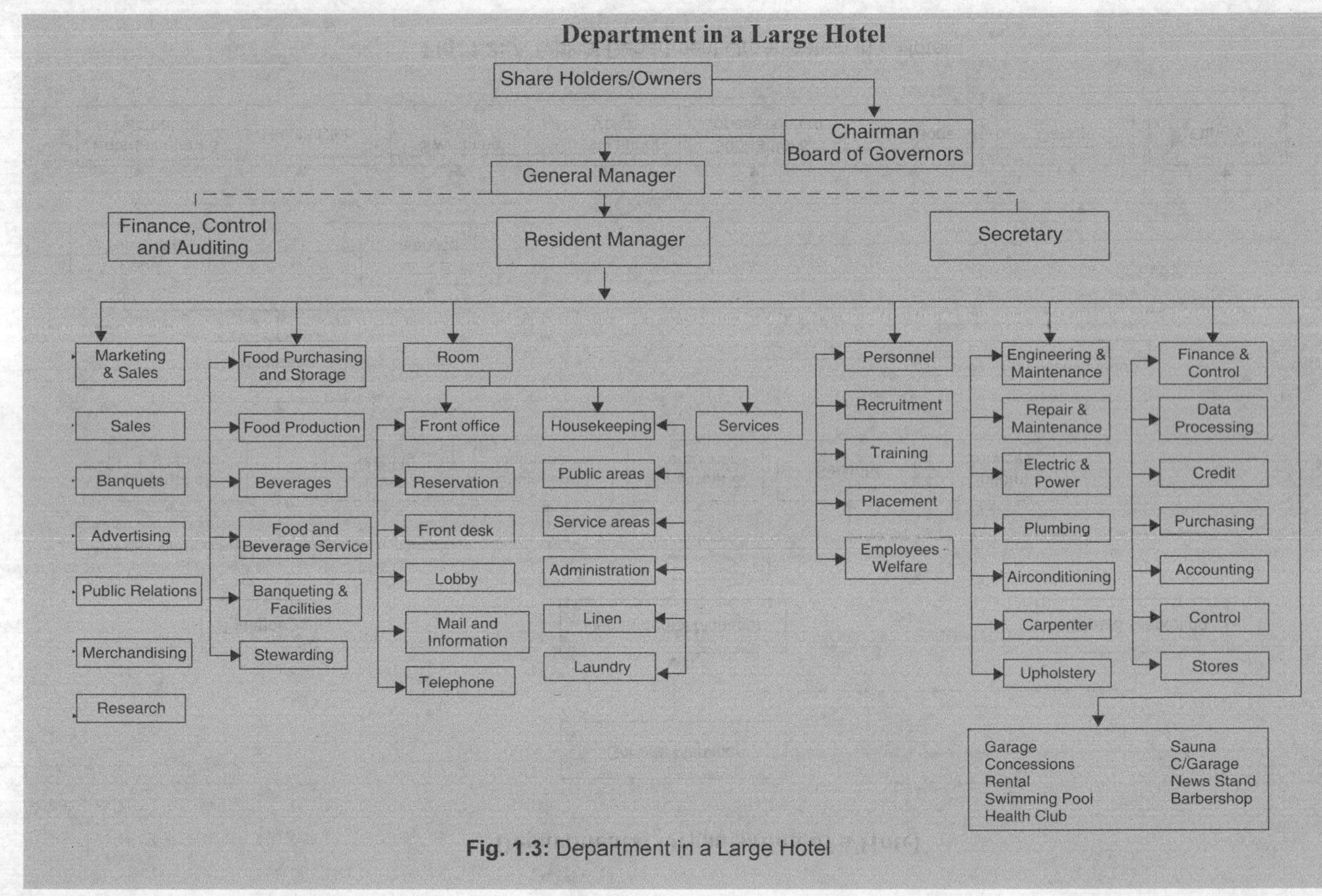

Fig. 1.3: Department in a Large Hotel

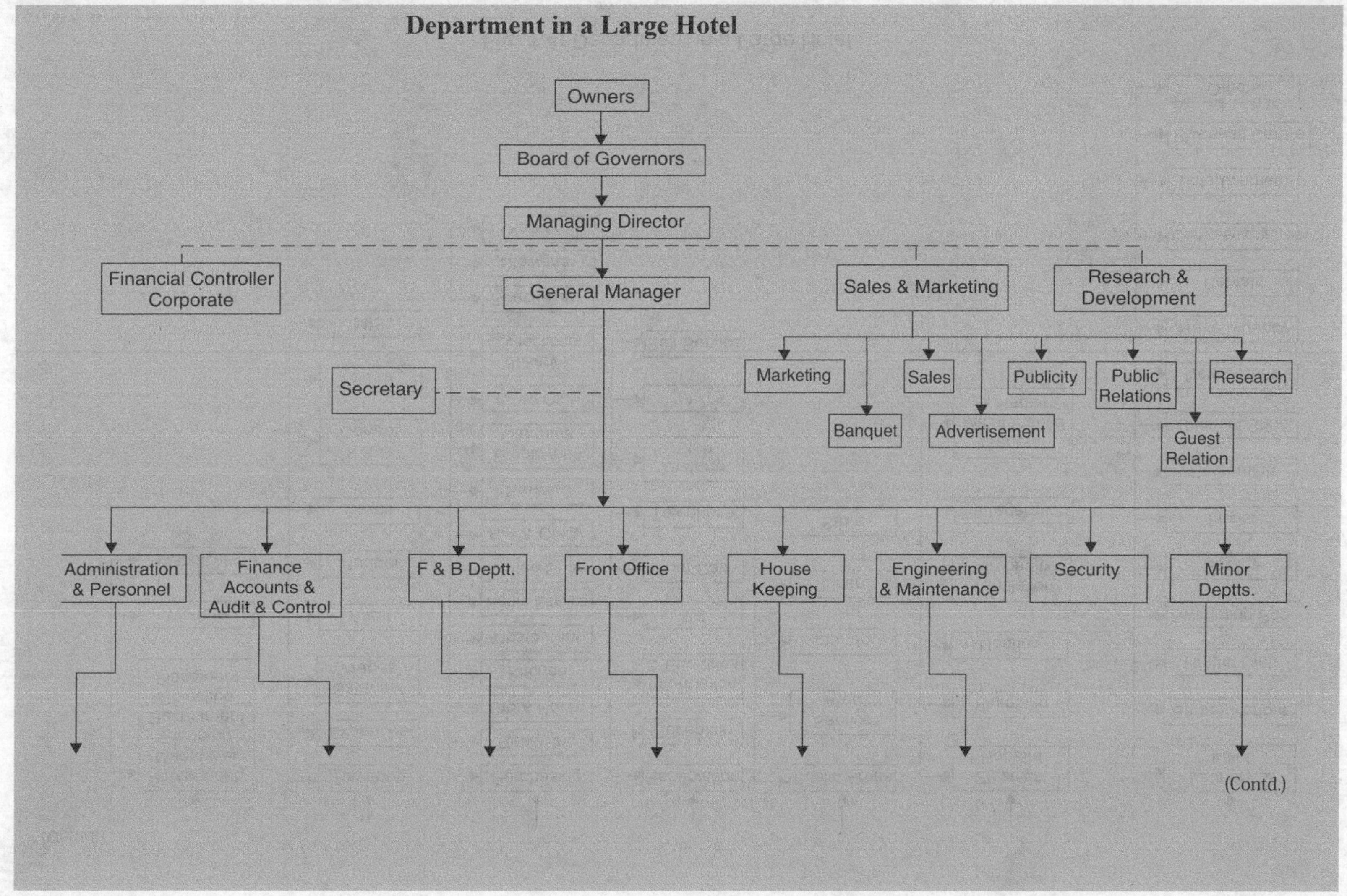
Department in a Large Hotel
Owners
Board of Governors
Managing Director
Financial Controller Corporate
General Manager
Sales & Marketing
Research & Development
Secretary
Marketing
Banquet
Sales
Advertisement
Publicity
Public Relations
Guest Relation
Research
Administration & Personnel
Finance Accounts & Audit & Control
F & B Deptt.
Front Office
House Keeping
Engineering & Maintenance
Security
Minor Deptts.
(Contd.)

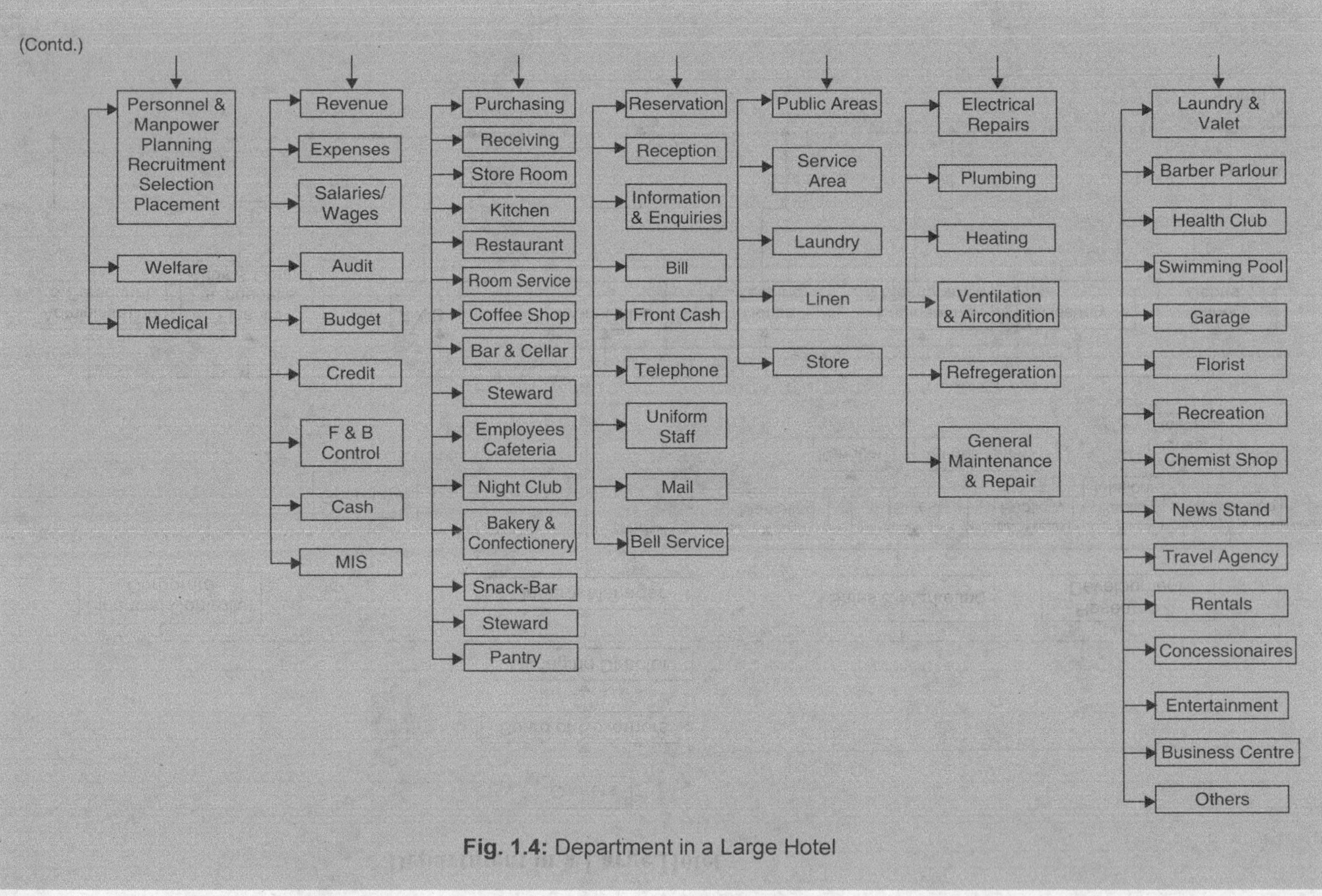

Fig. 1.4: Department in a Large Hotel

A knowledge of the various departments, their uses, functions and fields of responsibilities will enable the student of hotel management to recognise the internal operation and communication of hotel facilities. The departmental breakdown requires that top management know at each phase of the operation and during each day of operation, what is happening, where it is happening and the cost of performing such duties.

THE FRONT OFFICE

The front office includes all the offices which are situated in or near the front hall or lobby of the hotel. It is the nerve centre of the hotel. A well-known hotel personality, Mr. Charles O'Tool, pictures the hotel as a wheel, of which the front office is the hub. This department is the first that is contacted by an arriving guest and is the information centre during his stay. It is the last point contacted when he leaves. Thus, the main functions of a hotel's front office are :

1. Selling rooms	:	To process reservations and all communications with persons seeking accommodation in hotels.
2. Front desk	:	To register guests and assign rooms.
3. Service	:	To handle all mail, telegrams and messages for guests.
	:	To furnish information about the hotel, the country, and any special attraction or events of interest.
	:	Keeping the accounts of guests, rendering bills and receiving payments thereof.

Requests for reservation are received by telephone, telegram, teletype or across the desk. All inquiries relating to advance reservation and booking of accommodation and all the associated clerical work including correspondence is done in the advance reservation office. All particulars of booking are entered in the hotel diary. The advance reservation chart is used for allocating rooms for specific periods. An arrival list is sent to the reception office together with the file containing all reservation cards and correspondence relating to guest arrivals.

The work of the reception office is to receive, welcome and register the guests, and keep all other relevant departments in the hotel notified. All the guests arriving at the hotel must be registered. There is no legal obligation for the guest to write down the required information, the receptionist may do so on his behalf. As soon as the guests approach the front desk they are greeted by the receptionist. He/she inquires whether they have a reservation. Each guest is asked to give his full name and nationality. While the guest is filling out the registration card, the receptionist checks the reservation sheets, notes the arrival, and from the rack he/she picks out the room number blocked. The room number and the rates are recorded in the registration card. A room slip is prepared in duplicate. The bellmen are handed over their keys and the slips. The reception office informs the front office cashier and all departments and the information is noted down in the room rack. Once the guest is roomed, his chief contact with the front office will be through the mail and information.

During his stay at the hotel, the guest is charged several items. All these charges are sent by the individual departments concerned to the front office cashier, who posts it in the guest bill. At the chiecking out of the guest, the bill is presented and settled.

FOOD & BEVERAGES

The Food & Beverage Manager/Catering Manager is responsible for planning, co-ordinating and controlling all the food and drinks. There are as many as ten divisions under the control of the F&B Manager. This department alone can assure the success or failure of a hotel. The use of standard portion control and a general uniformity within the kitchen, from the purchasing department to the kitchen department, are the means by which a successful F&B operation is achieved. This department controls three thingsFood, Beverage and Service. Food and beverages are tangibles and with a certain amount of skill and supervision, they can be instrumentals in guest satisfaction. The service is intangible and it requires ability and versatility. Skill is highly essential in providing good service. A guest will not enjoy a meal when efficiency is lacking. To the student of hotel management, the F&B department presents an overall picture. Many people fail in the restaurant, not only due to lack of knowledge about the industry, but also because they hold this misconception that the restaurant business is a simple business. There are people who are most successful in this business but only those who know that good food and good service are the prime requirements, which get the success they are looking for.

This department represents a complex group in which there are many lines of authorities and various overlapping functions.

FOOD PURCHASING

The person who initiates this operation is called the purchase manager/purchase officer/purchase steward. He arrives in the morning and each day he follows a set routine. It is essential that all the food he purchases is as close as possible to the time it will be consumed in order to assure freshness and top quality. The purchase assistant looks into the perishable products and ensures that they are consumed when they are fresh. He checks the banquet menu, daily menu, forecasts of the number of covers or guests to be served that day, and accordingly decides the amounts and kinds of foods to be purchased. Staple items are generally purchased two or three times a month. Meat is purchased daily. The methods of purchasing vary according to the location and availability of merchandise.

FOOD RECEIVING

The responsibility of the person receiving the food is to ascertain quality and quantity based upon the quoted prices, orders and rèceiving articles. Every item received is weighted or accounted and checked. Once the quantity, qualities and the price are checked, the bill is approved. Items like meat, fish and poultry are listed on the receiving sheet and a meat tag is attached.

STORAGE AND ISSUANCE

After verification, the goods are entered into the respective registers. Food is kept in various types of storage : dry stores, vegetable, dairy, meat boxes and freezers. These are under the supervision of the storekeeper.

From the store, food is issued to the kitchen for preparation. At no time should any foodstuff be distributed, other than to those with the proper authority for the receipt of the merchandise. First a requisition is written and signed by the Chef'or his assistant and accordingly the food is given out. The requisitions are priced by the store-keeper and sent to the food controller. At the end of each day, the storekeeper should review the requisition, categorise them and issue a statement to the management on the quantity consumed. Periodically, a physical inventory is taken and checked against the requisition for the month.

BEVERAGES

Great caution is required in the purchase, receiving, storage and inventory of beverages due to very high cost. The basic aim is to receive the best quality at the lowest possible price. The purchase assistant of beverages must maintain a continuing inventory, co-ordinated with the needs of the various bars and cocktail lounges. Like for storage of food, each beverage has its unique requirement. Bottles of beverages in store must remain vertical or horizontal or according to specified temperature. The beverage controller must have complete knowledge of all the products under his control.

KITCHEN

The production side of food is delegated to the Executive Chef/ Chef de cuisine.'The next phase of food handling takes place in this section. Staffing requirement and the size of the section will depend upon the type of meals to be provided and the number of guests for whom they are prepared. The main kitchen is made of many small groups. Every section of the kitchen has a particular function in preparing food to be served. One section may prepare for the cooks, all meat, fish, poultry items etc. from the store room, the other may make salads and desserts and another may make delicious appetizers and canapes. There may be groups making soups, sauces and gravies, roasting, frying, boiling etc. There are also people who prepare vegetables for the cooks. Thus, there are several employees who contribute to the preparations of one dish in a hotel. The incharge of each section of the kitchen is called '*chef de parte*'or section head. He is specialised in that particular field. He is assisted by '*commis chefs*.'In small hotels the work of managing the different sections is combined.

The organization of kitchen in a medium-sized hotel may consists of :

1. *Chef de Cuisine* : He is the overall incharge of the kitchen. The chef's responsibilities begin with the purchasing of various foods. There are *Sous chefs* to assist him in the general organization and supervision. The work of chefs varies according to the size and the specialization of the kitchen.
2. Sauce Section : It is a place where all 'entrees 'and sauces are prepared.
3. Larder Section : All meat, fish, poultry and game are prepared for cooking, and all salads, *hors-d'oeuvres* and cold dishes are made in this section of the kitchen.
4. Roast Section : Roasting and grilling are done in this section.
5. Fish Section : It prepares and cooks all fish dishes and the appropriate fish sauces.
6. Vegetable Section : Prepares and cooks all the vegetables and egg dishes.
7. Pastry Section : Different types of sweets, puddings, *gâteaux* and pastries are prepared in the pastry section.

In addition to the above, under the *Chef*, there are other sections which may not form a part of the main kitchen itself, *e.g.* coffee shop, snack bar, grill room, etc.

KITCHEN STORE

It is a daily store. The store-keeper receives all the dry goods, and records the details on a card. Perishable goods such as meat, fish etc. are received directly into the kitchen. On receipt of an indent or requisition from the *Chef*, the store-keeper will issue the required store for use that day in the kitchen. The kitchen clerk assists the *Chef* in this work. He is also required to fill the job of a Caller (*Aboyeur*) during service time, *i.e.* calling orders as they are received from the waiters, so that each section knows what has been ordered and prepares it accordingly.

KITCHEN PORTERS

They are responsible for cleaning of all the areas of the kitchen and its equipment.

SCULLERY

It is an area in the kitchen for the washing and storing of pots and pans.

WASH-UP/PLATE ROOM

Here the waiters deposit dirty crockery and cutlery for washing, storing and re-use. The silver utensils are also washed here.

STILL ROOM/PANTRY

All beverages, bread and butter, sandwiches, toast, cereals, preserve, etc. are prepared and served from here.

SERVICE : FOOD & BEHERAGES

In a large hotel, there may be a number of different areas like the restaurant, dining room, grill room, snack bars, coffee shop, room service, lounge service and banquet hall, offering a variety of meals and services. Similarly, there are several bars within the same complex like cocktail bar, public bar, hotel bar, dispense bar, etc.

The incharge of a restaurant is known as Restaurant Manager. The room is divided into stations, each one consisting of a number of "covers" or place to set at a table. The incharge of each station is called *Chef de Rang*/Station Waiter. He takes the customer's order and writes out the necessary checks. He is assisted by *Commis* Waiters/*Commis de Rang*. *Commis* Waiter takes the checks to the kitchen and brings food and assist *Chef de Rang* to serve. *Debarasseurs*/Bus Boys help to carry and fetch food from the kitchen.

The beverage service within the restaurant is carried out by wine waiters (*sommeliers*). They take the orders from all the sections of the restaurant/bar and are assisted by Commis/ wine waiters (*Commis de Vin*). In a small restaurant the Head Waiter is incharge and is responsible for welcoming and seating all the guests and assists with the service of the food.

The Head Bartender is responsible for mixing all the drinks and maintains the beverage cost at the percentage decided upon by the management. At a briefing station before a meal, the special drinks for the day and the way it is to be served are discussed.

The restaurant cashier deals with the cash paid by the customers for the meals served. He prepares two or three copies of the bill under table numbers from the waiters/checks.

The waiter presents the original bill to the customer and obtains the money in return. The money is paid to the restaurant cashier who stamps it as "PAID". The waiter returns the bill to the customer. In case the customer signs the bills, the procedure is almost the same except that the original bill signed by the customer is retained by the restaurant cashier. The latter practice is applied to resident guests, those having credit cards or those who have an arrangement with the hotel to sign the bills. Accounts of such bills are submitted at a later date.

In large hotels, room service is a big business. Therefore, a separate section headed by the Waiter Floor (*Chef de etage*) assisted by *Commis* Floor Waiter (*Commis de etage*) is made responsible for the service. The orders are placed over the phone. The room service Order Taker takes down the room number of the guest and confirms it by writing the guest's name from the room rack. The order is written in the same order as it is placed. The order taker makes three copies of the Kitchen Order Ticket (KOT). The price of the food and drinks served in the room is generally higher than the equivalent served in the Restaurants or Bars.

BANQUETING

Banqueting denotes a multitude of private functions, conferences, cocktails parties, weddings, receptions, private and official luncheons and dinner parties, and many more besides. The Banqueting Manager is responsible for booking functions, helping the organizers to choose menus, provide efficient service, booking the banquet and cabaret, ordering and arranging of flowers, costing of the functions for hiring rooms, food and alcohol, and ensuring that the function is adequately staffed.

The type of service of beverages varies from hotel to hotel. The Bar Manager is responsible to the F&B Manager for the overall control of all barsLounge Bar, Cocktail Bar, Public Bar, Dispense Bar, etc. Each Bar has a Head Barman with Barmen/Barmaids to assist him. The Barmen/Barmaids are responsible to the management for the stock held within the Bar as well as for all cash taken. There is a great opportunity for pilferage in the Bar. The Management carries out spot checks of the stock in addition to regular stock-taking.

HOUSEKEEPING

It is the backbone of all the hotels. It is the busiest and most important department of the hotel. The head of the section is called as Executive Housekeeper. She is responsible for the cleanliness of most of the hotel rooms as well as neatness and orderliness of the guest rooms. She has an assistant and several supervisors to conduct her department. Duty Roasters are compiled by the Executive Housekeeper or her assistants. Room-maids and chambermaids are informed which rooms are due to be vacated or re-let so that linen can be changed and the room cleaned. All rooms are checked and bed occupancy lists, sleepers list and room station reports are prepared.

In large hotels, there is a Linen Room in which the linen is stored, sorted, checked and repaired. It is under the control of the Linen Keeper who is responsible to the Head Housekeeper. The number of staff to be employed in this department depends on the size of the hotel and the amount of work to be done. The main responsibilities of a housekeeper are:

1. To supervise the cleaning of all guest rooms, public halls and corridors.
2. To report necessary repairs to the engineering department.
3. To inform the room clerk of the status of each room and to prepare daily reports of the rooms occupied.
4. To keep the linen, draperies and curtains in good condition.
5. To be incharge of upholstery repairs.
6. To be responsible for day and night maids, housemen who do the vacuum cleaning, wall washing, painting, cleaning and furniture polishing.

UNIFORMS

The uniform service comprises the doorman, bellman, elevator operators, lobby porters etc. It comprises all those members of the hotel staff who wear a levered uniform. The head of this section is called Head Porter. He keeps a log book in which he records all the happenings of the day. Other staff of this department are the hall porters, linenmen, luggage porters, hotel valet, cloak-room attendants, lift attendants, inquiry clerk, page boy, night porters etc. The bellman escorts the newly arrived guests to their rooms. The bell captain is incharge of the bellmen.

TELEPHONES

In every hotel there will be telephones. The larger the establishment the greater will be the need for more outgoing links and internal extensions. It is a department that the guests will never see but one with which he may have frequent contact. It handles all intra-hotel, local and long distant calls.

SECURITY

Hotels and their guests are vulnerable targets for thieves, prowlers and other undesirables. Therefore, the Security Officer and his staff must be vigilant every hour of the day. The Security Officer must be having a law enforcement background. He must know in detail all local and state laws pertaining to hotels, and must actively co-operate with the police and authorities.

ENGINEERING

The chief engineer is responsible for effective control, repairs and maintenance. The work of this department is divided into seven main areaselectrical, plumbing, heating, ventilation, air-conditioning, refrigeration and building maintenance and repairs.

PERSONNEL

It has the duties of selecting, recruiting and improving the staff. Personnel management is a vital function of hotel management. The personnel manager must know the local labour market and must design a program that will attract qualified employees to the hotel. Hotels generally have a high turnover rate and this in turn magnifies the recruitment problem. Management looks to the personnel department for advice, suggestions and the latest development in the areas of wages, salaries, job evaluation study, service etc. As regards training, the only way to develop a competent staff is to train it. The personnel department must supply the techniques of training to supervisors, departmental heads and executives.

FINANCE ACCOUNTS AUDITING AND CONTROL

Accounting plays an integral part in the business and it holds prime importance. Every manager must have a knowledge and background of accounting procedures. The work of this department is categorised as revenue, expenses, payrolls and statistical reports. The head of this section is called the Financial Controller/Accounts Officer. Many of the accounts records are kept or originate outside the accounts office. The accounts of all guests are kept in the Front Office. The cashiers in dining rooms may record the services, present cheques and collect the cash, and the housekeeper should list the occupied rooms, the telephone and other departments record their sales, the receiving clerk prepares the lists of all goods received and the Time Keeper records the arrival and departure of all employees. The General Cashier receives cash from all cashiers and notes the deposit. He distributes payrolls, cheques and makes cash disbursements. The income auditor audits all the revenue and cash receipts of the hotel daily and checks the correctness of the guests accounts through the night auditor reports. There are clerks to look after the work of labour, accounts payable and payrolls.

SALES AND MARKETING

This department deals with the activities associated with the identification of markets for the hotel facilities and services and the advertising, sales and promotion personnel. In a small hotel there is a Manager while in a large hotel there is a Marketing Director who carries on these activities. In all sale rooms and public space, this department also promotes internal selling.

OBJECTIVES, STRATEGIES AND POLICIES

Every hotel has a set objectives or targets.In large hotels, objectives are arranged in hierarchy in which small unit constitutes the realisation of a large unit's objective. Strategies are the complex plans for bringing the hotel from a given posture to a desired position in the future. Policies are general statements which provide guidance in decision making to various managers. Policy means the art or manner of governing a nation, the line of conduct which rulers of a nation adopt on a particular question, relating to foreign countries, the principle on which any measure of close action is based. Considering these facts, in hotel operation, the definition of policy may be termed as a statement of general understanding which provides guidelines in decision making to members of an organisation in respect to any course of action.

'Strategy' may be defined as the determination of organisational objectives of a hotel in the light of environmental variables and determination of course of action and commitment of organisational resources to achieve those objectives.

Policies are the rules on which management bases its decision to conduct the business. These rules are supported by the philosophies of the hotel which may be termed informal rules and conventions. Plans and strategies are the instruments which direct management towards the attainment of the objectives with the use of different techniques such as Budgetary Control and Management by Objectives.

The top management executive committee, as indicated in Figure 1.5 is the hotel's policy making body.

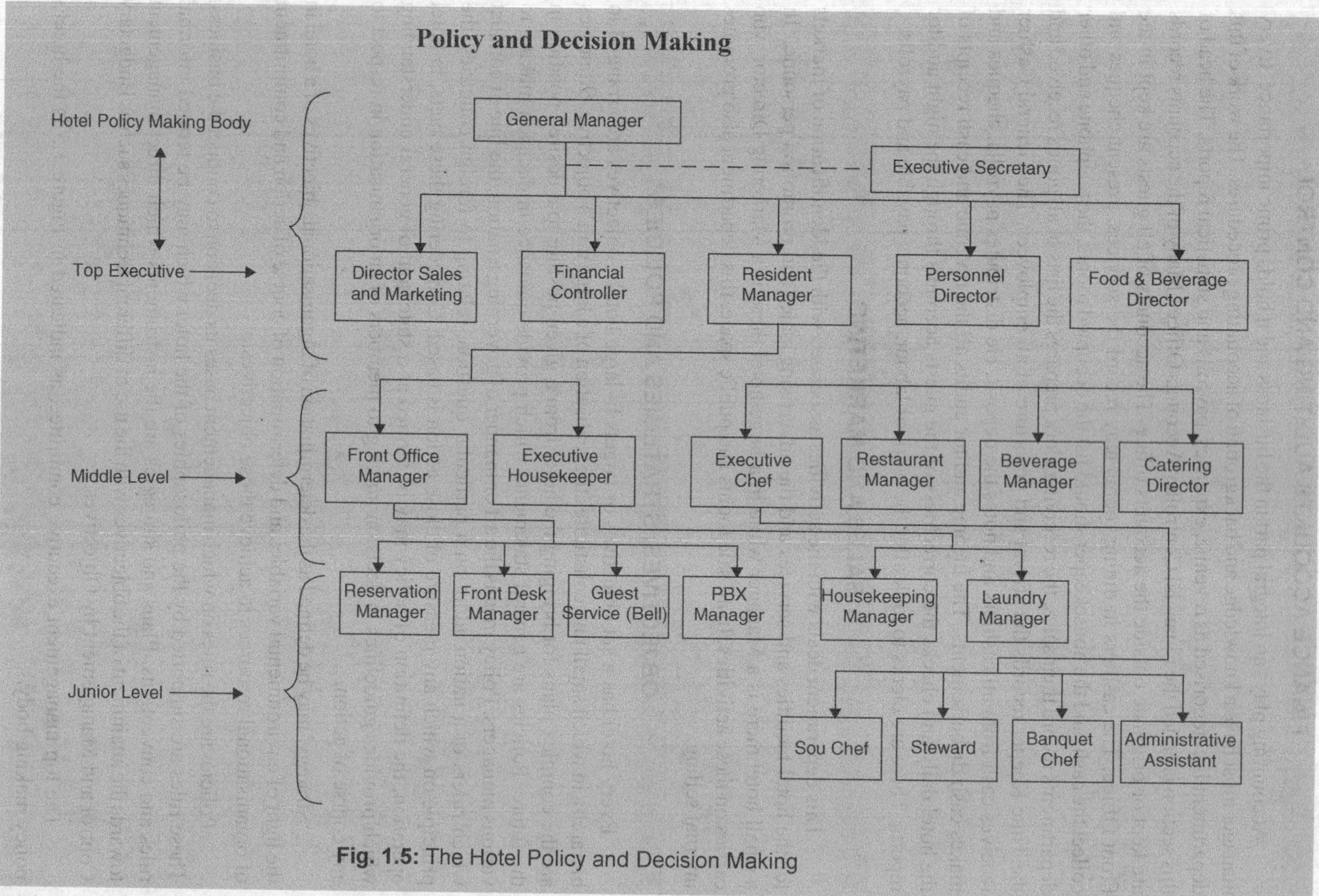

Fig. 1.5: The Hotel Policy and Decision Making

In any business, there are 'three 'main parties with one or more objectives. For the owner/shareholder the hotel business provides the return of investment. Thousands of people earn their living by owning and operating hotels. For employees a hotel is a source of income and for community and hotel customers, the purpose of the hotel is to provide certain facilities and services to its customers. Therefore, in a financial terminology, the hotel owners/shareholders are interested in high profit and security of their investments; employees with high salaries and wages and good working conditions; and customers have interest in low prices and high quality of facilities and services. Therefore, a careful analysis of these varying interests of three parties seems to be in conflict. A responsible management will endeavour to reconcile these compelling and conflicting objectives and accordingly, appropriate objectives of the hotel business and its operations. For sustained prosperity, the management must look into all aspects of running a hotel. Once objectives are clear the management must concentrate on actions and policies. Necessary guidelines or policies may be formulated whereinthe hotel defines attitudes and approach in its dealing with customers, employees, shareholders, suppliers etc. The general guidelines or general policy for the whole hotel is formulated by top management, i.e., the owner in small hotels, the partner(s) in partnership business, and Board of Directors, in the case of a company.

To clearly define the objectives and policies of the hotel, is the responsibility of the management, but this extends from the director to the managers, then departmental heads and supervisors. Management at all levels is required to contribute to the attainment of the objectives and for the implementation of policies. The owners/shareholders, employees, customers and suppliers are the main group of people who have direct dealing with the hotel. Departmental/sectional policies are formulated in relation to each of the parties in dealing with the internal and external aspects of the hotels. Thus,

1. A shareholders' policy defines what the owners are entitled to expect in terms of their rewards, information and participation in the business, and what is expected from them.
2. A personnel policy or employment policy indicates such as recruitment, selection, training, remuneration, condition of employment, welfare, promotion, termination, consultation, negotiation and handling of disputes.
3. A customers' policy clarifies what the hotel is aiming to do in terms of its markets and quality standards of what it provides, including its concept of goods, value and its approach to price, discount and credit. It also states the hotel's attitude to complaints and refunds.
4. A hotel suppliers' policy indicates what the hotel expects from them regarding the quality of supplies, delivery and terms.

In each of the above four relationships, the elements of the financial guidelines may be viewed as an extension of a policy to suppliers. Hotel departments having the responsibilities of accommodation, food, beverage and functions could be provided with a set of guidelines relating to each department.

In a small hotel, there is a high degree of personal contact between the owners, management, employees, customers and other parties. The aims and objectives of the hotel are often passed on informally by word-of-mouth. In a large hotel, these policies are statements in writing, to be followed at all times. They are relevant to all hotel employeees and partially to customers. Most of the hotel companies distribute these policies to those concerned. They feel that to tell their customers about their policies could be a powerful marketing tool. Similarly, the personnel policies communicated to the staff can have a favourable impact on their image, on employees, and on personal relations and to provide clear guidelines for all financial areas and departments, to those operating them. It is highly conducive to smooth and efficient operation of the hotel business.

The wide variety of provisions for recreation and leisure, provide new opportunities and changes keep occurring in the running of a hotel. New customer or employment legislation may require for changes in the determined policies of the hotel towards its customers, employees and outsiders. For example, new sources of supply may suggest changes in purchasing policies and departmental policies. The changes in the markets, environments and external and internal factors greatly affect the business of the hotel. Therefore, the management of the hotel has to keep their objectives and policies under constant review.

The main areas connected with the hotel policies are :

1. Employment
2. Rate Structure
3. Advertisement
4. Accounting
5. Credit
6. Catering
7. Financial
8. Operational
9. Purchasing
10. Receiving
11. Storing and Issuing
12. Preparation
13. Selling
14. Post-Operational Control.

EMPLOYMENT

Salaries and wages are the largest single expenses in the hotel's budget. The initial staffing of a new hotel requires top management decision. The position of the general manager, sales manager, personnel manager and controller are filled by interviews. Their salaries are predetermined. The salaries of other departmental heads and their assistants are flexible and depend on the availability of trained/experienced people. The salaries Of other staff including unskilled ones depend on the Minimum Wages Act, local customs, union contracts and the availability of labour. Fringe benefits, medical benefits, insurance, pensions, gratuity, saving plans etc. are generally uniform.

RATE STRUCTURE

The room rate is predetermined by the management in the initial planning stage of the buildings as per the style and the type of the hotel to be built, the appointment and facilities to be provided and the class of guests to be served. The location, availability of rooms, the potential volume of business and other guidelines developed in the feasibility study, help in the determination of room rates. Similarly, the prices of food and beverage menu are also fixed. In many independent hotels the rate schedule is prepared by the General Manager and the home office staff. Any change required are made by the General Manager with the consent of the control office. It is also imperative to lay the necessary guidelines for stores and concessions available for rental.

ADVERTISEMENT

The main objective of an advertisement policy is to popularise the name of the hotel based on the assumption that most travellers would stay or eat at well-known hotels. Room, food and beverages are common in all the hotels. Advertisements help in the desired publicity needed for each hotel, specially for banquet facilities, speciality restaurants, cocktail lounges, bars etc. The amount to be allocated in the budget for local advertising, the copy and the media to be used, must be properly decided.

The General Manager has the responsibility to project, develop and maintain the image of the hotel. He must be consulted before any copy is finally approved for publication. He is the person to establish contacts with the political leaders, influential citizens, press, and other media. He secures publicity for the hotel and builds and projects the desired image. His knowledge and familiarity with regional customers will help in initiating, recommending, supervising and assuming all responsibility for local advertising publicity.

ACCOUNTING

There must be a complete standardisation in accounting systems and information. Hotels do forecast, prepare reports, statistics and operating results. The comparison of this information to judge the operation of each hotel by the management will be meaningless unless they agree to the methods adopted to assemble the information.

CREDIT

Credit policy is similar in all the hotels of the same chain. All hotels in the group are required to honour certain credit cards. The rate of discount charged by credit card companies and banks varies accordingly to the volume of business generated by their clients. The credit card companies advertise to solicit new members and popularise the use of their cards. The credit card companies often include, in the monthly billing, the card holder's literature supplied by the establishments honouring the cards. The time and number of mailing is negotiable.

A liberal credit policy will tend to expand the hotel market, but it entails a certain amount of credit risk. A clear distinction must be made between a inhouse guest and non-house guest. Most of the credit privileges extended to inhouse guests are for room charges, food, beverages, laundering, valet, items purchased in the stores and concessions, telephone services, entertainment and cash, excluding city ledger billing, and the collection procedure should be covered by the credit policy. Therefore, the credit policy should cover the following periods :

1. Prior registration of guests and before the function starts
2. While the guest is in the residence and the function is in progress
3. At the check-out time of the registered guest or at the end of the function.
4. Prior registration of guests and before the function starts: The hotel should check the financial position of firms, associations, groups, industry and unknown companies.

Credit ranking should be given to each group as :

— High 1

— Good 2

— Fair 3

— Limited 4.

While the guest is in residence and the function is in progress. Suitable system should be evolved for :

1. Guest registration
2. Credit department billing procedures
3. Group and convention billing
4. Check cashing system :
5. Credit Card
6. Approvals
7. Registration :
   (*i*) Post-dated cheques
   (*ii*) Second party cheques
   (*iii*) Counter cheque
   (*iv*) Cheque payable to corporations, companies, firms and organisations
   (*v*) Money Orders
   (*vi*) Others
   (*vii*) Recording
   (*viii*) Traveller's Cheques
   (*ix*) Restaurants
   (*x*) Stamps
   (*xi*) Group and convention guests :
      (*a*) Guest charges
      (*b*) Charges for non-resident guests.

At the check-out time of the guest or at the registered end of the function. A basic policy must be observed regarding :

1. Check-out
2. Collection
3. Bad debts
4. Legal aspects of collection.

CATERING

The catering policy provides food facilities and describes the methods by which objectives are to be achieved. In this case, the management assesses the market and describes how it is to be catered to :

1. What type of customers is the hotel catering to :
   (*i*) Foreign tourists
   (*ii*) Domestic tourists

(*iii*) Local residents
(*iv*) Businessmen
(*v*) Managers/executives
(*vi*) Banquets
(*vii*) Others.

2. What are the requirements of the hotel's customers?
   (*i*) Type of menu
   (*ii*) *a la carte* menu
   (*iii*) *table d' hote* menu
   (*iv*) Both
   (*v*) How much variety do they require?
   (*vi*) Any specialities, e.g. regional dishes?
   (*vii*) Appropriate portion sizes
   (*viii*) Most suitable type of service
   (*ix*) Degree of comfort to be provided
   (*x*) Appropriate price level.
3. Thus, a catering policy basically will be concerned with :
   (*i*) Type of clientele
   (*ii*) The type of menu(s)
   (*iii*) The methods of buying
   (*iv*) Food quality standards
   (*v*) Type and quality of service
   (*vi*) Degree of comfort and decor
   (*vii*) Cost and profit targets as determined by financial considerations.

FINANCIAL

This policy sets out the intentions of the management/owner with regard to the envisaged profitability of the establishment. The financial policy involves :

(*i*) The setting of a profit target
(*ii*) The determination of departmental profit targets
(*iii*) The planning of a whole pattern of differential profit margins in respect of each item

1. Thus, a financial policy must specify :
   (*i*) What is the policy of the hotel with regard to capital and profitability?
   (*ii*) What is the requirement of fixed and working capital?
   (*iii*) How to obtain the financial requirements?
   (*iv*) What profit should be aimed at on capital?
   (*v*) What profit should be got from sales?
   (*vi*) What gross profit should be gained?
   (*vii*) How much margin should be given to different sections of sales?

2. Should the hotel impose :
   (*i*) Minimum charge ?
   (*ii*) Cover charge ?
   (*iii*) Service charge, etc ?
3. What volume of sales should the hotel achieve to secure the desired net profit?

   Thus, a financial policy should determine :
4. The return of capital invested i.e., overall profit target
5. The percentage of net profit on sales
6. The type of service and the degree of comfort to be provided
7. The percentage of revenue required to cover labour costs and overheads
8. The percentage of revenue available to cover the cost of sales
9. The cost of sales of each department of the business
10. The differential profit margins for each group of items offered on menu, wine list, etc.

OPERATIONAL

The operational policy consists of the total sum of the built-in system, technological procedures and clerical procedures. It should be planned so as to cover the whole cycle of hotel and catering operations. Operational policies are laid down relating to :

1. Purchasing
2. Receiving
3. Storing
4. Issuing
5. Preparing
6. Selling.

PURCHASING

Many of the big hotel chains have a Control Department. They do all the buying and selling of the merchandise for all the individual hotels. Bulk buying helps in reducing cost. Certain items can be purchased directly from the manufacturers which facilitates discount and reduction in costs. It also helps in quality control. In case of food items it is not possible to have central purchasing, as food is perishable, difficult to repackage and retransport. As regards to beverages, there are different regulations and licensing requirements. The central office establishes the brand of liquor that is to be used in the bars.

Hotels should not buy and store more food items and ingredients than is neccessary. The volume of items to be purchased depends on location and delivery schedules. The hotel needs to keep food in reserve to meet unexpected demands. It is not advisable to buy large amounts to take advantage of particular market situation. In hotel business, the amount saved does not make up for the money in storage costs, possible damage in storage and pilferage. In case the price of items is expected to go up, it is prudent for the purchase department to buy a little more than usual and pay the market price afterwards. The food store room inventory should turn over at least four times the amount every month.

Thus, a purchase policy sets out :

1. Technical procedures, for e.g. yield test in case of food items
2. Purchase specifications
3. Methods of buying
   (*i*) Open market
   (*ii*) Contracts
   (*iii*) Inviting suppliers to submit tenders.
4. Clerical procedures such as origin, sanctions, placing of orders and documentary evidence to be used.

   Similarly, in case of food and beverage items the following points may be clarified:

   A program of systematic yield testing in the hotel

   Use of purchase specifications

   Methods of buying in the hotel :

   (*i*) Contract
   (*ii*) Tender
   (*iii*) Cash and carry
   (*iv*) Wholesale and retail markets.
5. Obtaining most advantageous prices from the suppliers.

RECEIVING

Receiving policy includes three basic considerations :

1. Quality control
2. Quantity inspection
3. Clerical procedures

Thus, a receiving policy must clarify :

1. Staff responsible for controlling the quality of all incoming goods
2. Staff responsible for quantity inspection
3. Appropriate procedures for dealing with instances of short delivery and non-delivery of goods
4. 'Blinding Receiving', its uses and desirability
5. Purchase specifications and their use in the goods received department.

STORING AND ISSUING

A storing and issuing policy gives guidance about the daily recurring process of storing incoming goods and releasing or issuing them for use in the appropriate departments. The policy sets out the followings :

1. Stock records
2. Pricing of issues :
   (*i*) Actual purchase price
   (*ii*) Simple average price
   (*iii*) Weighted average price

(*iv*) Inflated price

(*v*) Standard price.

3. Clerical procedures.

Thus, the policy regarding storing and issuing must clearly determine :

1. Necessity of stock records
2. Staff authorised to requisition food
3. Use of written requisition notes
4. Methods of pricing stores issues
5. Records of food kept outside the food store
6. Frequency of stocktaking
7. Rate of stock turnover
8. Staff responsible for stocking
9. Procedure for writing off losses of stock
10. Availability of adequate storage space
11. Staff who has access to store keys outside normal working hours.

PREPARATION

In order to reduce over-production, loss from inefficient purchasing and excessive portion sizes, following four main stages may be helpful in planning and controlling the preparation of food:

1. Volume forecasting or production planning
2. Standard yields
3. Standard recipes
4. Standard portion sizes.

The management must specify :

1. The system of volume forecasting
2. Desirability of cyclical menus
3. Optimum length of the menu cycle
4. Sales histories and their use for volume forecasting purposes
5. System of pre-costing
6. Use of standard recipes
7. Preparation and approval of standard recipes
8. Establishment of portion control equipment
9. Familiarity of staff with correct portion sizes.

SELLING

Financial and catering policies define monetary aspects of the hotel. Therefore, the main factors involved, regarding sales, are :

1. Pricing problem
2. Billing problem

3. Control of cash and credit sales.

Thus, the sales policy of a hotel deals with the following :

1. Correctness of room tariff and pricing of menu keeping in mind the financial and catering policies
2. Staff responsible for room tariff and pricing of menus
3. Revision of room tariffs and menus
4. Size of the groups
5. Amount of advance deposit to be received
6. Commission to be paid
7. Requirements such as rooming lists, pre-labelling of baggage, reassignment of rooms and overall handling
8. Number of complementary rooms to be given to groups
9. Correct methods of pricing to achieve profit targets
10. Adequacy of operation of accounting and control procedures with regard to both cash and credit sales of the hotel
11. Daily intact banking of cash sales
12. Maintaining of sales histories
13. Availability of cash floats
14. Sales analysis : sales mix, sales per room, occupancy, average spending power etc.

POST-OPERATIONAL CONTROL

The main objective of post-operational control is to examine all the stages of the catering cycle, purchasing, receiving, storing and issuing, preparing and selling, ascertaining trading results and establishing remedial actions. This has three main aspects :

1. Cost reporting
2. Assessment of results
3. Corrective action where required.

The management should clearly lay down policies relating to :

1. Information required by the management for control purposes
2. Preparation of reports in respect to :
   (*i*) Sales volume
   (*ii*) Net profit
   (*iii*) Profit margin
   (*iv*) Cost levels
   (*v*) Departmental trading results
3. Use of reports sent to management
4. Assessment of current results in comparison to budget for previous periods
5. Establishment of permissible deviations from desired results to enable management by exceptions

6. Introduction of a current system of control
7. Periodic review of the current system of control.

In addition to the above policies, there are other fields which require policy decisions. It would be financially prohibitive to maintain a separate legal department in each hotel. These hotels need attorneys to handle the company's business and acquisition or sale of property. A central reservation office is also needed to complement the individual hotel reservation. It will process requests for information for rooms generated by chain advertising, channel them to the proper location and negotiate package deals and special group rates with associations, corporations, clubs, travel agents, etc.

A construction/engineering department can supervise the building or acquisition of new hotels. It is to direct and be responsible for any major improvement or alterations in the existing properties.

BASIC PRINCIPLES

As a hotel manager, you should know the principles of good management. There are some principles of management that cannot be violated. You should examine your own management ideas and that of your own operations and follow the following principles of management :

1. Every hotel should have a primary goal, usually dealing with long-term profit. Every person in the hotel should know the long-term objectives and try to help achieve them.
2. Each employee should have only one supervisor, should know who that supervisor is, and should be required to follow instructions only from his or her own supervisor.
3. No one can completely delegate responsibility. Work can be delegated.
4. Supervisors should not be held responsible for the work in their department unless they have enough authority to enforce what they say and do.
5. Organisation should be flexible.
6. The organisation should take planned steps to provide for its continued existence and survival.

OPERATING CONCEPTS

Howard Johnson, a leading hotelering of a largest organisation in food and lodging industry have suggested five basic operating concepts[1]

1. A standard product approach embracing a standard design and a standard basis of operation in the number of industrial organization.
2. Limited size resulting in more efficiency, greater dispersal, better service and better control.
3. Limited service–including featuring of speciality and convenience of foods.
4. Sensible pricing, moderate and reasonable prices and rates, based upon high volume of sales, with low unit profit.
5. Insistence that individual units, restaurants or hotels be identifed with and operated to the best interests of the communities in which they are located.

1. Howard Johnson, a leading hotelier, USA.

SUCCESS OF A HOTEL BUSINESS

The founder of the Hilton Hotel Chain, Conrad Hilton, named nine ways of success in the hotel business, which are: [2]

1. Turn waste into productive use, for example, conversion of a storage area to a coffee shop.
2. Maintain the distinctive character of accquired hotels.
3. Stress efficiency but not standardization.
4. Consolidate facilities, for example, storing linen supplies next to the laundry operation and repair room.
5. Achieve income from store rentals, for example, converting extra space in convention hotel's lobbies into income producing and guest-pleasing shops.
6. Emphasize guest service. The "Lady Hilton" service, offering specially designed rooms and amenities for female guests, exemplifies this concept.
7. Keep in personal touch with operations.
8. Diversify : The proverb of "not keeping all your eggs in one basket" is more applicable here. The profits from a coffee shop or small bar can make the difference between success and failure for a small operation. Large hotels can diversify by catering at a nearby ski resort, or airport or, if the business is a seasonal one, by acquiring property in a different climate. Larger chains diversify even further by acquiring travel agencies, bus lines and hotel supply firms, as well as campgrounds and other business.
9. Apply modern technology to hotel operation.

HOW TO BOOST PROFITS?

1. Cater to your Guests;
   (*i*) Learn their likes and dislikes
   (*ii*) Show genuine interest in them
   (*iii*) Give that extra bit of service.
2. Improve your Image
   (*i*) Use tools of advertising and publicity
   (*ii*) Build a reputation of quality and service.
3. Encourage Teamwork
   (*i*) Keep your employees informed
   (*ii*) Give them freedom in making decisions
   (*iii*) Teach them what to do, how to do it and when to do it
   (*iv*) Then let them do it.
4. Plan Ahead
   (*i*) Estimate your cash flow for the next five years
   (*ii*) Start now to make plans for financial growth.
5. Look for Profit Volume
   (*i*) Keep expenses under control
   (*ii*) Use break-even point, as a control total

2. Conrad Hilton, Chairman and founder, Hilton Hotel Chain.

(*iii*) Beware of the tendency to assume that big sales is necessarily equated with hight profit volume

(*iv*) Profit is what is left after the bills have been paid.

6. Pay your municipal rent

(*i*) Your hotel's growth and prosperity are closely related to the growth and character of your community

(*ii*) Take an active interest in organisations that work to build a good community.

MAJOR PROBLEMS

The future changes in the areas of technology and marketing may be the greatest challenge you all will be facing in the field of hotel management. The five major areas are identified below which will trouble you as a hotel manager :–

1. Managerial leadership shortage : The availability of individuals, with the requisite competency and capacity for growth.
2. Impact of automation and computerization, specially in areas such as decision making, long-range planning, organisational structure and motivation of employees.
3. New approaches to organisation and management : Temporary 'task force' grouping, bringing together highly skilled specialists and requiring a more supporting managerial style with more attention being paid to relationships than structure.
4. Inter-nationaliazation : The growth of international business and the limitation imposed by size, the need for such companies to develop the product mix, market techniques and technology to keep competition in a worldwide market economy.
5. Social problems: Population explosion, organisation, mass transit, low-cost, having environmental control, the poor and the aged, employed, handicapped, minorities and education.

MANAGEMENT BY OBJECTIVES (MBO)

Management by objectives is one of the highly effective tools for meeting the challenges facing you in this industry. MBO is, basically, a process of making and keeping promises. Periodically, you, as a manager and those reporting to you, agree on certain objectives and commit themselves to achieving them. MBO may be defined as a system of management that relates long-term plans and short-term goals and which is totally result oriented. It is thus a systematic and disciplined approach to objectives, using methods of analysis and management.

All the major hotel chains utilise management by objectives to some degree. You can set up budgets and hold management accountable for performance related to budgets. Similarly, management incentive plans are based on attainment of goals mutually agreed upon by you as a manager and your superior.

MBO PROGRAMMES

The five necessary elements in a successful MBO programme are:

1. Long-range planning
2. Clearly defined and attainable objectives
3. Commitment to specific results

4. Provision for periodic feed-back
5. Measurable goals.

MBO IN HOTELIERING

Some of the uses of MBO in the hotel business are:

1. Performance appraisal
2. Planning
3. Coaching and counselling
4. Self-development
5. Self-management
6. Salary administration
7. Incentive plan rewards
8. Manpower planning.

Let us take an example of application of MBO in the food and beverage department of a hotel. The Manager and the Food & Beverage Manager may agree upon the following goals:

1. Reduction in food costs to 40% of sales
2. Cut labour cost below 32%
3. Increase group business by at least 10% over the previous year
4. Increase cocktail lounge sales by 15%
5. Maintain employees' turnover at less than 10%
6. Develop an assistant capable of replacing Food and
7. Beverage Manager within a year
8. Prepare a procedure manual for Food and Beverage Department.

MANAGING BY RESULTS

Managing by results is an approach similar to MBO. It calls for resetting of higher but realistic profit objectives, and then lining up every function of the hotel business to support the profit target, and to permit it to be realized.

The principles of management by results are:

1. Top management must establish the major objectives for the enterprise. These furnish direction to all employees and facilitate delegation as well.
2. The responsibility for results must be delegated.
3. The results of all delegated responsibilities must add up to the total profit objectives sought.
4. Each manager in the hotel should be assigned definite profit improvement objectives, not only to give direction to his work, but to aid in the measurement of his performance.

TECHNIQUES

You may use a number of modern and sophisticated management tools and techniques in the management and operation of hotel business. Some of these techniques are:

1. System analysis
2. Management information system
3. Forecasting/futuristic system
4. Programme evaluation technique.

SYSTEM ANALYSIS

This is the most basic technique and involves a circular process of :

1. Defining objectives
2. Designing alternative systems to achieve those objectives
3. Evaluating the altenatives in terms of their effectiveness and costs
4. Questioning the objectives and other assumptions underlying the analysis
5. Opening up new alternatives
6. Establishing new objectives, and then repeating the whole process through new orders.

MANAGEMENT INFORMATION SYSTEM

Management information system in hotels could be made possible and successful by introducing advance computers. MIS will benefit from improved data acquisition, data processing, data analysis, data retrieval and data reporting. Through computers, you can convert raw data into information, to help the business more effectively, printing out payroll checks, mailing label's etc. Computers can also be used in reservation system, room management, finance and accounting, sales and marketing, food and beverage control and forecasting.

FORECASTING

Forecasting is a fundamental part of modern business planning. The main purpose of forecasting is to equip hotel managers to make better choices. It involves the following steps :

1. An examination of possible events and the probabilities of their taking place
2. An assessment of the interactions among these events
3. Identification of these events that can be controlled and the extent to which such control is possible
4. Evaluation of alternative future possibilities considering to what degree they might be controlled, and
5. Finally, arriving at an assessment of the impact of the possible future.

Through this process you may be able to forecast profit and loss, cash flows and the balance sheet statement for future years. The generating of 4-5-year detailed profit and loss projection takes only 45 minutes.

PROGRAMME EVALUATION TECHNIQUES

PERT identifies where, when and by whom decisions are made. It is a valuable management tool in reducing costs and improving planning and control. The technique is based on a graphic representation of the steps necessary to complete a particular job as well as the operations that connect the various steps. The graphic representation is expressed as the PERT network, wherein the steps or 'events' point in time marking the beginning or completion of specific tasks in the assignment. The operation of 'activities' are the physical process connecting one 'event' with another. Utilising this information, you, as a manager, can foretell the consequences of variations from a logical plane and take remedial measures, before the deviation takes place in the operation.

The graphic representation shows how certain tasks in a given job must be completed before initiating the other jobs. Under this technique identify the key activities related to main function (the critical path), pinpoint auxiliary activities which are required and may be performed concurrently, and highlight the slack or delay and lost time involving employees awaiting critical activity to be completed.

You may exemplify the PERT by the bar charts to keep track of construction progress. Inter-continental Hotels have bar charts to prepare staffing tables so the required people and skills are available as needed at various phases of construction and operations of a new property. You may also prepare program charts which may be helpful in planning for delivery and installation of furniture, fixtures, and equipment in the hotel.

Flow charts are very helpful in identifying the 'critical path' of operation and procedures followed in completing different jobs. You may use PERT in improving operating efficiency and employees' productivity. PERT can be applied in:

1. Night auditing
2. Accounting
3. Scheduling of housekeeping and maintenance
4. Room reservations
5. Laundry and kitchen production scheduling and
6. Other activities where time and cost relationships are important.

You may diagram the PERT network in night audit procedures. The various activities performed in the procedure, the sequence of 'events' representing the beginning or end of each activity and the time required to perform each activity may be diagrammed. Then you may identify the key activities relating to critical path, auxiliary activities and slack or delay time. This will eliminate delays and set up the fastest way of accomplishing critical activities. After the study of the PERT network, you may assign duties and balance the job functions. This will enable you to achieve considerable reduction in slack-float time and more efficient night auditing procedure/operation with fewer employees required.

Advantage of PERT may be summed up as:

1. Points out the way to more productive personnel
2. Simplifies procedures
3. Faster and more efficient operations and
4. Reduction in cost.

MODERN TOOLS OF MANAGEMENT

You should use the following management tools for the success of your hotel:

1. Electronic Data Processing (EDP): Use of electronic hardware and software for :
   (*i*) Compiling
   (*ii*) Sorting
   (*iii*) Processing and
   (*iv*) Reporting information.

2. Management Information System (MIS) : Use any specially designed, normal or computer based, method to get information on a regular basis for the use of management.
3. Management by Objectives (MBO): Establish specific objectives for:
   (*i*) The company
   (*ii*) Each of its major functions or departments
   (*iii*) Key individuals.
4. Organisational Development (O & D) :
   (*i*) Study the organisation, particularly its human resources
   (*ii*) Find the present and future weaknesses
   (*iii*) Take steps to effect necessary improvements.
5. Direct Costing/Marginal Costing:
   (*i*) Evolve methods to control cost between fixed and variable
   (*ii*) Identify costs as being directly associated and affected by the volume of individual profit centres.
6. Discounted Cash-Flow Analysis (DCFA) :
   (*i*) Examine the projected resources and/or expenses over a period of years resulting from a given investment plan or decision
   (*ii*) Discount them at a given rate (usually cost of capital)
   (*iii*) Determine their present value as a basis for facilitating comparison of various alternatives.
7. Systems Approach : Systems engineering applies this concept to planning and control of physical processes. View your organisation as an intergated complex of interdependent parts interacting among themselves and with their environment.
8. Job Enrichment
   (*i*) Change the nature or structure of jobs to make them more meaningful
   (*ii*) Give employees more responsibilities for planning and evaluating their own work
   (*iii*) Provide them with greater opportunity for participation in decision making.
9. Indirect Work Measurement
   (*i*) Measure re-work volume
   (*ii*) Measure the content of non-productive jobs
   (*iii*) Arrive at efficient staffing levels and
   (*iv*) Control productivity cost.
10. Modeling:
    (*i*) Simulate conditions in order to predict or control
    (*ii*) Use mathematical and electronic data processing.
11. Operational Research (OR) : Use of variety of mathematical techniques of analytical approach to a business problem.
12. Social Accounting:
    (*i*) Assign monetary values to non-economic consequences of decisions such as:
       (*a*) Effects on ecology
       (*b*) Community relations

(c) Company reputation.

13. Factor these values with profit and loss analysis in arriving at investment decisions and/or in appraising executive performance.

QUESTIONS AND ASSIGNMENTS

1. Discuss the basic and fundamental functions of management. (*MTA*)
2. Distinguish between :
   - (*i*) Centralization and Decentralization
   - (*ii*) Formal and Informal communication
   - (*iii*) Policies and Plan
   - (*iv*) Authority and Responsibility
   - (*v*) Line Managers and Staff Managers. (*IHMs*)
3. Explain Maslow's Theory of Hierarchy of Needs, giving the assumptions on which the theory is based. How can a hotel satisfy each of the staff needs listed in the theory? Give examples. (*IHMs*)
4. Explain the term, Management by Exception. How might a system a management by exception be operated at unit level ? (*MTM*)
5. Trace the evolution of 'management'. Who are the early management thinkers and how they have influenced the development of management concepts ? Explain briefly the different schools of management. (*MTM*)
6. Discuss the role and importance of management in the hotel industry (*MTA*)
7. "Management is an art of getting things done". Discuss this statement and describe briefly the important functions of management. (*IHMs*)
8. Explain the difference between a franchise and a management contract.
9. Discuss the situational theory of leadership of Hersey Blanchard. (*IHMs*)
10. What is 'direction' ? Explain the priniciples relating to direction process.
11. (*a*) What kind of decisions a manager is generally recuired to make in the organisational context ? Explain the relationship between managerial skills and managerial levels (*IHMs*)

    (*b*) Distinguish between operative decisions and strategic decision. (*IHMs*)
12. Compare and contrast Theory 'X' and Theory 'Y'. Discuss their relevance in Indian conditions. (*IHMs*)
13. Pressure is increasing for management to take account of social responsibilities of the firm. How might this affect the planning process with particular reference to hotel and catering activities. HCIMA (*London*)
14. Explain the full procedure required for project planning and approval for a deluxe hotel (*IHMs*)
15. Write short notes on any *two* of the following:
    - (*i*) Henry Fayol' contribution in management science
    - (*ii*) Family Vs. professional management
    - (*iii*) Social responsibility of management (*IHMs*)
16. Critically analyse money, power prestige and esteem as motivation from the viewpoint of Maslow's Hierarchy of Needs Theory. (*IHMs*)

17. In what situations are theory 'X' managers more effective than theory 'Y' Managers ? *(IHMs)*

18. Explain in detail the Maslow's Needs Hierarchy. *(IHMs)*

19. Explain the term, 'management by exception'. How might a system of management by exception be operated at unit level ? *HCIMA (London)*

20. Explain in detail the positive and negative impacts of tourism on economy. *(IHMs)*

OBJECTIVE TYPE QUESTIONS

1. State whether the following statements are **'True' or 'False':**

(i) Leaders are born not made.

(ii) 'A pat on the back has limited utility'

(iii) A good manager should always strive to achieve an appropriate integrations of employees needs and company needs.

(iv) A bed occupancy ratio is better indicator of capacity utilization than room occupancy ratio.

(v) Current ratio expresses a relationship between current assets and current liabilities.

(vi) A partially satisfied need continues to motivate.

(vii) Fund flow Statement is a better substitute for an Income Statement.

(viii) Capital budget is the planning of expenditure whose return will be available beyond one year time interval.

(ix) Cash flow statement takes into consideration only the changes in cash position whereas Funds Flow Statement is concerned with changes in working capital position between the two balance sheets.

(x) A preference share is one which carries a prior right to the payment of fixed dividend in preference to equity shares. *(IHMs)*

2. State wether the following statements are **'True' or 'False':**

(i) Total quality management (team) philosophies empowers its employees

(ii) Communication means only transfer of symbols

(iii) An achievement motivated person is not observed with the reward of success and prefers to work on a problem rather than depending on chance. They believe in task related, not attitudinal feed-back.

(iv) An open system approach stresses interaction with the environment and is a wholistic approach

(v) Contingency approach is a function of if-then relationship .

(vi) Captains of industry include, Durant, Rockfeller, Vanderbelt, Ford, JRD Tata, Birla, Goenka, Ambani among others

(vii) The west has reached a state of 'being' whereas India is still at the subsistence level.

(vii) A partially satisfied need continues to motivate.

(ix) Leaders are borne not made.

(x) Responsibility and accountability are the same thing.

(xi) People like to know what is expressed of them.

(xii) A pat on the back has limited utility.

(xiii) Delegation reduces a managers control on his subordinates.

(xiv) Goal activity reduces motivation.

(xv) The first step in problem solving is to find alternative solution to the problem.

(xvi) What do you understand by MBO ? Discuss by giving example

A CASE STUDY

Mr. G. Manoher, is nominated by the Himalayan Hotel Resort International for an advance course in Tourism and Hotel Administration. After attending the first few sessions he wants to plan a trip to the hotels in the Rishikesh and Doon Valley. The area is rich in cultural attractions and tourist attractions and well reputed educational and research institutions are located here. Group of students can visit a variety of tourists attractions. He asked you being one of his students, to appoint a group of students to assist him in setting up tours.

Ms. Kokila is a local residents of the area and suggested that they visit the famous Kampty Fall in Mussoorie and would like to see the hotels in Mussoorie. Mr. Kundan has worked in a tourist resort property in Dhanaulti. Ms. Dura knows about a cozy bed and break fast located in Dhakrani. Mr. Pearl is interested to get some information on resort hotel management. Mr. Jyoti is interest on forestry and botany. Mr. Chand is interested to see the Doon School and other important educational centre of the area. Mr. Arjun want to see the important hotel of the area specially Mussoorie, Dehradun and Rishikesh.

The group has sifted through all the requests and decided to form four teams to visit these places. Each team will appoint one spokeperson for a pannel discussion. The spokeperson will give a five minutes summary of what was learned from this visit.

What information, you think, each spokeperson will include in his or her summary to be presented before Mr. G. Manoher and the whole group of students.

CHAPTER 2

Planning Designing and Construction of Hotels and Restaurants

OBJECTIVES

After studying this chapter you should be able to :

1. *Know the objectives of the prospective hoteliers*
2. *Understand an ideal space management of hotel includingfurnishing of rooms, food and beverage areas; and*
3. *Understand the arrangement of bedrooms.*

LOCATION

Location is a crucial consideration in planning a new facility or improving an operative property. According to Ellsworth M. Statler, a great inventor of the lodging industry, the important factor in the success of a hotel is 'Location, Location and Location'. The location of a hotel mirrors the travel and traffic patterns of the times. Earlier accommodation facilities were established at trading routes. In the second stage of development, these are being established at waysides along roads, at inter-state interchanges and in the future, the trend will be near the airports. During the past few years many hotels have been established and built near places of special facilities such as parks, beaches etc.

You can check the site and relate items by visual inspection, such as:

1. Visibility
2. Traffic
3. Access
4. Intercepting position
5. Surroundings
6. Proximity of competition
7. Absence of interference
8. Typography
9. Cost of land: not more than 20 per cent of the total cost of the project should go into land acquisition and site development.

There is no ideal location for a hotel. The consideration for site requirements for a hotel in a city may be quite different to that of a resort properly. The basic considerations are the kind of guests the property is expected to attract, categories of transient guests which might influence location business, sporting events or other local attractions. You may have planned a hotel where guests would simply relax, enjoy the climate or sports facilities. In addition, a hotel connected with a franchise or referral chain, do well irrespective of location, because of the business generated by referral advertising within the chain. Therefore, a hotel planner needs to be aware of changing travel patterns and references such as movements of the hotel industry to the suburbs and rural areas.

FEASIBILITY STUDY

The feasibility study should be the first order of business in planning a hotel. It must be made by a competent professional organisation, that will do three things :

1. Determine if there is a market for a new hotel and what kind of market it is.
2. Recommend a site appropriate for the market.
3. Projection of income and expenses of the proposed property.

Gather all pertinent information about the community to determine and support a new hotel and what kind of property would have the best chances of success considering factors, such as,

1. Location in respect for other cities of the area
2. Mileages to major cities, resorts etc.
3. Community population and population trends
4. Transportation
5. Economic profile : which includes consideration of
   (*i*) Industries
   (*ii*) Colleges
   (*iii*) Military institutions
   (*iv*) Special events : fairs, retail trading areas and sales trends, bank deposits etc.
6. Make a detailed study of other hotels in the area to determine their occupancy, rate range, number of rooms, type and quality of accommodation provided, facilities for banquet and group functions and the existence of sites for potential competitors in the future.
7. Consideration needs to be given to :
   (*i*) Number of businesses
   (*ii*) Type of business
   (*iii*) Prosperity of local business
   (*iv*) Local employment
   (*v*) Type of residential areas, business and trade meetings
   (*vi*) Natural and man-made attractions.
8. Determine the economic feasibility of investment. Remember the land values are soaring and the cost of building and furnishing a hotel is well over ₹ 60,00,000 a room. Acquire the advice from experienced professional firms for this purpose.

Profitability is one the main objectives of any project investment analysis. Since the last few years many investors have started their entry into the hotel business. Most of these investors belong to the following categories :

1. Those buying an existing hotel property
2. Those converting private house into a fulfledged hotel
3. Those venturing a new hotel project.

All prospective hoteliers are confronted with many problems in the initial stages of hotel operation. There are certain basic rules,which if properly followed will definitely bring profitability and a good returns on the capital invested. It would be useful to understand some of these basic rules as given below :

1. The main objective of the hotel business is that the rate of return on capital should be comparable to any other comparable investment.
2. A hotel project is built to produce the expected return son investment.
3. The amount of investment should stay with in development forecasts.
4. The market is to be dictated by the capital invested.
5. Scope for future expansion and extension should betaken into account while building the hotel. It is an accepted fact that extension usually gives a better pro-rata return than constructing a new hotel building.
6. Efforts be made for installing labour saving devices, equipment and machinery at the start of the business.
7. The pricing policy must be economical for better return based on capital costs.

The hotel business is capital intensive in nature. The major part of the cost of building is involved in providing the bedrooms. This results in high building costs. The greater the building costs, the greater the overhead costs. Increasing costs of overheads forces a hotel to earn a large profit, as the same is required to meet over head costs and show an acceptable return on borrowed money and equity of the owners/shareholders.

Many hotel buildings with high costs have provision for large public areas, big bedrooms, wide corridors and provision for heating and lighting. These factors will lead to higher maintainance costs, with the result the cost of building dictates to a large degree the room rates of the hotel.

PLANNING, DESIGNING AND CONSTRUCTION

The hotel business makes its money from the building. It operates on a profit margin on the products sold daily. On an average the ratio of profit on individual sales are, rooms 70%, beverages 50%, commercial rental 15% and on food a very little percentage. Out of the total cost, 65% goes into the public and service areas, and 35% into rooms. The non-profit areas must be there to rent the room, rooms alone fail to meet the main demand of customers' food, lodging and entertainment.

The following are some rules from extensive hotel research and study based on 65% occupancy break-even point:

1. Room construction cost should not exceed ₹ 1,00,000 per ₹ 100 average room rate
2. The cost of land should not exceed 10% of the cost of the building

3. The number of necessary employees should not exceed the number of rentable rooms
4. Bedrooms (total floor area) should be at least slightly larger than public and service areas; and the more the better conditioned by those three basic demands again.

The planning, designing and construction of hotel is known as 'integration'.The design creates a lively atmosphere which sets the scene for hotel facilities and services. The modern day travellers seek 'experience' and more conveniences. The architects and designers create an ambience throughout the hotel premises. It begins with the exterior, is carried to the lobby and public areas, and continues to the guest rooms and usually reaches its peak in the speciality restaurant and night clubs.

Designer Henry End of the USA says that two-thirds of the hotel rooms in service to-day is dull and drab without charm. Architect F. Hennessy points out that changes in the means of transportation, vacation, and methods of conducting business, are creating new needs in hotel facilities.

The hotel history is full of examples of poor planning and construction. For example, in the Caribbean area, one large hotel built a second pool when it found that the original one was shaded all the time by the hotel itself. There has been cases where hotels have been built with only a few hundred guest rooms to occupy conventional facilities for more than a thousand, and without the ability to expand. In a large hotel in Pennsylvania with function space for several thousand on a single floor, no good toilet facilities are available on that floor ! The worst blunder occurred many years ago, when it was discovered, only a few days before a new hotel was opened, that the architect had failed to provide for a kitchen! The important question is, what does the public want or need? Ignoring what the public wants or needs can be very costly. A major hotel in the USA had to spend nearly $ 300,000 a few years after it was built to add a swimming pool not originally planned.

According to Morris Lapidus, noted hotel architect, responsible for some of Miamis most glamourous edifies, hotel guests fall into two categories:

1. Business travellers
2. Pleasure travellers.

The business travellers want a comfortable bed, easy accessible closet and drawers, space, good lighting for reading, excellent lighting for make-up or sharing and fast service.

The leisure travellers appreciate all these necessities, but above all, they want the atmosphere of their hotel and room, to reflect the ambience of the city or country in which they are visiting without detracting from the quality of the service. They want to feel as though they really are away from home. Thus both groups of travellers expect something different in the hotel than they all find at home. Now-a-days there is little demand from travellers for the 'home away from home' type of accommodation. Lapidus further states, the effort to capture the feeling of home in a hotel room is futile and expensive. Today, the hotelier should be guided by what will give him maximum occupancy with minimum maintenance cost. Fig. 2.1, 2.2, 2.3 and 2.4 are the various types of hotel plan.

MODULAR CONSTRUCTION

This is the most recent and promising development in the construction of hotel buildings. The technique is the answer to the drastic decrease in building costs. This has cut down the construction time and costs by as much as 40 per cent as compared to traditional construction methods.

In this method of construction, room units are constructed separately and hoisted into place by crane. The procedure followed is to place all necessary electrical and plumbing conduits along with reinforcing steel, and to pour concrete to form the room module. After curing, the unit is ready to be trucked to the site and placed into position. Thus, the buildings are relatively of low cost, time saving in construction, fire-resistant and virtually sound proof as well.

SLIP FORMING

This is another recent technique of concrete extension in the hotel construction. The technique was used to raise the exterior walls and some of the interior structure of a 15-story hotel in St. Peters-burg, Florida. It enabled the hotel to be 'topped out' in just eight days. In Norfolk, Virginia, the slip forming technique used in construction of a 14-story motor-inn enabled the builders to cut three months from the normal constructions time for a property of this size. In the Norfolk property a three-foot thick reinforced slab was poured for the foundation. Then using a specially constructed wood and steel form, workmen poured concrete into the form continuously at the average rate of 9-1/2 inch per hour. At the same time the form was raised by a number of electrically operated hydraulic jacks while steel re-inforcing rods were inserted into the concrete.

TRI-ARC DESIGN

Many advances are taking place in the configuration of hotel buildings. The idea of tri-arc style was introduced by Travelodge International. The main advantages of this type of designing are:

1. Each room has a view.
2. The wedge shape of guest rooms permits each to have an unusually large bath and dressing area.
3. The control core, containing elevators, linen rooms, utilities and ice cube machines, facilitates economies in construction and operation.

CYLINDER-LIKE STRUCTURE

The cylinder-like design of a hotel building have a distinctive appearance and have the following advantages :–

1. Concentration of service and utility equipment at the centre core.
2. Lower construction and operating costs.
3. All guest rooms on the outer-side with view.
4. Ready-made for the popular roof top revolving restaurant or lounge.
5. Minimum resistance to wind.
6. Suitable for sites where land costs are high and minimum area is available.
7. Compatibility with circumferential ramps leading to parking.

Pix 2.1: Burj Dubai Tower

Pix 2.2: Taj Mumbai

Pix 2.3: The Oberoi, New Delhi

Pix 2.4: Le Meridien, New Delhi

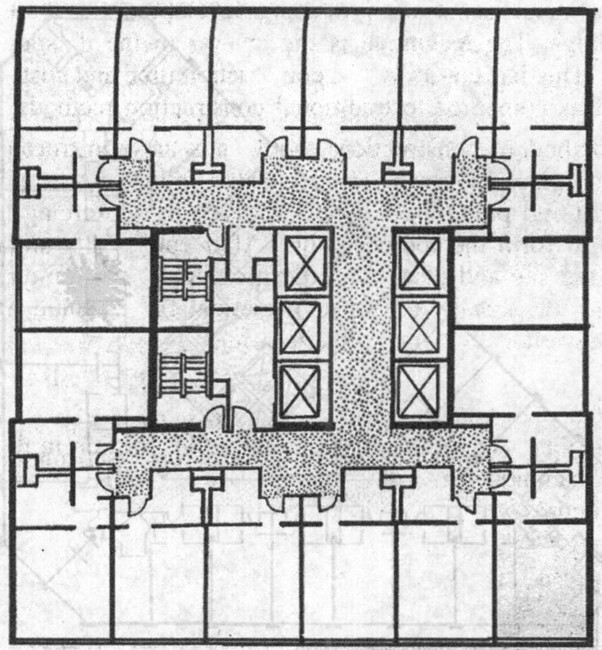

Fig. 2.1: A Square Hotel Plan.

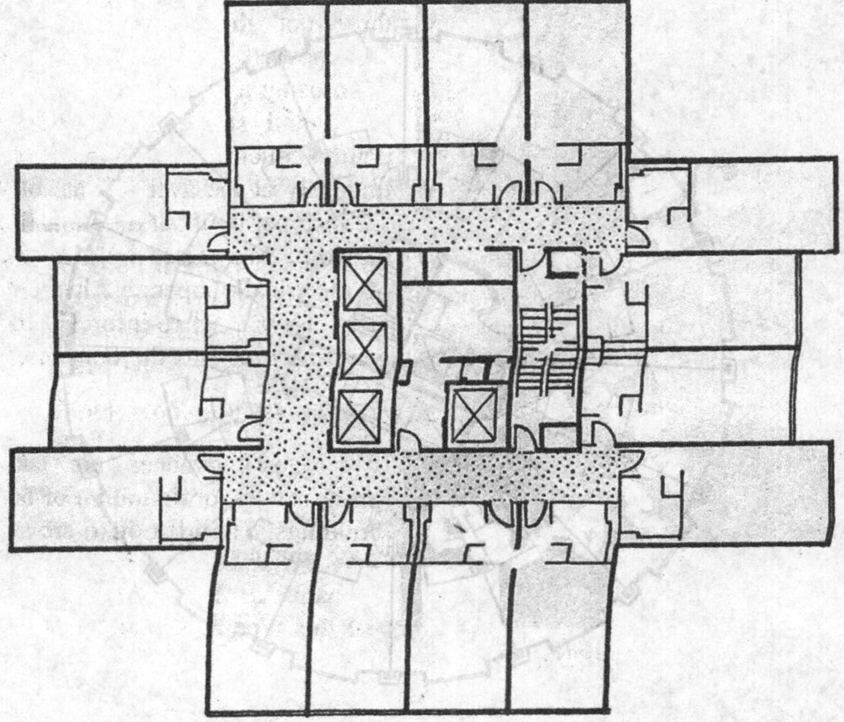

Fig. 2.2: A "Deformed" Square Hotel Plan.

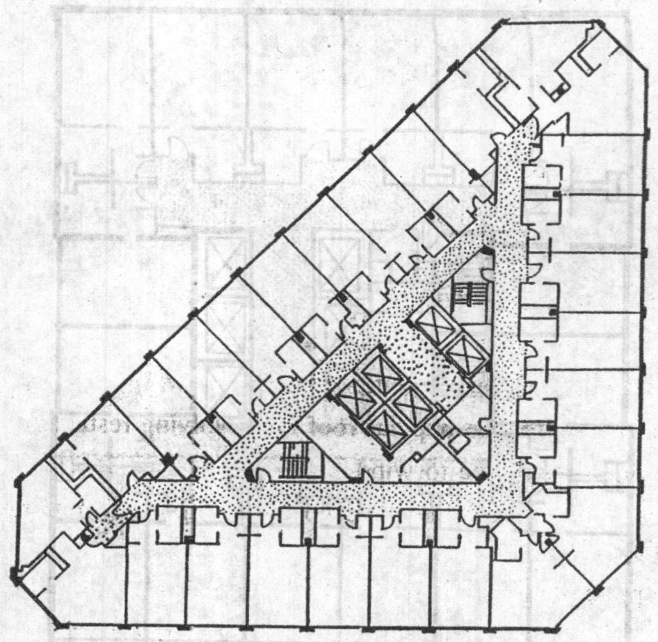

Fig. 2.3: A Triangular Hotel Plan with Interior Corridor.

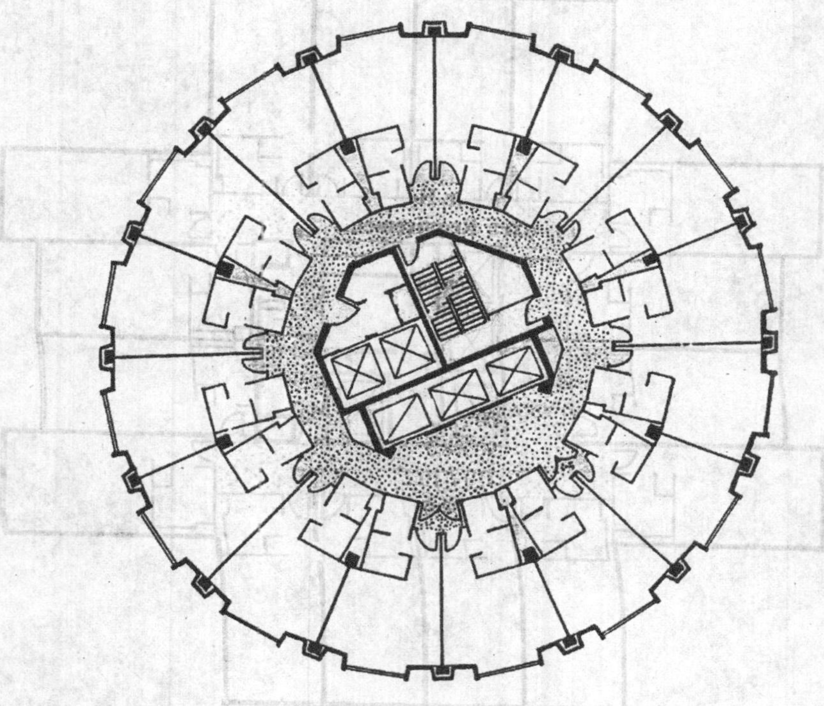

Fig. 2.4: A Circular Hotel Plan.

STANDARDS FOR ACCOMMODATION

Planning and designing of space requires due consideration. It determines the profitability of the hotel and restaurant business. A careful plan consideration to this aspect will benefit the hotel throughout its business operations. Some guidelines are given in Table 2.1 to prospective hoteliers and restauranters to enable them for an ideal space management and organisation.

Table 2.1 : Standard for Hotel Space Management Area Requirements

Sq ft/m²	Minimum Sq ft/m²	Standard Sq ft/m²	Luxury
1. **Bedrooms (including lobby and bath)**			
Single	60 / 5.5	70 / 6.5	–
Double	90 / 8.5	128 /12.2	–
Twin	110 / 10.2	215 / 20.0	260 / 24.0
2. Bath Rooms (if calculated separately)	43 / 4.0		
3. **Food and Beverage Areas :**			
Kitchen area	25-30% restaurant area		
Restaurant (Luxury)	18 ft² / 1.7 m² per person		
Medium Restaurant	14 ft² / 1.3 m² per person		
Coffee Shop	14 ft² / 1.3 m² per person		
Bar & Lounge	18 ft² / 1.7 m² per person		
Staff Canteen	12 ft² / 1.6 m² per person		
4. **Public Areas :**			
Banqueting rounds	10 - 12 ft² (1.1 m²) per person		
Banqueting springs	8 - 12 ft² (0.93 m²) per person		
Cocktail parties and Receptions	5 ft² (0.46 m²) per person		
Theatre seating	7 ft² (0.65 m²) per person		
Desk seating arrangement	16 ft² (1.49 m²) per person		
5. **Standard of performance as regards to production**			
Coffee Shop server	: 35 covers over lunch period		
	: 25 covers at dinner		
Restaurant silver	: 25 covers at lunch		
Service server	: 15 covers at dinner		
Dishwashers	: 110 cover per hour/per person		
Room attendants	: 12 - 15 occupied rooms per day per person		
Front office	: 55 occupied rooms per shift per person.		

Minimum standards for hotels and guest houses, including hotels andinns, were also drawn up by the British Tourist Authority, the English Tourist Board, the Scottish Tourist Board and the Wales Tourist Board.The BTA regards adherence to the minimum standards as a basic criterionfor the inclusion of establishments in its publications. Some of these standards are given in Table 2.2.

These minimum standards are applicable for accommodation in all licensed establishments and all other establishments with four or more letting bedrooms.

Table 2.2 : Minimum Standards for Accommodation

1. All bedrooms must conform to, or exceed, the following minimum dimensions for floor areas excluding private baths or shower area :

   (*i*) Single bedrooms 5.60 m² (60 sq ft)

   (*ii*) Double bedrooms 8.40 m² (90 sq ft)

   (*iii*) Twin-bedded rooms 10.20 m² (110 sqft)

   (*iv*) Family rooms :

   Minimum floor area of 280 m² (30 sq ft) plus :

   5.60 m² (60 sq ft) for each double bed and/or

   3.70 m² (40 sq ft) for each single adult bed, and/or

   1.85 m² (20 sq ft) for each cot.
2. All bedrooms must have reasonable free space for movement and for easy access to doors, drawers and beds.
3. All beds, other than those used by children, must conform to, or exceed, the following minimum dimensions :

   (*i*) Single beds : 183 cm × 76 cm (6 ft × 2 ft 6 in)

   (*ii*) Double beds : 183 cm × 122 cm (6 ft × 4 ft)
4. All mattresses must be spring interior, foam or of similar quality, and in sound condition. Bedding must be clean, and in sufficient quantity.
5. Beds must be made daily. Linen must be changed at least once per week and for every new resident guest.
6. All bedrooms must be equipped with a wash basin, having both hot and cold running water, either in the bedroom or in a private bathroom. A mirror must be above, or adjacent to the wash basin.

6. All bedrooms (or bathrooms) must be equipped with an electric shaver point.
7. All bedrooms must be supplied, for every new resident guest, with fresh soap and a clean towel and these must be replenished or changed as required.
8. All bedrooms must be provided with :

   (*i*) Dressing table or equivalent, and mirror

   (*ii*) Wardrobe, or clothes hanging space, equipped with at least four hangers per person

   (*iii*) Adequate drawer space

   (*iv*) Bedside table, or equivalent

   (*v*) One chair, or equivalent, per person (minimum of two in family rooms).

   (*vi*) Wastepaper container

   (*vii*) Ashtray

   (*viii*) One drinking vessel per person (minimum of two in family rooms)
9. All bedrooms must be equipped with bedside rugs or mats, where no carpet is provided.
10. All bedrooms must have at least one window and be adequately ventilated.
11. All bedrooms must be equipped with opaque curtains or blinds on all windows.

12. All bedrooms must be adequately heated, according to season, at no extra charge.
13. All bedrooms must be adequately lit, to the following minimum levels, with a light controlled from the bed :
    (*i*) Single bedrooms : 110 watts or equivalent
    (*ii*) Other bedrooms : 150 watts or equivalent.
14. All bedrooms must be fitted with a lock that will ensure privacy for guests and security for their property. Guests must be provided with a key to their bedrooms, duplicate or master keys being kept by the management.
15. All resident guests must be allowed access to their bedrooms at all reasonable times.

BATHROOMS

1. The establishment must have at least one bathroom, equipped with a bath or shower, for every fifteen resident guests (other than guests in bedrooms with private bathrooms).
2. Hot water must be available at all reasonable times, with no extra charge for baths or showers.
3. All private bathrooms must be equipped with a WC and either a bath or shower.

WCS

1. The establishment must have at least one WC for every ten resident guests (other than guests in bedrooms with private bathrooms).
2. Where there is only one WC, it must not be in a bathroom.
3. All WCs, including those in private bathrooms, must be equipped with toilet paper and a disposal bin.

GENERAL

1. The establishment must provide a residents' lounge or lounge area, appropriate to the type of establishment.
2. All public areas must be adequately heated, according to season, at no extra charge.
3. All public areas must be adequately lit for comfort and safety.
4. A telephone must be available for residents' use at all reasonable times.
5. The establishment must be kept clean throughout, and all exterior and interior decorations, furnishings, floor coverings and fittings must be maintained in good condition.

OPTIONAL STANDARDS : DISABLED GUESTS

The establishment may or may not be able to accommodate severely disabled guests (e.g. those in wheelchairs). Those that welcome disabled guests, and wish to be so designated in publications, must conform to the following minimum requirements :

1. At least one entrance must either have no steps or be equipped with a ramp whose gradient does not exceed 1 in 12.
2. All doors (including those of WCs, private bathrooms, etc.) must have a clear opening width of at least 74 cm (29 in.) with a head-on approach.
3. All essential accommodation, if not on the ground floor, must be served by an adequately sized lift.

4. Lift gates must be at least 80 cm (31.5 in.) wide; lifts must be at least 122 cm (48 in.) deep and 91 cm (36 in.) wide.
5. At least one bedroom and one public WC must be suitable for disabled guests.
6. In the bedrooms, private or public bathrooms and WCs used by the disabled, the clearance around beds, and to reach wash basins, WCs, etc. must be at least 75 cms (24.5 in.), and there must be turning space of 122 cm (48 in.) by 122 cm (48 in.).
7. The establishment must accept guide dogs, but may exclude them from dining or restaurant areas.

Although not required as minimum standards, it is strongly recommended that:

1. All beds, other than those for use by children, conform to, or exceed, the following dimensions :

Single beds	:	190 cm or 6 ft 3 in. x 90 cm or 3 ft
Double beds	:	190 cm or 6 ft 3 in. x 135 cm or 4 ft 6 in.

2. There be at least one bathroom for every ten resident guests (other than those with private bathrooms).
3. There be at least one WC for every eight resident guests (other than those with private bathrooms).

Pix 2.5: A Suite

Pix 2.6: A Double Room

GUEST ROOM DESIGNING

The location and type of guest served is to be considered in designing the type and size of a room in a hotel.

HIGHWAYS OR RESORT PROPERTIES

These hotels require a relatively high percentage of twin and larger rooms and connecting rooms that can be made into suites to accommodate family groups.

CITY HOTELS

These hotels require a higher number of singles although the trend overall is to larger rooms and larger beds. Two double beds in a room is becoming almost standard and even singles are likely to be furnished with a double bed since it is becoming increasingly common for an individual occupying a room to request a double bed. The studio-type designed rooms, serving as bedrooms at night and living rooms or temporary offices by day are not liked by businessmen.

We may analyse space utilization from the guest point of view. Most luxurious hotels found that as regards the in-room activities the guest wanted a suite rather than just a bedroom due to the following requirements:

1. Entertainment,
2. Working and relaxing atmosphere and
3. Sleeping.

According to an analysis, in traditional hotel rooms, there was an inordinate amount of wasted circular space and correspondingly awkward management of furniture. As a result of a study, Sheraton came up with a copyrighted room, in which the placement of bathroom is on the outside wall rather than along the corridors. This resulted in a room with considerably more living space and made possible the installation of each replacement of prefabricated bathrooms.

Sheraton considered the arrangements of furniture to improve space flexibility. It selected a new piece of furniture serving as a combination of chest of drawers, sofa and full double bed achieved by mounting conventional bed on an inclined track which can be looked into as a sofa or extended to serve as a second bed in the room. Given the potential flexibility of this convertible bed, Sheraton reasoned, that the first bed could be put up as a permanent base thus eliminating the need for carpeting or cleaning under it. The net effect of locating the bathroom, angling as well as to open up the view, and taking a new look at furniture designs and arrangements was to provide, essentially, the same overall area, more than twice the living space as could be obtained with the traditional layout.

FURNISHING

The trend, now-a-days, is to offer accommodation at low prices but there is a big category of visitors who still insist on amenities and are willing to pay for them. Below is a list of some items which are essential for a good hotel room:

1. Over-sized bed,
2. Coloured television

3. Selective piped-in music
4. Electric blankets and alarm clock
5. Black-out draperies
6. Game table with chairs
7. built-in refrigeration with ice-maker and
8. A balcony with furniture.

Early American, and 18th-19th century English styling in furniture are popular among tourists of all price ranges. Luxury establishments favoured French period furniture. The theme of integration, the furnishing of the guest rooms, the lobby, front desk, dining rooms, cocktail lounges, and meeting rooms should also blend together to create a merchandisiable atmosphere. Rather than each reflecting a different period of theme they should carry out the one such as English tavern, early American, French Provincial, or Scandinavian contemporary.

LIGHTING

The main object of lighting is not just to illuminate but to create a mood, an atmosphere which makes bedrooms more restful, public rooms more warm and friendly, and food more appetizing.

Exterior lighting requires illumination of the hotel sign so that it is visible at a distance and stands out from surrounding lighted areas. The entrance sign and entrance roadway of the hotel should be illuminated at a level considerably higher than street or highway lighting. The sign at a level from three to five times higher and the twice at least as bright. Ascent exterior lighting should be used to highlight landscaping and/or the facade of the building. Most hotels prefer colour corrected mercury vapour lamps mounted on aluminium poles for exterior lighting.

Lobby lighting has two main object, 'firstly,'to extend an invitation to the guest, and 'secondly,'to provide illumination for the work performed at the front desk. The higher level of illumination is required at the work area. It is usually best achieved by fluorescent light while the warmer, more subdued lighting in rest of the lobby, is got by the use of incandescent bulbs in attractive fixtures.

Poorly lighted hallways create a dismal atmosphere for guests. It may invite criminal activities.

The guest-rooms should have :

1. An overhead light controlled from the entrance
2. Lighted closet
3. Enough properly located wall outlets so long cords for lamps on TV are not necessary
4. Good lights over each chair
5. Lights conveniently placed for reading in bed and at least one light that can be turned on or off without getting out of bed.
6. The bathroom should have, in additon to an overhead light, fluorescent lamps with shields to illuminate the shaving mirror, and particularly, if it has two lavatories, an array of incadescent lights over a second make-up mirror.

Pix 2.7: A Typical Bed Room in a Hotel

Pix 2.8: A Bed Room

Pix 2.9: A Bed Room

Pix 2.10: A Bed Room

Pix 2.11: A Bed Room

Pix 2.12: A Bed Room

Pix 2.13: A Bed Room

Pix 2.14: A Bed Room

Pix 2.15: A Double Room

Pix 2.16: A Bed Room

Pix 2.17: A Deluxe Room

·**Pix 2.18:** A Suite

LIGHTING THE RESTAURANT

Basically, a food and beverage operation deals with merchandising a product to the sence of taste. Much of the success of these establishments depend upon the degree of appealing to the customers sense on sight. The light should keep food looking appetizing and reflect the kind of appreciation it deserves. For example, the break-fast room or coffee shop at noon, should be well-lighted not only for a cherry atmosphere, but to stimulate turnover in the restaurant. At dinner time, if you have subdued lighting it may encourage lingering but at the same time it may persuade guests to make an occasion of the meal by ordering more expensive items along with wine and other niceties of grand dining. In addition to the general area lighting of the food services operation, it is desirable to have some kind of extra light at each table. It may be provided by stops in the ceiling, cove lighting or lamps. For mood and atmosphere, lighting could focus on faces such as oil paintings, a brick wall, sculpture, grained wood etc. Proper and adequate illumination be provided in all areas of the restaurant.

QUESTIONS AND ASSIGNMENTS

1. What function could you bear in mind while planing a hotel in a developing tourist area ? How far do you think 'careful selection of site is important'.
2. What considerations should weight upon a promoter in selecting a site for establishing a 3-star hotel ? Explain fully. *(IHMs)*
3. **Write notes on :**
   (*i*) Certificate for Commencement of Business
   (*ii*) International Hotel Regulations
   (*iii*) Settlement of Guest Bills
   (*iv*) Functional Layout of a Kitchen. *(DTHM)*
4. Prepare in the form of a brief to an architect, a description of your principal requirements in terms of space, operation and environment for the design of a catering operation of your own choice. *(HCIMA London)*

5. As a catering manager you are a member of the design team concerned with planning the food production area for a new restaurant seating 120- customers. Define your role in such a team and describe the particular points on which you would seek to influence design criteria and layout proposals. (*HCIMA London*)

6. An improper layout causes endless problems in the operation of a commercial restaurant. Enumerate and explain in 300-words the points to be borne in mind while planning the layout of a commercial restaurant. (*DTHM*)

7. **Answer the following:**
   (*i*) Five star hotels are not only catering establishment in India. Write 5-lines each on 5-star catering establishments
   (*ii*) Name eight different types of restaurants
   (*iii*) Name six other food outlets
   (*iv*) What are the important steps to consider in choosing as hotel location
   (*v*) When a hotel/restaurant is for sale what are some of the questions that should be asked?
   (*vi*) What are the main advantages of buying and leasing a franchise ?

CHAPTER 3

Management and Organisation

OBJECTIVES

After studying this chapter, you should be able to :

1. *Identify the departments of a hotel*
2. *Understand organisational structure*
3. *Explain the facilities and services in a hotel*
4. *Know the different types of rooms in a hotel*
5. *Explain the basics of pricing policy*
6. *Analyse the determination of room tariffs and*
7. *Describe the methods of fixing room rates in Indianhotels.*
8. *Categorize the activities of a hotel under different departments and*
9. *Understand the level of professional development.*

ORGANISATION

Organisation is basically concerned with matters such as the decision of tasks within the hotel, position of responsibility and authority and the relation between them. It helps in introducing the concepts of span of control, level of management and delegation. Looking about 20 years back, a hotel used to have a large number of individuals and departments directly responsible to the manager. The hotel manager was mainly concerned with the guests and closely involved in all aspects of operations. There existed no authority on the *Chef*, the head waiter, and the house-keeper. The manager had most of the technical skills and his approach was that of a technician rather than the manager of the business. Financial matters and control was in the hands of the owner/proprietor. Personnel management was limited to hiring of the staff according to the requirements of the hotel.

Gradually, the whole profile started changing due to the growth in the travel market, increase in the number of hotels and the size of the ownership. New and scientific business techniques, management thought and commercial practices entered into the trade. Hotel education and training started flourishing. Higher quality of management found its place into the hotel world. The front office, uniformed services and house-keeping started getting recognised as departments. The front office manager, room manager, assistant manager, food and beverages manager and similar other positions specifically responsible for the specialist jobs, were appointed by the hotel. Now, we find hotels have positions for public relations, marketing and sales, purchasing, guest relations, entertainment, banqueting etc. Each hotel is trying to be self-sufficient in the provision of its guest services and supporting requirements.

The hotel is a business connected with several distant products, services and facilities which are offered in various combinations. Most effective organisation structures follow a classification and provide for clear profit and loss centre responsibilities. The following is a common pattern of uniform and standard systems of accounting practice in a number of hotels :

OPERATING DEPARTMENTS (Revenue Earning Departments)

1. Major (Primary)
   (*i*) Room
   (*ii*) Food
   (*iii*) Beverages
2. Minor ancillary (Minor Revenue Earning Departments)
   (*i*) Guest Telephones
   (*ii*) Guest Laundry and Valeting
   (*iii*) Guest Services.
3. Support Service Departments (undistributed overheads)
   (*i*) Administration and General
   (*ii*) Marketing
   (*iii*) Property Operation, Maintenance and Energy.

An organisation is a unified consolidated group of elements or a body of persons organised for some specific purpose. In order to function smoothly and to fulfil the objectives of hotel business, its various components must be systematically arranged. Therefore, there is no fixed ideal hotel organisational patterns as the best for a particular hotel.

The organisation of a numbers of hotels, large or small, deluxe or middle class, show that most of them have been organised on well defined principles of management. Traditionally, the hotel industry has been organised departmentally. In other words, individuals, who perform similar tasks, are grouped in a department, for example, housekeeping employees form the housekeeping department, front office employees form the front office department. The organisation chart of hotels varies. The larger the hotel, the greater the need for specialisation. In small hotels employees are expected to perform a number of different tasks. However, in luxury and deluxe hotels, employees are most specialised. They have some knowledge about other tasks in the different departments but they have to know a lot about their own special jobs. Thus in deluxe hotels there is a need for greater specialisation than in middle class hotels.

The scope, complexity and pattern of hotel organisation will vary according to the aims, objectives and size of an individual unit. A hotel organisational structure which would suit a large hotel may be wasteful and ineffective for another unit. The purpose of a suitable organisational structure is to be to fit in given objectives.

The main concepts forming the basis of any organisational structure are:

1. Duties : This comprises the activities by the individual by virtue of his employment in the hotel.
2. Authority: It is a right to acquire action from others and the ability to get things done. It results from a combination of sound knowledge, skill and personal attributes.

To frame the suitable organisational structure, the first priority must be given to establish the different levels of authority and a clear chain of command known as line management. It will help in the assignment, integration and delegation of responsibilities and duties. The organisational aspects of the different hotels from small to large reveal a lot of variation. The distribution of the authority and responsibility varies from hotel to hotel. This is because what helps in the smooth running of a deluxe hotel, may not be good for a middle class or small hotel. The organisation must be suited to the enterprise depending on the stage of its development.

As already mentioned, a model hotel organisation plan does not exist. It is affected by a number of factors, like its location, the type of service offered, the structural layout of the hotel, the background and the training of the manager, the type of the ownership, the degree of luxury as reflected in the extent of personal service, rate of occupancy, the basic design of the hotel in facilitating operations and to the extent to which the various services are contracted out. The number of employees in different areas of a hotel will vary with the sales mix of activities and extent of personal service.

In many countries hotels have been graded in order to give the potential customer an indication of service and style of facilities he can expect. For example, luxury hotels are marked as 5-star and 4-star or grade I, whilst modest hotels are as 3-star and 2-star or grade II, and the low class hotels as 1-star or grade III. Such grading is carried out by an official of an approved government body such as Department of Tourism or Hotel Division or a Classification Committee formed for this specific purpose. The facilities, the amenities, the comfort, the space, the number of rooms, the central heating and air-conditioning etc. are taken note of while grading the hotel.

The success of the hotel business depends mainly upon its organisational and functional capacity of each of the department. The goal of each department should be the overall goal of the hotel. The employees should be taught high standard of service and personal conduct which are essential for the successful running of the hotel. The practices of hoteliering vary considerably throughout the world. The requirement of greater efficiency and a better return from hotel investments have necessitated a new approach to traditional hotel operation. Japan follows the American practice not only in the construction of building but also in running the hotels. In India, hotel groups are trying to follow the latest and the most modern techniques of hoteliering. Personal supervision by the top management of the day-to-day hotel operations, is very common in the USA, with the result the hotel industry in the USA has built some of the best hotel companies in the world.

FACILITIES AND SERVICES

The gradual development of the hotel industry has led to the expansion of its activities. Earlier hotels provided lodging, food and protection of luggage. A modern hotel, besides these, offers a number of luxuries under the same roof. These facilities and services are operated and provided by the hotel itself while some others are provided by outsiders contracted by the hotel. Fig. 3.1 indicates the various activities of a hotel.

A hotel is defined as an establishment that provides goods and services to transit guests in search of over-night accommodation. The main functions of a hotel are provision of accommodation, sale of food and beverages and provision of entertainment. Although the hotel business all over the world presents a range of services, most of the key business activities of the hotels are common such as :

LODGING, ROOMS AND BEDS

Room sales are the most profitable source of revenue of a hotel. It yields the highest profit margins and as such constitutes the main source of hotel operating profit. Hotel

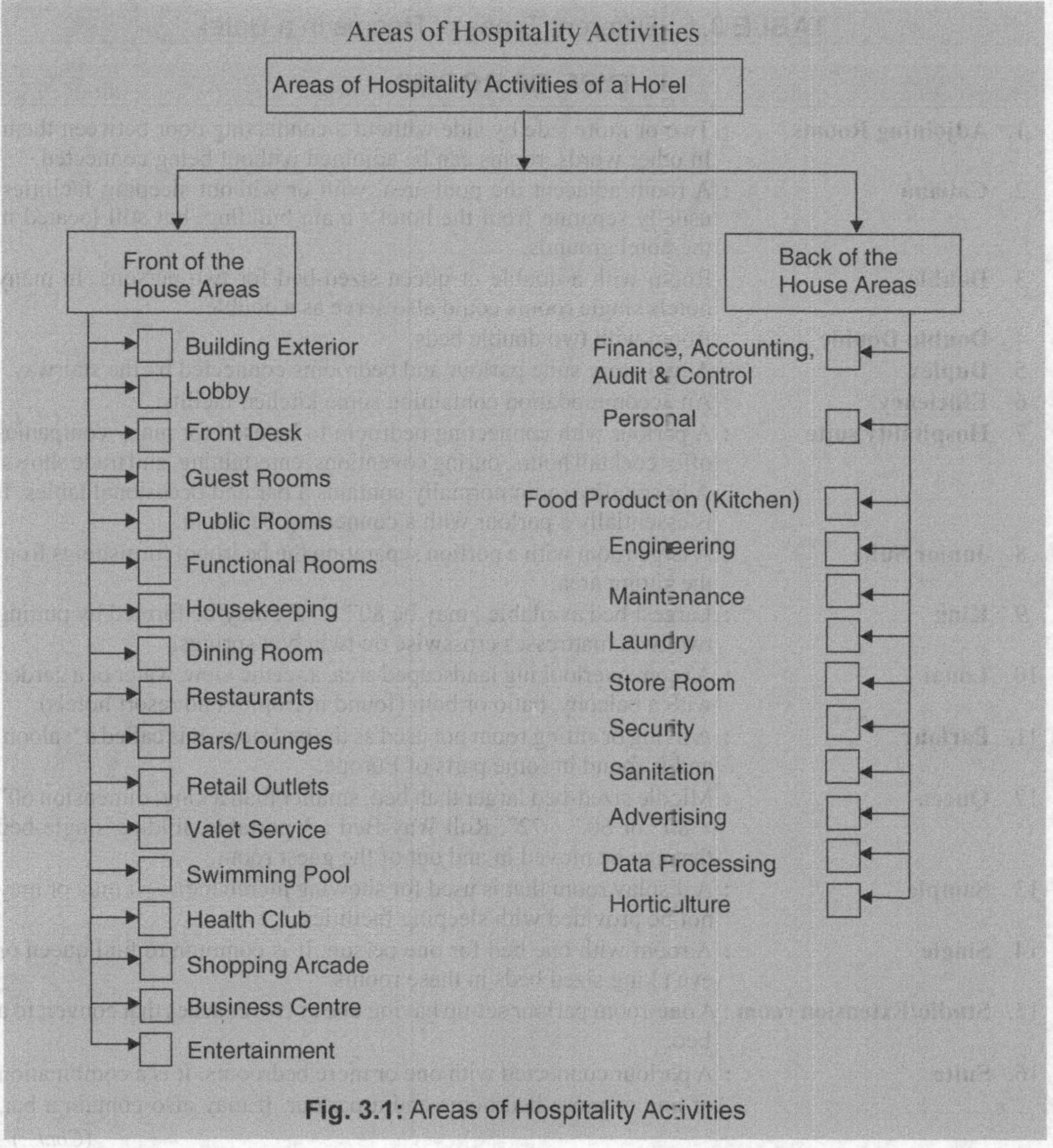

Fig. 3.1: Areas of Hospitality Activities

accommodation has changed over the years with the rising standard of living. Former 'luxuries' like private bathrooms or bedrooms even in top class hotels, are now commonplaces in modern simple hotels. In first class hotels, wealthy guests expect more than just a bed and bathroom. There are suites provided by the hotels which include additional lounge, sitting room and private dining room facilities. For modern single and double bedroom, 'studio' type accommodation is popular. Many hotel rooms come in a variety of sizes, shapes and decor. Various classifications of room and bed sizes available in hotels are given in Table 3.1.

The variety of rooms offered throughout the years were developed in response to customers' needs. As social and business needs change, the style of the hotel rooms must also change. Experienced hotels remain ahead of competition by developing and testing new concepts in rooms to meet needs of particular market segments. New room concepts may require design and engineering changes, deletion of furnishings and limited remodeling.

TABLE 3.1 : Different Types of Rooms in a Hotel

TYPE OF ROOMS	
1. **Adjoining Rooms**	: Two or more side by side without a connecting door between them. In other words, rooms can be adjoined without being connected.
2. **Cabana**	: A room adjacent the pool area, with or without sleeping facilities; usually separate from the hotel's main building, but still located in the hotel grounds.
3. **Double**	: Room with a double or queen sized-bed for two persons. In many hotels single rooms could also serve as a double.
4. **Double-Double**	: Room with two double beds.
5. **Duplex**	: A two-story suite parlour and bedrooms connected by the stairway.
6. **Efficiency**	: An accommodation containing some kitchen facility.
7. **Hospitality suite**	: A parlour with connecting bedroom to be used for many companies offer cocktail hours, during coventions, entertaining, and trade shows. A hospitality room normally contains a bar and occasional tables. It is essentially a parlour with a connecting bedroom.
8. **Junior Suite**	: A large room with a portion separating the bedroom furnishings from the sitting area.
9. **King**	: Largest bed available ; may be 80" × 72"; may be formed by putting two twin mattresses crosswise on twin box springs.
10. **Lonai**	: A room overlooking landscaped area, a scenic view, water or a garden with a balcony, patio or both (found in tropics and resort hotels).
11. **Parlour**	: A living or sitting room not used as the bedroom. It is called a 'saloon' and is found in some parts of Europe.
12. **Queen**	: Middle sized-bed larger than bed, smaller than a king; dimension 60" × 80" or 60" × 72". Roll Way Bed : A portable, folding single-bed that can be moved in and out of the guest room.
13. **Sample**	: A display room that is used for showing merchandise. It may or may not be provided with sleeping facilities.
14. **Single**	: A room with one bed for one person. It is common to find queen or even king sized beds in these rooms.
15. **Studio/Extension room**	: A one-room parlour set-up having one or two coaches that convert to a bed.
16. **Suite**	: A parlour connected with one or more bedrooms. It is a combination of one or more bedrooms and a parlour. It may also contain a bar,

(Cont...)

more than one bathroom, a small kitchen, and other facilities.

17. **Twin** : A room with twin beds/two single beds.
18. **Twin-Double/Family room** : A room with two double beds for two, three or four persons. This room may be referred to as a 'family' room or double room.
19. **Duplex** : A suite that separates into two stories joined by stairs.
20. **Pent House** : This opens on to the roof and might be accompanied by a swimming pool, patio, a tennis court and other amenities.
21. **Hotel within a Hotel** : It is a club suite floor with special amenities for executive class travellers.

ROOM RATES / TARIFFS

GUESS WORK APPROACH

Hotels may use different methods of determination of room rates. In fact most of the hotel room rates are based on simple guess work. These hotels base their room rates on the prevalent rates charged by their neighbouring hotels, and follow an annual increase in line with inflation. However, this method is not advisable for the newly established hotels. Each hotel should establish its own rate on a more scientific basis, which is a simple task.

RULE OF THUMB APPROACH

Rule of thumb approach is one of the oldest and universal methods of determination of room rates. It is found that whether a hotel was built in India, Japan, London or Chicago, there is always a direct relationship between the cost of the investment in hotel property and the average room rate. According to the rule of thumb formula, for every ₹ 10,000/- spent on building, a hotel should charge ₹ 10/- per room-night. For example, a hotel costing ₹ 200 lakh to build with 500 rooms gives a total cost of ₹ 4,00,000/- per room. A room rate of ₹ 400/- per night plus break-fast would, therefore, be appropriate.

This approach of calculating the average room rate is based on certain operating assumptions such as, that the hotel under consideration is a large unit, the average annual occupancy of the hotel varies between 65% and 70% and the hotel has additional income from other sources, such as food and beverage sale, store rentals, and other departmental incomes.

This approach of determining the room rates has some limitations as it does not take into account the occupancy, current rate of interest on capital, rate of inflation, the period of its application etc. All three assumptions mentioned in the formula, do not exist in the modern hotel operation. For instance, take the average annual occupancy. The annual occupancy percentage of most hotels in India does not fall in the range of 65% to 70%. In most of the hotels, occupancies have been fluctuating continuously. There is no income stability in the existing hotels, and new hotels have a very modest income from their food and beverage outlets. Owing to these limitations, this rule of thumb approach is no longer relied upon as an adequate guide in the determination of room rates. However, the formula may be adopted as a starting point in case of new hotel properties.

BOTTOM UP APPROACH

The bottom up approach to pricing is the most popular method of fixing the room rates in United States, United Kingdom, and several European countries. In this method, while preparing the profit and loss account in a vertical form, the usual practice is to start with the sale volume, deduct all the expenses and in the end arrive at the net profit required, project the expenses and in the end, arrive at the desired sales volume. This is why it is known as the bottom up approach. In brief, the bottom up procedure is explained as follows :

Step I : Determine the amount of profit aimed at. This will depend upon the profits achieved in recent years, current trends in hotel occupancies and pattern of costs behaviour.

Step II : Determine the operating costs for the next period. In case of an existing hotel, accurate projections of operating costs could be made on the basis of the past data/ information.

Step III : Arrive at the required volume of room sales on the basis of the profit and operating costs.

Step IV : On the basis of estimated percentage of room occupancy, calculate the desired average room rate.

This method is clearly a profit-oriented method. It is applied with the intention to ensure that the hotel seeks adequate profitability with the right marketing context. The rates so calculated should be compared to the relevant rates charged by similar hotels. One of the main drawbacks of the system is that in this case we assume a particular level of food and beverage departmental profit before actually determining on the level of room rates to be charged. In actual practice the volume of departmental profit secured from food and beverage operation depends, among others, on the room rates charged.

As regards to calculation of single and double room rates, there is no suitable formula available. In case the average room rate is calculated by per square footage / meter, single and double rates can easily be calculated; otherwise one will have to proceed by trial and error. Since the projected room rate is, say ₹ 500/-, the single room rate will be less than ₹ 500/- and double rate more than ₹ 500/-.

OPERATING COST APPROACH

Yet another method of calculating or determination of room rates is the operating cost basis. According to this approach, to be a profitable venture, a hotel should know its operating costs. This could be done by preparing a budget based on detailed estimates of room occupancy, overhead costs (wages, laundry costs, energy costs), variable expenses, and fixed charges. The total operating costs are calculated by adding variable overheads, fixed overheads minus profit from food and beverage and other departments. An estimate is made of the net costs to be covered by sales of the room division. This is calculated by adding operating costs and profit before tax. The total number of room-nights are calculated by the following formula :

$$\text{Room Nights} = \frac{\text{Total number of rooms} \times \text{Occupancy \%} \times 365}{100}$$

The room rate is calculated as follows :

$$\text{Rate} = \frac{\text{Net cost to be recovered}}{\text{Rooms to be sold}}$$

The room rates for functional areas in each of the hotel are fixed in an arbitrary fashion. The cost of these areas is not given any consideration. It is advisable to take the total cost of operating the whole hotel. From the annual financial report, one can take the variable costs, fixed costs, and the amount of wages directly attributable to the banqueting department.

Thus, in this method, a budget is made on the basis of an estimated room occupancy. Overheads such as wages, laundry costs, energy costs and other variable and fixed charges are calculated. An example of this calculation is given in Table 3.2 and Table 3.3

TABLE 3.2 : Average Room Rate

Calculation of Operating Cost :

Total Costs		(₹ in lacs)
Fixed Costs	15.19	
Variable Overheads	114.25	
Wages (excluding F&B deptt)	194.38	323.82
Less Profit from Food & Beverages		121.55
Operating Costs		202.27

Calculation Of Room Revenue :

Operating costs		202.27
Profit after tax (20% on estimated investment of ₹ 925,00,000) :		
Profit before tax assessment	308.33	
Less 40% tax	123.33	185.00
Estimated room revenue		387.27

Calculation Of Room Nights :

Number of Rooms	250
Budgeted Room Occupancy	65%

$$\text{Room Nights} = \frac{250 \times 65 \times 365}{100}$$

Calculation Of Average Room Rate :

$$= \frac{\text{Room revenue to be recovered}}{\text{Rooms to be sold}} = \frac{387,27,000}{59,312.50} = ₹\ 652.93/\text{- say } ₹\ 653/\text{-}$$

Thus, ₹ 653/- is the average room rate required to produce the budgeted profit. To reach this figure, the room tariff to be charged should be higher than ₹ 653/-. The hotel may increase this rate taking into account the prevalent market conditions.

For calculating double occupancy rate 20 - 25 % of single rate be added to this rate.

ROOM RATE BASED ON SQUARE FOOTAGE

This method is mostly used for letting the space for offices. A hotel may also adopt this method of determining the room rate. In this method the following basic information is required :

1. Total area of bedrooms
2. The size of each bedroom
3. The estimated amount to produce from each room to cover overheads.

EXAMPLE :

Let us assume a hotel of 250-bedrooms

Suppose total floor area of occupied bedrooms = 50,000 sq ft

which is broken-down as follows :

Single 150 sq ft (15 m^2) 125 = 18,750 (1,875m^2)

Double 250 sq ft (25 m^2) 125 = 31,250 (3,125m^2)

50,000 (5,000 m^2)

As per the Figure 3.7, the total budget revenue is ₹ 387.27 lakh, the revenue per night could be :

$$\text{Revenue per night} = \frac{387,27,000}{365} = ₹\ 1,06,101/-$$

Sales per square footage will be calculated as follows :

$$\text{Sales per sq. footage} = \frac{1,06,101}{50,000} = ₹\ 2.12 \text{ per sq ft}$$

or

$$= \frac{1,06,101}{5,000} = ₹\ 21.22 \text{ per m}^2$$

Therefore, the rate of single and double bed will be :

Single : 150 sq ft × 2.12 = ₹ 318/-

Double : 250 sq ft × 2.12 = ₹ 318/-

This could be accepted as the basis of charging the room rate.

ROOM RATES FOR LONG-TERM LETS/APARTHOTELS

Most of the operators charge these rates on the basis of guess work, which may result in under-charging or over-charging. In case of under-charging, the owner loses the money and in case of over-charging he will lose the business. Therefore, after taking care of the relevant rent control Act/laws, following guidelines should be used in determining the room rates :

1. Determine the cost of letting a room as described above in the example.
2. Re-work the room cost figure assuming a very low profit of 10% over no profit to break-even.
3. Assume that maximum booking for this type of accommodation is 25% of available rooms.
4. Determine the amount for meals to be charged to cover the expenses. In cost of average meal (lunch, dinner and break-fast), add 50% to cover staff cost, add the room rate and full board food cost plus tax, if any. The figure so calculated will be multiplied by seven in order to arrive at the weekly rate.

CALCULATION OF RATES FOR FUNCTIONAL AREAS

The rates for functional areas are fixed in an arbitrary manner. However, it is advisable to know the actual cost of functional areas and decide the rates taking into consideration the completion and the importance of the functional areas in the overall revenues of the hotel. The following procedure could be adopted :

1. Measure each functional area individually in square yard/meter
2. Find out the percentage of functional areas to the total space of the hotel

3. Find out the operating cost of the hotel
4. Find out variable and fixed costs plus wages directly attributable to functional areas
5. Charge the operating costs to the functional area on the basis of its percentage in hotel space
6. Add a fixed percentage of hotel profit after-tax
7. Calculate the cost per square yard for each functional area
8. Determine the occupancy level on usage
9. Calculate the new rate on the basis of occupancy level which will uplift the basic cost to cover the lost revenue days
10. On the basis of competition and the importance of the functional areas in the hotel business, determine the rate to be charged.

TABLE 3.3 : Calculation of Daily Room Rate

Suppose in a hotel there are three functional areas as follows :

Area A : 1,250 sq yards
Area B : 3,000 sq yards
Area C : 1,875 sq yards

Fixed overheads cost of the hotel	:	₹ 194.38 lakh
Variable overheads of the hotel	:	₹ 114.25 lakh
Wages directly attributable to functional areas	:	₹ 18.75 lakh

Assuming 10% of hotel profit after-tax, and 25% of the hotel space is occupied by functional areas, we will calculate the daily rate for each functional areas.

TOTAL OVERHEADS FOR FUNCTIONAL AREAS :

Total Fixed Overheads	:	₹ 194.38 lakh	
Total Variable Costs	:	₹ 114.25 lakh	
Total Overheads	:	₹ 308.63 lakh	
25% of ₹ 308.63 lakh to functional areas	:		₹ 77.16 lakh
Add Wages (functional areas)	:		₹ 18.75 lakh
Add 10% of Hotel Profit-after Tax (assumed)	:		₹ 18.43 lakh
Total Overheads for functional areas	:		₹ 114.34 lakh

Therefore, cost per square yard will be :

$$\frac{\text{Total Overheads}}{\text{Total Square Yardage}} = \frac{114,34,000}{6,125} = ₹\ 1,866.78$$

DAILY RATE FOR EACH INDIVIDUAL FUNCTIONAL AREA

Functional Area	Daily rate	Daily rates on the basis of 65% usage
A	$\frac{1,250 \times 1,866.78}{365} = ₹\ 6,393.08$	$\frac{6393.08 \times 65}{100} = ₹\ 4,155.50$

Cont.

B	$\frac{3,000 \times 1,866.78}{365} = ₹\ 15,343.40$	$\frac{15,343.40 \times 65}{100} = ₹\ 9,972.21$
C	$\frac{1,875 \times 1866.78}{365} = ₹\ 9,589.62$	$\frac{9,589.62 \times 65}{100} = ₹\ 6,233.25$

HUBBART FORMULA

A formula for computing guest room rates was developed for the American Hotel & Motel Association by its financial and accounting consultants and named after Mr. Roy Hubbart, who was the Chairman of the Committee in-charge of the work. Actually, it has been used for years prior to its publication by the association in 1952. Under the Hubbart Formula, an estimate is made of the number of guest rooms to be sold in a year. Then, a tabulation is made of the cost of operation, to which is added an amount representing the expected fair return on the investment, which total amount is then divided by the number of estimated occupied rooms to obtain the average rate that must be charged. Taking into account the risk of the business, a return of 10% to 15% on equity capital is considered by most investors to be reasonable. Rate computed under the Hubbart Formula is best explained by the following illustration given in Table which uses a 90-room and a 360-room hotel.

TABLE 3.4 : Average Room Rate Computation using Hubbart Formula

	90-room hotel	**360-room hotel**
Estimate of Annual Operating Costs :		
Payroll except Catering Deptt.	₹ 16,80,000	₹ 105,00,000
Payroll Taxes	1,25,000	8,00,000
House-keeping	6,00,000	33,00,000
Telephone	3,50,000	19,00,000
Administrative and General	5,00,000	33,00,000
Advertising & Promotion	3,60,000	18,00,000
Heat, Light & Power	3,50,000	25,00,000
Repair & Maintenance	3,00,000	20,00,000
Total Operating Expenses	₹ 42,65,000	2,61,00,000
Fixed charges and Return on Capital :		
Local Property Taxes	₹ 3,75,000	18,00,000
Insurance on Property	70,000	3,75,000
Depreciation	14,50,000	90,00,000
Interest on Borrowed Capital	9,00,000	59,00,000
Return on Equity Investment	15,00,000	30,00,000
Total Cost and Expected Profit	₹ 85,60,000	4,61,75,000
Deduct :		
Income other than Guest Room Sales :		
Profit on Catering Operations	:	85,00,000

(Contd...)

Telephone Sales	₹ 3,60,000	18,75,000
Store Rentals and Other Incomes	4,00,000	15,00,000
Total Credits	₹ 7,60,000	1,18,75,000
Amount to be provided by Guest Room Sales	₹ 78,00,000	3,43,00,000
Computation of Rent-necessary to cover total available room per year	32,850	1,13,400
Rooms based on 70% occupancy	22,995	91,980
Net cost divided by occupied rooms which is an Average Rate	₹ 1,018	1,119
Estimated Double Occupancy	50%	40%
AVERAGE RATE PER GUEST	₹ 679	₹ 799
Notes on values and financing assumed :		
Original cost of building, land and equipment	₹ 3,00,00,000	1,35,00,000
Borrowed Capital 6%	1,50,00,000	6,50,00,000
Debenture and Loan 5%	–	4,00,00,000
Equity Capital 10%	1,50,00,000	–
Equity Capital 15%	–	2,00,00,000
AVERAGE OCCUPANCY 70%		

DETERMINATION OF HOTEL ROOM TARIFFS (RATES) IN INDIA

In the years 1950's the government decided to rationalise the room tariff structure of hotels in the country. In pursuance of this decision a Hotel Standards and Rate Structure Committee was set up in 1957. The terms of reference of this Committee,'inter-alia,' stated: Taking into account the price level prevailing in India, the cost of hotel-keeping and other relevant factors to recommend rational rate structure for each category of hotels and other establishments."

The Hotel Standards and Rate Structure Committee submitted its report to the government in June, 1958. With regard to the hotel room rate structure, the committee observed that while each hotel determined the room tariff taking into account the construction cost, operational costs, value of land and building, prices of commodities etc., no uniform pattern had become discernible in arriving at the room tariff. The committee, therefore, expressed the views that it was essential that a formula be evolved for rationalizing the determination of hotel room tariff. The committee thus suggested the adoption of the Hubbart Formula followed by the American Hotel and Motel Association with appropriate modifications to suit Indian conditions. The modified formula was accepted by the government for determining hotel room tariff in the country.

In 1962, the government appointed a Hotel Classification Committee to classify hotels on the star category based on internationally accepted star system. For reviewing the rates charged by such hotels, as also to classify new hotels according to the star system, the government appointed the Hotel Review and Survey Committee in 1967 with the additional objective of determining a rational basis for standardising room tariff of each category. The committee recommended the continuance of the Modified Hubbart Formula for determining the room tariff of approved and classified hotels. Subsequently the Department of Tourism slightly amended the Modified Hubbart Formula for deleting the income-tax paid by the hotel from its operational costs.

The Modified Hubbart Formula was, thus, in operation for determining the hotel room tariff for almost 20 years. It was thus felt that a review of the formula was necessary as over the years certain ambiguities had crept in its application due to different interpretations of the Formula. For instance, in some cases the return on land and building was claimed twice, once at 6% or 8% on their value, and again at 10% on the capital employed which also included the cost of land and building. In some cases capital employed in hotel-keepingwas interpreted as only the working capital. To obviate such anomalies in the interpretation of the Modified Hubbart Formula, there was a need to undertake a review of the formula, as also to examine in depth the hotel construction and operational costs for determining, if considered necessary, a new formula on which hotel room tariff could be structured.

The following points have a bearing on hotel tariff structuring :

1. Whether the return on property, viz., land and building, should be calculated on the basis of its present-day fair value ?
2. Whether the return should be calculated on the historical value i.e. book value of the property after allowing for depreciation ?
3. Whether in case the return was calculated on the present-day fair value of the property, interest and income-tax should be allowed as expenditure ?

It is felt that the hotel room tariff formula should be based on the historical value or the book value of the property. However, those hotels operating for more than 10 years may be given an option to work out their tariff on the basis of their current fair value of the property, viz., land and building as certified by a government approved valuer.

The return on capital invested should be adequate enough to service the loan, pay interest on it, pay dividends to shareholders, and in addition, it should help to create sufficient reserves for meeting the cost of renovations, replacements, etc. since rapid obsolescence of equipment, decor, and wear and tear are only too frequent in the hotel industry.

Keeping all these factors in view as also the fact that hotel industry is highly capital intensive, a return of 12.5% on capital invested, after deducting interest, taxation (including income-tax), and actual depreciation as claimed for income-tax purposes excluding the initial depreciation on hotel building, if any, be allowed to hotels which work out their tariff on the basis of the historical value or book value of their property. In the case of hotels exercising the option to adopt the current fair value of the property, they may continue to be allowed, as at present, a return of 8% on the fair value of the land and building as certified by a government approved valuer and 10% on the depreciated value as per rates claimed for income-tax purposes of other assets.

The following will constitute the capital employed for the purpose of claiming return on capital investment :

1. Net Fixed Assets (after charging depreciation claimed for income-tax purposes) : consisting of land, building, plant and machinery, furniture, fixtures and other equipment, vehicles, etc., and

2. Current Assets minus Current Liabilities.

In view of the fact that in several cases hotels now enjoyed a high occupancy rate of over 80% to 90%, it no longer appeared realistic to work out the tariff at 60% as prescribed in the Modified Hubbart Formula being followed for determining the hotel room tariff. Hence, it would be more appropriate to adopt an occupancy ratio of 70% for this purpose. However, in order to ensure that hotels having less than 70% occupancy did not suffer any disadvantage, such hotels may be given the option of taking into account the actual average occupancy of three immediate preceding completed years. Further in the case of a new hotel, the occupancy ratio may be determined on the basis of the projected or anticipated occupancy depending upon its category, location and other related factors.

New formulas may be worked out on the basis of the following common denominators:

1. The return on investment should be calculated on the fair market value/replacement value.
2. The return on investment should be linked to the operating rates of banks and not in the manner in which the property is financed.
3. The occupancy ratio should be kept uniform at 60%.
4. The ratio of single and double occupancy should be kept at 80% and 20%, respectively.

The background to the fixation/revision of hotel room tariff is that in accordance with the regulatory conditions prescribed by the government, all hotels approved by it are required to fix/revise the tariff with the prior approval of the government. This regulatory function is being performed for the last over 25 years as it was felt necessary to control tariff of hotels in India so that as a tourist destination, India's competitiveness did not get eroded in the international market.

It was discovered during application of the existing formula that certain provisions of the formula led to a steep rise in tariff in the case of a number of hotels. The increase was found to be far in excess of the general inflation rate in the country. During the intervening period from 1980 the revision in room tariff was allowed on ad-hoc basis. To remedy the situation, a working group was set up to have a fresh look at the formula and to suggest necessary modifications so as to remove the anomalies. The working group submitted its report in March, 1986, suggesting a new formula called the modification formula for calculation of room tariff.

The modifications recommended in the new formula cleansed the old formula of the inflationary distortions which had crept into it and were detected during the course of its actual application. However, the Federation of Hotel and Restaurant Associations of India (FHRAI) made certain suggestions in some respects and after a series of meetings between the FHRAI and the government, the modified formula for calculation of room tariff was finalised and circulated to all approved hotels. The formula has the twin objective of ensuring value for money to the customers and a fair and reasonable return on investment.

The room tariff of a hotel of the higher star category is generally more than the tariff of hotels of the lower star category located at the small place, but the formula for the fixation/revision of tariff is related to the capital structure of a hotel in that it provides for a post-tax return of 15% on the capital employed (excluding borrowings) and a separate pre-tax return of 10% on long-term borrowings.

Except in the case of newly completed hotels, in which case the tariff is approved with reference to its approved star category and the tariff approved for hotels of the same star category at the similar station, the revision in tariff of old hotels is allowed only once a year which remains effective from 1st October to 30th September of the following year. Table 3.5 is the modified fomula for determination of the room rates in a hotel.

TABLE 3.5 : Modified Formula for Calculation of Room Tariff

All operating and overhead expenses under appropriate heads including depreciation (excluding initial depreciation on hotel building, if any) calculated either by the written down value method as allowed by the Income Tax Act, 1961 or straight-line method as permitted by section 205 (2) (b) of the Companies Act, 1956, subject to the condition that the method once adopted is consistently followed in the subsequent years.

Plus : Actual interest accrued for the period on all borrowings.

Plus : A net return of 15% on the net fixed assets (without revaluation) that working capital minus loans both short-term and long-term minus investment in other activities, after allowing for the national income-tax liabilities.

Plus : A pre-tax return of 10% on long-term borrowings only.

Note : Notional income-tax liability will be calculated on the basis of the rate of income-tax prescribed for the year for which tariff is being calculated. For example, if tax rate for a financial year for which the tariff is being calculated is 50% of income, the gross return on the basis of 15% pre-tax return will be 30%.

Less : Total gross revenue from all sources other than guest room sales, such as shop and storage rentals, food and beverages sales, cigarette and cigar sales, laundry and valet sales, telephone charges and miscellaneous income.

Balance : The balance is the amount to be realised from guest room sales.

Compute : Number of guest rooms multiplied by 365 days and assuming an occupancy ratio of 60%. However, in the case of hotels at hill stations and sea-side resorts occupancy ratio may be taken as the actual average annual room occupancy for the past two years or 60% whichever is less.

OPTION

1. Hotels more than 5 years old can claim :
   (*i*) Depreciation based on the replacement value of all the assets of the entire property, and certified by a government approved valuer.
   (*ii*) The fair market rental value as certified by a government approved valuer in the case of rented property as an expense.
2. The replacement value of the property/market rental value once adopted will remain in force for a minimum period of 5 years.
3. Provided that :
   (*i*) Hotels which follow the uniform system of accounts and can thus account for the operation of each department separately, may work out their room tariff by completely deleting the expenditure incurred and revenue earned on food and beverage operation.
   (*ii*) Hotels receiving management/consultancy fees may delete the amount so earned from gross hotel revenue while computing the hotel room tariff provided the expenditure incurred on rendering such a service is also deleted from the operating and overhead expenses.
4. Determination of single and double occupancy rate

(Cont...)

That shall be determined with reference to :

(*i*) Double occupancy ratio i.e., the percentage of rooms occupied by two or more than two persons in relation to the total number of room occupied, for the year for which the figure are furnished;

(*ii*) The difference in rupees as desired between the single occupancy and double occupancy rates as related to the average room rate worked out.

CERTIFICATION OF FIGURES

The figures furnished for purposes of fixing the tariff will be supported by the following Certificate from a Chartered Accountant/Cost Accountant :

We have verified the above statement prepared for the purpose of fixing the tariff, for the various single and double rooms in the hotel, from the books of account and certify that they are correct based upon the assumptions set out in the annexure to the statement. Further certified that wherever allocation of common expenses and/other funds are involved they are in accordance with the guidelines set in the tariff formula, if any, prescribed by the Government of India or otherwise in accordance with normal accounting practices."

EXPLANATORY NOTE

1. The Operating and Overhead Expenses other than depreciation will include :
   (*i*) Consumable supplies including cost of food and beverage sales.
   (*ii*) Payroll and related expenses.
   (*iii*) Entertainment, band, music, cabaret, laundry etc.
   (*iv*) Rent, rates, taxes, insurance.
   (*v*) Heat, light, power, gas.
   (*vi*) Repairs, maintenance and replacement.
   (*vii*) Commissions and discounts.
   (*viii*) Advertising and promotion expenses.
   (*ix*) Office and administrative expenses.
   (*x*) Directors' remuneration and meeting fees.
   (*xi*) Directors' travelling expenses.
   (*xii*) Auditors' remuneration.
   (*xiii*) Any other related expenses.
2. Room sales : The term room salesin the formula denotes guest room rent only.

ALLOCATION OF COMMON OVERHEADS

The overhead expenses of an entity that engages in activities other than hoteliering should be allocated in the proportion the Gross Revenue from such activity bears to the total turnover of the entity. The overhead expenses of any entity owning more than one unit of hotel should be distributed on the various operating units in the proportion, the turnover of each unit has to the total combined turnover of all operating units controlled by that entity.

ALLOCATION OF COMMON LOAN

In case where the long-term loan for each hotel is not specifically identifiable, the total long-term loan would be allocated in proportion to the next fixed assets of each hotel.

There are two major factors which are inter-linked with the determination of hotel room tariff. These are the need to introduce an uniform accounting system for hotels, and to bring about a rationalisation in hotel design. The government may consider :

1. Introducing the uniform accounting system in hotels on its approved list; and
2. Setting up a study group which should include an architect and an interior designer for formulating norms for the designs and construction of different categories of hotels of various sizes for ensuring optimum operational efficiency.

These measures will help to serve the interest of both the consumers and the hotels, and here again not only those of higher star category hotels in metropolitan cities, but also of hotels of all categories located at other centres in the country.

ROOM TARIFFS

The room rates are generally indicated through Room Tariffs, specimen of which are given in Fig. 3.2 and 3.3.

HOTEL ROOM TARIFFS

ABC HOTEL

City : ....

Hotel : ....

Address : ....

Telephone : ....

Telex/Fax : ....

Cable : ....

The hotel combining old-world panache with 20th century splendour.

ACCOMMODATION

Rooms .... Special luxury suites, duplex suites, pent houses. All rooms with telephones, attached baths, running hot and cold water and piped music.

INDIVIDUAL TARIFF

Single ₹ .... (U.S. $ ....)

Double ₹ .... (U.S. $ ....)

10% service charge extra

Suite rates on application.

DINING AND ENTERTAINMENT

A 24-hour Coffee Shop, Bars and several speciality restaurants.

SERVICES

24-hour Room Service, Laundry, House Doctor, Swimming Pool, Health Club and Beauty Saloon, Hair Dresser, Bank, Domestic and Internation Airlines Offices, Travel Agencies, Postal Services, Shopping Arcade, Florist, Art Gallery, Credit Cards : American Express Diner's Club, Bank Americard and Carte Blanche.

BANQUET AND CONVENTION FACILITIES

There are Banquet Rooms where functions ranging from small intimate gatherings to large internationl conventions can be held.

Fig. 3.2 : Specimen Room Tariffs

ROOM TARIFFS (*HOTEL ABC*)

LOCATION

.... km from shopping and entertainment areas (..... mins drive); ... km from airport (.... mins drive); ..km from railway station (.... mins. drive.)

ACCOMMODATION AND AMENITIES

.... rooms, centrally airconditioned with individual room-temperature control. TV and direct-dial telephones in all rooms. 5-channel stereo music. Attached baths with running hot and cold water. Round-the-clock room-service, Executive, Luxury and Presidential Suites, Beauty saloon and barber shop. Shopping Arcade, Airline, Travel counters, Bank, safe-deposit, 24-hour Money-Exchange. Doctor on call. Laundry and Dry Cleaning Service. Secretarial and Telex Services. Parking Facilities.

DINING

1. 24-hour restaurant overlooking the swimming-pool, snacks and light meals.
2. Roof-top Night Club, South-east Asian specialities. Live music. Dancing and entertainment.
3. Roof-top speciality restaurant serving foods from Spain, Italy and France.
4. Mughlai and Indian specialities.
5. Peshawari specialities from the Tandoor.
6. Restaurant overlooking water cascades, buffet meals.
7. Lounge Bar overlooking waterways.
8. Roof-top Bar.

RECREATION AND ENTERTAINMENT

1. Discotheque.
2. All-weather pool, heated in winter by solar energy.
3. Health Club and Yoga Centre.

BUSINESS AND BANQUETING

1. Banquet/Conference Hall. Divisible into 3 sections with pre-function area. Excellent acoustics. Latent audio-visual equipment. Simultaneous translation facilities.
2. Committee/Party Rooms.
3. Preview Theatre

INDIVIDUAL RATES EUROPEAN PLAN

Single Room	₹	US$
Double Room	....	....
Executive Room		
Dynasty Room	....	
Executive Suite	....	
Dynasty Suite	....	....
Luxury Apartment	....	....
Deluxe Apartment	....	....
Ashoka	....	....
Chandragupta	....	

(*Cont...*)

GROUP RATES

	Single ₹	Single US$	Double ₹	Double US$
European Plan	....	....	....	....
Modified	....	....	....	....
American Plan	....	....	....	....

Fig. 3.3 : Specimen Room Tariffs

FOOD AND BEVERAGES

The food and beverage department supplies food, beverages and drinks. These are tangible items and with a certain amount of skill and supervision, these can be provided to the guests' satisfaction. The traditional *table d'hote* and *a la carte* menus still form the basis for present-day eating. Each hotel has speciality restaurants and coffee shops.

SERVICE

It is an intangible item and requires ability and versatility. The hotel business is a highly personalized one. In addition to selling food, drinks and accommodation, it sells service to the public. Service element is a central factor in hoteliering. The service depends on the staff. The employees who render the service should be pleasant and courteous as well as skilful. The cost of staff and their skilled labour is a vital item while computing hotel charges. Service is the only product which cannot be purchased. It depends entirely upon its staff. Human behaviour in a free society cannot be standardised. It can only be guided and requires constant supervision, attention and training.

ENTERTAINMENT AND RECREATION

A hotel is concerned not only with bedrooms and restaurant facilities, the guest may also seek entertainment. Therefore, orchestras, cabarets, dance, drama, music etc. and other entertainment facilities are also inter-woven into the fabric of hotel services.

CONVENTION FACILITIES

Convention booking and selling is a highly competitive field. Conventions are held on local, national or international levels by large chains, companies, corporate, unions, educational institutions, etc.

OTHER FACILITIES

In addition to activities described above a hotel may provide :

1. Conference facilities
2. Business displays
3. Valet service
4. Television
5. Tennis courts
6. Squash
7. Shopping arcade
8. Handicrafts
9. Chemist shops
10. Car rentals
11. Travel agencies
12. Yoga and massage parlour
13. Notary public
14. Turkish bath and chiropodist
15. Saddle horses
16. Bookshops

17. Florists
18. Archery
19. Croquet and boating
20. Reservation service
21. Laundry and dry cleaning
22. Golf club
23. Computer services
24. Poolside barbeque
25. Instant Reservation
26. Tourist cars and garage facilities
27. Public stenographer and secretarial services.
28. Exhibition facilities
29. Guest laundry
30. Telephone
31. Swimming pool
32. Golf courts
33. Drugs store
34. Beauty parlour
35. Hairdresser
36. Tourist guides
37. Sight-seeing
38. Tobacco/cigars
39. News-stands
40. House physicians
41. Bath houses
42. Banking facilities
43. Landscape and gardens
44. Confectionery
45. Angling
46. Health club
47. Excursions
48. Airlines services
49. Telex and teleprinter
50. Business centre etc.
51. Jewellers
52. Boutique and discotheques.

The services found in majority of the deluxe hotels vary and change. However, all these facilities are not found in each and every hotel. Even the facilities offered by the same category of hotels differ. Every hotel decides what services should be provided based on public demands, the location, the size and character of the hotel and the class of patronage. In some of the hotels certain services are provided by renting space to other specialised agencies e.g. retail trades like beauty parlours, barber shops, check-rooms, valet service, drug stores, etc. The departments leased by the hotel are referred to as privileges or concessions and these leases are known as concessionaires. These concessionaires operate independently so long as they conform to the policies of the hotel. Furnishing of lodging and food is the principal business of each and every hotel and the extra services are merely necessary adjustments.

DEPARTMENTS

The hotel work is highly departmentalised and is truly a grouping of many types of business and professional services under one roof. Most luxurious hotels tend to demand a greater degree of departmentalisation and every one from the manager downwards may need, at times, to be more of an all rounder. The appearance of large hotels made imperative the need for delegation of authority and responsibility. The varied operating burdens are taken from the shoulders of manager and delegated to specialists; endeavour to find out in which way a hotel can be departmentalised, is subject to some variation.

Within a hotel there is a separation by the front of the house and the back of the house. The areas are those portions of the hotel with which the guest is likely to come into direct contact during his stay. The back of the house has those sections with which the guest is indirectly related. Figs. 3.4 to Figs. 3.11 depict the departmental organisation of various sizes of small and medium hotels.

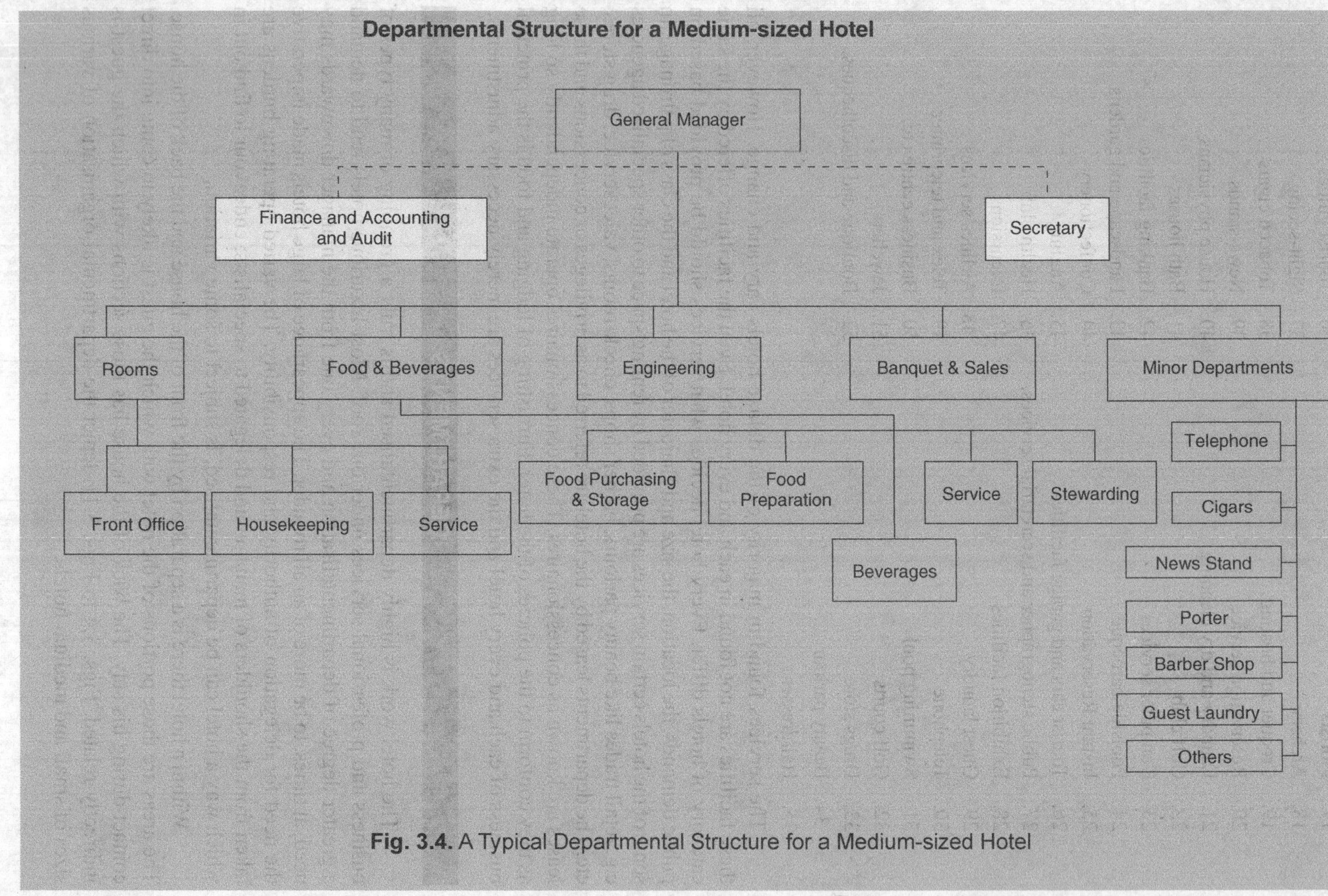

Fig. 3.4. A Typical Departmental Structure for a Medium-sized Hotel

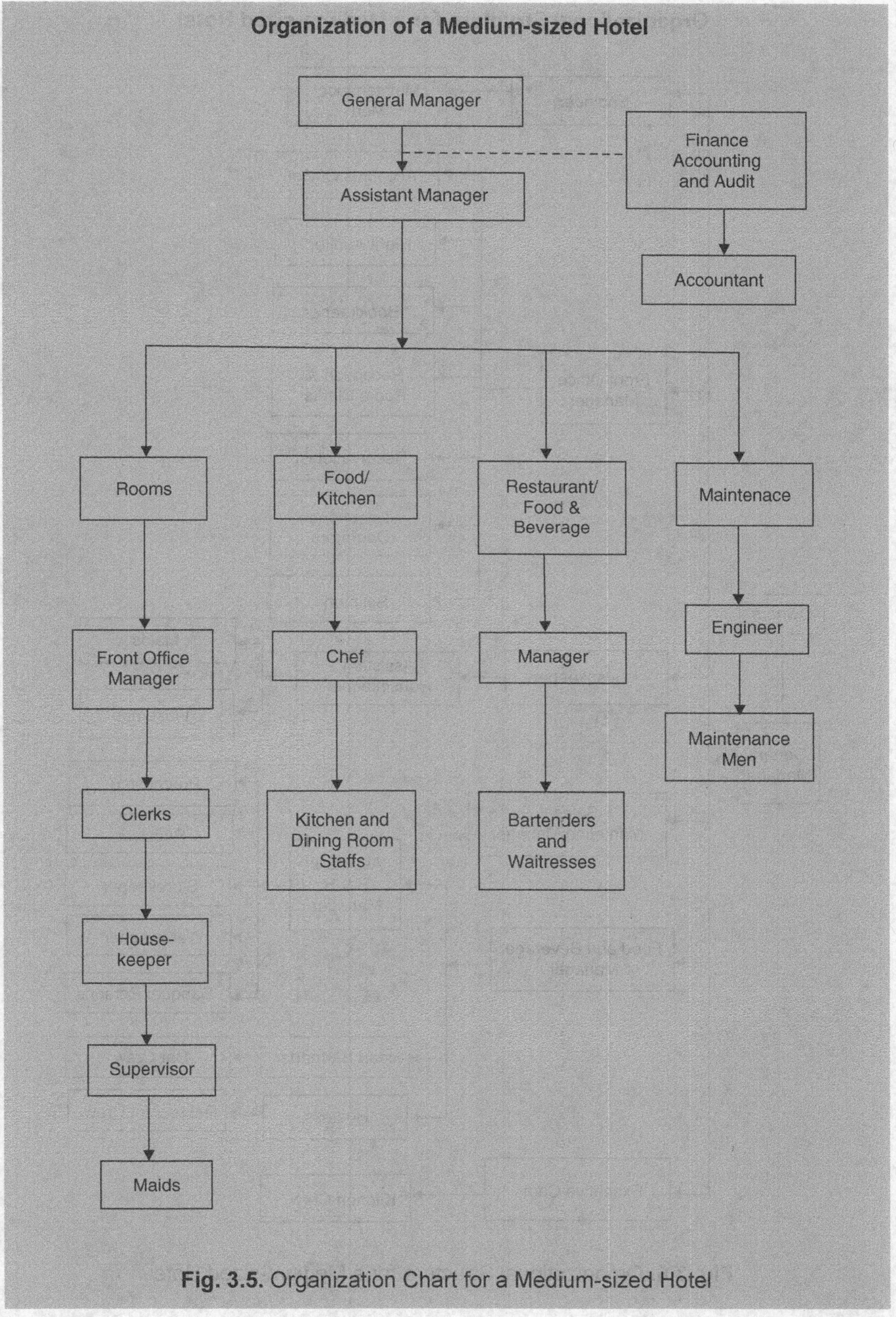

Fig. 3.5. Organization Chart for a Medium-sized Hotel

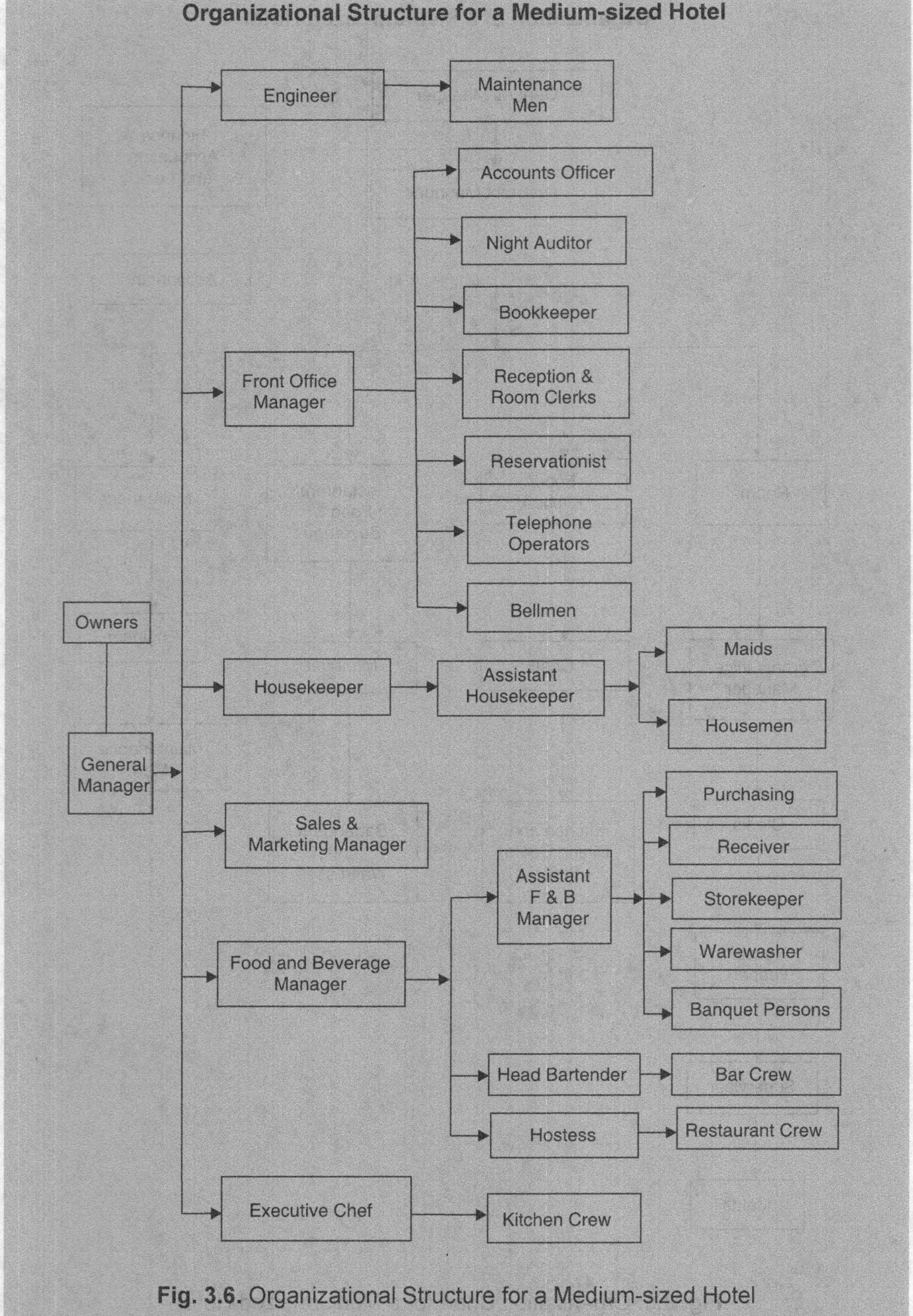

Fig. 3.6. Organizational Structure for a Medium-sized Hotel

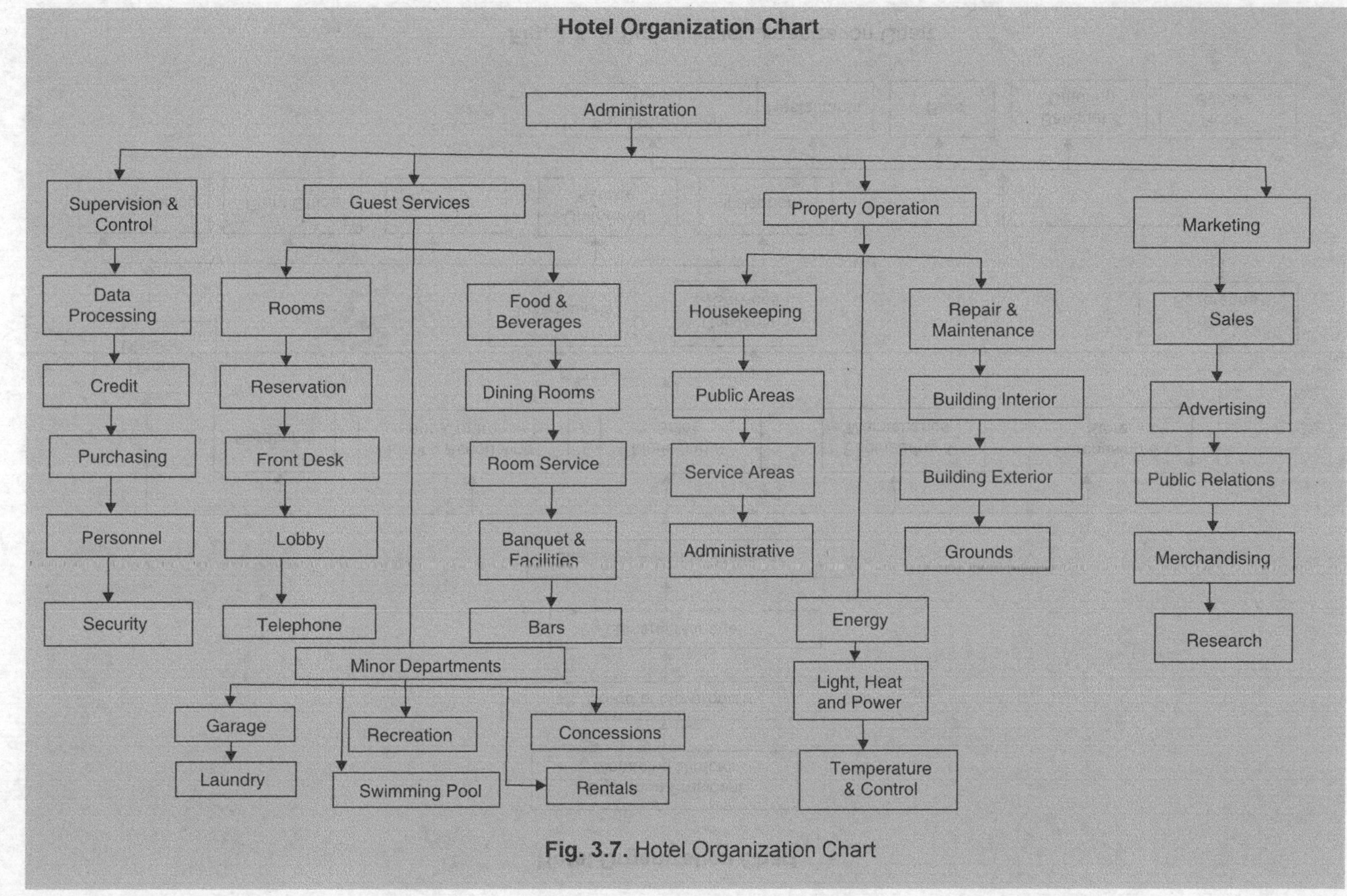

Fig. 3.7. Hotel Organization Chart

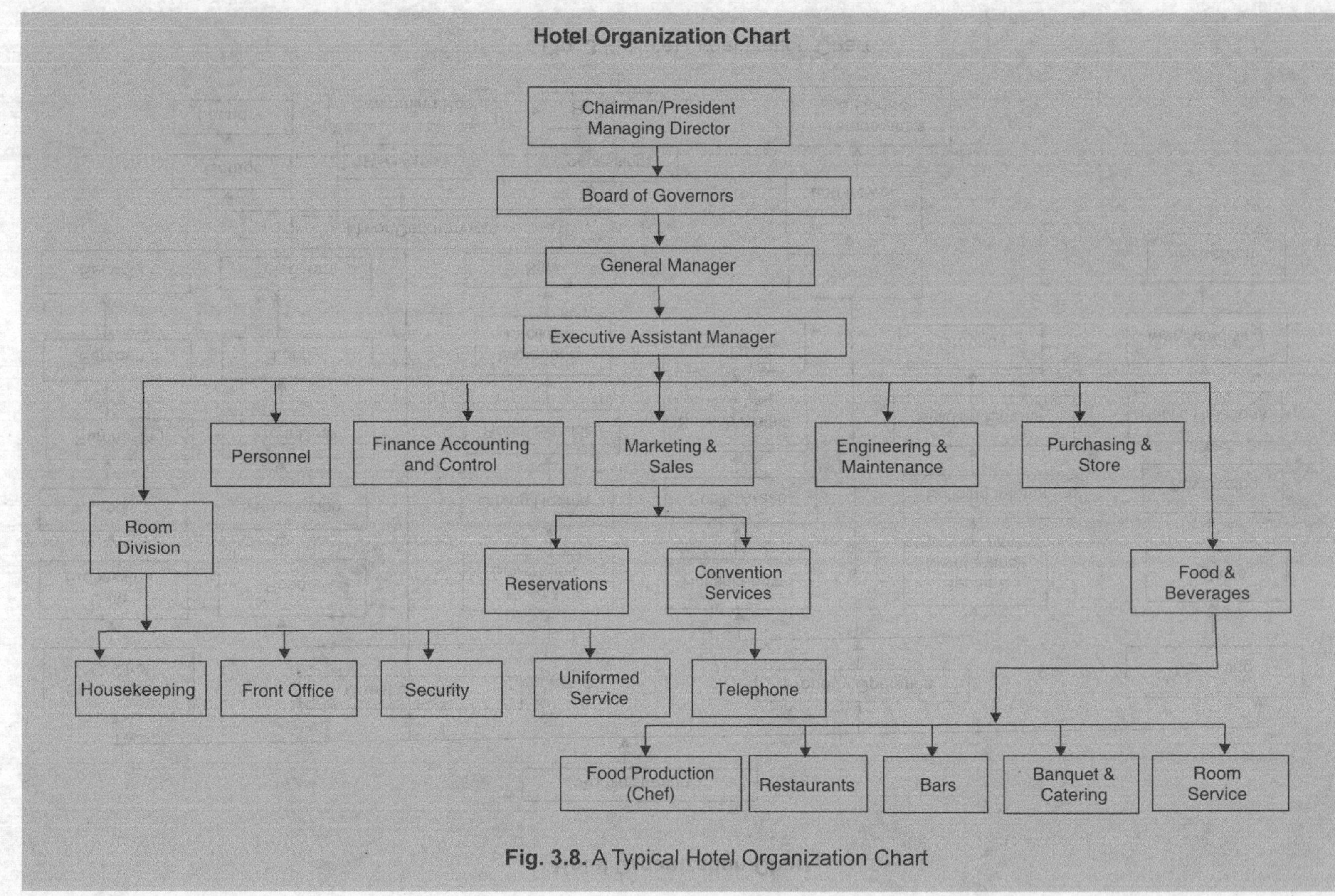

Fig. 3.8. A Typical Hotel Organization Chart

Departmental Structure for a Small Hotel

Owner/Proprietor

Manager

Accountant

Rooms

House keeping

Kitchen

Food and Beverage Service

Maintenance

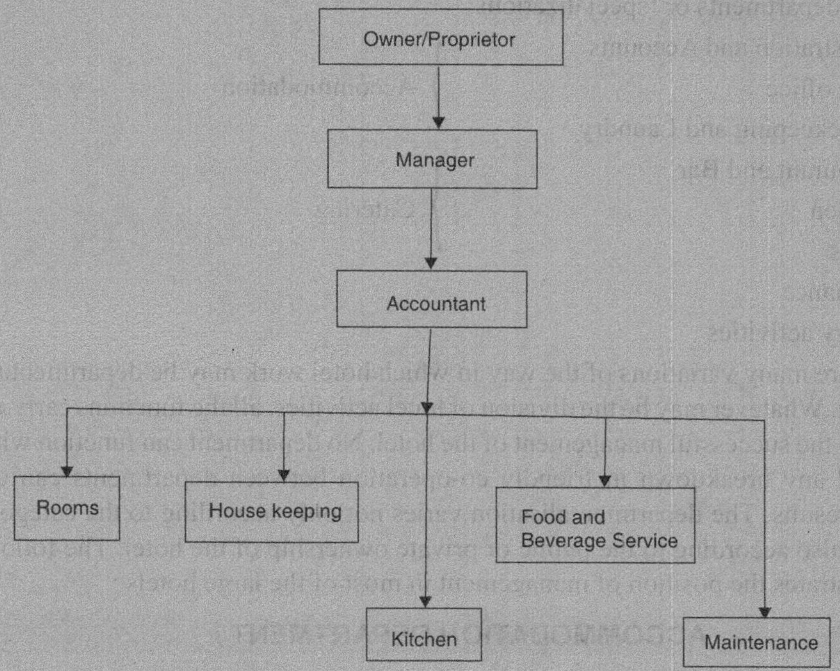

Fig. 3.9. Departmental Structure for a Small Hotel

The departments of hotels are arranged in a manner so as to achieve the objectives laid down as per hotel policy. Hotel work has been divided into the following[1] :

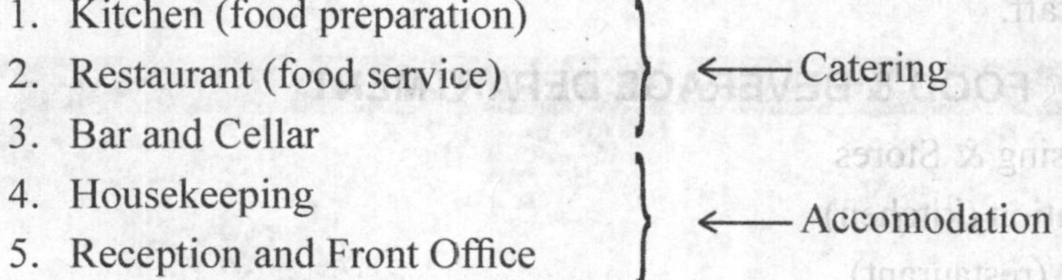

1. Kitchen (food preparation)
2. Restaurant (food service)
3. Bar and Cellar
4. Housekeeping
5. Reception and Front Office
6. Uniformed Staff
7. Maintenance and Engineering
8. Finance, Accounting, Audit and Control

In American hotels, the grouping is generally as follows :

1. Front Office
2. Catering
3. Housekeeping
4. Engineering and Maintenance
5. Sales and Advertising
6. Purchase and Control
7. Audit.

1. Careers in Hotel and Catering Sector, Page 3, ILO Publication.

According to ILO, the job break-down by function follows the traditional hotel structure consisting of departments or 'specializations'[1]

1. Administration and Accounts

Front office Housekeeping and Laundry	Accommodation
Restaurant and Bar Kitchen Stores	Catering

2. Maintenance
3. Auxiliary activities

There are many variations of the way in which hotel work may be departmentalised and organised. Whatever may be the division of hotel activities, all the functions carry equal importance in the successful management of the hotel. No department can function without the other and any breakdown in friendly co-operation between departments can cause catastrophic results. The departmentalisation varies not only according to the category of the hotel but also according to the public or private ownership of the hotel. The following break-up illustrates the position of management in most of the large hotels :

ACCOMMODATION DEPARTMENT

1. Administration
2. Personnel
3. Front Office
4. Housekeeping & Laundry
5. Uniformed staff.

FOOD & BEVERAGE DEPARTMENT

1. Food Purchasing & Stores
2. Food Preparation (kitchen)
3. Food Service (restaurant)
4. Beverages (bar).

ENGINEERING DEPARTMENT

1. Sales department
2. Security department (Protection).

FINANCE, ACCOUNTING, AUDIT AND CONTROL

MINOR DEPARTMENTS

1. Telephone
2. Cigar and Check Stand
3. Hairdressers
4. Check room

5. Porter
6. Guest laundry
7. Swimming Pool
8. Others.

The job break-down by hierarchical divisions i.e., levels of qualifications and responsibility in all these departments can be put as follows :

1. Manager
2. High level specialists
3. Medium level specialists
4. Basic level specialists
5. Miscellaneous labour apprentices.

The hotel staff could also be grouped into four main categories :

1. The general manager and departmental heads
2. Sub-departmental heads
3. Assistance department heads
4. General staff and operating personnel.

The organisation of a hotel points out the wide range in organisational structure within the hotel industry. The small hotel has a relativity simple structure. The organisation of a medium and large hotel is complex and varies considerably from one property to another. The organisation of a hotel is mainly dependent on the staff requirement of the hotel which in turn depends upon:

1. Size
2. Objectives and
3. Services.

SIZE

In a small hotel up to 50 rooms few persons may be employed. The various activities are put under the charge of one person only. In case of individually owned properties, the owner himself is the manager and performs much of the work himself. In these hotels, a simple system prevails and the number of activities are grouped under broad heads and minimum of staff is required. In case of medium and large-sized hotels there is a lot of specialisation and division of work, which necessiate the specialists for each and every work. It results in the increase of staff and creation of more departments for the smooth and efficient running of the hotel.

OBJECTIVES

The objectives of a hotel vary according to the type of properties. In a highly transient hotel, the average size of the guest's stay is short. Most of the guests stay only for one or two nights. Most of them check-out each morning. In the case of residential hotels, the guests' stay is longer, a week, a fortnight, or a month. In sea-side resorts, most arrivals and departures are concentrated between Friday and Sunday. Thus, the variation in the number of guests and their stay results in different members of staff requirement.

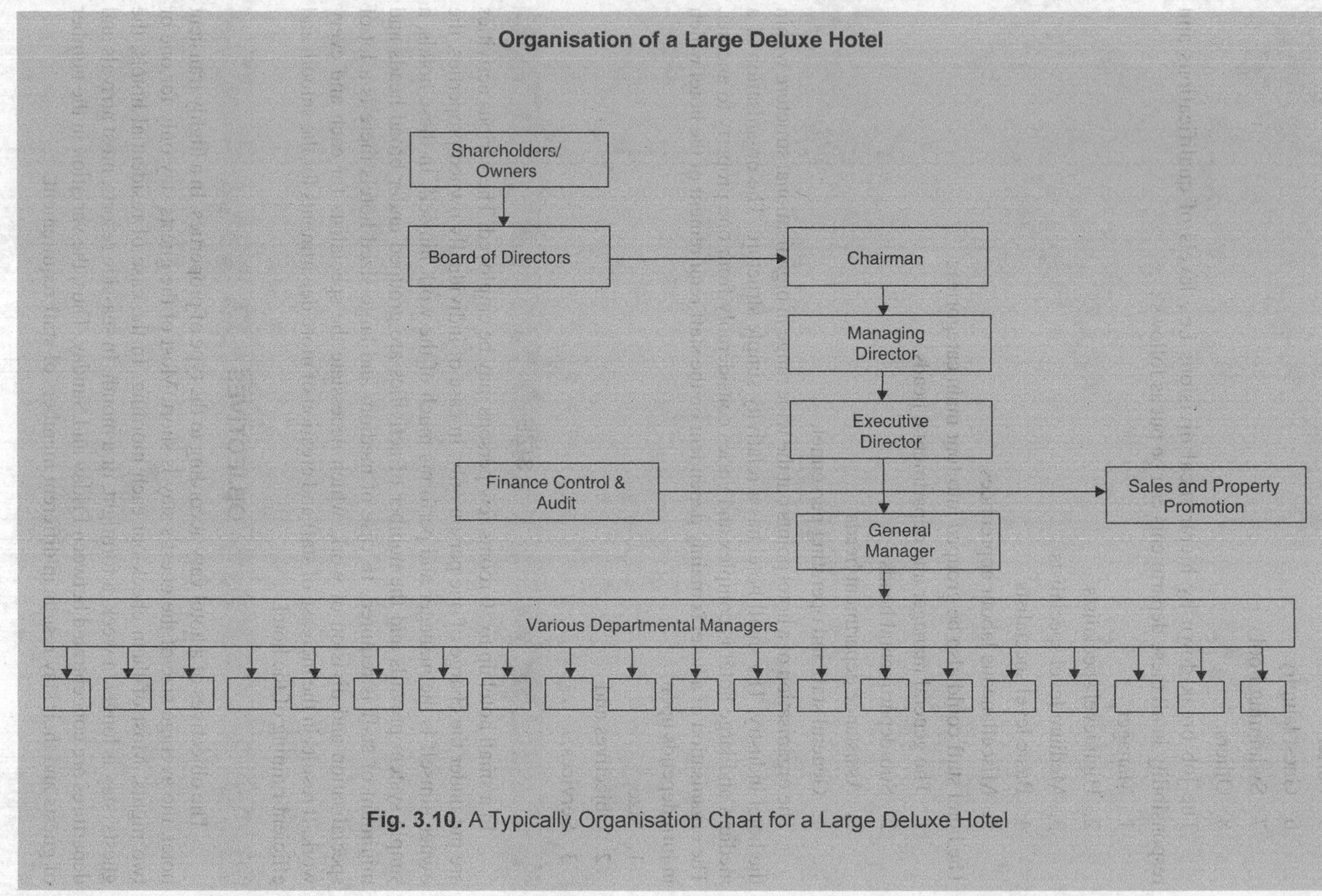

Fig. 3.10. A Typically Organisation Chart for a Large Deluxe Hotel

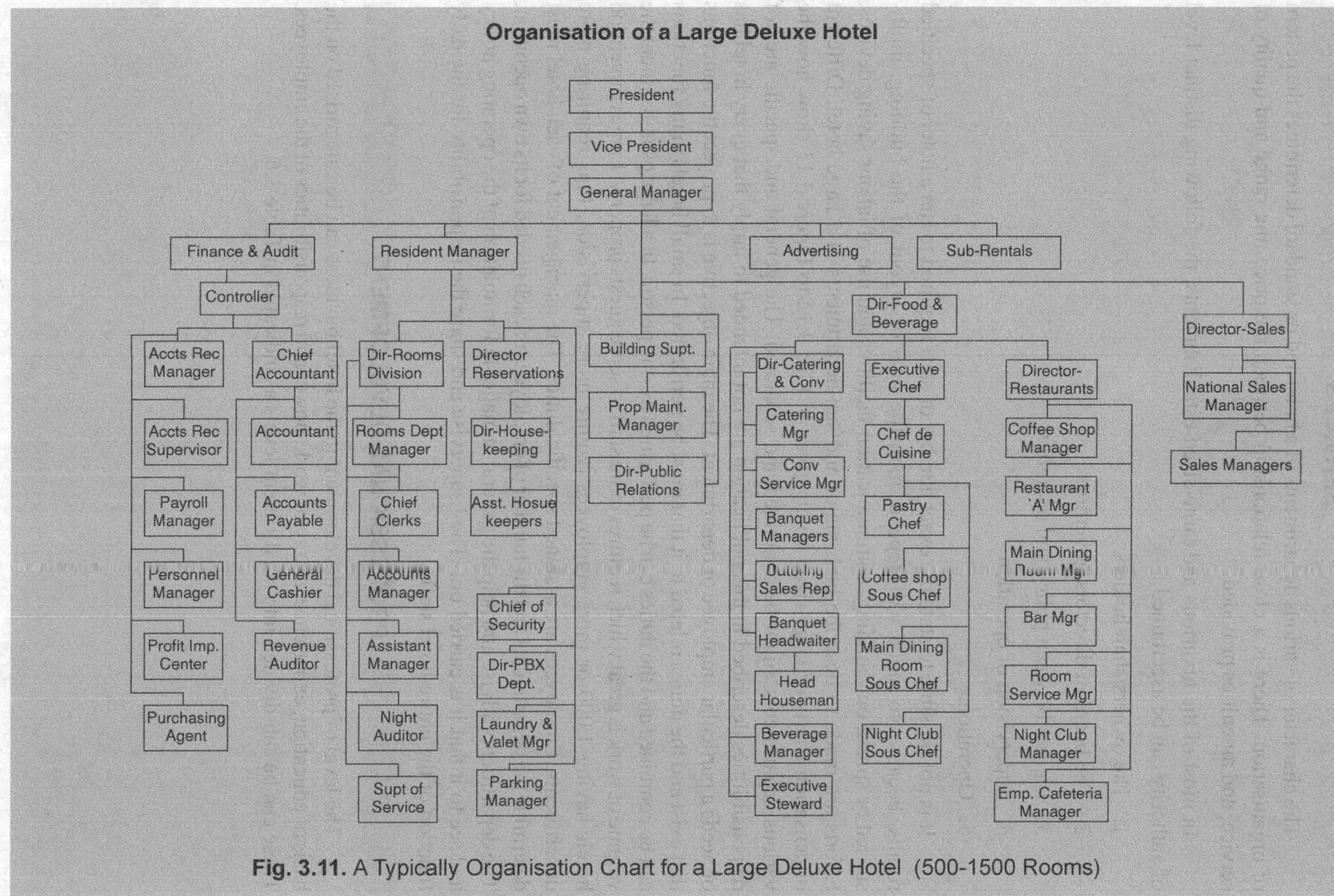

Fig. 3.11. A Typically Organisation Chart for a Large Deluxe Hotel (500-1500 Rooms)

SERVICES

The character of various departments of a hotel and its standard determines the pattern of organisation. There is a close relationship between the price, the range and quality of service, and amenities provided.

In most of the luxurious and large-sized establishments, the following distinct level of authority can be ascertained :

1. The owners/shareholders
2. The board of directors/governors
3. Liaison between policy and operation
4. Supervision of operation
5. Operation.

It is not possible to state the exact number of staff required to run a hotel of specified rooms, because so much will depend upon the interior layout of the building, multi-storied or spread out building, communication facilities and use of labour saving devices. Efforts are made to describe both major and sub-departments in a large hotel. Different organisation charts of large-sized hotels given in Figs 3.12 to Figure 3.13 show how the various departments might be combined and separated. The general and specific area of responsibilities described in this publication are not intended to imply that every hotel has or needs a particular employee or department. The main objective is to project the functions that exist and the duties related to it that must be performed. In small hotels many functions can be combined and the duties can be performed by one person. In a large establishment the volume of work is great which requires more staff to serve guests properly. Large convention hotels having 1,000 or more employees require more supervision, thus requiring more departments. Employees are assigned specific duties. The management of each hotel must determine the departments and the number of employees in each needed for its own operation. The departments advise and help the general manager in formulation of the operating policy and see to it that it is carried out. They supervise and share the responsibility for the daily function of the entire hotel staff.

PROFESSIONAL DEVELOPMENT

The level of professional development in the hotel business can be categorised on the basis of education, experience, nature of work, power and responsibilities of the employees. These can be sub-divided into six different levels as indicated in Table 3.6.

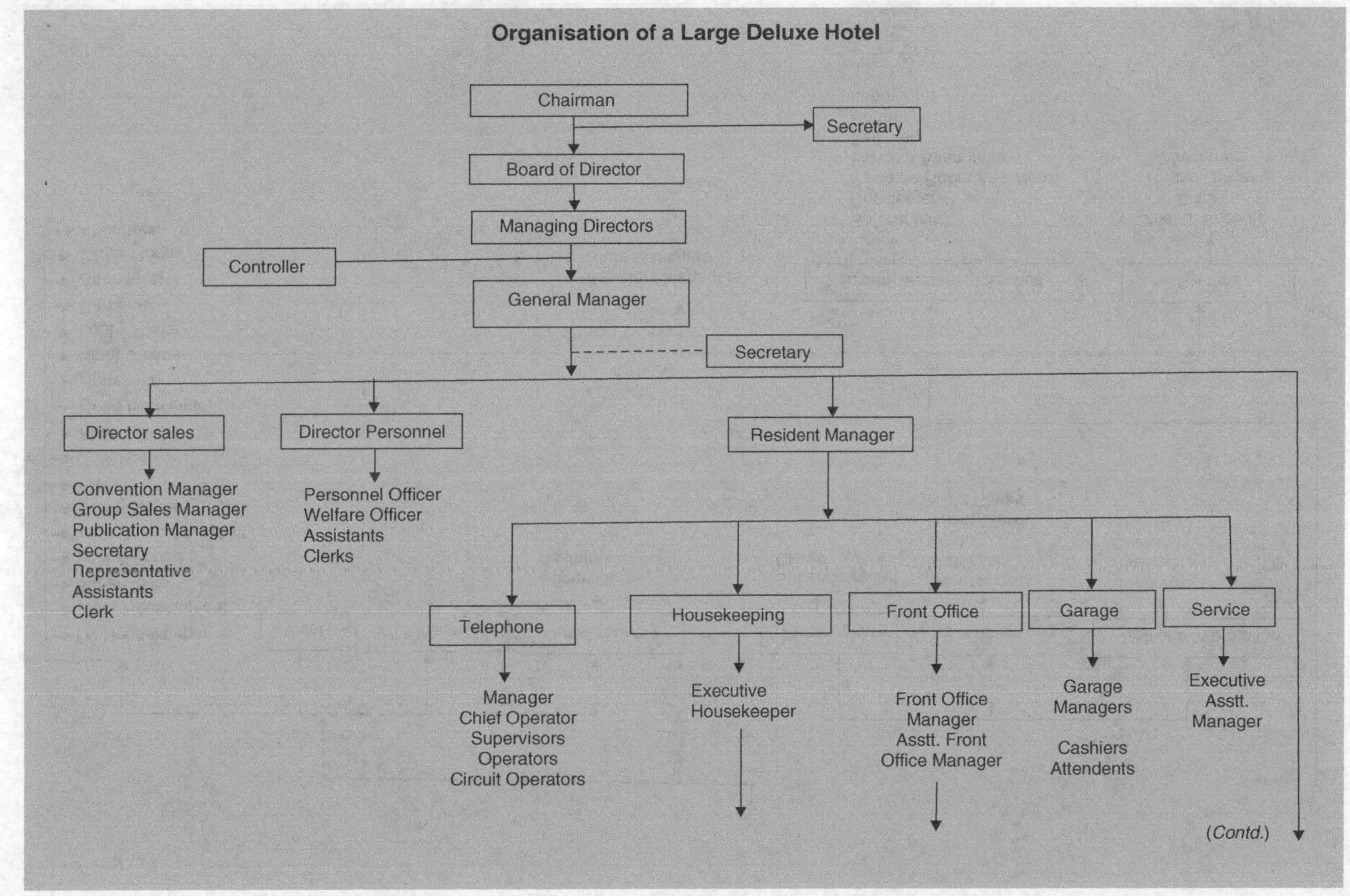
Organisation of a Large Deluxe Hotel
Chairman
Secretary
Board of Director
Managing Directors
Controller
General Manager
Secretary
Director sales
Convention Manager
Group Sales Manager
Publication Manager
Secretary
Representative
Assistants
Clerk
Director Personnel
Personnel Officer
Welfare Officer
Assistants
Clerks
Resident Manager
Telephone
Manager
Chief Operator
Supervisors
Operators
Circuit Operators
Housekeeping
Executive Housekeeper
Front Office
Front Office Manager
Asstt. Front Office Manager
Garage
Garage Managers
Cashiers
Attendents
Service
Executive Asstt. Manager
(Contd.)

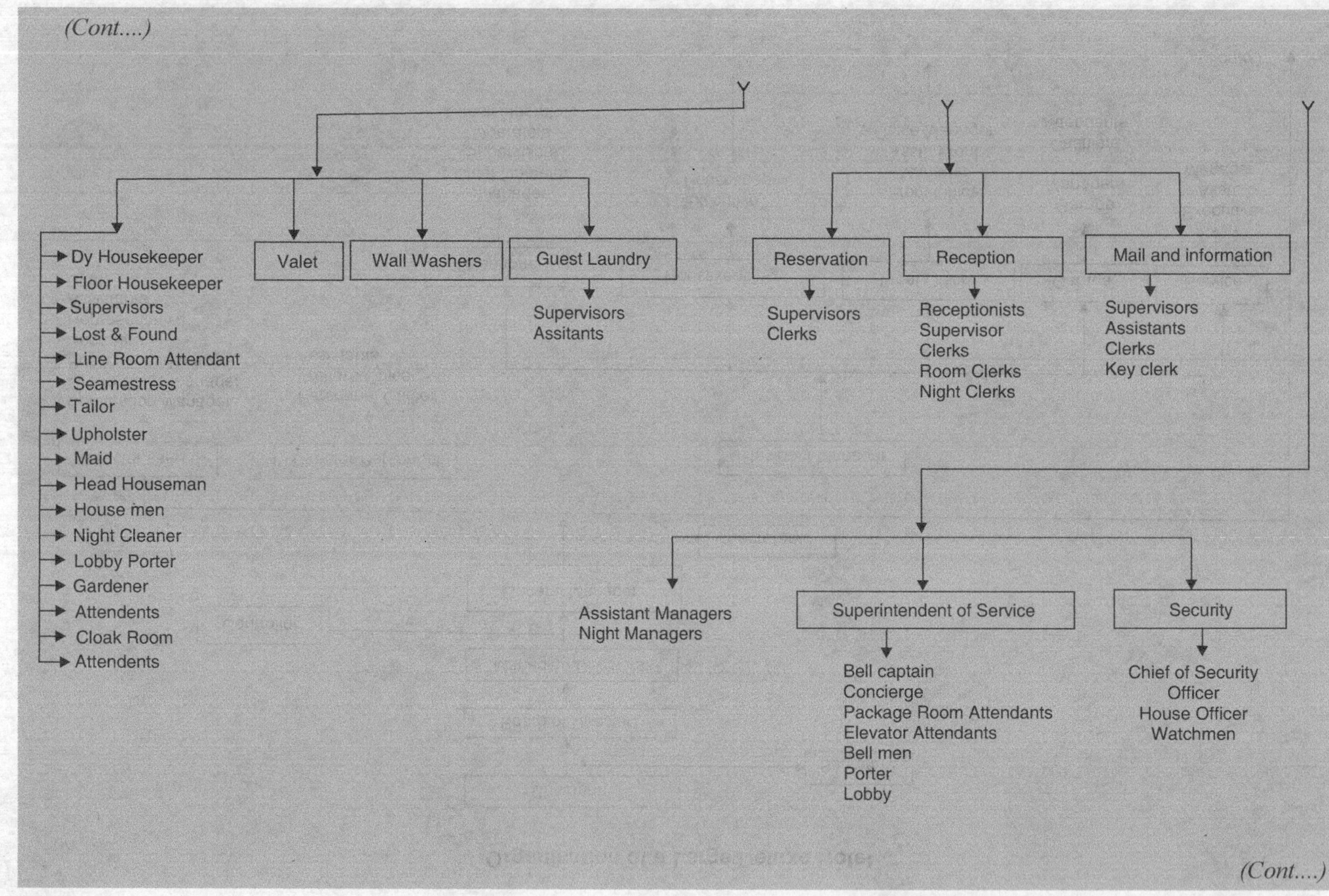
(Cont....)
Dy Housekeeper
Floor Housekeeper
Supervisors
Lost & Found
Line Room Attendant
Seamestress
Tailor
Upholster
Maid
Head Houseman
House men
Night Cleaner
Lobby Porter
Gardener
Attendents
Cloak Room
Attendents
Valet
Wall Washers
Guest Laundry
Supervisors
Assitants
Reservation
Supervisors
Clerks
Reception
Receptionists
Supervisor
Clerks
Room Clerks
Night Clerks
Mail and information
Supervisors
Assistants
Clerks
Key clerk
Assistant Managers
Night Managers
Superintendent of Service
Bell captain
Concierge
Package Room Attendants
Elevator Attendants
Bell men
Porter
Lobby
Security
Chief of Security
Officer
House Officer
Watchmen
(Cont....)

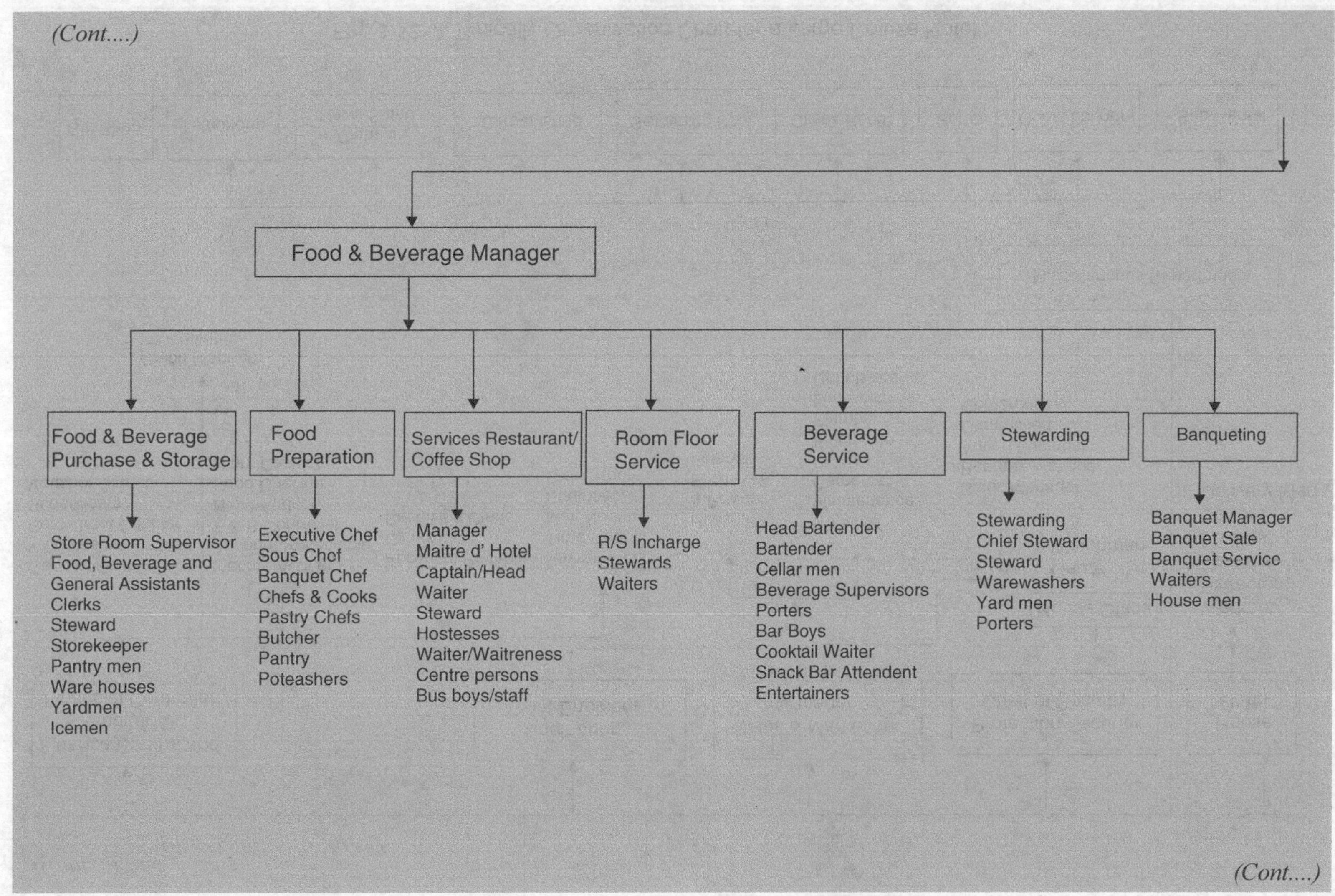
(Cont....)
Food & Beverage Manager
Food & Beverage Purchase & Storage
Store Room Supervisor
Food, Beverage and
General Assistants
Clerks
Steward
Storekeeper
Pantry men
Ware houses
Yardmen
Icemen
Food Preparation
Executive Chef
Sous Chof
Banquet Chef
Chefs & Cooks
Pastry Chefs
Butcher
Pantry
Poteashers
Services Restaurant/ Coffee Shop
Manager
Maitre d' Hotel
Captain/Head
Waiter
Steward
Hostesses
Waiter/Waitreness
Centre persons
Bus boys/staff
Room Floor Service
R/S Incharge
Stewards
Waiters
Beverage Service
Head Bartender
Bartender
Cellar men
Beverage Supervisors
Porters
Bar Boys
Cooktail Waiter
Snack Bar Attendent
Entertainers
Stewarding
Stewarding
Chief Steward
Steward
Warewashers
Yard men
Porters
Banqueting
Banquet Manager
Banquet Sale
Banquet Servico
Waiters
House men
(Cont....)

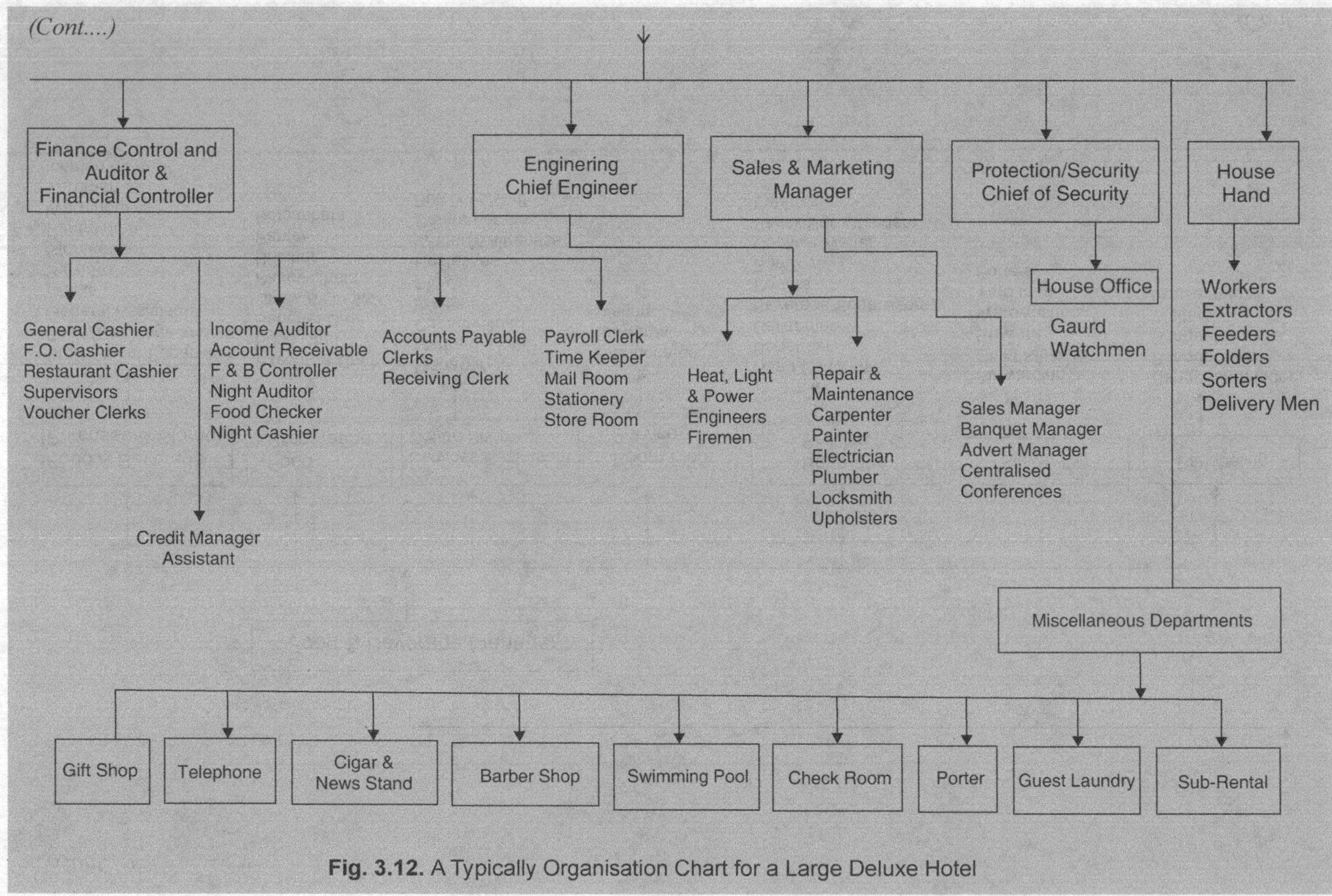

Fig. 3.12. A Typically Organisation Chart for a Large Deluxe Hotel

TABLE 3.6 : Levels of Professional Development in Hotels

Level/Grade	Explanation
Level 1 Grade I	*Trainees or Apprentice Stage :* This category includes trainees or apprentices who are new to the industry or start in a department in which they have no previous experience.
Level 2 Grade II	*Skilled Workers :* People at this stage are either workers or tradesmen, have an apprenticeship course of Food Craft with a diploma or certificate or have worked in similar positions for one to three years.
Level 3	*Supervisory Level/Semi-professional Level :* It includes people withconsiderable experience in their own field. They carry out supervisory functions as well as their respective job functions.
Level 4 Grade IV	*Departmental Heads :* They are responsible for their own departments or section of the overall operation. They require qualifications of the job and college experience.
Level 5 Grade V	*Management Level :* The work at this level requires planning, organising and controlling of other's work than dealing with guests or handling food and beverages. Extensive experience and training is mandatory.
Level 6 Grade VI	*Top Management or Executive Level :* They handle the overall management of the property and its human resources, with special concern for long-term planning of financing, marketing and staff development matters. A university degree, or Hotel School degree and extensive experience at the management level are basic qualifications for this level.

The management structure of a hotel comprises all the positions of responsibility and authority. The heads of management in any organisational structure are the representatives of the company or shareholders i.e., the board of governors or board of directors. Therefore, the hotel management team consists of the general manager, one or more deputy general managers/resident manager or assistant manager, and the heads of department. The chief executive of the hotel is designated in different styles such as Managing Director, Executive Director, President, General Manager or Hotel Manager. He participates in the formulation of the hotel policies and strategies. He is invariably responsible for their implementation and for the performance of the hotel.

In large hotels, this level is bifurcated into two: Managing Director and General Manager or Resident Manager. The Managing Director reports to the board and co-ordinates the work of the specialists departments and of the Resident Manager. The Resident Manager is responsible for the day-to-day management of the hotel activities. There are hotels where the positions of Deputy Managers exists, who have authority over the Departmental managers. Whatever may be the title of the positions, an effective system of hotel management requires a clear definition of responsibility and authority. Each title must describe the specific role and responsibilities appropriate to the job associated with the position concerned.

The managers heading specific departments are known as heads of the departments. They have direct lines of responsibility and authority to their superiors and to their subordinates of their respective departments. Heads of the department are specialists. They provide advice and service to line management.

The front office manager, head house-keepers, 'Chef,' and restaurant managers are treated as line management and purchase officers, accountant officers, personnel officers and other similar positions are treated as specialists.

THE HOTEL MANAGER

There must be one person responsible for the overall operation of the hotel. He is known as the General Manager. In the past the hotel manager was primarily a general host, personally greeting the guests and seeing to it that they were properly cared for. Now the successful general manager is a highly trained person capable of directing a complex business enterprise.

The hotel manager has to be a versatile, specialist, businessman and administrator, accountant and controller, a salesman and diplomat, a gastronomer, a personality and a competent man. The manager of a hotel includes any person in charge of the management of the hotel.[1] According to the Delhi Rent Control Act 1958, the manager of the hotel includes any person incharge of the management of the hotel.[2]

The Manager's duties can be multifarious but the main function of planning, budget and control should be carried out. The overall responsibility for the operation of a hotel rests with the manager. Representing the ownership interests, he directs the activities of the departments and gets involved into the day-to-day operations of individual sections of the establishment. He follows the policies and procedures prescribed for him by the proprietor or management. He must know how to organize and supervise. He is incharge of personnel, the money for operating the hotel and publicity about the hotel. He is responsible for operating matters such as rates of the rooms, use of guests' credit and the assignment of personnel. He has overall responsibility for operating hotel profitably and providing the best possible services and comforts for guests. It is his job to see that the guests are satisfied and an adequate profit is made. Accordingly, he must understand how each department operates and the duties of each employee. The hotel manager has many duties to perform, such as hiring personnel, buying and supervising the purchase of supplies, directing publicity, introducing improvements in service and determining rates and credit policies. In large hotels some of these duties are delegated to assistant managers. In small hotels, on the other hand, the manager who is frequently the owner may also do the work relating to the front office.

A successful manager should have cordial relations with the guests as well as the hotel employees in various departments. It is also important that the manager participates in the community affairs, since a good share of the hotel's business comes from local people. He should also come closely in contact with his fellow hoteliers for the improvement of the industry.

As an administrator he should have the ability to make quick decisions and device procedures which will help improve service. In large hotels, the ability to co-ordinate the operation of various departments with minimum of friction among staff members is a most important requirement. Under all circumstances he should be able to control his temper in settling problems with either guests or staff members. A considerable knowledge of all phases of hotel business gained by experience and training is necessary before a person can handle this. Long hours are often involved when civic or business groups are in convention.

1. FJ.J. Moral, Scientific Catering and Hotel Operating, Page 84.
2. F Delhi Rent Control Act 1958.

A great deal of physical endurance is also necessary. The duties of a hotel manager vary owing to the different methods of organisation found in hotels. His duties are varied and difficult but every task should be carried out efficiently. The main duty of a manager is to pass on the orders and ensure that they are properly carried out. He must pay great attention to expenditure and should draw conclusion from his observations. It is the responsibility of the manager to see that proper discipline is maintained in the hotel and that all the staff regulations are observed. He has to maintain proper co-ordination among the departments.

One of the biggest and more delicate jobs of a manager is in the field of human relations, particularly relations with the staff. Everyone must be handled differently according to his personality, age, position, background and outlook. While dealing with the Heads of Departments, the Manager should always remember their experience and professional skill. He must try to get himself accepted by them, which is possible by showing his hard work and intelligence in solving their problems. In certain circumstances he may be obliged to speak directly to a member of staff. In order to preserve the authority of the Head of the Department and respect his feelings, he should speak only to the person in charge of the department to which the concerned staff member belongs.

The manager must adopt a rigid code of conduct while dealing with suppliers and contractors. Quality and price are two important factors on which his decision must be based. Purchasing of goods and services should be carried out on a competition basis. He should take these decisions on the basis of price, taking into account any guarantees or condition, the date of delivery, details of payment, and after-sale service.

Running a hotel is a full–time 24–hours a day, seven-days a week operation. The hotel is never closed. There is no time off, no holidays. Some one representing management, and some members of the operating staff must be on duty every hour and every day of the year. There can be a broad policy laid down to cope with the many diverse situations that occur daily in hotels.

The general manager not only assembles a team but moulds them into a co-ordinated, co-operating group of people capable of working together for the common goal, i.e., making a guest satisfied.

The Hotel Manager will have to devote more attention to policy making, financial control, staff management, market research and business promotion. He must be given the means and the authority to do his job and must enjoy the complete confidence of the management. The hotelier or managers must offer an appropriate salary to the young man qualified to undertake these duties.

COMMUNICATION/REPORTS

Lack of communication between those who make decisions, and those who have to carry out routine tasks, may result in break-down of efficiency. There must be a two-way traffic of ideas. If the management alone is allowed ideas or introduce innovations, the rest of the personnel lose interest in the general well-being and running of property. Let there be an open policy by the manager to listen to ideas from all and to hold small meetings of departmental heads. Clear line of communications must be established and decision circulated to all departments. Test the paper work occasionally. It will help in eliminating some superfluous items. (Ref. Table 3.7 and Fig. 3.13)

Table 3.7 is a hotel report schedule which tells who gets report and when.

TABLE 3.7 : Hotel Report Schedule

S.No.	Report	Frequency	Distribution
1.	Arrival & Departure List	Daily	All departmental heads Hall porters Maintenance House-keeping
2.	Daily Report	Daily	Manager Assistant Managers
3.	Function List	Weekly	All departmental heads and Maintenance
4.	Room Occupancy Projection	Weekly	All departmental heads
5.	Weekly Report	Weekly	Manager Assistant Managers Head office
6.	Monthly Report	Monthly	Manager Assistant Managers Head office
7.	Food Stock Take Report	Weekly	Manager F & B Manager
8.	Beverage Stock Take Report	Weekly or Monthly	Manager F & B Manager
9.	House-keeper's Report	Daily × 2	Reception
10.	Wages Report	Monthly	Departmental heads
11.	Minutes of Meetings/Decisions	Weekly	All concerned
12.	Debtors List	Monthly	Manager Front Office Manager Head Office

For effective communication, your hotel should follow the guidelines given below :

1. Establish proper lines of communication
2. Construct and present a suitable management structure chart
3. Create detailed job descriptions for each position
4. Make a list of all reports, their frequency and distribution
5. Establish departmental meeting procedures.

Management Information (M/S)

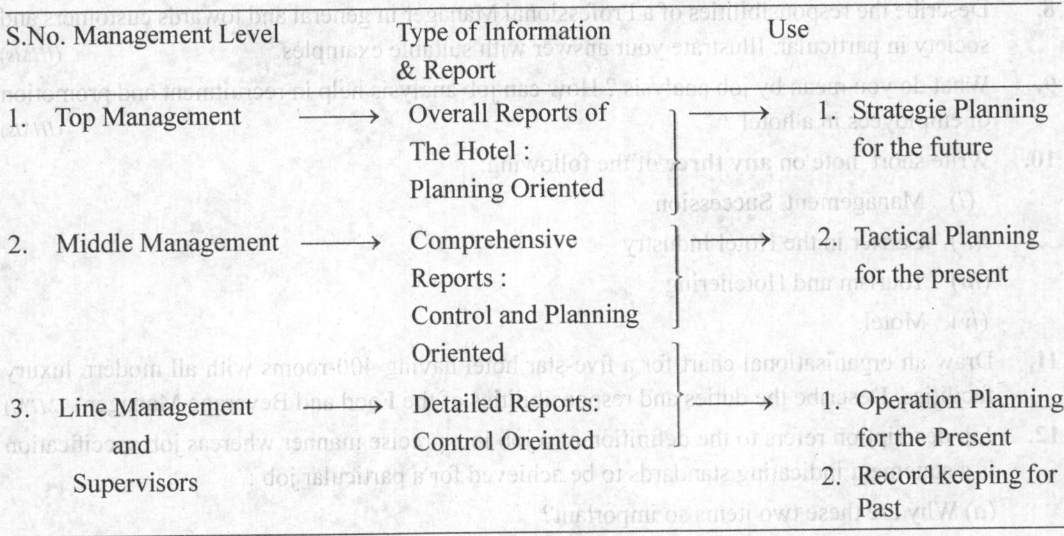

S.No. Management Level		Type of Information & Report		Use
1. Top Management	⟶	Overall Reports of The Hotel : Planning Oriented	⟶	1. Strategie Planning for the future
2. Middle Management	⟶	Comprehensive Reports : Control and Planning Oriented	⟶	2. Tactical Planning for the present
3. Line Management and Supervisors	⟶	Detailed Reports: Control Oreinted	⟶	1. Operation Planning for the Present 2. Record keeping for Past

Fig. 3.13. Classfication of Management Information Required in a Hotel

The system used in the different areas of the hotel can be brought together to exchange information and to avoid having to re-enter the same information twice. One system could be interfaced with another and thereby speeding up the task of information collection. Usually, a hotel may require varied information depending upon its use, and the management level.

QUESTIONS AND ASSIGNMENTS

1. Distinguish between :

(*i*) Memorandum of Association and Articles of Association

(*ii*) Hotel Accommodation and Supplementary Accommodation

(*iii*) Line and Staff Organisation

(*iv*) Internal and Exsternal Communication. (*DTHM*)

2. Draw an organisational chart of a classical kitchen brigade of a 500-room deluxe hotel. List the duties of a chef patisserie. (*DTHM*)

3. 'Job specification helps in recruiting the right personnel and job description helps in orienting the new personnel joining the industry.' Explain in detail. (*DTHM*)

4. Define partnership and joint stock company. How will you distinguish between them? (*DTHM*)

5. Distinguish between the following:

(*i*) Articles of Association and Prospectus.

(*ii*) Job Enlargement and Job Rotation.

(*iii*) Public Limited Companies and Private Limited Companies.

(*iv*) Backward Integration and Forward Integration.

6. What do you understand by job enrichment ? How does it differ from job enlargement ? (*IHMs*)

7. Define 'Partnership' What are the duties and rights of partners ? (*IHMs*)

8. Describe the responsibilities of a Professional Manager in general and towards customers and society in particular. Illustrate your answer with suitable examples. (*IHMs*)

9. What do you mean by job analysis ? How can job analysis help in recruitment and promotion of employees in a hotel ? (*IHMs*)

10. Write short note on **any three** of the following:
    (*i*) Management Succession
    (*ii*) Carrier in the Hotel Industry
    (*iii*) Tourism and Hoteliering
    (*iv*) Motel.

11. Draw an organisational chart for a five-star hotel having 400-rooms with all modern luxury facilities. Describe the duties and responsibilities of the Food and Beverage Manager. (*MTM*)

12. Job description refers to the definition of a job in a precise manner whereas job specification is a statement indicating standards to be achieved for a particular job :
    (*a*) Why are these two items so important?
    (*b*) Write the job description and job specification for a storekeeper in a Four-Star Hotel. (*MTM*)

13. Suggest an organisational chart for a medium-sized hotel say 200-rooms. (*PGDT*)

14. Explain the term 'organisation'. Give a suitable organisation chart for a deluxe hotel having 300-rooms. (*PGH&TM*)

15. "The organisation of an office of a hotel is particularly significant in large units." Explain. (*PGH&TM*)

16. Explain the salient features of a three star hotel and also give an organisational chart suitable for a medium sized hotel. (*PGDT*)

17. Give a brief account of the various departments of a hotel and explain in detail the functions of a housekeeping department. (*PGDH&TM*)

18. Successful operations in a hotel management depend on office management. What factors are kept in mind in setting up a good office organization? (*PGDT&HM*)

19. Describe a suitable management structure for a group of ten medium sized hotels situated within a 60-miles radius. Discuss the reasons for the creation of major posts indicating briefly the scope of their responsibilities and suggesting how problems of integration between them could be dealt with. (*MTA*)

20. Explain the nature of operating work and managerial work in hotel business and show how they are inter-related to each other ? (*MTA*)

21. Explain the following (any *five*) :
    (*a*) Strategic planning
    (*b*) Foreign collaboration in hotel
    (*c*) Heritage hotel
    (*d*) Banqueting
    (*e*) Tourism Finance Corporation of India (TFCI)
    (*f*) Induction. (*MTA*)

22. What factors would you keep in mind while deciding the organisation structure of a hotel ? Explain, with the help of flow chart the organisation structure of a five star hotel. *(DTHM)*

23. Write notes on:

(*i*) Memorandum of Association and Articles of Association

(*ii*) Hotel Accommodation and Supplementary Accommodation

(*iii*) Line and Staff Organisation

(*iv*) Internal and External Communication. *(DTHM)*

24. Give brief account of the revenue producing departments of a five star hotel.

25. Hotel managers usually agree that they have responsibilities to the public. Yet they also take profits and are strong for free enterprise. Are n't they talking out of both sides of their mouth at the same time ?

26. Is it true that you have to be capable middle managers if you decentralise ? Or, is this just an excuse to justify the boss deciding everything ?

27. Discuss the nature, benefits and limitations of organisational chart as a tool for organising planning.

28. Draw an organisation chart for a hypothetical hotel of any of the following category :

(*a*) A commercial hotel with limited service

(*b*) A commercial hotel of middle class

(*c*) A commercial hotel of luxury class

(*d*) A convention centre with limited service

(*e*) A convention centre with deluxe facilities

(*f*) A motel after middle class category

(*g*) A motel after luxury facilities

(*h*) A resort with limited facilities

(*i*) A resort with deluxe facilities.

29. Describe the main duties and responsibilities of the staff of each department on decision of a hypothetical hotel.

30. If you are employed in the hotel industry, describe the tasks your general manager performs on a daily basis. Also describe the task your departmental manager performs on a daily basis.

31. If you are employed in a hotel, sketch the organisation chart of the hotel. Have you seen this hierarchy change since you have been employed there ? If so, what do you think caused this change ?

32. With which departments of the hotel did you come into contact before, during and after your visit at the hotel ?

33. Prepare a typical organisation chart for a Front Office in a large commercial hotel located in a centre city area. How would this organisation chart differ for limited service property ?

34. Explain in brief the four departments in large hotel. Give a chart illustrating the organisational chart of a hotel. *(IHMs)*

35. Write notes on :

(*i*) Lay off and Discharge

(*ii*) Break-even Analyses.

36. You have been asked to work out the staff requirement in five star hotel of 350-rooms. Suggest a suitable organisation chart and give suitable records in support thereof.

37. In about 10-lines explain the difference between a job description and job specifications.

38. Organising is the establishing of effective authority relationships among selected workers persons and work places in order for the group to work together effectively comment and examine the scope of organisational activities in an enterprise.

39. Describe a suitable management organisation structure for a group of ten medium-sized hotels situated within a 60-mile radius. Discuss the reasons for the creation of major posts indicating briefly the scope of their responsibilities and suggesting how problems of integration between them could be dealt with. *HCIMA* (*London*)

40. Plan the operational staff requirement (service and production both) for a first class multi-cuisine restaurant with 80-covers and open for lunch and dinner only. (*IHMs*)

41. Make a duty roster for the staff working in the above restaurant to comply with the entire mise-en-place of the restaurant. (*IHMs*)

42. Prepare, in the form of a brief to an architect, a description of your principal requirements, in terms of space, operations and environment, for the design of a catering operation of your own choice. *HCIMA* (*London*)

43. Give a brief account of the revenue producing departments of five star hotels. (*IHMs)*

CHAPTER 4

Hotel Guest Relationship

OBJECTIVES

After studying this lesson you should be able to :

1. *Define the term guest.*
2. *Understand the various rules and regulations related to hotel operation.*
3. *Understandtal system of operation specially dealing with registration, stay guest property, cancellations, complaints, picences, consumer protection, hygines and sanitation bitting and gaming, death in a hotel etc,.*

THE HOTEL

A hotel is an establishment which receives all travellers and tourists who are willing to pay an adequate price to the sort of accommodation provided. There is an important legal distinction between a hotel/motel and a boarding/rooming house. A boarding house does not qualify as a hotel because it does not minister to any absolute public necessity. A boarding house is at liberty to deal with the customers on an individual basis, accepting and rejecting them at will. A hotel may have constraint not to vary the terms of acceptance of a guest, while a boarding house may make whatever arrangements it wishes with each guest on room rate, length of stay etc., subject, of course, to anti-discrimination laws.

An apartment house is a group or unit in a single building, each separate from the other, and arranged for independent housekeeping. Tenants have the right to exclusive possession of the occupied unit until expiry or breach of the lease. Even though certain services and conditions are furnished, the relationship between the property and the occupant is that of land lord/tenant rather than hotel/guest even if no housekeeping is done in the apartments. Some large city hotels in recent years have a small number of rooms which have been set aside for transient guests.

In addition there are a number of camping grounds or tourist camps which provide accommodation facilities. Accommodation of this type is of a 'casual' nature, and do not give rise to the hotel/guest relationship.

Knowledge of law has a direct bearing on the hotel business. A hotel manager needs to know his legal obligations to a guest as well as be aware of his legal rights in respect to the guests' responsibilities to the hotel. Misuse of this knowledge may lead to mistrust. Basically a hotel manager is concerned with :

1. Laws relating to buyers
2. Laws relating to sellers
3. Laws relating to landlords and tenants
4. Laws relating to unions and employees
5. Laws dealing with civil rights
6. Laws relating to liability and contracts
7. Laws relating to conditions and relationships
8. Laws of control, state and local bodies of a general nature, and those applying specifically to hotels.

Special laws relating to haltering are mostly based on precedents established in the past and judicial opinion since then. In addition, there are a number of laws enacted by legislative bodies at central, state or local levels, known as statute laws.

As a hotel manager there are some questions which you should be familiar with, such as

1. What is a hotel ?
2. Who is a guest ?
3. What are the duties and liabilities of the hotel ?
4. What protections are afforded by the hotel management by law?

According to the law, the owner of the property is legally responsible for what takes place there, but basically it is the manager who should be familiar enough with the law to avoid suits against him. The manager also should see that each employee is familiar with those laws that impinge directly on his job in the hotel.

THE GUEST

Primarily, there may be two types of persons who use the facilities of a hotel :

1. Invites, and
2. Licensees.

Everyone using the facilities of a hotel is not necessarily a guest.

1. Invites : They include
   (*i*) Registered guests
   (*ii*) Visiting guests and patrons of restaurants on the premises
   (*iii*) Visiting guests and patrons of bars on the premises
   (*iv*) Policemen and firemen
   (*v*) Others entitled by law to enter the hotel.
2. Licensees : Those who may be allowed to enter the hotel but not specifically invited or especially welcomed, such as,
   (*i*) News body
   (*ii*) Solicitor for charity
   (*iii*) Someone coming in off the street to a washroom.

Implicit permission to enter a portion of the hotel/property is not without limits. Any person who may venture beyond the area not allowed to enter becomes a trespasser.

There are three basic conditions which must be fulfilled to establish a hotel-guest relationships :

1. Element of a 'transient' : The person coming from or returning to his home, is a transient traveller.
2. Existence of a contract : A contract exists between the hotel and the person based on their consent, expressed or implied.
3. Agreement to pay : An agreement to pay is in effect.

It is the general opinion that a person does not become a guest of a hotel until he registers into the hotel. In actual fact the hotel/guest relationship can be and is established when each of the parties shows the intent to establish this relationship. One form of their intent could be by making a reservation. It is not necessary that a specific room be assigned to the person in order for the hotel/guest relationship to be established. Suppose a person's luggage is stolen while he is waiting to register. The hotel would have the same liability as if the person had already registered and been assigned a room.

A person using a hotel for an illegal purpose, as well as someone sharing a guest's room without the knowledge or consent of the hotel, forgoes the right he might have been entitled.

As a general rule, once the guest checks out and leaves the hotel, the hotel-guest relationship is automatically terminated. However, in many cases, the relationship may continue for a 'reasonable time' after the guest leaves and allows them to arrange for the removal of luggage, left at the hotel.

EXTENSION OF STAY

A guest may extend his stay beyond the period for which he made a reservation. This may result in the inability to accommodate incoming guests with reservations. Such situations may arise when hotels experience a spell of unpleasant weather or when transporters strike. The guest is forced to change his plans for departure under such circumstances. Most of the hotels seem to prefer to allow the guest to extend his stay beyond the reserved period. From a strictly legal point of view, the hotel is under no such obligation. At the end of the reserved period, there is an automatic expiry of hotel-guest relationship. If the guest attempts to remain without the consent of the hotel, he is termed a trespasser, and is subject to forcible removal if there is no more space available for incoming guests.

There is an important distinction in the law between various types of hotels. The name of the establishment does not always indicate its nature. An establishment held out by the proprietor as offering food, drink and, if so required, sleeping accommodation, without special contract, to any traveller presenting himself who appears to be able and willing to pay a reasonable sum for the services and facilities provided and who is in a fit state to be received."[1]

Without special contract implies that the hotel will be willing to accept chance guests without prior booking and any traveller implies that there will be no refusal solely on the grounds that the applicant for food or accommodation does not belong to any particular class or group of people the hotel proprietor desires to cater exclusively to. What is or is not, a reasonable sum is a matter for determination by the court in a specific case. Any hotel proprietor may be regarded as an hotelkeeper, even though he would prefer not to be, if he

1.The Hotel Proprietors Act 1956 (Britain)

accepts all comers and offers such accommodation, food and drink (not necessarily alcoholic drink, for it need not be licensed) as are available with him and he may thereby acquire certain obligations and liabilities as an hotelkeeper. The obligations and responsibilities of the hotel are :

1. Hotels' obligations to receive travellers.
2. Hotels' responsibility to ensure that the guest is properly cared for.

A hotel is obliged to receive travellers and their luggage, but not, if he does not wish, their vehicles or live animals, regardless of the hour at which they arrive. He is not required to serve hot food at a time when such foods are not normally served or to move out of his own bed or to improvise a bedroom when none is available. But, cases have occurred in which hotels have been successfully sued for damages when they refused to meet their obligations without sufficient cause.

The manager of an establishment which is not a hotel is not obliged to receive any one but faces the possibility of a complaint if he refuses to receive any one solely on grounds of colour, race or ethnic origins.

REFUSAL OF ACCOMMODATIONS

A hotel may legally refuse accommodation to a person due to any of the following reasons :–

1. When no accommodation is available in the hotel
2. When the hotel has reason to believe that the prospective guest might create disturbance, such as, intoxication or irrational actions
3. If the prospective guest is a known criminal or his language is objectionable
4. If the prospective guest refuses to make advance payment or asks for lower rates, the hotel may turn away the guest.

A hotel cannot refuse accommodation to a prospective guest on the basis of age, race, colour or creed. It can refuse admittance to a visitor or a guest for the same reasons it can refuse to accommodate the guest. Similarly, it can evict guests or the visitors for the same reason they might be refused admittance.

The right of eviction should be used with extreme caution to avoid damage suits and unfavourable publicity to the hotel. A hotel cannot legally evict guest if in so doing it violates any of his rights or if the eviction exposes the guest to an unreasonable risk of harm.

A hotel has the following responsibilities :

1. Legal responsibility to accept prospective guest unless he has a legal reason for refusing admission;
2. Legal responsibility for protecting his guests; and
3. Legal responsibility to care for guests' property.

GUEST PROPERTY

The hotel management is legally responsible for the loss of or damage to the property of a guest and this includes money, jewellery, clothing and any other movable effects, but is no longer responsible for his guests' vehicles or any property left by them. The garages and stables may come within the hospitium of the hotel and responsibility would extend to it, so that if a guest left a suitcase outside his car but in the garage, the management might be held responsible (unless the guest could be shown to have been negligent) whereas, if he locked the suit case inside his car the hotel could escape liability. Even though the loss or damage was in no way caused by the hotel management or its employees it is still liable unless the owner of the property has himself been negligent, that is, failed to exercise the ordinary care which a prudent man would show, or unless the guest, by taking excessive care, made it clear that he was relieving the hotel management of his liability and taking charge of his property himself.

In England the display of notices disclaiming liability does not relieve the management of responsibility but by displaying a copy of the relevant section of the Act can reduce its libility. The exceptions are where the management have been negligent or where the goods have been accepted for safe custody, or offered for safe custody and refused. The hotel is not only responsible for the loss of guest's property but is also responsible for damage thereto, except where the damage is caused by an act of God or the enemies.

It need hardly be said that, with obligations of this nature, prudent hotels cover themselves adequately by insurance.

The proprietor of an establishment which is not a hotel is not normally liable for his guest's property (except in cases of negligence) and neither the hotel nor the non-hotelkeeper is liable for the property of his employees, whether living on the premises or not unless this is specifically undertaken in the Contract of Employment.

In order to obtain protection the hotelier must exhibit a notice in the following terms in a conspicuous position near the main entrance of his hotel:–

LOSS OR DAMAGE TO GUESTS' PROPERTY

A hotel proprietor may in certain circumstances be liable to make good any loss of or damage to a guest's property even though it was not due to any fault of the proprietor or staff of the hotel. This liability however :

1. extends only to the property of guests who have engaged sleeping accommodation at the hotel;
2. is limited to a fixed amount for any one article and total amount fixed in the case of any one guest, except in the case of property which has been deposited, or offered for deposit, for safe custody;
3. does not cover motor-cars or other vehicles of any kind or any property left by them or horses or other live animals.

RESERVATIONS AND REGISTRATION

Provided it fulfils certain conditions, an agreement made between two or more parties is a legally binding contract. Perhaps the most important element in a contract (though there are others) is consensus. This means that both parties must be thinking of the same thing, that there must be an offer on one side and an unconditional acceptance on the other and that the agreement must be entered into freely and voluntarily and without misrepresentation or fraud.

A CONDITIONAL ACCEPTANCE

A conditional acceptance constitutes a counter-offer which requires acceptance before it becomes a contract. When a counter-offer is made the original offer lapses and cannot afterwards be accepted. For example, if 'A' offers to sell something to 'B' for ₹ 1,000 and 'B' counters with an offer of ₹ 900 which 'A' refuses, 'B' cannot then take up the original offer of ₹ 1,000. If he wishes to offer ₹ 1,000 he becomes the party making the offer and it is open to 'A' to accept or refuse. A mere request for further information does not consitute a counter-offer.

To supply information, for example, in advertisements or in a brochure, is not in itself an offer; it is merely an invitation to do business. In the same way, placing goods in a showcase or shop window, even with prices on them, is not an offer; the offer is made by the customer's tendering the price and it is accepted when the shopkeeper takes it. It has even been held that in a supermarket the contract is not completed by the customer's placing goods from the shelves in his wire basket; when the goods are taken to the cashier the customer offers to buy them and the cashier accepts the offer.

If an offer is conditional and the conditions are not fulfilled it has not been accepted. If an offer is made by telephone subject to confirmation of acceptance in writing it cannot be accepted in any other way. If the hotel-keeper writes: On receipt of a deposit of ₹ 1,000, I shall be glad to reserve the accommodation you require and the addressee replies confirming the booking but omitting the deposit, he has not complied with the conditions which eventuality must be accepted, if at all, subject to those conditions.

AN OFFER

An offer is made only when it is communicated to the offeree. An offer will lapse if:

1. either party dies before acceptance
2. at stipulated time or, failing stipulation, a reasonable time has elapsed.

Since it is open to question what is a reasonable time, disputes will be avoided if offers of accommodation, banqueting services, etc., stipulate a time for acceptance.

An offer can be revoked before acceptance but the revocation must be communicated to the offere before he has signified his acceptance. In one case an offer was made in a letter on 1st November by a man in Germany to another in India. The offer was received by the offere on 21st November. It was immediately accepted by cable. Two days earlier the maker of the original offer had sent a second letter withdrawing it but this was not received until 30th November. The court held that since the offer had been accepted before notice of revocation was received there was an enforceable contract.

An offer is accepted and the contract is made when the letter of acceptance is posted, even if it never reaches the addressee. A revocation takes effect only when brought to the notice of the person to whom it is addressed.

The revocation need not be in writing. If it is found that an error has been made and the offeree is notified by telephone before he has accepted the offer, there is no contract.

The contract need not be in writing unless there is made a condition. It is obviously more difficult to prove offer and acceptance when a contract is made orally but this can be implied. For example, if a customer in a restaurant, having seen the menu, orders a meal there is an implied contract to supply the meal at the agreed price on the one hand and to pay for it on the other. A guest arriving at a hotel and being presented with a room card indicating the tariff would probably be held to have accepted the offer at the price quoted even though he did not signify his acceptance in words or writing. If there were a notice on such a card saying A service charge of 10% is added to all accounts" he would probably be held to have accepted that condition if he did not protest at the time. This is not certain and has not been tested in a court of law. In a case concerning the purchase of a horse the intending buyer wrote (after disagreement about the price), If I hear nothing from you I shall consider that you have accepted my offer of ₹ 5,000 for the horse. The owner of the horse did not reply but it was held that he had not accepted the offer and there was no contract. However, in accepting the room card and the key of the room the guest would almost certainly be held to have made an outward sign of acceptance.

The Hotel Proprietors' Act in Britain makes reference to the acceptance of travellers without special contract. In Britain this does not imply that in accepting the offer of accommodation the traveller has not contracted to pay for it, but merely that it is not necessary that the offer should have been made and accepted in advance. As soon as the offer has been accepted, usually evidenced by his signing the register, a contract has been made and he can be compelled to pay even if he does not stay.

CONTRACTS MADE BY MINORS[2]

Under the Act certain contracts made by minors are void. In fact, they can be enforced by the minor but not against him. Such contracts include the goods supplied, or to be supplied, other than contracts for goods supplied, or to be supplied, other than contracts for necessaries. Goods, for this purpose, includes services, accommodation, etc. Necessaries have been defined as bought for the necessary use of the party in order to support himself properly in the degree, state and station in life in which he moves. The provision of lodgings for a person under 18-years could be the subject of an enforceable contract but might be voidable especially if it were luxurious or expensive. Even if accommodation and food were regarded as necessaries any special services, such as car hire or theatre tickets, might be regarded otherwise. It is immaterial that the minor misrepresents his age. There is no redress against him once he has received and disposed of the goods or services, nor can he be sued for deceit.

It would be very unwise to enter into a contract with an infant for a dance or reception, even if he purports to be acting on behalf of an incorporated club or association, since the debt incurred might be irrecoverable. An infant could, of course, be a traveller, and an innkeeper could not lawfully refuse him accommodation if it is available, but he could collect payment in advance.

CONTRACT BY MARRIED WOMEN

A married woman has power to hold property and can be sued independently of her

2. In law a minor is now a person under 18 years of age.

husband. A husband is not liable for the debts of his wife unless he has expressly or by implication authorised her to pledge his credit. A woman staying in a hotel with her husband, or, in the accommodation booked with his knowledge and consent, could safely be regarded as authorised to pledge his credit unless he had stated otherwise. However, in the case of a wedding reception, say, it might be possible for a married woman to incur substantial liabilities without the consent of her husband (especially if they were separated), in which event she alone would be personally liable.

CANCELLATIONS

From what has been said above, it is evident that when an offer (e.g. of accommodation) has been made and accepted there is a contract which cannot be rescinded by one party without the consent of the other. The law provides a number of remedies for breach of contract, including, in some cases, specific performance (i.e. the defaulting party is compelled to do what he undertook to do) but the normal remedy is the award of damages.

If an intending visitor has made a contract and wishes to cancel it, the hotel can claim damages. The contract may be to stay for more than one night, in which case staying for a lesser period than that agreed to would be a breach of contract. Similarly, if a banquet, or other service, has been offered and accepted, the customer cannot cancel without exposing himself to an enforceable demand for compensation.

The injured party (in this case the hotel) must minimise his loss as far as is reasonably possible. In the case of a room booked, for example, he must endeavour to re-let it and in the case of a banquet it must endeavour to cancel the order for food and the engagement of casual labour. In an action for damages, it be taken into account the time remaining between the cancellation and the date of the cancelled booking and any special circumstances, which might make it easy or difficult to reduce the loss. Even if it is not possible to re-let the accommodation, or let it on the same terms, the hotel cannot claim the full price as qutoed to the intending guest. A deduction must be made in respect of food included in the price but not supplied, linen not used, and any other expense which has been avoided by non-fulfilment of the contract.

If a deposit has been taken the repayment of the deposit can be withheld if the booking is cancelled. It would still be open to the customer to sue for the return of the deposit but he would rarely do so, since the hotel would counter-claim for damages arising from the breach of contract.

A contract made by offer and acceptance is binding on the hotel also. If he has promised to provide accommodation or services and his offer has been accepted or if the customer has offered to take accommodation and the hotel has accepted his offer, he is liable for not fulfilling his promise. This could apply when a particular room, or type of room, has been promised and only another room or type of room is available. For this reason it is unwise to make specific promises without qualification. In the case of over-booking it will usually be sufficient to reserve accommodation of a similar or superior type elsewhere and to provide suitable transport. If the substitute accommodation is more expensive, the hotel at fault shall have to pay the difference to avoid the possibility of legal action in respect of his breach of contract. Even then there might be other damages, for example, if the guest had arranged to meet someone or to eceive mail or telephone calls at the hotel, which could be the subject of a claim. Nevertheless, the court will always deal sympathetically with a defendant who has done his best to repair the injury he has caused.

Enquiry for Accommodation (not amounting to an offer)

Customer to Hotel

To ABC Hotel

I am arranging a tour in March and I should be grateful if you would let me know whether you can reserve 20 double rooms for the night of the 25th, for our team and supporters.

Your sincerely

(customer)

Hotel to Customer

Dear Sir/Madam

After your dinner-dance last year you asked me for a booking for the first Monday in Feburary again. I should be glad if you could let me know if this is to be treated as a firm reservation.

Your sincerely,

(ABC Hotel)

Supply of Information (not an offer)

Hotel to Customer

Dear Sir/Madam

In reply to your letter I am glad to be able to inform you that we can make available at the time of writing, the accommodation you require. The charge will be ₹ ....

Yours sincerely,

(ABC Hotel)

Provisional Booking of Accommodation (amounting to a conditional offer)

Customer to Hotel

To ABC Hotel

Please reserve a twin-bedded room for four or five nights covering ...... if we get knocked out in the first round we shall only want to stay until Friday morning; if we get into the semi-final we shall want to stay until Saturday, and if we should be lucky enough to get into the final we shall want the room for that night also.

Yours Sincerely,

(Customer)

Hotel to Customer

Dear Sir/Madam

I have provisionally reserved 30 twin-bedded rooms for your party, subject to cancellation not later than 15th March. If any rooms are not cancelled by then but are not required by you, it is agreed that you will pay three- quarters of the rate for any rooms we are unable to re-let.

Yours Sincerely,

(ABC Hotel)

Counter-offer : Conditional Acceptance (invalidating previous offer by the other party)

Customer to Hotel

To ABC Hotel

Thank you for your offer of a single room with bath-room at Rs. 1500 per night, but, I am afraid this is more than I wanted to pay. I do want a room for that night. Please let me know if you have any cheaper rooms.

Yours Sincerely

(Customer)

Hotel to Customer

Unfortunately we could not accommodate you for five nights commencing.......... We can offer you the accommodation for four nights only. I have reserved this for you.

Yours Sincerely

(ABC Hotel)

Request for further Information (not a couner-offer)

Hotel to Customer

Dear Sir/Madam

Thank you for your letter confirming the reservation referred to in our letter of the ...... You do not mention the ages of your children. Perhaps it would be good enough for you to let us know, as we have to make special arrangements in the dining room for your children.

Yours Sincerely,

(ABC Hotel)

Customer to Hotel

To ABC Hotel

I should be glad if you would let me know whether you can supply Bollinger NV or what the corkage charge would be if we brought our own.

Yours Sincerely,

(Guest)

Partial Cancellation (amounting to a breach of contract)

Customer to Hotel

To ABC Hotel

Last October I booked a double room for the last two weeks in January. Now, I find that I shall require the room for the first week only, commencing on the same date as previously arranged, namely......

Yours Sincerely,

(Customer)

Offer Apparently made by a Minor (contract not enforceable if accepted)

Customer to Hotel

To ABC Hotel

Last year you arranged our fourth form super. Now we are in the fifth and we would like you to book a similar event for the evening of ......

Yours Sincerely,

(Minor)

Letter from a Husband (repudiating liability for wife's debts)

I understand that my wife has booked room with you from .... you may hold me responsible for her accommodation and normal meals if necessary, but I cannot undertake to settle her drink bills, or any other expenses, if she is unable to do so.

Yours Sincerely,

(Customer)

Hotel to Customer

Dear Sir/Madam

On hearing from you by return post, I shall be happy to reserve a single room with private bathroom for the night of .... at a charge of .... including breakfast.

Yours Sincerely,

(ABC Hotel)

Customer to Hotel

To ABC Hotel

Further to our telephonic conversation I should be grateful if you would confirm that you can reserve a twin-bedded room overlooking the garden for three nights commencing ....

Yours Sincerely,

(Customer)

Acceptance of Offer

Customer to Hotel

To ABC Hotel

Thank you for your letter. The rooms you mention will suit us admirably and we shall be arriving in time for dinner on the...... We shall be staying at least three days and I hope that if we wish to extend our stay you will be able to accommodate us.

Yours Sincerely,

(Customer)

Hotel to Customer

Dear Sir/Madam

In response to the request contained in your letter of the ... I confirm that I have reserved our ballroom for your daughter's wedding reception on ... at a charge of .... which will include.... I note that the wedding will take place .... and that the guests will arrive here at ....

Yours Sincerely,

(ABC Hotel)

Conditional Offer for Accommodation

Hotel to Customer

Dear Sir/Madam

Provided your dog is small and well-behaved there is no objection to your keeping it in your bedroom, but dogs are not allowed in the public rooms. If the dog is one of the larger breeds we can accommodate it in the stables.

Yours Sincerely,

(ABC Hotel)

Customer to Hotel

To ABC Hotel

You may have a room available and I shall be glad to book it for the evening of the ... if you can assure me that it would accommodate sixty guests in comfort.

Yours Sincerely,

(Customer)

REGISTRATION

The name, nationality and date of arrival of every over-night guest over the age of 16 must be recorded, but not necessarily in a book or bound register. It is not necessary that each guest should enter his name personally. A courier, for example, could furnish information in respect of his entire party. It is quite in order to make a collective entry when the names are the same, as Dr and Mrs. S. and Miss Negi provided it is quite clear what are the names of each member of the party i.e., Dr A. Negi, Mrs S. Negi and Miss Negi and friend would not be sufficient if the friend were over 16, since the name of the friend has not been recorded.

The hotel is not obliged to ascertain that the name entered is the true name of the guest and cannot demand proof. If he suspects that a guest has given a false name in order to obtain credit by fraud he can either report his suspicion to the police or obtain payment in advance. But if he knows positively the true identity of a guest giving a false name it is his responsibility to record it correctly.

Nor is the hotel obliged to ascertain whether a couple purporting to be man and wife are, in fact, married. If the same woman repeatedly came to a hotel with different men claiming that each was her husband, then, the hotel might expose himself to the risk of prosecution for keeping a disorderly house.

In addition to furnish information about name and nationality, aliens are required to state particulars of their passport or registration certificate and, on leaving, their date of departure, and next destination.

Hotels are sometimes requested to make their register available for inspection by private detectives. Only a police officer, or someone authorised by a court, can demand to see the register. If a request is refused the person seeking information can apply to the court for an order, or can subpoena the hotel to give evidence.

The register of guests must be retained for at least 12 months.

OCCUPIERS' LIABILITY

Responsibility for loss of or damage to the property of guests relates only to keepers and to their guests (i.e. those who have reserved sleeping accommodation) and is applicable only between 0000 hrs. on the day of arrival to 2400 hrs. on the day of departure.

The Occupiers' Liability Act, 1957, in Britain, places responsibility for the avoidance of conditions which might lead to personal injury on the occupier of any premises to which the public is admitted. It applies not only to guests and customers, but also to enquirers, tradesmen and anyone else who may legally be on the premises.

The occupier is bound to take such care as in all the circumstances of the case is reasonable to see that the visitor will be reasonably safe in using the premises for the purposes for which he is invited or permitted by the occupier to be there".

What is "reasonable" will depend on the particular circumstances and people involved.

Example :

1. If an elderly man, following a sign pointing to the toilet, opened a door and fell down flight of unlit stairs leading to the cellar (such a case has occurred in Britain) the occupier might be liable for any injury he sustains, but if on the door it was clearly marked 'Private' or Staff Only or even Mind the Step it might be thought that sufficient precautions had been taken to avoid such an accident.
2. If a builders' merchant, delivering paint to the maintenance department, fell over a ladder it might be thought that he could have expected ladders or other obstructions to be in such a place; if a ladder were left in a dangerous position in the front hall, the position might be considered to be different.

Each case must be considered on its merits if and when a claim arises, but in general if hotel proprietors act with prudence and care and staff are trained to avoid dangerous practices and to report possible safety hazards, the effects of the Act will not be unduly rigorous.

A lien may be defined as a claim on some one's property as security for payment of money due. Traditionally, when a guest fails to pay for accommodations provided and services rendered, the hotel could put a lien on his personal belongings. Liens were allowed to be put on all guest baggage and unless excluded by law, on the automobile of the guest. Once a lien was put on a guest's property, the hotel was requried to exercise 'reasonable care' for the property and might be liable for negligence if it failed to do so. A Network court in Britain was of the opinion and declared the lien law invalid. The court said that, The inkeeper's right under lien law to seize a defaulting guest's property and to sell it at a public auction, is not questioned. All that is necessary is that the fundamentals of due process, be observed. By due process, the court meant that the guest should receive due notice and a chance to be heard before the property seizure.

The best way to prevent default on bills is to require advance payment, failing that, a hotel could obtain a temporary injuction to restrain a guest from moving out personal belongings.

THE HOTEL LIEN

A hotel can, if it wishes, demand that an intending guest pays in advance for the food and services to be supplied. If it does not do so and a guest is unable to pay his bill, the hotel has a lien on the property which the guest has with him; i.e. the hotel can seize the luggage of the guest, and that of his wife, until the bill is paid. He has no right to detain the guest himself or take off any clothes he may be wearing. Since vehicles, horses and other live animals have now ceased to be the hotel's unqualified responsibility these can no longer be held in such circumstances. This right of lien applies only to hotels although it is not uncommon for lessors of furnished accommodation to attempt to detain their tenant's property as security for unpaid accounts.

BAIL, PLEDGE AND LIEN

There is a clear distinction in law among bail, lien and pledge. A bailment is a delivery of goods from the owner to someone else in trust, or for a specific purpose. A pledge is anything put in the possession of another as security for the fulfilment of a contract of the payment of a debt and liable to be forfeited in case of failure. A lien is the right of a creditor to retain the property of a debtor until a debt is satisfied. Once the creditor has parted with the property he cannot reclaim it though he can, of course, seek other remedies for the recovery of his debt. If, for example, a hotel relinquishes possession of a guest's property on which it has a lien in exchange for a cheque it cannot demand its return if the cheque proves to be valueless, and if it gives up the property on part-payment of the debt it has lost its security for the remainder.

If goods have been in a hotel's possession as a lien for not less than six weeks without the bill's having been paid, the hotel may sell the goods by public auction.

The hotel must first endeavour to contact the owner, but if it is unable to do so (for example, if a letter addressed to him at his last known address is returned undelivered) it must, at least a month before the sale, advertise in one national and one local newspaper, giving the name of the owner, if known, and a brief description of the goods.

If the proceeds of the sale are more than sufficient to pay the outstanding account and the expenses (e.g. the cost of advertising and the auctioneer's commission) the hotel must pay the balance to the original owner of the goods on demand.

LOST PROPERTY

Although property which is left in public places (such as hotels and restaurants) may be dealt with by the police, there is no legal obligation on the hotels to report to the police details of anything they find on their premises. Obviously a good deal of property is left behind in the course of the year, and it would be a considerable nuisance to all parties if each such item was handed over to the police. However, it would be advisable to hand over to them valuables such as jewellery, furs or sums of cash over a certain amount, say, Rs. 500. Apart from relieving the proprietor of the responsibility for holding valuables, it would also be convincing evidence that as much as possible was being done to trace the true owner of the property.

In Britain the Theft Act 1968 gives some guidance in the handling of property left and unclaimed. The appropriate section states that one person's appropriation of property belonging to another is not to be regarded as dishonest if he appropriates the property in the belief that the person to whom the property belongs cannot be traced after taking reasonable steps.

Hence, the finding and keeping of lost property only becomes a criminal offence if the finder believes that he could find the true owner and return the goods, and if he fails to take reasonable steps to do so.

HANDLING LOST PROPERTY

As lost property accumulates, it becomes an embarrassment, particularly with storage problems, and there comes a time when there is no alternative but to sell, give or throw away unclaimed property. It is, therefore, important to draw up procedures for handling such goods.

First, it should be made clear that if any member of the staff, however senior, finds articles on the premises, these goods rightly belong to the employer and not to the finder. Lost property should, therefore, be handed over to a central office, where the security officer is incharge. He is the proper channel through which all matters concerning lost and found articles should be routed. Otherwise, the Manager or Assistant Manager's office is appropriate place, where a locking cabinet be used for the proper protection of goods. Every one should know where to take the items which he finds on the premises, and to make things as easy and quick as possible. It is obvious that a receiving place must be decided upon where someone is normally available. If the staff find they cannot hand over goods which, they find there develops misunderstanding and irritation, and the inclination might be to dump such property to a department drawer or cupboard.

RECORDS

Accurate records should be kept. When an article is handed over as 'found', a written report should be made and a receipt given to the finder. There are, of course, a variety of ways of drawing up such records, but a duplicate book along the following lines is suggested:

1. Date of finding
2. Place of finding
3. Name of finder
4. Private address of finder
5. Description of property.
6. Time of finding
7. Department
8. Signature of receiver
9. Signature of finder

The original copy should be detached and handed over to the finder; the carbon copy should remain in the book. The number of the top right hand corner of the duplicate copy should be so that it could be torn off and attached to the article and placed in the 'Lost Property' cabinet in monthly order. If the finder subsequently wanted to reclaim the goods on production of his original copy, the bottom number on the book copy would make for easy transaction.

DISPOSAL OF LOST PROPERTY

A 'resonable period' of holding should then be decided upon, and as the law gives no true indication of what this should be, it is usual for the employer to take the law into his own hand and make this decision himself. Six months would appear to be a reasonable time for holding, except for valuable goods and it would be wiser to retain them for a much longer period of time anything up to five years, in fact.

The Hotel or Restaurant Manager, who has legal claim on property found on his premises (other than the true owner), should reserve the right to destroy any article which he may consider unsuitable to return to the finder: for instance, a fur coat which had attracted moths and was contaminating other items or drugs which could become the basis for criminal action. Naturally, perishable goods should be disposed of as soon as possible.

CLAIMS : INFORMING THE FINDER

Everything possible should be done to find the rightful owner of lost items. If the item is claimed by the rightful owner, it is a good policy to inform the finder and a formal letter is recommended on the following lines:

Informing the Finder

Dear Sir/Madam.

I would like to inform you that the .... found by you in the .... Restaurant/ Lounge / Department (etc.) and handed over to the Security Officer has been claimed by ... to whom the article was handed over on ... against his/her signature, recorded in the lost property book in the Security/ Manager's office.

Your name and address, as the finder of the property in question has been supplied to the claimant.

Thank you for your action in handling the article in.

Yours faithfully,
(Authorised Signatory)

REMINDER TO FINDER

Although it is not necessarily the responsibility of the establishment to remind the finder that the property handed over by him now be claimed by him following the expiry of the time limit for holding, it is a courtesy much appreciated and does save verbal enquiries at inconvenient times. Here again a formal letter is suggested :

Reminder to Finder

To .... (finder)

Dear Sir/Madam,

The ..... found by you and handed over to the Security Officer/Manager has not been claimed.

You may now apply for its return and should call at the Security/ Manager's Office to sign a form when the article in question will be handed over to you.

If you do not wish to claim the article, please endorse this form accordingly and return it to the undersigned.

Yours faithfully,

....

(Authorised Signatory)

As it is possible that the true owner of lost property may turn up at any time in the future, the new possessor must be made aware of this fact, for it would then be necessary for him to surrender the property.

FORM OF INDEMNITY

It is a safeguard, therefore, for the new possessor of the article to sign a Form of Indemnity when he has taken back the property he originally found. This Form of Indemnity would be phrased thus:

Form of Identity

To ....

....

....

I, the undersigned, hereby acknowledge having received the ..... found by me on .... and I undertake to indemnify ..... (name of firm) against any claim or demand which may be made against the company in respect of this property.

Signed.............

Witness............

Date...............

SALE OF UNCLAIMED PROPERTY

Again, if you have kept goods for a reasonable time and the owner does not turn up, and the finder has either left your employ and cannot be traced, or alternatively does not want the goods, you may decide to sell them. It is important in this event to get the best possible price for them, for if the owner did subsequently claim them back, he would be entitled to the value of the goods or article.

Although there is often some doubt about what should be done with money which has been left behind, this may be treated in the same way as lost property. Where notes are involved, it would obviously be wise to keep a note of serial numbers to help in later, identification if necessary. Loose change might reasonably be put into some Charity Box after the expiry of the holding period.

NOTICES

Employees should be in no doubt about their responsibilities and duties in this matter, and as well as details written into rule books or staff handbooks. Notices should be displayed in staff quarters drawing attention to the fact that any article found on the premises should be handed over to the Security Officer or Manager, who guarantees to ensure its safe custody until the rightful owner claims it, or to return it to the finder after a certain period of time.

Apart from liability as a hotel, the management of an hotel or a restaurant may be liable for civil wrongs known as torts against property. A tort is a wilful and intentional act which does harm to another person without just cause or legal excuse.

TRESPASS TO GOODS

Trespass to goods consists of any direct act of physical interference with the goods of another person without justifiable excuse. Trespass is concerned not only with interference with the goods, but with depriving the owner of their use. Searching through a guest's luggage without justifiable cause could constitute trespass of property which is objectionable in itself and does not require proof of actual damage.

DETINUE

Detinue is the wilful interference with the goods or chattels of another person in such a way that the owner is deprived of them. As is pointed out elsewhere, a person who is not an hotelier has no right to detain the goods of a guest, even though money may be due from him and even though the hotel may detain the guest's property only till the outstanding account is paid. A refusal to allow a guest to take away his own property could lead to an action for detinue for which the guest could order the restoration of the property, or monetary damages, or both.

CONVERSION

Conversion is a wilful act which causes the owner of goods to be deprived of their possessions. It may consist of taking the goods away, selling them, destroying them or (perhaps most important for the hotelier) delivering them wrongfully to a third party. Thus, if someone is in possession of the goods of 'A' and delivers them to 'B' on 'B's representation that he is the true owner then the person delivering the goods will be liable to 'A' if 'B' acted without authority. If a customer, 'A', hangs up his umbrella on a hats- rack in a restaurant and another customer, 'B', takes it away, the proprietor of the restaurant is not liable but if, at the request of 'B' (or without being asked) a waiter gave 'A's, umbrella to him, the waiter and, therefore, his employer would probably be liable for conversion.

BAILMENT

A bailment is a delivery of goods to another person in trust for a specific purpose, for example, handing over goods to a warehouseman or carrier. If a guest hands over his property to a hotel servant, even outside the hotel (at a railway station, for example) for delivery to the hotel and the goods fail to arrive, the hotel will be liable as a bailee. Similarly, if a customer handed over a watch to the hall porter asking him to take it to a repairer, the hall porter (and thereby his employer) would be a bailee until he had delivered it back. It need hardly be said that when property is handed over for safe custody not only in a safe but also in a cloakroom, the recipient is a bailee and is responsible for restoring it to the owner on production of evidence of ownership, such as a ticket or receipt. This is why the limitation of liability does not extend to property which has been handed over for safe custody.

COMPLAINTS

Complaints are to be expected as part of the ordinary course of any business. As an expression of dissatisfaction or a grievance or anything that disturbs a guest they are to be taken seriously. They are in fact valuable because they direct attention to possible areas of improvement in operating efficiency, and give a chance for constructive action, whether it is in improving service, product or public image.

Although there are no procedures which can be laid down to cover the exact techniques for attending to every complaining guest or customer, there are certain rules and standards of behaviour which should be taught, understood, and applied, by every member of the staff from the Manager downwards.

COMPLAINTS : GUIDELINES AND PROCEDURES

Every hotel needs a policy for dealing with complaints which makes clear its desire to give the best possible service in every area of its operation, and that the staff must spare no pains to see that guests or customers are comfortable and satisfied. It must emphasize the fact that complaints which help to improve service, or organise a more efficient business, are welcomed, and that properly handled, they can be the cheapest form of advertisement, improving goodwill and possibly turning an irate guest into a customer for life.

To make no provision for training employees in dealing with complaints is short-sighted, for a 'brush-off' from a trainee or unskilled chambermaid could result in the complainant taking the matter further to a higher rank of management, and then the original complaint is doubled with the added accusation of rudeness or inefficiency by the member of staff concerned.

No complex system is necessary, just simple procedures, a few ground rules repeated often, and built into the induction training, so that no one is in any doubt about the management's thinking on the subject of complaints, and how they must be handled. Below are listed some guidelines for instruction :

1. Faced with a complaining or dissatisfied guest, the vital thing is a patient hearing. Let the guest tell the whole story, without interruption.
2. Listen sympathetically. Quite often a 'difficult' person's main motive is to find someone who respects his point of view. Having been satisfied in this respect, he does not seek anything further. There are outward and obvious signs that a listener is being sympathetic and understanding. The way he stands (e.g. arms akimbo, hand on hip, leaning); the way he looks (e.g. shifting eyes, half-smile); the movement of hands or feet (e.g. fiddling with pencil or cloth, flexing of muscles); shifting of feet all could indicate a truculence ill suited to the guest's mood, and likely to give rise to other complaints.
3. Say 'I am sorry this has happened'. Even when a complaint is known to be quite unjustified, the words, 'I am sorry' are soothing to the guest and can be said with sincerity: (a) because the guest is so upset and (b) because the guest has upset the person receiving the complaint !
4. Promptness in dealing with a complaint is a mark of courtesy. However, as time may be needed to get the facts, learn exactly what happened and the extent of the damage, which may take the investigator behind the scenes and out of the guest's presence, permission to do this should be courteously asked of the guest. This may appear to be an unnecessary courtesy, but it is a courtesy nevertheless.
5. While these enquiries are being made, see that the complainant is made comfortable and that any undue worries concerning trains, taxis, baggage etc. are looked after by other members of staff.
6. A drink might be offered or any other small service which may seem to be appropriate at the time in fact any little extra gesture which shows the guest that the complaint is being taken seriously and is important, will help to rebuild a feeling of justice and goodwill in the organisation.
7. Never take cover behind ambiguities such as,

   'We have never had a complaint like this before'

   'It is company's policy'

   'This was not dealt with by me'

   The guest does not care about excuses or the fact that it is not your particular fault; what he wants to know is whether something is going to be done about his grievance, and if so, what.
8. There are occasions when to defer to a complainant and ask, 'how best would you like us to deal with this, Sir'?, passes the onus back to the guest and gives the establishment the measure of the complainant's demands. If these demands are excessive, they at least form a basis for negotiation, or allow management to explain the reasons why they may not be able to comply with, while at the same time enlisting the guest's sense of justice.
9. Keep control of the situation. The more upset or unresonable the guest may be, the more necessary it is to keep calm and pleasant. Any complaint is a challenging situation

and a test of good human relations, and the more courtesy and charm are seen to be present, the more likely the complaining guest woud recognise a person of integrity and intelligence who will handle his complaint in a civilised and efficient manner.

10. Adopt a constructive, business-like attitude, making it easier to move out of the sphere of emotion and into reason.
11. Avoid being drawn into an argument, because whoever wins, you are in trouble. If the guest wins you may have had to give way on an important point or principle. If you win, you have probably lost goodwill and antagon sed a customer even if you are right. Never 'talk down' or humiliate a guest, however much you may be in the right track.
12. Give a decision as quickly as the circumstances allow. This is not difficult in restaurants when a complaint has been received about a meal. It is usually quite easy to replace. It must be stressed that no guest should be allowed to continue to eat a meal with which he is not completely satisfied. That way, he will always remember where he had a bad meal, even through an adjustment may have been made for it on the bill. There is a saying that 'Quality is remembered long after, pr ce is forgotten', and this applies to merchandise as well as service. Replace with a freshly prepared dish as soon as possible, in a friendly manner.
13. If delay in making an adjustment is necessary for example, an error on a bill, re-arrangement of a bedroom, a wrong booking, lost laundry etc., explain that there will be some delay and if possible state how long. Make helpful suggestions to occupy the guest's time meanwhile refreshment, rest-room whatever it is, make certain that he in comfortable and occupied so that he does not have to brood over his grievances and to magnify the sense of injury.
14. Hesitation in dealing with a complaint is a major mistake.
15. Finally, in settling the complaint, do so with a straightforward apology in a friendly composed way. An adjustment made grudgingly might as well not be made at all, because a very important object of the adjustment is to retain the customer's goodwill, and deepen it if possible.

Immediate action should be taken to put the complaint right. Particularly in serious cases, however, the underlying cause must be analysed to ensure that what has happened is not a symptom of some basic fault in the system and, therefore, liable to recur. A simple example of this would be where a guest complaints that his vegetables are cold. This could indicate:

1. A fault in the electricity or power supply to the hot dishes in the service area.
2. That they were placed on to cold serving dishes.
3. That the waiter was not working systematically through his tables, so that orders were piling up and getting cold.
4. That his service at the table was too slow.
5. That the Head Waiter was not doing his job of checking and surveillance efficiently.

It may also happen that an apparently unreasonable complaint is a disguise for something else that is not being openly expressed a vague dissatisfaction with charges, service or attitudes. Another point to watch out for is the query that looks like a complaint.

For instance, this may occur when an intending organiser of a function has received quotes from a number of establishments. He may want an explanation as to why one place charges more than another to justify queries in his own mind, or to have right answers to take back to a committee.

1. In order to analyse complaints, then, it is necessary to ask the following questions :
2. Is this a complaint of which the cause can be put right or is it a matter of company policy or principle?
3. Is a 'once-off' complaint or a symptom of some deeper fault, either in a person or a system?
4. Is it a genuine complaint or the product of a special situation a difficult or cranky guest, or some clash of personality with a particular member of the staff?
5. Is it a travel matter that has grown in size or intensity because of neglect?

INTERNATIONAL LAWS : WINES /ALCOHOL

There are numerous guides to the licensing laws, some of which are in lawyers' language and some written for laymen. The main points are outlined here, but in the major matters, such as applications for licences or alterations in licences, those concerned would be well advised to consult a solicitor experienced in these matters.

A licence can be held by one person or by two or more together or, in the case of limited companies, by a director or secretary of the company as an individual. In the case of tenanted premises it is the tenant, not the landlord, who holds the licence and whose name is, therefore, exhibited above the front door. Applications must be made to the concerned authority, with copies to the police, the rating authorities, and the fire authority.

ON-LICENCE

An on-licence, permitting the sale of liquor for consumption on or off the premises may, at the request of the applicant or otherwise, impose conditionsmaking the licence a Conditional Licence. Nowadays such conditions are normally limited to rendering a licence a six-day one (the establishment being closed on Sundays); early closing (closing the bar one hour earlier than the normal permitted hour in the evening); or seasonal (closing altogether for part of the year). When a renewal or transfer of a conditional licence is granted the competent authority must revoke the condition, if requested to do so. Such conditions can be applied to restaurant and residential licences also.

RESIDENTIAL LICENCE

Residential licences permit the sale of liquor only to residents or their friends (the resident must pay for the drinks) on the premises but if a meal (e.g. a packed lunch) is supplied for consumption elsewhere it is permissible to sell liquor for consumption with it.

RESTAURANT LICENCE

A restaurant licence permits the sale of liquor to persons taking table meals.

Provided the applicant is of full age and a fit and proper person, and the premises are suitable for residence or meals as the case may be. An application for such a licence, or for its renewal, cannot normally be refused. There are other grounds for refusal, such as where premises have previously been badly conducted or where a large proportion of the customers are under 18; and the holder of any type of licence can be disqualified on conviction for certain offences, some of which are detailed below in the note on the responsibilities of the licensee.

A restaurant licence may be for six days, early closing or seasonal. When the premises are open for luncheon only there may be a condition restricting the permitted hours so as to exclude the evening and when dinners only are served, the earlier period of the day may be excluded.

For both residential and restaurant licences the court may make other conditions such as that there shall be no bar or tap, and the availability of water and non-alcoholic drinks is an implied condition of a restaurant licence.

The permitted hours are prescribed by the local authorities.

Provided there is a break of 2-hours after mid-day the competent authority may help to vary the local hours and can add an extra half-hour to 11.00 p.m. if justified by local circumstance. Sometimes this is done only for certain days of the week (e.g. Fridays and Saturdays) or certain seasons of the year (e.g. the summer months).

Liquor may be consumed on the premises for up to ten minutes after the end of permitted hours, provided it was bought within permitted hours, and liquor so purchased may be taken away during this ten-minute period provided it is in a sealed container.

Liquor purchased for consumption with a meal (provided it was purchased within permitted hours) can be consumed within half-an hour after the end of permitted hours (afternoon or evening).

There are important arrangements whereby, apart from the drinking-up time allowed, the permitted hours of restaurants can be extended. In premises suitable for the purpose where drinks are supplied only as ancillary to a substantial meal, the competent authority cannot refuse the application for Supper Hour Certificate which permits the sale of drinks with meals for one hour after the normal closing time and up to 3.00 p.m. at lunch time. The competent authority must satisfy themselves in such a manner as they think fit that the conditions of the Act have been complied with (as to the premises being structurally suitable and bona-fide being used for the provision of meals) and could, if they wish, call for evidence or hear evidence to the contrary, but in practice they rarely do.

A notice must be displayed on the premises to the effect that such a certificate is in force.

A Special Hours Certificate can be applied for at any Licensing Sessions. It may be granted for only part of the week or part of the year and may specify the part of the premises to which it applies. It is only available when intoxicants are supplied as ancillary to a substantial meal where music and dancing is provided, and, of course, the premises must be licensed for music and dancing also. The Special Hours Certificate permits the sale of liquor with meals up to 2.00 a.m. provided the music and dancing does not end before then.

A notice must be exhibited outlining the details of the certificate.

An Extended Hours Order can be applied for when live musical or other entertainment is provided in addition to meals. This extends the permitted hours to 1.00 a.m. on weekdays. The competent authorities have discretion whether to grant an application for an Extended Hours Order or not, taking into account not only the premises, entertainment and meals provided, but also the comfort and convenience of neighbouring residents. As in other cases a notice must be exhibited on the premises if an Extended Hours Order is in force.

A General Order of Exemption can be granted for special occasions such as New Year's Eve. A General Order of Exemption may also be granted to allow premises in the vicinity of a public market, or where there is some other local need, to remain open beyond the permitted hours. In London these orders are granted by the Police.

A Special Order of Exemption can be granted to an no-licensee for a special occasion such as a wedding or a banquet. Hotels and restaurants doing regular banqueting business usually have a well-established procedure for applying for SOEs (Special Order of Exemptions) giving the required notice in advance. There may be difficulty in obtaining an exemption order for a Sunday in some special cases or for wedding receptions for actors or other workers who cannot hold the reception on a weekday.

THE RESPONSIBILITIES OF LICENSEES

There are a number of duties imposed on licensees. Many of these are matters of commonsense but in some cases the law might be infringed unwittingly and ignorance of the law is, or course, no excuse.

The sale of drinks on credit is forbidden but those taking meals may pay for drinks when they pay for the meal (which need not be immediately or on completion of the meal, or even before leaving the premises) and those who are resident may pay for drinks when they pay for their accommodation.

The sale of intoxicants to habitual drunkards within three years after conviction as such is an offence. Procuring, or assisting in procuring, liquor for consumption by a person who is already drunk is an offence. Being found drunk on licensed premises is also an offence.

Wages may not be paid in a public house except, of course, to the staff employed there.

It is a serious offence to harbour thieves or reputed thieves, policemen on duty, or prostitutes for an unreasonable time. If a licensee allows his house to be used as a brothel he is liable to a penalty, forfeiture of his licence and permanent disqualification for holding a licence.

In England under Town Police Clauses Act 1847, Section 35, every person keeping any house, shop, room or other place of public resort for the sale or consumption of refreshments of any kind, who knowingly offers common prostitutes or reputed thieves to assemble and continue on his premises[2] is liable to be fined[3]. Cases have been reported in which the proprietors of late-night snackbars have been fined under this Act.

CHILDREN AND YOUNG PERSONS

It is an offence for a licensee or his servant to sell intoxicating liquor to a person under 18 or to allow such a person to consume liquor in a bar, and it is an offence for any one to buy (or attempt to buy) drinks for young persons in a bar. Beer, port, cider or sherry may be sold to a person over the age of 16 for consumption with a meal in part of the premises set aside for meals. Cigarettes or cigarette papers may not be sold to a person apparently under 16–years of age but this prohibition is not, it seems, applicable to cigars.

3. Section 35, Tawn Police Clauses Act 1847, England

Children under 14 must not be allowed to be in a bar, or any other place wholly or mainly used for the sale and consumption of liquor, but children may be admitted to a licensed restaurant or part of a licensed house where meals are served.

A child over 5 or a young person of any age may consume beer, wine or spirits on licensed premises provided they do not themselves purchase the drinks and consumption does not take place in a bar.

WINES

There are numerous pitfalls to be avoided in descriptions of wines but if the supplier was a reputable wine merchant and the wine list said no more than the label on the bottle it might be possible to shift the blame. It would be less easy to excuse serving wine from a polythene bag and describing it as wine from the wood.

FOOD

There had been previous legislationwhich made it an offence to apply any false description to goods. There are many Acts which define a number of offences concerning the description of food. The '*Chef*' called upon to account for the origin of Aylesbury duckling or Norfolk turkey might have escaped by saying that these were merely descriptive terms like Dover Sole or Caneton Nantais or Chicken Maryland but it would have been more difficult to define the use of terms like Wye, Torridge, Tweed, or Tay to describe salmon which did not emanate from those rivers.

It has always been a breach of contract, for which damages might be awarded, to offer one thing and supply another but the Act now imposes on local authority's responsibility for enforcement.

In a suit for breach of control, of course, it was necessary for the plaintiff to show that he had suffered some injury or loss, however slight; in a prosecution for unlawful actions it is not necessary to prove that anyone has suffered.

CONSUMER PROTECTION

For centuries the tradition had gown up in common law that the sale of goods was governed by the principle ''caveat emptor" (let the buyer beware). As an eighteenth century judge put it, 'If the vendor says that a horse is sound in mind and limb and the buyer can see for himself, if he cares to look, that it has but one eye, then there is no fraud."

In the Consumer Protection Act 1986, India introduced some important new principles. One of these is that descriptions of goods given orally can be false descriptions within the meaning of the Act. Such descriptions may be related to the quantity, size or gauge of goods, what they are made of, their fitness for the purpose, strength, performance, behaviour or accurancy and any other physical attributes they may be said to possess. Where, when and by whom they were made and any other information regarding their history can, if stated incorrectly, lead to a prosecution. It would almost certainly be an offence to describe as 'morning gathered with the dew on them' mushrooms bought from Convent Garden without such a warranty and those offering Strasbourg foie-gras or Rillettes due Mans would be well advised to ensure that their origin was not other than as stated.

SERVICES

Another innovation of special importance to hotelkeepers is that it is now illegal to make false statements about services, accommodation and facilities, if such statements are made knowingly or recklessly. It would be an offence, for example, to say in a brochure that a four-poster bed was used by Queen Elizabeth I if that were not the case but it might be safe to say that it was reputed to have been so used. It would be an offence to describe a bedroom as spacious if it were clearly not so or to say that it had a sea view if the sea was never visible from it. False statements can be related not only to the provision of services, accommodation or facilities but also to their nature; the time at which they are provided; how they are provided and who provides them; their examination, approval or evaluation by any person; where accommodation is provided or what amenities it has. The statement can be spoken, or included in a letter or brochure or in an advertisement. The opportunities for falling foul of the law are almost boundless. A prosecution of a tour operator concerned a false description (concerning a hotel in Spain) made in a brochure which went to press twelve months or more beforehand, before the hotel was even completed.

Fortunately for those offering goods and services not every false statement is covered by the Act. Whoever made the false statement must be shown to have known that it was false at the time unless he made it recklessly, not caring whether it was true or not. If an offer is made in good faith and circumstances prevent its fulfilment, there may be a remedy in the civil court, by an action for breach of contract.

Courts have been given power to award compensation to persons suffering from a criminal act. It is, therefore, open to the court to make an award in respect of breach of the act. In order to avoid the odium of prosecution it is advisable, where an offence is likely to be proved, to endeavour to settle the complaint, if necessary, by an ex-gratia offer of compensation.

DISCRIMINATION

The long-term aims of these Acts are to achieve total elimination of discriminatory practices. Discriminationary is defined as a person discriminates against another if on the ground of colour, race or ethnic or national origins he treats the other, less favourably than he treats or would treat other persons. Segregating a person from other persons on any of the aforementioned grounds means treating that person less favourably than other persons are treated."

The hotelier, caterer and his guests are concerned with the following important aspects:

1. Goods facilities and services
2. Accommodation and land
3. Advertisement and notices
4. Incitement
5. Admission and segregation.

GOODS, FACILITIES AND SERVICES

It is unlawful to discriminate in the provision to the public, or a section of the public, any goods, facilitities or services by refusing or deliberately omitting to provide him with any of them. Examples of such goods, facilities and services would include:

1. Access to and use of any place where members of the public are permitted to enter

2. Accommodation in a hotel, boarding house, or other similar establishments
3. Facilities by way of banking or insurance or for grants, loans, credit or finance
4. Facilities for education, instruction or training
5. Facilities for entertainment, recreation or refreshment; transport or travel
6. The services of any business, profession or trade.

In the first case under the Act alleging discrimination in a public house heard at a country court, in England, five West Indians claimed that they were refused drinks on grounds of colour, race or ethnic origins. They were each awarded œ"5 damages, and costs, amounting to several hundred pounds, against the licensee.

ACCOMMODATION AND LAND

It is unlawful to discriminate in selling or letting housing accommodation, business premises or land, or in the treatment of tenants.

A person who has the power to provide or dispose of residential accommodation is exempted if he lives on 'small premises' and shares some of the accommodation with other people who are not members of his household. 'Small premises' are defined as those which,

1. normally provided separate residential accommodation for not more than two households under separate letting agreements in addition to the landlord's accommodation, or
2. provide accommodation for not more than 6 people in addition to the landlord and his household.

This exemption might apply to the small boarding-house where there is only accommodation for 6 people in addition to the landloard and his household.

ADVERTISEMENTS AND NOTICES

It is unlawful to publish or display disciminatory notices. In England the Act, sought to prevent the provocative and insulting notice such as 'White only' or 'No Coloured' makes it unlawful to display any advertisement or notice which implies discrimination.

Inevitably this has led to some irritation as the grounds for discrimination covered by the Act include national differences as well as colour, race and ethnic origin.

As an illustration, an Indo-Pakistan restaurant in England put up a sign which read 'No West Pakistanis will be served'. The Bengali owner when warned that he was infringing the Race Relations Act (if not under 'race and colour', certainly under 'National origin') took notice, and changed the wording to 'No supporters to the Pakistani repression in Bangala Desh will be served'.

Attention is again drawn to the use of the words 'type' or 'style', for whilst it would i ply discrimination to advertise a West

Indian Dinner Dance' (in other words the implication would be that it was just for West Indians), it would not be considered discriminatory to advertise a West Indian-style (or type) Dinner Dance".

INCITEMENT

It is unlawful deliberately to aid, induce or incite another person to discriminate unlawfully. Incitement to racial hatred (as distinct for unlawful discrimination) may be a criminal offence and, therefore, a matter for the police.

ADMISSION AND SEGREGATION

In England comparatively few cases have come before the courts of discrimination in places of 'public resorts' (which are mainly hotel, restaurants, cafes, public houses and clubs). However, it is important that all persons responsible for booking or admitting persons into the establishment are aware of their responsibilities and the dangers of discrimination.

An illustration is that of the linkman who was bribed to refuse admission to a certain coloured man. This, when brought into the open, was said to be contravening the law on incitement the linkman having been induced to discriminate unlawfully against another.

Unlawful behaviour could be the existence of two bars in a public place one presided over by a white barman and the other by a coloured man, where the white barman served only white people and the coloured barman served only coloured people. Segregation is against the law.

The owner of any establishment may, of course, exercise his Common Law rights and refuse admittance or eject anyone, whatever the colour of his skin, who is behaving in a manner to which the proprietor objects, so long as he can prove that he is not discriminating on racial grounds. For instance, it would not be unreasonable to ask drunk or abusive guests to leave and to take the same course of action with those who were misusing or causing damage to the premises, whether they were white or coloured.

CREDIT SALES

A hotel has to pay particular attention to avoid credit losses. It is a criminal offence to defraud the proprietor of a hotel by obtaining food or lodging without intending to pay for it or obtaining credit under false pretenses. An experienced hotel manager passes along the following suggestions for receipts by cheques :

1. Check positive identification. In endorsement the cheques must correspond to the payers' name and photo on the driving licences or other identification which resembles the passer. Even printed and government cheques can be forgeries. These may have been stolen and then forged. Credentials such as driving licences, credit cards etc. can be cancelled, lost, forged or stolen.
2. Cheque be endorsed in your presence while holding the identification card.
3. In a case of suspicion, call the bank, if possible.
4. Warn your employees that bad cheque passers are particularly active on weekends on holidays, and during the summer vacation months.
5. Look twice before cashing a rubber stamped cheque.
6. Check any alteration made on a cheque. Remember the payee's name can be altered, amount raised, and dates changed.
7. Record all identification dates before cashing cheques and necessary noting may be made on the back or face of the cheque.
8. Try to obtain multiple identification.
9. For identification get licence plate number of the cashier's car. Copy the licence data such as country/place, numbers and match the owners' description with that of the passer and the signature must also be identical.
10. You have to be cautious if the cheque offered is not more than the amount of the bill.

11. Don't be in a hurry, take your own time as bad cheque passers try to work fast.
12. Don't accept a social security card as identification document.
13. Don't let the stranger bluff you. Keep asking questions.
14. Don't accept a suspicious cheque simply because it is perforated, 'insured', this does not mean you have been insured.
15. A bad cheque may indicate the following signals :
    (*i*) Misspellings of makers' name
    (*ii*) Omission of the makers' name
    (*iii*) Unusually high serial number (five or more digits).

SKIPPERS

Skippers are a big problem in the hotel business. Therefore, the following precautions should be adopted to foil skippers:

1. Obtain complete and legible registrations
2. Ask for payment in advance particularly if you have reason to be suspicious and the guest is without baggage or checked-in late.
3. Make person to person telephone calls to the registered guest at the address given to check his bonafide.
4. Limit the amount of the bill to restrict the expenses from going up.

HYGIENE IN FOOD AND BEVERAGES

Hygiene is by definition concerned with the preservation of health. Apart from legal requirements, those who are engaged in the sale of foods have an obligation to the consumer to safeguard them against the dangers to their health and well-being which might arise through carelessness or ignorance in the storage, preparation and service of food. In training staff, it may sometimes be necessary to confine oneself to teaching basic rules of conduct but an understanding of the main causes of food poisoning and food contamination and the manner in which the dangers can be minimised is likely to lead to a more positive attitude towards hygiene than mere insistence on compliance with instructions and regulations.

In particular, it is important that all concerned with the handling of food should realise that food which looks and smells perfectly wholesome may nevertheless be a source of danger to health if it has been contaminated before or during preparation by harmful bacteria.

FOOD POISONING

Food poisoning is an acute gastro-enteritis contracted through consuming contaminated food or drink. It is characterised by diarrhoea, abdominal pain and, sometimes, by vomiting and fever. It is usually more alarming and unpleasant than dangerous, though acute cases can cause death, especially among infants, elderly people and those who are debilitated through illness. Food poisoning is a notifiable disease. Whenever an outbreak occurs the Medical Officer of Health will endeavour to trace its sources so that a recurrence may be prevented.

CAUSES OF FOOD POISONING

Food poisoning is usually caused by three main types of bacteria. These organisms require to grow in foodstuffs before there is a sufficient dose of bacteria or toxin to cause infection or intoxication. Many types of bacteria are not harmful and even the food poisoning bacteria can be present without harmful effects provided they are not allowed to multiply in a suitable food substrate which is warm and moist.

Some disease-producing bacteria reside in the human skin, nose, throat and bowel, and in animals. Food may be contaminated through careless handling, by bacteria brought in with raw foodstuffs which may be passed to cooked foods or may survive cooking, by dirty equipment, by vermin when storage conditions are unsatisfactory, and by insects, especially flies. Food handlers must be trained to wash their hands after handling raw foods, especially if they are to handle cooked food afterwards. Knives and surfaces for raw foods must never be used for cooked foods without thorough cleaning or sterilisation in boiling water. Ideally, separate equipment and preparation surfaces should be used.

Occasionally food poisoning is caused by toxic foodstuffs such as poisonous toadstools or by the action of food containing acids on galvanised containers. Chipped enamelware should not be used for cooking and the lining of copper pots should be renewed periodically.

Illness in individuals may be caused by allergies to certain types of foods but those concerned are usually aware of what upsets them and, if they are wise, avoid such foods.

The three most important types of bacteria responsible for food poisoning are : Salmonellae, Staphylococci and Clostridium welchii.

Salmonellae are the commonest causes of direct food poisoning by living bacteria. Their main reservoir is the lower bowel of humans and animals and they are often brought into the kitchen by raw foods, especially meat and poultry. They may be present in raw pet meat. The danger of spreading the infection can be greatly reduced by the practice of washing one's hands after handling raw meat and poultry and after using the toilet, and by keeping pet animals away from food stores and kitchens.

Staphylococci are carried mainly by humans in the nose, throat, skin and infections. Raw milk from cows and goats can also carry these bacteria. The illness arising from their presence in food is caused by the toxins they produce as they multiply in food before consumption. Handling food after touching the nose, mouth, hair or face (including handling cigarettes while smoking) can give rise to staphylococcal contamination. It should also be remembered that these bacteria are not always removed from the skin by washing.

Infected cuts, abrasions and boils are breeding grounds for staphylococci; even clean-looking wounds may be infected. When food handlers have cuts or sores on their hands, particularly, even covering them with a bandage may be insufficient to prevent the infection of food; it is best to remove the individuals concerned from food-handling duties altogether. The Food Hygiene Regulations stipulate that suitable and suficient waterproof dressings shall be supplied.

Clostridium welchii are carried in the human and animal intestines and in soil and dust. It may also, like other bacteria, be conveyed by flies. Cl.welchii is a spore-forming organism; the spores are capable of surviving cooking. Cl.welchii is an anaerobic organism (i.e. grows in the absence of air) and has high optimum temperature for growth, about 43-47°C. To prevent the rapid multiplication of Cl.welchi in cooked meat and poultry, the food should be cooled as quickly as possible followed by storage in the refrigerator.

The foodstuffs especially likely to contain and encourage the growth of bacteria include raw and cooked meat and poultry, food with a meat base such as soups and gravies, made-up and manufactured meat dishes, egg products, milk and milk products, fresh cream, some types of imitation cream and trifles and jellies.

FOOD HYGIENE REGULATIONS

The Food Hygiene Regulations relate mainly to:

1. The cleanliness of premises and shops used for the purposes of a food business and of the equipment used;
2. The hygienic handling of food;
3. The cleanliness of persons handling food and of their clothing;
4. The construction of premises used for the purpose of food business;
5. The provision of water supply and washing facilites;
6. The proper disposal of waste material;
7. The temperatures at which certain foods are to be kept on catering premises.

From the point of view of caterers, the most important regulations are firstly, which requires that no food business shall be carried on at any place the condition, situation or construction of which is such that food is exposed to the risk of contamination and secondly, which relates to the handling of food.

PROTECTION OF FOOD

A person who engages in the handling food shall, while so engaged, take all such steps as may be reasonable, necessary to protect the food from risk of contamination, and in particular (without prejudice to the generality of the foregoing) :

1. Shall not so place the food as to involve any risk of contamination;
2. Shall before offering any food for sale, ensure that any food which is unfit for human consumption is kept apart from any other food;
3. Shall not in or about any forecourt or yard, place any food lower than eighteen inches from the ground unless it is adequately protected from risk of contamination;
4. Shall ensure where reasonably necessary that open food while exposed for sale or during sale or delivery is kept covered or is otherwise effectively screened from possible sources of contamination;
5. Shall not keep in any food room any animal feed unless it is in a container of such material and so closed as to prevent the risk of contaminating the food in the room:

Provided that paragraph (*ii*) shall not apply where food is intended to be sold by wholesale either by sample or description.

PERSONAL CLEANLINESS

A person who engages in the handling of food shall while so engaged:

1. Keep as clean as may be reasonably practicable all parts of his clothing or overclothing which are liable to come into contact with the food;
2. Keeps as clean as may be reasonably practicable all parts of his clothing or overclothing which are liable to come into contact with the food;

3. Keep any open cut or abrasion on any exposed part of his person covered with a suitable waterproof dressing;
4. Refrain from spitting;
5. Refrain from the use of tobacco or any other smoking mixture or stuff while he is handling any open food or is in any food room in which there is open food.

HANDING OF OPEN FOOD

A person who in the handling of open food, other than raw vegetables, intoxicating liquor or soft drinks, shall while so engaged wear sufficient clean and washable overclothing, and every person who carries meat which is open food and which is liable to come into contact with his neck or head shall, while so engaged, also wear a clean and washable neck and head covering:

Provided that this regulation shall not apply:–

1. To waiters in catering businesses;
2. To any person so long as he is engaged only in the carrying of unskinned rabbits or hares or unplucked game or poultry;
3. To transport of food:–

   (*a*) by railway undertakers; or in the course of the business of a carrier other than

   (*b*) a railway undertaker; or

   (*c*) in which the vehicle used for the transport of food is not ordinarily so used;

   If in either case the person carrying the food takes all such other precautions as are reasonable and practicable to prevent the food from coming into contact with anyexposed part of his person or with any clothing other than overclothing.

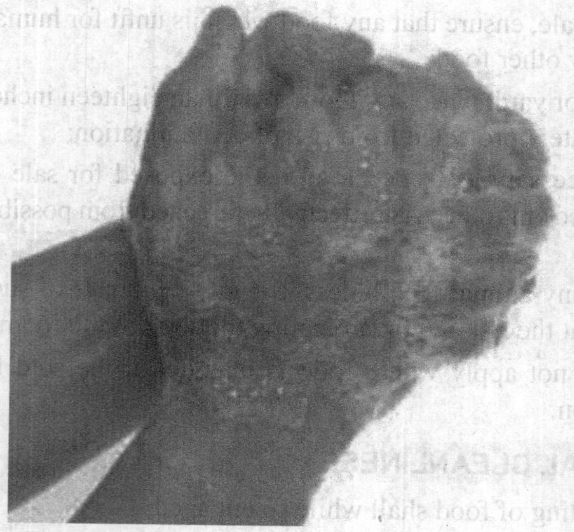

Pix 4.1: Washing Hands

Pix 4.2: Kitchen Hygiene : Washing Hands

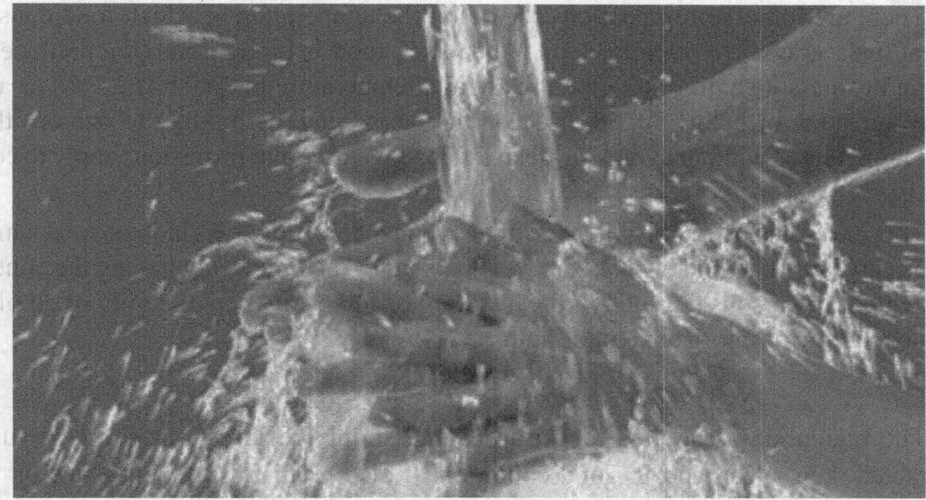

Pix 4.3: Kitchen Hygiene

Pix 4.4: Vegetable Cleaning

If anyone engaged in the handling of food becomes aware that he is suffering from, or is the carrier of, typhoid, paratyphoid, dysentery or any staphylococcal infection he shall inform the person carrying on the business immediately who in turn must notify the appropriate medical officer of health.

There are also regulations in the section relating to food premises, concerning soil drainage systems, water cisterns, sanitary conveniences, wash-hand basins (which must have an adequate supply of hot and cold water as well as soap or detergent, nail brushes, clean towels or other drying facilities), first-aid materials, accommodation for clothing and facilities for washing food and equipment. Lighting and ventilation must be suitable and sufficient. Food rooms must be kept clean throughout and kept in good order to prevent any risk of infection. The layout of the premises must permit waste and unfit food to be stored separately prior to disposal.

There are important regulations regarding the temperature at which food consisting of meat, fish, gravy, etc. is to be kept. When such food is brought into the premises of a catering business it shall, if it is not already at a temperature of 145°F (62.7°C) or above, on the one hand, or below 50°F (10°C) on the other hand, be brought to one or other of these temperatures without avoidable delay after arrival. Similar provisions apply to cooked food also.

Those who can be found guilty of offences under the regulations include food handlers, persons carrying on a food business and any person for the time being having the control or management of persons engaged in the handling of food. Any person guilty of an offence is liable to a fine or imprisonment or both.

GLASSWASHING

The regulation as applied to glasswashing, simply requires glasses to be suitably constructed, kept clean and in good condition. It also requires sufficient sinks or 'other facilities' to be provided and properly maintained. Sinks must be supplied with hot and cold running water or hot water at a suitably controlled temperature or cold water only if a suitable bactericidal agent is used. Adequate supplies of detergent, clean clothes or other suitable cleaning, and drying facilities must be on hand.

Clean glass to be provided on each serving and specifies how it must be washed that is, it must be either:

1. Washed in clean hot water and thereafter rinsed in water of 170°F minimum, or
2. Washed in clean hot water then washed in clean hot water with an efficient bactericidal agent in suitable quantity, and thereafter rinsed in clean water, or
3. Washed in clean hot water containing an efficient bactericidal agent in suitable quantity, and thereafter rinsed in clean water.

The term 'other facilities' enables machines designed for this purpose to be used. Machines currently available can be divided into two main categories:

1. Spray type machines
   (*i*) Spray type machines incorporate a cabinet into which wire baskets containing glasses are placed, the door closed and the machine turned on. Washing is affected by sprays and usually involves a wash with detergent and one or more rinses, sterilisation being affected by very hot water.

The advantage of the spray type machines is that they do not rely on the efficiency of the operator for consistent results. They take up more space and cost more to run than brush type machines.

2. Brush type machines
   (*i*) Brush type machines incorporate a number of brushes grouped around a central brush either immersed in water containing a detergent bactericide or by having sprays of water containing a detergent bactericide directed onto the brushes.

In addition to the above, various appliances incorporating static brushes for fitting in the sink are available.

Both spray type and brush type machines largely eliminate the need for cloth drying.

BETTING AND GAMING

Notwithstanding the relaxation of the law relating to betting and the opening of betting shops, it is still an offence to allow betting or the passing of betting slips on licensed premises except where a room is licensed as a betting shop and has a separate entrance to the street. Few licensing justices would grant an application for such a licence though they are not prohibited from doing so. It is not an offence for betting to take place if all those concerned either reside or work on the premises or are as bookmakers, but a licencee who encouraged or permitted betting in such circumstances would need to be very careful that these conditions were complied with.

The playing of games of chance for money or money's worth is permitted on licensed premises within certain limits.

Games of skill, including billiards, skittles, share-hipenny and darts, are allowed and there is no limit to the stakes that can be played for.

Dominoes and cribbage may be played, but not for high stakes. This applies only to fully licensed houses and not to restaurants which are licensed. It is an offence for a person under the age of 18 to take part in any gaming, even playing cribbages or dominoes, on licensed premises.

Other games of skill, or chance, or a combination of the two may be played and lotteries can be held for raising money for purposes other than private gain but there are restrictions contained in the Betting, Gaming and Lotteries Act, which must be studiously observed. Those contemplating such activities would be well advised to consult local trade association or a police officer before embarking on them.

Provided that permission has been obtained from the local justices any equal-chance game can be played under the conditions contained in the relevant Act. There is no fixed method of application and the concerned local authorities should be consulted as to the form and time of application.

LOTTERIES

It is not uncommon for a licensee to be asked for permission for a club or society, such as a darts club, to promote small lotteries. The society must first apply to the local authority and deposit the requisite fee.

When lotteries are promoted by a registered society some conditions must be observed:

1. The committee must nominate one of the society's members to be the promoter. He is not allowed to receive any remuneration.
2. No prize must exceed a fixed amount and no ticket may be sold for more than a pre-determined amount. After deduction of expenses the proceeds of the lottery must be devoted to the purposes of the society.
3. The total prize money must not exceed half the total proceeds and the expenses must be not more than 10%.
4. All tickets must be sold at the same price and the total sales must not exceed a certain amount.
5. No written notice or advertisement may be published except on the club premises (which might be the licensed house itself) or one circulated only to members.
6. Tickets may not be sent through the post, except to members.

7. Tickets must be sold only for cash (not refundable). Sales to persons under 16 are prohibited.
8. Expenses or prizes may not be provided from the funds of the society.

A return has to be submitted to the local authority not more than three months after the end of the lottery showing the proceeds and how they were disposed of.

Under the Act, taking part in a lottery is not gaming provided not more than three factors are involved in determining the winners. These are the result of a draw or other determination, or the outcome of an event such as a horse race, or an election.

BILLIARDS AND SNOOKER

A full on-licence includes permission for the playing of billiards (except between 1.00 and 8.00 a.m.). Holders of other licences must apply to a competent authority for a separate licence and must display a notice to the effect that they are licensed for billiards.

AMUSEMENT MACHINES

Applications for permit for an Amusement with prizes Machine must be made to the licensing authourity. Before a machine can be installed the permission of the owner of the premises, as well as the tenant, is necessary. The justices must afford a hearing to the application if they wish to refuse permission. There are certain conditions applied to the use of these machines.

These include:

1. No player may pay more than a certain amount;
2. The prize for any one play must not exceed a fixed amount in cash, or goods or token for goods.

GAMING MACHINES

Gaming machines with higher money prizes can be installed in rooms not open to the general public (e.g. in club rooms) but they must not exceed two in number and all stakes must be paid out either as winnings or for some purpose other than private gain (e.g. as a contribution to club funds).

MUSIC LICENCE

Licensed premises are exempt from the need to hold a music licence for music and singing if the music is provided solely from reproduction of radio or television entertainment, by recorded sound or by not more than two performers. A television licence is, of course, required for each set on the premises.

DANCING LICENCE

In other cases, like dancing, a licence is required. This is not necessary for private parties to which the public is not admitted and for which tickets are not sold at the door.

COPYRIGHT MUSIC

The use of a television set or radio where it can be heard by the public is a performance within the meaning of the Copyright Act 1956 in Britain, which also prohibits the playing of copyright music in any other way in public without the permission of the owner of the copyright. The playing of music as an accompaniment to a meal in a restaurant would be a public performance.

In order to simplify the granting of permission in performing in Britain Right Society may act on behalf of nearly all copyright holders for the purpose of collecting and allocating fees.

When music is habitually provided, the society may call for a return showing which items have been played. The band leader can normally supply this information but the occupier of the premises is responsible for collecting and forwarding it to the society.

Apart from copyright in the music, the makers of gramophone records have a copyright in the recording. If it is intended to play records in such a way as to constitute a public performance it is necessary to obtain (and pay for) permission from the organisation representing most of the owners of copyright in records.

Inclusive fees may be normally charged, based on the frequency of performances and/or the rateable value of the premises.

Infringement of copyright could lead to legal proceedings and to the award of damages and costs as well as an injuction to prevent further performance.

DEATH IN A HOTEL

In the unfortunate event of death in a hotel, procedures should be known and dutifully observed by everyone who has to deal with such an emergency. The following guidelines are suggested:–

1. If the guest is alone at the time of death (i.e. no doctor in attendance), the hotel doctor or other local doctor known to the establishment, should be called immediately. The doctor might, if the circumstances of death were not clear, need to call in the Police and/or the Coroner, but the doctor can be relied upon to take charge of the practical details such as the issue of the Death Certificate, and the contacting of the Undertaker and Nurse.
2. Relatives, or next to kin, should then be contacted. If there is difficulty in tracing the next to kin, details of the deceased's home, address etc., should be given to the local police who will make the necessary investigations.
3. Next to kin would eventually be asked to sign a list of the goods on removal. The room containing the body and personal effects should be double locked till the removal of the body and/or the arrival of relatives.
4. All luggage and personal effects should, if possible, be left till the arrival of the next of kin. If it is necessary for them to be removed, it is desirable that a careful inventory be taken in the presence of a witness before they are placed in storage.
5. It is wise to have a general understanding in an hotel or residential establishment, that nothing can be done regarding the removal of the body until after a certain time atnight, when activities are quietening down and when there is less danger of embarrassment to other guests.
6. The problems of bringing the coffin to the correct spot unobserved by other guests can usually be arranged with discretion and tact. However, once the body has been placed in the coffin, to observe the usual decencies of the occasion, the undertakers

would expect to proceed slowly out of the building to the waiting car. It is, therefore, important that members of staff are stationed in various strategic points along the route to restrict the movement of guests across the path of the coffin. At the same time, liftmen should be stopped from bringing guests to the particular floor, or automatic lifts stopped for a temporary period.

7. The disposal of the remains of a person whose relations or friends cannot be traced is the responsibility of the local authority. It is likely that in such cases the hotel would have the same right of lien over the property of the deceased as it would have had if the guest had left without paying his bill.

In the event of the death of a Foreign National, once a check had been made on the country of origin, the Consulate Officer at that Embassy should be informed. They, in turn, would report the death to their Minister of Foreign Affairs who would wish to know:

1. Date and time of death
2. Cause of death
3. Home address of the deceased
4. Name and address of relatives
5. Any information available regarding Travellers' Insurance.

Naturally, the wishes of the next of kin conerning the disposal of the body would be awaited, but the Undertaker would be responsible for negotiating whilst the body rested in his care. Apart from the Death Certificate, he would be required to provide a Certificate from the Public Health Officer to the effect that the transportion of the body presented no risk to public health (i.e. that death was due to causes other than such things as typhus, cholera, smallpox etc.).

QUESTIONS AND ASSIGNMENTS

1. Good management of any hotel depends on the balance between managing work and managing staff. Explain how a hotel manager would calculate an employees productivity ? *(MTA)*
2. Discuss the role and importance of management in the hotel industry. *(MTA)*
3. Explain the nature of operating work and managerial work in hotel business, and how they are interlinked with each other ? *(MTA)*
4. Over the past century there has been a considerable growth in the hospitality and catering industry. Discuss in about 250-words the role it has played in generating employment facilie.
5. Put a descriptive note on the development of accommodation industry through the ages. When and how hotels emerged on the scene ?
6. What is demand and what is demand potential ? What are the factors that affect demand of hotels ? Discuss the impact of these factors on demand. *(IHMs)*
7. Write a note upon modalities of hotel development and opening after completion of feasibility report. *(IHMs)*
8. Explain the contribution of hotel industry in the development of national economy. *(PGDT)*
9. Explain the term 'Hotel'. What are the different components of the Tourism Industry? Explain. *(PGDT)*
10. Give a description of the growth and development of the hotel industry in India. *(PGDT)*
11. 'No Hotels', 'No Tourism'. Do you agree with this statement ? Explain in detail. *(PGDT)*

12. Explain the significance of the hotel industry and its contribution in promotion of tourism in Nainital. *(PGDT)*

13. Define the term 'Hotel'. What are the special features of the hotel business ? Explain in detail. *(PGDT)*

14. Distinguish between 'HOTEL' and 'MOTEL'. Mentioning the supplementary accommodation facilities available in India, bring out the special features of the hotel business. *(PGDT)*

15. Explaining the terms, 'HOTEL MANAGEMENT' and 'CPERATION', clarify what you think is good Hotel Management Operation. *(PGDT)*

16. What are the problems and the prospects of the hotel industry in India ? *(PGDT&HM)*

17. What is "Supplementary Accommodation" ? Describe some of the principle forms of it. *(PGT)*

18. Write an essay on the "role of supplementary accommodation in the development of domestic tourism in India". *(PGT)*

19. "Hotel is a house for the entertainment of travellers." Do you agree ? Write the history of hotel concept in India. *(PGT)*

20. What do understand by classification and gradation of hotels ? What are the important factors taken into account while grading a hotel in a five star category? *(PGH&TM)*

21. Differentiate between :

(*a*) Hotel and Motel

(*b*) Three Star Hotel and Five Star Hotel

(*c*) Hotel Sales and Hotel Marketing. *(PGH&TM)*

22. Describe the special characteristics of hotel business. Explain the problems and prospects of hotel business in developing country like India. *(PGDH&TM)*

23. Define the term 'hotel'. Explain the different types of hotel and supplementary accommodation. *(PGT)*

24. Explain the contribution of the hotel industry in the development of national economy. *(PGDT)*

25. What steps would you like to take the establishment of a tourist class hotel in tourist centre like Nainital ? *(PGDT)*

26. Show your acquaintance with (*a*) present position and (*b*) future prospects of the hotel industry in India. *(PGDT&HM)*

27. 'The type of visitors (tourists, officers, businessmen, executive etc.) not only influence but determine3oped by Ashoka Group, Welcome Group, Oberoi Group, and Taj Group the chains to meet demands by market segments.

35. Investigate some of the properties hotel in your area. In what year they were built? What kind of competition did they have ? What services or facilities did they introduce to your community ?

36. List some of the hotels you have visited. What were some of the exciting things you noticed while you were a guest there ?

37. Define the term 'Hotel' classify hotels according to location., clientele, length of stay and facilities and explain each category. *(IHMs)*

38. Create a chronology for important events in the Indian hospitality industry.

39. You may select any of the following people of hotel companies and prepare a research project using the resources of your institute/college or library. Include a brief bibliography and discuss the person's/Company's contributions to the evolution of the modern hospitality industry.

(*a*) Conard Hilton
(*b*) Ellsworth M'Statler
(*c*) JRD Tata
(*d*) M.S. Oberoi
(*e*) Ram Prashad
(*f*) Oberoi Group of Hotels
(*g*) Taj Group of Hotel
(*h*) Welcome Group of Hotel
(*i*) Ashok Group of Hotel.

40. Discuss the history of hotel industry in relation to the needs of modern business and leisure travellers. In your discussion answer the following questions :
(*a*) Which social, economic and industrial factors influence the development of modern hotel industry ?
(*b*) Which individuals were the most influential in shapping the modern hotel industry? What were their important contributions ?

41. Define the term 'supplementary accommodation' and explain the various forms of supplementary accommodation.

42. Define the term 'hotel'. What responsibilities and liabilities are proprietors expected to assume with regards to their guests?

43. Classify different types of welfare catering establishments and explain each one of them in brief. *(IHMs)*

44. There a are various types of catering establishments. They can be categorised under profit oriented or non-profit oriented. List five establishments under each category and give a two or three line explanation of each. *(IHMs)*

45. Classify catering establishments as per the main branches of the industry giving appropriate examples and the salient features of each type. *(IHMs)*

46. Catering facilities are available on different modes of travel but these vary considerably discuss the salient feature of each type. *(IHMs)*

47. The hospitality and welfare catering services offer a wide range of career opportunities. Elaborate this statement in about 250-words. *(IHMs)*

48. Five star luxury hotels are not the only catering establishments in India. Write 5 lines each on 5 other catering establishments. *(IHMs)*

49. Review the development of fast food operation in the hotel and catering industry. Identify the essential characteristics of this type of business and give some indications concerning its future. *(HCIMA Lonodn)*

50. Outline the general responsibilities of the catering officer for the health and safety of people using catering premises. Indicate how he would engender a responsible attitude towards safety on the part of the staff. *(HCIMA London)*

51. Classify different types of welfare catering establishments and explain each one of them in brief. *(IHMs)*

52. Define the terms classification, approval and gradation of hotels. What factors are taken into account while grading a hotel ? Explain in the detail. *(PGDT&HM)*

53. Discuss the steps could you take to establish a medium size hotel in Nainital. *(PGDT)*

54. What factors should be taken into consideration in establishing a hotel ? Are there sufficient facilities to start and run a hotel business in Srinagar ? *(PGDT)*

55. What factors should be taken into consideration in order to establish hotels in India ?(*PGDT*)

56. "What are the main requirements for opening four and five star hotel in Kumaun region?" Describe in detail. (*PGT&TM*)

57. Define the term 'grading of hotel'. What do you understand by five star hotel ? Explain the main features of a five star hotel. (*PGDT*)

58. Explain the important laws and regulations relating to the operation of the hotel and catering business. (*MTA*)

59. Explain the various steps you would take into consideration while establishing a new deluxe hotel in a reputed tourist resort. (*PGDT&HM*)

60. In recent years specialist functions within hotel and catering organisations have become much more common. Describe the organisational problems they create and suggest ways in which these may be overcome. *HCIMA* (*London*)

61. Indicating by writing the facilities description of a hypothetical hotel of a luxury class include the following the list of:

(*a*) Physical facilities
(*b*) The total number of rooms
(*c*) Guest service
(*d*) Pet policy.

Indicate room type and room rates as well.

62. What do you think the major differences between chain and independent hotels are ?

63. Differentiate between franchises and company owned properties in a chain. What is the difference between franchises and referral groups ?

64. List various laws applicable to accommodation sector in the hotel industry. Give details of any five laws. (*IHMs*)

65. What type of accommodation facilities do you suggest for the development of accommodation facilities for tourist in the Uttarakhand region ? (*PGDT*)

66. What are the important laws governing operation of accommodation facilities ? Explain the relationship between the hotel management and their customers. (*PGDT*)

67. Describe the characteristics features of each of the following types of hotels: commercial resort, transit, and residential hotels. (*IHMs*)

68. List ten essential features for a hotel to be graded as a five star hotel. (*IHMs*)

69. An old palace is being converted into a four star hotel. It has 30-rooms of dimensions each. The rooms have high ceiling and small windows fever in number (visualize your own placement of windows). Suggest the layout plan for one room along with details of colour scheme flourishing and suitable accessories. (*IHMs*)

70. List 4-Indian chains and name four properties owned by each one of them. (*IHMs*)

71. Explain the following:

(*a*) Management by Objective
(*b*) Success Plan
(*c*) Decision Making
(*d*) Breakeven Point
(*e*) Performance Appraisal
(*f*) Arranging a Conference
(*g*) Public Relations
(*h*) Internal Control
(*i*) Cash Budget
(*j*) Trade unions
(*k*) On-the-job Training
(*l*) Group Section Procedure
(*m*) Partie System.

A CASE STUDY

72. Mr. G. Manoher, is nominated by the Himalayan Hotel Resort International for an advance course in Tourism and Hotel Administration. After attending the first few sessions he wants to plan a trip to the hotels in the Rishikesh and Doon Valley. The area is rich in cultural attractions and tourist attractions and well reputed educational and research institutions are located here. Group of students can visit a variety of tourists attractions. He asked you being one of his students, to appoint a group of students to assist him in setting up tours.

Ms. Kokila is a local residents of the area and suggested that they visit the famous Kampty Fall in Mussoorie and would like to see the hotels in Mussoorie. Mr. Kundan has worked in a tourist resort property in Dhanaulti. Ms. Dura knows about a cozy bed and break fast located in Dhakrani. Mr. Pearl is interested to get some information on resort hotel management. Mr. Jyoti is interest on forestry and botany. Mr. Chand is interested to see the Doon School and other important educational centre of the area. Mr. Arjun want to see the important hotel of the area specially Mussoorie, Dehradun and Rishikesh.

The group has sifted through all the requests and decided to form four teams to visit these places. Each team will appoint one spokeperson for a pannel discussion. The spokeperson will give a five minutes summary of what was learned from this visit.

What information, you think, each spokeperson will include in his or her summary to be presented before Mr. G. Manoher and the whole group of students.

CHAPTER 5

Accommodation Operation

OBJECTIVES

After studying this chapter, you should be able to :

1. *Understand the main activities engaged in the earning of room revenue*
2. *Describe the front of the house and the duties and responsibilities of the staff related to this department;*
3. *Describe the duties of the uniforms and guest services;*
4. *Explain the role of the house-keeping department, and*
5. *Understand the duties and responsibilities of the employees of the housekeeping department.*

ACCOMMODATION

Hoteliering is the art of pleasing people. It involves providing clean, comfortable accommodation, appetizing food and beverages. It requires graciousness in service, attention to details and dedication. Next in importance is 'courtesy of staff' and high on the list one pleasing people such as by arranging reservations, efficient checking-in and checking-out procedures and providing suitable atmosphere.

Room Division involves the letting and serving of guest rooms. It does not include public and banqueting areas. The departments and staff included in room division are the front office, including advance reservations, reception clerks, hall porters, luggage porters, linen-men, inquiry clerks, house- keepers, room-maids, floor and bathroom cleaners, house porters, linen porters, all laundry staff, linen room staff, assistant managers, rooms/front office managers, doorman, secretary etc.

There are three main hotel activities engaged in the earning of room revenue :

1. Hotel Front Office
2. Uniformed Services, and
3. House-keeping.

These are the main components of the accommodation function and are present in most of the hotels. Normally, these are organised in separate departments. The organisation and staffing of these departments will depend upon the size, type and standard of the hotel. The main components of the accommodation functions could be briefly outlined as :

1. *Hotel Front Office :*
   (*i*) Room Sales
   (*ii*) Guest Accounts
   (*iii*) Mail and other guest services.
2. *Hotel House-keeping :*
   (*i*) Servicing of guest rooms
   (*ii*) Servicing of public rooms
   (*iii*) Sundry house-keeping services.
3. *Uniformed Services :*
   (*i*) Servicing of arrivals
   (*ii*) Guest information services
   (*iii*) Arrangement for guests
   (*iv*) Sundry uniform services
   (*v*) Servicing of departures.

A close study of the departmental structure of different hotels indicates lots of variations in their organisational approach as regards reception, uniformed services and house-keeping :

1. Grouping of all three activities together as Room Department with its own head of department ;
2. Grouping of all three activities together as Room Department under an Assistant Manager ;
3. Grouping of reception and uniformed services together as front-hall or front-house department with its own head of department ;
4. Grouping of reception and uniformed services together as front hall or front-house under an Assistant Manager ;
5. Grouping all three activities as separate departments with their own heads of departments.

CODE OF CONDUCT FOR TOURIST ACCOMMODATION

There is a code of conduct for establishments providing tourist accommodation and is designed to ensure a fair deal for all guests. In addition to fulfil its statutory obligations, the management undertakes to observe the following code of conduct :

1. To ensure high standards of courtesy, cleanliness, catering, and service appropriate to the type of establishment.
2. To describe fairly to all visitors and prospective visitors the amenities, facilities and services provided by the establishment, whether by advertisement, brochure, word-of-mouth or any other means and to allow visitors to see accommodation, if requested, before booking.
3. To make clear to visitors exactly what is included in all prices quoted for accommodation, meals and refreshments, including service charges, taxes and other surcharges. Details of cancellation procedures and charges for additional services or facilities available

should also be made clear. In the case of establishments with four bedrooms or more, to adhere to the Hotel Industry Voluntary Code of Booking Practice.

4. To adhre to, and not to exceed, prices current at time of occupation, for accommodation or other services.
5. To advise visitors at the time of booking, and subsequent to any change, if the accommodation offered is in an unconnected annexe, or similar, or by boarding out and to indicate the location of such accommodation, and any difference in comfort and amenities from accommodation
in the main establishment.
6. To give each visitor, on request, details of payments due, and a receipt, if required.
7. To deal promptly and courteously with all inquires, requests, reservations, correspondence and complaints from visitors.

HOW TO INCREASE OCCUPANCY ?

In most of the hotels, occupancy turns down drastically on Friday, Saturday and Sunday. As an innovative hotelier you may be able to boost weekend occupancy. One of the most rewarding sales techniques is to increase weekend business in the 'package' i.e. room meals, some extra touches for glamour at a special price. The Vice-president of Sales and Marketing, W.W. Bud Grice says, Getting two-thirds or half of the price of a room and meal is better than having rooms and a restaurant, empty and still having to pay salaries, utilities and taxes."[1]

A letter addressed to businessmen who have been guests previously is a logical weekend profit. Direct mail letters and brochures are posted in promoting the special weekends. Newspapers, radio and T V advertising concentrates on the areas from which most guests, looking for new homes or apartments, club groups coming into the town, affluent shoppers and sports minded people (pool, sauna, tennis courts or golf courses) are drawn.

The main benefit drawn from weekend packages are:

1. Direct revenue attributable to the special weekend packages.
2. In a seasonal resort, it allows management to keep enployees on year round basis.
3. Hotel shops get extra business and this in turn increases rental for them from convention managers and other sources of group business.
4. Guest for special weekends often become regular patrons and provide word of mouth advertising among their friends and associates.

The following can make positive contributions to keep occupancy high:-

1. Travel agents
2. Tour operators : According to Arthur Tank, a leading tour operator, most conventions and meetings must be sold individually and this cost money. For tours, you sell the tour operator only once and, if you attend properly to his business, you receive it year after year like an annuity."[2]
3. Airlines
4. Your community :
   (*i*) Sales manager of real business

1. W.W. Bud Grice, Vice President, Sales and Maketing of a Leading Hotel Company, USA.
2. Arthur Tank, a Leading Tour Operator, U.S.A.

(*ii*) Secretaries to local executives
(*iii*) Civic club officers
(*iv*) Purchasing agents
(*v*) Clergymen/religious heads
(*vi*) Officers of women clubs
(*vii*) Service station operators
(*viii*) Rental car agents
(*ix*) Bus line personnel
(*x*) Vendors
(*xi*) Caterers
(*xii*) Nearby college and research centres
(*xiii*) Attractions.

A Case Study 5.1: Front Office

Situation

The front Office of a hotel appeared to be over staffed and yet had difficulty in getting work done.

Results of Analysis

Analysis of the jobs of room assistant and cashier showed a large portion of time lost through poor work planning. It was found that too often are room assistant and cashier wished to occupy the same space at the same time. By rearranging the front office and moving the assistant manager and reservation clerk from second-floor office to a space in the lobby near the front office, ₹ 5,000/- a week in salaries was eliminated. The reservation assistant or the assistant manager was available to cover relief and help in periods of usual activity. Moreover, the reservation assistant could perform additional duties such as typing feeding of front office account, and rack supplies.

LANGUAGE BARRIERS : COMMUNICATION

With travellers from all over the world visiting India either as tourists or on business, it is considered an asset for a hotel employee to have knowledge of at least one foreign language so that he/she can communicate with overseas visitors and make them feel welcome. Some useful words in English, Hindi, French, German, Spanish and Italian are given Table 5.1.

TABLE 5.1 : Useful Words in Other Languages

English	Hindi	French	German	Spanish	Italian
Do you Speak English?	Kya Aap angregi bol sakti hai ?	Parlez-vous anglais?	Sprechen Sie englisch?	Habla Usted ingle?	Parla inglese?
Yes/No	Ha/nahi	Oui/non	Ja/nain	Si/no	Si/no
Please	Kripaya	Sil vous plait	Bitte	Por favor	Perfavore
Thank you	Dhanyavad / Shukriya	Merci	Danke/Schon	Gracias	Grazie

(*Cont...*)

Good day, Sir	Namaste	Bonjour	Guten Tag	Buenos dias	Buon giorno signore
Good Morning,	Shubh Prabhat	Monsieur	Guten Morgen	Senor	
Good Evening Madam	Namaste Shrimatiji	Bon Soir Madame	Guten Abend Frau...	Buenos noches Senora	Buona sera Signora
Ladies	Shrimati	Dames	Damen	Sennora	Signore
Gentlemen	Shri	Messieurs hommes	Herren	Caballeros	Uomini
Today Yesterday	Aaj Kal	Aujourd shui Hier	Heute Gestern	Hoy Ayer	Oggi Ieri
Tomorrow	Kal	Demain	Morgen	Manana	Domani
Goody bye	Phir Milainge	Au revoir	Auf Wiedersehen	Hasta la vista !	Arrivederci
How much ..?	Kitna ?	Combien ?	Wieviel?	Cuanto...?	Quanto ...?
Service included	Bakshish Sahit	Service Compris	Bedienng einbevgriffen	Servicio induido	Servizio Compres so

INTERNATIONAL SYMBOLS : TRAVEL SYMBOLS OR SIGNS

To aid travellers who do not understand English or any other foreign language, the International Comittee for Breaking the Language Barrier had advocated the use of symbol signs (Ref. Figs 5.1, 5.2 and 5.3). According to ICBLB, the following are the essentials of good signs to overcome the language :

1. **Give information :** An example is the implementation in NewYork city of an ICBLB recommendation that route diagrams be put at bus stops. As a result, non-English speaking visitors can determine which bus to board and what route it will take.
2. Use Basic Vocabulary : The word Lounge, for instance, can confuse international visitors because it is used in USA for bar, lobby and also toilet.
3. **Make Multi-lingual Signs :** Keep in mind that since all major languages cannot be included because of space, graphic symbols should also be included. The airport at San Francisco and Seatle, for example, combine both symbols and language to indicate facilities.
4. **Make Objects Visible :** The language problem can be eased by showing the item itself rather than trying to describe it. For example, salt and pepper should be packaged in transparent envelopes. Some restaurants abroad display models of food they serve.
5. **Illustrate :** Rather than wait until international standardized symbols are universally agreed upon, use some form of graphics to convey messages. While graphic communication may not be perfect, it will be better than words which do not communicate at all.

Fig. 5.1. International Symbols (International Air Transport Association)

Sign Language: Tourism and Travel Facilities

Motel travellers Lodge Beach Resort Forest Lodge Tourist Reception				
Telephone Baggage Lockers Elevator Toilets, Men				
Toilets Women Toilets Information Hotel Information			?	?
Taxi Bus Ground Transportation Rail Transportation				
Car Rental Restaurant Coffee Shop Bar				
Hotel Shop Duty Free Shop Lost and Found				?
Ticket Purchase Baggage Check-in Customs Immigration				
No Smoking Smoking No Parking Parking			R	P
No Entry Entertainment Sound & Light Show Mail				

Fig. 5.2. Sign Language: Tourism and Travel Facilities

Sign Language: Tourism Hospitality Facilities

Contd...

Fig. 5.3. Sign Language: Tourism and Hospitality Facilities

6. **Use Maps :** They speak in universal language. Many places in Europe post large city maps in railway stations. In Tokyo, neighbourhood maps are posted at a major street intersections and at Police Stations.
7. **Use International Symbols :** Whenever practical, visitors from overseas complain about traffic signs because they vary between different states and cities. Today, many internationally-minded cities such as Tokyo, Montreal and Frankfurt, New Delhi, Bombay, Bangkok etc. use international symbols instead of the local language.

International Air Transport Associations have recommended some symbols for use in airports and in other locations where international travellers might be in need. These symbols are in black and white background except for some portion of signs which are in red.

ROOM REVENUE

Most of the guests reserve their rooms in advance i.e., a few hours to several days/ weeks or months before they actually arrive at the hotel. The mode of reservation is in person, by telephone, telegram, telex, by mail, through travel agents or through central reservation system. The reservation of hotel services creates a contractual relationship between the hotel and its guest. This relationship starts at the time each reservation is made and continues until the departure of the guest or till the settlement of accounts after his stay. Advance reservation has two vital aspects : legal aspect and business aspect. It requires an efficient and clean system which enables room reservations to be converted into room revenue.

On arrival, the guest is asked to register by providing the receptionist with certain particulars about himself. This register is maintained as per the requirement of the law and provides an internal record of guests for data analysis purpose. The allocation of accommodation could be done in advance or on arrival of the guest and immediately the guest account is opened. All the concerned departments such as house-keeping, uniformed, telephonists, and others are notified on arrival of guests.

The main records of the room sales in the front office are :

1. Reservation Form/Card
2. Reservation Diary/Daily Arrival Lists
3. Reservation Chart
4. Hotel Register
5. Reception Room Status Board
6. Guest Index.

There are basically two systems of recording room sales :

1. Selling by specific number : In this method rooms are sold and recorded by individual numbers. Allocate a specific room number, say 307, at the time the booking is made, even if it is a month or more in advance.
2. Selling by quantity : In this case rooms are sold from the density charge. Delete a room from the list of total rooms available in the required category. Mark off a specific room from the total of 50 left to sell.

The second system is most flexible and is practically used by most hotels.

Provision of accommodation facilities is one of the important activities of a hotel. The department looking after these facilities is commonly known as Room Department or Accommodation Department. In American-style hotels this consists the front office, the house-keeping and laundry department, the uniform services, and the security office. The responsibility for the well-being of the guest is delegated to the Resident Manager/House Manager/Room Assistant Manager, who is head of this department. From arrival to the departure of guests, some employee or the other of this department, is performing direct service for them. These employees need a thorough training as they come into personal contact with the guests.

Some hotels are experimenting with taking house-keeping out of the room division and making it a staff function, with the director of house-keeping reporting directly to the General Manager. Some other hotels are combining house-keeping and other property management functions along with maintenance and engineering.

THE RESIDENT MANAGER

The Resident Manager/Executive Assistant Manager/House Manager/Rooms Director/ Director of Room Operations carries out the daily routine management task as directed and assigned by the General Manager. He may be incharge of one department directly under his control. The sub-departmental heads which come under his supervision, are executive house- keeper, the executive assistant manager, the front office manager, the telephone operator, garage manager etc. They are responsible for reservation and registration of the guest, front desk, bell staff, PBX, transportation, concierge, maintenance and cleaning of rooms, providing information on the facilities of the hotel and local point of interest cultural, recreational and amusement etc. The Resident Manager is also responsible for handling guest complaints. He is most of the time in contact with the staff and guests as he moves around the operation and is available in case of queries, emergencies, complaints and special events.

The following forms are designed and printed to suit the requirements of this department:

1. Reservation Density Chart
2. Reservation and Registration Card
3. Rooming List
4. Arrival and Departure List
5. Whitney Slips and Racks
6. Room Cards and Key Cards, Numbers plus hotel facilities
7. Room Charge Advice Pads.

FRONT OF THE HOUSE

Pleasing people commences initially from the front. The guests first form a substantial evaluation of the hotel and its property. It is also a place where the guests come with their problems or complaints.

The main functions of this section are :

1. Process reservations and handling of communications with prospective guests.
2. Register guests and assign rooms
3. Make credit arrangements
4. Give information about local shopping
5. Arrange miscellaneous guest services.

In small hotels receiving guest payments is a function of the front office whereas in large hotels the cashier directly reports to the controller.

The front office is responsible for monitoring and co-ordinating the front of the house transactions and services. The front desk is the most visible segment of the front office and is located in the high traffic lobby area. The desk is the major source of guest information and is responsible for the maintenance of guest records. The front office is the logical connecting link between the guest and the hotel management. A typical layout of entrance, lobby, bell, front office, cash, etc., is given in Figure 5.3.

It is not the building and the interior decor or delicacies served in a hotel alone which make an individual accept the hospitality and comfort he is going to enjoy during his stay. The impression of the way in which he is received and the conduct of the staff play an integral part in the choice of a hotel. And this is where the front office staff comes in, because they are his first point of contact when he enters the hotel and the one last point of contact on his departure. It is, therefore, imperative on the part of the front staff to go all out to receive every guest with courtesy and induce in him a sense of belonging. His aim should be to make the guest feel at home, even though he is thousand miles away from his home. The front office staff must work like a team and make an all-out effort in achieving his standard of service and efficiency.

The front office is primarily responsible for the selling of the rooms. Besides rooms and sales, the front office is also responsible for accepting reservation, registering arrivals, handling keys and mail, dealing with messages, maintaining statistical information and preparing for guests on their departures.

Front of the House (Hotel)

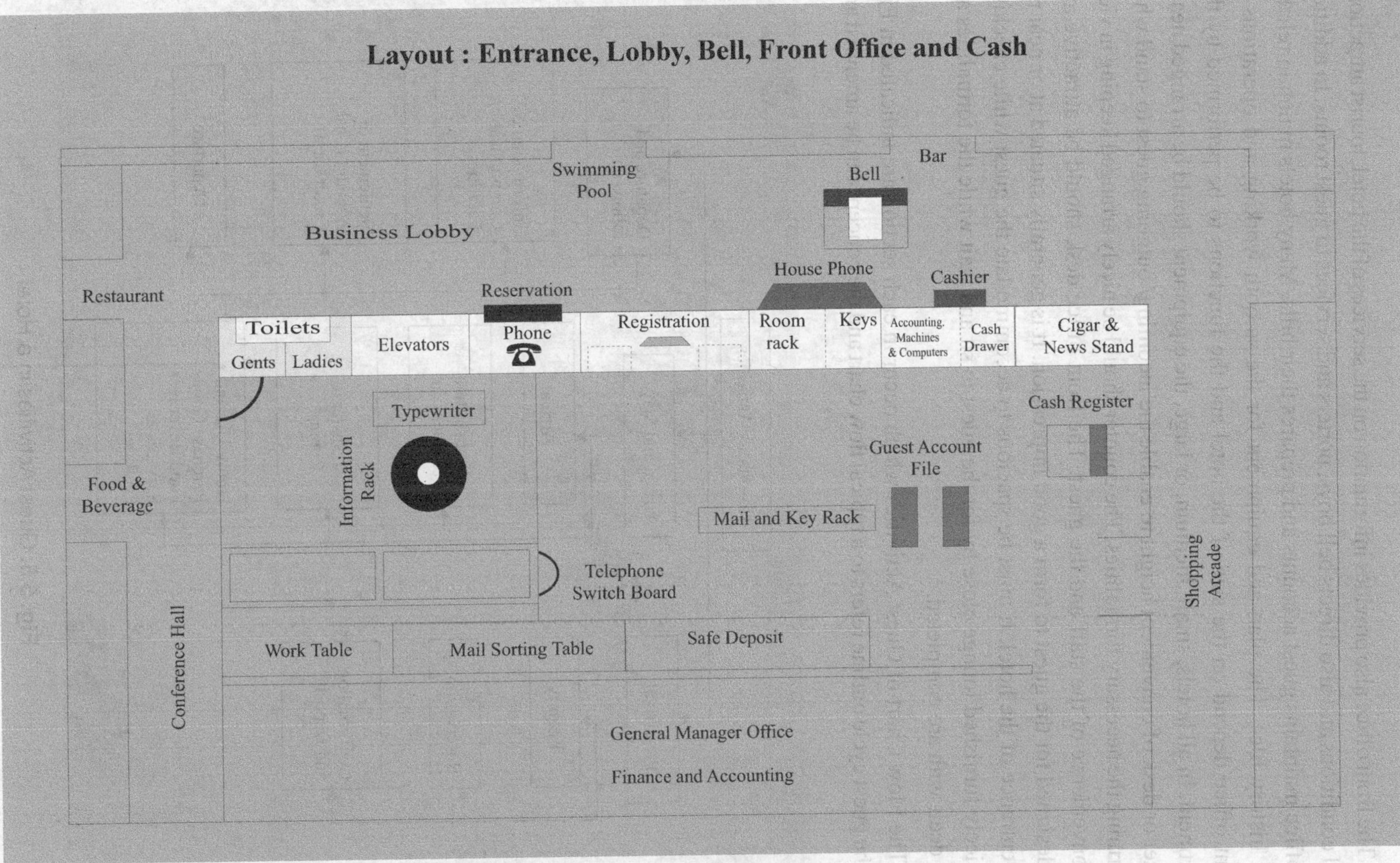

Fig. 5.4. Typical Layout : Entrance, Lobby, Bell, Front Office and Cash

The front office also provides information on the services of the hotel, tourist attractions, travel conditions and also directs bell boys, porters and services to guest rooms. In addition, this office maintains guest accounts and prepares their bills. Many hotels maintain reliable guest history files. The plan and equipment for the smooth working and operations of a front office depend on the size of the hotel and the functions to be performed by this department. In all hotels, small, medium, or large, the equipment should be arranged near a counter or desk of convenient height to enable the incoming/ outgoing guest to stand while performing the necessary formalities. The counter should be nicely arranged keeping in view the convenience of the staff and the guest. The front office desk should be attractive and well designed for the guest to form a good impression. It is generally situated at or near the main entrance of the hotel. It must be spacious to accommodate the guest while checking in a nicely furnished lounge close by for the guest to sit and wait while the formalities are being dealt with are completed.

The Flow Chart of Guest Activities which occur in each section are indicated in Fig. 5.5. The guest cycle outline refers to a typical flow chart and the concept can be amended and

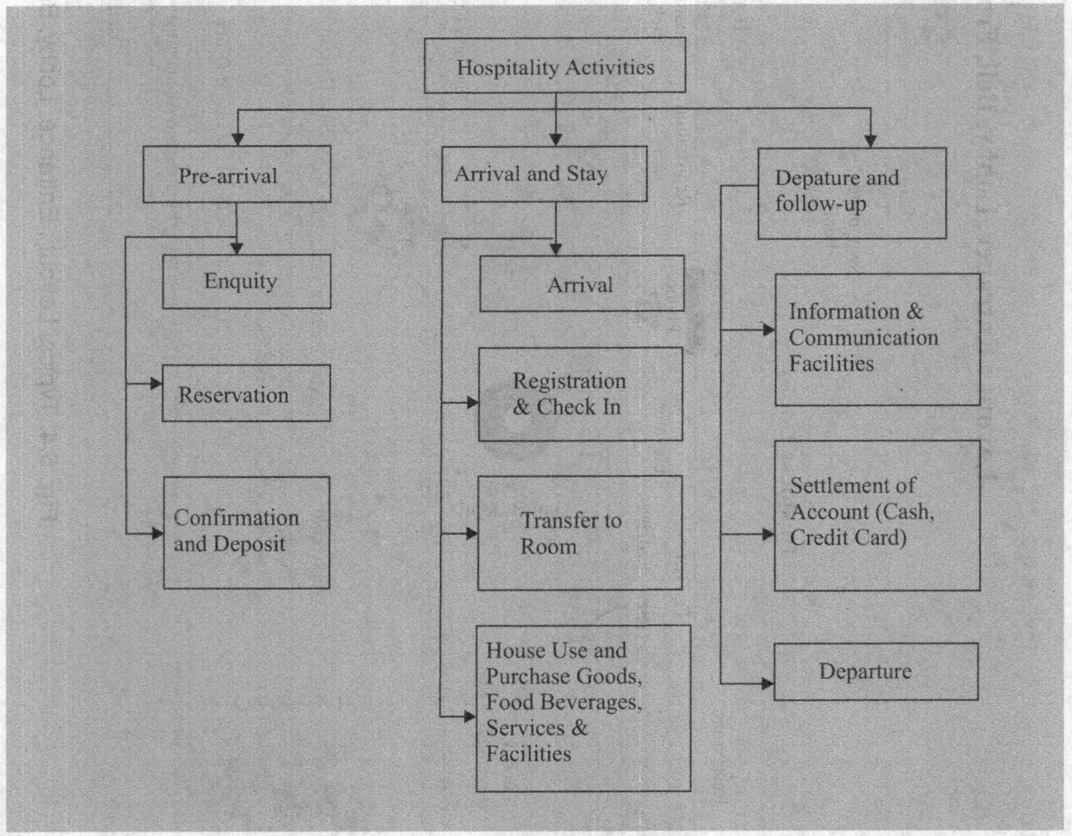

Fig. 5.5. Guest Activities in a Hotel

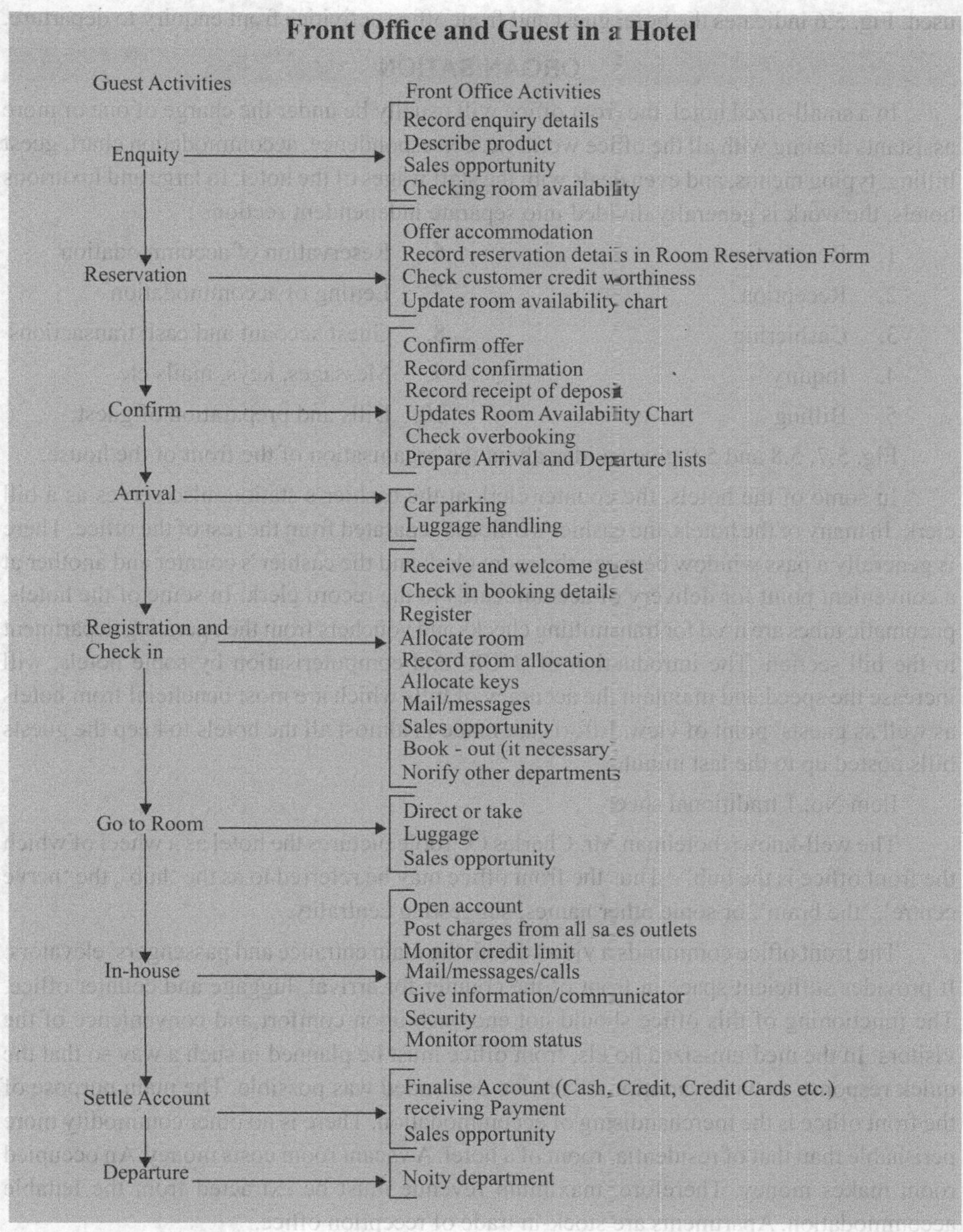

Fig. 5.6. The Front Office and Guest in a Hotel

used. Fig. 5.6 indicates the hotel guest and front office activities from enquiry to departure.

ORGANISATION

In a small-sized hotel, the front office will usually be under the charge of one or more assistants dealing with all the office work, i.e. correspondence, accommodation chart, guest billing, typing menus, and even deals with the staff wages of the hotel. In large and luxurious hotels, the work is generally divided into separate independent sections :

1.	Reservation	6.	Reservation of accommodation
2.	Reception	7.	Letting of accommodation
3.	Cashiering	8.	Guest account and cash transactions
4.	Inquiry	9.	Messages, keys, mails etc.
5.	Billing	10.	Bills and preparation of guest.

Fig. 5.7, 5.8 and 5.9 give an idea about the organisation of the front of the house.

In some of the hotels, the counter clerk at the cashier's station, also serves as a bill clerk. In many of the hotels, the cashier's office is separated from the rest of the office. There is generally a pass window between the room clerk and the cashier's counter and another at a convenient point for delivery of account cards to the record clerk. In some of the hotels, pneumatic tubes are used for transmitting checks and vouchers from the operating department to the bill section. The introduction of 'NCR' and computerisation by some hotels, will increase the speed and maintain the accuracy of bills which are most beneficial from hotels as well as guests' point of view. Efforts are made in almost all the hotels to keep the guests bills posted up to the last minute.

Item No. 1 traditional sheet

The well-known hotelman Mr. Charles O' Toole pictures the hotel as a wheel of which the front office is the hub".[3] Thus the front office may be referred to as the 'hub', the 'nerve centre', 'the brain', or some other names, suggesting centrality.

The front office commands a view of both the main entrance and passengers' elevators. It provides sufficient space in front of the counter for arrival, luggage and counter office. The functioning of this office should not encroach upon comfort and convenience of the visitors. In the medium-sized hotels, front office must be planned in such a way so that the quick response to wide variation of service demanded was possible. The main purpose of the front office is the merchandising of accommodation. There is no other commodity more perishable than that of residential room of a hotel. A vacant room costs money. An occupied room makes money. Therefore, maximum revenue must be extracted from the lettable accommodation. Apartments are stock-in trade of reception office.

From the operating angle, the dual role of the reception office, selling of accommodation and providing personalised service, being when the first contact is made with the customer. Inquiries are made by the guest and apartments are booked in advance by letters, phone,

---

3. Mr. Charles O'Toole, Modern Hotel and Motel Management, Gerald W. Lattin, Page 6.

cable or verbally.

THE FRONT OFFICE MANAGER

The front office manager must have organising and administrative ability. He must have knowledge of manners, customs, tastes and ways of life of the main tourist generating countries and must have knowledge of the regulations governing foreign exchange transactions, organisation of the hotel, hotel accounting, hygiene and safety regulations and relative labour legislation.

The duties and responsibilities of front office manager are :

1. To be responsible for the different services of his department.
2. To draw up the safety roasters and supervise discipline, conduct and appearance of his staff.
3. To be responsible for reservation, planning and for all operations concerning allocation of rooms.
4. To receive the guests on arrival and accompany the important guests to their rooms.
5. To decide on special rates of accommodation with the approval of the management.
6. To be responsible for ensuring a good relationship between the guest and the hotel staff.
7. To make suggestions for selection, recruitment, replacement, dismissal, change of duties, promotion and training of his staff.
8. To be responsible for maintaining co-ordination with other departments of the hotel.
9. To be responsible for the preparation of statistical reports of his department.
10. To assist the GM and keep him informed about the running of the hotel so that new policies could be formulated, if needed.
11. To be responsible for VIP bookings and arrivals and comfort in the hotel.
12. To exercise control over reservation.
13. To maintain control over desk operation.
14. To check status/occupancy reports and other statistical data for management information system and operational use.
15. To schedule the duty roasters and ascertain the reason behind determining the manpowers, strength of the department.
16. To co-ordinate sales promotion, banquets and house-keeping departments to have all accommodation ready for conventions and parties.
17. To do forecasting and budgeting for the department.
18. To liaison with travel agents, airlines and other business potential.

Subject to the requirements of individual hotel, a definite standard cannot be maintained and established as regards the qualification of a front office manager. In general, minimum requirements are to have a reasonable standard of basic education besides the hotel school

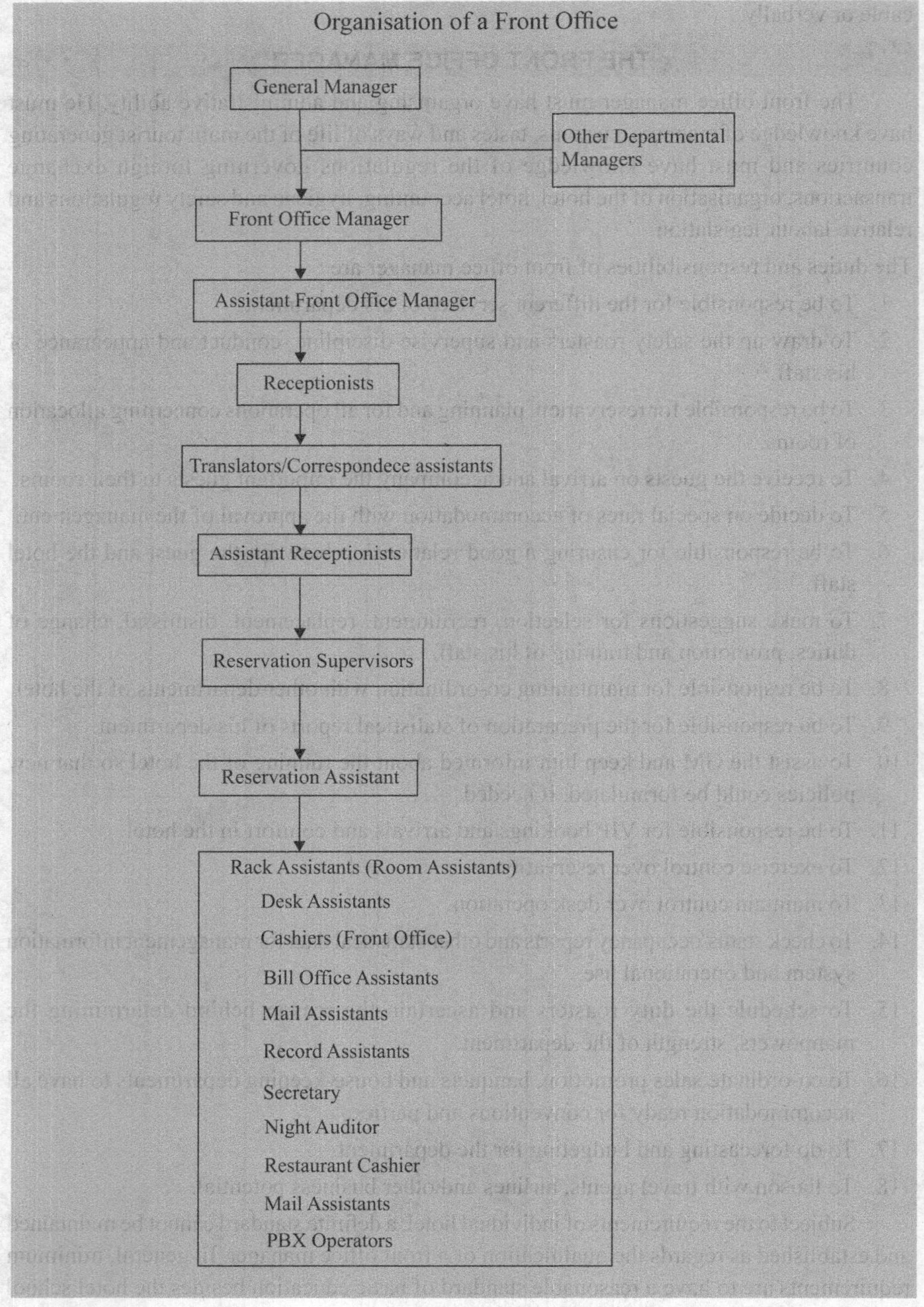

Fig. 5.7: A Typical Organisation of a Front Office

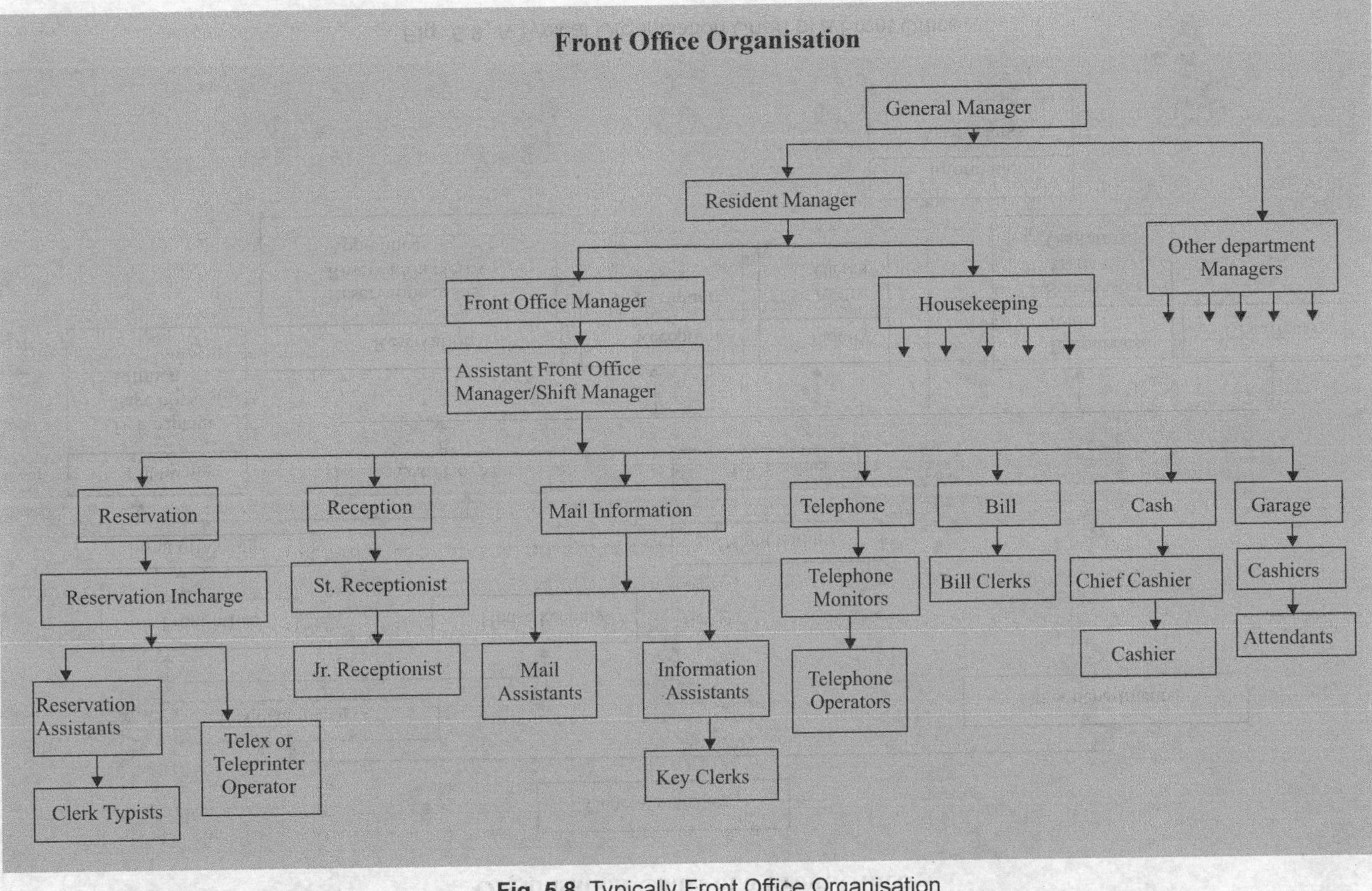

Fig. 5.8. Typically Front Office Organisation

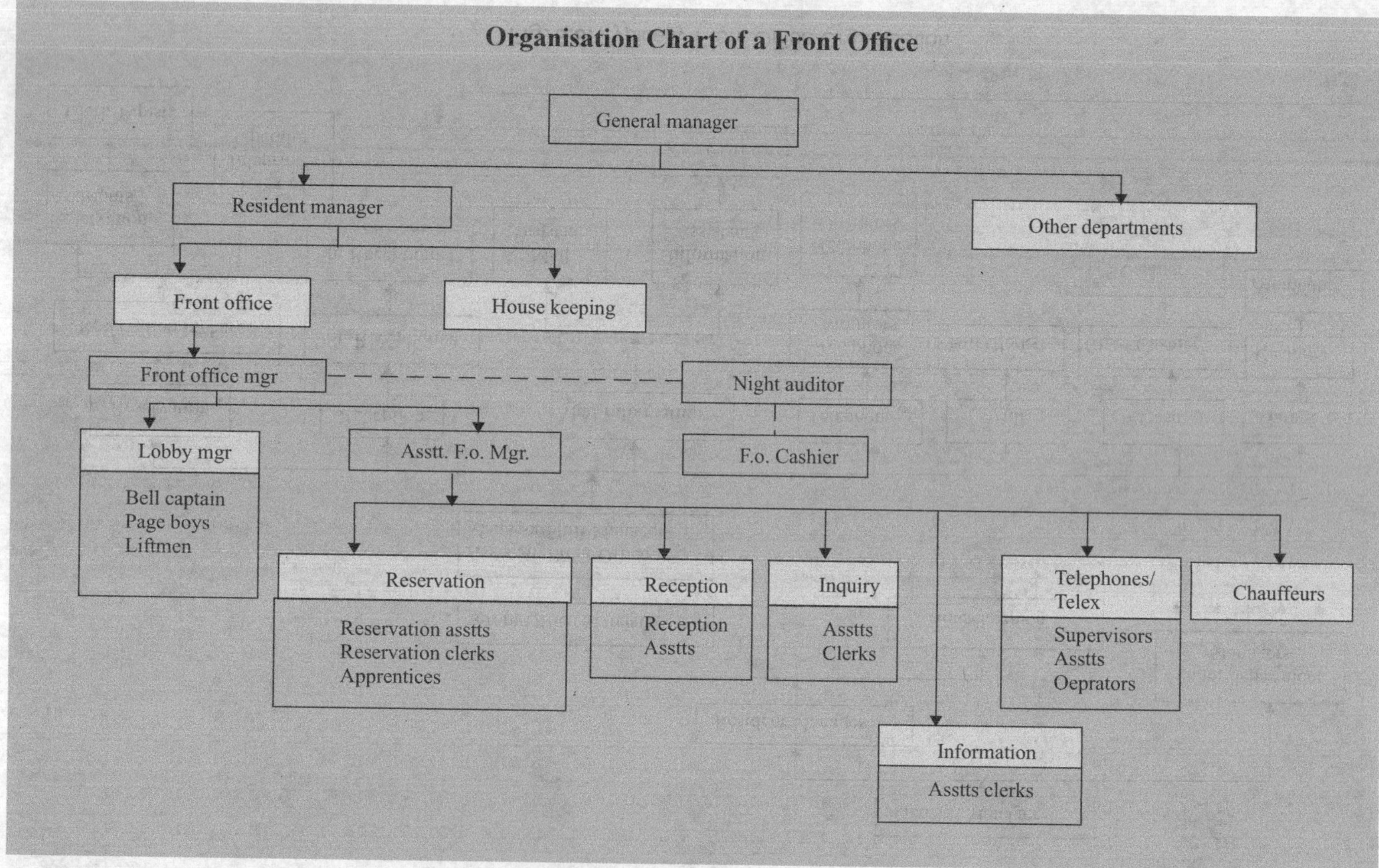

Fig. 5.9 A Typical Organisation Chart of a Front Office

education and knowledge of English and French, in addition to other foreign languages, is most essential.

ASSISTANT FRONT OFFICE MANAGER

In collaboration with and under the supervision of the front office manager, he is responsible for the smooth running of the department. He must have experience, good general education and a knowledge of foreign languages. His responsibilities and duties are the same as that of FOM and assists him in all daily activities. He replaces the FOM in the latter's absence. He assists the Front Office Manager in hiring, staffing, scheduling and training other front office personnel. He is responsible for monitoring the status of guest accounts and participates in the authorisation of checks, cashing and credit terms within the policy guidelines.

RESERVATION MANAGER

The reservation department of a hotel is headed by a reservation manager, who reports to the front office manager. In small and medium-sized hotels, these positions are combined like any other positions.

RESERVATION ASSISTANTS

The number of reservationists vary according to the size of the property. These are responsible for accepting reservations either by telephone or telegrams or telex or through mail. The reservation staff should have knowledge of total capacities of rooms and their break-up into singles, double twins and suites, special rates and discount applicable to groups, business houses, airline, VIPs, forecasting of room sales, tracing of reservation charts, reservation codes, 'no shows' problems, cancellations, deposits and refunds, guest complaints and redressal, systems of reservation racks etc. The main duties of reservation assistant are:

1. To handle guest correspondence concerning reservations.
2. To create and maintain reservation records for advance reservation.
3. To produce letters of confirmation of reservations.
4. To track future room availability.
5. To develop forecasts of room sales and occupancy levels.
6. To post reservations to reservation information chart.
7. To file and follow-up on reservations.
8. To co-ordinate with the instant reservation.

ROOM CLERKS/DESK CLERKS

The chief clerk reviews the night clerk's report to get an idea of the preceding day's occupancy and the number of vacant rooms available for assignment to new arrivals. He checks the rooms and the total number of projected departures for the day, on the basis of the list submitted by the night clerk or is prepared from the rack slips showing a departure date. The list indicates the room numbers of guests who paid their room rent in advance. The accounts of these guests are already cleared, therefore, they leave the hotel without stopping at the cashier's desk to check-out. The responsibility for checking out these guests rests with the credit manager.

The room clerk must check the reservations of the day. He also notes the approximate date of arrivals, special requirements, deposits etc. He blocks rooms for some of the expected arrivals by inserting a block out card, in the rack on top of the rack card, with guest's name and approximate time of arrival. The number of the room is noted on the reservation slip.

The room clerk also checks the supplies of registration cards, bills, pens, and other stationery. He checks the time stamp for the current date. The room rack is also checked against the house-keeper's morning report of the preceding night, occupied and vacant rooms. Discrepancies should be immediately investigated.

On departure of the guests, the room clerk clears the desk racks and gets the room made up so that they are available for new arrivals. The cashier informs the room clerk about guests' check out by giving the registration cards time stamped to show the actual departure time. The room clerk adjusts the room rack, informs the house-keeper and notifies the telephone operator and information desk. On receiving information from the house-keeper, the room clerk knows that the room is vacant. On room change, the room clerk changes the occupied room in the rack and notifies the house-keeper, cashier, telephone operator and information clerk.

Another important function of the room clerk is the registration of guest which varies according to categories he is handling individual guest and small groups with reservations, walk-ins, people without reservation, and group and convention guests. In brief, the duties desk clerks are :

1. To identify guest's room, rate and length of stay requirement.
2. To perform the registration procedure.
3. To assign guest rooms and rate.
4. To secure the guest's method of payment.
5. To be responsible for the handling of guest mail, information, messages and key services.

RECEPTION ASSISTANT/RECEPTIONIST

A receptionist must have good general education and thorough knowledge of the organisation of the hotel, guest billing, posting machines, labour legislations and foreign languages. He deals with the general public and other departments as such there is excellent opportunity for learning varied aspects of hotel management. There are three main aspects of the job of the receptionist :

1. Public relation : This involves good service and goodwill.

2. Sales or selling room : It involves the reasons of accomplishing these aims.
3. Technical : It involves the reasons of accomplishing these aims.

A receptionist, in most cases, is concerned with all of them at the same time. He should have a number of special abilities which are necessary for executing his work efficiently and successfully. While a pleasing personality is an asset, in a reception job, a good standard of education is equally important for a receptionist.

QUALITIES

There are certain attributes and qualities which are essential for a good receptionist. These are :

COURTESY

An inherent sense of courtesy is the key to success in reception work. He should have a genuine desire to do everything possible to make the visitor happy and comfortable. He must be courteous with the guest as well as his colleagues.

TACTFUL

The visitor and person making inquiries should be treated with courtesy and respect. There are many occasions when a receptionist has to refuse a request of the visitor due to hotel's rules. He should do it without offending the guest. It is the manner rather than the word which welcomes the arriving guest. The well-groomed receptionist who steps forward to greet the visitor in a cultured, well modulated voice with a gracious smile displaying simple courtesy and tact wearing a charming personality is a valuable asset for the hotel.

INTELLIGENCE

A receptionist needs intelligence and a good knowledge about different hotels, tourist spots and other places of interest. He should have the ability and desire to solve other people's problems. In addition, a receptionist must be capable of acting independently and taking decisions.

PSYCHOLOGIST

A receptionist must have the gift of intuition and be able to understand the difference between the various people he meets and to the most effective method of dealing with each of them.

SENSE OF RESPONSIBILITY

He must develop a sense of responsibility. He often has to deal with unforeseen situations, which require immediate decisions. He must always remember that his words and actions reflect not only his own but also the attitude of the hotel management. A receptionist must know by heart, certain essential facts such as :

1. Total number of rooms
2. Total check-out and check-in as per reservation
3. Position of accommodation, capacity, furnishing and price of every room in the hotel and its connection with other rooms
4. Rooms which are vacant and ready to be let
5. Number of rooms occupied

6. Name of visitor, date of arrival and date of probable departure
7. Room reserved for future engagement with date and name
8. Room which are out of order, reasons and the period till they are out of order, spring cleaning, renovation etc.
9. Room number and name of guest
10. Total number of visitors staying in the hotel and the amount of business done for rooms let.

The duties of a receptionist vary according to different classes and sizes of hotels. Every hotel evolves its own routine and makes some innovations to meet its particular requirements. The duties that have to be carried out by the receptionist should be planned in a methodical and systematic manner. Some of the duties are :

1. To assist the front office manager/assistant front office manager
2. To replace him in his absence
3. To make sure that all records are up-to-date
4. To keep the reception books up-to-date
5. To inform all the concerned departments of expected arrivals and departures
6. To prepare room status reports
7. To do actual reception of visitors on arrival at the hotel
8. To deal with the correspondence, take telephone messages and telegrams relating to the booking of accommodation
9. To prepare and maintain record cards of all visitors to the hotel
10. To complete guest registration, typing of guest folios, arrival slips 'C' forms etc.
11. To keep the safe custody of valuables on behalf of visitors
12. To prepare the tabular book which records all chargeable items to visitors account
13. To take out the letter for the following day's arrival, check them against the diary and place them in alphabetical order in the file for the next date
14. To send arrival lists to all departments
15. To prepare departure lists
16. To inform the house-keeping department about the arrival and departure timings of guests
17. To maintain a close liaison and co-operation between the various departments viz., lobby, front office, cashier, information room service and housekeeping
18. To attend guests' complaints and inform the concerned departments
19. To maintain proper records of complaints
20. To sell rooms
21. To prepare manager's report on daily turn over and rooms occupied
22. To prepare the index card both alphabetical and numerical
23. To supply various information which may interest the guest and indicate all services provided by the hotel
24. To keep mail and handle the messages

In medium-sized hotels, the receptionist may perform the following duties:

1. To carry out all cash operations

2. To keep records and be responsible for funds, preparation and checking of guest bills
3. To receive payment and carry out foreign exchange transactions
4. To keep the cash book up-to-date, preserve all vouchers
5. To prepare, issue and settle guest bills
6. To check and distribute cash float
7. To prepare and balance the cash book.

INFORMATION ASSISTANT

Hotels have introduced a system of design and control of the mail, message and telephone in the front office. The advent of 'over-night' mail and package service, fax-type document transmission and sophisticated telephone communications, the management of mail, documents, package and message service for guests is very important. The duties of the information assistant are :

1. To up-date the guest alphabetical rack
2. To be responsible for mail rack messages, distribution of letters, registered letters, parcels, telegrams and the hotel's liability in such matters
3. To liaise with the guest and front office cashier in particular
4. To handle guest and guest complaints
5. To be responsible for procedure of 'paging' guests
6. To be responsible for information board and its working
7. To look after preparation for groups and crew
8. To be responsible for mail checks and procedures
9. To reconcile the racks
10. To be responsible for receiving messages and the role of message lights.

ASSISTANT RECEPTIONIST

An assistant receptionist must have the knowledge of foreign languages and must be able to express herself/himself clearly. Knowledge of the organisation of the hotel, ability to use the electronic tabular ledger, to deal with the hotel's correspondence and to operate the switch board and to type, are some of the basic points which an assistant receptionist must know. He is also to assist the front office manager in all his activities. The assistant receptionist works under the supervision of the receptionist. His duties are :

1. To maintain the tabular ledger
2. To establish guest's bills and notify receptionists of unpaid bills
3. To receive guests on their arrivals, to assign rooms to guests and to accompany them to their rooms
4. To prepare room lists for groups/guests
5. To co-operate in keeping the various receptionist books up-dated
6. To type the hotel's correspondence
7. To replace the cashier, if necessary.

BILL OFFICE CLERK/POSTING CLERK

He must have a thorough knowledge of the organisation of the hotel and the experience of basic principles of accounting and hotel correspondence. He should be able to use machines which are needed in the office. The main duties of the bill office clerk are :

1. To maintain the tabular ledger, which is prepared on the basis of vouchers received from various departments
2. To open the guest bills on arrival
3. To bring to the notice of his superiors any unpaid bill
4. To monitor guest credit limits.

NIGHT RECEPTIONIST

The work of the night receptionist starts during the night. He is responsible for most of the work of the reception including other activities which are required to be completed during the night. The main duties and responsibilities of the night receptionist are :

1. To take charge from out-going persons
2. To check that room rack is current
3. To be responsible for early morning calls and departures
4. To check that all public areas and front office section, are rightly cleaned
5. To be able to provide the food items to a limited extent
6. To report to the General Manager in the morning regarding any happening in the hotel
7. To keep records of the room sales
8. To keep records of the house count and other occupancy reports, for the day
9. To prepare the night room sale report
10. To sort out the mail of the expected arrival for the next day
11. To check the key inventory report prepared by the information clerk
12. To sanction allowances up to a certain extent in case of a dispute
13. To check that all the windows, doors and ventilators of the ground floor and basement are properly closed and make the surprise check of the security from time to time.

CORRESPONDENCE CLERK

He must have administrative and drafting ability and knowledge of foreign languages, business correspondence and shorthand. He is responsible for the hotel's correspondence, particularly in foreign languages. He should assist the management in administrative matters.

INFORMATION CLERK/TELEPHONE CLERK

He receives all the daily mail and separates the guest and house mail. The house mail is forwarded to the proper departments and the guest mail is checked with the information rack. The mail of resident guest is marked with room number and placed in the mail rack. Mail addressed to the people expected to arrive is filled alphabetically by date of arrival after marking on it the date of arrival. On the indicated day, the mail is checked with the information rack for the guest's room number and placed in a mail box. As regards to guests after they check out, the clerk has a card for this purpose on which the guest is required to write his or her name and the forwarding address.

The information and mail clerk is also responsible for the room keys. The guests drop their keys at the desk when they go out and ask for them on their return. This system ensures that they receive their mail since the clerk will give them the keys plus any mail in the box. In addition, the information clerk is also responsible to answer questions regarding the guest rooms and other facilities of the hotel.

Other employees of this department include: night clerks, rack clerks, guest history/ file clerks, key clerks, typists, telegram clerk, safe deposit clerks etc.

THE CONCEPT

RESERVATION

The reservation of accommodation is made by the reservation section of the front office. Inquiries are received in person through telephone, telegrams, telex, letter or block booking list, etc.

Thus, the main sources of reservations are :

1. Telephone
2. Mail
3. Telegram
4. Person
5. Travel agencies
6. Hotel representatives
7. Airlines
8. Referrals from other hotels
9. Reservation system of which the property is a member.

THE PROCESS

The following are some of the steps required in reservation irrespective of its source :

1. Request for reservation must be accepted or refused by an authorised person.
2. Send a confirmation or refusal to the prospective guest as soon as possible.
3. Notify all the functions involved.
4. Maintain systematic records.

Figure 5.9 is a specimen of a Room Reservation Form.

THE SYSTEM

Reservation systems in the hotel industry should not be very time consuming and inconvenient for customers. Most of the travellers have to contact a number of the hotel in a given city/area to find available space.

1. **Manual Reservation :**

   Many hotels use manual reservation system which tend to be time consuming, inconvenient and error prone.

2. **Hotel Clearing Houses :**

   Under this system the space data concerning space available in a city/area is gathered and consolidated. The prospective guests could be provided with acceptable alternative accommodations if their first choice was sold out.

3. **Electronic System :**

   Under this system, in the lobby of each participating hotel there is a display board listing all member properties having vacancies in major cities. When a prospective guest calls a hotel for a room, and the hotel is full, check the display board, through which a hotel having rooms available could be referred to the caller.

4. **Automatic Reservation :**

   This system is most suitable for hotels, Doperated by a chain. The customer's choice is limited to the properties comprising the chain. An independent reservation services organisation may also offer limited customer service provided it has data on and makes reservations only in subscribing member properties.

5. **Integrated Reservation :**

   A total travel package could be available through an integrated reservation system. This enables the traveller to make reservations with one telephone call or at one place for hotel tourist accommodations, airline tickets, car rentals, attractions and other travel services. Many properties are making progress in evoling this system of reservations.

   Reservation systems have two main aspects :

   1. Internal reservation concepts
   2. External reservation concepts.

INTERNAL RESERVATION CONCEPT

The internal reservation function is basically concerned with record-keeping within the hotel properties to maintain room inventories and offer guest information. The following are some of the concepts relating to internal functions :–

1. On receipt of reservation, necessary entries are made in hotel's magnetic reservation file.
2. As reservations are entered into the hotel's computerized reservation system, the computer forms, letters of acceptance or rejection containing all necessary information which are sent to customers for verification.
3. Direct communication by remote reservation offices and special travel agents with the hotel's internal reservation system provides for direct processing by the computer system of reservation requests and confirmation with provision for automatic handling of close-out periods, travel agents' commissions, etc.

The other advantages of a computerized reservation system are:

1. Accuracy of reservation information and processing
2. Rapid information retrieved by desired classification such as :
   (*i*) Volume of business generated by different agents
   (*ii*) Number of cancellations
   (*iii*) Percentage of no shows, etc.
3. Easy detection of duplicate reservations
4. Fast retrieval of individual reservations
5. Provides information about status, reports on number of vacant rooms, expected checkouts, number of reservations to be picked up, etc.

6. Minimises problem of lost reservations
7. Eliminates multiple handling of individual reservation paper work.

In large hotels, advance reservation is a separate section of reception, but in an average-sized hotel, the head receptionist casually looks after the charts and allocation. The reservation section deals with the accommodation. Its main areas of activities are :

1. To deal with requests for reservation of rooms
2. To keep the reservation rack and charts current
3. To aim to attain maximum occupancy of the hotel at all times
4. To keep a liaison between the reception and reservation
5. To inform the FOM of the position of the house for 10 days in advance
6. To inform the F&B manager of all the group arrivals as soon as the booking is affected, giving details of the plan
7. To control the group bookings and direct activities of the tour/group co-ordinator to follow the terms and conditions of various contracts for rooms with airlines, travel agents and business houses
8. To deal with telephones, telex, telegrams, persons, letters etc. through which a request is made
9. To be courteous on the telephone avoiding use of slang etc.
10. To fill in a deposit advice each time a deposit is received
11. To prepare a daily chart and tray and send it to the reception
12. To make out the position of the house on each day
13. To inform the manager, F&B manager, house-keeping about the VIPs staying in the hotel
14. To receive complaints from guests, if any, and deal with them accordingly
15. To arrange duty rotations
16. To know full procedures concerning reception, reservation etc.
17. To prepare various statements, viz. statements to be sent to head office, materialization summary, room revenue, tour operators, status report, booking affected by chain hotels etc.
18. To update the position register, files to be checked and records to be maintained.

THE PROCEDURE

1. Receipt of booking requests by :
   (*i*) Letter : Check the chart. If accommodation is available, mark off on the chart. Head up copy letter with guest's name and date of arrival in capital letters. Confirmation should go out on the same day, as a request was received, if possible.
   (*ii*) Telex : Use the same principle. Start with reservation card, mark chart and reply by telex. Head up original request and copy of reply. File in date order.
   (*iii*) Telephone / in person : Check chart, create card and advise caller to confirm if time allows, or ask for deposit.
2. Every morning, or on the previous evening, take out and study the day's arrival, correspondence, check details against cards.
3. Put the registration card in the front of the drawer marked In-house file".
4. Write up the rooming listprevious night's guests should be brought forward. Enter today's arrival in pencil, showing number of persons, room rate, departure day.
5. Upon arrival of the guest (individual or group), they should each complete a registration card.

6. Each guest/couple could be issued with a room card. This must be produced whenever the key is required.
7. The name(s) etc., on the rooming list should be inked over in red.
8. Make up the bill folios, which must be typed showing as much details as possible. Add full details of account before it goes to ledger.
9. File registration card in alphabetical order in in-house file drawer. In the absence of Whitney Slip System, these cards can be placed in a rack. This will show which rooms are let, vacant and which is expected to be let that day.
10. Type up the Whitney Slips and distribute to telephone and porters.
11. File correspondence in current in-house file, remove upon departure.
12. At the end of the evening shift, type up Arrival & Departure List for the next day.

Fig. 5.10 is a specimen of Room Reservation Form. A list of all the expected arrivals of the next day is prepared and circulated to the concerned departments. Fig. 5.11 is a Reservation Procedure Flow Chart and Fig. 5.12 depicts the Room Reservation and Information Procedure in a hotel.

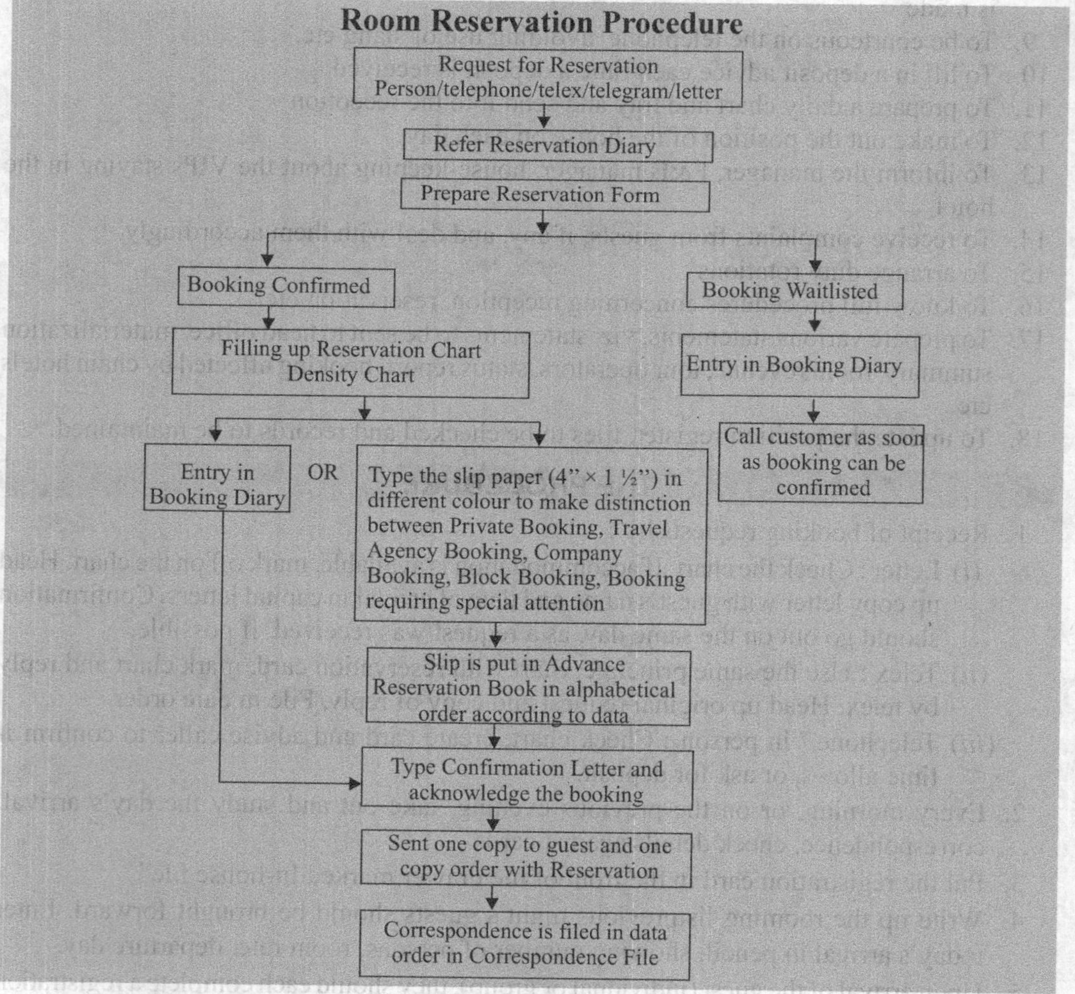

Fig. 5.10. A Typical Room Reservation Procedure Flow Chart

HOTEL ABC
ROOM RESERVATION FORM

FIT	FIT Sharer	Group Master

(Tick the correct entry)

Date : ....
Res. No.

1. Name : ____________________
2. Check in Date : ____________ 3. Check Out Date : ____________
4. Accommodation :

	Room	Suite 1	Suite 2	Suite 3	Suite 4
Unit					
Rate					

Shaper Present | Y | N | 5. PAX: [ ]

6. Company ID: ____________ 7. Repeat Guest : | Y | N | 8. Group ID: ________ (Tour op)
9. Arrival Rmks: ____________ 10. Dept Rmks : ____________
Flight/Train Time Fight/Train Time
11. Company Name ____________ 12. Designation: ____________
13. Hold Time ____________ 14 . TA Name & ID : ____________
15. Caller Name/Add/Tel : ____________
16. Permanent Address : ____________
Country City Street Addres
17. Biling Instruction : ____________
18. Comments : ____________
Registration Telephone Rest. Cashier/R.S. H.K.
19. Guest Class:

VVIP	VIP	RG	CB	GRP	CRW	Staff	Conf.	Other
1	2	3	4	5	6	7	8	9

20. Sex | M | F | 21. Nation Code: [ ]

22. Payment ID:

Cash	Cr. Cd	Chq.	Bill to Co.	Bill to T.A.	Staff	Misc Coup	Vou cher	Hotel Guest	Comp. GIT	Taj Del Cr. Cd.	Taj Grp. Cr. Cd	Others	Cham bers	Room Compl
1	2	3	4	5	6	7	8	9	10	11	12	13	14	15

23. Disc % : ____________ 24. Disc Remarks ____________
25. Sales Code:

Commr	Govt.	Crew	TR GRP.S	TR GRP (AH)	TR GRP (Inc)	Misc GRP	Cont	Lay over	Others
1	2	3	4	5	6	7	8	9	10

26. Mode of Bkg:

Commr	Tix/Tgm	Person	Latter	Others
1	2	3	4	5

27. Source Code: ____________ [ ] 28. Meal Plan : ____________
29. Deposit Ref.: ____________ 30. Deposit Amt. ____________
(Enter the original currency)

31. Expiry Date : [ ] [ ] [ ] Year Month Date 32.Rm to be Blocked: [ ] 33. Cofirm Letter?: | Y | N |

Reservation Taken By : Reservation Status : ____________

Reservation Entered By :

Detail Data Entered ?:

Fig. 5.11. Specimen Room Reservation Form

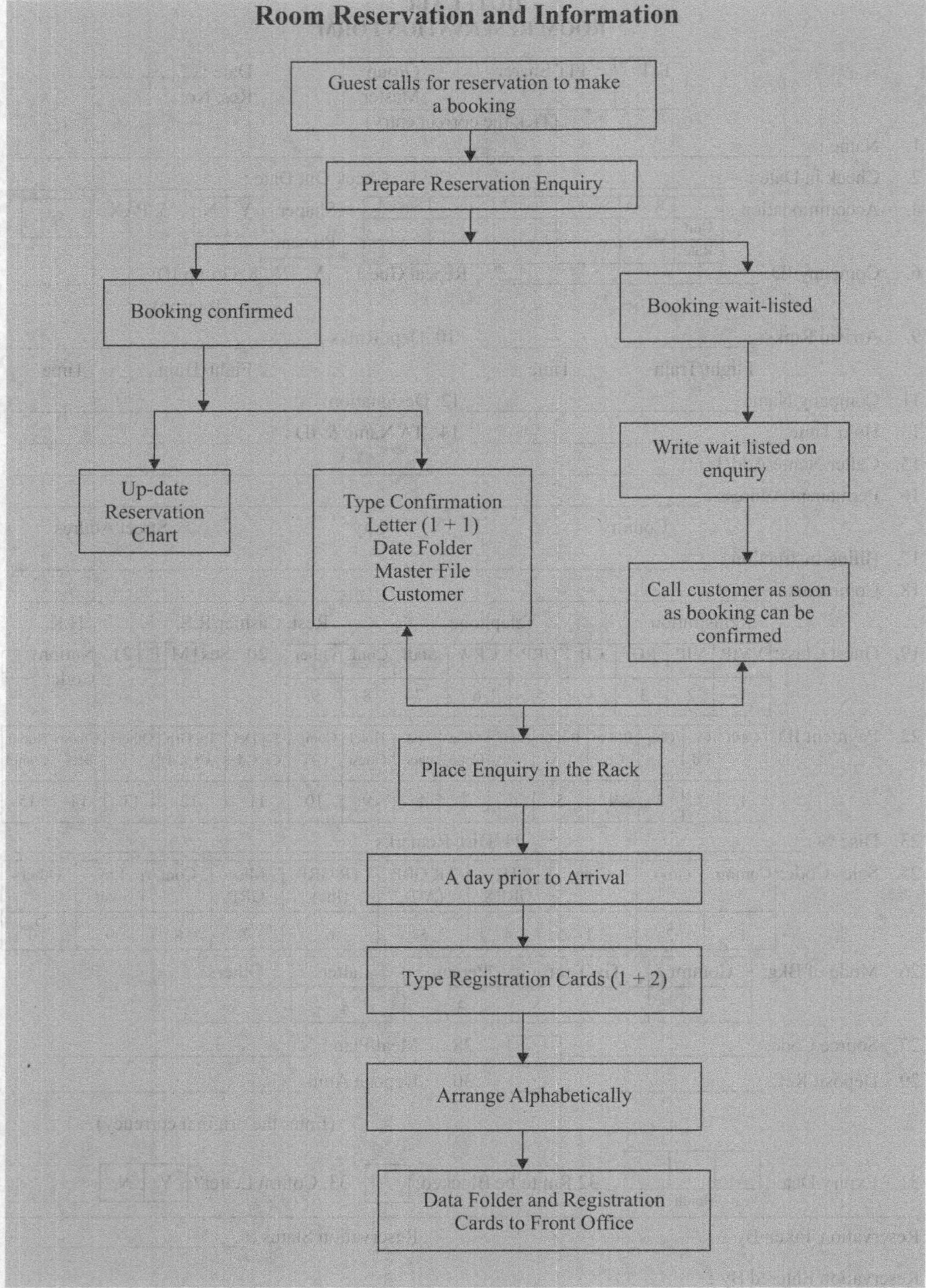

Fig. 5.12. A Typical Room Reservation and Information

Fig. 5.13 and 5.14 are a typical flow chart for a day before arrival of a guest fig. 5.15 is a guest check in flow chart and fig. 5.16 is a flow chart fo arrival of a guest

A Day Prior to Arrival of a Guest

Remove Files from Drawer
Type Reservation Card
Type Arrival List and Departure Lists (1 + 9)
Names and file numbers are written in the register and receptionist signs
Files and Arrival Lists to Reception

Note :

(*i*) Depature list is prepared from Reservation chart (*ii*) Distribution of Arrival lists:

(1) General Manager (2) Sales Manager (3) Head Housekeeper
(4) Head Waiter (Room service) (5) Lobby Manager
(6) Reception (7) Reservation (8) Chef (9) Telephone

(*iii*) Arrival List/Departure List and files are arranged alphabetically.

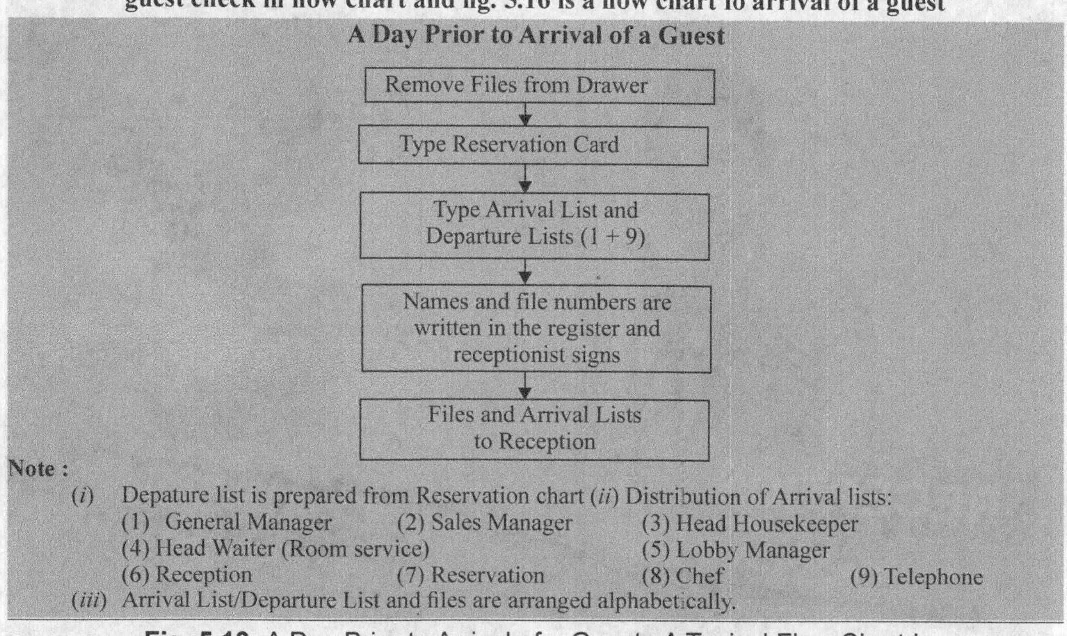

Fig. 5.13. A Day Prior to Arrival of a Guest : A Typical Flow Chart I.

A Day Prior to Arrival of a Guest

Remove file from the drawer
Correspondence is brought and sorted into alphabetical order, check against advance reservation rack
Prepare GRC-Type names, initial, number of people, of arrival and price quoted
Type Arrival and Departure Lists 1 + 9
GRC attached with correspondence
The next day's Correspondence File and Advance Registration Rack goes to Front Desk
The Advance Reservation Rack becomes the Front Office Desk's Arrival List
Reception Board contains the Whitney slips

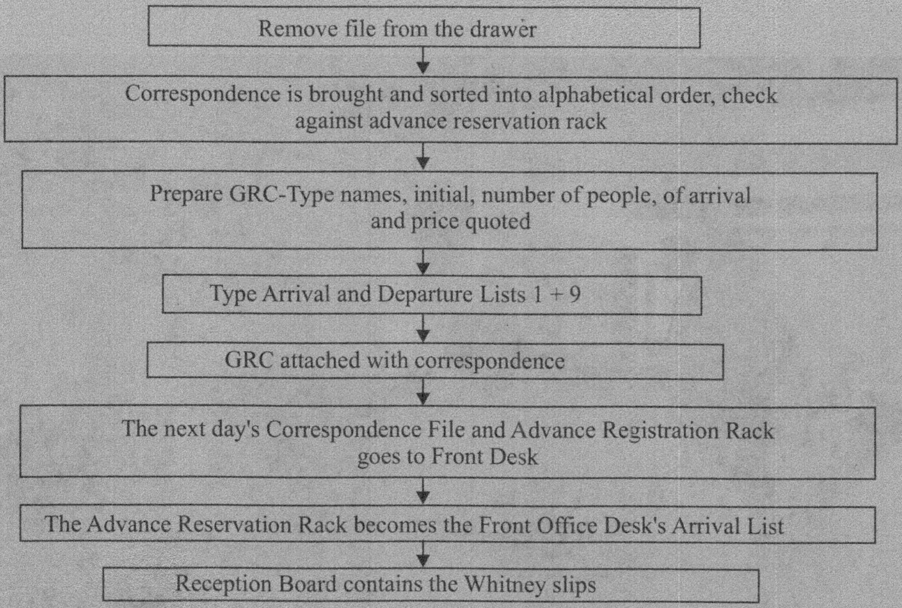

Note :

(*i*) Departure list is prepared from Reservation Chart (*ii*) Distribution of Arrival List

(1) General Manager (2) Sales Manager (3) Head Housekeeper
(4) Head Waiter (Room service) (5) Lobby Manager (6) Reception
(7) Reservation (8) Chef (9) Telephones

(*iii*) Arrival List/Departure list and files are arranged alphabetically

Fig. 5.14. A Day Prior to Arrival of a Guest : A Typical Flow Chart II.

Pix. 5.1. Telephone Handling

Pix. 5.2. Guest check in

Pix. 5.3. Welcoming a Guest in a Hotel

Pix. 5.4. Arrival of Guests

Pix. 5.5. Guests Arriving in a Hotel

Pix. 5.6. Guest Registration

Pix. 5.7. Reception and Guest Handling

Pix. 5.8. Guest Handling

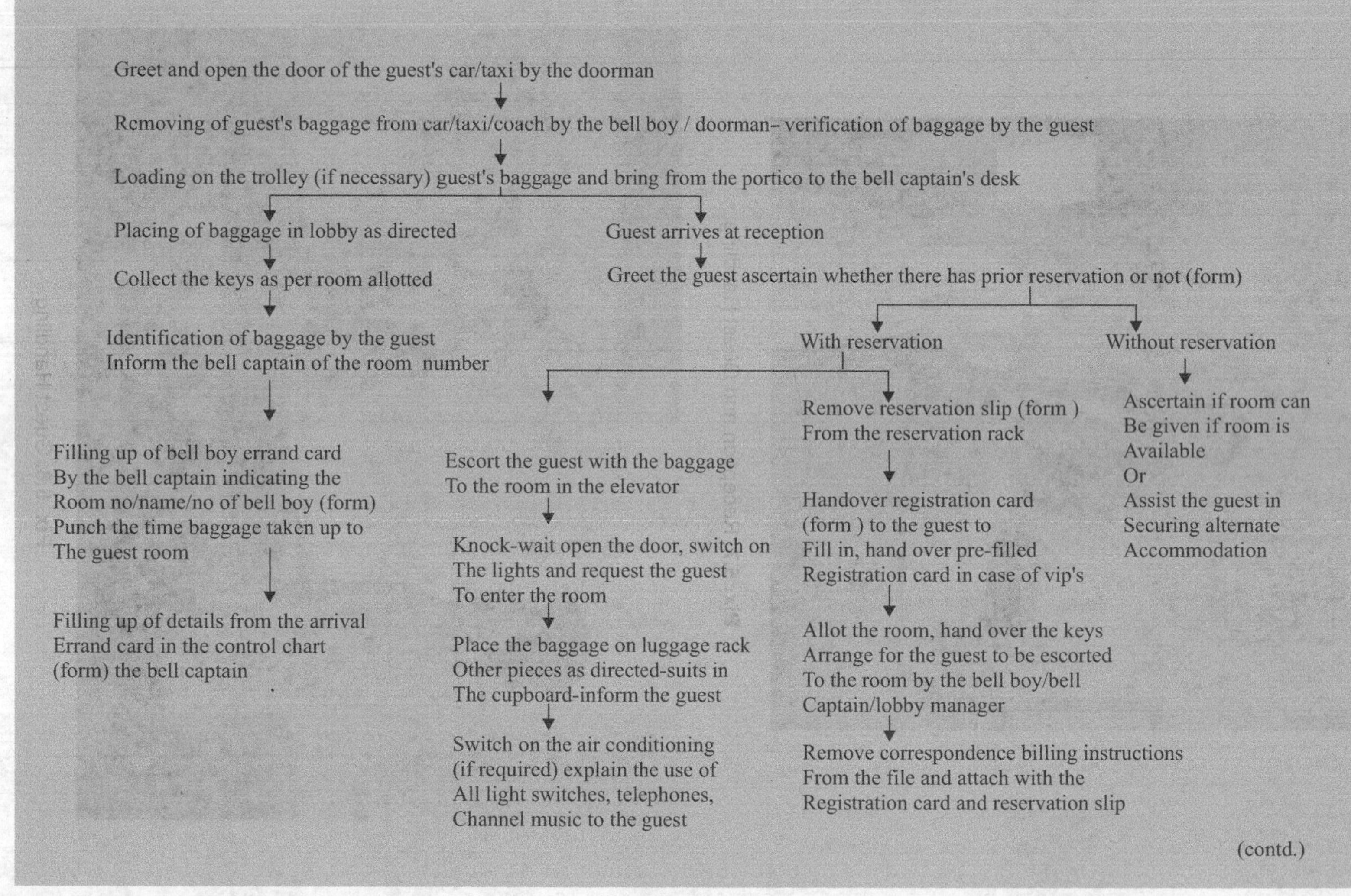
Arrival of Guest / Guest check in Flow chart
Greet and open the door of the guest's car/taxi by the doorman
Removing of guest's baggage from car/taxi/coach by the bell boy / doorman– verification of baggage by the guest
Loading on the trolley (if necessary) guest's baggage and bring from the portico to the bell captain's desk
Placing of baggage in lobby as directed
Collect the keys as per room allotted
Identification of baggage by the guest
Inform the bell captain of the room number
Filling up of bell boy errand card
By the bell captain indicating the
Room no/name/no of bell boy (form)
Punch the time baggage taken up to
The guest room
Filling up of details from the arrival
Errand card in the control chart
(form) the bell captain
Guest arrives at reception
Greet the guest ascertain whether there has prior reservation or not (form)
With reservation
Without reservation
Escort the guest with the baggage
To the room in the elevator
Knock-wait open the door, switch on
The lights and request the guest
To enter the room
Place the baggage on luggage rack
Other pieces as directed-suits in
The cupboard-inform the guest
Switch on the air conditioning
(if required) explain the use of
All light switches, telephones,
Channel music to the guest
Remove reservation slip (form)
From the reservation rack
Handover registration card
(form) to the guest to
Fill in, hand over pre-filled
Registration card in case of vip's
Allot the room, hand over the keys
Arrange for the guest to be escorted
To the room by the bell boy/bell
Captain/lobby manager
Remove correspondence billing instructions
From the file and attach with the
Registration card and reservation slip
Ascertain if room can
Be given if room is
Available
Or
Assist the guest in
Securing alternate
Accommodation
(contd.)

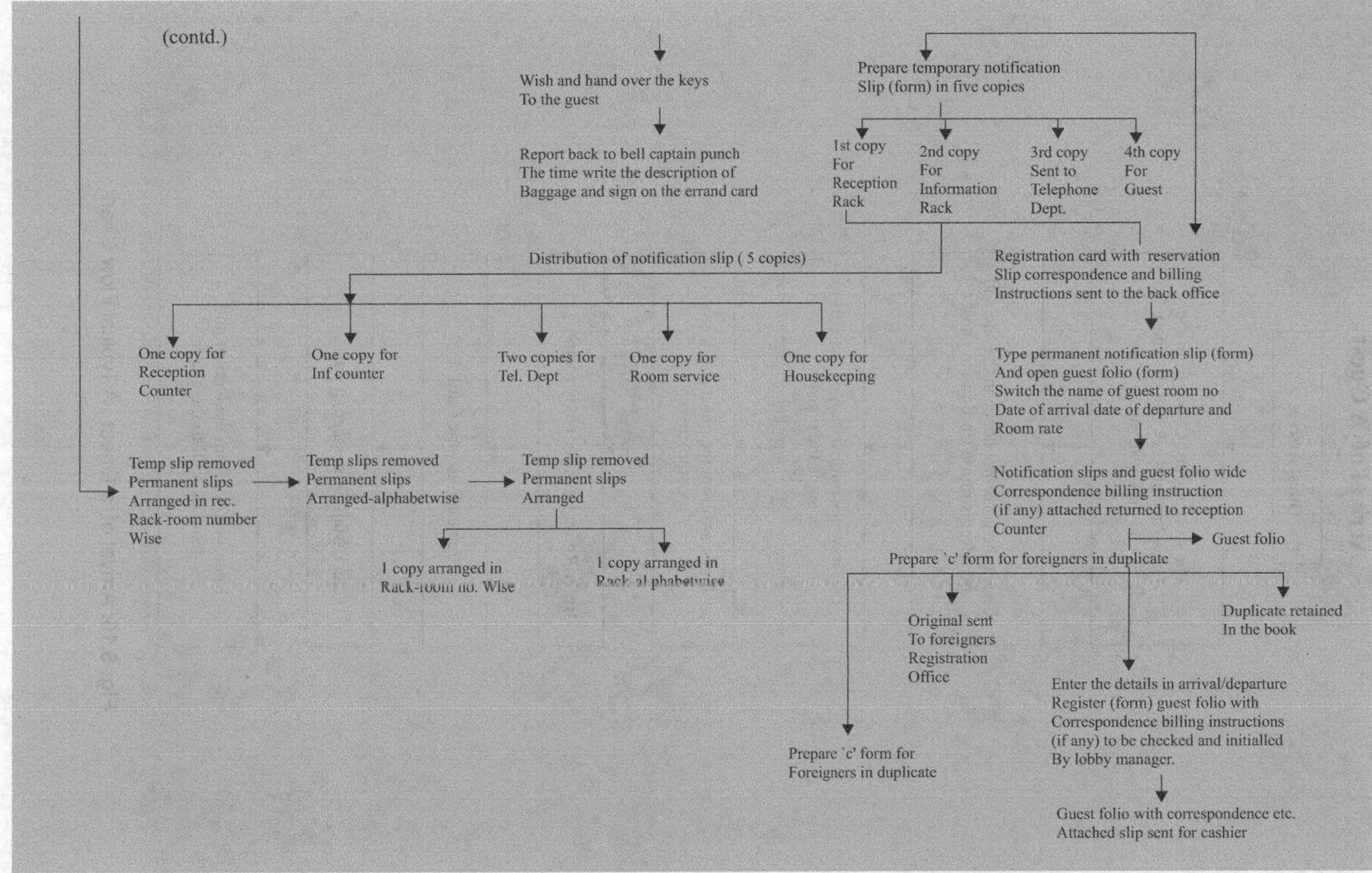

Fig. 5.15 Arrival of Guest / Guest check in Flow chart

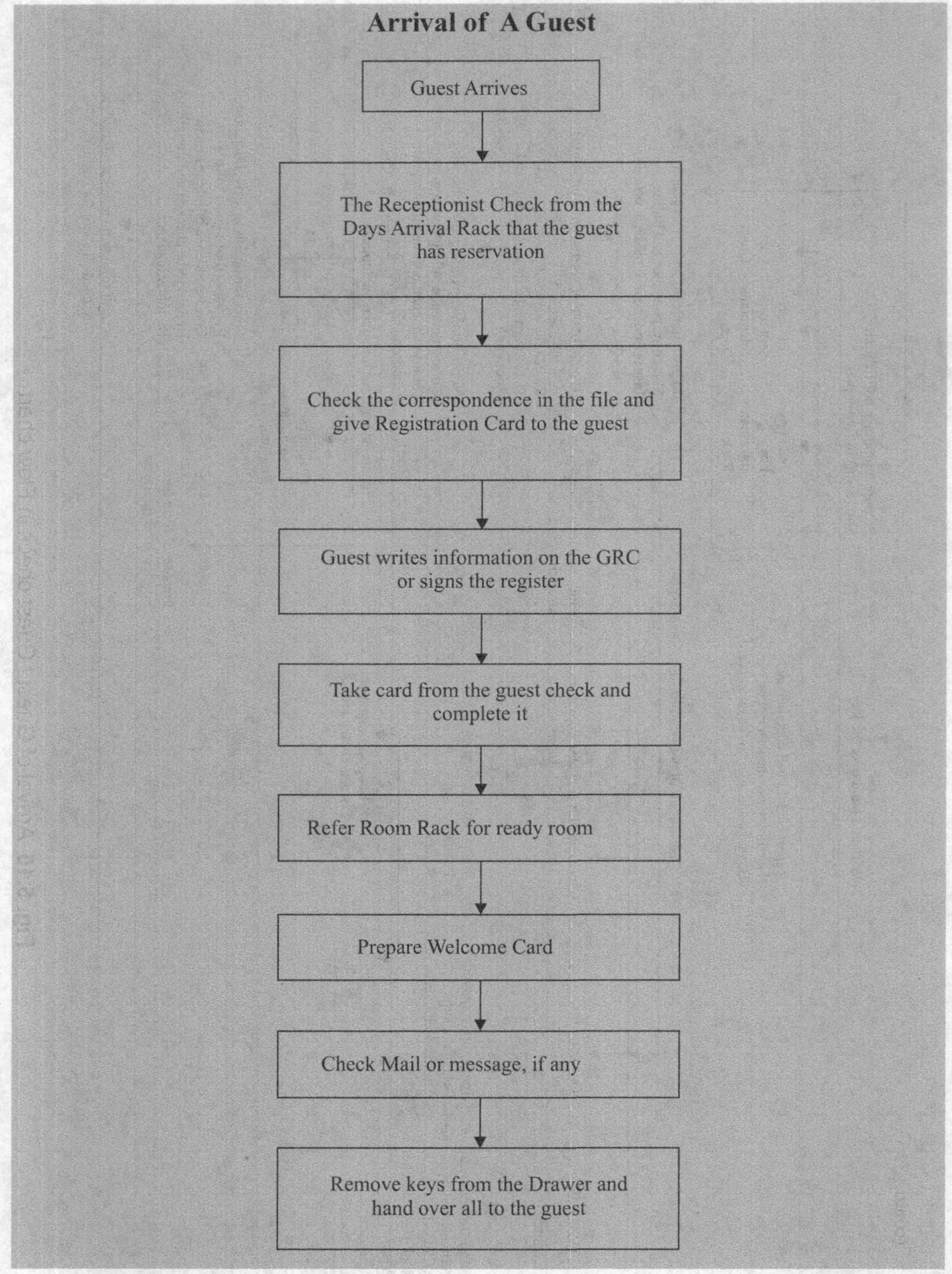

Fig. 5.16. Arrival of a Guest : A Typical Flow Chart

Reception :

The reception area is the registration desk. Guests, on arrivals, are greeted by room desk/receptionists and receive the first impression of the hotel, its staff and its service. A room clerk helps the guests to register and assign them their room. Figs. 5.17, 5.17 (a), 5.18 and 5.18(a) are the specimen of Guest Registration Form. Figure 5.18 is a specimen 'C' Form used for registration of the foreign guest. The work and preparation of this section starts early in the morning, when the employees of the eight hours shift on the registration desk report for duty.

The reception office is the 'show window' of the hotel. It needs to be well designed and well organised. It is the nerve centre of the hotel and is a contact point between the guest and the hotel. The reception office is the mirror of a hotel.[4] The key to the reception is the room chart which shows at a glance the state of the hotel. When a guest arrives and accommodation is allocated, the reception office issues, through a written voucher, all information to the bill office, house-keeper, head porter and the dining room, giving particulars of name, room numbers, rate and proposed period of stay. The bill office on receiving this information opens an account on the bill sheet. The other sections use this for adjustment of their record. The reception office enters all details on the 'arrivals' record and adjust the house-keeping chart. Departures notified to the various sections by a similar process.

A filing system giving the history of the visit of every guest, is kept in the reception office. In every large establishments, the information is passed on to the record room. Most of the small-sized hotels are operated with just two clerks, who perform the work done by reservation clerk, cashiers, bill clerks, telephone operators, mail clerks, record clerks, information clerks etc.

Pix 5.9: The Reception

Check-in and Check-Out

Queuing up during check-in and check-out specially during convention and business meetings is a source of irritation for customers and of frustration to the hotel manager. Most of the registration problems and delays can result from the following:

1. Inadequate room availability data

4. F.J.J. Marrel, Scientific Catering and Hotel Operating.

2. Inaccurate room availability data
3. Misplaced reservations
4. Lost reservations
5. Time consumed in filling out forms by both the guest and the front desk staff.

Similarly in the check-out process, delays may result because of :

1. Inadequate data on guest charges
2. Inaccurate data on guest charges
3. Delayed data on guest charges

Hotels have been trying to eliminate registration and check-out problems by reducing clerical efforts and improving accuracy of information by the introduction of computers, where the data are put into the computer when reservations are made. The same data are retrieved for use in registering the guest when he checks in. At this time an on-line computer guest ledger record is set up which can instantaneously records, room, food, laundry, valet and telephone charges. When the guest checks out, you can retrieve from the computer the complete and up to the minute statement.

Guest Registration Form

Account Number	Arrival Date	Arrival Time	Departure Date	Departure Time	No of Rooms	Room Type
....	....	....	....	....	....	....

Daily Rate	Number of Guests	Advance Deposit	Room Number	Package Plan
....	....	....	....	

Name	Natinality : ....
	Date of Birth : ....
Address	Designation : ....
	Arrived From : ....
Post Code	Processing To : ....
Company Name	Purpose of Visit : ....
CR Card No.	Employed in India : ....
	Passport No. : ....
T/A Name	Place of Issue : ....
	Date of Issue : ....
A/R Account	Date of Arrival in India : ....
Share With	Duration of Stay in India : ....

Booked By ....

Method of payment ☐ Cash ☐ Voucher ☐ Credit Card ☐ Company ☐

All Forign Nationals are required to settle their bills in Foreign Currency.

I Agree to abide by the Rules of the Hotel Which are printed on the Reverse.

....

Guest Signature

Fig. 5.17. Specimen Guest Registration Form

Back of Registration Form

(1) Check-out time is 12 noon. Please inform the Lobby Manager if you wish to retain your room beyond this time. Up to 6 p.m., if the room is available, you will be charged at half the normal tariff. After 6 p.m. the full normal tariff will be charged.

(2) In the case of default in payment of dues by a guest, the Management shall be entitled to a lien on the luggage and belongings, and to detain the same and to sell or auction such property at any time after the day of departure without reference to the party, and appropriate the net sale proceeds towards amount due from the guest.

(3) Luggage may be stored in the Left Luggage Room at the guest's sole risk as to loss or damage from any cause. Luggage may not be stored for a period of over 30 days.

(4) For the convenience of visitors, safe deposit lockers are available at the Front Office to ensure the safety of any valuables. Visitors are particularly requested to lock the door of their room when going out or when goint to bed, and not to leave the key in the key-hole. The Company will not in any way whatsoever be responsible for the loss of residents' goods or any other property not entrusted to the Management or for damage thereof whether due to neglect of hotel employees or agents or any other cause whatsoever including theft or pilferage.

(5) Storing of cinema films, raw or exposed, or any other articles of a combustible or hazardous nature in residential rooms or store rooms is strictly prohibited.

(6) Guests will be held responsible for any loss or damage to hotel property caused by them, their friends or by any person for whom they are responsible.

(7) The Management reserves for itself the absolute right of admission to any person into the hotel premises and to request any guest to vacate his or her room at any moment without previous notice and without assigning any reason whatsoever, and the guest shall be bound to vacate when requested to do so. In case of default the Management will be entitled to remove the luggage and belongings of the visitor from the room occupied by the guests and lock the room.

(8) Nothing herein above shall constitute or be deemed to constitute any tenancy, sub-tenancy or any right of tenancy or any right or interest in the hotel premises or any part of portion therof in favour of any guest or resident or visitor and the Company shall always be deemed to be in full and absolute possession and control of the hotel premises.

(9) Guests are requested to observe the Government Rules and Regulations in force from time to time in respect of registration, alcoholic drinks, firearms etc.

(10) The Management reserves the right to add to alter, or armend any of the above terms, conditions and rules.

WELCOME CALL ☐	Airline/Iapa Card No. ☐		Retention ☐	
Guest Escorted ☐	Registration		Special Billing ☐	
Sticker ☐	Certificate Number ☐			
Rnc ☐	Date of Issue ☐		Locker No ☐☐☐	
	Place of Issue ☐		During Stay ☐	
			Changing in Billing	

Ta I ☐ I Ta Ii ☐

Check In Receptionist	Lobby Manager

Fig. 5.17(*a*) : Back of Registration Form

Problems and delays in registration and check-outs can be solved by adopting the following measures :

1. Integrate registration with the reservation system.
2. Automatic accumulation and verification of all guest charges.
3. Establish separate check-in points by type of guest, confirmed reservation, walk-in, convention etc.
4. Use roving expediter in registration area to prevent bottlenecks.
5. Provide for separate handling of guests and their luggage. Introduce self-service luggage cart, or arrange for direct delivery of luggage from airport to hotel room.
6. Pre-register the guest arriving in groups or holding confirmed guranteed reservations.

Guest Ragistration Form

HOTEL ABC

Last Name First Name	Payment by Cash ☐ Travel Agency ☐ Credit Card ☐ Company ☐ Airlines Vouchers
Nationalty	Credit Card Expiry Date
Company	Date of Arrival in India
Permanent Address :	Proposed Duration of stay in India
Purpose of Visit	Particulars / Passport Details / Registration Certificate No. Number Date Place
Arrival Date : Time	
Department Date : Time	
Arrived From : Proceeding to :	Whether Employed in India
Check ion check out : Time 12 noon All Valuabies & cash should be Deposited with the cashier	I agree to able by the rules of the hotel which are printed on the reverse. Guest's Signature Manager's Signature

For Office Use Only : Natinality Code Payment Code Resv. No.

Room No.	No. of Person		Room Rate	Billing Instructions	Booked by	Initials of FOA
	Adults	Children				

THE ABC GROUP OF HOTELS

Travelling on in ABC Group has hotels in prime locations... Please tick your next detail and contract the Receptionist for assistance.

☐ Mumbai ☐ Madras

☐ Calcutta ☐ Banglore

Fig. 5.18. Specimen Guest Ragistration Form

SPECIAL TERMS & CNDITIONS FOR USE OF ROOM BY GUESTS

1. COMPANY'S LIEN ON RESIDENTS LUGGAGE AND BELONGING : In case of default in payment of dues, the mangement has a detain the same and to sell or auction such property and appropriate the net sale proceeds towards amount due to the guest.
2. Luggage Stoage Lauggae can be stored in the Luggage Room for a norminal charge at the guest's sole risk as to loss or damage from any cause. Luggage cannot be stored for a period of over 12 weeks. Any luggage left in the store Room or all unclaimed baggage left a period of 12 weeks are to be disposed of by management without any notice of intimation there of.
3. Visitors Belonging : The management of the Hotel is not in any way responsible for the loss of residents' goods or any property or for damage thereof whether due to neglect of Hotel servants or agents or any other cause whatoever including pilferage. For the convenience of Residents lockers are availables are available free of charge at the Front Office to ensure the safty of any valuables.
4. Hazardous Goods : Storing of Chinema Films, Raw and Exposed or any other articles of a combustible or hazardous nature in residental rooms or store room is strictly prohibited.
5. Damage to property and injury to guests : Guests will be responsible for any loss or damage to the hottel property caused by them, their friends or any person they are connected wit. The management of the Hotel shall not be responsible for any loss of guest's property or anu injury to the guests resulting from fire and/or natural calamities.
6. Management's right : Ther management reserve to itself the absoult right to refuse admission to any person in the hotel premises without previous notice and without assigning any reason whatsoever, and the guest shall be bound to vacate when requested to do so. In default the management will be entitled to make him or her vacate the room and remove the luggage and belongings of the visitor from the room occupied by him or her.
7. Relation between company and resident : Nothing herein above shall constitute or be deemed to constitute any tenancy or subtenancy or any right of tenancy or sub-tenancy or any right or interest in the hotel premises or any part or portion thereof in favour of any guest or resident or visitor and the company shall always be deemed to be in full nad absolute possion and control of the whole of the Hotel premises.
8. Government Rules and Regulation : Guests are requested to observe the Government Rules and Regulations in force from time to time in respect of registration, alcoholic drinks, fire-arms etc.
9. Amendent of Rules : The management reseves to itself the right to add to alter or amend any of the above terms, cvonditions and rules.

General Manager

Fig. 5.18(*a*). Back of Guest Ragistration Form

HOTEL ARRIVAL REPORT

HOTEL ABC

1. Name of Hotel/Rest House/Dak Bangalow
   Paying Guest House etc. ....
2. Name of foreign visitor in full
   (in Block Capitals, Surname first) ....
3. Nationality ....
4. Number, date and place of Issue
   of passport ....
5. Address in India (other than tourists) ....
6. date of arrival in India ....
7. Arrived from ....
8. Whether employed in India - Yes or No ....
9. Proposed duration of stay in India ....
10. Number, date and office from issue of
    Certificate of Registration, if any ....
11. Date and Tissue of Arrival at the Hotel ....

Date .... 20...........

Manager's/Visitor's Signature

Fig. 5.19. The Registration of Foreigners : Specimen Arrival Report

ROOMING

It consists of both distribution and allotment of rooms to the expected guests and rooming the walk-in. The vouchers are sent by different service centres of the hotel through pneumatic tubes or by sending staff members to the bill section. Fig. 5.20 indicates a typical guest check-in and check-out procedure.

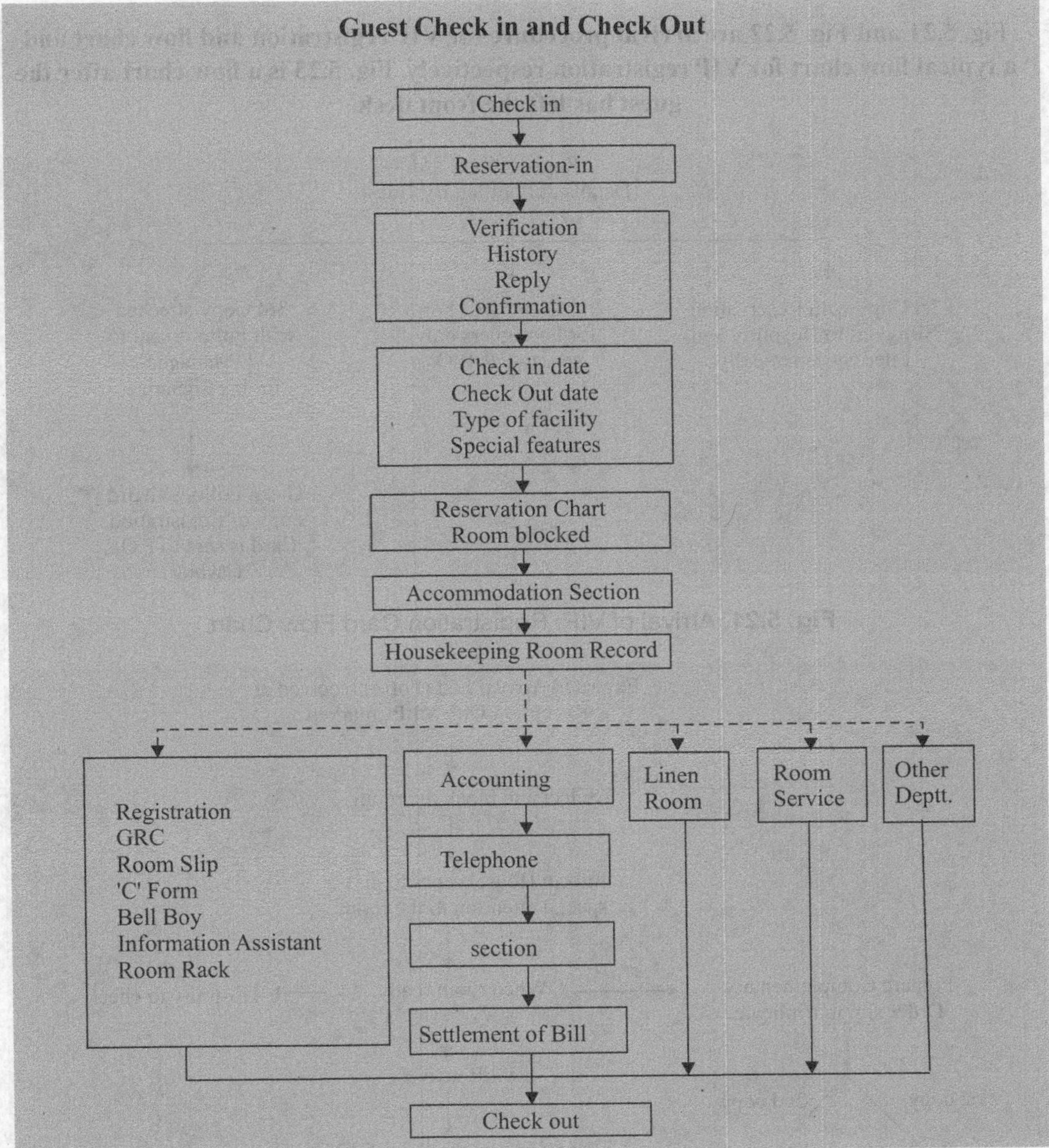

Fig. 5.20. Guest Check In and Check Out : A Typical Flow Chart

VIP CHECK OUT

There are some reputed chains which have provided convention guests with a 'VIP Check-out' form. These guests fill in this form with billing in formation and leave, along with their room key at the end of their stay in the hotel.

Thus, the front office is primarily responsible to meet guests and to promote the sales of room and other services of the hotel. This includes operating a booking system, answering letters and telephone inquiries and keeping up a chart of rooms. The daily tab and visitors bills are kept up-to-date for settlement.

Fig. 5.21 and Fig. 5.22 are arrival procedure for VIP registration and flow chart and a typical flow chart for VIP registration respectively. Fig. 5.23 is a flow chart after the guest has left the front desk.

Registration Card
(Details duly Filled By Guest)
Ist Copy with Reservation Slip goes to Hospility and Filed Systematically
2nd Copy is 'C' Form for Foreigners only sent to F.R.R.O.
3rd Copy atteched with Folio is sent to L.Manager for his Signature
Guest Folio with 3rd copy of Registration Card is sent to F.O. Cashier

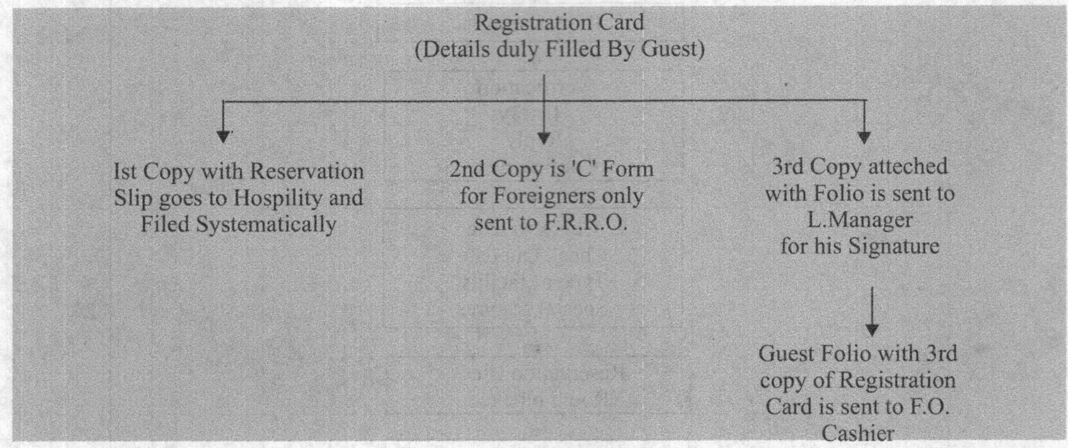

Fig. 5.21. Arrival of VIP: Registration Card Flow Chart

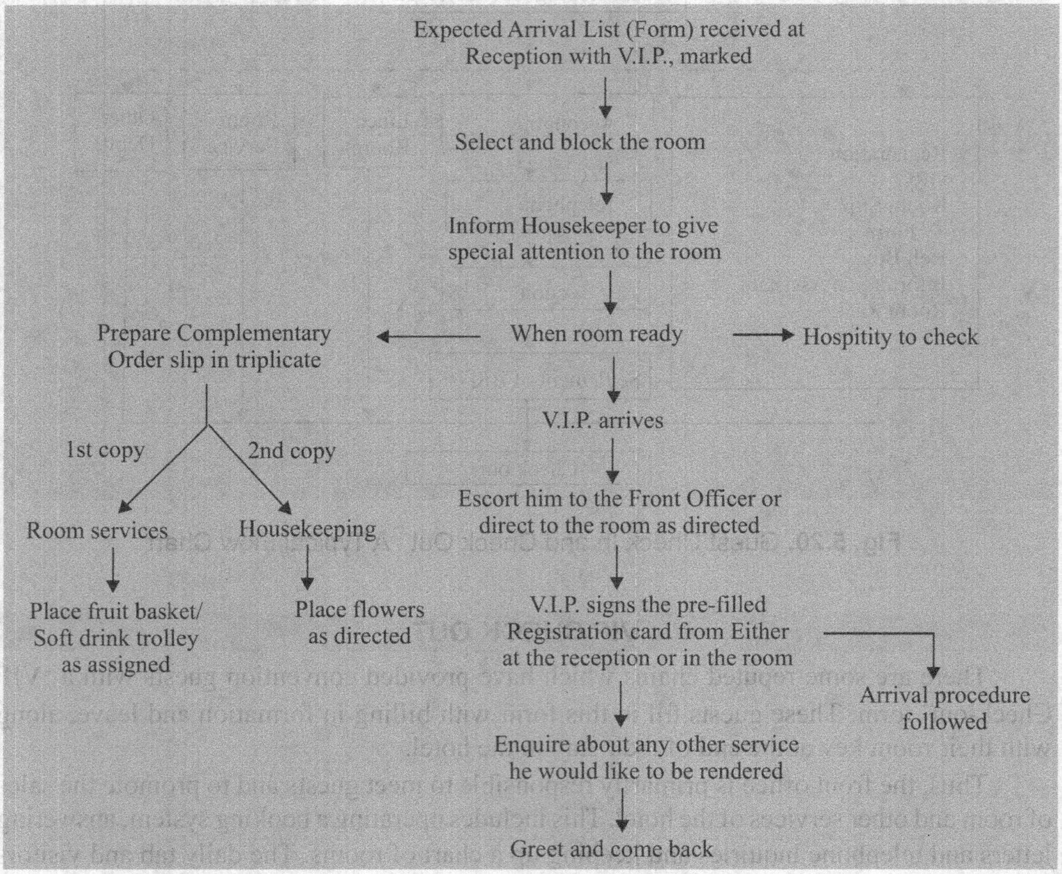

Expected Arrival List (Form) received at Reception with V.I.P., marked
Select and block the room
Inform Housekeeper to give special attention to the room
When room ready
Prepare Complementary Order slip in triplicate
Hospitity to check
1st copy
2nd copy
Room services
Housekeeping
Place fruit basket/ Soft drink trolley as assigned
Place flowers as directed
V.I.P. arrives
Escort him to the Front Officer or direct to the room as directed
V.I.P. signs the pre-filled Registration card from Either at the reception or in the room
Arrival procedure followed
Enquire about any other service he would like to be rendered
Greet and come back

Fig. 5.22. Registration Card : A Typical Flow Chart

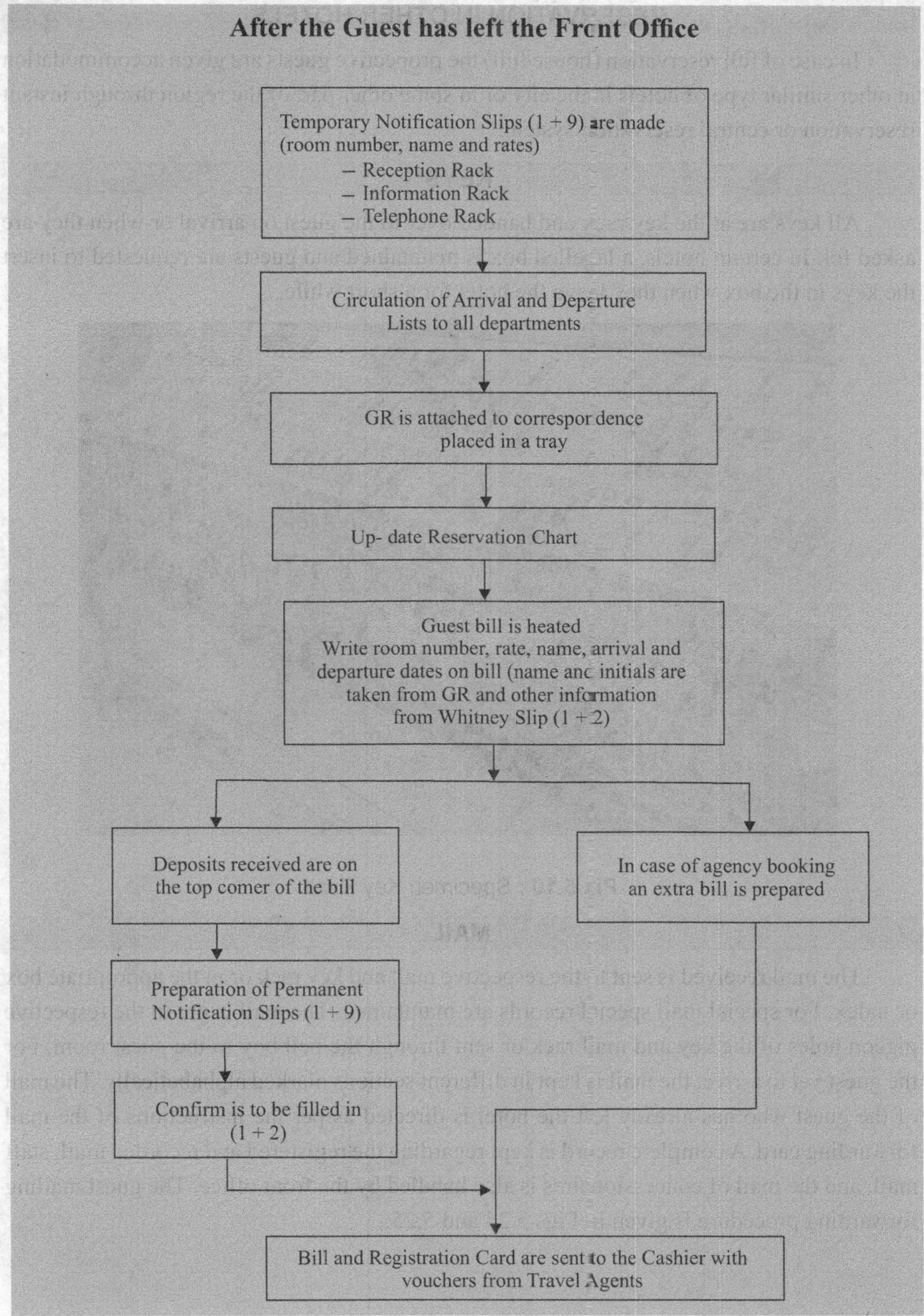

Fig. 5.23. After the Guest has left the Front Desk : A Typical Flow Chart

RESERVATION IN OTHER HOTELS

In case of full reservation (house full) the propective guests are given accommodation at other similar type of hotels in the city or in some other part of the region through instant reservation or central reservation system.

KEYS

All keys are at the key rack and handed over to the guest on arrival or when they are asked for. In certain hotels, a labelled box is maintained and guests are requested to insert the keys in the box when they leave the hotel for a short while.

Pix 5.10 : Specimen Key Rack

MAIL

The mail received is sent to the respective mail and key rack or in the appropriate box or index. For special mail special records are maintained. The mail is put in the respective pigeon holes of the key and mail rack or sent through the bell boy to the guest room. For the guest yet to arrive, the mail is kept in different sections marked alphabetically. The mail of the guest who has already left the hotel is directed as per the instructions of the mail forwarding card. A complete record is kept regarding the registered and recorded mail, staff mail, and the mail of concessionaires is also handled by the front office. The guest mailing forwarding procedure is given in Figs 5.24 and 5.25.

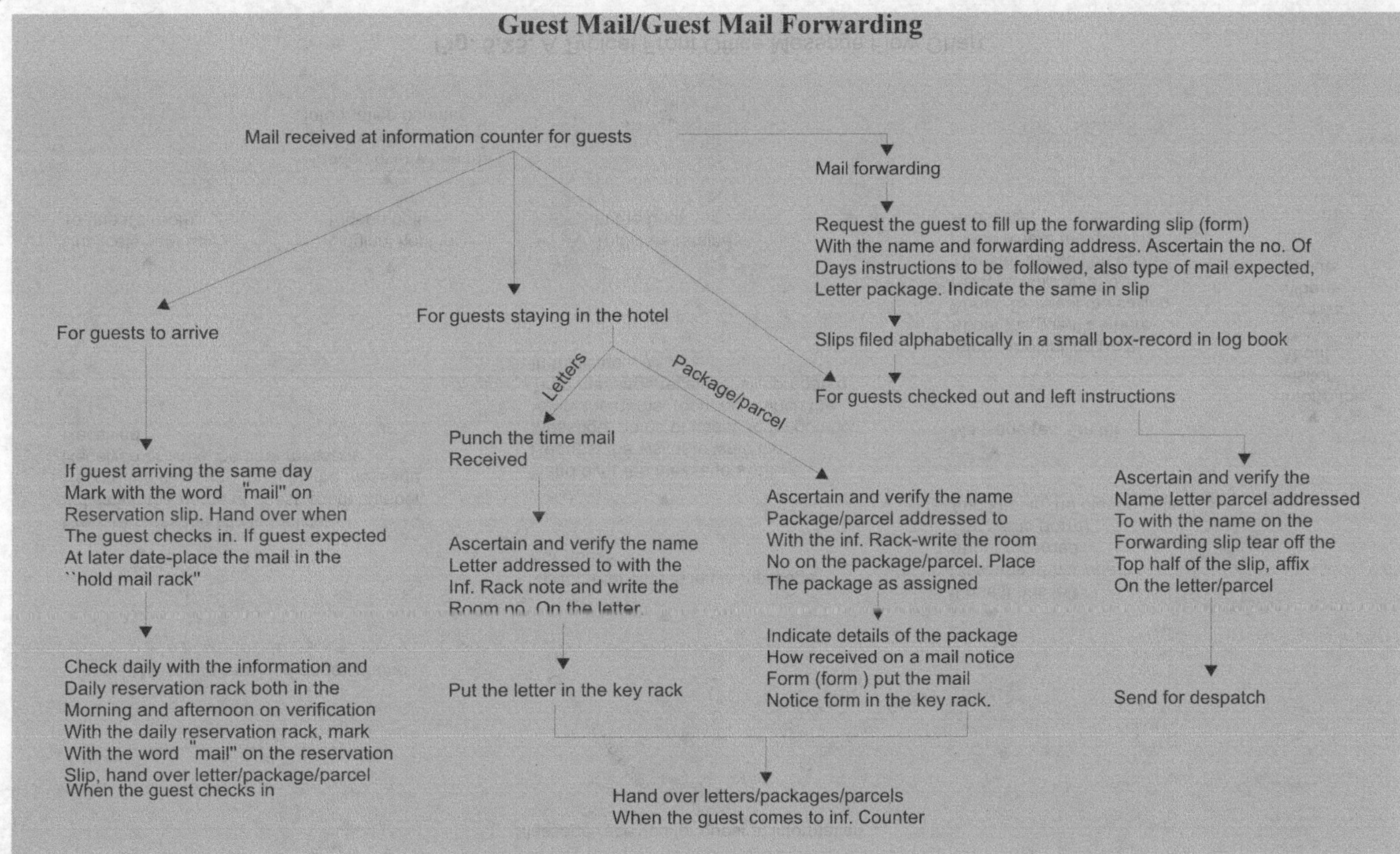

Fig. 5.24. A Typical Guest Mail/Mail Forward Flow Chart

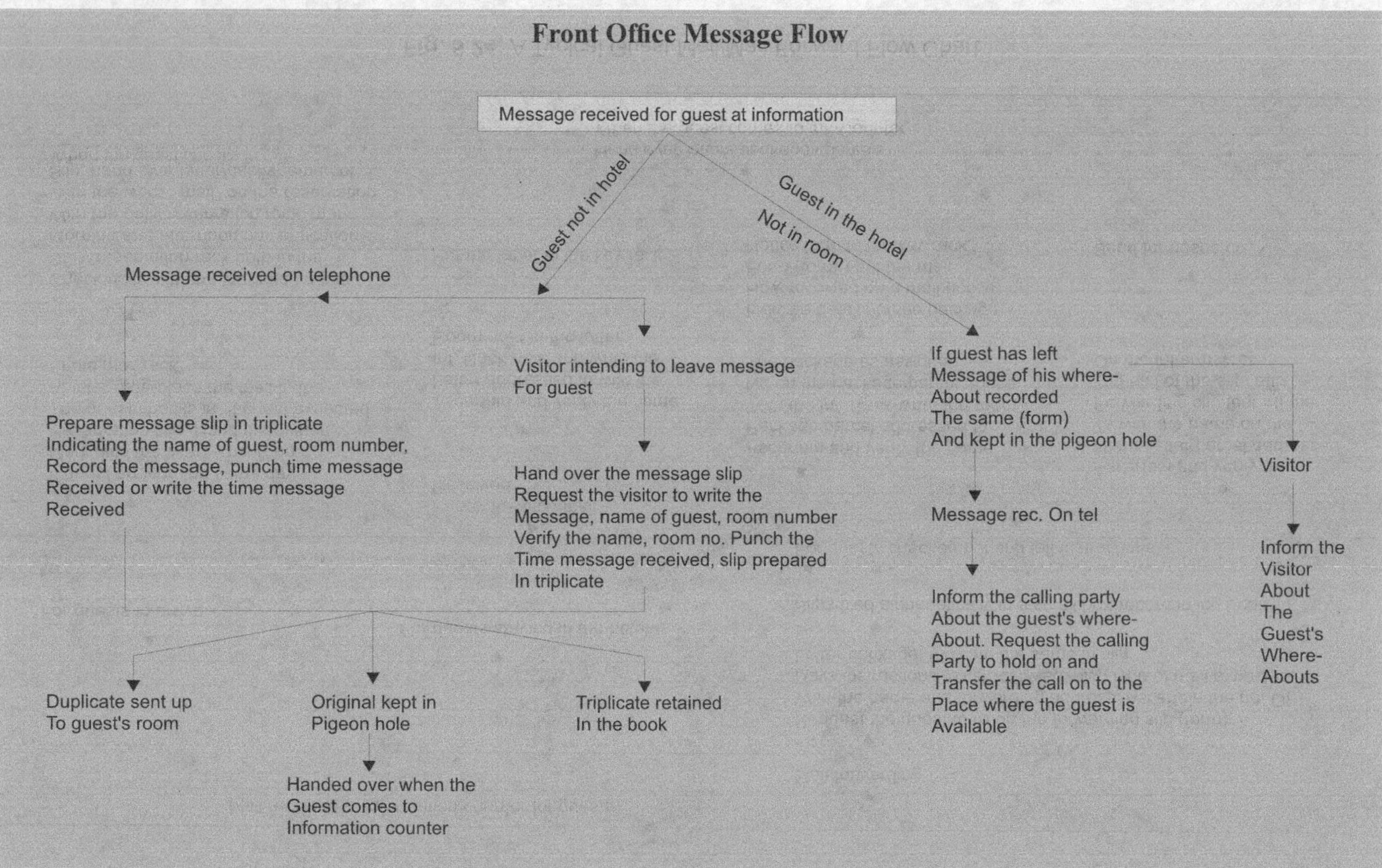

Fig. 5.25. A Typical Front Office Message Flow Chart

INFORMATION SERVICES

The purpose of information is to make aware of the various services offered in the hotel such as historical and tourist spots in the city, transport agencies and mode of entrainment, shopping centre etc. The information section is always in a position to attend the various queries and problems from time to time. The flow of reception information procedure as adopted by front office is given in Fig. 5.26 and a flow chart for front of teil harvesting information is given in fig. 5.27.

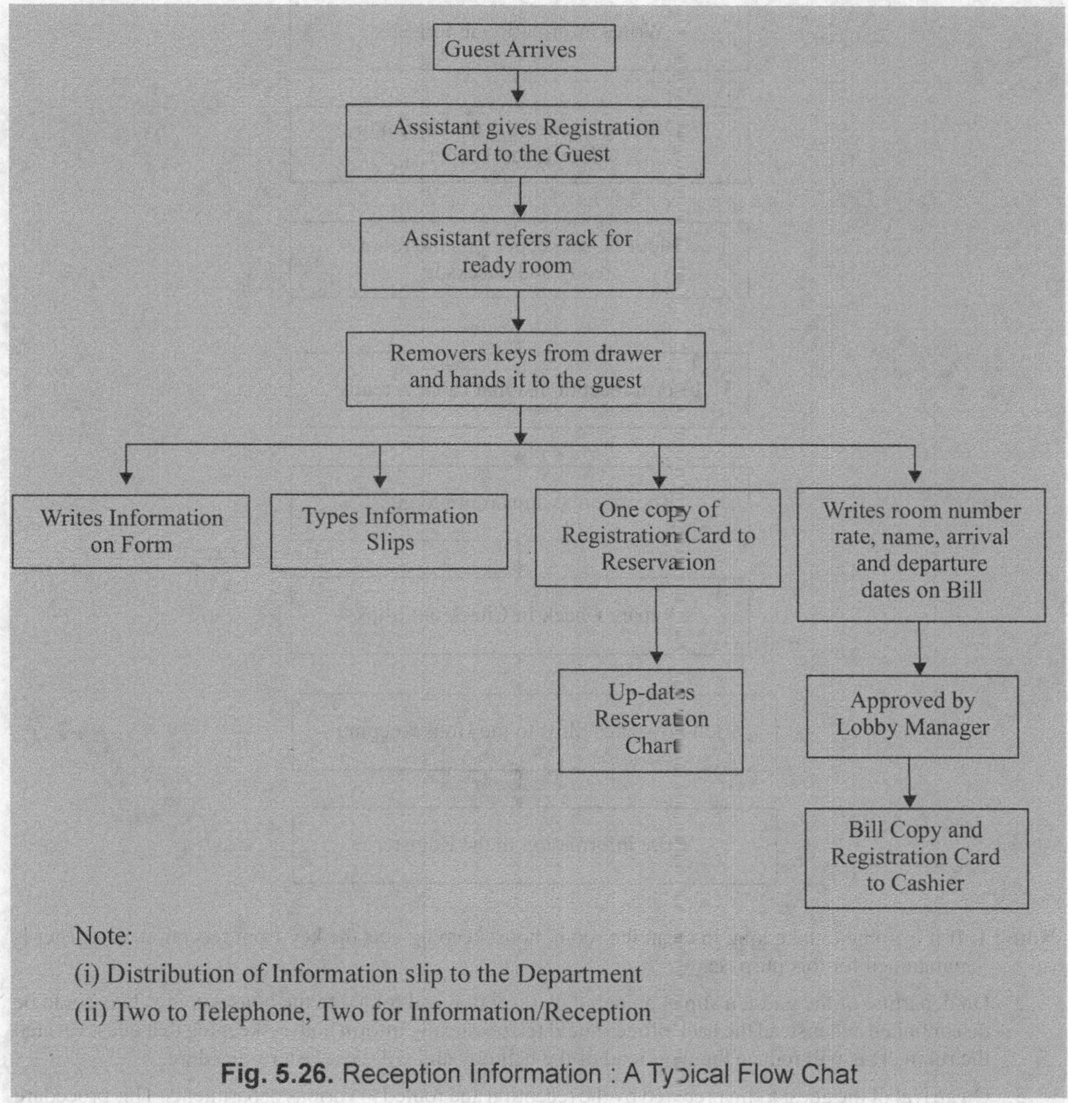

Fig. 5.26. Reception Information : A Typical Flow Chat

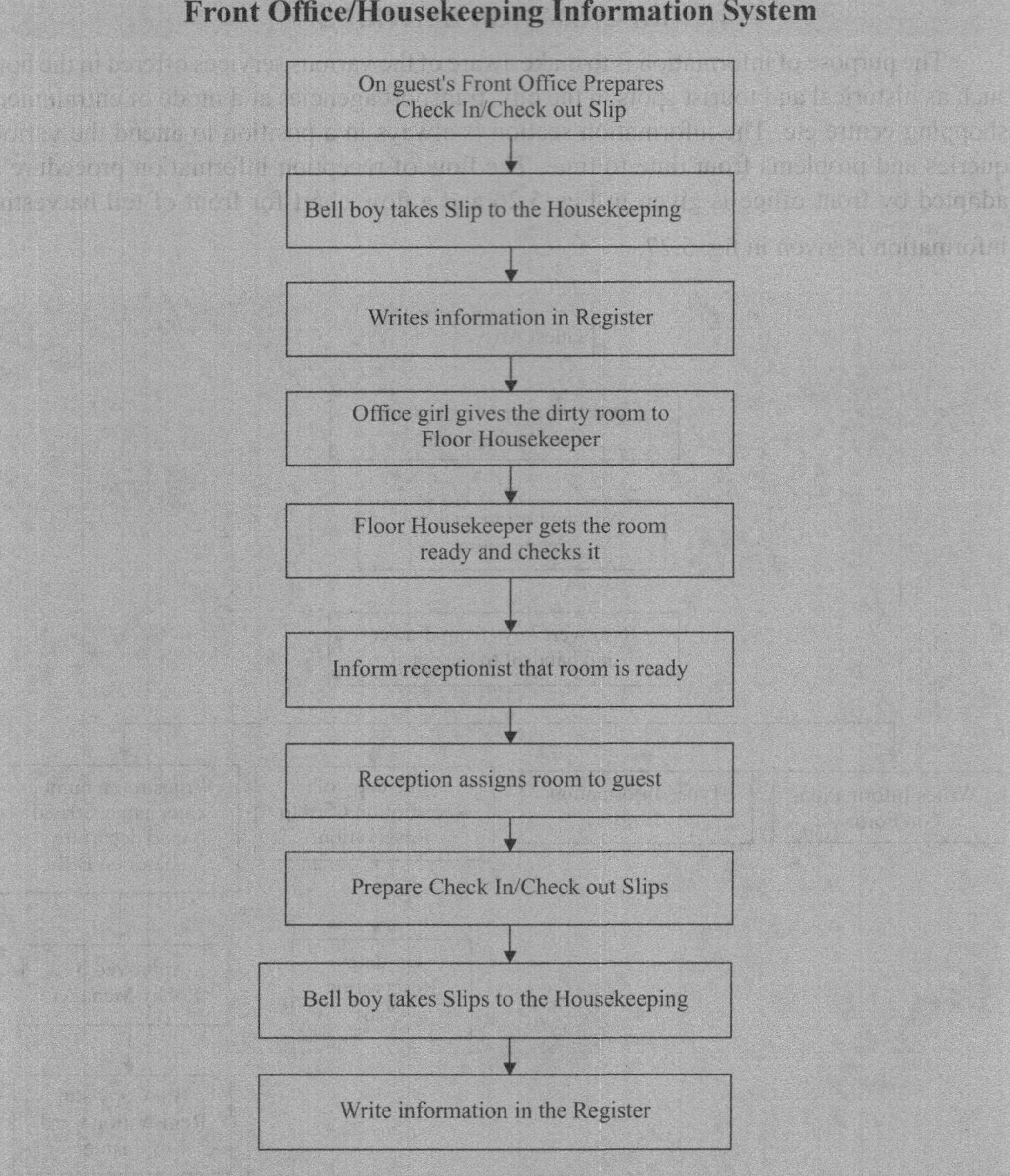

Note : 1. If it is going to take long to clean the room, housekeeping gets the key from reception. A register is maintained for this purpose.

2. On departure of the guest, a slip is prepared by reception and routed to the housekeping. This could be discontinued and instead the back office should telephonically inform house-' keeping that guest vacated the room. This will reduce the workload of the bell boy and will be a faster procedure.

3. On arrival of the guest a slip prepared by the reception and routed to various departments. This procedure does not serve any purpose and, therefore, should be discontinued.

Fig. 5.27 : Front Office/Housekeeping Information System : A Typical Flow Chart I

MAINTAINING STATISTICAL REPORTS

The house count, average daily rate, room occupancy report and bed occupancy report originate in this department.

COMPLAINTS

Complaints are received from the guests and concerned departments are informed accordingly. A patient hearing is given to the guests and adequate action taken to satisfy them. General complaints and suggestions are conveyed to the management and complaints regarding food service and bar service, are conveyed to the management through the front office manager.

MISCELLANEOUS JOBS

Arranging and preparing group itinerary, arranging cars on rental basis, providing information about the city, arrangement of tickets for entertainment, booking of air and railway seats, arrangement of bouquet and flowers, helping in mail, changing of foreign currency.

HANDLING CASH AND CREDIT

Collection of cash and credit for services rendered by the hotel is most important for the hotel's cash flow, its ability to pay its employees and creditors. The cashier must scrutinise personal checks and deal with foreign currencies either in cash or in the form of traveller cheques. The settlement through credit cards had made the cashier's function more streamlined but it requires careful attention.

LIAISON

One of the important functions of this department is to have close co-operation and liaison with the departments that provides guest services such as telephone, house-keeping, maintenance and engineering, food and beverage services, accounting, sales and marketing, manager's office and security.

BILLING

On registration of a guest, a guest account is opened. It will record all charges and credits pertaining to the guest's use of the hotel facilities and services. They include room charges, restaurants, beverages, laundry, valet, paid out and rebates. All checks made by different departments to guests are collected and sent to the bill section by name of vouchers. The guest account system has :

1. Visitors' Tabular Ledger (Ref. Figs. 5.28)
2. Guest bills (Ref. Fig. 5.29, 5.30 and 5.31)
3. Vouchers from sales outlets
4. Daily summary with :
   (*i*) Sales ledger
   (*ii*) Cash book and
   (*iii*) Receipt book

Pix 5.11 : Cashier's Counter

Pix 5.12 : Settlement of Guest Bill

Pix 5.13 : Cashiering

Pix 5.14 : Payment of a Hotel Bill by Credit Card

Pix 5.15 : Guest Handling

Visitor's Tabular Ledger

Room No.	101	102	103	104	105	106	107	108	109	110	Total
Name											
No. of Person											
GR No.											
Arrival Time											
Dep. Time											
Plan											
Rate:											
Apartment											
Board											
Apartment :											
Board											
EMT											
B/Fast											
Lunch											
A/Tea											
Dinner											
Tea/Coffee											
Soft Drinks											
Wine/Spirit Beer											
Service Charges											
Sales Tax											
Surcharge											
Room Service											
Local Calls											
Trunk Calls											
Laundry											
Tobacco											
News Stand											
VPO											
Misc											
Transfer											
Daily Total :											
Balance B/F DR CR											
Grand Total DR/CR											
Deposite/Cash											
Allowances											
Ledger											
Transfer											
Balance C/F DR-Cr											
Total DR/CR											

Fig. 5.28. A Visitor's Tabular Ledger

Guest Bill

HOTEL ABC

Have You Returned Key ?

ABC Group of Hotels

Guest Copy	Please collectarcelpt when paying cash	05211212

	Room No.	Rcsv. No
	Folio No	Arrival Date :
	Rate :	No. of Guests :
	Departure Date :	Arrival Time :
	Nationality	HIST No. :

S.No.	Date	Ref. No.	Description	Amount

Billing Instruction		L.No.
Cashier/LM	Bkd By	TA Name :
I agree that liability for this bill is not waived and agree to be held personally liable in the event that the indicated person, company of association fails to pay for any part of the full amount of these charges	Company Address Signature	For Office use Only Bill No. : AC. No. : Locker No.

Fig. 5.29. A Specimen of a Guest Bill

Guest Bill

HOTEL ABC

Phone :
Cable :

Continuation Sheet No........... of G.R No.

Name/s.. Room No..............G.R.No.......................

Date & Time of arrival.....................am./pm. Date of Time of Departure...........a.m./p.m.

No of Guests.. Rate..

Date	Rs.	P	Rs.	P	Rs.	P	Rs.	P	Rs.	P	Rs.	P	Rs.	P
Rooms														
Restaurants/Bar														
Telephone L'distance														
Telephone Local														
Telex														
Laundry														
Miscellaneous														
Paid outs														
Transfers														
Daily Total														
Brought Forward														
Grand Total														
Cash/Credit														
Allowances														
Balance C/Fd.														

Checked & Found Correct
Please forward bill to
M/s.......................................
....
....
Signature

Our Foreign Guests
Bills to be settled in convertible foreign exchange :
(*i*) Exchange vouchers No...
(*ii*) Exempted vide category No...

Amount Due ....
Cash Receipt No......................
Allowance Voucher No............
Transfers..................................
E.& O.E. Bill Clerk/Casher

Bills are payable on presentation. not accepted.

Fig. 5.30. Specimen of a Guest Bill

Guest Bill

Have You Deposited Your Room Key

And The Safe Deposit Locker Key

HOTEL ABC

Arrival............
Departure.............
No In Part.............
Rate

Account No. Room No

S.No.	Date	Description	Amount

	Company	Street
Bills Are Due On Presentation. Regardless Of Instruction, Guest Is Also Liable Until Balance Has Been Paid.	City State Pin Guest Signature	

Fig. 5.31. Specimen of a Guest Bill

AUDIT

The daily audit is done to ensure that all postings have been made correctly and that all guest accounts are up-dated. Different reports regarding the average rate, percentage occupancy, departmental revenues and their relationship to forecasts, are prepared and sent to the management and departmental heads.

DEPARTURE

A guest departure is the most critical phase of the guest cycle. On receiving the intimation of the guest to check-out from the hotel from the lobby captain or the guest himself, the customers bill is up-dated. The bill is presented to the guest for settlement. For departure a flow chart for information systm is given in fig. 5.32.

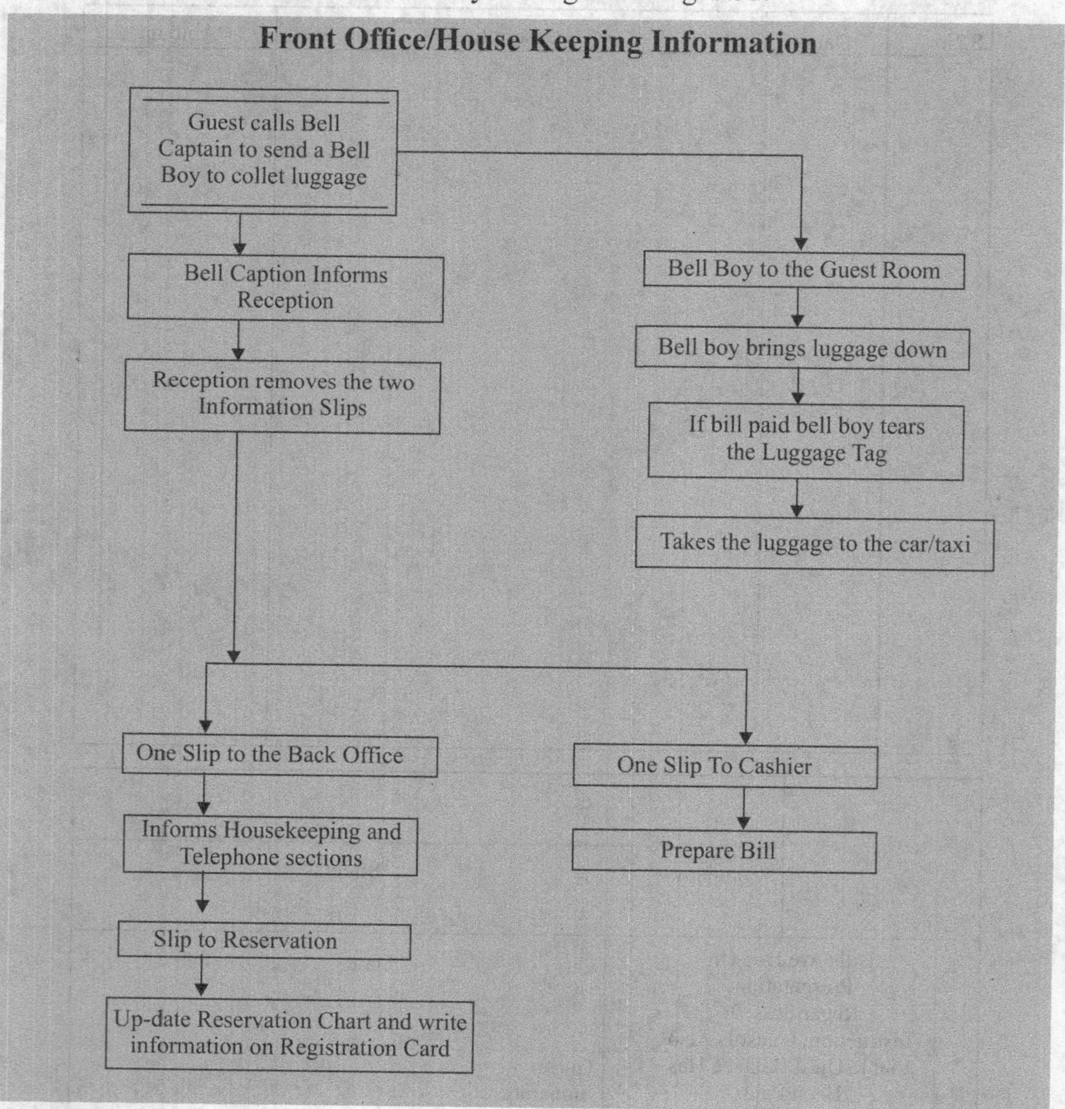

Fig. 5.32 : Front Office/House keeping Information System : A Typical Flow Chart II

The full procedure of guest departure or check-out are given in Figs. 5.33, 5.34 and 5.35.

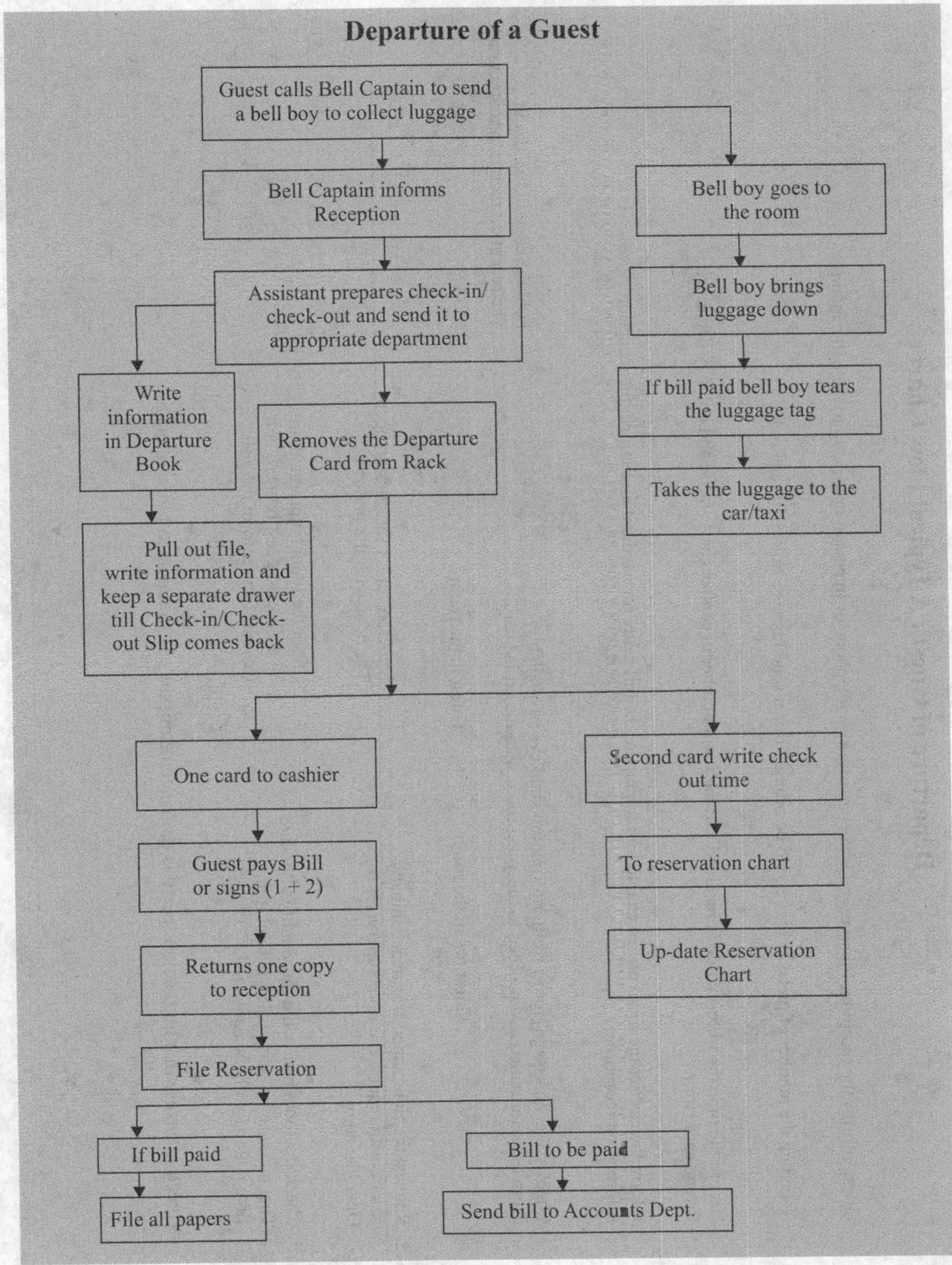

Fig. 5.33. Departure of a Guest : A Typical Flow Chart

Departure of Guest : A Typical Flow Chart

Guest informs the reception/lobby mgr. Of his departure on telephone or in person or directly to the bell captain

↓

Ascertain the number of piece of luggage to be brought down send luggage trolley (if required)

↓

Record the time the imformation is received and the room number in control chart (form) and bell boy departure
Errand card (form)

↓

Inform the cashier the room no. To enable him to prepare the bill ready for payment also inform the reception/
Information reception

↓

Check-collect message (form) from information and keys (if available)
From the information and proceed to the guest room with the errand card

Fold the edge of the slip in
The reception rack/information rack

Guest not in the room

Request the floor supervisor to accompany-
Knock-wait request the floor supervisor to
Open the door

↓

Check the room bath room thoroughly to ensure
That no guest property is left behind if any,
Take it along with the baggage.

Guest in the room

Knock -wait for the guest to open
The door-wish the guest

↓

Check the room bathroom thoroughly
To ensure no guest property left
Behind if any inform the guest

↓

Check to ensure that no hotel property is damaged or missing. If so report to lobby manager

(contd.)

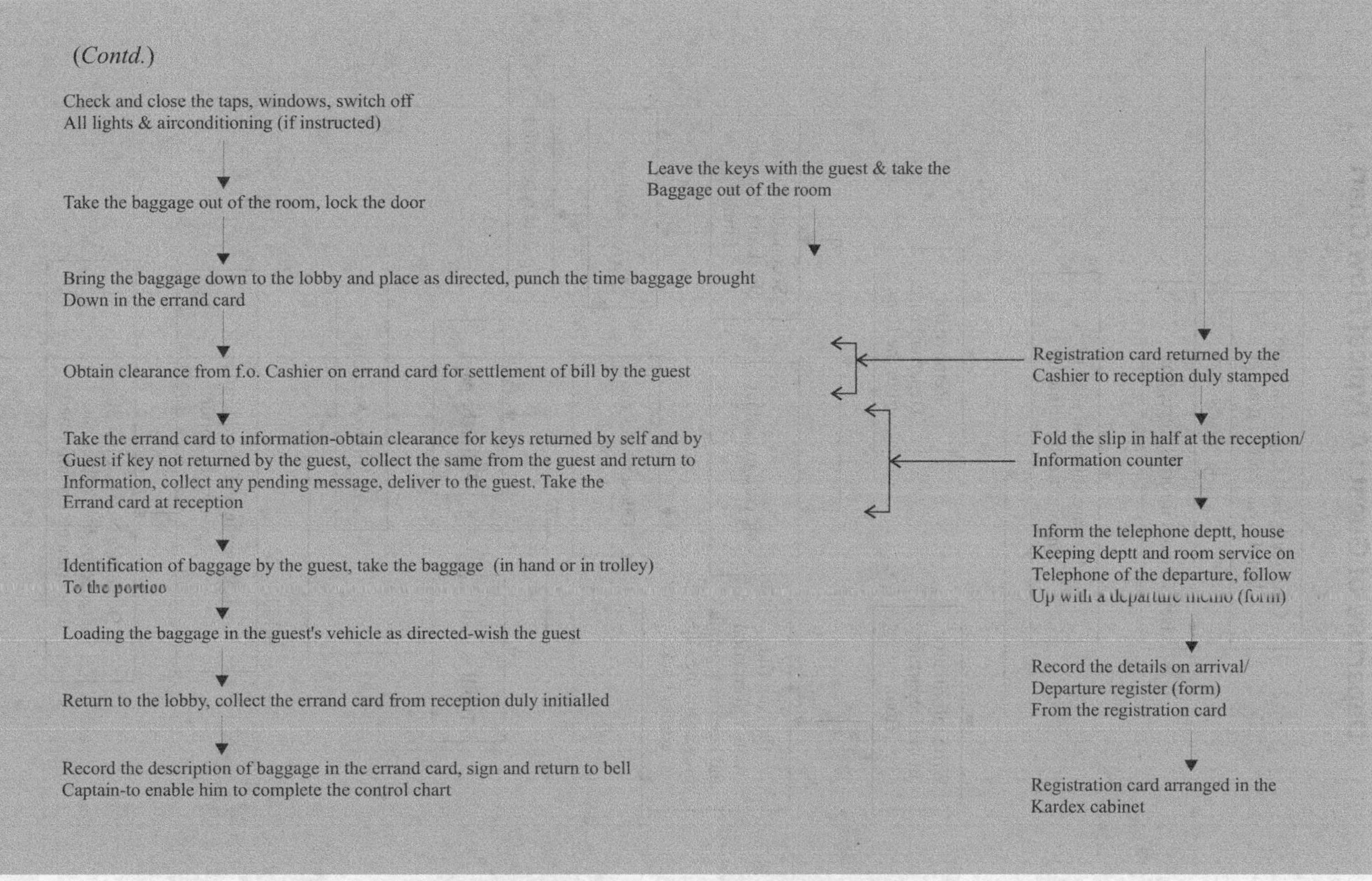

Fig.5.34 Departure of guest : a typical flow chart

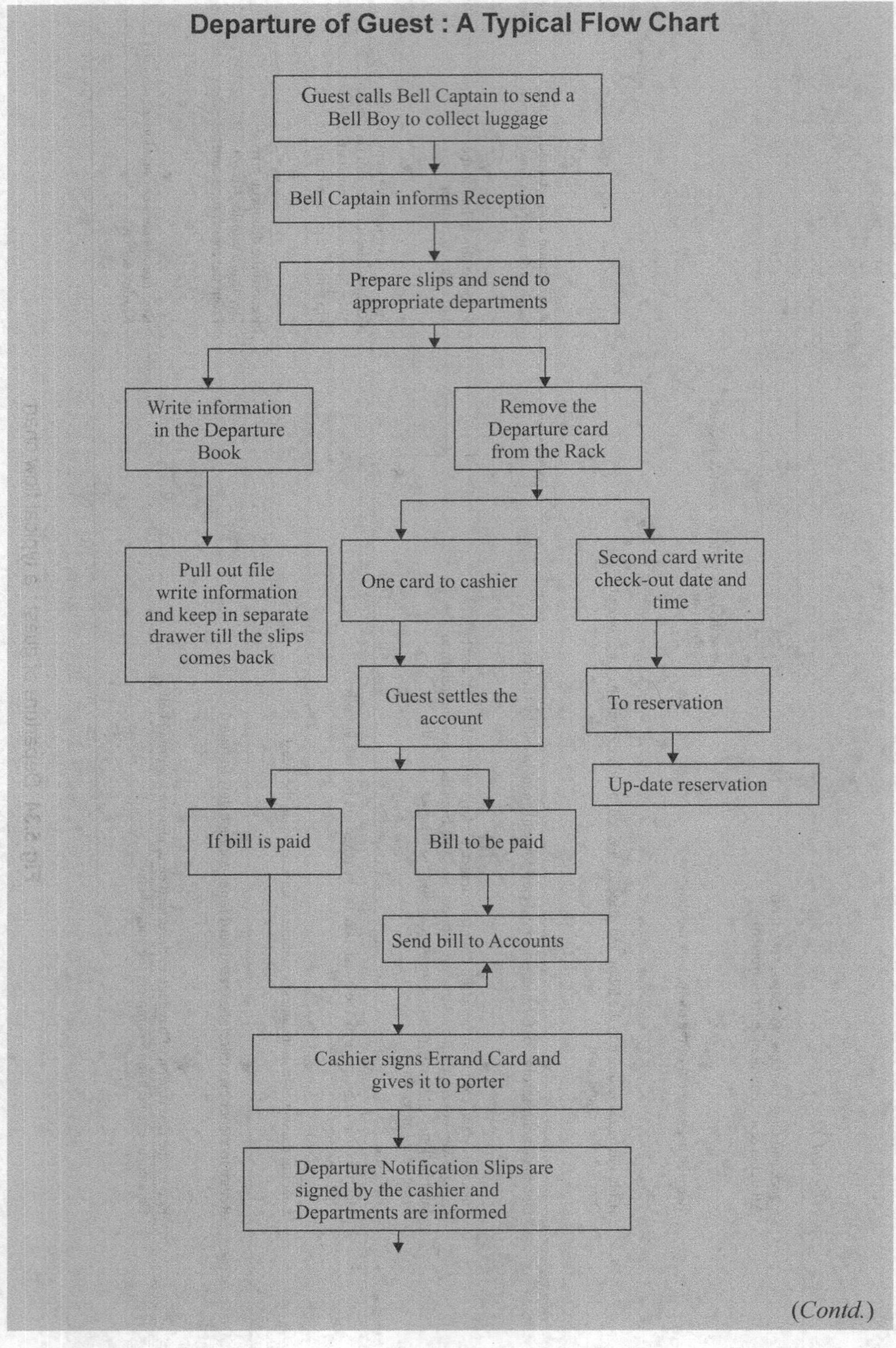
Departure of Guest : A Typical Flow Chart
Guest calls Bell Captain to send a Bell Boy to collect luggage
Bell Captain informs Reception
Prepare slips and send to appropriate departments
Write information in the Departure Book
Remove the Departure card from the Rack
Pull out file write information and keep in separate drawer till the slips comes back
One card to cashier
Second card write check-out date and time
Guest settles the account
To reservation
Up-date reservation
If bill is paid
Bill to be paid
Send bill to Accounts
Cashier signs Errand Card and gives it to porter
Departure Notification Slips are signed by the cashier and Departments are informed
(Contd.)

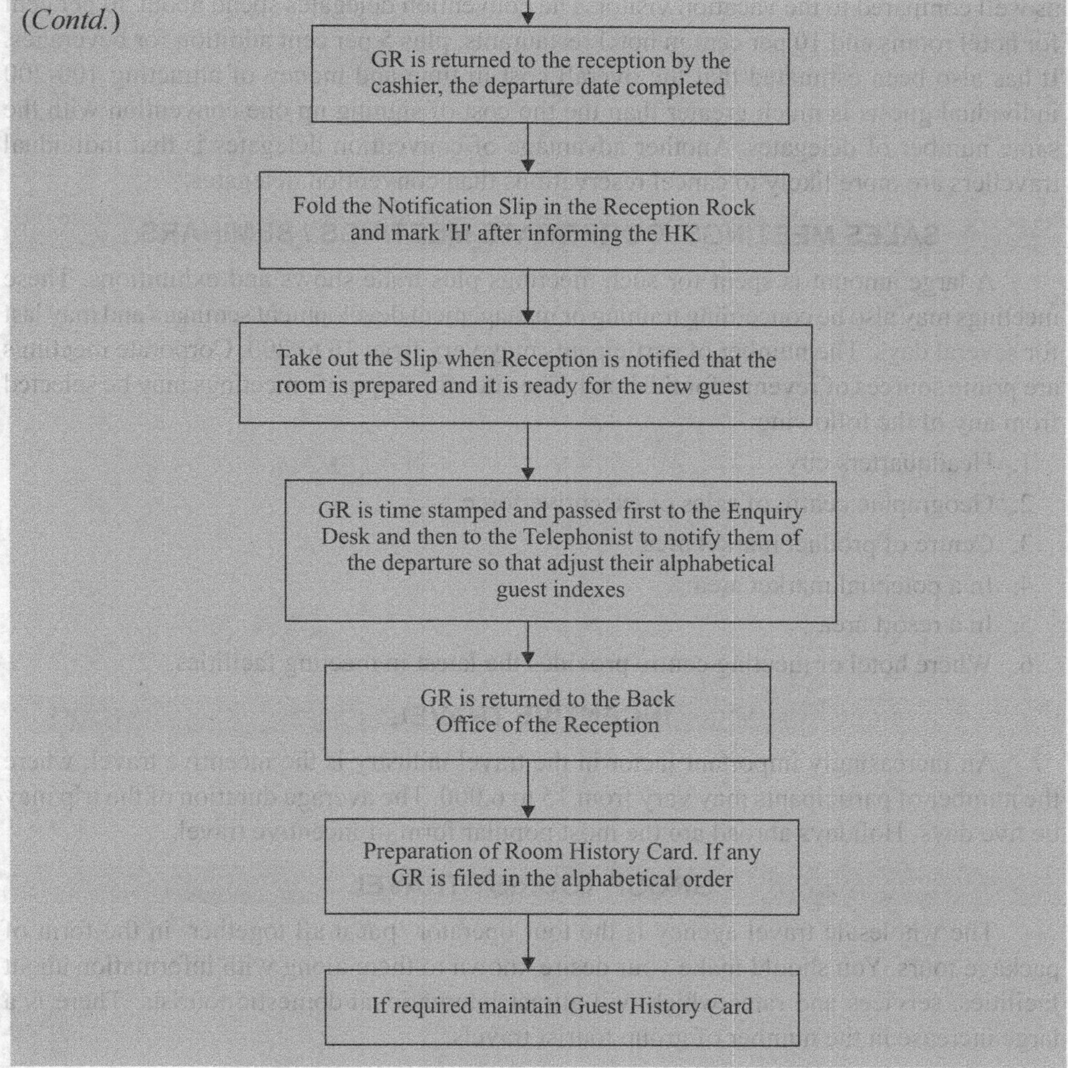

Fig. 5.35. Departure of a Guest : A Typical Flow Chart

GROUP BUSINESS

In large hotels, group business accounts for a large volume of sales. These group may be organised by a member. The travel agent may arrange or initiate the trip. An airline may provide the impetus where a hotel may be moving force. The group business may be classified under the following heads:

1. Conventions
2. Sales meetings, seminars etc.
3. Incentive travel groups
4. Special interests.

CONVENTION

Convention is a big business in itself. There are national, regional and intra-state conventions held annually. Conventions generate not only the direct sales but indirect sales as well compared to the vacation visitor. The convention delegates spend about 30 per cent for hotel rooms and 10 per cent in hotel restaurants, plus 5 per cent addition for beverages. It has also been estimated that the overall cost in time and money of attracting 100-200 individual guests is much greater than the the cost of signing up one convention with the same number of delegates. Another advantage of convention delegates is that individual travellers are more likely to cancel reservations than convention delegates.

SALES MEETINGS /CORPORATE MEETINGS / SEMINARS :

A large amount is spent for such meetings plus trade shows and exhibitions. These meetings may also be concerning training or management development seminars and may last for several days. The number of participants may vary from 10 to 200. Corporate meetings are prime sources of revenue for the hotel. The sites for corporate meetings may be selected from any of the following:

1. Headquarters city
2. Geographic centre of sales or executive force
3. Centre of product market area
4. In a potential market area
5. In a resort area
6. Where hotel or meeting centre provides the latest in meeting facilities.

INCENTIVE TRAVEL

An increasingly important factor in the travel industry is the incentive travel, where the number of participants may vary from 15 to 6,000. The average duration of the trip may be five days. Holidays abroad are the most popular form of incentive travel.

GROUP TOURIST TRAVEL

The wholesale travel agency is the tour operator 'put it all together' in the form of package tours. You should make your desire known to them along with information about facilities, services and rates which will attract international/domestic tourists. There is a large increase in the number of group tourist travels.

Pix 5.16 : Arrival of a Group on a Hotel.

SPECIAL INTEREST GROUP

The likely prospects are :

1. University seminars
2. University workshops
3. Technical meetings
4. Board of Directors' meetings
5. Sport, hobby groups, skiers, sky divers, golfers, amateur archaeologists etc.

DEVELOPING GROUP BUSINESS

Maximising profitability from group business requires to develop an effective sales programme. Convention Liaison Manuals and the Hotel

Sales Management Association's Convention Solicitation, provide detailed information on attracting and handling group business. Below are given the essentials in developing a sales programme designed to attract group business, as suggested by convention solicitation :

1. Top level participation :
   (*i*) The management should acquire a good knowledge of this type of business, its value and inherent problems.
2. Policy Consultation :
   (*i*) You should have a voice in policy formulation. advertising and other activities where experience and ideas can be of value.
3. Full access to information :
   (*i*) Sales staff should be told about operational problems which might affect standard of service committed to group business buyers. Especially important is that they be aware of the physical limitations of the facility, but also the point beyond which standard of service can't be raised without reducing or eleminating profits.
4. Keeping Sales Commitments :
   (*i*) Everyone in the hotel or motel has a responsibility to see that promises made to group business buyers are kept.

GROUP HANDLING

The hotel receives a large amount of business from groups. Special procedure required for group handling is given in Fig. 5.36.

The group and convention sale requires a long range planning. Handling of group reservation or block reservation, is one of the most important activities of the hotels. In large hotels, reservation for more than 25 rooms is confirmed with the knowledge of the front office manager. The reservation section will send the information about group reservation to the following departments :

1. House-keeping department
2. Maintenance department
3. Food and beverages department
4. Accounts department
5. Bell captain.

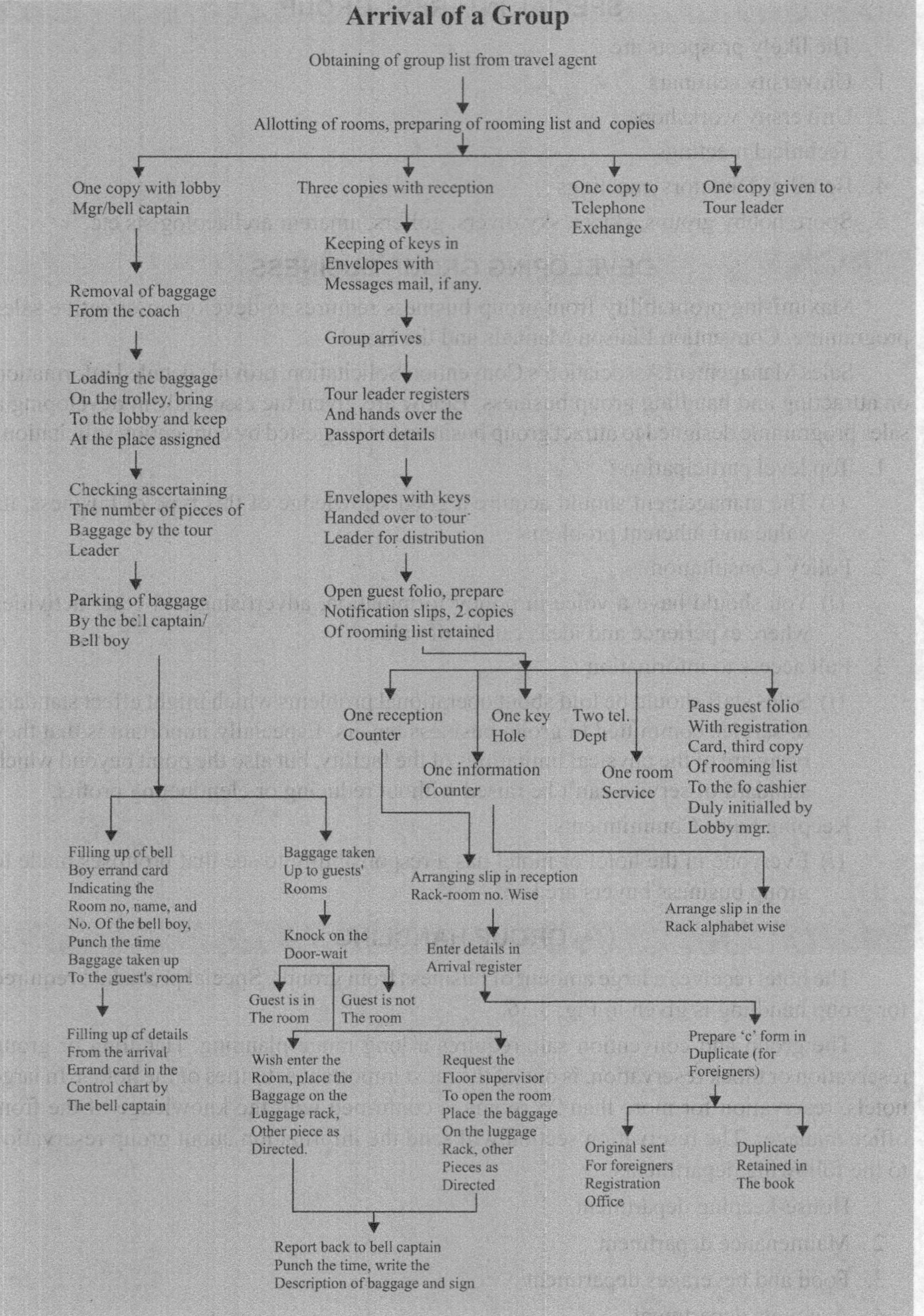

Fig. 5.36. A Typical Arrival of a Group : Flow Chart

Analyse the need of the companies and associations whose need and patterns meet your facilities and with intelligent staff training and a co-ordinated sales programme, group business could be effectively handled and successfully booked. Some guidelines for group handling are given below :

1. Pre-register participants whenever possible. Evolve suitable procedures and adequate numbers registration personnel to avoid long lines of people waiting for room assignment.
2. Be sure there is available to the group at all times, a member of the staff with full authority.
3. Don't depart from established rates.
4. Plan guest traffic. Avoid confusion and congestion at the conclusion of large meetings.
5. Have adequate functioning-equipment for audio-visual presentations (screens, room darkening equipment, public address system, light lanterns, etc.).
6. Provide detailed floor plans of meeting and exhibit areas.
7. Based on the design and physical facilities of hotels in India, we find that informational and educational type meetings are not yet being recognised.
8. Most of the hotel are not geared for to organise or provide the services required to successfully conduct group meetings.
9. Hotel salesmen must learn to sell the total community in which their hotels are located, not just their physical facilities.
10. Provide meeting planners with specifics on facilitiesexact room sizes and realistic seating capacities.
11. Give group business buyers information about meeting rooms, guest rooms, elevator service first. They are more intersted in the data than facts on cocktail lounges, lobbies etc.
12. Don't ignore the fact that the group business market is not a single market but a composite of many with different characteristics and requirements.

A guest may desire to change his room after he has checked into it; for reasons such as location of the present room not being too sunny or lack of it. The reception office informs the house-keeping department.

CHANGING OF ROOM

When a guest changes room a bell is sent with a change slip, together with the key. After completing the room change the bell boy gets the room slip signed by Telephone Exchange, Room Services, Laundary, Housekeeping and the Front Office Cashier so as all these departments are informed about the room change and they take necessary action.

A proper procedure is followed for shifting of rooms. The flow charts are given in Fig. 5.37 and 5.38 which shows the procedure for changing guest room on request.

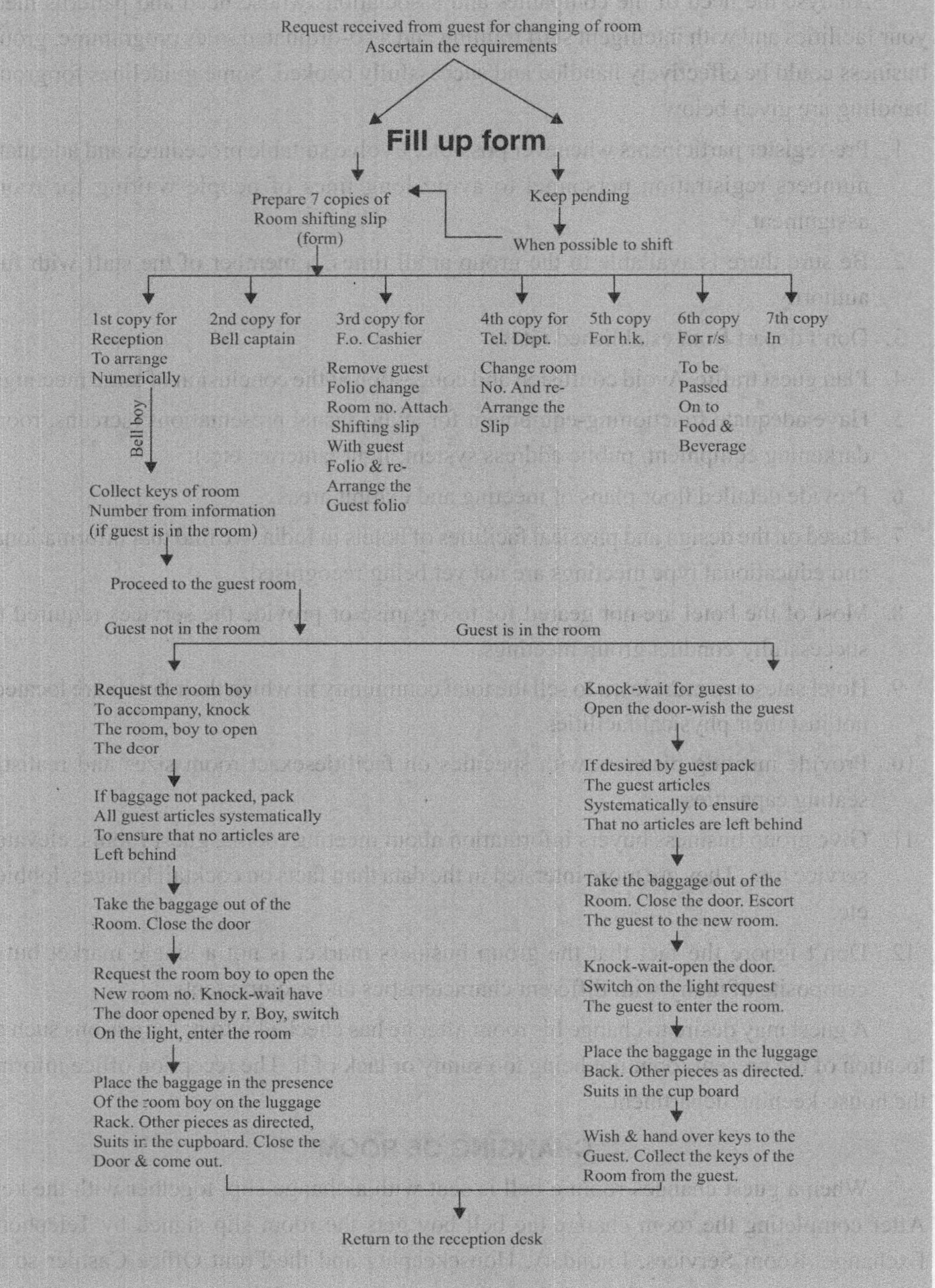

Fig.5.37. Changing of Room : A Typical Flow Chart

Shifting / Changing of Rooms : A Typical Flow Chart

Request received from guest for shifting of room
Ascertain whether the baggage is packed or not, also whether the guest is in the room or not.

→ Prepare shifting slip in quadruplicate with the guest's name, room no (form)

- 3rd copy → Laundry → To ensure that Any laundry given Is sent to the new Room no.
- 1st copy → Original slip given to Bell boy errand card (form) indicating The old and new room No. Punch the time In the errand card
  → Collect keys of new room No. From information (if Guest is in the room)
  → Proceed to the guest room
    - Guest not in the room → Request the floor Supervisor to accompany Request the floor supervisor To open the door →
    - Guest in the room → Knock, wait for guest To open the door-wish The guest →
- 2nd copy → Telephone dept. → Remove the slips from the Respective carrier Change the room no. Rearrange in carriers Systemically.
- 4th copy → Room service → (Remove the slips from the Respective carrier Change the room no. Rearrange in carriers Systemically.)

→ Indicate with a card (form) In the carrier at the reception Rack regarding shifting Prepare temporary notification Slip of shifting in triplicate.

- First copy for Rec. Rack
- Third copy with Previous slip sent To back office for Typing of copies (forms) And returned to Reception counter.
- Second copy For inf. Rack Remove Previous Slip

(contd.)

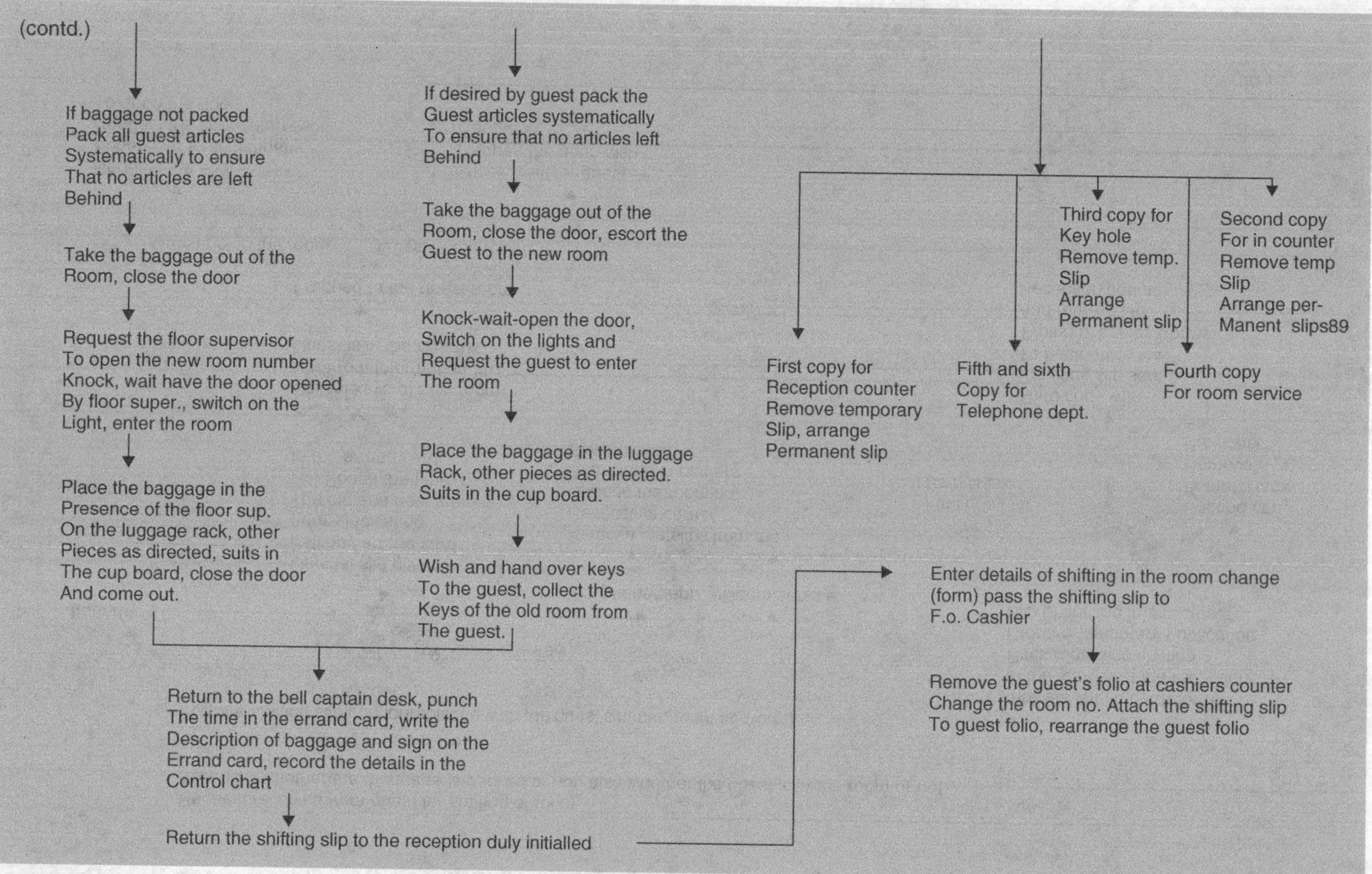

Fig. 5.38. Shifting / Changing of Rooms : A Typical Flow Chart

UNIFORM AND GUEST SERVICE

Hotel guest service is a very viable component that can include concierge, uniformed services, garage and specialised recreational and leisure activities. The bell staff, door greeters, garage and parking attendants and other uniformed staff are in many deluxe hotels an integral part of the guest service. Thus uniformed services form an integral part of the front hall functions of the hotel and provides a variety of potential services to guests.

Servicing arrivals and departures are the most common uniformed services. The meeting and greeting of arriving guests, their luggage and parking of their cars and a departure guest's, luggage and transportation are the primary responsibility of the uniformed staff.

The income of this department is derived from transfer of baggages and from messenger service in connection with the purchase of rail, road and airplane tickets. A record is maintained of the incoming and outgoing baggage, which serve as sales journals, so far as baggage transfer is concerned. The porters come in direct contact with guests and collect the cash. They receive considerable income from the gratuities, guests' pay in addition to charges made for the service. Some hotels lease this department. The porters receive nominal salary and keep all service charges. Very few hotels get profit from this department.

The main services provided by uniformed services could be classified as:

1. Servicing arrivals :
   - (*i*) Meeting and greeting of arriving guests
   - (*ii*) Luggage handling
   - (*iii*) Parking of cars
2. Servicing the stay of guests :
   - (*i*) Information about hotel
   - (*ii*) Locality
   - (*iii*) Arrangement for their tickets, tours, car hire and services
3. Other services :
   - (*i*) Newspapers
   - (*ii*) Small articles as per guest's requirements
   - (*iii*) To act as messengers, lift operator, men's cloak room attendants
4. In case of night duty :
   - (*i*) To provide all services which are provided by other departments during day time
   - (*ii*) To receive and register late arrivals
   - (*iii*) To serve light refreshments
   - (*iv*) To operate the hotel's switch board
   - (*v*) To arrange early morning calls
   - (*vi*) To clean public rooms
   - (*vii*) To ensure the security of the hotel

5. Servicing departures :

Depending upon the size, type and standard, the provision of uniformed services vary in hotels; the organisation of this department is also influenced by these factors and the established practices of the hotel. There are hotels, where information services to guests may be provided by reception office or uniformed services or both. Similarly cleanliness of public rooms may be assigned to house-keeping, uniformed services or outside contractors.

In large sized hotels there are many aspects of work which can be classed as 'General Service'. This classification will include :

1.	Pages	6.	Information clerks
2.	Doormen	7.	Bellmen
3.	Porters	8.	Elevator operators
4.	Parcel clerks	9.	Night porters
5.	Clock room attendant	10.	Hall porters etc.

The classification of employees of this section may be grouped as follows:

1. Service front :
   (*i*) Lobby manager/superintendents of service
   (*ii*) Assistants
   (*iii*) Bell captain
   (*iv*) Bell men
   (*v*) Pages.
2. Service elevators :
   (*i*) Elevator attendants
   (*ii*) Elevator operators.
3. Service floors :
   (*i*) Floor clerks
   (*ii*) Pages
   (*iii*) Lost and found employees.
4. Service doormen :
   (*i*) Doormen
5. Service package room :
   (*i*) Package room clerks
   (*ii*) Package room messengers
   (*iii*) Baggage porters etc.
6. Miscellaneous services :
   (*i*) Librarian
   (*ii*) Shopping guides

(*iii*) Lobby receptionists.

All these jobs are grouped under the single term 'uniform staff' and their classification often differs since the system varies according to the size and type of hotel in question. Most of the employees associated with this department are usually persons not necessarily possessing some skill but have a pleasing personality and a sense of service. To perform most of these tasks the individual should be physically strong though good educational qualification are not essential. This department, however, comes into direct contact with guests. Very often an active, alert and courteous department can contribute a lot towards the hotel's prestige and impression. Willingness, helpfulness, courtesy and smartness are some of the first and foremost qualities demanded of all uniformed staff from head hall porter to the smallest and most junior pages.

In most of the large-sized hotels the uniform staff comes directly under the hall porter and in smaller hotels it is generally less in number as many of the details of these services are performed personally by the hall porter.

Figure 5.40 indicates the organisation of uniform and guest services.

THE LOBBY

The lobby is an area located immediately upon entry into the hotel building. It is furnished with seating arrangements and is a meeting place common to all hotel guests. Being the first and the last area of contact of a guest with the hotel, the management makes the lobby attractive and convenient. The lobby desk, like front desk, is situated in the lobby and is the point of all co-ordination between guest and hotel services. (Ref. Fig. 5.39, organization chart Uniform Service and Fig. 5.40 is a Left Luggage Flow Chart).

The main functions of this department are :

1. To guide the guest to reception for registration
2. To carry guest luggage
3. To look after guest cars
4. To look after their personal jobs.

Pix. 5.17 : The Lobby

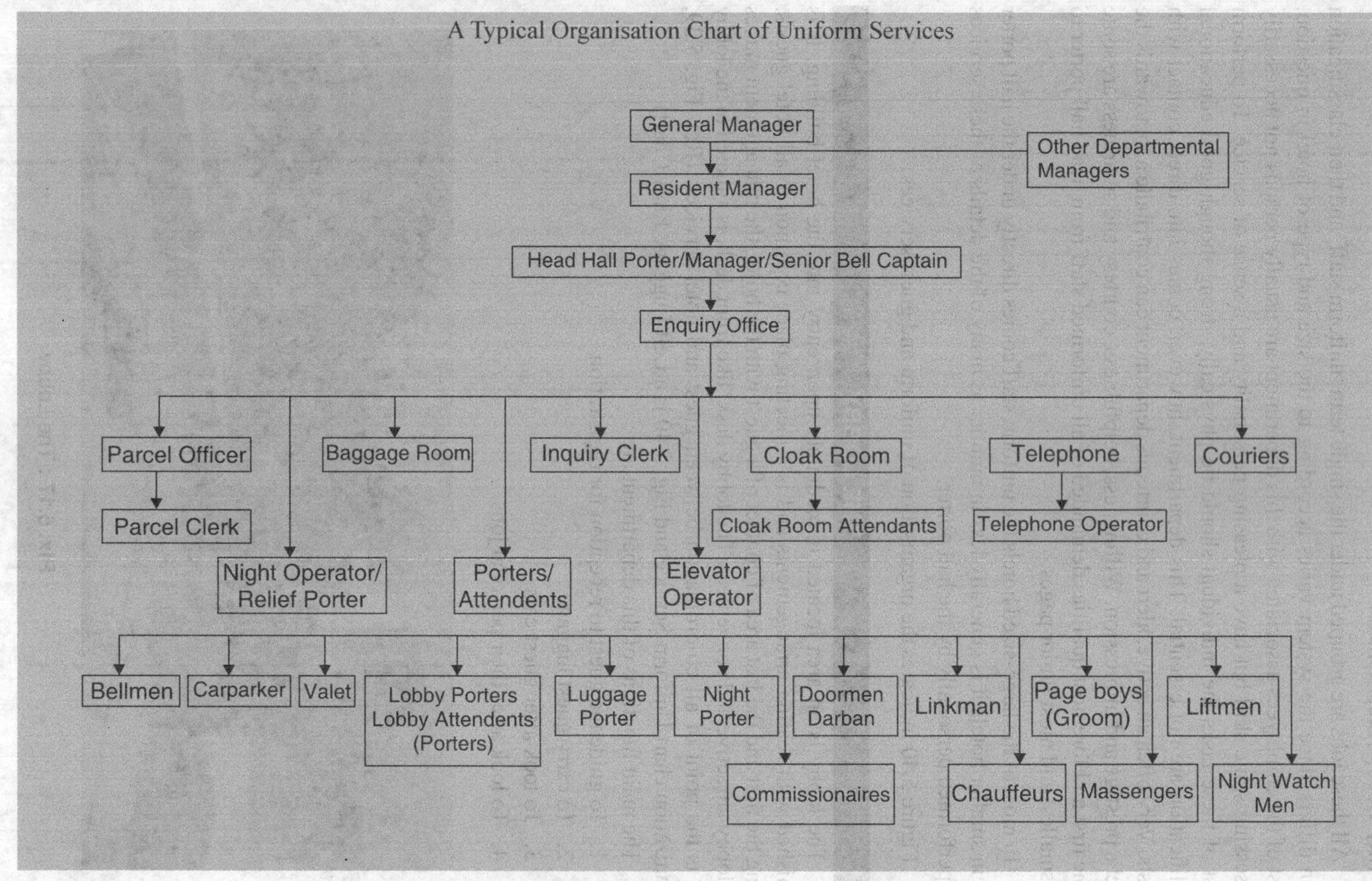

Fig. 5.39. A Typical Organisation Chart of Uniform Services

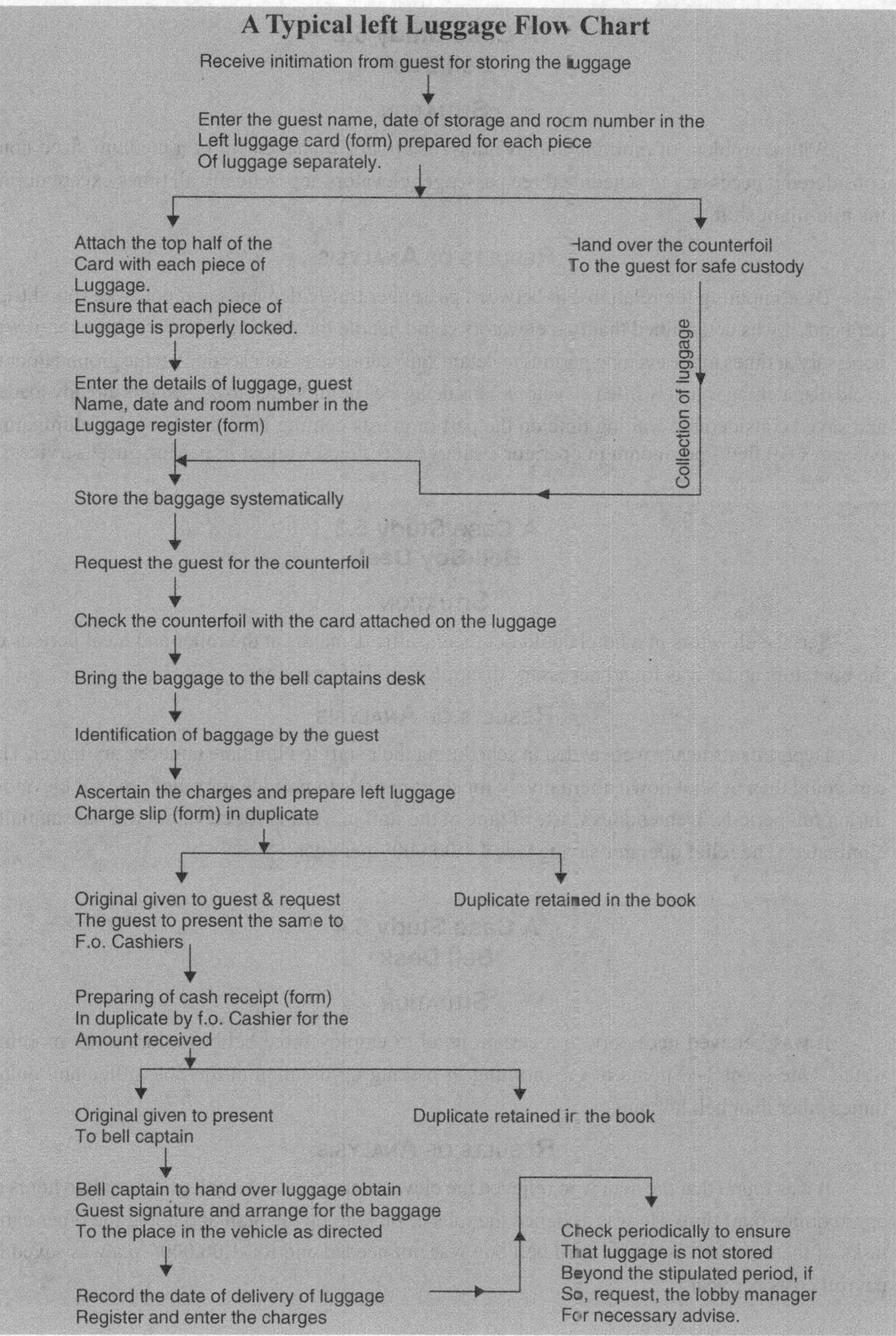

Fig. 5.40. A Typical Left Luggage Flow Chart

A Case Study 5.2
Bell Desk

Situation

With a problem of morning and evening rush hours, management of a medium sized hotel considered it necessary to schedule three passenger elevators at practically all times except during the mid-night shift.

Results of Analysis

By computing the relationship between passenger traffic demands and potential round trips per head, it was determined that two elevators could handle the passenger traffic. However, it was necessary at times in the evening periods to detain "up" cars two to four seconds at the ground floor to avoid dispatching sparsely filled elevators. This delay was unimportant to passengers already loaded and saved considerable waiting time on the part of guests coming in to the lobby. By eliminating one car, ₹ 10,000/- per month in operator's salarys was saved without impairing guest services.

A Case Study 5.3
Bell Boy Desk

Situation

Service elevators in a hotel could not meet traffic demands at the relief and meal periods of the operators and it was found necessary to employ a relief operator.

Results of Analysis

Departments heads were added in scheduling their staff to eliminate unnecessary travel. The cars could then be shut down alternatively for short periods to provide for relief time for elevators during full periods. Tremendous waste of time of the staff in waiting for elevators was substantially eliminated. The relief operator saving was ₹ 1,00,000/- per year.

A Case Study 5.4
Bell Desk

Situation

It was believed necessary in a certain hotel to employ three bellboys during the morning watch. One spent 1-½ hours of the morning in picking up the mail at the post office and doing duties other than bell hopping.

Results of Analysis

It was found that the man who relieved the elevator operator had a hell of almost two hours at approximate mail time. He was assigned the jobs of picking up the mail and doing the other extra tasks of the third bell boy. The third bell boy was not needed and Rs. 1,00,000/- p.a was saved in payroll costs per year.

LOBBY MANAGER

He is incharge of all the lobby area and represents the management all 24-hours. He should be well qualified, mature, experienced and diplomatic. Knowledge of hotel's rules is very essential as he has to be able to be effective in dealing with guest problems. He supervises a team of senior bell captains, bell captains and bell boys. Knowledge of one foreign language is essential apart from English. The lobby manager coordinates the front offices to house-keeping, food and beverage, engineering, security, telephones, stores etc. He might be required to meet the guests at the airport or at the railway station and escort them

Pix. 5.18. A Lobby of a Hotel

Pix. 5.19. A Lobby of a Hotel

Pix. 5.20. A Typical Hotel Lobby

Pix. 5.21. A Typical Hotel Lobby

to the hotel. In the night the lobby manager is known as 'Night Manager' and is directly incharge of the whole hotel. He is a problem solver and has the authority to handle all guest grievances. His work in the night is to check unauthorised persons. He also deals with all the unusual events which take place at night in the hotel. He is not a part of the front office staff, yet he must be included in reception area. He is stationed in the lobby area near the front office and he supervises the staff.

His duties and responsibilities include :

1. To schedule a duty roaster
2. To come into the contact of guests of different personalities, temperaments and various moods
3. To organise and supervise the uniform staff
4. To solve the guest grievances, give information about hotel tariff, discount, credit etc.
5. To know the full general layout, facilities provided to the guests, basic policies, hotel terms, places of interest in the city and other important events of the region
6. To be the management's representative for public and guest liaison to the front office
7. To assume direct control and authority in any department, where departmental heads are not present. Areas under his control are the lobby, but the whole hotel indirectly comes under his control.
8. He also helps sometimes in recruitment and training programmes particularly of his staff.
9. To receive the complaints, suggestions etc. of guests and pass it on to the management
10. To attend to the rooms of VIPs and welcome them at arrival in the lobby and then accompany them to their rooms
11. To co-ordinate with various departments of the hotel specially with reception, information etc. for effective handling, rooming and departure of guests
12. To liaison with airline offices, regarding arrival, departure of flights and organising wake-up calls
13. To take up reservations for other units of hotel belonging to the particular hotel chain and communicating the same to instant reservation
14. To make constant record at night of all operational areas to ensure their smooth functioning
15. To control the entire night operations
16. To pass credit bills in the absence of the front office manager
17. To train the lobby staff
18. To co-ordinate with the security
19. To verify all the guest folios
20. To be responsible for all the scanty baggage cases.

HEAD HALL PORTER/SENIOR BELL CAPTAIN

In most of the medium-sized hotels the head hall porter is responsible for the uniformed staff. As he has a very responsible job, he is one of the departmental managers in the hotel. He is constantly dealing with the hotel's patrons and must know the daily general movement and activities in the hotel. He keeps in touch with the arrival and departures of all transports liable to effect guest movements and should have a good knowledge of local affairs and entertainment. In large-sized hotels he looks after the inquiry department and often acts as a medium through which guests arrange to make their tourist trips, inquires about entertainments, shopping centres, names and localities of various medical services, secretarial and employment agencies, and other places of interest.

The head hall porter must have a knowledge of foreign languages and customers of the main tourist generating centres. He should have good knowledge of the town and its surrounding area, topography, transport, excursions, entertainment, shops etc. Knowledge of labour legislation, hygiene and safety standards is also essential. He should also be able to organise, conduct and supervise the training of the staff.

The main duties of head hall porter are :

1. To be responsible for various sections, parcel office, baggage room, cloak room, telephone
2. To draw up duty roaster and to supervise the discipline, conduct and appearance of his staff
3. To inform the management of arrivals and departures
4. To supervise the guest's information, service, travel arrangements and reservations
5. To keep account of the credit granted to guests
6. To be responsible to his staff and make suggestions concerning their recruitment, replacement, promotion and training
7. To organise and supervise the training of the uniform staff.

BELL CAPTAIN

He is directly responsible to the lobby manager. He organises the duties of bell boys and other staff members under him and is to ensure that the standard service of the hotel is maintained efficiently. He keeps the records of the staff for the purpose of control and the preparation of bills. The primary goals of the bell captain are to obtain economy of operation and time, maximisation of output with minimum of input and maintain the goodwill of the hotel. The left luggage room also comes under the direct control of the bell captain. The flow chart of the left luggage is given in Figure 5.41.

He makes sure that new staff members in his department are well conversant with the house rate, condition, services etc. laid down by the management. Some bell captains supply newspapers and the postage material to the guest, which calls for his full knowledge of the postal regulations of the country. He maintains a departure sheet/register and informs the house-keeping department about the departure which has taken place.

A bell captain should have good manners and good personality; he should be intelligent, honest and fully conversant with current affairs and must have full knowledge of the different hotel services and facilities. In addition, he should know at least one foreign language apart from English.

The bell captain is responsible for :

1. Supervision and scheduling of lobby attendants
2. Maintain baggage checkroom
3. Maintain the bulletin board in the lobby
4. Wake up call system for crew and groups

5. Proper recording of log book
6. House keeping discrepancy investigations
7. Handling of crews and group baggage at the time of arrival and departure
8. Look after newspapers/services required by guest
9. Scanty baggage procedures
10. Maintenance of lobby attendant work sheet
11. Liaison between lobby and other departments via. front office, front office cash, security and the doormen
12. To look after the work in the absence of the lobby manager.

HALL PORTER

He should have the knowledge of the town and its surrounding areas. The porter must also know about basic principles of accounting, foreign exchange transactions, legislation and police regulations concerning tourists, hygiene and safety regulations and labour legislations. He must also have the knowledge of the activities of the other departments and their relation to the uniformed department. The important duties of the porter are:

1. To give to the guest information on excursions, transport, travel, shops, theatres, museums, entertainment etc.
2. To make travel reservations
3. To be responsible for the mail and key service
4. To supervise the deposit, receipt and handling of baggage on arrival and departure of guests
5. To supervise the linemen, pageboys, and lift operators
6. To handle registration of guests
7. To be responsible for telephone operation and early calls to guests
8. To submit the daily report to the management
9. To replace the hotel hall porter during his absence.

Pix. 5.22. A Doorman

NIGHT PORTER

The night porter is required to have the knowledge of all the departments of the hotel. He is the sole representative of the hotel on duty during his hours of work. He has to handle all eventualities. For example, if needed he will call a doctor, police or the fire brigade. He performs the duties of the head hall porter, receives orders from the porter and is responsible for early calls to guests. He provides drinks or snacks requested during his hours of work. He also carries out if necessary inspections and reports every morning on anything that might have happened during the night in the hotel.

He petrols the hotel building periodically during the night. Guests requiring early morning calls generally place orders with the night porter. The room number, time and order is recorded in a book/sheet. A copy of it is sent to the chamber maid/floor services. The duties and responsibilities of the night porter are increased in hotels, where there is no night manager. In large-sized hotel due to heavy work during night, additional night staff is employed which is headed by a head night porter.

LOBBY PORTER

These are found in very large convention hotels. In other hotels this function is performed by a porter of the house-keeping staff. The lobby porter is responsible for the general appearance of the lobby during the day. He/she picks up loose papers or other debris of the floor, cleans the ashtrays, mops up spills etc. The importance of the lobby porter is reflected by the cleanliness of the hotel to the guest as well as to the general public.

PACKAGE ROOM CLERK

On receipt of the packages, the clerk logs it in a book called 'Log Book'. The log book contains the columns for the guest's name and room number, name of the sender, number of packages and a space for the bellman's signature. The guest is notified about the arrival of packages and is delivered to him through the bellman. The clerk is also responsible to pack and mail anything the guest wishes to send.

DOORMAN

The first hotel employee who meets the guests at the hotel gate is the doorman. His place of duty is outside the main entrance of the hotel. He greets all guests who arrive by cars or taxis and sees that their luggage is taken into the hotel. A smile and a pleasant greeting welcoming the guests will create the first impression. The work of the doorman is simple but very significant in an effort to make the guest feel at home and happy with their accommodation. During the stay of guests the doorman assists the guests in obtaining taxis, helps them in and out of the cars, gives directions to restaurants, when the guest checks out and leaves by car or cab, the doorman helps then to load their baggage and thus becomes the last employee to see them off.

Pix. 5.23. A Doorman

A Case Study 5.5
Doorman

Situation

Management of a hotel which has two entrances stationed a doorman at the main entrance and believed it necessary to station a doorman at the other entrance (an annex entrance) at least part-time basis.

Results of Analysis

An analysis showed that the guest traffic was negotiable at the annex entrance and that the entrance was used mainly for luncheon guests. The part-time service of a doorman at the annex entrance appeared to do more harm than good, since in the guest's minds it was inconsistent service. Doorman service at this entrance was discontinued with a saving of about ₹ 1,00,000/- per year.

The doorman is also responsible for cleanliness and order of the front door at the front entrance of the hotel. He wears a typical uniform which varies from hotel to hotel. He is responsible for calling the cars and taxis, for which purposes he uses a loud speaker and microphone. He is also responsible to see that only authorised members enter by the main entrance and other staff members use the staff entrance.

LUGGAGE PORTER

He unloads the luggage from the vehicle by which the guest arrives to the hotel and brings it to the lobby. Before taking it to the lobby, the luggage porter should take approval of the customer that all luggage is taken out and is in proper order. It is his duty to see that it is delivered to the guest room as promptly as possible. In case of the group's arrival, his responsibility increases. When the guest is ready to leave the hotel, it is the luggage porter who collects the cases from the bed room and brings them down to lobby or the porter lodge, and retains these with him until he receives a luggage pass. He calls the car/taxi and places these inside. It is his duty to ensure that a record is kept of all the luggage passing through the luggage room at the time of departure and the name of the member who handles it. In some hotels, he is responsible for the collection of keys at the time of departure from customers.

LINKMAN

He supervises the arrival and departure of vehicles. He keeps the guest with their luggage and summons cars and taxis when requested by guests. He also supervises all the incoming and outgoing luggage. He opens doors of cars and taxis and escorts the arriving guest into the hotel.

LIFT OPERATOR

He operates the lift and helps the guests in and out of the lift. He is responsible for the cleanliness of his lift but not for the service and maintenance of machinery which must be done frequently by the lift engineer. No unauthorised person should be allowed to operate the lift and the lift operator should never leave it unattended. He should make the lift unoperative before going away. No overloading should be allowed. He should be able to answer in a polite manner all the questions asked by the guests and should be able to show the way to the guest on the floors. Most of the modern hotels are equipped with self-service elevators. Elevator operators are found only in old hotels or in case of VIPs the lift operator may be used.

CLOAK ROOM ATTENDENTS

Gents cloak rooms comes under the hall porter, whereas the ladies cloak room goes under the house-keeping department. Guest cloak room attendants look after the hats, coats, overcoats, umbrella, brief cases etc. of guests. He should see that sufficient supply of hand towels, soaps and other toilet articles for customer's use are available in the cloak room always. He is also responsible for the cleanliness and upkeep of the place.

COURIER

He is assigned the regular external duties, which involve going out of the hotel for delivering of messages, parcels etc. Sometimes he is assigned the job of receiving guests at the airport.

VALET

His duties are to pack or unpack the suitcases when the guest is leaving or changing the room. He helps the guest in putting the uniforms, looks after the ironing of the clothes, polishing the shoes, shining of the decorations, medals, glassware and brassware.

BELLMEN

After the registration procedure has been completed and the guest has been assigned the room, the bellmen carry the guest's baggage and take them to his room. On way to the room, a well trained and experienced bellman can sense the guest's mood and carry on a conversation explaining the facilities available in the hotel. On reaching the room, the bellman should show and check for the guest the different types of facilities like TV, thermostat, bathrooms, the ashtrays, waste paper baskets, closets and all electrical equipment etc. Any disorder or mal-functioning of equipment in the room should be immediately brought to the notice of the house-keeper.

Pix. 5.24. A Bell Boy

During the stay of the guest in the hotel, the bellman asserts him in various ways which mostly depend on the policy of the management, delivery of messages and packages, take order for sandwiches, cocktails, snacks and beverages from the bar and deliver them in the room, when the room service is closed. Some hotels permit the bellman to buy food and beverages from outside for the guest when the hotel's outlets are closed. When the guests check out, the bellman carries down their luggage.

PAGE BOY

The Page Boy is known as 'groom'. He is a young boy and is available near the reception counter. He is always at the disposal of the guest and his department for undertaking rounds in and outside the hotels. In case the bell boy is not in the hotel, it is the duty of the page boy to guide the visitors to their rooms and explain in short the different facilities provided by the hotel and can make him familiar with the important persons of the hotel. In the corridor he should walk along the guest but towards the right side and not keeping too much distance. Any desired information must be provided immediately. In case he does not know about the information, he should politely tell the guest to contact the Reception Office. Sometimes due to heavy rush, he may be required to do the job of the luggage porter and valet.

His main job is to deliver messages, letters, telegrams etc., to guests or to run errands for them. To call a guest to the telephone or to meet a visitor, a page boy goes through the public rooms, calling quietly the name of the guest. If the guest cannot be found in the lounges, he enters the restaurants and takes permission to page. Thus, he is responsible for paging.

CHAUFFEUR

A driving licence is a must for chauffeur. He should have mechanical ability to keep the vehicle in his care in good repair. His main duty is to drive the hotel's vehicle car/bus. He should be a reliable person with a sense of responsibility. He comes under the control of the Lobby Manager.

Pix. 5.25. A chaufer waiting for a Guest

ENQUIRY CLERK

He is to answer the queries made by guests. His office is equipped with various reference books, which includes : street maps, road maps, telephone directories, post office guides, international hotel guide as well as local theatre, cinema, and other entertainment guides. All mail delivered at the hotel is sorted. The business mail is sent to the manager's office and the guest's mail is sorted to find the letters for resident guests. The room numbers are put and placed in the 'pigeon holes' of the key racks, so that guest receives his letter when he hands in or collects his keys. Any mail received for guests due to arrive, is kept in the file in alphabetical order and necessary note is made in the hotel's diary. Guests who have already left, their mail is re-addressed as per the forwarding address and details of re-directions, are noted in the mail forwarding book.

In case a guest wishes to send a telegram, cable, parcel or letter, the enquiry clerk can deal with this for him. Amount of money is paid out by the enquiry clerk on behalf of guests and is charged to the guest's account on the VTL by means of a 'VPO' cheque. All paid-outs are reimbursed to the enquiry clerk. The enquiry clerk is also responsible for the safe custody and issue of room keys to the guests.

HOUSEKEEPIN0G

The housekeeping operation has the main task of keeping the hotel rooms and public areas clean and attractive. Scientific housekeeping demands employment of the most effective cleaning material and procedures, attention to purchasing of the most suitable lines and cleaning supplies, decorating area of maintenance and proper organisation and supervision. Since the housekeeping budget accounts for nearly 20% of a property in total operating expenses, it is advisable to consider the following points.

1. Design guest rooms with maintenance in mind
2. Select furnishings with an angle of cleaning
3. Provide suitable equipment, facilities and supplies
4. Specify performance standard
5. Staff housekeeping function adequately
6. Organise the work efficiently
7. Explain procedures in writing
8. Provide both the theoretical and practical training
9. Supply motivation and recognition
10. Give continuing and supportive supervision
11. Hire temporary personnel for peak occupancy periods.

Housekeeping is one of the most vital and interesting departments in many aspects. The work of a housekeeping department in a hotel varies considerably according to the type and size of the hotel. This department in the large hotels is headed by an Executive Housekeeper, who is one of the busiest and most important departmental heads. She/he is assisted by a deputy housekeeper who will probably have under his/her assistant housekeeper, responsible for the work of chambermaids, cleaners, house-porters, linen maids, linen porters, office assistants, ladies cloak-room attendants, window washers, furniture polisher and seamstress. Also directly under the deputy housekeeper will come linen keeper, linen maids and a florist who have one or more assistants. Besides, there may be house porters or housemen, who work under the housekeeper and are usually responsible for the heavier work such as moving heavy furniture. This department is responsible for all the rooms and public areas of the hotel.

In small hotels the number of people working under the head house-keeper may be less and in others, there may be only one housekeeper, whilst in some other cases the job of housekeeper may even be combined with that of receptionist and even be integrated with both management and reception. The housekeeper not only handles all the supervisory duties by herself but in addition helps in the actual work. She is responsible for maintaining the inventory of linens, bedding, furniture, furnishing, accessories and cleaning materials.

Today's Executive House-keeper must have some knowledge of chemistry (cleaning agents and their uses), bacteriology (sanitation), interior decoration and textiles. A flair for colour exterior and interior decoration is ideal. Figs 5.41, 5.42, 5.43, 5.44, 5.45, 5.46, 5.47, 5.48, 5.49, 5.50, 5.51 and 5.52 show the organisational charts of a typical house-keeping department in small, medium and large hotels. The structure could be modified according to the size, type and standard of the hotel.

A Case Study 5.6
Housekeeping

Situation

In one hotel each maid's daily quota of rooms to be cleaned was 16. A check on the maid's performance showed an average of about 12 rooms cleaned per day. Extra payments had to be made from rooms cleaned above 13.

Results of Analysis

A study showed that 20% of maid's working time was spent in getting lenin from the Lenin Room. This was caused by a lenin shortage which did not allow proper stocking of the floor linen closets. A par system of stocking linen and other supplies was installed for floor closets. The maids were then able to report to their floors and to work uninterrupted. Maids were able to do their quota of 16 rooms and were saved considerable exasperation. Extra room payments were eliminated. Guests complaints subsided. Wear and tear on the service elevator was reduced and the hotel saved 10% of housekeeping payroll.

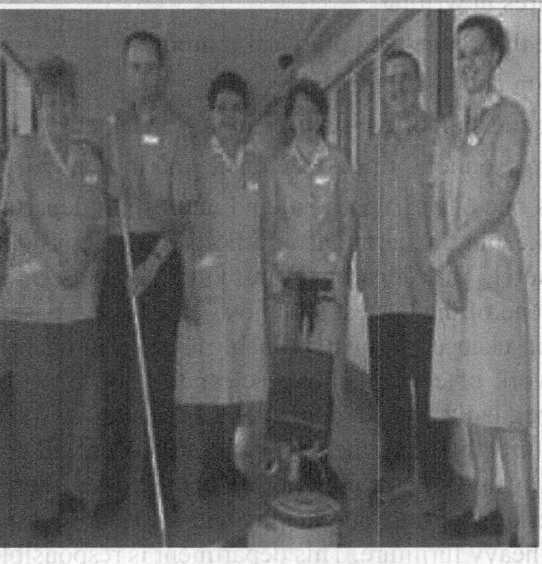

Pix. 5.26. Housekeeping Trainees

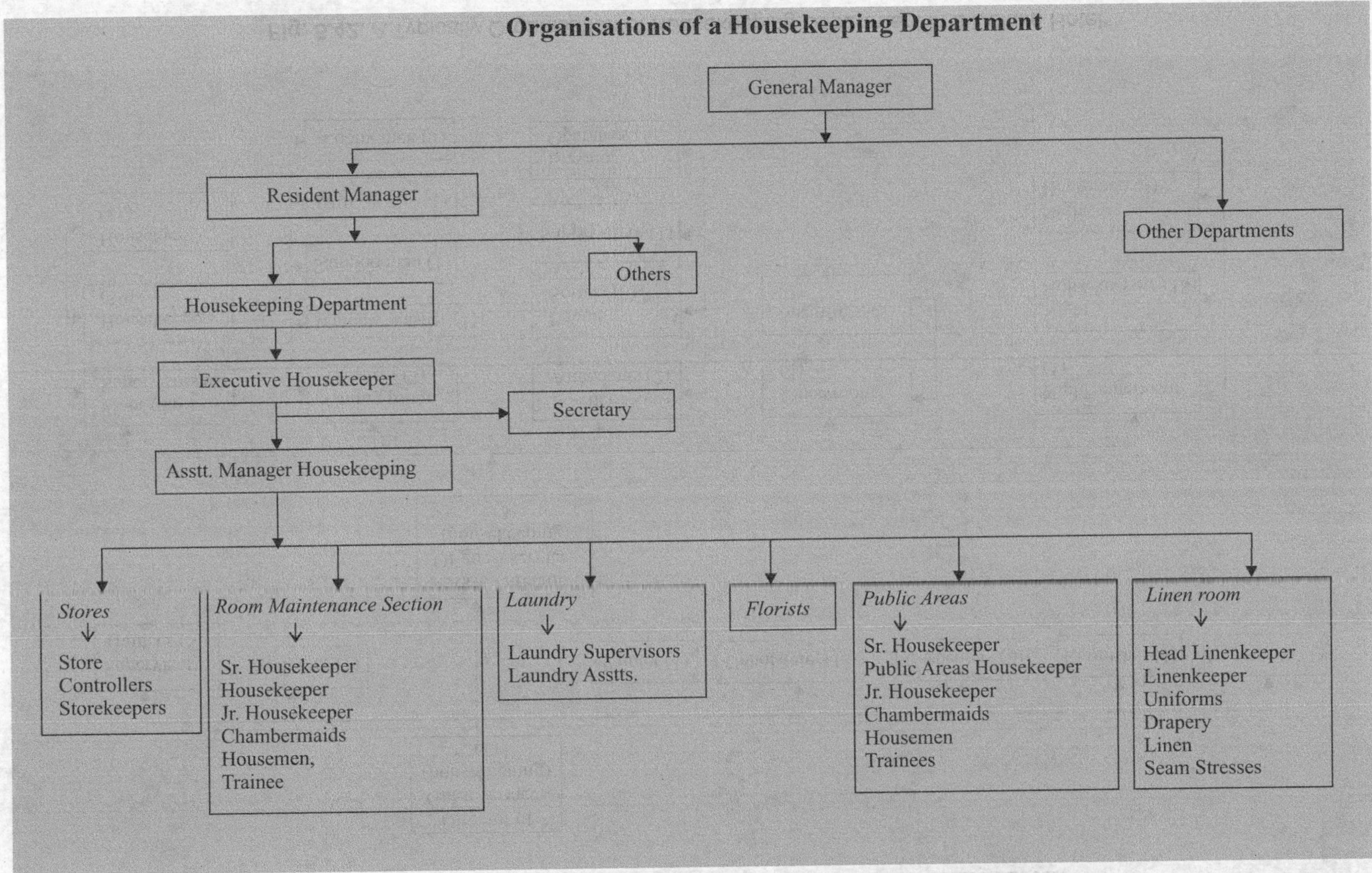

Fig. 5.41. A Typically Organisations of a Housekeeping Department

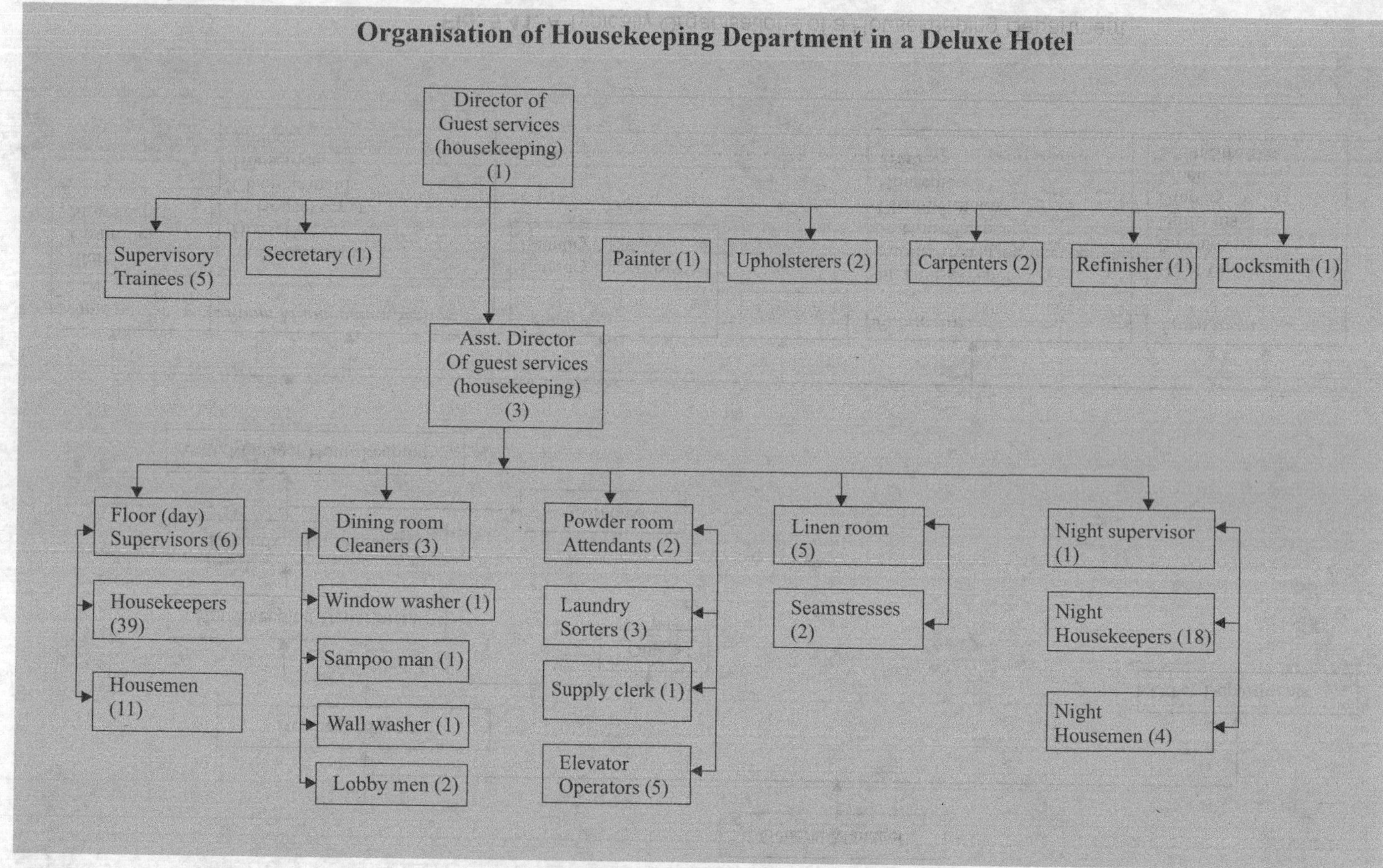

Fig. 5.42. A Typically Organisation of Housekeeping Department in a Deluxe Hotel

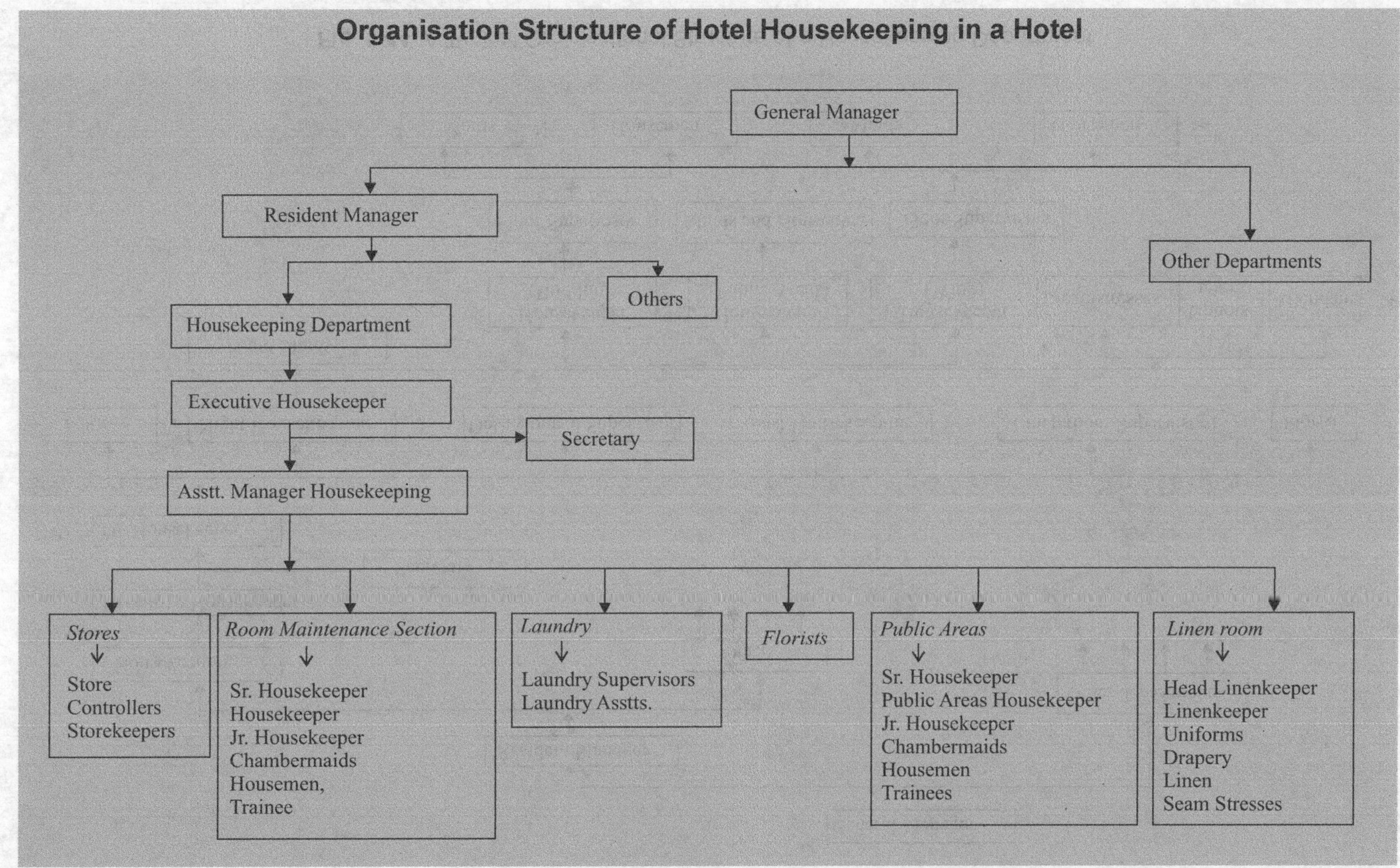

Fig. 5.43: Typical Organisation Structure of Hotelkeeping in a Hoel

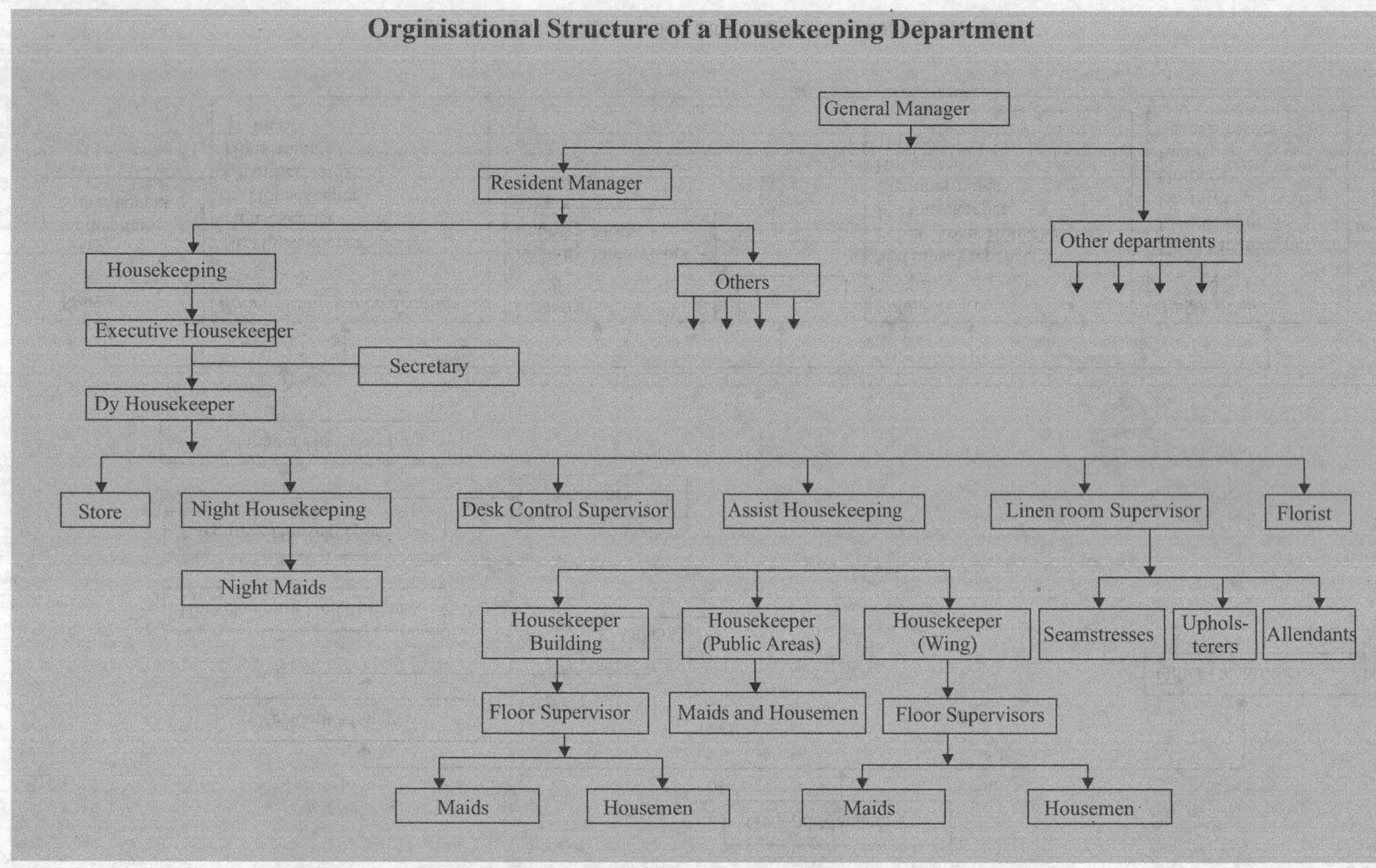

Fig. 5.44. A Typical Orginisational Structure of a Housekeeping Department

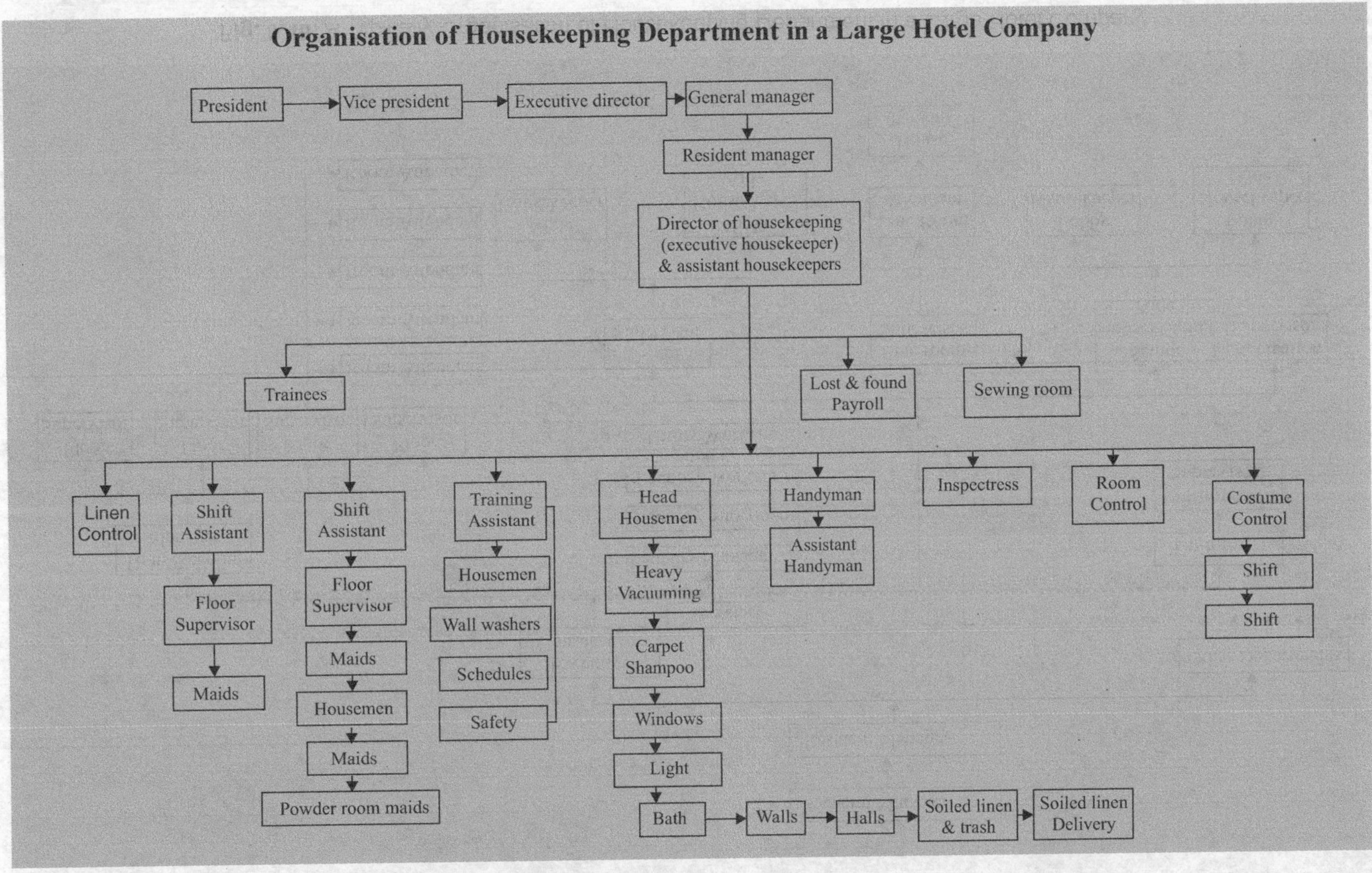

Fig. 5.45. A Typically Organisation of Housekeeping Department in a Large Hotel Company

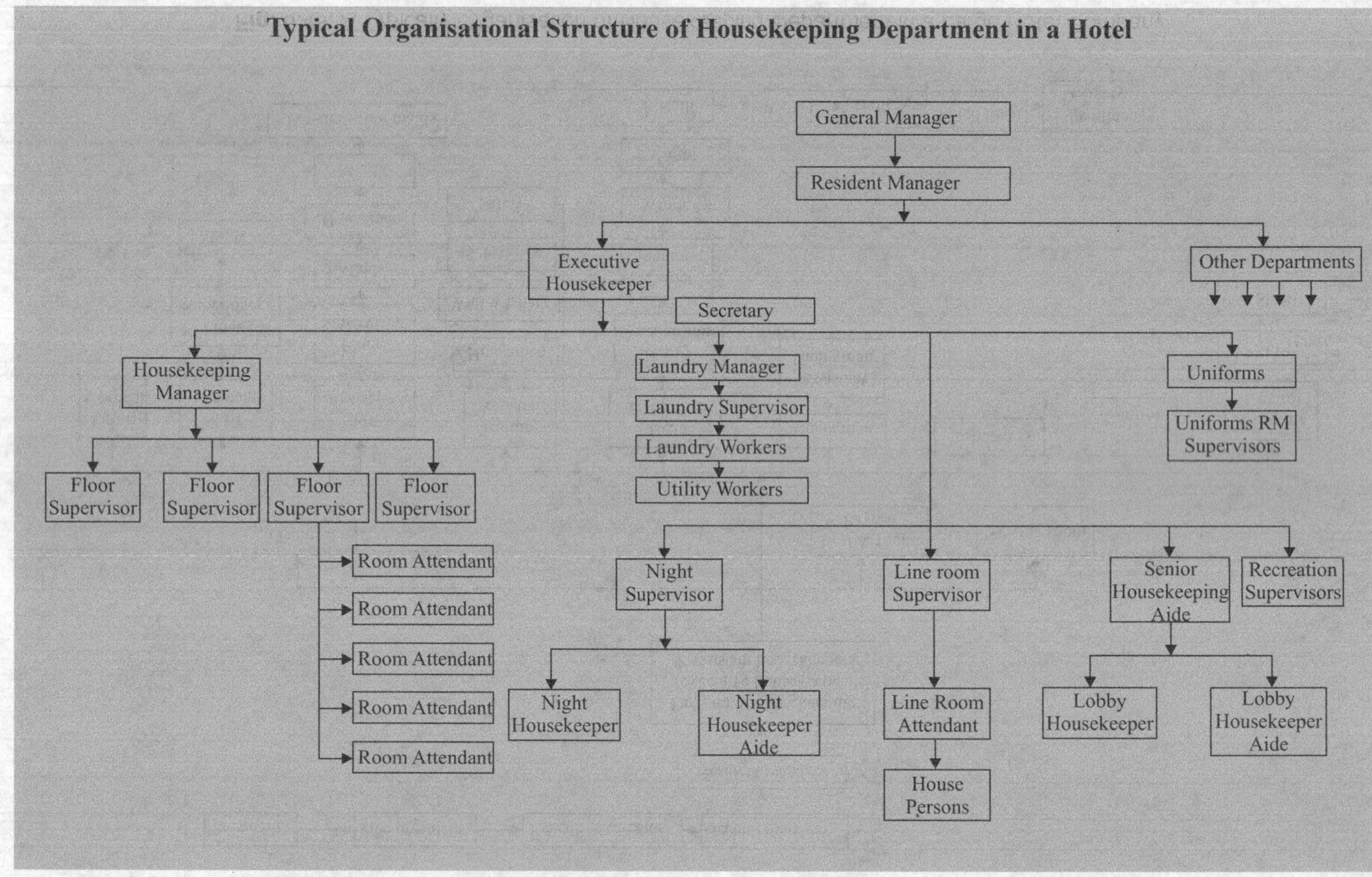

Fig. 5.46. A Typically Organisation of Housekeeping Department in a Large Hotel Company

Organisation Chart for 100-Room or Less Hotel
Owner/Manager
House keeper (may be owner's wife)
Assistant Hosekeeper
Laundress
Maids
Housemen (may also work as Bell men)

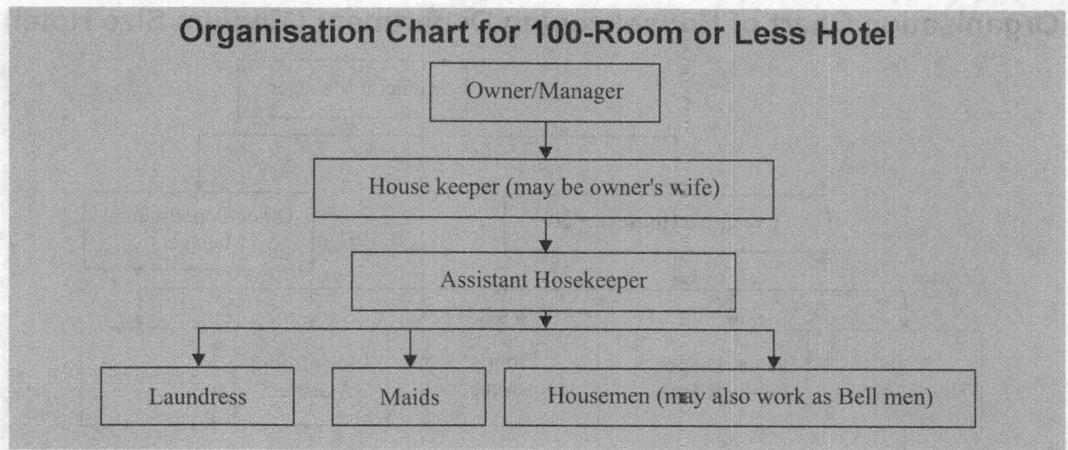

Fig. 5.47: A Typical Housekeeping Organisation Chart for 100-Room or Less Hotel

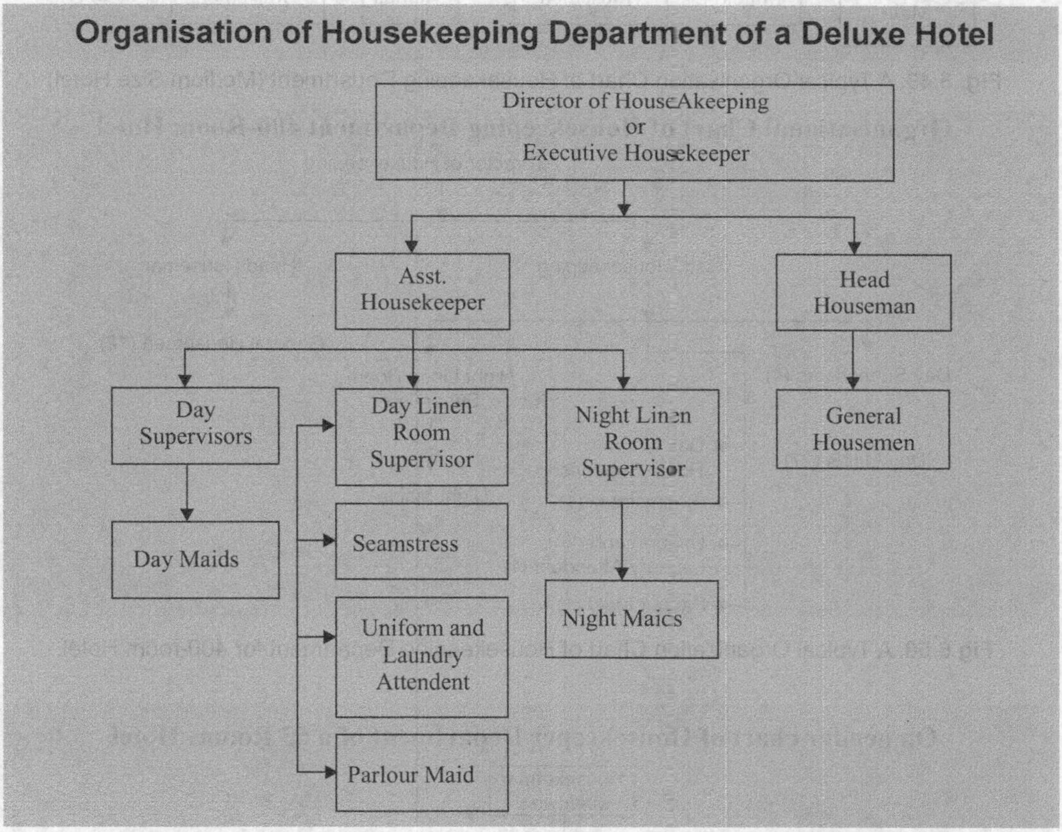

Organisation of Housekeeping Department of a Deluxe Hotel
Director of HouseKeeping
or
Executive Housekeeper
Asst. Housekeeper
Head Houseman
Day Supervisors
Day Linen Room Supervisor
Night Linen Room Supervisor
General Housemen
Day Maids
Seamstress
Night Maids
Uniform and Laundry Attendent
Parlour Maid

Fig. 5.48: A Typical Organisation of Housekeeping Department of a Deluxe Hotel

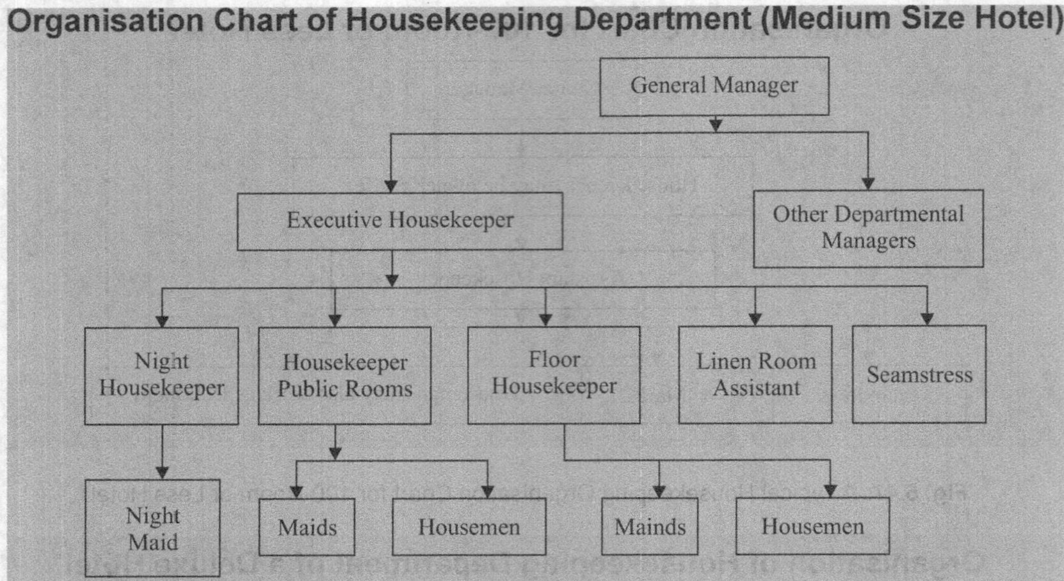

Fig. 5.49. A Typical Organisation Chart of Housekeeping Department (Medium Size Hotel)

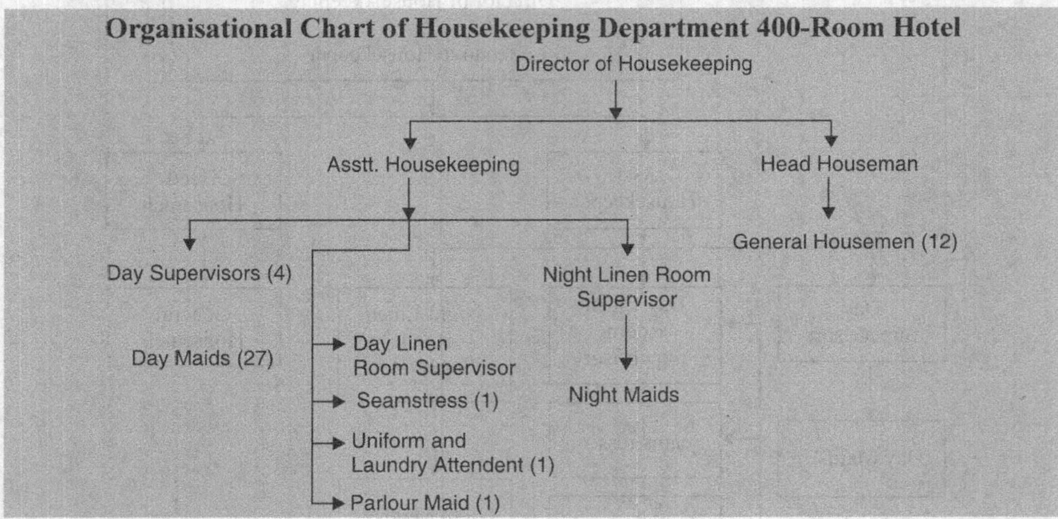

Fig.5.50. A Typical Organization Chart of Housekeeping Department for 400-room Hotel.

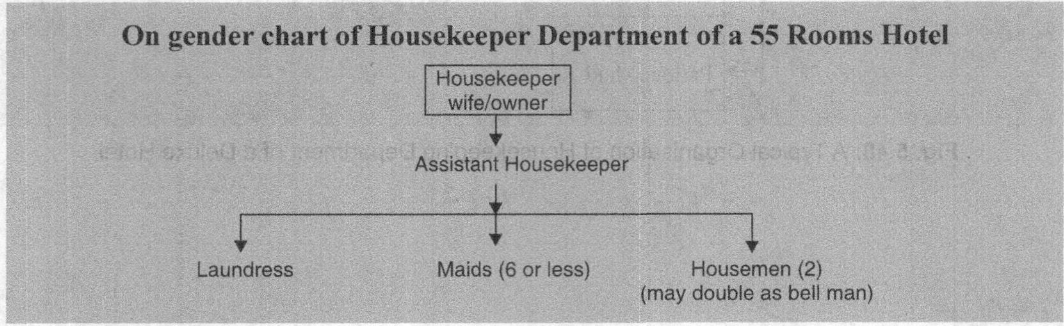

Fig.5.51 Typical Organisational for Housekeeping Department: 85 Room Hotel

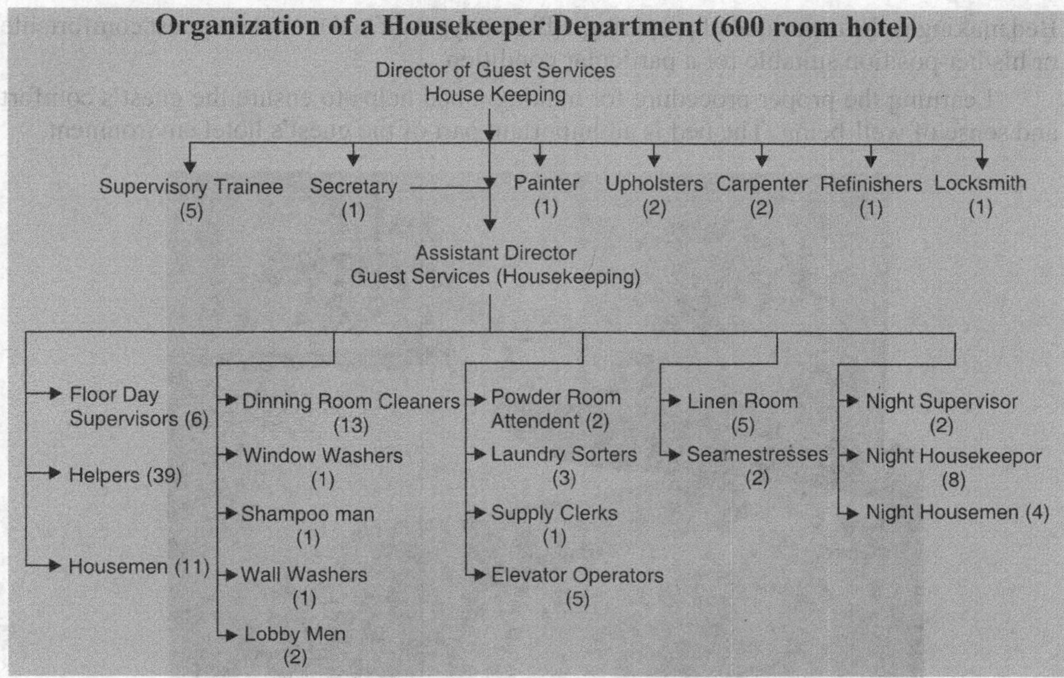

Fig. 5.52. Typical Organisation Chart for a Housekeeping Department: 600-Room Hotel

The exact outline of the hotel house-keeping activities and function will decide the organisational approach to be adopted. In some hotels a number of functions are integrated within this department, whereas in others these works/functions are assigned to different departments, largely on the basis of physical areas. In addition, many hotels have a practice of buying in certain prices from outside suppliers rather than operating them directly on hotel facilities.

The Executive House-keeper also investigates periodic storing, cleaning or redecoration which is found to be necessary. She maintains exact records showing when any given area was last decorated and where it is next scheduled for decoration. Depending upon the seasonal fluctuations of the hotel, she sets aside certain areas for thorough cleaning at different times of the year.

The different areas which come under the direct supervision of the Executive House-keeper are :

1. Guest rooms
2. Halls and corridors
3. Lobbies
4. Public areas
5. Offices
6. Stairways/cases
7. Windows
8. Stores, concessions and other leased areas.

BED MAKING PROCEDURE

A guest requires a comfortable bed to take rest, relax and enjoy. A bed that is well made will provide the required comfort. Bed making is a skill that requires to be developed by the housekeeper, as it not only provides comfort to the guest, but also adds to the pleasant ambience of a guest's room. Guests should not be able to tell if anyone has slept in the room, so a clean environment and perfect bed making is major consideration of this department.

Bed making is the technique of preparing different types of bed to make a guest comfortable or his/her position suitable for a particular condition.

Learning the proper procedure for making a bed helps to ensure the guest's comfort and sense of well-being. The bed is an important part of the guest's hotel environment.

Pix. 5.27. A Hotel Bed

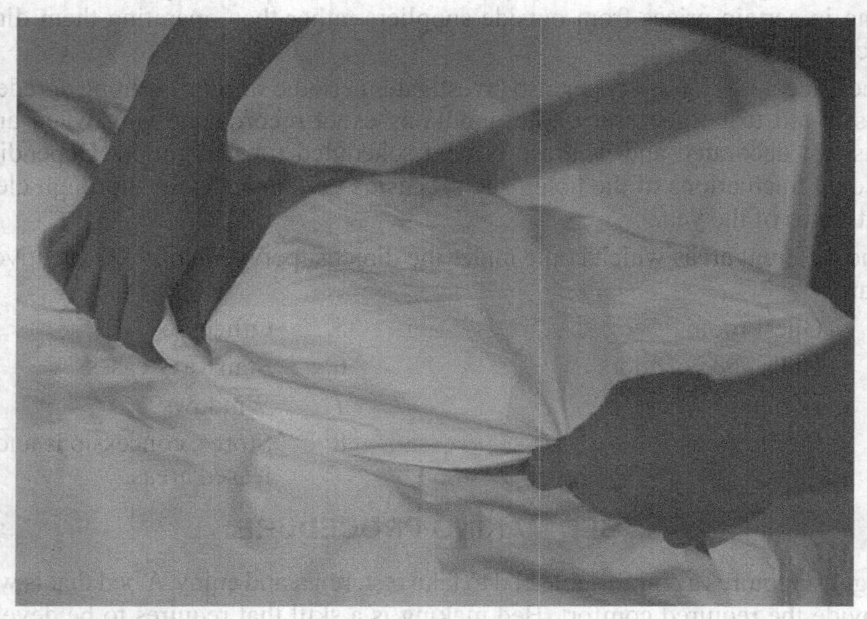

Pix. 5.28. 10 Steps for Bed Making

The main steps followed required in bed making are:

1. Remove soiled sheets and pillowcases and shake out individually. Check linens for dentures, hearing aids, jewelry, glasses, face tissues, or anything else belonging to the guest before stripping the bed.
2. Turn the mattress side-to-side on succeeding days followed by end-to-end turning. Smooth out the mattress to air it out.
3. Shake out the mattress protector and relay it on the mattress. Change the protector that is soiled or smelling.
4. Open out the fresh lower sheet evenly and puck it securely at the head, foot and the sides.
5. Open out fresh top sheet and distribute it evenly over the lower bed sheet. Ensure that the laundry creases are in the same line as the inner sheet for even distribution. The sheet hem should be evenly pulled up to the headboard. Tuck this sheet at the foot.
6. Open out the blanket and place it evenly on the top sheet using the crease as described earlier for even distribution. Ensure that the blanket labels are at the foot.

Pix. 5.29. 10 Style for Bed Making

7. Pull the blanket 4 inches from the headboard.
8. Fold the top sheet, at the head of the bed over the blanket and fold the sheet and blanket once again.
9. The blanket and the top sheet are together tucked uniformly on both sides while the comers at the foot of the bed are neatly mitered.
10. Cover pillows with fresh pillowslips. Fluff the pillow and even out pillowslips to look neat and tidy. Since pillowslips are larger than the pillow the excess slip should be neatly folded downwards. The side of the pillow, which has the fold, should be away from guest view.

11. Cover completed bed with the bed spread / bed cover ensuring that it is right side up and is falling evenly all around the bed. Keep extra bed spread toward the headboard to crease in between the pillows so as to make the bed look appealing. The bed-spread corners should be aesthetically done.

Put spare blankets in the upper most shelf of the wardrobe in case required by the guest. Blankets are folded in such a manner that the hotel logo appears on the top.

Pix. 5.30. Big Making in a Hotel

In large hotels, laundry, lost and found, seamstress, repairs and other maintenance functions come under the jurisdiction of the executive house-keeper. The important functions of a house-keeping department are grouped as:

1. Cleaning and maintenance
2. Supplies and equipment
3. Training of personnel
4. Preparation of schedules and reports
5. Other functions :
   (*i*) Flowers and floral decorations and arrangement
   (*ii*) Attending complaints and requests of guests
   (*iii*) Attending to lost properties
   (*iv*) First aid to guests and staff.

This department ensures that the amenities and bedrooms used by guests are maintained at a high standard. It has to work most closely with the front office. The house-keeping department must be informed as soon as guests check-out and in-turn must notify the front office immediately when a vacated room is ready for occupancy. The house-keeping office notifies floor house-keepers of all vacated rooms and the floor house-keeper will inform the executive house-keeping officer as soon as rooms are cleaned and inspected for re-letting.

Fig. 5.53 indicates the co-ordination and cooperation between the house-keeping and other departments of the hotel.

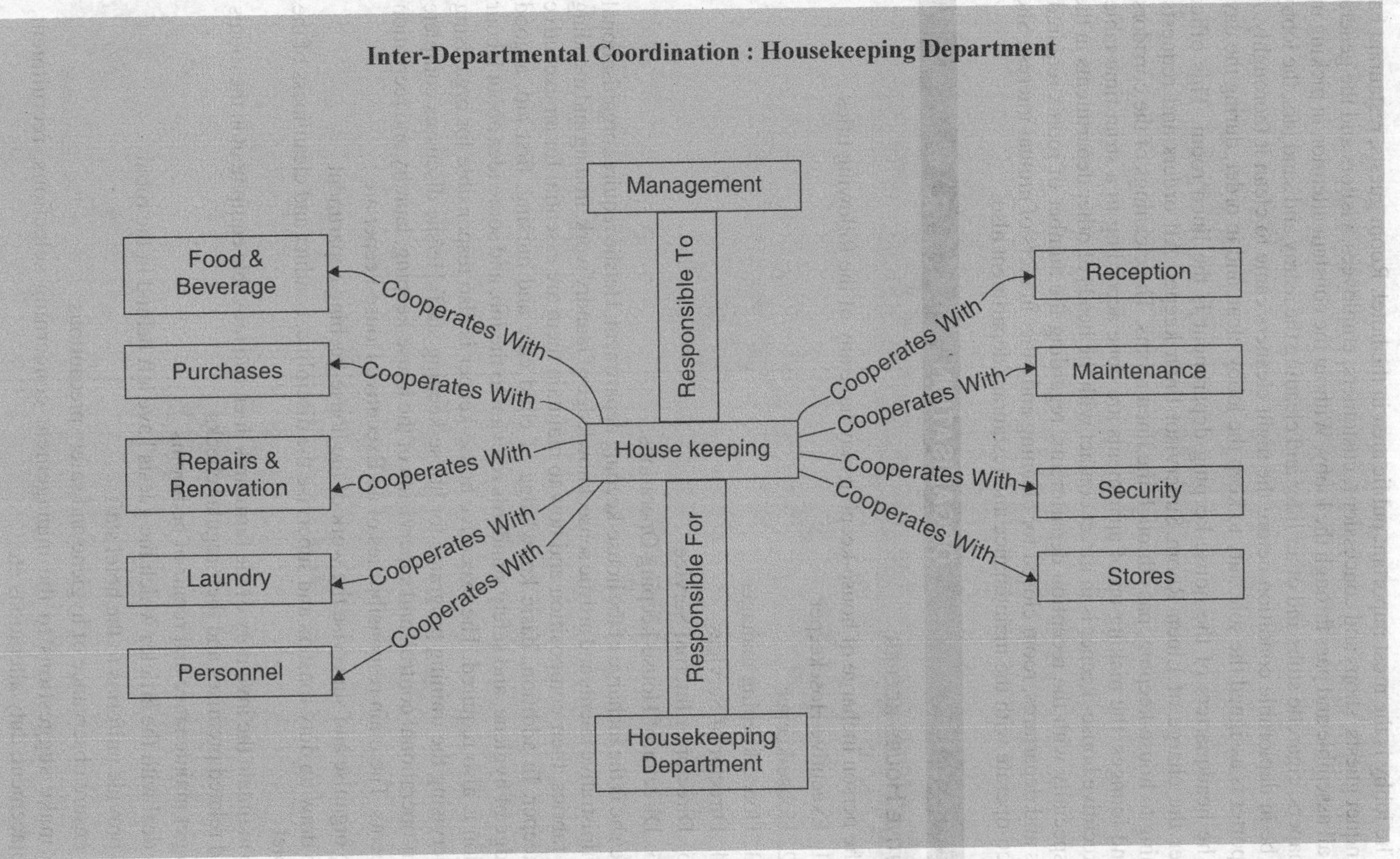

Fig. 5.53. Inter-Departmental Coordination : Housekeeping Department

The lobby is the most important public area in the hotel. Room guests, restaurant bar and banquet guests, shops and concessions, customers, employees, visitors and the general public all assemble and pass through the lobby. Without the constant attention in picking up loose papers, cigarette stubs and other litter and cleaning the astray and sand jars, the lobby would be in deplorable condition before the night cleaners came to clean it thoroughly. A lobby porter is assigned the sole duty to keep the lobby clean and in order, during the day.

The headquarters of the house-keeping department is the linen room. This office is under the charge of Linen Room Supervisor/linen keeper. All orders and requests, pertaining to house-keeping, pass through the linen rooms. The cleanings of the corridors, halls and lounges, the making up of apartments are done according to a strict time table. The Executive house- keeper is in direct contact with the heads of other departments in the hotel, specially with the reception departments, regarding the number of rooms required, arrivals and departures, room closed for cleaning and other matters of mutual interest. She has to co-operate with the maintenance and restaurant department also.

ORGANISATION

Executive House-keeper

The person incharge of house-keeping may have any of the following titles :

1. Executive Hosekeeper
2. House-keeper
3. House-keeping manager
4. Director of Services
5. Director of Internal Service
6. Director of House-keeping Operations.

He/she is the incharge of the house-keeping department. He/she requires organisational and administrative talents and artistic sense, knowledge of laundry work, ironing and mending various fabrics, their composition and how to maintain them are essential for an executive house-keeper. In addition, basic knowledge of child care and nursing, first aid, a good knowledge of hygiene, and safety standards relevant to the job, and some idea about labour legislation is also required. The executive house-keeper is also responsible for organising and supervising the training programs for house-keeping staff. He/she discusses complete direction-operational control, and supervision of the house-keeping, laundry and recreation departments. The main responsibilities of an Executive House-keeper are :

1. To organise and supervise the work of the house-keeping department
2. To draw up duty roasters and supervise the discipline, conduct and cleanliness of the hotel
3. To maintain the inventory of the furnitures linen and movable equipment in the rooms and related premises and their regular checks
4. To get maintenance and repair of bedrooms
5. To deal with the articles which the guests have left behind in the room
6. To provide uniforms to the hotel staff
7. To ensure observance of hygiene and safety precautions
8. To make suggestions to the management concerning selections, recruitment, replacement, duty alterations etc.

9. To organise and supervise the training of the staff
10. To liaise between maintenance and house-keeping department.

DEPUTY HOUSE-KEEPER/HOUSE-KEEPING MANAGER

The responsibility of the Deputy House-keeper will involve the daily supervision of specific areas within the hotel. In the large hotels, his/her work is supervision and control of room, maintenance, operations of bedroom floors. In the absence of the Executive House-keeper, he/she assumes the responsibility for the general administration of this department. He/she should have knowledge of laundry work, ironing and mending of fabrics, their composition and their maintenance. Like the executive house-keeper, an assistant house-keeper must have the basic knowledge of childcare and nursing, first aid, hygiene and safety standards and regulation, labour legislations and ability to train the housekeeping staff. The main duties of assistant house-keeper are :

1. To be responsible for the efficient and orderly management of guest room cleaning, servicing and repairing of room stations
2. To be responsible for the hotel linen and check its movements and distribution to chambermaids
3. To keep an inventory and check it regularly
4. To assist the chambermaids in their work
5. To provide the front office with a list of rooms ready for assignment to guests
6. To get arrangement of flowers
7. To arrange training of staff and replace the executive house-keeper in case of absence.

FLOOR HOUSE-KEEPERS/FLOOR SUPERVISORS/INSPECTRESS

Floor house-keepers are finally responsible for the conditions of the guest rooms. Each floor house-keeper is assigned three or more floors. She gives the maids their room assignment and floor master keys which are returned at the end of each day. She supervises, checks and approves the maid's work and makes periodical inspection of the physical conditions of all rooms on her floor. Any damage reported by maids or discovered, is referred to the executive house-keeper for transmission to the chief engineer for appropriate action. For decorating and refurnishing of the rooms, requests are made to top management. The floor house-keeper supervises the re-decorations, chooses the colour of the paints, upholstery etc. Close co-operation and co-ordination between the engineer and the house-keeper is required to keep to a minimum, the amount of time that the room is out of order.

Thus, the floor house-keeper must know the rooms to be handled, coordinate with front office and house-keeping desk and laundry, fire prevention and security system of floors, maintenance order procedures, lost and found procedure. She is responsible for :

1. Procedure of handling soiled linen to the laundry and requisitioning fresh ones from house-keeping
2. Supply of equipment and supplies to floors and public areas
3. Spring cleaning
4. Co-ordination with room service for cleanliness
5. Par stock on floor
6. Co-ordination with lobby manager
7. Provision of extra services to guests e.g. baby seaters, hot water bottles etc.

8. Scanty luggage
9. Preparation of occupancy report.

CHAMBERMAIDS/ROOM MAIDS/HOUSEMEN/ROOM ATTENDANT

He/she requires good knowledge of the methods of cleaning and care of rooms and furniture. Knowledge of hygiene and safety standards and labour legislation relevant to the work is also essential. The main jobs of the chambermaids are :

1. To clean and tidy the rooms and sanitary installation assigned
2. To change linen
3. To answer guest's summons promptly
4. To be responsible for cleaning, processing etc., of guest's clothes
5. To undertake the evening check of rooms
6. To hand over to the house-keeper any article which guests have left in their rooms

They undertake the servicing of the bedrooms and private rooms. They are each allotted a number of rooms, called sections.

DAILY CLEANERS/CORRIDOR MAIDS

They are responsible for the cleaning and maintenance of corridors, stair- cases, and cloak rooms, public rooms, corridors, halls, public bathrooms and the toilets and the various offices of the hotel. Her/his influence also extends throughout all areas of residential accommodation for staff.

FLOOR PORTER/HOUSE PORTER

The number of house porters depends on the size of the hotel and the amount of work to be done. All heavy work such as the moving of furniture or heavy linen baskets is done by the house porter. He is directly responsible to the head house-keeper.

OTHERS

It includes head housemen, sanitors, furniture polishers, polishers, paint cleaners, shademen, wall washers, vacuum cleaners, elevator cleaners, lobby housemen or porters, street cleaners, yardmen, carpet cleaners, shampooers, floor polishers, drapery hangers, curtain hangers.

They are responsible for :

1. Carpet cleaning and vacuum cleaning
2. Window panes and glass cleaning
3. Dumping soiled linen into laundry through chutes or by trolleys
4. Garbage and trash trolley cleanliness
5. Supplying clean drinking glasses to rooms
6. Cleaning of corridor
7. Cleaning of public areas
8. Uniform piling of carpet, brass work polishing, ashtray cleaning, mirror cleaning, elevator handling and elevator door cleaning, cleaning of staircases etc.
9. Stain removal of walls
10. Making of beds

11. Shoe shine
12. Co-ordination with the floor supervisor and the house-keeping desk.

CLEANING AND MAINTENANCE

Cleaning and maintenance of the areas under its supervision is the primary function of the house-keeping department. The guest rooms require cleaning, changing of the linen, and making up the beds which is done by the maids. The day-maid services and cleans the guest room. The house-men thoroughly clean bath rooms, wash the tiles, and floor fixtures. The nightmaids service the room in the case of late check-outs and is one called for extra supplies or other requests by the guests. The maid gives the bath-rooms and daily light cleaning, particularly the tubs, wall and fixtures, and a thorough cleaning is done periodically by the house-men.

Each maid is given a cart to carry her supplies. These carts are in front of the door, behind which the maid is working or where the maid's card is on the door handle. They are visible to every guest. Each morning these carts are cleaned before being equipped with linens and other supplies. These carts and supplies are kept under the charge of maids closed on every floor. The floor closet contains sheets, pillow cases, bath towels, wash clothes, bath mats, reserve for mattress pads, bedspreads, blankets and shower curtains to replace what has been stained, soiled or damaged. Other items required for equipping the hotel are : glasses, toilet tissues, facial tissues, shoe shine cloths, soap, ashtrays, matches, guest stationery, envelopes, post cards, pens, telephones, memo pads, laundry lists, guest laundry bags, room service memos, do not disturb card, and clothes hangers.

Room attendants are issued room trawlers and a basic set of work tools. Each trolley contains some basic items which are required by the room attendants for setting the rooms before they are re-let. The contents of the trolley for 12 rooms are estimated in Table 5.2.

The maid is required to inspect each room in her section for vacancies in the morning and afternoon, and prepare a room report. A good house-keeping procedure requires that a check-out be served first unless a guest requires early service.

Table 5.2 : Estimated Contents of a Trolley for 12 Rooms

The Trolley contents	
1. Sheets, double	4
2. Sheets, single	30
3. Pillow cases	30
4. Bath towels	24
5. Face towels	24
6. Bath mats	12
7. Under blankets	2
8. Book matches	20
9. Paper landry bags	12
10. Plastic landry bags large	12
11. Face tissue	3 boxes
12. Toilet papers	3 rolls
13. Soap bars	20
14. Clean new plastic tumblers	10

15.	Roll of cling wrap	1
16.	Glass ash trays	4
17.	Light bulbs (60 Watt)	2
18.	Stationary kits complete	5
19.	Restaurant promotional tent cards	5
The Stationary Kits Contents:		
1.	Guest note papers	4 sheets
2.	Envelope	4
3.	Shoe shine cloths	2
4.	Dry cleaning lists	2
5.	Laundry lists	2
The Maid's Tray Contents :		
1.	Spray bottle detergent	1
2.	Spray bottle glass/mirror cleaner	1
3.	Large sponge	1
4.	Shift hand brush	1
5.	Toilet bowl brush/stand	1
6.	Cleaning cloths (J cloths)	2
7.	Vaccum cleaners	1

Housemen give each room a general cleaning periodically i.e., the period depends upon the hotel's policy. It involves a thorough cleaning of the room and everything in it. It includes high wall dusting, cleaning the tiles in the bathroom, washing pictures and vacuuming the drapes, blinds, sofas, cushions and mattresses as well as the carpets. Housemen also carry furniture to and from the store room and from the guest room to another. They also help in setting up a banquet room from dinners, dances, meetings, etc. and strip the room after the function in over.

Cleaning Agents

Cleaning methods should be designed to remove dust, grit, grease and other foreign bodies which may have settled on or adhered to room surpaces. At the same time surfaces must not be harmed and the choice of cleaning method must yield an economic solution to the cleaning problem. The choice of cleaning method and cleaning agent is affected by two major factors :

1. The type of dirt or soiling to be removed
2. The nature of the surface to be treated.

Table 5.3 indicates the methods used for soiling and cleaning.

Table 5.3 : Soiling and Cleaning Methods

Stage	Type of Soiling	Cleaning Methods
Stage I	Litter, Cigarette, butts, Other discarded materials	Remove by hand
Stage II	Dust and loose dirt	*Furniture :*

		Remove with a dry duster walls etc.
		Remove with a soft wall brush.
		Hard floor :
		Remove with a soft floor brush.
		Carpeted floor :
		Remove with a vacuum cleaner
Stage III	Foreign matter adhering to surface straining	Select a cleaning method appropriate to the type of dirt or stain and with due consideration of the surface being treated.

Table 5.4 is a list of cleaning agents used in a hotel.

Table 5.4. List of Cleaning Agents used in Hotels

S.No.	Cleaning Agent
1.	Block soap, Powder Soap, Flake Soap
2.	Toilet soap
3.	Synthetic soapless detergents
4.	Washing soda
5.	Amonia
6.	Paraffin
7.	Vinegar
8.	Carbon tetrachloride
9.	Methylated spirits
10.	Hydrochloric Acid
11.	Bleaches
12.	Disinfections
13.	Toilet cleaners
14.	Abrasives (for removal of dirt from curtain hard and impervious surfaces)
	(*a*) Steel wool
	(*b*) Emery Powder or Paper
	(*c*) Nylon Scouring pads
	(*d*) Precipitated whiting and jeweller's powder
	(*e*) Souring powders
	(*f*) Souring paste
15.	Polishes
	(*a*) Floor polish (water based)
	(*b*) Floor Polish (spirit based in paste or liquid form)
	(*c*) Floor seals
	(*d*) Furniture polish
	(*e*) Metal polishes

GUEST ROOM CLEANING

All guest rooms within an hotel must be cleaned and prepared for incoming guests each day. It is evident that this is particularly important after guest departures. Even where accommodation has remained vacant overnight, superficial cleaning and airing will be needed to provide a fresh and inviting atmosphere for new visitor. When cleaning commences in one room, it should be followed through until completion. If room can be made available for reletting as speedily as possible, the sales function of the reception office will be eased.

Fig. 5.54 indicates the guest room cleaning procedure.

Fig. 5.55 is a flow chart for geust room cleaning.

Fig. 5.56 shows a bath room cleaning procedure.

Fig. 5.57 shows a typical stainway cleaning.

Fig. 5.58 procedure is a typical room cleaning procedure for a room maid.

Guest Room Cleaning Procedure

Stage	Room Cleaning Procedure
Stage I	Collect equipment from store or service room. It is wise to check that all necessary equipment, sufficient cleaning materials, and lenin are contained on the Room-maid's Trolley.
Stage II	Commence work on guest room. Freshern room by opening windows or ventilators
Stage III	Strip clothes off bed
Stage IV	Collect and remove all soiled linen Note: 1. If the guest is staying for a further night, linen should be removed according to house policy. 2. If the guest is due to leave, but has not vacated the room, hand towels may be left in the room until his departure. 3. Soiled linen should be collected from all rooms, sorted and exchanged for clean stocks. The timing of this operation should be determined by the Housekeeper.
Stage V	Remove litter empty and clean waste bins and astrays
Stage VI	Make up the bed (except in studio rooms, where bedding should be neatly stored for future use)
Stage VII	Clean and polish wash basin and toilet fittings. Check for dripping taps, blocked drains and report faults to the housekeeper. Replenish soap and towels.
Stage VIII	Dust furniture and fixtures, vacuum the carpet, mop the carpet surrounds and skirting. Check electrical fittings, telephone and radio and report deficienies. Replenish stationery, guide book, brochures etc. as required.
Stage IX	Adjust the window and ventilation as necessary.
Stage X	Make final inspection of the room and close door.

Fig.5.54 Guest Room Cleaning Procedure

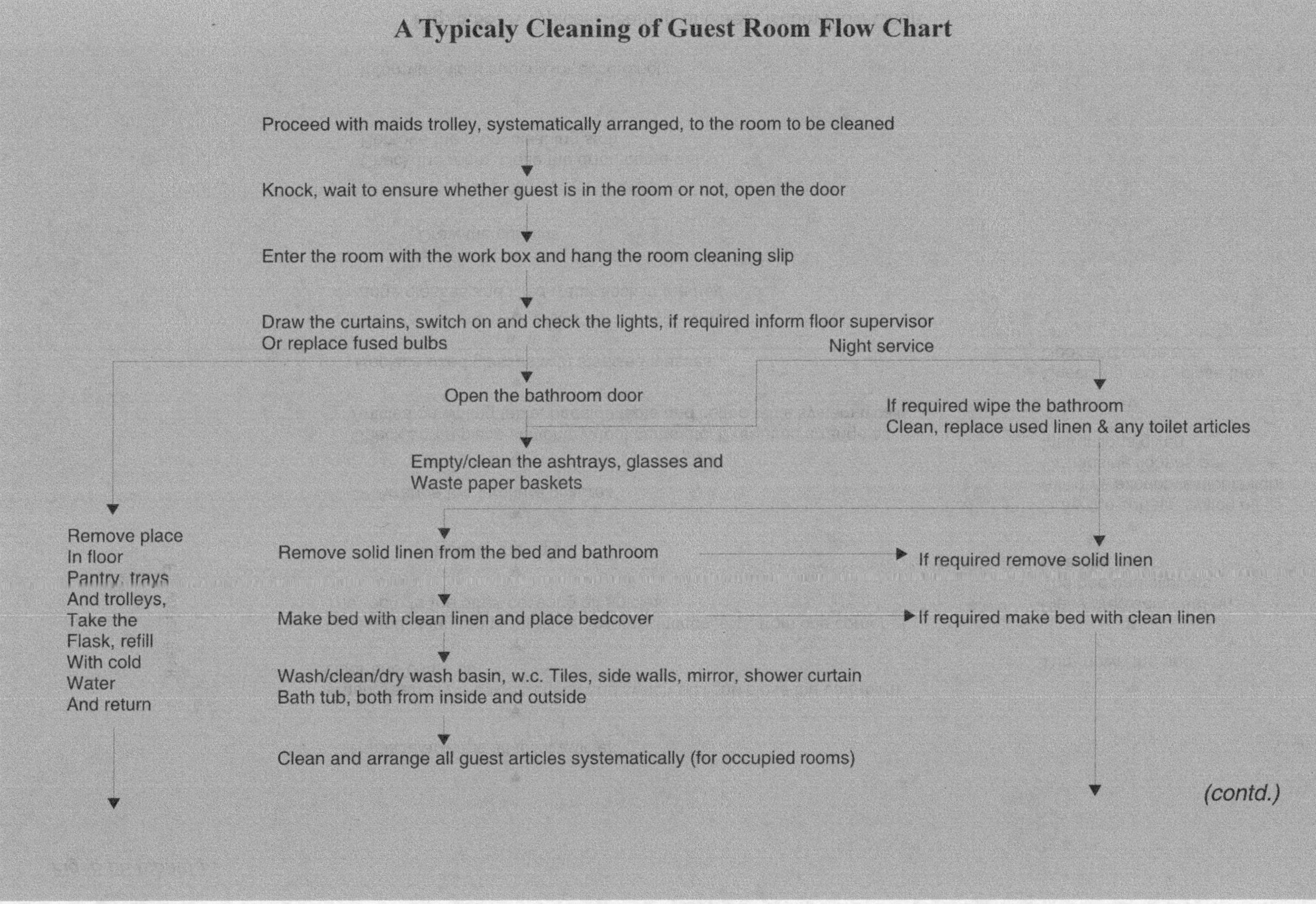
A Typicaly Cleaning of Guest Room Flow Chart
Proceed with maids trolley, systematically arranged, to the room to be cleaned
Knock, wait to ensure whether guest is in the room or not, open the door
Enter the room with the work box and hang the room cleaning slip
Draw the curtains, switch on and check the lights, if required inform floor supervisor
Or replace fused bulbs
Night service
Open the bathroom door
If required wipe the bathroom
Clean, replace used linen & any toilet articles
Empty/clean the ashtrays, glasses and
Waste paper baskets
Remove place
In floor
Pantry, trays
And trolleys,
Take the
Flask, refill
With cold
Water
And return
Remove solid linen from the bed and bathroom
If required remove solid linen
Make bed with clean linen and place bedcover
If required make bed with clean linen
Wash/clean/dry wash basin, w.c. Tiles, side walls, mirror, shower curtain
Bath tub, both from inside and outside
Clean and arrange all guest articles systematically (for occupied rooms)
(contd.)

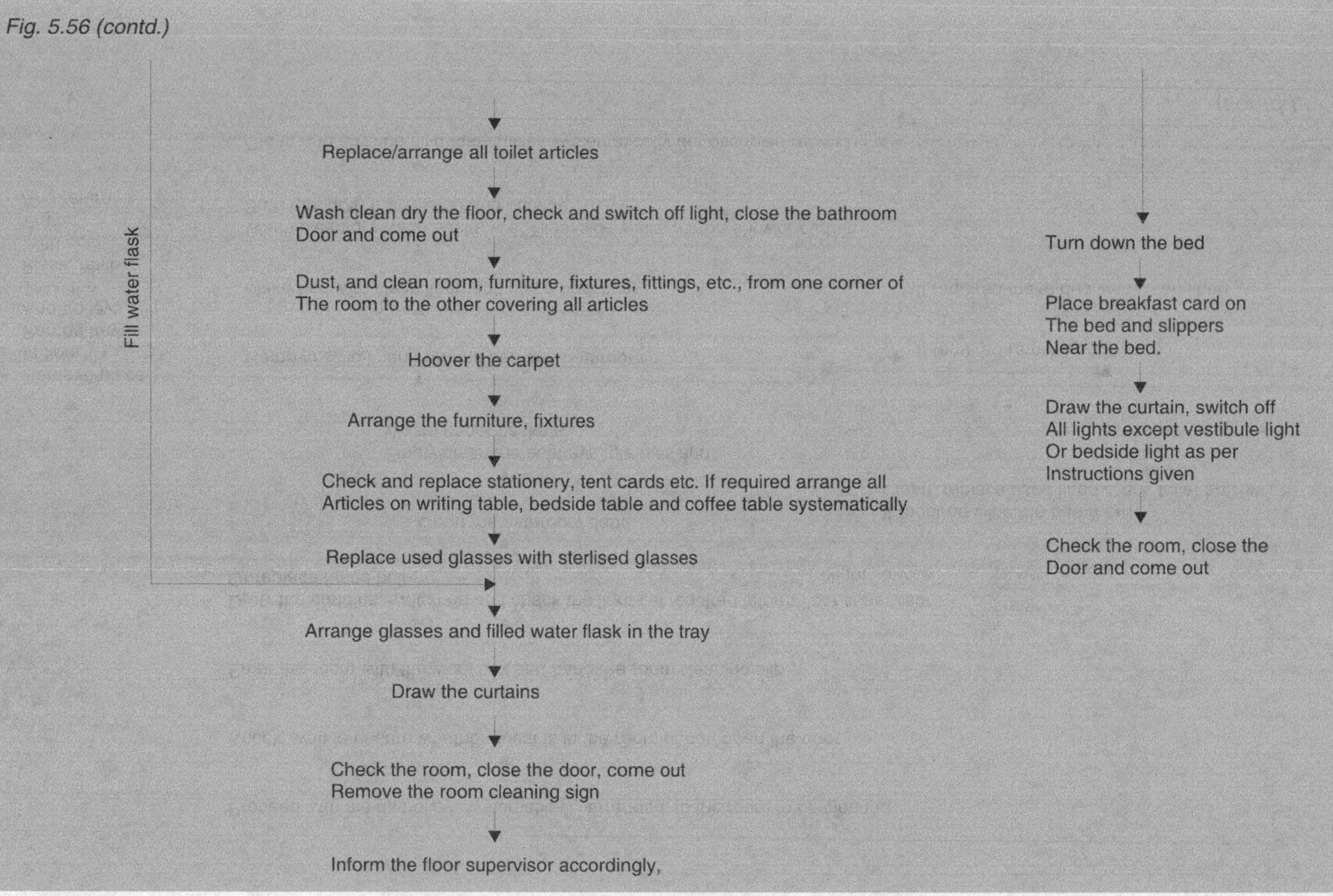

Fig. 5.55. A Typical Cleaning of Guest Room Flow Chart

Bath Room Cleaning Procedure

Stage	Description
Stage I	Collect equipment
Stage II	Open windows or ventilators
Stage III	Remove soiled linen
Stage IV	Remove litter, empty litter bin, Sani-bin and razor blade disposal box (if necessary)
Stage V	Wash bath surround and clean bath
Stage VI	Wash WC fitment and wash basin, clean surround and polish mirrors, sponze wall tiles, and clean other fittings. Dust telephone Check for blocked drain and faulty washers on taps
Stage VII	Sponge sweep floor
Stage VIII	Replace clean towels replenish toilet paper, tissues, toilet soap and other consumables such as washing powder sachets.
Stage IX	Check electric fittings
Stage X	Close window or ventilators
Stage XI	Make a final inspection of the room.

Fig.5.56. A Typical Bath Room Cleaning Procedure

Stairway Cleaning Procedure

Stage	Procedure
Stage I	Collect equipment
Stage II	Dust ledges, window sills, handrails etc. (working from the top most point to the lowest point of the stairway)
Stage III	Vacuum clean carpeted areas with vacuum attachments or dustette. Uncarpeted areas should be swept and washed as required.

Fig.5.57. A Typical Stairway Cleaning Procedure

Room Maid's Evening Routine

Stage	Descriptions
Stage I	Collect equipment–duster and other cleaning cloths, receptacles for rubbish).
Stage II	Knock on guest room door, if no reply, knock second time. Enter room.
Stage III	It dark, switch on light, adjust window if necessary, and close windows
Stage IV	Tidy room, empty waste bin and ashtrays, remove, straighten cushions and loose furnishings. (Note : It is important that Room-maids remove only those items which have already been discarded by the guest; in a doubtful situation, it is wiser to leave papers etc. undisturbed)
Stage V	Wipe the wash basin and fittings in the private bathroom, tidy and refold towels as necessary.
Stage VI	Remove bed spread and party fold down the top sheet and blankets and tuck in neatly. Layout night attire, dressing gown and slippers, according to hotel's custom or policy.
Stage VII	Make final inspection, switch off light. (It may be hotel practice to leave a light on inorder to create an inviting overcome to the incoming guest). Close door.

Fig. 5.58. A Typical Room Cleaning Procedure

Fig 5.59 is a service procedure for early morning tea.

Service Procedure for Early Morning Tea

State	Description
Stage I	Complete lay up of tea tray in service room. (Normally trays are kept laid up ready for use; milk jugs, tea and coffee pots are filled immediately prior to service)
Stage II	Take tray to guest room. Knock on door, await reply. Knock a second time if necessary and enter
Stage III	Switch on light
Stage IV	Act sociably towards the guest and say "Good Morning" (Note : It is important that room-maids are trained in social skills and are able to show a balance between shyness and embarrassment, and being too forward and talkative)
Stage V	Place tea tray, papers and mail (if this is the hotel practice) on the bed side table
Stage VI	If appropriate open curtains
Stage VII	Where shoes have been left outside the room for cleaning, these can be brought into the room.
Stage VIII	Check that the guest is still awake, and leave the room without banging the door.

Fig.5.59. A Typical Service Procedure for Early Morning Tea

EMPLOYEES TRAINING

The number of employees working in the house-keeping department varies from hotel to hotel. Numerically, this department has more unskilled workers (maids, porters, cleaners, housemen, wall washer etc.) than has any other department in the hotel. All of them are in direct contact with the guest, therefore, their arises a major need for training of these employees in their duties and there relationship with each other, with staff members in other departments and with the guests.

SUPPLIES AND EQUIPMENT

It includes the requisitioning, storage and control of the many operating supplies required for the daily routine of the department. The items in the guest rooms need replacement each day to maintain the standard set by the management. The maids and housemen need adequate supplies and proper equipment to clean and service the guest rooms, corridors and other public areas. Store room clerks should be instructed to record any item that falls below the needs of the operation. Effective control of the equipment should also be set up and maintained.

All guest supplies should be properly placed in each room. The items of guest supplies in each room are listed below :

1. Bed-room Doors :
   (*i*) Fire Notice/Room Rate Card
   (*ii*) Two Breakfast Order Cards
   (*iii*) One 'Do Not Disturb' Card

2. Dressing Table Top :
   (*i*) One Comment Card
   (*ii*) One Hotel Service Directory
   (*iii*) One Room Service Menu
   (*iv*) One Ashtray and Matches
3. Dressing table drawer :
   (*i*) The stationery kit (containing 4 sheets of papers, 2 envelopes, 2 post cards)
   (*ii*) Two shoe shine cloths
   (*iii*) One laundry list/dry-cleaning list
   (*iv*) One room service menu
   (*v*) One mending kit
4. Wardrobe :
   (*i*) Twelve coat hangers with bar
   (*ii*) Two laundry bags
5. Bedside Unit :
   (*i*) One ashtray
   (*ii*) Telephone
   (*iii*) Note pad and ball pen
   (*iv*) Luggage racks two
4. On Top of Television :
   (*i*) One restaurant card or other promotional material.
5. Wash Hands Basin :
   (*i*) One box cleaning tissues
   (*ii*) Two toilet rolls (one in holder/one reserve)
   (*iii*) One bar soap in bath soap holder
   (*iv*) Two bar soaps on the basin
   (*v*) Two glasses in cling wrap
   (*vi*) Ashtray
   (*vii*) Waste bin under basin
6. W.C. Unit :
   (*i*) Two sanitary bags
7. Twin Rooms :
   (*i*) Two bath towels
   (*ii*) Two hand towels
   (*iii*) Face towels
   (*iv*) One bath mat
8. Single Rooms :
   (*i*) One bath towel One hand towel
9. One face towel One bath mat.

Fig. 5.60 is typical housekeeping desk flow chart.
Fig. 5.61 is a work schedule for a hotel housekeeper
Fig. 5.62 incates the work programme for a room maid
Fig. 5.63 shows guidelines for houseman.

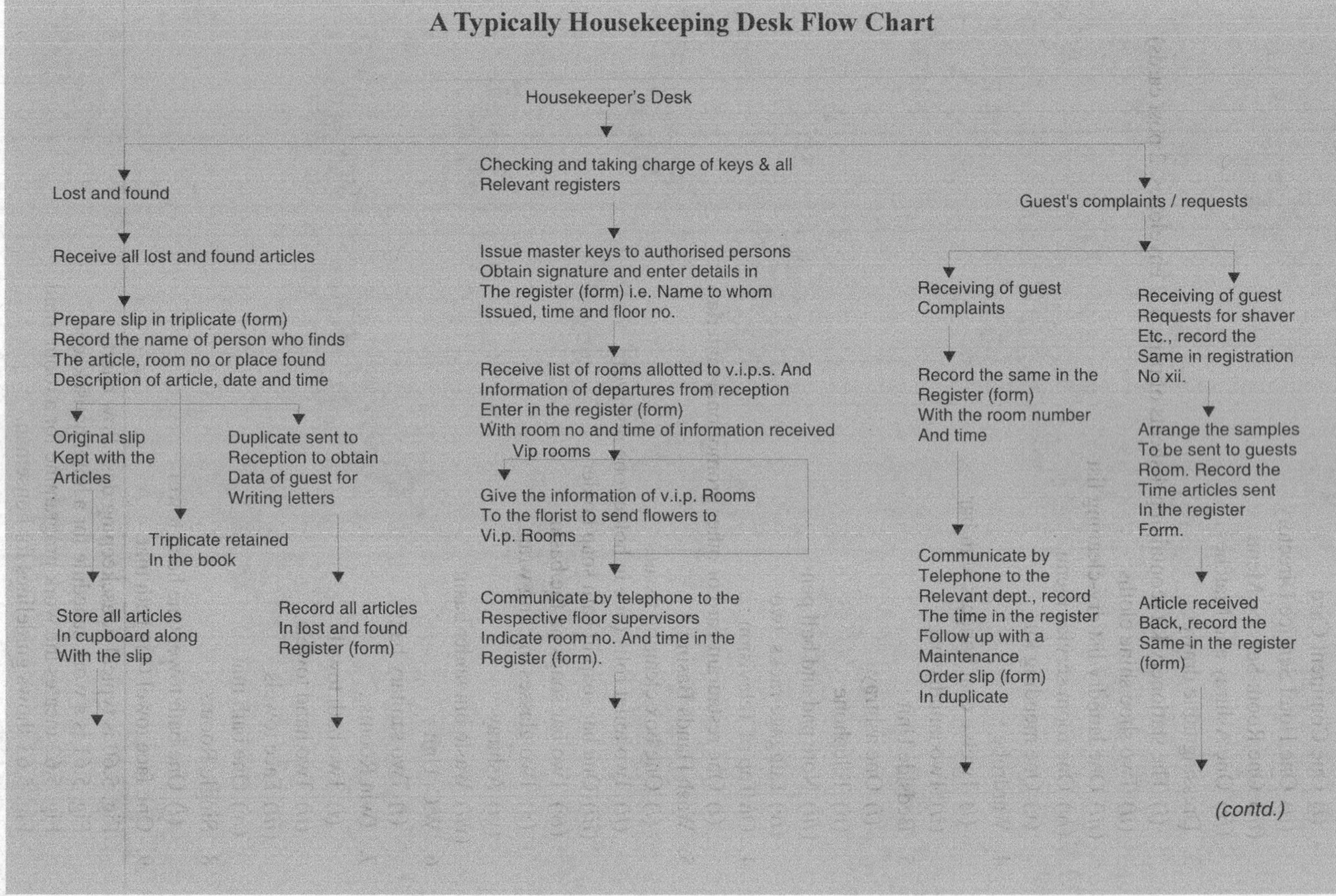
A Typically Housekeeping Desk Flow Chart
Housekeeper's Desk
Lost and found
Receive all lost and found articles
Prepare slip in triplicate (form)
Record the name of person who finds
The article, room no or place found
Description of article, date and time
Original slip
Kept with the
Articles
Store all articles
In cupboard along
With the slip
Triplicate retained
In the book
Duplicate sent to
Reception to obtain
Data of guest for
Writing letters
Record all articles
In lost and found
Register (form)
Checking and taking charge of keys & all
Relevant registers
Issue master keys to authorised persons
Obtain signature and enter details in
The register (form) i.e. Name to whom
Issued, time and floor no.
Receive list of rooms allotted to v.i.p.s. And
Information of departures from reception
Enter in the register (form)
With room no and time of information received
Vip rooms
Give the information of v.i.p. Rooms
To the florist to send flowers to
Vi.p. Rooms
Communicate by telephone to the
Respective floor supervisors
Indicate room no. And time in the
Register (form).
Guest's complaints / requests
Receiving of guest
Complaints
Record the same in the
Register (form)
With the room number
And time
Communicate by
Telephone to the
Relevant dept., record
The time in the register
Follow up with a
Maintenance
Order slip (form)
In duplicate
Receiving of guest
Requests for shaver
Etc., record the
Same in registration
No xii.
Arrange the samples
To be sent to guests
Room. Record the
Time articles sent
In the register
Form.
Article received
Back, record the
Same in the register
(form)
(contd.)

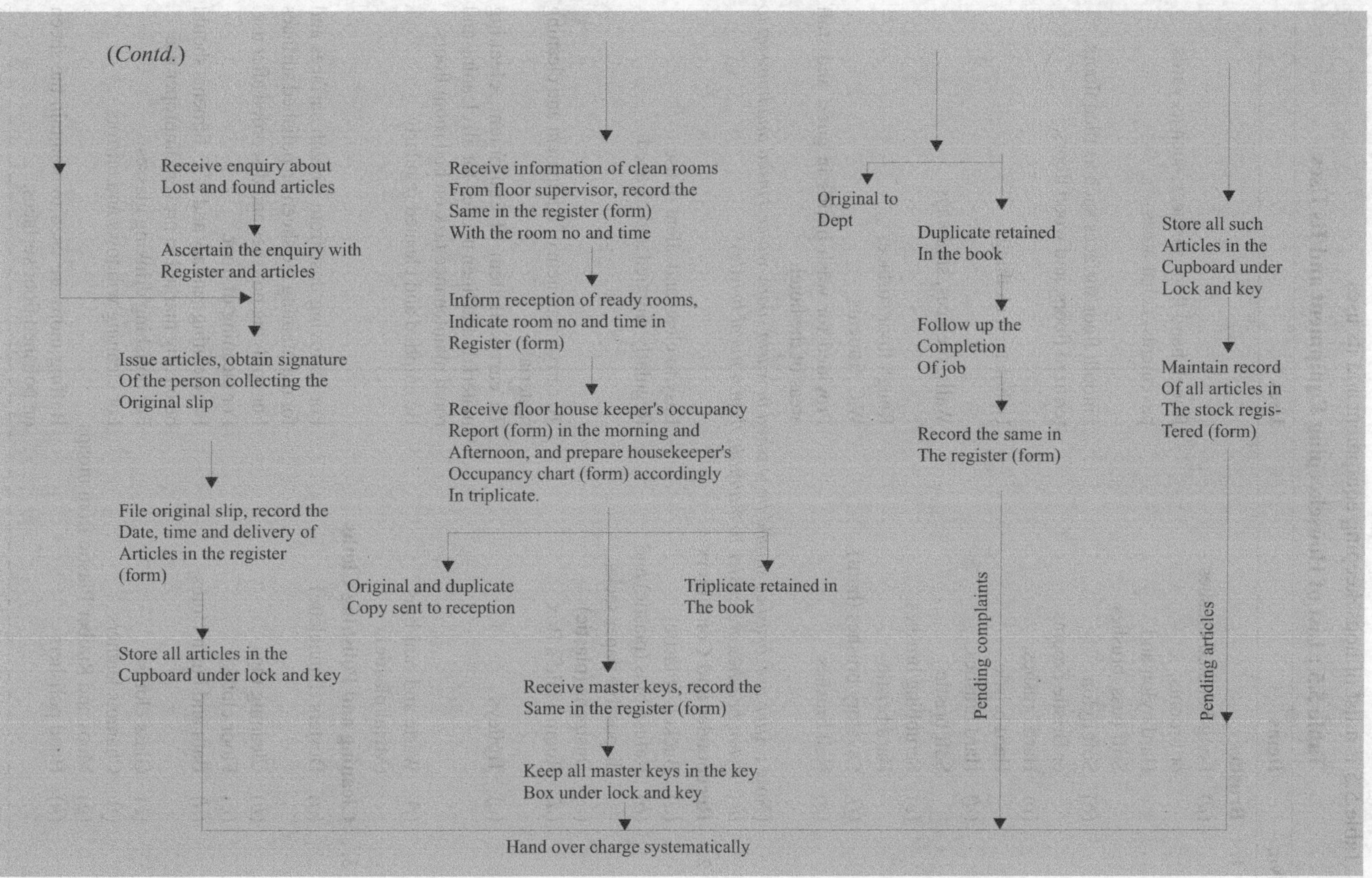

Fig. 5.60. A Typical Housekeeping Desk Flow Chart

Table 5.5 is a list of housekeeping equipment and its uses

Table 5.5 : List of Housekeeping Equipment and Its Uses

S.No.	Items		Uses
1.	**Brushes**		
	(*a*) Long-handled brushes or brooms, Hard nylon and Stiff bass brushes	:	Rough hand floor surfaces, such as yards, pavements, cellar areas
	(*b*) Soft nylon or Bristle brooms	:	Smooth floor surfaces such as tiled floors, terrazzo floors, and wood floors.
	(*c*) Hard brushes, Hard bristle	:	Upholstery, clothing
	(*d*) Hard brushes, Soft bristle	:	Walls, crevices, stairways
	(*e*) Scrubbing brushes Hard bristle	:	Rough floor surfaces
	(*f*) Lavatory brushes (hard)	:	W.C. fitments
	(*g*) Nail brushes	:	Provided for wash-basins in guest and staff areas of the hotel.
	(**Note :** *After use, brushes should be washed in warm soapy water, rinsed and hung up to dry. Nylon brushes are easier to maintain than natural bristl*e)		
2.	**Receptacles and Containers**		
	(*a*) Buckets (Plastic)		Easy to clean and silent in use
	(*b*) Refuse bins (plastic) and disposable paper sacks		Regularly emptied and cleaned
	(*c*) Dustpans (plastic)		
	(*d*) Room Maid's Box		To carry small item of equipment and cleaning materials.
	(*e*) Trolleys		To carry all item of equipment, cleaning materials and linen needed for all cleaning and room maintenance task on bed room floors.
	(*f*) Waste and sani-bins (Metal/plastic)		Be emptied and cleaned regularly
3.	**Cleaning and Polishing Cloths**		
	(*a*) Dusters (flannelette)		For removing dust from smooth surfaces and for maintaining the sheen on polished surfaces
	(*b*) Cleaning rags		For applying polishes and discorded after use.
	(*c*) Floor cloths		For cleaning of floor.
	(*d*) Bath and basin cloths		For cleaning sanitary and W.C. fitments should be clearly marked to prevent improper use
	(*e*) Glass cloths		For polishing drinking glasses
	(*f*) Chamois leathers		For cleaning windows and mirrors
	(g) Mops and Rubber/Plastic from moaps		
	(*h*) Hand polishers		Buffing mops are used to maintain the sheen on polished floor surfaces.

(*Contd...*)

4. Mechanical and Electric Equipment

(*a*) Vacuum cleaners	Used for carpeted areas. Attachment could beused for floors, ledges, upholstery cleaning
(*b*) Box sweeper	Manually operated for cleaning small floor areas
(*c*) Electric scrubbers and polishers	Used for very large floor areas, such as staff corridors, foyer/lobby area
(*d*) Central vacuum cleaning system	Suction inlets may be located throughout the hotel and a range of attachments can be used as required.

5. Sunday Items

(*a*) Dust sheets	For covering furniture and other fittings during major cleaning programs
(*b*) Stool-steps (as required)	For access to storage cupboards
(*c*) Protective Equipment	
Aprons, Overalls, and Gloves	Necessary for dirty cleaning operations.

Work Schedule for a Hotel Housekeeper

Timings		Description of Work
7 to 8.45 a.m.	:	Supervisions of subordinate's work routine viz., room service, cleaning of public rooms
8.45 – 9.15 a.m.	:	Break fast
9.15 – 12.30 p.m.	:	Main duties comprise : (1) Maintaining records Room occupancy Liaison with Reception Manager and others (2) Work supervision and inspection-bed room maintenance and cleaning Linen Room – issue of stocks, inspection of stock equipment (3) Department meetings Meetings with management Meeting with other departmental heads (3) Work scheduling of staff, Holiday reliefs Preparation of work records for wages department Selection and management of new staff
12.30 – 1.30 p.m.	:	Lunch
1.30 – 2.30 p.m.	:	Work supervision and inspection (as above)
either		
2.30 – 4.30 p.m.	:	Work supervision and inspection (as above)
or		
6.30 – 9.30 p.m.		

Fig.5.61. Specimen Work Schedule for a Hotel Housekeeper

Pix. 5.31. Cleaning in Process

Pix. 5.32. Dusting

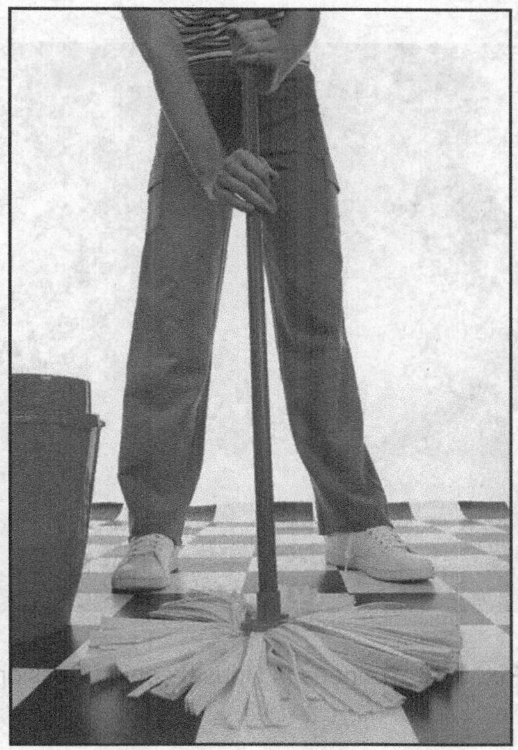

Pix. 5.33. Sweeping Activity

Pix. 5.34. Floor Scrubbing

Pix. 5.35. Trainees in Housekeeping Session

Specimen Work Program of a Room-Maid

Time		Description of work
7.00 to 8.45 a.m.	:	Report for duty
	:	Duties include :
		Service of early morning tea
		Service of breakfasts
8.45 – 9.15 a.m.	:	Breakfast
9.15 – 12.45 p.m.	:	Room cleaning duties,
		Changing lenin
12.45 – 1.30 p.m.	:	Lunch
1.30 – 2.30 p.m.	:	Room cleaning duties
		Tidying and cleaning work trolley
		Floor pantry and equipment
either		
3.00 – 4.30 p.m.	:	Afternoon tea duties
or		
7.00 – 8.30 p.m.	:	Evening duties (room preparation)

Fig.5.62. Specimen Work Program for a Room-Maid

A Typical Guideline Operating Procedure for Floor Housekeepers in Hotels

SCHEDULE FOR HOUSEMEN

While maids are taking room counts, assign houseman his work for the day as mentioned in Fig. 5.62.

1st Vacuum guest elevator foyer daily.

2nd Clean sand jars on guest foyer daily. (Refill sand jars once a week, on day before days off.)

3rd Vacuum out-of-order rooms going in order that day.

4th Vacuum "Special Arrivals."

5th Vacuum standard set-up of eight rooms a day; guestrooms and parlors four days a week.

6th Wash service landings once a week, sweep every day.

7th Day after days off, clean all glasses in guest corridors, glass covering indicator lights and face of clock in guest foyer; polish all brass such as fire extinguishers, etc.

You will help the Assistance Executive Housekeeper in preparing out-of-order rooms going in order that day or you may assign the making up of those rooms to maids, when possible.

Fig.5.63. A Typical Guideline for Housemen

DISTRIBUTION OF PASS KEYS TO MAIDS

1. Pick up your own pass key and maids' pass keys from Executive Housekeeper's Office before going to your floor.

   You are responsible for any pass key while it is in your possession.

   Do not unlock doors for anyone; courteously refer guests to assistant manager.

2. Give each of your maids her pass key and have her sign key slip when she reports to you for work. (Housemen do not have pass keys).

A typical key inventory flowchart is given in fig. 5.64.

Check appearance of each maid when you give pass key to her, making sure her uniform is clean, shoes polished, stockings without runs, hair neat, little or no makeup or jewelry on. Be sure to check for body odor which might be offensive to a guest.

PREPARATION OF SCHEDULES AND REPORTS

Records keeping for the control of payrolls is voluminous and important in this department. On the basis of monthly forecast of occupancy made by the front office, the house-keeping estimates the number of maids needed on any particular day and schedule them accordingly. The two departments constantly report the status of guest rooms to each other. The room clerk reports when a guest checks-out and house-keeping reports back as soon as the room had been serviced and is in order and can be resold. Permanent assignment of rooms cannot be made as it depends upon the number of rooms to be serviced each day,

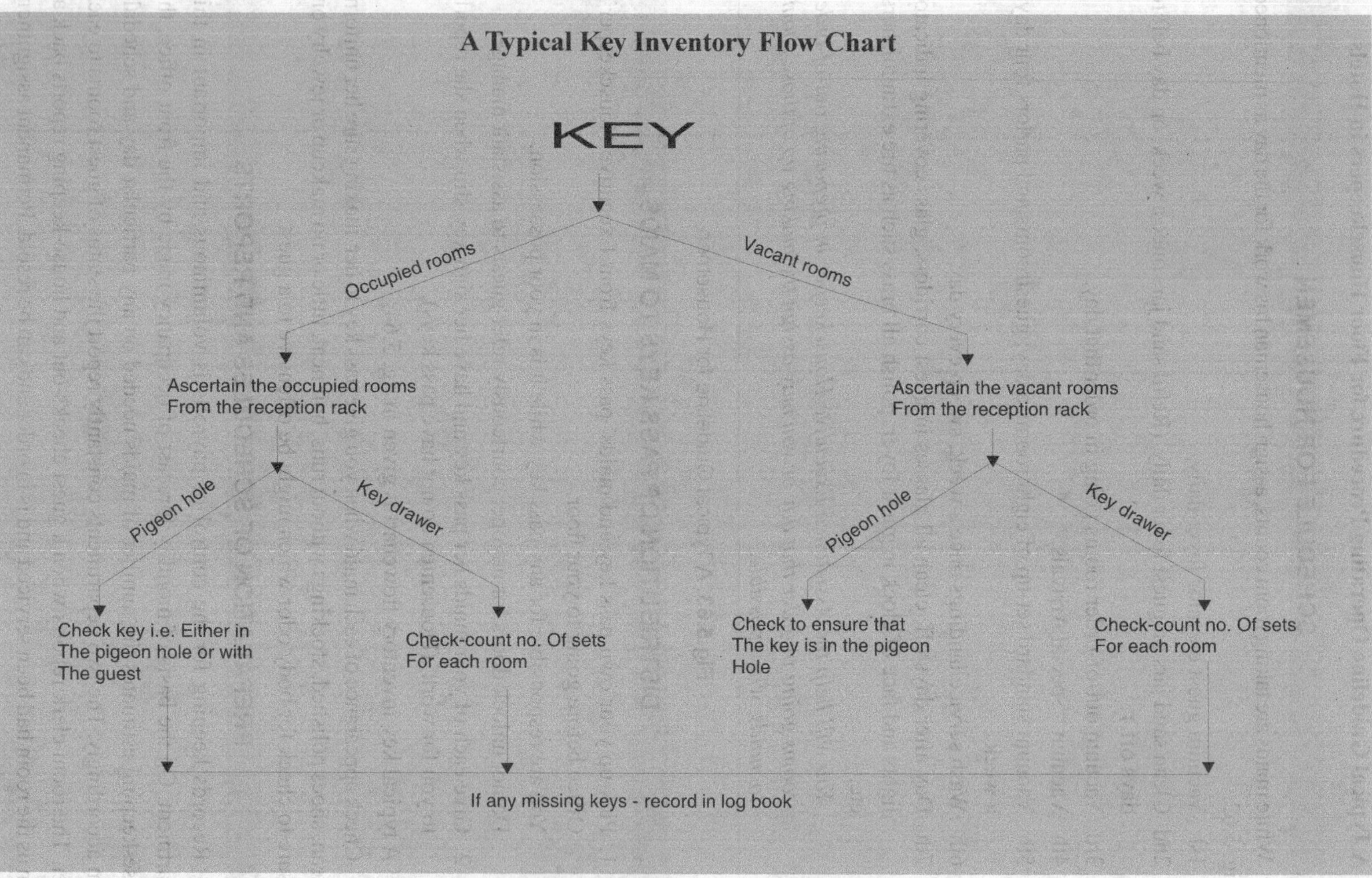

Fig. 5.64. A Typical Key Inventory Flow Chart

out of order rooms, vacant rooms, and sleep outs. It is advisable to assign all the rooms on the same floor to the maid, in order to save time.

HOUSE-KEEPER'S REPORT

The actual assignment of rooms is made by each floor house-keeper on the basis of the current status of room, which is obtained from the maids moving report. Before the start of work, each maid checks the rooms assigned to her and reports the status to the house-keeper. The House-keeper's Report (Figure 5.65) is made on a simple pre-printed sheet listing the room numbers by section or floor with a space for the code. The length of the house-keepers report depends on the size of the hotel. It ranges from a single sheet, listing every room in the hotel to separate sheets for each floor. It is usually prepared in duplicate. The original of the morning report is sent also to the accounts department where it is used to check the preceding nights, to room income. A similar report is also prepared each noon, before the end of the day maid's shift. In this case the original is sent to the front office where it is used to check the room rack, copies of all such reports are retained by the house-keeper. In hotels where the house-keeper's report is prepared in triplicate or in quadruplicate one copy each is sent to the front office, accounts department and the credit department. A HouseKeeper's Discrepancy Report (Figure 5.66) is also prepared which is signed by the reception and night auditor.

PREPARATION HOUSEKEEPER'S ROOM REPORT

1. As soon as all your maids have handed in their "Supplementary Housekeeper's Room Reports" to you, immediately prepare your "Housekeeper's Room Report," indicate by cross mark (X) in proper column and opposite room number on your report all information shown on maid's report.
2. Make out your report in triplicate; then take the three copies at once to :
   (*a*) Room Clerk in Housekeeping Office.
   (*b*) Executive Housekeeper's Office
   (*c*) Keep one copy until 4.30 p.m.

CHECKING PROGRESS OF MAIDS IN THEIR WORK

1. Check each maid's truck/trolly to see that it is properly equipped according to standard equipment listed in "Manual for Maid Training," and adequately supplied with linen and items listed on "Standard Guest room Requirements Card." If not properly equipped or supplied, have the maid equip and supply it properly (or as nearly as possible as sometimes laundry is delayed).
2. Inspect sink closets, fire closets, exit landings and stairway's, employees' lavatories, and service landing to see that they are clean and free of rubbish, and misplaced pieces of furniture; that lights on stairways, exit and service landings are; burning and of correct wattage as indicated on wattage list posted in maid's closet; and that service landing contains only standard equipment. Check rubbish and trash can area. If not clean, notify houseman. Every day a different maid cleans the maids' toilet, schedule to be posted in your linen room.

Housekeeper's Report

ABC HOTEL

Day	Month	Year

Hour	Minute	A.M
		P.M.

1			2			3			4			5		
Code	No. of Guests	Room No.	Code	No. of Guests	Room No.	Code	No. of Guests	Room No.	Code	No. of Guests	Room No.	Code	No. of Guests	Room No.
		301	O		401	O		601			701			801
		302	O		402	O		602	V		702	O		802
		303	O		403	O		603	O		703	O		803
		304	O		404	V		604	O		704			804
		305	O		405	R		605	O		705	O		805
		306	O		406			606	L		706			806
		307	O		407			607	O		707	O		807
		308	O		408			608			708			808
		347			547			647	O		747	V		847
		348	D		548			648	V		748	O		848
		349	L		549			649			749	O		849
		350			550			650			750	V		850

Code : O – Occupied
V – Vacant
D – Departure
L – Luggage Bed under
N – Occupied No-Luggage
R – Repairs
UM – Under Maintenance

Deputy Manager

Fig. 5.65. Specimen Format of Housekeeper's Report

Housekeeper's Discrepancy Report

The ABC HOTEL LTD.

Date ____________

Room	Per Reception Report	Per Housekeeper's Report	Remarks

Reviewed by ....

Prepared by

....

Fig. 5.66. Specimen Format of Housekeeper's Discrepancy Report

MAID'S ROOM REPORT

This report provides better control for the housekeeper. At the end of each shift the maid enters the required information and the housekeeper summarises, signs and forwards the report to the housekeeping payroll clerk, who uses it in preparing the link sheet. This report is sometimes used as the source for preparation of the payroll.

NIGHT-MAID'S REPORT

The reports prepared by the night-maids respond directly to guest's requests. The reports prepared by the nightmaids range from a simple entry in a log book of every call received from a guest and the action taken to a very detailed and elaborate night-maid's report. It is prepared with multiple copies, one copy is dropped off at the front desk so that the room clerk on duty can make a final check of the room rack.

OTHER FORMS

A number of other forms are prepared by the house-keeping staff to meet the requirements of management or the desires of the house-keepers, like :

1. Signature Sheets for Pass Keys issued Daily to Maids
2. Housemen's Daily Room Assignment Sheets for General Cleaning and Miscellaneous Duties
3. Housemen's Work Order
4. Travelling Maids Assignment Sheets
5. Overall Schedules for the Department
6. Time Sheets
7. Weekly Forecast of Payrolls.

CARE AND MAINTENANCE OF CARPETS

In addition to purchasing carpets with due regard to quality and standard, carpeting requires a planned maintenance programme in hotels, such as :

1. Daily light vacuuming to remove loose surface dirt and prevent soil build up.
2. Immediate attention should be paid to soil removal to avoid permanent staining.
3. Carpets should be thoroughly cleaned every week with particular attention to high traffic areas and even those rooms that are infrequently used.
4. Seasonal cleaning with wet shampoo at least once a year. While this can be done with the carpets in place, if practicable, the carpets can be picked up and processed in a commercial cleaning plant.
5. Finally, periodic maintenance include attention to permanently stained areas of carpet and such mechanical problems as open portions, loose ends, snags etc.

CARE OF OTHER FLOORING MATERIALS

Uncarpeted floor areas are in infinite variety in a hotel, for example, many types of demands coverings, formed in place and masonry. Each of these areas demands a different kind of maintenance, special and detailed instructions for keeping them effective as required.

SPRING CLEANING

Routine cleaning can maintain a guestroom's fresh and spotless appearance for a period of time. But after a while, a room will need deep cleaning. In some properties, room attendants on special project basis do deep cleaning; others use teams in which each employee does a particular deep cleaning task. Spring-cleaning removes the dust and dirt that accumulates from everyday wear and tear and attends to cleaning needs identified during a guestroom inspection. It includes activities such as turning mattresses, wiping down walls and baseboards and washing windows and casements. The dirty-ozen can also be perfectly cleaned.

The following are the spring-cleaning tasks that help the property shine are:

1. Flipping and rotating mattresses.
2. Shampooing carpets.
3. Removing soil and stains from wall coverings and baseboards.
4. Washing windows, casements, and shades.
5. Dusting high and hard to reach areas.
6. Cleaning vents and fans.
7. Vacuuming under furniture that requires heavy moving.
8. Cleaning and vacuuming drapes.
9. Cleaning carpet edges.
10. Washing sheer curtains.
11. Washing lampshades.

Spring Cleaning : A Typical Flow Chart

Spring Cleaning

↓

Ascertain-block the room for spring cleaning
record in Register (in co-ordination with Front Office)

↓

Place the furniture at convenient position in the room
and cover properly with old sheets

↓

Remove carpet (if required) and arrange
for stain removal and shampooing

↓

Remove curtains-lamp shades (if required) send
curtains for mending, dry cleaning -clean lamp shades

(*Contd...*)

↓

Clean-paint side walls, ceilling of
room. bath room as assigned

↓

Arrange for attending of services i.e., air- conditioning,
grills (fitters) exhaust grill, plumbing saintaryware,
bathroom fittings, electricalss points,
channel music and electrical fittings etc.

↓

Check-aatend to bathroom tiles, floor

↓

Check-attend to furniture repairs
(remove, if required), polish

↓

Check-clean mirrors, window panes,
glass tops, polish all brass articles

↓

Fix the curtains-rearrange the room as assigned.

Fig. 5.67. Spring Cleaning : A Typical Flow Chart

INSPECTION OF GUEST ROOMS

1. Look over "Housekeeper's Room Report" to find out which rooms are listed as "sleep outs" and O.K. Inspect these rooms first so they will be ready to sell (although obviously no: until the "sleep out" becomes a c/o).
2. Inspect a check-out room as soon as possible after it has been put in order. A check-out room should not be out-of-order" over an hour after a guest departs.
3. At least every hour during your shift, pick up list of check-out rooms to be made up. Turn in O.K. rooms as soon as possible.

Following is a list of items to inspect in an O.K. room (one that had not been occupied previous night):

4. **Inspection of Bathroom**
   (*a*) Floor: See that it is clean and that there are no broken or loose tiles.
   (*b*) Walls: See that they are clean and that there are no cracks or broken or loose tiles, and that ceiling is clean and has no cracks. Make sure top of tiling is clean.
   (*c*) Nickel fixtures : Check to see that they are polished.
   (*d*) Faucets and shower head: See whether they leak. (Be sure that shower head regulator is open so shower can drain.)
   (*e*) Soap recess: Grab handle part of soap recess in bathtub to see that it is not broken.

(*f*) Fixtures: Check toilet bowl, tub or shower and washbasin to be sure they are clean, not cracked, and that drains are working.

(*g*) Water pressure: Check water pressure by turning on faucets and flushing toilet. (Also check ice water faucet at this time.)

(*h*) Toilet seat: Check to see that it is thoroughly clean with sterilized band on it.

(*i*) Bath cabinet: See that it is clean, has no broken shelves, and that door works.

(*j*) Supplies: Check supplies such as towels, soap, etc., to see that bathroom is correctly supplied according to "Standard Guest Room Requirements Card.

5. Inspection of Guest room

(*a*) Check carpet to see that it has been properly vacuumed, has no tears or spots. Be sure: to look along baseboard and underneath beds, dresser, desk and chairs for dust and dirt.

(*b*) Move out furniture from wall when inspecting underneath. Backs of beds, dresser and desk are also to be inspected to see if they have been dusted by houseman.

(*c*) Inspect windows, sills and sashes to see that they are clean and undamaged; check draperies to see that they are clean, linings not torn, and drapery tiebacks attached on two separate hooks.

(*d*) Inspect furniture, being sure there are no stains on it.

6. In a check-out room:

(*a*) Inspect bathroom for same things as in an O.K. room.

(*b*) Inspect beds to see that linen has been changed and beds properly made. Lift spread and blankets to determine this.

(*c*) Inspect carpet in bedroom for same things as in an O.K. room.

(*d*) Inspect windows and draperies for same things as in an O.K. room.

(*e*) Inspect walls and ceiling in bedroom to see if they need washing or have cracks. Pictures on walls should be checked at the same time to see that they are clean, undamaged and hung straight.

(*f*) Check all lamps in bedroom to see that they are dusted, in working order, their shades in good condition, and that bulbs are of correct wattage as indicated on wattage list posted in maid's closets.

Note: *Lamps on dresser, desks, beds, etc., are checked when that piece of furniture is inspected by you.*

(*g*) Inspect clothes closet to see that walls/are clean and free of baggage marks, shelf and floor are clean (run hand over shelf for dust); clothes pole is dusted; pants hanger attached to wall or door and not bent out of shape; closet has standard set-up of hangers and laundry bag.

Note: *Twin bedroom has extra baggage rack in closet.*

(*h*) Inspect bureau to see that mirror is polished. Open drawers to see that they have been washed, a laundry bag is in bottom drawer, and that "Do Not Disturb" card and "Special Maid Service" card are in top drawer.

Note: *Metal fixtures on all furniture such as drawer handles, knobs, etc., should also be checked as you come to them. (This includes door knobs and door chains.)*

(*i*) Inspect night table to see that it has a memo pad, a breakfast menu, and reminder card to order breakfast the night before. Check telephone to see that it is working by lifting receiver; inspect mouthpiece for cleanliness. Check card to see that it is not frayed; check controls (1) and (2) on radio to see that they are working and radio compartment to see that it is locked; phone book (central section) with cover on night stand; yellow classified book in bottom dresser drawer.

(*j*) Inspect desk to see that it is correctly supplied according to "Standard Guest-room Requirements Card," and that pen is in working order.

Note: *At least one ash tray with matches to be on desk or dresser.*

(*k*) Inspect waste basket beside desk to see 'that it has been properly cleaned.

(*l*) Inspect all chairs and baggage rack to see that material is not worn, ripped or burned, springs not broken, wood free of splinters, and legs and arms not broken or cracked.

(*m*) Inspect servidor to see that it is clean, contains one hanger, and that locks work.

(*n*) Check ventilator over entrance door to see that it opens and closes easily, and that rate card is in holder on inside of door.

(*o*) Inspect thumb bolts on connecting doors to see that they are safely locked. Note: Keep a sharp lookout while inspecting rooms for articles left by guests that maid overlooked. If you find an article, attach paper with room number on it. Immediately take it to Lost and Found.

(*p*) Inspect all door frames as you come to them to see that they are clean.

7. In a reoccupied room—Inspect it the same way you do a regular check-out room except that the guest's belongings are not disturbed during inspection.

Note: *If guest is in room when you go in to inspect it, explain to guest that you were not able to inspect the room before his arrival but can inspect it now with his permission.*

8. In a parlor—Inspect it the way you do a regular check-out room except that there is no bathroom or bed in this type of room.

Note: *Be sure to lift up all loose cushions in room to see that they are clean and to see if any small articles have slipped down between side of cushion and chair or underneath cushion.*

9. In an occupied room—Inspect room to see that it is generally neat in appearance and that bathroom and desk are supplied according to standard set-up; guest's belongings are not disturbed, of course, during inspection.

Note: *As far as possible you should inspect all occupied rooms each day.*

PREPARATION OF TROUBLE REPORT

1. During inspection of rooms, make notes in your Memo Book of each defect or unsatisfactory condition which you find. Your notes will be of two kinds:

(*a*) Items for which you will need to make out a trouble report.

(*b*) Items which you can turn over immediately to your maid or houseman for prompt handling.

2. Prepare trouble reports as time permits during your shift as follows:

(*a*) Make out a separate trouble report for each craft (carpenters, electricians, etc.), listing all items needing attention.

Note: *Any furniture, plumbing, etc., reported to you by maid or housemen as needing repairs or cleaning is put on a trouble report.*

(*b*) If you find or learn of a defect or condition that must be taken care of at once, report it by "Tachography" to proper department.

Note: *Be sure and follow up your "Tachography" report to see that it is given immediate attention; if necessary, telephone executive housekeeper's office to see that it is being done.*

Note: *When a maid reports to you about guest damage to furniture, or you find such damage during your inspection of rooms, immediately report this by phone to executive housekeeper.*

(*c*) If, on inspection, you find a defect or condition which had been previously reported on a trouble report and not attended to, telephone department to which you sent report; find out if report was received; if so, find out how soon the condition can be cared for.

(*d*) Trouble report is prepared in triplicate; copies to be time-stamped and distributed as follows:

(*i*) One to department that will correct the trouble.

(*ii*) Second to executive housekeeper,

(*iii*) Third copy to be held till job is done, then taken to executive housekeeper's office.

3. If you find a room service table in the hall on your round of inspection, notify Room Service by phone to remove it.

4. Always be alert for suspicious persons on the floors, including employees who have no obvious business there. Report presence of such persons immediately to assistant manager.

REPORTING SICKNESS OF A GUEST

When a maid reports sickness of a guest to you, immediately notify Executive Housekeeper.

REPORTING LOSS OF LINEN OR BEDDING

When a maid reports loss of any linen or bedding to you, immediately notify executive housekeeper's office by phone.

REPLACING STAINED, TORN, BURNED BEDDING OR LINEN

(*a*) When maids bring your blankets, bedspreads, etc., that have been burned, torn or stained, give them clean, fresh ones from your supply closet in exchange; send stained or torn bedding down to Linen Room.

(*b*) When you need supply of clean blankets, go to the Linen Room on the Service Floor and take an ample supply to keep in your closets.

ORDERING SUPPLIES

When you bring down your cart for the next day's bathroom glasses, attach your requisition for supplies for the following day. The night linen room attendant will fill this order.

Note: *The removal of soap from occupied guestrooms before it is almost used up is controlled by you through checking the number of cakes distributed daily to a maid in relation to number of rooms occupied in her section.*

Note : *Old razor blaces and used soap are turned in to you daily by your maids. Keep these articles in closet during week, on Friday send to the linen room by the houseman.*

CHECK ROOMS WITH "DO NOT DISTURB" SIGNS

At 2:30 p.m. check rooms with "Do Not Disturb" cards on doors by first finding out from the maid if room has had room service; if not, telephone room and ask occupant how soon he wants room made up. If no answer to phone call, immediately notify assistant manager.

CHECK MAID'S ROOM SLIPS

Around 3:30 p.m. check each of your maids' room slips to find out which rooms they have not made up. List all rooms that will not be made up by 4:00 p.m., and 1urn in to executive housekeeper's office when you go off duty; also list on blackboard in Linen Room for the night maids.

CART AND CLOSET INSPECTION AT END OF SHIFT

(*a*) At end of shift, inspect maids' carts and maids' closets to see that maids are leaving them clean and orderly.

(*b*) Keep in mind that the company purchases only the best equipment, so it is important that all workers under you knew how to use each piece of equipment properly, and also how to take cart of it.

INSPECT GUEST ELEVATOR FOYER

Just before you leave your floor, inspect guest elevator foyer to see that it is clean and neat looking. Check sand jars to see that they are clean.

COLLECT PASS KEYS

At 3:50 p.m. collect all pass keys, take them to the executive housekeeper's office, place them in cabinet.

TRAINING MAID OR HOUSEMAN

When training a maid or houseman, use the training material and procedure as set up in the "Manual for Maid Training" or "Manual for Floor Houseman Training."

Although it seems, from the foregoing detailed instructions to the inspectors or floor supervisor, that nothing should go unattended to in a well-staffed hotel, it is still possible that the inspector will not) notice neglected duties because there simply is not time on all days to check every detail in a full quota of rooms.

Many maids build a reputation for doing a good job and supervisors do not bother to check up on them, preferring to spend their time inspecting those whose performance is less praiseworthy or consistent. But even that A plus maid may be interrupted in her work and forget to carry on where she left off, or, because she was hurried by a guest, she may neglect proper cleaning procedures.

For Example

1. Even a small spot on the lampshade is noticed by keen-eyed inspectress. After discovering it, above, she makes a note on the Repair Sheet that a handyman should bring a clean shade to room and return spotted one to Linen Room.
2. In a bathroom, she pays special attention to whether all guest's give-aways are in order, whether proper number of bath linens are in place, as pictured below, and whether fixtures arc clean and shining.
3. Inspectress is responsible for 60 rooms daily. She checks all V.I.P. rooms, "pre-reg's," c/o's as well as other rooms at random. Maids never know which of their rooms will be examined. Working like a white-gloved military inspector, inspectress, above, makes certain no item is dusty, even the tops of picture frames.

   Another reason an unclean or damaged room might accidentally be rented is because an inspectress has noted something on weekend that needs repair or redoing but, knowing that there is no help available there on a Sunday, does not bother to report it. Or, if he or she has reported the same damaged item before, and found, after several weeks, it still had not been repaired or properly cleaned, may simply stop trying to get action since it seems nobody cares. In the chapter on Controls we will consider ways to double-check these kinds of problems.

   In one of the hotel it was found that the supervisors and inspectors apparently are very observing and always alert because the hotel has abandoned all checklists– "there system of inspection is 'Follow your right hand around the room and train your eyes to cover ceiling to floor as you check."
4. Closer inspection covers items shown below to make sure that there are enough dangers; laundry bags are in place; mirror is clean. Each item is checked off on the "Please Do" form which is retained in files.

HOUSEKEEPER'S ROUTINE INSPECTION

Following the room maid's cleaning and other work routines, systematic inspection of complete work and of the condition and general state of furnishings should be installed. This takes the form of a check list so that the housekeeper or her assistant do not overlock any important features. A systematic approach to this activity is essential. One night start at the door and work methodically around the room as given fig. 5.68.

Housekeepers Business Routine Inspection Procedure

1. Entrance Door
   - (*a*) Cleanliness
   - (*b*) Condition of paint work,
   - (*c*) Condition of wood work
   - (*d*) Condition of furniture
   - (*e*) Check for 'Do not Disturb' card check for other notices
2. Entrance Area
   - (*a*) Cleanliness of Floor
   - (*b*) Cleanliness of walls
   - (*c*) Cleanliness of cupboard
   - (*d*) Cleanliness of luggage rack and light switches
   - (*e*) Check that switches function properly
3. Bathroom
   - (*a*) General Cleanliness
   - (*b*) Condition and working of all sanitary and other fittings
   - (*c*) Noting special mirrors
   - (*d*) Noting electrical sockets
   - (*e*) Noting toilet papers
   - (*f*) Noting Paper tissue holder
   - (*g*) Noting Tapes and washes
   - (*h*) Noting Toilet pipes (blockings)
   - (*i*) Noting Linen
   - (*j*) Noting Extract ventilation
   - (*k*) Noting Walls and floor
   - (*l*) Noting Shower curtain
   - (*m*) Soap and soapholder Drip dry clothes hangers
   - (*n*) Heated towel rail General decoration order Light fittings
4. Bedrooms
   - (*a*) Work around room in one direction (say anti-clockwise) noting the following :
   - (*b*) Cleanliness
   - (*c*) Cleanliness condition and working of all furnishing fittings and other items-neat appearance and make up of beds, bed side fittings (radio, telephone, direction, ashtrays etc.)
   - (*d*) Cleanliness Pictures, window, curtains
   - (*e*) Cleanliness Heated controls, loose chairs

(*f*) Cleanliness writing make up unildrawers wriling paper and other equipment

(*g*) Cleanliness wastebin walls ceiling,

(*h*) Cleanliness light fittings, flooring and

(*i*) Cleanliness general decoration

Fig. 5.68. Housekeepers Routine Inspection Procedure

LINEN

Whether to rent or buy linens is subject of continuous debate. Linen can be a major investment and the choice of this product is not easy. Small hotels generally decide to rent linens if the rental service is both reasonable and dependable. The increasing demand of particularly non-iron linens and uniforms goes in favour of owning linens in hotels.

LINEN ROOM AND UNIFORM ROOM

The linen and uniform room is the heart of the house-keeping department. Like store rooms for reserve linen and guest rooms for cleaning and other supplies, the linen and uniform room is adjacent to executive house-keeping's office. All articles are received and issued by linen room uniform personnel. Each day the linen room person counts and sorts the soiled linen and prepares it for the laundry. The night person counts and distributes the clean linen and all supplies to the maid's store rooms on each floor. Overstocking and understocking both are harmful for the hotel.

LAUNDRY

The form of contract between hotels and laundries may be the subject of agreement or standard conditions applicable in the case of domestic customers may apply. Some of the more usual provisions of these agreements are :

1. No article exposed to infection may be sent to a laundry; to do so would be an offence under laws.

2. The laundry has a general lien on article sent by a customer for all charges due.

3. Compensation for loss or damage of articles while in the possession of the laundry as the result of negligence of the laundry's employes may be subject to a maximum amount related to charge for washing.

4. A laundry may refuse responsibility for any of the following :

(*a*) Damage arising from defective manufacture, deterioration, unsuitable or faulty material, or incorrectly described articles

(*b*) Damage arising from fugtive colour, shrikages or distortion, unsuitable for faulty material, or incorrectly discribe articles.

(*c*) Damage to certains or blinds ;

(*d*) Loss of an articles not indelibly and distnctly marked with customer's name in full.

(*e*) Loss of any article not plainly described in the book or list bearing the customer's name and address sent to the laundry with the article;

(*f*) Loss of any money, jewllery or valuables included with any article sent to the laundry :

(*g*) Absence of proof that the article was duly received by the laundry.

Where an hotel installs a laundry machinary on its own premises and employees staff solely or mainly for this purpose, it is likely that Factory Act will apply, in which case certain obligation under that Act must be observed. The local factory inspector should be consulted. The wages of staff employes will be governed by the respective local muncipal/laws state.

LINEN ROOM

Location of linen room is an important factor. It must provide direct and easy occurs for laundry baskets rough the goods entrance and facilitate distribution of stocks with in the hotel.

The main functions of the central linen room are :

(1) Checking, inspecting, repairing and marking of linen.

(2) The issue of clean linen in good repair to staff and departments controlling return of soiled and covered item.

(3) Linen sorting preparation of records and the despatch of dirty linen to be laundry.

(4) Maintaining records of stock in uses, in store and the laundry.

(5) Scheduling the re-use of worn out linen.

(6) Storage and contract of hired linen stock and of disposable items used certain the department.

(7) Handling personal laundry of guest and staff.

The internal layout of the hotel linen room should consider point such as ease and cost of operation. Special feature to be taken into account include the problem of linen flow, adequate work space for inspection and repair work, storage space for laundry baskets, and open slatted shelf space for the storage of bed - linen, towels, conifoms, restaurant linen and other laundry stocks. Storage space requirements are affected by the size of linen stocks held in the hotel; quantilies are difficult to lay down as the size of stocks is affected by the rate of use, laundering time, and the period repaired for reordering new items. When an hotel hires all its linen requirement less storage space is generally required.

For close visual work and the temperature and ventilations of the store, adequate illumination must be provided. Store must be closely controlled in order to prevent stock deterioration. Frequent stock checks be made to show the, effectiveness of control measure used by the department. All stock should be checked on the same day. Details of stock held in the linen room raids and other members of staff, and by departments (*e.g.* restaurant table clothes, kitchens cloths, Waiter napkins and so on) Finally, details of linen sent to laundry should be added, and the final total should be entered in the Stock Book. The cause of major discrepancies must be investigated immediately and appropriate measure introduced cannot delay to prevent further loss. (Ref. Fig. 5.69).

Linen of Equipment Stock Book

Sl. No.	ITEM	Stock in Hand 9.6.2000	Stock Added	Sub-total	Conde -mned	Total	Discle Paneies	Stock in Hand 10.7.2000
1.	Towels :	...	...	...	...	...	...	...
	Face	...	...	...	...	...	...	...
	Rough	...	...	...	...	...	...	...
	Smooth	...	...	...	...	...	...	...
2.	Bath	...	...	...	...	...	...	...
3.	Lavatory	...	...	...	...	...	...	...
4.	Roller	...	...	...	...	...	...	...
5.	Bath Mats	...	...	...	...	...	...	...

Fig.5.69. Specimen of a Linen and Equipmtant Stock Book

CONTROL ISSUE

The room maid and the restaurant maintain their own stocks of linen for every day use or for emergncies. It becomes a responsibility of the members of the staff to account for their stocks and as required to exchange soiled linen for fresh supplies.

The procedure of 'Clean for soiled' works well for individual staff members as well as for departments and linen room staff can readily check for the loss or misure of individual items.

SOILED LINEN

Despatch lists must be made out for all linen sent to be laundry and returns checked carefully. Shortages must be reported to the laundry as soon as possible and satisfactory explanation obtained.

OVER STOCK

The linen requirement need frequent assessment and stock levels must be controlled accordingly. Before recording linen to replenish stock, access the suitability and wearing qualities of individual line, and make special notes for delivering periods for different items especially where particular instructions accompany an order.

RECEIPT OF NEW LINEN

On receipt of consignment of new linen, check each delivery and note down any descrepancies. Observation must also be made to verify quality, size in the case of sheets and table clothes and prices. On satisfying that each delivery for complete, the Housekeeper signs and pass the Delivery Advice to management.

STOCK

All linen must be examined after its return from the laundry and where possible damage should be required before further use. When linen is no longer suitable for normal case, it should be withdrawn from stock and either discarded or used for other purposes. The Housekeeper many wish to control the 'write off' of such items.

ROTATION OF STOCK

All item of linen held in stock be brought forward to care in rotation to ensure equal wear. Linen which remain unused for any length of time may attract dust and may become discoloured. Other symptoms of inadequate storage includes: *Rust mould*, *Mold dew*, *Moths*, *Other Stain* etc.

PERSONAL LAUNDRY AND DRY CLEANING

The work concerning guests and staff in personal clothing send to laundry is normally handled by the linen room. Clean linen received by the hotel is returned to the guest and special care must be taken to check that approval charge are placed on the green's hotel account. Members of staff are generally expected to pay for their own personal laundry. Laundrying and dry-cleaning of staff uniform is normally provided free of charge.

MARKING LINEN

All items of linen should be embroidered or neatly marked with the name or initials of the hotel. Figure or colour codes may be used to indicate the year and month each item of linen is put in to circulation.

HIRED LINEN

Some hotel hire their linen requirements from an outside conductor. The savings on storage space, heavey capital investment in stocks and or maintaining a repairs section in the linen room can be considerable.

MISCELLANEOUS ITEMS AND EQUIPMENT

A number of items for the use of the guests in addition to be stock of linen disposals, cleaning equipment and cleaning agents may be held by the hotel, such as :

1. Stationary – Writing pads, telephone directories, local events folders and other items for use in guest rooms.
2. 'Do not Disturb' and other hotel notices, laundry and dry cleaning lists.
3. Costs and emergency beds and bedding, bed boards.
4. Convector heaters for supplementary heating.
5. Candle for emergency lighting.
6. Garden furniture for are on guest room balconies.
7. Hot water bottles.
8. Book matches, emergency sewing and repair kits.
9. Waste bins.
10. Television sets.

Linen inventory control and laundering is the responsibility of the house-keeper. An operating par stock must be maintained. It is ideally five times the daily amount in use as determined by the number of beds and bathrooms in the hotel. This makes sufficient arrangement for one set in the rooms and one each in the laundry, the maids floor closet and the linen room and in transit. Circulating par stock for restaurant linens is more difficult to set up and maintain. Compared to the dining room, the banquet poses the real problem. Control of the reserve linen is very important. The store room must be properly and securely locked with access given to only authorised personnel. No item must be removed without a requisition approved by the house- keeper and a perpetual inventory must be kept reflecting purchases, issues and balance on hand. Frequent stock checks, physical counting of every item in stock after every six months must be done.

Fig. 5.70 is an organizational chart for Linen Room. Fig. 5.71 indicates Room Linen Flow Chart, Fig. 5.72 Restaurant Linen Flow Chart (Laundry Department), Fig. 5.73 Uniform Flow Chart, Fig. 5.74. Guest Room Linen Flow Chart and Fig. 5.75 shows the Uniform Flow Chart (Laundry Department).

Keeping track of the circulating linen is another problem. The linen is taken out for normal wear and tear, improper use, a carelessness in handling, losses in the laundry and theft.

The main functions of this department are :

1. Checking, inspecting, repairing and marking of linen
2. Issue of linen to staff and departments and control of the return of soiled and unused items

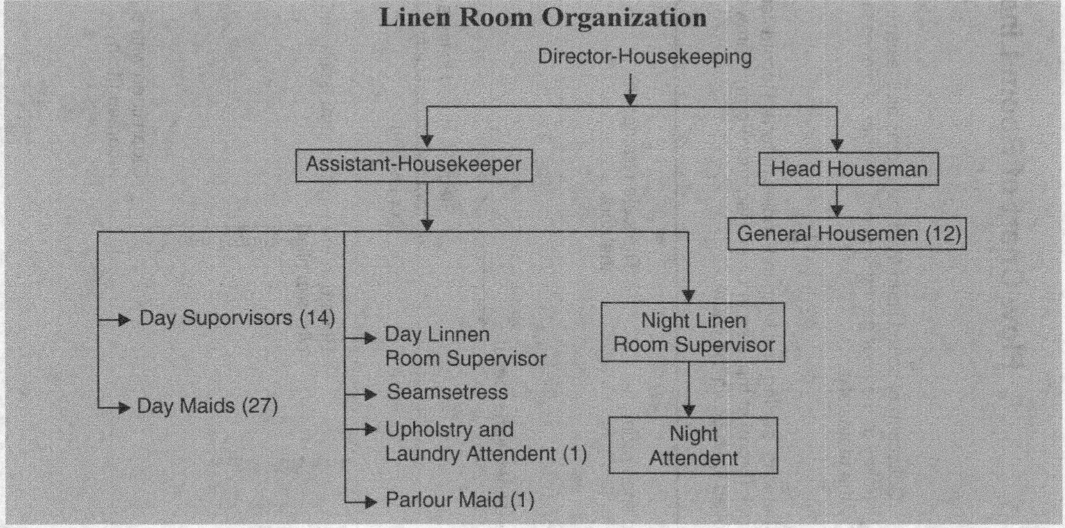

Fig. 5.70. Typical Organisational Chart for a Linen Room

3. Linen's sorting, preparation of records and despatch of dirty linen to the laundry
3. Maintain records of linen
4. Storage and control of hired linen
5. Handling personal laundry of guests and staff.

The staff of this section includes :

1. Head linen keeper
2. Linen room employees
3. Seamstresses.

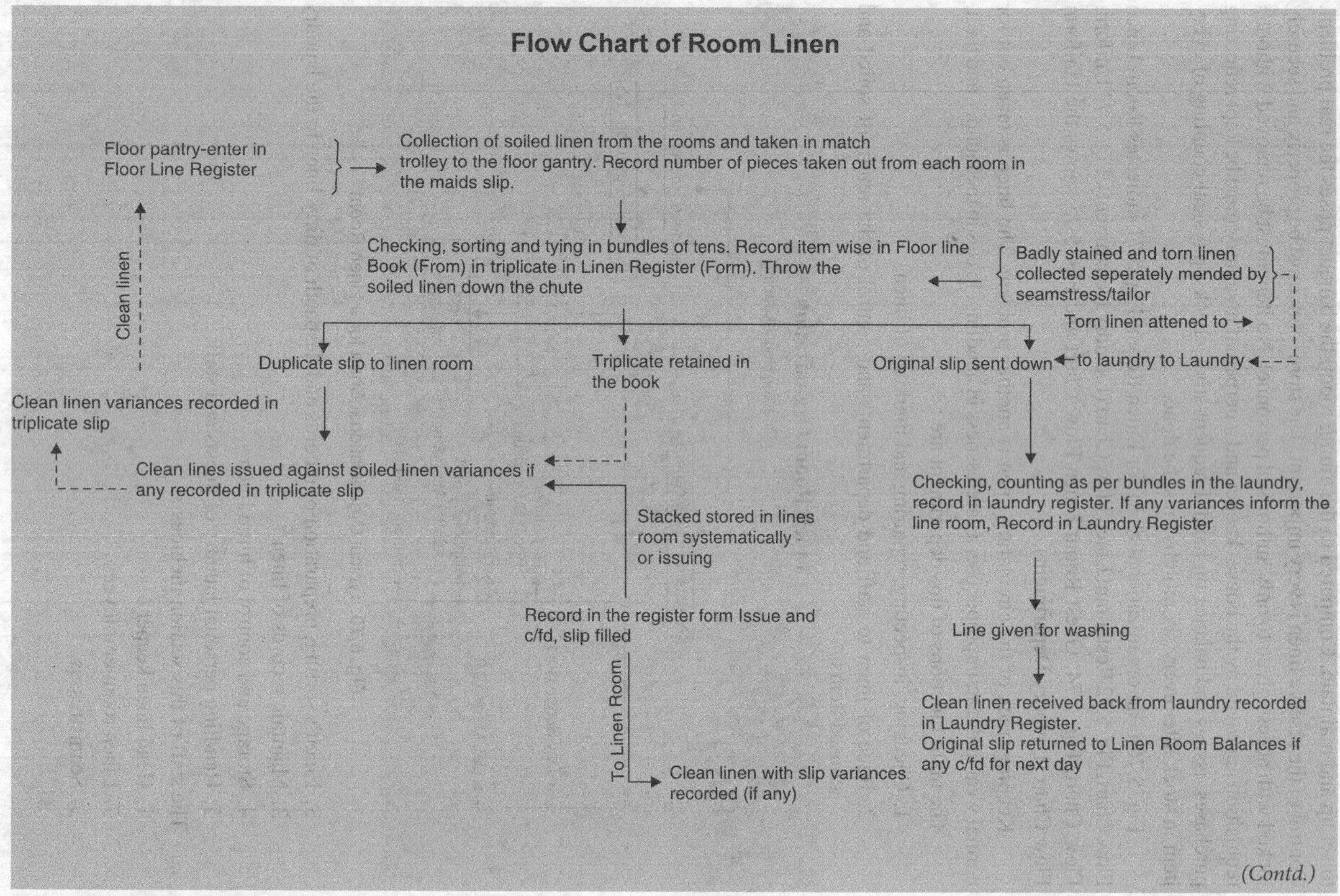
Flow Chart of Room Linen
Floor pantry-enter in Floor Line Register
Collection of soiled linen from the rooms and taken in match trolley to the floor gantry. Record number of pieces taken out from each room in the maids slip.
Checking, sorting and tying in bundles of tens. Record item wise in Floor line Book (From) in triplicate in Linen Register (Form). Throw the soiled linen down the chute
Badly stained and torn linen collected seperately mended by seamstress/tailor
Torn linen attened to
Clean linen
Duplicate slip to linen room
Triplicate retained in the book
Original slip sent down
to laundry to Laundry
Clean linen variances recorded in triplicate slip
Clean lines issued against soiled linen variances if any recorded in triplicate slip
Stacked stored in lines room systematically or issuing
Checking, counting as per bundles in the laundry, record in laundry register. If any variances inform the line room, Record in Laundry Register
Record in the register form Issue and c/fd, slip filled
Line given for washing
To Linen Room
Clean linen received back from laundry recorded in Laundry Register.
Original slip returned to Linen Room Balances if any c/fd for next day
Clean linen with slip variances recorded (if any)

(Contd.)

(Contd...)

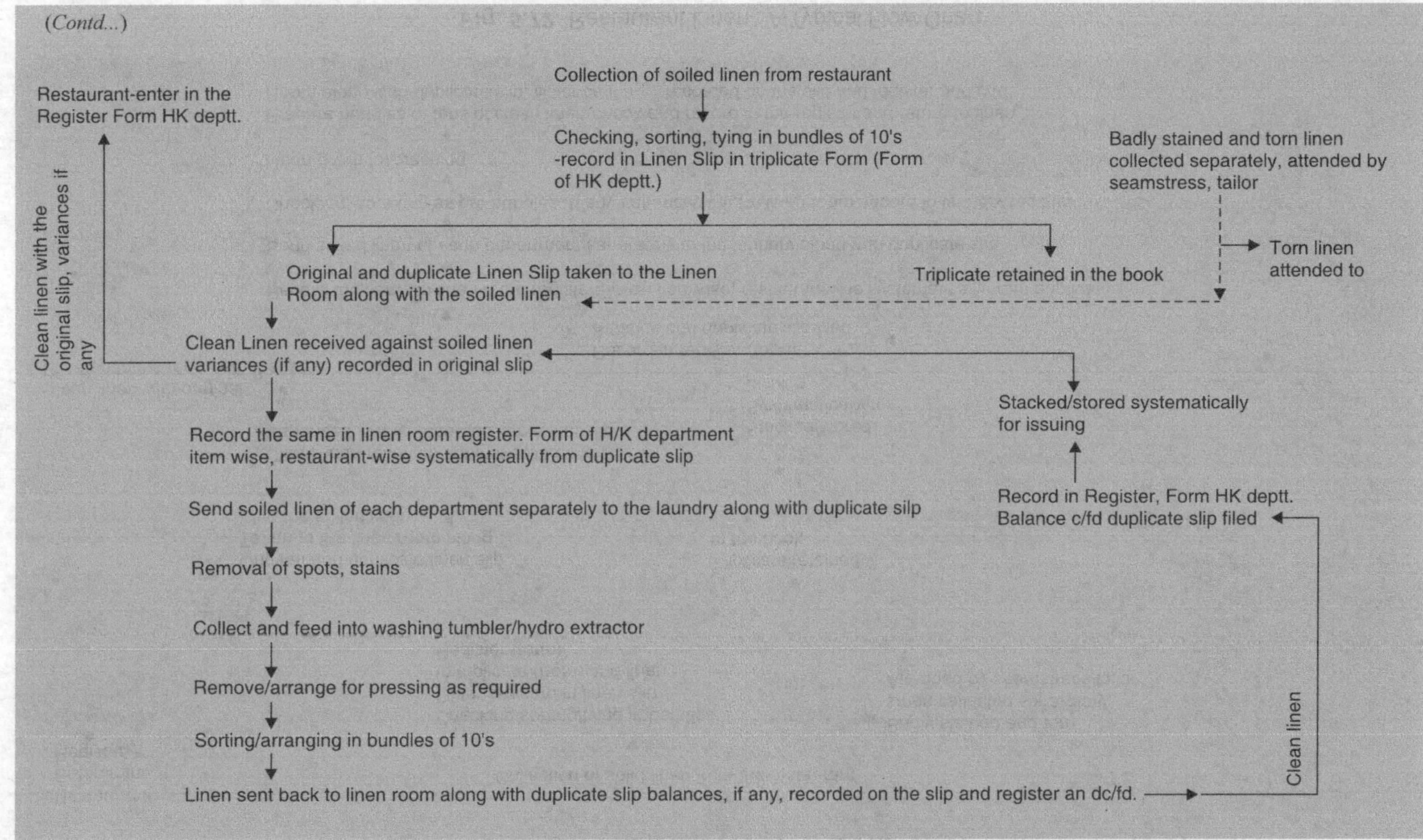

Fig. 5.71 : A Typical Flow Chart of Room Linen

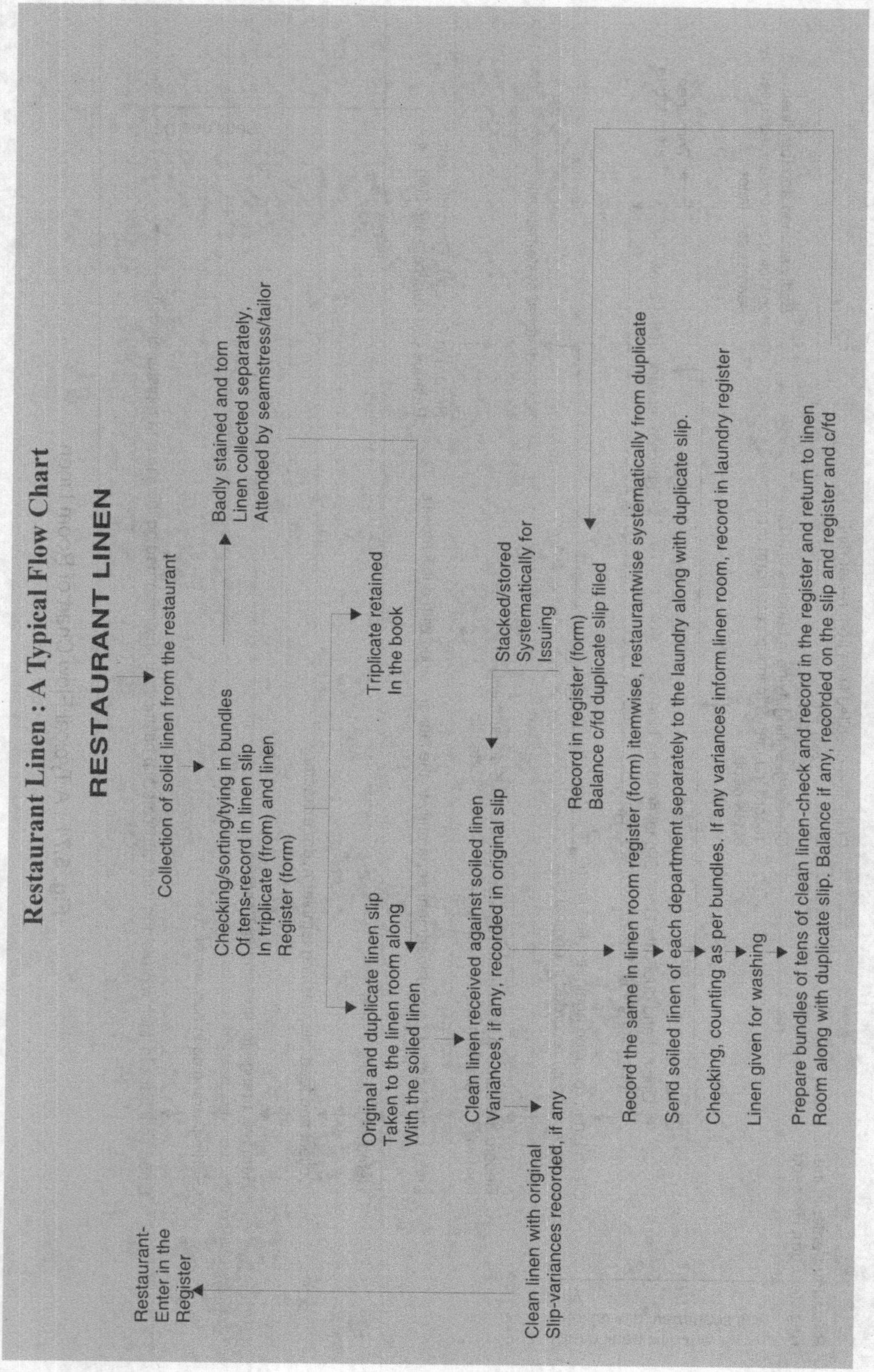

Restaurant Linen : A Typical Flow Chart

RESTAURANT LINEN

Collection of solid linen from the restaurant

Checking/sorting/tying in bundles
Of tens-record in linen slip
In triplicate (from) and linen
Register (form)

Badly stained and torn
Linen collected separately,
Attended by seamstress/tailor

Original and duplicate linen slip
Taken to the linen room along
With the soiled linen

Triplicate retained
In the book

Clean linen received against soiled linen
Variances, if any, recorded in original slip

Stacked/stored
Systematically for
Issuing

Clean linen with original
Slip-variances recorded, if any

Restaurant-
Enter in the
Register

Record in register (form)
Balance c/fd duplicate slip filed

Record the same in linen room register (form) itemwise, restaurantwise systematically from duplicate

Send soiled linen of each department separately to the laundry along with duplicate slip.

Checking, counting as per bundles. If any variances inform linen room, record in laundry register

Linen given for washing

Prepare bundles of tens of clean linen-check and record in the register and return to linen
Room along with duplicate slip. Balance if any, recorded on the slip and register and c/fd

Fig. 5.72. Restaurant Linen : A Typical Flow Chart

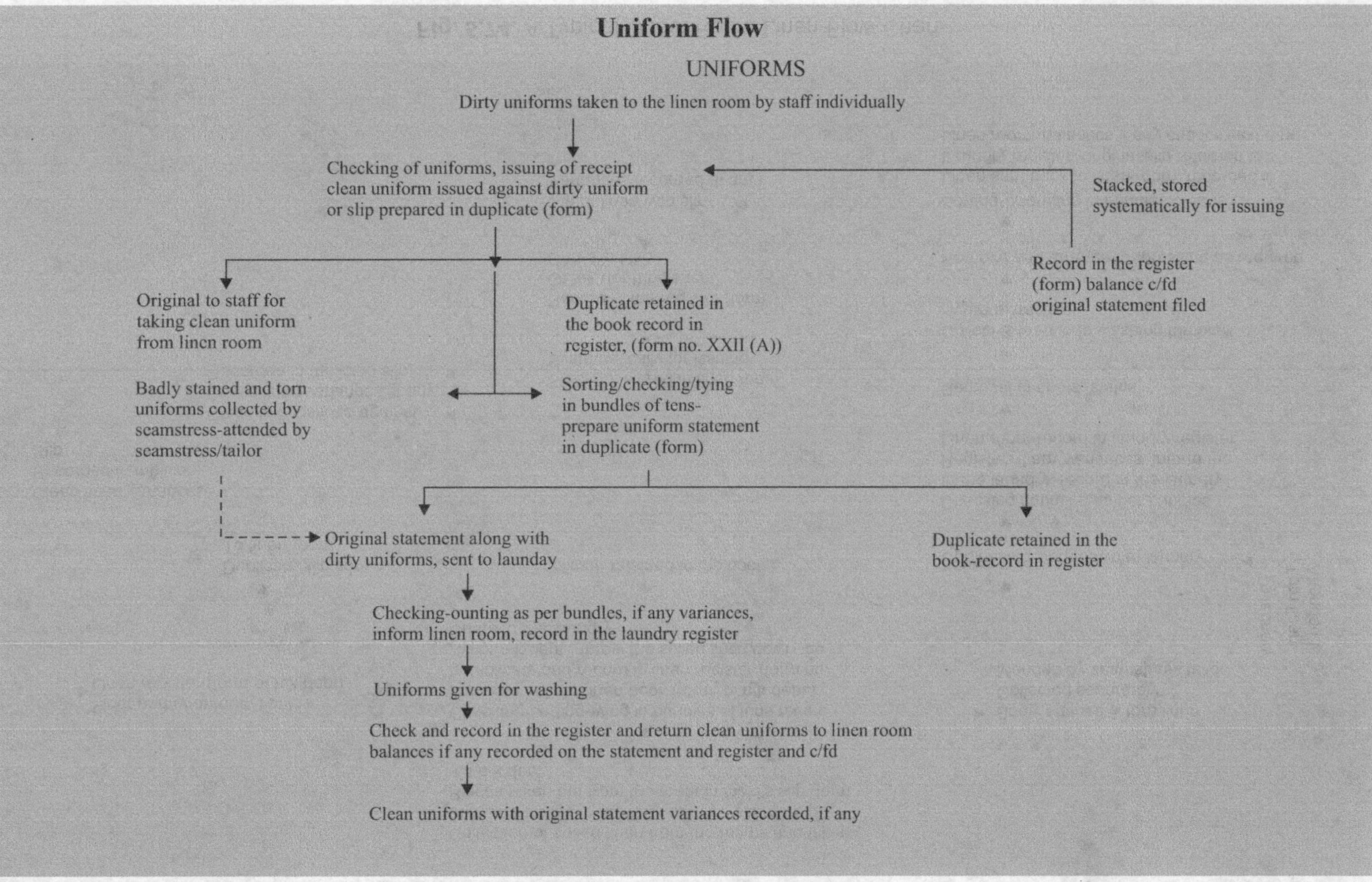

Fig. 5.73 : A Typical Uniform Flow Chart1

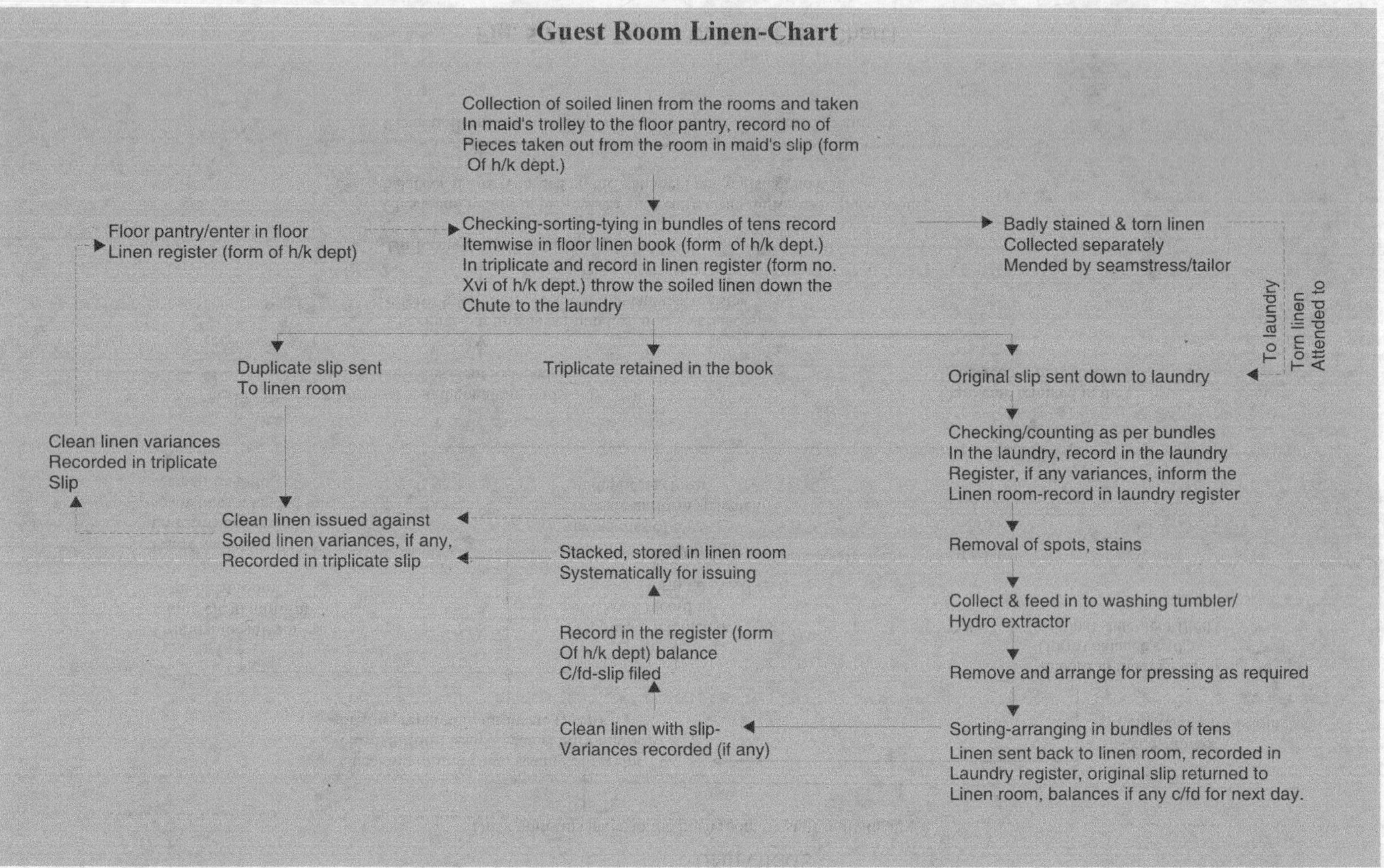

Fig. 5.74. A Typical Guest Room Linen-Flow Chart

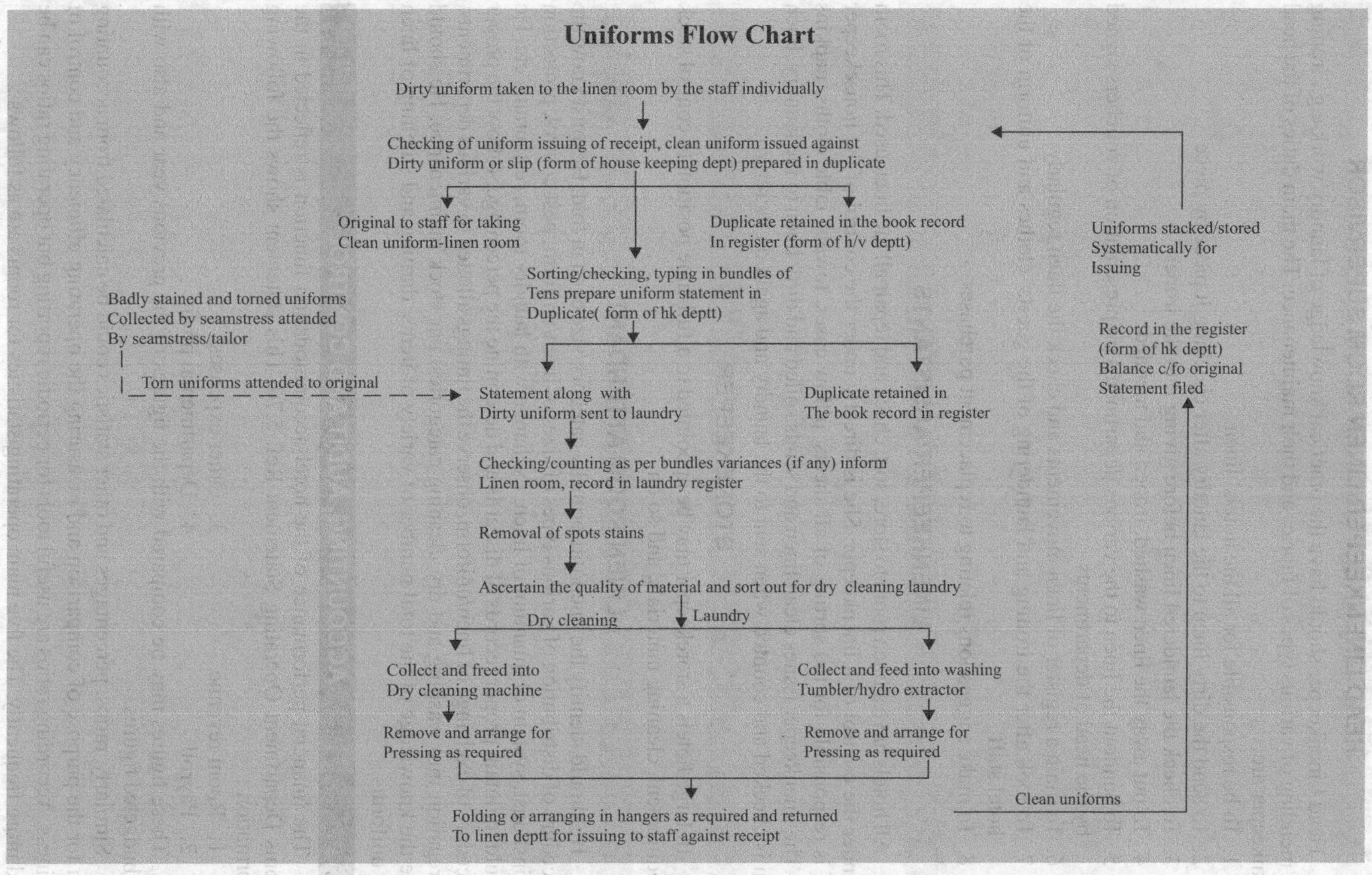

Fig. 5.75. A Typical Uniforms Flow Chart

HEAD LINENKEEPER/LINEN ROOM SUPERVISOR

Head Linenkeeper should have the practical knowledge of laundry work e.g., ironing and mending of various types of fabrics and their maintenance. The main duties of the head linknkeeper are:

1. To be responsible for all the hotels' linen.
2. To send the dirty linen to the laundry after checking it piece by piece
3. To check the laundered linen before giving it to the ironer
4. To put away the linen washed, ironed and mended
5. To handout the linen to the various departments on presentation of vouchers signed by the head of departments
6. To main a register of linen movements and check the linen regularly
7. To look after the ironing and laundering of the guests' clothes and uniform of the hotel staff
8. To make suggestions relating to replacement purchases.

LINENKEEPER/ASSISTANTS

All hotels have a linen room to store, sort, check and repair all the linen used. This room is under the control of a linenkeeper. She is directly under the control of the housekeeper and is responsible for the sorting of all sheets, pillow cases, towels, table cloths, napkins etc. The linenkeeper issues clean linen and sends soiled and dirty linen to the laundry. Each item is checked and counted when sent to the laundry and again on its return.

STOREKEEPER

In large hotels a storekeeper may be appointed to a full-time position to control stock of equipment, cleaning materials, and so on.

LINEN ROOM ATTENDANT

He should identify the linen/uniforms by category/size even in fold. He must know the procedure of distribution of various types of sizes of linen/uniform, pest control, protection against dust, system of quantum of linen, exchange with laundry room, restaurants etc. He should maintain proper records of discards and determine the percentage, follow the proper procedure of exchange of linen/uniform, observe the timings allotted to various departments, segregation into washing and dry cleaning categories, par stock maintenance. He should have the knowledge of the total number of variety of items, darning and stitching of linen and uniforms.

ACCOUNTING, AUDIT AND CONTROL

The financial performance of the hotel accommodation function is reflected in the Rooms Department Operating Statement Ref. 5.76. This statement shows the following information :

1. Room revenue
2. Payroll
3. Other expenses
4. Departmental profit.

These figures may be compared with the figures of the previous year and also with the budgeted figures.

Similarly, ratios, percentages and other statistics could be calculated from accounting data for the purpose of comparison and measuring the operating efficiency and control of business. According ratios are useful tools for periodic reporting but operating ratios can be used more frequently. The five main operating statistics for rooms are as follows :

$$\text{Room occupancy} = \frac{\text{Total occupied rooms}}{\text{Total available rooms}}$$

$$\text{Number of guests per room} = \frac{\text{Total number of guests}}{\text{Total number of rooms occupied}}$$

$$\text{Daily room rate} = \frac{\text{Room sales}}{\text{Total number of rooms occupied}}$$

$$\text{Rate per guest} = \frac{\text{Room sales}}{\text{Total number of guests}}$$

$$\text{Length of stay} = \frac{\text{Total number of guests days}}{\text{Total number of registered guests}}$$

The revenue from the sale of guest rooms, whether as bedrooms, meeting rooms or interview rooms is credited to this division. The wages and payroll taxes plus other staff costs and meals of all the staff in those departments should be charged to room division. Direct expenses such as laundry, linen hire, cleaning, cleaning materials, matches and other give away items put in guest rooms should be listed as variable overheads and analysed separately from room division. Tea and coffee materials are not included for this purpose.

INCOME FROM ACCOMMODATION

ROOM REVENUE

Revenue receipts from room rent and licence fee is one of the principal sources of income in a hotel business. The main source of income of this department may be classified according to the convenience of the hotel. The various alternatives are :

– Single – Transient

OR

– Double – Permanent

In hotels where guests are charged as per American plan or Modified American plan, clear distribution/allocation should be made of the sales between rooms and food.

PUBLIC ROOM RENTALS

Many hotels derive their income from rentals of public rooms. This will include public room rental which do not involve food and beverage sale

ALLOWANCES

It represents a concession or reduction allowed to the guests on room rates. It may be an adjustment in rates due to some reasons or complimentary accommodation provided to guests.

NET SALES (REVENUE)

The total of room revenue of guest rooms and public rooms (non-banquet) less allowances, will constitute the net sales of the room department.

EXPENSES

The main items of expenses of this department include :

SALARIES AND WAGES

The salaries and wages of the following employees will be grouped under this head :

1. Assistant Manager (Accommodation)
2. Front Office :
   (*i*) F.O. Manager.
3. Receptionists :
   (*i*) Room Clerk
   (*ii*) Night Clerk
   (*iii*) Information Clerk
   (*iv*) Register Card Clerk
   (*v*) Guest History Clerk
   (*vi*) Telephone Information Clerk
   (*vii*) Guest Card Clerk
   (*ix*) Telegram
   (*x*) Rack Clerk
   (*xi*) Reservation Clerk
   (*xii*) Mail Clerk.
   (*xiii*) File Clerk
   (*xiv*) Key Clerk
   (*xv*) Typists
   (*xvi*) Stenographer
   (*xvii*) Safe Deposit Clerk.
4. House-keeping and Linen :
   (*i*) Housekeeping
   (*ii*) Assistant House-keeper
   (*iii*) Clerk
   (*iv*) House-keeper
   (*v*) Inspectresses
   (*vi*) Store-keeper.
5. Linen :
   (*i*) Head Linen-keeper
   (*ii*) Others
   (*iii*) Linen Seamstresses
6. Maids :
   (*i*) Chambermaids
   (*ii*) Night-maids
   (*iii*) Lobby Cleaners
7. Housemen:
   (*i*) Head Housemen
   (*ii*) Sanitor
   (*iii*) Paint Cleaners
   (*iv*) Vacuum Cleaners
   (*v*) Lobby Housemen
   (*vi*) Yardmen
   (*vii*) Carpet Washers
   (*viii*) Floor Polishers
   (*ix*) Curtain Hangers
   (*x*) Housemen
   (*xi*) Furniture Polishers
   (*xii*) Wall Washers
   (*xiii*) Elevator Cleaners
   (*xiv*) Porters
   (*xv*) Street Cleaners
   (*xvi*) Shampooers
   (*xvii*) Drapery Hanger.
8. Services :
9. Front :
   (*i*) Head Hall Porter
   (*ii*) Bell Captain
   (*iii*) Pages
   (*iv*) Assistant
   (*v*) Bellmen.

10. Elevators :
    (*i*) Elevator Starters
    (*ii*) Operators
11. Floors :
    (*i*) Floor Clerk
    (*ii*) Lost and Found Employees
    (*iii*) Pages.
12. Door :
    (*i*) Doorman
    (*ii*) Taxi Starters.
13. Package Room :
    (*i*) Package Room Clerk
    (*ii*) Baggage Porter
    (*iii*) Messengers
    (*iv*) Handlers.
14. Miscellaneous :
    (*i*) Librarian
    (*ii*) Lobby Receptionists
    (*iii*) Shopping Guides.
15. Public Rooms (Non-Banquet) :
    (*i*) Entertainment Manager
    (*ii*) Page Girls
    (*iii*) House-keeper
    (*iv*) Cleaners
    (*v*) Captain
    (*vi*) Parlour Maids
    (*vii*) Housemen.

Some of the employees on the Room Department pay-roll may be providing services to other departments, the cost of services rendered by such employees should be allocated to the respective departments.

ROOM EMPLOYEES MEAL

This will include the cost of food and beverages consumed/provided to the employees of this department.

CHINA AND GLASSWARE

Items included under this head are :

1. Ashtrays
2. Candlesticks
3. Carafes
4. Dresser trays
5. Tumblers
6. Water pitchers

The amount of the charge of these items will depend upon the direct issues from stores and adjusted to actual inventories at the stated periods at a fair value in accordance with the re-valuation method.

There is an alternative method used in some hotels. On the basis of past experience, an amount per guest day or per cent of room sales of cost per room is calculated. This amount is credited to a Reserve Account. All issue of these items is debited to Reserve Account, the balance of Reserve Account (Debit /Credit) is adjusted to the actual inventory at the end of the financial year.

CLEANING SUPPLIES :

This account contains all the cost of cleaning supplies used in this department, like :

1. Acids
2. Ammonia Water
3. Belts and Equipment
4. Brass Polish
5. Carpet Sweepers
6. Chamois
7. Cleaning Fluids
8. Detergents
9. Dust Cloths
10. Dustpans
11. Floor Soaps
12. Fly Paper
13. Fly Swatters
14. Gasoline
15. Lumon Oil
16. Metal Polish
17. Mops
18. Pails
19. Rags
20. Sand Soap
21. Soda
22. Steel Work
23. Wall Washers
24. Washing Soaps and Powder
25. Ammonia
26. Alcohol
27. Brooms
28. Brushes
29. Carpet Washer Accessories
30. Cheese Cloths
31. Deodorants
32. Disinfectants
33. Dusters
34. Floor Polish
35. Floor Wax
36. Fumigators
37. Furniture Polish
39. Insecticides
40. Lye
41. Mop Handles & Wringlers
42. Mousetraps
43. Paint Cleaners
44. Sand
45. Soap for Cleaning
46. Soap Powder
47. Vacuum Cleaner Accessories
48. Window Cleaners

COMMISSIONS

To secure room sale business the hotel has to pay commission to the agents travel agents and rental agents for leases. The commission paid to rental agents for leases is spread-over the term of the lease.

CONTRACT CLEANING

In case the hotel gets contract cleaning of lobbies, public rooms, washing windows, exterminating and disinfecting, the expenses paid should be debited to this account.

DECORATIONS

It includes all items of decorations except those for banquets and dining room, restaurants. Cost of the following items is debited to this account :

1. Cut flowers
2. Ferns

3. Palms
4. Plants
5. Artificial flowers
6. Fibre bases used in guest rooms, the lobby, halls and corridors
7. Window boxes at the entrance and outside the building
8. Gold fish in aquarium
9. Song birds
10. Flags and bunting etc.

DRY CLEANING

This account includes all the amount relating to the cost of dry cleaning blankets, curtains, lamp shades, hangings, bedspreads, draperies etc. It includes washing or cleaning, window shades, awnings, carpets, rugs and furniture coverings in the rooms, lobbies, public rooms and corridors.

GARAGE AND PARKING

Many times hotels pay garage and parking charges to outside garage and parking lots for parking cars of patrons and guests using hotel facilities. The amount is debited to this account.

GUEST SUPPLIES

All costs relating to supplies furnished to guest room and writing desks are debited to this account. The items supplied to the guest room include:

1. Bathing caps
2. Bottle openers (loose)
3. Bridge scores, place cards and prizes
4. Candy
5. Corks crews
6. Facial tissues and holders
7. Fruits
8. Guest shop
9. Gift for guest
10. Hair nets
11. Inks
12. Magazines
13. Newspaper
14. Needles and thread
15. Playing cards
16. Pens
17. Talcum powder
18. Wash cloths
19. Writing supplies for guest rooms and writing rooms
20. Blotters
21. Buttons
22. Brushes
23. Combs
24. Face cloths
25. Flowers
26. Garments bags
27. Guest stationery
28. Hair pins
29. Hangers
30. Ink walls
31. Matches
32. Night apparel
33. Pins
34. Pokerchips
35. Shoe cloths
36. Toilet requisites

LAUNDRY AND DRY CLEANING

When the hotel pays laundry charges to outside agencies, the proportionate amount should be charged to the room department.

LINEN

The amount to be debited to this account is based on direct issue stores. This amount may be adjusted on the basis of evaluation at the end of each year.

In some of the hotels the usual practice is to create a reserve account with a certain fixed amount. This amount is determined on the basis of past experience, is calculated per guest day, per cent of room sales or cost per room, all issues and purchases relating to these items are debited to reserve account and any debit or credit balance in the reserve account at the end of the year is adjusted to the actual inventory. The items included under linen are :

1. Bath mats
2. Blankets
3. Towels
4. Matresses protectors
5. Sheets
6. Shower curtains
7. Spreads
8. Dress tops
9. Pillow cases.

LINEN RENTALS

In case the linen is arranged on rental basis, the amount would be charged to this account.

PRINTING AND STATIONERY

It includes the cost of printing forms, service manuals, stationery and office supplies used by employees of the room department etc. It does not include the printing and stationery supplies used by front office cashiers and bill clerks, as it is charged to administrative and general expenses. The items of printing and stationery include :

1. Binders
2. Book record
3. Charge vouchers
4. Desk pens
5. Floor plans
6. Guest register
7. Ink pad
8. Mucilage
9. Paste
10. Pen holders
11. Pins
12. Rubber bands
13. Stamp pads
14. Typewriter ribbons
15. Blotters
16. Carbon papers
17. Clips
18. Envelopes-safety
19. Fountain pen
20. Ink
21. Inkwell
22. paper clips
23. Pencils
24. Pen pints
25. Rack cards
26. Staples
27. Vouchers
28. Report for housekeeper and maids.

RESERVATION EXPENSES

All expenses relating to reservation service and control reservation system e.g., telephone, telegrams, teletype expenses etc., are debited to this account.

UNIFORMS

Expenses relating to cost of uniforms for employees of room department including the cost of repair and cleaning of uniforms, the cost of buttons, braid, badges etc., are charged to this account. The uniform includes :

1. Aprons
2. Shoes
3. Suits
4. Trousers
5. Blouses
6. Boots
7. Caps
8. Coats
9. Collars
10. Shocks
11. Ties
12. Umbrellas
13. Dresses
14. Gloves
15. Jumpers
16. Overall lain coats.

MISCELLANEOUS EXPENSES

In addition to the items of expenses described above, there are certain minor and sundry expenses which cannot be classified under a special head. All such expenses of room department are debited to this head. Some of these expenses are :

1. Books for guest library
2. Bulletin board supplies
3. Candles
4. Directories
5. Safe deposit box keys
6. Employees transportation
7. Firewood for apartments and lobby guide
8. Guides
9. Service of special officers
10. Signs for lobby and front desk
11. Time tables
12. Wrapping paper and twine for package room
13. Help wanted aid for room department
14. Licences and permits
15. Music for concerts in lobby
16. Postage due for guest's mail
17. Programmeconcerts in lobby.

ABC HOTELS LTD.

ROOMS SCHEDULE

	Current Period
REVENUE	
Transit Regular	₹ ....
Transit-Group	
Permanent other	₹ ....
Total Revenue	₹
ALLOWANCES	₹ ....
NET REVENUE	₹ ....
EXPENSES	
Salaries and Wages	₹ ....
Employee Benefits	₹ ....
Total Payroll and Related Expenses	₹ ....
Other Expenses	
Cleaning Supplies	
Contract Cleaning	
Guest Transportation	
Commissions :	
Travel Agency	
Others	
Operating Supplies	
Kitchenette Expenses	
Laundry and dry cleaning	
Linen	
Other Expenses	
Reservation Expenses	
Uniforms	
Total Other Expenses	₹ ....
TOTAL EXPENSES	₹ ....
DEPARTMENTAL INCOME (LOSS)	₹ ....

* Sales include ₹................ for trade advertising

Note : Various arrangements of additional columns for comparisons and percentages could be added.

Fig. 5.76 : Analysis of Income and Expenses of Room Division

QUESTIONS AND ASSIGNMENTS

FRONT OFFICE

1. Give the job description of a front office manager of 200-room five start hotel. Identify the various sections of the front office department. Briefly discuss their functions. *(DTHM)*
2. A tour operator wishes to book accommodation with a hotel for a group of 20-people on a package tour. Detail briefly the step by step procedure of handling the booking from the time the inquiry is made to the departure of the guests. *(DTHM)*

3. Explain in detail the procedure of control of room sales in a hotel. Give suitable diagram. *(MTA)*
4. What is meant by Occupancy Ratio ? What is its importance ? How will you calculate Room Occupancy Rate in a hotel ? Explain with imaginary example. *(IHMs)*
5. You are asked to project a eleven-day-room occupancy forecast for your hotel. What information you would require to proceed ? Explain in detail. *(IHMs)*
6. It is proposed to mechanize the accounting, reception, and control departments of a large hotel. You are asked to suggest what equipment would be of a value in these departments, and state the main application of each item of equipment. Make any suggestion you think necessary for the purpose of your answer. *(IHMs)*
7. Discuss the various basis for charging room tariffs ? Give the job description of a FO manager of a 200-room five star hotel.
8. Identify the various sections of the FO Dept. Briefly describe their functions. What are the essentials of a good telephone manners ?
9. What are the formulas for calculating:
   (1) Room occupancy %
   (2) Single " %
   (3) Bed " %
   (4) Local " %
   (5) Average rate per guest.
10. The FO manager heads the FO of a large hotel. Illustrate the hierarchy of the staff members under him in the form of a chart.
11. Explain the full procedure of reservation of accommodation, arrival (registration) and departure of a guest in a hotel. *(PGDT&HM)*
12. Explain the following :
    (*a*) Hubbart Formula of room rate determination.
    (*b*) Budget Hotels
    (*c*) Multinationals in Hotel Industry
    (*d*) Indian Cuisine. *(MTM)*
13. Writes notes on :
    (*a*) In room amenities
    (*b*) Excise laws as they are applicable to hotel industry
    (*c*) Food and beverage control
    (*d*) Density chart. *(MTM)*
14. When presenting a guest's account at the end of his stay what procedure would you adopt and what safeguard would you take in each of the following circumstances :
    He wishes to settle the bill:
    (*a*) By cash
    (*b*) By cheque, or
    (*c*) Have it sent by his company for payment at a later date. *(MTM)*
15. Explain the duties and responsibilities of a Receptionist in a middle class hotel. *(PGDT)*
16. What do you understand by Front Office management ? What are the main functions of Front Office in a deluxe hotel ? *(PGDT)*
17. What are the Front-Office Operations ? What are the roles performed by the various officials associated with them ? *(PGDT)*
18. Explain the factors you will keep in mind in preparing the layout plan of the front office in a medium-sized hotel. Give a suitable layout plan of a front office for a 100-room hotel. *(PGDT&HM)*

19. Differentiate between :

(*a*) Reservation and Registration

(*b*) Filling and Indexing

(*c*) Reception and Information

(*d*) Banquet and Outdoor Catering. *(PGDT&HM)*

20. "Hotel Receptionist is a salesman and builder of goodwill for the hotel and not merely a recorder of arrivals and departures". Comment. *(PGT)*

21. What do you understand by hotel room tariffs ? How will you fix the room rates in a hotels by Hubbart formula? Give a suitable example. *(PGH&TM)*

22. Give a description of the importance and operational procedure of the front office in a hotel. *(PGT&HM)*

23. Writes notes on :

(*a*) Communication in Hotel Business

(*b*) Hotel Sales and Marketing

(*c*) Travellers Lodge

(*d*) Reservation. *(PGDH&TM)*

24. Explain the following:

(*a*) Room Reservation Procedure

(*b*) Shop and Establishment Act as applied to Hotel and Catering business. *(PGDT)*

25. (*a*) Give the functions of a front office manager

(*b*) Explain the procedure of billing. *(PGDT&HM)*

26. Differentiate between any four of the following:

(*a*) Hall Porter and Bell Boy

(*b*) Reception and Information Clerk

(*c*) American Plan and European Plan

(*d*) Continental Dishes and Chinese Dishes.

27. Define the following :

(*a*) en pension

(*b*) demi-pension

(*c*) Rack Rate

(*d*) American Plan

(*e*) MAP

(*f*) Shoulder Period

(*g*) Back to back reservation

(*h*) Executive Chef. *(MTA)*

28. Give a brief account of International Hotel Regulations as applied to Indian hotels. *(MTA)*

29. Explain the following terms in not more than 70-80 words :

(*a*) Star Ranking

(*b*) In-room amenities

(*c*) Types of beds.

(*d*) Detergents

(*e*) Double lock room *(MTA)*

30. Explain Visitor's Tabular Ledger (VTL). Give a specimen of the same. Briefly discuss the advantages and disadvantages of mechanical billing and manual billing. *(MTA)*

31. What are the duties and responsibilities of a Front Office Manager in a luxury hotel having 300-rooms? *(MTA)*

32. A hotel prepares its Daily Report. You have been asked to suggest a suitable proforma of the daily report. Explain the main points which a daily report usually contains. *(MTA)*

33. Following information relates to a hotel :

(*a*)	Name of the hotel	:	ABC Hotels Ltd.
(*b*)	Capacity	:	300-double room
(*c*)	Room under repair on 1st May, 20..	:	10
(*d*)	Room occupied on 1st May, 20..	:	210
(*e*)	Room count on 1st May, 20..	:	330.

(*f*) On 2nd May, 20.., 10 room with double occupancy checked out while 20 rooms with double and 10 rooms with single occupancy checked in.

(*g*) The hotel earned a room revenue of ₹ 1,90,210 on 2nd May, 20.. .

You are require to calculate :

(*i*) Room occupancy (*ii*) House count
(*iii*) Double occupancy (*iv*) Bed occupancy
(*v*) Average room rate. *(MTA)*

34. Give a brief account of growth of credit cards in India. What are the advantages of credit card system ? *(DTHM)*

35. Write notes on :

(*i*) Certificate for Commencement of Business
(*ii*) International Hotel Regulations
(*iii*) Settlement of Guest Bills
(*iv*) Functional layout of a Kitchen. *(DTHM)*

36. What are the various sources through which reservations are made in a large hotel ? Explain by giving suitable flow chart. *(MTA)*

37. Identify the *three* types of detergents and explain the most appropriate uses for each type. Be sure to include the advantage and disadvantages of each type. *(MTA)*

38. A hotel follows the check-in and check-out system of charging room rent with 12-noon as a check-out time. Mr. Rajan checked in at 6.00 hours on Wednesday and checked-out on 5.00 hours on Thursday. For how many days will he be charged and explain why ? *(MTA)*

39. Explain the term Visitors Tabular Ledger (VTL). Explain the system of recording various transactions in this ledger. *(MTA)*

40. Write the notes on the following :

(*i*) Crib Rate (*iv*) House Count
(*ii*) 'C' Form (*v*) DND
(*iii*) Types of Bed (*vi*) KOT. *(MTA)*

41. Write in detail Front-Office Management of a five star hotel. How this office co-ordinates with other department of hotel? *(MTA)*

42. Differentiate between (any *four*) :

(*a*) Office site and Office layout
(*b*) Hotel and Motel
(*c*) American Plan and European Plan
(*d*) Food Service and Beverage Service
(*e*) Reception and Information Service
(*f*) Filing and Indexing. *(PGDT&HM)*

43. With a suitable illustration explain how a supervisor would go about checking a check-out room, after the room has been cleared by the room attendant. *(MTA)*

44. Describe in full the steps taken in preparing for guest arrival at (*a*) reservation section, and (*b*) at front desk.

45. In about 10-lines write about the following :

(*i*) Mode of Reservation
(*ii*) Standard Purchase Specification
(*iii*) Standard Yield
(*iv*) Foreign Exchange Regulations. (*MTA*)

46. The hotel Himalaya has 220-lettable room all twin bedded. House count on the Ist February, 20 was 305. On 2nd February, 20.., there were 200 check-ins and 180 check outs. Room revenue was ₹ 96000/-. All the room were sold out for the mid night of 3rd February, 20.. . Calculate :

(*a*) House count
(*b*) Double occupancy %
(*c*) Average rate per room.
(*d*) Room occupancy %
(*e*) Bed occupancy % (*IHMs*)

47. You are a front office manager and it is about to click after a tiring general shift at 6.00 P.M. You are called in by the General Manager and instructed to complete an urgent report by 9.00 A.M. next morning. You know that it would take at least 6-hours to plan, discuss and type the report. You need your reservation supervisor, two lady reservation assistants and the secretary of the Front Office who can all planning to leave for home.

Explain how will you tackle the problem of keeping them back with your reasons for each decision you take. (*IHMs*)

48. Describe briefly the basic function of the reception office enumerating the services it provides.

49. Draw an organisation chart of the Front Office Department of a 300-room five star hotel and list the duties of the Front Office Supervisor.

50. Front Office Manager heads the Front Office of a large hotel. Illustrate the hierarchy of the staff members under him in the form of a chart.

51. Hotel 'B' has 300-double rooms of which 10 are under repair. On 5th June, 20.., 210 rooms were occupied with a house count of 330. On 6th June, 20.., 10-rooms with double occupancy checked out, while 20-rooms with double occupancy and 10-rooms with single occupancy checked in.

The hotel earned a revenue of ₹ 1,90,710 on 6th June. You are required to calculate for the 6th June:

(*i*) Room Occupancy
(*ii*) Bed Occupancy
(*iii*) House Count
(*iv*) Average Room Rate.
(*v*) Double Occupancy

52. What is the process of reservation in the Whitney System from the time a reservation request is received at the time a guest arrives at the front desk ?

53. Explain the importance of Reservation Form and describe how it is used by the Front Office.

54. What is control of reservation system ? Explain its importance.

55. Ensuring maximum occupancy is of prime importance. How does the Front Office ensures them?

56. Explain the following terms in few lines each :

(*i*) Time Limit
(*ii*) Retention Charges
(*iii*) Crib Rate
(*iv*) Rooming List
(*v*) Miscellaneous Charge Voucher. (*IHMs*)

57. Draw a chart illustrating the organisation of a hotel. List out in details the duties and responsibilities of a Lobby Manager in a luxury hotel.

58. What do you understand by over-booking ? Why do hotels over-book ? Give the formula for calculating over-booking.

59. How will you deal with a guest who comes with a confirmed booking but do not have any room to allocate to him.

60. Handling group reservation is a lot of planning. What are the points you would bear in mind and discuss while handling group reservations?

61. Give the steps to be followed to process a reservation by the whitney systems of reservation. Give the relevant formula to be used.

62. List out the features of an efficient reservation system.

63. The Front Office Manager heads the Front Office of a large hotel. Illustrate the hierarchy of the staff members under him in the form of a chart.

64. Discuss the statement 'a room lost to day is lost for ever'.

65. What is the information recorded on a whitney slip in the reservation office?

66. Bring out the difference between those statements 'A room is reserved' and 'A room is assigned'.

67. What are the duties and responsibilities of a Front Office Cashier in a luxury hotel? What are the formulas for calculating :

(*i*) Room Occupancy (*ii*) Single Occupancy
(*iii*) Bed Occupancy (*iv*) Local Occupancy
(*v*) Average Rate per Guest.

68. Explain in few lines each:

(*i*) Density Chart (*ii*) Room Position
(*iii*) Cashier's Bucket/Well (*iv*) Hospitality Room
(*v*) Under Stay.

69. What are the various person through which reservations are made in a large hotel.

70. How do you assign room to (*a*) a guest ask a confirmed reservation (*b*) a group and (*c*) a walk in ?

71. Explain the use and importance of a Guest Registration Card with the help of a neat diagram.

72. Describe the role of Bell Desk Staff in (*a*) rooming a guest (*b*) guest departure.

73. Differentiate between:

(*i*) No show and Cancellation
(*ii*) Cheque and Travellers' Cheque
(*iii*) Room Rack and Information Rack
(*iv*) Sleeper and Sleep Out
(*v*) 'C' form and 'F' Form.

74. 'Turn Away' should be handled with care as they would be potential guests in the future. Explain.

75. Draw a neat diagram of a Key Card and explain its uses and advantages.

76. Identify the various sections of the Front Office Department of five star hotel. Briefly discuss their functions.

77. What do you understand by overbooking ? Why do hotel overbook ? Give the formula for overbooking. How will you deal with a guest who comes with a confirmed booking but you do not have any room to allocate to him.

78. Differentiate between:

(*i*) Stay Over and Over Stay

(*ii*) Density Chart and A.L.C.

(*iii*) Walk-in Guest and Walking Guest

(*iv*) Transient hotel and Destination Hotel

(*v*) Block a Room and Allocate a Room.

79. Define, describe, and explain the following terms:

(*i*) Franchise

(*ii*) Travel Agent's Voucher

(*iii*) Pneumatic Charts

(*iv*) Tour Groups.

80. Describe the limits of a hotel's liability towards guest valuables.

81. Explain the normal procedure followed in most hotels when occupying and returning guest valuables.

82. What are the formulas for calculating:

(*i*) Room Occupancy Percentage

(*ii*) Bed Occupying Percentage

(*iii*) Local Occupying Percentage

(*iv*) Average Rate per Guest.

83. Explain the construction, use, and functions of the following at the reception counter:

(*i*) Room Rack

(*ii*) Mail, and

(*iii*) Key Rack.

84. What special precaution's would you take when handling groups.

85. Write a letter in reply to a guest enquiry letters; informing him about your inability to accept a requested reservation.

86. Explain with the help of a diagram, the working of a Room Status Indicator and its case.

87. What are the tasks to be completed by the front office assistant after the departure of a guest.

88. Explain in detail how a good receptionist will deal with any two of the most common complaints.

89. How would you, as a receptionist proceed to assign a room to a walk in guest ?

90. Discuss the procedure for handling a guest with scanty baggage at the time of check in.

91. Give staff organisation of the Telephone Department and briefly described the duties and responsibilities of the senior personnels.

92. What are the functions and importance of Reservation section of the Front Office Dept. of a five star hotel.

93. Write a short paragraph on the desirable qualities of a good receptionist ?

94. What are the essential of a good telephone voice ? 'Attention to personal appearance and hygiene are of the out most importance to a receptionist. Discuss.

95. Define the following:

(*i*) Pension

(*ii*) Demi-pension

(*iii*) Rack Rate

(*iv*) American Plan

(*v*) MAP

(*vi*) European Plan

(*vii*) Shoulder Period

(*viii*) Back to Back Reservation.

96. Define the use and purpose of following using diagrams to illustrate your answers where necessary:

(*i*) The Conventional Reservation Chart
(*ii*) A Reception Board
(*iii*) The Hotel Diary
(*iv*) The Arrival and Departure List
(*v*) The Alphabetical Guest List.

97. A tour operator wishes to book accommodation with the JMS Hotel for a group of 20-people on a package tour. Detail briefly the step by step procedure of handling the booking from the time, the enquiry is made to the departure of the guests.

98. Detail some of the features of modern hotel communication systems.

99. Explain briefly the following terms:

(*i*) Telex
(*ii*) IDD
(*iii*) PABX
(*iv*) STD
(*v*) Free phone
(*vi*) PBX
(*vii*) ADC
(*viii*) Executive Bleeper
(*ix*) PMBX.

100. You are a head receptionist of a medium-sized hotel, instructing a new trainee receptionist, write briefly on how you would explain some of the task that have to be carried out

(*a*) On the morning shift 8.00 a.m. - 3.00 p.m.
(*b*) On the evening shift 3.00 p.m. - 11.00 p.m.

101. Neatly draw *any two* of the following forms and give an explanation of how it is used by the hotel :

(*a*) Mail Forwarding Card (*b*) Credit Card (*c*) Travel Agent Voucher.

102. Outline an efficient system of reservations for a 500-room three star hotel. Identify the forms you would use in the system with a description of the information required on each form and an explanation of how the hotel will use each form.

103. Sketch out a neat diagram of a five star hotel reception deptt. Indicate placement of tools of the Front Office on the sketch and describe rear functions in brief.

104. Explain with the help of a neat diagram, the lobby and counter layout of the F.O. Deptt. of a five star hotel.

105. Describe the effective systems of reservations of a 100-room four star hotel. Give reasons for your choice and identify all forms you would use.

106. Draw an organisational chart for the Front Office of a hypothetical luxury hotels having 450-rooms.

107. Define the term job description. Write a job description listing the responsibilities and duties of each employee of the Front Office of a hypothetical hotel.

108. Visit a five star luxury hotel in your area and observe the guest service staff performing its duties. Prepare a report on the staff, giving the name and location of the hotel, and describe the various job positions of the divisions.

109. Write a policy for the appearance and grooming of the guest services department of a luxurious hypothetical hotel ?

110. What is the importance of key control in the hotel? (*IHMs*)

111. Write down the procedure of key control and give the format of key control sheet. (*IHMs*)

112. What are incoming and outgoing mail ? How do you classify incoming mail ? Write in detail. (*IHMs*)

113. Explain the following :

(*a*) Call Barring
(*b*) Collect Call. (*IHMs*)

114. In which circumstances the message slip is used and in how many copies it is made ? Give its format (*IHMs*)

115. Explain the following:

(*i*) Franking Machine
(*ii*) Free Phone
(*iii*) Mail Forwarding Card.
(*iv*) Imprint Machine
(*v*) Mail Advise Slip
(IHMs)

116. Is key control essential ? If yes, then how will you have a track on movement of the keys if you are a receptionist. *(IHMs)*

117. What is computerized key system ? Is it more safer than manual key ? Why ? *(IHMs)*

118. What is a Credit Card ? At the time of departure of a guest, discuss the precautions to be taken while accepting credit card. *(IHMs)*

119. Explain any four:

(*i*) Flow Unit
(*ii*) U.S.P.
(*iii*) Mail Advise Slip.
(*iv*) Cancellation Bulletin
(*v*) Paging
(IHMs)

120. Discuss handling of incoming mail for the hotel.

121. Discuss how guest mail is distributed ? *(IHMs)*

122. If you are at information counter, what stationary will you require for this counter? Give proforma wherever required. *(IHMs)*

123. If a visitor has come to meet a guest (resident), what is to be done ? *(IHMs)*

124. Differentiate between:

(*i*) Wake Call and Guest Call
(*ii*) Transfer Call and Fixed Time Call
(*iii*) STD and IDD
(*iv*) Collect Call and Trunk Call. *(IHMs)*

125. What points are to be observed while accepting baggage for storage and delivering it? *(IHMs)*

126. List the various functions performed by Bell Desk. *(IHMs)*

127. With the help of a neat diagram explain the 'Message Slip'. *(IHMs)*

128. Discuss the function performed from the Bell desk with suitable examples. *(IHMs)*

129. Discuss the procedure for accepting left luggage from guest storage and handing it over. *(IHMs)*

130. What are the different ways by which guest can settle their total bills? *(IHMs)*

131. Discuss one reason for not accepting cheques from individuals and if accepted the precaution to be taken. *(IHMs)*

132. Draw the staff organisation chart of the uniformed staff of a 500-room five star deluxe hotel and explain importance of each of the service provided by the Front Office. *(IHMs)*

133. Explain briefly (*two* or *three* lines):

(*i*) PABX
(*ii*) Transfer Call
(*iii*) N/R Report
(*iv*) V.P.O.
(*v*) STD
(*vi*) Turn In
(*vii*) Franking Machine
(*viii*) ISD
(*ix*) Free Phone
(*x*) Imprinter
(IHMs)

134. Write short notes on (*any two*):

(*a*) Cashier's Report
(*b*) Type of Keys
(*c*) Sorting of Mail. *(IHMs)*

135. Explain briefly the working of a computerized keyboard. *(IHMs)*

136. With the help of a format explain the 'Baggage Check'. *(IHMs)*

137. Draw a neat format of the 'Key Control Sheet'. *(IHMs)*

138. To protect the hotel interest, the management frames certain condition for acceptance of left luggage of guests. Discuss these conditions. *(IHMs)*

139. Explain the complete procedure to be followed in a hotel while accepting credit cards for settlement of hotel bills. *(IHMs)*

140. Explain *any five* of the following is not more than 2-3 lines:

(*i*) Valet	(*iv*) Call Barring
(*ii*) Executive Bleeper	(*v*) Over and Short
(*iii*) Due Bank	(*vi*) Link Man. *(IHMs)*

141. Name five international credit cards that are accepted in India. *(IHMs)*

142. Name five international travel agents. *(IHMs)*

143. What are the various types of paidouts that feature on a Cash Sheet ? *(IHMs)*

144. With the help of neat diagrams, differentiate between cheques and travellers cheques. *(IHMs)*

145. List the categories of person exempted from paying their hotel bills of foreign exchange. *(IHMs)*

146. List the possible inquiries made by a guest to the receptionist. *(IHMs)*

147. "Turnaways should be handled with care as they could be potential guest in the future". Explain. *(IHMs)*

148. What is the Amenities Voucher and explain its purpose ? *(IHMs)*

149. Draw a neat diagram of a Key Card and explain its uses and advantages. *(IHMs)*

150. Give four examples of reports generated to a computerized Room Management Module. *(IHMs)*

151. Draw a staff organisation chart to the Front Office of a large hotel and list the duties of:

(*a*) Receptionist

(*b*) Lobby Manager. *(IHMs)*

152. List the steps involved in preparing for guest arrivals at the front desk and explain each. *(IHMs)*

153. Explain the term 'product knowledge' giving example. *(IHMs)*

154. What is USP for hotel and why is it used ? *(IHMs)*

155. Draw the format and discuss the purpose of :

(*a*) Housekeeper's Accupancy Report

(*b*) Welcome Slip Key Board *(IHMs)*

156. List the phases of guest account process and explain each briefly. *(IHMs)*

157. What are the various types of credit cards and discuss the procedure for checking the validity of a credit card? *(IHMs)*

158. In a tabular form compare and contrast the non-automated, semi-automated, and fully automated guest accepting modes. *(IHMs)*

159. Hotel Sea View has 55- Single rooms and 250-double room. The following figure each of the month of November 18,.....

Total single rooms sold : 660

Total double room sold : 3000

out of which 1750 had 2 people staying in them.

Total rooms sales : **₹ 5,50,000**

Calculate :

(*i*) Room Occupancy Percentage

(*ii*) Double Occupancy Percentage

(*iii*) Bed Occupancy Percentage

(*iv*) Average Room Rate

(*v*) Average Rate per Guest. *(IHMs)*

160. Discuss briefly how these situation could be handled :

(*a*) A guest inform the receptionist that he has accidentally broken the wash bashin.

(*b*) A guest arrives at the front desk at 7 a.m. with a confirmed reservation but the receptionist cannot give a room till 12-noon. *(IHMs)*

161. List the FIT departure procedure at the Bell desk. *(IHMs)*

162. Explain the housekeeping function of the computerized room management module. *(IHMs)*

163. Discuss with the help of flow chart the activities at the front desk at the time of group arrival. *(IHMs)*

164. How do you assign rooms to :

(*a*) A guest with a confirmed reservations

(*b*) A group

(*c*) A walk in ? *(IHMs)*

165. Discuss the role of the Bell Desk staff in:

(*a*) A rooming a guest, and

(*b*) Guest departure *(IHMs)*

166. Differentiate between :

(*a*) NO Shows and Cancellations

(*b*) Cheques and Traveller Cheques

(*c*) Room Rack and Information Rack

(*d*) Sleeper and Sleep Out

(*e*) 'C' form and 'F' form *(IHMs)*

167. Identify the various room/rate plans offered by hotels. Also identify which are suitable to the different kind of hotels. *(IHMs)*

168. List the duties and responsibilities of an information assistant. *(IHMs)*

169. What are the functions and importance of the reservation sections of the Front Office Department of a five star hotel. *(IHMs)*

170. What is Central Reservation System ? Explain it importance. *(IHMs)*

171. Ensuring maximum occupancy is of prime importance. How does the Front Office ensure this? *(IHMs)*

172. Explain these abbreviations :

(*a*) FHRAI (*d*) O.O.O.

(*b*) ARR (*e*) WTO

(*c*) ISD. *(IHMs)*

173. The hotel Ambadi follows the check-in and check out system of charging room rent with 12-noon as check out time. Mr. Oza checks in at 6.00 hrs. on Wednesday and checks out at 5.00 hrs. on Thursday. For how many days will be he charged and explain why ? *(IHMs)*

174. What are the merits and demerits of the Visitors Tabulator Ledger ? *(IHMs)*

175. Give the format of VTL. Give its merits and demerits. What is tariff card, give its uses and its format *(IHMs)*

176. List out the duties of a Front Office Cashier. *(IHMs)*

177. Discuss the duties of a Bell Captain. *(IHMs)*

178. Explain the Whitney System of reservation. *(IHMs)*

179. The check out time of a hotel is 12-noon. Mr. John check in at 5 a.m. on 4.4.2011 and checks out at 12 noon on 5.4.2011. The room rate is ₹ 2,200/-. How much did he pay without taxes, if he did not utilize any other services. *(IHMs)*

180. A hotel has 500-rooms. The members of occupied rooms on a particular day are 380. The house count is 550. The revenue earned ₹ 1,08,000. Calculate : *(IHMs)*

(*i*) Room Occupancy Percentage

(*ii*) Average Rate Per Person

(*iii*) Double Occupancy Percentage. *(IHMs)*

181. Define domestic tourist and foreign tourist as accepted by the Government of India. Give the main difference between domestic and international travel. *(IHMs)*

182. Explain :

(*a*) Suite

(*b*) Guaranteed Reservations

(*c*) Efficiency Room

(*d*) In house System

(*d*) Time Limit. *(IHMs)*

183. List out 5-international airport names in India. *(IHMs)*

184. List out 5-hill resorts in Southern India. *(IHMs)*

185. Give the format of VPO voucher. *(IHMs)*

186. Draw a chart illustrating the organisation of a hotel. *(IHMs)*

187. List out in detail the duties and responsibilities of a lobby manager in a luxury hotel. *(IHMs)*

188. Give the job description of a bell boy. *(IHMs)*

189. Hotel bank has 300-double rooms of which 10 are under repair. On 5th June 20.., 210- rooms were occupied with a house count of 330. On 6th June, 20.., 10 rooms with double occupancy checked out, while 20-rooms with double occupancy and 10-room with single occupancy checked in. The hotel earned a room revenue of ₹ 1,90,210 on 6th June.

You are requested to calculate for the 6th June :

(*a*) Room Occupancy

(*b*) House Count

(*c*) Double Occupancy

(*d*) Bed Occupancy

(*e*) Average Room Rate. *(IHMs)*

190. What do you understand by overbooking ? Why do hotels overbook ? Give the formula for calculating overbooking. How will you deal with a guest who comes with a confirmed booking, but you do not have any room to allocate to them. *(IHMs)*

191. Handling groups requires a lot of planning. What are the points you would bear in mind and discuss while handling group reservation ? *(IHMs)*

192. Give the steps to be followed to process a reservation by the Whitney System of reservation. Give the relevant format used. *(IHMs)*

193. List out the features of an efficient reservation systems. *(IHMs)*

194. Classify tourism based on the motives of travel and write about two lines on each. What is VTL ? Give its merits. *(IHMs)*

195. Differentiate between:

(*a*) Stay over and Over stay

(*b*) Density Chart and A.L.C.

(*c*) Walk in Guest and Walking a Guest

(*d*) Transient Hotel and Destination Hotel

(*e*) Block a Room and Allocate a Room. *(IHMs)*

196. What are the various food plans available in a hotel ? Which type of food plan is best for a resort hotel and why ? *(IHMs)*

197. Discuss the various basis for charging room tariff. *(IHMs)*

198. Identify and explain the various circumstances where special rates or discounts are offered on room rates by hotels. *(IHMs)*

199. What is the purpose of reservations in the Whitney System from the time a reservation request is reviewed till the time a guest arrives at the Front Desk ? *(IHMs)*

200. What do these terms mean :-

(*a*) Passing an Allowance

(*b*) Visitors Passed Out

(*c*) Rack Rate

(*d*) Guest Folio

(*e*) Visitors' Tabular or Ledger. *(IHMs)*

201. Give the definition of a foreign guest. *(IHMs)*

202. Tourism can be broadly classified into two different type based on the motives of travel, leisure, and business. Discuss. *(IHMs)*

203. Explain in a few lines each of the following:

(*a*) Density Chart

(*b*) Room Position

(*c*) Cashier's Bucket/Well

(*d*) Hospitality Room

(*e*) Under stays. *(IHMs)*

204. In a tabular form briefly classify hotels according to location, climate, length of stay and facilities. *(IHMs)*

205. The Front Office Manager heads the Front Office of a large hotel. Illustrate the hierarchy of the staff members under them in the form of a chart. *(IHMs)*

206. What is the information recorded in a Whitney slip in the reservations office. *(IHMs)*

207. Explain the terms 'A room is reserved' and 'A room is assigned'.

208. What are the duties and responsibilities of a Front Office Cashier in a luxury hotel? *(IHMs)*

209. What are the major sections of a guest folio? Give an specimen of the same. *(IHMs)*

210. Why is a posting machine necessary at a front desk ? What are the major features of a posting machine ? *(IHMs)*

211. Why would a front-desk set up include a cash register ? What is meant by the term 'cost effective' in relation to cash register at the front desk? *(IHMs)*

212.. What is difference between the a credit card imprinter and a credit card validater? What does the validater tell you? *(IHMs)*

213. Why are the vouchers used in a hotel ? Give an example of the use of a voucher. How are they controlled ? *(IHMs)*

214. When are paid-out slips used at the front-desk ? How are they controlled ? *(IHMs)*

215. (*a*) What is V.P.O. ?

(*b*) What is Cashier's Well ?

(*c*) What is the Cashiers Report ?

(*d*) What are Modes of Reservation ?

(*e*) What is the Deposit Reservation ?

(*f*) What is 'Adds' ? *(IHMs)*

216. Tourism has a great impact on a country. Explain the following with examples :

(*a*) Economic Impact

(*b*) Social Impact and Cultural Impact

(*c*) Impact on Employment Generation. *(IHMs)*

217. Write the importance and functions of National Tourism Organisation and Public Policy. *(IHMs)*

218. Explain the role of (*any three*)
(*a*) WTO
(*b*) PATA
(*c*) TAAI
(*d*) IATA. (*IHMs*)

219. Explain step by step procedure of handling VIP arrival at the reception (give all necessary formats)

220. Detail the duties and responsibilities of a Night Auditor. (*IHMs*)

221. How will you ensure internal control of cash ? Explain in terms of Incoming and outgoing cash. (*IHMs*)

222. Explain the following with suitable examples and necessary formats:
(*a*) Guest Ledger
(*b*) City Ledger
(*c*) Non-Automated Record Keeping System
(*d*) Guest Folio. (*IHMs*)

223. Explain the step by step procedure in handling guest complaints with suitable examples. (*IHMs*)

224. Hotel ABC has 263, rooms (all double-bedded). The following information was received from Front Office on 1st January 20.. :

On 1st Jan. rooms under maintenance	:	10
On 1st Jan. rooms occupied by executives	:	03
House count on 31st December 20..	:	436
Rooms occupied on 31st December, 20..	:	223
Departures on 1st January 20..	:	36 pax (20-rooms)
Arrival on 1st January, 20..	:	10 pax (05-rooms).

Calculate on 1st January 20.. :
(*a*) House count
(*b*) % of Room Occupancy
(*c*) % of Potential Room Occupancy
(*d*) % of Double Occupancy
(*e*) % of Bed Occupancy. (*IHMs*)

225. Describe in detail the procedure for key control and also give neat format of Key Control Sheet. (*IHMs*)

226. Draw a neat format of a message slip and explain how the Front desk ensures that the message reaches the guest, particularly when the guest goes out of the hotel with "Room Key". (*IHMs*)

227. List at least 20-entries in a Hotel Service Directory which provides essential information about the hotel and its services. (*IHMs*)

228. Write about 5-equipment required by the Bell desk to carry out its functions efficiently.

229. The Bell Desk handles guest baggage on arrival and departure. List 5-other functions performed by the bell desk staff. (*IHMs*)

230. Explain the procedure for allotting and surrendering a Hotel Safe Deposit locker. (*IHMs*)

231. Explain the conditions and process of accepting guest luggage for storage. (*IHMs*)

232. Explain the procedure while accepting a 'credit card':
(*a*) at the time of arrival when the guest indicates that he wants to settle his bills with a credit card.
(*b*) at the time of departure while settling guest bills. (*IHMs*)

233. List duties and responsibilities of a Doorman in a luxury hotel. *(IHMs)*

234. Explain *any five* of the following abbreviations:

(*a*) ISD (*c*) SFT (*e*) VPP

(*b*) MCV (*d*) PABX (*f*) HWC. *(IHMs)*

235. What are traveller cheques ? What are the procedures involved in making payment through them ? *(IHMs)*

236. What is Telex ? What are the procedure for incoming and outgoing messages. What is the difference between Telex and FAX ? *(IHMs)*

237. What is the left luggage ? What kind of records are maintained for it? What is the procedure for accepting baggage for store ? *(IHMs)*

238. (*a*) Draw a neat format of the Key Control Sheet.

(*b*) Explain the importance of Key Control in a hotel. *(IHMs)*

239. Explain the various modes of settlement of hotel bills. *(IHMs)*

240. Draw specimen formats of *any two* :

(*a*) Mail Forwarding Address Slip.

(*b*) Key Card (Welcome card.)

(*c*) Mail Advice Slip. *(IHMs)*

241. (*a*) Explain the functions of the bell desk.

(*b*) Give a comprehension list of equipment used at the bell desk of a five-star hotel. *(IHMs)*

242. What are the common enquiries guests make at the information desk ? List the sources of information for each of the enquiries. *(IHMs)*

243. What information is furnished by the Hotel Services Directory in a luxury hotel? Mention at least twenty items found in it. *(IHMs)*

244. Categorise mail received in a hotel. Explain the procedure for processing, distribution and storage of such mail. *(IHMs)*

245. Answering the telephone is an opportunity to portray a professional and a positive image for the property. Discuss the guidelines for enhancing the required skills. *(IHMs)*

246. Explain the procedure for accepting left luggage. Mention the precautions to be taken while receiving and delivering them. *(IHMs)*

247. (*a*) Give the organisation chart of the Front Office department of 3-star 200-rooms hotel. *(IHMs)*

(*b*) Give the duties and responsibilities of :

(*i*) Senior Receptionist

(*ii*) Front Office Cashier. *(IHMs)*

248. Write in details about the advance preparation for a guest arrival :

(*a*) at the Back Office; and

(*b*) at the Front Desk . *(IHMs)*

249. Differentiate between the following :

(*i*) "Walk In Guest" and "Walking a Guest".

(*ii*) Sleeper and Skipper.

(*iii*) Overstay and Stay Over.

(*iv*) Key Card and Card Key.

(*v*) Turn Down and Turn Away. *(IHMs)*

250. (*a*) Give a comprehensive list of equipment used at the Front Desk of a 5-star 300-rooms hotels.

(*b*) What is Room Rack ? Explain briefly.

(*c*) What is an Information Rack ? Explain briefly. *(IHMs)*

250. Give neat proformas of :
(*i*) 'C' Form
(*ii*) G.R. Card
(*iii*) Bell Captain Control Sheet
(*iv*) House Keeper's Occupancy Report
(*v*) Movement List. (*IHMs*)

251. Explain the phases in which the registration process can be divided.

252. Explain the various types of Registration records and also explain the Registration System. (*IHMs*)

253. Expand the following abbreviations :
(*i*) DNA
(*ii*) SPATT
(*iii*) FRRO
(*iv*) O.O.O.
(*v*) DND (*IHMs*)

254. What preparations are done for the departure of a guest at the :
(*a*) Bell Desk and
(*b*) Front Desk.

255. What are the duties of:
(*a*) Bell Boy and
(*b*) Cashier of a hotel at the time of departure of a guest. (*IHMs*)

256. With reference to "Computerised Room Management System" explain the following :
(*a*) Function of Room Management.
(*b*) Room Status Discrepancy
(*c*) Housekeeping Function
(*d*) Measuring Productivity
(*e*) Message Waiting System. (*IHMs*)

257. Explain the following :
(*a*) Pie Chart
(*b*) Pictograph
(*c*) Histogram
(*d*) Potential Room Occupancy %
(*e*) Ogive Curve

258. Define :
(*a*) Option Date
(*b*) Check Out Time
(*c*) Whitney Chart
(*d*) Retention Charge
(*e*) Paid Out.

259. Distinguish between :
(*a*) Junior Suite and Suite
(*b*) Hotel and Motel
(*c*) Guaranteed and Non-guaranteed Reservation
(*d*) Overstay and Stayover
(*e*) Turn away and Turn down. (*IHMs*)

260. Expand the following :
- (*a*) FHRAI
- (*b*) PSO
- (*c*) IATA
- (*d*) HRACC
- (*e*) TAAI (*IHMs*)

261. Answer *any four* of the following:
- (*a*) Illustrate through an examples the difference between the 12-Noon check-in/check-out system and the 24-Hour check-in/check-out system.
- (*b*) Discuss in brief the various plans used in hotels. Indicate their appropriateness in different types of hotels.
- (*c*) Illustrate through an examples the usage of the conventional booking chart. Give a neat diagram of the chart.
- (*d*) Discuss the types of hotels based on location, clientele, facilities offered and duration of stay.
- (*e*) Discuss the group reservation procedure. (*IHMs*)

262. Name at least *four* of each :
- (*a*) Bird sanctuaries in India
- (*b*) Hill resorts in India
- (*c*) Beach resorts in India
- (*d*) Historical momuments in India
- (*e*) Holy sites in India. (*IHMs*)

263. Hotel Dayton Inn has provided us the following data :

Total number of rooms	: 350
Room occupied last night	: 312
Today's expected departures	: 108
Today's expected arrivals	: 102
Total revenue for the last night	**: ₹ 1,87,200**
House Count :	: 420
(*i*) International guests	: 280
(*ii*) Domestic guests	: 140

Giving the formula and calculate :
- (*a*) Occupancy %
- (*b*) Average Room Rate
- (*c*) Average Rate per Guest
- (*d*) Multiple Occupancy
- (*e*) Domestic Clientele %. (*IHMs*)

264. Why is it essential to indicate the following on a Room Occupancy Report and how will they be coded :-
- (*i*) Room displaying a DND sign
- (*ii*) Room where there is a very little luggage
- (*iii*) Room which is occupied but the bed has not been slept in at night.

265. Differentiate between (any four):
- (*a*) Office site and Office Layout
- (*b*) Hotel and Motel

(*c*) American Plan and European Plan
(*d*) Food Service and Beverage Service
(*e*) Reception and Information Service
(*f*) Filing and Indexing. (*PGDT&HM*)

OBJECTIVE TYPE QUESTIONS

266. Choose the correct answer for each of the following:

I. The house keeping department of a hotel is not usually responsible for the cleaning of :
(*a*) Restaurants
(*b*) Banquet rooms
(*c*) Public clock rooms
(*d*) Kitchens.

II. In order to maintain standards an assistant housekeeper should inspect rooms at least
(*a*) Once a week
(*b*) Once a day
(*c*) Twice a day
(*d*) Twice a week.

III. The main purpose of a job description is to:
(*a*) Allocate working hours and meal times
(*b*) Clearly define the limits, responsibilities, and the authority of a particular job.
(*c*) Explain the correct procedure of carrying out task
(*d*) List the duties have to be carried out at times allocated.

IV. The housekeepers report or room status report is usually made at :
(*a*) Once a day
(*b*) Once a week
(*c*) Twice a day
(*d*) Twice a week.

267. State whether the following statements are **'true' or 'false':**

(*i*) 'C' form is made for all foreign guests.
(*ii*) Supporting vouchers are vouchers issued by travel agents to their clients.
(*iii*) The term 'No information guest' means a guest who did not sleep in hotel.
(*iv*) More room available than the expected arrivals for the day means plus position.
(*v*) RNA stands for 'rooms not available'.
(*vi*) Formula to calculate single occupancy % is :

$$2 - \frac{\text{House Count}}{\text{No. of Room sold}} \times 100$$

(*vii*) G R stands for 'guest registration card'.
(*viii*) Selling high means selling the rooms on the upper floor of the hotel.
(*ix*) Stay over and over stay means the same thing
(*x*) Floor limit means, the number of floors a hotel can construct.
(*xi*) A room that is taken, occupied, and paid for but not slept is known as 'slept out'.
(*xii*) An inter-hotel room status can only be used by hotels of the same chain.
(*xiii*) The guest registration card does not protect the guest's privacy.
(*xiv*) The hotel register is also called the 'red book'.

(*xv*) The tour leader of a group is also referred to as 'skipper'.

(*xvi*) A hotel adapts a fixed percentage for over-looking.

(*xvii*) The room change step slip is also known as movement list.

(*xviii*) The room rack is arranged alphabetically .

(*xix*) The GRE desk is also referred to as the hospitality desk.

(*xx*) The function room board is placed near the entrance of the lobby.

(*xxi*) Non-resident guests can also avail themselves of the hotels left luggage service.

(*xxii*) All out going mail is entered in the registered mail.

(*xxiii*) The bell captain records the movement of the bell boys with the help of the Bell captains control sheet.

(*xxiv*) The key control sheet is sent to the front office manager in the next morning for his investigation and action.

268. Fill in the blanks:

(*i*) Message slip is made in .... copies

(*ii*) Rack which is placed at reception is called a ....

(*iii*) The guest room keys are made .... sets in number

(*iv*) Change slip is used for .... of credit cards

(*v*) The staff mail is distributed from ....

269. True/False

(*i*) A bad occupancy ratio is better indication of capacity utilization from room occupancy ratio.

(*ii*) A room occupancy percentage is the same thing as a house count.

(*iii*) Liquidity ratio is an indicator of a bank balance of a company.

(*iv*) Current ratio expresses a relationship between CA & CL.

(*v*) The higher the room occupancy the higher the average room rate.

(*vi*) Industrial canteens have English service.

(*vii*) For Airline catering the cooking is done in the galley.

(*viii*) Maitre d' hotel is the French term for Head waiter.

(*ix*) The capacity of tea cup is approx. 200 ml.

270. State whether the following statements are 'True' or 'False' :

(*a*) Responsibility and accountability are the same thing.

(*b*) Delegation reduces a manager's control on his subordinates.

(*c*) The guest registration card does not protect the guests's privacy.

(*d*) The Room Rack is arranged alphabetically.

(*e*) The first step in problem solving is to find alternative solution to the problem.

(*f*) Goal activity reduces motivation.

(*g*) The Hotel Register is also called the Red Book.

(*h*) "Floor limit" means the limit of floor a hotel can construct.

(*i*) The Tour leader of a group is also known as a 'Skipper'. (*MTM*)

271. Fill in the blanks :

(*i*) A hotel situated near airport is called .... while one on the high way is ....

(*ii*) Food plan which includes breakfast and lunch or dinner with the room tariff is the ....

(*iii*) The key which opens all the rooms of a hotel is called ....

(*iv*) Mail the post guest is recorded with the help of the ....

(*v*) EPABX stands for ....

(*vi*) Before accepting a credit card the cashier should check for the .... date.

(*vii*) *Maite d'hotel* is a person who works in .... Department.

(*viii*) After seating the guest, the order is taken and slip is prepared known as ....

(*ix*) Grading of hotel in India is done by committee known as .... (*IHMs*)

272. State 'True' or 'False':

(*i*) The function Room Board is placed near the entrance of the Lobby.

(*ii*) The Care Desk in also referred to as the Hospitality Desk.

(*iii*) The Room Rack is arranged alphabetically.

(*iv*) The Room Change Slip is also known as Movement List.

(*v*) A hotel adapts to a fixed percentage for overbooking.

(*vi*) The tour leader of a group is also referred to as Skipper.

(*vii*) The hotel register is also called the 'Red Book'.

(*viii*) The Guest Registration Card does not protect the guest privacy.

(*ix*) An inner hotel room status can only be used by hotels of the same chain.

(*x*) A Room that is taken occupied and paid for but not slept is known as sleep out.

273. The following are short answer questions. Fill **in the correct** terms in the blanks provided:

(*a*) The four classification of style in flower arrangement are (*i*) .... (*ii*) .... (*iii*) .... (*iv*) ....

(*b*) The number of rooms checked by a supervisor in the regular shift is reformed to ....

(*c*) Key cleaning points for public area supervisor is check and encourage the staff to be alert to are 1.................. 2 .... 3 ....

(*d*) When a guest makes a request that the room maid put bottled water in his room each day, this information is recorded in which record book ....

(*e*) A scheduled of hours and shifts to be worked days off, early and late duty turns, split shift etc. for all members of housekeeping staff is called as ....

274. Fill in the blanks :

(*a*) The hotel staff mail is distributed from ....

(*b*) Charge slip is used for .... of credit cards.

(*c*) The guest room keys are made .... sets in number.

(*d*) Rack which is placed at reception is called as ....

(*e*) Message slip is made in .... copies.

275. State whether 'True' of 'False':

(*a*) The Key Control Sheet is sent to the Front Office Manager the next morning for his investigation and action.

(*b*) The Bell Captain controls the movement of the bell boys with the help of Bell Captain Control Sheet.

(*c*) The message centre is situated in the back office since the activity of taking down messages does not require any personal contact with the guests.

(*d*) All outgoing hotel mail is entered in the Registered Mail Book.

(*e*) Non-resident guests can also avail themselves of the hotel left luggage service. (*IHMs*)

276. Match the following :

(*a*) Vedanthangal	(*a*) Canteen
(*b*) Hertz	(*b*) Travel Agent
(*c*) Dumpukht	(*c*) Bird Sanctuary
(*d*) Air India	(*d*) Cuisine
(*e*) Cox and King	(*e*) TCI.

(*IHMs*)

277. Mix and match :

A	B
(*i*) Italy	Punjab
(*ii*) Lufthanse	Madurai
(*iii*) Vedenthangal	Hill Resort
(*iv*) Wildlife Sanctuary	Germany
(*v*) Trade Wings	Lira
(*vi*) Chandigrah	Bird Sanctuary
(*vii*) Kasauli	New Zealand
(*viii*) Wellington	Gir Forest
(*ix*) Kyat	Travel Agency
(*x*) Meenakshi Temple	Burma.

(*IHMs*)

278. Fill in the blanks : (*IHMs*)

(*a*) The .... boat race for the Nehru Trophy is held every year at the Vembnand lake in Kerala. (*IHMs*)

(*b*) The Kelkar museum of every day art is in .... Maharashtra. (*IHMs*)

(*c*) Kullu in Himanchal Pradesh and Mysore in Karnataka are famous of their yearly .... festival. (*IHMs*)

(*d*) Nalsarovar near Ahmedabad, Point Calimere in Tamil Nadu and .... in Rajasthan are well known water bird sanctuary. (*IHMs*)

(*e*) Nainital in Uttar Pradesh, Darjeeling in West Bengal and .... Shillong in .... are well known hill stations. (*IHMs*)

279. Answer the following questions

(*a*) If your package tour took you to the Prince of Wales Museum, the Hanging Gardens and the National Centre for Performing Arts, in which Indian city would you be ?

(*b*) During your last vacation's you had visited the ruins at Mandu, the Shivpuri National Park Centre, the Caves at Bhimbatka, which Indian state would you have tourned ?

(*c*) At which shop of science splendour across the river Sharaswati in Karnataka would you gaze at 'The Rocks', 'The Roarer' and the 'The Rani' ?

(*d*) If you are visiting the Surajkund Crafts Mela to looks at and buy ethnic handicrafts and handloom, in which Indian state would you be ?

(*e*) In which part of the country would you encounter these group of people 'The Ongoes', 'The Jarwahs', 'The Shompens', 'The Sentinelese'.? (*IHMs*)

280. Pick up the right answer :

1. Link man is also called :

(*i*) Bell Boy (*iii*) Doorman
(*ii*) Houseman (*iv*) Receptionist

2. Franking Machine is :
   (*i*) Hotel's Property
   (*ii*) Hired from P&T
   (*iii*) Hired from MTNL
   (*iv*) None of the Above
3. Bell Boy departure errand card is not signed by :
   (*i*) Bell Boy
   (*ii*) Lobby Manager
   (*iii*) Receptionist
   (*iv*) Cashier
4. Key Control Sheet is prepared during :
   (*i*) Morning shift
   (*ii*) All the shifts
   (*iii*) Night shifts
   (*iv*) Afternoon shift
5. Petty Cash paid on behalf of the guest to be charged in his bill is called :
   (*i*) Allowance
   (*ii*) Credit Advice
   (*iii*) Paid out
   (*iv*) Debit Advice. (*IHMs*)

281. State 'True' or 'False':

(*a*) Registration Card is also known as Form 'C'.
(*b*) House Count indicates the number of guests staying complimentary in the hotel.
(*c*) Commissionaire is the Chief of Police.
(*d*) Sleeper is one who sleeps out for the night.
(*e*) Foreigners must settle bills by payment in foreign currency only. (*IHMs*)

282. State 'True' and 'False':

(*i*) DNS means "did not stay".
(*ii*) Red Book and "F" Form means the same.
(*iii*) Certificate of Registration is needed for all guests staying at the hotel.
(*iv*) Bell Boy Errand Card and Lobby Attendant Errand Card are same.
(*v*) Chance guest is a guest who comes without prior reservation. (*IHMs*)

283. Give one word for the following :

(*a*) Rooms with a common wall but no connecting door.
(*b*) A hotel plan under which room charges include the guestroom and three meals.
(*c*) A hotel area that sells goods and services to guests.
(*d*) Array of metal file pockets displaying room status.
(*e*) A single room with a bed and a sitting area.
(*f*) A guest who has left the hotel without making arrangements to settle his/her account.
(*g*) The room is expected to became vacant after the following day's check out time.
(*h*) The collection of all non-guest accounts including house and unsettled departed guest accounts.
(*i*) A hotel with gambling facilities.
(*j*) The future time frame for which a property accepts reservations. (*IHMs*)

HOUSEKEEPING

1. Explain how internal control can be maintained in the House Keeping Department of a five star hotel. *(IHMs)*
2. Indentify the areas of responsibility of the HK dept., giving a detailed explanation of each.
3. Identify the categories of staff with HK dept. and explain the roles and duties of each. *(IHMs)*
4. What is the importance of the Housekeeping Department in a Hotel ? Explain the working of this department. *(PGDT)*
5. What are the Housekeeping Operations in a hotel ? Why is it considered important? *(PGDT&HM)*
6. What do you understand by house-keeping in a hotel ? Describe the importance of house-keeping department and the specific tasks carried out by the house-keeping department in a deluxe hotel. *(PGDT&HM)*
7. List out the functions of Housekeeping Department. Give a suitable organisation structure for a 300-room hotel. *(PGT&HM)*
8. What are the different methods of charging rooms rates in a hotel ? Explain the Hubbart formula of determination of room rates. *(PGDH&TM)*
9. Give in depth explanation of why housekeeping may be the most important department in creating the financial success of a hotel. *(MTA)*
10. Define Housekeeping Report. Explain in detail what information is on this report? Who prepares this report and how this information is used by the Front Office ? Give a specimen of a Housekeeping Report. *(MTA)*
11. What do you understand by 'house-keeping' operations' ? Explain the working of a House-Keeping department in a five star hotel having 350-rooms. *(PGDT&HM)*
12. Write in detail about the Housekeeping Report of a five star hotel. What are the important factors that should be taken into consideration by the Housekeeping Executive ? *(MTA)*
13. Discuss the statement 'A room lost today is lost for ever'. *(IHMs)*
14. Briefly discuss the advantages and disadvantages of mechanical billing and manual billing. *(IHMs)*
15. Give an in-depth explanation of why housekeeping may be the most important department in creating the financial success of a hotel. *(IHMs)*
16. Identify the areas of responsibilities of the housekeeping department giving a detailed explanation of each. Identify five category of staff in the housekeeping department and explain the role and duties of each. *(IHMs)*
17. Explain the following :
    (*i*) Star Ranking
    (*ii*) Double Lock Room
    (*iii*) In Room Amenities
    (*iv*) Detergents
    (*v*) Types of Beds. *(IHMs)*
18. What records must be maintained for lost and found articles ? If not claimed how are these articles disposed of? *(IHMs)*
19. Explain the following :
    (*i*) DND
    (*ii*) OOO
    (*iii*) SB
    (*vi*) N/P
    (*vii*) C/O
    (*viii*) S/O

(*iv*) D/L (*ix*) V
(*v*) P/L (*x*) OCC.

20. Give the description of the following :
(*i*) Executive Housekeeper
(*ii*) Houseman
(*iii*) Laundry Manager.

21. Give the format of the followings :
(*i*) Occupancy Report or Status Report
(*ii*) Maintenance Order and Job Order
(*iii*) Lost and Found Report

22. Explain the various services and facilities offered to VIP guests of various categories.

23. With a neat illustration explain how a supervisor would go about checking a check out room, after the room has been cleared by the room attendant.

24. Draw a work schedule for a floor supervisor in the morning shift.

25. List out five tasks that are essential part of a room attendant job specification. What should be the average time taken to perform each of them?

26. You have been asked to advise on the provision of bed and table lines for a new residential conference centre, bearing in mind new trend together with the cost of laundry facilities :
(*a*) discuss the reasons you would consider for new establishment
(*b*) giving reasons to support your recommendations prepare a report to be submitted to your manager offering your advice.

27. Why is it important for an Executive Housekeeper to take a systematic step by step approach to planning? (*IHMs*)

28. Enlist the various sequential steps that should be concluded while planning housekeeping operations in any hotel. Support your answer with brief explanations. (*IHMs*)

29. What are the basic responsibilities of an executive housekeeper in the budget process ? (*IHMs*)

30. What are the four basic methods an executive housekeeper can use to control expenses ? Explain each briefly. (*IHMs*)

31. What key areas should an executive housekeeper cover with a new employee in the letter's first day on the job ? (*IHMs*)

32. Employees generally welcome cross training. What are the benefits of cross training to both properties and employees ? (*IHMs*)

33. What items should a room attendant report to her supervisor or to security if they are spotted during guest room cleaning ? (*IHMs*)

34. Good management of an organisation depends on the balance between managing work and managing staff. Explain how an executive housekeeper would calculate maid productivity.

35. Because of high job profile in the Housekeeping Department, an executive Housekeeper spends a great deal of time in recruiting and interviewing employees. Identify and explain ten simple rules of interviewing a housekeeper must observe. (*IHMs*)

36. As an Executive Housekeeper, the hotel management has asked you to help them decide whether the seven year old hotel where you worked needs refurbishment. Explain what refurbishments means ? Give at least four questions. Ask full explanations you will need to take into consideration before giving the management your advice. (*IHMs*)

37. Identify four types of lighting and discuss the correct usages of each type in different areas of a hotel ? (*IHMs*)

38. Colour is an important aspect in creating the environment in which guest will spend time.

Identify the four major conservation factors you will need to take into account when dividing on a colour scheme the guest rooms. *(IHMs)*

39. What two factors can help the executive housekeeper predict a certain level of expense for each expense category? *(IHMs)*

40. The safety and security of hotel premises is essential for building up the same image. Discuss at least 10-different manners that can be taken to prevent theft and crimes. *(IHMs)*

41. In order that the work be carried out efficiently how would the linear room he laidout? Explain giving a typical layout of a linear room of a 400 rooms hotel.

42. Why is the coordination between laundry and housekeeping department is essential ?

43. List steps to be followed when planting a laundry.

44. Identify the four types of detergents and explain the most appropriate uses for each type. Be sure to include the advantages and disadvantages of each type.

45. You have just been hired as a floor supervisor is of 220-rooms 5-star chain hotel. Describe your daily routine and try to include at least 15 of the 24-activities you would engage in. Attempt as such as possible to put these in sequence in which they would be done.

46. Draw a typical work schedule for a Floor Supervisor in the morning shifts.

47. List five tasks that are essential part of a room attendant's job specification. What should be the average time taken to perform each of these tasks ?

48. Draw a layout of an on-premises laundry of a large hotel with 350-guest rooms offering valet services. List out the equipment and personnel required to ensure its smooth operations.

49. There are three basic areas in which housekeeping employees should receive training. What are their areas ? List several elements found in each area.

50. Draw the layout plan of a uniform room of a 400-rooms hotel. Briefly explain its essential features.

51. Discuss in detail where the HK Dept. fits into the organisation of a hotel ? Draw an organisation chart of a hotel company and support your answer.

52. It is impossible to eliminate all types of theft from taking place in a hospitality operation. However, management can enforce some measures in order to reduce the opportunities to steel. Enlist five such measures explaining each into 2-3 lines.

53. Discuss the following:

(*i*) Key Control

(*ii*) Lost and Found.

54 Draw an organisation chart for the housekeeping department of a luxurious hypothetical hotel.

55. Write a job description listing the responsibilities and duties of each staff members of the Housekeeping department.

56. Explain the terms 'Evening Housekeeping', servicing in 'Guest Rooms'. Indicate in your answer an explanation of why this service is done, when it is done, and the specific jobs to be done in the guest room.

57. Explain the following terms in not more than 70-80 words:

(*a*) Star Rating

(*b*) Double Lock Room

(*c*) In Room Amenities

(*d*) Detergents

(*e*) Type of Beds. *(IHMs)*

58. Answer briefly in *one* or *two lines* the following questions :

(*i*) When vacuuming a room, where should you begin in ?

(*ii*) What is the difference between a shower and a bath tub ?

(*iii*) Why should the trolley be parked against the wall ?

(*iv*) Why should soiled liner be folded ? Give at least two reasons.

(*v*) What type of cleaning materials should be used for cleaning badly stained toilets ?

59. List the major types of wall coverings and discuss their relative merits in terms of cost, care, and aesthetic appeal.

60. How will you clean and maintain the following :

(*a*) Chandelier in the Hotel Lobby

(*b*) Terrazo Floor

(*c*) Bath Tiles

(*d*) Bronze Statue

(*e*) Leather Upholstery?

61. Draw up a typical work schedule for a floor supervisor in the morning shift. (*IHMs*)

62. List five tasks that are essentially part of a room attendant's job specifications. What should be the average time taken to perform each of the tasks ?

63. Why is it essential to indicate the following on a room occupancy report and how will they be coded:

(*i*) Room displaying a 'do not disturb sign'

(*ii*) Room where there is very little baggage.

(*iii*) Room which is occupied but the bed has not been slept in at night.

64. Distinguish between built soap detergents and synthetic detergents. What is the polivit method of silver cleaning ? Briefly explain the use of any two of the following :

(*a*) High Pressure Spray and Soil Extraction Machine

(*b*) Brush floor Maintenance Machine

(*c*) Section Cleaner (Wet and day pick up)

(*d*) Carpet (box) Sweeper. (*IHMs*)

65. What is the following terms refer to :

(*i*) Bidet

(*ii*) Karaoke

(*iii*) All Suite Hotel

(*iv*) Dustette

(*v*) pH? (*IHMs*)

66. Compare three different methods of window cleaning in a tabular form under the following headings :

(*i*) Effort Required

(*ii*) Equipment Used

(*iii*) Costs Increased

(*iv*) Time taken

(*v*) Finished Effect. (*IHMs*)

67. What records must be mentioned for Lost and Found articles ? If not claimed, how are these articles disposed ? (*IHMs*)

68. Identify eight areas of responsibility of the Housekeeping Department giving detailed explanation of each. (*IHMs*)

69. Identify the five categories of staff in the Housekeeping Department and explain the roles and duties of each.

70. The success of the Housekeeping Department depends in part on the quality of inter-departmental cooperation that exists between Housekeeping and every other department in the hotel. An especially important area of cooperation is between Front Office and Housekeeping. List five forms (lists or reports) that help achieve effective communication between these two departments. Explain the information contained in these forms and how is it used by Housekeeping Department.

71. Explain in detail the difference between cleaning a departure room and a stayover room. Identify the specifications why the cleaning differs and what special consideration have to be taken into account. *(IHMs)*

72. "Supervising cleanliness in a public area is more complex than supervising the Guest Rooms on the floors". Comment. *(IHMs)*

73. What do the following terms refer to :

(*i*) Cut-downs

(*ii*) Mercerization

(*iii*) Twill Weave

(*iv*) Carding

(*v*) Seer Sucker. *(IHMs)*

74. Suggest a layout for liner room at a hotel having 500-rooms. *(IHMs)*

75. What are the salient features of a good linen room? *(IHMs)*

76. What are the advantage and disadvantage of sharing linen ? *(IHMs)*

77. List six functions that would be conducted in or from the linen room. *(IHMs)*

78. Why are the flower arrangements used in a hotel ? *(IHMs)*

79. (*a*) What are the various levels of placement of flower arrangements?

(*b*) What hints can be followed to ensure that the arrangement lasts longer?

(*c*) Clerical work in an integral part of the duty routine of the Housekeeping Department. *(IHMs)*

80. Justify with suitable examples and formats of at least five of them ?

81. "The level of risk caused by pest infestation in the catering and hotel business is clearly high and needs to be considered at the design stage". Discuss.

82. Enlist the common parts that infest bed rooms and bath rooms. How would you control and indicate them? *(IHMs)*

83. Explain the following terms

(*a*) Tentering

(*b*) Moireing

(*c*) Candle Wick

(*d*) Selvedge

(*e*) Suds. *(IHMs)*

84. What are the general rules to be followed while removing stairs ? *(IHMs)*

85. How will you remove the following stairs :

(*a*) Fresh Wine of Coloured Cotton

(*b*) Iron rust on Synthetic Coloured Curtains. *(IHMs)*

86. Briefly describe the facilities available in a club of various type of hotels. Explain the following terms in one sentence :

(*a*) Coffee Shop	(*e*) Chaise-longues	(*i*) Resident Manager
(*b*) Kiosk	(*f*) Disco theques	(*j*) Horticulture Manger
(*c*) Coiffeur	(*g*) Suite	(*h*) Motels.
(*d*) Jacuzzi		

(*IHMs*)

87. A maid finds a shoe in a check out room. Enlist the standard operating procedure to be followed. (*IHMs*)

88. Enlist the tasks for the daily cleaning procedure of the occupied room. (*IHMs*)

89. Discuss the points to be considered while training room attendants to clean hygienically the rooms and public areas.

90. Differentiate between check list and work cards. Give an example of each. (*IHMs*)

91. How is the Maid Trolley used in a housekeeping operations?

92. Suggest an alternative system to Maids Trolley for an establishment where the layout does not allow for use of a trolley. (*IHMs*)

93. With a neat illustration explain how a supervisor would go about checking a check out room, after the room has been cleaned by the room department. (*IHMs*)

94. Enlist the services and facilities offered to VIP guests of various categories. (*IHMs*)

95. How would the following surfaces be cleaned ?

(*i*) Bridle walls	(*vi*) Plastic
(*ii*) Wood walls	(*vii*) Upholstered furniture
(*iii*) Mosaic walls	(*viii*) Chandelier
(*iv*) Chrome fixture	(*ix*) Swimming pool area
(*v*) Brass and copper	(*ix*) Swimming pool area.

(*IHMs*)

96. What are the cleaning machines used for shampooing a carpet ? Describe them and how would the room be prepared for shampooing ? (*IHMs*)

97. Give the formats for the following :

(*i*) Occupancy Report or Status Report

(*ii*) Maintenance Order or Job Order

(*iii*) Lost and Found Record. (*IHMs*)

98. You have been hired as a floor supervisor in a 220-rooms 5-star chain hotel. Describe your daily routine and try to include at least 15 of the 24 activities you would engage in. Attempt as much as possible to put these in the sequence in which they would be done. (*IHMs*)

99. Why is the cooperation between laundry and housekeeping department essential? (*IHMs*)

100. Give three reasons for discrepancies between actual stock at stocktaking and the book stock. (*IHMs*)

101. In order that the work be carried out efficiently how should the linen room be laid out ? Explain giving a typical layout of linen room of a 400-room hotel. (*IHMs*)

102. You have been asked to advise on the position's of bed and table linen for a new residential conference centre. Bearing in mind new trends together with the cost of laundry facilities

(*a*) discuss the reasons you would consider for this new establishment

(*b*) give reason to support your recommendation. Prepare a report to be submitted to your manager offering your advice. (*IHMs*)

103. How will you treat the following spots on carpets :

(*i*) Bear

(*ii*) Dried Chocolate

(*iii*) Fruit Juice
(*iv*) Tea
(*v*) Coal Tea. (*IHMs*)

104. Draw up a classification of textiles fibres. State one possible care of each fibre in the hotel industry. (*IHMs*)

105. Draw a layout for a uniform room of a five-star hotel having 150-room and 600-employees. (*IHMs*)

105. What factors must be considered when designing a uniform ? (*IHMs*)

106. List the advantages and disadvantages of having on OPL (on premises laundry). (*IHMs*)

107. Draw a labelled diagram of chambermaids trolley. List the salient features of such a trolley as well as its approximate dimensions. (*IHMs*)

108. Prepare a Work Card for cleaning of a W.C. What criteria is used for inspecting the W.C. after cleaning ? (*IHMs*)

109. Differentiate between :
(*a*) Floor Cloth and Drugget
(*b*) Dimensions and Capacity of a Cleaning Equipment
(*c*) Brass and Powder
(*d*) Johny Mop and Dolley Mop
(*e*) Disinfection and Sterilization
(*f*) Granolithic Floors and Terrazzo Floors
(*g*) Surfactants and Suspending Agent
(*h*) Electric Broom and Box Sweeper
(*i*) Orthodox Cleaning and Block Cleaning
(*k*) Financial Benefits and Aesthetic Benefits of Cleaning Equipment. (*IHMs*)

110. List ten factors that affect the frequency of cleaning giving suitable examples. Indicate the suitable frequency of cleaning for the following :
(*i*) Chandellers
(*ii*) Formica surface
(*iii*) Upholstery
(*iv*) Brass handrails.
(*v*) Window panes. (*IHMs*)

111. Distinguish between a room attendant and a room maid. Draw the work schedule for a room attendant working in the morning shift. (*IHMs*)

112. What is the difference between recycled and non-recycled supplies ? What factor singularly affects the amount of supplies required ? Wherein a guest room would you be likely to find the following :
(*i*) A map showing the nearest fire exit
(*ii*) A good night chocholate
(*iii*) Laundry bags
(*iv*) A Dutch wife
(*v*) Bath Towels.

113. Define cleaning. List any three design features that can make cleaning easier. (*IHMs*)

114. Explain the difference between :

The soil bought into the building from outside and soil produced with in the building. Give examples. (*IHMs*)

115. How would you organise storage for lost and found articles ? Design a format for lost and found step to be attached to the article ? (*IHMs*)

116. In the 200-bedroom commercial city hotel in which you work as head receptionist, it is felt by management that the systems of dealing with advanced bookings and correspondence need attention.

With regards to advanced bookings, they feel that the system is too cumbersome, often inefficient in the letting of rooms, and needs streamlining.

With correspondence, they feel that letters are often too long in the system with delays in customers receiving replies.

You are asked to :

(*a*) Recommend an advance booking system suitable for the hotel, describing with appropriate diagrams, the component parts of the system.

(*b*) Suggest a procedure for dealing with and replying to a guest's letter requesting accommodation. *HCIMA* (*London*)

117. It could be said that there are three main types of guest accounting systems available in hotel today, manual, mechanical, and computer.

(*a*) With each of the above, suggest the criteria which would influence your choice.

(*b*) Comment on the main advantages and disadvantages of each of the systems.

HCIMA (*London*)

118. Your hotel is considering taking package tour during the next season.

(*a*) Prepare a report for the General Manager outlining the advantages and disadvantages to accepting group bookings.

(*b*) Produce a timetable showing the tasks to be carried out by the reception department both before arrival and during the stay of a group of overseas tourists. *HCIMA* (*London*)

119. In the planning of bedroom for a new hotel or hall of residence, it is most necessary to use all available space.

With this in mind, discuss the principles that would guide you in your choice when purchasing the furniture and fittings for the bedroom.

You should make specific recommendations on types, style, and quality you would think most suitable for the establishment of your choice. *HCIMA* (*London*)

120. As a management trainee with a company, you are requested to assist in the study of work organisation and the services offered to guests in the housekeeping department of an older type of hotel within the group.

Discuss your approach to this task and give your recommendations on the areas you may examine for greater efficiency in the department and the modern standards that can be attained with the limited amount of capital available. *HCIMA* (*London*)

121. You have been appointed the housekeeper in an old established hotel. A fire certificate has been granted.

Detail your responsibilities in the accommodation department and the methods you will use to ensure that the area you are responsible for is kept safe. *HCIMA* (*London*)

122. A well known local hostelry reputedly 400-years old and of considerable charm, is to be extensively modernised.

Much of the existing interior is to be improved as a direct result of the effects of localised rising damp and dry rot - **the extent of which cannot reasonably be assessed.** In addition, approval has been given for the existing building to be extended as part of the lounge bar improvements.

In terms of the most appropriate tendering method(s) and contract type(s), how might the building owner ensure that his modernisation proposals are to be effectively and efficiently carried out, giving reasons for your choice. *HCIMA (London)*

123. A large catering group has carried out a feasibility study with a view to extending one of its establishments. The extension will comprise of additional bedrooms and enlarged kitchen conference facilities, and an architect has been appointed who will prepare a scheme in accordance with the wishes of the client.

Outline the duties and responsibilities of the following personnel who will be involved in the project :

(*a*) The architect

(*b*) The local authority building inspector

(*c*) The representative of the management. *HCIMA (London)*

124. A new central heating system is to be installed in a large catering establishment and a decision has to be taken as to whether to install a solid fuel boiler or an oil fired boiler.

(*a*) From the information given below, calculate the cost of producing 1,000 mega joules of heat from each of those boilers. N.B. 1 tonne — 1,000 kilogramme.

Solid fuel boiler	:	Efficiency of the boiler	60%
		Calorific value	28 mega joules per kilogramme
		Cost of the fuel	£45.00 per tonne
Oil fired boiler	:	EFF/boiler	80%
		Calorific value	43 mega joules per kilogramme
		Cost of the fuel	£65.00 per tonne.

(*b*) Briefly discuss the conclusions as which you arrived. Outline the factors other than the cost of the fuel when assessing the running costs of the central heating plant.

HCIMA (London)

125. Identify the purpose of the following techniques used in maintenance planning for a large hotel building :

(*a*) Long-term programming

(*b*) Annual programming

(*c*) Short-term (*i.e.* monthly, weekly, daily) programming.

Briefly describe those factors which adversely affect accuracy when programming maintenance work. *HCIMA (London)*

126. The accountant is concerned that there seems to be a lack of control with guests' accounts. He has complained that

(*a*) there does not appear to be any check between reception and housekeeping as to whether rooms are occupied or not, nor by how many persons.

(*b*) guests can stay at the hotel without paying

(*c*) very few guest appear to be charged for breakfast, although many breakfasts are served.

(*d*) quite a number of cheques are being returned for representation or alternatively are not being honoured.

Discuss how you would try to resolve the above complaints and the remedies you would suggest for each. *HCIMA (London)*

127. You are concerned with a 100-bedroomes commercial hotel which has a 'more than usual' turnover of Front Office staff. It is felt that a prime cause of this is the lack of organisation and training in this area.

You are required to draw up for inclusion in the training manual :

(*a*) a job specification for the head receptionist.

(*b*) a procedure for a guest on arrival. *HCIMA* (*London*)

128. The hotel of which you are the reception manager has decided to investigate the possibility of setting up a central reservation system with other hotels in the area.

You are required to :

(*a*) suggest, as the lead hotel in this field, how you would set about this task.

(*b*) describe what you feel may be some of the advantages and disadvantages to be encountered in setting up and running an operation such as this. *HCIMA* (*London*)

129. A hotel group has decided to build a new hotel of 800-bedrooms with conference facilities near an airport. A report has to be made on

(*a*) which type of hire services are available, and a decision has to be made on

(*b*) which of these will be used.

As a Housekeeper with the group, you are asked to study the problems and report to the management on your findings. *HCIMA* (*London*)

130. The staffing budget of the establishment has been cut and it is necessary to streamline some of the operations in the Housekeeping department so that full use may be made of all staff employed.

Prepare a report on areas that you consider could be improved without reducing standards.

(You must specify the type of establishment to which you are referring). *HCIMA* (*London*)

131. Inter-departmental co-operation is necessary in the smooth running of any establishment.

Discuss the importance of this between the Housekeeping department and other departments in a hotel or residential establishment. *HCIMA* (*London*)

132. As manager of a 150-bedrooms, 40-years old hotel, you have been asked by the Board to submit an estimate of the expenditure required by your establishment for building maintenance during the next financial year. Explain fully how you would prepare such an estimate, indicating the areas to which, in your opinion, priority should be given. *HCIMA* (*London*)

133. A Hall of Residence is being planned for 400-students to provide accommodation for a nearby university. The total amount of cash which will be available for the project has not yet been finalised. Of the topics under consideration, the following points have emerged :

(*i*) after the initial costs of planning and completing the project have been met, the cash available for maintenance over the first 5 years will be limited.

(*ii*) the maintenance costs over the first 12 months will be met largely by the contractor's guarantee.

(*iii*) following the guarantee period, all maintenance costs must be budgeted for.

Bearing these points in mind, discuss the following:

(*a*) "low initial costs will lead to higher maintenance costs"

(*b*) ways in which the maintenance costs could be controlled. *HCIMA* (*London*)

134. A large catering establishment located near to a city centre is to be externally repainted. Specifications and tenders are to be invited from a number of suitable contractors.

Outline the procedure which should be adopted to ensure that the structure of the building has been thoroughly inspected prior to the commencement of the contract.

To what particular points in the specification should attention be given before a tender is accepted. *HCIMA (London)*

135. (*a*) What factors should be considered when setting 'par' for linen ?

(*b*) Explain step-by-step procedure for conducting physical inventory of linen in a round the year busy hotel. Support your answer with all relevant formats. *(IHMs)*

136. List the characteristics of fibres and weaves used in bedding and table linen. *(IHMs)*

137. (*a*) Draw up a list of Bath Linen that a five-star hotel would require for its guestrooms.

(*b*) State the purchase specifications for a bath towel in terms of fabric, size, colour and cost.

(*c*) What factors will affect the par stock of bath linen that a hotel maintains ?

(IHMs)

138. How will you deal with the following types of pest infestation in the hotel ?

(*a*) Rats

(*b*) Termites

(*c*) Ants

(*d*) Bed bugs

(*e*) Cockroaches. *(IHMs)*

139. A young boy is celebrating his 21st birthday. He has just become a cadet. Plan an invitation, cake design, centrepiece and decorations, and giveaways for this function. State the materials used for decorations and estimate the approximate total cost of decorations. (Assume and state additional data, if necessary) *(IHMs)*

140. Give one relevant reason for the following :

(*a*) White towels are more absorbent than coloured one.

(*b*) It is necessary to weigh linen before loading it into the washing machine.

(*c*) A fabric conditioner is used in the final rinse of the wash process.

(*d*) Blankets are napped.

(*e*) It is necessary to air articles, which have been dry cleaned before folding and storing them.

(*f*) There is lint left back on the garments after washing in the washing machine.

(*g*) Linen should be marked or monogrammed before laundering.

(*h*) The linen room should be situated near the service elevator.

(*i*) White cottons are starched.

(*j*) Flowers should be cut either early morning or late in the evening.

141. Explain the following terms (*any four*) :

(*a*) Suzzie

(*b*) Jupone

(*c*) Carding

(*d*) Mercerization

(*e*) Satin weave

(*f*) Sequestering agent. *(IHMs)*

142. What principles of interior decoration and elements are important aspect in creating an enjoyable environment for a guest room. Explain with suitable examples. *(IHMs)*

143. Differentiate and explain the following (*any three*):

(*a*) Classification and Properties of colour

(*b*) Job Description and Job Specification

(*c*) Wall Elevation and Floor Plan

(*d*) Refurbishing and Redecoration. (*IHMs*)

144. (*a*) **Why training is considered so important for the employees of an Hospitality Industry? Plan a training programme for a room maid.**

(*b*) **What is cross training ? What is the benefit of cross training to an employee?** (*IHMs*)

145. Why do accidents and injuries occur more in housekeeping and Maintenance Department ? What measures would take in preventing them ? (*IHMs*)

146. Enlist the type of contract services which are normally hired by housekeeping department of a hotel. What are the points considered before giving the contract? Enumerate the advantages and disadvantages of contract services.

147. What are the advantages of having the following (*any five*) :

(*a*) Duty Roster

(*b*) Procedure Manual and Master Manual

(*c*) Wholesale Buying

(*d*) Graphics

(*e*) Curtain Headings

(*f*) Bin Card. (*IHMs*)

148. You have been appointed as an Executive Housekeeper at a five star hotel in a Metropolis, which will be opening in due course. What steps would you take to ensure that the department is ready for full operation on the day it opens. (*IHMs*)

149. (*a*) Supervision in the Housekeeping Department calls for "Supervision". Justify the statement.

(*b*) How does a cleaning checklist assist this housekeeping function ?

(*c*) What are the criteria for inspecting the following items :

(*i*) the W.C.

(*ii*) the entrance door

(*iii*) the bed.

(*d*) List any four items/areas where the housekeeper has to depend on the room attendant for checking. (*IHMs*)

150. Classify the job titles in the Housekeeping Department in the categories of management, supervisory and operational staff. Using the format give the job description of a

Floor supervisor : ....

Job Description : ....

Responsibilities : ....

Responsible to : ....

Shift Timings : ....

Subordinates directly supervised : ....

Working in liaison with : ....

Basic duties : ....

Additional duties : ....

151. (*a*) Draw up a advertisement inviting applications for the post of an assistant housekeeper in a three-star hotel having 80-rooms.

(*b*) Prepare an outline interview for the job vacancy.

152. "A training programme should work from tasks to jobs instead of from jobs to tasks". Provide you viewpoint on this statement.

153. Explain how a monthly consumption sheet is useful for budgeting.

154. What is the work study ? How does it assist in assessing staff requirement when planning and organizing the Housekeeping Department ?

155. Explain the principles of interior design and their role in room decor.

156. What is a colour scheme ? List the different types of colour schemes with a brief explanation of each.

156. What factors must be considered when planning a duty roster ? The staff working in the Linen Room of a three-star hotel having 50-rooms and operating with an off-premises laundry, are a Linenkeeper, 2 Linen attendants, 2 Seamstresses and 1 Trainee Housekeeper.

Draw up a duty roster for the staff working in this area.

157. State any one advantage of :

(*a*) Contract cleaning

(*b*) Allocating the same group of workers to the same floor/section on a regular basis.

(*c*) Wall-to wall carpeting

(*d*) Lining curtains

(*e*) Purchasing items on a tender basis.

158. Indicate the essential difference between :

(*a*) Frequency schedule and Work schedule

(*b*) Redecoration and Refurbishing

(*c*) Floor plan and Wall elevation

(*d*) Floor finish and Floor covering

(*e*) The Value and Intensity of a colour

(*f*) Housekeeping in Hotels and Housekeeping in Hospitals.

159. On 1st January, 1995 a houseman Nandalal Shinde, slipped off a parapet while cleaning a window-pane from outside. The safety belt he was wearing was defective and snapped. Fortunately, his fall was broken by a ledge below and he suffered minor injuries.

Design an Accident Report form and as the Housekeeper in charge, fill in this form, assuming suitable additional data wherever necessary.

160. In the table below, tick the fire extinguisher that you should use for the type of fire listed.

TYPE OF FIRE	*CO_2*	*WATER*	*DCP*	*FOAM*	*OTHERS*
Electrical Fire	....	....	....	....	....
Gas	....	....	....	....	....
Kerosene	....	....	....	....	....
Wood	....	....	....	....	....

What systems of fire detection are usually installed in hotels?

161. Flower vases and flowers will become an arrangement when certain principles are adhered to. Would the same hold true if the room be compared to the vase and the furniture to the flowers ? Discuss.

162. Give a floor layout for a single bed room with attached bathroom (to scale) of a 4-star hotel.

163. You wish to be appointed as "Executive Housekeeper" of a five star hotel. List the responsibilities you have to undertake for such a job and also highlight the qualities which you possess to be fit for this appointment.

164. Good system of recruiting can reduce that turnover of employees. Discuss specifying :

(*a*) Recruitment and selection procedure

(*b*) Ways of reducing employees turnover.

165. (*A*) Answer briefly :

(*i*) List four ways in which a housekeeper endeavours to ensure security within her department.

(*ii*) List the different kinds of colour harmonies.

(*iii*) State two ways of preventing excessive wear in particular areas of carpet.

(*iv*) The wearing qualities of a carpet depends mainly on :

(*a*) Pile backing and fitting

(*b*) Density, height and weight

(*c*) Weight, colour and thread

(*d*) Pattern, colour and shading.

(*B*) Write short notes on any two :

(*i*) General procedure for removal of carpet stains

(*ii*) Ways of lighting

(*iii*) State the "Law of Chromatic Distribution".

166. What are main considerations in planning floor and carpet maintenance schedules and procedures ?

What are the basic components of a carpet ? What kinds of carpets would be most practical in

(*a*) Guestroom ?

(*b*) Lobby ?

167. Answer briefly :

(*i*) Give four reasons why the executive housekeeper should make daily tours of a new facility before opening ? Should these tours be made alone ? If not who should accompany the executive housekeeper ?

(*ii*) What key areas should an executive housekeeper cover with a new employee on the first day of his/her job.

(*iii*) Compare recycled and non-recycled inventories. What are some of the typical items in each category ?

(*iv*) What are the two main reasons that housekeeping and maintenance have more accidents and injuries than other hotel departments ?

168. Explain how a monthly consumption sheet is useful for budgeting ? Give a specimen form of a monthly consumption sheet.

169. What basic responsibilities does the executive housekeeper has in terms of purchasing operating supplies ?

170. State any two advantages of :

(*a*) Contract cleaning.

(*b*) Wall to wall carpeting

(*c*) Purchasing items on a tender basis.

(*d*) Allocating the same group of workers to the floor/section on a regular basis.

171. Indicate one main difference between :

(*a*) Frequency scheduled and work schedule

(*b*) Redecoration and refurbishing

(*c*) Floor plan and wall elevations

(*d*) Floor finish and floor covering

(*e*) Safety and security.

172. Answer briefly :

(*a*) What is the most important aspect of developing performance standards ? How are standards best communicated once they are developed ?

(*b*) What are some of the sources of information you might use to check an applicant's references ?

(*c*) What are the four 'basic methods' an executive housekeeper can use to control expenses.

173. Answer briefly :

(*a*) What is the last step of the four steps of training method and why is it important ?

(*b*) What three factors should be considered when setting "par" for linen.

(*c*) What are some of the things an executive housekeeper should do to prepare for an interview.

174. (*a*) What is the importance of guest room inspection and how should it be conducted ?

(*b*) Of what use is a room inspection checklist ?

(*c*) Mention at least four areas often overlooked during guest room cleaning.

175. (*a*) Explain the difference in the cleaning of an occupied stayover room and a checkout room.

(*b*) Give neat formats for the following :

(*i*) Maintenance Order Slip (MOS)

(*ii*) Lost and Found Record/form.

176. Briefly explain :

(*a*) DND

(*b*) Sanitary Unit

(*c*) Front of the office

(*d*) Service elevator

(*e*) Sanitized for use

(*f*) Shower curtain

(*g*) Bidet

(*h*) DL

(*i*) SB

(*j*) V.

177. How will you clean the followings :

(*a*) Brass door handles

(*b*) Wooden flooring

(*c*) Ceramic wall tiles

(*d*) Chrome fittings

(*e*) Upholstered sofa.

178. (*a*) What is 'tarnish' ?

(*b*) How would you clean EPNS articles used in your hotel ? Give at least two methods.

(*c*) Name two other metals commonly found in hotels and give the method of maintenance of each.

179. Write short notes on any FOUR of the following :

(*a*) Wall paper finishes

(*b*) Surfactants

(*c*) Role of housekeeping in the prevention of crimes in hotels

(*d*) 'Maids' service room

(*e*) Special cleaning

(*f*) Evening/turn down service.

180. (*a*) A clean lobby is the first moment of trust that a guest experiences in a hotel and this leaves a lasting impression on him". Explain the importance of keeping the lobby clean and it's cleaning method.

(*b*) Explain the working of a wet and dry vacuum cleaner OR a floor scrubber polisher.

181. (*a*) Give the job description of an Executive Housekeeper of a five star hotel.

(*b*) Explain the importance of inter-departmental cooperation between the Housekeeping and the Food and Beverage service departments.

182. Give reasons (why) :

(*a*) When cleaning a guest room, the maids' cart should be placed in front of the open door, facing into the room.

(*b*) The Room Occupancy Chart is prepared.

(*c*) Before taking a guest room under repairs, Front Office permission or approval is required.

(*d*) A floor seal enhances the life of the floor finish.

(*e*) The use of lacquer on brass helps prevent the formation of tarnish.

183. "Flower arrangement adds to the aesthetic appeal of an area". Justify this statement. Discuss the points to be considered for flower arrangements for the following areas with suitable diagrams :

(*a*) Lobby

(*b*) Coffee table

(*c*) Conference room

(*d*) Dressing table

(*e*) Hostess desk.

184. Classify fibres and give the suitability of the following for various purposes :

(*a*) Silk

(*b*) Nylon

(*c*) Cotton

(*d*) Kapok

(*e*) Jute.

185. 'Pests are uninvited guests in hotel premises'. Discuss various preventive measures that need to be taken at designing stage.

186. Explain the following terms in a line or two (*any ten*) :

(*a*) Flocking
(*b*) Merecerization
(*c*) Jacard
(*d*) Ticking
(*e*) Damask
(*f*) Jhvead Count
(*g*) Sat in Weave
(*h*) Scouring
(*i*) Condemned Linen
(*j*) Recycled Linen
(*k*) Suds
(*i*) Japone.

187. You have to organise a Christmas party for 50 people. Plan the layout, seating arrangement, materials required, and their approximate cost to make it a success.

188. At what temperature should the following items be laundered ?

(*i*) Woolen blanket
(*ii*) Dusters and Cleaning cloths
(*iii*) Coloured towels
(*iv*) Coloured Synthetic Uniforms
(v) Silken Bed Spread.

189. What is stock-taking ? Explain in detail the procedure adopted for stock-taking in the housekeeping department with formats used.

190. Draw an ideal linen and uniform for a 5-star hotel and explain the activities of the linen room and it's necessary features.

191. Give the classification of stain removal methods. What are general rules to be followed while removing stains ? How would you remove the following stains ?

(*i*) Lipstick
(*ii*) Milk
(*iii*) Tea
(*iv*) Chewingum
(*v*) Curry Stain.

192. What laundry symbols are used for the following terms :

(*i*) Cannot be bleached
(*ii*) Don't iron
(*iii*) Dry flat
(*iv*) Drip dry only
(*v*) Don't wash.

193. What are the rule of thumb method and the hubbast formula to establishing room rates? How effective do you feel each one is ?

194. Describe a system of monitoring room rates . If you are employed at a front desk, do you see your supervisor or manager using such a system ? How often ? How effective do you feel this is in maintaining effective room rates?

195. Describe the various type of room rates.

196. Make your application for the post of FRONT OFFICE ASSISTANT. With your Curriculum Vitae and Covering letter. (Do not reveal your identity or the identity of your Institute).*(IHMs)*

OBJECTIVE TYPE QUESTIONS

197. State whether **'True' and 'False'** giving reasons :

(*a*) Block cleaning is a system where a room attendant is incharge of a block of rooms and completes cleaning of each of room in the block before proceeding to the next.

(*b*) One of the distinguishing factors between a disinfectant and an antiseptic is that a disinfectant can be used only on in a minute objects while the antiseptics is used on human beings

(*c*) It is essential for a hotel to focus attention on the customer rather than a service.

(*d*) A burnishing machine is used by the kitchen stewarding for polishing floors to high lustre finish.

(*e*) Colour coding must be utilized to distinguish equipment used for toilet cleaning. *(IHMs)*

198. Give **one word** for each of the following sentences :

(*a*) A dense cotton fringe attached to a metal or wooden rod.

(*b*) A mixture of a clay, quartz or flint and fields par moulded and fired at high temperature.

(*c*) A soft leather used for polishing glass panes and silver.

(*d*) A floor consisting of marble chips band with cement and water and land in site.

(*e*) A napped cotton material used for butting of smooth surfaces.

(*d*) A rubber strip fixed for a metal holder and used in conjunction with a rod and handled designed to remove water from surface.

(*g*) This cotton sheet used to cover furniture during or in storage, after discarded item from linen room.

(*h*) Manually operated mechanical sweeper used for removal of light dust from carpeted areas.

(*i*) A term used to describe the process of destroying potentially harmful micro-organisms from a variety of surfaces.

(*j*) A general term that is used for a chemical that removes seals and polishes from surfaces.

199. Spot the **odd out** and give a reason, eg. bed-sheet, night- sheet, bath-sheet. Bath-sheet is the odd one out, bath-sheet is a bathroom linen and the other two are bed linen:

(*a*)	Duvet	Quilt	Blanket
(*b*)	Dust Sheet	Drugget	Dustette
(*c*)	Scrim	Swab	Sea Foam
(*d*)	OOO	OCC	WC
(*e*)	Bait	Silverfish	Cricket
(*f*)	Chamois	Jewellers rouge	Pumice
(*g*)	Harpic	Dettol	Savlon
(*h*)	Room attendant	Houseman	Valvet runner
(*i*)	Burnishing	Lacquering	Polivit
(*j*)	Bath towel	Face towel	Bathmat.

(IHMs)

200. Choose the correct answer for each of the following and write them to your answer book :

(*i*) The storekeeping department of a hotel is not usually responsible for the cleaning of:

(*a*) Restaurants

(*b*) Banquet rooms

(*c*) Public cloak rooms
(*d*) Kitchens.

(*ii*) In order to maintain standards an assistant housekeeper should inspect rooms at least :
(*a*) Once a week
(*b*) Once a day
(*c*) Twice a day
(*d*) Twice a week.

(*iii*) The main purpose of a job description is to :
(*a*) Allocate working hours and meal times
(*b*) Clearly define the limits, responsibilities and the authority of a particular job
(*c*) Explain the correct procedure of carrying tasks.
(*d*) List the duties to be carried out at terms allocated

(*iv*) A Housekeepers Report or Room Status Report is usually made out :
(*a*) Once a day
(*b*) Once a week
(*c*) Twice a day
(*d*) Twice a week.

(*v*) Sodium carbonate is :
(*a*) A disinfectant
(*b*) Washing Soda
(*c*) Bicarbonate of soda
(*d*) A sanitizer.

(*vi*) Toilet cleaners should never be mixed with any other cleaning agents as the combination could produce :
(*a*) Corrosion on the surface
(*b*) Heavy stains on the surface
(*c*) Harmful gases
(*d*) High inflammability.

(*vii*) Mild water stains on baths may be removed by uses of :
(*a*) Methylated spirit
(*b*) Deodorants
(*c*) Acitic acid.

(*viii*) The term dustettes refers to a :
(*a*) Gloved chamois leather
(*b*) Pedal bin
(*c*) Hand operated suction clearor
(*d*) Vacuum cleaner plant.

(*ix*) The piece of cleaning equipment which often provides ideal condition for bacterial growth is a :
(*a*) Wet suction machine
(*b*) Vacuum
(*c*) Box Sweeper
(*d*) Mop-head.

(*x*) The agent for cleaning marble wall is :
(*a*) Steel wool
(*b*) Abrasive powder

(*c*) Acid solution

(*d*) Neutral solution. (*IHMs*)

201. Give **one word** for the following :

(*a*) A floor mounted cistern with a hot and cold water tap attached at an ascending spray at centre of a bowl used for perineal washing.

(*b*) A cloth intended for polishing of glassware

(*c*) A lime stone metamorphosed by heat and pressure used at cut blocks for floors.

(*d*) A loosely women cotton cloth which is absorbent and does not leave lenters when used for cleaning.

(*e*) Linen, cotton or plastic sheets used to protect floor coverings from heavy spoilage during cleaning or renovations.

(*f*) Equipment used to remove debris soil and for water from surface by suction.

(*g*) A small portable light weight suction cleaner used for removal of dust from variety of surfaces.

(*h*) Keys that open doors that are double locked.

(*i*) A protective finish which form a film of parting on a surface and protects it.

(*j*) A general term that is used for a chemical that removes seals and polishes for a surface. (*IHMs*)

202. Choose the correct answer for each of following statements and write them out in your answer book :

(1) Certain establishment indicate that WC has been a sanitized. This establishes that the WC has :

(*a*) Received the attention of a plumber

(*b*) Received its weekly cleaning

(*c*) Been deodorized

(*d*) Been cleaned since the previous occupants departure.

(2) The tarnish which forms on silver is :

(*a*) Silver Sulphate

(*b*) Silver Oxide

(*c*) Vendigris

(*d*) Iron mould.

(3) A substance which rubs off stairs by the application of friction is referred to as :

(*a*) A disinfectant

(*b*) On abrasions

(*c*) A deodorant

(*d*) A sanitizer.

(4) Polivit plate is used for :

(*a*) Cleaning copper forms

(*b*) Sterlising stainless steal

(*c*) Washing crockery

(*d*) Asserting stain removal (one electroplated nickel silver)

(5) A combinations of five particles of purmice, synthetic detergent, and an alkali is reformed to as a :

(*a*) Biological detergent

(*b*) Soap powder

(*c*) Synthetic detergent

(*d*) Souring powder.

(6) One of these pieces of equipment is not electrically powered which one is it:
   (*a*) High speed polisher
   (*b*) Wet and dry pick up
   (*c*) Vacuum Cleaner
   (*d*) Box Sweeper.

(7) Which one of the following material could be used to construct a sub floor :
   (*a*) Terrazzo or Marble
   (*b*) Ruarry and Concrete
   (*c*) Bitumastic or Magnesite
   (*d*) Wood or Concrete.

(8) The best floor finish for a ball room floor is :
   (*a*) Marble
   (*b*) Block wood
   (*c*) Parquet
   (*d*) Terrazzo.

(9) A floor finish which may be laid as strip block and banquet :
   (*a*) Terrazzo
   (*b*) Granolithic
   (*c*) Marble
   (*d*) Wood.

(10) What is the main advantage of using a matt point rather the gloss ?
   (*a*) It increases reflection of light
   (*b*) It is easier to keep clean
   (*c*) Streaks are less noticeable
   (*d*) It absorbs light and reduces glare. (*IHMs*)

203. The following are short answer questions. **Fill in the correct terms** in the blanks provided

(*a*) The four classifications of styles in flower arrangement are :
   (*i*) ....
   (*ii*) ....
   (*iii*) ....
   (*iv*) ....

(*b*) The number of rooms checked by a supervisor in the regular shift is referred to as
   (*i*) ....

(*c*) Key cleaning points for the public area supervisor to check and increasing the staff to be alert to are :
   (*i*) ....
   (*ii*) ....
   (*iii*) ....

(*d*) When a guest makes a request that the room maid put bottled waters in his room each day; this information is recorded in which record book ?
   (*i*) ....

(*e*) A schedule of hours and shift to be worked days off, early and late duty-turns, split shifts etc., for all members of the Housekeeping staff is called the:
   (*i*) ....

204. Fill in the blanks :

(*a*) .... used by carpet cleaning were weighted.

(*b*) Sterling silver contains .... % silver and the rest is ....

(*c*) .... agent are based on caustic soda.

(*d*) Expensive tableware with lustre and reng is known as .... glass.

(*e*) Window cleaners are based on isopropyl ....

(*f*) Prepare bed for the night is referred to as " .... "

(*g*) Policist plat is used for ....

(*h*) A key which opens all doors including those which are double locked is a ....

(*i*) Borosilicete glass is made heat resistant by addition of ....

(*j*) High pressure washers are used for cleaning in .... *(IHMs)*

205. Give full form of :

(*a*) QUATS

(*b*) VFM

(*c*) EPNS

(*d*) E.M.T.

(*e*) W.C. *(IHMs)*

206. Using the proforma of a Form of Housekeeping Staffing Guide given at the end of this question, indicating the number of staff members that could be employed at various occupancy rates from 5% to 100%. Use the following information and guidelines to create the staffing guide:

(*a*) Total number of rooms in the hotel-1200.

(*b*) One housekeeper is required for every 15-rooms that are occupied

(*c*) One linen person is required for every 150-rooms that are occupied.

(*d*) One utility worker is required for every 400-rooms that are occupied

(*e*) One house person is required for every 150-rooms that are occupied.

(*f*) The minimum staff size is one housekeeper and one linen person regardless of occupancy.

Housekeeping Staff Guide

Occupancy %	Rooms	Housekeepers	Linen	Persons	Utility *Workers*	House *Persons*
100	....	....	....	....	....	....
95	....	....	....	....	....	....
90	....	....	....	....	....	....
85	....	....	....	....	....	....
80	....	....	....	....	....	....
75	....	....	....	....	....	....
70	....	....	....	....	....	....
65	....	....	....	....	....	....
60	....	....	....	....	....	....
55	....	....	....	....	....	....
50	....	....	....	....	....	....
45	....	....	....	....	....	....
40	....	....	....	....	....	....
35	....	....	....	....	....	....
30	....	....	....	....	....	....
25	....	....	....	....	....	....
20	....	....	....	....	....	....
15	....	....	....	....	....	....
10	....	....	....	....	....	....
5	....	....	....	....	....	....

207. As a Room Inspector you made the following **observations** on your rounds :

(*a*) Room nos. 502, 504, 505 and 409 are occupied.

(*b*) Room nos. 501, 503, 506 and 507 are vacant.

(*c*) According to the last status report 510 is supposed to be vacant but appears to be occupied.

(*d*) All of these rooms have been cleaned, except 509.

(*e*) The television of room no. 508 is not working.

(*f*) A night bulb needs to be replaced in 503.

Based on the above information you are required to prepare a Housekeeping Status Report, indicating the status of rooms 501 to 510 and room inspection sheets where necessary.

208. A partial housekeeping report is given below. You are required to review the same and answer the questions that follows :

Room No.	VAC	OCC	Room No.	VAC	OCC
200	VR			VC	
202		OCC			OCC
204	VR			VR	
206	VC				OD
208	VD				OD
210		OCC			OOO
212	V/O			VR	
214	VR				OD

(*a*) How many rooms are vacant and ready to sell ?

(*b*) How many rooms that are currently occupied by guests have been cleaned by the housekeeping staff ?

(*c*) How many room that are currently occupied have not yet been cleaned ?

(*d*) How many rooms are out of service and are neither occupied nor available to sell ?

(*e*) How many rooms are of uncertain status ?

209. Match the following :

(A)	(B)
(*a*) Damask	(1) Crinkle sheets
(*b*) Drill	(2) Theatre stage curtains
(*c*) Seersucker	(3) Bedspreads
(*d*) Net	(4) Napery
(*e*) Velvet	(5) Chef coats
(*f*) Candlewick	(6) Sheer curtains.

210. Match the following :

(A)	(B)
(*a*) Lipstick	(1) Ammonia
(*b*) Rust	(2) Acetone
(*c*) Paint	(3) Borax
(*d*) Blood stain	(4) Carbon tetrachloride
(*e*) Paan	(5) $KMnO_4$ and Oxalic acid
(*f*) Grease	(6) Turpentine.

211. Assess the accommodation and catering facilities in any one of the tourist resort/metropolitan of India. Also illucidate if the facilities are adequate there, or there is still some an exploited potential left ?

212. (*a*) What are the necessary qualities in the staff of a housekeeping department in a big hotel?

(*b*) Write the main points in the housekeeping operations which a manager must control.

(*PGDT&HM*)

213. Describe in full the steps taken in preparing for guest arrivals at :
(*a*) the reservation section, and
(*b*) at the front desk. (*MTA*)

A CASE STUDY 5.6

214. There are weekly manager's meeting in the Gangotri Hotel. In one of the meeting held on 15th January, Mr. Rajan, general manager, said that the wants to up-date all training manuals. He instructs the departmental head to involve the employees in this task, as employees participation will produce a quality product. On leaving the meeting, Raghu Nath, the front office manager, decides to start on the project right away. He decides to meet with his shift leaders and listen to their suggestions. The comments from the staff are most encouraging. However, they feel, the job will be a lot of work, They worked on the project for several days and Mr. Raghu Nath had developed a rough draft of a plan to revise the training manual for the front office. He has organised the major sections of the manual to follow the guests' experience at the hotel during the stay. Each point was thoroughly discussed with the staff, and a final draft of the plan is organised and agreed upon.

He assigns the revision of the guest checkout section to Amit, the head cashier. Amit has worked at the hotel for five years. He started as a waiter in the restaurant, progressed to the banquet department, worked for two years as a desk clerk, and has spent the past year as head cashier. His work has always been accurate. He extends hospitality very ably to departing guests. Several guests have sent, returned/comment, letter/cards praising his efficiency during busy check-in times.

Amit's first task him her to a step by step process of checking out a guest. Raghu Nath has instructed him to write this procedure as if 'nothing would go wrong'. You are reserved to answer the following:–

(*i*) Did Raghu Nath pick the right person for the job ?
(*ii*) Why?
(*iii*) What steps Amit should include in the guest checkout process ?
(*iv*) What are some safeguard he could include to ensure an efficient check out?

A CASE STUDY 5.7

215. Ms. Ritushka as a resident manager for the Mount View Hotel attended a meeting of the departmental heads with the executive director of the hotel. The main discussion in the meeting highlighted the short coming of the marketing and sales department of the hotel. The operations in the front office and housekeeping have been running quite smoothly but you decided to take a good hard look at her departments to avoid a similar situation. You have decided to examine the following:

(*i*) Is there a need to lighten up the financial areas ?
(*ii*) Are the employees of the front office and housekeeping delivering satisfactorily the hospitality as well as performing their functional roles ?
(*iii*) How cooperative is she with other departmental heads ?

You have compared your forecasts for the past three months against the historical figures and find that you were right up to 80% of the time. However you noted that a few times when you forget to enter a walk in count for a festival being held. You also find that labour costs are being held with in the budgetary guidelines. On some occasions you exceeded the guidelines when some college trainees and part-time employees did not show up for works and payment has to be made to regular employees for overtime.

You made an analysis and felt that there is a need of improvement in the area regarding the number of complaints from guest against two front office employees. Jamuna, the bell hop, has continuously been late for work for the past one month. On two occasion he did not show up at all. He has also been written up for his tardiness and absence. When questioned he claims, he will not be late again, Dhirju, the switch board operator is very terse and short with the guests. He has 12-years experience in the hotel. His approach to people has been very abrupt, not the smooth and caring personal touch. He has earned the outstanding employees award several times in the past.

You remember the incident with the sales and marketing department in the last meeting which has still not been smoothed over. You have told Mumtaz, the Director of marketing and sales, that the house was full on a weekend in September when it was booked for only 30%. This mistake caused him to loose a big amount of commission for the month. The sales and marketing office has questioned the front office clerk on information that has been requested.

You are well established in your position, but are willing to accept constructive suggestions for improving year approach to managing the front office and housekeeping. The executive Director of the hotel Mr. DPS Rawat, wants his departmental heads and supervisors to grow with the demand of the organisation. He is quite helpful and cooperative. Narrate all suggestion, Mr. DPS Rawat, could give in the above situation.

A CASE STUDY 5.8

216. Hotel Mandwa is a 500-room hotel situated in a small town of the same name near Jaipur. It is a family owned hotel. The Shahs bought the old palace from the ruler of Mandwa and converted it into a hotel. Some rooms have been redecorated in contemporary style while others have been left as they were, except that some kind of ethic furniture has been placed is the guest bed rooms. The elder son of a family, Sanjay Shah has been given the responsibility of managing this property. This is his first experience with the hotel business.

The initial response to this hotel was overwhelming. It was booked up to six months ahead for the coming winter. Travel agents were enthusiastic about this quaint little quite desert town and the old place.

Of late the hotel management has been receiving complaints from guests and travel agents that the housekeeping service and the standards are far below acceptable standards. The room look shabby, unkept, and a foul smell. The flooring is patched, the sofa worn out and the wardrobes are dirty and so the list goes on.

Repeated remands to the manager of the hotel have made no difference.

Group bookings are being cancelled one after another. There has been no repeat business and word about the hotel's deteriorating standards is spreading fast. The last straw was an article that featured in a trade journal, deriding the hotel. The writer of the article asks in his concluding sentence is the legend (Mandwa) dying a slow death ?

Prepare an action plan that Sanjay Shah must take to improve the housekeeping standards of the hotel. (*IHMs*)

A CASE STUDY 5.9

217. One of the regular guest who also is a VIP and fussy, complained the Lobby Manager that Rs. 5000/- were missing from his room something which had never happened with him. Lobby Manager gave the matter to security for investigation. The security on questioning the housekeeping boy come to know that the boy had opened the room for the glass cleaner who is a casual boy and also since the floor was under renovation and refurbishing, upholsterers with his boy had come to change the old sofa with the new sofa. This upholsterer was also on contract. On further questioning the boy said since the supervisor of the floor was along with these people, he did not stand and get the sofa changed.

On questioning the supervisor, she said that she was standing there with the contractor for some time but then after some time she left them on their own.

Questions :

(*i*) What was the details of the investigation ?

(*ii*) What action was taken ?

(*iii*) What are the role played by the :

(*a*) General Manager (*b*) Resident Manager

(*c*) Lobby Manager (*d*) Executive Housekeeper. (*IHMs*)

CHAPTER 6

Food and Beverages : Production Sales and Service

OBJECTIVES

After studying this chapter, you should be able to :

1. *Understand the importance of food and beverages sale in a hotel*
2. *Explain the functions of food and beverages department*
3. *Understand the important menus and courses and culinary terms, garnishes, accompaniments*
4. *Define food production and patisserie*
5. *Understand the organisation of food production and food and beverages service*
6. *Explain the duties and responsibilities of the food production and food and beverage service*
7. *Understand the various methods of food and beverage services.*

FOOD AND BEVERAGES

One of the basic requirements of a hotel is to offer food and beverage to all visitors. Many hoteliers have realised the importance of this activity. Much of the reputation of a today's hotel centres around its food and beverage service, much of the appeal of the hotel is in decor, atmosphere and service offered in the restaurants, bars and other sales outlets.

Food and beverage have become a potential source of profit in many hotels. Cash-generation, profitability, image building and giving a new look to the hotel, are the main perspectives of the food and beverage management. There are new developments taking place in the hotels, such as :

1. Profitable use of space
2. Recognising food and beverage facilities as a potential source of profit
3. Development of new styles and operating techniques in food and beverage
4. Introduction of street restaurant philosophies in hotel business
5. Indication of profit leverage due to investment in new food and beverage operations.

In majority of the hotels, food and beverage have become a second major activity. Figure 6.1 indicates the basic activities of the food and beverage section.

In many hotels the food and beverage service account for a large number of employees due to :

1. Meal and refreshments in these hotels may be supplied to non-residents as well as resident guests and include substantial functions of sales.
2. The provision of meals and refreshments has a relatively high labour content. Depending upon the size, type and structure, different organisational approaches for food and beverage outlets are adopted by the hotel :
   (*i*) Grouping all the food and beverage activities together as food and beverage department with its own head of the department.
   (*ii*) Grouping all food and beverage activities under the assistant manager.
   (*iii*) Grouping several of these departments together as one department under its own head of the department.
   (*iv*) Grouping purchasing, storage, bars and cellars, the back of the house activities including kitchen, under an assistant manager.
   (*v*) Treating each food and beverage sale outlet and supporting service as a separate department with its own head of the department.

The food and beverages functions in a hotel are closely related, but at the same time, these have inter-dependence on other activities of the hotel operation. The same employees handle both products food and beverages. Most of the goods and services provided in the same outlet, may not be identifiable as either food or beverages. The revenue of each function can easily be separated, but it is impracticable to separate all costs of operation other than the cost of sales.

Therefore, food and beverages are treated as one group and analysed by sales outlet and reflected in the organisational structure of the hotel.

Food and beverage control is another important activity and is an integral part of the total accounting function of the hotel. All restaurant cashiers, food and beverage control assistants, cost control clerks are part of the accounting department.

In hotels where the sales department is in existence, and food and beverage sales are monitored by that department and reservations for functions, banquet, conferences etc. fall under the responsibility of the sales department.

FOOD AND BEVERAGE DEPARTMENT

In many hotels this department is headed by a food and beverage director. It represents a complex group in which there are many lines of authority and over-taking functions. No hotels are alike specially in the case of organising Food and Beverage Department. They differ in regards to arrangement of authority and duties of personnel. Fig. 6.1. Shows the flow chart of basic facilities of food and beverage section. Figs. 6.2 and 6.3 show the different types of organisational charts of this department.

The main activities related to the Food and Beverage are :

1. Purchase and Storage of Food and Beverages
2. Food Production and Patisserie
3. Food Selling and Service
4. Beverage Service.

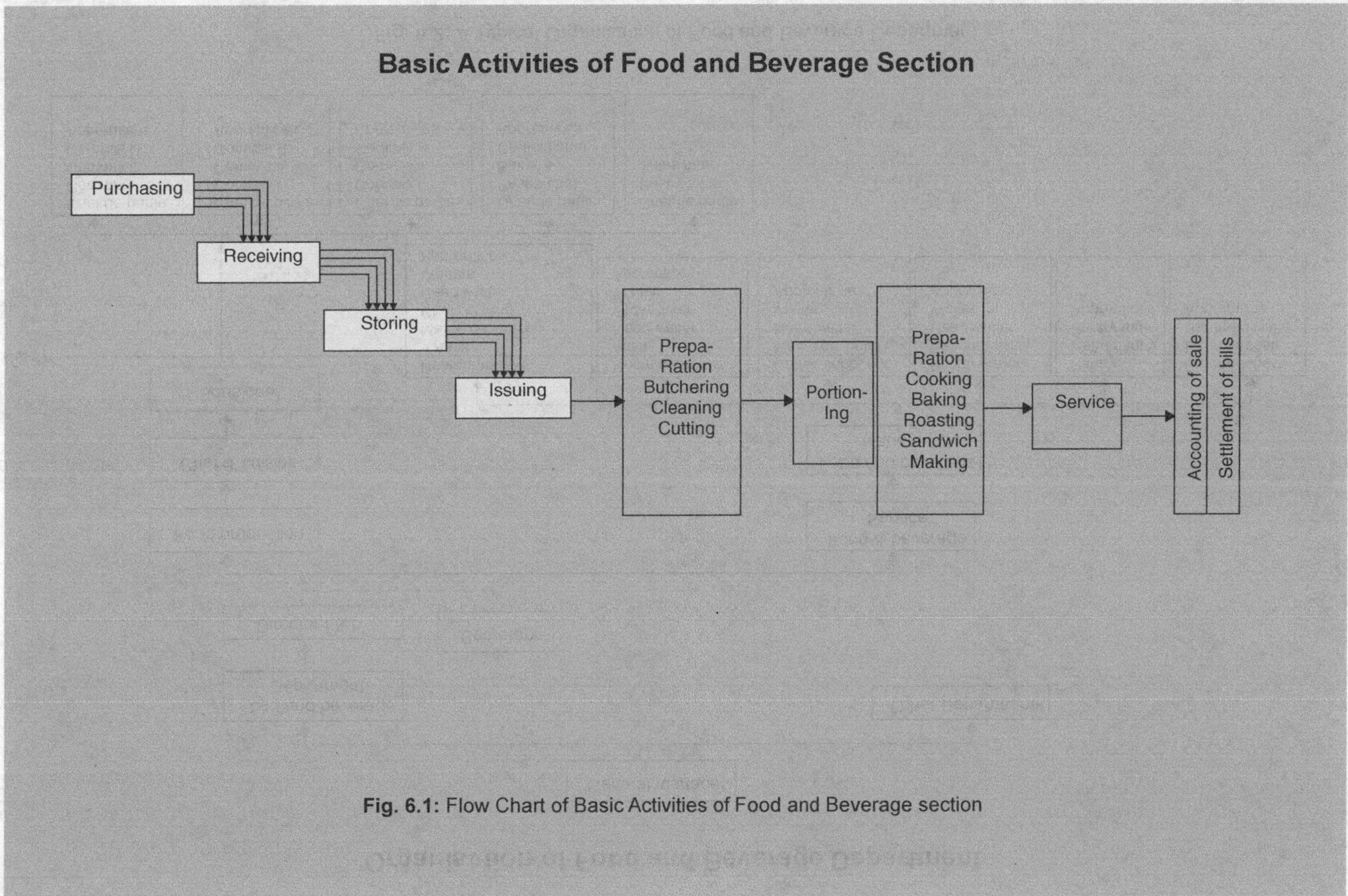

Fig. 6.1: Flow Chart of Basic Activities of Food and Beverage section

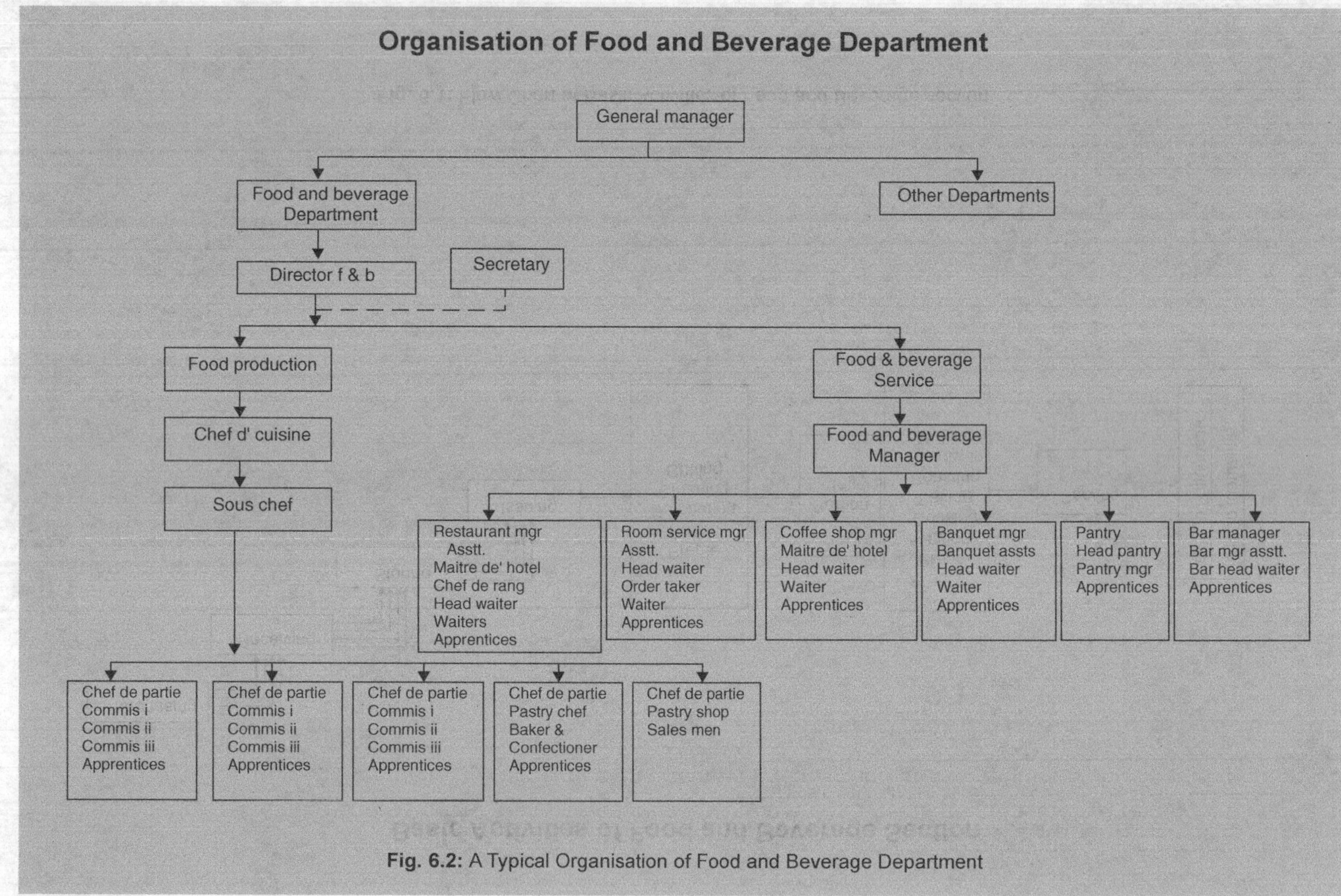

Fig. 6.2: A Typical Organisation of Food and Beverage Department

PURCHASE AND STORAGE

Food purchases are directed either by the Food and Beverage Manager or the Executive Chef. There are many variations in purchasing methods depending on the location and availability of merchandise. In most cases, a clerk receives the stores and distributes the food supplied.

FOOD PRODUCTION AND PATISSERIE

This is the next phase of food which takes place in the kitchen of the hotel. It is a place where artists and craftsmen work together under an Executive Chef (Master Chef) to achieve the most delicious combinations of food which must satisfy the appetite, the taste and the touch. A small kitchen might be divided into two areas : preparation and kitchen service. The preparation area will be for preparation of vegetables. Fish, meat and poultry as well as desserts such as cold starters, salads and decorative work. The kitchen service area will be the cooking and plating or service area. Large hotel will split preparation areas

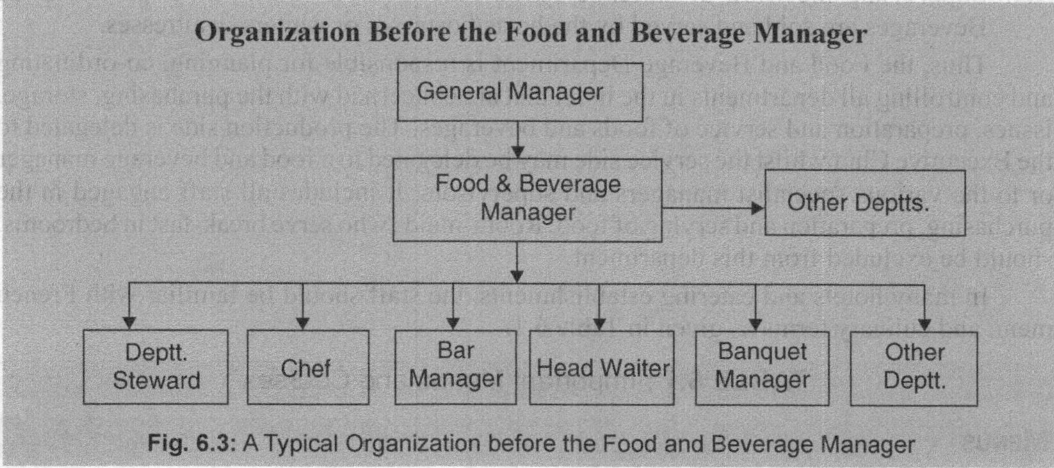

Fig. 6.3: A Typical Organization before the Food and Beverage Manager

into meat, fish and vegetable preparation and split the cooking area into sections or corners specialising in different methods of cooking preparation viz., soups, fish cooking, roasting, and grilling, vegetabls and potato cooking, sweets and larder where raw and cold preparation takes place. The Executive Chef is in-charge and plans the menus and supervises cooks and pantry workers who prepare food in the various sections of the kitchen. The department is divided into butcher-shop, kitchen, pastry and bakery. In smaller hotels, the Executive Chef is responsible directly to the manager, but in larger hotels, he reports to the food and beverage manager.

FOOD : SELLING AND SERVICE

In large hotels, the department in-charge of food and services makes arrangement for banquets and is called a Banquet Manager, Restaurant Manager or 'Maitre d'hotel'to distinguish him from the head waiters of the different restaurants. In small hotels, the in-charge of food service department is known as head waiter/head waitress. He/she is responsible for private dining rooms and banquet halls and the service of food and beverage in the guest rooms. In some typical hotels the head waiter is assisted by a staff of captains who directs the service-waiters and waitresses, who take orders and serve. Once a function is booked and all 'selling' arrangements have been made, the banquet service group takes over. The head waiter has a most important job and is responsible for a variety of duties. In addition to supervising the setting of the room, he must make sure that the banquet steward has the proper type and sufficient amount of glasses, china and silver available for the party. He must see the linen has been reserved and works very closely with the Chef.

BEVERAGE : SALE AND SERVICE

The wine steward handles the purchasing and receiving of the beverages. All liquor and wine is stored in the wine room or wine cellar and issued by a requisition. The requisition is made out and signed by the head bartender. Thus, the head bartender or wine steward, who reports to the food and beverage manager, is responsible for :

1. Purchasing, receiving and storing of wines and liquors
2. Preparation and service of mixed drinks
3. Requisitioning and ordering of beverages
4. Supervising the work of bartenders who must be able to mix all popular drinks. Beverages are sold and served by the hosts/hostesses or waiters /waitresses.

Thus, the Food and Beverage Department is responsible for planning, co-ordinating and controlling all departments in the hotel that are concerned with the purchasing, storage, issues, preparation and service of foods and beverages. The production side is delegated to the Executive Chef whilst the service side may be delegated to a food and beverage manager or to the various specialist managers and supervisors. It includes all staff engaged in the purchasing, preparation and serving of food. Room-maids who serve break-fast in bedrooms, should be excluded from this department.

In many hotels and catering establishments, the staff should be familiar with French menu and culinary terms as given in Table 6.1.

TABLE 6.1 : Important Menus and Courses

Menus

1. *á la carte :* from the card : All dishes are listed and priced separately. There are many dishes at different prices for the guest's choice.
2. *table d 'hôte :* This type of menu has a fixed number of courses, with or without a choice within each course. The selling price of the menu is fixed.
3. *plat du jour :* Speciality of the day. Individually priced dish or a frequently changed dish in an otherwise standard menu
4. *carte du jour :* This menu combines the *á la carte, table d 'hôte*, and *plat du jour* menus, each being priced according to type.

The Courses

1. *hors d' oeuvre* or appetizer course : a variety of sausages and dressed and pickled foodstuffs, designed to simulate the appetite
2. potage or soup course : vegetable soup
3. *consommé* : clear broth
4. *crême - veloute* : pure thick soup
5. *poisson(s)* : fish / fish course
6. *entrées* : well garnished meat dishes, frequently served as main courses

(*Contd...*)

7. *relièves or remove* : larger than entrees and take the form of joints that have to be carved
8. *sorbet* : water-ice perhaps flavoured with champagne or a liqueur
9. *rôti* : roast meat, game or poultry
10. *légumes* : vegetables course
11. *entremets* : the sweet, hot or cold
12. *savoureux* : savouries served hot on toast or as a savoury souffle
13. *fromage* : cheese
14. *dessert* : fresh fruits and nuts
15. *café* : coffee.

PRODUCTION OF FOOD

The modern kitchens in good hotels are air-conditioned, well ventilated, spotless and a pleasant place in which to work. The kitchen is the main production centre in a hotel. It has sub-divisions/sections/parts roast, pastry, butchery, larder and so on, supported by a production team known as kitchen brigade.

LAYOUT OF PRODUCTION AND SERVICES AREAS

The planning of kitchen equipment and layout needed depends upon :

1. The advance planning of market segments to be sought after
2. General menu contents and
3. Type of overall service planned.

The guiding principle for restaurant planning and designing is 'minimum of effort with a maximum of efficiency'. The equipment should facilitate rapid economic delivery to the guests. The right equipment must be of the right amount and at the right place. The configuration of basic equipment and storage facilities varies according to the spectrum ranging (non-convenience food to a gourmet cuisine). A meticulous system approach must be used to ensure that all the pieces fit to form a unified whole. The system adopted and practically used must translate the menu into its constituent elements, purchasing units, storage requirements and processing steps. A given level of sales of a given menu will determine both the amount of individual items needed and the nature and volume of individual work steps. A limited menu can hold equipment needs down, on the other hand, an eleborate menu calls for complex processing and storage equipment. Flexibility in the kitchen is required for adjustment in menu in the later stages.

In new food and beverage establishments, you require to translate the menu into work steps, storage requirements and equipment. Each menu item has its own logistical implications, from the receipt of food supplies, their storage and their issuance into production, through delivery of the meals to the table. Analysing the menu in term of the work steps involved is the basis for determining the processing and storage equipment and its placement for minimizing labour costs.

Storage equipment must be designed with consideration of nearness and accessibility for movement into storage from the receiver and issuing out of storage to production.

Menu also determines the kind of equipment needed for the most economic preparation of meals. It determines how that equipment is used. The efficient use of these equipment depends on the location on how the various pieces are located in relation to each others.

The food preparation process is composed of a greater number of individual work steps using variety of utensils, as well as the major pieces of equipment; therefore, facilities and layout is critically important point. The labour cost includes a substantial amount of time used just for moving supplies from one location to another.

The basic principle of a well-designed kitchen in a specialised food and beverage unit is the establishment of individual work centres for specific food preparation functions. In a normal type of restaurant the following work centres are generally required:

1. The Pantry to prepare salad, sandwiches and desserts
2. The broiler station
3. The fry/cook station.

Each of these stations operates with separate equipment and supplies. Each work is a self-contained unit, but not separated from others by walls or visual distractions, workers have no isolation. They are accessible to the necessary supervision and co-ordinations. Each work centre has its own crew workers, each of whom is trained to perform all the functions of that particular work centre.

A CASE STUDY 6.1 : KITCHEN

SITUATION :

A hotel formally peeled its potatoes by machine. When the Machine wore out, however, it was not replaced. Potatoes were agained peeled by hand. Data from both the hand and machine operations were compared as to cost of peeling and eyeing 100 pounds of identical grade potatoes.

RESULTS OF COMPARISONS:

	Cost when hand Peeled	Cost when Machine Peeled
Number of workers used	3	1
Average daily Wage Rate for Worker	$7.00	$7.00
Time of Operation (Minutes)	22.00	22.00
Total Man - Minutes	66.00	19.00
Waste in Peeling Port 100 Lbs	26.00	28.00
Cost Per 10 Pounds	$.963	$.273.

Since hand peeling cost more than three and one half-times as much as mechanical peeling, no time was wasted in the purchase of another mechanical of potato peeler.

Equipment in each work centre needs to be installed with a view to workers' convenience. All work surfaces, values control and appurtenances must be easily accessible and at right levels. The space allocated to individual work stations needs to be balanced between enough space and not too much. The greater the available space, the more workers have to move from one activity to another, and thus, the more time consumed. Equipment installation must also consider both workers' comforts and efficiency.

The relationship of each work centre must be carefully designed to flow from station to station and to the service area. The placement of facilities, the relationship to storage area and the dining area and the sequence with in the total meal need to be carefully planned. The kitchen should be able to operate as a production line. The food preparation should have smooth flow of work with successive stages of production accomplished as material move along.

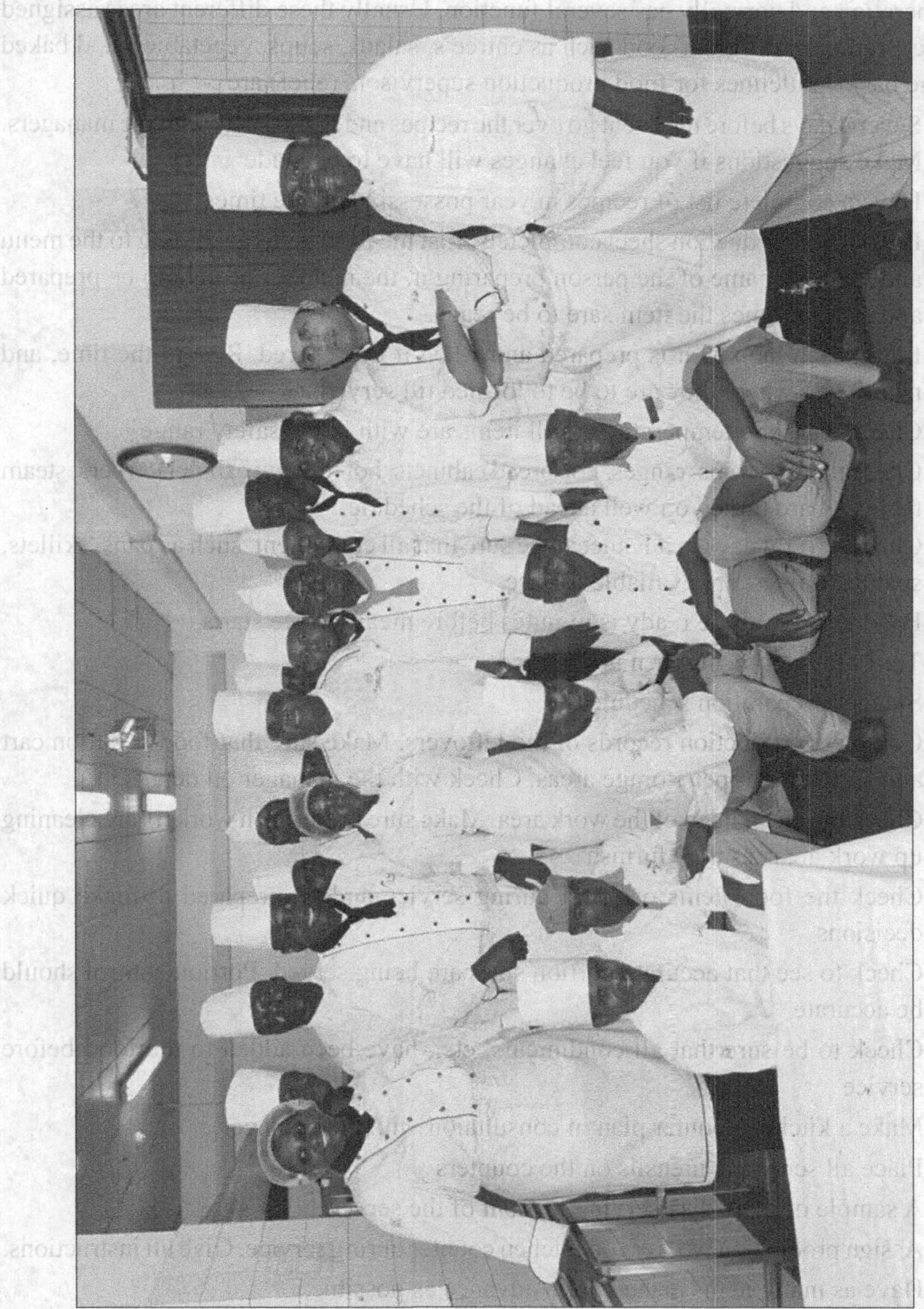

Pix 6.1 A Chef Brigade

KITCHEN SUPERVISOR–CHECK LIST

Production or preparation area is the principal activity centre of any food and average service operation and normally has several function. Usually these different areas assigned for the preparation of different food such as entree's, salads, soups, vegetables, and baked goods. The basic guidelines for food production supervisors (chef) are :-

1. Several days before the event go over the recipes and worksheets with the managers. Make suggestions if you feel changes will have to be made
2. Have a complete list of recipes in year possession all the times
3. Fill out the production sheet completely. List the food items according to the menu and with the name of the person preparing it, the member of item to be prepared and at what times the item sare to be ready.
4. Initial each item as it is prepared and when it is prepared. Record the time, and mentioned where they are to be to localed till served.
5. Check that time/temperature of all items are with in the safety range
6. Check that all ovens, ranges, hot-bread cabinets, hot holding cabinets, fryers, steam table etc, are turned on well ahead of the schedule.
7. Check several days in advance to be sure that all equipment, such as pans, skillets, spatula, knives, are available for use.
8. Food items must be ready is minutes before meal service starts
9. Turn off equipment when not needed.
10. Stagger preparation schedules.
11. Complete production records of the leftovers. Make sure that food is put on cart and sorted in proper storage areas. Check with the manager on details.
12. Check the clean linen of the work area. Make sure production workers are cleaning up work areas as they furnish
13. Check the food items on hand during service and be prepared to make quick decisions
14. Check to see that accurate portion sizes are being served. Portion control should be accurate
15. Check to be sure that all condiments, etc., have been added to the food before service
16. Make a kitchen counter plan in consultaion with the manager
17. Place all servicing utensils on the counters
18. A sample of plate/dish serving in front of the server
19. Assign production workers on kitchen counter during service. Give all instructions.
20. Have as many items dished up in advance as possible
21. Provide a wet cloths for wiping plates etc.
22. Be sure that the plates are nicely decorated prior to being taken with the dining room.
23. Coordinate timing for service of each course of the meal.

Finished meals also require a systematic kitchen layout design. Draw 'work overlap' diagrams as given in Figure 6.4 and Figure 6.6, by super imposing flow charts of the preparation steps of each menu items on a drawing of a planned layout, its position identified and eliminates flow problems before the installation of equipment. The figures clearly indicate the layout of production and service areas for the employees' food service facility in a service industry.

The layout of the kitchen relates direct to guest service. It determines the speed and efficiency with which guests' orders are received, processed and delivered. Thus, the kitchen layout flows direct into the layout of other facilities, such as :

1. Service areas, where servers deliver orders, price up foods, and assemble everything needed for delivering the complete meal to the guest
2. Supplies of linen, flatware, condiments, and other service related items
3. The dishwashing and storage facilities.

Figs 6.4, 6.5, 6.6 and 6.7 indicate the layout for food and beverage areas.

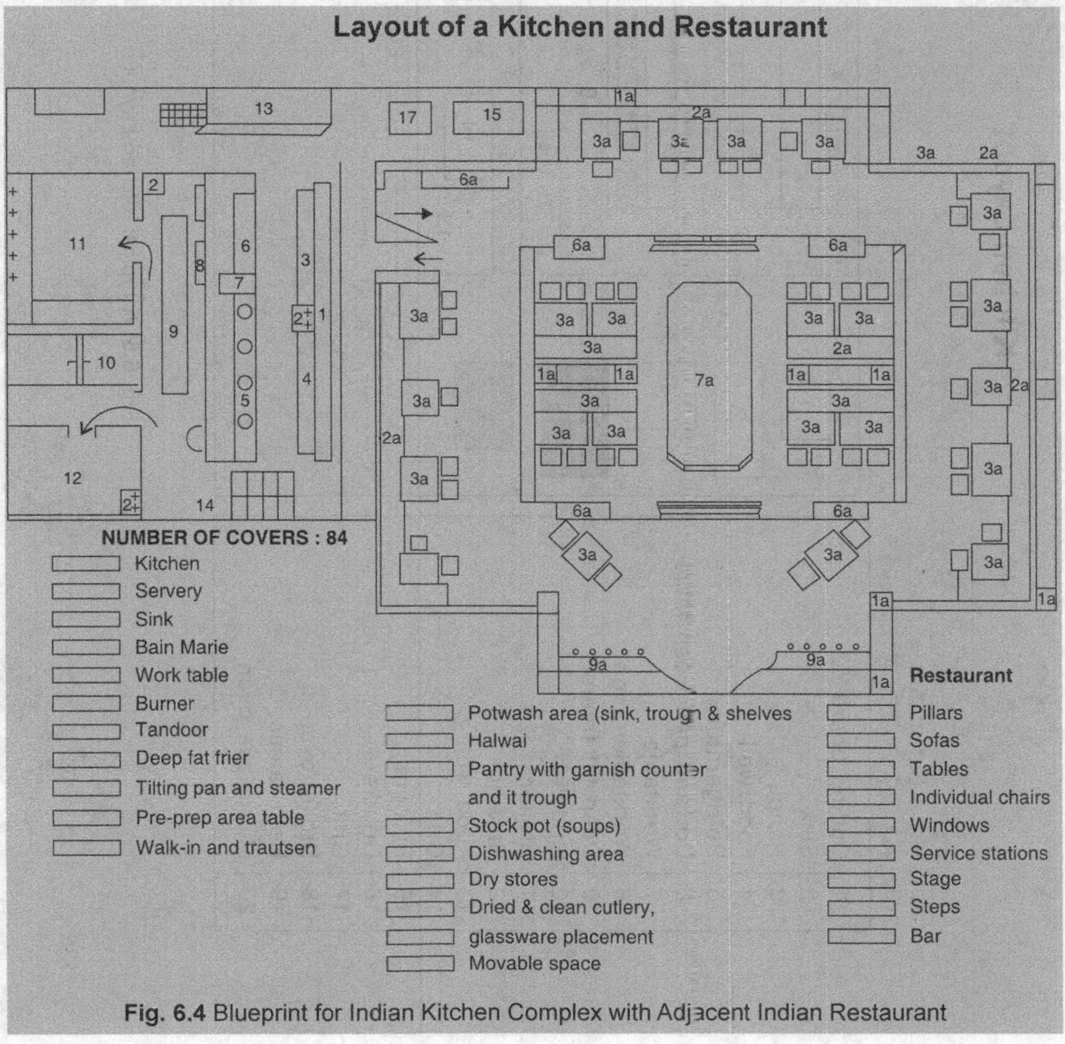

Fig. 6.4 Blueprint for Indian Kitchen Complex with Adjacent Indian Restaurant

Kitchen Layout

key

1	Cutting board
2	Sink
3	Range
4	Food well
5	Refrigerator
6	Dot and pan wash table
7	Worktable
8	Worktable/range
9	Deep fat fryers
10	Griddle
11	Broiler
12	Steamer
13	Food well
14	Grill
15	Burners
16	Griddle
17	Grill
18	Broiler/oven
19	Heat lamps
20	Microwave oven

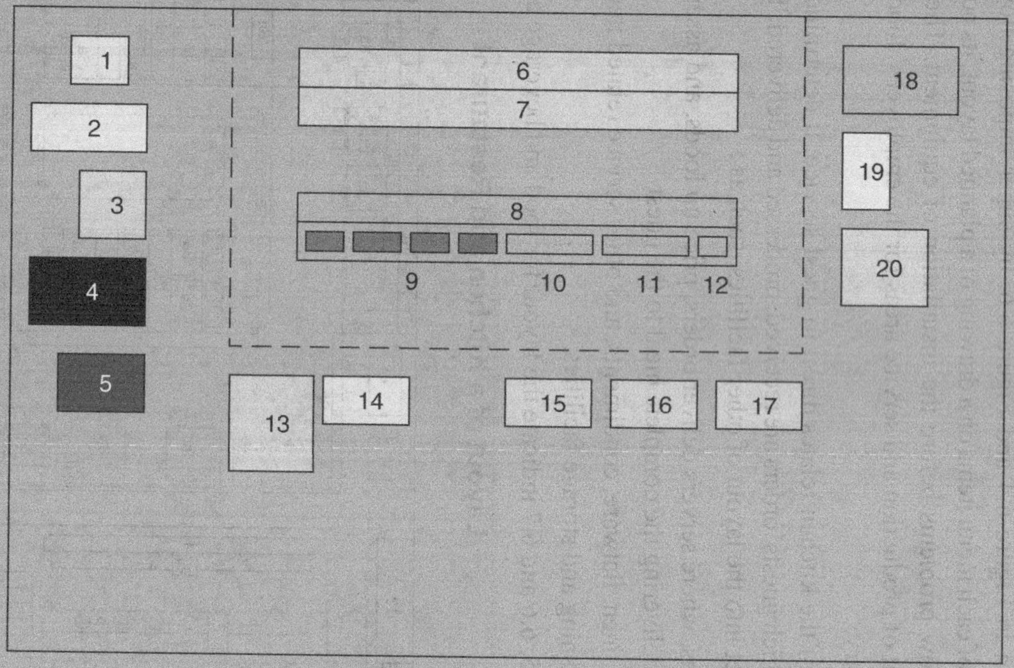

Fig. 6.5: A Typical Kitchen Layout

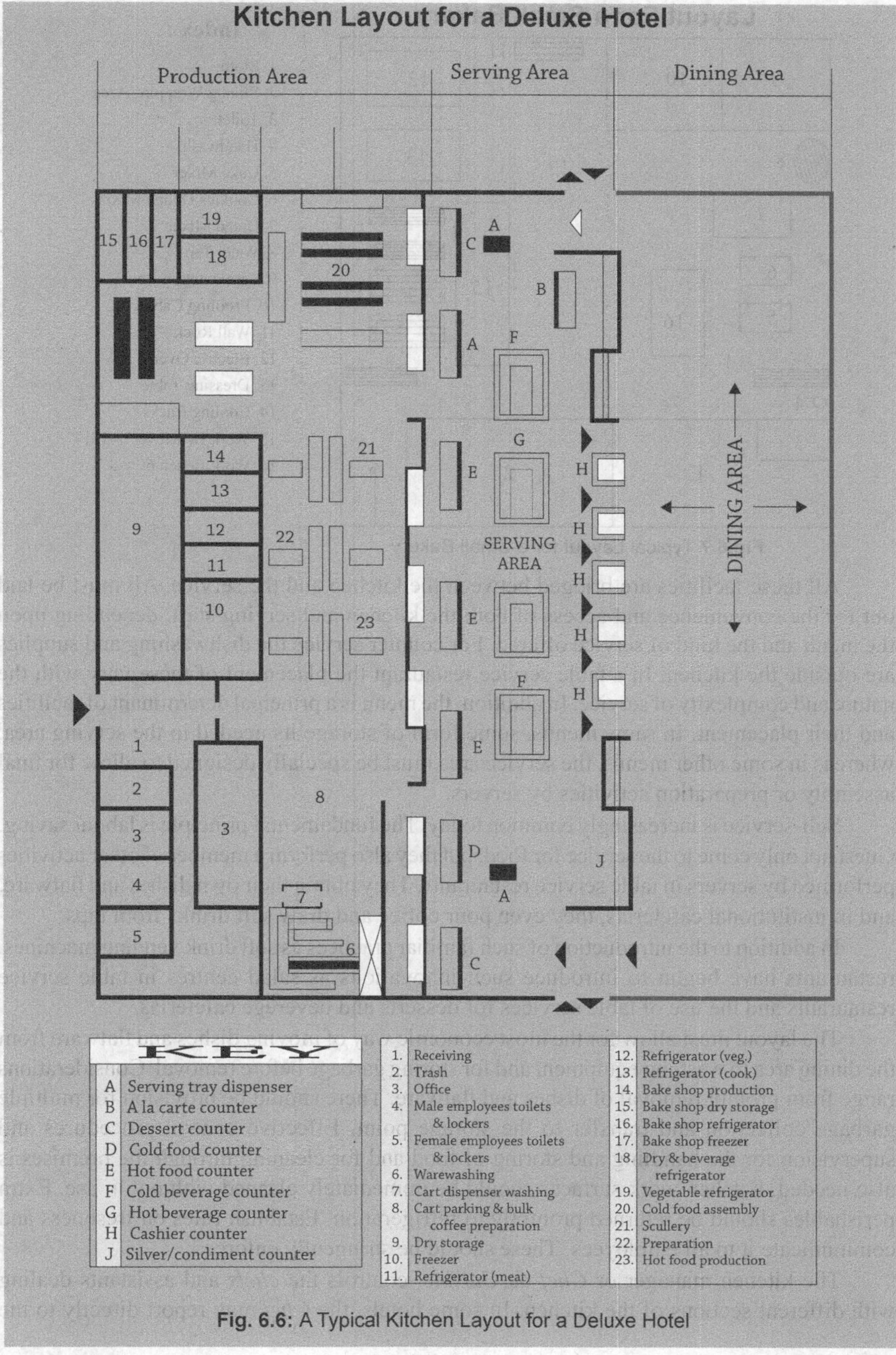

Fig. 6.6: A Typical Kitchen Layout for a Deluxe Hotel

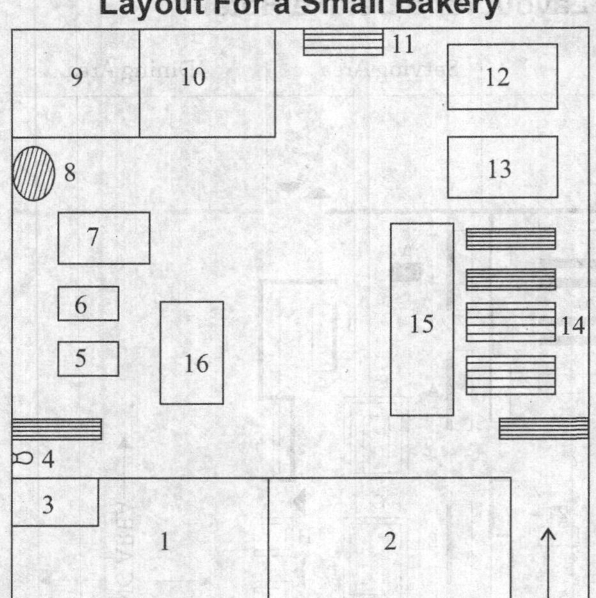

Index :

1. Store
2. Slicing Wrapping Area
3. Toilet
4. Handwash
5. Cake Mixer
6. Cookies Dough Mixer
7. Bread Mixer
8. Water Tap
9. Fermentation Room
10. Proofing Cabinet
11. Wall Rock
12. Electric Oven
13. Dressing Table
14. Cooling Racks
15. Work Bench 10” × 13½”
16. Work Bench 6” × 3”.

Fig.6.7 Typical Layout for a Small Bakery

All these facilities are bridged between the kitchen and the service. All must be laid out for the convenience and access of both the kitchen and serving staff, depending upon the menu and the kind of service offered. For counter service the dishwashing and supplies are outside the kitchen. In a table service restaurant the placement of these vary with the nature and complexity of service. In addition, the menu is a principal determinant of facilities and their placement. In same menus, some form of storage its needed in the serving area, whereas in some other menus, the service area must be specially designed to allow for final assembly or preparation activities by servers.

Self-service is increasingly common today. The fundamental principle is labour saving. Guest not only come to the service for food, but they also perform a member of other activities performed by servers in table service restaurants. They obtain their own dishes and flatware, and in institutional cafeterias, they even pour coffee and draw soft drinks from taps.

In addition to the introduction of such familiar practices as soft drink vending machines, restaurants have begun to introduce such innovations as salad centres in table service restaurants and the use of table services for desserts and beverege cafeterias.

The layout must allow for the most economic way of moving dishes and flatware from the dining area to washing equipment and for storing garbage before removal. Considerations range from prompt removal of dishes and flatware. There should be provision for multiple garbage collection and transfer to the storage point. Effective control procedures and supervision for the handling and storing of food and for cleaning through the premises is also needed. Kitchen work surfaces should be immediately cleaned with not in use. Extra perishables should be returned promptly to refrigeration. Establish rules on freshness and communicate it to all employees. These should be stringently enforced.

The kitchen manager or *Chef de Cuisine*, controls the *chefs* and assistants dealing with different sections of the kitchen. In some hotels, the *Chef* may report directly to the

Pix 6.2 : A Chef Garnishing a Dish

General Manager whereas in some other hotels, he reports to the F & B Manager, although he has direct communication with the General Manager.

The *chef*, during the time of Napoleon in France, was seen wearing a long floppy cap, on the order of a night cap as a symbol of his authority. Careme, who is credited with founding classical cookery, is credited with the tall starched cap that identifies the *Chef* or *Chief*. The height of the '*toque blanc*' is supposed to correlate with his rank in the kitchen.

The terms *Chef*, literally means 'Chief'. In kitchen parlance 'the Chef' means any member of the cooking staff, including apprentices, any one who wears a '*Chef's*' hat.

Great care is required in each stage of the kitchen operation planning, production, financial and quality control. The staff requirements of a kitchen depend on the size and type of the hotel and the type of meals to be provided and the number of guests for whom they are prepared. In a large organisation, the kitchen is divided into various sections (parties corners) and the number of parties depend upon the sizes of the kitchen. In addition, the organisation is contrasted for the traditional kitchen with its hierarchy of cooks and stewards and for the new institutional kitchen making great use of convenience products. In the convenience kitchen, minimum use is made of cooks and the butchers, bakers and most pantry workers are eliminated. Each section of the kitchen is led by a '*Chef de Partie*,' who is responsible for preparing certain kind of dishes. The number of assistants required under each 'partie' will depend on the amount of work handled.

The basic concept of food production is the conversion of the raw material (purchased food) into dishes and meals. This process of conversion passes through four main aspects :

1. Volume forecasting : A technique to predict the number of meals and particular items of menu to be served in each outlet of the hotel each day.
2. Yield test : A technique to postulate the quantity obtained from items of food after their preparation and cooking.
3. Standard recipe : The formula for producing particular dishes including the quantities and qualities of ingredients and the method of preparation used.
4. Portion control : It is the size or weight of food served to customers.

STYLE OF COOKING

The style of cooking practiced in most American, European restaurants and western style restaurants is called the international cuisine of the western world. Asian and Africans countries have their own styles of cooking of eating. The style of cooking (cuisine) of continental Europe is strongly influenced by the Italian and the French. The increase in travel trade and in the export and import of foods has made the modern restaurant cuisine basically the same all over the world. Because of this newly developed culture, the cooks and chefs of today have an opportunity to choose different areas and countries in which to practice their craft. Indian cuisine, Chinese cuisine, Thai cuisine, and similar other regional cuisine are getting popular all over the world.

MENU PLANNING

Menu studies show that 75 per cent of all 'entree'sale are luncheon and dinner menus and limited to six or seven items. If you offer two or three times this number of entries, the results are over-production, waste and expensive preparation costs. Therefore, limited menus make sense for all and have the following advantages :–

1. Less inventory is required, freeing working capital and reducing handling and storage charge
2. Less chance of spoilage and shrinkage
3. Less production is required, therefore, reduction in all pay costs.

FOOD COST

Inefficient purchasing, waste, over-production, pilferage, under-pricing, improper training and inadequate supervision all contribute to high food cost. Avoidance of waste can help a great deal in keeping food costs low. The following are some basic points to be considered :

1. Proper storage to prevent spoilage
2. Utilization of left-overs
3. Control of over-production
4. Curbing of over generous servings including extra rolls and butter
5. Use of standard recipes
6. Forecasting to adjust for special days and events.

A Case Study 6.2 :
KITCHEN

SITUATION

A study of a vegetable preparation section of a hotel restaurant showed that 35% of the time was spent in for peeling potatoes. The potatoes were pealed rapidly but the eyeing operation could not keep pace with the peeling machine.

Results of Analysis

A special table was designed for the eyeing operation which permitted the women doing the work to be seated. The table was provided with pans, one infront of each worker to catch the trimming and at hole made in the table through which eyed potatoes could be easily dropped in to G.I.cans.

The workers were delighted. Seating the women saved 14% energy expenditure. Production went up to 30% with less resulting fatigue. When one vegetable women resigned it was not necessary to replace her. Saving totalled ₹ 46,500/- a year. The table cost ₹ 5,000/- to build.

Pix 6.3 : Trainee Chefs and a Instructor

INDIAN CUISINE

The excitement and the sharp sensual pleasure of eating has inspired the creation of many great dishes in the Indian sub-continent. At its simplest, cooking brings one the flavour of a freshly baked 'chappatti'or the delight in the aroma and favour of a good "tarka"but at its height of excellence it results in the creation of great Indian dishes emanating from knowledge and technique evolved through the ages.

Indian food is influenced by its geography and history, religion and customs, economics and agriculture. As it is a vast country, food flavours and food habits vary from region to region.

Pix 6.4 : A Kitchen in a Hotel

The impact of the concept of '*Ahinsa*'(non-violence) found in Buddhism and Jainism resulted in a distinct and unique vegetarian cuisine. Whether in Punjab where only vegetarian food is prepared in most homes, or in Gujarat and Saurashtra, where the majority of the population is vegetarian, or in the South, the vegetarian repertoire is extensive.

While there are as many varieties of Indian food as there are dialects in our country, there is a certain uniformity in the diversity. All Indian foods are spicythe quantum and nature of spices varying from region to region. Strange as it may seem, although spices such as cardamom, cloves, cinnamon, nutmeg and pepper are grown in the South of India, there is a more generous use of these spices in the cuisine of the north. This may be attributed to the influence of the Mughal rule during which more expensive, rare and rich commodities such as nuts, rare spices, milk and milk products began to be used generously in North Indian cooking. In all Indian food the meal is built around one, or more than one cereal: rice in South India and Bengal, wheat in North India, and wheat or millets in addition to rice in Western India.

The use of spice grew out of the natural cooking techniques of India, China and South-east Asia, where herbs and spices are still widely employed. The spices indigenous to these areas, such as ginger and nutmeg, provide a lively and enjoyable accent to the blandness of rice and bring out latent flavours in vegetable, fish, poultry and meat dishes. In South East Asia, spices complement the fiery sambals and fermented fish sauces and are essential in the wide variety of curries prepared throughout the sub-continent.

There is no single style of Indian cooking. There is no one national dish. Styles of cooking and commonly used ingredients differ not only from region to region but from one household to another. Indian non-vegetarian curry is pieces of mutton, chicken or fish in a sauce based on onions, tomatoes, yoghurt or coconut milk into which as few, three or as many as twelve, cardamoms have been added.

Mutton, chicken and fish are even today served throughout the country. The frequency with which they make their appearance differs.

Some of India's best loved culinary traditions are in despair for the weight watcher, Tandoori cooking is an exception. Tandoori meats use no oil and are normally accompanied by yoghurt dips.

Some of the more celebrated culinary traditions of India originated in the royal courts of the Mughals, in Owadh and in Hyderabad. Distinguished by a succession of braised meats, rich sauces and flavoursome rice dishes steamed with meat, all three cuisines cater predominantly to meat eaters.

'*Dumpukhat*' cuisine, the origin of which dates back to the 1780's to the days of Nawab Asaf ud Daulah the erstwhile ruler of the state of Awadh or what is today, Lucknow, (U.P.), is one of the most ancient cuisines of the world. After tasting the varied specialities of gravy no one would never say that all Indian curries taste the same. Curries form the mainstay of almost all types of Indian cuisines. The basic art of any form of Indian cooking lies in the careful blending of different spices which yield subtle variations in flavour.

The '*Dumpukht*' cuisine is an example of ancient Indian culture and symbolises the culinary achme, not only in the food preparations but also in the service style and manner carried out in that region of our great land. The gastronomic delights of the cuisine were served in courses giving India the unique distinction of being a land of highly specialised cuisines, much before the West had a cuisine to talk about.

The popularity of the varied delicacies of this ancient cuisine among foreign guests in India and also among the Indian food outlets abroad truly insures its place marking the renaissance of Indian food on the international scale. It truly deserves its rightful niche among the great cuisines of the world and as the growing stimulation of the taste buds conveys, 'Dumpukht'cuisine is undoubtedly one of the most popular of India's numerous culinary delights.

The secret of '*Dumpukht*' cuisine lies in the unprecedented patience that its cooking style demands. The food is cooked on a slow fire in a sealed utencil. The meats and vegetables thus turn tender and soft within their own gravy and steam, with the addition of very little oil and spices. The food turns out deliciously different and not at all greasy.

The cuisine holds an unending variety for a food *connoisseur*, each stimulating and satisfying the palate in a different way. Some of the most popular dishes and delights include "*Murha Khushk Purdah*", comprising small chicken pieces marinated with herbs and baked in the '*tandoor*' with a flaky, pastry covering. Another delicacy is *Badal Jaam*, prepared with brinjal slices with a topping of tomato and garlic flavoured yoghurt. Surpassing all the other preparations in popularity and in taste are the melting *dokori kababs*. Savouring these with saffron coloured and small oval shaped *shirmal roti*, cooked in milk, holds a rich and unique eating experience. The dough for the *shirmal* or as it is more popularly known, the *lakhnavi roti* is prepared in *desi ghee*.

In Kashmir, mutton is a great favourite in the 24 course banquet, *wazwan*, each dish being special in its own way.

Some of the other regional specialities include Punjabi *'sarson ka sag'* or mustard green leaves simmered all night long on a coal fire. It is a seasonal favourite, being available only for a month or two in winter. Accompanied by thick unleavened bread made from cornmeal ('*makki de roti*'), its full bodies flavour works wonders on the taste buds.

Gujarat and Tamil Nadu have important vegetarian traditions, as meat is eaten only by a fraction of the population in these two states. However, because of the seemingly endless array of imaginatively cooked vegetables, lentiles and the succession of enticing accompaniments, the cuisine is relished even by confirmed non-vegetarians.

South Indian Cuisine stimulates the gastric juices and brings to mind the teasingly appetising *dosas* which are light on the stomach, 'idli, vada, uttappam'and the 'all accompanying' *'sambhar'*. There is also much else in the culinary category of state South of the Vindhyas.

The hottest curries come from Southern India and since most of the inhabitants of this part of the country are Hindus, vegetable dishes form the main course of their meals. Many of the spicy vegetable curries and even the recipes for stuffed aubergines and 'samosas'have originated from this region. Quite a few mouth watering varieties of meat and fish delights have their roots in south India.

The region is a temple oriented peninsla and many of the ancient and authentic dishes of the vegetarian flavour have been perfected by the temple cooks of the myriad fairs, festivals and feasts symbolising the gaiety of life. The tradition of eating on plantain leaves has also emerged from the South. Plantain leaves, apart from being the earliest discovered disposable plates, have been found as to not to interfere with the taste of food and eating out of them also has a practical advantage of water saving and freedom from the hassle of washing umpteen vessels.

The best way to begin a South Indian meal is to try to savour to appetiser which can be the water of tender coconut, lime, honey or mint. Coconut water is the most famous and nutritious beverage and prevents dehydrationin the hot climatic conditions. The main course can begin auspiciously with a rice sweet called '*payasam*', followed by vegetables served either as dry curries or with gravy. Rice, the staple food, is served with '*dal*, *ghee*, *appalams* (a small type of papad) and *sambar*. A tasty south Indian drink is '*rasam*'and as '*rasam*'rice is easy and light for the stomach, its close competitor, curd rice serves as a coolant.

The South Indian pickles add not only aesthetic appeal to a typical south Indian *thali* because of its varied colours but are a great favourite for those who like their food 'hot and spicy'. The dessert is *payasam* again and filter coffee is the best way to end a sumptuous meal. Of all the coastal states in the country, Goa, Kerala and Bengal have culinary traditions with a preponderance of fish. Goans and Keralites also make profuse use of coconuts. The Goan seafood delights include crab, lobsters, tiger prawns and shell fish, all accompanied with rice and washed down with excellent wine and vermouth of local manufacture. Kerala, in common with other Southern states, is noted for its variety of crisp pancakes and steamed rice cakes made from pounded rice.

The food of Kerala is distinctive for its extensive use of coconut oil and since the State has a vast population of Christians and Muslims, its cuisine is influenced by beef and pork, though the people also like to savour fish and prawns. A popular vegetable stew cooked in coconut gravy is Avial. For the sweet toothed, the sweet traditions of Bengal, Bikaner and Delhi are the nation's pride. While the regional differences in religion, culture and local produce have an influence on eating habits yielding an intriguing diversity of exotic, exclusive and tasty dishes, all add up to the rich diversity of unparalleled Indian cuisine.

The speciality from Andhra pradesh is '*Royya Vepunu*', prepared from succulent shrimps, marinated and cooked in a pungent paste of ginger, garlic and chillies. Since many Andhraites are habitual to chewing tobacco, as a result of which their taste buds become insensitive, their passion for chilly hot food is necessitated by the fact that chillies can reactivate their sense of taste and stimulate their appetite.

Some very specific but not so famous delights of each region include the non-vegetarian Kalyera curry of Tamil Nadu. It is a diced lobster in a coconut flavoured gravy spiced with traditional '*garam masala*'. Many Tamilians are noted for avoiding the use of garlic and other strong smelling spices in their cooking. The credit for ushering in the tradition of preparing rice mixed with vegetables and serving it with a dry, vegetable curry in the form of *palav* curry, goes to Karnataka. The hot and piping *chatni masala* and onion *dosas* are indeed a gourmet's delight and an epicurean's dream come true.

There are no hard and fast rules about what to serve in Indian food. Commonsense is the best guide to compiling a list of dishes. There must be a balance between protein and corbohydrate, richness and simplicity and mildness and high spicing. The number of dishes served at a meal varies from region to region. Traditionally, meals are eaten from a '*Thali*'. This can be a metal plate or an ordinary or porcelain plate. Each guest takes a small amount from each sample of food around the edge of the '*thali*'. The centre of the '*thali*' is used to mix the food. Rice is predominantly served with vegetarian meals.

Spices have always been an integral part of the Indian culture. They are mentioned in the holy book the Vedas. Spices are used not only in cooking but also an invaluable cures for every ailment.

Most popular Indian salads, cold foods, accompaniments, meat dishes, special dishes, fish dishes, vegetables dishes, snacks and drinks, and pudding and fruits are given in Tables 6.2, 6.3, 6.4, 6.5, 6.6, 6.7, 6.8 and 6.9.

Pix 6.5 : A tem of chefs working in a kitchen

TABLE 6.2 : Common Indian Salads and Cold Foods

Salad		Explanation
Jhinga Achar Salad	:	A piquant salad of prawn that can be used as a cooktail snack as well
Murg Salad	:	Cold tandoori chicken mixed with vegetables
Boti Ka Salad	:	A tandoori salad done in a clove flavoured mint and yoghurt dressing
Allo Salad Anarkali	:	A tartly sliced potato salad garnished with fish and pomegranate.
Kachumber	:	A common salad served with the main meal or as a garnish with innumerable delicacies.
Thandi Ajwani Machchli	:	Cold fish delicacy with exclusive use of 'ajwain.'
Murg Roshmi	:	A saffon flavoured chicken roll, spiced with pepper and nutmeg.
Murg Lajavab	:	Cold breast of chicken dressed in creamy mace 'n' cardamom flavoured sauce.
Raan-e-gulmarg	:	Nutmeg flavoured, cold leg of lamb spiced with Shahi jeera and coriander, and ganrnished with cashewnuts.
Khasta Keema	:	A cardamom flavored lamb plate spiced with cumin and garnished with almonds.
Mulligatwny Soop	:	Spicy soup.

Pix 6.6 : Chef Decorating a Dish

TABLE 6.3 : Accompaniments : Indian Cuisine

Accompaniment	Meaning
Chapatti/phulka	Unleavened Chapatti
Puree	Deep fried Chapatti
Naan	Leavened bread
Paratha	Shallow-fried bread
Aloo Paratha	Stuffed paratha
Tamatar ka Raita	Tomato cooler
Chapatti Malai	Chapatti with cream
Poppadum	Indian Crisps
Basini Roti	Chick pea bread from gram flour
Dahi	Yoghurt
Garam Masala	Home-mixed curry powder
Baigan ka Achar	Aubergine pickle
Tamatar Chatney	Tomato chatney
Nimboo ka Achar	Lime pickle
Dhaniake Chatney	Coriander Chatnee
Chatni	Chick pea chatnee
Podina ki Chatney	Nut sauce
Bombay Duck	Dried fish
Seb Sambal	Spiced apples
Piaz ke Bhajji	Onion fritters
Mushroom Bhajji	Mushrom fritters
Tandoor ki Roti	Unleavened bread cooked in tandoor
Khameeri Roti	Bread made from fermented flour
Bhatura	Fermented maida fried
Batti	Freshly prepared ball of wheat flour cooked in slow heated ash.
Kerala Paratha	A flaky paratha
Bakarkhani	Highly rich dough made of refined flour, butter, milk and nuts
Sheermal	Rice bread.
Virqui Paratha	A fluky, fried bread of Avadh.
Jalebi Paratha	An exotic fennel-flavoured multi-layered bread of Avadh.
Pickles	
Jhinga Achaar	A prawn pickle consumed as entree.
Muru Achaar	Sharp chicken pickle, in musturd and fenugreek seeds
Aam ka Achar	Mango pickle
Bharvan Lal Mirchi	Pickle of stuffed chillies
Nimbu Achar	Stuffed lemon pickle
Khatta Meetha Achar	A mixed vegetable relish, spiced with cumen and garam masala and sweetened with jaggery or sugar
Mirch Achaar	Chilli pickle

(Contd.)

Chatnees	
Aam ki Chatnee	Mango Chatnee
Piaz ki Chatnee	Onion Chatnee
Gajjar ki Chatnee	A sweet 'n' sour carrot chatnee with raisins
Thengai Thoiyal	Coconut Chatnee
Takkali Thoiyal	Tamato Chatnee
Vengayan Thoviayal	Onion Chatnee
Murrabaas	
Sookhe kale Angoor ka Murabba	Sultanas preserved in sugar and flavoured with red chillis, cardamom, cumin and fennel powder.
Aamle ka Murrabba	Aamla preserve rich in vitamin 'C'
Gajjar ka Murrabba	Carrots preserve
Adrak ka Murrabba	A ginger preserve
Keri ki Launjee	A piquant raw mango delicacy, spiced with fennel and kalonzi cooked in mustard oil.
Saunth	A chatnee made from mango powder

Pix 6.7 : Kitchen Traines

TABLE 6.4 : Meat Dishes : Indian Cuisine

Name of Dish	Meaning
From North Indian	
Murg dahi	Chicken with yoghurt
Shahi Murg	Royal Chicken
Murg ka Salan	Chicken Curry
Murg Tikka	Chicken Kabab
Murg Tandoori	Tandoori Chicken

(Contd.)

Murg Illachi	Chicken with Cardamom
Murg Biryani	Chicken beriyani
Murg Maida	Chicken with dumplings
Tali Kalejee	Fried Chicken livers
Nargesi Kofta	Indian Scotch eggs
Raan	Roast lamb with spices
Roghan gosht	Lamb with yoghurt
Shahi Korma	Royal lamb curry
Pullao Gosht	Lumb Pullao
Shakotee	Lamb with Coconut
Tikka Kebab	Lamb Kebab
Hussaini Kebab	Mince meat Kebab
Masala Chop	Spicy lamb chops
Pasanda	Mild beef Curry
Dahi Gosht	Beef in Yoghurt
Keema Pimento	Mince meat with pepper
Seekh Kabab	Minced Kebab
Khargosh ka Salan	Rabbit Curry
Teetar	Partridge
Jangli Murg Pulao	Pheasant Pulao

From South Indian

Gosht Molee	Beef with Coconut
Maadu Thukkali	Beef with Tomato
Gosht Madras	Hot Beef Curry
Taṣkebab	Baked beef
Gosht Chasnigarh	Sweet and sour beef
Shikar Chandigarh	Sweet and sour beef
Punny Valthumalai	Pork chops with almonds
Shikar ka Vindaloo	Pork with vinegar
Lamb Korma	Breast lamb
Altho-molee	Lamb with almonds and cocount
Masala Kalejee	Special liver
Pukkan	Kidney curry
Murg Madras	Hot chicken curry
Kholee Vindaloo	Chicken in vinegar
Kholee Coongee	Chicken with scrambled eggs
Dahi Gost	Beef in Yoghurt
Badam Gosht	Lamb and almonds
Gost Dopaiazah	Beef with onions
Vaathoo Pista	Duck with pistachios
Madras Anday	Hot egg curry
Moyal	Hare curry
Vaathoo Vindaloo	Duck cooked with vinegar

(*Contd.*)

From Central Indian

Murg Masale Wala	Chicken with Spices
Murg Dhansak	Chicken with Lentils
Delhi Murg	Delhi Chicken Curry
Murg Hyderabadi	Hyderabad Chicken Curry
Murg dopiaza	Chicken with Onions
Gosht dopiaza	Beef with Onions
Bund gobi gost	Beef with Cabbage
Calcutta Gosht	Calcutta beef Curry
Kofta Curry	Meat Ball Curry
Kofta	Stuffed Meat balls
Keema Karela	Meat with bitter gourd
Bombay Gosht	Bombay Lamb Curry
Budam Gosht	Lamb with almonds
Allo Gosht	Lamb with Patato
Bhuna Gosht	Dry Curry of lamb
Parsee ka Salan	Parsi stew
Masala Kalejee	Dry spiced liver
Anday Shikar	Pork with eggs
Baduk	Roast duck with Cashewnuts
Galina Xacutti	Chicken in a rich gravy
Vindaloo	Hot pork dish from Goa
Scorpotel	A pork and pork-liver deliecy
Kheema Sali	Spicy lamb mince topped with sali or straw potatoes
Dhansak	Mutton, Lentil and Vegetable Potpourri, Parsi National Dish

Pix 6.8 : Preparing Vegetables

TABLE 6.5 : Special Indian Dishes

Special Dish	Meaning
Tandoori and Kebab Preparations	
Tandoori Lobster :	Lobster roasted in tandoor
Tandoori Pomfret :	Pomfret roasted on tandoor
Murg Nawabi :	A creamy, gently spiced Chicken Kebab, flavoured with mace
Shan-e-murg :	Kebab of tender chicken breasts stuffed with black cumin-flavoured paneer
Murg Malai :	A creamy Kebab made from the breast of chicken
Kastoori Kebab :	An egg coated spiced with cream and flavoured with cardamom
Reshmi Kebab :	A tender kebab made from chicken mince and cashewnut paste.
Galouti Kebab :	Mace and cardamom flavoured royal kebab of minced spring lamb.
Malai Seekh :	Herbs and cashewnuts combine with Kebab of lamb mince.
Dumke Kebab :	Lamb mince is smoked, skewed and cooked in tandoor or over a charcoal grill.
Shikampuri Kebab :	Balls of lamb mince and other ingredients, filled and flatten into patties and deep fried.
Gosht Elaichi Pasanda :	Cardamom flavoured Kebabs made from picatta of lamb.
Handi Preparations	
Muglih Navrattan :	Chicken preparad in a handi, flavoured with mace and cardamom.
Methi Murg :	Chicken prepared in a Handi with fresh fenugreek.
Achaar Korma :	Semi-dry lamb done in combination of mustard oil, musturd seeds, Kalonji, and Jaggery cooked in a Handi.
Gosht Aur Vadi Biryani :	Lamb and 'urad dal'dumplings, simmered in an exotic gravy cooked in a Handi.
Kachchi Mirch Ka Gosht :	A delectable lamb dish, done in a creamy, but 'hot' green pepper corn, flavoured with suffron and fennel cooked in a handi.
Khade Masale Ka Gosht :	Leg of spring lamb cut into 'boti'and cooked in a Handi.
Kadhai Preparations	
Kadhai Jhinga :	'Ajwain'flavoured prawns done in tomatoes cooked in a Kadhai.

(Contd.)

Kadhai Murgh :	Kadhai cooking chicken delicacy cooked in tomatoes predominantly flavoured with femugreek and coriander.
Narial Ka Gosht :	Lamb cooked with coconut and flavoured cooked in a Kadhai.
Kadhai Gosht Hussainee :	Kadhai preparation of lamb chunks with use of yogurt, almond paste and cream.
Dahi Ka Kheema :	Lamb mince cooked with yoghurt and flavoured with the combination of cloves and cinnamon powder, cooked in a Kadhai
Tawa Preparations	
Jhinga Masala :	Ajwain elevated prawn delicacy prepared in a Tawa
Samudri Khazana Tak A Tak :	Prawns, crab and fish stewed over heat in a Tawa
Murg Tawa Masala	A chicken meat done in smooth sauce with crushed pepper corns, cooked in a Tawa
Gosht Pasanda Paya Ras :	A delicacy of lamb picatta, applied in a 'masala' rich in herbs and spices, simmered in pay 'ras' trotter (stock) and cooked in a 'tawa.'
Gosht Banjara :	A Hyderabadi style of cooking of lamb cubes cooked in spices in a 'Tawa.'
Gosht Ke Khaje :	A delicacy made from brain, liver and kidneys, cooked in a Tawa.
Dumpukht Preparations	
Gulnar Jalpari :	Jumbo prawns marinated in unique batter and then put on 'dum'
Khuroos-e-tursh :	A tangy chicken delicacy, saffron flavoured and spiced with black cumin and put on 'dum'
Ahd-e-changezi :	A leg of lamb delicacy cooked in 'dum' served with an exquisite peppery gravy.
Zaqand-e-kababi :	Clove favoured lamb picatta cooked on stone (marble red) before being put on dum.
Firdaus-e-barein :	A delicacy of meat balls stuffed with Sunflower seeds and raisins, simmered in an aromatic gravy and put on 'dum'
Subz Gosht :	Combination of lamb, turnips (or Zucchini) and spinach cooked in mustard oil and put in a 'dum'.
From Avadh	
Dudhia Bataer :	Magnificent delicacy of fried quail
Murgh Mussalam :	Shallow fried chicken and stuffed
Murg Wajid Ali :	Saffron flavoured chicken breast done in a rich almond based gravy.

(*Contd.*)

Gosht Korma :	Lamb assorted cuts with thick gravy
Chandi Kaliyan :	A delicacy of cardamom flavoured lamb with white gravy
Nahari Gosht :	Gravy lamb delicacy
Lazeez Paslian :	A delicacy of single rib lamb chops cooked in a thick, yoghurt based gravy

From Goa

Goa Prawn Masala :	A pungent sea food delicacy which also makes an excellent cocktail snack.
Goa Balchao :	Pickled prawn
Goa Curry :	Chilli hot fish curry
Gulina Xacutti :	Speciality chicken made in combination of three sets of 'masalas'whole spice, dry roasted, and tempered.
Vindaloo :	Pork dish from Goa
Sorvpotel :	A pork and liver delicately cooked in butter
Kolmino Patio :	Prawn Curry sharp (chillies) sweet (jaggery) and sour (tamarind and lemon juice)
Dhan Dal Patio :	Fish curry served with rice and lentils.

From Punjab

Amritsari Machchi :	Ajvain flavoured fish delicacy
Mugewala Kukarh :	Tikka of chicken skewered with tomatoes, capsicum and mint leaves cooked in a shahi jeera flavoured 'masalas'.
Patiala Shahi Meat :	Lamb 'boti'cooked in a Handi
Meat Belli Ram :	Lamb chunks cooked in Handi
Masalewalian Chaampan :	Cumin flavoured lamb chops cooked in their own fat
Raarhameat :	Lamb chunks cooked in a Handi

From Rajasthan

Maas Ke Sule :	Kabab made from game (vension, wild boar, sand grouse, quail, patridge) lamb, chicken and fish.
Safed Mass :	White meat a Rajasthani delicacy
Lal Mass :	Lamb chunk preparation
Makki Ka Soweta :	Spicy combination of corn and lamb
Maas Ki Kadhi :	Lamb delicacy done in Gram flavoured 'n' yoghurt gravy.
Khad :	A multitiered cake of lamb mince
Amrud Ki Subzi :	A delicacy of guava simmered in a tangy tomato and yoghurt masala

From South

Iggaru Royalu :	Sea food delicacy, spiced with cumin, fenugreek and pepper

(*Contd.*)

Erha Kari :	A coconut flavoured prawn curry redolent with corriander powder as well as the herb
Kerala Nandu Masala:	A coconut flavoured crab curry
Pomfret Mappas :	Fillet of pomfret (or sole or halibut) marinated in tamarind and simmered in a delicately spiced gravy.
Kozhi Vartha Kari :	Tender boneless cube cooked in a palate tickling combination of herbs and spices.
Milagu Kozhi Chettinad :	Chicken curry done in a black pepper sauce.

From Hyderabad

Hyderabadi Murg Korma :	A cashewnut based chicken curry, flavoured with nutmeg.
Murga Nizami :	A semi-dry chicken 'masala 'cooked with nuts (chashew, nut, peanuts and coconut) and seeds (sunflower and sesame)
Murg Do-piaza : Hyderabadi	A mild chicken curry cooked with an abundance of onion and garnished with cashewnut and sunflower seeds.
Sofyani Biryani :	A saffron-flavoured rice delicacy mild and easy to digest
Dalcha Gosht :	A sour lamb stew, simmered in a lentil puree.

Pix 6.9 : Preparation Vegetables

TABLE 6.6 : Fish Dishes

Fish Dishes	Meaning
Bengal, Goa and Kerala	
Machi Ka Salan	Fish curry
Meen Tamatar	Fish with tomatoes
Bombay Meen	Bombay fish curry
Dum Machli	Steamed fish with courgettes
Machli Ka Tikka	Barbecued Fish
Machli Kofta	Fish ball curry
Machli Kebab	Fish patties
Machli Saffron	Sole with Saffron
Tale Machli	Stuffed Halibut
Jhinghe Ka Salan	Prawn Curry
Prawn Pakora	Prawn in butter
Jhinghe Karela	Prawn with courgettes
Jhinghe Ballachow	Spiced prawn pickle
Jhinghe Saag	Prawn with Spinach
Jhinghe Kebab	Prawn patties
Jhinghe Sambal	Prawns with lemon and coconut
Jhinghe Bhajji	Dry curry of king prawn
China Conee Mootay	Prawn curry with Eggs
Chinaconee Meen	Prawn with coconut and egg
Choti Muchli Masala	Spiced Herring
Jhinghe Ka Tikka	Barbecued Bengal prawns
Teesrioka Salan	Mussel curry
Dum Teesrio	Steamed Mussels
Kurbachi Ka Salan	Crab curry
Goa Prawn Masala	A pungent Seafood delicacy
Prawn Balchao	Fried prawn with 'masala'
Goa Curry	Chilli hot delicious fish Curry Galina Xacutti
Jhinghe Ka Tikka	Barbecued Bengal Prawn
Parsee Dishes	
Kolmino Patio :	Sharp (chillies), Sweet (jaggery) and sour tamarind and lemon juice, in Prawns
Dhan Dal Patio :	Fish Curry served with rice and lentils
Patrani Machchi :	Steamed Fish
Peethiwali Machchi :	Sole, dipped in rice batter, fried in mustard oil and then simmered in a typical Avadhi gravy.

Pix 6.10 : The Style of Cooking

Pix 6.11 : Student Trainers

Table 6.7 : Vegetarian Dishes : Indian Cuisine

Name of Dish	Meaning
From East	
Kela Kofta	Curried banana balls
Matar Paneer	Peas with cream cheese
Chotee Gobi	Brussel sprouts
Kicheree	Breakfast Rice
Subzi Pillao	Vegetable Pillao
Chawal Safran	Rice with saffron
Kabli Channa	Bengal Beans
Kathi Dal	Sour Lentils
Urad Dal	White tentil curry
Channa-dal	Chick-pea curry
Kela Sambar	Chilled Banana Spice
Selgum	Turnip Curry
Shahi Dal	Royal lentil Curry
Tali Saag	Dry Fried Spinach
Saag Bhajji	Dry Spinach Curry
Mushroom Bhagar	Dry Fried Mushrooms
Dum Ka Sabzi	Steamed French beans
Subzi Nimboo	Leeks with lime
From South	
Subzi Ka Salan	Vegetable curry
Masoor Dal	Indian lentils
Bhindi Bhajji	Okra curry
Aviyal	Mixed vegetable curry
Gobi Dal	Lentils with cauliflower
Goodhi Bhajji	Marrow curry
Dum Arvi	Steamed yam
Allo Bogar	Dry Potato curry
Narial ka Salan	Coconut curry
Cabbage Foogath	Cabbage cooked with coconut
Khatti Meeti Gobi	Sweet and sour cabbage
Chawal Dhania Pudina	Rice with coriander and meat
Chawal Samabal	Coconut salad
Baigon Masale	Special aubergines
Baigan Bhagar	Aubergines with tamarind
Akoori	Parsee egg curry
Uppama	Semolina with vegetables
Pakora Ka Raita	Fritters with Yoghurt
Kela Ka Raita	Bananas with Yoghurt
Chuchumher	Indian Salad

(Contd.)

From North

Chawal	Rice (Boiled)
Aam Chawal	Mango Rice
Kesari Chawal	Saffron Rice
Pillao	Spiced Rice
Saag Aloo	Spinach and potato chutney
Talnatan Ka Salan	Tomato curry
Gajjar Bhajji	Carrot, with cashewnuts
Palak ke Dal	Lentils with spinach
Murg Piaz	Onions studded with chicken
Tark Dal	Lentils with spicy topping
Beans	Mixed vegetable curry
Aloo Bhindi Bhajji	Okra with potatoes
Aloo Gobi	Potato and cauliflower curry
Aloo Chop	Potato chips
Raita	Yoghurt cooler
Baigan Tamatar	Aubergines and tomatoes
Baigan Bhurta	Dry cooked aubergines
Keema Bairan	Stuffed aubergines
Baigan Masala	Spiced aubergines
Karela ka Sabzi	Stuffed aubergines
Goodhi Bhajji	Marrow curry
Pimento Keema	Stuffed peppers

Tandoori Preparation

Paneer ka tikka	Exotic Kebab of India

Handi Preparation

Khumb Hara Dhania :	Mushroom in green corriander leaves cooked in Handi
Aloo Chatnewale :	Potatoes stuffed with paneer and simmered in a tangy chutney cooked in a Handi
Raspberry Mutter :	Paneer balls cooked and peas cooked in mild and rich gravy in a Handi
Kale Moti Biryani :	Bengal gram simmered in gravy and basmati rice, cooked on a Handi

Kadhai Preparation

Laziz Khumb :	Combination of mushroom, cabbage and capcicum, cooked in a *Kadhai*
Makki-Khumb Masala :	A colourful Maize and mushroom combination cooked with fresh herbs in a *Kadhai*
Kadhai Paneer :	Chilli hot, semi-dry and colourful paneer cooked in a kadhai
Kadhi Choley :	White gram cooked in a Kadhai

(*Contd.*)

Dal Ka Bila :	Tomato based lentil delicacy cooked in a Kadhai

Tawa Style Preparation

Paneer Tawa Masala :	Spiced cheese simmered in a rich gravy and flavoured with Ajwain cooked in a Tawa.
Pao Bhaji :	Potato 'n' Tomato dish, cooked in a Tawa.
Dal Be Aab :	A dry lentil delicacy, cooked in butter and spiced with cumin in a tawa

Dumpukht Preparation

Guncha-o-bahar :	Cauliflower vegetable cooked in a handi put on dum
Dhaldari Kofta :	Raw banana balls cooked in a rich gravy put on 'dum'
Badal Jaam :	Aubergine delicacy, dressed in a creamy coriander flavoured yoghurt, put in 'dum'

Avad Style

Lauki Mussalam :	While marrow stuffed with a rich Khoya nuts seeds, dry fruit filling, coated with yoghurt and gramflour and then finished in the oven.
Dhingri Dulma :	A colourful combination of musrooms and paneer, cooked with tomatoes and tempered with black cumin.

Punjabi Style

Sarson Ka Sag :	Muster leaves cooked in white butter.
Masale Dar Karele :	A bitter gourd delicacy stuffed with the stuffing and onions
Bartha :	A charcole smoked aubergine delicacy cooked with onions and tomatoes.
Kadhi :	A preparation of gramflour dumplings simmered in a yoghurt based gravy.
Punch Rattani Dal :	A combination of five lentils.
Dal Amritsari :	A lentils low cooked delicacy
Dal Makhani :	A lentil delicacy

Rajasthani Style

Mungodi Ki Subzi :	Grape sized dumplings napped in a spicy masala
Besan Ke Gatte :	Gramflour dumplings cooked in a sharp cumin and asafoetida gravy
Moong Dal Khilama :	Dry preparation of pulse tossed in a tempered mixture of spices.

(Contd.)

South Indian Style

Bataani Kaal Kari : A delicious combination of peas and mushroom in a thick, rich gravy.

Murugakkai Sambhar : A lentil delicacy flavoured with asafoetida.

Vandakka Masala Pachchadi : Okra simmered in thick coconut flavoured, yoghurt based gravy.

Rasam : Juice of extract of tomato/lemon

Bisi Bhela Huliyana : A rice 'n' sambhar delicacy cooked with a special huliyonna masala, garnished with cashewnut.

Hyderabadi Style

Subz Khada Masala : A chilli hot mixed vegetable dish with a prominent flavour of fenugreek.

Nawabi Tarkari Biryani : Mild and light basmati rice cooked with vegetables, almonds, yoghurt and suffron.

Pix 6.12 : Final Touches on a Dishes

TABLE 6.8 : Snacks and Drinks : Indian Cuisine

Name of the Snack and Drinks	Meaning
Samosa	Staffed pastry cases
Pakoras	Frillers
Shami Kebabs	Ground meat patties
Kachori	Nut puffs
Tali chawal	Fried rice balls
Suji Pakora	Semolina fritters
Alebele	Stuffed coconut pancake
Dosa	Rice pancakes
Masala Dosa	Stuffed masala rice pancakes
Num Keen Koti	Savoury toast
Sev gatia	Savoury biscuits
Lassi	Yoghurt Drink
Lussi Namkeen	Salted Yoghurt drink
Sharbats	Sherbets
Podina ka Sharbat	Mint drink
Doodh ka Sarbat	Milk drink
Sarabh Sandal	Sandalwood drink
Nimboo Pani	Lemonade
Imli ka Pani	Tamarind water
Chai	Tea
Coffee	Coffee
Bonda	Spicy potato-balls dipped in gram flour batter and deep fried
Jhinga Til Tinka	Ajivain flavoured prawns, coated with sesamum seed and spiced with mace and cardamom.
Jaane Man	Tender chicken pieces, simmered in saffron and fennel flavoured milk, skewered, dipped in rice batter and deep fried.
Kanjeevaram Idli	Steamed Rice Cake of Kanjeevaram.
Chaurasia Kathi	A herbal lamb masala rolled in a square paratha
Goolab Kabab	A Kashmiri snack of meat balls stuffed with a tangy chutney of raisins and mint 'n' coriander.
Allo Tikki	A potato patty stuffed with variety mince lentils, white gram or green peas of fillings and then shallow fried and deep fried.
Pakora	Fritters of anything veg and non-veg.
Samosa	Stuffed with a variety of fillings, mincemixed vegetables, lentils or special peas and potatoes.
Mathi	Ajvain flavoured crisp savoury laced with pepper.
Kachori	Crisp, stuffed snack

(Contd.)

Dosai	Rice pancake preparation served with samber
Masala Dosa	Dosa stuffed with every variety of fillings such as patatoes, lamb mince
Urla Kazhangu Bonda	Spicy potato balls in a gram flour batter and deep fried
Idli	A steamed rice cake with Samber and Chutney or a knot of white butter.
Kanjeevaram Idli	Steamed rice cakes
Medu Vada	A doughnut shaped savoury spiced with black pepper corns

Pix 6.13 : Practical of Food

TABLE 6.9 : Puddings and Fruits : Indian Cuisine

Name of Pudding and Fruit	Meaning
Phirni	Grounded rice pudding, the dessert is set in Shikoras (earthenware bowls) and flavoured with cardamom and saffron
Sewain	Vernicelli
Kesari Kheer	Indian rice pudding
Rasgullah	Cream chesee balls
Kulfi	Ice cream
Nariyal ka Halwa	Coconut cake
Beveca	Coconut pudding
Gulab Jamun	Sweet dumplings in syrup

(*Contd.*)

Jalebi	Fritter whirls in syrup
Bombay Halwa	Nut fudge
Gajrela	Carrot pudding
Meetha chawal	Sweet Rice
Chickoree	Sweet dumpling with cream
Suji halwa	Semolina pudding
Pista burfee	Pistachio sweet meat
Gajoar ka halwa	Carrot pudding
Sheheed Tukra	Honey snacks
Safran anday	Saffron egg
Malpua	Indian pancake
Shai Tukra	Khoya bread pudding
Aam Illaichi	Mango aroma
Kayla Pustholes	Banana puffs
Chat	Spicy fruit salad
Aam	Mangoes
Ganna	Sugar cane
Papita	Papaya
Leechee	Lychee
Amrood	Guavas
Ananas	Pineapple
Tarbouz	Water Melon
Rabarhi Rasmalai	Thickened milk sugar with nuts and chilled.
Shrikhand	Suffle flavoured with saffron and cardamom.
Sueh ki Kheer	Creamy and aromatic saffron and cordamom apple dessert
Ananas ka Muzaafar	Rice and ananas
Musthq-e-Tanjan	Sweet lamb rice
Murg ki Burfi	A chicken Sweet meat/Sweet lamb mince
Falooda	Noodle like garnish
Paal Poli	Flavoured puffs soaked in cardamom flavoured milk.
Shahi Tukra	A sterling stuff garnished with dry fruits and covered with sheets of pure silver
Kulfi	A creamy and rich ice cream made in saffron, pistachio and mango flavour.
Rasmalai	Chena cakes cooked in sugar and milk syrup and chilled.

GUIDELINES FOR USE OF FRENCH MENU

The function of language on the menu is to inform the customers, the kitchen and the serving staff. The choice of the language will depend upon the establishment. If the workforce consists of many nationalsties or if the clientile is sophisticated or international this will have a bearing on the language used. Traditional menus are in French language.

In some cases there is a practice to have menus in French with an English translation, but it is not advisable to use a mixture of French and English. The main objective is to describe the dish accurately so that that customer can identity the dish. Avoid over elaboration as it causes disappointment. Use the language easily understood. As the majority of customers now-a-days are English speaking, it is logical to use the English language. For example, the following indicates the clear distinction of the informative and communicative aspects of the two terms:

French	:	*English*
Poulet saute chasseur	:	Chicken pieces fried and served in a white onion, mushroom , tomato, and tarragon flavoured sauce.

or

Sauted chicken Hunter Style

However, French has been the traditional international language of professional chefs and kitchens. Many French words cannot be exactly translated in to English. For example, as hors-d' oeuvre, roux, canapé and flucuriste.

If French is to be used in menu it must be used correctly. The spelling grammar and pronunciation must be accurate. If a dish is named traditionally then it must be authentic. For example, if 'meunier' is stated then it should be shallow, fried, served with lemon, chopped parsely and nut-brown butter.

Hotel catering and tourism industry has its own particular terminatory and the students of catering should know basic French words and phrases in addition to the knowledge and use of English.

RULES FOR WRITING OF MENUS IN FRENCH LANGUAGE

Below are few rules for the writing of menus, but accuracy of gender, agreement and spelling are required.

Use of 'The' i.e., le, la or les:

'The' in French is translated by different words according to be gender and matter (*i.e.,* singular and plural).

Gender	**Number** *Singular*	*Plural*
Masculine	: Le melon	Les melons
	l'abricot	les abricots
	l'hôtel	les hôtel
Famine	: la tomote	les tomates
	l' orange	les oranges

If the singular noun begins with a vowel then the '*le*' or '*la*' changes to *l* :-

The water	:	Eau (*f*)	*l'*eu
The garlic	:	Ail (*m*)	*l'*ail

In some cases the noun begins with an '*h*' and the same rule applies :

The hotel : Hôtel (*m*) *l* 'hôtel

When the noun is plural that is, when more then one item is considered, the French for the 'The' is 'les', for example :

les saumons, les homards, les hôtels

When using '*le*', '*la*' or '*les*' on a menu before a cut, part or joint then the gender used in that of the cut part or joint and not that of the food of which it is part :

La darne de la selle de : le trongconde

La coeur de le suprême : la ris de

Le dêlice de les goujons : la paupiette de.

METHODS OF COOKING

The method of cooking the cut or piece must also agree with the cut or piece.

Les filet de sole frits

La selle 'd' agneau rôte

le gigot d' agneau rôte

Verbs are often used to describe the cooking method. In the menu the verbs are given in the past tense (past participles) and follow the noun and agree with it. like an adjective, in gender and in number. For example,

To toss : Sauter

Tossed : Sauté, Pommes sautées

To set alight : Fambler

Set alight : Flambé, Pêche flambée

To cut roughly : Concasser

Cut roughly : Concasse, Tomates Concasées.

With a masculine singular noun the verb is left unaltered e.g.,

Saumon fumé

With a masculine plural noun add '*s*' :

Champignons grillés

With a faminine singular noun add '*e*' :

Anguilee fumée

With the famine plural noun add '*e*' :

Pommes persilees.

Most verbs to do with cooking will end in 'er' but some in 'ir', 're' or 'ire' and these take different spellings in the past tense. For example,

To fry : Frire

Fried : Frit

To melt : Fon

Melted : Fondu

To boil : Bouiller

Boilled : Bouilli

To stuff : Farcir

Stuffed : Farci.

The agreement rule still applies

Beurre (masc. sing) : Beurre fondu

Boeuf (Masc.-sing) : Boeuf bouilli

Cabillaud (Masc.sing) : Cabillaud frit

Tomates (Fem.sing) : Tomates farci

USE OF '*A*'

The word '*a*' has several meanings, but on the menu the usual ones are 'with' and 'in'. Changes in the translation of 'with the' and 'in the' take place according to the gender and number of noun used :

à la : is not changed

à l is : not changed

à les : becomes aux

Therefore, 'tart with apples' (tarte a les pommes) must be written : Tarte aux pommes

Skate with black butter (raie à le beurre noir) must be written : Raie au blurre noir

'Homard à la Américane' becomes Humard à l Americane

' Crêpes à la citron becomes crêpes au citron

'Chou-fleur a la grecque' remain choufleur a la grecque.

USE OF NOUNS

Nouns eg. as used below, apple, butter, and chocolate, when following the name of the main ingredient of main dish can be singular or plural :

Rai au beurre noir

Profite role au chocolate

Tarte aux pommes.

'De' means 'of', and '*e*' is replaced by an apostrophe before words meaning with a vowel or '*h*' as with 'le' and 'la'

'Gilot de agneaú becomes Gigot d' agneau

Table de hôtel becomes table d' hote

Rable de lièvre is unchanged

Longe de veau is unchanged

Filet de beuf is unchanged

Bisque de homard's unchanged.

USE OF 'OF'

When translating 'of' between two nouns, 'de' is the only correct form :

Beignets de pommes

Darne de saumon

Délice de sole

Raviers de hor-s d'oeuvre

Salad de tomates

Suprûme de turbot

Paupiette de boeuf

Purré de mavrons

Trençon de barbue.

On the menu the term 'of' (de) or 'then' is used to describe the composition of a dish. If the main ingredient of the dish is discribed, 'de' is used :

Beignets de pommes

Salade de tomates

If the term is only part of the dish, 'au' is usually used :

Crêpes au citron Dinde aux marrons Omelette au Jambon.

USE OF 'IN THE FASHIONS OF'

The phrase 'a la mode' mean in the styling or fashion of and is often left out of the name of the dish but the word which describes the fashion must agree with the noun 'la mode', which is feminine.

Petits pois à la mode francaise becomes – Petits pois à la française

The shortening of the phrase is even taken so far that it is not even written, but understood :

Chou-fleur à la mode polanaise becomes chou-fleur polonaise.

Polonaise is femine because it is describing a 'mode', which is femnie, it is not describing

Chou-fleur which is masculine.

When a dish is dedicated to a particular place or person the 'a la' is omitted :

Pêche Melba poire conde

'A la' can also describe a method of cooking :

Biftech a la poêle Pommes à la vopeur Haddock au four

USE OF 'EN'

'En' used on the menus, means 'in' :

Consomme' en soup–consomé en tesse

Leaf Spinach	:	Epinards en branche
Sole in small strips	:	Sole en goujons
Curled whiting (with tail in mouth)	:	Merlin en colère.

'Pommes purée is written in this way because full, name would be 'Pommes deterre en pureé. The puree remains singular because it is not an adjective but a noun.

Care should be taken to ensure that 'various hors dòeuvre is translated as 'hors d'oeuvres.

USE OF CAPITAL LETTERS

Trade practice is to capitalise all major words in the dish. A capital letter should be used for the first word and the names of people, eg. Pêche Melba, and places, 'Crème Crecy'. If it is in the style of place eg. 'Petits pois à la francaise' 'then a small letter is used.

The words used to describe a dish or a menu must agree in gender and number. For example,

A fillet of sole	:	Le filet de sole
Two fillets of sole	:	eux filets de sole
Two fried fillets of sole	:	Deux filets de sole frits
Lamb	:	Agneau (m)
Lamb cutlets	:	La côtelette d' agneau
Two Lamb cutlets	:	Dêux cotellettse d' agneuu
Grilled lamb cutlet	:	Côtellette dàgneau grillée
Two grilled lamb cutlets	:	Deux côtelettes d' agneau grillées.

It will be noticed that the agreement is made with the cut or joint. The definite article, 'le' or 'la' if used with one dish on a menu should be used on all dishes; for example, the menu given below on the left is correct, and the one on the right is not :

Le Saumon fumé	:	Le Saumon fumé
La selle dàgneau rôti	:	Selle dàgneau rôtie
Le Chou-fleur ; Sauce hollandaise	:	Le Chou-fleur, sauce hollandaise
Les pommes perisienne	:	Les pommes parisienne
La Pêche Malba	:	Pêche Melba.

Care should be taken of the use of the term 'a la' which means 'in' or 'after the style of'. This means that it can be used when a dish is prepared in the style of a certain place, town or country, for example.

Horsd' oeuvre a la grecque

Poulet sauté à la partugaise

Filets de sole frits à la francaise

Petit pois à la flamande

(As stated, the last word does not have a capital letter).

When a dish of food is named after a person or place the name usually follows the food, and a capital letter is used :

Name after Dame Nellie Melba	:	Pêch Melba
Name after Madame Dubarry	:	Crème Dubarry
Name after Waldorf Astoria Hotel, New York.	:	Salade Waldorf.

When using classical garnish names see that any vegetable which is included in the garnish is not repeated as a vegetable. For example, Chou-fluer Morney would not be put on the menu on a vegetable to be served with 'selle däugneau Dubarry'

Some of the term used in a menu, are given below. These signify that a specific item of food will be served. For example, parmentier indicates that potatoes will be used. Therefore, parmentier is potato soup; omelette parmentier is an omlet garnished with potatoes :

Bruxelloise	:	Brussels sprourts
Clamart	:	Peas
Dubarry	:	Cauliflower
Doria	:	Cucumber
Florentine	:	Spinach
Lyonnaise	:	Onions
Princesse	:	Aspagarus
Portugaise	:	Tomatoes
Provencale	:	Tomato and garlic
Washington	:	Sweet corn.

MASCULINE AND FEMININE WORDS

When you look at the words in French you will see that almost all of them have 'le', la' or les', which means 'the', in front of them. When learning French, it is a good idea to learn the le, la, or l' with each word. This is because all words in French, like giraffe and camel, as well as woman and man, are feminine or masculine. When you see la, the word in feminine. *Le* means the word is masculine. If the *le* or *la* comes before a word which begin with an *a*, *e*, *i*, *o*, *u* or *h*, then the *le* or *la* usually become *l'*. *les* can be either masculine or faminine but becomes before words that are plural, that is, more than one, such as giraffes or camels.

LOOKING AT THE WORDS

Some French words also have accents on the letters. These change the sound of the word. When the ascent is on the last letter, that letter is then said. In French the last letter is not usually pronounced.

SAYING THE WORDS

There are some sounds in the French language which are quite different from any sound in English. They may look funny or strange. To say them as a French person would say them, you have to hear them spoken. Listen very carefully and then try to say them like that yourself. But if you say them as they are written, a French person will understand you even if your French accent is not quite perfect. Just read them as if they are English words, except these special rules :

g = is said like *g* in game

j = is said like *s* in treasure

r = is made by a roll in the back of your mouth and sounds like a little like gargling. When there is an *r* it is always said like this, except when it is in brackets, like this (*r*).

n = means that the *n* is not said but the vowel before it is nasalised. This means that you made the sound through your nose and your mouth at the sametime. These are not sounds like this in English, so you have to hear someone say them before you can pronounce them correctly.

e = is said like '*e*' in 'ten' except when followed by '*r*'.

er = sounds like the '*er*' in 'her' except that '*r*' is pronounced.

e(*r*) = means that the *e* sounds like the *e* in the (not thee). The *r* is not said.

ew = is a sound which we do not have in English. To make it, round your lips as if to say '*oo*', then try and say *ee*.

a = is said a little longer than *a* in 'cat' but not as long as the *a* in car.

ay = is like *a* in date.

TRANSLATING THE SENTENCES

When you look the English translation of the French sentences, you will see that the words do not always match. This is because in French sometimes the words are in a different order, sometimes there are more a less words, and same things are said on different ways. If you translate the sentences word or words, you would have very strange English.

MENU LANGUAGE

Many menus in English speaking countries are written in English. When menus are written in French or Hindi many establishments provide an English translation or explanation. To understand the French terms and their complexities study some text books.

Some of the common menu terms are :-

a la : After the style or fashion of, for example
à la francaise (french style)
à la russe (Russian style)
It also means : with or dressed in, for example
à la creme (with or in cream)

à la carte : On the menu (literally card) : It implies many dishes at different prices for the guest's choice. Normally, cooked to order (as distinct from *table d'hote*, q.v.)

au : Masculine form of a la (q.v)

Biscotte : Rusk

Café : Coffee

Cafe au lait : Coffee with milk

Cafe double : Double strength coffee for lunch and dinner

Cafe noir : Coffee without cream or milk, that is, black coffee

Carte du jour : Menu of the day

Chauffe-plats : Side board hot-plates

Couvert : Cover or place setting

Dejunner : Lunch

Demit-tasse : Literary half cup, small coffee cup

Diner : Dinner

Entreé : A composed garnished dish served before the roast or main meat course in a luncheon, served as main course

Entremets : Sweet course formerly entremet sucre's, as an entremets de légume, separate vegetable course was equally frequently served.

Fromage : Cheese

Guêridon : Side table (for service), Now-a-days may be a wheeled table or cart

Mise en place : Literary 'put in place' to waiting, implies pre-preparation of side boards, table

Petit dejeuner : Breakfast

Plat du jour : Special dish of the day

Rechoud : Lamp or small spirit stove for restaurant heating or cooking

Souper : Supper

Table d' hote : A set meal, usually of service course, at a fixed inclusive price

Timbale : A round deep dish of straight sides.

Vol au Vent : Puff pastry case usually filled with diced chicken, fish, etc. dressed in sauce

Voiture : Carriage or trolley, for example for horsd òeuvre or pastries

Wagon : Alternative name for voiture.

FRENCH MENUTERMS

The French are considered to produce the ultimate in fine cooking. The best restaurants take pride in engaging a French Chef and serving French food, which has influenced both the language of the menu and the language of the kitchen. A waiter finds it helpful to know at least basic French menu terms their pronounciations and meanings are given in Table......6.1.

TABLE 6.10 : French Menu Terms, Definition and Pronounciation

French Term	Pronunciation	Definition
Agneau	*ahn-yo*	Lamb
Aigre	*aygr* Sour	
Ail	*eye*	Garlic
Aileron	*ay-luh-rawn*	Wingbone
Allumette	*ah-loo-met*	Match stick potatoes
Alsacienne	*ahl-sah-seeyan*	Alsatian style; usually served with saurkraut
Amandine	*ah-mawn-deen*	With almonds
Américaine	*ah-mair-ee-ken*	American style
Ananas	*ah-nha-nah*	Pineapple
Anchois	*awn-schwah*	Anchovy
Andalouse	*awn-dah-loos*	With tomatoes & peppers
Auguille	*awn-ghee*	Eel
Argenteuil	*ahr-zhawn-toy*	With asparagus
Artichaut	*ahr-tee-show*	Artichoke
Asperges	*ah-spayrge*	Asparagus
Aspic	*ah-speek*	Decorated jellied piece
Aubergines	*oh-bare-zheen*	Egg Plant

(*Contd.*)

Béarnaise	*bair-nez*	In America, a sauce similar to hollandaise, fortified with meat glaze, and with tarragon flavor predominating
Bécasse	*bay-khace*	Woodcock
Béchamel	*bay-shaw-mel*	Cream sauce
Beignet	*bayn-yay*	Fritter
Beurre	*burr*	Butter
Bifteck	*bif-teck*	Beefsteak
Bisque	*beesk*	Thick, rich soup
Blanc	*blawnk*	White
Blanquette	*blawn-ket*	Stew with white wine
Boeuf	*buff*	Beef
Boisson	*bawh-sawn*	Drink, Beverage
Boullabaisse	*bwee-yuh-baze*	Fish stew
Bouillon	*bwee-yawn*	Broth
Bouquetiére	*boo-ket-yer*	With mixed vagetables
Bourguignonne	*boor-geen-yawn*	With onions and red Burgundy wine
Bouteille	*boo-tie*	Bottle
Café	*kah-fay*	Coffee
Canard	*kah-nahr*	Duck
Caneton	*kah-nuh-tawn*	Duckling
Carré	*kah-ray*	Rack
Cervelle	*sir-vel*	Brain
Champignon	*shawn-peen-yawn*	Mushroom
Chapon	*shah-pawn*	Capon
Chateaubriand	*shah-to-bree-yawn*	Thick Filet Mignon
Chaud	*show*	Wavvvvrm, Hot
Cheveruil	*shuv-roy*	Venison
Chou-Fleur	*shoo-flure*	Cauliflower
Choux de Bruxelles	*shoo-duh-brewzel*	Brussel sprouts
Cochon	*ko-shawn*	Suckling pig
Coeur	*koor* Heart	
Compote	*kawn-pawt*	Stewed fruit
Concombre	*kawn-kawmbr*	Cucumber
Confiture	*kawn-fee-toor*	Jam, preserve
Consommé	*kawn-saw-may*	Clear soup
Coquille	*ko-kee*	Shell for baking
Cote	*kaw*	Rib, Chop
Crème	*krem*Cream	
Créme Fouettée	*krem-fo-et-tay*	Whipped cream
Crèpe	*krepp*	Pancake
Crevette	*kruh-vet*	Shrimp

(Contd.)

Croquette	*kro-ket*	Patty of meat
Déjeuner	*day-zhoo-nay*	Breakfast, Lunch
Diable	*dee-abl*	Deviled
Dinde	*dand*	Turkey
Du Barry	*du-bahree*	With cauliflower
Eau	*oh*	Water
Ecrevisse	*ay-kruh-veece*	Crayfish
Entreote	*awn-truh-kawt*	Sirloin steak
Entremets	*awn-truh-meh*	Sweet, Desserts
Epinard	*ay-pee-nahr*	Spinach
Escargots	*es-kahr-go*	Snails
Faisan	*fay-zawn*	Pheasant
Farce	*fahrce*	Ground meat
Farci	*fahr-see*	Stuffed
Filet	*fee-lay*	Boneless ribbon
Flambé	*flawn-bay*	Flamed
Foiefwah	Liver	
Foie Gras	*fwah-grah*	Goose liver
Fondue	*fawn-doo*	Melted cheese
Forestière	*faw-rest-teeyer*	With musaroom
Four	*foor*	Oven baked
Fricandeau	*free-kahn-doe*	Braised veal morsels
Fricassée	*free-kah-say*	Chicken or veal stew
Frìt	*free*	Deep fat fried
Froid	*frwah*	Cold
Fromage	*foo-mahge*	Cheese
Fumé	*foo-may*	Smoked
Gateau	*gah-toe*	Cake
Gelée	*zhuh-lay*	Jelly
Gibier	*zhee-bee-yay*	Game
Gigot	*zhee-go*	Leg
Glacé	*glah-say*	Ice, ice, cream
Gratin	*gran-tan*	Brown, baked with Cheese
Grenouille	*gruh-noo-ee*	Frog
Grillé	*gree yay*	Broiled
Hereng	*ah-rawng*	Herring
Haricot Vert	*ah-ree-ko-ver*	String beans
Hollandaise	*aw-lawn-dez*	Sauce made with egg yolk, melted butter, and lemon
Homard	*oh-mar*	Lobster
Hors d'Oeuvres	*or-durve*	Pre-dinner tidbits
Huitre	*wheatr*	Oyster

(Contd.)

Jambon	*zhahn-bawn*	Ham
Jardiniére	*zhahr-dan-yer*	With vegetable
Julienne	*zhool-yen*	Thin strips
Jus	*zhoo* Juice, gravy	
Lait	*lay*	Milk
Langouste	*lawn-goost*	Sea crayfish or rock lobster
Lapin	*lah-pan*	Rabbit
Légume	*lay-goom*	Vegetable
Macédoine	*mah-suh-dwahn*	Mixed fruits
Maitre d'hotel	*maytr-doe-tell*	With spiced butter
Marmite	*mahr-meet*	Pot; Stew
Meringue	*meh-rang*	Beaten egg white
Meunière	*moon-yer*	Pan fried and served with brown butter
Mignon	*mee-yawn*	Dainty
Mornay	*mor-nay*	Cheese sauce
Mousse	*moose*	Whipped foam
Mouton	*moo-tawn*	Mutton
Nantua	*nahn-too-ah*	Lobster sauce
Naturel	*nah-tew-rel*	Plain
Noirnwah	Black	
Noisette	*swah-zet*	Hazelnut
Nouille	*noo-ee*	Noodle
Oeuf	*uf*	Egg
Oeufs Pochés	*uf-paw-shay*	Poached eggs
Oie	*wah*	Goose
Oignon	*awn-yawn*	Onion
Pain	*pan*	Bread
Patépah-tay	Meat pie	
Patisserie	*pah-tee-suh-ree*	Pastry
Pêche	*pesh* Peach	
Petit	*puh-tee*	Small
Poire	*pwahr*	Pear
Poispwah	Peas	
Poisson	*pwah-sawn*	Fish
Poitrine	*pwah-treen*	Breast
Pomme	*pawn*	Apple
Pomme de Terre	*pawn-duh-ter*	Potato
Potage	*poh-tahge*	Soup
Pot Au Few	*paw-toe-foo*	Boiled beef with a va riety of vegetables and broth served as a meal

(Contd.)

Poulet	*poo-lay*	Chicken
Purée	*poo-ray*	Sieved food
Quenelle	*kuh-nel*	Dumpling
Ragout	*rah-goo*	Stew
Ris	*ree*	Sweetbread
Riz	*ree*	Rice
Rognon	*rawn-yawn*	Kidney
Roti ro-tee	Roasted	
Roulade	*roo-lahd*	Rolled meat
Saumon	*saw-mone*	Salmon
Sauté	*saw-tay*	Pan fried in butter
Sel	*sell*	Salt
Selle	*sell*	Saddle
Sorbet	*sawr-bay*	Sherbet
Soufflé	*soo-flay*	Whipped pudding
Tasse	*tahce*	Cup
Tête tet	Head	
Tournedos	*toor-nuh-do*	Two small tenderloin steaks
Tranche	*trawnsh*	Slice
Truite	*trew-eet*	Trout
Veau	*vo*	Veal
Veloute	*vuh-lootay*	White sauce made from fish, chicken, or veal stock
Vichyssoise	*vee-shee-swahz*	Hot or cold potato and leek soup
Viennoise	*vee-yen-wahz*	Vienna style, breaded
Vinaigrette	*vee-nay-gret*	Dressing with oil, vinegar and herbs
Volaille	*vo-lie*	Poultry
Vol au Vent	*vole-oh-vawn*	Patty shell.

TABLE : 6.11 : Commonly used Cookery French Terms with their Pronunciations

Term	Pronunciation	Meaning
à la	ah-lah	After the style or fashion
àl la carte	ah-lah-cart	Prepared as ordered
à la king	ah-lah king	Served in a cream sauce of mushrooms, green peppers, pimentos
amandine	ah-mawn-deen	With almonds
au gratin	aw-grat'n	With cheese
au jus	ah ju	Served in natural juice or gravy
beãrnaise	bair-nays	Sauce of tarragon, shallots egg yolk, butter
groochette	bro-shet	Meat boiled on a skewer
canapé	kah-nah-pay	An appetiser of small piece of toast or fried bread spread with savory foods

(Contd.)

chateubriand	sha-toe-bree-yawn	Thick filet mignon
carte dujour	kahrt-du-jour	Menu of the day
cocoth	kau-kaht	Small earthern-ware pan
compôte	kom-pote	Fruit stewed in syrup
consommé	kon-so-may	Clear meat stock served hot or jellied
créôle	kray-ol	Prepared with tomatoes, green pepers and onions
croustade	kroo-stahd	Hot crisp patty
crouton	kroo-tohn	Small pieces of fried toasted bread to accompany soup or salad
demitasse	deh-mee-tahss	Small cup of coffee
éclair	ay-klair	French choux pastry with a cream filling and iced
entrée	ahn-tray	A main dish served before the roast or meat course. As commonly used, however, includes all main dish
en casserol	ahn-kash-rol	Based or served in an individual dish
escargots	es-kahr-go	Snails
filet	fee-lay	Boneless loin cut of beef, veal, pork or bonelss strip of fish
fricassée	free-kah-say	Meat or chicken stewed and served with thickened creamy sauce
gas pacho	guz-pah-cho	Cold Spanish soup, tomatoes base with peppers and spices
glace	glah-say	Frozen or glazed
horsd'oveuvres	ohr-deo-rv	Savory food served as appetizers
jardiniére	zhar-da-nee-air	A mixture of green vegetables
julienne	zhu-lee-air	Cut in thin strips
maître d'hôtel	maytre-doe-toll	With fresh melted butter
marmite	marh-meet	Small earthen ware dish for onion soup
mayonnais	may-on-ays	A salad dressing made with egg, oil and lemon juice or vinegar
maringue	mah-ran-g	A baked dessert made of white of egg and sugar or the topping of the pastry
meringue glace	mah-ran-g-glah-say	Meringue shells on ice cream
mulligatawany	mull-i-ga-taw-nee	Cold cream soup chicken
newburg	new-burg	Lobster sauce with cream and sherry
purée	puray	A thick sieved vegetables fruit or soup
ragoût	ra-goo	A rich stew of highly seasonal meat and gravy
rissole	ree-so-lay	Browned
sauté	sah-tay	Fried in a small amount of fat
soufflé	soo-flay	Light, puffed, a light egg mixture, served as an entree or some time as dessert when sweetened
table d'hôte	table	A meal served in several courses at a set price

(Contd.)

therminder	ther-ma-dohr	Sea food cooked with cream and wine
vinaigrettee	vee-nay-gret	With oil, vineger and herbsa salad dressing

Table 6.12 indicates some of the French culinary terms, which are very important for any employee working in the hotel. These are a few simple and basic French culinary terms which could prove useful to the hotel staff.

TABLE 6.12 : Important French Culinary Terms

French Term		Meaning
agneau	:	Lamb
américane	:	Dishes cooked with herbs and tomatoes
asparagus	:	Asparagus
aspic	:	Savoury jelly
abuergine	:	Egg plant/brinjal
bechamel	:	White sauce
bordelaise	:	Sauce flavoured with red wine
brioche	:	Yeast roll
canapés	:	Tasty food on small piece of toast and bread
caneton	:	Duckling
cardinal	:	Lobster sauce and garnish
champignons	:	Mushrooms
chantily crême	:	Whipped cream
chasseur	:	Garnish of mushroom and shallots cooked in white wine sauce
châteaubriand	:	A thick steak from the middle of the fillet
cog.coquelet	:	Cockeral
courert	:	Cover, place setting, cover charge
crêpes	:	Think pancakes
corquettes	:	Balls of various foods (e.g. mashed potato, fried and crispy)
croutons	:	Dried bread used as a garnish
demi-tasse (cofé)	:	Small coffee cup
entrecôte	:	Serloin steak
escalope	:	Flattened thin slices of veal or beef
filet mignon	:	A piece of steak from the fillet
flamber	:	To pour brandy or fortified wine over food and ignite
foie-grass, pâtéde	:	(plate of) liver of goose or duck
fraises	:	Straw berries
frappé	:	Chilled
fricassee	:	Cut of meat or poultry cooked in sauce and gravy
gâteau	:	Cake
glace	:	Ice (cream)
glacé	:	Candied, glazed with sugar
gratin'an	:	A dish sprinkled with grated cheese and butter and browned on top in an oven or under grill

(Contd.)

hollandaise	:	A sauce made with yolk of egg and butter
hûitres	:	Oysters
italienne	:	Dish with chopped mushrooms
jambon	:	Ham
julienne	:	Fresh vegetables cut up finely
kebab	:	Small pieces of marinated meat threaded on skewers and grilled
kirsch	:	A liqueur distilled from wild cherries
lapin	:	Rabbit
macédoine	:	Mixture of diced vegetables or fruits
marons	:	Chestnuts
meuníère	:	(fish) flavoured and fried in butter
mise en-place	:	Pre-service preparation
mornay	:	Sauce made from bechamel sauce, cream, parmesan or Gruyere cheese
mousse	:	Light, whipped sweet or savoury with whites of eggs.
newburg	:	A method of preparing shellfish
noisettes d'agn eau	:	Small round slices from the cutlet or saddle of lamb
normade	:	Poultry or meat cooked in cider and cream
pâte	:	A fine savoury mixture made from liver, pork or game and served cold
paupiettes	:	Thin slices of meat stuffed, rolled and wrapped in bacon
petits pois	:	Green peas
petits four	:	Small fancy cakes and biscuits
pomme	:	Apple
pommes de terre	:	Potatoes
polonaise	:	With chopped hard boiled eggs
portugaise	:	Tomato fondue with onion and garlic
poulet	:	Chicken
poussin	:	Small young chicken (spring)
praline	:	Burnt almomd flavouring
purée	:	Cream or blended thick sauce or soup
ragôute	:	A rich stew of meat or poultry
roulade	:	Rolled piece of meat
sauerkraut,	:	Pickled white cabbage choucroute
sauté	:	Tossed in fat or butter
soubise	:	Accompaniment of smooth onion pulp
suprême	:	A creamy white sauce made with chicken stock
tartare sauce	:	Cold mayonnaise sauce with egg
tarte	:	Tart, flan, pie
vinaigrette	:	A spicy dressing of oil, vinegar, chopped shallots, gherkins, and capers
vol-au-vent	:	A small putt pastry case
wieners-chhitzel escalope vienncise	:	Thin piece of veal or chopped pork dipped in flour, egg and bread crumbs and fried in fat.

GARNISHES

Garnish can be defined as food items placed around or on top of a principal dish for adornment of relish". Classical dishes are garnished by its creator for the naming of public personalities, whether political, professional or merely a name of the establishment. The popularity of an establishment has often been made by the'Chef'(head cook, specialising on his garnishings alone).

The constituents of garnishes are supplied by farinaceous products, quenelles of all kinds, cock's combs, kidneys, truffles, mushrooms, plain or stuffed olives, shellfish, bone marrow etc. Vegetables for garnishing are treated in accordance with the use and shape, implied by the name of the dish e.g. for Consomme Juliennes, the vegetables will be cut into juliennes.

A careful selection of garnishes that have flavour, colour and eye appeal is appreciated and it is accepted as a finished dish. The purpose of garnishing food is to supply some appropriate and suitable adjunct to the dish e.g. 'Maitre d'hotel'and straw potatoes with mixed grill.

It makes the dish attractive in appearance and enhances flavour e.g., lemon wedges and parsley with fried fish. It helps to improve the colour of the principle dishes and it is seen that the colourful ingredients blend well with the dish. The subtle touch of colour well used will increase the attractiveness of a dish whereas if uncontrolled the result can be disastrous. Omission of any constituent is to be avoided, as the garnish would thereby be out of keeping with its specified character. The neatness is of prime importance and from the service point of view, arranging of garnish must be planned to facilitate the servicing. Many a dressed and garnished dish has been spoilt by its appearance after only one portion having been served; simply because the garnish has not been carefully considered with the service in mind. There is no specific design to work to, although the classical dishes are always garnished as its originator intended.

There are two types of garnishes, simple and composite. Simple garnishes consist of a single element most commonly vegetable, braised, sauted or fried, rice, croutons, flutes, e.g. Tomato soup with croutons. Composite garnishes are made from a number of ingredients varying according to the basic dish e.g. Chicken Maryland with corn galettes (thick corn pancakes) Bacon rashers, banana fritters, potato croquette and grilled tomatoes.

The garnishes for cold buffet for decorating cold dishes must be glazed with aspic jelly before they are arranged on the dish. After the garnish has been arranged on the dish, a final coating of aspic jelly will ensure that they become set on the dish and do not move when being carried for service. A few specific garnishes for cold buffets are eggs, stuffed tomatoes, barquettes with various fillings, fanciful shapes, cuts of vegetables, used wherever appropriate. Their important role is that the garnishes are neat, tastefully decorated, and in keeping with the item of food which they accompany. The number of piece should be in keeping with the number of portions of the dish.

While compiling menus, it should be borne in mind that the garnish used must be in keeping with the nature of dish. The garnish should not be repeated between courses nor should it form an accompaniment to any course. Some of the common garnishes are given in Table 6.13.

Pix 6.14 : A Chef Working in a Kitchen

TABLE 6.13 : Garnish for Some of the Dishes

Name of Garnish	Meaning
1. Tomato juice	Lemon wedges.
2. Shellfish cocktail	Parsley, lemon, boiled egg.
3. Fruit cocktail	Cherry.
4. Soups	Juliennes of vegetables, brunoise of vegetables, egg royal, cooked tongue, ham, spaghetti, vermicelli, crouton rice etc.
5. Fish	Parsley, lemon, truffles, prawns, shrimps tomatoes, grapes and bananas etc.
6. Meats :	
7. Grills	*Maitre d'hotel'* butter and straw potaotes.
8. Stews	Dices or turned vegetables, grilled tomatoes, mushrooms, peas, French beans.
9. Roast	A salad, orange, greens etc.
10. Sandwiches	Lettuce or water-cress
11. Tandoori Murgh	Slices of onions, green chillies, lemon slices.
12. Seekh Kabba	Slices of onions, lemon wedges and chatney.
13. Pulaos	Silver foil, fried cashewnuts and fried onions
14. Curries	Silver foil, chopped coriander leaves.
15. Masala Fish	Lemon wedges and coriander leaves
16. Dals	Whole red chillies or fried onions, coriander leaves.

ACCOMPANIMENTS

Many dishes have separate accompaniments whose flavour, taste and colour blend or give contrast to the principal dish. Food items such as sauces, vegetables, salads and certain meat items, cheese or bread are accompaniments that make a dish complete. They add to the bulk of the dish and give greater satisfaction, improve the satiety value and enhance the taste e.g. bland poached fish accompanied by Holladaise sauce. They also help to digest food, sometimes provide moistness, and give piquancy to the dish e.g. roast lamb accompanied by mint sauce, fried fish with tartare sauce, etc. Some of the important food items and their accompaniments are given in Table 6.14.

TABLE 6.14 : Foods and their Usual Accompaniments

Food items	Accompaniments
1. Grape Fruit	Castor sugar.
2. Melon	Castor sugar and ginger powder.
3. Oysters	Tabasco sauce (commercial) chilly vinegar, cayenne
4. pepper, brown bread and butter. Pepper Mill, lemon.	
5. Tomato Juice	Worcestershire sauce (commercial sauce).
6. Caviare	Hot buttered breakfast toast.
7. Smoked Valmon	Red pepper, pepper mill, brown bread and butter.
8. Foie gras	Hot buttered breakfast toast.
SOUPS	
1. Puree Soups	Croutons (fried)
2. Bortsch a la russe	Sour cream, beet root juice, duck force meat bouchees
3. French onion soup	Slices of dry French bread, Parmesan cheese
4. Potage Bonne Femme	Flutes
5. Minestrone	Parmesan cheese.
6. Petite Marmite	Sippets, Parmesan cheese.
FISH	
1. Fried Fish (egg and bread crumbed and deep fried)	Tartare sauce, lemon slices.
2. Fish Orly (Only batter and deep fried)	Tomato sauce.
3. Grilled Fish	Tartare or Hollandaise sauce or Lemon butter sauces.
4. Poached Fish	Hollandaise sauce or egg sauce and melted butter.
5. Poached Fish salmon or cold salmon	Cucumber salad, Hollandaise sauce.
6. Fish Meuniere	Tomato sauce, Noisette butter.
7. Cold Lobster or any other fish	Mayonnaise.
MEATS	
1. Roast Beef	Yorkshire Pudding, Horse radish sauce and roast gravy.
2. Roast Lamb	Mint sauce, roast gravy.
3. Roast Mutton	Onion sauce or Red currant-jelly, roast gravy.
4. Roast Pork	Sage and onion stuffing, apple sauce, roast gravy.

5. Roast veal	Savoury herb stuffing, grilled bacon, roast gravy.
6. Roast Venison Hot	Red Currents jelly, roast gravy
7. Boiled Mutton	Caper sauce, (mashed turnips) Mustard.
8. Boiled Fresh Beef	Rock salt, gherkins and grated horse radish.
9. Braised Ham	Spinach, Maderri or Peachs auce
10. Grilled Ham	Sauce will appear on the menu.
11. Cold Meats	Mustards, pickles, chutney, relishes and proprietary sauce.

POULTRY AND GAME

1. Roast Chicken	Bread sauce, roast gravy, roast potatoes.
2. Roast Duck	Sage and onion stuffing, apple sauce roast gravy.
3. Roast Turkey	Herb stuffing chestnut stuffing, chipolatas, cranberry sauce, roast gravy.

VEGETABLE

1. Vegetables served hot	Hollandaise sauce melted butter.
2. Vegetable served cold	Mayonnaise or vinaigrette sauce.

IMPORTANT TERMS WHICH FEATURE DISHES

When the featured dishes are served they must match the build up provided by the menu description. Here is a selection of standard terms which are understood the world over. These standard terms and their indicators are useful in food production, given in Table 6.15.

TABLE 6.15 : Standard Terms which Feature Dishes

Terms	Indicators
Africaine	Egg plant, tomatoes and mushrooms.
Americaine	Tomatoes, bacon, watercress.
Argenteuil	Asparagus
Bohemienne	Onions, tomatoes, rice.
Boquetiere	Carrots, turnips, peas and beans and Cauliflower
Bourgeoise	Carrots, small onions, lardons.
Clamart	Green peas
Conti	Lentils.
Danoise	Cucumber.
Daria	Cucumber.
Dieppoise	Shrimps, nussels, mushrooms.
Dubarry	Cauliflower.
Fiananciere	Cock-combs, kidneys, mushrooms, olives, Quenelles.
Fleuriste	Carrots, turnips, peas, beans.
Florentine	Spinach.
Hongroise	Paprika.
Indienne	Curry sauce, rice.
Jardiniere	Carrots, turnips, peas, beans.
Judic	Stuffed tomatoes, braised lettuce, chateau potatoes.
Marechalle	Aspargus, noisettes, potatoes truffles.
Maryland	Sweet corn, banana, bacon, potatoes, croquettes.
Milanaise	Spaghetti, ham, tonque mushrooms.
Montmorency	Cherries.
Nicoise	Tomatoes, beans, chateau potatoes.
Parmentiere	Potatoes.
Perigueaux	Foie-gras, truffles.

Portugaise	Tomatoes, chateau potatoes.
Princesse	Aspargus, artichokes, noisette potatoes.
Reforme	Ham, tongue, gherkinm mushrooms.
Rossini	Foie gras, truffles.
Soubise	Onions
St. Germaine	Green peas.
Toulousaine	Cocks comb, kidneys, sweet bread, quenelles.
Tyrolienne	Tomatoes, onions.
Vichy	Carrots.
Viennoise	Lemon, hard boiled egg, Olives and anchovy.
Walewska (Fish)	Slices of lobster tails and truffles.
Washington	With poultry and egg sweet corn.
Zingara	Julienne of ham, tongue, mushrooms, truffles.

KITCHEN ORGANISATION

The best kitchen organisation could be brought about by making a careful study of the work procedures involved in the light of facilities, products and techniques.

The famous French Chef Auguste Escoffier is credited with organising kitchens into well defined stations called the *Chef de Partie* specialised in specific type of food preparation and a specific plate had component made by different station *Chefs*[1].Modern kitchen can't adopt the original *partie* system but they can apply some basic principles of organising their own production systems taking into account the type of menu and style of service desired, the staff and customers involved and the equiptment and layout of the kitchen. The quality and skills required will be determined for the menu. Each type of operation will need its own unique organisation for best results. Only a few luxury hotels have a brigade of cooks divided into parties that include every section.

In most of the hotels, the *garde* manger either with one or small staff handles all the tasks relating to meat, poultry and fish. Two or more parties such as soup preparation and vegetable cookery are combined. There are basically three broad divisionslarder, pastry and main kitchen and intermingling of the branches of work. In small kitchen are employed one chef and one assistant cook, who do at most the full range of tasks.

Fig. 6.8, indicates kitchen organisation in a small hotel, Fig. 6.9, is a typical kitchen organisation in a medium hotel. Fig. 6.10 the role of Executive 'Chef 'within the organisation. Figs 16.17 and 18 are typical organisation chart for a kitchen.

Today kitchens are organised in a variety of ways according to different needs of food and services. The broad features of a kitchen organisation are based on :

1. Storage
2. Preparation of meat, fish, poultry
3. Preparation of desserts and parties
4. Assembling and cooking of prepared food.

From organisational point of view the main section of a kitchen are :

1. Main production centre
2. Ancillary food production
3. Administration
4. Pantry
5. Cleaning.

---

1. Chef Auguste Escoffier, French Chef.

Kitchen Organisation : Small Size Hotel
Kitchen
Chef de Cuisine (Working)
Sous Chef (Sauce and Fish Combined)
Larder Cook
Chef de Parte For Preparation of Soups Vegetables and Rast
Vegetable Hand
Pastry Chef
Kitchen Porter

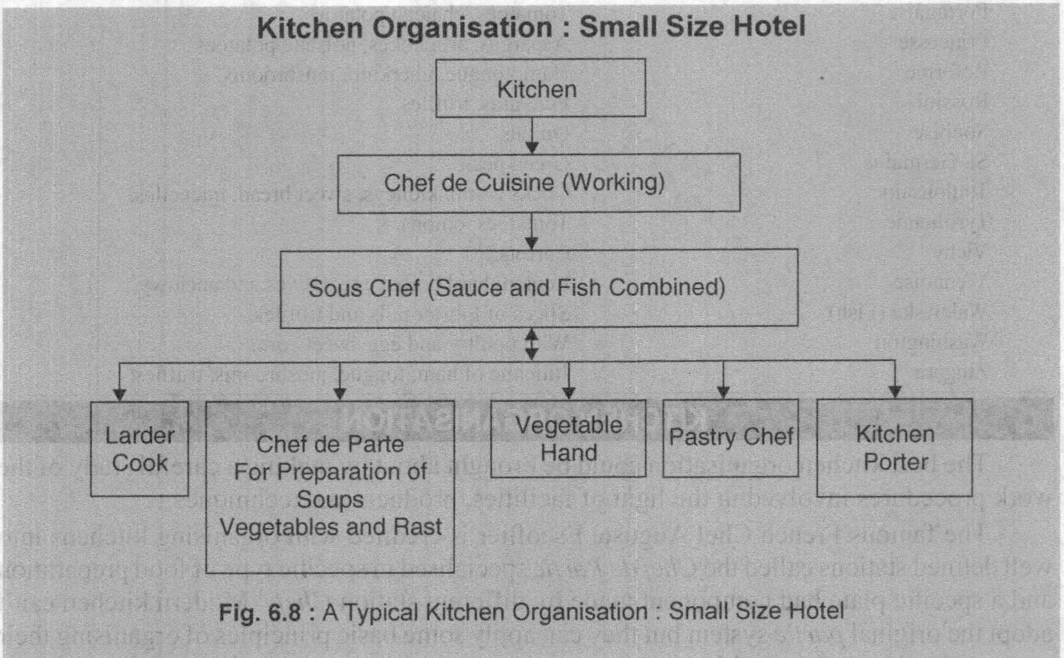

Fig. 6.8 : A Typical Kitchen Organisation : Small Size Hotel

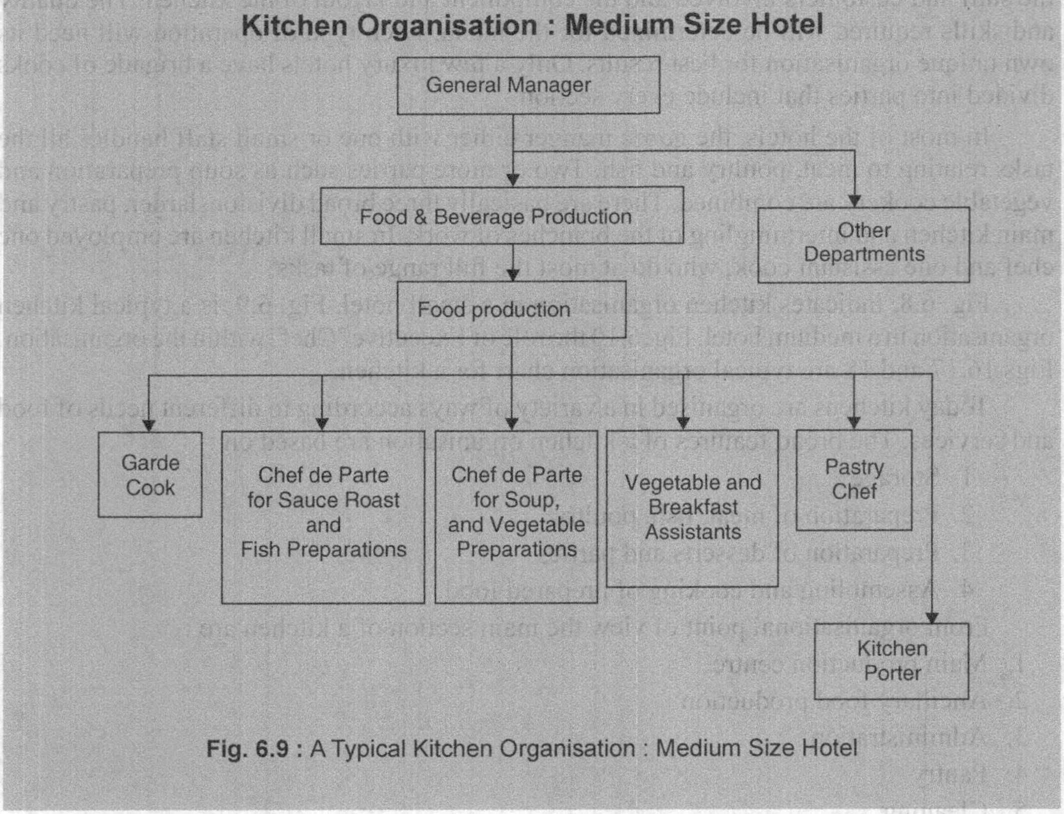

Kitchen Organisation : Medium Size Hotel
General Manager
Food & Beverage Production
Other Departments
Food production
Garde Cook
Chef de Parte for Sauce Roast and Fish Preparations
Chef de Parte for Soup, and Vegetable Preparations
Vegetable and Breakfast Assistants
Pastry Chef
Kitchen Porter

Fig. 6.9 : A Typical Kitchen Organisation : Medium Size Hotel

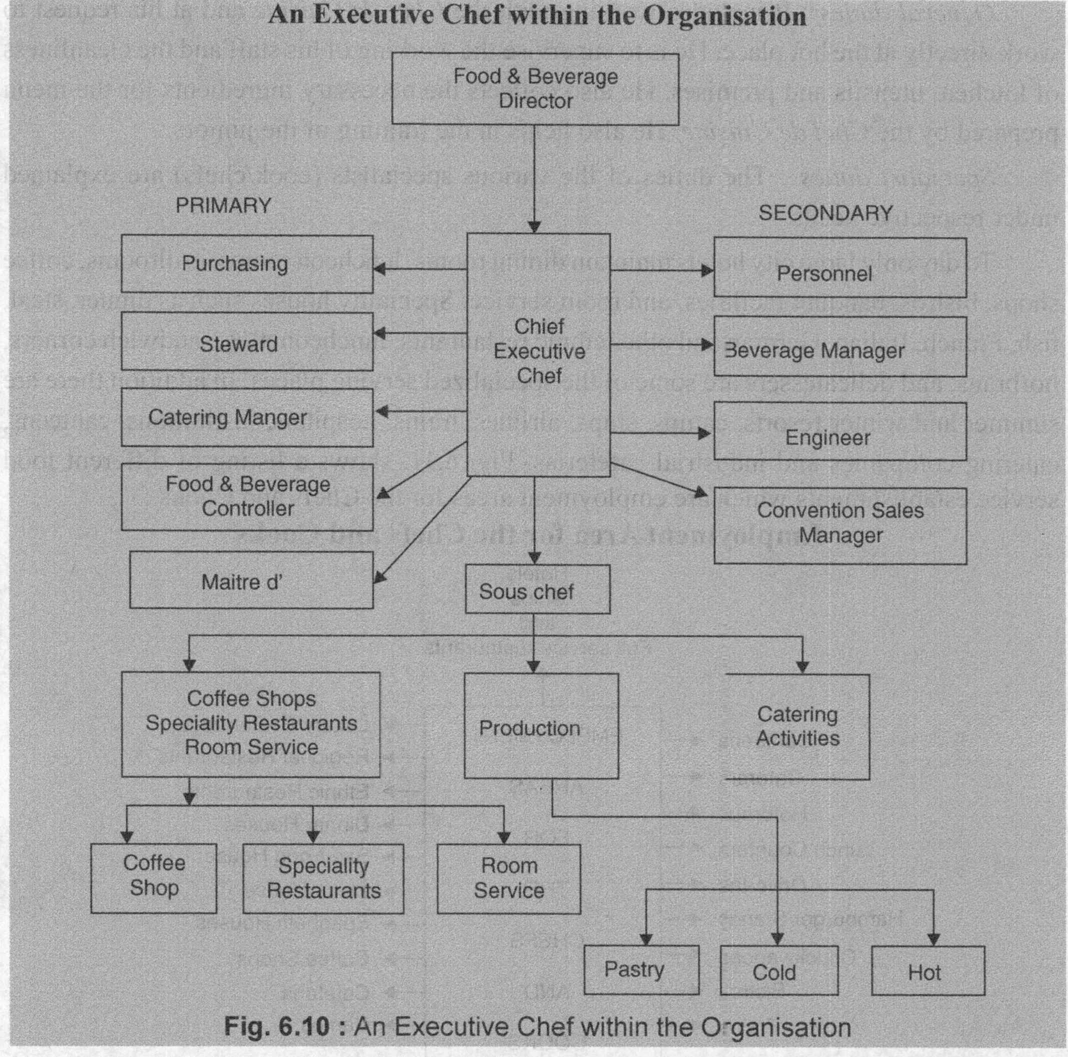

Fig. 6.10 : An Executive Chef within the Organisation

MAIN PRODUCTION CENTRE

'*Partie*' is a French word meaning 'part' (of a whole) or section. A *partie* system is one in which the kitchen space, equipment and jobs are divided into sections. The partie system operated by Escoffier remains an integral part of culinary craft's traditions and illustrates the enduring principle involved in determining task groupings. Each section has clearly defined tasks to be performed and co-ordinated by a supervisor.

Section Chefs/Chef de Parties work in close co-operation with the *Chef de Cuisine*. They must have adequate kitchen training and a great deal of practical experience. *Chef de Partie* must have almost all those qualities and knowledge which are required for the assistant *Chef*. They should have a good knowledge about the different frozen foodstuffs and their utilisation. In the case of pastry cook, he must have drawing ability and practical knowledge of designing. In case of larder cook, perfect knowledge of the quality, cutting up and presentation of meat, poultry, game fish etc. is required. The duties of the *Chef de Partie* can be divided into two categories :

General duties : It includes working with the *Chef de Cuisine* and at his request to work directly at the hot place. He is to supervise the working of his staff and the cleanliness of kitchen, utensils and premises. He also collects the necessary ingredients for the menu prepared by the *Chef de Cuisine*. He also helps in the training of the juniors.

Specialist duties : The duties of the various specialists (cook/chefs) are explained under respective heads.

To day only large city hotels maintain dining rooms, luncheon rooms, grillrooms, coffee shops, bistros, banquet facilities, and room service. Speciality houses such as dinner, steal, fish, French, Italian, German and other ethnic restaurants; luncheonettes, sandwich corners, hofbraus, and delicatessers are some of the specialized serving places. In addition there are summer and winter resorts, camps, ships, airlines, trains, hospitals, institutions, canteens, catering companies and industrial cafeterias. Fig. 6.11. shows a listing of different food service establishments which are employment areas for the Chefs and Cooks :

Employment Area for the Chefs and Cooks

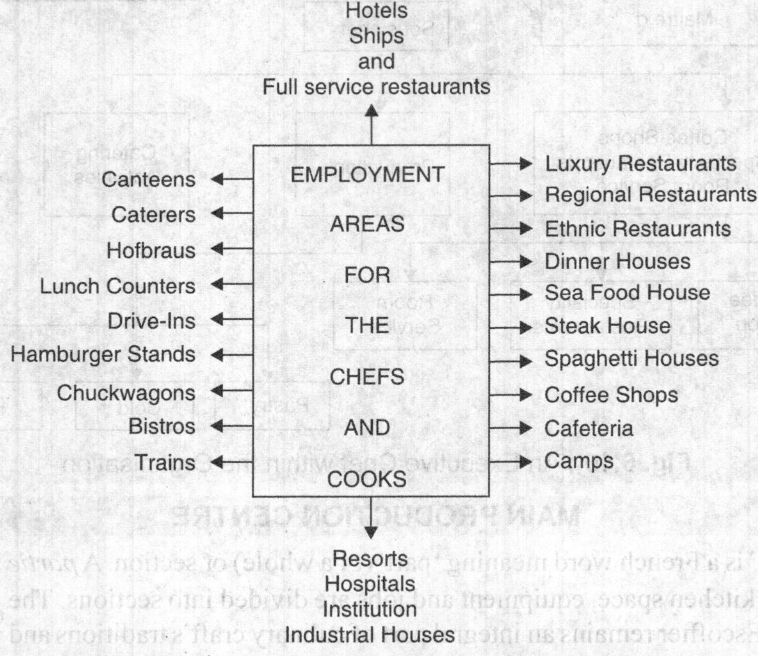

Fig.6.11: Employment Area for the Chefs and Cooks

SKILLS LEVELS AND RANKS

Skills levels and ranks go hand in hand. Elevation in rank comes as reward for service. Skills alone even though matched with professional knowledge, is not enough, to be promoted. Personality, reliability, and honesty are qualities just as important. A good sense, as capability of public relations, and a cool head are as important in a chef as his top culinary performance. The shortage of good chef is so great that many hotels and restaurants are satisfied with chef whose business sense is greater than his culinary know-how. Fig. 6.12 Shows the rank of cook brigade generally found in a good hotel.

Ranks of Cooking Brigade

Rank	French Equivalent Rank
Executive Chef	Chef de cuisine
Sous Chef	Sous chef
Station Chef	Chef de partie
Station Cook (Commis I)	Premier commis
Cook's Helper (Commis II)	Deuxieme commis
Cook's Helper Assistant (Commis III)	Trisomieme commis.

Fig. 6.12. A cook's Brigade

The rank of a cook brigade may not be exact the same in difficult areas or regions. They are influenced by union classification and management preferences. In many cases two or three station are combined and the work is supervised by one chef. For example, in many establishments, there is a combination of Sous Chef, saucer. Etremetier and Postager, and is commonly known as Second Cook. Figs 6.13 shows the Ranks of Cooks Brigade in hotels, and restaurants :

Cooks Brigade in a Restaurants

Large Hotels	Medium	Small
1. Executive Chef	1. Head Chef	1. Chef
2. Day Chef (Sous chef)	2. Night Chef	2. Broilerman
3. Night Chef (Sous chef)	3. Second Chef	3. Pantryman
4. Banquet Chef (Sous chef)	4. Broiler-short Order Man	
5. Second Cook	5. Pantryman	
6. Chef-Garde-manger	6. Steamable-Fryman	
7. Station Cook		
8. Broiller man-short Order Cook		
9. Cook's Helper-Fryman		
10. Steamableman-Carver		
11. Pantryman –		
12. Pastry Chef		

Fig. 6.13. Cooks Brigade in American Style Hotels

Fig. 6.14 shows the comparative English, French and American equivalent name along with station divisions generally found in hotels and restaurants.

Ranks and Corresponding Skill Levels (American and French Hotels)

English Name	French Style	American Station or Rank Equivalent	
1. Sauce Station Cook	Saucier		
2. Fish Station Cook	Poissonier	Sance Cook	Second Cook Station
3. Soup Station Cook	Potager		
4. Vegetable and Egg	Entremetier	Vegetable Cook	
5. Station Cook			
		Broiler-shortorder	
6. Roast and Broiler Station Cook	Rotisseur	Break fast Cook	
7. Cold Pantry Cook	Grade mangei	Salad and Sandwich	
8. Buffet Carver Cook	Buffetier	Pantry Cook	
9. Pastry Station Cook	Patissier	Pastry and Dessert Pantry Cook	
10. Relief	Tournant	Swing Shift Cook.	

Fig.6.14. Station Division or Sections of a Kitchen

The ranks and corresponding skill levels found in American and French style hotel are given in Fig. 6.15.

Rank and Corresponding Skill Levels (American and French Style)

American style		French Style	
Rank	Skill Levels	Rank	Skill Levels
1. Executive Chef	Master Chef and Administrator	Chef de cuisine	Master Chef and Administrator
2. Day Chef-Night-Sous Chef	Skilled Chef	Sous Chef	Master Chef
		Chef-de partie	Master Chef or Skilled Cook
3. Banquet Chef-Chef grade Manger	Master Chef	Premier Commis	Skilled Cook (5 year) minimum experience)
4. Second Cook	Skilled Cook	Deuxieme Commis	Skilled Cook (1–5 years experience)
5. Station Cook	Skilled Cook	Trosiemee Commis	Skilled cook (First year after apprenticeship).
6. Broiler-short order Man	Semi-skilled Cook		
7. Pantryman	Semi skilled Cook		
8. Cook's Helper-Fryman	Unskilled Labour		
9. Steam table-Carver			
10. Vegetable Helper			

Fig. 6.15. Ranks and corresponding levels (American and French style)

A Typical Organisation of a Large Culinary Section/Kitchen

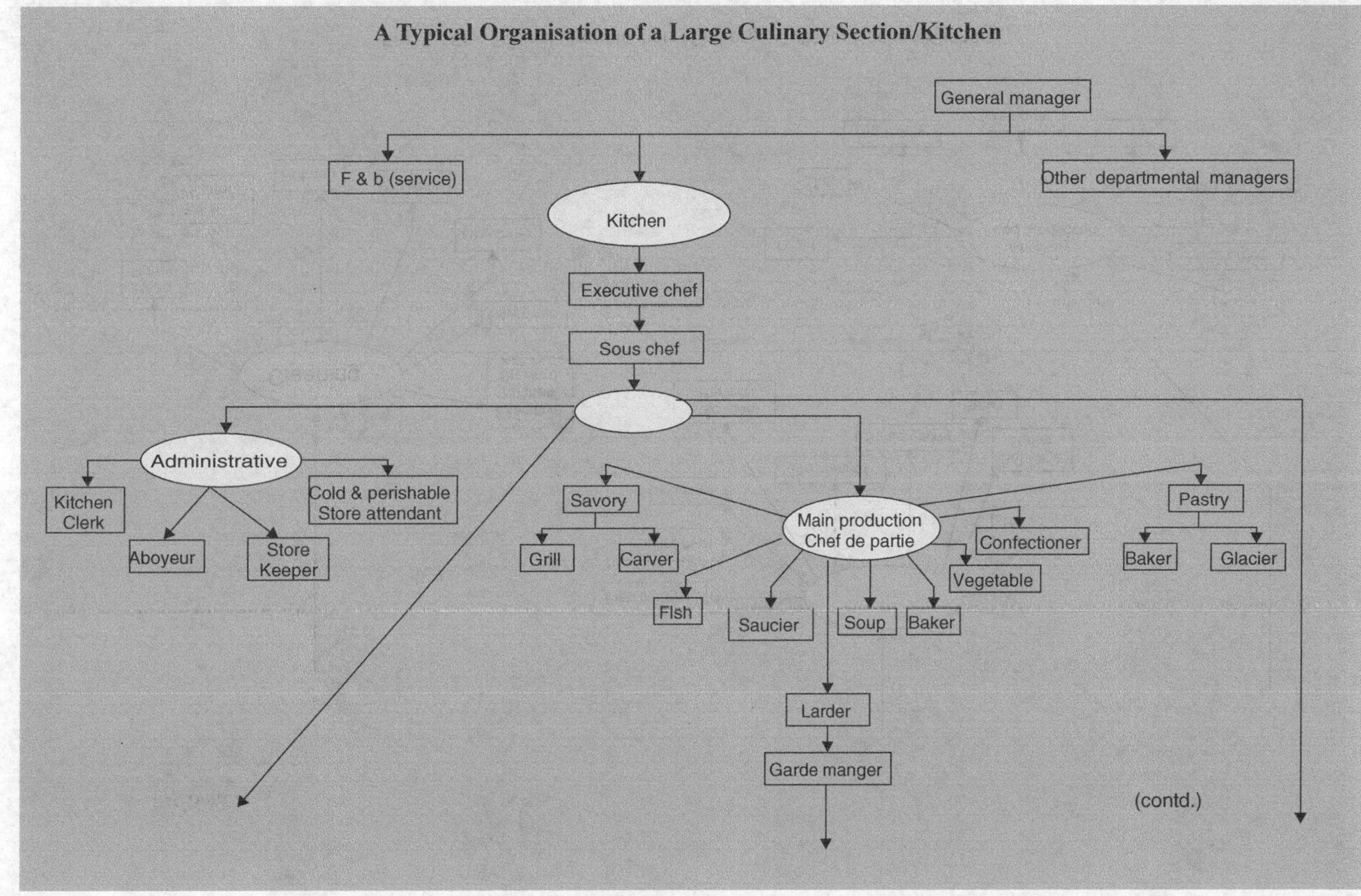

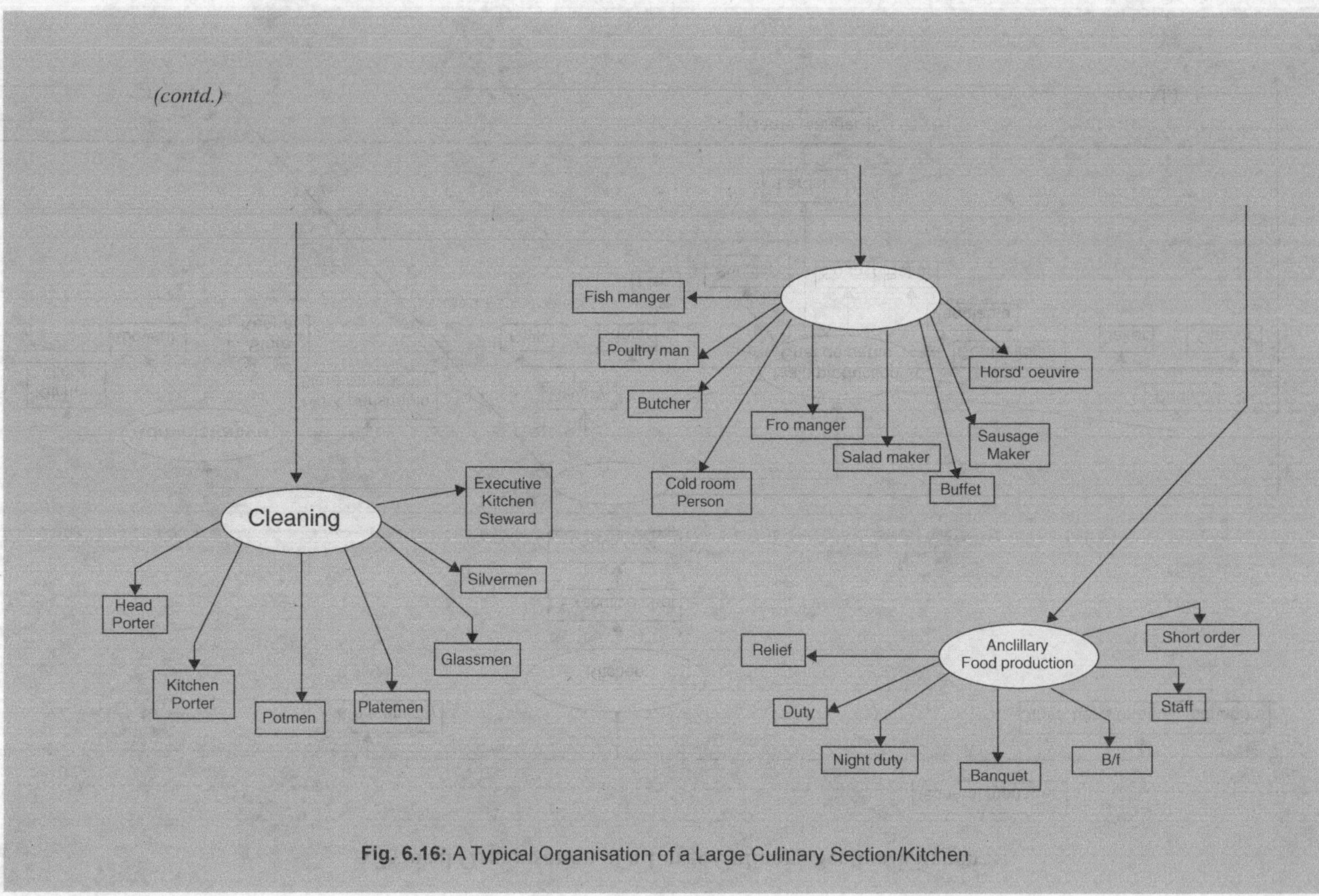

Fig. 6.16: A Typical Organisation of a Large Culinary Section/Kitchen

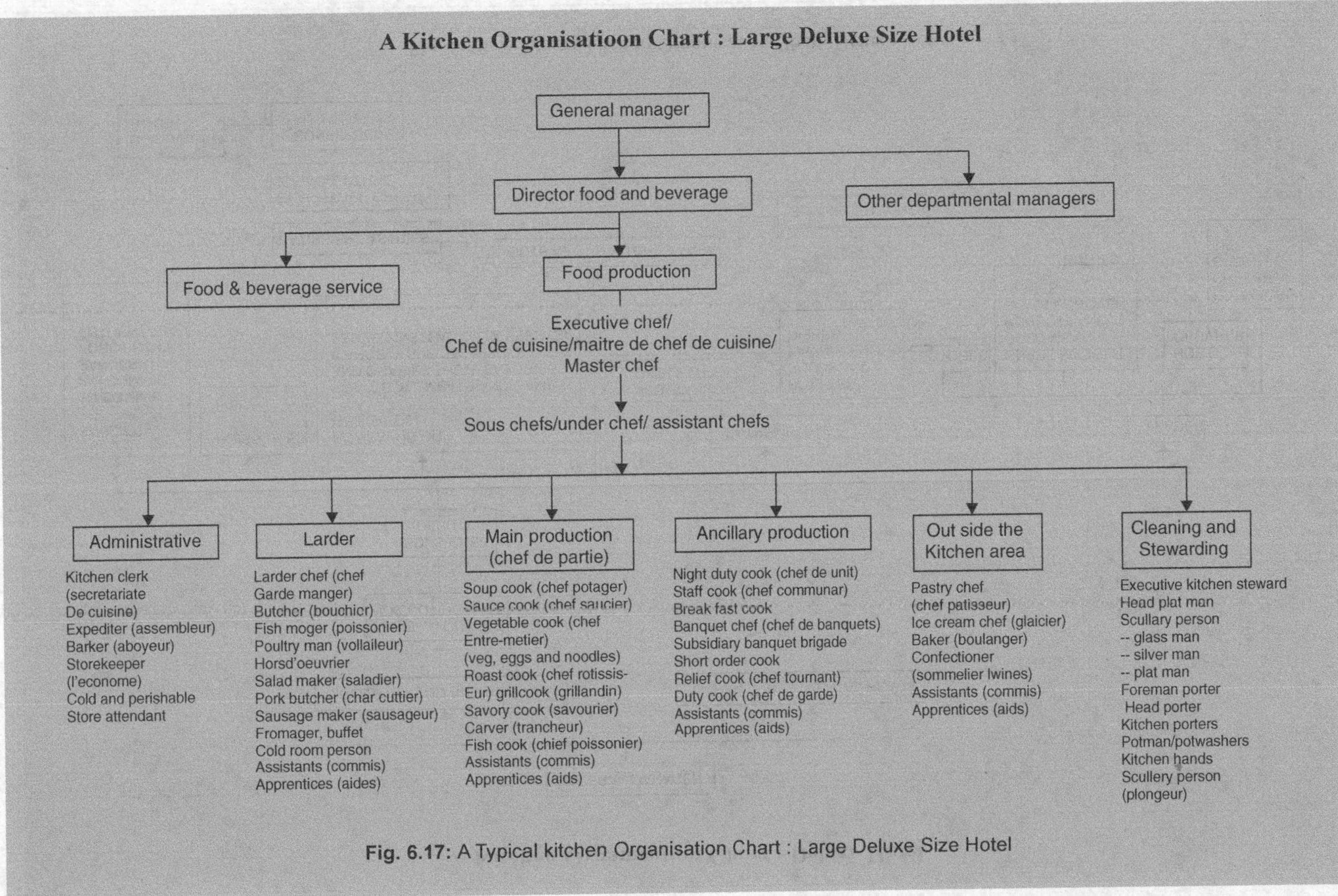

Fig. 6.17: A Typical kitchen Organisation Chart : Large Deluxe Size Hotel

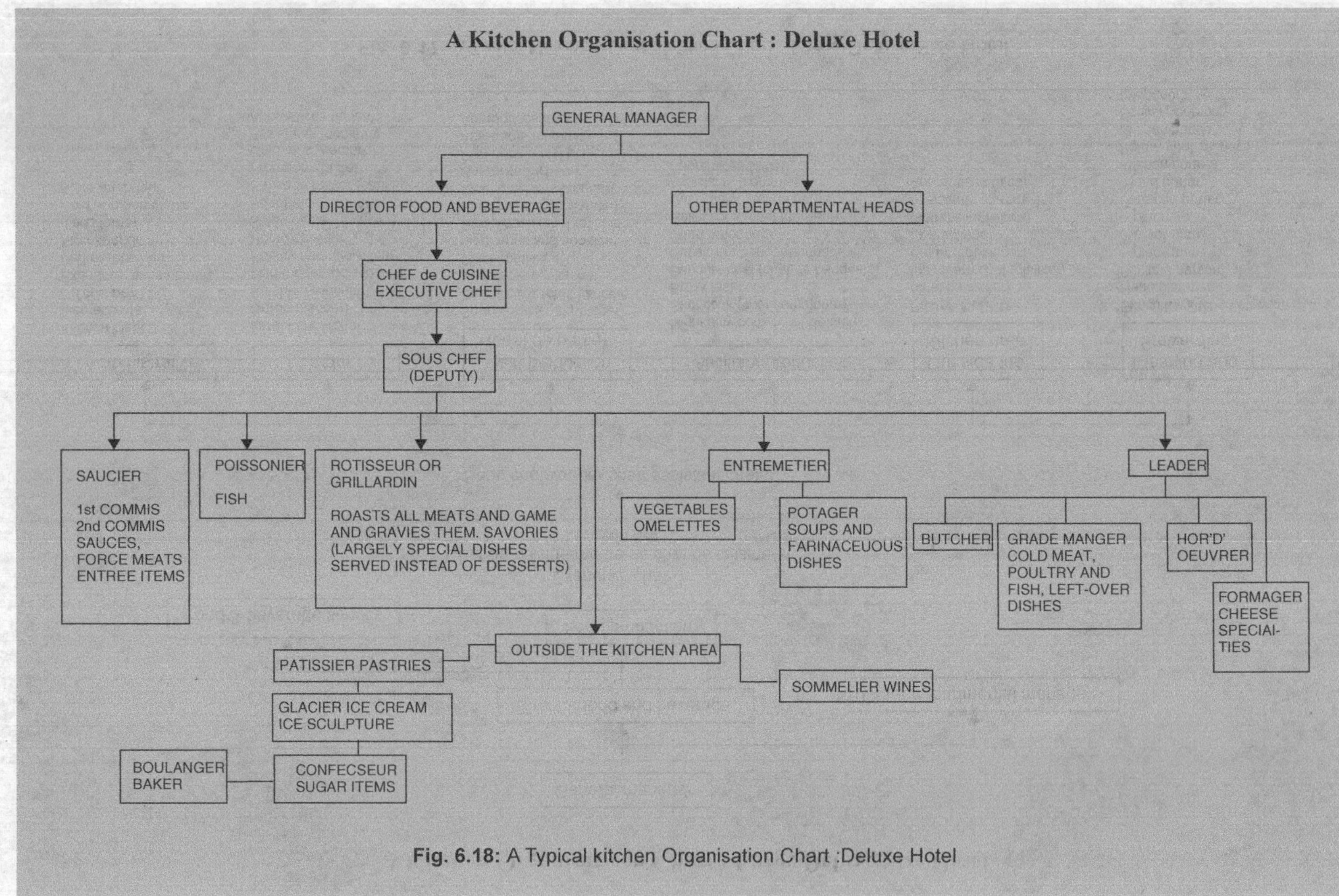

Fig. 6.18: A Typical kitchen Organisation Chart :Deluxe Hotel

EXECUTIVE CHEF/HEAD CHEF/*CHEF-DE-CUISINE*

He is the commander of the kitchen. In large hotels he is more a department manager than a working craftsman. He has the responsibility for the organisation, planning and supervision of the kitchen. He prepares the menu for the management in accordance with the costing and catering policies laid down by the management. He has full responsibility for staffing within general kitchen, labour post policy, or will have major responsibility for staff selection and dismissal in conjunction with the personnel department. A *Chef* must have good health, a sense of responsibility, organisational ability, special inclination towards the culinary arts. He must have extensive practical experience in all branches of cooking, knowledge of foodstuffs and their marketing. He must have a sound knowledge of French phraseology and terminology used in kitchens and the names and composition of all dishes, characteristics of various countries. He must have ability to use kitchen equipments, knowledge of hygiene and safety standards and regulations and labour legislation relevant to the work of kitchen staff is also essential for a successful *Chef*. The *Chef* is a person with varied skills and normally commands a high salary.

In addition to the craft skill and technical knowledge acquired as a result of apprenticeship, technical training and experience, the *Chef-de-Cuisine* must acquire managerial qualities and administrative knowledge particularly in regards to the organisation of work, control of staff, efficient use of machinery, costing, and food control. He must be aware of modern development in manufacturing and processing food for his use and perfecting equipments for the kitchen. He must concern himself with the techniques of meal presentation. He must have good experience of controlling staff as the stores wash up, still-room and kitchen staff are all under his supervision.

The duties of executive chef include :

1. Food cost control techniques
2. Use of kitchen equipments
3. Hygiene and sanitation
4. Preparation of Standard Recipes (Figs 6.19 and 6.19 (*a*))
5. Performance appraisal of kitchen staff
6. Kitchen staff problems and disciplinary action
7. Maintenance of files and formats
8. Co-ordination with service out-lets
9. Co-ordination with kitchen stewarding for supplies and maintenance of equipments
10. Organisation of kitchen operations and delegation of duties to the staff.
11. Menu planning in consultation with F & B Manager.
12. Drawing up of duty roasters
13. Staff and scheduling
14. Testing of new food items
15. Control of received merchandise
16. Supervising food preparation
17. Control operation throughout the service
18. Inform the buying office and stores in advance of all items needed
19. Check weight and quality of goods on arrival

A Standard Recipe Card

ABC Hotel Ltd.

Side 01 Serial No..........

Standard Recipe Card

Name of the Dish .... No. of Portions ....

Portion Size ....

S.No.	Ingredients	Unit	Quantity	Cost I		Cost II		Cost III	
				Unit	Total	Unit	Total	Unit	Total
	SPECIAL INSTRUCTIONS	**Total**							
		% to Sales							

Fig. 6.19 : Speciman of a Standard Recipe Card

20. Decide on the staff menu and supervise its preparation
21. Organise and conduct training
22. To advise management on purchase of kitchen equipment requirement
23. To be responsible wholly or partially for the stores, still-room and wash-up unit
24. To ensure that required kitchen profit target is attained
25. To provide management with full information on the efficiency of kitchen operaiton.

Most of the American hotels use a modified version of the European organisation design for their culinary departments. The primary modification has been the addition of food and beverage director who is responsible for all activities related to food and beverages. The *Chef* is incharge of quality of food production, food preparation for banquet and catering, satellite centre such as coffee shops, speciality restaurant and room service. He has extensive dealings with other departments such as purchasing, stewarding, catering and '*maitre d*'.

A Standard Recipe Card (Back)

<table>
<tr>
<td>

SIDE 02

METHOD OF PREPARATION :

....

....

....

....

SERVICE SPECIFICATION

....

</td>
<td>

Standard Yield Cards used :

ITEM **S.No.**

1. ....
2. ....
3. ....
4. ....

Prepared by : .... Date ....

Prepared by : ....

Sampled by : 1..

2. ....

3. ....

3. ....

APPROVED ( ) NOT APPROVED ( )

RECOMMENDATION:

....

....

....

....

</td>
</tr>
</table>

Fig. 6.19. (*a*) : Specimen of a Standard Recipe Card (Back)

As a departmental head the *Chef* is involved in the managerial function of planning, organising, directing and controlling as indicated below:

Planning :

1. Budgeting
2. Forecasting
3. Decision making
4. Departmental policy making
5. Interpreting
6. Analysing.

Organising :

7. Recruiting
8. Staffing
9. Hiring
10. Indoctrinating
11. Training
12. Assigning.

Directing :

1. Initiating
2. Leading
3. Motivating
4. Supervising
5. Communicating
6. Providing.

Controlling :

7. Auditing
8. Reporting
9. Observing
10. Comparing
11. Evaluating
12. Adjusting.

ASSISTANT CHEF/SECOND CHEF/*SOUS-CHEF*/DEPUTY-CHEF

Sous means under in French and the *Sous Chef* is the second chef in command of the kitchen. He is the principal assistant of the *Chef De Cuisine* in general administration, supervision of the work of preparing food and in seeking its service.

In large hotels, the assistant 'chef'has a supporting role to the *Chef de Cuisine*. He helps him in his varied duties. His position is, of course, regarded as an intermediate step between control of a part and the ultimate control of a kitchen. In small hotels, one of the principal *chef de partie* (*chef saucier/chef grade/larder chef*) may act as a *Sous Chef*.

He acts as a *Chef de Cuisine* in his absence. When *Chef de Cuisine* is engaged at work with his office i.e. occupied by menu planning, checking records, figures or in similar administrative routines, *Sous Chef* directly supervises all the practical kitchen activities. He is able to supervise at the meal service times and can make ad-hoc staff changes during the working day to relieve pressure. In large hotels there may be as many as four to six *Sous Chefs* particularly when separate kitchens are set up for grill room, restaurant, floors and banquet service.

Some of the major duties of a *Sous Chef* are :

1. Co-operation with the *Chef de Cuisine*
2. Replace *Chef* in supervision and control of kitchen operation
3. Replace *Saucier* on days off
4. Work in each kitchen department
5. Preparation of Sunday buffet etc.
6. Menu planning
7. Direct supervision of kitchen practical activities
8. Direct supervision of service during meal service
9. Ad hoc staff changes, during the working day to relieve pressure.

LARDER COOK/LARDER CHEF/'CHEF GARDE MANGER :

He is incharge of the larder, the place where the raw material of cookery are prepared and dressed. In large hotel 'Garde Manger'is often broken into sub-sections of the larder. He prepares *hors d'oeuvres*, jellies, aspics, cold sauces, salad and all dishes for the cold buffet. He is incharge of the larder a place where food is stored and raw material of cookery are prepared and dressed. In large hotels larder work may be broken into sections, and the sub-sections may have an independence of the *Chef Garde Manger* i.e. Boucherie might be directley controlled by the *Chef de Cuisine* or *Sous Chefs.*

The garde manger is normally accommodated adjoining the main kitchen and have its own cooking facilities. Depending upon the size of the kitchen its sub-sections too will be separate to a greater or smaller extent. This also incorporates the *hors d'oeuvres* section and a salad room and a fruit room where items such as compotes, melon grape pint, fruits salad, etc. are prepared.

He keeps a complete record of all materials received and used. His own dishes include all those commonly found on a cold table and comprises not only cold joints but also galantine, ballotines and cold dishes and salads. Sandwiches are his responsibility with the exception of the hot or toasted sandwiches such as club sandwiches. Mayonnaise and its derivatives, vinagnette sauce and other dressings, and saucer for cold food are made by the garde manger. Thus his duties and responsibilites include pre-preparation of cold meat trays, pates, galantines, salads, canapes, aspic and other special hors d'oeuvers, with special emphases on :

1. Marination of meats
2. Preparation of *mayonnaise* and vinagrette sauce
3. Use of *chaud* and *froid* sauce for decoration specially for poultry, fish, and sukling pig.
4. Ice carving and butter sculptures
5. Equipment and working temperatures
6. Handling of blast freezers and freezing/chambers.

FISH MANGER/*CHEF POISSIONIER*

He must have the raw material ready for the appropriate *Chef*, either for *Chef poissionier* or in some instances for cold dishes for chef garde manger. Products of sea, river and lake come to him for treatment which includes skinning, filleting and portioning. Fish such as eel, oysters, lobsters and crab will demand his attention as well as the ordinary range of river, sea, and shell fish.

BUTCHER/*BOUCHIER*

His jobs is to dissect the quarters of beef and carcasses of lamb and sides of pork. It also includes the dressing of meat either for joints such as courtrefillet or small cuts like noisette, cotelettes or tournedoes. He works under the supervision of the larder/chef. His duties and responsibilities include:

1. Knowledge of basic, whole sale, and retail cuts of various carcasses beef, veal, lamb, chicken, pork, fish etc.
2. Cleaning and deboning of carcass.
3. Yield of each carcass and recording the same on butcher yield cards.
4. Preparation of special cuts of chicken, *a la kiev*, steaks, fish, *fillets*, etc. and their weights.
5. Use of bones and timings for various stock soups and sauces.
6. Storage temperature for various meats and the manner in which they are stored.
7. Use of special knives and equipments in the butcher shop.
8. Number of butcher per shift and their work load.
9. Sanitation and hygiene condition.

SALAD MAKER/*SALADIER*

He is responsibile for the preparatory work and assembling of salads.

HORS D'OEUVIRE / HORS D'OEUVIER

He prepares all hot and cold *hors d' oeuvre* appetizers. The range of dishes for this section can be great and involve the regular preparations of commodities e.g. preparation of various varietiers of vegetables, salads, varieties of meat and fish dishes found on *hors d'oeuvre* viture trolley. He receives stock from the *Chef Poissionier* for fish soups. However, this section involves a substantial amount of garnish preparation involving skilful use of the knife and other ordinary tools, particularly producing vegetables of a wide variety of shapes and sizes. He needs right judgement for a potáge. Personal judgement as well as technical skill is required. He works like a *Saucier*in a section of the main kitchen.

POULTEUER/VOLLAILEUR

He is responsible for the plucking, cleaning and dressing of the poultry, game brids, hares and rabbits.

SAUSAGE MAKER/PORK BUTCHER/*CHARCUTIER*

He is responsible for speciality pork butchery and preparation of pork products and sausages and also for the rending and classifying of dripping.

ROAST COOK/BROILER CHEF/CHEF ROTISSEUR

This is one of the most important positions in the kitchen. The finest roast cooks are found in England, as roasting has always been renowned in England as a specialisation. Roast is quite popular and entails complex work.

This *Partie* is responsible for deep frying of foods of all kinds including fried potatoes and the *Rotisseur* may have an assistant called for this task who is known as Frying Cook / *friturier*.

The roast corner is situated in the main stores section and all necessary cooking apparatus for roasting, for deep frying, for finishing of savourises under a salamander are grouped together and make this section. Some of the dishes require handling both by the *Rotissuer* and by the *Saucier.*

Foods like poultry game and meat need roasting. The joints, poultry and game to be cooked by the *Rotissuer* are given the basic preparatory treatment like plucking and preparation, for the oven in the larder by the Butcher or *Vollaileur*. Sometimes *Commis* from the roast corner may help the larder for cleaning and trussing of poultry or the dissection, trimming and tying of joints of the butcher's meat. In brief, the *Chef Rotisseur* is responsible for :

1. Roasting poultry and game/feathered and furred
2. Preparation of all deep fried fish dishes, pomfrets, etc.
3. Preparation of all deep fried fish dishes, e.g. if separate grilled pommes pôelé, must be prepared by the *Rotisseur.*
4. These are used as garnish on certain grills.
5. Preparation of hot sandwiches e.g. club sandwiches.
6. Preparation of steaks and gravies which accompany roast.
7. Savouries e.g. oysters rolled in bacon grilled or skewered, welsh rabbit, certain types of savouries, scotch wood cock, scrambled eggs are prepared by the 'Entremetier', but it is completed and served at the last minute by the *Rotisseur.*

GRILL COOK/SAVOURY COOK/CHEF *SAVOURIER/ CHEF GRILLANDIN*

His duties are cleaning, while grilling, using either the traditional media like charcoal, electricity or gas. Where a separate grillandin is established, he might deal with the savouries and combine the function of Grillandin with that of Savourier.

CARVER/*TRÂNCHEUR*

He is generally under the control of the *rotisseur*. He is skilled in both serving and cooking. He may operate behind the scene at the hot service counter.

PASTRY CHEF/*CHEF PÂTISSIER*

This *Chef* has quite a different status but certainly not less than the *Chef Saucier* and the *Chef Garde Manger*. The work of this department is normally separated from the main kitchen and is self-contained in the matter of cold storage, machinery and equipment. It has its own baking and cooking facilities. This *Chef* is responsible for all hot and cold sweets for lunches, dinners and functions and for pastries served at tea time or other occasions. He is responsible for the making of pastes like short and puff pastry, fritter, batters, noodles and Italian passtes for supply to other corner of the kitchen, pies, cakes, special desserts, rolls, special breds, petits fours, souffle, biscuits, puddings, compotes, fruit salads, preserved fruits dough for noodles, rissoles macaroni, etc. In addition a sorbets and water ice items are made in the pastry section. The service of ice and those sweets which are based upon ice cream are prepared and assembled in the Patisserie. They include, sweet omlete and souffles peach melba, poire, helene, spun, sugar, ice cream with hot meringue exterior, and souffle, dipped fruits etc.

The main duties and responsibilities of a pastry *Chef* include :

1. Preparation of basic doughs pastes, sponge, pastry mixture and their recipe.
2. Methods of preparation of various recipe and the ingredients to be used.
3. Methods of preparation of chocolates and toffees and the ingredients to be used.
4. Preparation of sorbets (flavoured ice) and carving of ice blocks for decorative purposes.
5. Storage of pastriestime and environment preparation and decoration of special cakes, supply of bakery products to the pastry shop.
6. Milk cake recipe and its preparation.
7. Operation of special equipments of bakery and its utility.

The art of making pastry includes work like coloured sugars to make flower baskets and similar decorative centre, work with icing sugars, gum paste, fashioning of praliné into boxes and decoration objects containing chocolates and the carving of blocks of ice into sculptured pieces using heated irons. The work of *Pâtissier* has always been high-lighted by the beauty of the cold sweets, ices and their accompaniments. The *Chef Pâtissier* requires great skill, imagination and experience.

In large hotels one or more cuisinnier will do no more than prepare pastry itself like short and puff pastry for making of pies, flans etc. Semi skilled assistants will prepare fresh fruit for fruit salad for service at lunch, dinners and breakfast. Thus, the *Chef Pâtissier* is like the garde manger or *Chef de Cuisine* of a speciality kitchen. In addition to his own skill, he must co-ordinate and organise the work of a number of subordinates.

Thus, main duties and responsibilities of a Pastry Chef are grouped into two:

1. Preparation of basic doughs, pastes, sponge, pastry mixture and their recipe.
2. Methods of preparation of various paste.

BAKER/*BOULANGER*

He is a baker working under *Chef Pâtissier* and as such responsible for all baking items like bread rolls, bread croissants, etc.

ICECREAM CHEF/*GLACIER*

He prepares all kinds of icecream, water ices, mouses, biscuits glaces and icecream foundation including other varieties of icecream. He is one of the assistants of the *Chef Pâtissier.*

FISH COOK/*CHEF POISSONIER*

He is responsible for the cooking, garnishing and sauce making for fish courses, with the exemption of deep fried fish. *Chef Poissonier* is also responsible for the cooking, garnishing, saucing and dishing of fish dishes featuring fresh-water fish, sea-water fish, shell fishes like crab, cray, fish, shrimps, lobsters and mussels. Oysters are served either direct from the fish manger or a convenient cool place, if they are cooked. They are dished directly from the *Chef Poissonier's* corner. Method of cooking fish including poaching *a la meuniere*, en pôele and elaborate dressing are varied and done by *Chef Poissonier*. *Veloute de poisson* is a fundamental sauce produced only by *Poissonier* made from a *soux and fon de poisson*. He is also responsible for making stock and then veloute, the fish bones are supplied by garde manger.

He should have the knowledge of various types of fishes (sea water, river fishes etc.) and the cooking temperature for various types of fishes/dishes. His duties and responsibilities include :

1. Skinning, filleting and portioning of fishes
2. Preparation of sauces for fish courses
3. Preparation of all fishes (except deep fried fish dishes)
4. Garnishing of fish dishes
5. Preparation of fish stocks from fish trimmings
6. Preparation and service of special items like lobsters, shrimps, oysters etc.

SAUCE COOK/*CHEF SAUCIER*

He is the person who supervises the kitchen in the absence of the *Sous Chef*. He makes note of the day's menu prepared by the *Chef de Cuisine* and accordingly obtains the ingredients needed for the *Fonds de Cuisine* and the various soups and prepares all fundamental sauces i.e. bechamel, tomato sauce, veloute. He also prepares all sauce saultees, saulted meat, fish special soups. He prepares light and heavy *entrees*, for example, *value vent* (light entrees), heavy *entrees* (steaks) i.e. meat, paultry and game dishes which are not roasted and grilled. He is considered to be the senior *Chef de Partie* and takes over the responsibility of the *Sous Chef* when absent. He requires special knowledge because his work covers an extensive variety of dishes, specially sauces.

According to Escoffier, The sauce makes the dish. The garnish of a dish changes the whole appearance. A dish must taste good and look attractive to be appreciated. Application of sauce and garnish can make or mar a dish.The work of the Sauce Cook comprises cooking, garnishing of all meat poul- try and game dishes with the exception of those that are plainly grilled and roasted, which are cooked by the *Rôtisseur*. Thus, he is responsible for braises, entrees *pôeles*, bouillis etc. The *Saucier* is responsible for at least one of the *plats de jour* or specialities of the day. He is assisted by one or more commies and apprentices. He prepares his own *mise-en-places* and receives prepared commodities from other sections.

In brief, he is responsible for :

1. Preparation of various stocks and sauces
2. Knowledge of weights and volumetric measures of the ingredients consistancy of products and its final appearance

3. Garnishing of stocks and sauces and their derivatives
4. Preparation of all light and heavy *entree* dishes e.g. *vol an vent* (light entree) and steaks (heavy entrées), meat and poultry dishes which are not roasted and grilled.

SOUP COOK/*CHEF POTAGER*

He is responsible for the preparation and making of all the soups, and for the garnishes, accompanying the soup. This chef may be assisted by commis and apprentices according to the size of the establishment/hotel. *Chef Potager* and his assistants sometimes began their duty a little earlier than the other cooks. The work of the potager is important as soups give an impression of meals to follow.

He can be supplied by other parties with some of the garnishes required. His importance in the kitchen is supported by the fact that the repertoire of soups including consume, cremes and velouteés, purees, broths, bisques and many speciality and nationality soups is extensive. Consomme alone can be composed with differing flavouring essences and garnished in hundreds of ways. Besides, all basic stocks are prepared by him.

His duties and responsibilities include :

1. Preparation of basic soups and veloutes and their derivates
2. Preparation of stocks
3. Garnishing of soups
4. *Du jour soup* preparation,
5. Consistency and garnishes
6. Balancing and blending of soups
7. Service of soups and use of containers
8. Equipment used.

VEGETABLE EGG AND NOODLE COOK/*CHEF ENTREMETEUR*

This corner employs the largest number of staff as the variety of vegetables is quite large and there are very bussy times of the year when certain vegetables are in season e.g. asparagus. *Chef Entremetteur* is responsible for all vegetable dishes, all potato dishes, other than deep fried, all egg dishes and all farinaceous dishes. He is responsible for passing vegetable garnsih to another parties for completion of a dish e.g. accompaniments including tomato and French beans in case of tournedos. Italian pastes but not noodles are also cooked by vegetable cooks. Items like cooked spaghette and rice may be sent to another chef for garnishing. The cooking of eggs forms an integral part of the work at this section, particularly omelettes of various typesplain, garnished, stuffed and flat round omelette. The cooking of pancakes for service from the kitchen or cooking from guericon are prepared by this chef. Butter for these pancakes are supplied by *Chef pâtissier*. Vegetables prepared and cooked as accompaniments to the main meat, poultry and game dishes are also prepared by this section. The operations in this section are assembling, cooking, garmishing and flavouring, etc.

His duties and responsibilities include :

1. Preparation of all vegetable dishes.
2. Preparation of all potato dishes except deep fried.

3. Preparation of all egg dishes.
4. Ration of farinaceous dishes (except noodles)

In many hotels and restaurants where a Chef Potager is not engaged, the job of *Soup Chef* is performed by *Chef Entremetier*.

ANCILLARY FOOD PRODUCTION

RELIEF COOK/*CHEF TOURNANANT*

His duty is to take over from any *Chef de Partie* in his absence as demanded by the normal incidence of holidays and days off. This appointment generally goes to an older man of long experience as a prelude to appointment as *Sous Chef*.

DUTY COOK/*CHEF DE GARDE*

During the break hours, when the bulk of the kitchen staff are off duty, this chef remains with appropriate *commis* and apprentices which cannot be delayed until the other employees return to duty. In large hotels separate *chefs* or *commis* de garde remain in one Patisserie and in the Garde-Manger as well as in the more section of the kitchen. Each may see the affairs of more than one of the kitchen parties.

NIGHT DUTY CHEF/*CHEF DE NUIT*

His main duty is to take over the responsibility when the main kitchen staff leaves. Night duty chef does not necessarily remain on duty throught the night but until such time till the late meals have ceased. The duties of *Chef de Nuit* are sometimes carried out by a *Sous Chef*. The *Sous-Chef* doing the service of dinner only is responsible for all the work when the normal brigade has gone off duty. The *Sous Chef* must make sure that he has all the necessary facilities and that the correct *mise-en place* is left by the *Chef de Partie* before they go off duty.

BANQUET CHEF/*CHEF DE BANQUETS*

The chef given special duty responsibilities for special service of banquets is known as Banquet chef. He is given the responsibility for the assembly and service of banquet and functional meals.

The work of this department is normally separated from the main kitchen and is self-contained in the matter of cold storage, machinery and equipment for making ices and with its own baking and cooking facilities.

His duties and responsibilities include :

1. Organisation of service
2. Co-ordination with *chef de parties*
3. Knowledge of time and service
4. Total number of persons to be served
5. Co-ordination with the banquet manager.

BREAK-FAST COOK/*CHEF DE PETIT/DEJEUNER*

The cooking and service for breakfast in hotels is commonly entrusted to this speciality cook. He does not rank as a full *Chef de Partie*. He works along with *commis* and porters.

After finishing the breakfast, he attaches himself with the roast corner, and prepares *mise-en place* and cooks roast and grills for late service lunches when the *Chef de Partie* and staff go off. The *mise-en place* for breakfast and boning and slicing of bacon and preparation of the various types of fish eaten at breakfast time, is done by a subordinate of the Garde Manger and similar skilled assistants. Preparation of fruits compotes and fruit salads is made by assistants in *Pâtisserie*. Thus, the breakfast cooks and helpers are concerned with simple taste assembling and cooking of eggs, grilling and frying of fish and bacon.

In brief his duties and responsibilities include :

1. *Mise-en-place* for breakfast service
2. Various preparations of eggs with accompaniments and presentation
3. Preparation of variety of vegetarian items
4. Quality production for large groups.
5. *Mise-en place* for *dej our* dishes (special dishes of the duty)

STAFF COOK/*CHEF COMMUNAR*

He is responsible for the preparation of staff meals which implies meals for the rank and file uniformed staff, chamber maids, waiters and low grade clerical staff. He requires the knowledge of the preparation of main dishes and the techniques of collective cooking. He must have the same qualification as that of the *Chef de Partie*. He works as per instructions of the *Chef de Cuisine*, obtains the necessary ingredients, and prepares the food for the two daily meals of the staff. He usually comes under the kitchen stewarding section which looks after the staff meals. However, in many hotels this job position has been clubbed with the kitchen brigade, because of his nature of duties.

SHORT ORDER COOK

He requires same qualities as the staff cook and performs all those duties of the staff cook. He serves all light luncheon items and hot sandwiches.

STAFF

There are various subordinate personnel of different types working under the various chiefs.

COMMIS COOK/ASSISTANT COOKS

They are the cooking artisans, have the knowledge of main dishes and their names in various languages. They must have ability to use kitchen equipment and good knowledge of hygiene relevant to their work. They follow the instructions of their *Chef de Partie* and help them in preparing and cooking dishes. They prepare simple dishes by themselves. The *Commis* should have completed their apprenticeship or training but will still be gaining experience before taking full *partie* responsibilities. The first *commis* should be capable of taking charge when his *Chef the Partie* is off.

APPRENTICES/APPRENTIS/*AIDES DE CUISINE*

These are the trainee *chefs* who move from section to section of the kitchen during their training period. On completion of the training, they are competent to work as *Commis Chefs*. In French brigades learners and apprentices were styled *aids de cuisine*.

CREATIVITY IN COOKING

Creativity isn't just about coming up with the next best idea. Creativity is the consistent forefront in global culture today. This is the driving factor in our global economy and essential to free enterprise. The art of creativity has enabled many brands to carry distinction over time. Without such titles, a consumer would not know the difference between Burger King and McDonald's. It has helped define corporate institutions through the use of image and colour. This alone has helped the consumer identify itself with such brands. For example, what brands do you consider when you are going to make your famous spaghetti? If you are not one to step foot in the kitchen, then what restaurant would you pick to satisfy that spaghetti craving?

The ability to utilize the creative mind has helped consumers differentiate brands, and create a sense of loyalty for many. If you take a quick look around your surroundings, you can identify which people are following trends, and which individuals create their own flair. Fashion has allowed individuals to create a trend or follow one. It is as simple as finding inspiration, which can find its way into mainstream pop culture.

Even those who genuinely enjoy home cooking will find that the need to produce quality food on a daily basis can put pressure on the imagination. The aim is to encourage creativity and fun in the kitchen: to promote great home cooking.

Creative Cooks is a range of premium quality pre-prepared ingredients designed to help you skip straight to the creative jobs that make cooking (and eating) so enjoyable - more of the tasting, seasoning, stirring, drizzling, mixing and less of the peeling chopping, soaking, boiling, steaming.

Today and in the future, a commitment to excellence requires openness to all resources that can help us give pleasure and meaning to people through the medium of food. In the past, cooks and their dishes were constrained by many factors: the limited availability of ingredients and ways of transforming them, limited understanding of cooking processes, and the necessarily narrow definitions and expectations embodied in local tradition. Today there are many fewer constraints, and tremendous potential for the progress of our craft. We can choose from the entire planet's ingredients, cooking methods, and traditions, and draw on all of human knowledge, to explore what it is possible to do with food and the experience of eating.

Cooking and the creation of new recipes provide us then with an altogether more helpful, accurate and more economically relevant metaphor for ideas and the creative process than any "thinking outside the box".

Cooking is all about relationships. Just as in the composition of music, it requires understanding harmonies and juxtapositions. Any fool can put on an apron and mix two random sets of ingredients together, but not any fool can cook. Understanding the relationships between the ingredients and their interactions is crucial, as the food writer McGee notes:

To understand what's happening within food as we cook it, we need to be familiar with the world of invisibly small molecules and their reactions with each other.

Similarly, Tania Sanchez recognizes the fundamental importance of understanding the ampersand for the creator, reminding us that creating a new perfume isn't simply a question of throwing together random ingredients. The skill and artists of the perfumer – and one of the reasons why it takes many years to become a successful one – lies in understanding the and he breathless claims of fragrance marketing to the contrary, it is just not true that fine ingredients guarantee a great perfume. Imagine chucking a fresh Maine lobster, a wheel of top-notch Camembert, and a pound of artisanal Venezuelan chocolate in a kettle and simmering in Chartreuse until Wednesday. Yummy? It doesn't work for perfume.

Pix 6.15

Pix 6.16

Pix 6.17

Pix 6.18

Pix 6.19

Pix 6.20

Pix 6.21

Pix 6.22

Pix 6.23

Pix 6.24

Pix 6.25

Pix 6.26

Pix 6.27

Pix 6.28

Pix 6.29

Pix 6.30

Pix 6.31

Pix 6.32

Pix 6.33

Pix 6.34

Pix 6.35

Pix 6.36

Pix 6.37

Pix 6.38

Pix 6.39

Pix 6.40

Pix 6.41

Pix 6.42

Pix 6.43

Pix 6.44

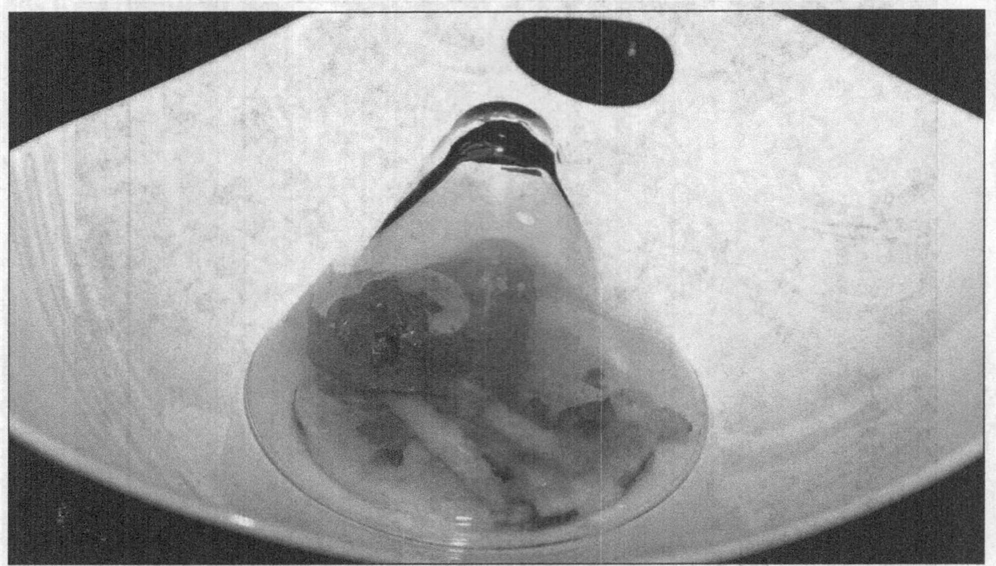

Pix 6.45

Pix 6.46

PANTRY

Most of the large hotels and resort hotels have their own independant pantry. It is an auxiliary section situated between the kitchen and the restaurant. It may be an independent unit or may be the part of the kitchen. It should be located as near as possible to the actual consumer and is invariably found attached to the dining room or in the banquet area. The man responsible for the pantry is known as Pantry man/wash-up. He must have knowledge of the operation of the machine part at his disposal. He is responsible for the cleanliness and that of his work places. He has to remove or destroy the garbage. His duties are :

1. To prepare hot beverages like tea, coffee according to specific standards
2. He should know how to prepare shakes, cold coffee, fresh lime soda, ice cream, juices etc.
3. Preparation of toasts, sandwiches, milk, break-fast cereals etc.
4. Services of fruits
5. Positioning of butter with the help of butter pot machine to ensure standard position.

A CASE STUDY 6.3 : WORK SCHEDULE

Situation

A small dish pantry was staffed for four years on the basis of service for three meals a day. Later when the morning meal was eliminated management neglected to change the work schedule.

Results of Analysis

A bar graph was drawn up which plotted the work schedule and rated the amount of work done by periods throughout the day.

PLAT ROOM

All the silver dishes and cutlery are cleaned, polished and supplied to kitchen from the Plat Room.

STILL ROOM HEAD/*CAFETIER*

The still room is regarded as an ancilliary department of a kitchen for in it are prepared non-alcoholic beveragestea, coffee, chocolates, horlicks and other warm drinks. Toast, bread rolls and butter are also prepared in the still-room. Therefore, a still-room hand must have thorough knowledge of the different blend and different ways of making coffee, tea and herb tea. He prepares the equipment of coffee pots, tea pots and kettles required for the staff and guest's breakfasts. He prepares coffee and tea or hot chocolate and breakfast food, hot beverages ordered during the day, takes order and sends vouchers to the administration department.

PLATMAN/SILVERMAN/GLASSMAN

His nature of duties are similar to that of the pantry man. He carries out washing, cleaning and takes care of restaurant equipment. He is also responsible for polishing silver.

ADMINISTRATION/NON-COOKING STAFF

The kitchen department includes number of functionaries who are an integral part of the kitchen brigade but they belong to the non-kitchen category :

KITCHEN CLERK/*LE SECRETAIRE DE CUISINE*

Apart from the supervision of the checking system, clerical work in the kitchen is mainly a matter of recording the receipts and issues of goods. The kitchen clerk sometimes works as a personal assitant in the office duties falling to the *chef*.

ORDER ANNOUNCER/HOT PLATE CLERK/BARKER/*ABOYEUR*

His job starts at the time of service of meal and on receipt of written orders/chits from the waiting staff. He stamps the time of receiving the order on the check and usually has a board fitted with hooks or waiter stations to which the order relates. He calls out the orders at the hot plate as they are received from the waiter so that each section knows what has been ordered by the customers and can prepare it accordingly. When an order has been completed and removed from the hot plate, by the waiter, the *Aboyeur* removes the check from its hook and places it through a slip into a locked box, which at the end of the service goes to the control office, where the key is kept for control purpose. The *Aboyeur* must ensure that the box remains secured and is safely conveyed to the control office.

The *Aboyeur* must be a person of some culinary knowledge and must have command of cookery repertoire and be able to recognise the appropriate garnishes for all dishes. In some of the hotels the *Sous Chef* may undertake the duties of the *Aboyeur*.

STORE KEEPER/*L'ECONOME*

A storekeeper is not only responsible for receiving, recording and issuing of stores but also must have a good knowledge of grocery as he has to deal with the wide range of commodities under his control.

COLD AND PERISHABLE STORES ATTENDANTS

The placement of meat, poultry and soforth in refrigerated storage and fruits and bulk butter in cold storage is generally separated from the main storage operation and placed under the control of separate functionary, a person who has received good training in the care and issue of goods of perishable kind needing cold storage. He is responsible for the perishable items like meat, poultry, fish etc. The storage attendant must have received on the job training in the care and management of perishable foods.

KITCHEN HAND HELPERS

These are helpers employed in the kitchen for taste ranging from butter pats, vegetable peeling, fruit and salad preparation, replenishing *hors d'oeuvres* and *raviers*.

MAN FOR FLOOR SERVICE LIFT

He is responsible for service of food which is supplied to customers in their rooms.

KITCHEN PORTER

He must be able to use kitchen equipment and should have the knowledge of the preparation of food. His duties are to take care of kitchen burners, to heat water, to layout the utencils and equipment required on the table, to wash and peel vegetables, to clean fish, to change dirty linen, to wash the kitchen, and tidy up. He is responsible for unskilled work in the kitchen under a head porter who acts as foreman responsible for the head chef.

APPRENTICE/*AIDES DE CUISINE*

Apprentices are attached to each *Chef de Partie*. They are the trainers who, whilst learning, also help in the practical day-to-day work of food preparation.

RUNNERS/UTILITY PERSON

Heavy physical cleaning work as well as transporting goods or supplies to different parts of the kitchen is done by runners or utility persons. Often same cleaning chores are also handled by them.

OTHERS

Unskilled work in the kitchen is undertaken by the porters, helpers, kitchen hands, vegetable preparers, etc.

FOOD AND BEVERAGE FACILITIES AND SERVICES

The provision of food and beverage facilities must be based on detailed analysis of market considerations and economic feasibility. Examination of surveys should provide a basis for assessing :

1. The type of food and beverage facilities
2. Pattern of demand, hours of use, peak demand etc.
3. Menu choice
4. Method of service
5. Staffing requirements
6. Size of the restaurant
7. Seating capacity
8. Seat occupancy over meal periods
9. Flexibility in use and space separation
10. Changes in service and arrangement.

Entry to a restaurant should be through a reception launge or foyer. This area may be little more than a widening of the entrance corridor to provide space for seats and tables and will be used as an assembly point before entering or on leaving the restaurant and as a lounge for cocktails and other drinks. The bar should be on the remote side of the lounge extension so that the guests entering the restaurant do not need to cross directly along the front of the bar and the guests can use the bar without having to pass through the lounge cloakrooms and toilets should be near the entrance lobby. All entrance and exist should be positioned to allow proper vision and control.

Pix 6.47 : A Restaurant in a Hotel

Restaurant layout should take account of the features of the room, external vistas and internal displays and entertainment, circulation patterns of customers and staff, method of food service, seat groupings and type of furniture to be used.

Restaurant areas require sophisticated environmental control. Depending on location and case, windows may be provided to take advantage of the view and/or to attract outside attention as a form of merchandising. For example, in resort areas the windows may be an important feature of the restaurant's attractions by opening on to swimming pools, gardens or vistas of the land or natural scenery. In case of other type of restaurant intended for mainly evening dining, these may be completely enclosed within the interior of the building. Provision must be made for adequate ventilation and air-conditioning. Lighting is an important feature of design and atmosphere. Incandescent lamps should be used rather than fluorescent types, but the latter may be sociable as background lighting in coffee shops and fast food operations provided the colour balance is corrected for display purposes. Light with a spectrum of greater emphasis towards red must be selected and infra-red-luminescent lamps may be maintainted over hot counters. Within the restaurant use a wide variety of light fittings. Indirect light be frequently employed around the parameter to emphasise wall texture and other features. Background lighting may be provided within or immediately below the ceiling. Local lighting over tables, recesses and seating enclosures serve to create individuality. It is necessary to provide several lighting circuits with dinner switches for control purposes.

Ceilings should normally be at least 2750 mm (9 ft) high and should provide sound absorption and sound damping of machinery vibrations and transmission noise. The ceiling construction may be based on panels, to allow access, or continuous surfaces, with relief provided by mouldings and architraves. Alternative wall surfaces include dry linings of laminated plastic, panels of glass, plastered surfaces, slabs of stones/marble and exposed brickwork. The main points to be considered are :

1. Resistance to damage
2. Resistance to staining
3. Safety
4. Replacement.

Floors and floor coverings require special attention. Most restaurants are carpeted to reduce noise and to create a sense of comfort and warmth. Floor toiling are appropriate for tourist or economy class hotels. These may be used in coffee shops and bars, particularly in the heavily used areas in front and behind the counters. Stone slabs and mosaics may be introduced. Wood block or strip flooring provide an intermediary effect. Strip flooring is most suitable for dance areas. Wood construction is also advisable for stages and entertainment areas.

The furniture must complement the theme and decor of the restaurant. The main features and considerations to be taken into account are :

1. Dimensions
2. Spacing
3. Adaptability
4. Durability
5. Safety
6. Appearance
7. Comfort
8. Fixed and movable
9. Construction material.
   (*i*) Frameworks
   (*ii*) Surfaces
   (*iii*) Upholstery finishes.

The table design must be considered in terms of its total effect. This must be reflected in the choice of table appointments, linen, cutlery, china and glassware and in the style of staff uniforms, menu holders and other specific features of restaurant operation. There is

Fig. 6.20, Fig. 6.21, Fig. 6.22, Fig. 6.23, 6.24, 6.25 and 6.26 are typical arrangements for tables and chairs for different rooms.

Pix 6.48: A Speciality Restaurant in a Hotel

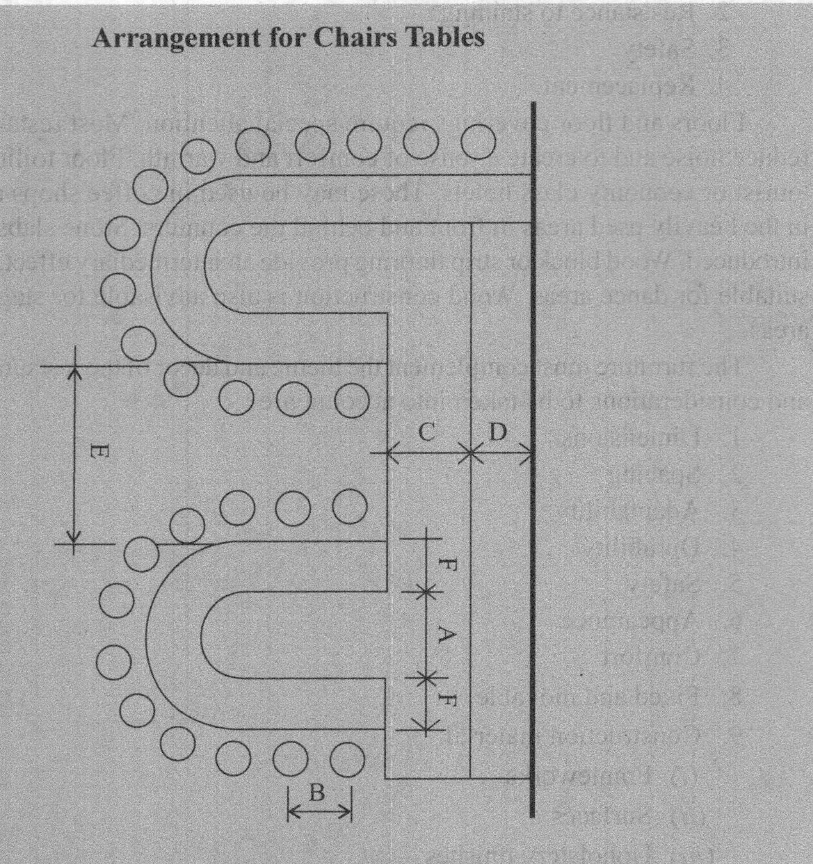

Fig. 6.20. A typical Arrangement for Tables and Chairs

Type of Room	Max.
Banquet	10 – 11
Tea Room	12 – 14
Din. Rm/Rest.	14 – 15
Cafeteria	15
Lunchrms :	
Counter & Chair–table	
types incl. counters chairs, tables	20

Fig. 6.21. Maximum Capacity for Different Rooms

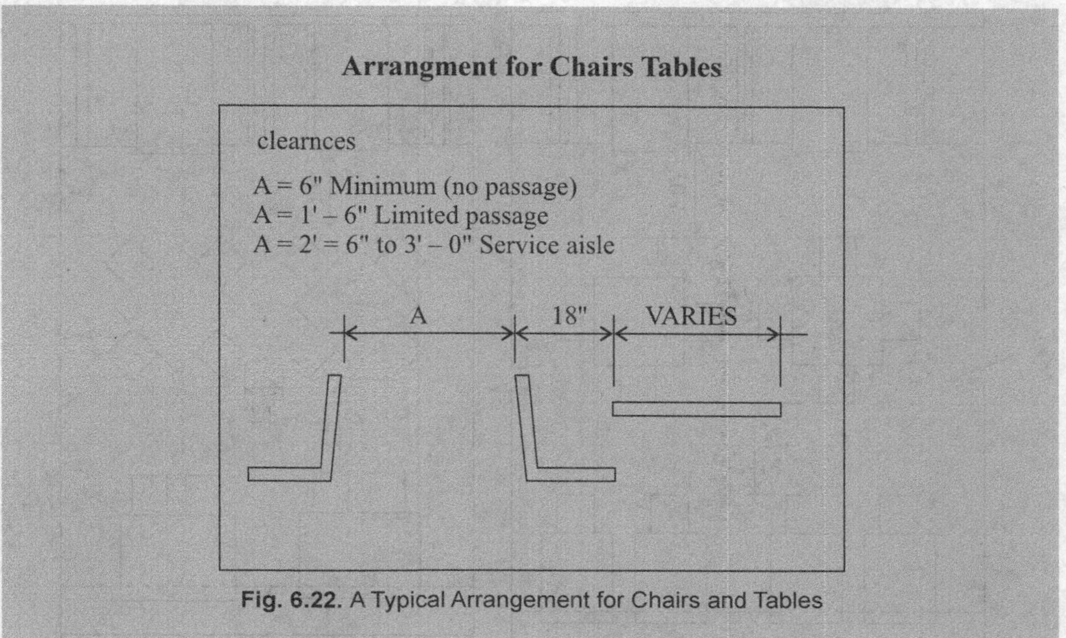

Fig. 6.22. A Typical Arrangement for Chairs and Tables

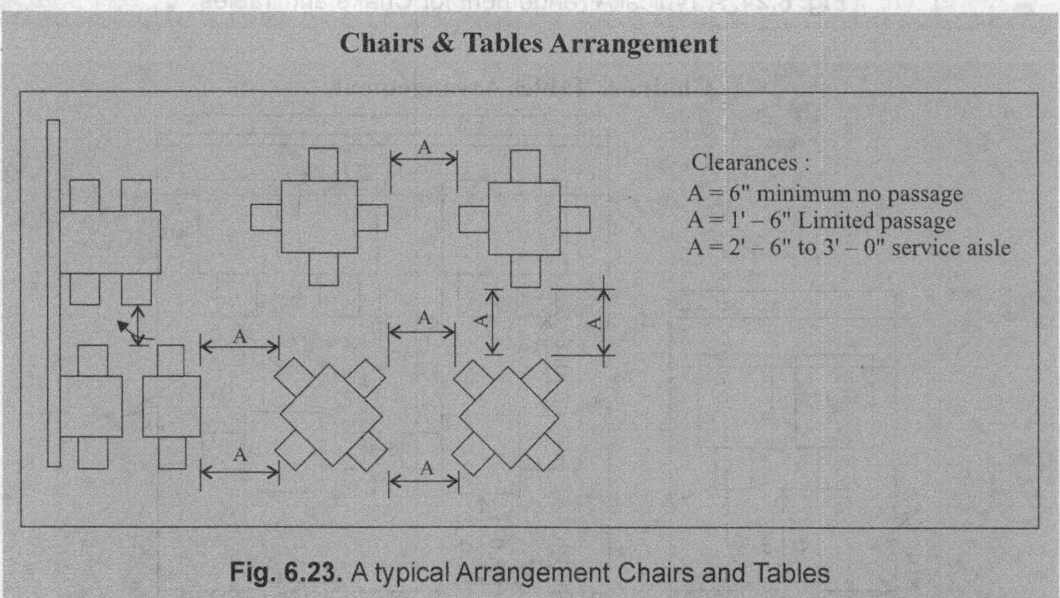

Fig. 6.23. A typical Arrangement Chairs and Tables

Chairs & Tables Arrangement

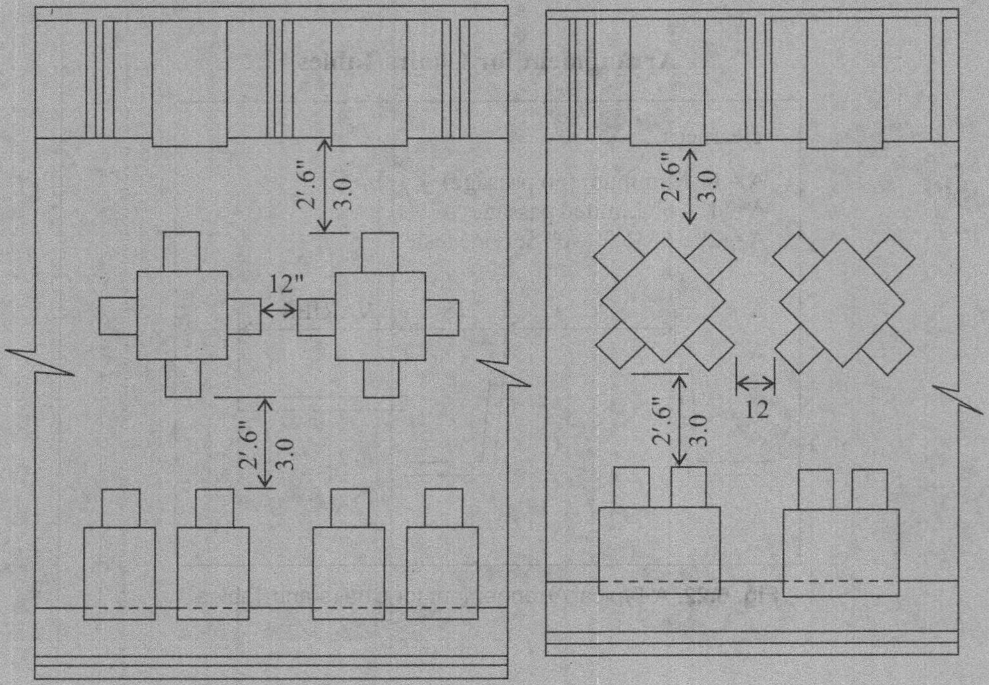

Fig. 6.24. A Typical Arrangement for Chairs and Tables

Chairs & Tables Arrangement

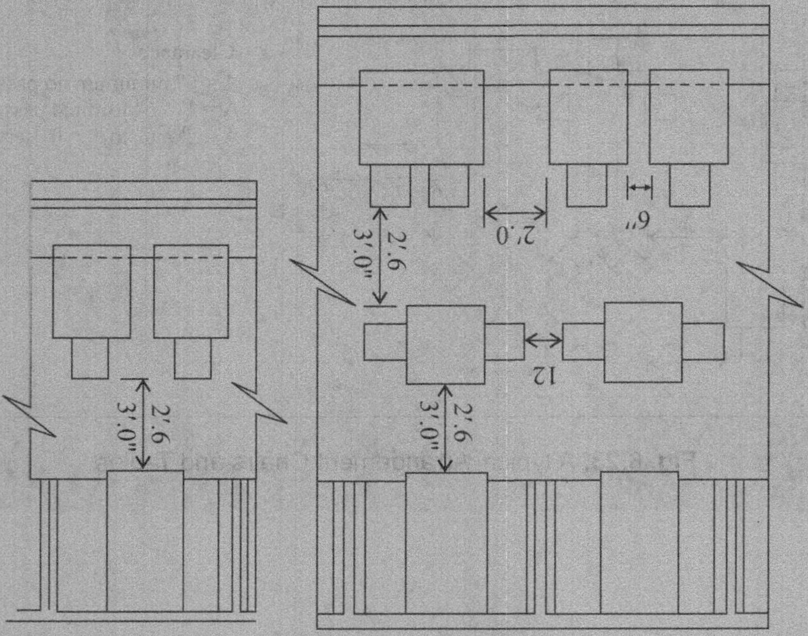

Fig. 6.25. A Typical Arrangement for Chairs and Tables

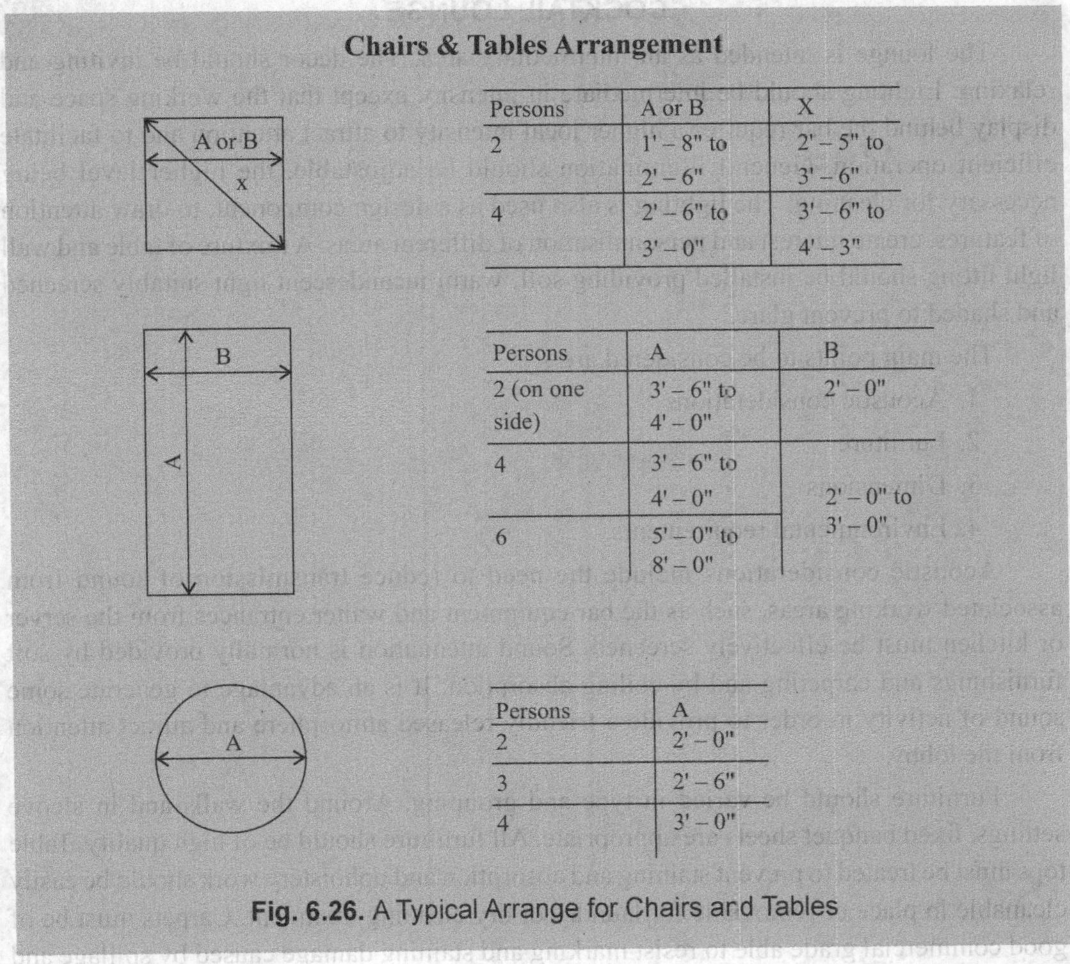

Persons	A or B	X
2	1' – 8" to 2' – 6"	2' – 5" to 3' – 6"
4	2' – 6" to 3' – 0"	3' – 6" to 4' – 3"

Persons	A	B
2 (on one side)	3' – 6" to 4' – 0"	2' – 0"
4	3' – 6" to 4' – 0"	2' – 0" to 3' – 0"
6	5' – 0" to 8' – 0"	

Persons	A
2	2' – 0"
3	2' – 6"
4	3' – 0"

Fig. 6.26. A Typical Arrange for Chairs and Tables

There is a need for rationalisation in the range of equipment and tableware used in the hotels. For each items of china or glassware in use there are, on an average, one to two replacements in reserve, and perhaps more where designs are manufactured to specific order. For table linen and uniforms the stocks are even greater to allow for delays in laundering, and a ratio of 1 in use, 5 or 6 in circulation and reserve. In determining the choice of table ware, consider the following points :

1. Standard catalogue range are suitable to facilitate replacement,
2. The range of items can be reduced, having regard to the menu range and
3. Multi-purpose use in other areas of hotels, restaurants or room service.

Table appointments and decorations, menu holders and certain tableware items associated with speciality dishes, should be specific to each restaurant. In many chain hotel and catering operations tableware are used as a means of merchandising. In these hotels, insignia, emblem and other representations are standardized throughout the group.

COCKTAIL LOUNGE

The lounge is intended as an intermediary area. The decor should be inviting and relaxing. Lighting should be intermediate in intensity except that the working space and display behind the bar requires a higher local intensity to attract attention and to facilitate efficient operation. General illumination should be adjustable, the higher level being necessary for cleaning. The lighting is also used as a design component, to draw attention of features, create interest and personalisation of different areas. A mixture of table and wall light fitting should be installed providing soft, warm incandescent light suitably screened and shaded to prevent glare.

The main points to be considered are :

1. Acoustic considerations
2. Furniture
3. Dimensions
4. Environmental requirements.

Acoustic considerations include the need to reduce transmission of sound from associated working areas, such as the bar equipment and waiter entrances from the server or kitchen must be effectively screened. Sound attenuation is normally provided by soft furnishings and carpeting and by ceiling absorption. It is an advantage to generate some sound of activity in order to provide a friendly released atmosphere and attract attention from the lobby.

Furniture should be varied in type and grouping. Around the walls and in alcove settings, fixed banquet sheets are appropriate. All furniture should be of high quality. Table tops must be treated to prevent staining and absorption and upholstery work should be easily cleanable in place or removable for laundry or dry cleaning treatment. Carpets must be of good commercial grade able to resist marking and staining damage caused by spillage and cigarette butts.

Dimensions must be related to the number of people likely to use the area and be suitably proportioned. Ceiling heights should be 2750 mm (9 ft) or more over the general area. Lower ceilings in alcoves or under mezzanines help to provide better proportion and more interesting seating areas. Space requirements range from 1.1 to 1.7 sq. m (12 to 18 sq. ft) per seat.

A high standard of air-conditioning is essential. Variable heating and cooling control should be provided, regulated automatically to maintain correct temperature and humidity.

A Case Study 6.14: Customer Handling

Customers Can be Very Difficult !

Don't underestimate how difficult customers can be. This is an extract from 'Business at the Bear', a series of real-life articles written by John and Amanda Willmott, then the proprietors of the Bear Hotel, Wantage, Oxfordshire, for a weekly catering industry newspaper.

(Contd..)

Every hotelier must have had one of those disastrous days when he believes that things cannot possibly become any worse – and then they do.

We had one such day last Saturday. Our problems began in the evening, at the commencement of our regular Saturday night dinner dance. A party of 22 had booked, wishing to eat early at 7.30 p.m. We had agreed to this and the band were due to begin at 7.30 p.m. However, at 7.45 p.m., as the party were being served with the main course, the band had still not arrived. They eventually turned up at 8 p.m. and spent the next 40 minutes setting up the equipment and establishing that their amplifier was faulty – it was emitting a high pitched buzzing noise at regular intervals.

By this time, our other large party of 15 people had arrived and things began to hot up.

We suggested to this party that they might like to congregate in the bar and we would take their orders there. Their 'organiser' seemed to assume that we were delaying their dinner for some reason and, having seen the party of 22 already seated in the restaurant, complained that it was unfair that his party should be unable to sit down until other people had left. We assured him that this was not the case, and that his table was already prepared.

He accepted this and returned to the bar, although, as we later discovered from our bar staff, he omitted to pass on the information to the other members of his party.

Having successfully served the first course to this group, our next big hitch came with the main course. The same gentleman waited until all the dishes had been silver–served and the vegetables passed round, and then called us over. Without even picking up his knife and fork to taste his food he demanded that all the meals should be returned to the kitchen as they were stone cold (some of his party had already begun to eat their dinner, and with obvious enjoyment).

Chaos reigned for the next few minutes as plates of food were hurtled back into the kitchen, the other large party clamoured for more coffee, the band's amplifier buzzed, and our 'awkward' customer told everyone in the restaurant that his meal had obviously come straight from the freezer.

In order to make amends to those people who had their meals whisked from under their very noses, we provided the party with additional complimentary wine. The meal was reserved, and despite a number of sarcastic comments to members of our staff, all 15 people ate it.

Comments continued throughout the service of the sweets, although at all stages in the meal no wasted food was returned to the kitchen.

The chain of events was completed by a disastrous mistake over the bill – the complimentary wine was charged for.

Despite our apologies, the atmosphere created by these few unpleasant people permeated the restaurant and the smaller parties were also affected. The 15 left declaring they would not return – a sentiment of which we heartily approved.

We certainly never wish to relive that night. After a post-mortem of the evening's events, we agreed that we had all learnt some valuable lessons about human nature.

We feel sure that none of these 15 people would have behaved in a similar way in a bank, shop or in their own homes, but good manners are sometimes not preserved for hoteliers.

To make matters worse, when we expressed our dissatisfaction to the band they refused to accept any responsibility for their faulty equipment and the resulting poor performance. We wish we could deal with complaints in a similar fashion – although we should soon be out of business.

We were delighted when one of the smaller parties present that night returned later in the week for dinner – and made a point of telling us how badly behaved they considered the party of 15 had been. We are hoping that others present on that fateful night also thought along those lines!

FOOD AND BEVERAGE MANAGER

The person responsible for this department is known as Food and Beverage Manager. He heads department that involves guest relations as well. He is concerned with the smooth flow of foods and service before they reach the guest. He must have organisational ability and foresightedness. He must have thorough knowledge of hotel organisation, supervisory techniques in the catering field and labour legislation. In addition, a food and beverage manager must have the knowledge of commerce and accounting and a perfect and up-to-date knowledge of the preparation of dishes and prices of food- stuffs. He is directly responsible to the general manager for all service activities, bars and restaurants. In small properties he is responsible for the buying, receiving and storing of foodstuffs and beverages. He is to organise banquets and put forward proposals to the general manager, regarding the marketing and pricing. He and the Executive Chef work together on menu designing, pricing, catering, banquet arrangements and staffing.

A typical layout of a hotel restaurant is given in Figure 6.27.

The duties and responsibilities of the food and beverage manager depend on the size and type of the establishment. He is either responsible for the implementation of agreed policies or for contributing to the setting of catering policies. The larger the organisation the less likely the manager is to be involved in policy setting. In brief, the food and beverage manager is responsible for :

1. Ensuring that required profit margins are achieved
2. Up-dating and compiling new wine list
3. For compiling menus in liaison with the kitchen
4. The purchasing of food and drinks
5. Ensuring that quality in relation to price paid is maintained
6. Determine the portion size in relation to selling price
7. Maintenance of the professional standards
8. Departmental training and promotions
9. Discipline of the staff
10. Holding regular meetings with sectorial heads to ensure all areas are working efficiently
11. Coordination with other departments.

The food and beverage manager should concentrate on the short-term and long-term needs of the operation in the confines of hotel's needs and objectives. He is responsible for personally supervising the daily food and beverage operation entirely including :

1. Quality and consistency of service and product
2. All cost factors
3. Cleanliness of F & B areas
4. Final selection and training of staff
5. Production of department profit

6. The implementation and exercise of all policies and procedures.
7. He should also be involved in the financial planning including :
8. Preparation of monthly and annual forecasts and budgets
9. Development of recommended concept changes
10. Development of profit potentials.

In order to give good service, a restaurant employee must have the thorough knowledge of the menu. Each day before going on duty, he should review the menu to determine those items specially prepared for the day including entreés, daily *entree* from kitchen, salads, soups and desserts.

He should know the principal method of cooking such as :

1. *Boiling* : It refers to cooking by moist heat of foods at either below or above the boiling point. Other terms used are 'simmering', 'poaching', 'stewing', 'steaming.'
2. *Braising* : It is a method which combines both dry and moist heat.
3. *Broiling* : It is a quick cooking by direct flame or heat and gas, electricity, or charcoal may be used.
4. *Plain-broiling* : In this method food is cooked in a hot frying pan or on a griddle without the use of fat.
5. *Frying* : In this method food is cooked in fat or oil and may be either pan fried or deep fat fried. There are three methodssaute, shallow frying and deep frying.
6. *Roasting* : It is cooking in the oven with dry heat in an uncovered pan. Knowledge of cooking time is a must in order to advise guests, the time required for preparing *a la carte* food, and to plan assembling of orders. For example, for steaks, the timing are 10 minutes. Similarly boiled lamb chops require about 15 minutes.
7. *Grilling* : Grilling is a dry heat method of cooking where prepared food is cooked mainly by radiated heat in the form of intra-red waves.
8. *Baking* : Baking is a dry heat method of cooking where prepared food and food products are cooked by convected heat in a pre-heated oven.
9. *Cold Preparation* : Cold preparations are cold items which have been prepared and assembled and are either raw, or cooked, then cooled.

In addition to the knowledge of the meaning and correct pronunciation of commonly used foreign terms, he should know the different types of food preparations and their accompaniment, such as :

Food Items	**Accompaniment**
1. Steak	1. Steak sauce
2. Roast pork (hot or cold)	2. Apple sauce
3. Ham steak	3. Mustard
4. Lamb chops	4. Mint sauce
5. Fried fish	5. Lemon and tarter
6. Boiled fish	6. Lemon wedge
7. Lobster	7. Lemon wedge
8. Shrimp cocktail	8. Cocktail sauce
9. Tomato juice	9. Lemon wedge.

A Layout of a Hotel Restaurant

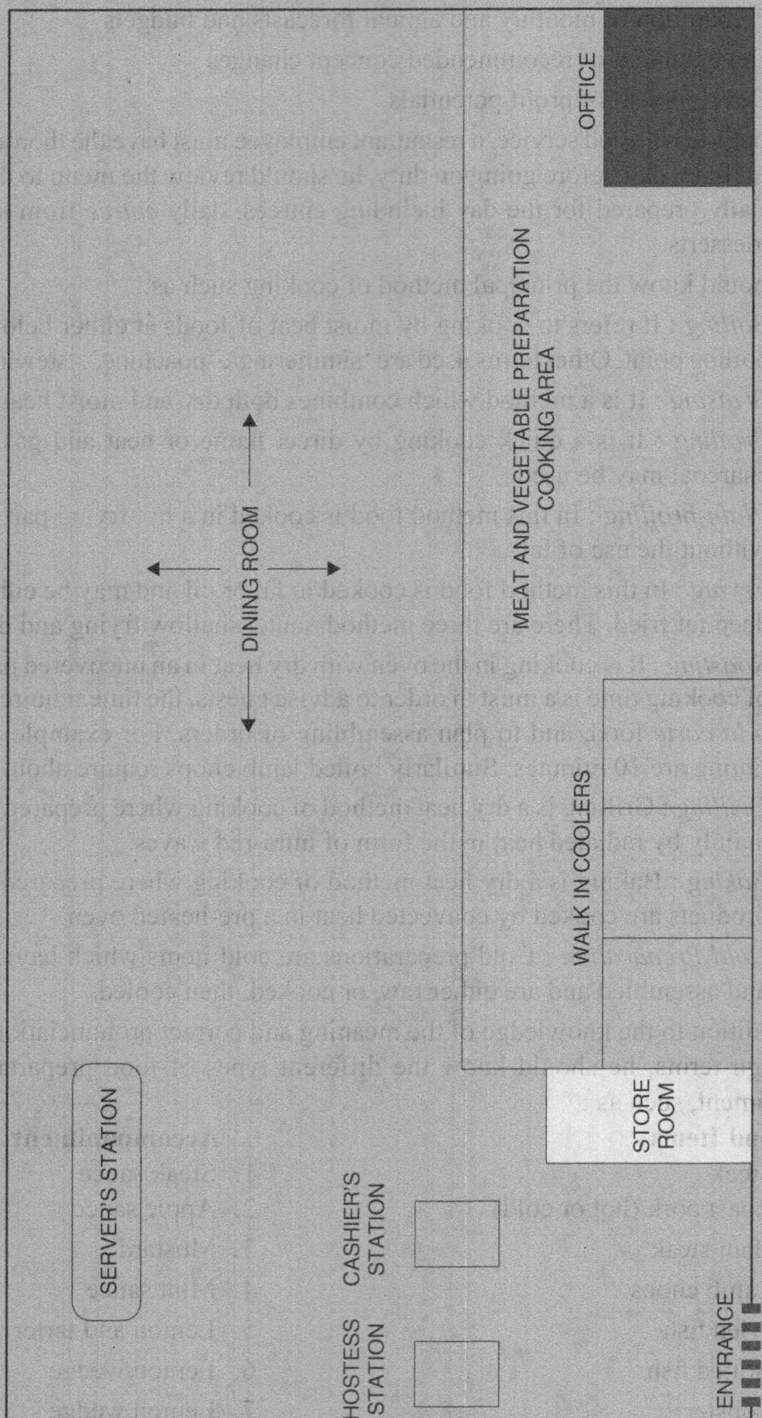

Fig. 6.27. A Typical Layout of a Hotel Restaurant

Pix 6.49 : A Speciality Restaurant

All food and beverage personnel, generally, fall under the jurisdiction of the F & B manager, who reports directly to the food and beverage director or general manager. He is responsible for the scheduling of service personnel, the reporting of hours worked, the control and distribution of all the administration function in the service area. The importance of this department will depend on the number and size of outlets available in a hotel. For example, in many hotels a variety of different types of restaurants, bars and banqueting facilities are aimed at the registered guests and outside customers, while in others, a restaurant and a bar may be exclusively for resident guests.

The service of staff in the restaurant, coffee shop, room service, lounge service, grill room, bars and banquet rooms come into direct contact with the resident guest as well as with the general public who use the hotel facilities other than the sleeping room. Service is the prime objective of this department. Good food well cooked and beautifully presented, can be easily, spoiled by a careless waiter/waitress. Proper attention to the table set-up (silverware, china glasses, etc.) and proper attention to the guests' needs are very important in hotel business.

Basically, food is served from the left, beverages from the right, with the simple reason that glasses and coffee cups are normally placed on the right side of the customer, and dirty dishes are removed from the right. These rules are applied when practicable otherwise concern for the guest's comfort is more important than any rule.

Most of the hotels lost the repeat business by poor service rather than by poorly cooked food. Word-of-mouth advertising is the most powerful medium in this service industry. Repeat business in the hotel is the most important factor in the success or failure of the hotel as a profit making enterprise. There is a need for organisational training and supervision in this department.

In a large establishment, there may be different areas offering variety of meals and service :

1. The restaurants There may be a number of speciality restaurants Continental, Chinese, Indian, executive club, room service, roof top restaurants, barbeque, coffee shop, snack bars, lounge service and banqueting.
2. The bars, cocktail bars, public bars, hotel bars, dispense bar, S/R bar, lounge bar.

RESTAURANT

Traditionally, it is said that 'you can't make money on food' and to some extent it is true even today because in many accommodation units food service is strictly a 'Loss Leader' proposition provided as a convenience for guests. But in the hotel business, many of them have turn a nice profit in their restaurants, coffee shops, food and beverage out-lets and bars. Now-a-days, to be successful in hotel business, a hotel should conceive of and operate its food facilities and restaurant competing with other food and beverage establishments rather being merely as adjuncts to their room business. Since all people do not want the same thing, there is no one best product for each market segment a category of people you hope to serve. A well-known hotel designer in hotel field Jac Lessman asserts that each patron has four senses that must be satisfied if his dining experiences to be enjoyable. What he sees, what he smells, what he hears, as well as what he tastes, all are important. Psychology has a great deal to do with a diner's mood and response.[1]

A hotel may prefer to lease out a restaurant or coffee shop rather than operating them by the hotel. This will be a profitable arrangement for the hotel to provide needed food facilities for guests without operating botherations to run it. Great care should be taken in choosing the restaurateur to whom the space will be leased as the quality of food served, price and service standards will reflect on the hotel.

According to a operations bulletin of the American Hotel and Motel Association one should follow the following advice[2] :

1. Make surveys, including a rental market appraisal, to determine which type of rental agreement will be of greatest benefit to the landlord.
2. Determine basis for computing rentals :
   (*i*) Fixed rental uniform payments throughout terms of lease
   (*ii*) Graduated lease : rent graded upward as lease matures
   (*iii*) Percentage lease rent paid according to :
   - Fixed or sliding percentage of sales or profit
   - A minimum fixed retail or a percentage of sales or profit, whichever is greater.
   - A minimum fixed sum plus a percentage of sales or profit
3. Reappraisal rental value lease :
   (*i*) After a short-term during which rent is fixed, it is increased or decreased according to a reappraisal of the value of the space occupied or gross sale annually. The most satisfactory arrangement is one giving the landlord a minimum rental plus a percentage of gross sales.

1. Jac Lessman, well known Hotel designer.
2. The American Hotel and Motel Association, USA.

4. Spell out in the lease who pays for maintenance and other changes. If an adequate return on value of the space is to be earned, the tenant should pay for:
   (*i*) Installation and up-keep of furnishings, fixtures and equipment.
   (*ii*) Silver, glass, china, kitchen utensils and all other movable items.
   (*iii*) Cleaning, repairing and maintaining the lease space.
5. Require that the tenants provide certain services for the hotel such as room service, meals for staff, banquet and other catering services, fixed service, food service, if the property offers American or Modified American plans.
6. Avoid a long-term lease a 10-year term usually works out best from the landlord's point of view.
7. If possible, do not include a renewal option clause in the lease.
8. Be sure the lease retains for the landlord the right approval of any sub-lease or assignment of the original lease, and, if possible, that it includes a cancellation clause favouring the landlord.

Besides the rental arrangement, a lease should include :

1. Detailed description of the premises
2. Plans and space
3. Clauses covering the services and facilities that the landlord is supplying
4. List of duties and responsibilities of the tenant
5. Percentage of real estate tax tenant is to pay
6. How utility charges are to be handled
7. Water and sewage cost allocation
8. Control of access from and to space
9. Insurance requirement, fire liability, etc.
10. Provision covering partial and complete loss via condemnation or fire
11. Agreement on hours and days of operation
12. Determination of the quality of product
13. Range of retail price of items to be sold
14. Disposition of receipts form vending, counter and other sales.

RESTAURANT ORGANISATION

The number of employees required will depend upon the size and the nature of amenities of the hotel. However, some of the positions found in a food and beverage service are described below :

RESTAURANT MANAGER/DIRECTEUR DE RESTAURANT/DINING ROOM MANAGER:

The Restaurant Manager is responsible for the overall operation of the establishments which serve food. He coordinates and directs the work of the employees. He is responsible for the food and equipment necessary for the restaurant. Periodically he inspects the restaurant to ensure the maintenance of health and sanitation regulations.

He performs many clerical and financial duties such as keeping records, directing payroll operations, handling large sums of money and taking inventories. His work usually envolves a constant contact with the customers taking their suggestions, handling complaints and creating a friendly atmosphere. A number of hotels employ specially trained assistants, often called food manager or assistant managers who supervise the kitchen staff and are responsible for the preparation of food served.

Figure 6.28 indicate the Organisation of F & B Services in a hotel.

Servers primarily take the order for service of food and beverages, make out customers food checks / KOT (Ref. Figure 6.29) and in some cases serve as a cashier in the smaller hotels. They have varied duties depending on the size and kind of hotel in which they are employed. They present menus to the customers after they are seated, assist in suggesting choices from the menu, inform the customer of special preparation and seasoning of food and sometimes suggest beverages that would be complementary to the meal. They check to see that correct silver is on the table and try to attend to any special requests the customers to make their dining more pleasurable. They follow the more formal and correct protocol procedures for serving food. Captain, waiters or head waiters may greet and seat the guests and supervise the service, bus-boys or girls may assist in cleaning table, refilling water glasses, pouring coffee, setting tables and removing dishes and soiled linen to the kitchen.

The Restaurant Manager is responsible for planning and organising all the service activities of the restaurant such as staffing, scheduling, training, promotion of team spirit, motivation to achieve targets. In brief he has :

1. To have keen sense of observation power
2. To look after the operational policies, hours of operation, main meal periods, type of food and service required, decor and atmosphere, table lay-out and seating capacity.
3. To co-ordinate with engineering, house-keeping and other departments for the maintenance and up-keep of all equipment/furniture used in restaurants
4. To liaise with other departments with special reference to food production department
5. To do their daily staff briefing
6. To maintain effective guest relations; know regular VIPs by name/ guest service comments and their redressal
7. To maintain service standards and specifications in different food and beverage out-lets
8. To understand the full procedure, forms and files used in restaurants
9. To assess daily performance of the restaurant through number of covers sold, total F & B sales, turn-over/covers; menu items, sale summary, sales expectancy, plate wastage, popularity of particular item
10. To exercise cost control techniques for reducing breakage, spoilage and pilferages to arrange suitable entertainment facilities.

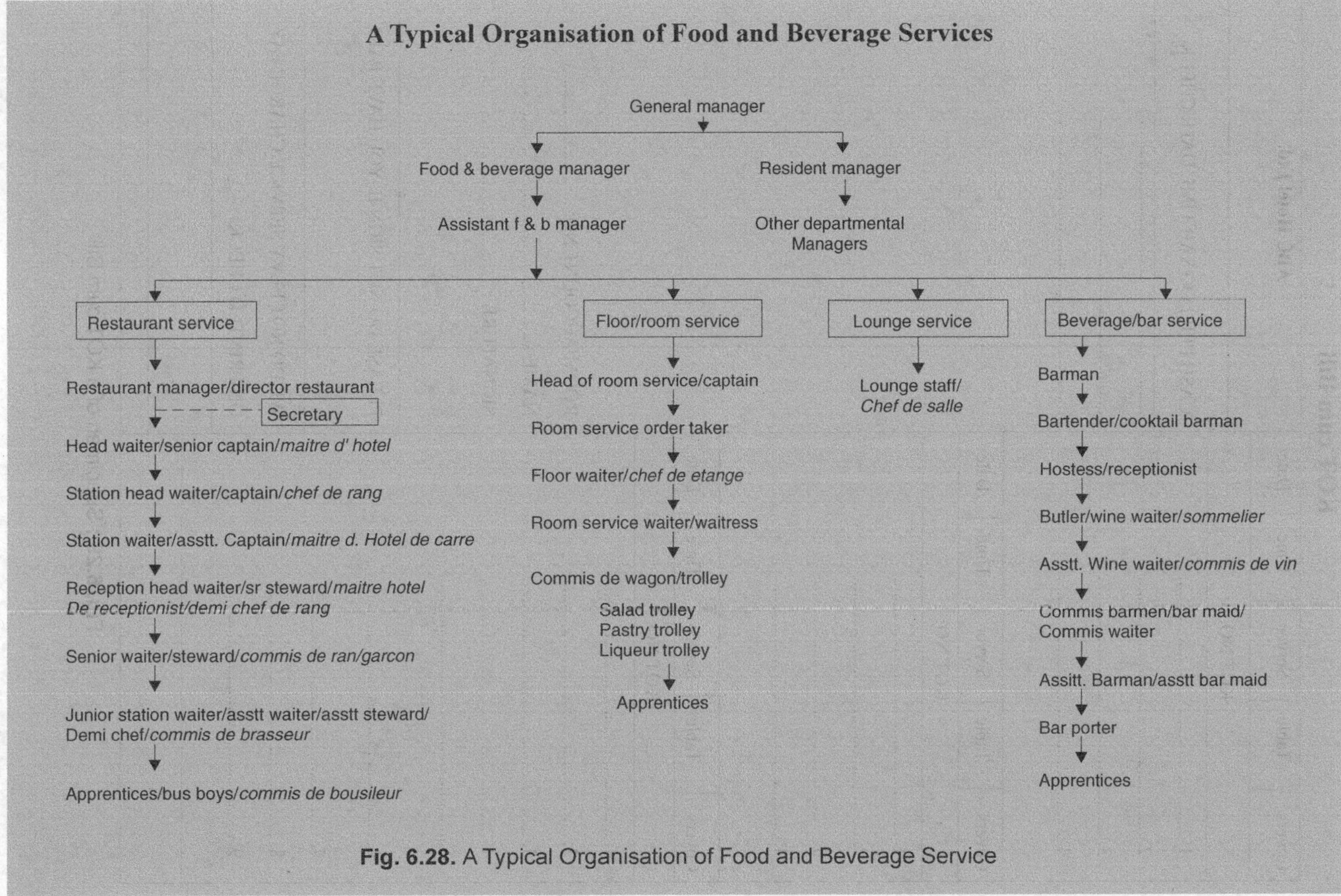

Fig. 6.28. A Typical Organisation of Food and Beverage Service

KOT cum Bill

Covers	Table	Server	Time	Date
KOT NO:				

1. ....
2. ....
3. ....
4. ....

Covers	Table	Server	Time	Date
KOT NO:				

1. ....
2. ....
3. ....
4. ....

Covers	Table	Server	Time	Date
KOT NO:				

1. ....
2. ....
3. ....
4. ....
5. ....
6. ....
7. ....
8. ....
9. ....

ABC Hotel Ltd.

CASH PER LOG TAB TIME DATE CHECK

....

....

....

ROOM/ACCOUNT NO: ....

NAME : ....

SIGNATURE : ....

PLEASE DO NOT SIGN IF YOU HAVE PAID

WE DO NOT LEVY SERVICE CHARGE PAY ON PRINTED CHECK

Fig. 6.29 : Speciman of a KOT cum Bill

Pix: 6.50 A Restaurant

SENIOR CAPTAIN/SUPERVISOR/*MAITRE D'HOTEL*

He must have the knowledge of foreign language and a knowledge of foreign and national specialities, wines and tastes of clients of different nationalities. He is also responsible for organisation and administration of food and beverage. and conducting training for staff. He must have the sound knowledge of hygiene and safety standards and principles of organisation. His duties and responsibilities are :

1. The service of the restaurant
2. Daily training and hiring of staff
3. Scheduling of employees
4. Supervision of the service of each meal
5. General maintenance of area and equipment
6. Draw up duty rosters and supervise discipline
7. Take part in the preparation of special tariffs and prices
8. Inform the *Chef de Cuisine* of probable day of request
9. Assist the management in the preparation of normal dinners, receptions, parties etc.
10. Ensure the observance of hygiene and safety standards and regulations
11. Be responsible for his staff and give suggestions, concerning their recruitment, change of duties, promotion and further training
12. Look after operational policies, hours of operation, main meal periods, type of food service required, decor, atmosphere, table lay-out and seating capacity
13. Maintenance and upkeep of all equipment/furniture
14. Service standard and specification in different out-lets
15. Assess the daily performance of the restaurant through : number of covers sold, total food and beverage sales, turn-over per cover, sales summary of plate, wastage, seating capacity restaurant, sales and promotion
16. Cost control reducing breakage, spoilages and pilferages

17. Provision of entertainment facilities and the equipment and accoustics required
18. Procedure, forms and files used
19. Co-ordinatation with engineering, house-keeping etc.
20. Liaison with other departments, with special reference to food and production department
21. Effective guest relation
22. Knowledge of regular guests, VIP by name, guest service comments and types of complaints and redressal.

Pix 6.51 : Wine and Plated Service

CAPTAIN/HEAD WAITER/*MÂITRE D'HOTEL*

He should have knowledge of foreign languages and thorough knowledge of various dishes. He assists the head waiter in receiving the guests and taking orders. He should have knowledge of different dishes and should be able to explain the dishes to the customers. In most of the deluxe restaurants, game birds are carved in front of the guests by the station waiter. Whenever the station head waiter is busy in receiving, the station waiter is responsible for all tables, he will do the gueridon service. He is incharge of a *'rang'* or group of about 5 tables to seat approximately 20 guests. In the absence of the station head waiter he performs all his duties. His main duties and responsibilities are :

1. To take customer's order, to present them dishes and to service them.
2. To carve meat, poultry and game
3. To take account of the time required to prepare dishes with a view to regulate the space of service
4. To supervise commis and waiters/waitresses

To see that station is clean and that all tables are properly laid to prepare the bill

To receive complaints from guests and answer them

To return to the kitchen any dishes he considers unsuitable

To be responsible for all the equipment in the station

To do guest service and guest handling

To do *mis-en-place* of his station

To do staff handling and work head distribution

To get familiarisation of menu items

To do KOT control and bill presentation

To observe the number of covers at each station and determine the number of covers per steward

To liaison between restaurant staff and kitchen.

STATION HEAD WAITER/*MAITRE DE HOTEL D CARRE'/ MAITRE-D-HOTEL DE RANG*

In a large restaurant he is incharge of 100-125 covers. He is responsible for the cleanliness of tables, chairs etc. He allocates stations, tables to the station waiters/waitresses. He also checks the lying of the covers, tables and side boards. He receives the guests either directly or through the head waiters and seats them on their respective seats. He takes the order of the guests and passes it to the station waiters, waitresses for the service of food. He is responsible for smooth service and also attends to all the guest complaints. He also looks after the gueridon service as it requires lot of skill.

ASSISTANT CAPTAIN/RECEPTION HEAD WAITER/*SENIOR STEWARD/ DEMI CHEF DE RANG*

Knowledge of foreign language and national specialities are essential for reception waiter. In a large restaurant the 'Maitre de hotel'is busy as he is responsible for a number of duties and cannot always welcome the patrons and lead them to their respective tables. To perform these duties a reception head waiter is employed. He will have a plan of the room with the table number. He reserves the table and the place for the guests. He greets the guests upon arrival and will take them to the table and seat them, leaving them in the charge of station head waiter.

SENIOR WAITRESS/STEWARD/*COMMIS DE RANG*

He/she should have sound knowledge of foreign and national cooking specialities and wines and of the tastes of clients of different nationalities, language, and of labour legislation. He should have knowledge of taking orders from the kitchen and service and cleaning. His duties and responsibilities are :

1. To carry out the *maitre de hotel's* instructions
2. To supervise discipline in his department and the cleanliness of the dining rooms, pantries and equipment
3. To receive the guests, present the menu, advise the guests and take their orders
4. To supervise and assist his subordinates and perform all the duties of the *maitre de hotel* in the latter's absence
5. Laying of covers and *mise-en-place* of his station
6. Service of food and beverages in conferences with the standards and specifications laid down by the management

7. Knowledge of menu items, brief idea of preparation of menu items, ingredients gone into the making of the dish, preparation time, accompaniments and the final appearance
8. Service equipment and its usage
9. Methods of check preparationcash and credit.

JUNIOR STATION WAITER/*DEMI CHEF*

The duties of a Junior Station Waiter are similar to that of a station waiter, the main difference being that in the beginning he has a small station comprising 8-10 covers. He serves the food and also removes the soiled dishes himself.

WAITER/SERVERS/*GARÇON*

He should have good knowledge of national and international dishes and should be able to handle restaurant equipment efficiently. Knowledge of hygiene and safety regulation is essential. His duty is to take the guest order direct or through *Maitre de hotel* or *Chef de Rang*. The order is passed on to the kitchen where he assembles the foods, carries it to the restaurant and serves it to the guests. If the waiter is busy, the *Commis debarrasseur* helps him in all his work except that of service. On the allotment of station, the waiter should check and wipe the cutlery, crockery, glasses and the side-board. In addition to this, the waiter lays the table cloth, folds the napkins, makes sure that the cruet set is filled, the ashtrays are clean, fills the sauce bottle, checks that oil and vinegar stands are ready for service and there is adequate stock of linen. Quite often, he polishes the cutlery and silver. He is also responsible for the presentation of the bill, when the guest departs, removes the dirt and cleanse the table. The main duties of the waiter are :

1. Preparing table according to the instructions of his station waiter
2. Obtaining drinks from bar or dishes from the kitchen and placing them on the table
3. Removing dirty plates if there is no *Commis* waiter
4. Assists in cleaning restaurant and bar equipment material
5. Serving drinks and dishes to clients at their table.

Thus, the waiter is responsible for the service of all food and beverages to the guests seated within his station and also for the maintenance of that station.

ASSISTANT WAITERESS/*COMMIS* WAITER

An assistant waiter must have the knowledge of various dishes. His/her main duties are :

1. To take orders from the station waiter on the basis of order vouchers
2. To obtain the dishes from the kitchen and place them on appropriate tables
3. To clear the table.

ASSISTANT TROLLEY WAITER/*COMMIS DE WAGON*

He brings the trolley to the restaurant. Passes on the trolley to the station head waiter or to the station waiter for the actual service. He is also responsible for arranging the *hors d'oeuveres*, pudding, desserts, etc. and also sets the gueridon service of flambe dishes.

ASSISTANT WAITER (CLEANING)/ASSISTANT STEWARD/BUS BOYS/BUS PERSONS/*COMMIS-DEBARRASSEUR*

This is the junior most position in the restaurant. The main duties of the Assistant Cleaning Waiter are to carry soiled dishes, dusting and sweeping of floor, cleaning of carpet, tables and chairs.

The busboy assists the waiter/waitress and serve bread rolls, coffee and other items and clears dirty dishes, sets up the table, changes table cloths, picks-up crumbs, fills water glasses and repolishes silverware when necessary.

CARVER/*TRANCHEUR*

Carver is usually under the kitchen department but included among the *Maitre-d-hotel* team. The duties of a carver are to lay the buffet tables for roast and cold meals, carve saddle or barn of beef, roast legs of mutton and roast turkey at the table as required. He tries to get the maximum number of positions, from each joint with as little wastage as possible.

TRAINEE WAITER/THE *COMMIS-DE-RANG*

He mainly fetches and carries and does a little service of vegetables, sauces, offering rolls and placing plates upon tables. He clears the table after each course and acts under the intimation of the *Chef-de-rang*.

APPRENTICES/*DEBARRASSEUR*

Apprentice is the learner who has joined the hotel wishing to take up waiting as career. In continental brigades, young waiters and apprentices are known as '*Piccolo*' which means little one in Italian. During pre-preparation periods he carries out the cleaning task and will keep the side-board well filled with equipment. He also helps to fetch and carry items as required.

FOOD AND BEVERAGE SERVICE

The different types of service found in modern restaurant are explained in the following paras.

FOOD SERVICE PROCEDURE

The decisions on the style and standard of service must be efficiently communicated to the managements and staff working in food service. These are usually covered in procedure manuals, instructions to staff and training sessions. Operating manner are an essential management tools. They ensure that everyone knows what to do, how to do it, when to do it and to what standard. They ensure that employees work consistently in some agreed manner.

One to two hours period before service commences, serving staff usually lay up the side boards and tables and fill cruets, pepper mills, sauce bottles and sugar balls. In small restaurant, the service staff is also responsible for cleaning the dining room and for simple food preparation such as preparing plated side salads, making dressing or melba toast, butters, preparing coffee and tea, setting up cold butter, sweet trolleys and cheese boards.

Pix 6.52 : Food and Beverage Service

A Case Study 6.5 :
Restaurant

Situation

A restaurant maintained a staff of five bus boys. It appeared that only four were needed.

Results of Analysis

It was found true that four boys could handle, all bus boys, tasks. When one boy left the remaining crew readily absorbed his work. Management saved ₹ 80,000/- per year.

A Case Study 6.6 :
Dinning Room

Situation

In one dining room it was found that the average production per waiter fall three covers below that which reasonably could be expected.

Results of Analysis

Each waiter was given an additional day off per week. As a result each waiter could do more cover per day and to his average daily earnings cover higher. The hotel saved ₹ 90,000/- per year. Its service did not suffer and the waiters earned approximately, the same in five days as they formerly did in six.

The staff must know exactly the type of service expected such as silver service, a plate service, combination of silver and plate service or family service.

On completion of service the restaurant must be ready for the next service. Therefore, the duties of the staff are as under :

1. To ensure that all used plates, cutlery and glass one cleared to the wash up
2. To put all used clothes and napkins in the laundry basket

3. To count the number of table cloths and napkins for the laundry list
4. To clear away all condiment sets ready for filling the following day. Empty and soak English Mustard Pots
5. To empty sauces back into main containers so that small containers can be washed
6. To hand in bill books and check pads with bill control slip
7. To clear away buffet to kitchen where appropriate
8. To ensure that side boards are all clear of rubbish or dirty items
9. To switch off light
10. Where still room duties are carried out by the waiting staff, empty and clean coffee making machinery and serving jugs. Return mill and cream to the refrigerator
11. To return biscuits and melba toast to tins
12. To return cheese boards to refrigerator storage
13. To ensure that what area is clean and tidy and ready for the preparation team to start work for the next service/day.

Large hotels provide several type of food services. These include a restaurant offering an extensive *a la carte* and *table d'hote* menu, based on French cuisine, a specialist restaurant, a grill room and a coffee shop. The surroundings of a restaurant will normally be luxurious and restful, as the customers would wish to take their time whilst enjoying the meal, the atmosphere, music, cabaret etc. Restaurants in hotels are generally of luxury type. They have elaborate decor, personal service and elegant cuisine. They attract people who want to be entertained as well as fed, who want a pleasant all-round experience in dining out. Many of the speciality restaurant serving steaks and prime ribs, sea food, polynesian food or French cuisine are included in this class.

Pix 6.53 : Guest taking food

FRENCH SERVICE/SILVER SERVICE

French service means service at the table. All food is brought to the table on platters and in shafling dishes. It is individually serviced to the guests by the waiter or captain. In some instances, the actual preparation of food takes place at the table side. Speciality dishes requiring flambe, such as a steak, Diana and desserts and salads are prepared by the captain. This service is uncommon as it requires more space and more staff and is offered by most of the first-class restaurants. Figure 6.30 is an organisation of a French style restaurant.

Organisation of a Restaurant : French System

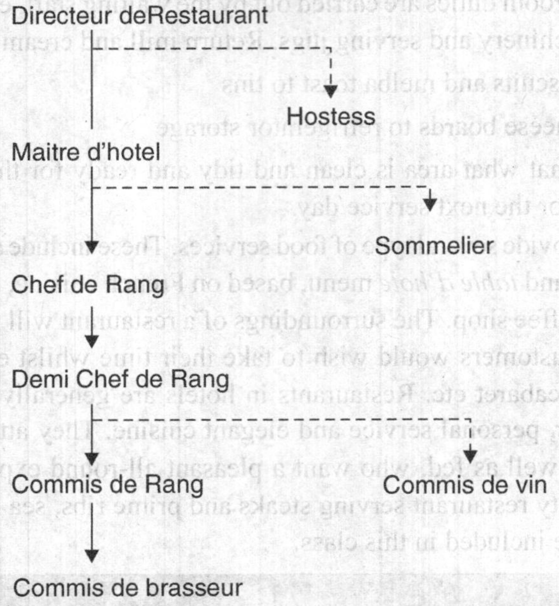

Fig. 6.30. A Typical Restaurant Organisation (French System)

Under French Service the following points are observed :

1. The table is set for appetizers, soup, main course and sweet.
2. The food is prepared and portioned in the pantry.
3. The portioned food is put on the platters and brought in the restaurant.
4. The waiter then places hot or cold plates as per the food in front of the guests.
5. He then picks up the platter and with a service spoon and fork, serves the food from platter to plate from the left side moving clockwise.
6. The rule of the service is to serve the food from the left and clear the dirties from the right moving clockwise.

ADVANTAGES OF FRENCH SERVICE

1. Only one waiter is needed on each station.
2. It is faster than the English service.

3. It is an elegant form of service and gives personalized service to the guests.
4. There is comparatively less wastage since the unused food goes back to the kitchen.

DISADVANTAGES

1. There is a large investment in silver equipment.
2. If many guests are to be served from the same platter the last to be served will see a very unappetizing display.
3. If every guest at a table orders a different dish, then it becomes difficult for the waiter to carry a heavily loaded tray.

AMERICAN SERVICE

In this method the casual practice of service is as follows :

1. Portioned food is plated in the pantry by the kitchen staff.
2. The per-plated food is then served to the guests from the right side.
3. The rule of this service is that all the beverages as well as food is served from the right side and the clearing is also done from the right side.

Figure 6.31 is a typical organisation structure in an American style restaurant.

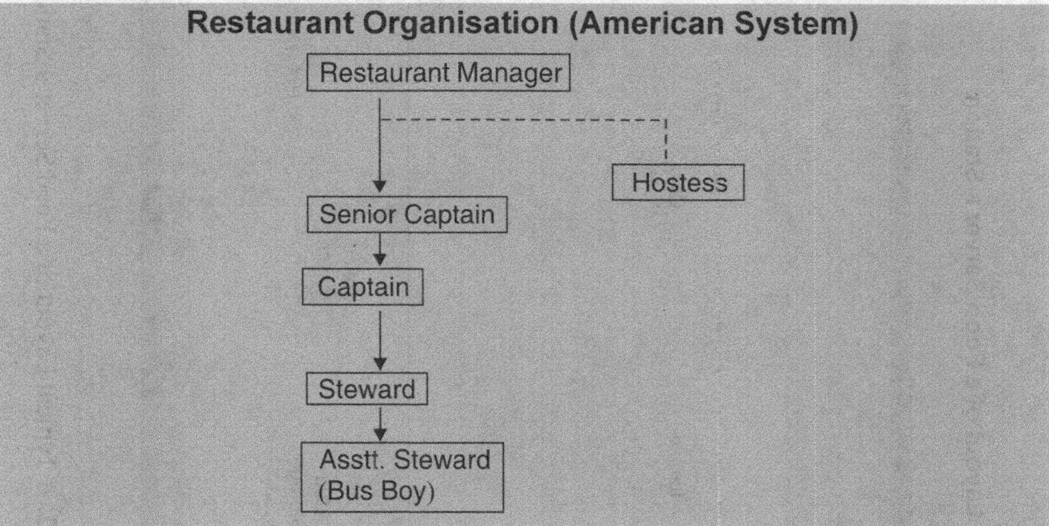

Fig. 6.31. A Typical Restaurant Organisation (American System)

ADVANTAGES

1. Time consumed in this service is less.
2. It is an inexpensive service.

DISADVANTAGES

1. It is not a personalized service.
2. There is lot of wastage of food.

Figure 6.32 shows the layout of a typical side station. The server is responsible for keeping his/her side station fully stocked.

The staff also need to know the detail about the following :

1. The size of plates that should be used for each at each course.
2. The cut way to be used for each dish.
3. The composition and price of each dish
4. The correct accompaniments to each dish.

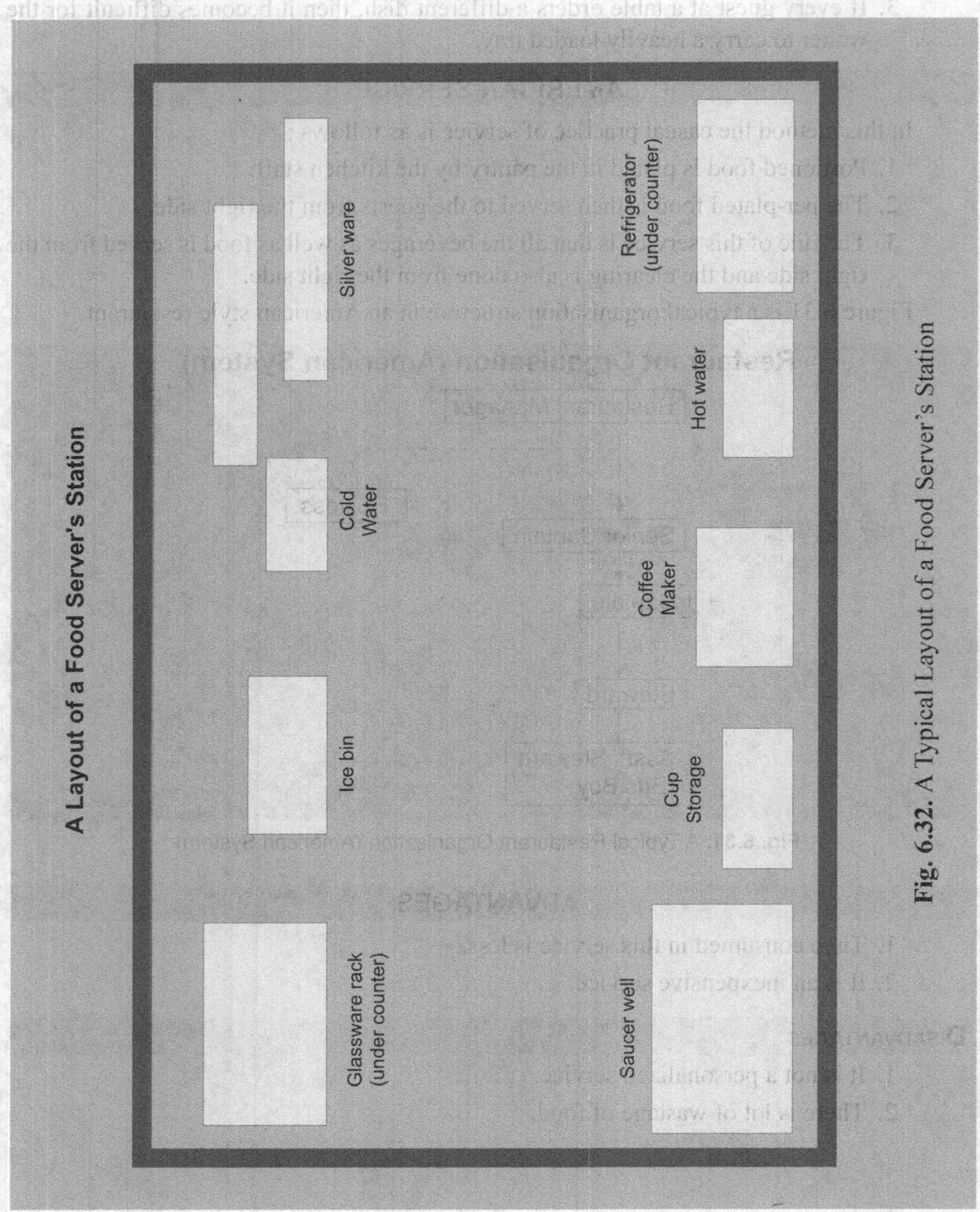

Fig. 6.32. A Typical Layout of a Food Server's Station

The order of service in a restaurant may be summarised as follows :

1. Meet and greet customers as they come in. In a large restaurant the jobs is assigned to restaurant hosts/hostesses.
2. Offering water, rolls and butter
3. Taking of order
4. Serving of all items of food to the left of the customer and clearing from the right
5. Serving beverages to the right of the customer and clearing from the right
6. Serving ladies first
7. Clearing should start out after every member of the party has furnished eating the course
8. Paying regular attention to rolls and butter and refilling of water glasses
9. Offering coffee or tea
10. Presenting the bill.

RUSSIAN SERVICE OR PLATE SERVICE

It involves directly plating of all good food in the kitchen. Some of the hotels have adopted the combination of plate service and French service. They prepare certain speciality items like soups, bread rolls and salads at the table or service them from a service cart. Most of these items are relatively easy to handle on a table service basis.

BUFFET SERVICE

In this system the customers mostly serve themselves. Buffet service is adoptable to limited hot dishes where the cover count can easily be controlled like breakfast dishes. The composition of lunch buffet should be carefully planned to prevent cost of customer excesses and wastage from exceeding the payrolls. This type of service is getting very popular mainly because it speeds up turnover which results in a greater number of covers and reduces the number of staff requirement.

ENGLISH SERVICE

The system followed is as follows :

1. The butler brings the food on platters and sets in front of the host.
2. The host portions out the food and passes the plates to the hostess who serves the accompaniments.
3. Then the butler placesthe plates in front of the guests.
4. In restaurants the dish is first presented to the host. The waiter then portions out the food on the side-board and sets the pre-plated food in front of the guests, serving the host last.
5. The pre-plated food is served from the right side and cleared from the right side.

The organisation structure under this system is given in Figure 6.33.

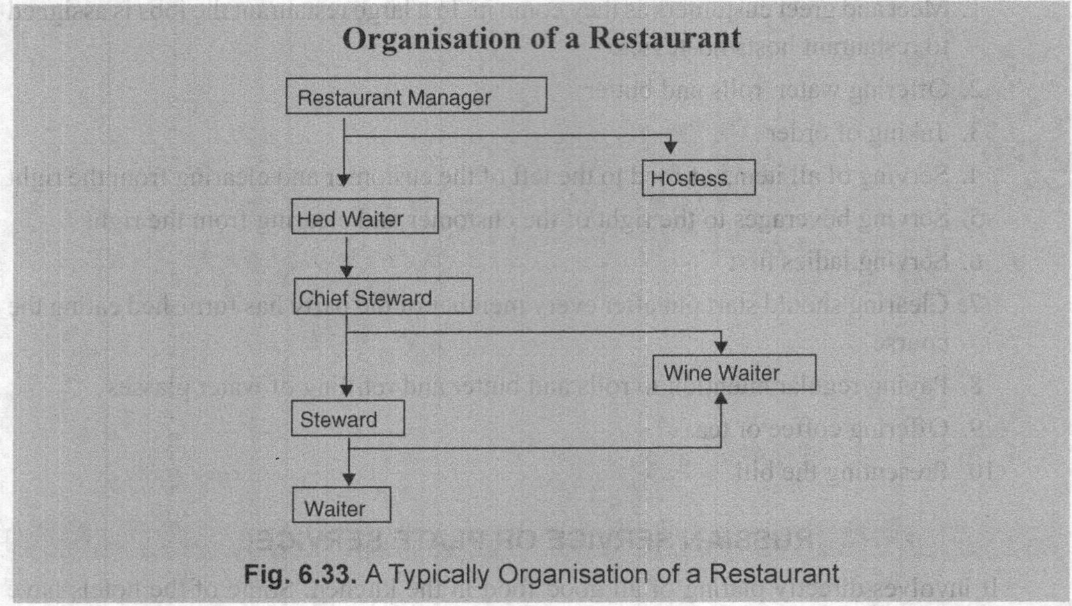

Fig. 6.33. A Typically Organisation of a Restaurant

THE GRILL ROOM

In addition to a grill, a grill room may carry a far more comprehensive menu usually *a la carte menu*. In hotels where restaurants and grill rooms operate side by side, it is usual to find that the latter offer simple dishes mainly grills and perhaps snacks. The type of service determines the type of and number of staff.

ROOM SERVICE / FLOOR SERVICE

It involves the service to guest rooms of both food and beverages operations. The peak period for room service is during the morning hours when the resident guests prefer breakfast in their room. Orders are taken on phones which require an order-taker, a cashier, supervisory personnel, and service personnel. Removal of dirt dishes is a big problem in the room service. The room service requires the maintenance of number of service staff to handle this fluctuating service, therefore, results in an unproductive payroll costs. It is the most unprofitable area of food and beverage operations. In many hotels, in order to plan efficiently, an advance breakfast order form is placed in each room, which indicates the order and the time at which the breakfast is to be served. The guest hung it on the door before retiring and the service personnel collect it in the early hours of morning.

To be a first class hotel, room service must be available even though that room service may constitute a loss operation. Room service is a hall- mark of a first class hotel. These hotels maintain floor pantries from which room service operates. Press a button and in a second a room service waiter appears. Successful room service depends on getting the food to the room as quickly as possible.

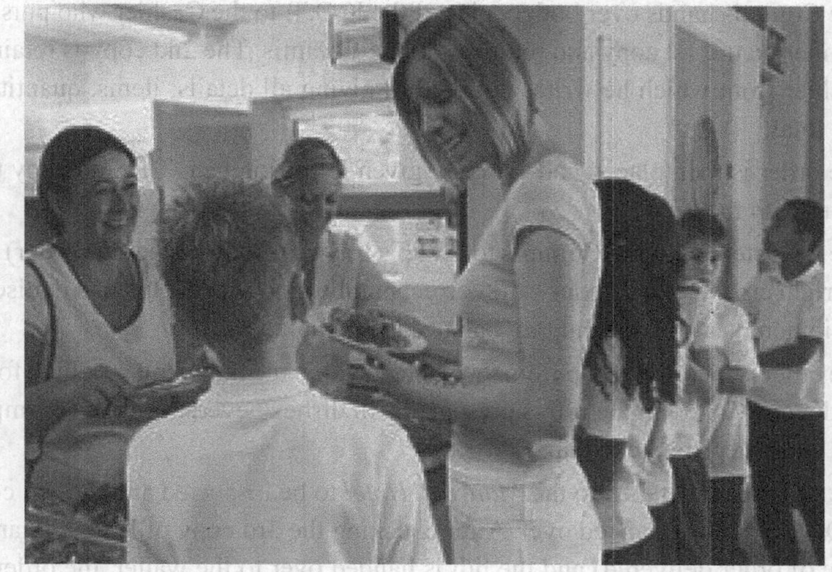

Pix 6.54 : Customer's in a Restaurant

In large hotels, captain oversees each room service shift. In the small hotels the bellman, busboys or regular waiters make the room service delivery. A Floor Waiter (*Chef d'etage*) assisted by *Commis d'etage* is responsible for food and beverages in the bed rooms or private suites. The number of staff required for room service depends on the size of the hotel and the demand for this service. In many hotels, floor waiters have their own service room or floor pantry connected directly to the kitchen by means of 'dummy waiters'.

Thus, room service is serving of food and beverage in guest rooms of the hotel. Small orders are taken on trays and his wonder in trollies.

The step by step room service procedure of receiving order and serving it to the guest (Ref. Figure 6.34 and Figure 6.35 and) is explained below :

1. Order taker should attend the telephone on the 2nd or 3rd ring.
2. Respond to the call by identifying the department and then wishing as per the time of the day.
3. Take the order on the K.O.T.
   (*i*) Ensure beforehand that the carbons are placed between all 3 copies.
   (*ii*) Write the room number and order of the guest (with special request) clearly.
   (*iii*) Fill in all the details like date, time, number of covers and signs.
   (*iv*) Repeat the order to the guest to re-check and close the conversation by saying 'Thank You'.
4. All 3 copies of the KOT are handed over to the *Maitre d'Hotel* or duty *Chef de-rang*.
5. The *Maitre d' hotel* or Duty *Chef de-rang* then hands over the order to the Commis and retains the 3rd copy with the Commis name on it.

6. The Commis hands over both copies of the K.O.T. to the Cashier who puts the check number on the 1st copy and returns it to the Commis. The 2nd copy is retained by the Cashier from which he writes out the bill giving all details; items, quantity, amount and total.
7. The order is then placed and 1st copy given to the kitchen. The 2nd copy to Cashier along with the bill.
8. The next step is for the Commis to set up a tray or trolley (as per the order) and select the right crockery and cutlery, the correct number and also the linen. All miscellaneous equipment is also kept and tray balance is maintained.
9. The order is then picked up from the kitchen within the time limit specified for the item. At the pick-up point the bill is presented. All dishes/beverages with accompaniments and garnishes are picked up.
10. The order is then taken to the *Maitre d' Hotel* to be inspected and the 3rd copy of the K.O.T. and bill is handed over. After checking the 3rd copy of K.O.T. (stamped with time of order delivered) and the bill is handed over to the waiter, the ordertaker fills in the control sheet from the 3rd copy of the K.O.T.
11. After the order is inspected, the waiter, after announcing the room to the *Chef de rang* proceeds to the guest room.
12. For complete check on the waiter and the service of order, the name of the waiter, time in, time out and type of order is entered in the control sheet.
13. The waiter in the meantime before entering the guest room check the room number on the door against room number on the bill to ensure the correct room. If there is no DND sign then the door is gently knocked and Room service is announced.
14. If there is a DND sign or there is no response then the guest is contacted from the floor telephone. If still no response then the Room service ordertaker is informed and he checks with the Reception.
15. When the guest opens the door, 'wish' according to time of day and place the tray or trolley where the guest indicates. Lift the dish covers and announce names of the dishes. If the guest wishes to be served, serve, otherwise leave the tray/trolley.
16. Present the bill along with a pen. If guest pays in cash check amount discreetly and if he signs, check all the bills have been signed.
17. After enquiring if the guest requires anything else the waiter then returns to the room-service, clearing any dirties from the corridor on the way.
18. On return to the room-service the transaction is settled with the cashier and the ordertaker is informed that the service is completed.

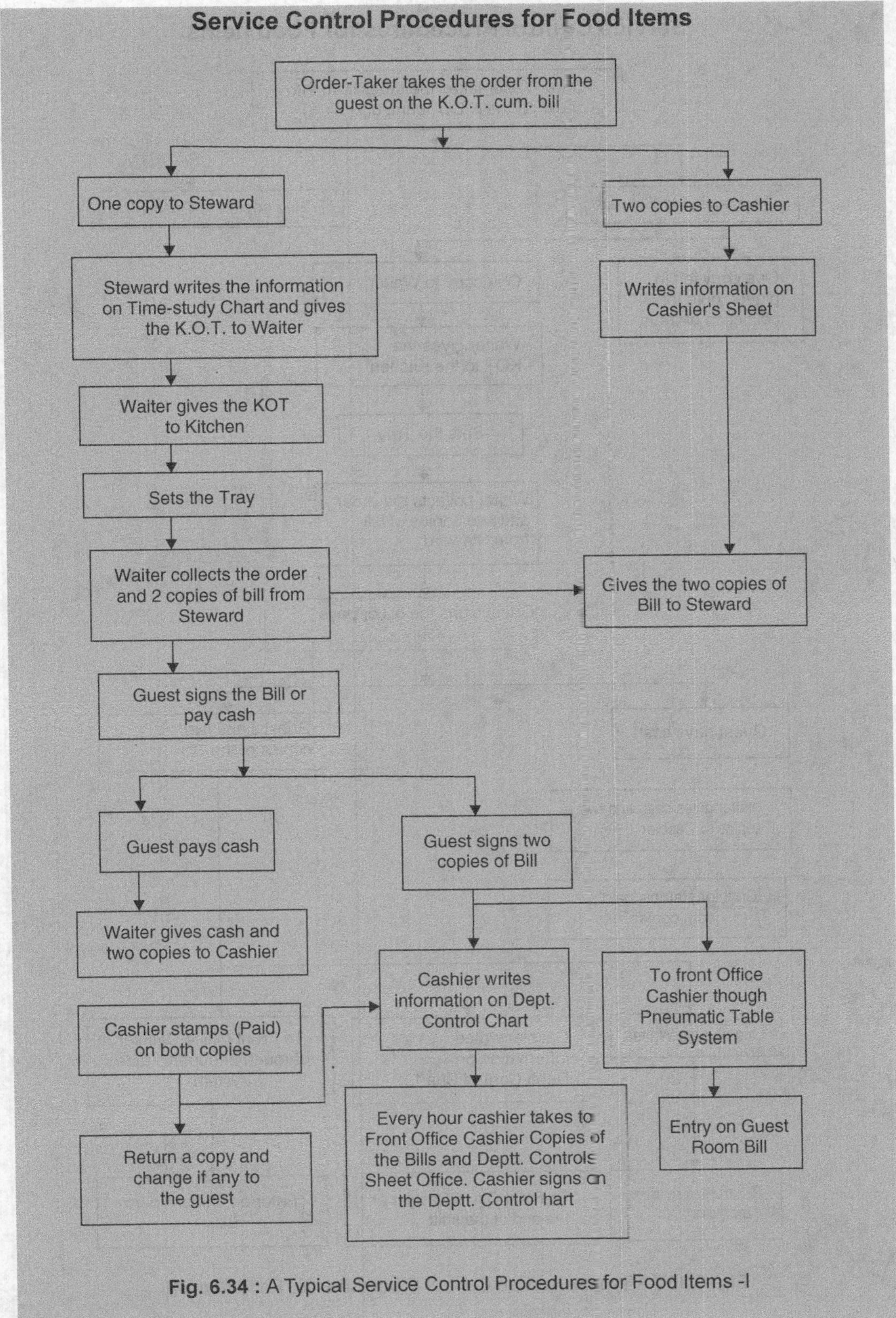

Fig. 6.34 : A Typical Service Control Procedures for Food Items -I

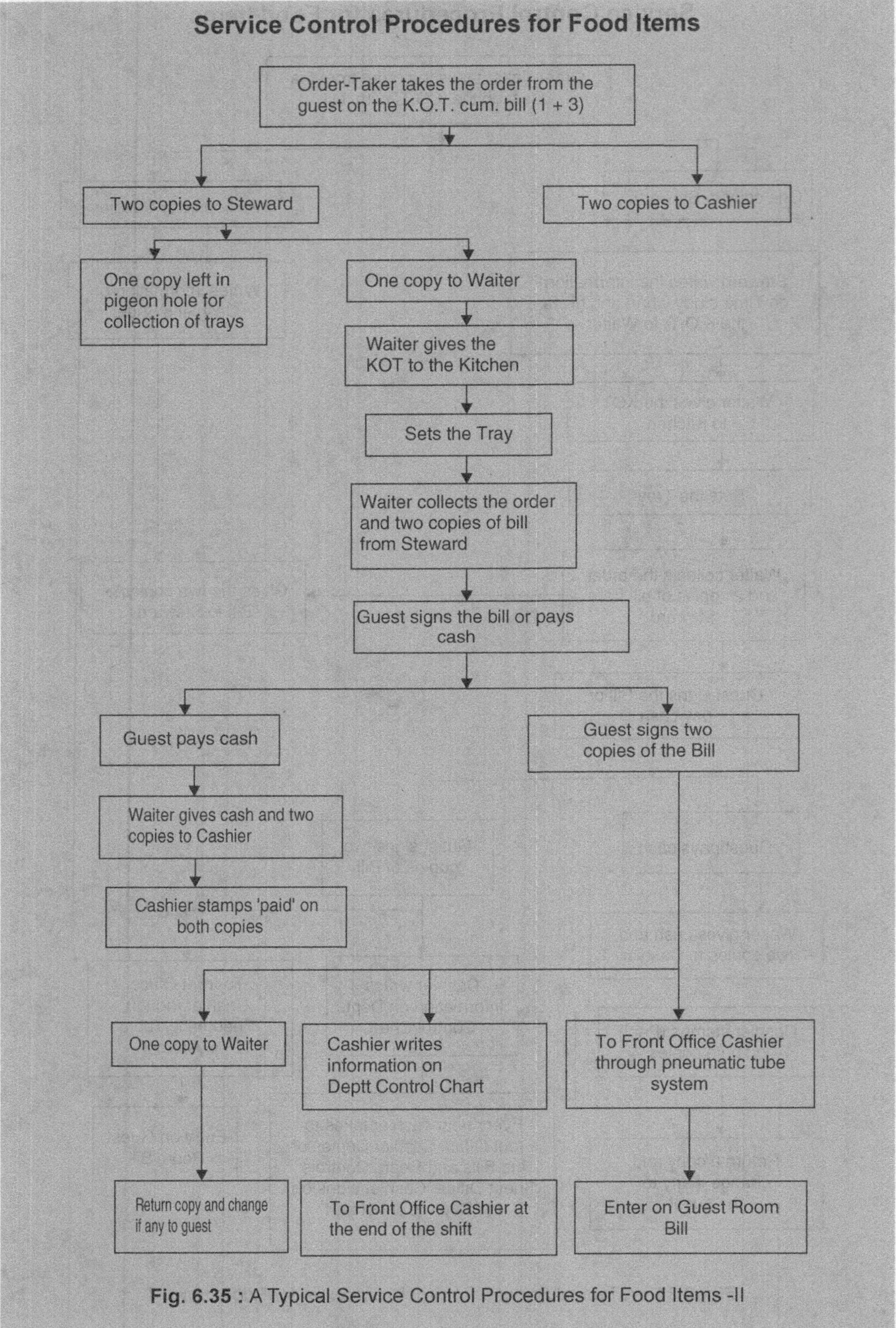

Fig. 6.35 : A Typical Service Control Procedures for Food Items -II

THE COFFEE SHOP

It is a place where guests (hotel and chance customers) can obtain beverages (tea, coffee etc.) light snacks, cakes, pastries etc., throughout the day and late evening, or sometimes throughout the night as well. A typical organisational structure of a Coffee Shop is given in Figure 6.36.

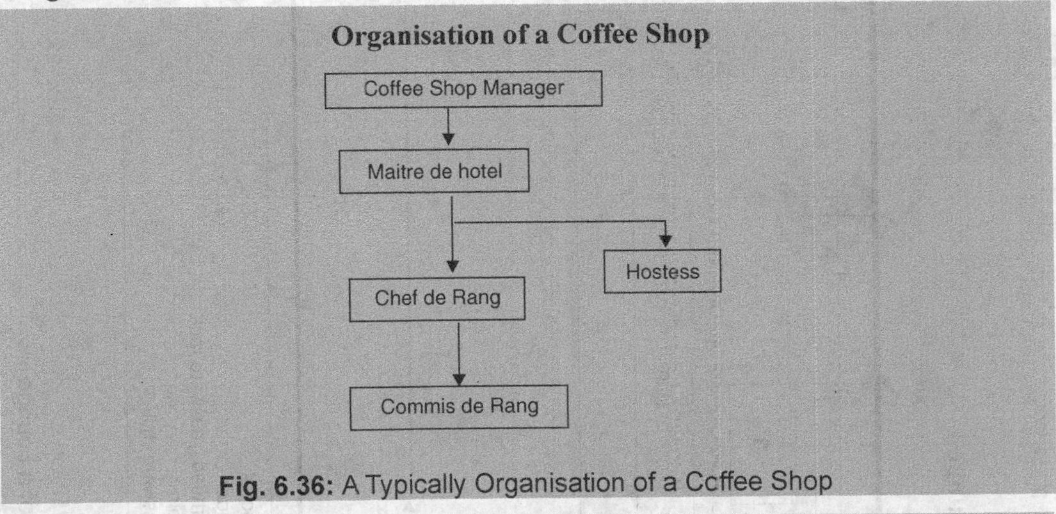

Fig. 6.36: A Typically Organisation of a Ccffee Shop

THE LOUNGE

In the absence of a 24-hour coffee shop, a lounge service facility is offered to the guests to obtain snacks, beverages and other drinks outside the usual hours of service. In a lounge service area, it is usual to have two lounge waiters or waitresses. They divide the day between them when the lounge waiters go off duty at the end of the day, the Night Porter usually assumes the responsibility for this service.

Generally a lounge is divided into two main areasthe table service area and the bar. Tables and chairs are arranged in the service area for consumers who do not wish to sit at the bar and those who wish to be served at the bar. The chairs or stools are arranged in front of the bar counter. Order and service are provided by a table attendant or when the attendant is off duty, by the bartender. The cash register is also kept behind the bar accessible only to the bartender or bar attendent. Figure 6.37 is a typical layout of a lounge.

BUFFETS AND BARBEQUE

This service is provided on an outdoor pool side or terrace. These are self-service operations with some staff behind the buffet table or barbeque helping to service the guests with their choice of food. There is also staff employed for serving drinks and cleaning the tables. The indoor buffet is an excellent way of catering a function. The buffet meals are becoming popular at lunch time as with minimum of service a busy guest can get quick and reasonably inexpensive food.

BANQUET SERVICE

It covers conferences, cocktail parties, wedding receptions, dances, private and official luncheon and dinner parties. The banquet manager is responsible for booking functions, helps the organisers to choose menus and the type of service required, deals with order and

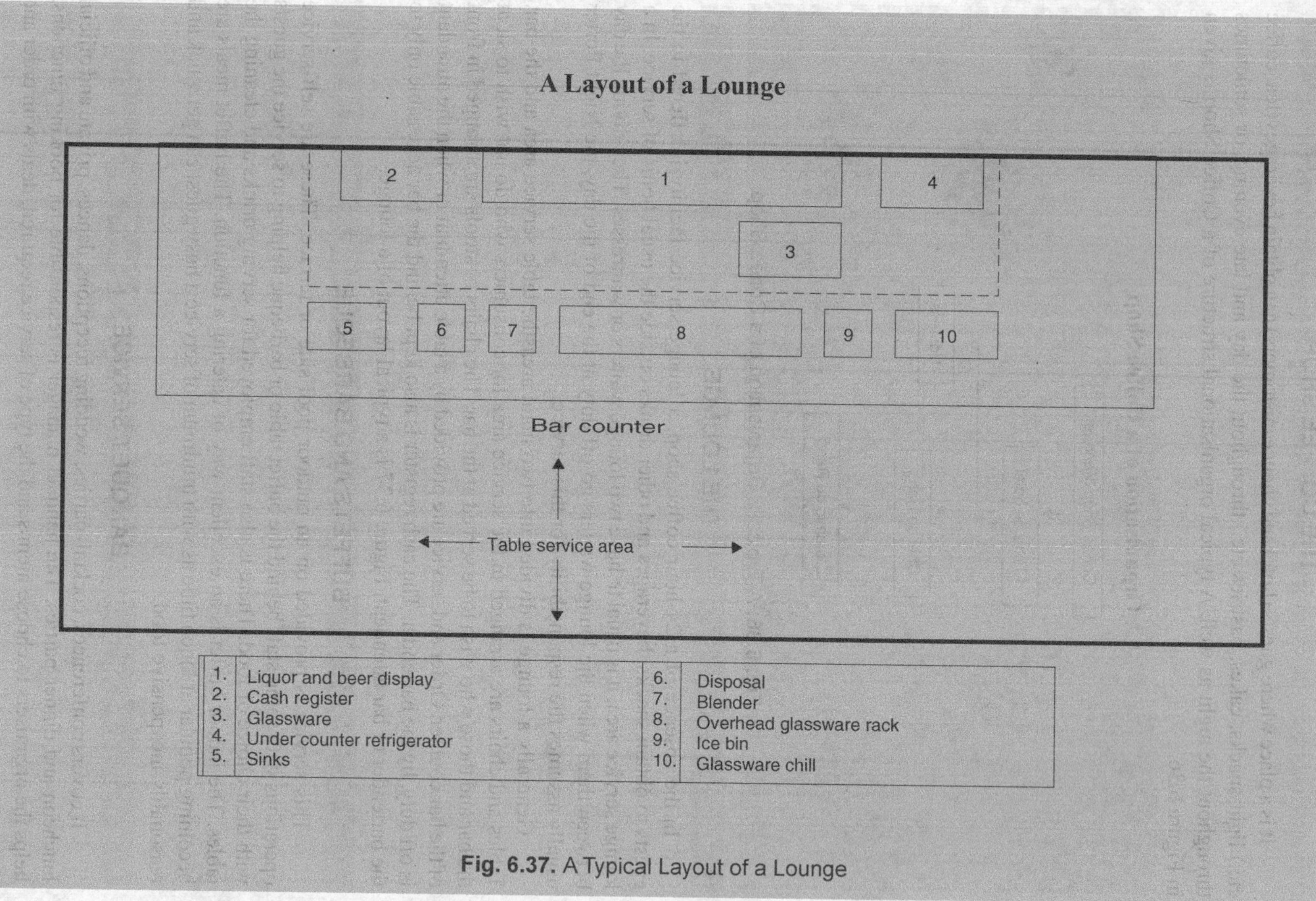

Fig. 6.37. A Typical Layout of a Lounge

arrangement of flowers, costs of the function of hire or rooms, as well as food/alcohol and staffing of the function. A full-time banqueting brigade of waiters is employed which is supplemented during the period when larger functions are held.

GUERIDON AND FLAMBE

It is one of the speciality service in deluxe restaurant. Gueridon service means side table service work that is carved out on a side table before the service is included under gueridon service. For example :

1. Making a salad dressing
2. Salad carving
3. Preparing a grape fruit etc.
4. Flambe work and flambe service.

One of the main advantages of gueridon serivce is that it provides a visual appeal to the customer. Guests are impressed by the skills shown in gueridon performances. Flambing is a reliable means of attracting the attention of other tables in the restaurant, and has the effect of provoking repeat orders. The flickering lamp, the gleaming silver, the *mis-en place* on the gueridon added substantially to restaurant atmosphere. The customers in the deluxe restaurant continue to appreciate and demand similar visual services, in particular individual scene service at the gueridon and on the lamp.

In addition to general equipment, a gueridon service requires the following special equipment :

1. Gueridon trolley
2. Table cooking lamps or chaffling lamp
3. Crêpe suzette pan or chaffling pans
4. Steak pans
5. Other tools special carving knife, forks etc.
6. Shaslik swords.

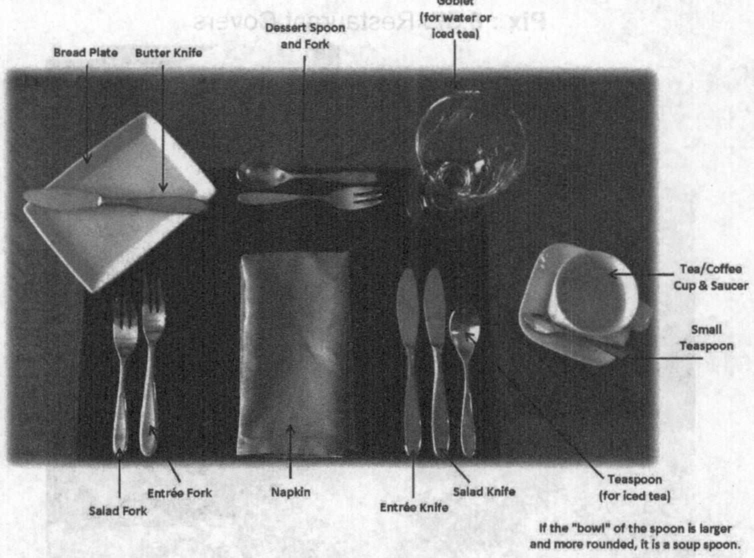

Pix : 6.55: Table Setting for Lunch and Dinner

Pix : 6.56: A Cover

Pix : 6.57: Restaurant Covers

Pix : 6.58: Table Setting

THE COVER

Cover is the space on a table for keeping all cutlery, crockery, glassware and linen required for a guest. Each cover requires 27" × 15" in space.

A typical layout of a typical standard cover is given in Fig. 6.38

CHARACTERISTICS

1. Each cover must be well balanced and should not be crowded with cutlery, glasses and china. Keep only the required cutlery, glasses and china on the cover.
2. All cutlery and table appointments must be placed at least 1/2 m. away from the edge of the table.
3. Knives and spoons are kept on the right hand side and forks are kept on the left hand side. If only a fork is to be used for a dish, then keep it on the right hand side.
4. The cuting edge of all the knives should be towards the left hand side.
5. The water glass is kept at the tip of the large knife.
6. The butter dish is kept on the under-liner with a butter knife.
7. The napkin is kept in the centre of the cover.
8. Cruet set is kept on top of the cover.
9. All covers must be laid directly opposite each other.
10. While placing the cutlery or crokery on a cover, ensure that the monograms are facing the guest.
11. Before laying a cover, check that tables and chairs are clean and not wobbling. Spread a fresh table cloth.

WAITING AT THE TABLE

BEFORE GUEST ARRIVAL

1. Report 15 minutes before time in order to study any menu changes and for briefing.
2. As soon as station is allotted, check your station for cleanliness and whether the covers and sideboard area is complete.
3. Study the menu to make sure you know the description of all the dishes. Also ensure that you know the specialities of the day and non-available items if any.
4. While in the restuarant stand erect, with the waiters cloth hanging evenly on the hand.

ON ARRIVAL

1. When the guests come to your table greet them politely and help them to be seated. Pull chairs specially for ladies and children.
2. Fill the glasses with iced water and present the menu.

Pix : 6.59: Order Taking

Pix : 6.60: Launch and Dinner Service

GENERAL RULES FOR SERVICE

1. If the table is set for more persons than the actual number sitting, clear the extra covers.
2. Adjust covers as per order, e.g., if the soup spoon is kept on the cover and the guest does not order soup, then remove the soup spoon before starting service.
3. If any piece of cutlery falls on the floor replace it with a clean one.
4. Check that crockery and glassware being used is not chipped or cracked.
5. When about to serve, if the guest has his hand on the cover say 'Excuse me Sir/Madam'.
6. Serve ladies first and then the men. Serve anti-clockwise.
7. Serve food in proper sequence of the menu, checking to see that proper cutlery is in place.

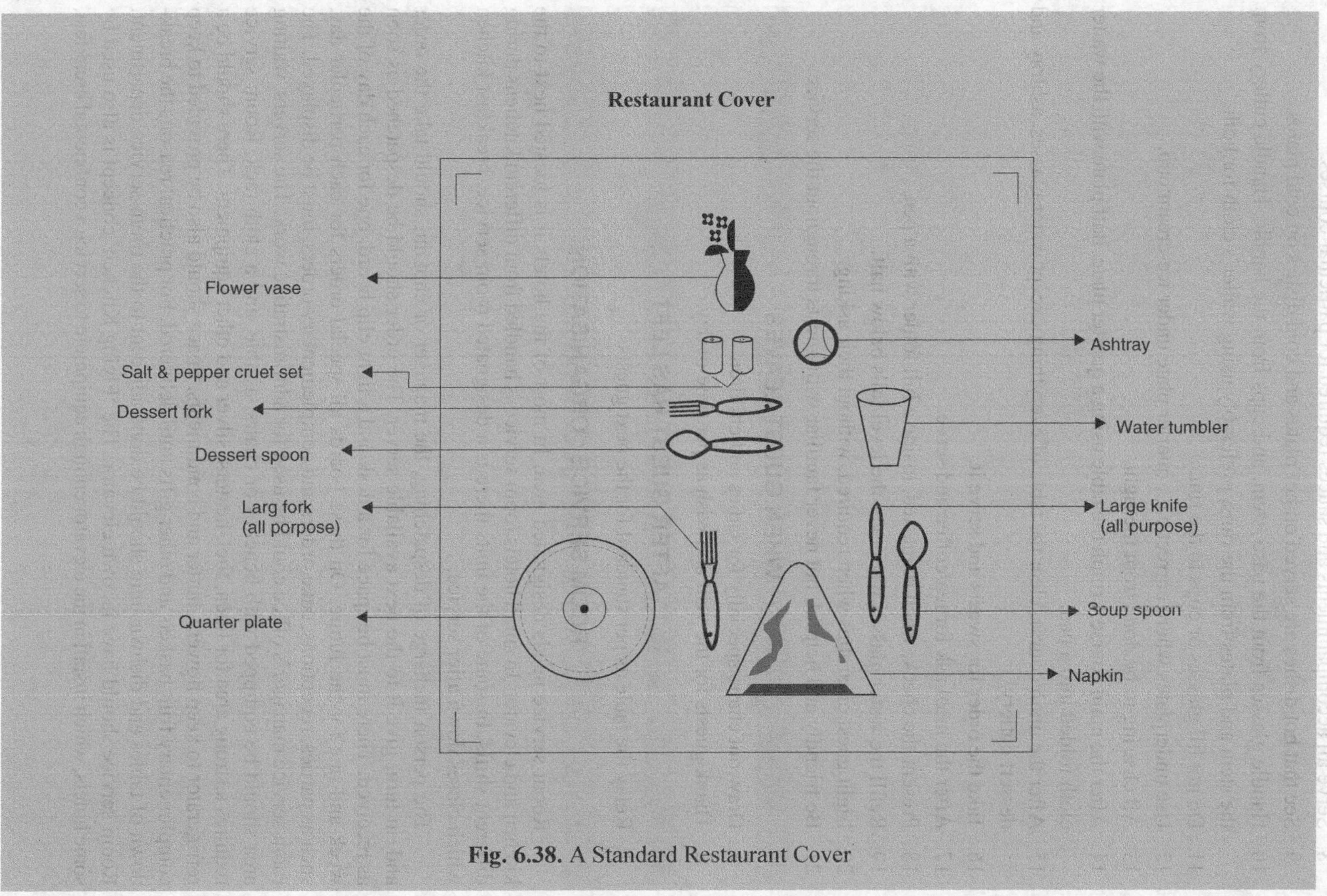

Fig. 6.38. A Standard Restaurant Cover

8. Serve all accompaniments and sauces required for particular courses.
9. See that hot dishes are served on hot plates and cold dishes on cold plates.
10. Handle glasses from the base /stem, and cups from the handle. Handle cutlery from the stem and plates from the rims, preferably using waiter's cloth for both.
11. Do not fill glasses or cups to the rim.
12. Use underplates where correct e.g., quarter plate under ice-cream cup.
13. All clearing to be done from the right.
14. After the main course, crumb the table using a quarter plate, half plate with the waiter cloth folded into a pad.
15. After the main course, clear the table of everything except water glasses, ashtray and dessert cutlery.
16. Take the order for sweets and serve it.
17. After the meal ask for tea/coffee and serve.
18. Present the check, when requested, inside a bill folder with a pen.
19. Refill the water glasses whenever the level falls below half.
20. Light guest cigarettes when required, without their asking.
21. Be friendly and helpful, but never familiar with guests throughout the service.

WHEN GUEST LEAVES

1. Draw out chairs specially for ladies and children.
2. Thank guests for the visit and wish as per time of day.

AFTER GUEST HAS LEFT

1. Relay the table as per standard for the next guests.

ROOM SERVICE : ORGANISATION

Room service needs designated area. In most of the hotels it is located next to the kitchen and elevator. In small hotels room service is handled from different kitchens during different shifts. In some of the units there is a designated room service, breakfast kitchen which closes down after service.

The person incharge of despatching, the manager or captain, should take the order and, in turn, give it to the next available server. The order should be despatched as soon as received. There must be space for a desk and a light clip board, one for each day of the week and one for the future. On these boards all special orders for each particular day, such as parties, receptions, cake orders and complementary orders, must be displayed. The room service manager's office could be used for administrative work. The servers, waiting area should be equipped with benches or chairs, a table, and a cloth rack. Room service requires a strong area for linen, fuel, heaters, silver and other equipment. There should be a refrigerator to keep flowers, butter and condiments. Space should also be provided to keep complimentary fruit baskets and other gifts until delivered. For practical reasons the break-down of tables and dishwashing should be done adjacent to the room service department. Room service should have its own elevator. The 'Flying Kitchen' concept is also used by some hotels, which install in the elevator enough equipment to service a continental breakfast.

ROOM SERVICE MANAGER/HEAD OF THE ROOM SERVICE/CAPTAIN

He is known as room service captain. He is a very crucial employee for the smooth operation of room service. A successful captain must know a foreign language, knowledge of national and foreign beverages, hygiene and safety standards, cleaning techniques. He should have a good idea about dishes and types of service in each restaurants. His duties include :

1. To co-ordinate the initial preparation and set up of equipment
2. To schedule the orders and their pick-up with the waiters
3. To carefully oversee each tray or chart for completeness and correctness and in general to be totally responsible for the room service operation during his shift
4. To be responsible for clerical work such as scheduling of waiters' time, keeping sample studies such as cover counts and menu abstract.
5. To remove all restaurant and bar equipment from guest room after service
6. To supervise and assist his staff
7. To be responsible for training of new employees.

ROOM SERVICE ORDER-TAKER/FLOOR WAITER/*CHEF D'ETAGE*

He handles all calls from guests, takes their food and beverage orders and coordinates the service of these with the room service waiters and captains. In addition he also reserves table for the various restaurants. He is responsible for the restaurant manager.

ROOM SERVICE WAITER/WAITERESS/ASSISTANT FLOORWAITERS/*COMMIS D'ETAGE*

The room service waiter is basically a food and beverage waiter specially trained to service food and drinks into the room. He also writes checks and collects the money from guest. The room service waiter is responsible for the equipment he uses while executing his duties.

LOUNGE WAITER/*LE GARÇON DE (LA) SALLE*

He serves light refreshments, afternoon tea and drinks in the lounge and other public areas of the hotel.

A BAR

BAR MANAGER

All matters concerning liquors, wines and beers are coordinated by a separate function within the food and beverage department called Bar or Beverage. The Bar Manager is responsible for all activities relating to liquor, wine and beer. He is responsible for :

1. Purchasing, receiving, storage, issuing of liquor, wine and beer
2. Controlling inventory
3. Hiring, training, scheduling and control of all beverages and bar personnel
4. Promotion of beverage services
5. Coordination with other departments
6. Compliance of all central, state and local laws and regulations relating to these activities.

BARMAN/*GARÇON-DE-COMTOIR*

He is also known as head bartender. He handles the purchasing and receiving of beverages. He should have the ability to prepare alcoholic drinks, mixed drinks and cocktails and some idea of the taste of the foreign visitors. Knowledge of hygiene and safety standards, labour legislation and price regulations is absolutely essential. The important responsibilities of a barman are :

1. To supervise the entire bar operation including ordering, stock taking, issuing of all liquors, beers and other bar items
2. To draw up daily roasters
3. To prepare bills, receive payment and register the snacks and beverages sold
4. To prepare and mix drinks and cocktails
5. To maintain all time keeping and bar stock books
6. To be responsible for the preparation and service of mixed drinks
7. To supervise the work of bartenders who must be able to mix all popular drinks
8. To ensure that bars are properly stocked and that ice, bar napkins, coasters, swizzle sticks and the like are in proper supply

To instruct, train and supervise all the product workers in all the bars.

Pix : 6.61: A Bar

BARTENDER/COCKTAIL BARMAN

He makes cocktails according to prescribed hotel's formulas and procedures, serves cocktails to waiters and guests, maintains healthy sanitary conditions in the bar, accepts money and gives changes for the guests. He must be a responsible person well versed in the skill of shaking and stirring cocktails and should have good knowledge of all alcoholic drinks, the ingredients, and of the licensing laws. He is responsible for *mise-en-place*, storage facilities, inside the bar, and decorative arrangements of liquor bottles. His duties include : Provision of different types of garnishes with different drinks

1. Processing of all guest checks
2. Inter-bar transfer and kitchen to bar transfers
3. Bar cleaning and closing
4. Storage and service temperature of various beverages
5. BOT control
6. Guest relations
7. Coordination with store and billing section
8. Liaison with F &B control for daily inventory.

WINE BUTLER/WINE WAITER/*SOMMELIER*

He must be good salesman and sell as much liquor as possible as it is one of the main source of incomes in a hotel. He is responsible for the service of all alcoholic drinks during the service of the meals. Knowledge of the foreign languages, beverage laws and laws relating to wines is a must for wine butler. He requires complete knowledge of national and foreign wines, the good vintages and good years, the wine suitable for various dishes and handling and care of good wines. He must be proficient with wine lists. He must have the knowledge of making and bottling of the wines. He should know how and when to serve the wines at room temperature or chilled. In addition he should have the knowledge of stock-taking and also mixing of cocktails. His duties include :

1. To carry out *maitre's* instructions
2. To present the wine list to customers
3. To assist them in selection
4. To fetch the wines ordered with the help of the *commis* waiter
5. To uncork the bottles in the presence of guests.

ASSISTANT WINE WAITER/*COMMIS-DE-VIN*

He should have good knowledge of wines and drinks and must know the correct methods of washing, drawing and handling of glasses. He should keep the wine tables, wine glasses, ice buckets ready for service. He takes the order of wines, spirits and beer either directly from the customers or from the wine butler. Thereafter, he collects the drinks from barman and serves them.

COMMIS BARMAN/BARMAID/*COMMIS WAITER*/WAITER/BARWAITER/BUS BOYS

His job is to supply dining rooms with all items necessary for service, setting up of the dining room, assisting his waiter(s) in service and general maintenance of the dining area, relating to the preparation of client's order and organisation of equipment and stocks. He obtains supplies from the still room and kitchen and replaces the barman during the latter's absence.

ASSISTANT BARMAN/BAR MAIDS

He needs a good knowledge of national and foreign beverages. He must be proficient in the use of bar equipment. Knowledge of hygiene, safety standards and regulation and labour legislations relevant to job are also essential. He carries out the barman's order.

BAR PORTERS

Generally assists the bartender in all phases of service and preparation of drinks e.g. he cuts fruits, hauls ice and cleans the bar. This is a position for trainees who after a start as bar porter go on to become bartenders.

BEVERAGE SERVICE

For purpose of beverages, a hotel may have different types of bar depending upon its requirement. Usually four types of bars are found :

1. Public bar
3. Portable bar
2. Service bar
4. In-room bar.

PUBLIC BAR

It is also known as 'Front Bar'. In these bars the guest can interact with the bartender and other service personnel. There are provisions for guest seating at the bar itself and there may be separate room or areas for the purpose.

SERVICE BAR

This is also known as hidden bar. It is designed for the hotel's food and beverage service staff only and serves more or more food service areas and/or room service. Most of these bars are centrally located in the back of house spaces within and out of guest view.

IN-ROOM BAR

It may also be called Mini-bar or Horor bar. The beverage manager is deeply involved in the design of these bars and is responsible for their marketing and control. As regards the responsiblity of inventory, it rests with the room service.

The staff should know exactly which measures and glasses to be used for different types of drinks. They must know the correct temperature at which to serve the various drinks, garnishes, and presentation and the prices. Their duties prior to service include :

1. Stocking and laying up the bar with lemon, slices and other garnishes.
2. Putting out nibbles such as crisps, nuts and olives or more elaborate canapes.
3. Washing glasses, locking up the bar at the end of service.
4. Cleaning and restocking for the next service.

BAR CONTROL

For proper control of bars it is essential to set up systems to cover the following areas :

1. Billing and checking system for the bar
2. Cash handling and control
3. Cellar work
4. Handling complaints
5. Handling emergencies
6. Licencing laws.

The bar must be properly equipped with corkscrews, crown cork opener, and sharp knife and measures. Spirits such as gin, whisky vodka, brandy and liqueurs are sold in measures of 1/3, 1/4, 1/5, 1/6 of a gill or 25 cl. or multiple thereof. Drought beer or cider are sold in multiples of half a pint in standard size glasses. Wines are served in any size of glasses.

The range of drinks stocked in a bar will depend on factors such as storage space in the bar and cellar, availability of funds, and the feature of them in your restaurant. Usually the beverage items include the following:

1. Whiskey
2. Rums
3. Brandy
4. Vodka
5. Port
6. Sherry
7. Vermouths
8. Mixers
9. Red and White wine
10. Beer and Cider
11. Champagne
12. Vintage Port
13. Liqueurs
14. Other ingredients for a range of cocktails.

The bar should be fully stocked. Check the whole bar to make sure that everything is clean and tidy and everything works properly. New stocks should be placed behind old stocks to ensure that old stocks are used first. There must be a proper system for moving stock from cellar to bar.

The distribution of the Purchase Order Form is made in 4 copies, as per following requirements:

1. The Purveyor (2 copies)
2. The Receiving Department
3. The Accounting Department
4. The Bar Manager.

The copy forwarded to the Receiving Department may have the last two columns, which list the unit and extended prices, blacked out or eliminated from the form. This distribution is done so that each of the person involved understands exactly how much merchandise has been ordered, when it is to be delivered and the other arrangements that may have been made. (See Figure.6.39.)

Distribution of Purchase Order Form

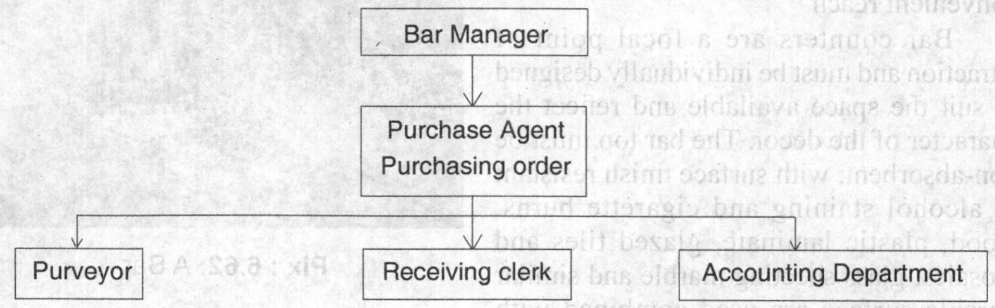

Fig. 6.39 Distribution of Purchase Order Form

EXCISE LAWS

The management and the members of staff who disperse and serve alcoholic drinks must know the relevant sections of the laws that immediately affect their work. The relevant sections of the law must be set down in writing and the staff should be trained accordingly. They should be given a copy of the relevant law, appropriate training should be imparted and should be told about the penalties for transgression.

These regulations are concerning :

1. Permitted hours for the service of alcoholic drinks
2. The difference between residents and non-residents in a hotel
3. Statutory measure to be used
4. Dilution and pasing off
5. Underage drinking and the purchase of cigarettes
6. Drinking up times
7. Betting, gambling and lotteries
8. Prostitution
9. Price indication regulations
10. Drinking and smoking on duty
11. Gratuities
12. Over-rigging/under-rigging cash register.

BAR DESIGN

The design of a bar should enable drinks to be served over the counter and by waiter service. Seats are required for patrons wishing to drink at the bar and may be in the form of seats or stoolsthe latter being provided with footrests. Bar counters are usually constructed with two levels of surface. The first level is the working counter with preparation space, sinks etc., at a convenient height in the bartender and the second level is the higher serving counter, providing screening, which is also within convenient reach.

Pix : 6.62: A Bar

Bar counters are a focal point of attraction and must be individually designed to suit the space available and reflect the character of the decor. The bar top must be non-absorbent, with surface finish resistant to alcohol staining and cigarette burns, wood, plastic laminate, glazed tiles and mosaics, glass sheeting marble and similar durable surface are used combined with softer panelling of leather or polyvinyl chloride and decorative facings. The effect of wetting on glued joints and plies must also be taken into account.

The working area behind the serving counter should have facilities for glass storage, washing and draining glasses, drink dispending and cash registering. An aisle space of at least 750 mm (2 ft. 6 in.) should be spillage resistant and non-slip. The back bar behind the servery combines the functions of a supplementary dispensing area and display for drinks. Mirror, glass work, and decorative metal work are used to provide reflection and sparkle.

Bottle storage must be accommodated in strong locable cabinets below and or behind the counter, with sufficient capacity for one day's requirements unless direct access to the main store is provided. Equipment requirements in an adjacent to the bar include one or more refrigerators, chilled dole plate, ice-maker and temporary storage for empty cans, bottles and garbage.

To provide security at night, and to next licensing requirements where hours of drink service are limited by law, the whole area must be capable of being screened.

A bar could be a small lounge. It may be a complex of cocktail public lounges and dispense bars. In the cocktail bars a great deal of experience is required, first to memoirs and then to blend and mix the many composite drinks, like cocktail, slings and fizzes which an experienced barman is expected to prepare in front of the customers.

The bar service means simply a drink which includes non-alcoholic and alcoholic drinks. The term 'dispense bar' is recognised to mean any bar situated within a food and service area. All alcoholic drinks are served by that member of the restaurant team. The bar must be located near the heart of the hotel. Robert Sage, President of the Fenway Motor Hotels of Boston, found on moving a bar from the back of one of his motor hotels to the front that sales increased 250 per cent.[1]

Pix : 6.63: A Bar-wine Mixing

Wine waiting is a specialised function and the wine waiter must know the background and how to serve each of the wines on the hotel's wine list. The service of wines and other drinks with the large restaurant is carried out by one or more wine waiters ('sommeliers'), who generally take orders from all stations in the restaurant. The 'commis'wine waiters serve the customers. In small restaurants the head waiter is incharge and is responsible for the welcoming and seating of guests. The head of large bars is known as Head Bar Man. He is assisted by barmen/barmaids, if the volume of business demands. In large hotels having several bars and a large volume of business there is a Bar Manager, who looks after all bars and is directly responsible to the food and beverage manager.

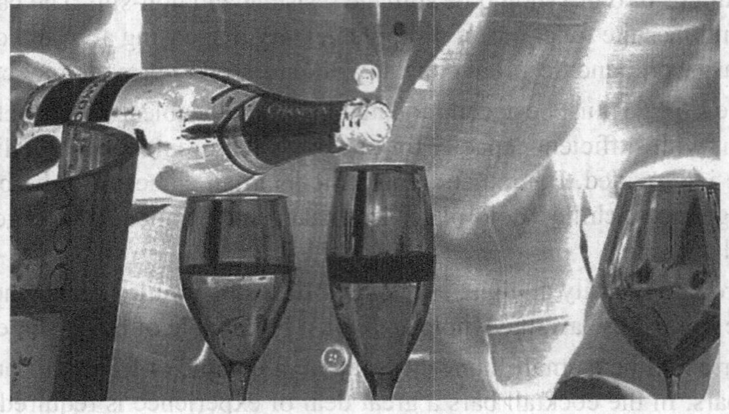

Pix : 6.64: Wine Service

WINE SERVICE

Place all wine glasses on the table in the same order as the wine is served. All wine glasses should appear to the right of the water gobletthe only glass to the left of the water is the cordial glass and port wine glass. In a formal setting, the glasses would appear as follows, starting at the right:

1. Sherry glass
2. White wine glass
3. Champagne saucer or goblet
4. Water goblet
5. Port wine glass
6. Cordial glass

Always serve wine from right and food from left. The wine stand should always be placed to the right of the host or person orders the wine. Below are given some guidelines regarding :

1. What type of wine to serve?
2. What type of wine to serve when?
3. What type of wine to serve with what food?
   (*i*) *Sherry Wine* : A fortified wine served before a meal instead of a cocktail, also with certain appetizers and soups.
   (*ii*) *Dry White Wine* : May also be served with certain appetizers and soups, particularly sea food, caviar, and other non-sweet appetizers. Served in an all purpose wine glass.
   (*iii*) *Dry or Semi-Sweet White Wine* : May be served with all fish dishes and shell fish. Served in an all purpose wine glass.

1. Robert Sage, President of the Fanway Motor Hotels, Boston, USA.

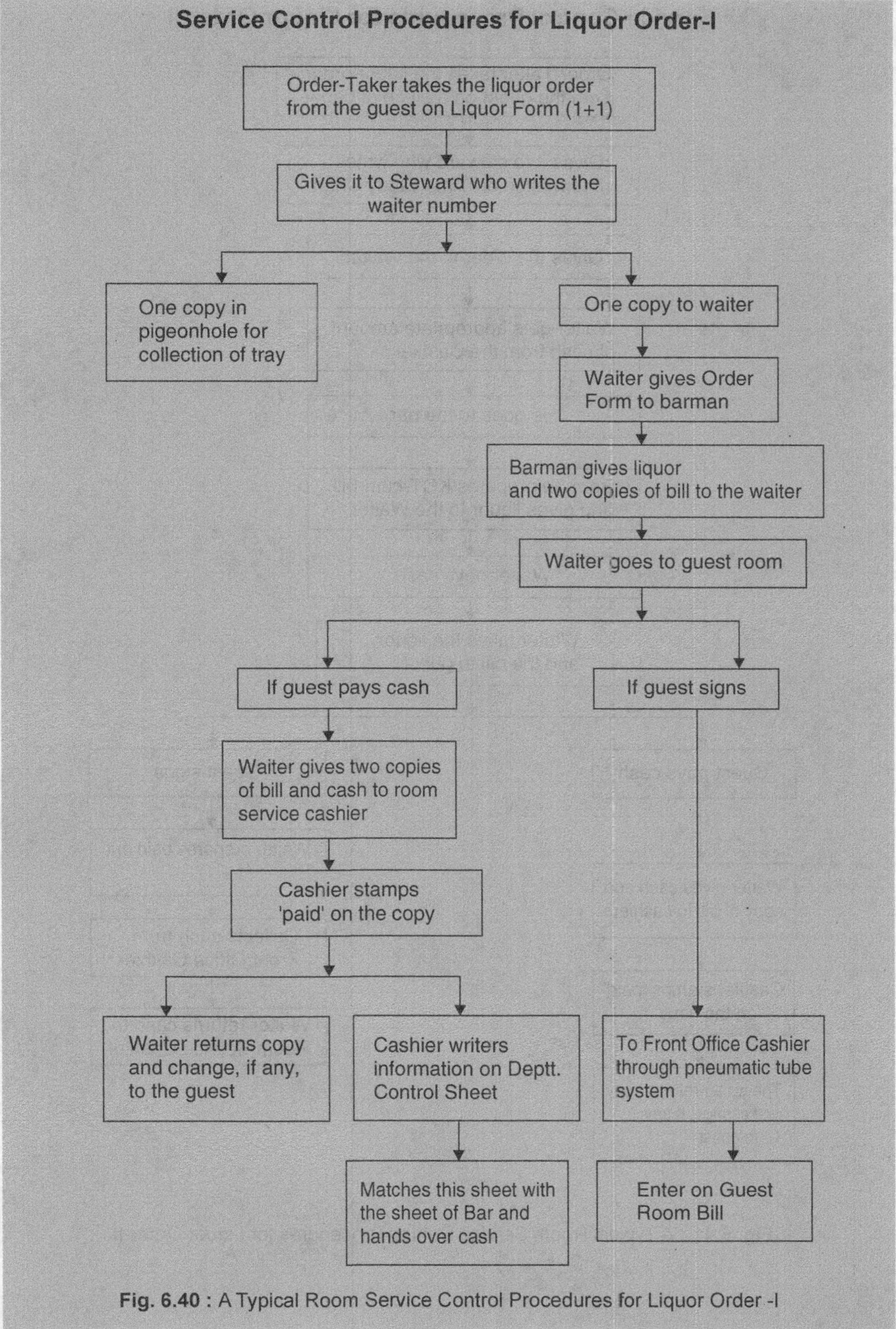

Fig. 6.40 : A Typical Room Service Control Procedures for Liquor Order -I

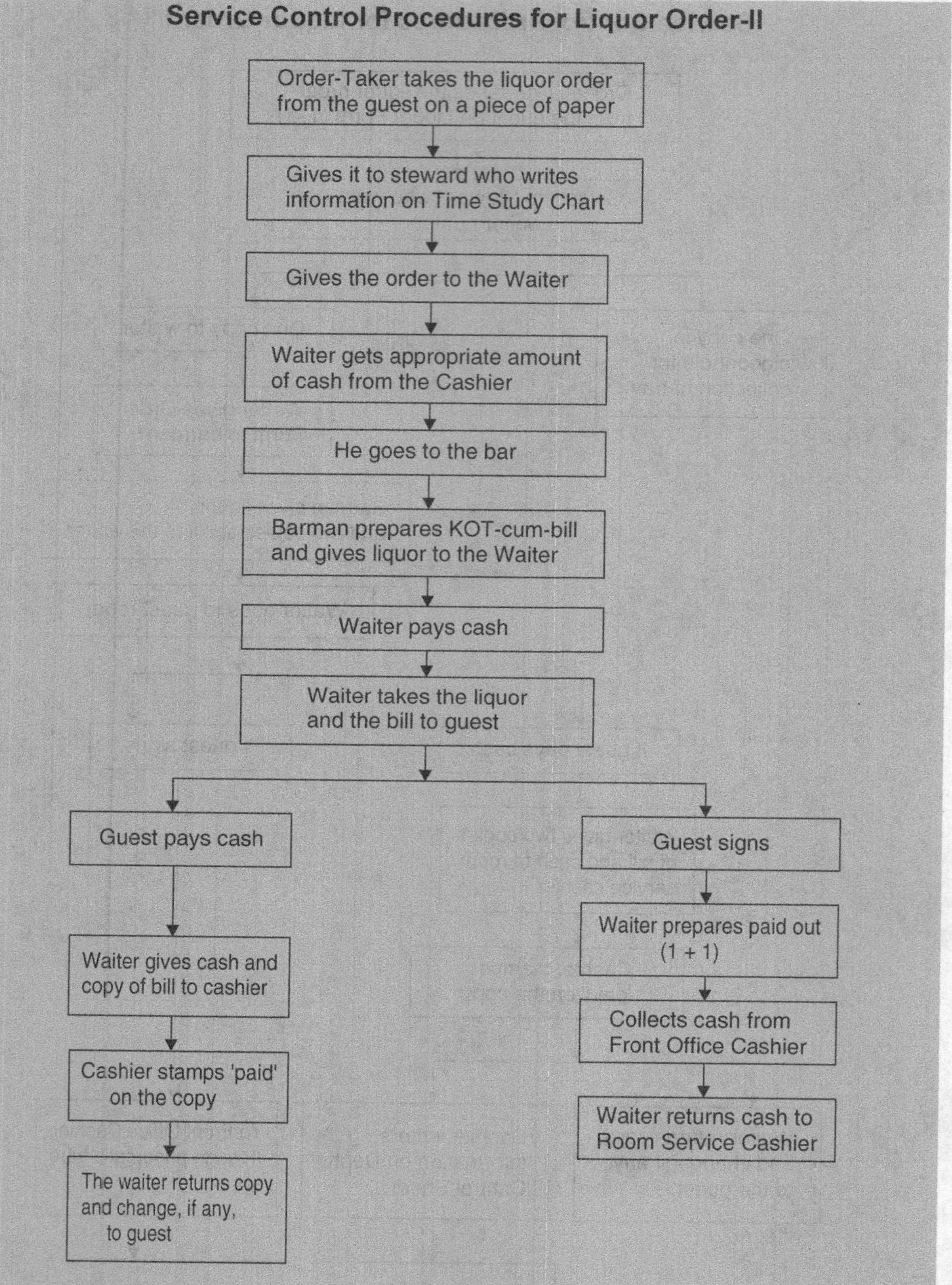

Fig. 6.41 : A Typical Room Service Control Procedures for Liquor Order-II

(*iv*) *Dry, White Wine, Light Red Wine, or Rose Wine* : May be served with all white meat poultry and light meat such as veal. Served in an all purpose wine glass.

(*v*) *Full-Bodied Red Wine* : May be served with all red meat, game, and dark meat poultry. Served in a wine wine glass.

(*vi*) *Rose Wine, Sparkling Burgundy and Champagne* : May be served with all meals and with all courses. Rose wine is served in an all purpose wine glass, sparking burgundy and champagne are served in a champagne goblet or champagne saucer.

(*vii*) *Dry Red Wine* : May be served with cheese. Serve in an all purpose wine glass.

– Wines can be served only after they have been sold. It must become a standard procedure to ask the patron after the food order has been taken, if he desires some wine. And with this question, present the wine list, or draw his attention to the wine selection on the menu.

– Once an order for wine has been taken, the server must proceed immediately to prepare for such service so that the wine may be served when it is appropriate. The proper glassware must be placed on the table immediately and the ordered wine obtained from the bar. Wine glasses, except for the port wine glasses, are always placed to the right of the water goblet.

(*viii*) *White Wine, Rose Wine, Sparkling Burgundy, and Champagnes* : Take the selected wine to the table and present it to the person who has made the choice so that he may "approve" the bottle. After approval, place the bottle into the wine bucket on stand next to the table. The wine bucket should be filled three-quarters with ice and some water, this facilitate the bottle sliding into the ice. Place napkin, folded lengthwise, over the bucket and let it stand until needed. White and rose wines may be opened just prior to serve the meal or course. Champagne and sparking burgundy may only be opened immediately after the given course or meal with which the wine is to be served has been served.

– First, serve a sip to the host to try the quality of the wine. When approved, proceed around the table serving the ladies first, then the gentlemen and last the host. Wine glasses are filled only three-quarters full and never to the rim. After serving, return bottle to the wine bucket.

(*ix*) *Red Wine* : Take the selected wine to the table and present it to the person who has made the choice so that he may approve the bottle. (When red wine is served, it must be placed into a wine basket immediately and should be moved as little as possible in order not to stir up any possible sediments.) After approval, proceed to open the bottle immediately and leave standing on the table in the wine basket. Red wine is opened immediately and left standing so that the wine may "breathe". Actually, the wine absorbs oxygen from the air, and this oxidation process activates the development of the bouquet and the aroma.

– Red wine is served at room temperature or at approximately 65 degrees. Immediately after the meal or course has been served with which the wine is to be served, proceed with the wine service in the same way as for white wine.

(x) *Opening the Wine Bottle* : First of all, provide yourself with a good corkscrew. A good corkscrew has sharp thin screw edges that bite into the cork and pull it out. A cheap corkscrew has rounded edges, and since it cannot bite into the cork, it will pull out of the hole without pulling the cork. When cork is removed, it should be placed above the set plate of the person ordering the wine or the host.

All still wines are opened exactly the same way. Place bottle on firm level support and immediately cut, not tear the tin foil around the neck of the bottle with a sharp knife, just below the protruding edge. Wipe the top of the bottle, particularly the now-exposed cork, keeping the bottle at all times in an upright position. Insert the corkscrew all the way straight into the cork as far as it will go and pull out in one smooth movement. After removal of the cork, wipe the inside of the bottle neck for any possible particles inside it. When opening champagne and sparkling burgundy, first remove all foil or tin foil around the cork and upper part of the neck of the bottle. Remove the wire holding the cork in place. Hold bottle at a 45-degree angle and proceed to push the cork out with the thumb, turning the bottle slightly. At all times, keep the bottle at the same angled position after the cork is forced out, to allow inside pressure to adjust to outside pressure. Holding the bottle at an angle, to avoid spillage of the wine, proceed to serve the same way as for a still wine.

The bar serves the customers a requested brand if it is stocked. The bartenders should know the recipe for the standard cocktails and a recipe guide for the unusual drinks. Standard measurements should be prescribed. The actual physical control of wine is in the hands of the bartender. Red wine will be available in racks while white wines and roses are stored in chilled department.

STEWARDING

The stewarding function of a hotel kitchen is essentially charged to maintain and preserve the cleanliness and condition of the china, silver, glassware, equipment and working area of the kitchen. In doing so the steward department maintains inventories and supplies of all equipment, china and silver and further, scrubs and cleans all the working surfaces and floors of the entire kitchen. Also the care of the employee's cafeteria is the charge of the steward department. This section is thus responsible for :

1. Storage and issue of cutlery, cookery, halloware to the kitchen and restaurant
2. Cleaning and washing of above items and routine maintenance of all kitchen equipment, silver plating of cutlery etc.
3. Garbage disposal and kitchen sanitation. Large deluxe hotel may require a large team for machine operation, banquet, night staff etc.

Figure 6.42 indicate s the brigade of stewarding required in large sized hotel.

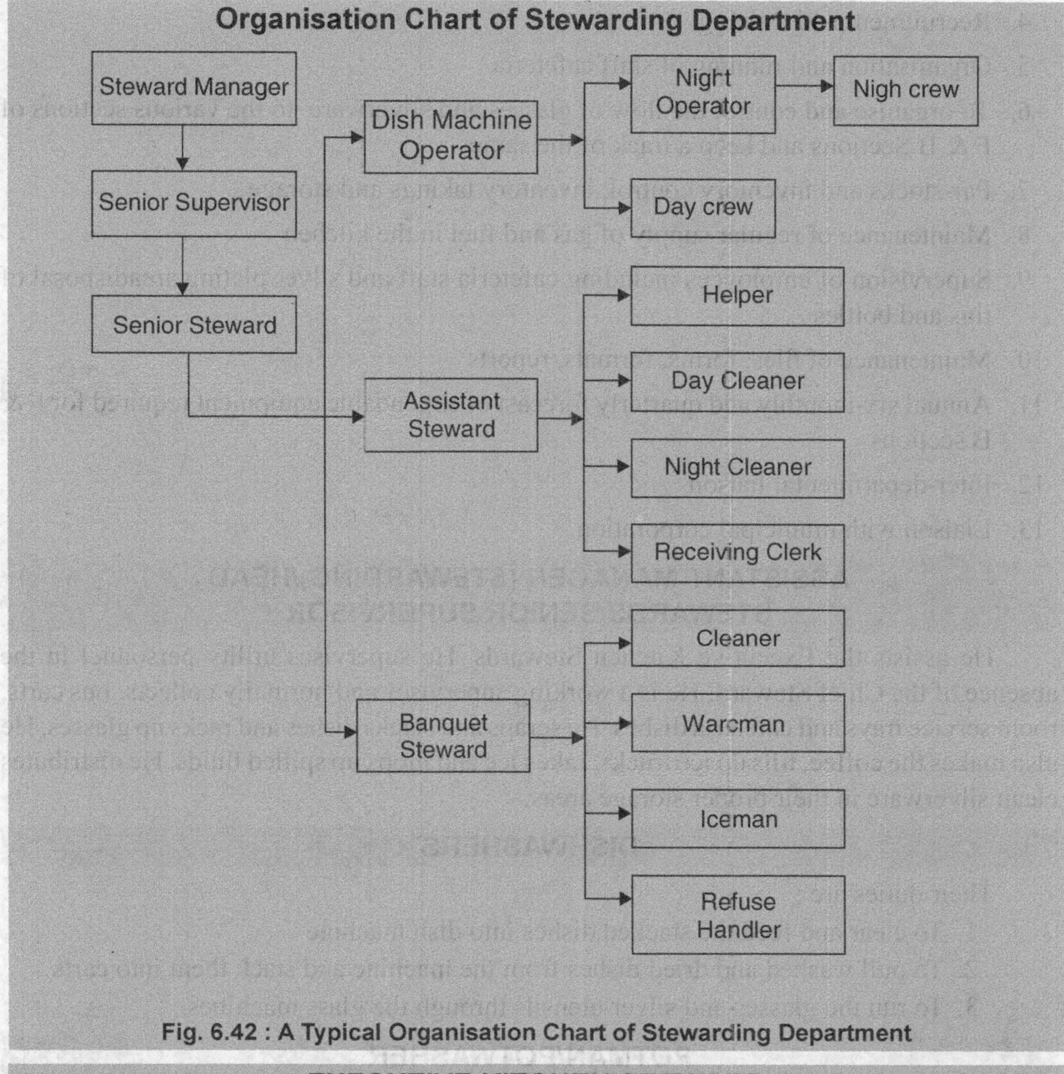

Fig. 6.42 : A Typical Organisation Chart of Stewarding Department

EXECUTIVE KITCHEN STEWARD

He is responsible for all silver, dish and glass washing and the maintenance of high standards of kitchen cleanliness. He reports directly to the Executive Chef.

EXECUTIVE KITCHEN STEWARD

He should be familiar with all kitchen and service equipment, their usage, procurement, maintenance and storage, government laws enforced by health and sanitation department. His duties and responsibilities include :

1. Preparation of schedule of sanitation programs for kitchen and other areas
2. Maintenance of cleanliness as per the standard specifications laid down by the management
3. Preventive maintenance and up-keep of kitchen machines and equipment

4. Recruitment and training
5. Organisation and running of staff cafeteria
6. To organise and control the flow of glasses and silverware to the various sections of F & B Sections and keep a track of the same
7. Par-stocks and inventory control, inventory takings and storage
8. Maintenance of regular supply of gas and fuel in the kitchen
9. Supervision of employees including cafeteria staff and silver plating areadisposal of tins and bottles
10. Maintenance of files, forms, formats, reports
11. Annual six-monthly and quarterly forecast of expendable equipment required for F & B sections
12. Inter-departmental liaison
13. Liaison with municipal corporation.

ASSISTANT MANAGER (STEWARDING)/HEAD STEWARDS/SENIOR SUPERVISOR

He assists the Executive Kitchen Stewards. He supervises utility personnel in the absence of the Chief Steward. He is a working supervisor and normally collects, bus carts, room service trays and cafeteria dishes. He scraps and stacks dishes and racks up glasses. He also makes the coffee, fills up ice trucks, rakes ice and mops up spilled fluids. He distributes clean silverware in their proper storage areas.

DISHWASHERS

Their duties are :

1. To clear and feed the stacked dishes into dish machine
2. To pull washed and dried dishes from the machine and stack them into carts
3. To run the glasses and silver utensils through the glass machines.

POTMAN/POTWASHER

He cleans all pots used by kitchen and soup kettles. During slack periods, he empties the kitchen garbage.

SILVERWARE

He clears, polishes and burnishes all silver flatware and hollow-ware. During slack periods, he clears all copperware.

SCULLERY MAN (PLONGEUR)

He is responsible for the wash up of metal kitchen vessels and implements. The kitchen scullery is known as the *plonge* and the scullery man as the *plangeur casserolier*.

NIGHT DUTY STEWARD

The peak work load occurs at different sections at different times during the work shift, therefore, the related steward in each section will pitch in and help each other out under the direction of the supervisor on duty. His main duties are :

MAIN RANGE

1. To clean thoroughly all grilled plates, trough, grease traps, edges and corners
2. To clean with oven cleaner all oven and salamanders
3. To clean steam tables, steam table stands and shelves below steam tables
4. Clean dust strong below steam tables
5. Clean shelves above steam table
6. Scrub down duck board and scrub below them.

SOUP KITCHEN

1. To clean all pots, steam kettles, large steamers and electric pots
2. To clean all fixtures and exposed pipes
3. To clean all shelves and wipe all boxes and cans and arrange neatly
4. To remove items from shelves below all work tables and remove and scrub all grill shelves
5. To wipe and polish sinks and pots of all work tables
6. To scrub floor
7. To thoroughly clean can opener.

BUTCHER SHOP

1. To dismantle and clean thoroughly the meat saw
2. To clean and protect with light coating and grease the food chopper
3. To remove and clean drawers of fish box steam inside and below the fix box
4. To scrub with soap and very hot water all other working surfaces
5. To scrape and cleanse thoroughly the chopping block and wood table
6. To remove items below tables and scrub the lower shelves thoroughly
7. To wash wall shelves and work sink thoroughly
8. To wipe refrigerator door
9. To scrub floor.

PANTRY

1. To remove and scrub duck boards
2. To scrub top of all working tables
3. To scrubs all wall shelves and shelves in all front areas
4. To wipe down coffee urns
5. To remove items from below work tables and scrubs the shelves below the table
6. To wipe down drinks and stainless steal edgings
7. To scrub floors.

FRONT OF KITCHEN

1. To scrub all stainless steel areas including shelves and egg machine
2. To thoroughly scrub floors.

GARBAGE

1. All garbage cans can be emptied and steamed out and scrubbed both inside and out
2. Garbage rooms to be cleaned and floor to be thoroughly scrubbed

BAKE SHOP

1. To clean sinks all work areas, below work tables
2. To clean stove and ovens, inside and out
3. To scrub floor
4. To clean and polish stainless steel surfaces

ICE

1. Ice is to be raked in the morning
2. All the ice troughs are to be filled in the morning.

Coordination is of great importance not only between the various service staff members but also between them and the kitchen. It requires proper layout of the kitchen, as would facilitate the systematic and easy pickup of food by the waiter/waitress. Pick up areas should be clearly defined. Entrance and exists should be paid out to establish a standard format for traffic flow. In many hotels, a buffer zone is provided between the service and preparation staff by having a side man, mostly the chef, who transmits all order to the cooks.

ACCOUNTING, AUDIT AND CONTROL

The Food and Beverage Operating Statement shows the financial performance of the food and drinks service. It includes :

1. The revenue from food and beverages
2. The cost of sales of food and beverages
3. The payroll of this department
4. Other expenses of the department such as china and glassware, cleaning supplies, decorations, guest supplies, laundry, linen, music, entertainment, menus and beverage lists, silver and uniforms. (Ref. fig. 6.44).

For the purpose of control the main operating ratios are :

1. Daily seat turnover or rate of seat occupancy
2. Average sales per seat or average sales per customer
3. Average annual restaurant occupancy.

The wages and salaries of chefs, wash up, storemen and waiters in restaurants, grill rooms or coffee shops, room service staff and staff of other food-lets such as buffet service in bars, should be included in the food department. The wages of the staff in canteens used only for employees, should be debited to administration and general.

Some of the staff such as storemen and room service staff also issue or sell beverages. Half of their salaries on the proportion of food to beverage sold should be debited to beverage department.

The cost of materials used in food production i.e., food and liquor used by the kitchen is counted in the total of food consumption.

The revenue from sales of food in any department, plus an allowance for tea and coffee making items supplied to the bedrooms should be credited to the food department.

The wages and cost of barmen, bar-wash up, bar waiters, cellarmen, wine waiters, and bar cleaners should be debited to the beverage department. If the restaurant has a wine waiter or designated beverage server, their wages should be debited to the beverage department. In the case of staff serving food and beverage, an allowance of one-third or whatever the ratio of food to beverage is, should be made to the appropriate wage bill.

The cost of all materials used in serving drinks, such as vegetables, fruits, consomme and actual liquor including soda tonic etc., is debited to the beverage department.

Food and beverage division needs constant monitoring. Food is the most difficult to control. It is essential to establish detailed controls for all aspects of food and beverages purchasing, receiving, issuing, preparation, serving and stock-taking. A food control procedure could be established as given in Figure 6.43 :

INCOME FROM FOOD AND BEVERAGES

Incomes connected with F & B can easily be identified with food and beverages. There are some incomes and expenses which are applicable to both the heads. All such joint incomes and expenses may be segregated by using a equitable method of allocation. The basis of allocation may be based on estimated percentages applied to the total amount of joint income and expense accounts. Thus separate operating results can be calculated for both food and beverages.

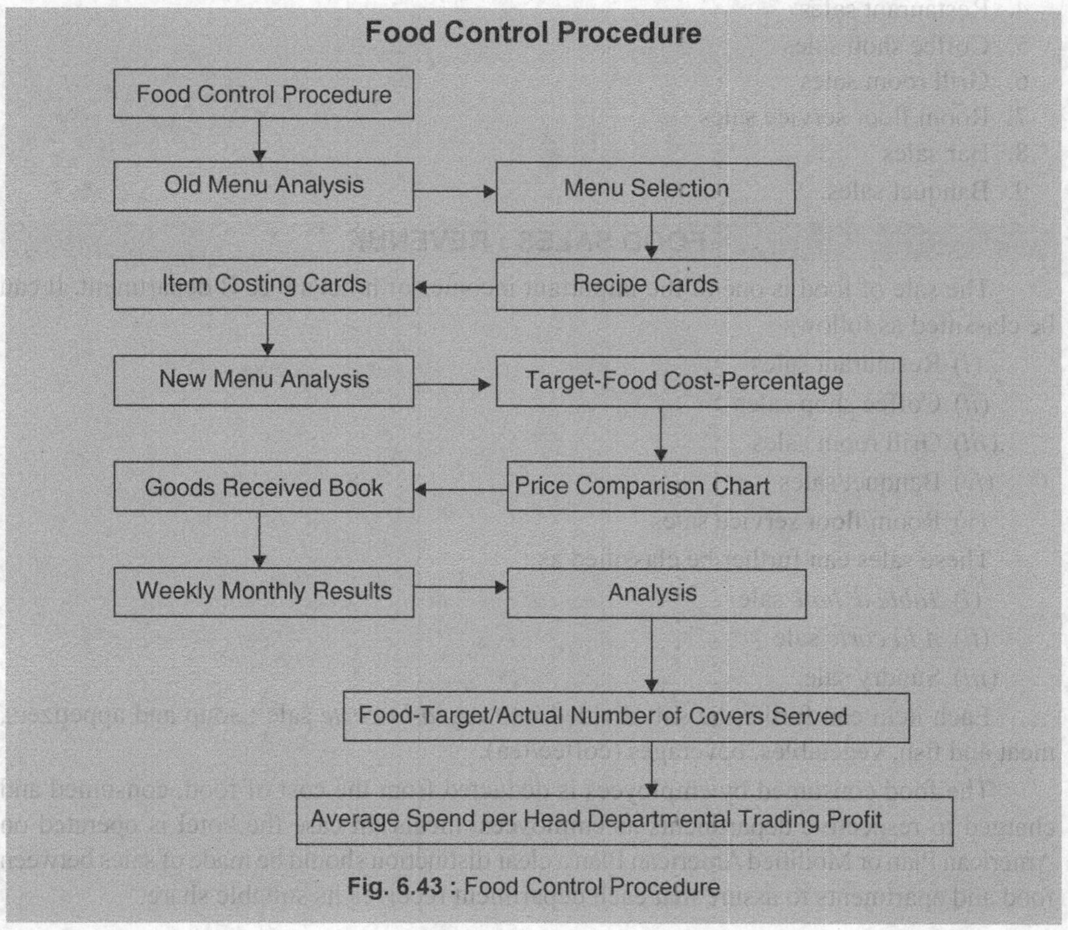

Fig. 6.43 : Food Control Procedure

The main incomes of this department can be classified as :

1. Income from Food Sale
   (*i*) Break-fast
   (*ii*) Lunch
   (*iii*) Dinner
   (*iv*) Supper
   (*v*) Food sundries.
2. Income from Beverage Sale
   (*i*) Beer
   (*ii*) Spirit
   (*iii*) Wine
   (*iv*) Liquors.
3. Other Incomes
   (*i*) Public room rentals
   (*ii*) Cover charges
   (*iii*) Sundry banquet incomes
   (*iv*) Miscellaneous incomes.

These incomes can also be divided on the basis of sales point :

4. Restaurant sales
5. Coffee shop sales
6. Grill room sales
7. Room/floor service sales
8. Bar sales
9. Banquet sales.

FOOD SALES : REVENUE

The sale of food is one of the important incomes of hotel's F & B department. It can be classified as follows :

(*i*) Restaurant sales
(*ii*) Coffee shop sales
(*iii*) Grill room sales
(*iv*) Banquet sales
(*v*) Room/floor service sales

These sales can further be classified as :

(*i*) *Table d' hote* sale
(*ii*) *A lâ carte* sale
(*iii*) Sundry sale.

Each item can further be sub-divided into e.g. *a la carte* sale : soup and appetizers, meat and fish, vegetables, beverages (coffee/tea).

The food consumed by employees is deducted from the cost of food, consumed and charged to respective departments as employees' meals. In case the hotel is operated on American Plan or Modified American Plan a clear distinction should be made of sales between food and apartments to assure that each department receives its suitable share.

All restaurant and food service establishments have the same basic functions : purchasing, receiving, storage, preparation, and services. These functions need to be systematically planned and executed otherwise any deficiency can adversely affect sales. Where food sales decline, it may be due to one or more of the following factors:-

1. Overpricing of products
2. Poor menu planning
3. Poor food quality
4. Indifferent service
5. Poor sanitation and lack of hygiene
6. Unattractive, noisy atmosphere
7. Inconvenient access
8. Inadequate or ineffective promotion.

BEVERAGE SALES : REVENUE

All beverage sales are credited to this account. The cost of beverage served on employee checks, are deducted from cost of merchandise consumed and charged to the respective department as employees' meals, entertainment etc. All beverage sales may be classified as :

1. Restaurant/dining room beverage sales.
2. Room service beverage sales
3. Banquet beverage sales
4. Public bar sales.

A detailed analysis could be made by further analysis such as :

1. Wine
2. Spirits and liquors
3. Beers
4. Mineral waters.

ALLOWANCES

Allowances allowed on beverage sales include rebates and over-charge not known at the time of sale, but adjusted at a subsequent date.

NET FOOD OR BEVERAGE SALE : NET REVENUE

It is the difference between food sales/beverage sales and allowances.

COST OF FOOD/FOOD COST

1. It includes the cost of the food served to guests. The cost of food includes :
2. Invoice price of material and provision after deduction of trade discount
3. Transport charges on material
4. Storage and delivery charges.

The cost of employees' meal is deducted from the cost of material consumed and an extra entry is passed against the respective departments whose employees are served. In large hotel the cost of employees' meal is calculated by a systematic cost system whereas in small hotels it is computed at a fixed price per meal.

BEVERAGE COST

It is debited with the cost of all merchandise consumed e.g.

1. Cost of wines, beers, liquors, mineral water, fruits syrups, sugar bitters, and other materials served or used in the preparation of mixed drinks served to both guest and employees at invoice price less trade discount
2. Import duties
3. Transportation charges
4. Storage and delivery charges
5. Taxes.

The deposit refunds and sales of bottles, barrels and other materials previously charged as a cost to this account is credited to beverage cost.

As regards to the cost of employee's beverage, the amount is debited to beverage cost and the contra entries are made in the respective department.

NET COST OF FOOD/BEVERAGE SALES

It is the difference between the cost of food/beverage and the cost of employees meal.

GROSS PROFIT ON SALES

It is the difference between the net sales and cost of sales.

OTHER INCOMES

1. **Meeting room rentals**

Incomes derived from the rental of meeting rooms used for banquets or functions involving food/beverage sales is credited to this account. Rentals of public rooms not used for food/beverage service (non-banquet) is debited to room department.

All other expenses related to payroll and other expenses applicable to this revenue should also be debited to food and beverage department.

2. **Cover charges**

It is an admission charge derived from charging a specific rate per person. It is a revenue for the hotel and is intended to defray such expenses as music and entertainment. Cover charges for bread and butter should be included in gross food sales.

3. **Sundry banquet income**

This account includes all occasional sales of goods or service made in connection with banquets. The respective music, decorations, souvenirs etc. should be credited to the food/beverage department.

4. **Miscellaneous income**

This head will include all other incomes or revenues not covered under the above heads e.g., ice service to guest room.

F & B EXPENSES

The expenses of the food and beverage department can be apportioned between food and beverages. The basis of apportionment will depend upon the nature of use of the expense item.

EMPLOYEES' REMUNERATION AND BENEFITS

Salaries and wages paid to employees in food and beverage department are debited to this account. The employees included in this group are :

1. *Maitre d' hotel*
2. Manager
3. Assistant
4. Secretary and
5. Clerk
6. Coffee shop : all employees
7. Kitchen :
   (*i*) Chefs
      (*a*) *Sous chefs*
      (*b*) Night chefs
   (*ii*) Secretaries
      (*a*) Announcers
      (*b*) Cooks
      (*c*) *Saucier*
      (*d*) Grade manager
      (*e*) Tournant
      (*f*) First commis
   (*iii*) Miscellaneous
      (*a*) Firemen
      (*b*) Utility men
      (*c*) Runners
   (*iv*) Restaurants :
      (*a*) Stewards and assistants
      (*b*) Chefs and assistants
      (*c*) Head waiters
      (*d*) Captains
      (*e*) Waiters and waitresses
   (*v*) Pantryware washing
      (*a*) Cleaning
   (*vi*) Stewarding :
      (*a*) Stewards
      (*b*) Assistant stewards
      (*c*) Kitchen stewards
      (*d*) Secretaries.
8. Bar :
   (*i*) Bartenders
   (*ii*) Public and
   (*iii*) Service bartenders

9. Banquet service :
   (*i*) Charges from other departments like cost of services of public room employees, housemen and other employees carried on payrolls of other departments but charged to banquet service.
10. Public rooms (banquets) :
   (*i*) Entertainment manager
   (*ii*) Clerks
   (*iii*) Captain
   (*iv*) Page girls
   (*v*) Ushers
   (*vi*) Parlour maids
   (*vii*) House-keeper
   (*viii*) Housemen
   (*ix*) Cleaners.
11. Food cost control :
   (*i*) Food cost accountant
      (*a*) Accountant
      (*b*) Sales analysis clerk
      (*c*) Stock budget clerk
      (*d*) Issue sheet clerk
      (*e*) Stock ledger clerk.
12. Charges from other departments :
   (*i*) Cost of services of linen seamstresses
   (*ii*) Window cleaners
   (*iii*) Night cleaners.

COST OF F & B EMPLOYEES MEALS

The account is debited with the cost of food and beverages furnished to employees included in this department.

BANQUET EXPENSES

All expenses in connection with banquets which cannot be included in other groups are debited to this account.

BAR EXPENSES

Expenses relating to the following items are included under this head :

1. Cost of bar utensils
2. Other expenses
3. Gratis food (not used in the preparation of mixed drinks)
4. Mixers
5. Shakers
6. Squeezers
7. Stainers
8. Supplies to bar
9. Cork screws
10. Openers
11. Spoons
12. Stoppers
13. Swizzle sticks.

CHINA AND GLASSWARE

The amount of expenses relating to china and glassware to be debited to this head will be based on direct issues from stores and adjusted to actual inventories at stated periods in accordance with the revaluation method. In some hotels a fixed amount is credited to a special reserve account, which is provided on as a monthly charge between inventory periods based on amount per cover or per cent of food sales determined by previous experience. All issues or purchases are debited to reserve account. The balance (debit or credit) of this account is debited or credited to the asset account which is adjusted to the actual inventory at the end of the year. The items included under this head are :

1. Food expenses
   - (*i*) Bowls
   - (*ii*) Saucers
   - (*iii*) Goblets
   - (*iv*) Compotes
   - (*v*) Trays
   - (*vi*) Plates
   - (*vii*) Drinking glasses
   - (*viii*) Coffee pots
   - (*ix*) Teapots
   - (*x*) Pitchers
   - (*xi*) Cups
   - (*xii*) Tumblers.

COST OF BEVERAGE GLASSWARE

Various types of glasses used in the serving of wines, liquors and other beverages.

CLEANING SUPPLIES

Cleaning expenses relating to food and beverage department include:

1. Acids
2. Alcohol
3. Ammonia
4. Ammonia water
5. Brass polish
6. Brooms
7. Brushes
8. Buffing compound
9. Carpet sweepers
10. Carpet washers and accessories
11. Chamois
12. Clearing fluids
13. Deodorants
14. Detergents
15. Disinfectants
16. Dust cloths
17. Dusters
18. Dustpans
19. Floor polish
20. Fumigators
21. Gasoline
22. Insecticides
22. Floor soaps
23. Floor wax
24. Fly paper
25. Fly swatters
26. Lemon oil
27. Metal polish
28. Mop handles and wranglers
29. Mops
30. Mouse traps
31. Pails
32. Paint cleaners
33. Rugs
34. Sand
35. Sand soap
36. Shot (BB)
37. Silver wash
38. Soap for cleaning
39. Soap powder
40. Soda
41. Steel wool
42. Vacuum cleaner accessories
43. Wall washers
44. Washing soap and powders
45. Window cleaners, belts and equipment.

COMMISSIONS

Commissions allowed or payment made to individual agents for receiving business for the hotel is debited to this account. The amount paid to credit card holders is not debited to this account.

CONTRACT CLEANING

In hotels where contract cleaning is done, all expenses connected with cleaning the restaurants, public rooms and pantries, washing windows in restaurants exterminating and disinfecting are debited under this head.

COST OF ACCOUNTING

Fees paid to professional accountants for supervision of cost and control accounting are debited to this account.

DECORATION

Expenses relating to following items are debited to this account :

1. **Cut flowers**
   (*i*) Ferns
   (*ii*) Palms
   (*iii*) Plants
   (*iv*) Flags and bunting used in for banquets and restaurants.
   (*v*) Artificial flowers :
   (*vi*) Fibre vases used in restaurants
   (*vii*) Gold fish in aquariums
   (*viii*) Song birds.
2. **Dry cleaning**
   The cost of the following items is debited to this account :
   (*i*) Dry cleaning of curtains, draperies, hangings, lamps shades, etc.
   (*ii*) Washing or cleaning of awnings, carpets and rugs, window shades and furniture coverings in the various restaurants and public rooms.
3. **Garage and parking**
   (*i*) Payments made by the hotel to outside garages and parking lots for parking cars of guests using the food and beverage facilities are debited to this account.
4. **Guest supplies**
   All expenses relating to the supplies furnished to guests in various restaurants is debited to this account e.g. :
   (*i*) Boutonnieres
   (*ii*) Bride scores, place cards and prizes
   (*iii*) Candy
   (*iv*) Cigarettes
   (*v*) Cigars
   (*vi*) Car sages

(*vii*) Fans (paper & straw)
(*viii*) Favours
(*ix*) Gifts to guests
(*x*) Matches
(*xi*) Newspapers
(*xii*) Souvenirs
(*xiii*) Toothpicks.

5. **Cost of ice**
   (*i*) Cost of ice purchased used and sold by the hotel is charged to this account.
6. **Kitchen fuel**
   (*i*) This account is charged with the cost of fuel and electricity used for cooking :
7. **Fuel**
   (*i*) Charcoal
   (*ii*) Coal
   (*iii*) Food warmer supplies
   (*iv*) Gas governors
   (*v*) Steam.
8. **Electricity**
   (*i*) Expenses relating to electricity where cooking and baking is done by electricity.
9. **Laundry**
   (*i*) Expenses of laundry charged to F & B outside laundries are debited to this head.
10. **Licence fee**
   (*i*) Licence fee paid to municipal bodies, state government and central government debited to F & B is debited to this account.
11. **Linen**
   (*i*) The linen expenses relating to F & B department should be based on direct issues from stores and adjusted to actual inventories at stated period at a fair value on the basis of revaluation method. In some hotels a reserve account is created by crediting a monthly charge between inventory periods based on an amount per cover or per cent of food sales determined by previous experience. All issues and purchases are charged to reserve account and any credit or debit balance of this account is debited or credited to the asset account, which is adjusted to the actual inventory at the end of the year. Items of linen included in this group are :
   (*i*) Doilies
   (*ii*) Table cloths
   (*iii*) Table tops
   (*iv*) Napkins
   (*v*) Table protectors
   (*vi*) Towels.
12. **Menus and wine lists**
   (*i*) The cost of purchased menus, bills of fare and cardboard stock and printing thereof, whether done by outside concerns or produced by the hotel's own print shop are debited to this account.
13. **Music and entertainment**
   (*i*) Films

(*ii*) Radio reception (not including maintenance of radio equipment)

(*iii*) Mechanical music

(*iv*) Piano recital

(*v*) Programs

(*vi*) Royalties

(*vii*) Tuning piano.

(*viii*) Music licence

(*ix*) Professional entertainers

(*x*) Records

(*xi*) Sheet music.

14. **Paper supplies**

(*i*) Cupboard boxes

(*ii*) Doilies

(*iii*) Foil wrapping

(*iv*) Liquid containers

(*v*) Pastry bags

(*vi*) Sippers

(*vii*) Waxed papers.

(*ix*) Chop frills

(*x*) Fibre covers

(*xi*) Holders

(*xii*) Napkins

(*xii*) Plates

(*xiv*) Souffle cups

(*xv*) Cups

(*xvi*) Filter papers

(*xvii*) Liners

(*xviii*) Narchment

(*xix*) Ramekins

(*xx*) Tortoni cups.

15. **Printing and stationery**

(*i*) Cost of printing the forms, service manual, stationery and office supplies used by food and beverage department. The stationery includes:

(*i*) Adding machine tape

(*ii*) Announcements

(*iii*) Blotters

(*iv*) Carbon paper

(*v*) Checking supplies

(*vi*) Desk pad holders

(*vii*) Ink

(*viii*) Inkwells

(*ix*) Paper clips

(*x*) Pencils

(*xi*) Pen points

(*xii*) Pins

(*xiii*) Rubber bands

(*xiv*) Signature book

(*xv*) Staples

(*xvi*) Vouchers

(*xvii*) Waiter's checks.

(*xviii*) Announcement cards (on table)

(*xix*) Binders

(*xx*) Book-(records)

(*xxi*) Charge vouchers

(*xxii*) Clips

(*xxiii*) Desk pads

(*xxiv*) Ink pads

(*xxv*) Mucilage

(*xxvi*) Paste

(*xxvii*) Pen holders

(*xxviii*) Pens

(*xxix*) Restaurant checks

(*xxx*) Rubber stamps

(*xxxi*) Stamp pads

(*xxxii*) Typewriter ribbons

(*xxxiii*) Writer books.

These items are used in the food and beverage department by the following staff :

(*i*) Beverage controllers

(*ii*) Chefs

(*iii*) Hostesses

(*iv*) Restaurant cashier

(*v*) Steward

(*vi*) Checkers

(*vii*) Food controllers

(*viii*) *Maitre d' hotel*

(*ix*) Restaurant manager

(*x*) Waiters.

SILVER

The items of silver include :

(*i*) Flatware
(*ii*) Platters
(*iii*) Trays.
(*iv*) Ladles
(*v*) Serving dishes.

The charge for silver is made on the same basis as of the linen, china and glassware.

UNIFORMS

It includes :

1. The cost of uniforms for employees of the food and beverage department
2. The cost of repairing and cleaning of uniforms
3. The cost of buttons, braid, badges, including

(*i*) Aprons
(*ii*) Blouses
(*iii*) Buttons
(*iv*) Braid
(*v*) Badges
(*vi*) Caps
(*vii*) Coats
(*viii*) Collars
(*ix*) Dresses
(*x*) Gloves
(*xi*) Shirt fronts
(*xii*) Shoes
(*xiii*) Socks
(*xiv*) Suits
(*xv*) Ties
(*xvi*) Trousers.

UTENSILS

The charge for utensils is made on the same basis as that of china, glass and silver and includes the cost of replacing and repairing tools and small equipment used in kitchen such as :

(*i*) Batter bowls
(*ii*) Veaters
(*iii*) Kettles
(*iv*) Lemon squeezers pots
(*v*) Mixing spoons
(*vi*) Pans
(*vii*) Sharpening of knives
(*viii*) Batter mixers
(*ix*) Can openers
(*x*) Kitchen knives
(*xi*) Markets
(*xii*) Molds
(*xiii*) Pots
(*xiv*) Skewers.

WINE CELLAR EXPENSES

This head includes the cost of minor equipment supplies and other expenses including the following :

(*i*) Bin card
(*ii*) Containers for mixing
(*iii*) Measuring rules
(*iv*) Small tools
(*v*) Cases
(*vi*) Corking equipment
(*vii*) Paper
(*viii*) Wire.

MISCELLANEOUS EXPENSES

All items which cannot be grouped under above head will be classified as:

MISCELLANEOUS FOOD EXPENSES

(*i*) Coffee bags
(*ii*) Food inspection
(*iii*) Garage cans
(*iv*) Laboratory costs
(*v*) Twine.
(*vi*) Employees' transportation
(*vii*) Galax leaves
(*viii*) Gas range rental
(*ix*) Rock salt.

MISCELLANEOUS BEVERAGE EXPENSES

(*i*) Employees' transportation
(*ii*) Sawdust
(*iii*) Warehouse costs.
(*iv*) Laboratory costs
(*v*) Signs.

Abc Hotels Ltd.
Food And Beverages Schedule

	Current period		
REVENUE	Total	Food	Beverages
Restaurants	₹	₹	₹
Grill	....	....	....
Cafe	....	....	....
Room Service	....	....	....
Bar	....	....	....
Banquets			
Total Gross Sales	₹	₹	₹ ....
ALLOWANCES			
NET REVENUE	₹...........	₹	₹..........
Cost of Food and Beverage Sales	....	....	....
Cost of Food and Beverages	....		
Consumed	₹.........	₹	₹..........
Less Cost of Employees' Meal			
Net Cost of Food Sales			
and Beverage	₹	₹...........	₹ ....
GROSS PROFIT ON SALES	₹	₹	₹ ....
OTHER INCOMES			
Meeting Room Rental	....	....	....
Miscellaneous Banquet Income - Net	....	....	....
Cover Charges	....	....	....
Miscellaneous Other Incomes	....	....	....
Other Cost of Sales	....	....	....
Other Income	....	....	....

(*Contd.*)

GROSS PROFIT (LOSS)	₹	₹	₹ ....
EXPENSES	₹	₹	₹ ....
Salaries and Wages			
Employees' Meals			
Employee Benefits			
Total Payroll & Related Expenses	₹	₹	₹ ....
Other Expenses	₹	₹	₹ ....
Bar Expenses			
China and Glassware, Silver and Linen	....	....	....
Cleaning Supplies	....	....	....
Commission	....	....	....
Contract Cleaning			
Cost Accounting	....	....	....
Decorations	....	....	....
Dry Cleaning	....	....	....
Garage and Parking	....	....	....
Guest Supplies	....	....	....
Ice	....	....	....
Kitchen Fuel	....	....	....
Licences	....	....	....
Laundry and Drycleaning	....	....	....
Linen	....	....	....
Menus & Beverage Lists	....	....	....
Miscellaneous	....	....	....
Music and Entertainment	....	....	....
Paper Supplies	....	....	....
Printing and Stationery	....	....	....
Silver	....	....	....
Uniforms			
Utensils			....
Wine Cellar Expenses	....	....	
Total Other Expenses	₹	₹	₹ ....
TOTAL EXPENSES	₹	₹	₹ ....
DEPARTMENTAL INCOME (LOSS)	₹	₹	₹ ....

NOTE : Various arrangements of additional columns for comparisons and percentages could be added.

Fig. 6.44 : Analysis of Income and Expenses of Food and Beverages

QUESTIONS AND ASSIGNMENTS

FOOD PRODUCTION

1. What do you understand by production management and its functions ? What are the various techniques which may be used for improving productivity for efficient production management? *(DTHM)*
2. Should a hotel have one kitchen to cook all meals for the whole hotel ? Or should you have several kitchens, specialising in one way or another ? If they specialise, on what basis ? *(MTA)*
3. The person who controls the hot plate at service time is known as the
   (*a*) *Abouyer*
   (*b*) *Chef de rang*
   (*c*) *Chef de partie*
   (*d*) *Trancheuer.*
4. In about 200-words explain the necessity for close cooperation between the Food and Beverage dept. as the other operating departments of a hotel.
5. Write notes on (any Four) :
   (*a*) *Chef-de Cuisine*
   (*b*) Brochure Writing
   (*c*) Bell Captain
   (*d*) Guest Registration Form
   (*e*) Interior Decoration
   (*f*) Courses of Menu
   (*g*) Storage of Food. *(PGDT&HM)*
6. Write notes on :
   (*a*) Motels
   (*b*) Front Office
   (*c*) *Chef-de Cuisine*
   (*d*) Menu *(PGDT)*
7. "Vitamins are not so important for the growth of the body." Do you agree and why ? *(PGDT)*
8. Describe the duties and responsibilities of an Executive Chef in a deluxe hotel. *(PGDH&TM)*
9. What do you understand by food production? Suggest an organisational chart of a food production department in a medium sized luxury hotel having 300-rooms and being run on MAP terms. *(PGDT)*
10. Explain the following terms :
    (*a*) *Maitre d'hotel*
    (*b*) *Chef de cuisine*
    (*c*) *Sous Chef*
    (*d*) *Sommelier*
    (*e*) *Chef-d-rang.* *(MTA)*
11. What do you understand by the term 'main kitchen' and 'Satellite kitchen' ? What factors should be kept in mind while planning a kitchen. *(DTHM)*

12. Give a kitchen organisation chart of a 5-star deluxe hotel. Discuss the duties and responsibilities of the Executive Chef. (*MTA*)
13. Write notes on (any *four*) :
    (*a*) *Chef-de-Cuisine*
    (*b*) Brochure Writing
    (*c*) Bell Captain
    (*d*) Guest Registration Form
    (*e*) Interior Decoration
    (*f*) Courses of Menu
    (*g*) Storage of Food. (*PGDT&HM*)
14. Neatly draw a kitchen organisation chart of a continental kitchen located in a five star hotel. Describe the duties and responsibilities of the Executive Chef.
15. Should a hotel have one kitchen to cook all meals for the whole hotel ? Or should have several kitchens, specializing in one way or another ? If they specialize on what basis ?
16. Plan a menu for a college hostel of 250-students concern the following factors:
    (*a*) Allowance of ₹ 4.50 for breakfast, ₹ 6.50 for lunch and dinner each
    (*b*) The griddle plate and the puffer are not functioning.
    (*c*) 30% of the sandwitches are foreigners
    State any other factors you have taken into account while planning the menu. (*IHM*)
17. Compare and contrast the cuisines of north and south India in relation to
    (*a*) Staple Foods
    (*b*) Dietary Habit
    (*c*) Geographic Influence
    (*d*) Equipment
    (*e*) Religious Sentiments.
18. With the help of a flow chart highlight the operational features of a flight kitchen operation. (*IHMs*)
19. Write short notes on (any three):
    (*a*) Micro-wave Cooking
    (*b*) Hyderabadi Cuisine
    (*c*) Convenience Foods
    (*d*) Gujrati Snacks (*IHMs*)
20. (*a*) 'Today's Indian cuisine is a result of continues blending of different cultures over the centuries'. Discuss.
    (*b*) Both speciality restaurants and coffee shops cater to varied heads of the guests but they are completely different to their operational modes and methods. How and why ?
21. Kitchen stewarding is a major supporting section of the F & B force. Elucidate.
22. Compare the cuisine of Punjab with Bangalore, Tamil Nadu with Kashmir. Limit your answer within 250-words. In three or four lines each, explain *any five* of the following:
    (*a*) Hollandaise
    (*b*) Sorbet
    (*c*) EPNS
    (*d*) Garnish
    (*e*) Canape
    (*f*) K.O.T.

(*g*) Gueridon

(*h*) Baize.

23. In two or three lines each list the differences (*five*)

(*a*) Huitre and Escargot

(*b*) Yoghurt and Lassi

(*c*) Chef de rang and Chef de vin

(*d*) Still Room and Ante Room

(*e*) Scotch Broth Scotch Egg.

(*f*) Furniture and Fixture

(*g*) Petits pains and petit fours

(*h*) Buffet and Gueridon.

24. Describe briefly the duties and responsibilities of the Chef Grade Manger. (*IHMs*)

25. Describe the various type of sandwiches. Explain the different components of sandwiches. (*IHMs*)

26. Larger kitchen may be countered to be the 'Heart' of kitchen. How would you substantiate? (*IHMs*)

27. What are the essentials of a Lader kitchen and what are the various functions and responsibilities of a good grade manger chef ? (*IHMs*)

28. What are the various utensils used in a Chinese kitchen and write a short notes on Szechwan style of cooking ? (*IHMs*)

29. Give the standard purchase specification for the following :

(*i*) Mutton Leg (for curry cuts)

(*ii*) Whole fish (for fillet and space by the fish you choose)

(*iii*) Cauliflower

(*iv*) Sweet Lime

(*v*) Milk (cow).

30. Describe the following on few lines and mention the state/region it comes from:

(*i*) Oandhiu

(*ii*) Srikand

(*iii*) Sandesh

(*iv*) Errussery

(*v*) Dhokla

(*vi*) Lapsi

(*vii*) Thepla

(*viii*) Double ka meetha

(*ix*) Bepinea

(*x*) Kala Jamun. (*IHMs*)

31. Differentiate between :

(*i*) Shami Kabab and Shikarpur

(*ii*) Naan and Kulcha

(*iii*) Phirnee and Gille Firdose

(*iv*) Boti Kabab and Chelo Kabab

(*v*) Kalji and Rabri

(*vi*) Soup and Shorba.

32. Describe briefly 'Maharashtra cuisine' revision, it various regimes eating habits and festivals. (*IHMs*)

33. Give the recipe of the following (*any two*):

(*a*) Mohan Thal

(*b*) Gulab Jamun

(*c*) Jhangeri. (*IHMs*)

34. As a chef how could you utilise the following left-over from banquet function:

(*a*) Mughlai Paneer

(*b*) Potato Bhajee

(*c*) Mixed Vegetable Jhalfrezi

(*d*) Tandoor Chicken

(*e*) Boti Kabab. (*IHMs*)

35. Describe briefly in not more than 200-words:

(*a*) Vegetarian Food

(*b*) Microwave Cookery (*IHMs*)

36. Describe in one line each of the following:

(*a*) Rasmalai

(*b*) Chicken Chetlinad

(*c*) Tomato Shorba

(*d*) Shikarpoori Kabab

(*e*) Kulf

(*f*) Muttan Biryani

(*g*) Missi Roti

(*h*) Dhokla

(*i*) Samosa

(*j*) Kala Jamun. (*IHMs*)

37. Define soups.

38. Clarify soups with appropriate examples.

39. (*a*) Discuss the components of sauce.

(*b*) Explain the mother sauces with two derivatives of each.

40. Give the recipe for preparing one dozen bread rolls. Explain the role of each ingredient.

41. List and explain briefly:

(*a*) Cuts of fishes

(*b*) Cuts of vegetables.

42. Discuss the role of gelatin for cookery and bakery products. Differentiate between:

(*a*) Short crust pastry and flaky pastry.

(*b*) Fritter batter and Savarin batter.

43. Draw a kitchen organisation chart for a five star hotel. Describe the duties and responsibilities of chef 'saucier'.

44. List the basic stocks and their elements.

45. List the ingredients and the method to prepare a 'consomme'.

46. Give the recipe for one litre of brown stock.

47. Define the cheese, and

(*a*) Describe how cheese is manufactured

(*b*) Classify cheese giving two examples of each.

48. (*a*) Classify fish listing two examples of each

(*b*) List the cuts of fish

(*c*) How would you select, store and cook shell fish.

49. Write short notes on (*any five*):

(*i*) Marbling in meat

(*ii*) Thickening agents

(*iii*) Moist methods of cooking

(*iv*) Structure of an egg

(*v*) Laminated pastries

(*vi*) Emulsion sauces

(*vii*) Raising agents.

50. (*a*) Give the recipe to prepare one batch of bread rolls.

(*b*) Explain the role of each ingredient in the above recipe.

51. (*a*) With the help of a neat diagram explain the cuts of lamb stating the use of each.

(*b*) What do you understand by 'quality' in meats.

52. Draw a kitchen organisation chart of a medium sized hotel. Discuss the duties and responsibilities of the Executive Chef.

53. Define sauces. Give the elements of sauces. Classify sauces with appropriate examples.

54. Classify vegetables.

55. Draw organisation chart of a classic kitchen brigade. List the duties of Chef Patissier.

56. How do you preserve the colour of vegetables while cooking? Illustrate and explain the cuts of vegetables.

57. What are the various cuts of fish. How do you select and store the same. What are the different methods of cooking fish? Give examples of each.

58. Write short notes on (*any two*):

(*a*) Salad dressing

(*b*) Stages in cheese processing

(*c*) Kitchen equipment.

59. Neatly draw an organisation chart of kitchen located in a five star hotel. Describe the duties and responsibilities of *Chef Saucier* and *Chef Patissier*.

60. How would you select the following nd what precautions will you take while cooking them.

(*i*) Potatoes

(*ii*) Spinach

(*iii*) Green peas

(*iv*) Fresh mushroom

(*v*) Beet root

(*vi*) Parsley.

61. List the different cuts of fish. How would you select, store and cook shell fish?

62. (*a*) Chinese food is said to be a 'Healthy Cuisine'. Justify in about 100-words whether or not you agree with this statement.

(*b*) Contrary to conventional cooking methods, the Chinese have a more elaborate classification. Define in one or two lines ten methods of cooking that the Chinese employ.

63. (*a*) The Larder or Garde Manger is one of the more important departments of a well organized kitchen. Briefly outline the different sections and what work is carried out in each.

(*b*) Explain the following Larder terms: (*any five*)

(1) En papillote	(5) Darne	(9) Cloute
(2) Chapelure	(6) Tammy	(10) Foie gas
(3) Fricadelles	(7) Gepinett	
(4) Farce.	(8) Fumet	

64. Explain the following:

(*i*) an gratin	(*ix*) sabayon
(*ii*) blanch	(*x*) beignets
(*iii*) cro quettes	(*xi*) minepoix
(*iv*) liason	(*xii*) zest
(*v*) cocotte	(*xiii*) aspic
(*vi*) diane	(*xiv*) famet
(*vii*) estouffade	(*xv*) mousse.
(*viii*) meat glaze	

(*IHMs*)

65. Lay the diagram of cuts of lamb. State the uses of each. (*IHMs*)

66. Explain the salient differences between : (*any five*)

(*i*) Pate and Terrine
(*ii*) Open Sandwich & Zakuski
(*iii*) Bombe & Coupe
(*iv*) Aspic & Gelee
(*v*) Galantine & Ballottine
(*vi*) Saltillage & Pastillage
(*vii*) Zampone & Mortadella.

67. Modern food trends reveal a growing consciousness of the need and importance of health food, especially salads. Plan a salad Bar Menu for a 'A' grade restaurant to promote their lunch sales. Explain briefly your choice of items and draw a rough sketch (not to scale) of the layout of the counter.

68. You have been invited as a Guest Chef on a luxury Cruise Liner to promote Indian Cuisine. Plan a 5-Course plated menu which will reflect the variety and diversity of our cuisine. Give a brief description of each course and its presentation. Bear in mind the following points:

(*a*) All passengers are foreigners;
(*b*) Limited space in the galley;
(*c*) No live fires are allowed on board - all equipment is electric; and
(*d*) Food costs is not a limiting factor.

69. Answer the following in one or two lines only:

(*a*) Name three stuffed pastas.
(*b*) What is 'docking' ?
(*c*) What is an icing comb ?
(*d*) What is a carbonnade ?
(*e*) What is barding ?
(*f*) What is Haggis ?
(*g*) What is overrun ?
(*h*) What is oven spring ?

(*i*) What is gum paste ?

(*j*) What is rigor mortis ?

70. Besides basic meats and fat, various additives are used in production of charcuterie goods. List the various additives and the role that they play.

71. 'Curing' and 'brining' are established methods of preservation. Explain each one, the process involved and the advantages.

72. (*a*) What are standard purchase specification ? How do they contribute towards :

(*i*) Standardisation

(*ii*) Food Cost Control

(*iii*) Guest Satisfaction.

(*b*) What signs would you look for to indicate high quality products in the following items:

(*i*) Mutton Chops (for Gravies)

(*ii*) Indian Spring Chicken (for Tandoor)

(*iii*) Margarine (for Bakery)

(*iv*) Apples (For Fruit Baskets)

(*v*) Prawns (For Seafood Platter).

73. What are the external and internal faults you could find in a loaf of bread and what are they due to ?

74. (*a*) Describe briefly the duties and responsibilities of the "Chef Garde Manger".

(*b*) Explain the following larder terms :

(1) Cornichon

(2) Chippolato

(3) Bouchee

(4) Vol-au-vent

(5) Lardoons

(6) Crepinette

(7) Centre fillet

(8) Cloute

(9) Ramekins

(10) Tammy. (*IHMs*)

75. For a cuisine so varied and extensive, the equipment, used in Chinese cuisine is very basic and simple. List and briefly describe the various equipment used in Chinese cookery. (*IHMs*)

76. Discuss the different regional styles of cooking which dominate Chinese cuisine. (*IHMs*)

77. Write short notes on (*any two*) :

(1) Sandwiches

(2) Icecream

(3) Cures & Brines (*IHMs*)

78. Give salient differences between :

(1) Aspic & Gelee

(2) Larding & Barding

(3) Mousse & Mousseline

(4) Ham & Gammon

(5) Zakuski & Canapes. (*IHMs*)

79. (*a*) List and explain the role of various additives used in charcuterie

(*b*) Give reasons for the following faults often observed in bread.

(*i*) Lack of volume

(*ii*) Excess crust colour

(*iii*) Corres, seams and streaks

(*iv*) Crumbly texture

(*v*) Tunnels in the loaf.

80. (*a*) Complete the following chart with reference to vegetable cookery: (*IHMs*)

Colour	*Pigment*	*Effect of Acid on Cooking*	*Effect of Alkali on Cooking*
White	....	....	....
Green	....	....	....
Yellow	....	....	....
Orange	....	....	....
Purple	....	....	....

(*b*) Discuss briefly the steps involved and the equipment you would require to prepare an Ice Soccle. (*IHMs*)

81. (*a*) What are the essentials of Larder Control?

(*b*) Explain the contribution of the Garde Manger to the success of a buffet of a five star hotel with suitable examples. (*IHMs*)

82. How would you practically go about standardising recipies in a running establishment where it is needed ? (*IHMs*)

83. (*a*) Draw the organisation chart for a three star hotel Kitchen.

(*b*) Discuss the duties and responsibilities of Chef Garde Manger. (*IHMs*)

84. (*a*) Draw an organisation chart of an Indian kitchen serving lunch and dinner. The kitchen is attached to a restaurant having 100-covers.

(*b*) Suggest the number. of people required at each level.

(*c*) Describe the duties and responsibilities of the Executive Chef. (*IHMs*)

85. What are the factors that influence the food habits of people ? Outline the traditions, uniqueness, and service of Bengali Cuisine. List five speciality dishes of the region and describe them briefly. (*IHMs*)

86. What do you understand by the term "Indenting" ? Explain the various factors that affect indenting. (*IHMs*)

87. (*a*) What are the factors that need to be considered while selecting equipment for a kitchen. (*IHMs*)

88. What are the characteristics of snacks ? Name 4-snacks each from the four regions of India giving brief description of each. (*IHMs*)

89. Explain the various reasons for the limited use of convenience foods in Indian mass catering establishments. Name five companies manufacturing convenience foods in India. (*IHMs*)

90. Compare the cuisine of Punjab with Bengal or Tamilnadu with Kashmir. Limit your answer within 250-words (*IHMs*)

91. Give appropriate accompaniments for *any five* of the following :

(*a*) Poisson Colbert

(*b*) Huitre

(*c*) Dindon Roti

(*d*) Mutton Curry

(*e*) Cream of Tomato

(*f*) Chicken Maryland

(*g*) Coffee (after Dinner)

(*h*) Stilton. (*IHMs*)

92. (*a*) Draw an organisational chart of an Indian kitchen serving lunch and dinner. The kitchen is attached to a restaurant having 100-covers

(*b*) Suggest member of people required at each level.

(*c*) Describe the duties and responsibilities of the Executive Chef. (*IHMs*)

93. Explain between stewarding along with the importance of the department and mention duties and responsibilities of the manager of the kitchen stewarding department. *(IHMs)*

94. List reasons why standard yield, standard portions, and standard recipes are important for the success of a restaurant in a five star hotel. *(IHMs)*

OBJECTIVE TYPE QUESTIONS

95. Match the columns 'A' with state they come from:

A	B
(*a*) Machel Jhol	(*i*) Rajasthan
(*b*) Bagaru Baigan	(*ii*) Kashemerie
(*c*) Dal Batti Kurma	(*iii*) Goa
(*d*) Tabaq-Maz	(*iv*) Gujarat
(*e*) Sorpotel	(*v*) Maharashtra
(*f*) Avial	(*vi*) Bengal
(*g*) Osaman	(*vii*) Punjab
(*h*) Amti	(*viii*) Andhra
(*i*) Makkai ki Roti	(*ix*) Tamil Nadu
(*j*) Bisi-Belo Hulliana	(*x*) Karnataka.

(IHMs)

96. Fill in the blanks (form the choice ven after each)

(*a*) Carte du juor is a .... (speciality item, day, menu, restaurant trolley).

(*b*) Plat room is the place for .... (electroplating of cutlery, storing crockery, staff dinning).

(*c*) Bell boy is a member of the .... staff (Bell desk, conducted tour, restaurant).

(*d*) The size of a guest's serviette is approximately .... cm.sq. (32,50,62).

(*e*) .... is a stew of white meat (Blanquette, Barquette, Bisque).

(*f*) .... sauce is the accompaniment for roast lamb (apple, cranberry, mint).

(*g*) The capacity of a demitasse is .... cl. (12, 8, 10).

(*h*) .... is a type of melon (panieer, cantaloupe, potiron).

(*i*) Dhansak is a speciality .... dish (Parsi, Bengali, Punjabi).

(*j*) Sommelier is the .... waiter (trolley, wine, station).

97. Fill in the blanks:

(*i*) The Indian name for onion seed is ....

(*ii*) The area where food is stored on board the air craft is called ....

(*iii*) .... oil predominates Bengali cuisine.

(*iv*) Kashmiri banquet is called ....

(*v*) Goan cuisine has a domain of .... and ....

(*vi*) Gujrati snacks are also known as ....

(*vii*) Kakori kebabs originating from a small town near ....

(*viii*) .... and .... are two common Bengali mithais. *(IHMs)*

98. Fill in the blanks:

(*a*) .... is a safron flavoured rice cooked in cream and butter.

(*b*) .... is a fried bread in carbon flavoured sweet milk.

(*c*) Fish covered with masala and wrapped on a banana leaf is called ....

(*d*) Thepla belongs to .... cuisine.
(*e*) Staple food if Punjab is ....
(*f*) A Kashmiri banquet is called ....
(*g*) The main ingredients in Jhangiri are .... and ....
(*h*) Sarpotel is prepared from ....
(*i*) Heat in microwave to produce by the .... molecule.
(*j*) The formula for food cost % is .... (*IHMs*)

99. State whether 'True' or 'False':

(*a*) Sugar strengthens the cellulose in cooking fruits and vegetables.
(*b*) Red vegetables are covered to retain red colours.
(*c*) Baking powder and yeast are chemical leavening agents.
(*d*) Anti-pasta are well known Italian pastas.
(*e*) Fat in meat makes an important contribution to flavour.
(*f*) Hard boiled eggs are cooked for five minutes.
(*g*) A cut of fish on the bone is referred to as darne.
(*h*) Seventy percent of wheat grain consists of endosperm.
(*i*) Vinegar helps in coagulation while poaching eggs.

100. Fill in the blank (*answer any ten*)

(*a*) Braising is a combination of .... and ....
(*b*) Tomato contains .... pigment.
(*c*) Emulsified sauces are made with the base of .... and ....
(*d*) .... is found in green vegetables which is destroyed by the presence of ....
(*e*) The accompaniments for minesterone soup are .... and ....
(*f*) Chocolate eclairs are the derivatives of ....
(*g*) Fond de cuisine means ....
(*h*) Bolognaise is the mixture of .... and ....
(*i*) Consomme celestine has a garnish of ....
(*j*) Sauce mayionise + gherkins + shallots + parsley is = to sauce ....
(*k*) The traditional accompaniments poisson is ....
(*l*) A conical strainer is also called a ....
(*m*) Gluten contains .... and .... protein.

101. Fill in the blanks:

(*a*) Spinach *hors d'oeuvres* are also called ....
(*b*) Italian *hors d'oeuvre* varies are also referred to as ....
(*c*) .... is a cold soup from the Andalusian region of Spain.
(*d*) .... is the Belgian equivalent of Bouillabaisse.
(*e*) .... is an example of an Italian blue veined cheese.
(*f*) Sauce Aurore = ... + Fish veloute.
(*g*) Hollandaise + Tomato Puree = Sauce ....
(*h*) Sauce maltaise = ... + orange juice.
(*i*) Sauce Bigarde = Demi glace + ...
(*j*) Sauce Bercy could be a derivative of sauce Espagnole or Sauce ....

102. (*a*) Give correct baking temperatures for the following :

(*i*) Bread loaf
(*ii*) Puff Pastry
(*vi*) Fruit Cake
(*vii*) Sponge Cake

(*iii*) Jam Tarts
(*iv*) French Bread
(*v*) Croissants
(*viii*) Choux Pastry
(*ix*) Bread rolls
(*x*) Macaroons.

(*b*) Give acceptable standards for high quality products of the following :

(*i*) Caramel custard
(*ii*) Quiche Lorraine
(*iii*) Consomme.
(*iv*) French fries
(*v*) Swiss Roll.

(*IHMs*)

FOOD AND BEVERAGE SERVICE

1. You are required to cater for a wedding buffet for 250–300 pax at ₹ 150-per head (inclusive). Plan an Indian menu giving the recipe for any one vegetarian dish. (*DTHM*)

2. With the help of a flowchart explain the role of KOT in controlling sales in the Food and Beverage Department of a five-star hotel. (*DTHM*)

3. Every category of room service personnel have an important role to play in providing personalised service, bringing about guest satisfaction and achieving sales targets. Discuss in about 250-words. (*DTHM*)

4. How is the food sale of a restaurant attached to a large hotel recorded ? Explain clearly with the help of diagrams. (*IHMs*)

5. An effective control system is necessary for maximising food and beverage sales. How do K OTs contribute in achieving this end ? (*IHMs*)

6. The F and B Deptt. is one of the most important revenue producing department of the hotel. Draw an external chart of the F and B Deptt. of a Five Star Hotel and explain the importance of line and lateral relationship with in the deptt. in about 200–250 words.

7. As a person working in the F of B Deptt., how important do you think it is to maintain a good liaison between the other departments and why ? Explain your reasons in about 250-words.

8. Taking into account that 50% of the clientele are Indians plan a suitable break-fast menu which is to be utilised both for the coffee shop and room service.

9. Classify catering establishment as per the main branches of the industry giving appropriate example and the salient feature of each type.

10. With the help of a flow chart illustrate the control cycle in a restaurant using the duplicate checking system.

11. In a 5-star hotel the F & B deptt. has several food service areas. In about 4 – 5 lines each describe the type of operation that exist in these areas.

12. Human resource is a major component of any major hotel and a large part of this resources is utilized in the F& B Dept. Justify this with the help of a chart and support with appropriate explanations.

13. Explain the staff organisation and function in a food and bererage department. Give a organisation chart for 300-room hotel. (*PGDT&HM*)

14. Differentiate between :

(*a*) Counter Service and Gueridon Service

(*b*) Mis en place and Mis en scene

(*c*) Hotel and Motel

(*d*) American Plan and European Plan. (*MTM*)

15. The Food and Beverage Department is one of the most important revenue producing department of a hotel. Draw an organisational chart of the Food and Beverage Department of a five-star hotel and explain the importance of line and literal relationship within the department in about 200-250-words. (*MTM*)

16. Write note on :

(*a*) Courses

(*b*) Executive Housekeeper

(*c*) Chef-de Cuisine

(*d*) Type of Menu. (*PGDT*)

17. Writes notes on :

(*a*) Food and Beverage Deptt.

(*b*) Supplementary Accommodation. (*PGDT*)

18. Explain the organisation and management of a restaurant. What are the prospect of a restaurant business in a tourist centre like Nainital ? (*PGDT*)

19. Writes notes on **any three** of the following :

(*a*) Compilation and Display of Menu

(*b*) Methods of Purchasing for Stores

(*c*) Maintenance of Stores in Hotels

(*d*) Youth Hostels.

(*e*) Maintenance of internal and external Hygiene for Hotels. (*PGDT&HM*)

20. Explain the importance of staff organisation and structure in a Food and Beverage Department. Give a suitable organisation chart for a 350-room hotel with modern facilities. (*PGDT&HM*)

21. Define the term 'Catering'. Explain the activities involved in catering services. What are the requirements of a good catering services in a hotel of an international importance? (*PGDT&HM*)

22. Write notes on any two of the following :

(*a*) Menu planning

(*b*) Classification of alcoholic beverages

(*c*) Chef-de-cuisine

(*d*) Star ranking of hotels. (*PGDT&HM*)

23. (*a*) "Catering has no important place in the development of tourism." Comment.

(*b*) Describe the organisational chart of a restaurant in a place like Almora. (*PGDT*)

24. What is K.O.T. ? Suggest proper form of it and describe the utility of K.O.T. in the proper control of a restaurant. (*PGDT*)

25. Write short notes on any four of the following :

(*a*) Visitor's Card Index

(*b*) Bell Captain

(*c*) Pentry

(*d*) *A'Lá'Carte* and *Table-de-hôte*

(*e*) Cigar

(*f*) Kumaon Mandal Vikas Nigam. (*PGT&TM*)

26. Describe the duties and responsibilities of a Food and Beverage Manager in a hotel. (*PGH&TM*)

27. What do you understand by Food and Beverage Service ? Explain the different functions and irresponsibilities entrusted to this section of the hotel. (*PGT&HM*)

28. Writes notes on (any three) :
(*i*) Menu Planning
(*ii*) Buffet Caterings
(*iii*) Interior Decoration
(*iv*) Guest Weekly Bill
(*v*) Hotel Health and Hygiene. *(PGH&TM)*

29. Explain the following :
(*a*) Youth Hostels
(*b*) Hotel Garni
(*c*) Camping sites
(*d*) Resorts
(*e*) Food and Beverage Service. *(PGDH&TM)*

30. Briefly describe the organisation and management of a restaurant in a medium-size hotel. What are the main functions of a restaurant operating in a hotel ? *(PGDT)*

31. Write notes on the following:
(*a*) KOT
(*b*) Pantry
(*c*) Information Rack
(*d*) Lobby Manager
(*e*) Vitamin Deficiency *(PGDT)*

32. Differentiate between the following:
(*a*) *à lâ carte* and table *de-hôtel*
(*b*) Hotel and Motel
(*c*) American Plan and European Plan
(*d*) Food Service and Beverage Service.

33. Writes notes on :
(*a*) Courses
(*b*) Executive House Keeper
(*c*) Chef-de-Cuisine
(*d*) Type of Menu. *(PGDT)*

34. Draw a stepwise buffet catering plan for a marriage dinner for estimated 500 ± 50 guests invited in your hotel. Other requirements: time 8.00 p.m.; vegetarian as well as non-vegetarian food; no hard drinks. *(PGDT&HM)*

35. 'Menu planning is an art as well as a science'. Explain. *(PGDT&HM)*

36. Purchasing is the stepping stone of the Food and Beverage Control of a hotel. Explain in 300 words the control procedure required in this area including supplier's rating, supplier's selection, purchase requisition, and purchase order and method of purchasing. *(MTA)*

37. As a *maitre d'hotel* of a first class restaurant (international), what responsibilities do you have during the bench *mise-en place* operation ? *(MTA)*

38. You are required to cater for a wedding buffet for 250-300 pax at ₹ 150 per head (inclusive). Plan an Indian menu giving the recipe for any one vegetarian dish. *(DTHM)*

39. With the help of a flow chart explain the role of KOT in controlling sales in the Food and Beverage Department of a five star hotel. *(DTHM)*

40. As a maitre d'hotel of a first class continental restaurant located in a 5-star deluxe hotel, what responsibilities do you have during the lunch mis-en place operation ? Explain in detail.

41. (*a*) Write a job specification for the Food and Beverage Manager of a 5-star hotel.
(*b*) Give the Job description of Food and Beverage Controller of a 5-star hotel. (*MTA*)

42. Explain the difference between the following :
(*a*) Mis-en place and mise-en scene
(*b*) Industrial and Institutional Catering
(*c*) Counter Service and Gueridon Service
(*d*) Restaurant and Cafeteria. (*IHMs*)

43. Draw the organisational chart of Food and Beverage Department of a five star deluxe hotel having 300-rooms and describe the duties and responsibilities of any two senior personnel. (*IHMs*)

44. Give appropriate accompaniments for *any five* of the following:
(*a*) Poisson Colbert
(*b*) Huitre
(*c*) Dindon Rôti
(*d*) Mutton Curry
(*e*) Cream of Tomato
(*f*) Chicken Marryland
(*g*) Cofee (after dinner)
(*h*) Stilton.

45. Give a neat illustration of a s*ix course* continental *table d'hotel* menu card with all necessary and relevant details.

46. Briefly explain the concept of fast food operations in India. List the equipment required and explain the need of standardized recipes in a fast food outlet. (*IHMs*)

47. Food service in institutions differs for some aspects from those in hotel industry. How is it different from Airline catering. Explain. (*IHMs*)

48. Write short notes on (*any two*):
(*a*) Railway Catering.
(*b*) Indian Breads.
(*c*) Outdoor Catering.

49. (*a*) Explain the importance of a Dumb waiter in a restaurant.
(*b*) Illustrate it with a diagram. (*IHMs*)

50. The cardiological association is arranging a whole day seminar in a 5-star hotel banquet suite. No. of pax-80, Non-vegetarian-60 and veg.-20, Time 09.00 Hrs. to 1800 Hrs. The chief organiser wants 6′ × 3′ tables and a herring bone arrangement for the participants and a podium with a table for the three speakers.
(1) Illustrate the complete table arrangements.
(2) Plan a suitable days menu for the function keeping in mind a working lunch, the two tea break, and an S.P. of ₹ 165/- per head exclusive of taxes. (*IHMs*)

51. Why is stainless steel used for cutlery and flatware in hotel and restaurants in preference to silver ? Can stainless steel be used in silver service ? (*IHMs*)

52. For an efficient service, breakfast buffet is a necessity in hotels. Plan a breakfast buffet menu for ₹ 150.00 and also explain the layout of the buffet table in right sequence. (*IHMs*)
(*a*) Name 10 proprietory sauces used in restaurant.
(*b*) Give accompaniments of tomato juice and fresh fruit juice. (*IHMs*)

53. Enlist the 14-possible courses of a french menu. Give two examples of every course along with a brief translation. (*IHMs*)

54. Plan a 5-course TDH menu to be served for 20-covers for a group in a continental Restaurant. Suggest a suitable cover layout and prepare cutlery, crockery, glassware, linen and other items including the side board and service equipment requirements, to serve the TDH menu for 20-covers. *(IHMs)*

55. Translate the following french menu into English. Mention the 5-main points that make it a badly planned menu.

Cocktail
Potage Tortue Clarie aux Xeres
Filet de Pomfret Colbert
Sauce Tartare
Poulet Maryland
Dommes Duchesse
Choufleur Mornay
Glace de Vanille
CAFE *(IHMs)*

56. Explain the difference between the two basic types of menus and the factor considered while planning these. *(IHMs)*

57. Differentiate between (*any five*) :

(*i*) Buffet and Gueridon
(*ii*) Continental and English Brakfast
(*iii*) Cafe Simple and the Complet
(*iv*) KOT and Bill
(*v*) Crockery and Cutlery
(*vi*) Classical hors' doeuvre and Horsd' oeuvre Varies
(*vii*) English and America Service
(*viii*) Carte du jour and plot du jour. *(IHMs)*

58. State the accompaniment of the following (*any five*):

(*i*) Chilled melon
(*ii*) Real turtle soup
(*iii*) Caviar
(*iv*) Asparagus
(*v*) Oysters
(*vi*) Pate de foie gras
(*vii*) Dotted shrimps
(*viii*) Grape fruit. *(IHMs)*

59. Explain in about 10 – 15 lines the difference between *tabled hote* and '*a la carte*'. Give one example of well planned '*carte du jour*'. *(IHMs)*

60. What is the difference between a full English breakfast and Continental Breakfast? Give sample menus of both. *(IHMs)*

61. Menu balance is an important part of deciding what to put on a menu – the season of the year – colour and flavour. What other factors must be considered to make up a balanced menu ? *(IHMs)*

62. Give appropriate accompaniments for any of the following:

(1) Caviar
(2) Pate Maison
(3) Mullgatwany
(4) Sole Orly
(5) Roast Pork
(6) Edam
(7) Oysters
(8) Gamebirds. *(IHMs)*

63. Give the explanation of *any five* of the following in one or two lines:–

(1) Pomme Alumettes
(2) Bouteille a vinaigre
(3) Cafetiere
(4) Chateau Briand
(5) Ciseaux a raisins
(6) Maitre d' hotel Beurre
(7) Molleton
(8) Paupiettes. *(IHMs)*

64. Taking into account that fifty per cent of the clientele are Indians, plan a suitable break fast menu which is to be utilized both for the coffee shop and room service. *(IHMs)*

65. Give the accompaniments for any 5 of the followings :–

(*i*) Artichoke (cold)
(*ii*) Melon
(*iii*) Consomme (hot)
(*iv*) Pomfret Colbert
(*v*) Roast Lamb
(*vi*) Roquefort
(*vii*) Asparagus (hot)
(*viii*) Poulet Roti. *(IHMs)*

66. 'Todays Indian cuisine is a result of continuous blending of different cultures over the centuries'. Discuss. *(IHMs)*

67. In two or three lines each, list the differences (*any five*) :

(*a*) Huitre and Escargot
(*b*) Yoghurt and Lassi
(*c*) Chef de rang and chef de vin
(*d*) Still Room and Ante Room
(*e*) Scotch Broth and Scotch Egg
(*f*) Furniture and Fixture
(*g*) Petits pains and Petits fours
(*h*) Buffet and Gueridon. *(IHMs)*

68. Give a neat illustration of a six-course continental *tabel d' hote* menu card with all necessary and relevant details. *(IHMs)*

69. List and describe the factors you could consider in framing the menu policy for either a commercial self-service restaurant in a city centre or an institutional food service operation (each serving approximately 600-main meals per day). How important do you rate the menu as an aid to promoting sales ? *(IHMs)*

70. (*a*) Give the F & B service staff requirements in all categories for a 120-covers first class speciality restaurant.

(*b*) Form a duty roaster for the stewards waiting at the above restaurant stating the daily *mise in place* jobs to be carried out. *(IHMs)*

71. List down the attributes of a good waiter. *(IHMs)*

72. Determine the F & B Service staff requirements in all categories of french restaurant having 100-covers, providing silver and gueridon service. The restaurant also has a stand up bar attached. Plan a suitable duty roaster for the staff of this restaurant. The restaurant operates 7-days a week and is open only for lunch and dinner. *(IHMs)*

73. In 5-star-hotels the food and beverage department has served F & B Service areas. In about 4 to 5-lines each describe the type of operation that exists in these areas. *(IHMs)*

74. (*a*) Identify the Staff requirements for a five star hotel coffee shop (service staff only) and prepare a duty role for two weeks with the following assumptions:

(*i*) 100-covers divided into 4-stations

(*ii*) seat turn over : for break fast (Buffet only)

(*iii*) 1.5 lunch, dinner and evening snacks 1 each;

(*iv*) after dinner snacks-0.5

(*v*) Hours of operation:

Breakfast	: 07.00 to 11.00 hrs.
Lunch	: 11.00 to 15.00 hrs.
Evening snack	: 15.00 to 19.00 hrs.
Dinner	: 19.00 to 24.00 hrs.

Midnight snacks from 0000 to 0700 Hrs. and Assume additional date if required.

(*b*) Explain in brief, how the manpower planning considerations differ for a coffee shop to that of other restaurant. (*IHMs*)

75. Both speciality restaurants and coffee shops cater to varied needs of the guests, but they are completely different in their operational modes and methods. How and why ? (*IHMs*)

76. Profit is the main motive of commercial establishments . In about 250-words describe how a waiter contributes in achieving this objective. (*IHMs*)

77. In two or three line differentiate between :

(*a*) Baize and Slip cloth

(*b*) EPNS and SS

(*c*) Chef de rang and Chef d' etage

(*d*) Hollaware and Flatware

(*e*) Cafe complet and the simple. (*IHMs*)

78. Illustrate the necessary cover for a room service order being executed and tray to a single occupant in a double room :

(*a*) Lassi

(*b*) Masala Dosa

(*c*) Coffee. (*IHMs*)

79. Give your assessment of the view that in food service establishments too little time and attention is given towards effective supervision. How do you see the role of the supervisor in the food service situation ? (*HCIMA, London*)

80. Examine current trends in food production and service. To what extent do you feel technology will influence the catering industry in the future ? (*HCIMA, London*)

81. Gueridon service has a tremendous marketing advantages. Explain. (*IHMs*)

82. (*a*) Draw a neat gueridon top diagram indicating therein different types of equipment required for the preparation of 'CREPE SUZETTE' for two person.

(*b*) Name the ingredients and quantities required for two persons. (*IHMs*)

83. " Explain in detail step by step method you would adopt for the preparation of CREPE SUZETTE for two person". (*IHMs*)

84. What is 'Door knob' style of ordering. Give a sample of an ideal room service door knob menu format. (*IHMs*)

85. Illustrate with the help of a diagram how a guest requiring a Room Service Breakfast Order would indicate his preferences an a door knob menu ? (*IHMs*)

86. Write notes an *any three*, in about 100 words :

(*a*) Banquet

(*b*) Buffet

(*c*) KOT

(*d*) Menu planning considerations. (*IHMs*)

87. Differential between (*any five*):

(*a*) Mise-en-place and mise-en-scene

(*b*) Chef de rang and chef de etage

(*c*) Sommelier and Aboyeur

(*d*) Continental Breakfast and English Breakfast

(*e*) Cona coffee and Espresso coffee

(*f*) Brunch and Supper.

88. Explain the following in not more than 2-3 lines (*any five*):

(1) Socle

(2) Berg

(3) Fine maison

(4) Speed rack

(5) Darne

(6) Wedding cake

(7) Impulse buying. (*IHMs*)

89. Give accompaniments and cover for *any two* of the following :

(*a*) Pâte de foie grass

(*b*) Les huitres

(*c*) Caviare. (*IHMs*)

90. Trolley service is prevalent in restaurants. Name the different types of trolleys and give examples of 10-different foods served off any two of them. (*IHMs*)

91. Room service operations are of different types. Explain centralized and decentralized types bringing out the differences between them. (*IHMs*)

92. The 'Dummy waiter' is very important piece of restaurant equipment. Explain its uses briefly and make a diagram of what you think would be the perfect working design. (*IHMs*)

93. Give French equivalents of *any five* of the following phrases :

(1) Lemon press

(2) Dinning Room

(3) Mayonnaise based sauce served with fried fish

(4) Corkscrew

(5) Oil and vinegar dressing for salad

(6) Water jug. (*IHMs*)

94. Explain in about two lines the difference between the following :

(*a*) Mis-en place and mis en scene

(*b*) Industrial and institutional catering

(c) Counter service and gueridon

(*d*) Cafe simple and cafe complete

(*e*) Restaurant and cafeteria. (*IHMs*)

95. You are a restaurant waiter serving at a table with 10-covers. Whilst silver servicing the soup, a guest accidentally bumped your arm and you spill the hot soup over the table and the dress of a lady guest. In about 10–15 lines describe your reaction to this accident and what method you would employ to rectify it ? (*IHMs*)

96. In three or four lines each, explain *any five* of the following :–

(*a*) Hollandaise

(*b*) Sorbet

(*e*) Canape

(*f*) K.O.T.

(*c*) EPNS (*g*) Gueridon
(*d*) Garnish (*h*) Baize. (*IHMs*)

97. Give reasons in about 4 or 5-lines for each situation as to what the waiter should say and do in the following:
(*a*) A male guest arrives at your dinning area wearing no jacket. His dress therefore does not meet the standards laid down by your establishment.
(*b*) The guest is in a hurry and wishes to order his meal be served, eat and leave within 20-minutes.
(*c*) You suspect that a prospective guest asking for a table has had too much to drink. (*IHMs*)

98. Answer the following :
(*a*) If the allowance along the cover is 2 feet per person, the member of people who may be seated at a round table 3-feet in diameter is .... ?
(*b*) What is the correct overlap of a table cloth allowed all around the table ? The size of a table cloth to fit a table 2' 6" (76 cms) is .... ? (*IHMs*)

99. There are various forms of food service. What factors would influence the different patterns of services for a coffee shop as opposed to a continental speciality restaurant. (*IHMs*)

100. As a restaurant manager emphasise in 10-sentences the importance of briefing and de-briefing function to your maitre d' hotel and in another 10-sentences discuss some of the points that must be considered in a briefing of F & B waiters in an Indian speciality restaurant. (*IHMs*)

101. Explain the following in not more than 2-lines each :
(1) Ullage (6) VSPO
(2) Chaptalisation (7) Decanting
(3) Vintage year (8) Supper
(4) Cafe complet (9) Spumante
(5) Criaderas (10) High Tea. (*IHMs*)

102. Differentiate between the following (*any five*)
(1) Corky and Corkage
(2) Cider and Mead
(3) Blanc de Blanc and Blanc de Noir
(4) Sekt and Sec.
(5) Moet et Chandon and Marques de Pompadour
(6) Congeners and Lees. (*IHMs*)

103. Mis-en place is an essential part of the restaurant operation, in any F & B Service outlet, in about 20-lines describe the mis-en place in a busy city restaurant prior to lunch. (*IHMs*)

104. (*a*) Gueridon service restaurant incorporates the use of various trollies. Name at least 4 important trollies used for guerideon service.
(*b*) With the help of a diagram of a flambe trolley, explain the mis-en place required for the flambe trolley.
(*c*) Give three examples of flambe dishes with the appropriate spirit/wine to be used for flambeing the dish. (*IHMs*)

105. Differentiate between 'Fork Buffet' and 'Finger Buffet'. (*IHMs*)

106. Answer briefly:
(*a*) How many metres of table cloth material required to stitch 100 table cloths for 36" × 36" table and 50-table cloths for 36" × 60" table, if the table cloth material selected is of 54" width ?

(*b*) What are the accompaniments for Tomato Juice and Fruit Juice ?

(*c*) List the items in a room service tray to serve tea for 2-persons

(*d*) Name 10-properietory sauces used in the restaurant and explain why they are not recommended to be served in the sauce boat.

(*e*) Explain the service of espresso coffee. (*IHMs*)

107. Gueridon service has its merits and demerits, however, in about 20-lines discuss the factors to be borne in mind to provide good gueridon service. (*IHMs*)

108. The various forms of buffet service can be an asset to the F &B service department. However there are certain drawbacks, with this kind of service. Give your opinion on the advantages and disadvantages of buffet service in about 20-lines. (*IHMs*)

109. 'A proper briefing before the service plays a very important role for the success of any service operation'. Elaborate. (*IHMs*)

110. How does a supervisor plan his job for supervising a meal service ? (*IHMs*)

111. Gueridon service has a tremendous marketing advantage through impulse buying-elucidate in brief . (*IHMs*)

112. Give the recipe for the following flambe dishes (*any two*):

Steak Diane, Steak Tartare, Monkey Gland Steak (*IHMs*)

113. A buffet service has more advantages than disadvantages- explain in details. (*IHMs*)

114. Give the recipe of any two of the following :

Steak Diane, Banana Flambe, Crepe Suzette. (*IHMs*)

115. For an efficient service, Breakfast Buffet is a necessity in hotels. Plan a Breakfast Buffet menu for ₹ 150.00 and also explain the layout of the buffet table in right sequence. (*IHMs*)

116. Give accompaniments and cover for any two of the following :

(*a*) Pâté de foie gras.

(*b*) Les huîtres.

(*c*) Caviare.

117. Food & Beverage department is split into several sections, working towards a similar goal of good food and service. In about 5-lines each describe these sections and the type of operation that exists there. (*IHMs*)

118. Discuss in about 200-words, the various methods employed for the cleaning silver flatware and holloware used in the restaurant. (*IHMs*)

119. In about 15-lines, differentiate between 'table 'd' hôtel' menu and 'á la carte' menu. Give one example of each menu type, well planned and suitable for a luxury restaurant (one dish for each course only).

120. The 3-basic types of room service operations are centralised, decentralised and mobile. For a 250-rooms City Hotel, catering mainly to business clientelle, what would be your choice of room service operation ? Explain in not more than 150-words. (*IHMs*)

121. State the accompaniments of *any five* of the following :

(*a*) Les huîtres

(*b*) Pétit Mermite

(*c*) Bortsch Polonaise

(*d*) Caneton Rôti

(*e*) Horsd'oeuvre Varies

(*f*) Saumon Fumé. (*IHMs*)

122. Give reason, about 5-lines for each situation, as to what the waiter should say and do in the following :

(*i*) A guest suggests that the fish dish served is 'off' ; and

(*ii*) A waiter finds a wallet under a chair, recently vacated by one of the clients. (*IHMs*)

123. Examine current trends in food production and service. To what extent do you feel technology will influence the catering industry in the future ? *HCIMA* (*London*)

124. A busy catering operation comprises a restaurant with full table service, a self-service grill bar, a cocktail bar, a public bar with snack counter, and banquet accommodation. Indicate how you would set about establishing a pricing structure for each of these outlets and show the need for and how you would develop a forward pricing policy. *HCIMA* (*London*)

125. List and describe the factors you would consider in framing the menu policy for either a commercial self-service restaurant in a city centre or an institutional food service operation (each serving approximately 600 main meals per day). How important do you rate the menu as an aid to promoting sales ? *HCIMA* (*London*)

126. Assess the importance of training for personnel involved in the service of wines and other drinks. What should be the objectives of such training schemes and how would you recommend that they be conducted ? *HCIMA* (*London*)

127. As catering Manager you are a member of the design team concerned with planning the food preparation area for a new restaurant seating 120-customers. Define your role in such a team and describe the particular points on which you would seek to influence design criteria and layout proposals. *HCIMA* (*London*)

128. Give your assessment of the view that in food service establishments too little time and attentions is given towards effective supervision. How do you see the role of the supervisor in the food service situation ? *HCIMA* (*London*)

129. How would each of the following adversely affect the average sale in a restaurant

(*a*) Deterioration in service standards

(*b*) Inadequate sales promotion. (*IHMs*)

130. State eight practices that help to increase the efficiency of a refrigerated storage. (*IHMs*)

131. Explain the following in not more than 100 words (*Any three*) :

(*a*) ABC Analysis

(*b*) Contribution

(*c*) Menu Merchandising

(*d*) Menu Engineering

(*e*) Supplier rating and Supplier Evaluation.

132. The budgeted details of two companies are as follows:

	Company A	*Company B*
Budgeted sales in units	: ₹ 100,000	₹ 100,000
Budgeted Selling price/unit	: ₹ 20.00	₹ 20.00
Budgeted Variable cost/unit	: ₹ 15.00	₹ 10.00
Budgeted Fixed Expenses (Total)	: ₹ 30,000.00	₹ 80,000.00
Budgeted Capacity	: 80%	80%

Compute for each company :

(*a*) The budgeted net profit

(*b*) The budgeted breakeven point in units

(*c*) The budgeted margin of safety expressed as a percentage of total capacity. (*IHMs*)

OBJECTIVE TYPE QUESTIONS

133. Choose the correct answer:

(1) Plat du jour is :
(*a*) The soup of the hause
(*b*) An EPNS Platter
(*c*) Soup of the day
(*d*) None of the above.

(2) The Still Room is a :
(*a*) Resting place for staff
(*b*) Room for storing lines
(*c*) Part of the pantry
(*d*) None of the above.

134. Match the following:

(1)	Entree	(*a*)	Grilled Salmon Steak
(2)	Poisson	(*b*)	Gazacho
(3)	Entremet	(*c*)	Sphepherd Pie
(4)	Potage	(*d*)	Smoked Salmon
(5)	Hors doeuvres	(*e*)	Baked Alaska.

135. Fill in the blanks:

(1) 'A pleasant................means waiter and waitresses will be tactful, courteous and have an ability to smile

(2) The team brigade is check to denote that t............. of s............. working together in the dining room in the same shift.

(3) A form of service which supplements other system might often he A............. V.............

(4) All food orders to the *aboyer* showed be.............so that there is..............in calling up a particular dish

(5) When taking order at the table, recognition of the.............is an important factor in effective communication

136. Fill in the blanks:

(1) Carte du jour is a............. (speciality item, day's menu, restaurant trolley).

(2) Plate room is the place for .... (electroplating of cutlery, storing cutlery, staff-dinning).

(3) Bell boy is a member of the .... staff (bell disk, conducted tour, restaurant).

(4) The size of guests serviette is approx .... c.m. sq. (32,50,52).

(5) .... is the team for the penty of commercial aircraft.

(6) The first IHC was hotel was established in ....

A CASE STUDY

137. Write answers as directed:–

(*i*) A table of 2-meters in diameter can accommodate .... covers for a formal banquet.

(*ii*) The maximum aisle space between the two chairbacks for a formal banquet is .... meter (*iii*) The best serving temperature for serving coffee is .... °C

(*iv*) On the craveny, the meat is maintained at a temperature of around .... to ....°C by the use of overhead infra-red heat lamps.

(*v*) The suggested area allowance for sit down functions per persons is approximately 1.0–1.4 square metres (true or false)

(*vi*) Write the English equivalent of the main dish 'cuissot de porc roti, purée de pommes'.

(*vii*) A meeting or formal assembly of representatives or delegates for discussion of an action on particular matters of common interest is: (Choose the right answer):

(*a*) Conference

(*b*) Convention

(*c*) Workshop

(*d*) Seminar.

(*viii*) The dish used on buffets to keep hot food hot is ....

(*a*) Chaffing dish

(*b*) Chefing dish

(*c*) Chafling dish

(*d*) Chaffer.

(*ix*) Pick the odd one out :

(*a*) Dais

(*b*) Lactern

(*c*) Rostrum

(*d*) Platform.

(*x*) Pick the odd one out

(*a*) Chef de rang

(*b*) Commis-de rang

(*c*) Chef d'etange. (*IHMs*)

138. Write the full forms of the following abbreviations:

(*a*) 'C'

(*b*) EPNS

(*c*)'CC'

(*d*) 'M'

(*e*)'CCC'

(*IHMs*)

139. Delete the odd one out. Support answers with proper reasoning:–

Example : (*a*) Lobster bisque (*b*) Consomme celestine (*c*) Cream of Tomato

Answer (1) (*B*) Consomme celestine is odd one out as it is a thin clear soup and the others are thick soups)

(*i*) Clam	Oysters	Crab
(*ii*) Corona	Ponatella	Colorado
(*iii*) Latakia	Oranege Pekoe	Earlgrey
(*iv*) Stilton	Parmesan	Roquefort
(*v*) Welsh Rare Bit	Deche Melba	Cana Pé Diana

(*IHMs*)

140. Match the following:

(*a*) Confiture (*i*) Oyster

(*b*)	Riz	(*ii*)	Duck
(*c*)	Crépe	(*iii*)	Pancake
(*d*)	Oeuf	(*iv*)	Water
(*e*)	Eau	(*v*)	Strawberry
(*f*)	Vin	(*vi*)	Milk
(g)	Fraise	(*vii*)	Snail
(*h*)	Huitre	(*viii*)	Rice
(*i*)	Loit	(*ix*)	Wine
(*j*)	Canard	(*x*)	Jam.
(*i*)	Egg		

(*IHMs*)

141. Rearrange the following items in the correct sequences, give alternatives for vegetarians where necessary and appropriate accompaniments:–

(*a*) Shrimp cocktail
(*b*) Chicken a la Kiev
(*c*) Fish meunire
(*d*) Coffee
(*e*) Chocolate and mint-mousse
(*f*) Cream of corn soup. (*IHMs*)

142. Make the odd one out:–

(1)	Hors D'oeuvre Trolley	Room Service Trolley	Gueridon Trolley
(2)	Escargots	Estragon	Huitres
(3)	Mirabelle	Kirsoh	Slivovitz
(4)	Margarita	Tequila Sunrise	Pina Cloada
(5)	Lanson	Tattinger	Tio Pepe
(6)	Peter Scot	Glenfiddich	J&B
(7)	Mead	Perrier	Cider
(8)	Isinglass	Cutglass	Crystal
(9)	Anjou	Pommard	Trave
(10)	Snake Coffee	Cafe Royal	Pousse Cafe.

(*IHMs*)

143. Match the columns :

A	B
(*a*) Entree	(*i*) Grilled Salmon Steak
(*b*) Poisson	(*ii*) Gazpacho
(*c*) Entremet	(*iii*) Shepherds Pie
(*d*) Potage	(*iv*) Smoked Salmon
(*e*) Hosd' oeuvres	(*v*) Baked Alaska.

(*IHMs*)

144. 'True' Or 'False'

(*i*) Turtle Soup is served with port wine
(*ii*) Industrial canteens have English service
(*iii*) For airline catering the cooking is done in the galley
(*iv*) Maitre d' hotel is the french term for head waiter
(*v*) The capacity of a tea cup is approx. 200 ml.

(*vi*) Silver cleaning with the help of aluminium sheets is called burnishing
(*vii*) A cereal plate is crescent shaped
(*viii*) Wine is served in Paris goblet
(*ix*) Waitress' shoes should be high heeled and fashionable
(*x*) A side board is also called service console or a dummy waiter. (*IHMs*)

145. Match the following :–

A	B
(*a*) Courvoisier	(*i*) Roast Pork
(*b*) Tomato Juice	(*ii*) Italy
(*c*) Turtle Soup	(*iii*) Jewish
(*d*) Apple Sauce	(*iv*) Florentine
(*e*) Parsnesan	(*v*) Brandy Balloon
(*f*) Kosher	(*vi*) Sherry
(*g*) Spinach	(*vii*) Binder
(*h*) Franindises	(*viii*) Duck
(*i*) Cigar	(*ix*) Coffee
(*j*) Aiguilette	(*x*) Worcestershire Sauce.

(*IHMs*)

146. Fill in the missing words :–

(*a*) A pleasant .... means waiters and waitress will be tactful, courthouse and have an ability to smile.
(*b*) The term brigade is used to denote the t.................. of s.................. working togather in the dinning room on the same shift.
(*c*) A form of service which supplements other systems might often be A ....V...... ....
(*d*) All food orders to the abouyer should be ...., so that there is .... in calling up a particular dish.
(*e*) When taking order at the table, recognition of the .... is an important factor in effective communication. (*IHMs*)

147. State whether true/false:

(*a*) Expresso coffee is traditionally served in a small cup.
(*b*) The term Germain denotes cauliflower.
(*c*) Escalope is normally a french menu term relating to pork.
(*d*) Darne and delice are terms relating to cuts of fish.
(*e*) The most suitable glass for the service of champagne is Elgin. (*IHMs*)

148. Choose the correct answer:–

(1) What is the definition of the term 'gueridon'?
(*a*) Dumb waiter
(*b*) A movable service table or trolley
(*c*) A style of menu
(*d*) A style of food service used in hospitals.

(2) Melba toast is :
(*a*) Offered as an accompaniment with pâté maison.
(*b*) Only served with breakfast and afternoon tea.

(*c*) Offered as an accompaniment with all forms of fruit melba.
(*d*) Offered as an alternative to bread rolls

(3) A polivit plate would be correctly used to:–
(*a*) Serve special fish dishes on
(*b*) Clean wood block flooring
(*c*) Clean silver
(*d*) Heat food in a microwave.

(4) The hot water in a sterilizing tank should be maintained at a temperature of:
(*a*) 75°C
(*b*) 85°C
(*c*) 65°C
(*d*) 56°C.

(5) The term used to indicate a steak required to by cooked 'medium' is :
(*a*) Saignant
(*b*) A point
(*c*) Baveuse
(*d*) Bien cuit.

(6) The term 'plat du jour' indicates :
(*a*) First class dish
(*b*) Main course dish
(*c*) A sweet dish
(*d*) A speciality coffee.

(7) With which of the following 'starter' dishes should a waiter not offer in a 'hot breakfast toast'?
(*a*) Pate de foie gras
(*b*) Caviare
(*c*) Escargots
(*d*) Potted shrimps.

(8) The name Duke Henry of Brunswick has connection with:
(*a*) Classical meat garnish
(*b*) The origin of menu
(*c*) An old established brewery company
(*d*) The french classical menu.

(9) You should normally find 'high tea' served in :
(*a*) Outdoor catering operation
(*b*) Buttery
(*c*) Departmental store
(*d*) The first class hotel.

(10) The person who controls the hot plate at service time is known as:–
(*a*) Abouyer
(*b*) Chef de rang

(*c*) Chef de partie
(*d*) Trancheur. (*IHMs*)

149. Choose the correct answer:

(1) Plat du jour is-
(*a*) The soup of the house
(*b*) An E.P.N.S. platter
(*c*) Soup of the day
(*d*) None of the above.

(2) The still room is a:
(*a*) Resting place for staff
(*b*) Room for storing linen
(*c*) Part of the Pantry
(*d*) None of the above.

(3) Chinese tea or green tea is best served:
(*a*) Without sugar or milk
(*b*) With sugar only
(*c*) With milk only
(*d*) None of the above.

(4) A K.O.T. is prepared by the :
(*a*) Cashier
(*b*) Chef de partie
(*c*) Station Head Waiter
(*d*) None of the above.

(5) Burnishing is used for:
(*a*) Cleaning service
(*b*) Cleaning glassware
(*c*) Polishing brass
(*d*) None of the above. (*IHMs*)

150. Match the following:

(1)	Consome Royal	(*a*)	Beverage
(2)	Evian	(*b*)	Bread crumbs
(3)	B.O.T.	(*c*)	Scissors
(4)	Colbert	(*d*)	Water
(5)	Grapes	(*e*)	Savoury egg custard. (*IHMs*)

151. Fill in the blanks:

(1) Blinis are an accompaniment for ....
(2) *Table d' hote* means ....
(3) Dhoklas are a speciality of ....
(4) Angels on horse back are served with ....
(5) The size of a slip cloth is ....
(6) ...., ..., ... are the three best types of chinaware.

(7) .... consists of tea or coffee, rolls/ croissants/ toast, butter, jams and occasionally fruit juice.

(8) Entremet is a course in which .... are served.

(9) A wine waiter is known as a ....

(10) A copy of the KOT is retained by the .... for preparing customer preference reports. *(IHMs)*

152. In this question you are given three words or phrases, two of which are related and the third is the odd man out. You are required to write down the one that does not fit with the other two:–

Example : Chef de rang – Sommelier – Sous chef. Sous chef is the odd man out. He belongs to the kitchen brigade –the other two are in restaurant brigade.

(*a*)	Croutons	Grated cheese	Chipolata
(*b*)	Consomme Royal	Lobster Bisque	Cream of spinach
(*c*)	Lancashire	Gorgonzola	Camembert
(*d*)	Cherry	Cardamom	Cashewnuts
(*e*)	Hollandaise	Vinaigrette	Mayonnaise. *(IHMs)*

153. Match the following:

(1)	Minestrone soup	(*a*)	France
(2)	Shrimp cocktail	(*b*)	Entremet de sucre
(3)	Roquefort	(*c*)	Italy
(4)	Oeuf a La neige	(*d*)	Stew.
(5)	Lancashire hot pot	(*e*)	Hors d' oeuvre. *(IHMs)*

154. Fill in the missing words:

(1) Burnishing is a method of cleaning ....

(2) Scotch Broth is a ....

(3) Borstch is the national soup of ....

(4) Tartar sauce is a derivative of ....

(5) Preparation of the restaurant is called ....

(6) The french term for snail is ....

(7) Egg plant is another name for ....

(8) Broceoli is a kind of ....

(9) Herring is a variety of ....

(10) .... is the french term for shrimps. *(IHMs)*

155. State 'true' or 'false':–

(*i*) Bombay duck is an Indian game bird

(*ii*) Service board is known as dumb waiter

(*iii*) Yorkshire pudding is an accompaniment for roast beef

(*iv*) Sweet breads are a collection of cakes

(*v*) Doiley is an under liner used in the service of tomato juice.

(*vi*) While laying a cover for spaghetti, the fork should be placed on the right hand side of the cover.

(*vii*) Beer Tankard is used to store beer

(*viii*) Pantry is an auxillary section between the kitchen and service doors.

(*ix*) Coffee still is decaffeinated coffee. *(IHMs)*

156. Fill in the blanks (from the choice given after each):

(*a*) Carte du jour is a .... (speciality item, days menu, restaurant trolley)

(*b*) Plate room is the place for .... (electroplating of cutlery, storing crockery, staff dinning)

(*c*) Bus boy is a member of the .... staff. (bell desk, conducted tour, restaurant)

(*d*) The size of the guest serviette is approximately .... cm. Sq. (32, 50, 62)

(*e*) .... is a stew of white meat. (blanquette, barquette, bisque)

(*f*) .... sauce is the accompaniment for roast lamb (apple, cranberry, mint)

(*g*) The capacity of demi tasse is .... cl. (12, 8, 10)

(*h*) .... is a type of melton. (panier, cantaloupe, potiron)

(*i*) Dhansak is a speciality .... dish. (parsi, bengali, punjabi)

(*j*) Sommelier is the .... waiter. (trolley, wine, station). (*IHMs*)

157. State whether 'true' or 'false':

(*a*) A mobile pantry can be used in the lobby area

(*b*) The tarnish on EPNS cutlery is silver sulphide

(*c*) Glass cloth should be made of cotton

(*d*) Dumb waiter is a restaurant side-board

(*e*) Gorgonzola is a blue- veined cheese

(*f*) Petis fours are a type of pastry

(*g*) The BOT is an essential control measure

(*h*) Cheese is always accompanied by cream crackers

(*i*) Cafe complete is coffee with biscuits and brandy

(*j*) Bird's nest is the national soup of Ireland.(*IHMs*).

158. Match 'B' with column 'A' :

Column 'A'	Column 'B'
(*a*) Cream of tomato	(1) Worcestershire
(*b*) Entremet	(2) Yorkshire pudding
(*c*) Gueridon	(3) U.S.A.
(*d*) Reachaud candles	(4) Crepe suzette
(*e*) Tomato Juice	(5) Sommelier
	(6) Buffet
	(7) Black forest.

(*IHMs*)

159. Delete the odd out – e.g., (*a*) Consomme Royal; (*b*) Lobster bisque (*c*) Cream of spinach, (*a*) is the odd one out as it is a clear soup and the other two are the thick.

A	B	C
Plate Room	Still Room	Ante Room
Pheasant	Turkey	Patridge
Table d' hote	Plate du jour	Carte du jour
Clam Oyster	Crab	
Roquefort	Stilton	Edam.

(*IHMs*)

160. Match column 'A' with column 'B'

A	B
1. Les noix	(*a*) Finger Bowl

2. Spinach Soup	(*b*) Bread Sauce
3. Tomato Juice	(*c*) Crepe Suzette
4. Roast Chicken	(*d*) Tureen
5. Orange Juice	(*e*) Worcestershire
6. Dessert	(*f*) Apple Sauce
7. Chateau briand	(*g*) Nut Cracker
8. Gueridon Dish	(*h*) Speciality Restaurant
9. Battery	(*i*) Pony Tumbler
10. Roast Pork	(*j*) Grape Scissors
	(*k*) Sandwiches. (*IHMs*)

161. Fill in the blanks:–

1. .... is the term for the pantry of commercial aircraft.
2. The first IHC hotel was established in ....
3. .... is the method of cleaning silver by using aluminium and washing soda.
4. Another name for egg plant is ....
5. Restaurant trolleys move with the help of .... (coasters, ball bearings, casters).
6. Hospital and school catering fall under ....
7. The analysis at the end of the meal session by a mitre d' hotel is known as ....
8. Castor sugar and ground ginger are the accompaniments to ....
9. Cream crackers are .... (pastries, waffles, biscuits, porkrind).
10. Diameter of a large plate is .... cms. (*IHMs*)

162. State whether 'true' or 'false':–

1. Hot case is an important component of a room service trolley,
2. Roquefort is made from ewes milk
3. Coffee still is decafeinated coffee
4. Butter milk is prepared from whey.
5. Garlic sauce is served with snails.
6. The accompaniments to ice tea are milk and sugar.
7. A show plate is used for presenting the bill in the absence of a bill folder.
8. Petits fours are served at the end of a meal along with coffee.
9. The thickening in Scoth broth is corn flour
10. Vichy is mineral water. (*IHMs*)

163. Delete the odd one out. Support answers with proper reasoning :

Example (*i*) (*A*) Lobster Bisque; (*B*) Consomme Celestine; (*C*) Cream of Tomato.

Answer (*i*) (*B*) - Consomme Celestine is odd one out as it is a thin clear soup and the others are thick soups.)

(*i*)	Clam	Oysters	Crab
(*ii*)	Corona	Ponatella	Colorado
(*iii*)	Latakia	Orange Pekoe	Earl Grey
(*iv*)	Stilton	Parmesan	Roquefort
(*v*)	Welsh Rarebit	Pêche Melba	Canapé Diana (*IHMs*)

164. State whether "True" or "False" :

(*i*) Service lift is known as Dumb Waiter.
(*ii*) Sweet breads are served as an entremet.
(*iii*) Grogonzola is a blue cheese from Germany
(*iv*) A side board is also called a service console.
(*v*) While lying a cover for spaghetti the fork should be placed on the right hand side of the cover. (*IHMs*)

165. Pick the odd one out (stating reasons) and write down that does not fit with the other two :

(*a*) Fish Plate	Soup Plate	Cheese Plate
(*b*) Roly Poly	High ball	Collins
(*c*) Chef de Rang	Sommelier	Sous Chef
(*d*) Mise-en-place	a la carte	Plat du jour
(*e*) Orange Pekoe	Rombouts	Tisanes
(*f*) Hollandaise	Vinaigrette	Mayonnaise
(*g*) Consommé	Chowder	Bisque
(*h*) Buck Wheat	Shreded Wheat	Wheat flakes
(*i*) Croutons	Grated Cheese	Chipolate
(*j*) Evian	Ginger beer	Tonic water. (*IHMs*)

166. Anxious Limited is a factory employing 1,000-people (800-day shift), it is prosperous, has good management/staff relationship, and is regarded locally as a good employer.

A firm of contract caterers, Bogus Limited, has responsibility for feeding the staff and management etc. Bogus Limited has held this contract for three years, taking over from Anxious Limited who previously managed their own catering. Pressure of work on the Personnel Department at Anxious Limited led to Directors's decision to off-load the responsibility of catering to experts in the field, so relieving the pressure and yet providing greater expertise. The Cook in Charge and the staff of Anxious Limited were retained by Bogus Limited on takeover.

Usage of the catering facilities has been dropping steadily, if not considerably, over the past 18-months. A usage rate of 35% of the total workforce has fallen to 17% . These figures are mentioned by the Personnel Manager at Anxious Limited as part of a complaint made to the Caterers, Bogus Limited. More specific complaints were made by a Senior Shop Steward, who is vice-chairman of the Canteen Committee. They are :

(*i*) lack of variety of food
(*ii*) food too expensive
(*iii*) slow service
(*iv*) table not cleared
(*v*) poor presentation of food
(*vi*) obviously bad portioning of food
(*vii*) vending machine often not working (used for small items-cigarettes, sweets, etc.).

The catering facilities, whose only local competition for lunchtime trade is a nearby pub, offer a 24-hour service, providing morning snacks and trolley service to offices. Cups of tea are served during the afternoon. Two women (one cook and one general assistant) operate the night shift (10 pm - 6 am) 5-nights per week and serve approximately 30-full meals per night plus beverages.

The catering staff are all female with the exception of the Head Chef and the Assistant Head Chef. At the present time, there is no manager, the previous incumbent left recently after only three months service, and has yet to be replaced. The Catering Supervisor — Mrs. Briggs — is acting manager, a role she has filled on each of the four previous occasions when the manager has left. Mrs. Briggs had been 'Cook in Charge' for Anxious Limited before Bogus took over.

Staff turnover rate varies according to the nature of employment, apart from the instability of the Unit Management Position, the other area of concern is the annual 200-250% turnover rate of the eleven general assistant positions.

The Area Manager for Bogus Limited begins to investigate the complaints.

You are required to:

(*a*) Describe how the Area Manager might effectively carry out his investigations emphasising the manner in which he would gather relevant information.

(*b*) Suggest the most likely areas requiring attention and outline proposals to deal with them quickly.

(*c*) Indicate what action might be taken in the longer term to ensure an efficient operation and to minimise complaints. *HCIMA* (*London*)

BEVERAGES

1. Explain the full procedure for obtaining various licences required by a hotel for running bars and holding parties in the hotel under the existing excise laws. Indicate the dry days which are in vogue at present ? (*DTHM*)

2. What are the different types of bar generally found in hotels ? Explain each type. (*MTA*)

3. Write notes on the following :
   (*i*) Linen Inventory
   (*ii*) Project Report
   (*iii*) Alcoholic Beverages
   (*iv*) Density Chart. (*MTA*)

4. Explain the following terms :
   (*i*) Maitre d' hotel
   (*ii*) Chef de Cuisine
   (*iii*) Sous Chef
   (*iv*) Sommelier
   (*v*) Chef de vang
   (*vi*) Chef de partie
   (*vii*) Chef d' tange.

5. What are the type of Bar generally found in Indian hotels ? Explain each type.

6. Classify non-alcoholic beverages with suitable examples. Describe the beverage-Iced Tea.

7. (*a*) Give the check list of information required prior to setting up of a public bar in a five star hotel
   (*b*) What are the proceedings for purchasing foreign liquor ?
   (*c*) "State the formalities to be carried out for setting up a temporary bar or banquet.
   (*d*) What are the factor to be considered for opening a new restaurant ? Explain in detail. (*IHMs*)

8. Explain the following terms :

(*a*) Varietal wine

(*b*) Generic wine

(*c*) Proprietary name of wine. (*IHMs*)

9. Name the five (5) main still wine producing regions of France, giving examples of two wines from each region. (*IHMs*)

10. Describe the processing of vodka, emphasize the 'pure spirit' aspects and re-distillation. List five brands of vodka. (*IHMs*)

11. 'The ingredients used in bear processing are of primary importance'. Elucidate with step by step process of manufacturing of larger bear. (*IHMs*)

12. Explain how liqueurs are made and classify the different categories with examples. (*IHMs*)

13. (*i*) Cognac quality is indicated by letters. What following letters stand for :

(*a*) VSOP (*b*) VO (*c*) XO.

(*ii*) Explain the terms Grande fine Champagne and Fine Champagne (*IHMs*)

14. Distinguish between :

(*i*) Ruby Port and Tawny Port

(*ii*) Champagne and Fire Champagne

(*iii*) Malt whisky and Grain Whisky

(*iv*) Italian Vermouth and French Vermouth.

(*v*) Porter and Stout. (*IHMs*)

15. (*a*) Why does 'Natural spirits' make the best cocktail ingredients as opposed to 'aged-spir its'?

(*b*) What are the three essential components of cocktail. Briefly explain each method. (*IHMs*)

16. Explain the following wine terms:

(*i*) Racking

(*ii*) Fining

(*iii*) Lees

(*iv*) Bouquet

(*v*) Corky. (*IHMs*)

17. Write brief notes on:

(*i*) Chianti

(*ii*) Tequila

(*iii*) Single Malt

(*iv*) Apellation Controlee

(*v*) Solera System. (*IHMs*)

18. (*a*) Define the terms 'bloom' and 'verification'.

(*b*) Write three main types of yeast found with in the boom, giving 3 to 4 lines explanation of each type. (*IHMs*)

19. Name the principal grape varieties used in producing :

(*i*) Beaujolaise

(*ii*) Champagne

(*iii*) Alsace. (*IHMs*)

20. Differentiate between:

(*a*) Cognac and Armagnac

(*b*) Malt Whisky and Grain Whisky

(*c*) Bear and Ale

(*d*) Sherry and Port

(*e*) Campari and Vermout. (*IHMs*)

21. What are the basic steps and procedures involved in the opening and serving of the following wines:–

(*a*) Charles Heidsieck

(*b*) Vosne – romanée (*IHMs*)

22. (*a*) What are liqueurs ?

(*b*) List down six liqueurs with their predominant flavour ?

(*c*) Write a short note on the three basic methods of liqueur preparation. (*IHMs*)

23. (*a*) With the help of flow chart explain the various steps involved in the manufacture of the scotch whisky

(*b*) List down six brand names of deluxe scotch whiskies.

24. Explain in a line or two the origin of the names of *any two* of the following:

(*a*) Vodka

(*b*) Rum

(*c*) Gin

(*d*) Cocktails.

25. Illustrate with a flow chart the sequence of cocktail dinner order for two persons served through room service, specifying the items and quantities involved. (*IHMs*)

26. Describe the manufacture of sherry. List the different types of sherry with examples of each.

27. Describe 'methode champenoise', list ten champagne shippers. (*IHMs*)

28. Define aperitifs and give an alternative name. Name and explain briefly any four aperitifs. (*IHMs*)

29. Describe the manufacture of rum. Name two Indian brands of :

1. White Rum
2. Darkrum
3. Gin
4. Vodka
5. Mineral Water
6. Soft Drink
7. Beers
8. Diet Bears
9. Premium Whiskey
10. Brandy. (*IHMs*)

30. (*i*) Define the term spirit.

(*ii*) What are the different types of stills used in the distillation of spirits.

(*iii*) Name the five main spirits.

(*iv*) Explain the basic steps involved in the manufacture of whiskey. (*IHMs*)

31. Give four brand names of the following :

(1) Indian premium whiskies

(2) Cognacs
(3) Indian wines
(4) International brands of vodka
(5) Clarets. *(IHMs)*

32. Discuss in detail the various points to be considered for the successful operation of the main bar of 5-star hotel. *(IHMs)*

33. List 5-electrical and 5-non-electrical bar equipment along their uses in not more than 4 lines each *(IHMs)*

34. List 10 small equipment used in a bar. *(IHMs)*

35. The correct tools and the sequence in which they are set in the bar are essential for smooth and efficient bar service. List 10 such bar items describing each in about 2 lines *(IHMs)*

36. In about 10-lines list and explain the different types of requisitions used for smooth and efficient bar operations. *(IHMs)*

37. There are many different shapes and sizes of glass used in a Bar/Restaurant. Give the approximate capacities in centilitres of *any five* of the following:

(1) Collins Glass
(2) Brandy Balloon
(3) Zombie or a Long mix
(4) White Wine Glass
(5) Water Goblet
(6) Delmonico Glasses
(7) Beer Tankards. *(IHMs)*

38. Classify non-alcoholic beverages with suitable examples. Describe the beverage Iced Tea. *(IHMs)*

39. Assess the importance of training for personnel involved in the service of wine and other drinks. What should be the objectives of such training schemes and how would you recognise that they be conducted ? *(HCIMA, London)*

40. Indicate the area and origin and the colour of the french wines :

(*a*) Pouilly Fuisse
(*b*) Gewurtztraminer
(*c*) Chateau d' Yquem.
(*d*) Hermitage
(*e*) Chateau Cheval Blane *(IHMs)*

41. List the wine glasses and equipment for service of wine and discuss the use of each in turn. *(IHMs)*

42. (*a*) Define wine.
(*b*) Classify wines with the help of a neat diagram.
(*c*) Name 5-black and 5-white grapes. *(IHMs)*

43. (*a*) Explain the storage conditions of different types of wines
(*b*) What is the purpose of "racking wines" ?
(*c*) What does the "body of wine" mean ? *(IHMs)*

44. (*a*) What is Bourbon Whiskey ?
(*b*) How it is matured ?
(*c*) What are the specialities of 'Tennessee' Whiskey ? *(IHMs)*

45. (*a*) What is Fine Champagne ?
(*b*) What is the speciality of an Armagnac Still ?
(*c*) What are Marc and Grappa ? *(IHMs)*

46. (*a*) Vodka is a "neutral spirit" Justify.
(*b*) How is Vodka filtered ?

(*c*) Give the recipe, garnish, glass and the method of preparation of a popular cocktail with tequila as the base spirit. (*IHMs*)

47. (*a*) What is tequila sourced from ?

(*b*) List the step involved in making tequila.

(*c*) Give the recipe, garnish, glass, and the method of preparation of a popular cocktail with tequila as the base spirit. (*IHMs*)

48. (*a*) What is a humidor ? Explain its special features.

(*b*) List and briefly explain the three different parts of a cigar.

(*c*) Name the three most popular sizes of cigar. (*IHMs*)

49. (*a*) What are the temperature range and humidity range for storage of cigar ?

(*b*) What precautions should be taken while lighting a cigar ?

(*c*) Give any three terms which classify a cigar according to colour. (*IHMs*)

50. (*a*) What are the principal ingredients for manufacturing beer ?

(*b*) What are the effects of each on the final product ?

51. (*a*) What is draught beer and how is it different from bottled or canned beers ?

(*b*) Explain the facility-requirements for installing draught beer service in a bar. (*IHMs*)

52. Compare and contrast (*any two*)

(*i*) Dutch Gin & London Dry Gin

(*ii*) Pot Still & Patent Still

(*iii*) Fino & Oloroso. (*IHMs*)

53. Briefly explain the following (*any five*):

(*i*) Pernod

(*ii*) Kirsch

(*iii*) Slivovitz

(*iv*) Schnapps

(*v*) Sake

(*vi*) Aquavit

(*vii*) Pastis. (*IHMs*)

54. Give any name of the following :

Hock Wine, Burgundy White Wine, DOCG wine from Italy, Cream Sherry, Vintage Port, Madeira, Indian White Wine, Premier cru Wine from Médoc, Brut Champagne, Golden Sweet Wine from Sauternes. (*IHMs*)

55. Calculate the space required for a 120-pax format comb shape seating arrangement with a neat drawing of the arrangement in which the top table has 11-covers. (*IHMs*)

56. Explain the following :

(*i*) Finger Buffet;

(*ii*) Fork Buffet; and

(*iii*) Sit-down Buffet. (*IHMs*)

57. Single the odd word out (give reasons for each) :

(*i*) Herring bone shape/comb shape/class room shape of eating arrangement

(*ii*) Moet et chandon/Perrier Jouet/Marquis de pompadour

(*iii*) Function Prospectus/Function Enquiry Sheet/Letter of Confirmation
(*iv*) Pastry Trolley/Hors d'oeuvre Trolley/Flambe Trolley
(*v*) Bar Spoon/Tea Spoon/Measuring Spoon. (*IHMs*)

58. Explain the following in few lines only (*any three*) :
Cocktail Bar, Dispense Bar, Mobile Bar, Pub (*IHMs*)

59. Give a 3 or 4-line description of the following (*any five*) :
(*i*) Jigger
(*ii*) Toasting
(*iii*) Toto
(*iv*) Copita
(*v*) Seminar
(*vi*) Angel's wing
(*vii*) Catwalk. (*IHMs*)

60. What are the procedures for taking physical inventory in a bar-both opening and closing inventory ? Explain in about 100-words.

61. Give the job description and job specification of a Bar Supervisor. (*IHMs*)

62. Name the five main Still Wine producing regions of France giving examples of two wines from each region. (*IHMs*)

63. Describe the processing of Vodka, emphasize the "Pure Spirit" aspect and re-distilation. List five brands of Vodka. (*IHMs*)

64. "The ingredients used in beer processing are of primary importance" Elucidate with step by step process of manufacturing of lager beer. (*IHMs*)

65. List the wine glasses and equipment for service of wine and discuss the use of each in turn. (*IHMs*)

66. What are the two main method of making a cocktail, briefly explain each method. (*IHMs*)

67. Explain the following wine terms :
(*i*) Racking (*ii*) Fining (*iii*) Lees
(*iv*) Bouquet (*v*) Corky. (*IHMs*)

68. Write brief notes on :
(*i*) Chianti (*ii*) Tequila (*iii*) Single Malt
(*iv*) Apellation controlee (*v*) Solera System (*IHMs*)

69. Give the checklist of information required prior to setting up of a public bar in a five star hotel. (*IHMs*)

70. What are the proceedings for purchasing foreign liquor ? (*IHMs*)

71. Explain the following terms :
Varietal Wine, Generic Wine, Proprietory name of wine. (*HTMS*)

72. List down the attributes of a good waiter. (*IHMs*)

73. (*a*) Explain the importance of a Dumb Waiter in a restaurant.
(*b*) Illustrate it with a neat diagram. (*IHMs*)

74. Trace out the history of Railway Catering and role played by Spencer's in Railway Catering in India. (Limit your answer to 200-words only). (*IHMs*)

75. Review the development of fast food operations in the hotel and catering industry. Identify the essential characteristics of this type of business and give some indications concerning its future. *HCIMA* (*London*)

76. Explain the full procedure for obtaining various licences required by a hotel for running bars and holding parties in the hotel under the existing excise laws. Indicate the dry days which are in vogue at present. (*DTHM*)

77. Calculate the length of the top and spring table for a format sit down banquet of 250-packs with 11-person on the top table. Illustrate with the help of a neat diagram. (*IHMs*)

78. Explain kitchen stewarding along with the importance of the department and mention duties and responsibilities of the manager of the kitchen stewarding department.

79. Draw an organisation chart of a 100-seater à la carte restaurant of a 5-star hotel offering continental and Chinese dishes. The restaurant is open for lunch and dinner only. Several items featured on the menu are flambeéd or gueridon serviced. (*IHMs*)

80. Draw the layout of a still room connected to a restaurant of 150-covers and is open for 3-major meals. In not more than 50-words explain the importance of a still room. (*IHMs*)

81. To what extent do you judge that in order to satisfy profit targets today, the catering industry has misjudged long-term consumer expectations by reducing 'service' so drastically that it could never be reintroduced ? *HCIMA* (*London*)

82. Write short notes on *any two* (100-words each):

(*a*) Faults in Cakes

(*b*) Chaud Froid

(*c*) Sandwiches

(*d*) Non-edible (Buffet) Displays.

83. You are celebrating the birthday party of a 5-year old girl using clowns as a theme. Plan an invitation, cake designs, centre piece and decoration and give aways for this function. State the materials used for decoration and an approximation of the total cost of decoration (Answer suitable additional data if necessary and state the assumption)

84. Every category of room service personnel has an important role to play in providing personalized service, bring about guest satisfaction and achieving sales targets. Discuss in about 250-words. (*IHMs*)

85. As Catering Manager of a food and beverage unit of your choice, suggest steps you would take to increase and sustain the volume of profitable business. *HCIMA* (*London*)

OBJECTIVE TYPE QUESTIONS

86. Match the following liqueurs with their flavours and country of origin:-

Liqueur	*Flavour*	*Country*
(*i*) Kahlua	(*a*) Various Herbs	(*i*) Sweden/Denmark
(*ii*) Charereuse	(*b*) Caraway	(*ii*) Mexico
(*iii*) Advocat	(*c*) Coffee	(*iii*) Scotland
(*iv*) Drambuie	(*d*) Brandy/Egg Yolk	(*iv*) France
(*v*) Kummel	(*f*) Whiskey & Honey	(*v*) Holland.

87. There are various wine producing countries of the world, and each produces certain well known varieties, for which the areas are famous:

In a tabular form, list at least 3 wines of each country along with their characteristics, in the given format:

Country		*Name of the Wine*	*Nature*	*Colour*	*G.L.*	*Serving Temperature*	*Food served with*
France	1	....	....	....	....	....	....
	2	....	....	....	....	....	....
	3	....	....	....	....	....	....
Germany	1	....	....	....	....	....	....
	2	....	....	....	....	....	....
	3	....	....	....	....	....	....
Italy	1	....	....	....	....	....	....
	2	....	....	....	....	....	....
	3	....	....	....	....	....	....
Spain	1	....	....	....	....	....	....
	2	....	....	....	....	....	....
	3	....	....	....	....	....	....
Portugal	1	....	....	....	....	....	....
	2	....	....	....	....	....	....
	3	....	....	....	....	....	....
Or any other country of Your choice	1	....	....	....	....	....	....
	2	....	....	....	....	....	....
	3	....	....	....	....	....	....

(IHMs)

88. Fill in the blanks:

(*a*) Size of a 4-cover square table is ....

(*b*) Name five banquet tools (1) .... (2) .... (3) .... (4) .... (5) ....

(*c*) Banquet Memorandum means .... (Function sheet / Banquet Diary / Function Prospect us)

(*d*) Capacity of margarita (a stamware) is .... ($5^1/_4$oz, /$5^1/_2$oz, /6oz).

(*e*) Airspace at top of a wine barrel due to evaporation or leakage is called ....

(*f*) In a formal, banquet testing is done at the beginning of dinner or at the middle with rest course or at the end of dinner (choose the appropriate one).

(*g*) Hery Charpentier accidently invented flambe dish in the year ....

(*h*) For a buffet service of 300-pax total space required would be .... sq. ft. *(IHMs)*

89. State whether the following statements are 'true' or 'false' :

(1) Fine champagne is a well matured champagne wines.

(2) Liqueurs are served after meals.

(3) Tomato shorba is garnished with croutons

(4) Rose wines are served after red wines

(5) Vermouths are made from wines

(6) Perry is a wine made from pears.

(7) In a restaurant right way to move a trolley is to push it and not pull it.

(8) 'High land Queen' is an aperitif wine

(9) 'Forbidden Apple' is a liqueur

(10) Caviare is shell fish. (*IHMs*)

90. Complete the following :

1. Brandy + Lime juice + Cointreau = ...
2. Gin + cointreau + Lime juice + Sugar + Egg white = ...
3. Rum + Coca = ...
4. Vodka + Vigin Marry = ...
5. Black Coffee + Whisky + Cream = ...
6. Scotch + Dram buie = ...
7. Rum + Sugar + Egg = ...
8. Vodka + Orange Juice + Galliano = ...
9. White Cream + Lime Juice + Banana = ...
10. Brandy + White Rum + Cointreau + Lime Juice = ... (*IHMs*)

91. Translate into English :

1. Beignets d' Ananas
2. Corbeille de Fruits
3. Cocktail de Fruit de Mer
4. Ragout d' Homard Et Ris de Veau
5. Sorbet Au Cassis Et Au Frambise
6. Gelee A Fraises Avec Glace de Vanille
7. Jambon C.R.U. Avec Une Mousse de Noix
8. Scampis Saute Au Beurre d' Orange
9. Coteletties de Pommes de Terre Avec Sauce de Tomato
10. Rongnons Saute Bercy. (*IHMs*)

92. Complete the following:–

(1) .... system is used for maturing sherries.

(2) The cup used for tasting wine is called ....

(3) .... is a red wine served chilled.

(4) .... is an example of neutral spirit.

(5) Port wine gets its name from the town of .... (*IHMs*)

93. Choose the correct answer:–

(1) The abbreviation B & B stands for :–

(*a*) A Bartender's Beaker

(*b*) Benedictine and Brandy

(*c*) Babycham and Baccardi

(*d*) Barbecued Beef. (*IHMs*)

(2) Which wine its composed only of Sherries ?

(*a*) Tarragonna, Montilla, Bual, Ratafia, compari

(*b*) Muscadet, Alto Douro, Sercial, Mead, Schnapps

(*c*) Malmsey, Marsala, Malaga, Madera, Verdelho

(*d*) Fino, Manganilla, Amontillado, Sack, Olorosso.

(3) The person who serves wine is called a:
(*a*) Debrasseur
(*b*) Truncheuer
(*c*) Sommelier
(*d*) Commis-de-rang.

(4) Cocktails are usually served:
(*a*) Before the meal
(*b*) During the meal
(*c*) Between meals
(*d*) After the meal.

(5) Components of liqueurs are:–
(*a*) Wines, spirit, and Herbs
(*b*) Spirits, Herbs and Gomme
(*c*) Spirits, Flavourings, and Sugar
(*d*) Flavourings, Bitters, and Fortified Wines. (*IHMs*)

94. Delete the odd one out giving examples:–

e.g., Magnum Keg Nip

Keg is the odd one out as it indicates a cask and the other two are bottles.

(1)	Medoc	Graves	Maconnals
(2)	Sherry	Madeira	Port
(3)	Sekt	Marsala	Spumante
(4)	Benedictine	Kahlua	Chartreuse
(5)	Angel's Wings	Beeswings	Fliers

(*IHMs*)

95. Choose the correct answer to fill in the blank :

(*a*) Armagnac bottles are known as .... (bocksbeutel/basquaise/fiasco).
(*b*) Virgin Mary is a .... (beer/cocktail/mocktail)
(*c*) Calypso Coffee is flavoured with .... (Tia Maria/Cointreau/Kahlua).
(*d*) .... is an ideal accompaniment with poached fish (Morgan/Barolo/Pouilly Fuisse).
(*e*) .... is an aromatized wine (Dubonnet/Robert Pepi/Linderman).
(*f*) The process of adding sugar to the must is known as .... (Vinification/ Chaptalization/Fortification).
(*g*) Grand Mariner is a .... liqueur (plant/generic/fruit).
(*h*) The process of disgorging the debris from a champagne bottle was introduced by .... (Dom Perignon/Veuve Cliquot/Romanee Conti).
(*i*) Demerara rums are made in .... (Guyana/Jamaica/Puerto Rico).
(*j*) .... is the name of an Irish Stout (Lowenbrau/Guinness/Carlsberg).

96. Find the odd one out :

(*i*) Islay, Speyside, Hampshire, Campbelltown, Highland.
(*ii*) Grenadine, Cassis, Citronelle, Gomme, Orgeat.
(*iii*) Ricard, Ouzo, Lillet, Pernod.
(*iv*) Marsala, Sherry, Soave, Malaga, Port.
(*v*) Meursalt, Montrachet, Chablis, Fleurie. (*IHMs*)

CHAPTER 7

Sales and Marketing Techniques

OBJECTIVES

After studying this chapter, you should be able to :

1. *Define the terms : sales and marketing*
2. *Distinguish between sales and marketing*
3. *Understand the sales and marketing techniques*
4. *Understand the role of public relations, guest relations and press relation, and*
5. *Explain the organisation of the department.*

COMPETITION

The sales and marketing has assumed greater importance and with increased competition and increasing number of hotels full-time Sales Directors/Marketing Directors are being appointed in many hotel companies. Sales and marketing is called as the life and blood of the organisation. To quote Earnest Henderson III, President of the Sheraton Corporation, In England, if a man wants to reach the Presidency of an organisation, he usually goes through the finance division. In Germany, the fastest road up is through production. In the United States, the glory road is through sales and marketing."[1] Sales and marketing has become one of the most vital functions of the hotel business and an integral part of the modern hotel management. It includes packaging for selling, sales promotion, advertising, and public relations.

The organisation of this department depends upon the size and location of the hotel and the policy and goals of the management. Figs. 7.1 and 7.2 indicate the organisational break-up of sales and marketing in a hotel. In small hotels, the manager looks after the sales but in large hotels it is not possible and hotels have Vice-President (Marketing) or Director Marketing or Sales Manager depending upon the size of the property. He is responsible for the functions of the sales department. He looks after the banquets and conventions promotion, food and beverage promotion, guest history, advertising, publicity, and other internal selling. It is the staff members' responsibility to do continuously search for convention business and to encourage the use of the hotel's facilities. This department encourages the use of hotel facilities. It searches its customers through well-organised and coordinated advertising and sales efforts. The department is on a constant look out for group or tour business. The staff

1. Earnest Henderson III, President of the Sheraton Corporation, USA.

should have good knowledge and experience in advertising, marketing, public relations and publicity.

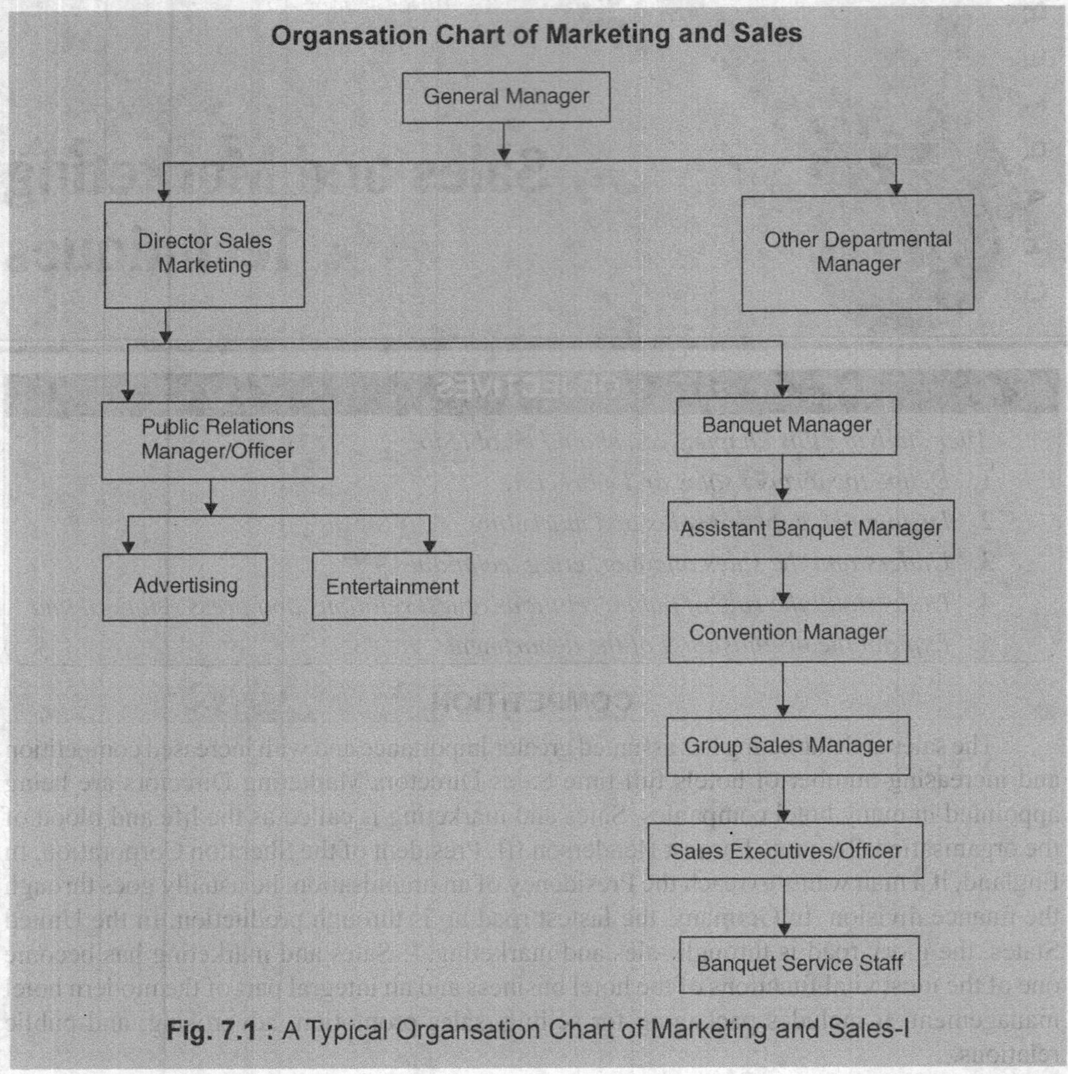

Fig. 7.1 : A Typical Organsation Chart of Marketing and Sales-I

The prime responsibility of the director of marketing is to generate new business for rooms, food and beverage departments of the hotel. This may involve direct sale calls to corporate head offices, travel agencies and other places. Advertisement, sales promotion, public relations and publicity activities are directly under the control of the Director.

Other employees of this department include advertisement manager, publicity manager, press representative, sales manager, secretaries, stenographers, assistants, clerks etc.

The large hotels having convention banquet facilities could not exist without the business generated by their sales and convention staff. In the Hilton Corporation, every new management trainee will have his first assignment as sales respesentative. Obviously, Hilton believes in sales minded managers. C. Dewitt Coffman, a leading hotel sales expert, lists the following specific responsibilities for any hotel department : sales planning, sales policies,

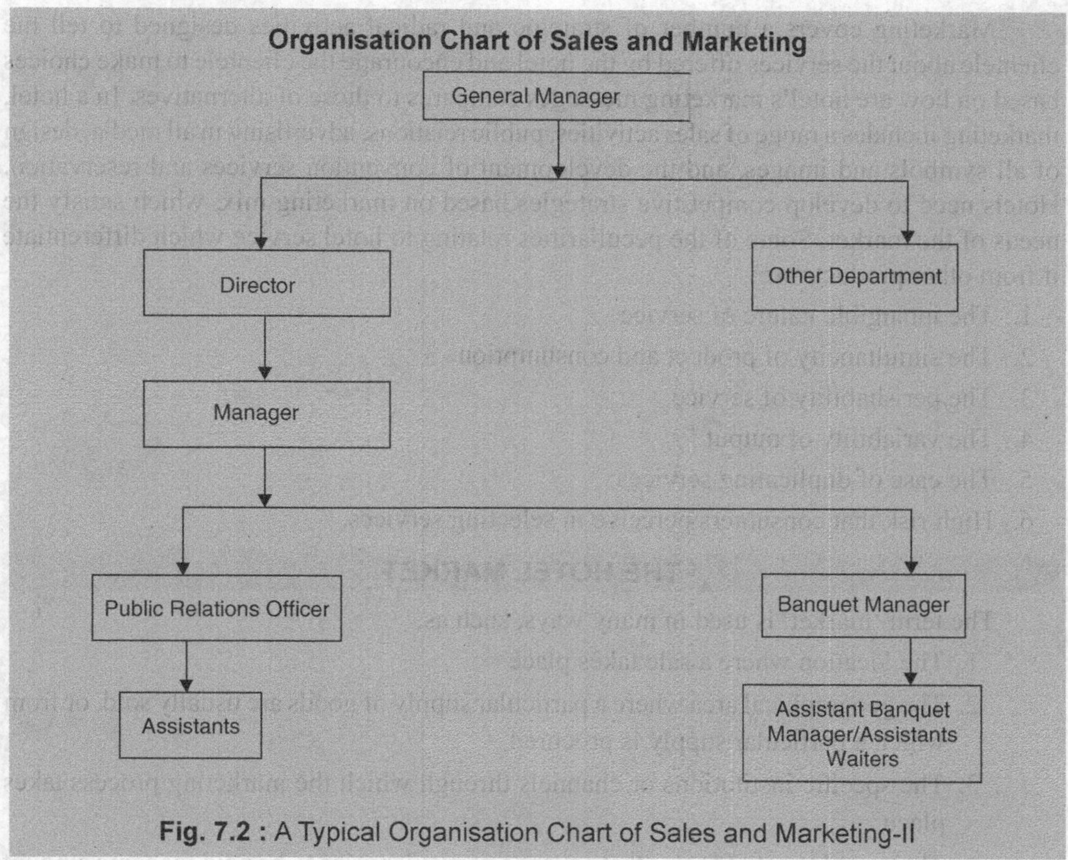

Fig. 7.2 : A Typical Organisation Chart of Sales and Marketing-II

sales budget, inter-departmental cooperation, research and training, sales departmental management, selling stimulus, personal selling, display advertising, internal selling, direct mail, general advertising.[2]

Marketing is the total process by which goods and services are designed, presented, merchandised and delivered to the ultimate consumer. It is the key to success in the hotel industry. According to Philip Kotler, marketing may be defined as sensitively serving and satisfying human needs[3]. Management consultant Peter Drucker supports the distinction that selling focuses on the needs of the seller, while marketing focuses on the needs of the buyer.[4] According to C. Dewitt Coffman, Get the confidence of the public and you have no dificulty in getting their patronage. Inspire your whole force with the right spirit of service; encourage every sign of the true spirit. So display and advertise wares that customer shall buy with understanding. Treat them as guests when they come and when they go, whether or not they buy. Give them all that can be given fairly, on the principle that to them that giveth shall be given. Remember always that the recollection of quality remains long after the price is forgotten.[5]

2. Ref. C. Dewitt Coffman, a leading sales expert. Modern Hotel and Motel Management, Gerald W. Lattin, Page 173.
3. Philip Kotler and Sindey Levy, Broadenings the Concepts of Marketing, Journal of Marketing, Vol. 33 (January 1969), Page 15.
4. Peter Drucker, Management Consultant.
5. Retailing, 'Great' H. Gordon Selridge.

Marketing covers a number of strategic and radical activities designed to tell the clientele about the services offered by the hotel and encourage the clientele to make choices based on how are hotel's marketing messages compares to those of alternatives. In a hotel, marketing includes a range of sales activities, public relations, advertising in all media, design of all symbols and images, and the development of convention services and reservation. Hotels need to develop competitive strategies based on marketing mix, which satisfy the needs of the market. Some of the peculiarities relating to hotel service which differentiate it from other products are:

1. The intangible nature of service
2. The simultaneity of product and consumption
3. The perishability of service
4. The variability of output
5. The ease of duplicating services
6. High risk that consumers perceive in selecting services.

THE HOTEL MARKET

The term 'market' is used in many ways, such as,

1. The location where a sale takes place
2. The geographical area where a particular supply of goods are usually sold, or from which a particular supply is procured
3. The specific institutions or channels through which the marketing process takes place
4. The complex set of forces that causes a particular price to be paid for some amount of goods and/or services.

COMPONENTS OF MARKETING SYSTEM

The former President of Treadway Inns and Resorts, Dewitt Coffman asserts that there are six components of marketing :[6]

1. People
2. Product
3. Package
4. Price
5. Promotion
6. Performance.

In developing a marketing plan for a hotel, each of these elements must be considered as part of an integrated marketing system.

PEOPLE

1. Who are the present or potential customers ?
2. Where are they ?
3. What are their needs, desires and constraints?

PRODUCT

1. What are the existing or planned facilities and services?

6. Dewitt Coffman, former President of Treadway Inns and Resorts, USA.

2. How closely do they match?
3. Can they be made to correspond with what guests want?

PRICE

1. Consider the hotel's needs to operate at a profit while offering product which are competitive not only with other comparable hotel facilities but with other products such as vacation abroad, second homes, camping, jewellery and furs.

PROMOTION

1. Utilise all appropriate communication media and merchandising tools.
2. Attract the attention of the prospects.
3. See that the product and price are right.

PERFORMANCE

1. Living up to what has been promised in every respect in order to maximize the guests, length of stay and amount of spending, the customer will become a repeat customer and an ambassador of goodwill.

MARKETING MIX

The three elements of the marketing plans are :

1. The Customer or Prospect Mix
   (*i*) Who are present customers?
   (*ii*) Who are desired as customers?
2. The Service Mix:
   (*i*) What needs and wants of each group are now being met?
   (*ii*) What needs and wants of each group should be met in future?
3. The Promotion Mix :
   It deals with assessing
   (*i*) How the demand is being cultivated and sustained?
   (*ii*) How it should be ?
4. The Promotion Mix include :
   (*i*) Advertising
   (*ii*) Promotion
   (*iii*) Merchandising
   (*iv*) Personal selling etc.

SALES TECHNIQUES

This department is responsible for administering and directing sales efforts within several areas into which the sales function is normally divided. Selling of hotel products/ services may be done through a marketing group or directly with the public through travel agencies. The important responsibilities of this department are :

1. Planning is the most important responsibility of this department. Group and convention sales, travel agents' sales and banquet sales are booked in advance, which require proper planning.

2. Process of selling must be done with certain policies in mind. Clear policies must be laid down for rates and tariffs for future bookings, size of groups, amount of advance deposits, commission to be paid, complementary rooms, allotments of rooms, rooming lists, pre-labelling of baggage, pre-assignment of rooms and overall handling procedures.
3. Detailed research must be carried out to ascertain and develop the possible sources of business.
4. To administer and manage the departmental activities.
5. Cooperation with other departments of the hotel is fundamental to the proper delivery of the services that are sold.
6. Proper training of the staff which is less experienced must be arranged.
7. The department must prepare its own budget and must be responsible to see that it operates within it.
8. To communicate with possible sources of business by direct mail.
9. Attempts are made to develop hotel business by selling facilities to employees of other segments of the overall corporation.

The total travel market consists of three basic elements :

1. Domestic tourists.
2. Foreign tourism incoming tourists.
3. Foreign tourism outgoing tourists.

The demand for tourist accommodation within the country is made up of the first and third categories. In most of the countries accommodation facilities are mostly designed to cater for the domestic as well as the foreign market. Hotels and other tourist accommodation facilities predominate in countries with high volume of foreign visitors in relation to the volume of internal travel. For most of the users of touristic accommodation, hotel rooms and services are a means to an end and not an end itself. The supply of the hotel room is fixed in time and place. In the short-term the number of rooms cannot be changed and location is part of the highly perishable product, which cannot be stored for future sale or follow the customer. The demand for hotel product fluctuates from day to day, wall to wall, month to month and from one part of the year to another. There are slack and peak seasons which lead to waste and increase in volume of business, respectively.

The bulk of the hotel investment is in fixed assets, combined with the continuity of hotel activity, which give rise to high fixed costs. This is to be recovered irrespective of the volume of business. The key factors for a successful hotel operation are the right location, correct capacity and a high level of utilisation. In the hotel operation, marketing can contribute through a continuous process of market research, product development promotion, selling, monitoring and review. All hotel services are tangible and cannot be easily defined and described in terms of clearly measurable products and their qualities. All these services are brought individually or as part of the package. According to American Uniform System of Accountants for Hotels(64), The efforts of a hotel to obtain and retain customers for its products or services may include many activities. Among them are :

1. Building the image of operations
2. Developing an awareness by the customer for the hotel's products and

3. Stimulating customers to patronise its various service outlets.

These activities are interrelated and make up what is generally termed the marketing effort of a company. In the new schedule .... the various expenses associated with the marketing programme are listed. Combined, they show the result of using all of the techniques of merchandising, selling, promoting and public relations, by both the internal staff and various outside agencies, to produce business for the hotel.

According to T. C. Levitt in 'Marketing Myopia' (Harvard Business Review, July/August 1960), the difference between marketing and selling[7] is more than semantic. Selling focuses on the needs of the seller, marketing on the needs of the buyer. Selling is pre-occupied with the seller's need to convert his product into cash, marketing with the idea of satisfying the needs of the customer by means of the product and the whole cluster of things associated with creating, delivering and finally consuming it.

Similarly R. Doswell in Towards an Integrated Approach to Hotel Planning states, The paradox is that when the marketing concept is observed and carried through in the entire planning process of a new service, the sales effort required in the long-run should be minimal. Where great emphasis is on sales required, it usually means that the hotel marketing concept has been disregarded, it is an enormous task to try and sell something which people neither need nor desire. This does not mean marketing replaces sales but they are complimentary to each other. If marketing establishes what people need, then sale function demonstrates that their needs can be fulfilled.[8]

The marketing function is seen not merely as a department of business, but as coordinating all aspects of the business and it exists to achieve the overall objectives of the business. According to the British Institute of Marketing, Marketing is the management function which organises and directs all those business activities involved in assessing and converting customers' purchasing power into effective demand for a specific product or service and in moving the product or service to the final customer or user so as to achieve the profit target or other objectives set by the company.[9]

THE APPROACH

The essentials for marketing approach may be outlined as follows:

1. Know your market:
   (*i*) Your potential customers' feelings by research, such as
   – Travel patterns
   – Guest preference studies
   – Guest histories.
2. Know your competitors:
   (*i*) Hotels
   (*ii*) Motels
   (*iii*) Friends and relatives where travellers stay
   (*iv*) Camping areas

7. T. C. Levitt, Marketing Myopia, Harvard Business Review, July/August 1960
8. R. Doswell, Towards an Integrated Approach to Hotel Planning.
9. British School of Marketing.

(*v*) Competitors such as sellers of jewellery, fur, colour TVs, automobiles etc.

3. Know your product :
   (*i*) Limitation
   (*ii*) Capabilities.
4. Redesign your product
   (*i*) Changing market
   (*ii*) Competition
   (*iii*) Modernisation
   (*iv*) Redecorating
   (*v*) Installation of new products
   – In-room motion pictures
   – Automobile food dispensers
   – Creation of package plans
   – Arrangements for inclusive tain package with airlines and travel agents.
   – Right pricing
   – Cararante for facilities and service advertised.
5. Use all the marketable tools effectively
   (*i*) Techniques of advertising
   (*ii*) Direct mail
   (*iii*) Sales promotion
   (*iv*) Publicity.

The visitors from abroad are the primary sources of business for hotels.International tourism is developing more rapidly and both governmentand the private sector are making substantial efforts to attract visitorsfrom abroad. There are many ways through which hotels at littlecost can cash on opportunities being offered by international tourism.Some of these methods are:

1. Contact the wholesalers to include your hotels in theirpackage tours.
2. Co-operate with airlines and other organisations bringingforeign tourists and travel writers on familiarization tours.
3. Make promotional material available for distributionoverseas in the language of the country where it is to be disseminated.
4. Special interest groups are an important source ofbusiness. Wildlife tours, adventure tours, historical site's tours,have bright possibilities.
5. Provide special promotional rates for internationalvisitors specially encouraging them during slack periods.
6. 'Extend the invitation' by advertising in directorieswhich are used by travel agents to increase markets in planning hotelaccommodation for their clients.
7. Write directly to those overseas travel agents sendingsignificant number of their clients.
8. Utilize the services of hotel representatives operatingabroad.
9. Ask business clients to urge international groupsto hold their conventions. Make a direct approach to the head of foreignassociations and their convention holders.

The American Hotel & Motel Association has offered the following suggestionswhich are practicable while servicing international visitors:

1. Correspondence from abroad should be answered promptlyand in the language of the person who has written.
2. Do something about the language problem, such as
   (*i*) Utilize the language skill of your employees as interpreters
   (*ii*) Provide employees and foreign guests with phrase bookswhich have English translations for travellers, of words commonlyused.
   (*iii*) Have menus available at least in French, German, English,Spanish and local version.
   (*iv*) Provide for easy and fair currency exchange.
   (*v*) Make available tape recorders with foreign languagetapes to be used on local tours
   (*vi*) In handling group tours, pre-register members of theparty, be sure all members of the group understand meal and tippingarrangements and that all accounts are settled before departure.

GROUPS AND CONVENTIONS

It is the largest divisions of the sales department both in terms of time and efforts and number of people employed. The hotel must evaluate the number of rooms it wishes to allot to group sales. After making an estimate of the transient business, the rest of the anticipated available rooms can be allocated to group sales. There must be continual communication with such organisation to learn of decisions made in respect of dates and geographical areas being considered for future conventions/conferences. The member of the group and convention sales department of the hotel must continually travel and visit the travel agents and their operators whose principal business is the handling of incentive groups and other groups and convention sales.

TRAVEL AGENT

Travel agents are spread across the length and breadth of the country. It requires substantial travel by sales staff. Sales calls must be made even in small towns which are potentially good sources of business. The representatives personally visit the retail and wholesale travel agencies. From retail agencies they can ascertain that brochures and rate sheets for their property/properties are displayed there. The staff of the retail travel agency must be made familiarised with the characteristics of the property and motivate them to sell the property or recommend it in preference to others. The wholesalers should be persuaded to incorporate the property into their packages which requires negotiations on sales and room allotment. Some of the hotel use direct mailings of promotional literature to agents as a means of developing interest and business. The degree of discount and complementary offer must be given to the travel agency personnel on the basis of the importance of the agency, its location and the amount of potential business that may be developed.

Many large hotels employ a group or Convention coordinator for proper handling of business that is already booked. He works closely with the group leader or leaders to ensure that the entire event is handled properly from beginning to end. He resolves problems, soothes angered guests and meets all emergencies. He has the responsibility for handling of airport arrivals, baggage handling, proper running of all the functions and verifies with the group leader daily charges to the group master account 'Calls reports' and 'Group Booking Sheets' are prepared. The Call Report is a record of results of a sales call on a prospective customer and the Group Booking Sheet records the details of a prospective sale on an estimated, or tentative or final. These forms are prepared in several copies to permit follow up or to advise those people who should be aware of the bookings or sales calls.

Cocktail parties must be offered to the staff of the travel agencies in various cities throughout the year. This will provide an opportunity for the sales staff to meet the agents. A presentation can be made in these parties, setting out the features the hotel has to make.

BANQUET

The type and nature of functions of the banquet business consists of weddings, dinners, dance and social events, cocktail parties, meeting of business firms, companies, etc. Pre-established menus and prices should be used so that the potential customer could select an appropriate menus (Refer : Figure 10.9 Banquet Menus). The main source of business is the local community in which the hotel is located. Proper relationship and close contact with the community must be maintained with major companies in the area, fraternal and charitable organisations. Such organisations and associations have periodic meetings, dinners and other functions.

OTHER AREAS

Other sources of business of the hotel trade also need to be tapped and the work could be assigned to the local sales manager. Important among them are airlines, travel agents and tour operators, secretaries, taxi drivers, professional people and embassies. Good relations and close contact with the following segments will help to promote business. Social packages should also be promoted to obtain weekend business.

1. Airlines
2. Travel and Tour Operators
3. Secretaries
4. Professional people
5. High Commission and Embassies
6. Local taxi drivers.

ADVERTISING

Advertising is one of the most common ways of promoting a hotel. Advertising must be effective and should be seen by the public the hotel wishes to attract. The theme of the hotel should be carried through, to give it individuality and make it easily recognised. If budget permits, advertising agencies may be approached as they have a flow of ideas and are able to give advice on the layout of the advertisement, the timing and the placing in the newspapers and magazines.

PROMOTION CAMPAIGN

The Koehl, Landis & Landan. Inc., a New York advertising agency, with many hotel/motel clients prepared a comprehensive checklist for advertising promotion campaign. You may use it to serve as a guide in improving the extent and the impact of your hotel property's advertising campaign:[10]

1. Magazine Advertising
2. Outdoor Advertising
   (*i*)Highway
   (*ii*)Railway
   (*iii*) Station Poster
3. Radio
4. Television
5. Direct Mail
6. Car Cards
7. Trade Papers
8. Rack Folder
9. Menus
10. Beverage List
11. Table 'Tent' Card
12. Menu Flyers
13. Service Directories
14. Stationery
15. Post Cards
16. Match Boxes
17. Convention Signs and
    (*i*) Display Material
18. All Inclusive Package
    (*i*) Promotion
19. Banquet and Convention Brochures
20. Novelties
21. Wash Cloths
22. Razor Black Cloths
23. Laundry Bags
24. Entertainment Promotion
25. Special Material for
    (*i*) Fire Promotion
    (*ii*) Water Conservation, etc.
26. Employees Operating Manuals
27. Rate Sheets
28. Daily Function Boards
29. Desk Calendars
30. Photography
    (*i*) Black and White
    (*ii*) Colour
31. Interior Promotions for Concessionaires
32. Trade Mark & Emblems
    (*i*) For Printed Material,
    (*ii*) Uniforms, service plates,
    (*iii*) Lines etc.
33. Slogans
34. Coordination of colour and design
35. Special Promotions
    (1) Fashion Shows
    (2) Holiday Parties, etc.
    (3) Elevator Cards
    (4) 'Do Not Disturb Cards'
    (5) 'Maid' Cards
    (6) Registration Cards
    (7) Reservation Forms
    (8) Business Cards
    (9) Sales Letters
    (10) Key Tag Designs
    (11) Letter Stickers
    (12) Cocktail Napkins
    (13) Cocktail coasters
    (14) High Ball Stirrers
    (15) Shipping Labels
    (16) Baggage Stikers & Tags
    (17) Shoe Cloths
    (18) Design and Preparing
    (19) Telephone Book
    (20) Covers
    (21) Time Table Advertising
    (22) Speeches by Excutives,
    (23) Articles etc.
    (24) Labels for Private Bottling
    (25) Remembrance Advertising
    (26) Publicity
    (27) Travel Agency
    (28) Promotional Material
    (29) Advertising Display
    (30) Material for Travel Agents
    (31) Gasoline Stations, etc.
    (32) Production of Sound Motion
    (33) Pictures
    (34) Roof Signs

10. The Koehl, Landis and Landan, Inc., a New York Advertising Agency.

(a) Personnel (Elevator Operators,
(b) Bellmen, Waiters, Telephone Operators etc.)
(c) Birthday Cards
(d) Christmas Cards
(e) Credit Cards

36. Exterior Displays
37. Advertising valances for Marquees
38. Naming New Rooms and
39. Restaurants.

BASICS FOR ADVERTISING-PROMOTION SALES

The most efficient results from advertising promotion sales could be achieved from the guidelines given below :

1. Cultivate those who have been customers in the past.
2. Concentrate on a few effective marketing tools, use them well rather than try to do everything at once. In other words, 'use a rifle instead of a shotgun'.
3. Stick with the tried and true.
4. Talk the language of the customer. Use those medium which get through to them and emphasize the appeal that are most meaningful to them.

You must observe the following rules to get the most out of your advertising :

1. Have an advertising plan.
2. Be flexible
3. Synergize : Take advantage of the help offered by other companies. Tie in with their ads and promotions.
4. Simplify
5. Don't go off the deep end
6. Exaggeration and overselling make poor advertising and unhappy customers
7. Be customer oriented and use examples
8. Test the results :
   (*i*) Ask guests if they have seen your advertisement.
   (*ii*) What they think of them?
   (*iii*) Whether they are influenced by the advertisement?

It is advisable to use a professional advertising agency when planning a major campaign. An outline can be given to the advertising department of the local paper or radio station, which will then prepare the finished advertisement. The key messages which must be included in an advertisement are:

1. The name of the hotel
2. Whether the hotel is a part of the national chain ?
3. The address, telephone and fax numbers
4. What is an offer-room, restaurant, catering, leisure club
5. Opening and closing hours
6. The style of food and drinks on offer
7. Special features, such as jazz etc.
8. Whom to contact for what ?

The written brief should cover the following:

1. The objective of the advertisement
2. The menu message
3. The target customers
4. The use of colour or mono
5. The selection of media to reach the target
6. The timing of the advertisement
7. The budget.

The choice of media depends on budget and the target audience. There are various media of advertisement :

1. TV
2. Newspapers (national and local)
3. Magazines and Colour Supplements
4. Static Poster sites.
5. Mobilesbuses and taxies
6. Radio and Cinema
7. Sponsorships
8. Local clubs
9. Charity brochures etc.

Large hotel compaines organise their own local campaigns. This requires that the hotel progresses and reviews the various stages in the preparation of effective advertisements and be aware of the advertising production cycle.

1. Advertising brief
2. Production of visual and draft copy
3. Review and amend
4. Revised visual copy
5. Approval and minor amendment
6. Art work
7. Art work amendment (minimal)
8. Revised art work
9. Art work apporved and to publication.

ADVERTISING BUDGET

Hotels spend about five per cent of room sales income on advertising and sales promotion. The break-down of this normally spreads into different media depending on a number of factors, such as :

1. Size of the hotel/property
2. Age of the hotel/property
3. Location
4. Indentified market.

A typical break-down of media utilized, expressed as ratio to room sales is given below :

Media Utilized	*Percentage of Room Sales*
Printed Materials	0.5%
Franchise fees	0.7%
Signs	0.8%
Radio and Television	1.1%
Newspapers and Magazines	1.0%
Miscellaneous	1.7%
Total	5.8%

DIRECT MAIL

Direct mail advertising is the second only to newspapers as an advertising medium in the hotel industry. It is the most widely used promotional tool because of the following advantages:

1. Selectivity : Pick-up the people you want your message to reach.
2. Timing : Choose the timing when your message will be received.
3. Flexibility : Control the size, shape and format of the material.
4. Cost Efficiency : It is the least expensive in terms of reaching a selected group, although it is the most expensive medium in terms of what it cost to reach an individual prospect.
5. Versatility : You may use it for a wide variety of purposes.

The success of the direct mail campaign depends 'firstly,'on attractive and carefully selection list of names and 'secondly,'on a well written, attractively produced letter with a compelling sales messages. Compile mailing lists from your files and utilize sources such as local telephones and city directories, organisation membership lists, etc.

Direct mail is the most cost-effective way of communication with a target audience. The recipient of a direct mail shot, want details of the service offered and endorsement of a few satisfied customers.

Selling in the hotel starts with the telephonist or receptionist who takes the initial enquiry and continues through all contact with the prospective client until the details of a sale are agreed. Corporate business opportunities include:

1. Hospitality organisers :
   (*i*) Public Relations Managers
   (*ii*) Personnel Managers
   (*iii*) Personal Assistants
   (*iv*) Senior Secretaries
2. Travel Agents
3. Tour Operators
4. Associations and societies organising regular meetings
5. Conference and Exhibition Organisers.

The key to effective selling is organisation, planning and timing. The sales person must have well defined sales plans taking into account the following elements:

1. What is to be sold ?
2. To whom it is to be sold ?

3. What is the price ?
4. What are the benefits over the competitors ?

The plan must be backed up with good product knowledge and an effective presenter.

OUTDOOR ADVERTISING

Different modes of outdoor advertising are :

1. Poster or bill boards
2. Painted walls or buildings
3. Transportation advertising
4. Marquees
5. Window displays and
6. Signs on the property itself.

Keep your letter style simple and avoid script or italic letters except in unusual circumstances. As a rule of thumb, each two inches of letter height adds about a hundred feet to the distance at which a letter can be seen and read. An eight inch letter should be readable, therefore, from a far way as 400 feet. Letters and words must be properly spaced. To get full effectiveness from your sign at night it must be planned to stand out from traffic lights, car headlights and nearby lighted signs. Advertising experts are of the opinion that internally illuminated signs are the most efficient and effective for both day and night.

NEWSPAPER AND MAGAZINE ADVERTISING

Newspaper and magazine advertising calls for use of the best professional talent. The production aspects must be left to the experts. Observe the following guiding priniciples :

1. Media selection : The number of prospects who will see an advertisement.
2. Repetition : Advertising gain in effectiveness by repetition.
3. Objective : Each advertisement should give a specific purpose, such as,
   (*i*) attract conventions
   (*ii*) develop week-end business
   (*iii*) promote food and beverage facilities.
4. Appearance : Advertisement should reflect the image of the property/ hotel and copy should be appropriately worded for the target audience.
5. Distinctiveness : Each advertisement should be made to create and stay with a personality that will be easily recognised. This may be achieved through use of symbols or logotype copy style, illustration or type style.

YELLOW PAGES

In view of low cost of this medium, hotels should consider yellow pages advertisement in local telephone directories.

SALES LETTERS

Sales letters should be tailored to the audience and reflect the personality of the writer. Here are some practical points for good sales letters :

1. Plan your letter first
2. Write as you would talk
3. Use simple action words
4. Edit carefully.
5. Capture the readers' attention
6. Be clear, concise and brief
7. Be friendly and positive.

PERSONAL SELLING

Personal selling is the most potent method for promoting hotel sales. The seller has an opportunity to make a complete presentation of his sales story, to answer all objections and follow through to the computation of a sale with a signed order. All this can occur in one meeting with the prospect. You must coach the entire hotel staff and they should be required to offer sales suggestions. The following are some of the examples :

1. *Front Office* : When the guest registers, the room clerk should suggest a more expensive room for view, additional comforts, mention food facilities, in room motion pictures etc.
2. *Bell Desk* : While rooming guest, Bellman should mention speciality of the restaurant, hotel entertainment facilities, etc.
3. *Bar / Restaurant* : While serving meals waitress/waiter should suggest speciality of the house, beverages with meal, featured desserts etc.

The Intercontinental prepared a manual for its sales manager which contains the following suggestions regarding effective personal selling:[11]

1. Have a specific reasons for making the call. Don't just drop into exchange pleasantries.
2. Study the organisation you plan to call on its products, organisation, eating habits, etc.
3. Plan your selling approach to emphasize benefits to the customer and how your property and service are superior to competitors.
4. Work out your sales presentation carefully and reherse it, so that interruptions will not throw you off the track.
5. Strive to get
   (*i*) A definite commitment
   (*ii*) At least a tentative booking
   (*iii*) A commitment from the prospect to inspect your facilities.
6. Leave something with the prospect to aid his recalla rate card, folder, a small souvenir.
7. To be on time for your appointment
8. Make sure your prospect knows who you are and the property you represent. Hand him your business card.
9. Be concise. Get to the point, don't overstay your welcome.
10. Use visual aids such a floor plans, photographs and simple menus to drive your point home.
11. Look at things from the prospect's point of view.
    (*i*) Find out his needs
    (*ii*) Let him set the place, if he wants details, give him details
    (*iii*) Listen
12. Don't oversell leave when you have made the sale or finished your presentation.

---

11. Interncontinental Hotel, USA.

SELLING BY TELEPHONE

The manual prepared by the Intercontinental for its sales managers, give the following advice for effective telephone selling :

1. Be available, make sure incoming sale calls are routed straight to the sales office. Let assoicates know where you can be reached.
2. Speak the prospect's language.
3. Ask questions, find out all you can about the prospect's needs and plans. He may require facilities or services beyond what he is inquiring about.
4. Take notes, don't trust your memory for correct spelling of a prospect's name, his address and phone number, his requirements and essential follow up.
5. Don't take 'No' for an aswer. Try to get an appointment for a personal visit or a commitment to inspect your property.

RADIO AND TELEVISION ADVERTISING

Advertising on the air i.e. radio and television, is quite reasonable and more effective in small communities. Room on food and beverage sales could be promoted from spot advertisement. Through radio and TV, you get opportunities to sponsor or participate in variety of activities such as local sporting events, speeches by distinguished individuals, tie-ins with local promotions of other businesses or organisations.

ADVERTISING-PROMOTION-SALES

Advertising requires careful planning, organisation and execution. The following guidlines would be valuable :

1. Set aside funds for information gathering and research
2. Set attainable market and advertising goals
3. Find out what your guests want
4. Select the most communicative media
5. Don't cut your advertising budget in lean years
6. Carry your messages to your specific market
7. Measure the results of your advertising programme
8. Regularly review your budget, goal and media mix.

PUBLIC RELATIONS AND GUEST RELATION

Public relations is the art of keeping a hotel's business favourable in the public eye. It extends into the possible structuring of relations with members of the public as to leave a favourable impression of hotel's activities and create a favourable image for their properties. The public relations in a hotel may have numerous audiences, the public, employees, the financial community, and specialised segments, such as entertainment industry and travel industry. In small hotels the work is assigned to resident manager or assistant to general manager. In large hotels the job is assigned to full-time employees. One of the jobs of a public relations representative is to act as a source of reliable information.

Public relations is being a good neighbour, a good citizen, as well as a good business executive. Ninety per cent of public relations is simply the knack of establishing and maintaining good relationships, the other ten percent is being recognised for your activities and contributions. Public relations may be discribed as the planned effort to influence opinion through socially responsible performance based on mutually satisfactory two-way communication. If a hotel is favourably known in the community, on the national scene and to other hotels, it can get a lot of business.

Given below are some examples of public relations:

1. Smiling at people;
2. Shovelling snow off the front side walk;
3. Having a staff of neat and efficient employees.
4. Having an attractive awning over the front of the establishment on afternoons;
5. Saving an old display item for that freckled-faced kid down the street;
6. Asking a father how his children are;
7. Interest in community activities and taking dynamic part in local, state and national associations.
8. Remembering a man's name when he comes into your establishment after not having been there for some time ;
9. Stopping to talk with a customer;
10. Being an active temple/church member and a civic leader;
11. Lending your support to a student, scout or other worthwhile community campaign.

The basic tool for public relations is the press kit. The press kit facilitates the job, assists in contact with the media and is generally the mark of a professional at work. Some of the elements of a press kit are :

1. The fact sheet about the hotel :–
   (*i*) Name, address, telephone number
   (*ii*) Name of general manager
   (*iii*) Number of rooms and suites
   (*iv*) Number of restaurants
   (*v*) Number of bars and lounges
   (*vi*) Special feature and guest amenities such as swimming pools, health clubs, massage, sauna baths, beaches etc.
   (*vii*) Ball rooms and meeting room and their capacities, etc.
   (*viii*) Parking and garage facilities
   (*ix*) Name of resident manager
   (*x*) Name of Executive Chef.
2. Location of the hotel
3. Special features of the hotel architecture, decor, suite etc.
4. Description about hotels, restaurant, and lounges
5. Interior and exterior photograph of the hotel
6. A brief bibliography of hotel's general manager.

Hotels use a large number of public relation activities, for example, activities, such as:

BEFORE THE LAUNCH

1. Announcement of planning consent
2. Appointment of architect and designers
3. Cutting the first rod.
4. Foundation stone and topping out ceremony
5. Appointment of key staff
6. Launch party and press launch.

ON OPENING OF THE HOTEL

1. Announcement of special promotions
2. Write-up on visiting chiefs and VIPs
3. Publication of a diary of special events
4. Monthly newsletter.

You may use the following check list to ensure that the right information has been included in all the above activities:

1. A short headline incapsulating the subject of the story
2. An introductory paragraph setting out main elements of who, what why and where.
3. Three, four paragraphs developing these elements in order of importance.
4. If appropriate, a quotable quote from the personality incharge.
5. Contact name, address and telephone number for further information.

SPECIAL OFFERS AND EVENTS

Special events in the calendar and seasonal dishes represent an opportunity to add variety to the basic menu. It creates a reputation for excitement and fun. The regular customer is keen to try the 'special' and may well advise friends to also try the dishes. Special offers and events may include:

1. A regular dish of the day
2. Seasonal menus
3. Independence/Republic day
4. Menus for children
5. Culinary festivals
6. Cultural weeks, with special guests
7. Fashion and art festivals
8. Open days with schools and colleges.

PUBLIC RELATIONS PROGRAMMES

Public relations programmes/activities would provide the business, build employees' morale and productivity and generate goodwill in the community. Suggested below are some of the programmes and activities you can arrange in your hotel :

1. The annual day celebrations inviting retarded children.
2. Community relation programmes to unify students and corporate citizens.
3. Sponsorship for publicity and coverage on a nation-wide
4. TV network.
5. Celebrity sports leads to extensive pictures, news, features and radio coverage.
6. Cultivating local secretaries : To encourage the secretaries to book accommodations, meetings and food and beverage functions. Mail a monthly newsletter to the secretaries of the various departments/organisations and ministries.
7. Assistance to visitors from abroad : Establish a multi-lingual national toll-free travel information centre to provide answers in appropriate language to foreign visitor or attract public transportation, airways, accommodation, sight-seeing, adventure sports and any other travel topics. Similarly, organise interpreter service for visitors from abroad with answer by telephone to question about attractions, dining, accommodations and travel and general information.
8. Programme to improve/boost employees' morale : If required, the following activities are organised to improve the employees' communication, morale and productivity :–
   (*i*) Set up an employees' council to facilitate upward communication and to involve employees' participation.
   (*ii*) Publish employees' magazine/journalInitiate an improved employee orientation programme
   (*iii*) Special programme to honour employees for unusual loyalty or dedication.

PUBLIC RELATION OFFICER

The public relation officer should have a good knowledge of how the various services in a hotel operate. He must have the knowledge of foreign languages. He works under the direct responsibility of the management and assists in increasing the clientele and makes contact for the purpose. He reports and makes suggestions to the management. The important job of this department is to organise publicity, receptions and to represent the manager at outside reception. Publicity and preparation of brochures and folders is also under the charge of this department.

Hotel companies have fierce competition to attract large groups, companies and organizations. As regards to convention sale, these are booked in advance and hotels are called upon to guarantee minimum room rate/tariffs and offer other inducements such as free meeting rooms and discount on banquets. In many hotels we find public relation directors or guest relation directors who are responsible for promoting the image of the hotel.

The entertainment of VIP visitors is one of the major duties as it results in pictures and publicity in newspapers and publications.

The public relation department is also responsible for fashion shows, beauty contests and other activities. It also handles the hospitality desk in the hotel.

With increased operating costs and competitions, all the hotel companies try to ensure that each of the facilities they provide is fully utilised. This results in the appointment of more marketing and sales staff, which need to have efficient training and education in selling and public relation areas rather than a background in hotel management.

GUEST RELATIONS EXECUTIVE

In most of the large sized hotels a guest relations executive is appointed to handle the public relations with guests. He/she is responsible for receiving VIPs and attending to any coordinational aspect regarding them.

Advertising and sales promotion includes all costs incurred in connection with the maintenance of the present goodwill of the hotel and the creation, promotion and furtherance of new business, whether paid for in cash or in hotel trade. Many hotels enter into contracts for advertising for long periods. The cost thereof should be prorated over the term of the contract, and the unexpired portion carried as a deferred asset in the balance sheet.

PRESS RELATIONS

The American Hotel and Motel Association's Public Relations Director, Al Kudrle, offers some valuable suggestions concerning good public relations.[12] Some of these are :

DOES :

1. Do keep in touch frequently with representatives of all news media:
   (*i*) Daily newspaper editors
   (*ii*) Weekly newspaper editors
   (*iii*) Radio and television news editors.
2. Do contact these people only when you have solid factual news, such as
   (*i*) Plans for improvement
   (*ii*) Rehabilitation programme
   (*iii*) Appointment of key personnel
   (*iv*) Open house programme
   (*v*) Career day programme for undergraduates/students etc.
   (*vi*) Others.
   Always give date, time, place, etc.
3. Do be fair : Supply same information to all news media at the same time.
4. Do make sure the names are spelled correctly and the news release is accurate in every respect.
5. Don'ts
   (*i*) Don't call the editor to ask if he has plans to use the material
   (*ii*) Don't ask to use a copy of the story before it is printed
   (*iii*) Don't ask for a sheet containing the article. Buy a copy of the paper yourself.

You must develop a press fact sheet/memeographed sheet giving the essential data about your hotel property. They may be very useful aid to ensure accuracy in the media whenever they have occasion to refer to your hotel. The press fact sheet may contain :

1. Data and type of construction
2. Assessed valuation

12. Al Kudrle, Director Public Relations, American Hotel and Motel Association, U.S.A.

3. Number of rooms/beds
4. Name and residential phone numbers of top management
5. Ownership sole trade, partnership, corporate, cooperative, public etc.
6. Room rates double, single, suite etc.
7. Significant event in the history of the property
8. Number of employees
9. Total payrolls
10. Local taxes paid
11. Any additional information of value in writing a feature story about the hotel.

Keeps in touch/contact with radio, news departments and programme directors. Arranges talk shows of key staff such as a Chef or of important guests. TV also offers good publicity opportunities. Look for material with visual impact such as,

1. How to prepare an exotic dish demonstration
2. Speaking appearances by well known people
3. Athletic tournaments.

Contact prominent clubs, civic and social organisations to offer the services of an appropriate member of the hotel staff as a guest speaker; you may suggest talks on a number of interesting hotel-tourism related subjects.

PUBLICITY

Many local newspapers will be interested if you are elected as a president of a reputed club, to attend a chamber of commerce meeting or a sales and marketing seminar, or to a talk or to plan an unusual display or event. In all such cases you should send your story typed, double spaced, on one side of the page to the editor of the newspaper. Put your name, address and phone number on the left-hand corner of the page. Put below this 'Release on Receipt' or 'Hold or Release (date)' as desired by you. In the 'lead' the first sentence or two tell the most important facts and thereafter, follow this with more and complete details.

In case your story carries photographs it is advisable to have them on glossy black and white pictures of 8" × 10" with good contrast. All captions, identifying people on the photo should be from left to right and pasted on the back or at the bottom of the photo. Never write on the back of a photo. Always put a piece of cupboard in the envelop with the photo to keep it from being cracked in the mail.

A news release should confine itself to the following facts:

1. What happened ?
2. When did it happen ?
3. Where did it happen ?
4. How did it happen ?
5. Why did it happen ?
6. Who was involved ?
7. Writer's viewpoint,
8. Give spokesman's views or analysis of the happening or situation.

On the other hand in a feature story, the main object is to dramatise. From the point of view of the writer, provide human interest, appeal by colourful description of an event or person.

You may be having the ability to write or there may be someone in your staff to prepare a suitable press release. In the absence of both, you may call an editor from the newspaper office and tell him what happened or what is going to happen depending upon the event. If required you may bring a reporter or a photographer to the scene. If you are for or against something controversial, you require support for which you should pay a personal visit to the office of the paper's editorial writer.

A SOURCE OF NEWS AND FEATURE STORIES

Your hotel may be situated/located at the hub of the community. It operates 24 hours a day i.e. 365 days in a year. Therefore, your hotel should be an inexhaustible source of news and feature stories. In such hotels, there are possibilities of the followings :

1. Prominent or unusual guests
2. Important meetings/seminars/conferences, etc.
3. Significant speeches by prominent personalities
4. Social and cultural events balls, weddings, charity lunches, etc.
5. Community activities, exotic hobbies or praise-work achievement of employees.
6. The physical requirements and consumption of the hotel such as meters of carpets in the rooms, number of light bulbs, sheets, towels, etc. used weekly.
7. Heroic acts of employees or special help given to handicapped guests.
8. Community groups using facilities without charge meeting room, swimming pool etc.

PRESS CONFERENCE

As a hotel manager or head of an institution/establishment, you may have to hold a press conference on many occasions. Below are given some valuable guidelines for staging a press conference :

1. The best time to hold a press conference is 10 a.m. on Tuesday, Wednesday and Thursday. Get the advice of the newspaper editor on the best time and day. Both morning and evening newspapers, should get its share of news 'breaks'.
2. All invitations to the press conference should be sent out a week ahead of time. They should cover who, where, when, what and why as well as mention of any photo opportunities.
3. Personal phone calls should be made to all invitees, a day before the press conference.
4. Selection of room for press conference :
   (*i*) Large enough for the expected attendance
   (*ii*) The acoustics are good
   (*iii*) Well ventilated
   (*iv*) Air-conditioned or heated as appropriate
   (*v*) The PA system is in good working order
   (*vi*) Adequate electric current is available for TV, floodlight and other electric equipment

5. Tell radio and TV newsmen, when they arrive and where to set up equipment. Arrange special area where each can interview principals in the press conference afterwards.
6. Keep the conference short and to the point :
   (*i*) Hand out news releases and scripts as invitees come in
   (*ii*) Introduce principals
   (*iii*) Make presentation following format of news release and script.
   (*iv*) Questions and answers period
   (*v*) Thank invitees for coming.
7. If some media fails to attend the press conference, arrange for hand delivery of the news release.

OPENING CEREMONIES

You may have to handle an opening ceremony. It may be a pre-view of the opening of a new or expanded facility in your hotel. The hotel will first have a 'soft' or unpublished opening. It will accept 'walk ins' and some VIP guests. This will keep the 'bugs' out of operation. The official opening can be the occasion for considerable ceremony. To be successful in handling such opening, you are advised to observe three important rules :

1. Invite the press, local hoteliers, civic leaders and representatives of companies and organizations that may be potential sources of business. Don't invite the general public.
2. Keep the guest list small enough so facilities will not be overtaxed.
3. Check that all facilities and services are in good order. Rehearse ceremonies, reception, service of food and beverage etc. Your invitees may be limited to the representitive of following organisations :
   (*i*) National and International airlines
   (*ii*) Auto-rental agencies
   (*iii*) Realtors and property dealers of repute
   (*iv*) Restaurant/food and beverage outlet owners
   (*v*) Service station operators
   (*vi*) Tourist attraction managers
   (*vii*) Religious heads
   (*viii*) Neighbouring defence installations
   (*ix*) Universities/colleges and private schools.

ENVIRONMENTAL CONCERNS

Public relation counsists of 'doing good and getting credit'. All states are much concerned about the environment and hotels have great responsibility in supporting efforts to preserve a quality environment in and around the property as well as in the community. To guide the hotelieres in this mutually beneficial activity, the AH & MA's Committee for a Quality Enviornment has developed the following pledge :[13]

"As an inkeeper, my success depend on a clean environment as well as on service and a quality product. Not only do depend on the environment for today's business, but I

13 . The American Hotel and Motel Association's Committee for a Quality Environment.

recognise the importance of maintaining a quality environment for permanent future growth. I am aware that depends on nature, and that man must work with, not against nature.

"Whenever I plan new facilities, I must acknowledge my responsibility to give approval and direction to architects and building contractors that will minimise contribution to pollution and visual blight. This is an obligation to my neighbours as well as to future progress.

"Therefore, with full recognition that these requirements might increase project costs, I agree to accept all even points of the following pledge :

1. My construction plans will specify that as many trees and shrubs or as much ground cover, will remain untouched, as possible. Should trees have to be removed, healthy new trees will be planted in other areas of the site.
2. Attractive landscaping will be planted.
3. The contractor will be required to schedule his work so that as little raw earth as possible will be exposed to the elements for the shortest possible time. If the construction site is large, or the schedule prolonged, to minimise erosion, vegetation, a mulch will be placed on earth, and sediment basins will be built to keep neighouring ravines, streams, rivers and the like free from silt pollution.
4. At all times, the contractor will be encouraged to keep the building site neat and clean. This decreases visual blight as well as minimises windblown trash that night degrade neighbouring property.
5. There will be no trash burned at the site. In this way the project will not contribute to air pollution. Also, whenever possible, the contractor will be asked not to burn trees or timber.
6. When poisonous chemicals must be used for termite control, to avoid polluting the soil, application will be directed by qualified, bonded expert.
7. The least possible amount of ground will be paved to minimise water run off that causes erosion and kills plants, trees and grass. When a large area of pavement is required for functional areas, trees, and a plant beds will be built into the area.

ACCOUNTING, AUDIT AND CONTROL

EMPLOYEE REMUNERATION AND BENEFITS

Salaries, wages and other benefits paid to the following employees are debited to this account :

1. Advertising manager
2. Publicity manager
3. Press representative
4. Sales manager
5. Sales representative
6. Secretaries
7. Stenographers
8. Clerk.

EMPLOYEES' MEAL

This account is debited with the cost of food furnished to employees of this department.

EXPENSES RELATED TO ADVERTISING

1. **Agency Fee :**
   It includes advertising agency retainer fee and special fees.
2. **Car Cards :**
   All cost of advertising in rail, road, trains, street cars, sub-way trains, tax cabs, buses or any other transportation conveyances are included under this head.
3. **Due Bills :**
   Many times the expenses of advertisement are paid for by contract in rooms, food or other equivalent. The sales price of room, food etc. should be charged to this account and complete record should be maintained including the nature of such purchase, such as newspapers, magazines, outdoor, radio, television, etc.
4. **Magazine and other Publications :**
   The cost of advertising in journals, magazines, directories, special issues, telephone directories, guide books and theatre programmes are debited to this head.
5. **Newspapers :**
   The cost of advertising in newspaper is debited to this account.
6. **Preparation of Copy :**
   This account includes all creative and mechanical costs, art work, typograph, copy engraving mats, electors, etc. purchased for advertising purposes.
7. **Printing and Stationery :**
   The cost of printed forms, service manuals, stationery and office supplies used in advertising are debited to this account.
8. **Radio and Television :**
   The cost of radio broadcasting and television advertising are debited to this account.
9. **Steamship and Foreign :**
   It includes the cost of advertising in connetion with steamships or foreign countries.
10. **Miscellaneous :**
    All other expenses connected with advertising are grouped under this head.

EXPENSES RELATED TO SALES PROMOTION

1. **Civic and Community Projects :**
   It includes all costs and expenses connected with the cost of convention bureau activities, contribution to specific or general convention funds, promotion of civic community projects such as fairs, expositions etc.
2. **Entertainment :**
   The cost of entertaining for the purpose of promoting business are debited to this account. It does not include complementary rooms, accommodations, meals and other services.

3. **House Publication :**
   The cost of purchasing a house periodical issued at regular intervals for publicity purposes are debited to this account.
4. **Letter Service :**
   All expenses or costs relating to mailing lists, letter mailing, letter sealing, letter signing, envelope or card addressing etc. done by outside agency are debited to this account.
5. **Literature :**
   The cost of printed promotional matters such as circulars, pamphlets, blotters, announcements, notices, calendars etc. are debited to this head.
6. **Photo Service :**
   All expenses relating to photographers' bills, bills for photographic prints, reprints, etc. used for sales promotion are charged to this account.
7. **Postage :**
   The postage expenses in connection with sales promotion are included under this head.
8. **Printing and Stationery :**
   The cost of printed forms, service manuals, stationery and office supplies used by this department are charged to this account.
9. **Outside Sales Representation :**
   The costs of maintaining outside sales representation for the hotel are included in this account. For example, monthly fee paid to outside sales organisations for representation in conjunction local sales effort.
10. **Travel Expenses :**
    This head will include the cost of maintenance and transportation of executives or employees whose efforts are devoted to sales promotion including entertainment in route.
11. **Miscellaneous :**
    Sundry expenses relating to sales promotion which are not distributable are included under this head.

DISTRIBUTION OF ADVERTISING AND SALES PROMOTION

All advertising and sales promotion expenses are allocated on the basis of sales. In case where a particular programme of advertising or promotional is directed to a particular activity of the hotel, the hotel amount may be charged to the department operating that activity.

Figs 7.3 and 7.4 schedule indicate the expenses relating to advertising and sales promotion and marketing.

ABC Hotels Ltd.

Advertising and Sales Promotion Schedule

		Current period
Salaries and Wages	₹	
Employees' Meals	....	
Employee Benefits	....	
Total Payroll and Related Expenses		₹ ....
Advertising		
Agency Fees	₹	
Car Cards	....	
Due Bills	....	
Magazines and other Publications	....	
Miscellaneous	....	
Newspapers	....	
Outdoor	....	
Preparation of Copy	....	
Printing and Stationery	....	
Radio and Television	....	
Steamship and Foreign	....	
Total Advertising		₹ ....
Sales Promotion		
Civic and Community Project	₹	
Entertainment	....	
House Publications	....	
Letter Service	....	
Literature	....	
Miscellaneous	....	
Photo Service	....	
Printing and Stationery	....	
Postage	....	
Outside Sales Representation	....	
Travel Expenses	....	
Total Sales Promotion		₹ ....
Total Advertising and Sales Promotion	....	₹ ....

Note: Various arrangements of additional columns for comparisons and percentages could be added.

Fig. 7.3. Analysis of Expenses of Advertising and Sales Promotion

ABC Hotels Ltd.
Marketing Schedule

	Current Period
Sales	
Salaries and Wages	₹ ....
Employee Benefits	....
Total Payroll and Related Expenses	....
Other Expenses	....
Total Sales	₹ ....
Reservations	
Salaries and Wages	....
Employee Benefits	....
Total Payroll and Related Expenses	....
Other Expenses	....
Total Reservations	....
Advertising And Merchandising	₹ ....
Direct Mail	....
In-house Graphics	....
Outdoor	....
Point-of-Sale Material	....
Print	....
Radio and Television	....
Selling Aids	....
Other	....
Total Advertising and Merchandising	₹ ....
Fees and Commissions	....
Agency Fees	....
Franchise Fees	....
Others	....
Total Fees and Commissions	....
Miscellaneous Marketing Expenses	₹ ....
Total other Expenses	....
Total Marketing Expenses	....

Note : Various arrangements of additional columns for comparisons and percentages could be added.

Fig. 7.4 : Analysis of Marketing Expenditure

QUESTIONS AND ASSIGNMENTS

1. As a Manager of a hotel, how will you develop a conceptual framework for public relation of your property ? *(IHMs)*

2. Develop a Public Relations Programme for a new bakeshop. *(IHMs)*

3. "Public relations cannot be a substitute for good performance or good reputation and cannot disguise the fact that an organisation is not well run, well managed or unprofitable"- Comment. *(IHMs)*

4. What do you mean by public image ? What actions can be taken for improving public image in a five star hotel ? *(IHMs)*

5. What are the major environmental trends of Indian market likely to affect the growth of hotel industry in the coming decade ? Critically evaluate the impact of these trends. *(IHMs)*

6. Write notes on :

(*a*) Co-operative marketing

(*b*) Demographic segmentation

(*c*) Qualities of a good market segment. *(IHMs)*

7. What is product positioning ? How a marketer can analyse its existing position for effectively positioning its hotel ? *(IHMs)*

8. Differentiate between :

(*a*) Five Star Hotel and Three Star Hotel

(*b*) Commodity Market and Hotel Market

(*c*) Project Planning and Feasibility Study. *(IHMs)*

9. Produce a brief report, which demonstrate how the various type of hotels reach their market in India and abroad. *(IHMs)*

10. Write notes on :

(*a*) Public Relations

(*b*) Product Positioning

(*c*) Tourism Market Segmentation. *(IHMs)*

11. Distinguish between the following :

(*a*) Palace Hotel and Heritage Hotels

(*b*) Hotels and Motels

(*c*) Four Star and Two Star Hotels

(*d*) Sales and Marketing. *(MTM)*

12. Imagine yourself as the advertising manager of a middle class hotel located in your market:

(*a*) Prepare a list of potential advertising media that could be used to promote a hotel both locally and nationally. Identify the media by name.

(*b*) Prepare a list of public relation media. *(MTM)*

13. What steps would you suggest for increasing the sales of a hotel in a backward area with lot of tourists attraction facilities ? *(PGDT)*

14. Write short notes on :

(*a*) Market Research

(*b*) Information Processing

(*c*) Target Setting in Marketing. *(MTA)*

15. Discuss the role and importance of a Public Relations Officer in a hotel. *(IHMs)*

16. Which promotional policy do you consider the best for the Staff in a five-star hotel and why? Discuss. *(IHMs)*

17. How do you decide how much you can afford to spend on :

(*a*) a new product

(*b*) developing a new product

(*c*) advertising.

18. Discuss the proposition that many of the problems which face hotel and catering operators arise from being product rather than market orientated. *HCIMA (London)*

19. What role marketing play in today's business world ? Discuss the same with special emphasis on marketing of hotel business. *(IHMs)*

20. How would you identify the market for a hotel business ? Discuss it in detail. *(IHMs)*

21. Write short notes on any two of the following :

(*a*) Target Setting in Marketing

(*b*) Market Research

(*c*) Information Processing. *(IHMs)*

22. Explain clearly the concept of personal selling, publicity and advertisement. Which one would you recommend for hotel and why ? *(IHMs)*

23. Describe the difference between marketing and selling.

Show how marketing techniques could be applied in a sector of your choice within the field of hotel and catering activity. *HCIMA (London)*

24. What do you understand by Eco-Tourism ? Explain the following environmental issues on tourism.

(*a*) Water Pollution

(*b*) Air Pollution

(*c*) Habitat Destruction. *(IHMs)*

25. Distinguish between (*any four*):–

(*a*) Macro competition and Micro competition.

(*b*) Formal Product and Informal Product.

(*c*) Marketing and Selling.

(*d*) Loss Leader Pricing and Diversionary Pricing.

(*e*) Services and products. *(IHMs)*

26. (*a*) Explain the concept of product life-cycle.

(*b*) What are the marketing objectives in each of the stages ?

(*c*) Discuss the difference between consumer goods and hospitality product at the introduction or launch stage. *(IHMs)*

27. Write short notes on (*any four*):-

(*a*) Internal Marketing

(*b*) Relationship Marketing

(*c*) Environment Scanning

(*d*) Opportunities analysis

(*e*) Branding. *(IHMs)*

28. Write short notes on (any four):-
(*a*) What are the different elements of the communication mix ?
(*b*) Explain *any three* with reference to the hospitality industry. (*IHMs*)

29. (*a*) What is the importance of pricing in marketing?
(*b*) What are the objectivies of pricing?
(*c*) List common mistakes in pricing and how they can be rectified? (*IHMs*)

30. Discuss the argument that the marking of services is different from the marketing of goods, Give examples both for and against from your experience. (*IHMs*)

31. (*a*) What are the qualities of a good salesperson ?
(*b*) Explain the terms:
(1) Sales Call
(2) Cold Call
(3) Prospect
(4) Close
(5) Open & Closed Probes. (*IHMs*)

32. Explain the importance of hiring good, competent and effective sales persons to represent your organisation. (*IHMs*)

33. Explain how product differentiation is used as a strategy to make your product more attractive to your target market ? What part does segmentation play in a differentiation strategy (*IHMs*)

34. Explain any 5-elements of the communication mix. (*IHMs*)

35. Answer Briefly – (*any five*)
(1) What are the four basic qualities that separate goods from service ?
(2) Differentiate between sales & marketing.
(3) What is primary & secondary data ?
(4) What are sources of internal and external information ?
(5) What are the four types of organisational customers ?
(6) Define marketing. (*IHMs*)

36. Political impacts on the hospitality business environment can be enormous. Discuss some present potential impacts. (*IHMs*)

37. What do you understand by buyer behaviour ? Which are the factors in the micro environment and macro environment which affect the buyer behaviour. (*IHMs*)

38. Consider Maslow's hierarchy in terms of a hotel and of a restaurant. In each case, name as many attributes as you can that fit each level of the hierarchy. (*IHMs*)

39. What is a marketing information system ? (*IHMs*)

40. Which are the four stages of a product life-cycle ? How is the product life-cycle different in case of a goods industry than in case of a service industry ? (*IHMs*)

41. (*a*) Write short notes (*any four*) :
(1) Market Research
(2) Indirect and Direct advertising
(3) Publicity versus Public Relations
(4) Marketing and Selling
(5) Difference between need, want and desire. (*IHMs*)

42. Give one word for the following :
(*a*) The totality of all benefits received or experienced by the customer when purchasing the product.

(*b*) Gaining a verbal or written commitment from the customer.

(*c*) The analysis of trends that may affect both the production and the purchase of a product by the customer.

(*d*) Demand for which even the customer does not yet recognize there is a need.

(*e*) A consumer term identifying those who are first to try a new product.

43. Define and give an example :

(*a*) Mission statement.

(*b*) Penetration pricing.

(*c*) Relationship marketing.

(*d*) Innovative marketing.

(*e*) Product life cycle. (*IHMs*)

44. Answer any five :

(*a*) Discuss briefly the goods/ environment/services trichotomy of the hospitality product.

(*b*) What are the key differences between strategies and tactics ? List at least one example of each.

(*c*) What is differentiation ? List at least three examples of how differentiation of intangibles is accomplished.

(*d*) What are the bases of market segmentation. List at least one example of each.

(*e*) List the circumstances under which a differentiation strategy is most appropriate and also list the circumstances when a segmentation strategy is most appropriate.

(*f*) What is target marketing ? What are the strategies for selecting target markets?

(*g*) How does the Hospitality Industry distribution channel work ? (*IHMs*)

45. Explain in detail the concept of Environmental Scanning giving relevant examples. (*IHMs*)

46. Explain the various steps in the market research process. (*IHMs*)

47. What is positioning ? Discuss briefly the concepts of Subjective and Objective positioning. (*IHMs*)

48. What is repositioning ? List the steps in the procedure of repositioning with a brief description of each step. (*IHMs*)

49. The hospitality marketing, according to Lao Renaghan, contains the sub mixes: the product / service mix, the presentation mix and the communications mix. Discuss each mix in brief giving relevant examples. (*IHMs*)

50. Discuss in brief the three major types of pricing objectives with suitable examples. (*IHMs*)

51. Why is the Front Office aften considered an extension of the marketing and sales department?

52. Is it possible to direct energies of the Front Office staff to support the efforts of the marketing and sales department ? Explain.

53. Discuss the role of the Guest History in the marketing and sales department.

54. Give one word for the following :

(*a*) The totality of all benefits received or experienced by the customer when purchasing the product.

(*b*) Gaining a verbal or written commitment from the customer.

(*c*) The analysis of trends that may affect both the production and the purchase of a product by the customer.

(*d*) Demand for which even the customer does not yet recognize there is a need.

(e) A consumer term identifying those who are first to try a new product. *(H&M)*

55. Define and give an example :

(a) Mission statement

(b) Penetration pricing

(c) Relationship marketing

(d) Innovative marketing

(e) Product life cycle. *(H&M)*

56. Define marketing. Discuss how tourism marketing has been provided in the last few years in India. *(IHMs)*

57. Multiple choice :

(a) The three types of pricing objectives are financial, volume and ....

(i) Demand (ii) Supply (iii) Competition

(b) A .... strategy is when the incentive to buy is given to the customer.

(i) Push (ii) Pull (iii) Positioning,

(c) A common way of expanding your distribution network by not owning or managing is ....

(i) Franchising (ii) Atmospherics (iii) Consortiums

(d) Planned management of media perspective is known as ....

(i) Publicity (ii) Advertising (iii) Public Relations

(e) Marketing communications that serve specifically as incentives to stimulate sales on a short-term basis are known as ....

(i) Promotions (ii) Discounting (iii) Yield management

(f) The four different stages of a Product Life-cycle are introduction, growth, maturity and ....

(i) Decline (ii) Demise (iii) Revival

(g) .... is the study of population

(i) Pneumatics (ii) Psychographics (iii) Demographics

(h) Three approaches to the market are a product orientation, sales orientation and .... orientation.

(i) Marketing (ii) Segment (iii) Differentiation

(i) In a goods market traditional channels of distribution are wholesaler, retailer and ....

(i) Consumer (ii) Broker (iii) Seller

(j) Research Motives are Descriptive, Exploratory and ....

(i) Searching (ii) Exploding (iii) Diagnostic *(IHMs)*

CHAPTER 8

Engineering and Maintenance

OBJECTIVES

After studying this chapter you should be able to :

1. *Appreciate the role of engineering and maintenance in hotel business*
2. *Explain the various functions of this department and*
3. *Understand the organisation of the department and duties and responsibilities of the employees.*

ENERGY AND COST

The energy crisis throughout the world have given a great importance to the engineering department of a hotel. This department provides on the day-to-day basis the utility services, electricity, hot water, steams, air-conditioning and other services and is responsible for repair and maintenance of the equipment, furniture and fixtures in the hotel. The former are grouped in the financial statement under the head Energy Cos tor Heat, Light and Powerand the latter as Repair and Maintenanceunder the Profit and Loss Statement. Proper maintenance and provision of hotel services have a significant effect on the attitude of guest towards the hotel. The engineering department has an important role in satisfying the guest-demand and helping to maintain the profit level of the hotel.

The cleaning, up-keep, repair, replacement, installation and maintinance of property and its furnishing, machinery and equipment are the joint responsibilities of Engineering/ Maintenance and the Housekeeping Department.

ORGANISATION

The organisation structure of this department is given in Figs. 8.1 and 8.2.

CHIEF ENGINEER

Chief Engineer or Director of Building Operation or Maintenance Engineer is the title usually given to the head of this department. He is concerned with the appearance and physical condition of the building and is responsible for the maintenacne and running of all machinery in the operation: steam plants, heating, refrigeration, ari-conditioning elevators, lighting and others. He directly supervises the staff of technicians. He has two principal functions :

1. To provide the hotel with heat, electric power, air-conditioning, refrigeration, water etc., and
2. To maintain the building and equipment in good conditions.

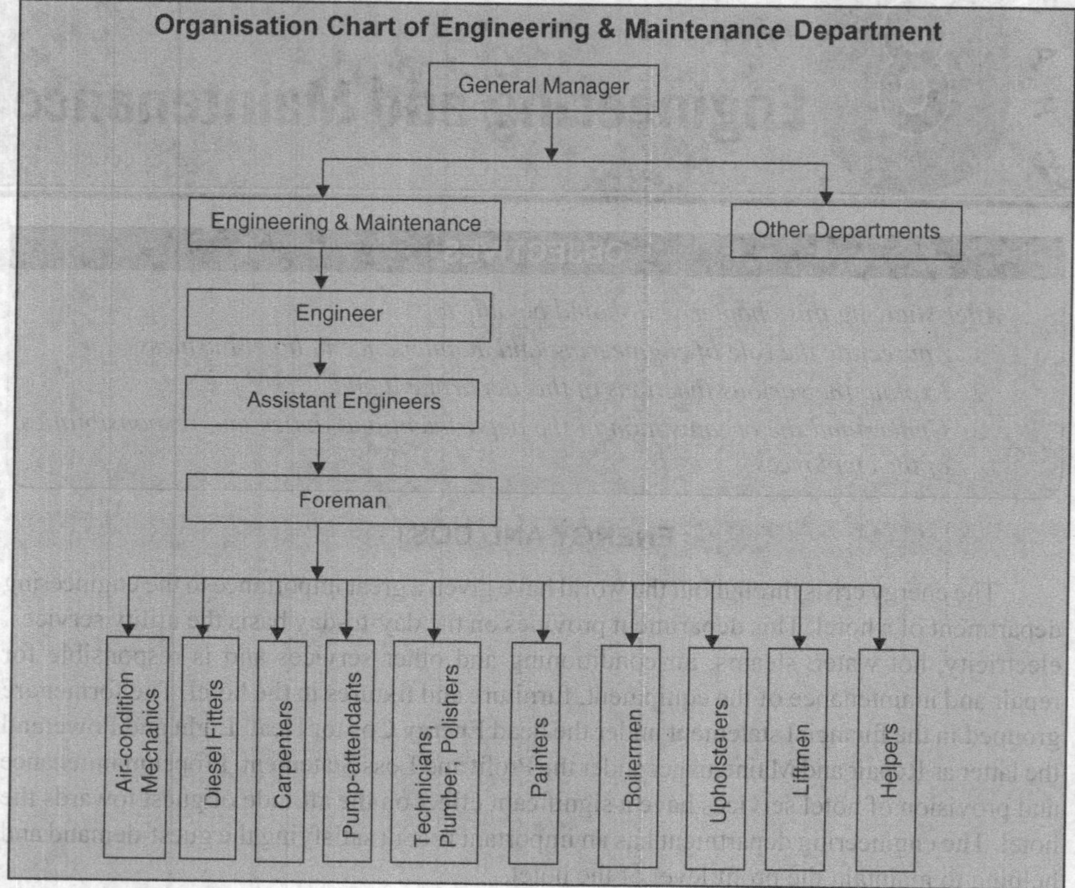

Fig. 8.1: A Typical Organisation Chart of Engineering & Maintenance Department

The size of the maintenance crew will again depend upon the size and age of the hotel's building. Some hotels have the repair work done by outside contractors which is more economical than having a complete department. Large hotel usually divide the activities into two departments : an engineer for electrical and mechanical and heavy equipment. These hotels employ plumbers, painters, polishers, carpenters, steam fitters, upholsterers, air-conditioners, electricians, cabinet makers, silver platers and some time even masons.

The chief engineer purchases all supplies necessary for the operation of his department and supervises his own storeroom. All matters relating to refrigeration, internal communication, radio and television maintenance contracts, come under the chief engineer. The laundry, garage and all the machinery are also under his charge. The work of the engineering department is divided into six main areas :

1. Electric system
2. Air-conditioning plant
3. Plumbing
4. Refrigeration
5. Ventilation
6. Repair and maintenance
7. The elevator.

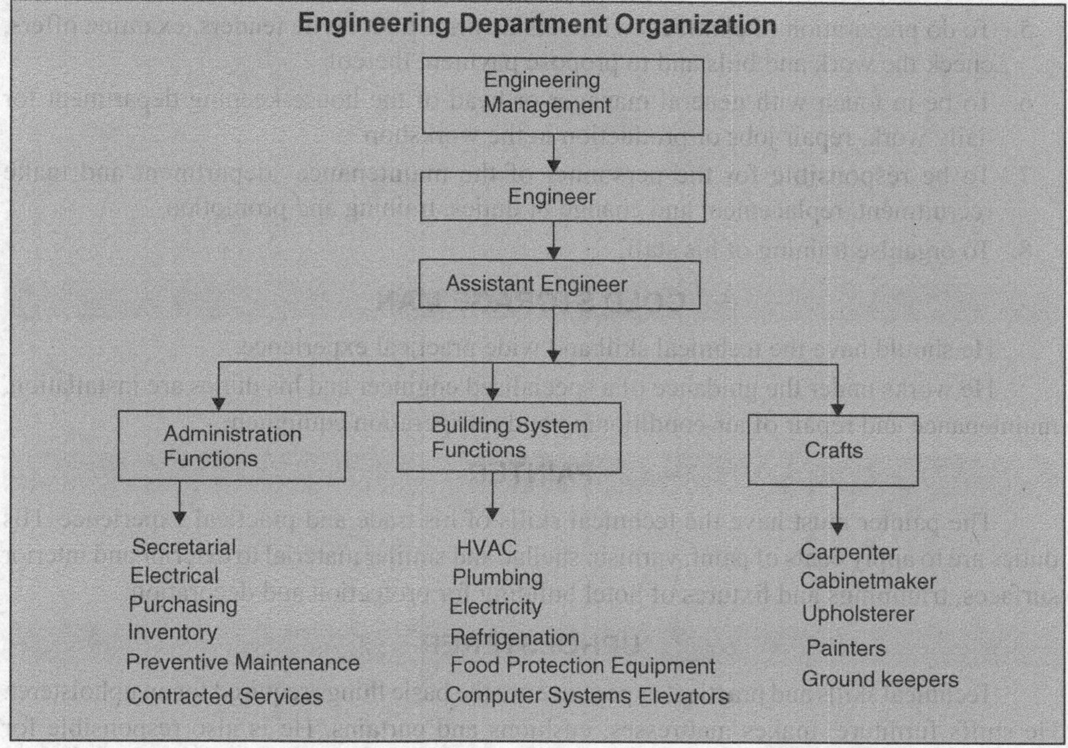

Fig. 8.2 : A Typical Engineering Department Organization

In addition to this he is also incharge of the safety programmes and of protecting the building against fire. This includes insuring that fire buckets, hoses and extinguishers are in right place and in working order. The chief engineer's office receives daily maintenance complaints from the various hotel departments like Food and Beverage, Executive House-keeper, Executive Chef and is responsible for carrying out speedy and efficient normal routine work. In large hotels, the conference, convention and exhibition work and other public functions require close cooperation with the banqueting department.

This department is also responsible for public address system, all kitchen equipment including walk-ins, the television as well as the inhouse VCR equipment, the piped music, the standby power generating plant and looking for the guest complaints.

The salaries paid to chief engineer, assistant egineer, office and store room employees, engineers, firemen, refrigeration are included under the head Heat, Light and Powerand the salaries of others are included under Repairs and Maintenance.

In addition to general education, a chief engineer must have to carry out repairs, maintenance and preventive maintenance. He should also have the ability to plan the installation of equipment and to draw up estimates for extensive maintenance work and repairs. The responsibilities of chief engineer are :

1. To give direction to different sections of the maintenance department
2. To draw up and check the daily work programme of the staff
3. To prepare orders for maintenance and supplies
4. To be responsible for such supplies
5. To do preparation of contracts with outside firms and invite tenders, examine offers, check the work and bills and to propose payment thereof
6. To be in touch with general manager or head of the house-keeping department for daily work, repair jobs or production in the workshop
7. To be responsible for the personnel of the maintenance department and make recruitment, replacement and change of duties, training and promotion
8. To organise training of his staff.

COLD STORAGE MAN

He should have the technical skill and wide practical experience.

He works under the guidance of a specialised engineer and his duties are installation, maintenance and repair of air-conditioning and refrigeration equipment.

PAINTER

The painter must have the technical skills of his trade and practical experience. His duties are to apply coats of paint, varnish, shellac and similar material to exterior and interior surfaces, trimmings and fixtures of hotel building for protection and decoration.

UPHOLSTERER

Technical skills and practical experience are the basic things required for an upholsterer. He stuffs furniture, makes mattresses, cushions and curtains. He is also responsible for making and installing textiles or leather covers, upholstery and interior decorations.

CARPENTER AND FURNITURE REPAIRERS

A carpenter must have technical skill in carpentry and sufficient practical experience. His main duties are to cut out shape, fit and assemble wooden parts. He makes and repairs woodwork and wooden fixtures, doors, windows, staircases, panelling and simple furniture. He selects suitable wood and repairs wooden articles such as cabinets and other furniture.

ELECTRICAL FITTERS

Technical skill and practical experience are pre-requisite for an electrical fitter. His duties are to fit, adjust, assemble and repair in workshop or place of use the various electrical machinery and apparatus needed in the hotel.

MAINTENANCE ELECTRICIAN

He requires same knowledge as the electric fitter. The job of a maintenance electrician are to repair and maintain the electrical equipment of the establishment, checking of the electrical wiring and equipments and to see that the wiring in equipments are in conformity with safety standards and regulations.

PLANT MAINTENANCE MECHANIC

He also requires the technical skill and practical knowledge for his job. He repairs and maintains machinery, plumbing, installation and mechanical apparatus of the establishment. In addition he may also install simple electrical equipment and make repair of wooden structure and paint walls, floors and woodwork.

BOILERMAN

A boilerman must have the thorough knowledge of the operation of boilers and safety regulations. He must also have the licence to practise this activity. He is responsible for the functioning of the boilers for heating and hot water. He maintains the boiler equipment and installations and checks the fuel supply, records consumption and reports any malfunctioning of equipment.

MAINTENANCE HAND

A maintenance hand must have all-round knowledge of sanitary, plumbing, carpentry, painting, electricity, cabinet making and upholstery. He is to carry out the orders of the Head of Maintenance Department. He carries out repairs in his workshop or on the spot, including the guest rooms. He is also to be on all night duty to do emergency repairs.

GARAGE WATCHMEN

Knowledge of the various types of cars and their service is very essential for a garage watchman. He is responsible for the hotel's garage and looks after the guest's car and official vehicles. He has to register car movements and services to guests such as washing cars and petrol or oil supplies. He has to write vouchers and send them to the administration.

The following are some of the major works which fall under the engineering and maintenance :

1. General maintenance and repair including :
   (*i*) Structural maintenance
   (*ii*) Grounds and swimming pool care
   (*iii*) Heavy cleaning
   (*iv*) Carpet servicing
   (*v*) Furniture moving
   (*vi*) Trash removal
   (*vii*) Minor repairs
   (*viii*) Maintenance and cleaning of tools and equipment used by the department
   (*ix*) Painting
   (*x*) Upholstering and
   (*xi*) Cabinet making.
2. Maintenance of :
   (*i*) Heating

(*ii*) Ventilating
(*iii*) Refrigerating and
(*iv*) Airconditioning systems
(*v*) Electrical system
(*vi*) Radio and television systems
(*vii*) Communication system
(*viii*) Motor appliances
(*ix*) Electrical appliances
(*x*) Water Supply
(*xi*) Plumbing fixtures
(*xii*) Sewage systems

3. Fire safety and protection :
(*i*) Fire protection
(*ii*) Fire prevention
(*iii*) Maintenance of fire equipment
(*iv*) Establishment of fire protection procedures.

PLANNING FOR MAINTENANCE

Hotels' property needs to be maintained and managed properly. Proper property maintenance will depend upon a number of factors such as :

1. The size of the hotel and its property
2. The construction of the hotel
3. The general condition of the premises
4. The functions of the property
5. The condition of the plumbing, the gas, the electric and mechanical equipment, the paint work, decorations and frabrics.
6. The size and scope of the business now and in the foreseeable future
7. Alterations required and purchase of new equipment
8. The proximity of the property to others
9. Possibility of noise pollution in residental area
10. Legal requirement and constraints
11. The practical and theoretical knowledge of the management team.

The maintenance plan should take into account capital planning so that improvement, renovations and expansions can be brought on line. The plan should detail the work likely to be carried out during the coming year together with a budget cost figure. The plan should be reassessed every six months. Simple day-to-day maintenance can be carried out by the management or employees. But more technical work should be carried out by professionally qualified technician. Maintenance of lifts and hoists, boilers, ovens, air-conditioning systems, refrigerators, washing machines, extractor fans, pumps, cooking towers, ventilation and water system, fire arms and electric protection equipment and sprinkler systems are all of technical nature.

The maintenance plan must concentrate on the following points :

1. The aspect of the property requiring regular maintenance
2. Standard of maintenance
3. Regularity of maintenance work
4. Requirement of skilled workers and unskilled workers
5. Availability of expertise within the operation
6. Full-time/part-time help required
7. Provision for a contract with an outside agency.

ENERGY MANAGEMENT

Careful and prudent care of gas, electricity and water is the most simplest form of energy managements. Selection of most efficient equipment and use of time clock must be made for proper energy management.

WASTE MANAGEMENT

Safe storage and disposal of waste in hotel varied according to the size of the hotel. Small hotel may use strong plastic sacks, which are tied securely and stored until collection. Large hotels may use compactors of different sizes for waste apart from bottles. The best method of safe storage and disposal of waste will depend upon the following factors :

1. Type of waste items :
   - (*i*) Food scraps
   - (*ii*) Used fat or oil
   - (*iii*) Card board/paper
   - (*iv*) Tins
   - (*v*) Plastic
   - (*vi*) Bottles
   - (*vii*) Broken glass
   - (*viii*) China.
2. The volume of waste in each area
3. The frequency and cost of local municipal services
4. The cost of private contractors
5. The space available for handling and storage of waste.

Proper care must be taken of cleaning of waste storage area and waste bins. Transfer notes and description of waste must be prepared and kept for future reference.

MAINTENANCE SYSTEM

Repair and maintenance cost can be a sizable item for a hotel. Large hotels have higher repair and maintenance costs per available room due to higher rates charged, more services offered and greater preparation of public space. To keep the property up and repair and maintance costs down, preventive maintenance and periodic routine inspection and repair is essentially required.

Sheraton Corporation has developed a unique maintenance request system, which they claim, if properly implemented, may eliminate most causes of guest complaint before the problem comes up and shall ensure prompt response to guest complaint due to maintenance problems. Before installing this system by Sheraton, it was evaluated by chief engineers representing more than 60 hotels ranging in sizes from 100 to 1,500 rooms.[1]

1. Sheraton Corporation, U.S.A.

A specially designed three-page maintenance request form is used. The main contents of the form are :

1. Date for request for work
2. Person or department requesting
3. Description of problem
4. To whom assigned
5. When completed
6. Time spent on work
7. Remark by person doing the work.

On the back of the form there is a check list of things to be inspected while on the primary service call.

THE PROCEDURE

The procedure followed for maintenance request is detailed below :

1. The originator of a maintenance request fills out three-page form:
   (*i*) Top copy (original white) is retained
   (*ii*) Second and third copy are sent to engineering/maintenance department.
2. Head of the Department assigns the job and places both copies of the form on the 'assignment' both under the repairman's name.
3. The repairman puts one copy of form (blue) on the 'In process' hook and takes the third copy (on heavier buff stock and with check list on back) along with him to place where repair is to be made.
4. On completion of repair, he inspects the area for other maintenance deficiencies as noted on the check list and remedies them, if possible.
5. On return to the assignment board, employee removes the blue form from the 'In process' hook and staples it to the buff form which he has filled out.
   (*i*) If assigned work has been completed, both tickets are placed on 'Complete hook'.
   (*ii*) If work could not be finished, the reason why is noted and the tickets are placed on the 'Not Complete' hook.
   (*iii*) If maintenance deficiency was noted, but not corrected, the tickets are placed on the 'Complete–Inspecton Deficiency hook'.
6. When forms are removed from 'Report' section of board, disposition is as follows :
   (*i*) If job is completed, the blue copy is sent back to the originator of maintenance request.
   (*ii*) If problem was not solved, needed materials are secured and the Maintenance Request Form is reissued.
   (*iii*) If an inspection deficiency was noted, and not corrected, a new form is written up and the job is assigned to some one with the skills and equipment to do the job.

Thus, the 'Backlog' section of the assignment board makes it easy to spot when work build up for particular trade, such as painters or electricians indicating the possible need for additional help or contracting out work of that type.

ADVANTAGES

The main advantages of this system are

1. It provides a complete record of each problem from report to solution.
2. It reduces oral requests and assignments
3. It is easily understood
4. It eliminates duplications of effort and record
5. It reveals staffing problems
6. It ties inspection in with repair call.

WATER CONSUMPTION

A leading hotelier and an administrator at Harvard University, Stephen S.J. Hall, has suggested the following ways to cut water consumption charge in a hotel:[2]

1. Make sure the hotel system has cross-connections between high and low level service, allowing water from the high level to flow into low level service and back into the city system.
2. If your establishment has two or more meters connected to the city supply, there should be no cross-connections. If pressures in the service differ even slightly, this could allow water from a high pressure line to flow back into a lower pressure line and then back into the city supply after being metered. Wherever possible, use one city service, even if a new impeller or a longer pump is necessary to supply house tank.
3. If tanks are located on the roof, make sure, when increase in pressure is necessary, that this does not cause the house tank to fill and overflow.
4. Consider reducing the size of supply lines or installing orifice plates in lines to reduce flow.
5. If faucets are frequently left open in service and kitchen areas, install pressure-operating faucets.
6. Explore ways to recapture clean waste water for possible use in the laundry or elsewhere where health department requirements will not be breached.
7. Check all plumbing fixtures frequently for leaks and repair immediately.
8. Where city water is for condensing of air-conditioning and refrigerating compressors, investigate use of cooking tower water for both summer and winter operation. There are some 1/2 2 gallons per operating minute per ton of refrigeration. If it is economically impractical to connect the condensing unit to cooling tower water, regulating valves should be installed and kept accurately adjusted. The water coming from the condenser should approach 95 degrees. Any cool water indicates waste.
9. Investigate leaks in the laundry and the possibility of using control valves on water. If control valves have been installed make sure they are operating properly and are not leaking.
10. When making periodic inspection for leaks in toilet bowls, also be sure that toilet flushometers are adjusted to allow flushing time of seven second. Urinal flushometers should be set to provide a flushing time of 4-5 seconds. Such tanks should be regulated for 4 gallons per flushing.

2. Stephen S.J. Hall, a leading Administrator at Harvard University.

11. Make sure the blow-downs or boilers are not leaking. All possible steam condensate should be returned to boilers. If blow-down valves are leaking or steam condenstate is wasted, this means additional make-up water will be needed.
12. Check water softeners to see if use of high capacity resin would produce a savings by reducing the frequency of regenerations.Inspect cooling tower during operation to determine whether the loss of water due to windage is above normal. If tower has exceptionally bad cross draft, it might be desirable to install a wind screen.
13. Packing gland on pumps should be checked frequently for excessive leakage.
14. Make sure that potato peelers are equipped with a solenoid valve to shut the water off when not in use. Garbage disposal units can also be fitted with a solenoid with a time delay to shut the water off a minute or so after the unit is turned off.
15. Check efficiency of hot water circulating system by noting the time it takes to get hot water from opened tap. If system is faulty or undersized, an excessive amount of water will be run before guests receive hot water.
16. Check make-up tank to see that they are of proper size. If they are overflowing, either larger or additional one should be installed.
17. Be aware of water problems. Log your meters hourly during period of high and low occupancy and over weekends. What are your periods of peak load? Where is the water going ? Attempt to isolate portions of your load. Get the facts.

HEAT CONSUMPTION

As an engineering cost control cousultant of American Hotel & Motel Association, Stephen S.J. Hall, suggested the following checklist to keep reduce heating costs in hotels :[3]

1. Take stack measurement of boiler's CO_2 level often, keep record of adjustment required. If you do not have an analyzer, ask your fuel supplier to make the test for you. (If you heat with oil, the boiler's CO_2 level should approach 13 per cent. If you heat with gas, the boiler's CO_2 level should be between 10-11 per cent).
2. Check needless loss of condensate; recover it all if you can. Frequently the expenses of condensate storage tank plus piping is less than the cost of fuel saved in heating cold make-up water.
3. Check return water for blowing traps.
4. Use low pressure steam where possible to reduce losses because high pressure systems tend to leak more easily.
5. Insulate all pipes and boilers.
6. Remove unused piping which would otherwise be wasting heat.
7. Consider zoning heating system so that entire building is not heated to satisfy demand in one room area.
8. Consider seperating function room and dining room heating from the guest room heating system.
9. Steam traps should be inspected at least once a year and rebuilt if required.
10. Replace steam pumps with electricity.
11. Consider these additional ways to reduce heat loss :

3. Stephen S.J. Hall, Engineering Cost Control Consultant, American Hotel and Motel Association, U.S.A.

(*i*) Keep temperature in unoccupied function and guest rooms at 50-60 For turn off heat.

(*ii*) In occupied rooms, keep temperature not more than 72F.

(*iii*) Use 100% return air when heating function rooms before use. Shut off outside air takes used for ventilating when heating unoccupied areas. Fresh air is required when heating occupied space.

(*iv*) Install vestibules and revolving doors.

(*v*) Tighten loose windows and check weather-stripping

(*vi*) Stop use of unessential exhaust fans and fresh air fans.

12. Reclaim as much heat as possible from laundry waste water by installing a heat exchanger. The hot waste water will pre-heat the make up water for the hot water generator. In hotel which purchase steam, the condensate and/or its heat can often be utilized.

FUEL COST

Incomplete combustion in fuel oil fired heating systems can increase fuel bills (by 15%) and also due to oil not being fully burned, result in an accumulation of soot in the boiler reduces the heating efficiency of the system. Combustion engineers suggest the following three steps to prevent supplies going up in smoke :

1. Observe the fuel-air ratio
2. Keep fuel oil temperature at burner tip at suggested level
3. Be sure burners are properly adjusted and nozzles clean.

PLUMBING

The plumbing system poses a number of frequent and frustrating maintenance problem in a hotel. Presented below are suggestions for solving the pumbing problems:

1. **Assure proper hot water temperature :** You can obtain optimum efficiency from hot water heating equipment if it is set to produce water at 135. If the hotel produces water at a higher temperature it will accelerate problem with valves and washers and may prove annoying and dangerous for guests.
2. You may also install a circulating pump on the hot water return line. It has the effect of making all the hot water piping in the system reservior and improves the availability of hotwater for guest use. It eliminates the water wasted for the flow of hot water. If the circulating pump still does not help in making the required amount of hot water available, the tubes may need cleaning for increased heat transfer. The only other solution is to get a larger water heater.
3. **Proper Faucet Pressure :** Excess pressure at faucet is hard on washers. The gush of water which result when a faucet is turned on can also cause water hammer and sediment filled water. It may be that showers will need slightly higher pressure than sink faucet to operate properly, but expert advise that no more pressure should be provided for shower heads than actually needed for proper operation.

   The following are recommended flow pressures :

Gauge (absolute pressure)		*Flow : Gallon per minute*
Basin Faucet	8	3.0
Bathtub Faucet	5	6.0
Shower Faucet	12	5.0
Sink Faucet	10	4.5

4. **Minimise Pipe Corrosion :** Every hotel has a water pipe corrosion problem. You have to replace water tubing in as little as five years or install numerous clamps on pipes to stop leaks. Thorough investigation should be made of the water supply system to determine the rate of corrosion taking place. Hotels with pipe embedded in the walls or concrete floors need to be alerted to the problem of corrosion because the expense of replacing such tubing generally involves major structural and repairing charges in addition to the expense of the new piping.

Check hot water tubing first because hot water is more corrosive than cold water. Soft waters are usually more acid and generally have a more corrosive action on the pipes than most hard waters. When repairs or partial replacement are made in piping systems, pipes and fittings of the same materials as those already installed should be used.

The rusty water can be cleared and corrosion curtailed by proper treatment of water supply. This requires the careful introduction of suitable chemicals into the water system by specially designed chemical practising devices. Pipe that are already clogged with corrosion can be cleared so that the supply presure and flow of water through them is made satisfactory.

5. **Reduce water consumption :** One minor faucet leak producing only a thin stream (1/32 in.) can result in a loss of up to 52,000 gallons water a year. One leaky lavatory fixture will ordinarily waste as much as 75,000 gallons a month. Leaks in water pipes running through inexcavated sections under the floor of a hotel may go on for years without being discovered. Investigate regularly all water lines embedded in the earth. Blow-down valves of the boiler be maintained in tight condition. When leaky, these valves can waste tremendous quantities of hot water.

ELECTRIC LIGHTING

Unplanned and improrer lighting may cost large amount to hotels, therefore, observe the following hints to save money on lighting :

1. Provide adequate but not excessive illumination.
2. Select the most appropriate fixtures and illumination level for each purpose.
3. Choose lamps with switches at the base to lessen the chance of accidental breakage. Wall and hanging unit will be most suitable.
4. All fixtures should have the seal of the reputed laboratories for fire prevention and longer life.
5. Fluorescent light provide more illumination than incandescent bulbs for each unit of power consumed with only 1/3 of the wattage.
6. Bulbs on their 'last legs' provide less light. Replace regularly as per the schedule based on life expectancy.
7. When buying fixtures, keep the cost of maintenance in mind.
8. Instruct employees to turn off lights when not needed.

9. Remind guests to turn off lights, when leaving their rooms.
10. Bulbs and fluorescent tubes be cleaned with a damp cloth occasionally to ensure the full utilization of and delivery of illumination.
11. Reduce excessively high lamp wattages whenever lower wattages furnish acceptable lighting.
12. Reduce and then standardardise the size of lamps in guest rooms. Have maid and bellmen turn off light when not in use.
13. Consider using long life bulbs to reduce bulb cost and labour costs to change them.
14. Consider use of mercury exceptionally useful in parking lots, this type of lamp is also inexpensive lamps.
15. Use time clocks for automatic switching of signs, motors, building light, heater and warmers, air-conditioning, water pumps, fans.
16. Experiment with alternate light switching and automatic transformer dimming to reduce the amount or intensity of night time corridor lighting.
17. Replace resistance dimmers with tranformer type.
18. Use photo electric cells to switch off lamps when same light provides adequate illumination.
19. Investigate the possibility of installing short time (twist on) timers controlling light in store rooms and walk in boxes or other time use areas where light are apt to be left on needlessly.
20. Turn off large motors when not needed. Turning-off one 50 horse power motor saves as much as 100-400 watt light bulbs.
21. Turn off banquet refrigerators and ice maker when not in use.
22. Turn off lights in function areas when functions are ended. Lock panels so night cleaners cannot turn on every light when only a few are required.
23. Turn off central vacuum system after housemen have finished morning cleaning.
24. Turn off elevator motor generators when not in use.
25. Turn off some automatic elevators during low traffic periods.
26. Reduce speed of motor for light service duty. If the fan or pump must run, it may be worthwhile to replace a single-speed motor with two speed motor. A motor operating at ½ speed consumes only 1/8 as much power as at full speed.
27. In single speed motor, reduce the drive (motor pulley) when full speed is not required. This will cut wattage consumed.
28. Enlist the aid of all staff-members in turning off unused equipment and lighting.
29. Ask power company representative to explain how power factor can be costly and how to improve the power factor.
30. Reduce demand and sudden increase in current consumption. Ask the power company to install recording meters to analyse the loads. If large load can be juggled so that not all equipment is started up at once in the demand period, they should save money. Large motors should lave reduced voltage starters. Demand limiting or alarm equipment is available for airconditioning or heating equipment.
31. Be sure your wiring is adequate in capacity for peak loads.

32. Check with the electric company to make certain that the service provided is the one that afford the most economical rate.
33. Check all electrical bills :
    (*i*) Is rate schedule properly applied ?
    (*ii*) Is arithmetic correct ?
    (*iii*) Are they in line with past experiences, if not why not?
    (*iv*) Are you receiving discounts for which you are eligible?

A Case Study 8.1 : Maintenance

Situation :

In a particular hotel, outside contractors had previously been engaged to paint a block of rooms. Now painters in the hotel staff do the same job.

Results of Analysis :

The hotel's staff required twice as many manhours to paint a given area as did the crew of outside contractor. Although the hotel painters received considerable less wages per chair, the total cost of painting was almost as great using hotel painters as it was to engage to outside contractor. Including the fact that the hotel painters took longer and consequently reduced revenue by keeping room unrentable, the outside contractor may have been more economical. It was concluded that poor supervision and training accounted for the inefficiently of the hotel painters.

A sample form as given in Fig. 8.3 was devised which could be used for aiding supervision of all maintenance employees.

XYZ Hotel

JOB TICKET

Date ....

Name of Employee : ....

Time No: .... Location...

Time Job Commanded ....

Describe Nature of Job Briefly Time Job Concluded..............................

....

....

Fig. 8.3 A Specimen of a Job Ticket

The form permits the supervisor to appraise the industriousness of the employee and to spot soldiering on the job. For example, if an employee has taken an hour and a half to replace a washer in a faucet, probably one of the three thing is wrong, the employee is loafing; he is incompetent; or the wide faucet needs replacing.

ACCOUNTING, AUDIT AND CONTROL

PROPERTY OPERATION AND MAINTENANCE

This head includes all costs incurred in connection with the repairs and maintenance of building, equipment, furniture and fixtures to keep them in proper and efficient working condition (Ref. Figs. 8.3 and 8.4). The following are the usual expenses connected with this head:

EMPLOYEES' REMUNERATION AND BENEFITS

It includes the salaries, wages and benefits paid to : Carpenter and furniture repairers, cabinet makers and wood finishers, upholsterers, mattress makers and repairers, shade makers and repairers, upholstery seamstresses, carpet repairers, carpet layers and sewers, painters and paper hangers, sign painters, general mechanical elevator, mechanics, machenists, tinsmiths, clocksmiths, locksmiths, electricians, motorman, masons, tile setters and plasterers.

EMPLOYEES' MEALS

The cost of food employees included in the repairs and maintenance payroll is included under this head.

BUILDING SUPPLIES

The cost of material used in repairing the building including the following are debited to this account:

1. Ceilings
2. Doors
3. Floors
4. Side walks
5. Water proofing
6. Masonry
7. Fire escapes
8. Plaster
9. Smokestacks
10. Windows
11. Strairways
12. Fire hose
13. Roof
14. Walls.

CONTRACTS

The cost of work let to outside concern is debited to this head.

CURTAINS, DRAPERIES AND SCARFS SUPPLIES

It includes the cost of materials used in repairing, hangings and covers and other items such as :

1. Arm rests
2. Cretonnes
3. Doiles
4. Draperies
5. Lace curtains
6. Portres
7. Rods
8. Tassels
9. Window hangings
10. Bureau covering
11. Curtains
12. Door hangings
13. Hangings
14. Poles
15. Rings
16. Table covers
17. Valances.

ELECTRIC AND MECHANICAL EQUIPMENT

The cost of material used in repairing equipment is debited to this account.

Air-conditioning and Refrigeration

1. Air-cooling systems
2. Pipes
3. Valves
4. Ice plant and refrigeration
5. Pumps
6. Equipment.

GENERAL ELECTRICAL AND MECHANICAL EQUIPMENT

1. Ammeters
2. to-truck repairs
3. Boards instrument
4. Cash register
5. Dynamos
6. Electric system
7. Vacuum cleaners
8. Generators
9. Keys
10. Office equipment
11. Loks
12. Typewriter–inspection and maintenance
13. Swimming machines
14. Tags-key
15. Television
16. Time clock
17. Time stamps
18. Fans
19. Wiring
20. Incinerators
21. Machinery
22. Pneumatic tubes
23. Radios.

KITCHEN EQUIPMENT

1. Coffee urns
2. Dishwashers
3. Food trucks
4. Kitchen equipment
5. Mixers
6. Ranges
7. Soda fountain.

LAUNDRY EQUIPMENT

1. Laundry plant

PLUMBING AND HEATING

1. Boilers
2. Heating plant
3. Pipes
4. Fillings – steam
5. Plumbing
6. Pumps.

ELEVATORS

1. SUPPLIES : The cost of materials used in repairing elevators.
2. CONTRACTS : The cost of work let to outside concerns, including inspection service.

FLOOR COVERING

1. SUPPLIES : The cost of materials used in repairing floor coverings for guest rooms, corridors, dining rooms and public rooms, including the following :
   (*i*) Carpets
   (*ii*) Linoleum
   (*iii*) Padding
   (*iv*) Rubber tilting
   (*v*) Thread
   (*vi*) Dye
   (*vii*) Lining
   (*viii*) Paste
   (*ix*) Rugs
   (*x*) Felt
   (*xi*) Mats
   (*xii*) Rubber mats
   (*xiii*) Tape.
2. CONTRACTS : The cost of work let to outside concern.

FURNITURE

1. SUPPLIES : The cost of materials and supplies such as textiles, fibres, timber, metal, parts and glass used in the repair of furniture including beds, tables, dresses, chairs and other articles of similar nature.
2. CONTRACTS : The cost of work let on contract to outside concerns.

GROUND AND LANDSCAPING

Maintenance of ground is debited to this account.

PAINTING AND DECORATING

1. SUPPLIES : It includes cost of material and supplies including :
   (*i*) Alcohol
   (*ii*) Brushes
   (*iii*) Burlap
   (*iv*) Canvas
   (*v*) Enamel
   (*vi*) Glue
   (*vii*) Gold leaf
   (*viii*) Ladders
   (*ix*) Lincrusta
   (*xi*) Pails
   (*xii*) Paint
   (*xiii*) Scrapers
   (*iv*) Sponges
   (*v*) Steel wool
   (*vi*) Turpentine
   (*vii*) Varnish
   (*viii*) Wall paper
   (*ix*) Oil.
2. CONTRACTS : The cost of work let to outside concern.

PRINTING AND STATIONERY

It includes the cost of printed forms, service manuals, stationery and office supplies used in this section.

SPRINGS, MATTRESSES AND PILLOWS

1. SUPPLIES : The cost of materials and supplies used under maintenance heads, such as:
   (*i*) Bed springs
   (*ii*) Ticking and fabrics
   (*iii*) Hair and wool
   (*iv*) Feathers and down used in the maintenance of bed equipment.

2. CONTRACTS : The cost of work let to outside contracts.

UNIFORMS

Same basis as the uniforms in Room Department.

WINDOW SHADES, SCREENS AND AWNINGS

1. SUPPLIES : The cost of materials and supplies including the following :
   - (*i*) Blinds
   - (*ii*) Shades
   - (*iii*) Canvas
   - (*iv*) Card
   - (*v*) Frames
   - (*vi*) Rollers
   - (*vii*) Screening
   - (*viii*) Springs
   - (*ix*) Venetian blinds
   - (*x*) Weights
   - (*xi*) Hook
   - (*xii*) Rings
   - (*xiii*) Rope.
2. CONTRACTS : The cost of work let to outside contracts.

CREDITS

All credit to this department should be divided into two sections :

1. **SALES DEPARTMENT :**
   - (*i*) Materials
   - (*ii*) Mechanic's services
   - (*iii*) Miscellaneous
2. **CHARGES TO OTHER DEPARTMENT :**
   - (*i*) Food and beverages
   - (*ii*) Banquet expenses, sundry banquet income and
   - (*iii*) Miscellaneous

MISCELLANEOUS

All other expenses are included under this head.

DISTRIBUTION OF REPAIR AND MAINTENANCE

The allocation of expenses relating to repairs and maintenance could be made on the basis of estimates made by the Chief Engineer. The various types of expenses may be allocated individually to the respective department involved and certain expenses on the basis of square foot or cubic foot of area.

Figs. 8.4 and 8.5 are schedules of xpenses for repair and maintenance and properly operation and maintenance respectively.

ABC HOTELS LTD.
PROPERTY OPERATION AND MAINTENANCE SCHEDULE

		Current period
Salaries and Wages	₹	....
Vacation and Holidays Pay		....
Employees' Meals		....
Payroll Taxes and		....

(Contd...)

Employees' Benefits	
Total Payroll and Related Expenses	₹ ....
Other Expenses	
Building	₹ ....
Curtains, Drapes and Scarfs	....
Electrical & Mechanical Equipment	....
Air-conditioning & Refrigeration	....
General Electrical & Mechanical Equipment	....
Kitchen Equipment	....
Laundry Equipment	....
Plumbing and Heating	....
Elevator	....
Floor Covering	....
Grounds and Landscaping	....
Miscellaneous	....
Printing and Stationery	....
Painting and Decorating	....
Springs, Mattresses and Pillows	....
Uniforms	....
Window Shades, Screens and Awnings	....
Total Other Expenses	₹ ....
Total Direct Expenses	₹ ....
Credits	
Sales	₹ ....
Charges to Other Departments	....
Total Credits	₹ ....
Net Cost	₹ ....
Adjustment of Deferred Account	....
Repairs & Maintenance	....
Charged to Operations	₹ ....

Note: Various arrangements of additional columns for comparisons and percentages could be added.

Fig. 8.4 : Analysis of Expenses of Repair and Maintenance

ABC HOTELS LTD.
PROPERTY OPERATION AND MAINTENANCE SCHEDULE

	Current Period
Salaries and Wages	₹ ....
Total Payroll and Related Expenses	....
Other Expenses	....
Building Supplies	....
Electrical and Mechanical Equipment	....
Engineering Supplies	....

(Contd...)

Furniture, Fixture, Equipment and Decor		....
Group and Landscaping		....
Operating Supplies		....
Removal of Waste Matter		....
Swimming Pool		....
Uniforms		....
Others		....
Total Other Expenses		....
Total Property Operation and Maintenance	₹	....

Fig. 8.5 : Analysis of Property Operation and Maintenance

QUESTIONS AND ASSIGNMENTS

1. Explain types of maintenance. *(IHMs)*
2. What are the advantages and disadvantages of Maintenance Contract ? Explain the concept of Cost + Percentage in relation to such contract. *(IHMs)*
3. Explain how is energy conserved at management levels. *(IHMs)*
4. Explain any two reasons under which equipment is replaced. *(IHMs)*
5. Answer any four of the following in two lines each: *(IHMs)*
   (*a*) Scale Formation
   (*b*) Emergency Exit
   (*c*) Running Cost
   (*d*) Inspection
   (*e*) Pollution.
6. Describe the duties and responsibilities of the Engineering Department of a hotel. *(IHMs)*
7. Explain the work undertaken under preventive maintenance. Is preventive maintenance better than breakdown maintenance? *(IHMs)*
8. (*a*) What is alternating current ?
   (*b*) What is the usual voltage and frequency of single phase electric supply in India ?
   (*c*) Explain why all electrical appliances must be earthed.
   (*d*) Why is a miniature circuit breaker better than a Kit Kat Fuse. *(IHMs)*
9. Discuss the various electrical lighting devices used in hotels, mentioning their average life and other features. *(IHMs)*
10. What are the various causes of dampness in a building ? *(IHMs)*
11. Describe the maintenance of swimming pool of a hotel. *(IHMs)*
12. With the help of a neat sketch explain the hot water circulation system in a hotel. *(IHMs)*
13. Discuss the comparative advantages and disadvantages of the various fuels used in a hotel. *(IHMs)*
14. With the help of a neat sketch explain the working of a LPG gas stove. *(IHMs)*
15. With the help of a neat sketch explain the working of vapour absorption cycle of refrigeration. *(IHMs)*
16. Explain the installation, use, and maintenance of a refrigerator. *(IHMs)*
17. Define the following :
    (*a*) Calorie
    (*b*) British Thermal Unit
    (*c*) Calorific Value of a Fuel

(*d*) Relative Humidity
(*e*) Due Point
(*f*) Air Conditioning
(*g*) One ton of Air Conditioning
(*h*) Latent Heat of vapourization. (*IHMs*)

18. Discuss the importance of maintenance department in a hotel. Draw the organisation chart of the department and explain their duties and the responsibilities.

19. Define airconditioning. Explain the working of a window type airconditioner with emphasis on its maintenance (*IHMs*)

20. What do you mean by hardness of water ? State the disadvantages of hard water. (*IHMs*)

21. In one or two lines explain **any five** of the following:
(*a*) Short Circuit
(*b*) Therm
(*c*) Expansion valve
(*d*) Calorifier
(*e*) Class 'B' fire
(*f*) Defrosting
(*g*) Sensible heat
(*h*) P.V.C.
(*i*) Commercial units of electric energy. (*IHMs*)

22. Define the term kilo calories and British thermal unit and give relationship between them.

23. State the desirable properties of refrigerant (*IHMs*)

24. Define refrigeration. Discuss the basic scientific principle behind it ? Explain functions of an absorption type refrigeration system, with the help of a neat diagram with emphasis on its care and maintenance. (*IHMs*)

25. 'The engineering department work almost completely behind the scenes, but it fulfils a tremendous important function. Explain. (*IHMs*)

26. Define calorific value :
10,00 litres of water is to be heated from 25°C to 75°C. Find the cost if fuel used is :
(*a*) LPG and (*b*) Electricity
Cost of one cylinder of LPG is ₹ 100/-
Cost of 1 KWH of electricity is ₹ 1/- (*IHMs*)

27. Briefly describe the duties and responsibilities of maintenance department. (*IHMs*)

28. Explain various types of fuses. (*IHMs*)

29. In one or two lines explain **any five** of the following :
(*a*) Thermostat
(*b*) LPG
(*c*) Class 'C' Fire
(*d*) B.T.U.
(*e*) Critical Temperature
(*f*) Earthing
(*g*) Degree of hardness
(*h*) Thermo
(*i*) Method of Transmission of Heat. (*IHMs*)

30. Explain the compression refrigeration cycle with the help of neat diagram with emphasis on its care and maintenance. (*IHMs*)

31. State the prevention maintenance required for window air-conditioner. (*IHMs*)

32. Explain the importance of 'earthing' in electricity. (*IHMs*)

33. In one or two lines explain any five of the following :

(*a*) Latent Heat
(*b*) Class 'C' Fire
(*c*) Fire Hazards
(*d*) D.P.C.
(*e*) Calorific Value
(*f*) HRC Fuse
(*g*) Thermostat
(*h*) Methods of Cooling Condenser
(*i*) B.T.U. *(IHMs)*

34. What is defrosting ? Explain the different methods of defrosting. *(IHMs)*

35. Explain the different types of portable fire extinguishers *(IHMs)*

36. Explain the difference between temporary hardness of water and permanent hardness of water. How is hardness of water expressed ? Describe one method of removing permanent hardness of water. *(IHMs)*

37. What does maintenance of cold water cistern, flushing cistern, and swimming pool comprise of? *(IHMs)*

38. Define refrigeration. State the basic scientific principles used in refrigeration with the help of a neat switch. Explain the working of a vapour absorption type of refrigeration system.*(IHMs)*

39. Describe the care and maintenance of :
(*i*) A refrigerator
(*ii*) Refrigeration equipment
(*iii*) A water cooler. *(IHMs)*

40. Explain the necessity of earthing all electrical equipment. Compare a miniature circuit board with a Kit Kat Fuse. Give 10 points to be taken care of in maintenance of electric circuits and equipment. *(IHMs)*

41. Explain the care and maintenance of fire detection alarm and fire extinguishing equipment. *(IHMs)*

42. State 10-steps that can be taken to make a hotel building more fire safe. *(IHMs)*

43. Define any five of the following:
(*a*) British Thermal Unit
(*b*) Kilocalorie
(*c*) Calorific Value of Fuel
(*d*) Latent Heat of Vapourization
(*e*) Class 'C' fire
(*f*) One tone of Refrigerator
(*g*) Relative Humidity
(*h*) Fool Canole. *(IHMs)*

44. In one or two sentences explain the following:
(*a*) Thermostat
(*b*) Break-down Maintenance
(*c*) Preventive Maintenance
(*d*) Ignition Temperature
(*e*) Commercial unit of Electricity
(*f*) Alternating Current
(*g*) Horsepower
(*h*) Convector
(*i*) Radiator
(*j*) H.P.G. *(IHMs)*

45. With the help of a neat diagram explain the hot water circulation system for a large hotel. *(IHMs)*

46. In one or two lines explain **any five** of the following:
(*a*) Calorific value of fuel
(*b*) Earthing
(*c*) Methods of softening water
(*d*) Latent heat
(*e*) Refrigerant.

47. What is the object of energy conservation within the hotel industry ? Discuss in detail the various steps which are necessary for developing a good energy conservation programme. *(IHMs)*

48. List the circumstances under which you will think of replacing an equipment. A dish washing machine costs ₹ 80,000. Its value if sold is ₹ 48.000 after one year, ₹ 36,000 after 2 years, ₹ 27,000 after three years and so on, i.e. after the heavier depreciation in first year. It looses 25% of the remaining value in each subsequent year. Its operating costs in estimated at ₹ 10,000/- in the first year, ₹ 12,000 in the second year and soon increasing by ₹ 2,000 each year, when should the machine be replaced. *(IHMs)*

49. What you mean by contract maintenance ? Describe its advantages. Explain different types of contracts. *(IHMs)*

50. Define preventive maintenance. Briefly describe the procedure of preventive maintenance programme. *(IHMs)*

51. Briefly state the sewage pollution problem. *(IHMs)*

52. Explain the following terms in one or two lines:–

(*a*) Salvage Value
(*b*) Probability
(*c*) Break-down maintenance
(*d*) Refuse
(*e*) Base Exchange Method
(*f*) Planned Maintenance
(*g*) Timmer
(*h*) Net Present Value
(*i*) Scheduled Maintenance.

53. "Timely decision of equipment replacement is important before break-down". Discuss. *(IHMs)*

54. Define the term "contract". Discuss the advantages and disadvantages of contract maintenance. Explain item rate contract. *(IHMs)*

55. Answer the following (Any five) in one or two line:

(*a*) Ventilation
(*b*) Insecticuter
(*c*) Electricity
(*d*) Salvage value
(*e*) Deposting
(*f*) Scale formation
(*g*) Energy audit
(*h*) Probability
(*i*) Circuit
(*j*) Air conditioning
(*k*) Sanitary trap
(*l*) Sewerage
(*m*) Incineration.

56. Discuss about the replacement decision related to capital equipment. *(IHMs)*

57. Initial cost of a laundry machine is ₹ 60,000/-. Its value (if sold) is ₹ 40,000/- after one year, ₹ 32,000 after two year, ₹ 25,600 after three years and so on *i.e.* after the initial heavy depreciation in the first year it loses 20% of the remaining value in each subsequent year. Its operating cost includes maintenance, cost of scrap and loss of output is ₹ 3000/- in the first year, ₹ 5000/- in the second year and so on increasing by ₹ 2000/- a year each. When should the machine be replaced ? *(IHMs)*

58. List 10-points to be followed for saving energy while using cooling appliances. *(IHMs)*

59. Describe different type of maintenance. Explain each one with suitable examples. *(IHMs)*

60. The following mortality rates have been observed for certain type of light bulbs:

Week	1	2	3	4	5
Percentage failing by the end of the week.	10	25	50	80	100

The cost of replacing an individual bulb is ₹ 5/-. The decision is made to replace all bulbs simultaneously at fixed intervals and also to replace individual bulbs as they fail in service. If the cost of replacement is ₹ 2/- per bulb, what is the optimum interval between group replaced? *(IHMs)*

61. Discuss various types of contract maintenance. Illuminate the basic steps involved in establishing a maintenance contract. *(IHMs)*

62. Name 10 points to be followed for saving energy in the kitchen. *(IHMs)*

63. Briefly discuss the water pollution problems. *(IHMs)*

64. Answer the following (any five) in one or two lines :

(*a*) Service contract
(*b*) Air curtain
(*c*) Grease trap
(*d*) Net present value
(*e*) Replenishment
(*f*) Warranty
(*g*) Thermostat
(*h*) Ozone Lamp.

65. Write short notes on any *two* of the following :

(*a*) Hotel Industry in India
(*b*) Internal and External Communication
(*c*) Manpower Planning
(*d*) Functions of Maintenance Department of a Hotel. *(DTHM)*

OBJECTIVE TYPE QUESTIONS

66. Fill in the blanks:

(*a*) The units used to measure intensity is in CGS system.
(*b*) .... is good conductor of heat but a bad conductor of electricity.
(*c*) Oil fires are known as .... class fires.
(*d*) .... chemical is used in basic exchange method of water softner .
(*e*) The boiling points of a substance will change depending on the ....
(*f*) The part of a refrigerator which gives away heat to the atmosphere is known as...............
(*g*) The low current fuse wire is of an alloy consists of ....
(*h*) Single phase supply voltage in India is .... V.
(*i*) .... is the symbol used for earthing
(*j*) Motor is used to current electric energy into .... energy. *(IHMs)*

67. Fill in the blanks:

(*a*) Heat is transmitted in a liquid medium by .... method.
(*b*) The method by which the ice accumulated on the vaporater is removed, is known as ....
(*c*) One British gallon is equal to .... litres.
(*d*) The outside body of electric equipment is maintained at zero potential by means of ....
(*e*) One horse power is equal to .... khws.
(*f*) 50°C is equal to .... °F.
(*g*) .... tap is used in wash basins.
(*h*) Generator is used to current mechanical energy to .... energy.
(*i*) .... acid is used in soda acid type extinguishers.
(*j*) .... oil is used in boilers. *(IHMs)*

68. Fill in the blanks :

(*a*) Commercial unit of electric energy is............... .
(*b*) .... unit is used to measure power.
(*c*) Relative humidity is the ratio of .... :
(*d*) .... colour wire is always neutral in electricity.
(*e*) Three phase voltage in India is .... volts.
(*f*) The unit of illumination is............... .
(*g*) .... extinguisher is used on electrical fire.

(*h*) Dampers regulates the flow of................ in various ducts.

(*i*) Defective foundations are caused by .... and ....

(*j*) .... refrigerant is used in modern refrigerator .... (*IHMs*)

69. Fill in the blanks:

(*a*) .... extinguisher is used for electric fires

(*b*) L.P.G. is a mixture of .... and ....

(*c*) ICTP stand for .... switch

(*d*) Frequency of three phase supply in India is ....

(*e*) .... symbol is used for earthing

(*f*) .... unit is used to express electric power.

(*g*) The boiling point of a substance will change depending on the ....

(*h*) Two way switch is used for ....

(*i*) .... is used to control water level in storage tank.

(*j*) .... wire is used to make filament of a bulb. (*IHMs*)

70. Write 'true' or 'false' against each of the following statements:

(*a*) Preventive maintenance is nothing but corrective maintenance.

(*b*) Stop replacement is the most expensive form of replacement.

(*c*) Pollution mostly is a result of inefficient use of energy.

(*d*) Burners smaller than kettle placed on them with help in saving energy.

(*e*) The entrance to a walk-in type freezer through the cooler will help to save energy.

(*f*) The high diesel is the cheapest fuel as compared to either electricity or LPG.

(*g*) Group replacement method is used for gradually deteriorating equipments.

(*h*) Water sprinklers are not used in painting workshop. The only cause for replacement is excessive maintenance.

(*i*) The average energy cost of the hotel in India it around one percentage of total sales. (*IHMs*)

71. Write 'true' and 'false' against each statement:

(*i*) Break-down maintenance can be under planned maintenance.

(*ii*) Maintenance contract with outsides is always a better proposition.

(*iii*) Sewage and sewerage mean same.

(*iv*) Use of fluowresent tube light in place of incandescent lamps is one way to save energy.

(*v*) Using flat bottom pots and pans will help to maximum heat transfer.

(*vi*) Increase of number of doors opening of a refrigerator save energy.

(*vii*) Contract maintenance is always better than department maintenance.

(*viii*) Fire can be eleminated either by reducing the temperature or eliminating oxygen.

(*ix*) Canvass pipe is preferred than rubber pipe because of flexibility for fire fighting.

(*x*) Insecticuter is used for waste disposal. (*IHMs*)

72. Write 'true' or 'false' against each statement:

(*i*) Group replacement is always cheaper than the individual replacement.

(*ii*) Preventive maintenance is always better than breakdown maintenance.

(*iii*) Change to design of a product is one reasons for replacement of equipment.

(*iv*) Energy by consumption of cooling appliance will decreases if it is located away from the heating appliances.

(*v*) Feed precooled and chilled water into ice making machine to save energy.

(*vi*) Non-resistance type dimmers are used to save energy while controlling illumination level.

(*vii*) Timber is used to control the temperature in the oven.

(*viii*) Covering pots and pans will save energy.

(*ix*) LPG is lighter than air.

(*x*) For extinguishing oil base fire soda acid extinguisher is used.

(*xi*) Burner should always be small than the kettle placed on them.

(*xii*) Regular defrosting of cooling appliance will help to increase the careful life of appliance.

(*xii*) About 25% of the sales in a hotel are spent in energy. (*IHMs*)

CHAPTER 9

Administration and Human Resources Development

OBJECTIVES

After studying this chapter, you should be able to :

1. *Understand the role of administration and human resource management*
2. *Understand the personnel policies of the hotel and personnel control system and*
3. *Explain the role of training and human resource development.*

ORGANISATION

The employees need to contribute their full skill, care and effort to the activities and operation of the hotel. To achieve this objective it is required that the management be knowledgeable about needs and desires. It must provide the communication, incentives, recognition and rewards. It is often seen that the problem of employee motivation gets complicated because of the widely disparate view of the management and employees on what individuals want from their job. For example, management thought material considerations ranked uppermost in the mind of employees as regard to job satisfaction on the other hand, employees rated the psychological satisfaction more important.

Admistration department in a hotel is usually supervised by a Director (administration). He is responsible for all the work connected with administration, personnel, manpower, employees' welfare, medical, health and security of the hotel. In large hotel the work is sub-divided and separate departments are created to look after human resource development, administration and security.

Hotel industry offers relatively limited opportunities for the application of improved technology, therefore, improved productivity and performance on the part of the employees represent the best chance for realizing, operating, saving and improving profits for the hotel. The industry is becoming dominated by chain operators, convenience food and standardized operating techniques. This requires ability, training dedication, involvement, interest and service orientation of employees.

The management of hotel has to depend totally on the employees for guest satisfaction which is the most important ingredient for success of a hotel. In addition, payroll and related expenses account for approximately one-third of the distribution of the rupee income. Thus the money and effort expended in obtaining, training and retaining qualified and highly motivated personnel is one of the most rewarding investment in a hotel business.

In small hotels the various aspects of personnel functions are the responsibility of the hotel manager. Medium-sized hotels delegate these responsibilities to assistant manager. Whereas in large hotels due to increase in the size of operation, the personnel function is the responsibility of a separate personnel department headed by a Personnel Manager.

Some of the positions in this department are :

1. Personnel Director
2. Personnel Research and Development Officer
3. Recruitment Officer
4. Training Officer
5. Welfare Officer

Figs 9.1 and 9.2 indicate the break-up of the employee working in the various section of this department.

DIRECTOR PERSONNEL

He is one of the several specialists reporting directly to the General Manager. The day-to-day operation of the department is divided between several subordinates who are

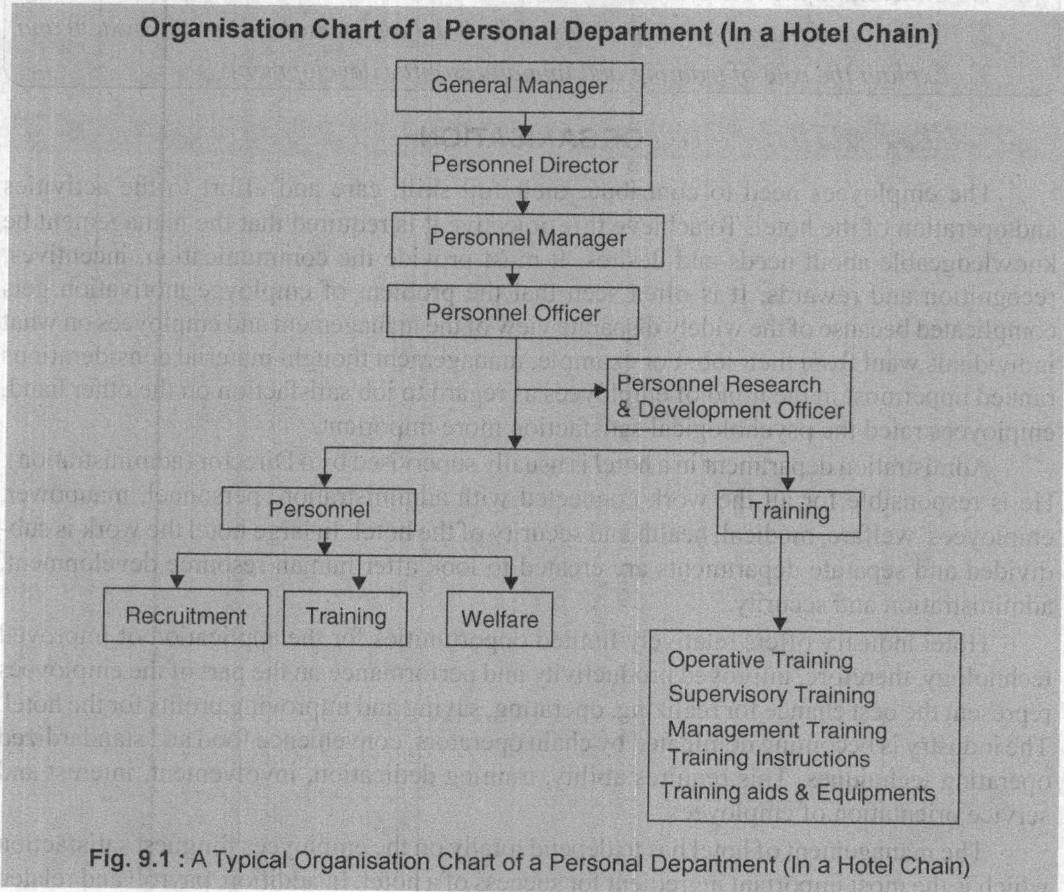

Fig. 9.1 : A Typical Organisation Chart of a Personal Department (In a Hotel Chain)

responsible to the Personnel Manager. His job takes in the recruitment and selection of staff, employment contracts, grievance procedures and trade union contact as well as the training, development and motivation of staff.

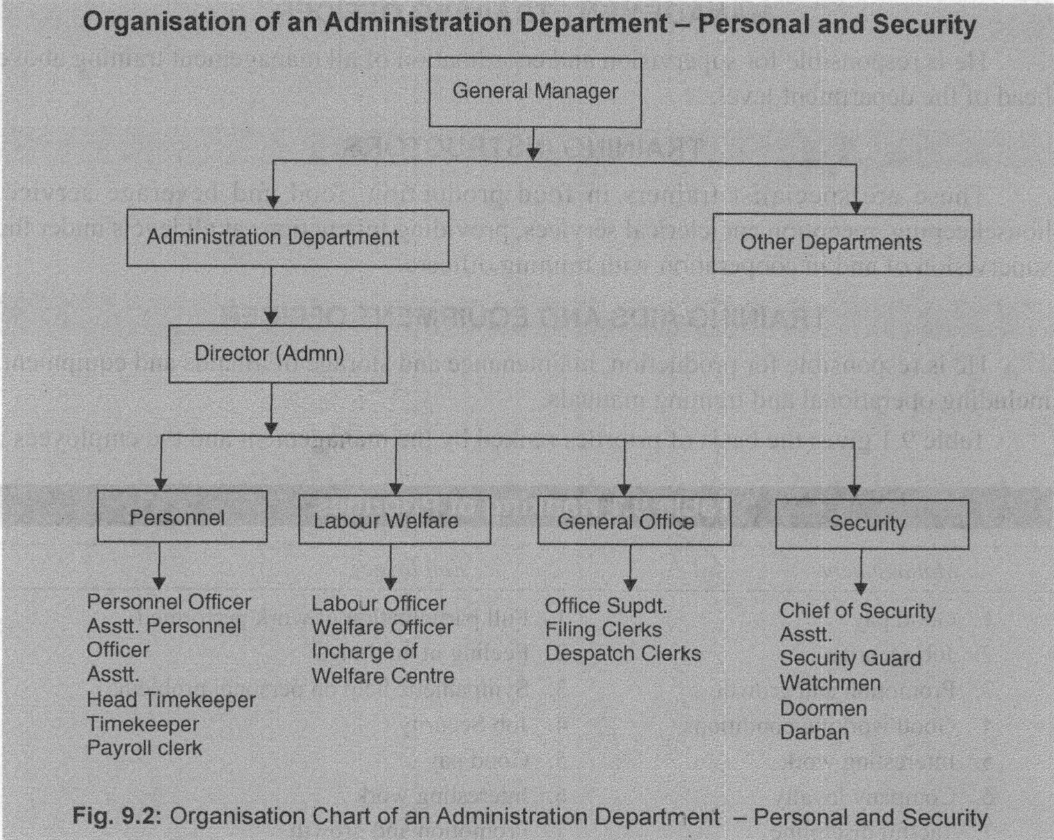

Fig. 9.2: Organisation Chart of an Administration Department – Personal and Security

He is concerned with all the personnel functions such as :

1. Employment policies
2. Issues of employment
3. Management of his department
4. Cooperate with personnel department in establishing and maintaining an inventory of management and supervisory personnel
5. Preparation, operation and training manuals and other publications, teaching aids and material for employee's training
6. Representing the hotel in all matters concerned within and outside the hotel and advise the General Manager and top management.

TRAINING OFFICER

He directs and coordinates all training and maintains close liaison with concerned officer related to welfare, recruitment and personnel.

OPERATING TRAINING OFFICER

He is responsible for supervision and coordination of all operative training below the level of assistant head of the department.

SUPERVISORY TRAINING OFFICER

He is responsible for supervision and coordination of all training above operative and below assistant manager level, i.e. head and assistant head of departmental training.

MANAGEMENT TRAINING OFFICER

He is responsible for supervision and coordination of all management training above head of the department level.

TRAINING INSTRUCTORS

These are specialist trainers in food production, food and beverage service, housekeeping, reception and clerical services, providing instructions at all levels under the supervision of and in cooperation with training officers.

TRAINING AIDS AND EQUIPMENT OFFICER

He is responsible for production, maintenance and storage of all aids and equipment, including operational and training manuals.

Table 9.1 gives the basis of priorties ranked by the management and the employees :

Table 9.1 Ranking of Priorities

Management	*Employees*
1. Good pay	1. Full participation of work performed
2. Job security	2. Feeling in on things
3. Promotion and growth	3. Sympathetic help on personal problems
4. Good working conditions	4. Job Security
5. Interesting work	5. Good pay
6. Company loyalty	6. Interesting work
7. Tactful discipline	7. Promotion and growth
8. Full appreciation of work performed	8. Company loyalty to workers
9. Sympathetic help with personal problems	9. Good working conditions
10. Feeling in on things	10. Tactful discipline

A Case Study 9.1 : Disciplinary Accident

THE DUBBINGTONS CASE

Chrissie is a relatively new 17-year-old waitress at Dubbingtons, a large department store. One Saturday afternoon Store Security Officers stop her as she is leaving, search her bags and find 11 Ib of sliced ham and half-a-dozen eggs in them.

Chrissie admits that these came from the store restaurant's stocks, but claims that she was given them by Fred, the chef, in return for her helping out over her lunch break in the kitchen, which was short handed. Fred denies her story emphatically. 'She's a lying little ****,' he says. 'You know I've no authority to make that sort of deal!'

Fred has been employed at Dubbingtons for the past twelve years. He is a big, genial man of 45, well liked by the other middle rank departmental staff and undeniably possessed of excellent craft skills. However, the catering department (which comprises the customer restaurant, tea-room, coffee bar and staff canteen) has suffered for several years from higher than average food cost percentages and labour turnover.

(Cont.)

The store has recently created the post of Catering Manager to control this side of its operations, and you have been appointed. You have been in the post for three weeks, and this is your second confrontation with Fred. The first was over the board's decision to close the senior staff dining-room and require staff to eat in the staff canteen: Fred apparently thinks you initiated this policy, and resents the fact that he will no longer be able to produce a limited number of high-quality meals and thus ingratiate himself with the senior staff.

There are few records, and those available throw little light on the reasons for the high food costs or the labour turnover in the catering sections. Fred's attitude of surly non-cooperativeness makes further investigation difficult. The other catering staff are noncommittal, and it is very unlikely that they will be prepared to 'tell tales' against either Chrissie or Fred.

How would you deal with this situation?

Well, how should you? As it happens, this is one of those cases where you can use the classic problem-solving approach more or less as it stands.

The first thing to do is to re-read the case thoroughly until you are confident that you have assimilated all the facts (this isn't too difficult with a short case like this one, but is a bit harder with the longer ones). Some students find that it helps them to make a brief precis of the situation, though you shouldn't waste too much time in writing out points which you already have set down in front of you.

The second stage is to see what conclusions you can draw from the facts: in other words, to try to fit these into a pattern that makes sense. What has really been going on in this establishment? The facts - that Chrissie has been caught taking food home, the higher than average food costs, etc. – show that things haven't been going entirely according to plan, but what are the *cause*? Answering this kind of question will inevitably involve you in a certain amount of guesswork, because you can't know for certain what has been going on, but some assumptions are more likely than others. For instance, there is a whole range of factors which *could* lead to high food costs, including bad purchasing, storage or portion control, but there isn't any supporting evidence in the case itself for most of these. On the other hand, there is some supporting evidence for an explanation based on pilferage. Ask yourself whether the other facts are consistent with this explanation, and see whether you can come up with a pattern of events which makes sense in terms of ordinary human nature.

The next stage is to identify the problems. As we have already said, make sure that you list them as well. Don't make the mistake of concentrating just on the immediate problem. This is a wellknown pitfall in real life as well as in case studies. Keep in mind that your real objective is to get this unit running smoothly and efficiently.

Next, you have to consider the options open to you and their likely consequences. Remember that one of these options is to do nothing, though you may well feel that this is one of those cases where this course of action (or inaction) would simply make matters worse. Clearly, you have to make up your mind what to do about Chrissie, and you should also think hard about Fred, the chef. Be careful, though. It's no good writing something down as an option unless you actually have the power to do it. And be realistic. It isn't much good writing 'I would carry out a thorough investigation and get to the bottom of this whole business . . .' The case has already given you Fred's answer, and what you are told about Fred suggests (deliberately) that he is a pretty tough, hard-bitten sort of character. How likely is it that he would change his story? The case has already told you that the records are incomplete. How likely is it that the other staff would volunteer information, especially about practices in which they themselves might have been involved?

Once you have established what your options are, you should go on to produce a specific recommendation or set of recommendations. Try to make these positive, and if possible try to manage with the resources already available to you. It is tempting to write 'If I had my way, I'd fire all the staff and start all over again', but top management doesn't usually look very kindly on

(*Cont.*)

this kind of approach. One of your problems in this case is Fred, the chef: no doubt you would like to see him replaced by someone else who is equally skilled but a lot easier to work with. However, you will get more credit if you can put forward a solution which allows you to operate effectively with the staff you already have. Try to make your recommendations practical. If you decide (as you might) that part of the answer lies in changing the system within which the staff are working, then you should outline what changes you propose to make and how you would introduce them to staff, both present and future.

Finally, a word about presentation. We have already indicated that this case can be answered along the classic problem-solving lines, which gives you a ready-made structure for your answer. How long should it be? Well, as a very, rough approximation, you ought to be able to get 3–4 pages of answer out of every page of case study text. This probably sounds horrifying, but once you start, you'll find it very difficult to answer this one adequately in under 3–4 sides. Remember that the facts are only the starting point: you will have a number of assumptions to justify and several courses of action to consider before you submit your final recommendation. Obviously, this last stage shouldn't involve too much repetition: if you're already identified the reasons why this is the best course of action you don't have to repeat them all over again. However, you *could* usefully add some details as to how you would implement your proposal.

You will find an outline 'answer' to this introductory case. However, we do advise you, very strongly, to try it yourself first. As we have said, you can only develop a skill by practising it.

As we said in the introduction, your response to this case can be organized in terms of the classic problem-solving structure. This also provides a useful framework for a report-style presentation. This is bound to be somewhat artificial, since the obligation to show all the stages of your reasoning forces you to appear rather more introspective than you would be in real life, but it still provides good practice in arranging and presenting material in an acceptable style. It might go along the following lines:

To: General Manager, Dubbingtons
From: P. Abbott and J. Shepherd,
Joint Catering Managers, Dubbingtons
Date: Today's date
Subject: *Report on Disciplinary Incident*

1. Facts

On Saturday afternoon store security officers stopped Chrissie................, a waitress, as she was leaving, searched her bags and found 11 lb of sliced ham and half-a-dozen eggs in them. Chrissie admitted that these came from the store restaurant's stocks, but claimed that she was given them by Fred................, the chef, in return for her helping out over her lunch break in the kitchen, which was short-handed. Interviewed, Fred denied her story emphatically, pointing out that he had no authority to make that sort of deal.

As the management will be aware, Fred has been employed at Dubbingtons for the past twelve years. He is well liked by the other departmental staff and undeniably possessed of excellent craft skills. However, the catering department has been suffering from higher-than-average food costs and labour turnover rates for several years now, though the available records do not disclose any obvious reasons for these. In consequence, the Board has recently created the post of Catering Manager to control this side of its operations, and we have been appointed.

We have only been in post for three weeks, but this is our second confrontation with Fred. The first was over the Board's decision to close the senior staff dining room. Fred apparently thinks we initiated this policy, and resents the fact that he will no longer be able to produce a certain number of high-quality meals.

(*Cont.*)

The paucity of the records makes further investigation difficult. The catering staff are non-committal, and it seems very unlikely that they will be prepared to 'tell tales' against either, Chrissie or Fred.

2. Assumptions

It is not immediately clear whether or not Chrissie is telling the truth. If she is, then the problem of the higher-than-average food costs would appear to be explained, assuming that the practice she describes has been common. If she is lying, then we still have to find some other explanation. Chrissie is relatively young and inexperienced, and while she may be a hardened liar and criminal, we feel the balance of the probabilities is that she is telling the truth. This clearly implicates Fred. However, the facts still fit two alternative scenarios:

(*a*) Fred has been encouraging pilferage over a long period. Not only have food costs been above average, but the labour turnover has been relatively high, which is a little odd since Fred is generally considered to be genial and well liked (though we must add that we have found no evidence that this is true as far as his staff are concerned). Many people do not like working in an atmosphere of petty theft, and while they may not actually inform on their colleagues, they might well have taken the first opportunity to leave. This point helps to explain why there do not appear to have been many actual dismissals for pilferage (we assume that we would have been told if there had been an abnormally high incidence of these), but we would still have expected there to be some if pilferage *has* been common, particularly since store security is not under Fred's control. The fact that there have not leads us to consider a possible alternative explanation.

(*b*) Food costs have been high in the past because Fred has not been as efficient as he might have been (he certainly seems to have neglected his record-keeping!), and his action in letting Chrissie take the food was motivated by his resentment at being demoted. This explanation fits the facts and is psychologically plausible.

Either explanation is reasonable, but the essential point is that both clearly point to poor control.

3. Problems

We have divided these into two groups:

(*a*) *Short term*:

- What to do about Chrissie?
- What to do about Fred?

(*b*) *Long term*:

- What to do about control (this covers both pilferage and inefficient production methods)?
- What to do about the high labour turnover?
- Finally, how can we establish our authority over this department?

4. Alternative Courses of Action

(*a*) *Do nothing*. Fairly obviously, this is not one of those situations where this is an acceptable solution. Doing nothing solves none of our problems and, by encouraging Fred, is likely to make most of them worse.

(*b*) *Prosecution and/or dismissal*. It is dangerous to simplify law, but our understanding is that to convict someone of a serious crime like theft, we normally have to prove not only that they committed the alleged act, but also that they knew it was wrong. Chrissie cannot deny that she took the items, but she might well argue that she thought Fred had the authority to let her have them, and unless we can show that she had been told otherwise

(*Cont.*)

our prosecution might well fail, especially since the law traditionally recognizes that 'perks' are a feature of the catering industry. As for Fred, we have to remember that it is Chrissie's word against his, and that he is entitled to the benefit of any doubt. So it is unlikely that we could successfully prosecute either of them, even if we were willing to accept the expense and loss of time involved.

The same arguments apply to termination. Fred is protected against unfair dismissal, and in the absence of any previous official (i.e. provable) warnings he is likely to win in the event of an appeal. Chrissie is not protected to the same extent because she has not worked for long enough, and there may be grounds for dismissal.

Let us assume for a moment that we could indeed fire her: should we? We have to consider staff attitudes and morale. On the one hand, they may think it unfair if we dismiss Chrissie and retain Fred. On the other, a dismissal would show that we were in earnest about stopping pilferage. The arguments would appear to be evenly balanced, but we must also consider whether Chrissie and Fred are likely to work well together in the future after she has 'informed' on him.

In our view, this tips the scales against Chrissie, though we recognize that there is room for argument here.

(*c*) *Set up a proper control system.* Neither prosecution nor dismissal really solves the underlying problems, and our emphasis must be on establishing control. This must include a proper system of recording orders, stocks, issues, consumption and wastage. It should also include issuing a statement of policy regarding 'perks', to form part of all present and future contracts of employment, together with an intensified programme of random checks to show that we really mean what we say. What this does is:

- It helps to solve our problems with Chrissie and Fred by making it clear that we are doing something about the food costs.
- It should lead to a reduction in the food costs themselves.
- It *may* help to improve the labour turnover figures by improving morale, though this is not certain. We would recommend additional measures such as termination of employment interviews in order to establish the real reasons for the increase.
- It establishes our authority as catering managers, since we are shown to be not only in charge but doing something positive.

5. Recommendations

Fairly obviously, it is Alternative 4(*c*) which points the way forward. We would couple this with an investigation to discover the real cause or causes of the high labour turnover (which may turn out to have nothing to do with the immediate problem). We would also suggest an attempt to conciliate Fred by returning the responsibility for special functions to him. After all, he is competent and well liked, and we should try to retain him if possible. If he accepts the new system, well and good. If he does not, then it is up to him to resign, which avoids any problems with unfair dismissal and allows us to recruit a new chef who will start with a clear idea of his position and responsibilities.

Notes

1. This uses the 'memo heading' format we mentioned earlier. There is no need to invent imaginary names: in fact, if you were doing this report as an assignment, you could put your tutor's name opposite the 'To'.
2. This kind of summary is possible with a relatively short case, but you will find that it becomes progressively more difficult with the longer ones. In fact, it doesn't earn many marks, if any, and you should reduce it to the minimum. We have included it here because it is required by the context (i.e. a disciplinary report).

(*Cont.*)

3. This gets round the case's failure to provide some important background facts. Most cases have this kind of 'hole' in them, and it is useful to be able to circumvent them smoothly.
4. A common-sense assumption, so obvious as not to need labelling as such. Practically all stores reserve the right to search employees and their baggage as a matter of course.
5. This is by far the most important conclusion you can come to in this section. The temptation is to concentrate on trying to find some way of proving Fred's guilt or innocence. In fact, the real point is to get this department functioning efficiently.
6. This is probably too introspective (*i.e.* self-critical) to be included in a real-life report, but it is a genuine problem none the less, and you need to show that you have recognized it as such.
7. Again, this is a little too 'introspective' for inclusion in a real-life report. At this stage, however, you are only practising decision-making, and it is useful to set out all the stages of your thinking. Common sense should tell you what is likely to strike an employer as unduly negative.
8. These two paragraphs provide a fairly bald summary of the legal position. They could be 'enriched' by references to the statutes involved and possible precedents. However, don't get carried away to the extent of seeing this as a purely legal problem. The real point is still control.
9. You will see that we have followed our own advice and climbed down off the fence here. As markers, we would be happy enough to see you argue either way as long as you recognized that there is indeed room for argument over this point.
10. These ought to be set out in much more detail in a complete answer. The necessary measures are obvious enough, and you should be familiar with them from your work on food and beverage control.
11. You might draft a specimen statement and show it as an appendix. This would certainly 'enrich' your answer. Remember that one of the things we are looking for is the ability to *implement* solutions.

PERSONALITY AND MOTIVATION

The employees in the modern time are far different in terms of value, life-style, needs and motivations. You will find them better educated and qualified, more sophisticated and more demanding. Dr. Abraham Maslow, an eminent psychologist in his essay of personality and motivation, stated that there need be recognisation that all humans are motivated by 'hierarchy of needs'. According to him, man is motivated to reach a certain goal because he has own internally generated needs to reach it. All human needs can better he ranked from the most primitive and urgent (psychological needs) to the needs for self-actualization at the top of his scale as following :[1]

1. Pshychological needs.
   (*i*) Food
   (*ii*) Shelter
   (*iii*) Warmth
   (*iv*) Sleep
   (*v*) Water
   (*vi*) Sex
   (*vii*) Other physical requirements.

1. Dr. Abrahm Maslow, an eminent Psychologist.

2. Safety needs :
   (*i*) Freedom from threat of
   – Physical injury as well as
   – Emotional Security
3. Need for belongingness and love :
   (*i*) Relationships with other people
   (*ii*) Social needs.
4. Esteem :
   (*i*) Self-respect
   (*ii*) High regard of others
5. Self-actualization:
   (*i*) Making the most of one's objectives and talents.

According to this hierarchy of needs, until a given need is satisfied a person is not motivated by a need higher in Maslow Scale as given in Fig. 9.3. For example, take the case of a hungry man. He would care for less for maintaining his self-respect than for satisfying his hunger. After some time, 'a satisfied need is no larger a motivator of behaviour' The same hungry man, having his appetite satisfied, ceases, at least for the time being, to be motivated by the needs for food.

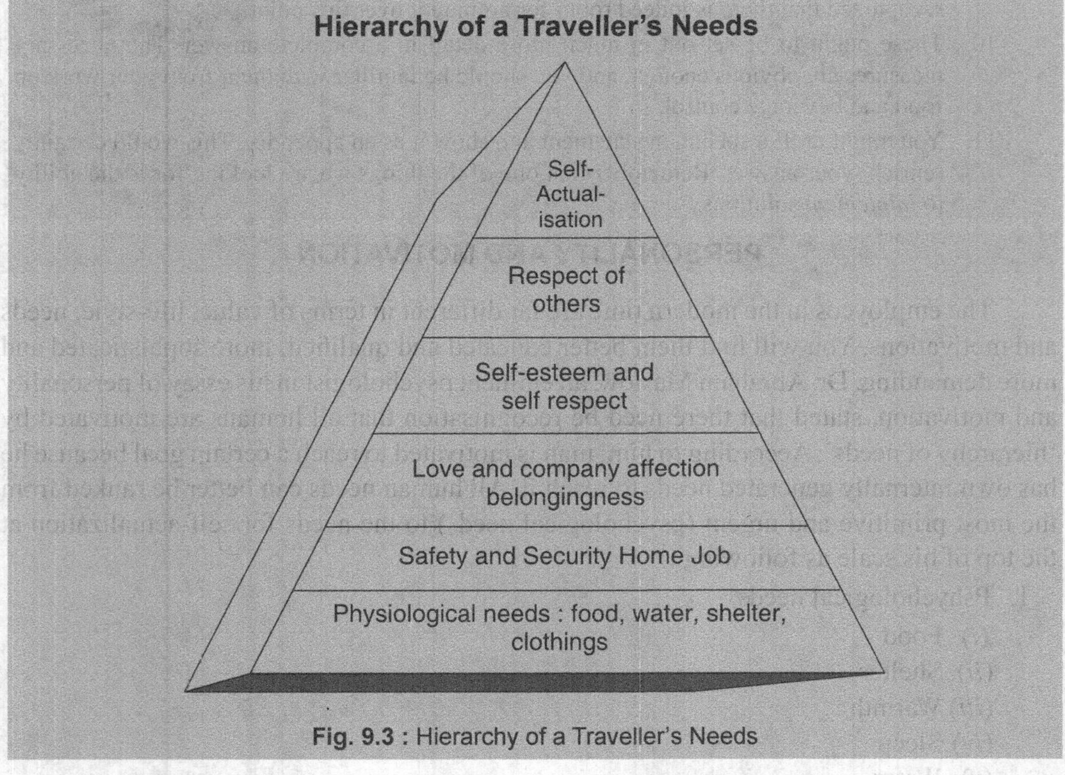

Fig. 9.3 : Hierarchy of a Traveller's Needs

In travel, vacation and leisure, travellers are motivated by the desire to satisfy needs. People who lack money for food, shelter and clothings can't travel for pleasure. Once the basic physical and emotional needs have been met, travel meets people's needs for esteem, respect and self-actualization.

Travellers who need to be with other people may purchase a group tour or a cruise with many planned activities. Travellers who feel a need for respect may purchase a travel product that will impress their friends and associates, such as a trip to an exotic destination or a stay in a ritzy resort hotel.

Travellers who feel a need for self-actualization are beyond trying to impress their friends they want a travel product that will help them develop physically, mentally and spiritually such as a cycle tour, study tour, or a pilgrimage trip.

The hierarchy needs of travellers operate on different levels for different activities at different times.

Many theories relating to employees' motivation have been developed by behavioral scientist. Let us discuss the famous 'X' and 'Y' theory of management'. This theory was propounded by Douglas McGegor. The theory deals with two sets of fundamental beliefs, manager hold about what people are like and which dictate their management style, to be identified as :[2]

1. Theory X Manger
2. Theory Y Manager

In theory X, manager believes that people dislike work and will avoid it if at all possible, shirk responsibility, are ambitious and excessively security conscious. Therefore, such employees respond only to threats of punishment, strict control and demanding supervision.

In theory Y, manager, on the other hand, has a more positive attitude towards people. He believes that work is natural and inherently pleasurable activity, that employees can and will provide their own motivation to achieve organisational objectives. They seek rather than avoid responsibility. They have vast resources of ambition, imagination and creativity which most organisations and managers fail to tap effectively.

According to the theory X vs. theory Y of management, in theory Y employee is self-motivated and that his needs can best be met by working towards fulfilment of the organisational goals. McGegor obviously favours theory Y as per the management strategies evoked by it and permissive supervisory style it engenders.

PERSONNEL POLICIES

The personnel function in a hotel includes many activities such as :

1. Consideration of leadership style
2. Relationship
3. Responsibilities
4. Philosophy
5. Social orientation and
6. Organisational structure.

In all the large hotels, personal policies are put into writing. These policies are distributed to key and responsible executives to provide guidance and ensure consistent application. Periodically you must review the policies in the light of changing conditions. The personnel policies concern with each of the following areas:

1. Employment
   (*i*) Recruitment

2. Douglas McGegor, propounder of 'X' and 'Y' Theory of Management.

(*ii*) Interviews.
(*iii*) Psychological and aptitude tests
(*iv*) Selection
(*v*) Medical examination
(*vi*) Administration and transfers
(*vii*) Promotions and terminations
(*viii*) Responsibilities for adherence to indiscrimination laws.

2. Education and Training
(*i*) Orientation of new employees
(*ii*) Educational needs for employees
(*iii*) Training of both employees and supervisors
(*iv*) Educative development programmes and
(*v*) Communications.

3. Health and Safety
(*i*) Occupational health
(*ii*) Emergency medical care
(*iii*) Safety programme
(*iv*) Perventive medicine

4. Employees' Services
(*i*) Cafeteria
(*ii*) Vending Machines
(*iii*) Employees' lounge
(*iv*) Lockers
(*v*) Counselling
(*vi*) Suggestion system

5. Wage and Salary Administration
(*i*) Salary structure
(*ii*) Performance standards and job evaluation
(*iii*) Salary surveys

6. Benefits
(*i*) Group insurance
(*ii*) Sick-pay plan
(*iii*) Hospitalization
(*iv*) Major medical coverage
(*v*) Key man insurance
(*vi*) Pension plan/scheme
(*vii*) Social security

7. Labour/Industrial Relations
(*i*) Presentation elections
(*ii*) Collective bargaining
(*iii*) Grievance procedures

8. Administration
   (*i*) Personnel records
   (*ii*) Turn-over statistics
   (*iii*) Security
   (*iv*) Holidays and vacations
   (*v*) Office layout and services
   (*vi*) Work rules

In small and medium-sized hotels the personnel function is still regarded as a minor function and delegated to an Assistant Manager connected with some other activity. In the large hotel, there may be a separate department under Director who will look after personnel and manpower planning, administration and security.

This department has the specialised duty of selecting, serving and improving the human team. It is observed that in most of the small, medium and large-sized hotels only one person is assigned the duties of personnel department. He is known as Personnel Officer or Personnel Manager or Personnel Director. He deals with all aspects of employees' relations which includes employees' training and development. This department is entrusted the task to attract good people to various jobs of the hotel and is responsible for recruiting employees at level of skill. It is seen that compared to other industries hotels have a high turnover rate which increases the problems of the recruitment. The personnel department should try to reduce the rate of turnover. The head of this department must also conduct job evaluation studies and wage surveys and the various benefits and incentive system. In addition, there is a need for training of hotel employees. Therefore, he is to supply the technique of training to all the persons connecting with the training department of the hotel. Besides, he is the architect of company's morale and unites all the human elements by minimising the misconceptions and by discussing the problems of the hotel employees.

The personnel control system is given in Fig. 9.4.

The person incharge of this department must have the thorough knowledge of all hotel work and must have competence in legal and trade union matters. His main duties are to cooperate with the management in establishing terms of appointment and to direct and supervise the conduct of personnel. He has to establish general instructions, duty shifts, days of rests etc. He is also to receive and examine requests and complaints.

The Personnel Manager/Director also handles many problems and minor disputes with and among the employees that occur in the daily operation of the hotel. The Personnel Manager meets the union delegates and resolves their differences. The general manager steps in only when a dispute is serious or cannot be settled at the hotel level and requires arbitration or court action.

Top management sets policy and the management team defines the duties of each category of employees. The Personnel Manager as a member of this team, assists by recommending and finally formalising these duties. It is then up to this department to administer, interpret and implement. The important duties or function of the personnel department are :

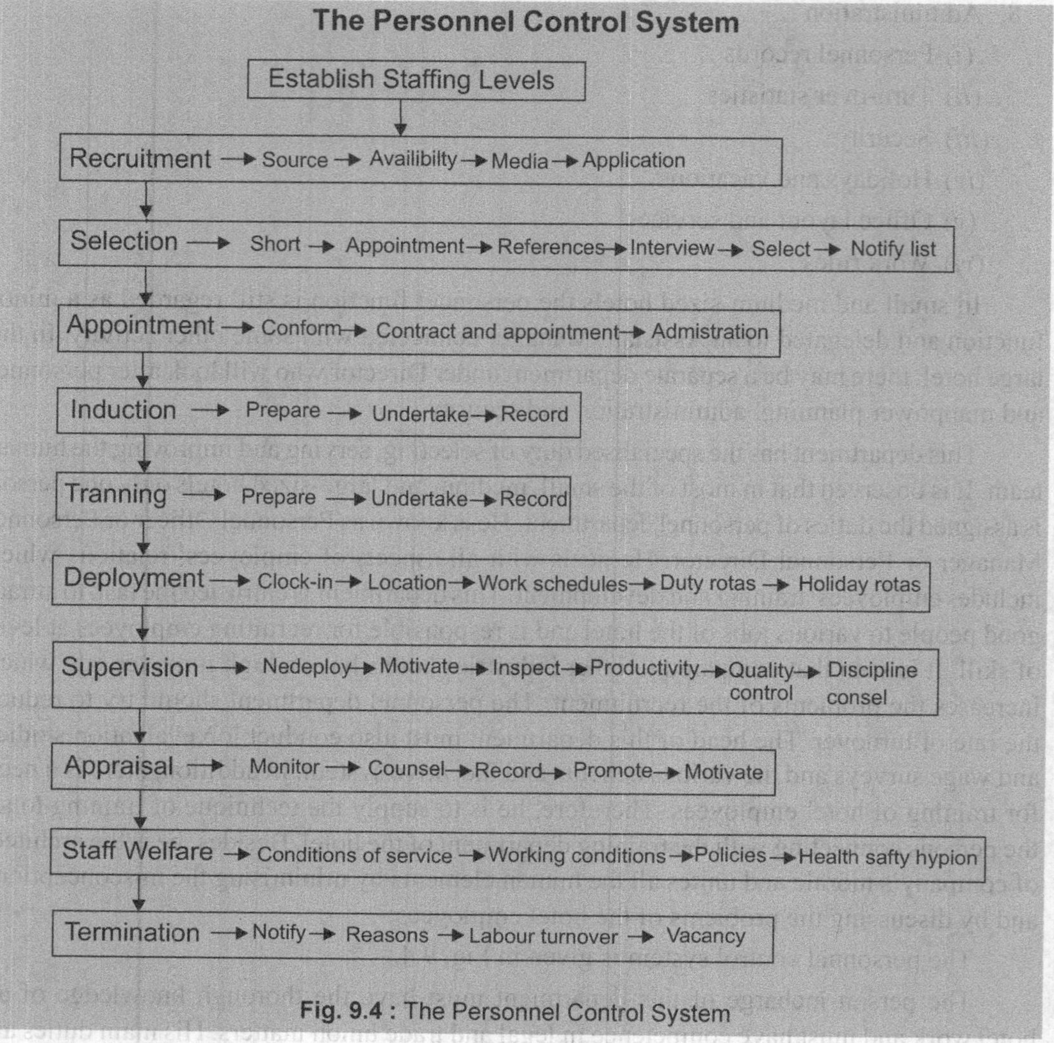

Fig. 9.4 : The Personnel Control System

1. Recruitment of staff
2. Interviewing and screening of applications
3. Verification of references
4. Referral to departmental heads
5. Processing of successful applicants
6. Training programs which is a constant and unending process
7. It states the employees not only what to do and how to do it, but also what to say and how to say it
8. Safety programmes
9. Benefit programmes, hospitalization, major medical group insurance and saving, pension plans, etc.
10. Union relations and agreements
11. Introduction and implementation of labour laws and regulations
12. To look after the health, recreation and entertainment of the employees.

The various functions handled under personnel and human resource development are :

1. Manpower planning
2. Recruitment
3. Training programmes
4. Developmental training
5. Centralised appraisal
6. Industrial relation
7. Wage and salary administration.

In addition to the general recruitment of employees in large hotel, recruitment and training is conducted under various schemes such as :

1. Trainee steward scheme
2. Kitchen training scheme
3. Hotel operational training scheme
4. Management training scheme
5. Graduate training scheme
6. Miscellaneous training scheme.

In all large hotels, there is a well established training division of the personnel department. Its objectives are :

1. To increase output and sales
2. To improve employees' knowledge, skill and attributes to work
3. To improve recruitment
4. To improve employees' loyalty
5. To improve the image of the company
6. To reduce breakage, waste of material and misuse of equipment
7. To reduce accidents
8. To reduce absenteeism
9. To reduce labour turnover
10. To reduce stresses on management.

The main functions of this division are :

1. To formulate a training policy
2. To prepare annual budget
3. To identify qualitatively and quantitatively the training requirements and keep them under review
4. To maintain close liaison with educational institutions and training centres and arrange for new courses
5. To establish and operate induction, orientation, refresher and other appropriate courses for different grades of employees.

COMMUNICATION

Communication is the interchange of facts, viewpoints, and ideas which bring about unity of interest, unity of purpose and unity among all members organised to achieve specific mission. The objective is to achieve mutual confidence and understanding between employees and management. Communication is a two-way street. There must be opportunities for two things.

1. Management to employees' communication channels
2. Employees to communicate upward.

The existence of upward channels helps in the following ways :

1. Provides management with information needed for decision making.
2. Employees relieve the pressures and frustrations of the bore situation.
3. Enhance the employees' sense of participation in the hotel.

You may adopt the following media as a channel of upward communication :

1. Employees' attitude serveys
2. Personal contact by supervisors and managers
3. Informal grievances procedure for non-organised employees
4. Exit and transfer interviews
5. Performance appraisal discussions
6. Question box or 'rumour clinic' variant of the suggestion system.

Communication exists only when a person has received what the sender has tried to convey. Therefore, while choosing the media of downward communication, you must know that people generally remember :

10% of what they read
20% of what they hear
30% of what they see
50% of what they hear and see
70% of what they say and
90% of what they say as they do a thing.

Below is a best of sampling of downward communication media, both written and oral appropriate for a hotel :

Written communication	**Oral communication media**
1. Policies, procedure and reports	1. Regular staff and information meetings
2. Bulletins	2. Orientation
3. Employees' publication	3. Assignment giving
4. Letters to employees homes	4. Performance appraisals
5. Literature racks	5. Counselling
6. Bulletin Boards	6. Walking the shop and office.
7. Reports to employees	

THE TRAINING PROGRAMME

Employee training and management development are key elements in creating and maintaining effective work force. Before planning training programme a number of questions need to be answered, such as :

1. What should be taught ?
2. When should training take place ?
3. Where should training be done ?

4. How should it be done ?
5. Who should to be the trainer ?
6. How much training should there be ?
7. How will the training be measured ?

BASIC PRINCIPLES OF LEARNING

You must keep in mind the six basic principles of learning while planning and administering a training programme :

1. Motivation
   (*i*) Create a desire to learn on the part of the employee
2. Objective
   (*i*) Learning is more rapid and complete when the learner knows exact what he is expected to learn as well as the purpose of the exercise.
3. Doing
   (*i*) The student must actually perform the operation
4. Realism
   (*i*) The more realistic the situation the more efficient the learning process.
5. Background
   (*i*) New learning is based on past knowledge and experience.
6. Appreciation
   (*i*) Show the student how what he is being tought has practical application in his/her daily life and on the job, as well as by pointing out the direct benefits enjoyed as a result of his newly acquired knowledge and skill.

EMPLOYEES' RELATIONS

Good job environment and effective leadership are very important for sound employees' relationship. The following points will help to a great extent in establishing good employees' relations :

1. Introduce competitive pay structure and benefits package.
2. Provide confortable and pleasant working conditions.
3. Provide facilities of communication network which will let employees know what is going on, their part in and benefit from this, what is expected from them and which provides opportunities for upward communication.
4. Provide an opportunity to employees for discussing their problems with levels of supervisors higher than their immediate boss.
5. Authority commensurate with responsibility. Delegate decision making authority to the lowest practical level to encourage a sense of participation and involvement among all employees.
6. Recognise achievement.
7. Introduce facilities for social and recreational programmes.
8. Introduce well planned training and development opportunities for present jobs and future growth.

EMPLOYEES' ASSOCIATION

A hotel may often competitively pay good benefits and working conditions and enlightened management practice; it does not mean that it has immuned itself to unionization in the establishment. The management has to conduct effective two-way communication with employees to get the credit for the good job it provides. The employees require an out-let to express their job frustration and dissatisfaction. These two objectives could be achieved though employees' association.

The Management should provide the following assurances to employees:

1. Fair treatment : Fair treatment to every employees regardless of race, sex, age, colour or creed.
2. Selection and assignment : Assign job to employees according to their aptitude and experience and the work which will offer maximum growth and advancement. In filling vacancies select the person best qualified for the job.
3. Compensation : Compensate employees for work performed. General business conditions and pay and benefits for comparable work offered by other hotels must be given appropriate considerations.
4. Advancement : Qualified present employees be considered for promotioin before considering applicants from other hotels.
5. Training : Help employees to improve their ability to handle their present job and to up-grade their skills for future advancement
6. Communication : Inform employees about policies and plans effecting them and their work. Provide employees opportunity to express themselves on their jobs and relationships within the orgnisations. Let them suggest improvements in work methods and working conditions. Make continuous effort to learn and consider employees' interest, ideas and attitudes.
7. Grievances : Give full and fair hearing to employees on their grievances.
8. Job Security : Provide steady work and continuous employment to employees.
9. Health and Safety : Insure that the work places and working conditions must protect employees' health and to prevent injury.
10. Dismissal or lack of avancement : Tell every employee, frankly and fully the reason of his failure to succeed with the organisation.

TRADE UNIONS AND PERSONNEL POLICIES

In the historical perspective and present status of the hotel business, there are very bright chances that sooner or later employees' union may get a powerful status in this industry. Therefore, you must be sure that all personnel policies of the hotel are being fair and fully implemented.

You must watch for the following :

1. Festering employees' grievances
2. Favouritism
3. Poor morale
4. Lagging wages and benefits
5. Deteriorating working conditions

6. Capricious disciplinary actions
7. Lack of recognition.

EMPLOYEES' ASSOCIATIONS AND COMMUNICATION

You must be prepared to counter in oral and written communications to employees the organiser's main arguments for union membership :

1. Job security to employees
2. Improved wages and benefits
3. Representation of grievances
4. Participation in management.

Be on your guard against the following activities while union's organising effort is being made :

1. Offering wage increases or other inducements to employees unless the increases are part of one established pattern.
2. Threat to fire, suspend or otherwise discriminate against an employee for joining or being in favour of a union
3. Discharge of an employee for union activity
4. Linking promotions or raises to how an employee votes.
5. Questioning employees on how they intend to vote on union activities
6. Holding a stray vote
7. Saying or employing that a union victory would result in a strike
8. Other actions which the legal expert advises you are illegal.

NEGOTIATIONS

You may be negotiating a contract either individually or as a member of a multi-employer bargaining team. Keep in mind that the day to start preparing for negotiation on your next contract is the day your present contract goes into effect. Everything that happens under your present contract may become a factor in your next negotiations.

Prior to beginning negotiations you should :

1. Study the contracts of other hotels which might have a bearing on you
2. Review wages, benefits, working conditions and personnel practices and
3. Get recommendations from your superiors

For successfully concluding contract negotiations you should adhere to the following bargaining principles :

1. Establish a positive bargaining attitude
2. Recognise the point of view and the security of the union bargaining committee
3. Provide the bargaining committee with information to change their views
4. Keep in mind that management and union representatives see many things in different perspectives
5. Remember that in bargaining, you get in return exactly, what you give
6. Keep putting the burden of profit on the union
7. Keep negotiations moving and on target
8. Keep employees informed on the progress of negotiation.

STRIKE HANDLING

Negotiaitons may fail and you may have to face up the possibility of a strike. A strike is a test of economic strength as well as a clash of wills between management and the union. Strike threats should not be taken lightly. Immediately secure the help of a competent labour legal advisor. In case strike seems inevitable consider the following hints :

1. Inform employees of the circumstances and their rights
2. Arrange to keep in operation delivery of supplies obtaining replacement employees, security, maintenance etc.
3. Distribution of back-pay to strikers
4. Payment of group insurance premiums
5. Handling of unemployment claims, if any
6. Recording accident during strike
7. Getting community support
8. Getting police protection
9. In anticipation of the eventual end of the strike, continue employment of replacements, recall of strikers, effect on employees' benefits of strike absence, etc.

THE TRAINING

Training within a hotel provides the best opportunity to influence the attitude and performance of employees. The training programmes include are as such as introduction, fire, food hygience, control of substances hazardous to health, manual handling first-aid, technical skills, product knowledge, customer service. In many other areas, there is a statutory requirement to carry out training.

ACCOUNTING AUDIT AND CONTROL

ADMINISTRATIVE AND GENERAL EXPENSES

All expenses incurred in connection with the general administration of the hotel are included under this head. Administration and general expenses are indicated below :

1. **Salaries and Wages**

(*i*) Manager's Office

(*a*) Managing Director
(*b*) Resident Manager
(*c*) Executive Manager
(*d*) Secretaries
(*e*) Stenographers
(*f*) Clerk
(*g*) Reception Clerk
(*h*) Office Boys.

2. **Accounting Office and Data Processing**

(*a*) Chief Accountant
(*b*) Assistants
(*c*) House Treasurer
(*d*) General Cashier
(*e*) Pay Masters and Assistants
(*f*) Book Keepers
(*g*) Income Auditors
(*n*) Payroll Clerks
(*o*) Statisticians
(*p*) File Clerk
(*q*) Computer Operator
(*r*) Stenographers
(*s*) Typists
(*t*) Clerk

(*h*) Controllers
(*i*) Data Processing
(*j*) Analyst
(*k*) Programmers
(*l*) Data Processing Clerk
(*m*) Code Clerk
(*u*) Office Boys
(*v*) Supervisor
(*w*) System Personnel
(*x*) Operators
(*y*) Key Puncher.

3. **Front Office Book Keeping**
   (*a*) Front Office Book Keeping
   (*b*) Cashiers
   (*c*) File Clerk
   (*d*) Bill Clerk
   (*e*) Voucher Clerk.
4. **Night Auditors**
   (*a*) Chief Night Auditor
   (*b*) Night Auditor
   (*c*) Transcript Clerk
5. **Credit Office**
   (*a*) Credit Manager
   (*b*) Credit Investigators
   (*c*) File Clerk
   (*d*) Assistants
   (*e*) Stenographers.
6. **Receiving Clerk**
   (*a*) General Receiving Clerk
   (*b*) Clerk Receiving Food and Beverage Supplies
7. **Personnel Office**
   (*a*) Personnel Manager
   (*b*) Stenographers
   (*c*) Assistant
   (*d*) Clerk.

COST OF EMPLOYEES' MEALS

This account is debited with the cost of food and beverages furnished to the employees included in the administrative and general expenses account.

ACCOUNTANTS' FEES

The cost of public accountant's services, including fees, travelling expenses and maintenance are debited to this account.

CASH OVERAGES AND SHORTAGES

All overages and shortages of cash section which are not recovered are debited under this head.

COMMISSION ON CREDIT CARD CHARGES

Commission paid to credit card companies is debited and rebate received from them is credited to this account. Volume rebate payments received from credit card organisations should be credited to this account. When these amounts are primarily incurred for sale purposes notation of the amounts applicable to the various operating departments particularly rooms and food and beverage should be made to the respective departmental schedules.

EXECUTIVE OFFICE EXPENSES

It includes the salaries and expenses relating to the executive and corporate officers, billed to hotel. It may include directors' fee and expenses etc.

INSURANCE

All expenses relating to general insurance (except those of workmen compensation insurances fire insurances on building and contents and social insurances) including the following are debited to this account :

1. Boiler liability
2. Elevator liability
3. Flywheel liability
4. Fraud
5. Lost and damaged goods
6. Products liability
7. Public liability
8. Burglary
9. Fidelity bonds
10. Forgery
11. Holdup
12. Parcel lost
13. Property damage
14. Robbery and
15. Use and occupancy.

INTERNAL AUDIT EXPENSES

The cost of audit made by the central organisation of a chain of hotels, the salaries of auditors, travelling expenses and maintenance are included under this head.

INTERNAL COMMUNICATING SYSTEM

This account should be charged with the cost and supplies applicable to the followings :

1. Cost of automatic telephone
2. Cost of telautograph
3. Cost of dictagraph
4. Cost of pneumatic tubes service
5. Cost of other internal communicating systems.

LEGAL EXPENSES

It includes all legal fees, and legal expenses excepting the cost of collection.

LOSS AND DAMAGE

Amount paid to guest regarding the lost or damaged property and the payment made for guest property lost or damaged in excess of the amount recovered from insurance company.

MANAGEMENT FEES

Fees paid to management organisation for executive supervision or management service.

POSTAGE AND TELEGRAMS

Cost of postage, telegrams, cables, radiograms (except expenses applicable to advertising).

PRINTING AND STATIONERY

It includes all the printing and stationery expenses incurred by manager's office, accounting office and other related employees. Cost of printed forms, service manuals, stationery and office supplies etc. are debited to this account. The items included are :

1. Adding machine paper
2. Bank checks
3. Billing machine supplies
4. Binders
5. Blotters
6. Books of account
7. Book records
8. Carbon paper
9. Clips
10. Envelopes
11. Fountain pens
12. Guest ledger
13. Ink
14. Ink pads
15. Mucilage
16. Inkwells
17. Office supplies
18. Paper clips
19. Paste
20. Pencils
21. Pen holders
22. Pen points
23. Pens
24. Pins
25. Report covers
26. Rubber stamp
27. Rubber bands
28. Stamp pad
29. Staples
30. Stationery
31. Transcripts
32. Typewriter ribbons.

PROVISION FOR DOUBTFUL DEBTS

A provision is made for the probable loss in collection of amount receivables. A monthly percentage of total receivable is charged to this account.

TRADE ASSOCIATION DUES

It includes all fees and cost of the representation of the hotel in different business organisations and members of the staff when authorised to represent the hotel.

TRUSTEES' AND REGISTRATION FEES

The fees and expenses of trustees and registrars should be included under this head.

TRAVELLING EXPENSES

The cost and maintenance of transportation of officers and employees of the hotel, travelling on the hotel business, should be charged to this account, except that travelling in connection with promotion should be charged to 'Advertising and Sales Promotion'.

UNIFORMS

Same basis as the uniform charges in the Room Department.

DISTRIBUTION OF ADMINISTRATIVE AND GENERAL EXPENSES

These expenses may be allocated either of the two bases :

1. On the basis of sales : The sales of a particular department to total sales of the hotel.
2. Payroll basis : The ratio of the departmental payroll of an operated department to total payroll. (Ref. figs. 9.5, 9.6, 9.7 and 9.8).

ABC Hotels Ltd.
Administrative and General Expenses Schedule

	Current period
Salaries and Wages	₹ ....
Employees' Meals	....
Employee Benefits	....
Total Payroll and Related Expenses	₹ ....
Other Expenses	
Accountants' Fees	₹ ....
Cash Overages and Shortages	....
Commission on Credit Card Charges Net	....
Credit and Collection Charges	....
Executive Office Expenses	....
Insurance General	....
Internal Audit Expenses	....
Internal Communicating Systems	....
Legal Expenses	....
Loss and Damage	....
Management Fee	....
Miscellaneous	....
Postage and Telegrams	....
Printing and Stationery	....
Provision for Doubtful Account	....
Trade Association Dues	....
Trade Publications	....
Travelling Expenses	....
Trustees' and Registrars' Fees	....
Uniforms	....
Total Other Expenses	₹ ....
Total Administrative and General Expenses	₹ ....

Note: Various arrangements of additional columns for comparisons and percentages could be added.

Fig. 9.5 : Analysis of Administrative and General Expenses

Abc Hotel Ltd.
Administrative and General Expenses Schedule

	Current Period
Salaries and Wages	₹ ....
Employees' Benefits	....
Total payroll and related expenses	....
Other Expenses	
Credit Card Commissions	....
Data Processing	....

(Contd...)

Dues and Subscriptions	....
Human Resources	....
Insurance General	....
Operating Supplies	....
Postage and Telegrams	....
Processional Fees	....
Provision for Doubtful Accounts	....
Travel and Entertainment	....
Others	....
Total Other Expenses	....
Total Adminstrative and General Expenses	₹ ....

Fig. 9.6 : Analysis of Administrative and General Expenses

ABC Hotel Ltd.
Administrative and General Expenses Schedule

	Current Period
Salaries and Wages	₹
Employee Benefits	....
Total Payroll and Related Expenses	
Other Expenses	....
Dues and Subscriptions	....
Employees' Housing	....
Employees' Relations	....
Medical Expenses	....
Operating Supplies	....
Recruitment	....
Relocation	
Training	
Transportation	
Others	
Total Other Expenses	....
Total Human Resorces Expenses	₹ ....

Fig. 9.7 : Analysis of Human Resources Expenses

ABC Hotel Ltd.
Transportation Schedule

	Current Period
Salaries and Wages	₹ ....
Employee Benefits	....
Total Payroll and Related Expenses	....
Other Expenses	....
Fuel and Oil	....

(Contd...)

Insurance	
Operating Supplies	....
Repairs and Maintenance	....
Uniforms	....
Others	....
Total Other Expenses	....
Total Human Resoruces Expenses	₹............

Fig. 9.8 : Analysis of Transportation Expenses

QUESTIONS AND ASSIGNMENTS

1. What are the provisions relating to fixation and review of wages as provided under the Minimum Wages Act, 1948 ? Also mention the procedure for fixation and revision of the minimum wages. ***(DTHM)***
2. You are a personnel manager in a five star hotel. How would you discharge your function of procurement of personnel to man the hotel ? ***(DTHM)***
3. What is manpower planning ? Discuss the procedure of recruitment of employees. ***(IHMs)***
4. Define trade union. How can a trade union contribute in labour welfare and effective hotel management ? ***(IHMs)***
5. Suggest a suitable system of internal check for the following : ***(IHMs)***
   (*i*) Sales
   (*ii*) Stores Department.
6. Explain the different methods of Performance Appraisal System and also state why it is necessary for the organisation. ***(IHMs)***
7. Write short notes on:- ***(IHMs)***
   (*a*) Induction
   (*b*) Performance Appraisal
   (*c*) Training Programme.
8. (*a*) Develop an integrated recruitment system for a new property. ***(IHMs)***
   (*b*) Prepare a checklist for identifying training needs for the Front Office Staff of a hotel.
9. Write short notes on the following:- ***(IHMs)***
   (*i*) Pre-recruitment Process
   (*ii*) Selection Techniques
   (*iii*) Orientation Goals
   (*iv*) Human Resource Information System.
10. (*a*) How do you distinguish between Education, Development and Training? ***(IHMs)***
    (*b*) Design a suitable performance appraisal for evaluating the performance of a Front Office Manager. ***(IHMs)***
11. Define Training. What is the difference between training objectives and training criteria? ***(IHMs)***
12. "Recruitment is a positive approach while selection is a negative approach to manpower". How ? Why ? ***(IHMs)***
13. Briefly examine in not more than 150-words advantages at M.B.O. for evolving a more objective performance appraisal system. ***(IHMs)***

14. Discuss the pre-requisites for the success of collective bargaining. ***(IHMs)***

15. What is the rationale for worker's participation in management ? ***(IHMs)***

16. What is the purpose of training ? Discuss the characteristics of a good training programme. ***(IHMs)***

17. (*a*) What is meant by Performance Appraisal ?
    (*b*) Explain the process of recruitment and selection of employees. ***(IHMs)***

18. From training point of view, does it really matter whether you say that principles and generalisations are different kind of things or are just different degrees of the same thing ? ***(MTA)***

19. What are the important personnel policies formulated by hotel enterprises ? Discuss any two of them. ***(MTA)***

20. Explain the following:
    (*a*) Future trends in hotel sector
    (*b*) Growth of public sector hotels in India
    (*c*) Tourism and hotel education in India. ***(MTA)***

21. What is the importance of training of executive staff in hotel management ? What are the various methods of training ? ***(IHMs)***

22. What is the importance of good labour relations in the management of a hotel ? What steps will you take to improve labour relations in a hotel in which you are the manager? ***(IHMs)***

23. Distinguish between (any five):
    (*a*) Job analysis and Job Description
    (*b*) Budget and Forecast
    (*c*) On-the-job training and Off-the-job Training
    (*d*) Recruitment and Selection
    (*e*) Apprenticeship Training and Vestibule Training
    (*f*) Distinguish between Private and Public Co. ***(IHMs)***

24. In present corporate environment formal manpower planning in essential for all big organisations. In the light of above what is the significance of manpower planning. What are the steps involved in manpower planning ? ***(IHMs)***

25. What is selection and discuss the selection procedure ? ***(IHMs)***

26. Discuss in about 150-words the importance of a Training Deptt. or HR division of a five star hotel.

27. Describe Job specification helps in recruiting the right personnel whereas job description helps us inviting the new personnel joining in the industry.

28. Explain different types of maintenance contract with reference to Cost + Upper Limit. ***(IHMs)***

29. Differentiate between Personnel Management and Human Resource Management. ***(IHMs)***

30. Human Resource is a major component of any major hotel and a large part of this resource is utilized in Food and Beverage Department. Justify this with the help of a chart and support with appropriate explanations.

31. With the help of a flowchart illustrate the cost control cycle in a restaurant using triplicate checking system. ***(MTM)***

32. There are currently strong pressures towards workers, increasing participation in industry. Discuss this statement and explain the various forms that workers, participation could take. Make an assessment of potential value of workers participation in the hotel and catering industry. ***(MTM)***

33. Writes notes on :

(*a*) Housekeeping Department

(*b*) Front Office Manager

(*c*) Communication in Hotels

(*d*) Supplementary Accommodation. ***(PGH&HM)***

34. 'Hotel and catering industry is facing problem of shortage of technically qualified personnel.' Do you agree with this statement ? If yes, what steps do you suggest to improve the training facilities ? ***(MTA)***

35. Writes notes on :

(*a*) Motor-hotel

(*b*) Hotel Corporation of India

(*c*) Tourism Finance Corporation of India

(*d*) Hotel Education in India

(*e*) Manpower Planning. ***(MTA)***

36. What do you mean by personnel management ? What are its objectives ? Discuss. ***(MTA)***

37. What is the process involved in selection of staff ? What are the benefits of an induction programme ? Describe with examples. ***(DTHM)***

38. Why is training and development of personnel essential in the hotel industry ? What factors does one keep in mind while developing a training programme ? ***(DTHM)***

39. What do you understand by workers' participation in management ? Why and how can it be implemented in hotel industry ? ***(IHMs)***

40. "Managers are not born but made"— How far do you agree with this statement ? In this connection, discuss the importance of training. ***(IHMs)***

41. Write notes on :

(*a*) Induction

(*b*) Performance Appraisal

(*c*) Training Programme.

42. From a training point of view does it really matter whether you say that principles and generalisation are different kinds of things or are just different degrees of the same thing ?

43. Explain in detail what are considered to ensure effective listening. ***(IHMs)***

44. How does one being about good upward communication? ***(IHMs)***

45. Write brief notes on the following:

(*a*) The process of effective communication

(*b*) The planning process

(*c*) Styles of leadership

(*d*) Internal and external factors that effect management

(*e*) The benefits of delegation. ***(IHMs)***

46. Analyse the pros and cons of downward, upward and horizontal communication. ***(IHMs)***

47. Explain in detail at least five barriers to effective communications. ***(IHMs)***

48. You are a Personnel Manager in a five star hotel. How would you discharge your function of procurement of personnel to man the hotel ?

49. Discuss in about 150-words the importance of a Training Department in Human Resources Division of a Five Star Hotel.

50. What are the important personnel policies formulated by hotel enterprises ? Discuss any two of them.

51. Explain briefly the followings :

(*i*) Organisational goal and objectives

(*ii*) Personal values and beliefs

(*iii*) Professional ethics and standards

(*iv*) Social delegations and responsibilities.

52. What is the importance of effective communication for a manager ? Identify and discuss the barriers of effective communication in an organisational environment. As a manager how would you remove the barriers to improve communication in the organisation ? ***(IHMs)***

53. Explain the principles of work study. Give examples of work study techniques and indicate how these might be applied to good effect in the hotel and catering industry.

54. Discuss the value and limitations of using interviews techniques for :-

(*a*) Employee selection

(*b*) Employee appraisal. ***HCIMA* (*London*)**

55. "An authoritarian approach may not be the best way for management to deal with personnel". Discuss this statement, suggesting alternatives. ***HCIMA* (*London*)**

56. Concluding the importance of communication, discuss modern communication system for a hotel. ***(IHMs)***

57. Human resource is a major component of any major hotel and a large part of this is resource is utilized in the F & B Department. Justify this with the help of a chart and support with appropriate explanations. ***(IHMs)***

58. Discuss the view that successful catering today seems to rely increasingly on the use of statistical and financial analysis to the extent that managers can no longer afford the time to develop their personal flair and traditional skills. ***HCIMA* (*London*)**

59. As labour costs continue to rise, suggest how the Catering Manager might respond in order to make full and effective use of his human resources. ***HCIMA* (*London*)**

60. Describe the principal areas of management control relevant to a busy catering operation. Suggest in broad terms, the methods by which control might be applied in order to provide an effective measure of all aspects of performance. ***HCIMA* (*London*)**

61. Write a job description listing the responsibilities and duties of each staff position of the marketing and sales department of a well established independent chain. ***(MTM)***

OBJECTIVE TYPE QUESTIONS

62. Match the following:

(1) List of employees abilities and career goals.	(*a*) Socialization.
(2) Measures the applicant ability to perform the entire job.	(*b*) Attitude Surveys.
(3) Also known as learning the ropes.	(*c*) In-basket Training.
(4) A company's critical values, beliefs and norms.	(*d*) Skills Inventory.
(5) Used to determine need for behavioral training.	(*e*) Valence.
(6) Training method in which group members evaluate each other's behaviours.	(*f*) Proactive Response.

(7) Results in more favourable ratings than normal. — (*g*) Halo Error.

(8) Strength of an Individual's preference for a particular outcome. — (*h*) Critical Questions.

(9) Assessment method that asks broad questions about ethical conduct. — (*i*) Content Validity.

(10) Results when an employee is logged on a single positive trait. — (*j*) Leniency Error.

(*k*) Sensitivity Training.

(*l*) Organizational Culture.

63. (A) Choose the correct alternative:

(*a*) Suppliers, competitors, customers, labour and globalisation are components of:

(*i*) Political-legal environment
(*ii*) Technological environment
(*iii*) Economic environment
(*iv*) Cultural environment.

(*b*) Demand Forecasting and Supply Forecasting are techniques of:

(*i*) Human Resource Accounting
(*ii*) Job Evaluation
(*iii*) Manpower Planning
(*iv*) None of the above.

(*c*) A Manpower demand forecasting technique based on estimates made by managers in each department

(*i*) Top-down forecasting
(*ii*) Bottoms-up forecasting
(*iii*) Career planning
(*iv*) None of the above.

(*d*) Which of the following is not a function of the Human Resources Department?

(*i*) Job Analysis and Job Evaluation
(*ii*) Layout Planning and Equipment Purchase
(*iii*) Performance Appraisal and Training
(*iv*) Induction and Placement.

(*e*) The best-selling book "Seven Habits of Highly Effective People" is the basis for many management development programmes. The book is written by :

(*i*) Stephen R. Covey
(*ii*) Norman Vincent Peale
(*iii*) Deepak Chopra
(*iv*) None of the Above.

(*f*) Skill inventories which list each employee's current skills, ability to learn new skills, qualifications, career goals, etc. is a useful tool for Manpower Planning, as it helps in:

(*i*) Demand Forecasting
(*ii*) Supply Forecasting
(*iii*) Trend Analysis
(*iv*) None of the Above.

(*g*) The factor which is a good predictor of human resource demand using the Trend Analysis method of demand forecasting is:
(*i*) Staff Turnover Percentage
(*ii*) Occupancy Rate
(*iii*) IQ level of Employees
(*iv*) None of the Above. (*IHMs*)

A CAUSE STUDY 9.2 :

64. Mr. J.M. Dhir, Resident Manager of the Tourist Hotel is in the process of organising an orientation programme for new employees on the front office, food production, food and beverage service, and housekeeping staff. Part of the programme will include an introduction to kitchen equipment and assorted paper work. Further training on each piece of equipment will be scheduled at a later time.

Mr. Dhir begins by listing and describing the function of all the equipment. He also indicates how each piece of equipment relates to the total function of the various department of the hotel. Since most members of the staff of the various department are relativly new, he decides he must deliver the orientation programme himself. As he begins to work through the details of the plan, he realize the time that is required - time that he does not have. He calls one Professor Rawat at IHM to ask if he would like to do the project for extra credit. Prof. Rawat deputed you for the assignment. List the equipment you would include for a manual and semi-automated front desk operation. List the paper work you would include for a manual or semi automated operation in various departments. Briefly outline how to operate one of the pieces of equipment of front office and how to fill out one of the forms. Include the following:–

(1) Who uses the equipment ?
(2) When is the equipment used ?
(3) Where is the equipment used ?
(4) Why is the equipment important ?

CHAPTER 10

Safety and Security

OBJECTIVES

After studying this chapter, you should be able to :

1. *Know the importance of safety and security systems in a hotel business and*
2. *Understand the duties and responsibilities of the staff/employees of this department*

HOTEL SECURITY

In United States of America, it is estimated that at least $ 10 billion is lost annually by American business due to theft, that 30% of all business failures each year are the result of employees' dishonesty and that 7% of all bankruptcies in the country are due to pilferage. Therefore, security is one of the most important responsibilities of a hotel.

The main point to be considered in a hotel security are:

1. Preventing thefts and pilferages
2. Avoiding malicious waste on the part of the employees and
3. Development of emergency plan for the protection of guests in the event of civil disturbances.

The following are some of the tips to prevent finanicial loss and physical injury to employees :

1. Keep an eye open for suspicious persons loitering on the premises.
2. Maintain complete record of and description of all valuable properties:
   (*i*) Serial numbers of bills
   (*ii*) Identification of cash register
   (*iii*) Identification of office equipment
   (*iv*) Serial number of TV sets.
3. When large amount are to be deposited with the bank keep on changing your routes and the trips should be made at different times of the day.
4. Don't open the safe in the presence of strangers.
5. Don't keep too much cash in the register. Use the safe for large amount of money and send surplus cash to the bank as often as convenient.

6. Install an alarm such as electronic beam or other non-obvious type. This can be tripped unobtrusively by the casheir in case of an emergency situation. The burglary alarm system is the best one having silent central station type which does not warn the thief.
7. Keep all areas well lighted specially where the mony is kept.
8. Keep a little 'bait money' in the safe and cash register.
9. This is the money from which the serial numbers have been copied, 'marked money' which will make good evidence if found on a suspect.
10. Use closed circuit television to monitor areas such as parking lots and supply rooms which are generally not under instant direct observation.

ORGANISATION

The organisational structure of the Security Department is given in Fig. 10.1.

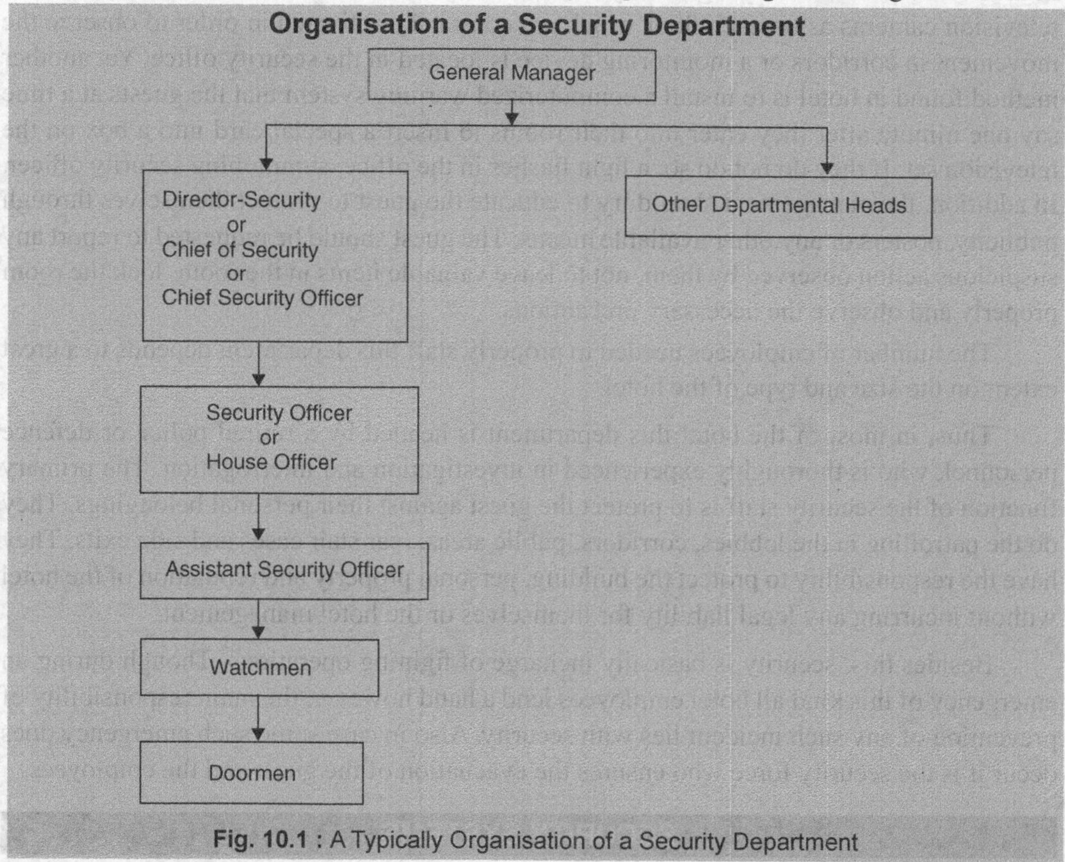

Fig. 10.1 : A Typically Organisation of a Security Department

DIRECTOR-SECURITY/CHIEF SECURITY OFFICER

He reports most often directly to general manager. In some hotels he is responsible to the resident manager. He handles the safety and security of the operation.

SECURITY OFFICER

The security officer is responsible to protect the hotel and well-being of guests and staff. In brief his duties include :

1. To supervise the issue of all master or sub-master keys to such personnel as are authorised by the management
2. To spot all undesirable or suspect guests and bring any suspicious behaviour to the attention of the management
3. To maintain friendly working relations with the local police officer
4. To be responsible for lost property
5. To supervise security precautions in the handling of cash within the hotel
6. To supervise correct maintenance of fire fighting equipment and carry out periodic training of security staff.

Most of the hotel built up their security department and staff them with retired defence or law-enforced officer. Sophisticated devices are installed to protect the guests. The name of the hotel is printed in key tags or keyless locks may be installed. Some deluxe hotels have television cameras as on each floor which are constantly activated in order to observe the movement in corridors or a monitoring device is located in the security office. Yet another method found in hotel is to install a computerized warning system that the guests at a time say one minute after they enter into their rooms to insert a special card into a box on the television set If they do not do so, a light flashes in the office, summoning security officer. In addition, the management should try to educate the guest to protect themselves through publicity, posters or any other available means. The guest should be requested to report any suspicious action observed by them, not to leave valuable items in the room, lock the room properly and observe the necessary precautions.

The number of employees needed to properly staff this department depends to a great extent on the size and type of the hotel.

Thus, in most of the hotel this department is headed by a retired police or defence personnel, who is thoroughly experienced in investigation and interrogation. The primary function of the security staff is to protect the guest against their personal belongings. They do the patrolling in the lobbies, corridors, public areas, rear stair cases and side exits. They have the responsibility to protect the building, personal property and reputation of the hotel without incurring any legal liability for themselves or the hotel management.

Besides this, security is basically incharge of fighting operations. Though during an emergency of this kind all hotel employees lend a hand however, the main responsibility of prevention of any such incident lies with security. Also in case some such emergency does occur it is the security force who ensures the evacuation of the guest and the employees.

SECURITY SYSTEMS

WALLET-SIZED PLASTIC CARD

The wallet-sized plastic card substitutes the traditional metal room key. When the guest registers at the hotel, a special machine codes several cards at random. Only card, the 'control card', is inserted in a master console, while one 1/2 or more cards are given to the guest. When he wishes to unlock the door to his room the guest insert the card into a slot near his door.

The card he inserts is electronically compared with the corresponding card in the slot matching his room number. If the code matches, the door opens with a click. It is virtually impossible to inadvertently duplicate a code. In the case of lost or stolen cards, what amount to an instantaneous change of lock sets can be accompained simply by coding a new set of cards.

Another system utilizes a keyboard to change key and lock combinations by remote control. The keyboard is wired to every lock in the hotel. When the guest registers, his key is 'validated' by the keyboard, in effect changing, in less than a second, the key and lock used by the previous occupant of the room.

THEFTS AND EMBEZZLEMENT

Thefts and embezzlement by employees can easily be controlled by effective methods of internal control. The Fireman's Fund American Insurance Company suggests the following 'do' and don'ts to check and control thefts and embezzlement by employees:[1]

DO'S

1. Do keep important job functions separated : Don't let the same person make up invoices, bank deposit, check payment and reconcile bank statements. Purchasing should also be separated from receiving responsibilities.
2. Do make frequent, surprise spot checks. Account receivable, inventory, account payable, sales and marketing department should also be subject to examination without warning, as should every other department where cash transactions or valuable goods may be handled.
3. Do eastablish printed control on forms. It should be mumbered serially at the printers. Delivery tickets should also be pre-numbered and duplicate copies of all forms should be sent to the accounting department for sales and inventory records. Check should be printed on 'safety' paper that will not erase.
4. Do establish personnel controls : Check the job reference of prospective empployees for the past 10 years. If the staff is adequate, rotate employees between jobs.
5. Require passes for after-hours entry to certain areas and check excessive overtime claims.
6. Without being excessively negative or harmful to moral, let all employees know dishonesty will be prosecuted to the full extent of the law.

DONT'S

1. Don't let customers' unpaid balances accumulate. To prevent embezzlement of incoming payments, regular notices with return postage paid should be sent to the customers with consistent unpaid balances. These can be worded not to offend the customer and they should be returned to some one other than the person who ordinarily receives payments.
2. Don't let audit be routine. If an audit is only perfunctory, or if audits are held on regular and unvarying schedules, the embezzler can plan around it, kitting fund to lower bank balances or juggling records to hide inventory losses.

---

1. The Fireman's Fund Americal Insurances Company.

3. Don't ignore large balances due to your suppliers. Bills you have paid still show as due are suspect. Payment from you may be siphoned off in your paymaster's office or in the supplier's account receivable department.
4. Don't economise on loss prevention :
   (*i*) Use a reputable CA/CPA firm for an extensive audit, preferable at least annually;
   (*ii*) Consult with layout experts and security architects about protective measures for inventory, equipment and important records;
   (*iii*) Ask your insurance company's loss prevention engineers for assistance in developing an overall programme to prevent theft; and
   (*iv*) Make certain you have enough insurance to cover your potential for loss.

LIABILITY FOR PROTECTING GUESTS

A hotel has liability for protecting guests from harm embraces the following :

1. Protection against danger caused by the defecticondition of equipment or the premises of the building itself, walks, driveways, swimming pool etc.
2. Protection against the carelessness of the employees.
3. Protection against improper language or discourtesy of employees.
4. Protection against defamation of character or invasion of privacy.
5. Protection against physical harm caused by other guests.
6. Protection against the serving of unwholesome or poisonous food.

LIABILITY FOR PROPERTY OF GUEST

A hotel's liability for guest's property usually is contingent on two conditions :

1. That at the time of the loss the hotel guest relationship existed and
2. That the property was under the administrative control of the hotel.

Generally, hotels are liable for guest's property entrusted to their care and such a liability is limited if loss or damage to the property is caused by:

1. 'An act of God'. Occurrence over which man has no control such as,
   (*i*) A torrential rain
   (*ii*) Tornado or lightning
2. The public emergency : It includes,
   (*i*) Action during a civil disturbance
   (*ii*) Action by many soldiers in wartime.
3. Guest's own negligence : This contributory negligence results from the failure of the guest to exercise appropriate prudence with regard to the safeguarding of his own possessions.
4. Additional exceptions to strict liability arise from :
   (*i*) Acts of public authority such as police.
   (*ii*) The inherent nature of the property which may lead to spoilage.
   (*iii*) A fire not caused by the hotel.

In many countries there are laws which limit the hotel's liability. For guest's property notices of statutory limitation be posted on the premises in such a case.

If the valuables of a guest are stored in a hotel safe, the liability is generally limited. The guest must be informed of the limitation. In case the guest choose to retain his valuables instead of depositing them in the hotel safe, it is not considered negligence and does not relieve the hotel of liability. You will find that in many hotels notices are put in guest rooms advising patrons of measures available for protection of their property and person.

One of the first laws affecting hotel keeping was the establishment of the hotelier's responsibility for the protection of guest's personal safety and property. Now a days, there are dual responsibility of protecting both the guests and the hotel from harm as both are vulnerable targets for thieves, prowlers and other undesirables. In small hotels this function is assigned to a watchman who records his regular rounds on a clock to prove his presence in every part of the building. During his rounds he is also responsible for noting and reporting anything which may seems unusual or undesirable. In large hotels this function is often assigned to a person known as Chief Security Officer or Chief House Officer. Figure 10.1 shows the organisation structure of the security department of a hotel. The hotels for obvious reasons prefer not to have the methods and techniques of their security force publicized. In general the security department must deal with :

1. The problems of doors being left unlocked or keys being left in the lock
2. Any potential hazard or indication of fire
3. The problem of inebriated-intoxicated persons and
4. Illegal occupants of the hotel rooms.

Thus the main functions of the security in a hotel are :

1. To safeguard guests and their property
2. To guard the hotel's property
3. To guard employees and their property.

The principal ingredient in the security programme's effectiveness is the ability to respond promptly to security problems. Large hotels have security men in uniforms and plainclothes walking in the hotel lobby and around the hotel. Now, a number of security systems are being introduced by modern hotels.

HOTELS' ASSETS

The most important aspect of property control is an adequate locking system with key control. Entrance keys, front, back and side doors are normally held by the owner or general manager with spares held by a senior trusted employee. Internal keys will be required to control store rooms, chillers, fridges and freezers, internal doors to public areas, different sections of kitchen and preparation areas and store rooms. With internal keys it is good to work on master key, sub-master and single door key system. The master key is held by the general manager, the sub-master key by middle manager or supervisors or head of the department and single door keys or grouping of single door keys by junior employees who are authorised to have access. Many deluxe hotel, install electronic digital systems with available code numbers. Windows need to be considered from security point of view.

CAR PARK

Hotel should display notices for guest and staff using car park that cars are parked at owners' risk and that the hotel will not accept any responsibility for loss or damage to vehicles or contents. However, hotel management do have a duty to ensure that customer's property is safeguarded as much as reasonably possible.

CLOAK ROOMS

Many hotels accept coats and bags from customers for safe keeping. A disclaimer notice covering loss or damage to property while in management care must be properly displayed. All receipts must be numbered and property returned on presentation of receipt; a disclaimer on the reverse of the ticket could also to printed.

ALARMS AND SURVEILLANCE

There are many hotels which have installed the intruder or burglar all over and closed circuit TV surveillance system. These are very useful devices and include comprehensive rides recording with date and time logging of accident.

The main safe should be controlled by more than one key or combination lock. In a large hotel, two senior managers should be present to open the safe, each having one key or one knowing the combination and the other having the key. The safe room must also be controlled by two keys. Cashiers should be the subject of detailed background enquiries. Fidelity insurance should to considered for management and those handling large amount of cash or stock. Keys for cash for cash boxes holding float or takings and cash register keys must be controlled. For proper security of cash specially for handling cash following steps could be adoped :

1. Use of modern cash registers.
2. Milk 'tills' regularly throughout the day and deposit in the main safe or bank.
3. Do not bank monies at the same time every day.
4. Do not alter the rota of personnel visiting the bank.
5. Employ a cash in transit collection service for banking and collection of payroll.
6. Install surveillance system.

PROPERTY

Security of property of customer and staff as well as food, drink and items of equipment need to be properly maintained. The following steps ccould be taken to prevent theft:

1. Never allow any deliveries where there is no one to receive them.
2. Do not leave goods outside the back door unattended
3. Ensure that delivered goods are not taken off the van and put straight back again
4. All store rooms, wine cellars, large fridges and freezers should be kept under lock and key
5. Minimum required quantities be delivered from store to kitchen
6. Lock up all expensive items and mark with an identify code
7. Restrict the number of people who have access to stores and kitchen
8. Consider routines for issuing keys and authority levels allowed to have access to keys
9. Maintain proper stock records
10. Maintain a register for all items of equipment
11. Efficient cost control
12. Regular training of staff in all security matters

13. Watch for staff acting suspiciously
14. Hotel's property should not leave the premises without an official 'passout'
15. Spot checking and its record.

LOST AND FOUND PROPERTY

The found register and lost register are maintained to manage lost and found property. Any property reported lost on the premises must be checked against the found register and if it is not there, it must be recorded in the lost register indicating :

1. The description of the article
2. The day, date and time it was found
3. The location of the find
4. The name of the finder
5. Name and address of claimant.

The finding of valuable property should be reported to the police. Effort should be made to restore found property to rightful owner without delay. Property not claimed after a reasonable period of time can be disposed of by selling to raise money for staff fund or returning to the finder or giving to charity.

PERSONNEL AND CUSTOMERS

The hotel has a duty to have proper security and care of its personnel and customers. The management and staff must be prepared to deal with possible emergencies such as :

1. A fire in the hotel
2. A bad cut caused by the knife
3. Slipping and breaking or knocking head
4. A customer choking of a fish bone
5. Stroke, heart attack, epileptic fit
6. Loss of water, gas or electricity
7. Bomb threat.

All allegations by customer of accident involving injury, loss or damage to their property, and finding of foreign bodies in food must be fully recorded. This report should indude :

1. The name, address and telephone number of the customer involved
2. The name and position of the person who dealt with the accident
3. The date, time and place of the accident
4. A description of the accident
5. The value of the article
6. The action and decision taken
7. Who else was informed ?

The hotel should set up procedures to protect the safety of their staff and customers. Identification of possible suspect object or packages and procedures to be adopted if there is a specific warning of terrosist activity should be established. Employees should be trained for emergency, fire prevention, fire fighting and evacuation drill.

QUESTIONS AND ASSIGNMENTS

1. Outline the general responsibilities of the Catering Officer for the health and safety of people using catering premises. Indicate how he would engender a responsible attitude towards safety on the part of his staff. ***HCIMA* (*London*)**
2. Explain different methods of disposing solid waste. **(*IHMs*)**
3. Explain safety precautions that are generally taken in a kitchen. **(*IHMs*)**
4. List eight steps that should be taken to make a hotel to reduce the fire hazard to a minimum. **(*IHMs*)**
5. Explain briefly the maintenance of fire detectors, fire alarms, and fire extinguishers. **(*IHMs*)**
6. Describe the various types of fires. Explain the importance and function of fire detectors. **(*IHMs*)**
7. Explain different types of fire extinguishers. **(*IHMs*)**
8. Explain the various waste disposal systems used in hotels. Explain one system in detail. **(*IHMs*)**
9. Discuss the problem of noise related to the hotel industry. **(*IHMs*)**

A CASE STUDY

10. Ms. Nath, front office manager of the Valley View Hotel has scheduled an appointment with the Director of security, Captain Bahadur. Captain Bahadur has just received word that a nearby hotel, the Sea View, recently received a bomb threat that required the evacuation of all guests and employees, The situation caused a great deal of confusion and panic. Several employees were screaming, "Bomb ! Bomb! Run for your life". While other employees and guests were absolutely stunned. Although the bomb threat was of no substance, 4 employees and 3 guests had to be treated in the emergency room for shock and broken limbs caused by the crash to evacuate the building.

    After reviewing the film in the security department, captain Bahadur feels he and Ms. Nath should develop an emergency communication procedure to be sure that the situation that occurred at the Sea View Hotel will not be repeated at the Valley View Hotel. Ms. Nath agrees, her prior experience at a hotel on the east coast makes her realize the importance of such a plan.

    You are asked to give Ms. Nath and Captain Bahadur some suggestions for developing an emergency communication plan.

CHAPTER

11

Hospitality and Facilities

OBJECTIVES

After studying this chapter, you should be able to :

1. Understand the various guest services offered in a hotel
2. Explain the role of :
   - (*i*) Laundry and Linen
   - (*ii*) Guest Laundry
   - (*iii*) House Laundry
   - (*iv*) Sub-rentals and Concessions
   - (*v*) Telephone and Telex
   - (*vi*) Garage and Parking Lots
   - (*vii*) Swimming Pool, Cabanas and Baths
   - (*viii*) Valet
   - (*ix*) Tobacconist, Cigar and News Stand
   - (*x*) Gift Shops and Souveniers
   - (*xi*) Barber Shop/Hairdressing Saloon
   - (*xii*) Beauty Parlour
   - (*xiii*) Concierge
   - (*xiv*) Florist/Horticulture
   - (*xv*) Entertainment and Recreational Facilities
   - (*xvi*) Secretarial Assistance and Business Centre
   - (*xvii*) Check Rooms and Wash Rooms
   - (*xviii*) Banquets, Functions, Conferences, Connections and Exhibitions
   - (*xix*) Other Incomes :
     - (*a*) Rentals
     - (*b*) Concession
     - (*c*) Interest
     - (*d*) Foreign Exchange
     - (*e*) Commissions

(*f*) Vending Machines
(*g*) Cash Discount Earned
(*h*) Salvage
(*i*) Miscellaneous, and
(*x*) Other Operated Departments.

GUEST SERVICES

There are a number of other hospitality facilities other than accommodation, food and drinks which are provided by modern hotels to their guests. Some of these facilities and services are operated by hotel itself and for some of them the space is rented out to outsiders to run their business and provide services to guests. The persons to whom these spaces are rented out for a specified period are known as concessionaires. These services whether provided by hotels or by the outsiders can be grouped under any department. These departments are created as a source of additional income to reduce operating costs and provide more efficient service to the guests. (Ref. Fig. 11.1)

In most of the hotels the organisational approach for miscellaneous guest services may be shown as :

1. **Minor departments directly operated by the hotel :** It provides a closer direct control and supervision by the hotel and greater fexibility in operation.
2. **Minor departments operated by outside firms/agencies :** This arrangement relieves the hotel from operating unfamiliar services and allows it to concentrate on its primary activities.

Figure 11.1 shows the minor departments of a hotel. Some of these departments are:

1. Guest laundry and dry cleaning
2. Sub-rental and concessions
3. Telephone
4. Garage parking lots
5. Swimming pool
6. Cabana and baths
7. Valet
8. Tobacconist, cigar and news stand (newspapers and magazines)
9. Gift shops/Souvenirs
10. Sundry banquet income
11. Barber shop
12. Beauty parlour
13. Concierge
14. Florists/horticulture
15. Secretarial services
16. Entertainment and recreation
17. Other incomes :
    (*i*) Rentals
    (*ii*) Concessions
    (*iii*) Commissions
    (*iv*) Vending machines
    (*v*) Cash discount earned

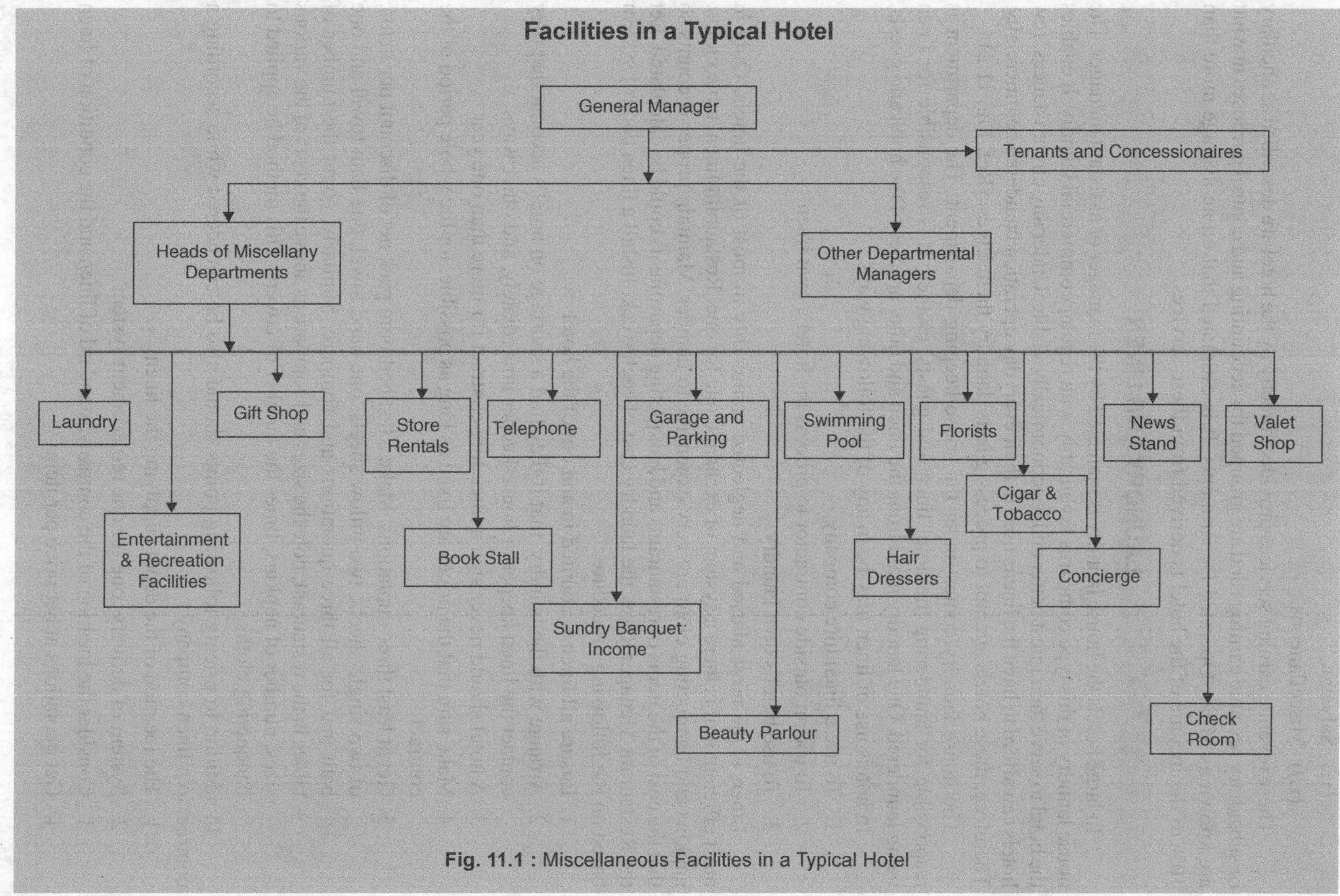

Fig. 11.1 : Miscellaneous Facilities in a Typical Hotel

(*vi*) Salvage

(*vii*) Miscellaneous.

These revenue earning services provided directly by the hotel are described as ancillary or subsidiary revenue earnings and are grouped for accounting and control purposes in what are known as Minor Operated Departments. It is estimated that on an average more than 10% of the income of the hotel is derived from these services.

LAUNDRY AND LINEN

In large hotels the house laundry is managed by the manager or assistant manager. The house laundry of this type compares favourably with regular commercial laundry. It enables the hotel to serve their guest better and is economically viable. Under any circumstances, few hotels can afford to have the linens used in their everyday operation laundered commercially. Therefore, these hotels attempt to process guests' laundry themselves. (Ref. Fig. 11.2)

The house laundry comes under the house keeping department. The department is responsible for laundering the hotel linen and guests' clothes. It is responsible for linen being laundered. One laundry maid irons the linen and other articles of the hotel and guests.

In hotels use of linen may be in any of the following ways :

1. To use a linen hire company
2. To use an outside contractor to process the hotel's own linen
3. To use hotel's own laundry.

Linen is the most abused and neglected commodity in most of the hotels. Only in most efficient unit is there a system of exchange one for one. Restaurant linen, table cloths, napkins and banqueting cloth are very expensive to launder. Maintain proper accounts so that the cost of the items of restaurants and banqueting departments could be calculated. Let the Restaurant Manager know the laundry cost of each week. Install a linen control system based on the following procedure :

1. Ensure all linen is counted in and out of the hotel
2. Arrange with the laundry, that if they find a shortage on hotel's account that they contact the linen keeper or house-keeper immediately, and other ways
3. A hotel should never sign a linen hire contract for more than one year
4. Make sure that the prices are fixed as long as possible, for the whole period of the contract
5. Get at least three quotations. Make a test bedroom pack net of discount per items, of two single sheets, two pillow sheets, one hand towel, one bath towel and one bath mat for all three quotations and compare. Similarly, count the number of tables in the restaurant, note the sizes and compare as above the costs of the various sizes, number of napkins, times the number of covers. This method be applied to banqueting cloths.

In addition to pricing following points should also be considered while according a contract to a linen company :

1. The location of the depot supplying the linen
2. System of delivery one for one replacement system
3. Consider the location of the company, standard of linen and the condition of linen
4. Get quotations at net price per item

5. The laundry costs to room revenue, excluding restaurant usage, be 2.5% per deluxe hotels and 8% for medium tourist operations. Check this cost every week
6. Stocking must be done on a regular basis and often as practicable
7. Hotel must have sufficient stock for a minimum of six times the number of hotel beds. There should be adequate provision to cover all beds from stock, if there is a failure in delivery. Linen room can count and check all incoming linen before issue. In off-season return surplus items.
8. Calculation of number of table cloths required :

Assumptions	:	24-hour service daily service three-day allowance for weekends
Table cloths	:	3-4 per table
Napkins	:	9-12 per table.

Table cloths with 'tops' or slips : 4 table cloths 12 tops per table 'slips'

1. All torn and soiled linen send back by the laundry should be set aside when being checked and return separately for a credit note
2. When negotiating a contract there should be no minimum charge in it
3. Never accept an automatic percentage charge of the total account in an assumed stock losses clause.
4. Guidelines for ordering table cloths :

	Table Size	Cloth Size
Table for 2	30 × 30in (76 × 76 cm)	54 × 54in (135 × 135 cm)
Table for 4	45 × 45in (112 × 112 cm)	63 × 63in (158 × 158 cm)
Table for 6	30 × 54in (76 × 135 cm)	54 × 72in (135 × 182 cm).

GUEST LAUNDRY

In hotels having their in-house laundry, the guest laundry and cleaning services are provided by concessionaires. The concessionaire is given a space in the building and allowed to install necessary equipment. Concessionaires do not accept the cash payment from guests. All laundry charges are processed through the front office. The total daily readings in the NCR machines represent the gross laundry and valet sales for that day. (Ref. Fig. 11.2 and 11.3)

In small hotels the volume of such laundry transaction is limited, therefore, they deal with an outside valet. In return for the exclusive right to handle the guest's laundry and dry cleaning requirements, the outside firm pays the hotel a commission. The amount of commission is a fixed percentage of the total guest.

The price list of laundry charges is agreed on by the valet and placed in each room by the hotel maids. Agreement is also made regarding the laundry bags, charge slips or any other supplies.

All sales relating to laundry are posted on the guest bills. The concessionaires operating within the hotel maintains a staff to pick up and deliver the guest packages. If the guest are out, these employees are entrusted with pass keys and enter the room and leave the clothing. Outside valets are not allowed to enter the guest room. Pick-up and delivery are handled by the bellmen or house-keeping department employees. All the items are gathered in one space and outside valet employees pick them up and deliver them there.

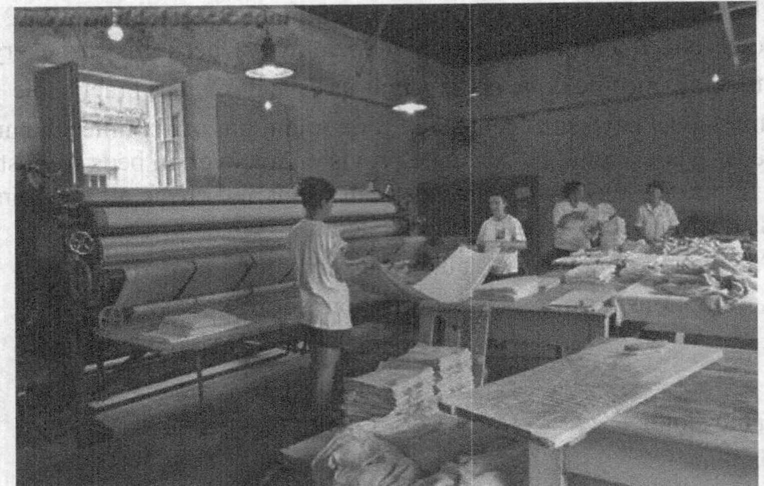

Pix.11.1 A Laundry Service

A Layout of a Laundry for a Small Hotel

24.0"
42"
12.0"
18"
6.0"
24"
3
2
2
1
4
V G JB V 4 JB
D CW HW JB
ON HW
LEGEND
1 90 LIST WASH MASTER
2 50 GH DRY MASTER
3 STACK TABLE
4 SOAK SINK
JB JUNCTION BOX
D DRAIN
CW COLD WATER
HW HOT WATER
G GAS
V VENT

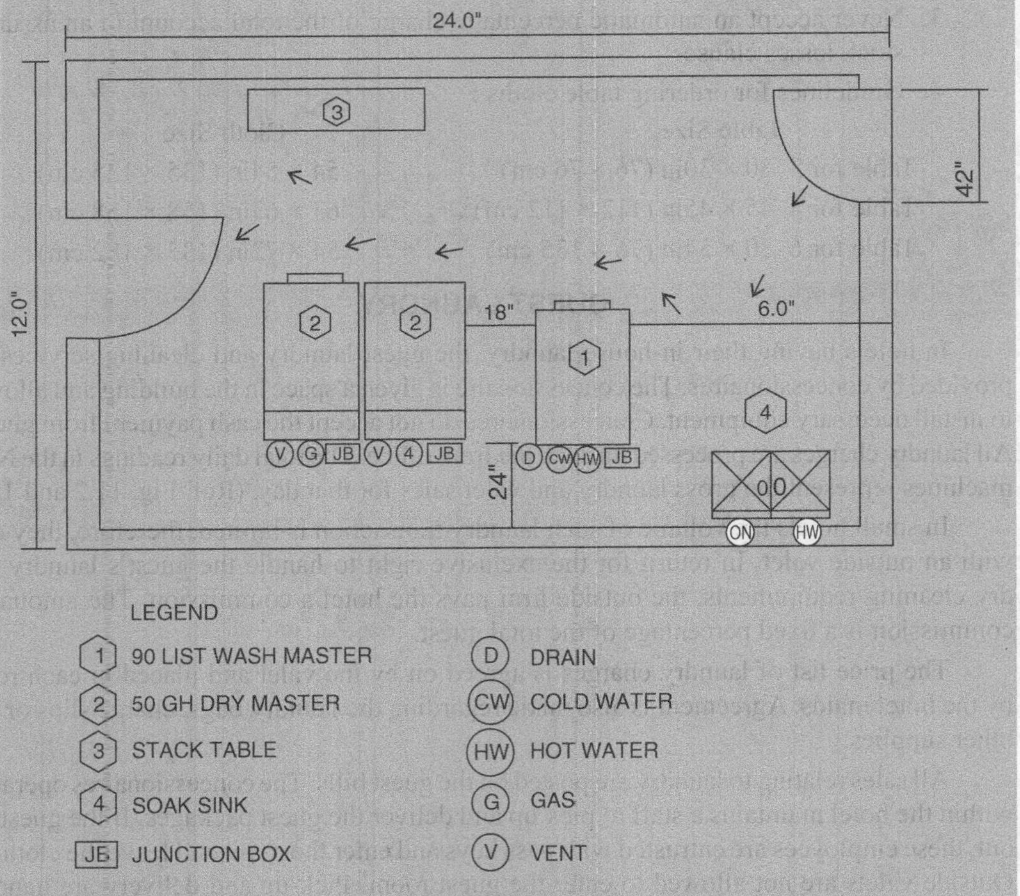

Fig 11.2 A Typical Layout of a Laundry for a Small Hotel, Hotel (80 – 90 Rooms) Using One Employee.

STAIN REMOVING

Stain removal presents considerable problems and especially with present day hand made materials. Extreme care must be taken not to damage the fabric. Where potentially harmful chemicaly are used, an experienced Housekeeper or should control their use. Figure Indicates some methods suitable for application on traditional white and colourfast materials. (Ref. Tables 11.1 and 11.2)

TABLE 11.1. Stains and Stain Removing Techniques

S. No.	Stains	Method
1.	Blood (fresh)	Soak in cold salted water
2.	Blood (dried or left after laundry)	Oxalic acid or Sodium dithionite
3.	Lipstick	Carbon tetrachloride. Use with extreme care; this chemical is highly volatile and adequate ventilation is important.
4.	Ink	Removed by sponging or running under cold water. For white and color fast materials are oxalic acid or sodium dithionite.
5.	Ball-point ink	Apply methylated spirits except for stains on rayon accepted fabrics acetone may also be used.
6.	Rust Mould	Application of oxalic acid or sodium dithionite.
7.	Mildew (caused by exposing linen to damp conditions)	1. Wash in warm soapy water OR Use a hot week solution of potassium permanganate. 2. Treat the linen with a week acid before normal washing.

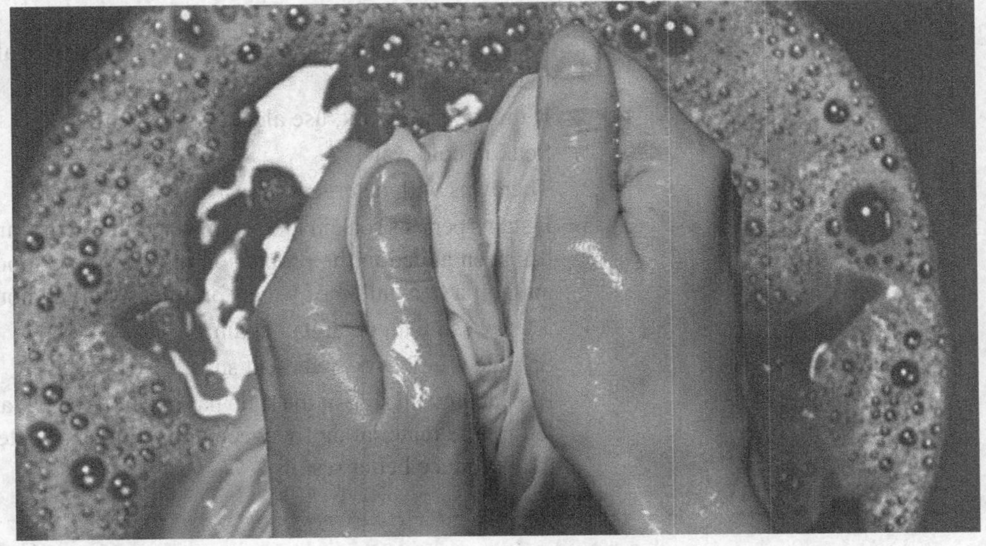

Pix.11.2 Stain Removing

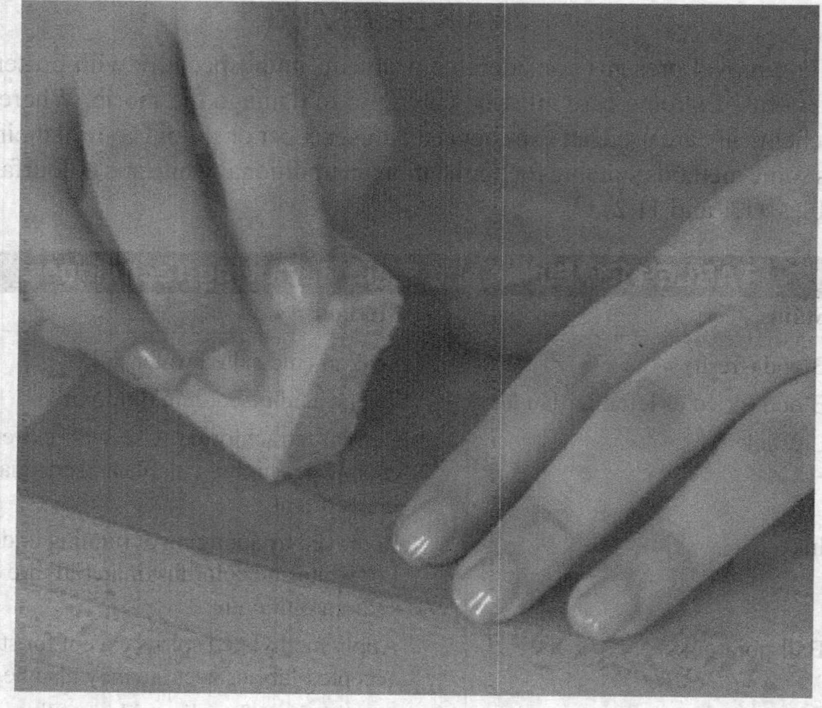

Pix.11.3 Stain Removing

Table 11.2 Common Stains and Removing them from Washing Fabrics

S.No	Stains	Methods of Removal
1.	Alcoholic Beverages	1. Soak in cold water before stain has a chance to set 2. Then sponge with liquid detergent and rinse, putting a few groups of vinegar in rinse water 3. Launder 4. If stains persists, sponge with solution of one part of alcohol to two of water 5. If that doesn't work, use alcohol full strength.
2.	Blood	1. Soak in cold water 2. Then was with detergent in warm water 3. If stains persists soak in lukewarm water to which ammonia has been added in the proportion of three table spoons of ammonia to a gallon of water for at least half an hour. 4. Then wash with detergent again.
3.	Cosmetics	1. Sponge with heavy detergent suds 2. Repeat until all sign of the stain has gone. On same fabrics, letting the material dry between applications of detergent may produce better results.

(Contd...)

		3. If cosmotics are greasy, follow directions for remaining grease stains.
4.	Egg	1. Be careful to use hot water, or stain may become parmanently set
		2. If stain has dried, scrape off a much as possible, then sponge with cold water
		3. Work detergent into stain,
		4. Then launder as usual, using beach of recommended
		5. Fabrics with special finishes may need further treatment with a spray stain remove for washable fabrics.
		6. Treat stains from meat juice the same way
5.	Fruit	1. Sponge with cold water first
		2. If stain persists and boiling water will not damage fabric, stretch cloth over a bowl and pairboiling water through the cloth.
		3. If stain remains stubborn, sponge with hydrogen peroxide or a lemon-juice solution
		4. If boiling water can't be used soak in cold water, then rub stain with glycerine and let it remain on fabric for at least three hours
		5. Rinse thorough in water to which several drops of white vinegar have add, then launder.
6.	Grass	1. Work detergent into stain and launder using bleach recomended for that fabric.
		2. If stain presists let fabric dry and sponge with robbing alcohol, using one to two parts of water on coloured fabrics be sure to test solution on scrap first.
7.	Grease	1. Scrap off as much as possible, sponge with liquid detergent, then launder as usual.
		2. Non-iron fabrics may also be treated with a solution of two table spoons of washing soda to a cup of warm water.
		3. Rub it into dampened spot and allow to remain for not more than five minutes
		4. If stain persists after either method, sponge with cleaning fluid, let dry and repeat until stain is gone.
		5. Another method is to use one of the new spray stain remover, Spray it on stain and launder according to directions on package.
		6. This is particularly useful for specially-finished frabrics, which, although strain-resistant, are very hard to get clean once a stain has penetrated the finish.

(Contd...)

8.	Ink Ball point	1. Ordinary laundering (with black, if recommended, will wash out some types of ball point ink, other need special treatment and may be set by washing. 2. To determine which type the stain is, mark a similar piece of fabric with the same ink and wash 3. If laundering does not remove Work, pour denatured alcohol through fabric (testing first on scrap) or rub white petroleum Jelly into stain and soak in detergent solution; then launder. 4. You can also spray with hair spray until soaking wet, then scrub by hand, using, a thick solution of liquid detergent (If fabric is not likely to be harmed by a small amount of abrasion, rubbing the stain with an eraser specially designed to remove ball point ink before you any of the other methods may do the trick.)
9.	Ink regular	1. Run cold with through stain until it runs clear. 2. Then rub in thik detergent suds 3. Let stand, then launder, using bleach, if recommended 4. If stain persists sponge with chlorine bleach of hydrogen peroxide, and baking soda stain and steam, however, all of these methods may affect the colour. 5. You might also try a solution of one part of alcohol to two parts of water, then full strength alcohol. 6. Some ink is permanent and can not be removed.
10.	Paints	1. Stains must be treated before they dry or they will be almost impossible to remove 2. If they are from a oil based paint, sponge with turpentine (testing fabric first) 3. Then launder, using bleach, if recommanded 4. If stains are from a water-based paint, Sponge with liquid detergent and launder 5. In either case, if traces remain, soak overnight in liquid detergent and launder again.
11.	Perspirations	1. Sponge fresh stains with ammonia, older ones with veneger 2. Rinse and wash in water as hot as fabric can take using bleach, if recommended. 3. If there is any residue of the stain, sponge with cleaning fluid. 4. Since perspiration may weaken a fabric and change the colour, it is not always possible to remove effect completely.

ORGANISATION

Depending upon the size of the laundry, the staff includes assistant manager, assistants, clerks, bundle and hand washers, starchers, wringlers, extractors, pullers, tumblers, mangle workers, folders, curtain girls, press machine operators, finishers, flat workers, shakers, feeding receivers, checkers, delivery employees, cleaners, utility men, linen men, cutmen, porters, markers and sorters, delivery clerks, plain, fancy, collar and shirt ironers etc.

Fig. 11.3 indicates the Organisational Structure of a Laundry, Fig. 11.4 shows the Laundry System and Fig. 11.5 shows the Guest Laundry Flow Chart.

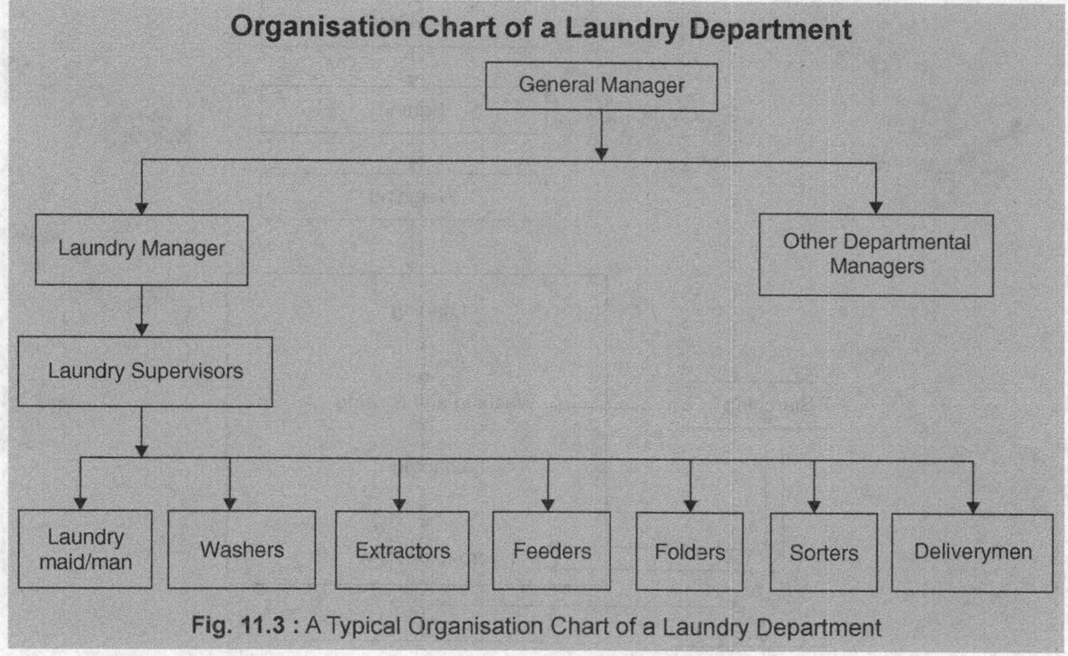

Fig. 11.3 : A Typical Organisation Chart of a Laundry Department

LAUNDRY MANAGER

The laundry manager is responsible for the laundry. He must have thorough knowledge of the planning, organisation, direction, control and coordination of various activities of the laundry department. He should have high morale and the need of human relation approach. His duties and responsibilities include :

1. Preventive maintenance and constant care of the laundry equipment and coordination with engineering department
2. Scheduling of department personnel
3. Ensuring utmost operation efficiency and minimum payroll
4. Adherence of dry cleaning formulas and use of proper detergents
5. Inter-departmental cooperation specially with house-keeping department
6. Selection and quality control of materials, textiles, carpets, factories and furnishings
7. Adherence to the regulations of factories Act

8. Control over use of chemicals, detergents, etc.
9. Liaison with chief factory inspector
10. Working conditions and fatigue factors of employees
11. Preparation of operational reports and its submission to general manager.

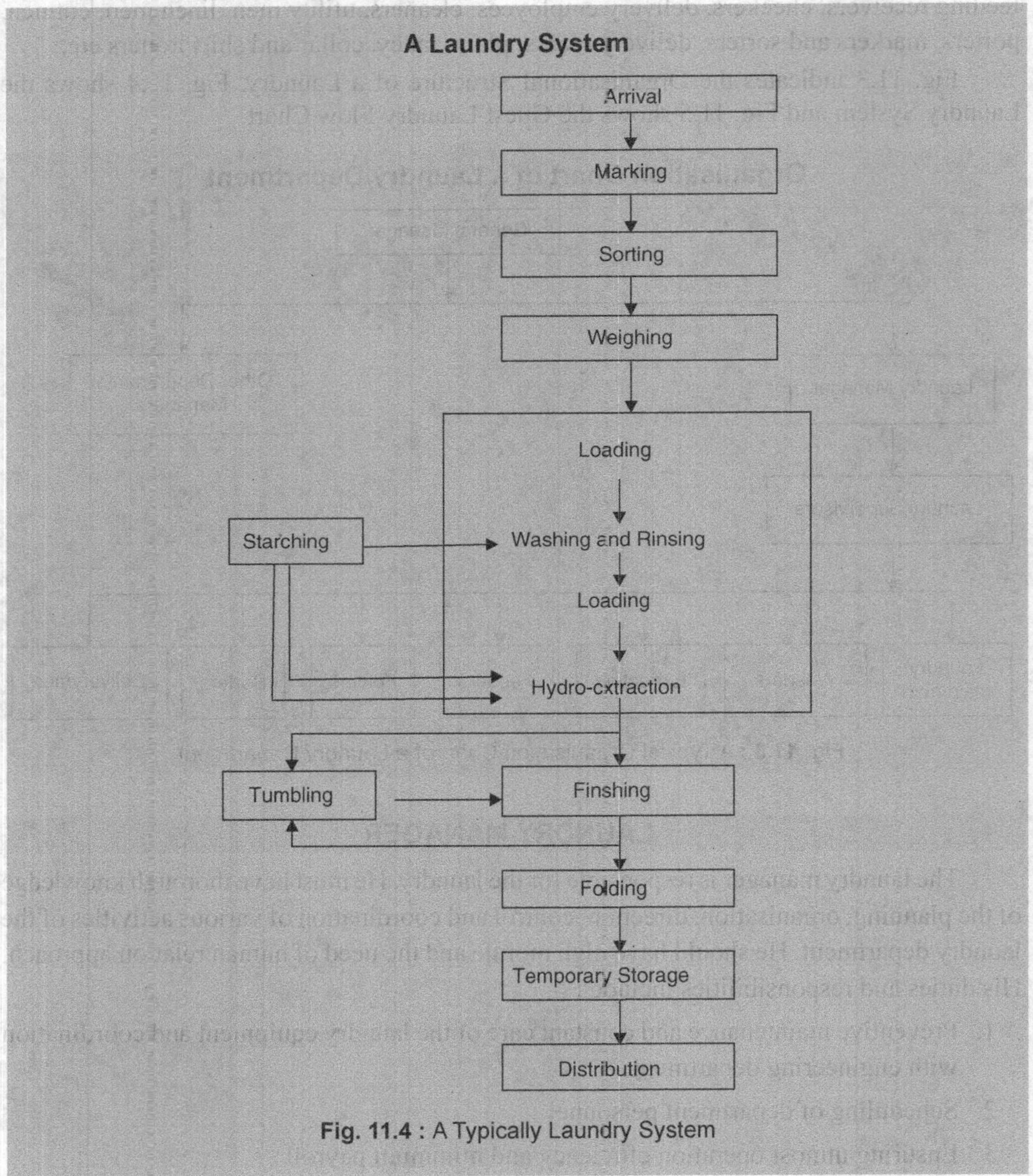

Fig. 11.4 : A Typically Laundry System

Laundry Supervisors

He supervises the activities of laundry attendants. He works as the head washing person and is incharge of the use of all major washing equipment and chemicals.

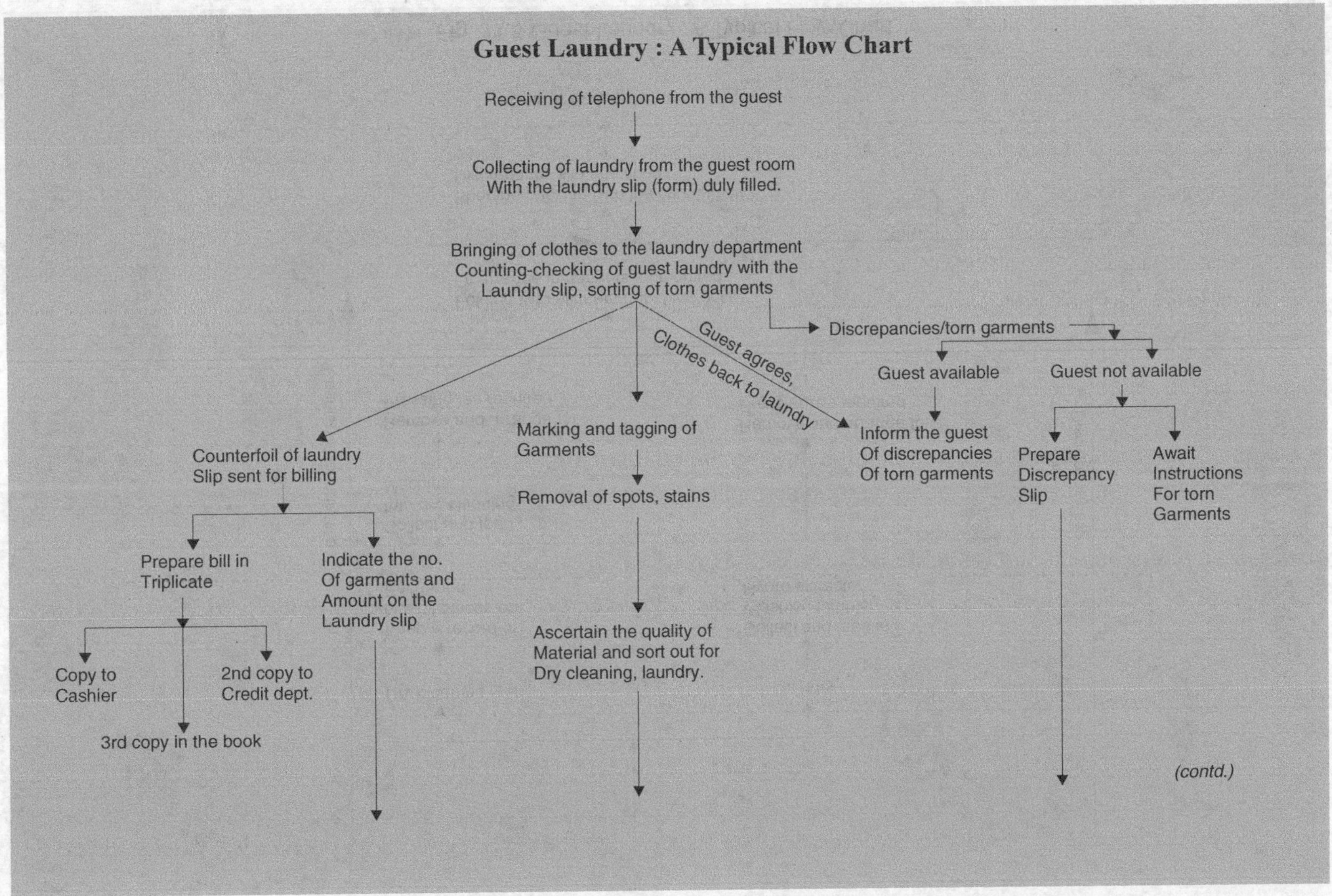
Guest Laundry : A Typical Flow Chart
Receiving of telephone from the guest
Collecting of laundry from the guest room With the laundry slip (form) duly filled.
Bringing of clothes to the laundry department Counting-checking of guest laundry with the Laundry slip, sorting of torn garments
Discrepancies/torn garments
Guest available
Guest not available
Guest agrees, Clothes back to laundry
Inform the guest Of discrepancies Of torn garments
Prepare Discrepancy Slip
Await Instructions For torn Garments
Counterfoil of laundry Slip sent for billing
Marking and tagging of Garments
Removal of spots, stains
Ascertain the quality of Material and sort out for Dry cleaning, laundry.
Prepare bill in Triplicate
Indicate the no. Of garments and Amount on the Laundry slip
Copy to Cashier
2nd copy to Credit dept.
3rd copy in the book
(contd.)

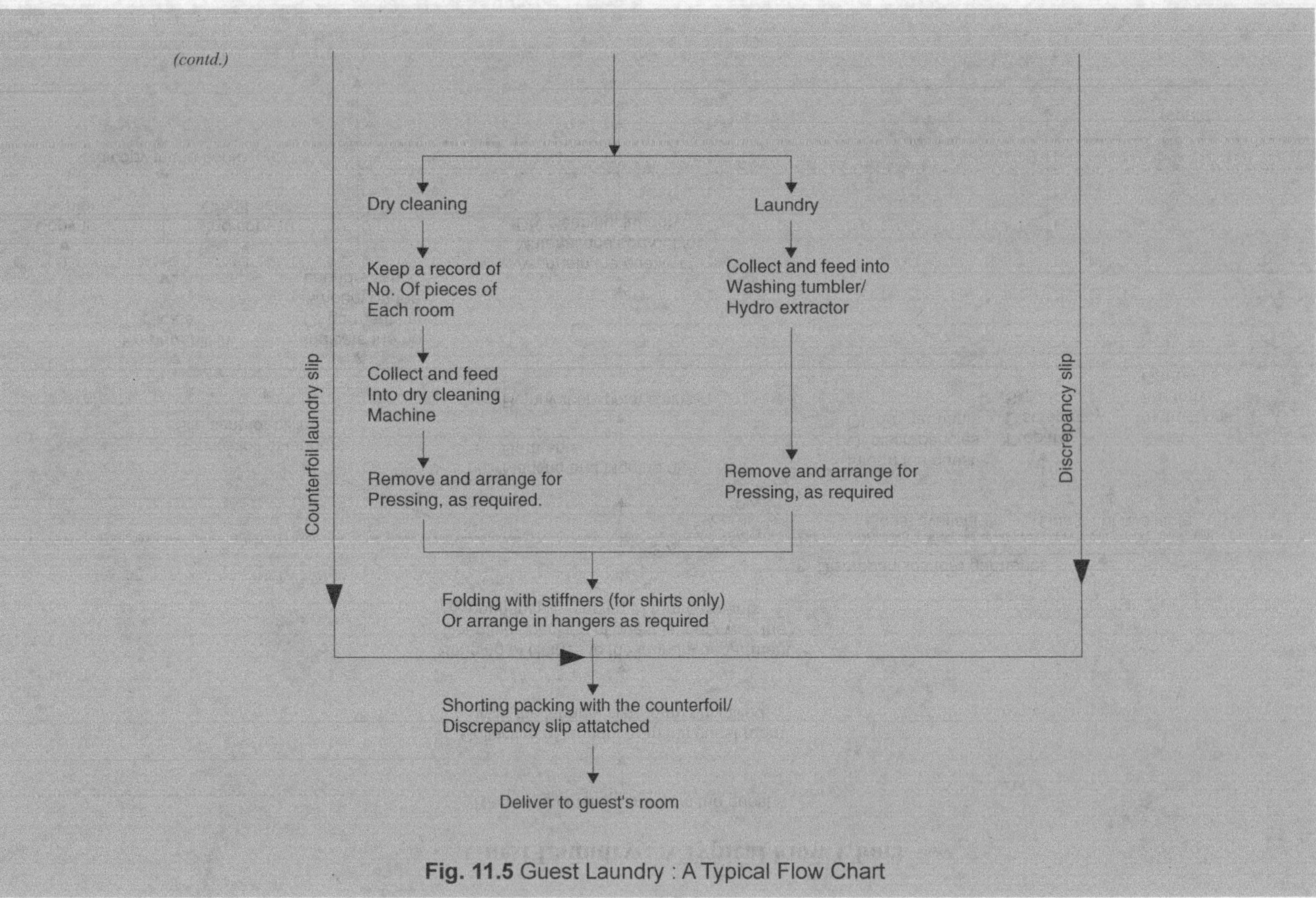

Fig. 11.5 Guest Laundry : A Typical Flow Chart

Pix.11.4 Ironing Service

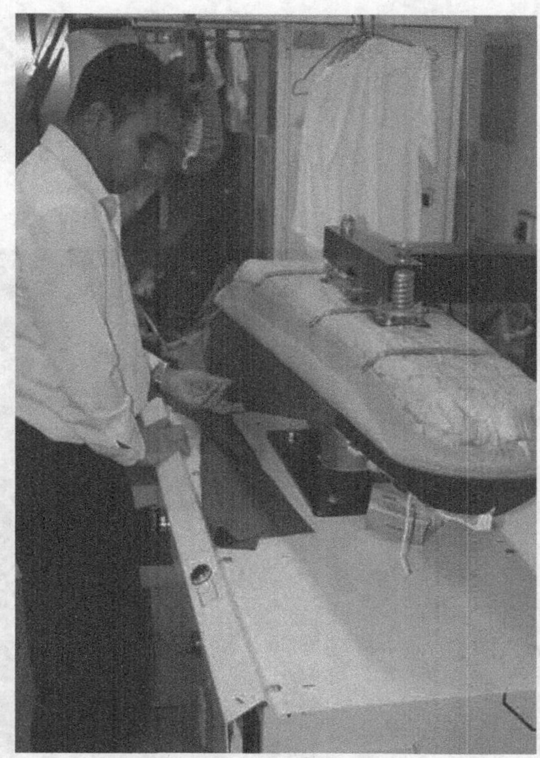

Pix.11.5 Ironing of Clothes

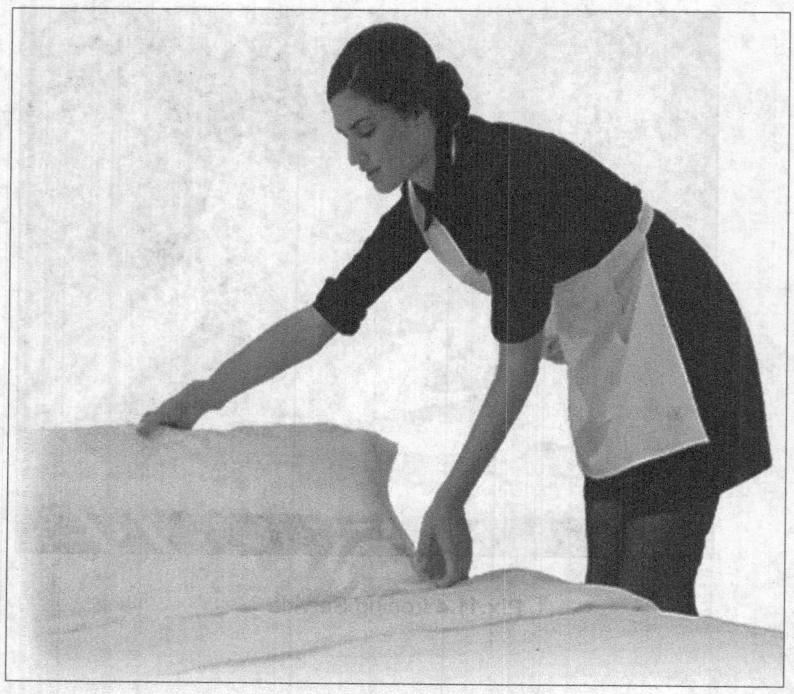

Pix.11.6 Lenin Keeping

Pix.11.7 Lenin Management and Control

HEAD LAUNDRY MAID

She/he should have a good knowledge of the systems and techniques of hand and machine laundering and the use of detergents. The main duties of the Head Laundry Maids are :

1. Laundering of both hotel and guest clothes
2. Control and proper use of the laundering and ironing machine equipment and product
3. To keep stock of linen being laundered.

LAUNDRY MAID/IRONERS

His/her duties are to iron the linen and other articles of the hotel and guests.

LINEN MAID

She/he is responsible for washing and laundry of the hotel's linen and articles of clothing. The duties of the linen maid are to wash and launder the linen and other articles of the hotel and guest and put away the clean linen and to check the incoming and outgoing linen.

CLEANERS

She/he helps various personnel of the different departments to clean and tidy up.

LAUNDRY ATTENDANTS

They work for their respective jobs.

ACCOUNTING AUDIT AND CONTROL

Although the same laundry facilities may be used by guests and by the hotel, each has its own revenue and its own costs. The cost of room linen are treated as part of the room cost and cost of table linen as part of the restaurant cost. The former is included in the room and the latter in the meal price. The costs of guests' own laundry and dry cleaning are received through a separate charge to the guest's account. This normally includes a mark up on the price charged to the hotel as a handling charge if an outside firm is used to the hotel laundry. In case of a group laundry, it is to be decided whether the profit element accrues to the laundry or to the hotels or whether it is to be shared by two. Guest laundry is a service to the guest. Therefore, it is to be treated as to cover its direct costs. In large hotels, laundry charges are treated as revenue earning activity, as such the revenue and costs are monitored and guest laundry operating results are calculated separately. Since hotel incurs costs in providing the laundry service, it is advisable to charge these costs to those guest availing these services, rather than charging higher prices to all guests for their stay. (Ref. Figs 11.6 and 11.7)

REVENUE FROM LAUNDRY

All revenue derived from guest service are credited to this account.

ALLOWANCES

Rebates and overcharges adjusted at a subsequent date are grouped under allowances.

NET

The total gross sale, less allowances will represent the net sales of guest laundry.

COST OF LAUNDERING

In hotels where only one laundry is operated by hotel management in which both house and guest work is done and no division of cost is practical, the cost of the laundering charged with 60% of the total revenue and a like sum credited against the cost of the operation of the house laundry. This percentage can be adjusted according to the experience of the hotel and it should be sufficient to include the cost of boxes, card board, shirt bands, shirt fronts, buttons, pins, tags and laundry bags.

The total expenses of house laundry minus all credits, represent cost of laundry. This cost must be distributed to the department in percentage basis:

1. Rooms
2. Food and Beverage
3. Gift Shop
4. Check Rooms and Wash Rooms
5. Barber Shop
6. Beauty Parlour
7. Swimming Pool/Cabana and Baths.

EMPLOYEES' MEALS

This account is debited with the cost of food furnished to employees of this department.

CLEANING SUPPLIES

Same basis as in Room Department.

LAUNDRY SUPPLIES

It includes items such as :

1. Acids
2. Bags
3. Boxes
4. Card board
5. Duck
6. Ecru
7. Felt padding
8. Marking ink
9. Shirt bands
10. Soaps
11. Tags
12. Wrapping paper.
13. Aprons for mangles
14. Bluing
15. Buttons
16. Chemicals
17. Salt
18. Erusticator
19. Laundry bags
20. Pins
21. Shirt front
22. Soda
23. Twine.

PRINTING AND STATIONERY

All expenses relating to the cost of printed forms, service manuals, laundry lists, stationery and public supplies are debited to this account.

UNIFORMS

Same basis as in the room department.

MISCELLANEOUS

All sundry items which are not distributable under other captions, including delivery expenses are included under this head.

ABC Hotels Ltd.
Guest Laundry Schedule

(Where separate laundry is operated for guest work)

	Current period
Revenue	₹ ....
Allowances	....
Net Revenue	₹ ....
Expenses	
Salaries and Wages	₹ ....
Employees' Meals	....
Employee Benefits	....
Total Payroll and Related Expenses	₹ ....
Other Expenses	....
Cleaning Supplies	₹ ....
Laundry Supplies	....
Miscellaneous	....
Printing and Stationery	....
Uniforms	....
Total Other Expenses	₹ ....
Total Expenses	₹ ....
Departmental Income (Loss)	₹ ....

Note : Various arrangements of additional columns for comparison and percentages could be added.

Fig. 11.6 : Analysis of Income and Expenses of a Guest Laundry

ABC Hotels Ltd.
Guest Laundry Schedule

(Where only one laundry is operated)

	Current period
Revenue	₹ ....
Allowances	....
Net Revenue	₹ ....
Cost of Laundering	....
Departmental Income (Loss)	₹ ....

Note: Various arrangements of additional columns for comparisons and percentages could be added.

Fig. 11.7 : Analysis of Income and Expenses of a Guest Laundry

HOUSE LAUNDRY

Many of the hotels have their own in-house laundries. The large hotels operate a complete laundry which compares favourably with regular commercial laundry. It enables the hotels to serve their guest better and is economically viable. Under any circumstances, few can afford to have the linens used in their everyday operation laundered commercially. Large hotels attempt to process guests' laundry themselves.

In the event of a hotel having its own laundry, this section comes under the House-keeping department. The department is responsible for laundering the hotel linen and guests' clothes. It is responsible for the linen being laundered. The laundry-maid irons the linen and other articles of the hotel and guests. A typical layout of a laundry is given in Fig. 11.8.

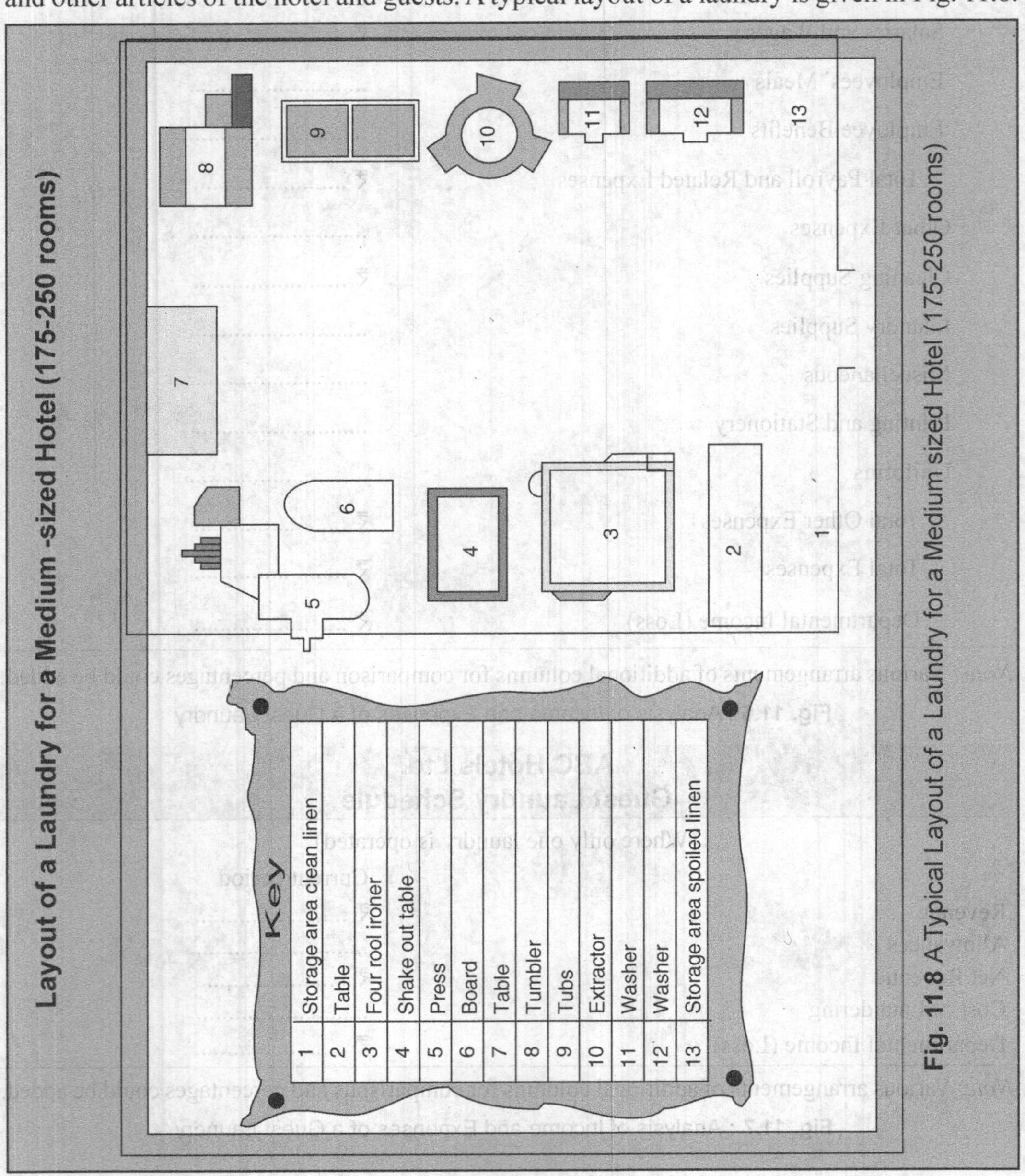

Fig. 11.8 A Typical Layout of a Laundry for a Medium sized Hotel (175-250 rooms)

An in-house laundry should be more economical to run using the existing hotel infrastructure i.e. management, accounts, staff already employed, rather than paying either for someone else to wash hotel's linen or hiring linen. Hotel need not have to pay for the outside laundry overheads and their elements of profit. In addition, hotel eliminate the need of carrying large stocks to allow for break-downs in delivery. In installing an in-house laundry, following basic conditions must be fulfilled :

1. The space is available and is not revenue producing or could be used in a more productive way.
2. The cost of conversion of the area i.e. plumbing, ventilation etc. does not make the capital investment impracticable.
3. In addition to a manager or a regular full-time staff for overall incharge, the hotel should have sufficient staff.
4. If space is available buy or lease the equipment and the linen.

In deluxe hotels (four and five star hotels) guests do not accept any thing but real cotton or linen sheets.

Fig. 11.9 is an estimate of equipment and size of area required for an in-house laundry to cater for various bed-room members, assuming only one non-iron linen is used :

EQUIPMENT AND SPACE FOR AN IN-HOUSE LAUNDRY

		20-30 Roomed Hotel	40-60 Roomed Hotel
Area Equipment	:	225 sq. ft. (22.5 sq. m.)	300 sq. ft. (30 sq. m.)
		1) one 25 lb washer extractor	1) one 25 lb washer extractor
		2) one 75 lb drying tumbler	2) 18 lb washer extractor
			3) one 75 lb drying tumbler
			4) one non-iron sheet folder clip.
Labour	:	One full-time employee 5 hours per day 5 days per week	one full-time employee 8 hours per day 5 days per week.

Note : When calculating the size of the machines required to cater for any particular unit one must know the weight of the linen items and from this, the total weight of linen at various levels of occupancy can be calculated.

Fig. 11.9 : Estimation of Equipment and Space Required

ADVANTAGES

1. Saving on linen costs.
2. Flexibility : In low occupancy period washer can be scheduled over the week, thus using fewer part-time staff and saving on energy costs. When high occupancy, linen turn-round can be as quick as 2-3 hours, if required.

3. Hotel requires less stock to worry about.
4. A higher standard of finished linen.
5. Reduction in waste.
6. No threat of minimum charges.
7. There is no question of shortages.
8. Economy in transport costs of linen hire, including an area for garaging, separate offices and administration.

DISADVANTAGES

1. Large capital investment
2. Lack of suitable area/space
3. Addition of an extra staff
4. Problems of availability of staff
5. Control of energy costs
6. Loss of linen.

ACCOUNT AUDIT AND CONTROL

EMPLOYEES' REMUNERATION AND BENEFITS

The salaries, wages and other benefits paid to employees related to this department are included in this group. It includes the following employees:

1. Manager and assistantsmanager, assistant manager, clerk
2. Washing washers, wringlers, extractors, pullers, tumblers
3. Finishing mangle workers, folders, curtain girls, starters, press machine operators, liners, finishers, flat workers, shakers, feeders, receivers
4. Miscellaneous sorters, markers, checkers, collectors and delivery employees, cleaners, utility men, linen men, cutmen, bundle worker, porters.

EMPLOYEES' MEAL

This account is debited with the cost of food furnished to employees of this department.

CLEANING SUPPLIES

It is to be treated in the same manner as in the case of room department.

LAUNDRY SUPPLIES

The costs of the following items included are :

(*i*) Acids
(*ii*) Bags
(*iii*) Boxes
(*iv*) Card board
(*v*) Chemicals
(*vi*) Ecru
(*xiv*) Aprons for mangles
(*xv*) Bluing
(*xvi*) Buttons
(*xvii*) Chloride of lime
(*xviii*) Duck
(*ixx*) Erusticator

(*vii*) Felt padding
(*viii*) Marking ink
(*ix*) Pins
(*x*) Shirt bands
(*xi*) Soaps
(*xii*) Tags
(*xiii*) Wrapping paper
(*xx*) Laundry bags
(*xxi*) Oxalic acid
(*xxii*) Salt
(*xxiii*) Shirt front
(*xxiv*) Soda
(*xxv*) Twine.

PRINTING AND STATIONERY

It includes the cost of printed forms, service manuals, stationery and office supplies.

UNIFORMS

The cost of uniform used in this department should be treated on the same basis as in the Room Department.

MISCELLANEOUS

It includes all the petty expenses connected with this department including delivery charges.

CREDITS, COST OF GUEST LAUNDRY

In hotels where no separate guest laundry is maintained this account should be credited with 60% of the total revenue derived from work done for guests and outside parties. This percentage can be adjusted according to the experience of the hotel.

COST OF CONCESSIONAIRES LAUNDRY

The house laundry renders services to concessionaires such as barber shop, beauty parlour, swimming pool, cabana and baths. The revenue derived from these concessionaires is credited to this account and deducted from the departmental expenses.

Have laundry schedule is given in Fig. 11.10.

ABC Hotels Ltd.
House Laundry Schedule

	Current period
Expenses	
Salaries and Wages	₹ ....
Vacation and Holidays Pay	....
Employees' Meals	....
Employee Benefits	....
Total Payroll and Related Expenses	₹ ....
Other Expenses	....
Cleaning Supplies	₹ ....
Laundry Supplies	....
Printing and Stationery	....
Uniforms	....
Miscellaneous	....
Total Other Expenses	₹ ....
Total Expenses	₹ ....

(Contd...)

Credits		
Cost of Guest and Outside Laundry		₹ ....
Cost of Concessionaires Laundry		....
Total Credits		₹ ....
Cost of House Laundry		....
Charged to		
Rooms	(Schedule)	₹ ....
Food and Beverage	(Schedule)	
Fountain and Gift shop	(Schedule)	
Check Rooms and Wash Rooms	(Schedule)	
Barber Shop	(Schedule)	
Beauty Parlour	(Schedule)	
Swimming Pool, Cabana & Baths.	(Schedule)	
Total		₹ ....

Note : Various arrangements of additional columns for comparisons and percentages could be added.

Fig. 11.10 : Analysis of House Laundry Expenses

COST OF HOUSE LAUNDRY

The total expenses of house laundry minus all credits represent cost of house laundry. This cost must be distributed to the departments on percentage basis :

1. Room
2. Food and Beverages
3. Gift Shop
4. Checkrooms and Washroom
5. Barber Shop
6. Beauty Parlour
7. Swimming Pool
8. Cabana and Baths.

SUB-RENTALS AND CONCESSIONS

Rentals from stores and concessions are good source of revenue in many hotels. Hotel executives should consult real estate brokers and attorneys, regarding the type of tenants and consideration should be given to kind of tenants or concessonaires, the fair rental value of the premises and the type of leases to offer. The kind of tenants depends on the location of the hotel, the facilities and shops available in the areas and other competing hotels. Reliable tenants who can provide the goods and services required by the guests will contribute more in the longrun to the financial success of the hotel than the immediate increase in income realised by just renting to the highest bidders.

All stores should have an entrance providing direct access to and from the hotel. Hotel's reputation will be directly affected by the success or failure of the tenants' business. Hotel lease should clearly define the responsibilities of the tenants in the areas of cleanliness, hours of opening, signs, prices, control of personnel etc.

The type of agreements will depend on the kind of tenants, the product they sell, the service they perform. Usually there are three methods of agreements :

1. Straight rentals
2. Minimum rentals plus a percentage of the gross receipts over a specified amount
3. Straight percentage of the goods sold.

The tenants and concessionaires should permit the guest to charge their purchases or fees for services to their hotel bills. The management must agree to accept the charges and reimburse the tenants in full for them. These charges are processed through the hotel's accounting and collection system at no cost of the tenants and concessionaires. Problems arise when the guest disputes the charges on checking out. The result is that the hotel has to pay collection charges, commission to credit card companies, collection agencies or attorneys and legal fees and court costs for law suits and in some cases it writes off the amount as bad debts. Solution of such problems can be reached only by the direct initial negotiation between the two parties.

The income from rental arises mostly from :

1. Flats and apartments let to tenants for residential purposes on a long-term basis
2. Offices let to business and other organisations for their purposes
3. Shops let to retailers
4. Club rooms let for purposes of a member's or proprietary club
5. Display rooms let to others
6. Show cases let to others for display of their wares.

Services to guests may also be provided by concessionaires. The concessionaires are given right to operate on hotel premises with a view to undertaking services to guests. These may include those provided by news agents, hairdressers and souvenir shop, cloak room etc.

The rental denote greater independence for the tenant than the licence to use the premises on certain conditions, which is the essence of the concession. Rental and concessions are seen as alternative means of providing services to guests. This relieves the hotel from operating unfamiliar service and concentrate on its primary activities. There is a recent trends in the hotel, under which even the primary activities such as restaurant facilities are entrusted and operated by an external organisation.

GROSS RENTALS

This account should be credited with the revenue derived from the rental of stores. In this connection a store is defined as any space on the ground floor or any space on other floors rented to others for operations which are not ordinarily operations of a hotel as part of usual hotel service.

GROSS STORE RENTALS/STORE RENTALS

Income from rentals of all stores space should be credited to a separate account 'Store rentals'. This space may also be occupied by a concessionaire or used for any other purpose.

STORE RENTALS

A store is defined as any space on the ground floor or space on other floor, rented to others for operation which are not ordinarily operation of a hotel as part of usual hotel service.

RENTAL COMMISSION

The commission paid to renting agents for different leases obtained is debited to this account. The amount is prorated over the terms of the respective leases.

Profit before the addition of store rental is called as total house revenue and after the inclusion of the store rental will be known as 'Gross Operating Profit'. (Ref. Fig. 11.11)

ABC Hotels Ltd. Store Rentals Schedule	
	Current period
Gross Rental	₹
Rental commission	₹
Net Store Rental	₹

Note : Various arrangements of additional columns for comparisons and percentages could be added.

Fig. 11.11 : Analysis of Incomes from Rentals

TELEPHONE AND TELEX

Prompt, efficient and accurate telephone service is an important element in building and maintaining good guest relations. Courtesy, efficiency and helpfulness in handling guests' requirements and prompt and effective demands, make a great contribution to the efficiency of hotel operation. Generally two basic types of telephone equipment are used as :

1. Manual system, and
2. Dialling system

In a manual system all outgoing calls must be made by the hotel operator whereas in a dial system the guest can dial their own calls.

TELEPHONE COSTS

A look on the income statement in Fig. 11.12 of a hotel indicates that cost of providing telephone services has been a sizeable drain on hotel's profit. Use the following check list to control telephone costs:

1. Is each item of equipment used and necessary ?
2. Eliminate some trunk times and extension lines if possible
3. Reduce the number of operators required by using more sophisticated equipment
4. Ask the telephone department for a detailed itemization of all telephone equipment
5. Check that everything is listed and is properly working
6. Check whether you have received all toll commission which you are entitled
7. Take advantage of deductions allowed on charges for toll calls made by guests who leave without paying their bills
8. Take advantage of suspended service rate if there is a sharp second drop in switch board use
9. Ask the telephone department to make free, periodic, trunk busy studies
10. Eliminate extra cost options much as seldom used extensions, private lines, dial intercom call director etc.

11. Provide facility to guest to use coin telephone for local calls
12. Keep a light rein on use of hotel telephones for personal call.
13. Take advantage of savings possible through direct dialling and station calls instead of person to person.
14. Investigate positive saving through WAT service flat rate billing for long distance calls, both incoming and outgoing
15. For high traffic service to a particular city use tie lines
16. Check all changes on telephone bill carefully
17. If necessary avail the services of a communication consultant.

In a small hotel, the telephone department reports to the front office manager whereas in a large hotel, it reports to the resident manager. In both the cases the responsibilities of this department are :

1. To handle all incoming and outgoing calls
2. Cleanliness and maintenance of all public areas
3. Maintenance and repairs to telephones in guest room
4. To ensure that all messages are dealt correctly
5. To maintain information on all functions, banquets, conferences etc. in the hotel
6. To check all telephone accounts
7. To control the volume of outgoing calls
8. To maintain a complaint book
9. To liaise with the telex operator
10. To supervise the effective training of present staff as well as induction of new personnel.

ORGANISATION

Chief operator, supervisors, operators, cashiers and messengers are some of the employees working in this department.

CHIEF OPERATOR

He is the departmental head and is responsible for the quality of service, work schedule, supervision and recruitment and dismissal of the operators. In large hotels there are day and night supervisors, who assist the chief operator as telephone requires continuous 24 hours a day coverage.

TELEPHONE OPERATORS

The job of the telephone operator is mostly handled by females. She should have the knowledge and good command of foreign language and complete knowledge of telephone service regulations. Technical education and experience is essential. Promptness and responsibilities are among the attributes of a telephone operator.

Her main duties are :

1. To put through calls to guest rooms and other concerned departments.
2. To book long distance calls for the customers to reply.
3. To attend inquiries to guests from time to time and record the same to be entered on guest's bill by filling out a special form for transmission to the front office.

4. To maintain information rack current to avoid confusion.
5. To remember more frequently used telephone numbers like cinema, banks, travel agents, and other hotels.

OPERATORS

The practical role of the operator is to service incoming calls and handle all incoming house calls. They answer the telephone calls and connect the callers with the desired parties. They must have access to an alphabetical rack which contain rack slips that display the name and address of guests. It must be up-to-date at all times. This rack is placed near the switch board.

Due to room changes, arrivals and departure, it is difficult for the operator to keep the rack in a large hotel. Therefore, an electronic system is installed which replaces the rack. On receipt of a call for a guest, the operator punches the surname of the guest on a vending machine installed at each station. The computer automatically flashes/lashes on a screen the room number, name and address of the guest and the operator completes the call.

CIRCUIT OPERATORS

For faster and more efficient handling of all rack changes, the circuit operators are located in the front office near the room racks. All incoming calls requiring room numbers are referred to these employees. They question the caller and obtain the room number and give it to telephone operator.

MESSAGE OPERATOR

If the guest is not available and a message is to be conveyed, the caller is switched to message operators. They take verbal messages and note it down. All such messages are forwarded to the mail and information desk to be placed in the respective mail slot. The bellman delivers a copy to the guest room.

CONSOLE OPERATIONS

In some hotels the consoles are installed. It is a device through which a light in each room can be activated. The light is a signal to a guest that there is a message left for him and if required, he can obtain it by dialing the console operator. Once the message is delivered the light is disconnected.

TELEX OPERATOR

The telex operator must have the knowledge of various codes, framing of messages, system of accounting, proper debit and tallying of monthly bills. He should have liaison with overseas communication service.

ACCOUNTING AND AUDIT CONTROL

The telephone facilities are used by guest as well as by the hotel for its own communication purposes. These are clearly costs attributable to guests' use. There are fixed costs of the premises, semi-fixed costs of equipment rentals and staffing and variable costs of individual calls and messages through the external systems. All incoming calls and messages are available to guest free but most hotels seek to recover the variable cost of outgoing calls, telex messages and other costs by mark-up in the prices charged to guests. Thus telephone and related services have their own incomes/revenue and cost of sales, payrolls, direct and indirect costs. In large hotels telephone and related services are regarded as a revenue earning activity and as a cost centre for which the operating result may be periodically computed in the same way as for other activities of the hotel. If the telephone switch board operator has also other duties, the payroll cost can be apportioned between the departments concerned. All costs could be apportioned between guest use and the hotel use of the service.

GROSS REVENUE

Income from telephone is derived from the cost of telephone facilities by guests. It does not include any amounts for telephone services used by management or other departments of the hotel. The gross sales from telephone may be divided into three main categories :

1. Local calls
2. Long distance calls/trunk calls
3. Service charges.

ALLOWANCES

These allowances are allowed to guests as rebate or due to overcharge and are adjusted at a subsequent date from the gross sale.

NET REVENUE

The difference of the gross telephone sales and allowances is known as net sales.

COST OF TELEPHONE CALLS

The gross cost of telephone calls is the sum total amount of bill charged by the telephone company for local and long distance calls.

The cost of telephone calls is the difference of gross cost of telephone calls and the commission received on long and local calls.

The total cost of telephone calls is the total of cost of telephone calls, the cost of switch board, and telephone equipment in guest rooms or other places of the hotel charged by telephone company.

GROSS PROFIT

The difference of the net sales and the cost of sales is called as gross profit.

EXPENSES

The employees' remuneration and benefits, salaries and wages and other benefits paid to employees of telephone department are debited to this account. These employees are :

1. Chief Operator
2. Supervisors
3. Cashiers
4. Operators
5. Messengers

COST OF EMPLOYEES' MEALS

This account is debited with the cost of food and beverages furnished to employees of this department.

EQUIPMENT CHARGES

The telephone company goes on changing the telephone equipment and charges the bills to the hotel.

PRINTING AND STATIONERY

It includes the cost of printing and stationery used by the employees of the telephone department, e.g.

1. Printed forms
2. Service manuals
3. Traffic sheets
4. Telephone vouchers
5. Message envelopes
6. Stationery and office supplies

The Telephones schedules with analysis of income and expenses are given in Fig. 11.12.

ABC Hotels Ltd.
Telephone Schedule

	Current period
Revenue	
Local	₹ ....
Long Distance	....
Service Charges	....
Pay Station	....
Total Revenue	₹ ....
Allowances	
Net Revenue	₹.................
Cost Of Calls	
Local	₹.................
Long Distance	
Total Cost of Calls	₹ ....
Less Commissions	
Local	₹ ....
Long Distance	
Total Commissions	₹ ....
Net Cost Of Calls	
Rental of Equipment	....
Total cost of calls	₹.................
Gross Profit/Loss	....
Expenses	....
Salaries and Wages	....
Employees' Meals	....
Employees' Benefits	....
Total Payroll and Related Expenses	....
Other Expenses :	....
Equipment Charges	....
Printing & Stationery	....
Uniforms	....

(Contd.)

Miscellaneous	....
Total Other Expenses	₹ ....
Total Expenses	₹ ....
Other Income	....
Pay Station Commissions	₹ ....
Miscellaneous	....
Departmental Profit (Loss)	₹ ....
Cost Of House Calls	....
Local	₹ ....
Long Distance	₹ ....

Note : Various arrangements of additional columns for comparisons and percentages could be added.

Fig. 11.12 : Analysis of Income and Expenses of Telephone Department.

UNIFORMS

This account is debited with the cost and repairing, and cleaning charges of the uniform used by the employees of this department.

MISCELLANEOUS

It includes all other expenses which cannot be classified under any of the above heading e.g. cost of covers and holders of telephone directory, cost of out of town directories etc.

GARAGE AND PARKING LOT

Many of the garages are operated either as concessions or on a management fee basis by car rentals or garage operating companies. Hotels within house garage offer parking to the general public at the prevailing rates of their locality. Controlling garage revenue is required in every hotel. A clear distinction is required to be made between the guest cars, which park free and those of the paying public. In case the garage is operated by an outside firm, it is the responsibility of the firm to thoroughly check the revenue as per its natural procedure. The verification of revenue and an actual inspection of the parked car is required to be made.

The manager, parking attendants, starters, drivers, mechanics, helpers, workers, cleaners, deskmen, clerks, etc. are the employees connected with this department.

Hotels with in-house garage make arrangement for parking cars. An agreement with the operators of a nearby garage or parking lot is made. The guests are required to pay for parking their cars and the hotel receives a percentage of the total charges as a commission. The guest leaves the car with the doorman, who calls the garage to send one of the employee to pick up the car and, when desired by the guest, to deliver it to the hotel. Parking fees are charged to the guest accounts. For daily postings, a garage attendant delivers each night, to the front office cashier or night auditor, a list of the guest cars in the garage. The list shows the room numbers, guest name and the amount due. Reimbursement for the parking charges can be made in full to the garage attendant delivering the charges and treating the charge as paid out and posted in the guest bill or these charges are accumulated for a specified period and the net amount after deducting the commission is sent to the garage operator. Some hotels offer free parking to their guests even though they have no in-house garage. The procedure for parking the car are the same except that the hotel assumes the responsibility for parking charges. Similar agreements are also negotiated with car rentals, firms, photographers, telegraph companies, vending machines and leasing companies.

ACCOUNTING AUDIT AND CONTROL

MERCHANDISE SALE

Revenue realised from the sales of merchandise are credited to this account.

COST OF SALES

It represents the purchase price of merchandise sold and is calculated by taking into account the opening and closing inventory and the total purchases.

OTHER REVENUE

It includes the charges for storage and parking and other revenue primarily of a service nature.

EXPENSES

Employees' remuneration and benefits : Salaries, wages and other benefits paid to employees of this department are debited to this account. The employees include are :

1. Manager
2. Starters
3. Mechanics
4. Washers
5. Deskmen
6. Parking attendants
7. Drivers
8. Helpers
9. Cleaners
10. Clerks.

EMPLOYEES' MEALS

This account should be charged with the cost of food and beverage furnished to employees of this department.

GAS AND OIL CONSUMED

It includes all the expenses relating to the cost of gas and oil used in the preparation of garage parking lot for autos and equipment owned by the hotel.

LICENSEES

All fees relating to licences and permits necessary for the operation of this department are debited to this account.

PRINTING AND STATIONERY

Expenses relating to the cost of printed forms, service manuals, stationery and office supplies used by the department are debited to this head.

SUPPLIES AND PARTS

All expenses relating to the cost of supplies and parts used in the operation of garage and parking lot for autos and equipment owned by hotel are debited to this account.

UNIFORMS

It includes the cost of uniforms for employees of this department as well as the cost of repairing and cleaning uniforms, the cost of buttons, braid, badges, etc.

WATER

All specified water bills applicable to this department are debited to this head.

MISCELLANEOUS

Small and petty expenses which cannot be categorised under above head are debited to this account.

CHARGES TO OTHER DEPARTMENTS

In many hotels, there are passenger cars, limousines, station wagons etc. which are used for general purpose of the hotel such as transporting guests, handling goods, bringing employees for work etc. Similar other garage parking service facilities and equipment are used for hotel purposes. Accurate data relating to the same can be maintained and charged to other departments. All such amounts related to other departments would be entered as a credit to the garage parking operation and charges as 'garage and parking' expenses in the respective departments to which they are apportioned.

The account presentation as shown is intended for use when the garage and/or parking lot operation is primarily for the purpose of parking cars and servicing hotel guests. In those instances where a garage is operated as a separate unit and services hotel guests as part of a major garage operation the account presentation would include accounts for utility services, telephone, insurance, real estate taxes, etc.

Fig. 11.13 is a schedule for Garage and Parking showing analysis of income and expense of garage parking lot Fig. 11.14 is a schedule Garage and Parking lot showing anaysis of garage and parking.

ABC Hotels Ltd.
Garage And Parking Lot Schedule

	Current period
Revenue	
Gas and Oil	₹ ....
Parts and Accessories	....
Total	₹ ....
Cost Of Sales	....
Gas and Oil	₹ ....
Parts and Accessories	....
Total	₹ ....
Gross Profit Of Merchandise Sold	....
Other Revenue	....
Storage and Parking Income	₹ ....
Washing and Polishing	....
Sundry Repairs	....
Miscellaneous	....
Total Gross Profit	₹ ....

Departmental Expenses	....
Salaries and Wages	₹ ....
Vacation and Holiday Pay	....
Employee Meals	....
Payroll Taxes and Employee Benefits	....
Total Payroll and Related Expenses	₹ ....
Other Expenses	....
Gas and Oil Consumed	....
Licenses	....
Miscellaneous	....
Printing and Stationery	....
Supplies and Parts	....
Uniforms	....
Water	....
Total Other Expenses	₹ ....
Total Expenses	₹ ....
Departmental Profit (Loss) Before	....
Charges To Other Departments	₹ ....
Add : Charges To Other Departments	....
Departmental Income (Loss)	₹ ....

Note : Various arrangements of additional columns for comparisons and percentages could be added.

Fig. 11.13 : Analysis of Income and Expenses of Garage Parking Lot

ABC Hotels Ltd.
Garage And Parking Lot Schedule

	Current Period
Revenue	
Parking and Storage	₹ ....
Merchandise	....
Other	....
Total Revenue	₹ ....
Allowances	....
Net Revenue	₹ ....
Cost Of Merchandise Sold	....
Gross Profit (Loss)	....
Expenses	....
Salaries and Wages	....
Employee Benefits	....
Total Payroll and Related Expenses	₹ ....
Other Expenses	....
Licences	....
Management Fee	....
Operating Supplies	....
Uniforms	....
Others	....
Total Other Expenses	₹ ....
Departmental Income (Loss)	₹ ....

Note : Various arrangements of additional columns for comparisons and percentages could be added.

Fig. 11.14 : Analysis of Garage and Parking Lot

SWIMMING POOLS, CABANAS AND BATHS

Swimming pools are built to attract guests. The hotel may have outdoor or inorder or on-premises swimming pool. Some of the hotels have the facilities of health club which provides facilities like sauna and massage. The facilities of swimming pool are generally available to the public on payment of a daily admission fee. As regards to massages, it can be run by the hotel or given to concessionaires. The employees are paid salaries plus a commission of a percentage of their sales. In case, these services are given to concessionaires, they collect their fee directly from the guests and pay to the hotel a fixed rental or a percentage of the gross income.

Fig. 11.15 indicates the break-up of the staff at the swimming pool and Fig. 11.16 shows the income and expedition of this section.

Pix 11.8 : The Swimming Pool

Pix 11.9 : The Swimming Pool

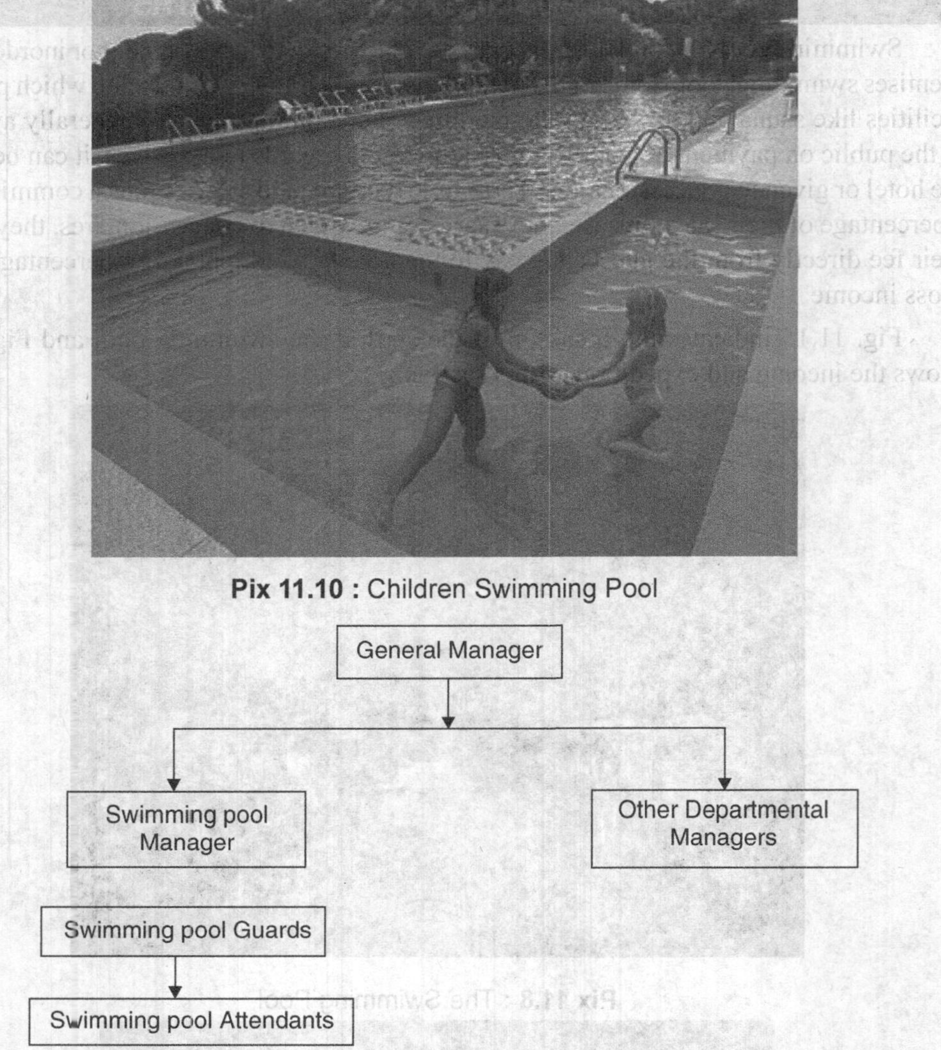

Pix 11.10 : Children Swimming Pool

Fig. 11.15 : A Typical Organisation Chart of a Swimming Pool

ACCOUNTING AUDIT AND CONTROL

INCOME FROM SWIMMING POOL

The income from swimming pools, cabanas and bath include :

1. Rental receipts
2. Revenue from the operation of Turkish, Russian, Sun or other baths, swimming pool, solarium
3. Services of masseurs, rubbers, chiropodists, swimming pool instructors
4. Sale of merchandise and
5. Income from cabanas and lockers.

EXPENSES

1. **Employees' Remuneration and Benefits :** It includes the salaries, wages and other benefits paid to managers, cashiersclerks, masseurs, steam room boys, linen handlers working in this department.
2. **Employees' Meals :** The cost of the meals furnished to the employees of this department are debited to this account.

CLEANING SUPPLIES

Same basis as in the Room Department.

LAUNDRY

The cost of laundry chargeable to this department is debited to this account.

LINEN

Same basis as in the Room Department.

OPERATING SUPPLIES

The cost of supplies of the following items is debited to this account:

1. Alcohol
2. Oils
3. Soaps
4. Lotions
5. Powders
6. Tonics.

PRINTING AND STATIONARY

Same basis as in the Room Department.

UNIFORMS

Same basis as in the Room Department.

MISCELLANEOUS

All items which are not distributable under other captions.

Fig. 11.16 is a swimming pool cabanas baths schedule analysing the income and express.

ABC Hotels Ltd.
Swimming Pool Cabanas Baths Schedule

	Current period
Rentals	₹ ....
Revenue From Service	....
Sales of Merchandise	₹ ....
Allowances	....
Net-Revenue	....
Less Cost of Merchandise Sold	....
Gross Profit on Merchandise Sales	₹ ....
Expenses	....
Salaries and Wages	₹ ....
Employees' benefits	....
Vacation and Holiday Pays	....

(Contd.)

Payroll Taxes and Employees' Benefits	....
Total Payroll and Related Expenses	₹ ....
Other Expenses	....
Cleaning Supplies	₹ ....
Laundry	....
Linen	....
Miscellaneous	....
Operating Supplies	....
Printing and Stationery	....
Uniforms	....
Total Other Expenses	₹ ....
Total Expenses	₹ ....
Departmental Income	....
Departmental Profit (Loss)	₹ ....

Note : Various arrangements of additional columns for comparisons and percentages could be added.

Fig. 11.16 : Analysis of Income and Expenses of Swimming Pool, Cabanas, Baths

VALET

The practice of employing valet is hardly seen in any hotel in modern times. The process is almost dead as the house-keeping staff arranges a quick dry cleaning and pressing services from outside the hotel. Guests who wish to undertake their laundry and ironing, for them the dry racks and irons are available in the room maids pantry. The usual practice in all the hotels is to provide pack of needles, thread and buttons for guests' emergency repairs.

The income of the valet department is derived from the pressing, cleaning and repairing of guest's clothes. In some hotels shoe shining is added to this, when a guest calls in for the service from his room. Valet also keeps a small stock of collars, collar buttons, shirts or similar articles for the convenience of guests. The sale of such items is an income of the department. In small hotels there is only one employee in this department, who renders the service and records the sales. In many hotels the bellmen answer all calls for the valet and deliver the garments after they have been pressed or delivered. In large hotels, the valet department is very active and a clerk is employed for keeping all records.

Head valet, tailors, pressers, dry cleaners, clerk runners, delivery boys etc. are the employees of this section.

ACCOUNT AUDIT AND CONTROL

REVENUE/GROSS REVENUE

All revenue derived from the following services are credited to this account :

1. Pressing
2. Dry cleaning
3. Sales of haberdashery
4. Shoe-shining etc.
5. Cleaning
6. Repairs of wearing apparel
7. Rental of clothing.

ALLOWANCES

It represents rebates and overcharges adjusted at a subsequent date.

NET SALES

The gross sales less allowances constitute the net sales of valet shops.

EXPENSES

Employees' Remuneration and Benefits : Salaries, wages and other benefits paid to head valet, tailors, pressers, dry cleaners, clerks, runners, delivery boys etc. are debited to this account.

Employee meals : The cost of food furnished to employees of the valet shop are debited to this account.

Outside Work : It includes the expenses incurred by establishments for repairing and renewing of clothing, repair of shoes etc.

Valet Schedule analysing all income and expenses are given in Fig. 11.17.

ABC Hotels Ltd.
Valet Schedule

	Current period
Gross Revenue	₹ ....
Allowances	....
Net Revenue	₹ ....
Expenses	....
Salaries and Wages	₹ ....
Employees' Benefit	....
Payroll Taxes and Employee Benefits	
Total Payroll and Related Expenses	₹ ....
Other Expenses	....
Miscellaneous	₹ ....
Outside Work	....
Printing and Stationery	....
Supplies	....
Uniforms	....
Total other Expenses	₹ ....
Total Expenses	₹ ....
Profit (Loss) Before Charges to Other Departments	₹ ....
Charges To Other Departments	....
Departmental Income (Loss)	₹ ....

Note : Various arrangements of additional columns for comparisons and percentages could be added.

Fig. 11.17 : Analysis of Income and Expenses of Valet

Printing and Stationery : It includes the cost of printed forms, service manuals, charge sheets, vouchers, tickets, envelopes, stationery and office supplies, whether purchased from outside printing concerns or produced by the hotel is print shop, when used by the employees of this department.

Supplies : It includes the cost of the following :

1. Buttons
2. Clothes brushers
3. Cost of haberdashery
4. Linings
5. Cleaning fluids
6. Coat hangers
7. Gas
8. Pressing machine covers.

Uniforms : This account is debited with the cost of uniforms including repair and cleaning furnished to employees of this department.

Miscellaneous : It includes all the sundry items not distributable under other captions.

Charges to other departments : There are some charges which are credited to this department. It includes the amount charged to departments for serving hotel uniforms or other wearing apparel of hotel employees. Pricing of these could be compared with rates of similar outside commercial concerns.

TOBACCONIST' CIGARS AND NEWS STAND

Guest may avail the services of cigars and news stand from the respective sale points. These sale points are recorded separately. The sale of cigar or cigarettes are generally made at the stand direct to guests or other customers for cash. The cigar clerk keeps the record. This record is prepared in a form of report and forwarded each day to the income auditor, who compares it with the report prepared by night auditor. The cigars and cigarettes are also sold in the restaurant from a tray carried to the tables. The cigar clerk controls such sales by recording the issues and returns and calculates the quantity sold and the amount of sales. These sales must be charged on the waiter's checks, so that the guest may have such purchases charged on his account, together with the charges for meal. In some hotels, the waiter has to pay at the cigar stand when he obtains cigars or cigarettes, and collects from the guest separately without any record of such sales on his (waiter's) check.

Cigars and cigarettes issued for banquets on requisitions of the banquet department are recorded in the same way as sales by waiter in the restaurant. Sales of packages of candy, chewing gum, smokers' supplies and other small marchandise are included in the total sales of cigar stand. The method of checking foods and beverages may also be used to check the sale of cigars and cigarettes.

If the cigar stand is operated by a lessee, only the sale charged to guests enter into the hotel's records. These charges are treated in the records in the same manner as sales, except that the total for the month is credited to the lessee instead of to a sales account. If the lessee pays a certain percentage of the sale as rent, the hotel should verify the cash sales.

All income conel expenses of cigars and new stand are analyzed in a fig. 11.18 of cigars and News stand schedule.

ACCOUNT AUDIT AND CONTROL

REVENUE

The amount received from sale of various items is included under this head :

1. Sale of cigars
2. Sale of smokers' accessories
3. Sale of magazines
4. Sale of candy
5. Sale of tobacco
6. Sale of newspapers
7. Sale of books
8. Sale of novelties.

ALLOWANCES

Rebate and overcharges, adjusted at subsequent date, are debited to this account.

NET SALES

The total sales less allowances will constitute the net sale of this department.

COST OF GOODS SOLD

It includes the following :

1. Purchase price of merchandise and commodities sold less trade discount
2. Transportation charges
3. Storage and delivery charges.

The actual cost is calculated by taking into account the opening and closing inventory and the total purchases.

GROSS PROFIT

The total net sales minus the cost of goods sold is represented as gross profit.

ABC Hotels Ltd.
Cigars And News Stand Schedule

	Current period
Revenue	₹ ....
Allowances	₹ ....
Net Sales	₹ ....
Cost of Goods Sold	....
Gross Profit (Loss)	₹ ....
Departmental Expenses	....
Salaries and Wages	₹ ....
Employees' benefits	....
Total Payroll Taxes and Employee Benefits	....
Total Payroll and Related Expenses	₹ ....
Other Expenses	
Commission on Sales	₹ ....
Matches	....
Miscellaneous	....
Printing and Stationery	....
Total other Expenses	₹ ....
Total Expenses	₹ ....
Departmental Income (Loss)	₹ ....

Note : Various arrangements of additional columns for comparisons and percentages could be added.

Fig. 11.18 : Analysis of Income and Expenses of Cigars and News Stand

EXPENSES

Employees' Remuneration and Benefits : Salaries, wages and other benefits paid to the manager, sales clerk and inventory clerk is included under this head.

Employees; Meals : This account is charged with the cost of food and beverages furnished to employees of this department.

Commission on Sales : The commissions or other profit sharing remuneration paid to employees or others is debited to this account.

Outside Work : This account includes charges for work done by outside cleaning establishments for repairing and reweaving of clothing, repair of shoes, etc.

Printing and Stationery : All expenses relating to printing and stationary used by employees of this department are debited to this account. It includes cost of printed forms, service manuals, cigar lists, tickets, stationery and office supplies, cash register supplies etc.

Miscellaneous : It includes sundry items which are not distributable under other captions, such as :

1. Benzine
2. Cigar bags
3. Licences
4. Ribbon
5. Wrappers etc.
6. Cellophane
7. Delivery charges
8. Paper
9. Twine.

GIFT SHOPS AND SOUVENIRS

Sales from gift shops are recorded separately. These may include the sale of candies, confectioneries, mineral waters, soda, ice-cream, sandwiches, food products, novelties, fancy goods etc.

ACCOUNTING AUDIT AND CONTROL

REVENUE OF GIFT SHOPS

It includes the sales of various items such as :

1. Candies
2. Soda/mineral waters
3. Sandwiches
4. Novelties
5. Other commodities.
6. Confectioneries
7. Ice-cream
8. Food products
9. Fancy goods.

ALLOWANCES

It represents the rebates and overcharges adjusted at a subsequent date.

NET REVENUE

The total gross sale less allowances is known as net sales.

COST OF GOODS SOLD

Cost of goods sold includes :

1. Purchase price of merchandise, commodities and products less trade discount
2. Transportation charges
3. Storage and delivery charges

The amount is determined by taking into account the opening and closing inventory and the total purchases.

This account is also charged with the cost of food transferred to the gift shop from the hotel's kitchen. It may also include charges such as carbonated gas, the cost of boxing candy and the tax on candy.

GROSS PROFIT

The cost of goods sold deducted from net sale represents the gross profit.

EXPENSES

Employees' Remuneration and Benefits : Salaries, wages and other benefits paid to employees of this department are included under this head. The employees include the manager, sales clerks, soda dispenser, bus boys, ware washers, messengers etc.

Employees' Meals : This account is debited with the cost of food furnished to the employees of this department.

Fig. 11.19 is a schedule for fountain and gift shop containing analysis of all income and expeneses of fountain and gift shop.

ABC Hotels Ltd.
Fountain and Gift Shop Schedule

	Current period
Revenue	₹ ....
Allowances	....
Net Revenue	₹ ....
Cost of Merchandise Sold	....
Gross Profit (Loss)	....
Expenses	....
Salaries and Wages	₹ ....
Employees' Meals	....
Employee Benefits	....
Total Payroll and Related Expenses ;	₹ ....
Other Expenses	....
Operating Supplies	₹ ....
China and Glassware	....
Laundry	....
Linen	....
Miscellaneous	....
Printing and Stationery	....
Silver	....
Uniforms	....
Total Other Expenses	₹ ....
Total Expenses	₹ ....
Departmental Income (Loss)	₹ ....

Note : Various arrangements of additional columns for comparisons and percentages could be added.

Fig. 11.19 : Analysis of Income and Expenses of Fountain and Gift Shop

China and glassware : The charges of these items are treated in the same way as similar title in the food department.

Laundry : The account is debited with the cost of laundry as designated by bills of outside laundries are chargeable to this account.

Linen : The charges to this account should be handled in the same manner as the similar title in the food and beverages department.

Paper Supplies : The items included under this head are similar title as in the food department schedule.

Printing and Stationery : The cost of items whether purchased from outside printing concerns or produced by the print shop should be charged to this account when used by employees of this department. These items are:

1. Cost of printed forms
2. Service manuals
3. Stationery and office supplies.

Silver : The charges to this account should be handled in the same manner as described in the account of similar title in the food department schedule.

Uniforms : The charges to this account should be handled in the same manner as described in the account of similar title in the food and beverages department schedule.

Miscellaneous : Items which are not distributable under other captions, including delivery charges, signs, rock salt, twine or other expenses peculiar to this department.

BARBER SHOP / HAIR DRESSING SALOON

Hair dressing saloon or barber shop is one of the minor revenue producing departments of a hotel. In some hotels, this department does only cash business. The barber or cashier collects from the customers and records all sales on the cash register. The charges for manicure service and shoe shine are recorded on the same check but shown separately so that the sales can be properly analysed. The cashier enters all the checks on the alysis sheet.

In addition to a fixed salary, the barber and manicurists are paid a certain part of their sale above a fixed amount. Each barber is credited only with the amounts earned for his services. Charges for shoe-shine and occasional sale of tonics and other supplied should be listed separately, as the barbers do not receive any part of such sales. (Ref. Fig. 11.20)

ACCOUNT AUDIT AND CONTROL

REVENUE

Revenue from Services : This section provides number of services to the guests. These include services of barbers, chiropodists, boot blacks and manicurists and other beauty parlour services.

Sale of Merchandise : Sale proceed from brushes, combs, cosmetics, lotions, tonics etc. are credited under this head.

COST OF MERCHANDISE SOLD

This is computed as follows :

1. Cost of merchandise less trade discount
2. Cost of transportation
3. Storage and delivery charges.

The actual amount is calculated by this value of inventory at the beginning of the period plus total purchases less closing inventory.

GROSS PROFIT AND MERCHANDISE SALES

It is the balance after dedicating the cost of merchandise sold from thesales.

EXPENSES

Employees' remuneration and benefits :

Salaries, wages and other benefits paid to employees of this department are debited to this account. The employees include are :

1. Barbers
2. Cashiers
3. Chiropodists
4. Coat rack attendants
5. Manicurists
6. Clerk
7. Boot blacks.

Employees' Meals : All cost of food and beverages furnished to employees of this department are debited to this account.

Cleaning Supplies : All expenses relating to cleaning supplies applicable to this section should be debited to this head.

Laundry : The cost of laundry chargeable to this department should be debited to this account.

Linen : The term to linen charges should be debited in the same manner as linen charges of room department.

Operating supplies : It includes are :

1. Alum
2. Brushers
3. Cloth brushers
4. Cosmetics
5. Fruits
6. Hones
7. Lotions
8. Powders
9. Scissors
10. Shoe clothes
11. Shoe polish
12. Tweezers
13. Boot black supplies
14. Clippers
15. Combs
16. Eggs
17. Hair brushes
18. Licences
19. Oils
20. Razors
21. Shoe brushers
22. Soaps
23. Tonics
24. Vibrators.

Printing and stationery : Cost of printing and stationery used by this section when purchased from outside printing concerns or produced by the hotel's print shop, are charged to this account when used by the employees of this department :

1. Printed forms
2. Vouchers
3. Stationery
4. Service manuals
5. Envelopes
6. Office supplies.

Uniforms : Cost of uniforms and repairing and cleaning of uniforms used by the employees.

Miscellaneous : Any other items of expenses not distributable under other captions.

Fig. 11.21 is a schedule for Barber shop indicating analyses of all income cave expenses of Barber shop.

ABC Hotels Ltd.
Barber Shop Schedule

	Current period
Revenue from Services	₹ ....
Pales of Merchandise	₹ ....
Dst of Merchandise Sold	....
Gross Profit on Merchandise Sales	₹ ....
Total Income	....
Expenses	....
Salaries and Wages	₹ ....
Employees' Benefits	....
Total Payroll Taxes and Employee Benefits	....
Total Payroll and Related Expenses	₹ ....
Other Expenses	....
Cleaning Supplies	₹ ....
Laundry	....
Linen	....
Miscellaneous	....
Operating Supplies	....
Printing and Stationery	....
Uniforms	....
Total Other Expense	₹ ....
Total Expenses	₹ ....
Wrtmental Income (Loss)	₹ ....

Note : Various arrangements of additional columns for comparison and percentages could be added.

Fig. 11.20 : Analysis of Income and Expenses of Barber Shop

BEAUTY PARLOUR

In most of the deluxe hotels beauty parlour is one of the main source [income. Income from hair dressing saloon, chiropodists, manicurists, and eurs are recorded separately.

REVENUE FROM SERVICES

It includes the amount received from the various services rendered to guests :

1. Hair cutters
2. Manicurists
3. Chiropodists
4. Masseurs

SALES OF MERCHANDISE

It includes the receipts from sale of brushes, combs, cosmetics, lotion. tonics etc.

COST OF MERCHANDISE SOLD

It includes :

1. The cost of merchandise less trade discount
2. Transportation charges

3. Storage and delivery charges.

The value of opening inventory, total purchase and closing inventor are taken into account to find out the cost of merchandise sold.

GROSS PROFIT ON MERCHANDISE SOLD

It is a difference between the sale of merchandise and cost of merchandise sold.

EXPENSES

Employees' remuneration and benefits : Salaries, wages and other benefits paid to employees of this department are debited to this account :

1. Barbers
2. Cashiers
3. Coat rack attendants
4. Manicurists
5. Clerks.

Employees' Meals : Expenses relating to the cost of food and beverages furnished to the employees of this department are debited to this account.

Cleaning Supplies : Same as the cleaning charges of the Room Department.

Laundry : The expenses of laundry chargeable to this department as designated by bills of outside laundries are debited to this account.

Linen : The linen charges should be treated in the same manner as described in the account of similar title in the Room Department Schedule.

Operating supplies : It includes :

1. Alum
2. Clippers
3. Combs
4. Curlers
5. Fruits
6. Hair nets
7. Licences
8. Lotions
9. Powders
10. Razors
11. Tonics
12. Vibrators
13. Brushers
14. Cloth brushers
15. Cosmetics
16. Eggs
17. Hair brushes
18. Hair pins
19. Hones
20. Oils
21. Scissors
22. Soaps
23. Tweezers.

Printing and stationery : The cost of printing and stationery relating to the items whether purchased from outside printing concerns or produced by the hotel's print shop, when used by the employees of this department is to this head :

1. Cost of printed forms
2. Vouchers
3. Stationery
4. Service manuals
5. Envelopes
6. Office supplies.

Uniforms : Cost of uniforms and expenses relating to repairs and cleaning of uniforms used by this department.

Miscellaneous : It includes all such items and expenses which cannot be grouped under other captions.

ABC Hotels Ltd.
Beauty Parlour Schedule

This schedule is identical with BARBER SHOP schedule as given in Fig. 11.21.

Note: Various arrangements of additional columns for comparison and percentages could be added.

Fig. 11.21 : Analysis of Income and Expenses of Beauty Parlour

CONCIERGE

The concept of concierge has been traditionally practised in Europe. Now it is being introduced in all the reputed hotels. These hotels usually have concierge in the main lobby, but also have a person designated as a concierge' specifically for the upper level. In some of the hotels the bell captain also holds the concierge title. A concierge is the orchestrator who maintains control of the lobby, sets the tone of the hotel and monitors the mannerisms and habits of the individual employees. He sees that in every operations functions of hotel standards are maintained. He makes certain that the guest is not lost from sight after checking in. The concierge calls the guest to make certain that all is well and to find out if the guest has any requests.

The concierge provides directions to points of interest, recommends for restaurants or night clubs outside the hotel, armnges tickets to the tf and tours and other similar type of services. Most of the guests turn to concierge for any kind of service required.

Thus he assists guests with most problem concerning their acorn dation, takes keys when they leave the hotel and handle their mail, I concierge's log is more than a record of the converge actions, it is a *sums* of the activities in the hotel. Thus, the concierge has become part of the management structure of the hotel. With the growing sophistication of trveller and the increasing efforts of hotel to differntiate, in a competitive market the services of a concierge has become important to the hotel's position in its market.

In brief a concierge provides the following services :

1. Direction to point of interest
2. A recommendation for restaurants or night clubs outside theft
3. Ticket to the theatre
4. A run-down of the tour offered and tickets for them
5. The purchase of airline tickets
6. Other related services.

Thus, a concierge is the equivalent of the Superintendent of Service. He also works as an assistant manager, mail and information clerk, doorman and travel agent, so far as the functions of guest relations are concerned.

FLORIST / HORTICULTURE

An outside firm may be contracted to supply floral arrangen The house-keeper should make fully aware of the terms and condition of such contract. Large hotels have their own horticulture department managed by a Horticulture Manager with a number of supervisors, senior gardeners and gardeners. The composition of this department is given in Figs 11.22 and 11.23.

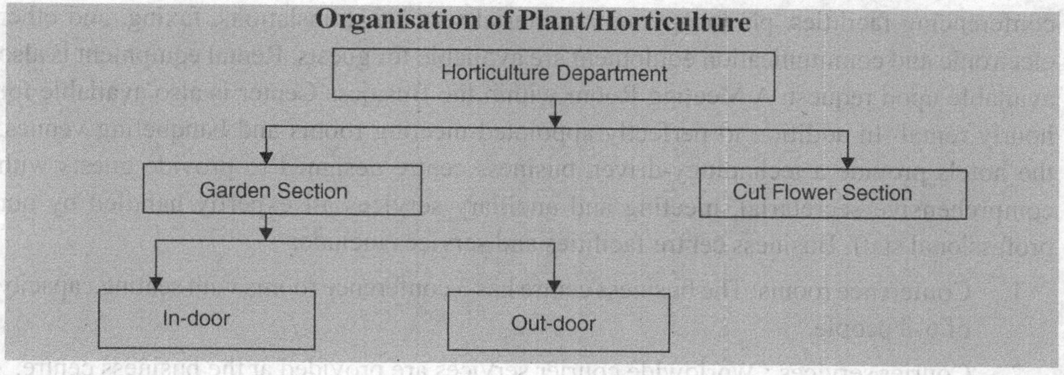

Fig. 11.22. Depicts the organisational structure of the department in a large hotel.

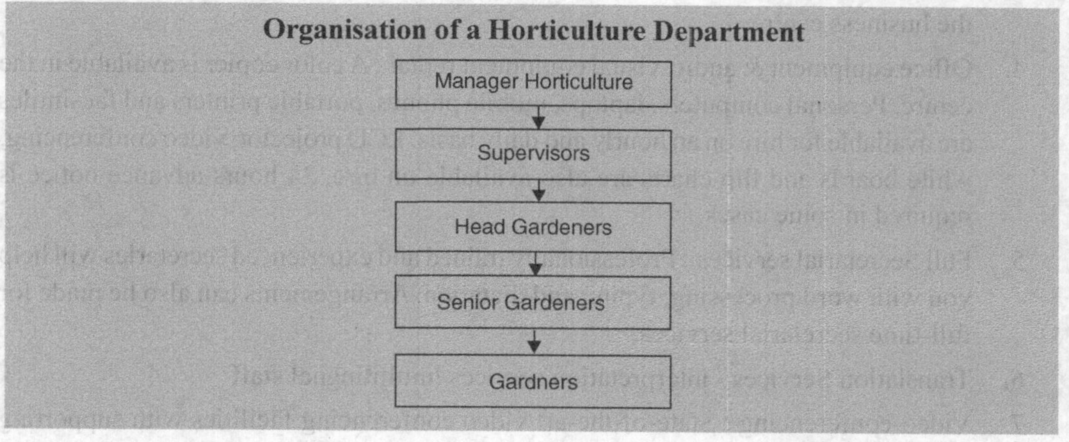

Fig. 11.23 : A Typical Organisation of a Horticulture Department

ENTERTANMENT AND RECREATION FACILITIES

On the basis of location and type of clientele, a hotel provides different of recreational facilities to its guests, such as

1. Golf
2. Horse riding
3. Cushions.
4. Tennis
5. Game rooms
6. Movies
7. Squash courts
8. Billiards

These services are managed by a manager for entertainment and recreation. He is responsible to keep the guest occupied in pleasurable activities and frequenton the spot checks and surprise audits are very essential procedure is required to control the revenue received from these activities and frequent on the spot checks and surprise audits are very essential in order to control the income.

SECRETARIAL ASSISTANCE AND BUSINESS CENTRE

Hotels may provide meeting and conference services to ensure the highest levels of creativity, convenience and efficiency for every business need and event. In addition to conference rooms, hotels may provide a 24-hour, technology-driven business centre. Video conferencing facilities, photocopying, secretarial services, translations, faxing, and other electronic and communication equipment are available for guests. Rental equipment is also available upon request. A Meeting Room within the Business Center is also available for hourly rental In addition to perfectly appointed meeting rooms and banqueting venues, the hotels provide a technology-driven business centre designed to provide guests with comprehensive secretarial, meeting and ancillary services all expertly handled by our professional staff. Business centre facilities and services include:

1. Conference rooms: The business centre has 3 conference rooms with seating capacity of 6-8 people.
2. Courier services : Worldwide courier services are provided at the business centre.
3. E-mail / internet : Access to high-speed broadband Internet and wi-fi is available at the business centre.
4. Office equipment & audio-visual equipment rental : A color copier is available in the centre. Personal computers, laptops, mobile phones, portable printers and facsimiles are available for hire on an hourly and daily basis. LCD projector, video conferencing, white boards and flip charts are also available on hire. 24 hours advance notice is required in some cases.
5. Full Secretarial services : Professionally trained and experienced secretaries will help you with word processing, typing and dictation. Arrangements can also be made for full-time secretarial services.
6. Translation Services / interpretation services /multilingual staff
7. Video-conferencing : State-of-the-art video conferencing facilities with supporting computer software as well as advanced Internet services are available at the business centre.
8. Telepresence: Some hotels provide video-conferencing facility for hotel public use.
9. Legal library : The business centre has a comprehensive legal library. Some hotels also have the SCC (Supreme court cases) online facility.
10. Telepresence: Some hotels provide video-conferencing facility for hotel public use.
11. Wi-fi cards : Just insert your wireless Internet card into a laptop and you can begin surfing from any location, be it in the hotel lobby or at the pool.

Thus, the business centre is available around the clock and offers:

(*a*) A private office

(*b*) Computer/ Fax facilities and services

(*c*) International news

(*d*) Photocopying facilities and services

(*e*) Shipping and receiving services

(*f*) Technology Butler

(*g*) High speed Internet access, both wired and wireless

(*h*) Facsimile
(*i*) Scanner
(*j*) Mac and IBM computers available
(*k*) Apple and Microsoft software available
(*l*) Workstations
(*m*) Secretarial services
(*n*) Full-service shipping and receiving office
(*o*) Notary Public at Concierge desk
(*p*) Electric current Voltage is generally /110-220.

Pix. 11.11 : A Business Center

CHECK ROOMS AND WASH ROOMS

It covers revenue received by the hotel from sources such as :

1. Coat rooms
2. Parcel rooms
3. Coin clocks
4. Shoe shining service
5. Weighingmachine
6. Vending machines in public lavatories.

In large hotels there is no fixed charge for checking coats but the revenue consists of gratuities from the guests. The coat room attendants receive fixed salaries and all cash collected by them goes to the hotel. In many hotels the coat room attendants are required to drop all receipts through a slot in the counter into a locked box.

In the coat rooms there is no fixed charge for checking coats and hats. The income of this room consists of gratuities from the guests. The attendants are paid fixed salaries and all cash collected by them goes to the hotel. The attendants are required to drop all receipts through a slot in the counter into a locked box. The income from the parcel room is of the same nature as that from coat rooms. There are the charges made for shoe shining service and a cash register is used for recording the receipts. The attandants are required to account only for the fixed charges and retain the gratuities. Coin locks in public lavatories are equipped with a counting device which show the number of coins dropped in. The cash is collected from the locks by head cashier accompanied by an assistant of the auditor who records the readings of the counting device. The cash from weighing and vending machines is collected in the same manner as that from coin locks. The nature of these personalised services is such that they never involve any charges to guest's account. A report for the sale is made at each point, which are varified by register readings wherever a cash register can be used.

Many hotels lease these personal services and thus receive a fixed income. In some hotels, the income from this source is insufficient to pay the salaries of the attendants, therefore, these attendants receive only a nominal fixed compensation and retain all gratuities.

ACCOUNTING AUDIT AND CONTROL

NET REVENUE

This account is credited with revenue derived from the following items:

1. Coat rooms
2. Coat racks
3. Parcel Checkrooms and washrooms
4. The collections from lock machines in public lavatories
5. Receipts from shoe-shining service

In case the checkrooms and washrooms are operated by a concessionaire, the expenses in connection therewith should be charged against the income received for the concession in the other Income Schedule. What there is no income, the expenses should be included in the room departmeiil expenses.

EXPENSES

Salaries and wages of the following employees are included :

1. Manager
2. Check form and washroom attendants
3. Boctblacks.

The account is also charged with vacation and holiday pay of these employees. Other amounts paid to employees such as bonus, severance pay, etc. may also be included. A proportion of payroll taxes, social insurance and other related expenses may also be grouped under this head.

EXPLOYEES' MEALS

This account should be charged with the cost of food furnished to employees of the checkrooms and washrooms.

Cleaning Supplies : The charges to this account should be handled in the same general manner as described in the account of similar title in the, room department schedule.

Guest Supplies : It includes the cost of toilet requisites supplied to guests in the washrooms, including paper towels.

Laundry : This head includes the cost of laundry chargeable to the checkrooms and washrooms, as designated by bills of outside laundries.

LINEN

The charges to this account should be handled in the same general manner as described in the account of similar title in the room department schedule.

MISCELLANEOUS

Items not distributable under other captions are grouped under this heads, such as,

1. Bootblack supplies
2. Clothes brushes
3. Coat hangers
4. Shoe brushes
5. Shoe clothes
6. Whisk brooms.

PRINTING AND STATIONERY

The cost of the following items whether purchased from outside printing concerns or produced by the hotel's print shop, when used by employees of the checkrooms and washrooms should be charged to this account :

1. Cost of printed forms
2. Cost of service manuals
3. Cost of vouchers
4. Cost of stationery and office supplies.

UNIFORMS

The cost of uniforms for employees of this department should be charged to this account. It also includes the cost of repairing and cleaning uniforms.

Fig. 11.24 is a schedule for check room and washroom containing analysis of all income and expressed check room and washrooms.

ABC Hotels Ltd.
Checkrooms And Washrooms

	Current period
Net Revenue	₹ ....
Expenses	
Salaries and Wages	₹ ....
Vacation and Holiday Pays	
Employee Benefits	....
Total Payroll and Related Expenses	₹ ....
Other Expenses	
Cleaning Supplies	₹ ....
Laundry	....
Linen	....
Miscellaneous	....
Printing and Stationery	....
Uniforms	....
Total Other Expenses	₹ ....
Total Expenses	₹ ....
Departmental Income (Loss)	₹ ....

Note : Various arrangements of additional columns for comparisons and percentages could be added.

Fig. 11.24 : Analysis of Income and Expenses of Checkrooms and Washrooms

BANQUETS, FUNCTIONS, CONFERENCES, CONVENTIONS AND EXHIBITIONS

Banqueting or functional catering may be defined as the service of special functions for specific group of people at specific times, the food and beverage being predetermined. In a small hotel where there are fewer functions, the functions normally take place in a room set aside for the purpose, The hotel manager or assistant manager is responsible for all such functions He may employ the banqueting staff on casual basis. In large hotels, banqueting or function forms the most important activities. All functions take place with-in the banqueting suite or banqueting halls. The Banqueting Manager has the administrative control of all such functions. In addition, theremay be one or two assistant banqueting head waiters, a dispensing barman and a secretary to the banqueting manager.

Banqueting and functions are getting interestingly popular and their style and purpose are changing specially because of the high sophistication in tastes and higher standards of food and comfort demanded by guests.

Pix. 11.12 : Preparation for a Banquet

The functions may be categorised as follows :—

1. Banquest (formal meals)
   (*i*) Luncheon—company, clubs etc.
   (*ii*) Diners
   (*iii*) Wedding break-fasts.
2. Buffet Receptions
   (*i*) Wedding receptions
   (*ii*) Cooktail parties
   (*iii*) Buffet teas
   (*iv*) Dances
   (*v*) Anniversary parties
   (*vi*) Conference—National, international seminars, training courses.

A detailed break-up of functions could be as follows :

1. Social Function:
   (*i*) Dinners
   (*ii*) Cooktail parties
   (*iii*) Lencheons
   (*iv*) Charity performance
   (*v*) Reception
   (*vi*) Fashion shows
   (*vii*) Rentals
   (*viii*) Balls.
2. Conferences/Functions
   (*i*) Political conference
   (*ii*) Trade union conference
   (*iii*) National sales conference
   (*iv*) International conferences
3. Public Relation Functions :
   (*i*) Press parties to launch a new product t Fashion parade
   (*ii*) Dealers' meeting
   (*iii*) Seminars
   (*iv*) Exhibitions.
4. State Banquets :
   (*i*) Intra-governmental for head of states
   (*ii*) Inter-governmental for head of states
   (*iii*) National Days.

Income from the banquet varies from hotel to hotel. The usual method of dealing with the sales in connection with banquets and selling parties is to record it in the respective selling departments. In case there are some banquet sales of goods and services not sold in the ordinary course of business by any selling department of the hotel, there are two alternatives to deal with such sales :

Pix. 11.13 : Preparation for Banqueting

In case of occasional banquet sales are of negligible amount: The amount is credited to the various expenses account to which the cost should be charged. For example, revenue earned from sale of music should be credited to music and entertainment account. There may be some other expenses/cost of goods and services sold in connection with banquets, which are not applicable to any expensive item in food schedule, these may be debited to banquet expenses account and the relative sales are also credited to same account.

If the banquet sales are of large amount: A separate banquet income account is opened. The profit/loss is calculated and the same is carried over to the food schedule as 'sundry banquet income'.

ORGANISATION

BANQUET MANAGER/DIRECTOR OF BANQUET SERVICE

A banquet manager must have thorough knowledge of banqueting, banquet booking, banqueting facilities, scope, menu and price structure, type of banquet layouts and equipment, furniture and fixtures. He must have the number of service personnel required for varied functions and services. His duties and responsibilities include :

1. Supervision of banquet services
2. Motivation of the staff
3. Organisation of banquet service
4. Menus and price structure
5. Guest comments and complaints
6. Coordination with house-keeping, kitchen stewarding, F & B control and kitchen
7. Banquet facilities and optimum utilisations of the same
8. Public relations
9. Banquet selling— personnel mail, advertisement, contact with embassies, high commission and study of regular clients
10. Liaison with excise personnel regarding
11. Maintenance of banquet functions, history files.

DIRECTOR OF CATERING/CATERING MANAGER

He should be a good administrator and be able to sell. Many individual start in the sales department and later transferred to the catering department. Some have general hotel management background but all should have a food and beverage background. In addition to administrative duties, this department is required to do revenue forecasting, preparation of sales reports and marketing plans. In order to sell food and beverages effectively, knowledge of food and beverages is needed. Hotels have to practise of having printed suggested menus i.e. canned menus, which offer many choices and possible combinations. The tastomers could be advised in the selection of choices, as per the capabilities of the kitchen, seasonal availability of items, the service limitations, the availability of equipment, etc. In brief the director of catering , is responsible for :

1. Sales figures
2. Labour costs
3. Food costs
4. Marketing plans
5. Strict observance of all safety regulations with special emphasis on fire regulations
6. General upkeep of all function space and for scheduling repairs
7. Maintaining strong support with all department heads in the food and beverages department, specially the Executive Chef
8. Suggesting interesting menus to the customers
9. Administrative work of his department
10. Selling of food and beverages.

FUNCTION/BANQUET SALES MANAGER

He should have a hotel sales and food and beverages background. He assists the director of catering. In large hotels, the banquet sales manager tend to specialise. Each manager may specialise in different menus such as:

1. Commercial business :
   (*i*) Meetings
   (*ii*) Trade shows
   (*iii*) Seminars.
2. Large social dinners.

The function sales manager is responsible for the sale of banqueting facilities of the hotel. He makes the initial approach and contact and refers the client to the banqueting manager. He must have an extensive knowledge of accommodation of space, locations, size, light switches, electric points, height of doorways, maximum floor load etc. The client is usually given a well presented booklet containing menus and price range pi as all details about the faciliites available in the hotel. He should have photograph of the various table lay-outs for different members.

BANQUET/CONFERENCE MANAGER

He is the administrative head for all the banquet and functions such as:

1. The meeting of prospective clients
2. Discussing arrangements with the clients concerning menus, table plans, costs, wines, bands, toast master and soon.
3. Once the booking is confirmed, he should note down the following points :
   (*i*) Type of function
   (*ii*) Date
   (*iii*) Time
   (*iv*) Number of covers (final number 24-72 hours before)
   (*v*) Price per head
   (*vi*) Name and method of service
   (*vii*) Wines inclusive on cash
   (*viii*) Type of organisation
   (*ix*) Table plan.

4. To decide about
   (*i*) Toast mater
   (*ii*) Band, cabaret, dancing
   (*iii*) Plan card
   (*iv*) Seating plans
   (*v*) Type of menus of printing-format,
   (*vi*) Special information : vegetarian, non-vegetarian, ethnics etc.

In addition to above a check list of the following requirements should be prepared :

(*i*) List of toast-who is proposing ? Who is replying ?
(*ii*) Floral decoration—tables, room reception areas, button holes
(*iii*) Audio-visual equipment required
(*iv*) Special licence—occasional licence
(*v*) Fraindises
(*vi*) Car parking
(*vii*) Cloakrooms
(*viii*) Artists
(*ix*) Changing rooms
(*x*) Cigars and Cigarattes
(*xi*) Accommodation
(*xii*) Telephones
(*xiii*) Special light arrangement
(*xiv*) Lectern
(*xv*) Secrectaria! facilities
(*xvi*) Syndicate rooms
(*xvii*) Photographers
(*xviii*) Sign posting
(*xix*) Private bar facilities
(*xx*) Function
(*xxi*) Date of final inspection by client
(*xxii*) Security
(*xxiii*) Marketing—press briefing and realease.

SECRETARY

She/he works with the banquet manager and is responsible for :

1. Handling al incoming and outgoing mails.
2. To send the dictated menus to the appropriate department
3. Take provisional bookings for functions in the absence of banquet manager and enter all details in banquet memorandum
4. Handle all telephone calls
5. Correct filling of all documents/correspondence.

BANQUET CAPTAIN

He assists the director of banquet service. He supervises the service operation. In large functions, one captain and floor captains are put incharge of a specific function, who work closely with the client in all aspects of service, timings and other requests. Captains rely on the information received from the floor captain when co-ordinating the plating of the food with the banquet Chef. Floor captain conducts an informal head count at the beginning of the meal in order to have the right amount of portions prepared.

BANQUET HEAD WAITER/SUPERVISOR

He is incharge of banqueting suites and the organisation required to prepare for various form of functions. He is responsible for the following:

1. The engagement staff on casual basis
2. To cover the various duties at the function
3. To have a list of names and address and telephone numbers of the best casual staff and ensure that they are well employed.

Their duties and responsibilities are :

1. To allocate bar staff for stock of various functions
2. The setting up of bars
3. The organisation of bar staff
4. Control of stock and cash during service
5. Stock taking of stock and cash on completion of network
6. To do the restocking of the banquet dispence bar.

BANQUETING HEAD WINE WAITER

He works in conjuction with the dispence bar staff. If hotel has no permanent dispence bar staff, the responsibilities and duties of banquet head waiter are same as that of dispence bar staff.

PERMANENT WAITING *STAFF/CHEF DE RANG*

These are experienced *Chef de rang.* They can handle any jobs concerning banqueting, most of the *mise en place* before the function (the laying of the table is done by the *Chef de Rang).* Their main job during the service is the wine waiting. They may aso help to clear after the wine servicing is completed.

BANQUET SERVERS

They have a difficult job which is hard and hectic. They are always on call. They perform individual jobs or functions.

MEETING ROOM ATTENDANTS

They handle smaller service functions such as coffee breaks, supply of materials, and ice water etc.

BANQUET ROOM ATTENDANTS/HOUSE-MEN

The cardinal rule of the catering department is that the room must be cleaned and set up after every party, regardless of when the function ends. Therefore, the work of these attendants is physically very hard. They move carpets and furniture to change a function room from a meeting to a ball room.

TECHNICIANS

The catering department requires audio equipment. Audio equipment service is crucial for the success of a meeting. Many hotels provide these services through an outside contractor. In case the hotel has equipment built-in or own the equipment, the audio equipment technician is a hotel employee.

CASUAL STAFF

The number of casual staff to be employed will depened upon the size of the function. They report few hours before the function commences. They are allocated stations and briefed with regard the procedure for serving of a particular function. As soon as the function is over they are paid off.

PORTERS

Hotels with banqueting facilities require two or three permanent porters in banqueting in their staff. They are essential staff. A great deal of heavy work is reouired during banqueting/ functions.

BANQUET FUNCTION

A large part of hotel business is concerned with letting room for varies types of functions. This is a direct source of revenue and intends to increase revenue from other hotel facilities such as guestrooms, bars and restaurant It ensures greater utilization of kitchens, engineering plant and staff. Room intended for this purpose are usually designed to the multi-functional to sure frequent use and justify the high cost of providing the space. A la oom may be adapted as a ball room, banquet hall, convention or exhibn hall. To provide even further flexibility the room may be divided by sepa partitions into smaller areas providing accommodation for a number of m ings or functions held at the same time.

In planning for multi-functional use of rooms consider the follow important factors :

1. Additional car parking space
2. Access and circulation routes, including fire safety requirement
3. Clockrooms and toilet facilities
4. Entrance foyer, provision of drink and other service
5. Space determination for different uses
6. Method of dividing rooms, standards of sound insulation
7. Separation of public access for each area
8. Service facilities and staff access to each area

9. Storage for furniture, carpets and special equipment
10. Stacking and handling feature of chairs and tables
11. Storage for china, utensils, serving equipment and trolleys
12. Engineering plant services, environmental control
13. Communication equipment, telephone connections, music and paging.
14. Construction features and acoustic design
15. Dance floor provision, security and protection
16. Exhibition and projection services
17. Water, drainage, gas and electricity services
18. Music and amplification control, local sand systems
19. Closed circuit television and cine projection
20. Band stand and stage provisions (permanent or temporary)
21. Changing rooms, access for speakers or performers
22. Translation, press and reporting both facilities
23. Access for exhibition or other equipment such as vehicles, etc.
24. Legal requirement for fire and user safety.

MEETING ROOMS

Requirements for meeting rooms usually depend on external demand and are influenced by the character and location of the hotel. These rooms are multi-functional, being used for business activties, lectures, private parties, meetings of societies and many other purposes. The need is for arrangement of furniture and facilities, including built-in audio-visual aids equipment, adjustable engineering services, large furniture storage areas and efficient food and beverage services. To provide flexibility, a larger room may be divisible by sliding or folding partitions into separate areas, each self-contained and having a separate entrace and independent service facilities. The division of rooms in this way is an expensive investment.

Pix 11.14 : A Meeting Room

Movable portion must provide a high degree of sound insulation and this involves special attention to the design of panels, joints and supports. In additon, lghting, air-conditioning, sound systems and other engineering services must be capable of separate operation and control with provision for balancing when the room condition change. The advantages of room division by movable partitions include wide range of room sizes made available common storage, kitchen service, and engineering facilities and easy control and management.

One method of increasing space utilization is to combine daytime use of rooms for small business meetings etc. Rooms for multiple purposes must be larger than normal guestrooms and provide facility for family use during vacation periods. The room must be easily converted with minimum of effort and disturbance features such as sliding or swivelling bed recesses, convertible divans, closets for desks and furniture may also considered.

Meeting room must be conveniently and directly accessible from hotel lobby without any need to pass through the guest reception area. Large function rooms be situated at or near the street and may be approached through stairs or escalators leading directly to the entrance foyer. Smaller rooms may be near the main elevator service and located on one or several floors. Separation from the guestrooms is important to facilitate management and reduce noise disturbance. Clear sign posting and direction control is essential and this should also apply at the main or secondary entrances and at the car park.

The requirement of cloak rooms, toilets and entrance areas will depend on the number involved on location and on the relative importance of function/business. Meeting rooms may have individual cloak rooms and toilets or use the facilities provided elsewhere such as near main lobby, restaurant approaches, etc.

An entrance foyer is usually necessary to provide a reception area. If required provision may be made for various services such as cocktails, coffee etc., to supplement functions.

These rooms should be designed for multipurpose use and a natural decor with minimum ornamentation is usually adopted. Walls are often pannelled to allow access to service voids and suspended ceilings are necessary to accommodate the engineering services. Ceiling heights should be at least 2,750 mm (9ft.). Depending on size and access, the ceiling construction may be plastered or acoustic tiled and paneled. Recessed light fittings, ventilation grilles and deflectors, speaker panels and automatic fire detector and sprinkler equipment will usually need to be built into ceiling. Wall construction will involve a combination of different materials to provide a balanced decor, acoustic properties, noise insulation, resistance to impact and scraping.

An important aspect of de-sign involves sand control which may have noise attenuation and noise insulation. Space allocations per person depend on the size and use of the room and furniture layout. Special attention should be paid for engineering services such as ventilation and air-conditioning, lighting and communication.

Tables will usually be rectangular with provision for linking together to meet banquet needs. In large rooms some circular tables may also be provided. Seat spacing is usually based on width of 600 mm (2ft) per diner. To allow easy arrangement and storage furniture should be :

1. Light weight but strong
2. Fitted with protective ends to legs
3. Stockable into mobile carrier, if possible
4. Inter-changeable
5. Replaceable
6. Linkable to form rows
7. Resistant to marking
8. Durable resisting, scraping and impact
9. Styled to suit character of room and hotel.

Furniture requirement will also include serving trolleys and mobile side boards and other meal sources equipment. There is also a need to install a temporary bar either in the meeting room or on the entrance foyer. Carpet and furnishing are movable.

Special requirements of meeting room include :

1. Dance floor
2. Stag, band stand, or dais
3. Audio visual aids equipment
   (*i*) Cine projection for 8 mm and/or 6 mm with remote control
   (*ii*) Slide projector with remote control and tape/speaker extension
   (*iii*) Projection screen
   (*iv*) Portable microphone connections
   (*v*) Tape and disc connections
   (*vi*) Chalk board, pin board and-display board
   (*vii*) Remote lighting control and dimming
   (*viii*) Portable closed circuit TV camera and projection equipment.

CONVENTION HALLS

The principles as. applied to meeting rooms are also applicable to large halls, balls, banquets, conventions, exhibitions and other large-scale facilities This provision may be

Pix 11.15 : Banqueting

Pix 11.16 : A Convention and Gathering

made within the hotel and be of sufficient size to accommodate the delegates and visitors or as a part of a larger complex. Direct access for public users is essential and access requirements for food and beverage services and for exhibition or stage material must be determined. Stringent legal requirements will apply to places of assembly and multiple fire exits will normally be stipulated.

Public cloakroom, toilets and powder room facilities must be designed to meet the intensive peak periods of use before, after and during intervals of an event without creating conjestion in the rooms or in adjacent circulation areas.

The entrance foyer serves many purposes such as a gathering and waiting area, for cocktail and bar service, for coffee and light refreshments and as a social annexe. An area between one-tenth (l/10th) and one-third (1/3rd) of the main hall is usually allocated for this purpose, the latter including entrance corridor and circulation areas. Provision be made for :

1. Cocktail bar and storage
2. Coffee bar, meal service
3. Separation and direction
4. Illumination signs
5. Noise reduction
6. Air-conditioning
7. Lighting
8. Fire safety
9. Emergency lighting
10. Sound systems.

The entrance and exit doors must be suitably positioned, proportioned and protected. Special attention should be given to location and positioning of the main entrance door, exit doors and service doors.

Division by movable partitions is usually warranted to provide for flexibility in size and use. A ceiling height of at least 4600 mm (15 ft) is normally required. In addition to general engineering equipment and fittings, separate booths or cubicles for slide and cine projection must be provided and the separation must meet local fire and safety code requirements. This also applies to storage and operating areas. Other storage space will be required for audio-visual and equipment furniture and the tableware and utensils required Jor banquets or functions in the area. Electric installations, lighting, commu-ations and mechanical servic. es need special attention. For furniture same isiderations apply as for meeting rooms. For ball room use, large spring floor is required.

The planning of furniture layouts should be related to service entrances. The service entrances must

1. Provide baffling for kitchen and party activity and noise
2. Minimise distraction
3. Suits decor of room
4. Be positioned to minimise crossing of room and interruption of speeches.

CONFERENCES AND BANQUETS

The success or failure of any conference or banquet in a hotel must ulsy depend on the quality of the speakers, the amount of help or in-tion and the degree of learning which participants received. All these ents are out of the control of hotel management.

ARRANGEMENT FOR CONFERENCE

The more thought and care be given to the arrangements for receiving and treating conference guests and to the efficiency and care given to the set-up of the conference area. The organisers and leaders of such meetings are likely to be impressed with the fact that the hotel staff knows what they are doing. Confidence in the smooth running of these arrangements will doubtedly lead to more business in the future.

You must prepare a checklist of the sort of information which will be i needed from the conference organisers in order that a systematic plan of campaign can be set up. The checklist given below may serve as a basic guide which may need to be augmented by details which will vary with the domestic needs and arrangements of individual hotels:

CHECKLIST FOR INFORMATION

1. Dates to be set
   (*i*) Majority of group arrive
   (*ii*) Majority of group leave
   (*iii*) Late arrivals
   (*iv*) Release of reserved room not taken up.
2. Attendance to be ascertained
   (*i*) Total number of guests expected, plus wives and children, if any
   (*ii*) Total number of conference members
   (*iii*) Total number of wives
   (*iv*) Total number of children (if any)

(*v*) Grand total of those attending the meetings to include organisers, receptionists, speakers or other conference visitors.

3. Sleeping accommodation to be ascertained
   (*i*) Number of double rooms with bath
   (*ii*) Number of double rooms without bath
   (*iii*) Number of single rooms with bath
   (*iv*) Number of single rooms without bath
   (*v*) Number of suites.
4. Meeting requirements and equipment
   (*i*) Conference room(s)
   (*ii*) Annexe(s)
   (*iii*) Cloakroom(s)
   (*iv*) Changing room(s)
   (*v*) Number of tables
   (*vi*) Number of chairs
   (*vii*) Notices/flags/banners
   (*viii*) Flowers/plants
   (*ix*) Microphone
   (*x*) Projector or other visual aids
   (*xi*) Ash trays
   (*xii*) Paper, pencils, notepads etc.
   (*xiii*) Lectern
   (*xiv*) Platform
   (*xv*) Carpet.
5. Organisation of food and beverages and other breaks
   (*i*) Menu sections
   (*ii*) Members per table
   (*iii*) Shape of tables
   (*iv*) Bar facilities
   (*v*) Appetisers with drinks
   (*vi*) Tea/coffee facilities
   (*vii*) Starting and finishing times of meals and breaks
   (*viii*) Place of meals and breaks.
6. Basic costs
   (*i*) Double rooms with bath
   (*ii*) Double rooms without bath
   (*iii*) Single rooms with bath
   (*iv*) Single rooms without bath
   (*v*) Suites
   (*vi*) Children's rates

(*vii*) Conference Room(s)

(*viii*) Additional rooms (i.e. changing rooms etc.)

(*ix*) Garaging

(*x*) Drinks ("by the drink" or "by the bottle")

(*xi*) Main meals

(*xii*) Coffee/Tea.

7. Other services to be costed

(*i*) Provision of special equipment, i.e. projector, typewriters, microphone etc.

(*ii*) Provision of personnel for servicing of above

(*iii*) Provision of flowers

(*iv*) Complimentary meals and/or accommodation

(*v*) Sign/place cards

(*vi*) Cigarettes, if requested

(*vii*) Gratuities.

8. General information

The hotel should be prepared to make suggestions and arrangements for the entertainment of wives and possibly children, if and when they attend conferences with their husbands. In this connection, it would be helpful to have a list of facilities which are available in the area, to hand to the conference organiser. The sort of information to be listed would be:

(*i*) Shops and stores of special interest near by

(*ii*) Restaurant facilities

(*iii*) Theatre and cinema programmes

(*iv*) Any special exhibition or event in the area

(*v*) Bus or other transport facilities available

(*vi*) Taxi firms

(*vii*) Special tours

(*viii*) Baby sitting facilities (where necessary)

(*ix*) Availability of guides.

On occasions it may be possible for hotel to arrange a special event, such as a fashion show within the hotel. Opportunities for promotion of this nature can be a means of increasing income from the conference.

THE CONFERENCE ROOM

The organisation of conference facilities means that the hotel has to consider the needs of a special sort of guest — a guest who is on the premises in the role of a student to study, listen and absorb information.

A good conference room will never of itself result in learning something more quickly. The physical surroundings do have a marked effect on the responses of students, whatever their age.

You shculd select and equip a room which will ensure a comfortable, awake audience, not distracted by outside disturbances, undue extremes of temperature or inconvenient tables and uncomfortable chairs. The room should be pleasing to the eye, comfortable to be in and above all flexible. Symbols and clues which could remind the adult student of school days should be kept to a minimum.

The size of the room select will depend on the maximum number of participants at the conference. A room which at first sight may appear to be too large should not be rejected out of hand for although small groups could feel uncomfortable in a very large room as uncomfortable in fact as a group that is over-crowded in a small room. Conditions can always be improved by the use of screens or curtains to partition off to the right size. There is nothing which can be done with a room that is too small, other than reduce the number of residents/students/guests.

SERVICES

The ideal conference room would preferably be windowless, artificially lighted and air-conditioned and the following points will indicate why this should be so. It amounts to the fact that the speaker or instructor can then control all these factors.

WINDOWS

The attention of participants at any lecture or meeting will tend to move to the light source-the window. Attention be diverted when there is something esle to look at outside these windows—other activities causing movement and noise will be a most disturbing influence, so it is for this reason that curtains or blinds should be pulledxiver existing windows to allow for greater concentration.

LIGHTING

A professional lighting specialist be employed to advise on the types and placement of light fittings. The minimum requirement in this respect is an adequate number of electric points in convenient place. Extension cords are a nuisance and dangerous. People can trip over them and valuable equipment toppled and broken. All light switches should be located for the conference organiser, labelled and checked just before the meeting.

Check on doors to see that when people come in or go out during a film or slide presentation, the light from the open door does not fall directly on the picture. A screen or curtain would be sufficient to overcome any difficulties in this respect.

Keep light fittings as simple as possible. Fussy design or an attempt to be too clever in the grouping of light fittings is likely to cause distraction.

The eye is always drawn to either the highest luminous point or the one which has the highest colour intensity. Therefore, it is important that the speaker should be illuminated and seen against a very simple background which is preferably darker than the rest of the room. Beware of a concentration of light, if, which can cause glare, forcing the speaker to step aside to avoid this painful experience or give his talk in some discomfort. It is a simple matter to shield or cover the light source.

HEATING

The success of any central heating plan or any other form of heating is not to know that it is operating. The noise of a bad air-conditioning or heating system in operation can be very disturbing. People initially react favourably to a sound which indicates that something is happening to ensure their comfort.

There should be proper air-conditioning to control the 'climate' of the room and to give constancy to the temperature, especially bearing in mind the fact that there will be occasions when what windows are there, are either covered to cut out outside goings-on, or blacked out for the projection of films.

An audience will be more responsive mentally if they are seated in a slightly lower than normal temperature, the temperature of the air plus five degrees Fahrenheit is considered suitable. There should be an awareness of a flow of air across the room, or at least a movement of air. A 'warm day in spring' perfectly exemplifies the conditions which should exist.

The duty manager should constantly check the temperature especially after lunch when a return from a meal or a drinking spree at the bar would tend to raise body temperatures, so that a cooler room would be more comfortable. After a tea-break at the end of the day, a few degree warmer would be comforting.

NOISE CONTROL

There are no means of measuring the degree of annoyance caused by sound. In order to help concentration it is important that distractions such as typewriters, lift operations, constant door openings and closing and people walking about or talking, are cut down to a minimum.

Noises which are continuous or recurrent and do not change in frequency do not necessarily form a distraction for the mind adapts to them and finally accepts them. This is better than the creation of a sound-proof room which could be rather frightening in its lifelesseness.

COLOUR

The effect of colour on human being is the subject of much study. Every individual has a very personal attitude towards it and, therefore, a wise policy would be to 'play safe' by choosing pastel shades and plain fabrics for curtains and coverings. Patterned materials can be very disturbing and distracting.

CHAIRS

Chairs should be comfortable with semi-padded seating but without I hard front edge. They should not be very comfortable, otherwise they induce sleepiness. There is a case for a special chair for the lecturer which should be covered in a brighter coloured fabric to keep him the important target in the audience's field of vision.

Consideration should be given to chairs of the stacking kind so that the room may be more easily cleared when it is necessary to set up display equipment. Accommodate some of the large visual aids used in training, or even on occasions have a session which calls for some audience participation.

TABLES

Flat-topped tables of uniform size are better than one or two large ones. They can be arranged in a *greater* variety of ways. Check that the tables are of light weight material; possibly of the folding kind; that there are no obstructions for the knees and that ideally they have a rod underneath for the feet to rest on.

The professional-looking student desk is comfortable and practical. The combination of relaxed seating and note-taking at the slightly angled top of some of the desk tops is combined with a lightweight, sturdy and effcient piece of equipment.

DISPLAY MATERIAL

Make as much pin-up space as possible around the walls of the room. Ply-backed felt squares and ordinary peg board are ideal surfaces on which to pin and hang display material.

PLATFORM

Have a raised speaker's platform available. Apart from the advantage of being able to see a lecturer, some of the problems governing sound direction are overcome. Sound travels across a room and decreases towards the back and as the ceiling acts as a conductor of sound it is obvious that the nearer the speaker is to the ceiling, the better will the audience at the back of the room be able to hear.

GENERAL

The lay-out of the room in which the meetings are to be held should be discussed and planned beforehand. It is not always appropriate to have a theatre-style arrangement as the delegates may be expected to split into working groups around separate tables or partake in a more general discussion around a conference table.

A series of diagrams of seating arrangements should be drawn up and checked with the conference leader before each meeting. For detailed study on planning and arranging conferences and banquet refer the case study of Taj Mahal Hotel, New Delhi, as given in Appendix J.

Further points for checking are, therefore :

1. Seating arrangement :
   (*i*) School-style with tables
   (*ii*) U-shaped conference table
   (*iii*) Theatre-style
   (*iv*) Top tables and for how many persons.
2. Size of Conference Room:
   (*i*) Length
   (*ii*) Width
   (*iii*) Height.

   Is this adequate (comfortable) for the group, if seated as required?

   (*i*) Is there space in Conference Room for coffee and tea break service, or will it be served in an outside area or room?
   (*ii*) When may all necessary equipment such as microphone, screen, projector etc. be set up; the night before, the morning or the afternoon of the conference? This may depend on the event which immediately precedes the actual conference meeting.

BEFORE EACH MEETING

Before each meeting, the following points need to be checked:

1. The seating is arranged as planned
2. The location of any additional chairs and tables

3. The room temperature
4. Water pitcher, glasses at lecture table and conference tables
5. Ash trays, pencils, notepads, name places (where provided)
6. Signs directing members to the conference room
7. Acoustics; to be checked for echoes or dead spots
8. All plug-in equipment is working
9. Microphone cords long enough
10. Where film screen provided — is it level and steady?
11. Spare fuses or standby circuits ready?
12. Sufficient extension cords and adaptors
13. Is the room dark enough for projection?
14. All heating, air-conditioning and fan controls working
15. That eveyone can see platform when all the seats are filled
16. That 'In the Event of Fire' notices are promiently displayed.

AT THE END OF MEETING

1. For lost or forgotten property.
2. The removal of organiser's property for safe keeping.
3. The return of any hired equipment.
4. The removal of promotional material relating to the last session.

The hotel should be of sufficient size to accommodate a conference without inconvenience to other guests. It is of vital importance that their comfort is ensured. It is more irritating and disturbing from the regular visitor's point of view to find a whole hotel's activities geared to the needs of a conference. It is courteous and very necessary that guests should be warned of the conference and of the times the delegates will be taking their meals and separate arrangements made for the comfort of all other guests staying at the same time.

Functions include banquets, conferences and similar hotel services. Their |users require accommodation and other services of the hotel. Special banquet penus are prepared for such occasions. Analysis of some of the banquet menus is given in Fig. 11.25, and 11.25.

HOTEL ABC
ANALYSIS OF A BANQUET MENU

SOUP (OPTIONAL)

1. **Cream of Almond :** Rich almond paste blended with cream and garnished with Juliennes of almonds.
2. **Cream of Asparagus :** Chopped asparagus blended with cream.
3. **Cream of Chicken :** Diced boiled chicken blended with cream.
4. **Cream of Mushroom :** Finely chopped mushrooms blended with cream.
5. **Potage Minestrone :** Italian style garlic and tomato flavoured broth garnished with vegetables, kidney beans and macaroni.
6. **Tamattar Shorba :** Indian style soup of fresh tomatoes pureed and spiced, topped with cream.
7. **Sultani Shorba :** Pureed lentil and vegetable soup.

SALAD (SELECT ANY HIREE)

1. **Cucumber with Dill Salad :** Creamed cucumber salad with dill.
2. **Tossed Green Salad :** Fresh green vegetable salad with French dressing.
3. **Russian Salad :** Green peas, diced boiled potatoes and carrots bounds in mayonnaise garnished with boiled eggs.
4. **German Potato Salad :** Diced boiled potatoes bound in the Chef's special dressing garnished with parsley.
5. **Italienne Salad :** A combination of potatoes, carrots, turnips, beans, eggs, tomatoes, salami, mayonnaise, olives, capers and anchovy fillets.
6. **Waldorf Salad :** Apples and celery bound with mayonnaise and topped with walnuts.
7. **Cheese and Salami Salad :** Quarters of cheese and salami served with an Italienne dressing.
8. **Mixed Masala Kuchumber:** Chopped tomatoes, cucumber, radish, onions and carrots in a lemon dressing with piquant chaat masala.

NON-VEGETARIAN (SELECT ANY THREE)

CHICKEN

1. **Murg Kadhai :** Tender cuts of chicken cooked in a kadhai, flavoured with garlic, freshly crushed pepper and coriander in a tomato gravy.
2. **Murg Mughlai** : Chicken cooked in rich dry nut gravy topped with a flat masala omelette.
3. **Murg Begum Bahar**: Tender cuts of chicken cooked in methi flavoured yellow gravy.
4. **Murg Mukhani**: Tandoori chicken cooked in a buttered tomato gravy blended with cream and cashewnuts.
5. **Chicken Marengo** : Souted chicken deglazed in brandy/white wine, cooked in a derniglazed tomato puree with mushrooms and garnished with French fried eggs.

MUTTON

1. **Saag Meat** : Curried lamb cooked with spinach.
2. **Keema Mattar** : Green peas and lamb mince cooked in Indian herbs and spices.
3. **Nahari Gosht** : Lamb pieces cooked in onions flavoured with nutmeg and ittar.
4. **Bhuna Gpsht** : Mutton cooked in its own juices with garlic and garam masala,
5. **Mutton Do Piaza** : Succulent larnb pieces cooked with onions and tempered with whole fed chillies.
6. **Kadhai Gosht** : Lamb cooked with garlic, freshly crushed pepper corns and coriander in a tomato gravy.
7. **Fried Fish with Tarter Sauce** : Fillets of fish marinated in lemon juice, crumbed and deep fried.
8. **Fish Masala** : Seasonal fish cooked with hand ground spices.
9. **Fish Afghani** : Boneless fish marinated in garlic, black cumin, lemon juice, creamed youghurt and cooked in the tandoor.

VEGETARIAN (SELECT ANY ONE FOR NON-VEGETARIAN AND ANY TWO FOR VEGETARIAN MENU)

1. **Paneer Do Piaza** : Cottage cheese and onions cooked Mughlai style.
2. **Paneer Malai Kofta**: Fried cottage cheese dumplings simmered in a mild gravy.

3. **Mattar Paneer**: Green peas and cubes of cottage cheese cooked in a thick spiced gravy.
4. **Mattar Mushroom** : Green peas and mushrooms in a yellow Indian gravy.
5. **Shah! Paneer** : Cottage cheese in a delicately blended cream and dry nut sauce.
6. **Paneer Pasanda** : Sliced cottage cheese in a tomato based gravy, topped with cream.
7. **Paneer Birbali** : Layers of cottage cheese slices stuffed with chillies, oniora, coriander and dry nuts, rolled in gram flour, shallow fried and served in a tomato based gravy.

VEGETABLES (SELECT ANY THREE OF VEGETARIAN MENU)

1. **Chukki Mattar** : Green peas and cumin cooked dry.
2. **Dum Aloo** : Small potatoes deep fried and cooked in a mildly spiced gravy.
3. **Jeera Aloo** : A delightful combination of cumin and potatoes.
4. **Bhindi Masala** : Ladyfingers cooked dry with spices.
5. **Bhindi Do Piaza** : Ladyfingers with onions and red chillies.
6. **Gobhi Korma** : Flowerets of cauliflower coated in a rich creamy gravy.
7. **Gobhi Mussallam** : Whole cauliflower baked and coated with a mild cashewnut and poppy gravy.
8. **Gobhi Masala** : Dry preparation of cauliflower in spices.
9. **Lacheele Aloo** : Potatoes mildly spiced and cooked dry combined with vermicelli.
10. **Aloo Mumtaz :** Fancy-shaped potato slices cooked in a golden gravy with sultanas.
11. **Lauki Musallam :** Baked whole bottle gourd with an exotic stuffing.
12. **Baghare Baingan :** Small egg plants cooked in youghurt and Indian masalas.
13. **Punjabi Kadi :** Preparation of yoghurt and gram flour tempered with methi seeds, cumin, turmeric powder, whole red chillies and curry leaves served with pokodas.

DAL (SELECT ANY ONE)

1. **Rajma :** Curried kidney beans cooked with tomatoes and ground spices.
2. **Urad Dal :** White washed lentil, cooked dry and tempered.
3. **Pindi Channa :** Chick peas cooked and tempered with channa masala and topped with tomato quarters, green chillies and coriander, tempered with cumin and red chillies.
4. **Urad Dal Rajma :** Black lentil cooked overnight over slow charcoal fire along-with rajma, blended with tomato paste, cream, butter and garlic paste.

ROTI (SELECT ANY ONE)

1. Tandoori Roti
2. Kulcha
3. Naan
4. Tandoori Parantha
5. Stuffed Kulcha
6. Mughlai Parantha
7. Roomali Roti

PULAO (SELECT ANY ONE)

1. **Peas Pulao :** Basmati rice cooked with ghee, whole spices and peas,
2. **Vegetable Pulao :** Basmati rice cooked with ghee, whole spices and assorted vegetables.
3. **Mushroom Pulao :** A combination of rice and fresh mushrooms cooked together.

4. **Navrattan Pulao :** A pulao of stewed fruits and dry fruits.
5. **Sultana Pulao :** A pulao of stewed fruits and dry fruits. I Noormahal Pulao : A pulao of stewed fruits and dry fruits.
6. **Sultana Pulao :** Pulao rice, garnished with raisins.
7. **Noomahal Pulao :** Pulao rice and small cottage cheese dumplings with saffron.
8. **Pickles, Papad and Chutney**
9. **Dahi/Raita/Pakori/Bhalla**

DESSERT (Select any two)

1. **Fresh Fruit Salad :** Diced fresh fruit in sugar syrup.
2. **Fruit Jelly :** Diced fruits in jelly (strawberry, raspberry, lemon).
3. **Savarin Mousse :** Yeast leavened flour cakes soaked in rum-flavoured syrup.
4. **Trifle Pudding :** Layers of sponge cake and flavoured custard filling, decorated with sweetened whipped cream and jam.
5. **Black Forest :** Layers of cherries, whipped cream and chocolate sponge on a short crust base topped with flaked chocolate.
6. **Gulab Jamun :** Roundels of khoya deep fried to golden brown, served in sugar syrup.
7. **Rasgulla :** Milk dumplings in syrup, served chilled.
8. **Handi Kheer :** Blended saffron flavoured milk and rice, sweetened, and served garnished with nuts.
9. **Moong ka Halwa** : Ground moong dal cooked with fat and sugar syrup, topped with dry fruits.
10. **Savian ka Muzafar** : Golden vermicelli cooked in syrup and topped with khoya and saffron, served hot.
11. **Diplomat Pudding** : Multi-flavoured cream bavarois topped with jelly.
12. **Phirni** : Reduced sweetened milk, thickened rice flour, set in earthen moulds and decorated with pista and almonds.
13. **Profiterole Suchard** : Profiteroles stuffed with cream and topped with chocolate sauce.
14. **Baba Au Rhum** : Moulded sponge cakes soaked in rum flavoured syrup.
15. **Charlotte Russe** : Vanilla mousse topped with orange fruit jelly, barricaded with sponge fingers.
16. **Souffle** : A very light dessert with a choice of flavours.
17. **Kulfi Kesar Badaam Pista** : Reduced milk mixed with almonds, frozen and served in earthen moulds.
18. **Rasmalai** : A cold dessert of reduced milk and cheese balls.
19. **Apple Pie** : Sliced apples, raisins and crumbled cake baked in a flan mould lined with pastry and twin glazed with jam.
20. **Cream Caramel** : Caramelized custard served cold after steaming.
21. **Mille Feuille Gateau** : Layers of puff and flaky pastry, topped with cream and custard fillings.
22. **Tea/Coffee**

Fig. 11.25. Analysis of a Banquet Menu

Analysis of a Banquet Menu
HOTEL ABC

SOUP (Select any one)

1. **Cream of Mushroom** : Consomme Carmen : Bean consomme flavoured with tomato juice garnished with rice and strips of green pepper.
2. **Hungarian Goulash** : A paprika-based hashed tenderloin soup with fresh herbs and kidney beans.
3. **Cream Princes** : Cream of chicken blended with cream of asparagus and garnished with diced asparagus tips.
4. **Mulligatawny** : A curry flavoured lentil soup garnished with boiled rice and chicken dices.
5. **Potage Minestrone** : Italian style garlic and tomato flavoured broth garnished with vegetables, kidney beans and macaroni.

SALAD (Select any three)

1. **Tomato Vinaigrette** : Blanched tomatoes with vinaigrette dressing.
2. **Cucumber Salad** : Sliced cucumbers served with cream dressing.
3. **Tossed Green Salad** : Fresh green vegetable salad with French dressing.
4. **Russian Salad** : Green peas, diced boiled potatoes and carrots bounds ir mayonnaise garnished with boiled eggs.
5. **German Potato Salad** : Diced boiled potatoes bound in the Chef's specia dressing garnished with parsley.
6. **Beetroot with spring Onions** : Pickled dices of beetroot garnished with sliced spring onions.
7. **Chiffonade Salad** : Lettuce, celery, beetroot, tomatoes a watercress in an American dressing.
8. **Bean Sprouts Salad** : Bean Sprouts tossed in French dressing.

HORS D'OEUVRE (Select any one)

1. **Mixed Seafood Cocktail** : Prawns, mussels, shrimps, varieties of fish seasoned with salt, pepper, mustard, lemon and coated with a brandy flavoured cocktail dressing.
2. **Pate Maison** : A home-made pate of meats, jellied and cooked in a mould, sliced and served cold.
3. **Stuffered Eggs** : Hard-boiled eggs pealed, halved, scooped and stuffed with cream mousse and garnished.
4. **Assorted Cold Cut Platter**: Cold cuts of cooked meats, sliced and garnished.
5. **Chicken Liver Terrine** : Chicken liver mousse mi^ed with cream and brandy filled in an aspic lined mould.

VEGETARIAN (Select any three)

1. **Fried Eggplants** : Marinated roudels of eggplant dipped in batter and deep fried.

2. **Mushroom Florentine** : White mushroom sauce coated over creamed spinach topped with Hollandaise sauce and glazed under the salamander.
3. **Carrots Vichy** : Fancy slices of carrots glazed with batter.
4. **Choufleur a la Polonaise** : Cooked cauliflower topped with Polonaise sauce, comprising of parsley, butter, chopped boiled eggs and fresh bread crumbs.
5. **Epinard a la Cream** : Chopped boiled spinach, sauted in onion and garlic with an addition of a wholesome quantity of cream.
6. **Petit Pois a la Francaise** : Boiled peas sauted with button onions and cooked over a slow flame, finished with cream.
7. **Pommes de Terre Lynonnaise** : Sauted sliced potatoes topped with slices of onions and moistened with stock or consomme.
8. **Vegetable Au Gratin** : Cooked dices of potatoes, carrots and green peas in white sauce and gratinated.
9. **Bauquetiere de Legumes**: Garden fresh vegetables, tossed in butter, decora-tively served by sprinkling chopped parsley and glazed tomatoes on the side.
10. **Aubergine au Gratin** : Deep fried aubergine coated with homemade tomato sauce topped and gratinated.
11. **Ratatouille Nicoise** : Courgettes, aubergine, capsicum and whole fresh mushrooms, tossed together and placed in the oven to cook in its own juices, and tomato concasse added to it.
12. **Haticot Verte Provencale** : Boiled green beans, topped with a thick tomato fondue.

NON-VEGETARIAN (Select any three)

CHICKEN

1. **Chicken Mexicane** : Chicken cooked in a red wine souce with capsicum and mushrooms.
2. **Supreme de Votaille Princess** : Breast of chicken, grilled and placed on a bed of spaghetti. Topped with mushroom sauce and garnished with asparagus tips.
3. **Coq au Vin :** Sauted chicken swilled with red wine sauce, granished with bacon dices, onions and button mushrooms.
4. **Southern Fried Chicken** : Tender pieces of chicken dipped in batter and deep fried.

LAMB :

1. **Lamb Leg Boulangere** : Sliced, roasted leg of lamb decoratively interspersed with slices of potatoes and onions. Coated with its own juices.
2. **Lamb Moussaka** : A dish of oriental origin. Lamb mince cooked in red wine sauce with demiglazed and fried aubergine slices and white sauce layered in between.
3. **Navarin Printainer**: A brown stew of selected cuts of lamb deglazed with red wine and cooked over a slow flame with garden fresh vegetables.

FISH

1. **Fried Fish with Tartar Sauce :** Fillets of fish marinated in lemon juice, crumbed and deep fried.
2. **Bekti Bonne Femme :** Fish poached in white wine and topped with fish mush-. room veloute.

3. **Fillet de sole Bedford :** Grilled fillet of sole topped with spinach and mushroom puree garnished with croutons, coated with mornay sauce, and gratinated.

RICE/PASTA (Select any one)

1. **Rizau Blanch** : Plain boiled rice— sparkling white.
2. **Rissi Bissi**: Boiled rice, concassed tomatoes and peas tossed in butter, topped wth cheese and placed in the salamander.
3. **Rissotto Con Fungi**: Boiled rice, mushrooms, tomato concasse tosssed together in butter.
4. **Lasgne Catalaise** : Pata mixed with tomatoes and aubergine in a sauce.
5. **Spaghetti Burmese** : A spicy tomato-based sauce tossed with spaghetti and served with fried, slit whole chillies.
6. **Noodles Alfredo** : Boiled noodles tossed with concasse and cheese with mild seasoning.

DESSERT (Select any two)

1. **Fresh Fruit Salad** : Diced fresh fruit in sugar syrup.
2. **Caramel Custard** : Egg and milk custard topped with caramel sugar bcked in the oven.
3. **Black Forest**: Layers of cherries, whipped cream and chocolate sponge on a short crust base topped with flaked chocolate.
4. **Ice Cream (one flavour)** : Vanilla, Strawberry. Chocolate.
5. **Diplomat Pudding** : Multi-flavoured cream bavarois topped with jelly.
6. **Mousse** : Whipped cream and custard set in moulds and topped with cream flavoured to your choice.
7. **Fresh Fruit Gateau** : Layers of sponge, custard cream and fresh fruits.
8. **Mocha Gateau** : Coffee flavoured rich cake.
9. **Chocolate Mont Blane** : Profiteroles filled with whipped cream and topped with chocolate.
10. **Chocolate Mille Feuille Gateau** : Layers of puff and flaky pastry with chocolate cream and custard filling.
11. **Tea/Coffee**

Fig. 11.26. Analysis of a Banquit Menu

BUSINESS MEETINGS

Business meetings in hotels are getting very popular and are turning an important source of revenue for many hotels. The modern meeting planner are requiring different types of equipment and facilities. You could have minimum requirements in a meeting room, such as:—

1. The required number of chairs arranged in the form requested
2. A platform
3. A presiding officer's table and chairs
4. A lighted lectern (either table or floor type)

5. A gavel
6. Ice water and glasses on the speaker's table
7. A black-board
8. Chalk
9. An eraser
10. A pointer
11. A national flag (for public gathering)
12. Audio-visual tool
13. Any other latest sophistication.

Below are listed some of the key points which should be considered by the hotel hosts and meeting planners for the success of these meetings :

1. Entrance and exit facilities for material and properties, as well as guests, facilitating movement without delay.
2. Provision for adequate parking varies for guests and meeting sponsors.
3. Provision of safety features including properly marked fire exits, properly fused circuits, adequate floor load capacity and flame-proofed draperies.
4. Provision for adequate electric circuit, 20-amperes minimum capacity with outlet, both at front and rear of room. You can control all room lights from a single switch, preferably at the rear of the room where projection equipment could be located. This switch should also not turn off projection equipment outlet or the heighted speaker's lectern. Dimmer controls to allow partial illumination for note taking during film projection are a desirable features.
5. For the comfort and convenience of the audience, air-conditioned and heating should be controlled by a room thermostat which can easily be adjusted without the services of the hotel managers.
6. Ventilation should be provided and washing rooms and drinking fountains should be arranged near by.
7. Chair should be more comfortable than the folding type.
8. Special room darking facilities rather than Venetian blind and draperies should be provided.
9. Ceiling heights should be adequate to accommodate a large server above the stage. Room with low ceilings cause restlessness to the audiences and usually have poor acoustics.
10. Top quality soun systems are a must. In addition to lectern mike, there should be provision for "lavaliere', microphones for panelists and portable microphones for audience participation."
11. A usual complement of 'props' will include easels and black board, tables and chairs for panelists and speakers, and an adequate size screen. It is recommended that screen

be at least 6' × 8' for room less than 40' long, 8' × 10' for 40' long rooms and 10' × 12' or larger for ball rooms.

12. House staff must be readily available to help in setting up the room and equipment for a meeting.
13. Provide fast food and beverage service for 'breaks' and meals. Hotels having large meetings should have a separate wing with its own kitchen for meetings.
14. At the end of the meeting room, provide a projection table, plate form or both depending on the size of the room and the lavishness of the facility. The main purpose of this is to provide convenient outlet and space for projection equipment and to keep audience distraction to a minimum.

In a large and luxurious hotel, you may require the following:

1. Tape and videotape recording equipment
2. Play-back equipment
3. Record player
4. Two-way closed circuit television
5. Rear-screen projection.

In a small hotel it is uneconomical to own meeting equipment. These hotels should arrange this equipment with local suppliers on rental basis. The equipment demanded in these hotels may indude :—

1. 16-mm sound projector
2. Slide porjector
3. Tape recorder and
4. Sound amplificication equipment (PA).

No hotel can exist without booking groups, conventions, meetings, trade shows and social business such as seminars, lunches and dinners for many occasions. The selling of the entire hotel, with emphasis on guest room sales, is done by the sales department. The banquet and meeting space not sold in conjunction with room and group sale, is sold by catering department to the local market for social parties. Large hotel may having convention facilities handle many meetings and trade shows require a separate convention service department to handle all meetings room demands not related to food service and social business.

The revenue generated by the catering department can be substantial and it is seen that in many hotels, the food and beverage department could not be profitable without the revenue from this department.

The booking and billing procedures followed in a banquet department are indicated in Fig. 11.27 and 11.28.

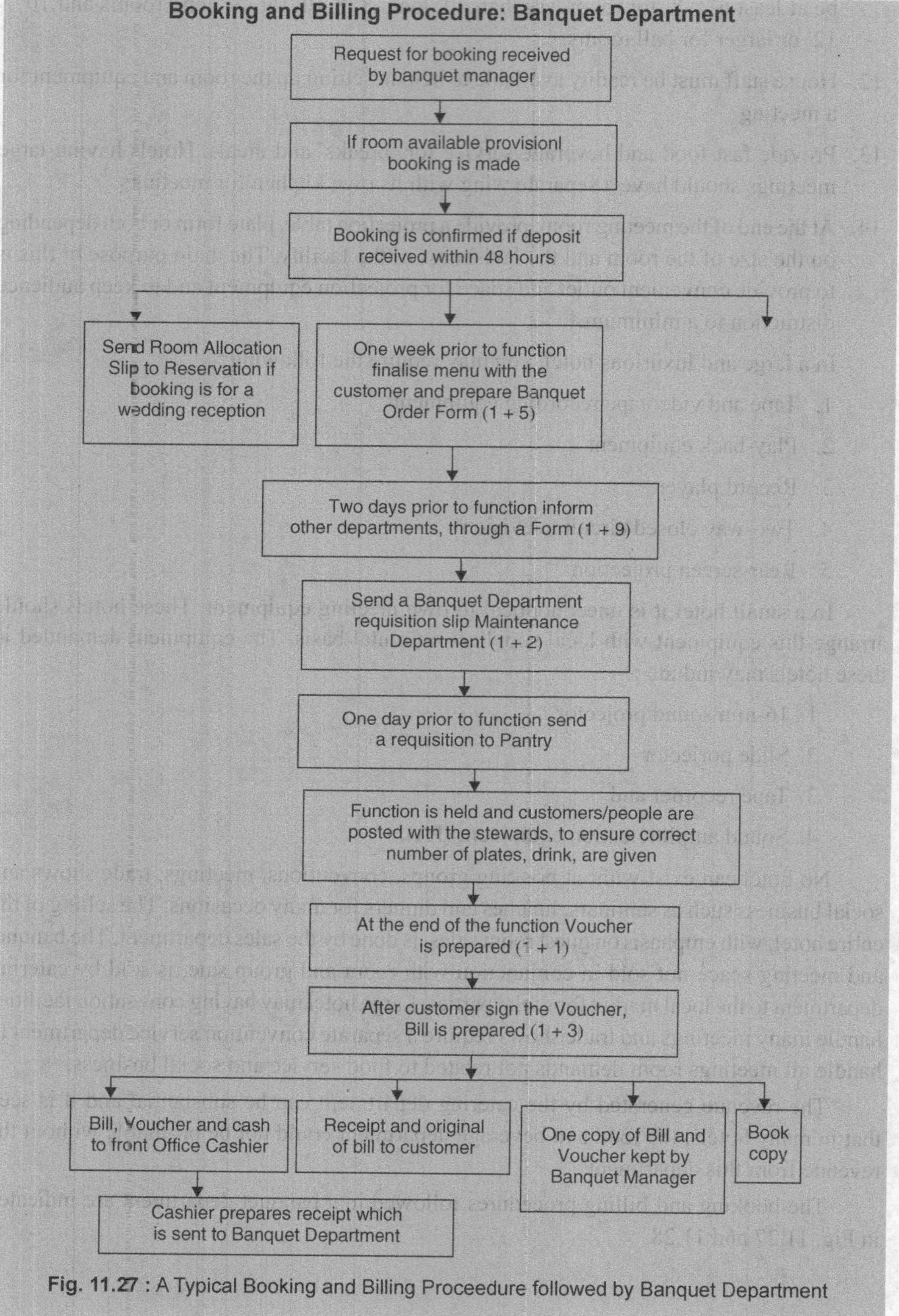

Fig. 11.27 : A Typical Booking and Billing Proceedure followed by Banquet Department

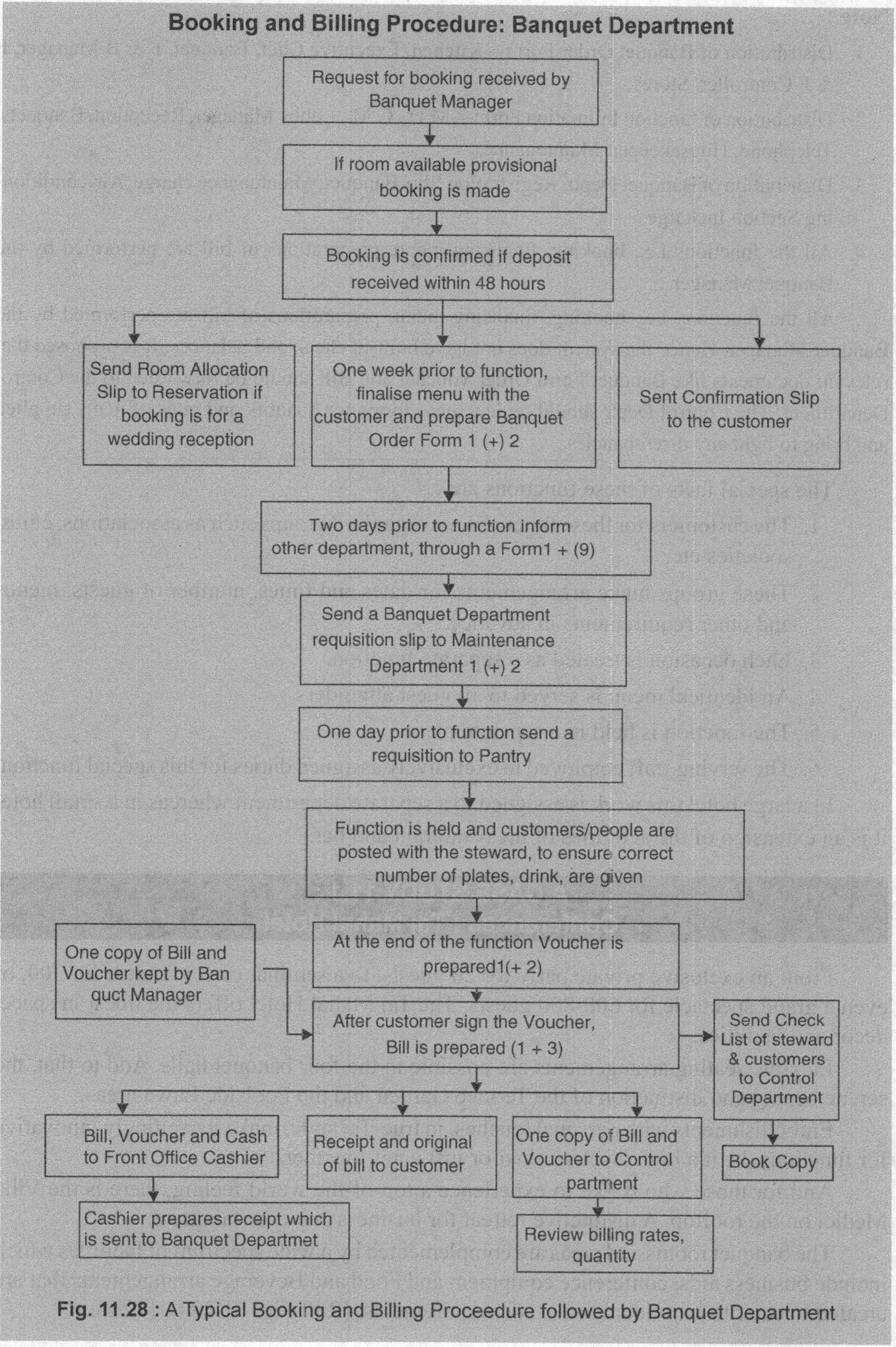

Fig. 11.28 : A Typical Booking and Billing Proceedure followed by Banquet Department

Note :

1. Distribution of Banquet Order Form—Kitchen, Executive Chef, Banquet, F & B Manager, F & F Controller, Stores.
2. Distribution of function Intimation Form—M.D., G.M., Lobby Manager, Reception, Banquets, Telephone, Housekeeper, Maintenance.
3. Distribution of Banquet Deptt. Registration Slip-Banquet, Maintenance charge, Air-conditioning Section Incharge.
4. All the functions i.e., booking, finalising menu, preparations of bill are performed by the Banquet Manager.

All the functions i.e., booking, finalising menu, preparations of bill are performed by the Banquet Manager. Hence the system does not have built-in check and balances. It is proposed that relevant documents like Banquet Form Order Voucher and Bill should be forwarded to the Control Department. The Control Deptt should review these forms for quantity and rates of items supplied and bring to light any discrepancies.

The special facts of these functions are :

1. The customers for these functions are organised groups such as associations, clubs, societies etc.
2. These groups make arrangements for dates and times, number of guests, menus and other requirements in advance.
3. Each occasion is treated as a separate function.
4. An identical menu is served to all guest attainders.
5. The function is held in a separate place.
6. The serving staff employed in exclusively assigned duties for this special function.

In a large hotel this work is assigned to a separate department whereas in a small hotel it is an extension of the activities of the restaurant and bar.

A CASE STUDY 11.1 : Conferences : Taj Mahal Hotel

From an exclusive private party for 20 guests, to a seminar or conference for 300, or even a grand spectacle for 600-800 guests, The Taj Mahal Hotel offers the finest in space, decor and facilities.

Flexible seating arrangements are possible in the four banquet halls. Add to that, the serene beauty and distinction of the Terrace Garden and the Poolside Lawn areas.

Embellishments with personal touches, in true-Taj style, make it excitingly innovative for functions, be it a high level seminar or just a get-together.

And for those who'd like to experience a top-of-the world feeling, there is the Villa Medici on the rooftop. A distinctive retreat for business and entertainment.

The banquet rooms and areas are complemented by a wide spectrum of facilities which include business aids, conference equipment and Food and Beverage arrangements that are created to cater to individual tastes and requirements. (Ref. Figs 11.29 to 11.52).

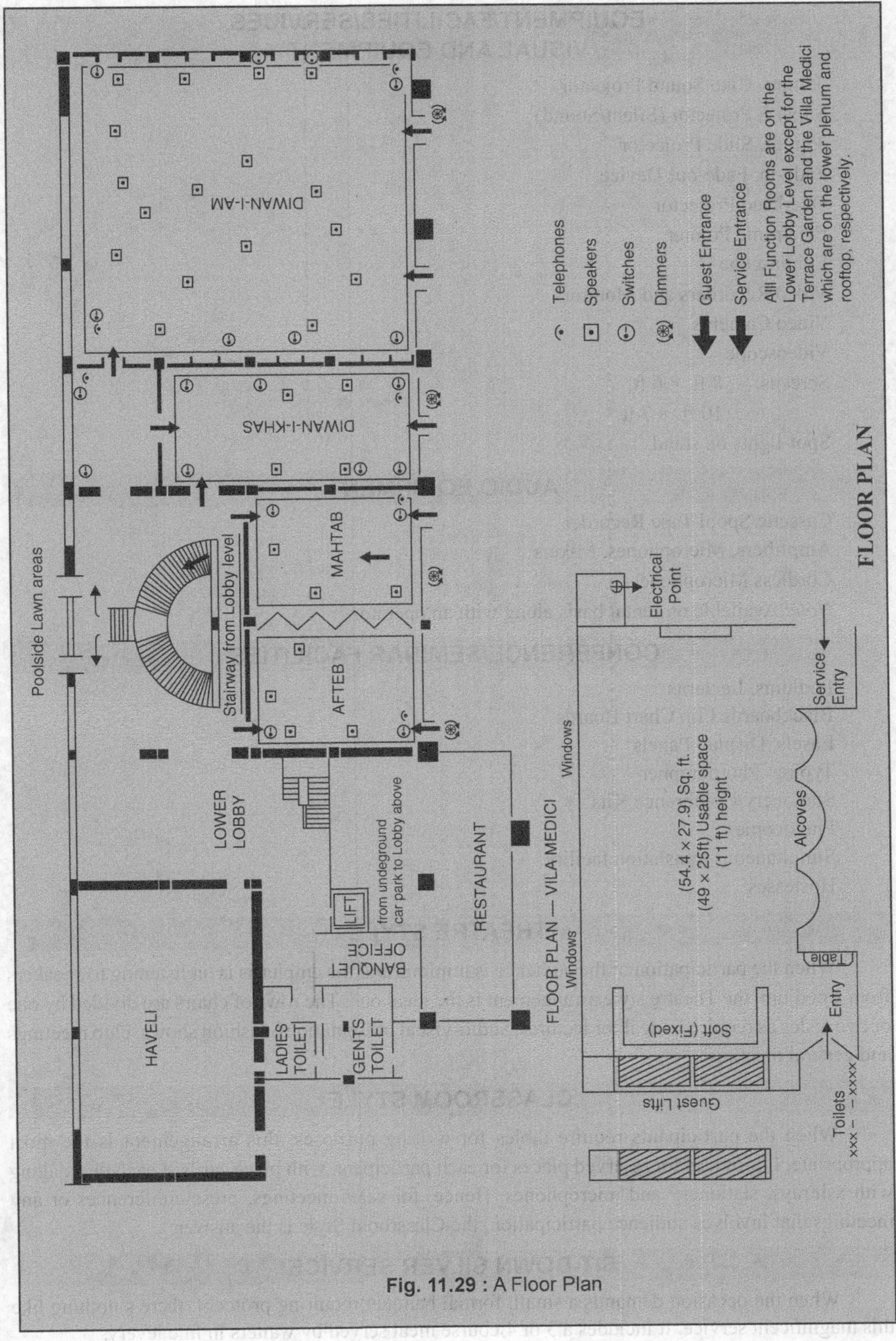

Fig. 11.29 : A Floor Plan

EQUIPMENT/FACILITIES/SERVICES VISUAL AND EQUIPMENT

35 mm. Cine Sound Projector
Super 8 Projector (Silent/Sound)
35 mm. Slide Projector
Fade-in, Fade-out Device
Overhead Projector
Electronic Pointer
Epidiascope
Video Recorders and Monitors
Video Cameras
Videoscope
Screens: 8 ft. × 6 ft.
10 ft. × 7 ft.
Spot-lights on stand.

AUDIO EQUIPMENT

Cassette/Spool Tape Recorder
Amplifiers, Microphones, Mixers
Cordless Microphones
Note: Available on rental basis along with an operator.

CONFERENCE/SEMINAR FACILITIES

Podiums, Lecterns
Blackboards/Flip Chart Boards
Easels, Display Panels
Typing, Photographer
Stationery/Conference Kits
Photocopies
Simultaneous translation facility
Hostesses.

THEATRE STYLE

When the participation of the audience is minimal and the emphasis is on listening to speakers from a podium, the Theatre style arrangement is the ideal one. The rows of chairs are divided by one or two aisles as required. Ideal for lectures, audio-visual presentations, fashion shows, club meetings and general meetings.

CLASSROOM STYLE

When the participants require tables for writing purposes, this arrangement is the most appropriate. It provides for reserved places for each participant, with place cards at each desk, along with ashtrays, stationery and microphones. Hence, for sales meetings, press conferences or any meetings that involves audience participation, the Classroom Style is the answer.

SIT-DOWN SILVER SERVICE

When the occasion demands a small, formal banquet requiring protocol, there's nothing like this magnificent service. It includes a 3 or 4 course meal served by waiters in fine levery.

SIT-DOWN BUFFETS

When the evening involves cocktails, during which guests have been standing, followed by dinner, this arrangement is convenient and friendly. If you like, you can also group people the way you want to, by placing name cards at each place on the table. So, if it's a company meeting-cum-dinner, staff get-togethers, a private party or a semiformal function, make your evening memorable with a Sit-down Buffet.

SEATING ARRANGEMENTS

STANDING BUFFETS

When you want guests to mingle freely, a standing buffet creates an informal atmosphere. Be it a cocktail party, a press function or even a business get-together.

SOME SPECIAL ARRANGEMENTS

In addition to those listed, The Taj Mahal also provides some special arrangements devised for specific needs.

Banquet style seating for conventions, seminars and conferences.

For receptions, where space is required for a free flow of guests and the seating is casual and limited, there is the Lounge style arrangement.

You may, however, have some of your own specific requirements. Do let it know. The hotel's experienced staff will be glad to work out the details.

THEME PARTIES

The aim of these parties is to turn dreams into reality. And the Taj Mahal staff specialises in creating just the ambience that's required. Ranging from an ethnic Indian village, a Rajasthani folk evening, Goan carnival, to the internationally popular Caribbean extravaganza, cafes in Paris....may be even a page out of Arabian Nights.

There are many themes to choose from. And, given adequate notice, The Taj Mahal is willing to create themes according to individual tastes.

SPECIAL SERVICES

The Taj Mahal Hotel, New Delhi, has a rich tradition of warmth and hospitality complemented by a personalised touch.

The following is a list of the special services offered :

1. *Conference kit with the company logo embossed.
2. *Special working lunch menu, to cater to various individual tastes.
3. *Special ambience by way of music or light entertainment, to provide a welcome break.
4. Complete conference detailing, right down to cocktail napkins.
5. Charming and helpful hostesses to welcome and escort guests.
6. *Speical effects for product launches, like life size models of product and special display boards.
7. *Facilities to make banners of your choice.
8. *Special themes for parties, be it ethnic or western, depending on your requirement.
9. Cookie platters on the table.
10. *Personalised stationery, match boxes, pencils.

Name of the Company ....
Tel & Add. of Co. ....
Venue ....
Date of the Conference ....
No. of Participants ....
No. of Registration Counters ....
Seating Arrangements ....
Telephone required ....

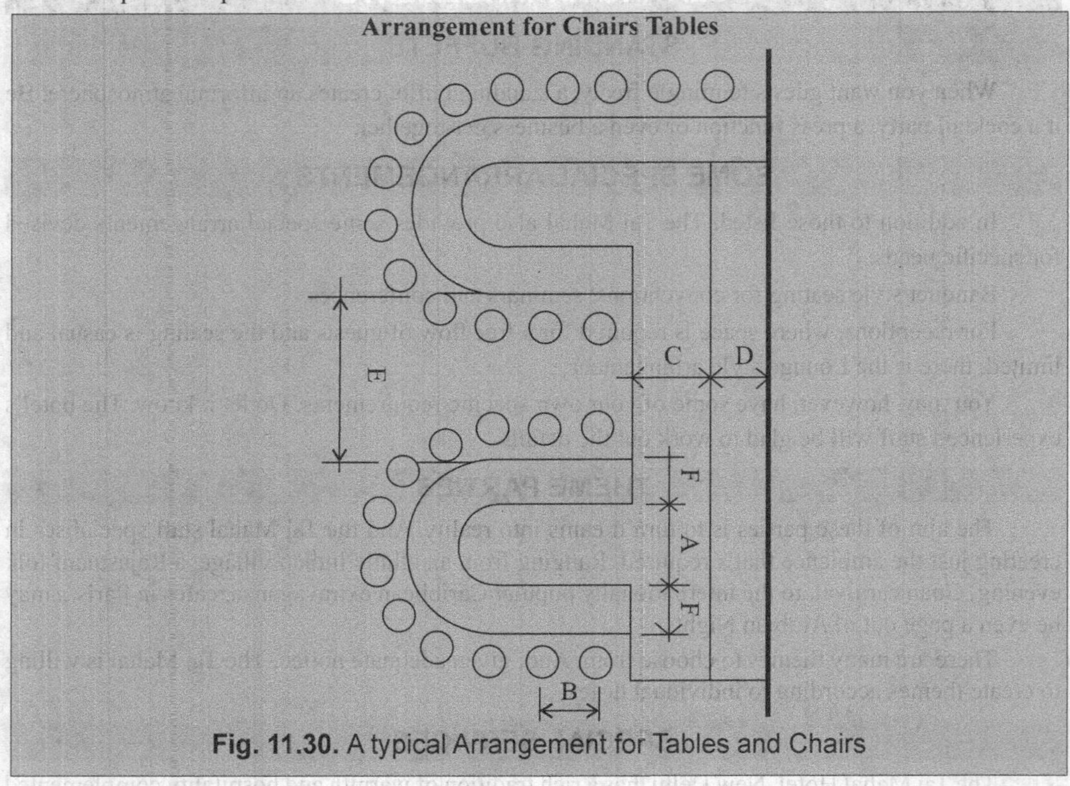

Fig. 11.30. A typical Arrangement for Tables and Chairs

Capacity of Different Rooms

Type of Room	Max.
Banquet	10 – 11
Tea Room	12 – 14
Din. Rm/Rest.	14 – 15
Cafeteria	15
Lunchrms : Counter & Chair–table types incl. counters chairs, tables	20

Fig. 11.31. Maximum Capacity for Different Rooms

* AT least 15 days' notice required

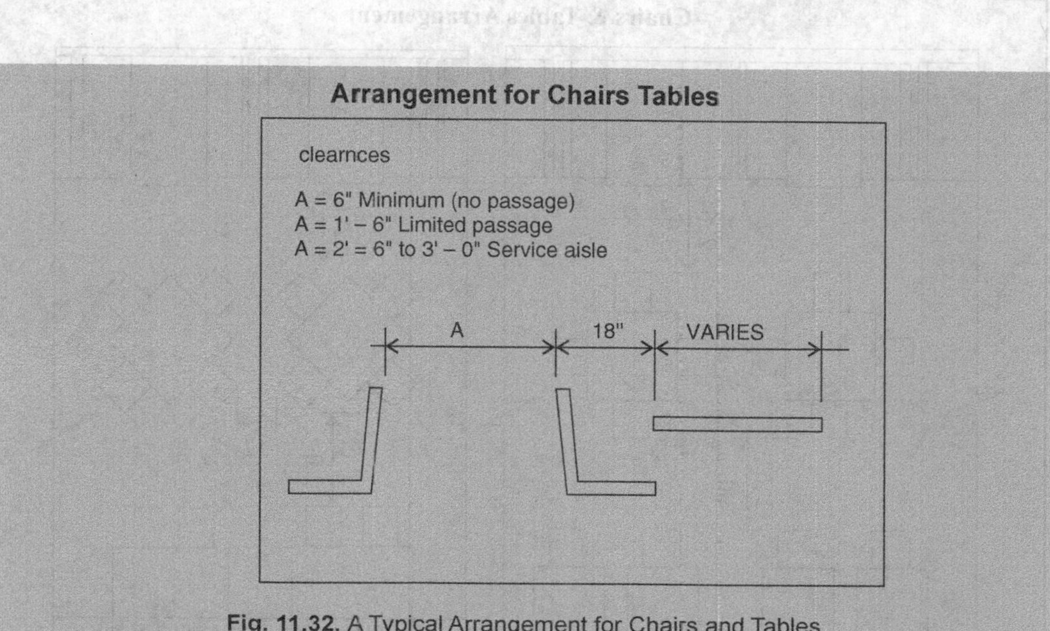

Fig. 11.32. A Typical Arrangement for Chairs and Tables

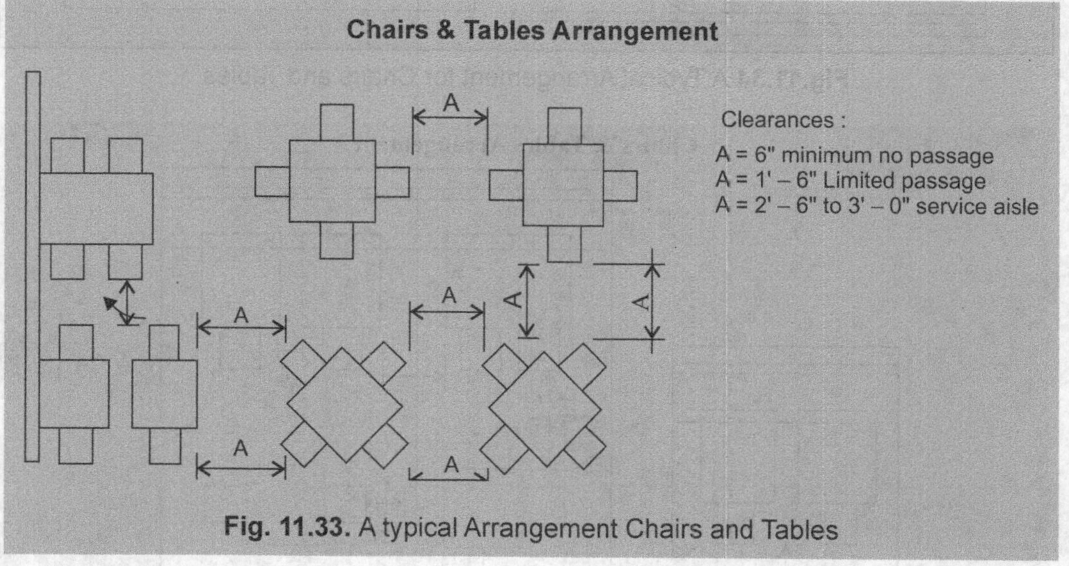

Fig. 11.33. A typical Arrangement Chairs and Tables

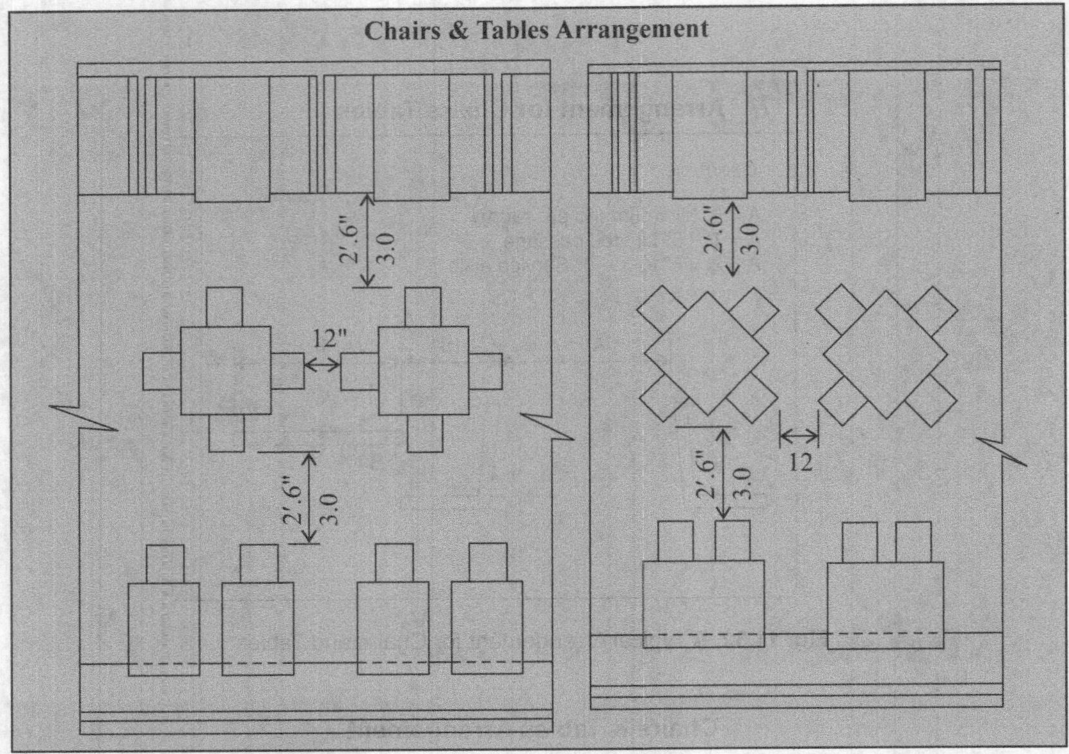

Fig.11.34 A Typical Arrangement for Chairs and Tables

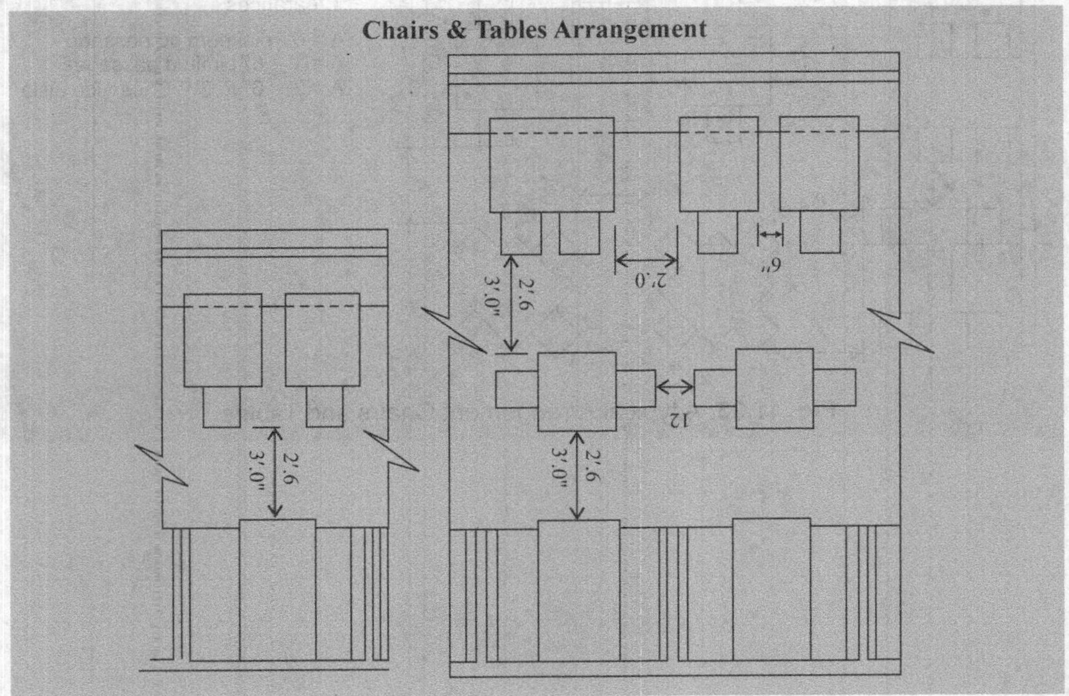

Fig.11.35. A Typical Arrangement for Chairs and Tables

Chairs & Tables Arrangement

Persons	A or B	X
2	1' – 8' to 2' – 6'	2' – 5" to 3' – 6"
4	2' – 6" to 3' – 0"	3' – 6" to 4' – 3"

Persons	A	B
2 (on one side)	3' – E" to 4' – C"	2' – 0"
4	3' – E" to 4' – C"	2' – 0" to 3' – 0"
6	5' – C" to 8' – C"	

Persons	A
2	2' – 0"
3	2' – 6"
4	3' – 0"

Fig.11.36. A Typical Arrange for Chairs and Tables

Main Table Banquest Requirement (Meeting)

No. of Persons	....
Chief Guest	....
Arrival/Inaugural Time	....
Blackboard with chalk	Yes/No.
Flipchart with Charts	Yes/No.
– Screen(s)	Yes/No.
– Slide projector(s)	
with–Caroussel(s)	Yes/No.
– Overhead projector(s)	Yes/No.
– mm. film projector(s)	Yes/No.
– Lapel/Cordless Mike(s)	Yes/No.
– Table mike(s)	Yes/No.
Podium mike(s)	Yes/No.
– Standing mike(s)	Yes/No.

Dias	Yes/No.
– Garland(s)/Bouquet(s)	Yes/No.
Photographer	Yes/No.
Place cards	Yes/No.
Display board	Yes/No.
Pocium	Yes/No.
– Reserved row(s)	Yes/No.
Room for secretariat	Yes/No.
Table for Press	Yes/No.
Video recording facility	Yes/No.
Taping facility	Yes/No.
Extra electric load/electrical points	Yes/No.
Electrician	Yes/No.
Carpenter	Yes/No.
TV / V.C.R.	Yes/No.
– Video scope(s)	Yes/No.
– Movie projector(s)	Yes/No.
– Extension cord(s)	Yes/No.
– Spot light(s)	Yes/No.

– Please indicate the number required

Other Extra Services ....

Fig. 11.37. Required for a meeting

(Contd...)

Arrangements and Capacity

HALL NAME	Theatre Style	Class Rooms Style	U-Shape	Rec-tangular	Flow of Guests	Sit-down Banquet	Buffet With Seating	Board Room Style	Area In. Mts. And Sq. Mts.	Area In Ft. And Sq. Ft.	Ceiling Ht. Mts. And Ft.
Diwan-I-Am											
With Buffet	200	100	90	100	500	—	150	—	18.5 × 21.4	61 × 70	3.6(M)
Without Buffet	400	175	120	120	600	200	—	60	396	4270	11.9(Ft.)
Diwan-I-Khas											
With Buffet	50	25	30	40	60	—	35	—	8.1 × 15.5	26 × 51	3.6 (M)
Without Buffet	80	35	40	45	80	40	—	30	125.5	1326	119. (Ft.)
Aftab and Mahtab											
With Buffet	70	30	40	50	100	—	50	—	159 × 107	52 × 34	—
Without Buffet	130	50	60	65	150	80	—	40	170.1	1768	11.0(Ft.)
Villa Medici											
With Buffet	40	20	30	30	70	—	45	—	—	49 × 25	—
Without Buffet	70	35	45	40	90	50	—	32	—	1225	111.0 (Ft.)
Terrace Garden											
With Buffet	—	—	—	—	450	—	225	—	—	—	—
Without Buffet	—	—	—	—	—	—	—	—	—	—	—
Poolside											
With Buffet	—	—	—	—	1000	—	200	—	—	—	—
Without Buffer	—	—	—	—	—	—	—	—	—	—	—

Fig. 11.38. Arrangement and capacity

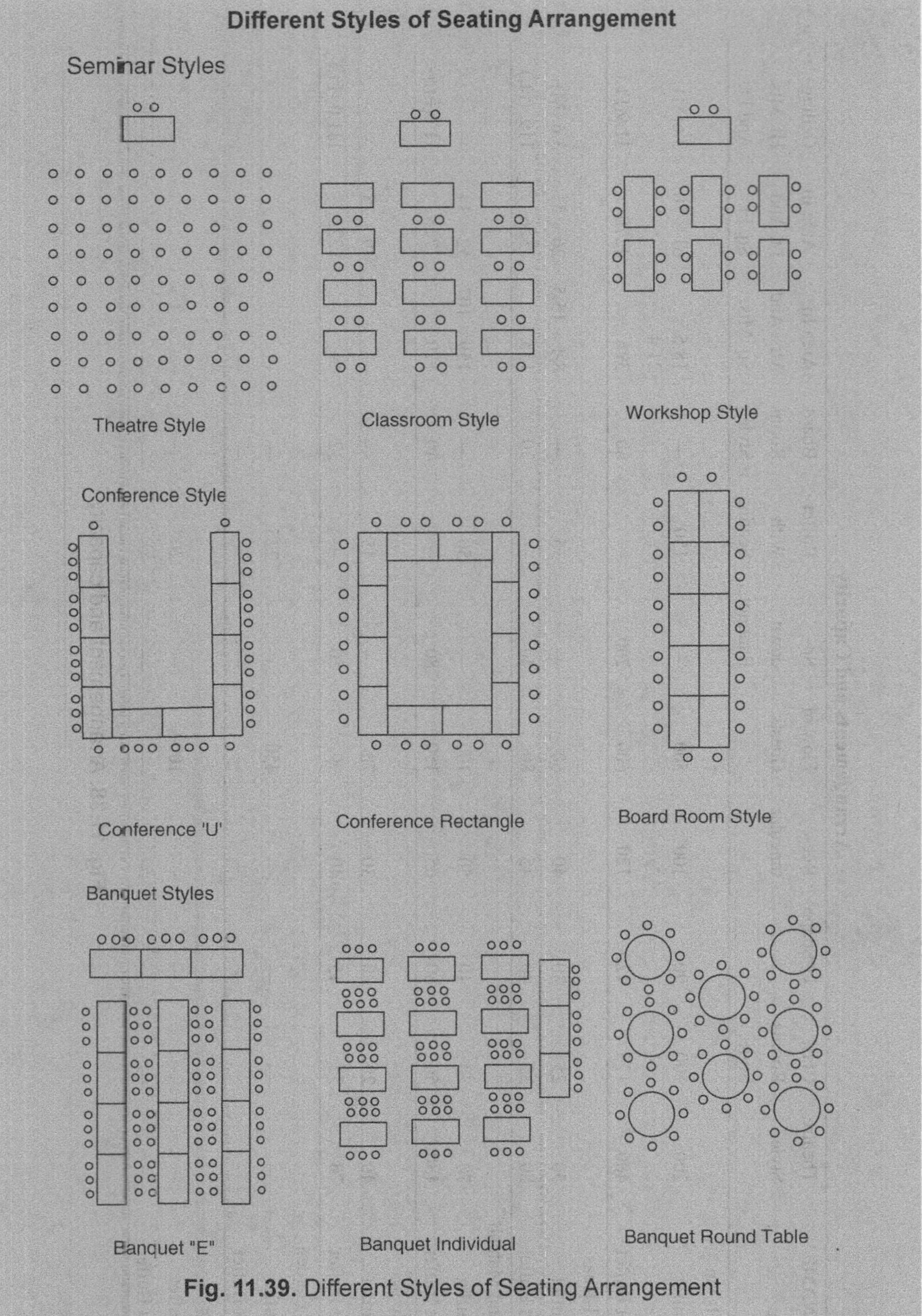

Fig. 11.39. Different Styles of Seating Arrangement

Banquet Halls

Aftab And Mahtab

Whether for work or entertainment, the Aftab and Mahtab provide an imaginative setting. They have two different guest entrances and one reserved for the service staff. A clever mix of tradition and modernity, the Aftab and Mahtab halls are a superb example of grace and style.

DIWAN-I-KHAS

A more intimate setting, the Diwan-I-Khas is perfect for smaller gatherings. A companion to Diwan-I-Am, it is ideal for all kinds of seating arrangements. Stately in decor, Diwan-I-Khas has one guest entrance and a separate one for the service staff.

Diwan-I-Am

The largest of the four banquet halls, the Diwan-I-Am has played host to a variety of occasions, celebrations and conferences.

You enter through a compact but plush ante-room, into the majestic ambience of Diwan-I-Am. The warm, elegant decor is complemented by trained staff, excellent business facilities and a wide selection of cuisines, both Indian and International. Its perfect blend of convenience and comfort make conferences, exhibitions and conventions truly successful.

Villa Medici

This compact, neat hall is an experience in quiet elegance. Away from the maddening crowd, situated at the rooftop, it offers a private and secluded place for exclusive business meetings, conferences or for celebrations of a personal nature. Special attention to detail and service of a high standard, make the Villa Medici a choice venue for the corporate world.

Outdoor Venues

Terrace Garden

Imaginatively located on the Mezzanine level, the Terrace Garden overlooks the blue waters of the pool. It can accommodate as many as 500 guests.

For special receptions, exclusive gatherings, the Terrace Garden is an out-of-the ordinary venue. It's ideal for lunches and dinners on winter afternoons and summer evenings.

Poolside Lawns

When you want to give your celebrationpersonal or corporatethat unique touch, the Poolside Lawns are perfect venues. The two lawns can be used separately or together and each accommodates 300-400 guests. It provides a natural canvas for receptions and bar-be-ques.

FORMAL BANQUETS

Non-Vegetarian	Vegetarian

MENU ONE

Non-Vegetarian	Vegetarian
Sour of Spiced Lamb, French Beans and Coriander	Wild Mushroom Soup
Pan Roasted Chicken served on a Sauce of Sharp Mustard and Cabernet Paprika	Cauliflower, Zucchini, Peppers, Tomatoes and Garlic Casseroled with Olive Oil and Herbs

Selection of Fresh Vegetables and Potatoes

Dobos Cake

Coffee with Friandises

MENU TWO

Potage Hongroise

Non-Vegetarian	Vegetarian
Kentucky Fried Chicken	Kidney Bean Hot Pot
Tuna Fish Sandwich	Grilled Vegetables
Lamb Shashlik	Fettucine Trieste

Jacket Potatoes

Caramel Custard

Coffee

MENU THREE

Non-Vegetarian	Vegetarian
Murg Golishorba	Sabz Golishorba
Mutton Tikka Peshawari	Tandoori Paneer
Khatta Murg	Aloo Tamatar Ka Cut
Kaju Khumb Curry	Kaju Khumb Curry
Dal Makhani	Dal Makhani

Kashmiri Pulao

Dahi Bhalla

Achar, Papad, Chutney

Kulfi Falooda

Coffee

MENU FOUR

Badam Ka Shorba

Non-Vegetarian	Vegetarian
Tandoori Machali Irani	Tandoori Gobhi
Murg Hyderabadi	Paneer Makhan Masala

Zeera Aloo
Dal Kabila

Zeera Aloo
Dal Kabila

Vegetable Pulao
Dahi Bhalla
Achar, Papad, Chutney
Rasgulla
Coffee

Fig. 11.40. Banquet menus

MENU ONE

Essence of Seasonal Vegatables
with Black, Orange and Green Pearls

Panfried King Prawns
seasoned with Thyme
and Lemon, finished
with a light Saffron
Butter Sauce

Toretellini filled with
Garden Vegetables
and served with
a Cheese, Caper and
Pimento Sauce

NON-VEGETARIAN

Grilled Lamb
Mignonnettes
accompanied with
Leek Mousse and served
with Grape Sauce

VEGETARIAN

An Island of Spinach
and Mushroom Duxelle
surrounded by
Morel Sauce

Selection of Fresh Seasonal
Vegetables and Potatoes
Homemade Ice Cream and Fresh Fruit served on a
bed of Wildberry Coulis Coffee

MENU TWO

Timbale of Smoked Salmon
filled with Prawns and
Poached Eggs, finished with
Gherkins and Thousand
Island Dressing
Potage Villars
Sauteed breast of Chicken
glazed with Cream and
Diced Root Vegetables

A cold Asparagus and
Spinach Terrine with
Green Goddess Sauce
Minestrone Milanese
An exciting mould of
Egg Plant and Tomatoes
cushioned on a Herbed
Cream Sauce

Selection of Fresh Seasonal
Vegetables and Potatoes
Prune Pancakes with Cherry Sauce
Fresh Fruit
Coffee with Friandises

MENU THREE

Paya Ras
Tandoori Prawns
Murg Tikka Masala
Gosht Badam Pasanda
Kadi Pakodi

Tamatar Ka Shorba
Subz Kabab
Palak Paneer Kofta
Guchhi Mattar Curry
Kadi Pakodi

Zafrani Pulao
Dahi, Kachumber
Achar, Papad, Chutney
Badam Kheer
Gulab Jamun
Fresh Fruit

MENU FOUR

Tamatar Dhania Shorba

Achari Murg Tikka
Kachi Mirch Ka Gosht
Khumb Rizalla
Rajmah Masala

Dahi Ke Kabab
Palak Paneer
Khumb Rizalla
Rajmah Masala

Zeera Pulao
Mixed Raita
Achar, Papad, Chutney
Kesari Rasmalai

MENU FIVE

Minced Chicken Noodle Soup
Lemon Chicken Hakka style
Shredded Lamb Hot Garlic Sauce
NON-VEGETARIAN
Seasonal Vegetables Hakka Style

Roasted Bean Curb and Vegetable Potage
Cabbage Dry Red Chilli
Seasonal Vegetables Hakka Style
VEGETARIAN
Shredded Capsicum with Bean Sprouts Cantonese Style

Vegetable Fried Rice
Singapore Rice Noodles
Fried Lychees
Strawberry Ice Cream
Jasmine Tea

Fig. 11.41. Banquet menus

Banquet Menus

MENU ONE

Corn and Sea food Bisque
with Thyme
Collop of Lamb panfried
served with Asparagus and
Grapes with an essence of
Terragon and Madeira

A Delicate Cream of
Artichoke with Morels
Leaf Pastry filled with
Ratatouille
accompanied with
Mushroom Sauce

Selection of Fresh Seasonal Vegetables and Potatoes
Peah Yoghurt Cream
with Curacao Sauce
Coffee with Friandises

MENU TWO

Home made Pasta
with Smoked Salmon
and Caviar
Supreme of Chicken
filled with Gruyere
Cheese and Pimentoes,
topped with fresh Basil
flavoured with Red Wine Sauce

Home made Pasta
with Asparagus and
Mushrooms
Grilled Cottage Cheese
flavoured with Mint
and served with
Choron Sauce

Selection of Fresh Seasonal Vegetables and Potatoes
Vanila Ice Cream with Walnuts
and Raisins, topped with Truffle Sauce,
served in a Bricelet
Coffee with Friandise

MENU THREE

Nariyal Shorba

Khaas Seekh Kabab
Murg Masala
Vegetable Kofta Curry
Dal Masala

Tandoori Salad
Khumb Palak
Vegetable Kofta Curry
Dal Masala

Dry Fruit Pulao
Cucumber Raita
Achar, Papad, Chutney
Ras Gulab
Coffee

MENU FOUR

Jehangiri Shorba
Sikandari Raan

Dal Shorba
Paneer Kar Soola

Murg Tikka Lababdar
Dal Gosht
Rajmah Rasila
NON-VEGETARIAN
Gosht Biryani

Moong Pakodi Curry
Aloo Dum Kashmiri
Rajmah Rasila
VEGETARIAN
Sabz Tahri

Dahi Bhalla
Kachumber
Achar, Papad, Chutney
Kulfi Falooda
Khoya Malpua
Fresh Fruit
Coffee

MENU FIVE

Sweet Corn Chicken Soup
Dry Chilli Chicken
Prawn Soya Bean and Chilli
Sliced Chicken, Green and Red Pepper
Braised Lamb

Sweet Corn Asparagus
Batter Fried Mushrooms
Stir Fried Vegetables with Almonds
Eggplant with Chilli
Sweet and Sour Vegetables

Steamed Rice
Vegetable Hakka Noodles
Date Pancakes
Vanilla Ice Cream
Fresh Fruit
Jasmine Tea

Fig. 11.42. Banquet menus

Banquet menus

MENU ONE

Asparagus and Sea Food Salad with Tarragon Cream Dressing
Grilled Supreme of Pomfret with Tomato Concasse and Parsley Butter
Medallions of Lamb with Minted Aubergine Mousse and Green Pepper Sauce

Salad of Fresh Fruits and Celery served with a mild Ginger and Curry Sauce
Baked Crepe of Garden Vegetables masked with Cheddar Sauce
Cabbage Darioles served with Herbed Tomato Sauce

Selection of Fresh Vegetables and Potatoes
Rum Truffle Pastry in Tulip Biscuits with Vanilla Sauce
Fresh Fruit
Coffee and Friandises

MENU TWO

Baked Asparagus Tart with Artichoke
and Herb Butter Sauce

Non Vegetarian	Vegetarian
Consomme Brunoise	Potage Saint Cloud
Panfried Pomfret in Oatmeal served with Caper Lemon Sauce	Aubergine, Chilli, Garlic, Tomato and Shiitake Mushrooms with Tagliarini
Charred Escalope of Duck with Spiced Orange Sauce	Vegetable Timbale with two Sauces

Selection of Fresh Vegetables and Potatoes
Pineapple filled Profitroles on a base of Chocolate Sauce
Fresh Fruit
Coffee and Friandises

NON VEGETARIAN **VEGETARIAN**

MENU THREE

Dahi Ka Shorba

Non Vegetarian	Vegetarian
Fish Tikka	Sabz Seekh Kabab
Murg Lababdar	Kadhai Paneer
Mattar Korma	Mattar Korma
Dal Masala	Dal Masala

Navrattan Pulao
Dahi Pakodi
Achar, Papad, Chutney
Kala Jamun
Malai Chop

MENU FOUR

Mulligatawny Soup

Non Vegetarian	Vegetarian
Reshmi Kabab	Bharvan Tandoori Aloo
Aloo Tamatar Gosht	Paneer Do Piaza
Mixed Vegetable Kali Mirch	Mixed Vegetable Kali Mirch
Dal Maharani	Dal Maharani

Green Pea Pulao
Pudina Raita
Achar/Papad/Chutney
Kulfi Falooda
Moong Dal Halwa

MENU FIVE

Sour Pepper Vegetable Wonton Soup

Vegetable Spring Rolls	Vegetable Spring Rolls
Cripsy Fried Pork Red and Green Chilli	Spinach with Chilli Garlic
Diced Lamb with Cashewnuts	Okra Black Bean Sauce
Shredded Pctato	Shredded Potato Hot Garlic Sauce

Hot Garlic Sauce
Ginger Fried Rice
Hakka Noodles
Sesame Cake
Vanilla Ice Cream
Jasmine Tea

Fig. 11.43. Banquet menus

Banquet menus

NON-VEGETARIAN	VEGETARIAN
MENU ONE	
Dahi Ka Shorba Machli Chutney Wali Murg Do Piaza Elaichi Gosht Dal Makhani	Vegetable Jalfrezi Malai Kofta Gobhi Mattar Aloo Kaali Mirch

Dal Makhani
Kashmiri Pulao, Pineapple, Raita
Achar, Papad, Chutney,
Kheer, Jalebi, Coffee

MENU TWO

Carrot and Coriander Soup

NON-VEGETARIAN	VEGETARIAN
Fillet of Pomfret with Juliennes of Vegetable served with White Butter Sauce Chicken Roulade with Pistachio and served with Cream Sauce	Ravioli of Spinach and Pimento served with Cream Sauce infused with Nutmeg Mosaic of Cottage Cheese smothered with Basil and Tomato Concasse

Baked Lemon Tartlets with Italian Meringue and Brandy Sauce
Fresh Fruit
Coffee with Friandises

MENU THREE

Dal Shorba

Tandoori Murg Tikka
Achar Gosht
Paneer Lababdar
Sookhi Moong Dal

Tandoori Shimla Mirch
Aloo Dum Chutney Wala
Paneer Lababdar
Sookhi Moong Dal

Subz Biryani, Boondi Raita
Achar, Papad, Chutney
Gajar Halwa
Vanilla Ice Cream
Fresh Fruit, Coffee

MENU FOUR

Murg Shorba
Goan Fish Curry
Assortment of Kababs
Khoya Mattar Curry
Dal Hariyali

Tamatar Shorba
Radaa Paneer
Baingan Patiala
Khoya Mattar Curry
Dal Hariyali

Safed Chawal
Aloo Mint Raita
Achar, Papad, Chutney
Gulab Jamun
Rasmalai
Fresh Fruit
Coffee

MENU FIVE

Chicken Clear Soup
King Prawns with Greens
Cheng Du Chicken
Smoked Lamb Sesame with Black Mushroom

Vegetable Clear Soup
Egg plant Hong Kong Style
Plain Fried Spinach with Asparagus
Vegetable Hot Garlic Sauce

Steamed Rice
Chilli Garlic Noodles
Fresh Fruit Salad
Vanilla Ice Cream
Jasmine Tea

Fig. 11.44. Banquet menus

VEGETARIAN

Banquet menus

BUFFET LUNCHEONS AND DINNERS

CHOOSE ANY FOUR

Green Salad

Potato Salad

Sliced boiled potatoes, chopped onions and thin mayonnaise.

Chiffonade Salad

Lettuce, cucumber and quartered tomatoes mixed with French dressing, sprinkled with chopped beetroot, egg and parsley.

Coleslaw Hawaiian

Very fine shredded cabbage and carrots seasoned with salt and pepper with pineapple, chopped nuts and mayonnaise.

Kuchumber

Onions, tomatoes, cucumber, green chillies, coriander leaves, chopped ginger and lemon.

Russian Salad

Cooked cubes of carrots, beans, potatoes and green peas mixed with creamed mayonnaise.

Caprice Salad

Lettuce, sliced pineapple and tomatoes, with French dressing.

Cucumber SaladSwedish Style

Thin slices of cucumber with salt, pepper, sugar, chopped parsley and wine vinegar.

Tossed Salad

Sliced cucumber, tomatoes, green and red pepper tossed in lemon dressing and served on a bed of crisp lettuce.

Grand Union Salad

Coleslaw, green peppers and tomatoes served with French dressing.

CHOOSE ANY ONE

Lentil Soup

Combination of lentil and cream with croutons.

Sweetcorn Asparagus Soup

A soup with a combination of sweetcorn and asparagus.

Vegetable Broth Saffron

Vegetable soup flavoured with saffron.

Fig. 11.45. Vegetarian menus

BUFFET LUNCHEONS AND DINNERS

Cream of Tomato Soup

Puree of tomato mixed with bechamel sauce and cream, garnished with bread croutons.

Cream of Mushroom Soup

Puree of mushrooms mixed with cream and egg yolks and garnished with mushroom slices.

CHOOSE ANY FOUR

Vegetable Au Gratin Princess

Diced fresh vegetable baked with asparagus and gratinated with cheese.

Pasta with Four Season Sauce

Italian pasta with a creamy tomato and cheese sauce.

Alu Mattar

Potatoes with fresh green peas in a thick gravy.

Kaju Mattar Makhane

Cashewnuts, green peas and makhanas cooked in a korma sauce.

Palak Paneer

Puree of spinach and cottage cheese cooked together with spices.

Alu Dum Kashmiri

Deep fried potatoes cooked in a thick gravy.

Paneer Pasanda

Batter fried paneer cooked in a rich tomato gravy.

Lasagne Napolitaine

Blanched sheets of pasta placed in layers with vegetables and tomato sauce and baked in the oven.

Mushroom Fine Herbs

Mushroom cooked in a cream sauce with French herbs.

Malai Kofta

Deep fried creamy cottage cheese and vegetable balls cooked in a delicately flavoured gravy.

Khumb Mattar

Mushrooms and fresh green peas cooked in a rich gravy garnished with freshly chopped coriander.

Dry Seasonal Vegetables

Dal Makhani

Mah ki dal cooked with rajmah and channa dal and tempered with ginger, garlic and asafoetida.

Chana

Chana cooked in traditional Punjabi spices.

Rajmah

Rajmah cooked and garnished with onions, cumin seeds and green chilli.

Rice

Green Pea Pulao/Vegetable Pulao/Zaffrani Pulao/Kashmiri Pulao.

Naan/Paratha/Prui/Kulcha.

Raita, Achar Chutney, Papad.

DESSERT

CHOOSE ANY THREE

Queen of Puddings, Sevain Kheer, Gajar/Moong Dal Halwa,

Caramel Custard, Pineapple Gateaux, Gulab Jamun, Ice Cream, Pudding a Taj.

Fig. 11.46. Buffer Lunch and Dinner

Buffet Luncheons and Dinners NON-VEGETARIAN

CHOOSE ANY FOUR

Green Salad

Potato Salad

Sliced boiled potatoes, chopped onions and a thinned mayonnaise.

Chiffonade Salad

Lettuce, cucumber and quartered tomatoes mixed with French dressing, sprinkled with chopped beetroot, egg and parsley.

Coleslaw Hawaiian

Very fine shredded cabbage and carrots seasoned with salt and pepper with pineapple, chopped nuts and mayonnaise.

Kachumber

Onions, tomatoes, cucumber, green chillies, coriander leaves, chopped ginger and lemon juice.

Russian Salad

Cooked cubes of carrots, beans, potatoes and green peas mixed with a creamed mayonnaise.

Caprice Salad

Lettuce, sliced pineapple and tomatoes, with French dressing.

Cucumber Salad–Swedish Style

Thin slices of cucumber with salt, pepper, sugar, chopped parsley and wine vinegar.

Tossed Salad

Sliced cucumber, tomatoes, green and red pepper tossed in lemon dressing and served on a bed of crisp lettuce.

Grand Union Salad

Shredded cabbage, green peppers and tomatoes served with French dressing.

CHOOSE ANY ONE

Sweetcorn Chicken Soup

A soup with a combination of sweetcorn and diced chicken.

Tomato Egg Drop Soup

Cream of tomato broth with threaded egg.

Cream of Chicken Chartreuse

Veloute of chicken garnished with dices of tomato and small ravioli filled with spinach mushrooms.

Murg Shorba

Chicken soup, flavoured with Indian herbs and garnished with dices of chicken.

CHOOSE ANY ONE

Fish Colbert Tartare Sauce

(Contd.)

Fried fish fillets served with maitre d'hotel butter and tartare sauce.

Mixed Grilled Fish

Fresh fish marinated and grilled, served with lemon butter.

Tandoori Machli Tikka

Pieces of fresh fish marinated and cooked in the Tandoor.

CHOOSE ANY ONE

Kofta Kashmiri

Lamb Koftas flavoured and served with Kashmiri masala.

Lamb Chop Romarin

Lamb chops cooked with red wine, flavoured with garlic and resemary.

Lamb Steak Helder

Mutton Steak Cooked in Wine Sauce, garnished with tomato cubes and potato Parisienne.

Gosht Do Piaza

Tender mutton pieces cooked with freshly ground spices and onions.

Gosht Palak

Mutton pieces cooked with spiced minced spinach.

Mutton Chop Masala

Mutton chops lightly bar-be-qued and simmered in a thick gravy

CHOOSE ANY ONE

Roast Chicken Stelline

Roasted spring chicken, coated with wine sauce and star shaped dumplings.

Bhuna Murg Masala

Tender pieces of chicken, cooked in a freshly ground masala.

Murg Shahi Korma

A mid chicken korma prepared with Indian spices, condiments and curd.

Rogan-E-Murg

Chicken pieces in a tomato and curd based gravy with traditional Kashmiri spices.

Hyderabadi Chicken Curry

Chicken cooked with green coriander and condiments.

Rice

Green Pea Pulao/Vegetable Pulao/Zaffrani Pulao/Kashmiri Pulao.

Naan/Paratha/Puri/Kulcha.

Raita, Achar, Chutney, Papad.

DESSERT

CHOOSE ANY THREE

Queen of Puddings, Sevain Kheer, Gajar/Moong Dal Halwa,

Caramel Custard, Pineapple Gateaux, Gulab Jamun, Ice Cream, Pudding A La Taj.

Fig. 11.47. Buffet Lunch Dinner-non vegetarian

RECEPTIONS AND COCKTAILS

MENU ONE

Cold Canapes

Egg and Ham Mousse
Roast Beef and Gherkins
Tunna Fish
Chicken Liver Pate
Cucumber and Gherkin
Baked Beans
Mixed Pickles

Hot Canapes

Chicken Fingers
Batter Fried Prawns
Mutton Samosa
Chilli Cheese Toast
Vegetable Kabab
Mushroom Filled Croustade

MENU TWO

Cold Canapes

Chicken Gallantine
Creamed Egg
Salmon Mousse
Ham and Asparagus
Pickled Onion and Tomato
Cheddar Cheese and Olive
Corn Relish
Swedish Cucumber

Hot Canapes

Batter Fried Chicken
Ham and Tomato Pizza
Seekh Kabab Roll
Vegetable Pizzas
Vegetable Samosas
Cheese Balls
Masala Wafers

MENU THREE

Cold Canapes

Ham Mousse
Egg and Tomato
Pickled Fish
Chicken Loaf
Asparagus and Pimento
Tomato and Cheese
Creamed Cottage Cheese
Pickled Mushrooms

Hot Canapes

Seekh Kabab
Fish Goujons
Chicken Quiche
Mushrooms on Toast
Vegetables Seekh Kabab
Chutney Filled Paneer
Tostados

MENU FOUR

Cold Canapes

Beef Roll
Ham and Pineapple
Egg and Olive
Chicken Gallantine
Tomato and Cucumber
Kidney Beans
Corn Relish
Mixed Pickles
Hot Canapes
Shammi Kabab
Sausage Roll
Chicken Tikka
Fish Amritsari
Paneer Fingers
Chutney Filled Potato Balls
Cashewnut Rolls
Masala Green Pea Bouches

MENU FIVE

Cold Canapes

Cheese Onion Olive Sticks
Egg with Caviar
Chicken Gallantine with Pistachios
Roast Beef with Fried Onion
Pork Pate with Pickled Cabbage
Pickled Fish

Asparagus and Pimento
Corn Relish
Rainbow Canape Wheel
Tomato and Cucumber.

Hot Canapes
Golden Dragon
Chicken Tikka Barquettes
Khaas Seekh Kabab
Pork Wonton
Channa Chaurasia
Mushroom Duplex
Artichoke Quiche
Vegetable Pizza.

MENU SIX

Cold Canapes
Caviar and Sour Cream Bouches
Prawn Basil Sticks
Ham Mousse
Chicken Liver Pate
Smoked Salmon Roulette
Peanut Butter and Chopped Pickle
Pickled Mushroom
Tomato and Cheese.

Hot Canapes
Crumb Fried Chicken Quennels
Raan Chaurasia
Mixed Meat Dumplings
Prawns Nest
Mini Anchovy Croissant
Paneer Coins
Claret Mustard Cheese Toast
Vegetable Dumplings
Dal Vada.

MENU SEVEN

Cold Canapes
Salmon Mousse with Dil
Egg and Anchovy
Tuna Fish with Pickle
Chicken-Ham and Olive
Caviar on Toast
Roast Beef with Fried Onions
Asparagus and Pimento
Rainbow Canape Wheel
Corn Relish
Baked Beans
Creamed Cottage Cheese and Chutney
Cucumber and Olive.

Hot Canapes
Batter Fried Prawns
Chicken Prune Stick
Golden Nuggets
Pork Wonton
Seekh Kabab Roll
Vegetable Turnover
Mushroom Feuillette
Vegetable Shashlik
Fried Rice Cheese Balls
Paneer Coins.

Fig. 11.48. Reaffion's and cocktails

Conference Lunches

MENU ONE

Russian Salad
Beansprout Salad
Red Beans in Sweet and Sour Sauce
Consomme Xavier
Roast Lamb Polonaise
Chicken Sandeman or Grilled Chicken Diable Sauce
Cannelloni Neapolitana
Vegetable Shashlik
Spaghetti Burmese
Mont Blanc
Seasonal Fresh Fruit Tart
Tea/Coffee.

MENU TWO

Potato Salad
Coleslaw Hawaiian
Grand Union Salad
Minestrone
Seekh Kabab rolled in Roomali Roti
Machli Kababs
Tandoori Paneer rolled in Roomali Roti

Mushrocm Rissoles in Tomato Sauce
Macaroni Mexican
Flavoured Yoghurt
Peach Melba
Orange Souffle
Tea/Coffee.

MENU THREE

Rice & Pimento Salad
Kimchi
Sweet Cucumber Salad
Hot & Sour Pepper Soup
Diced Chicken Hong Kong Style
Lamb Shashlik
Spinach and Cabbage Chilli Garlic
Stir Fried Mushrooms
Bamboo Shoots and French Beans
Vegetable Spring Rolls
BeansproutsChinese Style
Date Pancakes with Ice Cream
Gorlee Banana
Tea/Coffee.

Fig. 11.49. Conference Lunches

OUTDOOR CATERING

It is also known as off-premises catering. The hotel providing outdoor catering facilities should make it a continuing activity to ensure the fuller utilization of its equipment and staff. A full and comprehensive sales service such as, meals, drinks, confectionery, cigarettes, hot dog kiosks and so on should be provided in these functions. The following points should be included in the initial survey to be conducted for proper planning of outdoor catering :

1. Type of function
2. Size of function
3. Date
4. Site and distance from depot
5. Local transport facilities
6. Local commodity supplier
7. Availability of staff
8. Layout of site
9. Number of people expected
10. Availability of water, gas, electricity, refrigerating
11. ASP of people attending
12. Kiosks and stand details
13. Time allowance for setting up catering units and dismantling
14. Type of licences required
15. Provision of mobile units adaptable to hot and cold food
16. Communication facilities to ensure coordination and control of staff and continuous supplies of commodities
17. Arrangement for photographers
18. Press and the media
19. Provision for changing rooms and toilets
20. Insurance against fire/weather etc.

21. Provision of first-aid
22. Estimate of cost of overhead
23. Type of service received
    (*i*) Buffet style
    (*ii*) Restaurant service
    (*iii*) Takeaway service
    (*iv*) Supply of hot dishes
    (*v*) Drink services
    (*vi*) Washing up facilities
    (*vii*) Containers for little and disposable items.

The person incharge of outdoor catering needs to be decisive, quick to command and adaptable to various situations. He need to have the respect of the staff, most of whom are taken on casual basis. Prior to every event each employee should receive an engagement pack consisting of :

1. Casual workers Registration Form.
2. Legal requirement Form.
3. Acceptance of offer of employment.

EXHIBITIONS IN HOTELS

Now a days hotels are increasingly being asked for exhibition facilities. The main advantages from the exhibition organiser's point of view are -under one roof an air of luxury is added to the attraction of bars, dining rooms and sleeping accommodation. The hotel should, therefore, study and give through to the available accommodation recognising that exhibition facilities could be a source of additional income, particularly during its off peak periods.

Many of the precautions mentioned earlier in the Conference section apply to the planning of an exhibition. Stridently patterned carpets can instantly destroy the quality of a display. Air-conditioning must not only be adequate, but constantly checked, as considerable heat is generated by the extra lighting needed and people - much more heat than is generated during a dance function. The hotel accommodation is small in exhibition terms and if well attended could result in very cramped conditions, so it is important to provide some over-flow area to which people can escape. Public rooms, usually adjacent to the area in use, should be made available for this purpose to raise the level of pleasure of efficiency for both exhibitors and the attendees.

Thought should be given to storage space. Every exhibition, small or large, will carry with it crates, packing materials and articles which will not be put on display. Because of this factor, extra porterage can be useful. Exhibitions bring bulky things with them and although contractors and exhibitors may have their own staff, but if space is to be cleared and set up in short time, they need hotel staff standing by for help.

The role of the local fire officer must be given due importance in arrangements. His advice is of vital importance. The chances are that the exhibition organisers may try and force more stands into the area than are safe from a fire and escape angle.

Lighting can be a grave problem if the hotel has not made adequate arrangements before offering its accommodation for use as an exhibitionarea. Lighting must be flexible, with points ideally in the middle of the room, either at floor or ceiling level. Extra points laid at the last minute can cost extra and the organisers are unlikely to look very favourably on the hotel who has provided the accommodation, but has to ask the organiser to pay for extra points to be installed and then finds that the wiring is insufficient to carry the extra load.

A simple paging system should be arranged to avoid the use of tannoy relayed into the exhibition room causing disturbance to everyone in the exhibition.

Care should be taken over the sign-posting system. Information which is well designed, prominent, flexible and clear can save a great deal of irritation to members of the staff and~to all those involved in the exhibition.

Finally, the hotel would not use bedrooms for exhibition purposes. Apart from the particularly cramped conditions, visitors are likely to feel 'trapped' once inside the door, with little hope of escaping unobserved. Freedom of movement is essential to the creation of an overall sense of luxury.

ACCOUNT, AUDIT AND CONTROL

BANQUET INCOME

Sales in connection with banquets and private parties should be accounted for in the respective selling departments. Sale of goods and services not sold in the ordinary course of business by any selling department of the, hotel, except in connection with banquets, may be accounted for in accordance with one of the following methods :

1. Credit to the various expense accounts : If such sales are only occasional, or if the profit on them is negligible or not practically de-terminable, the sales should be credited to the various expenses accounts to which the cost would be naturally charged. For example, under this method, an occasional sale of music would be credited to music and entertainment and an occasional sale of flowers to decorations. The cost of goods and services sold in connection with banquets which are not regularly sold by any department and are not applicable to any specific expense items in the food schudule, should be charged to banquet expense and the relative sales credited to the same account.
2. Credit to 'Sundry Banquet Income' : If the sundry sales in connection with banquets are of suffcient importance to make it desirable to determine the profit on such sales, accounts should be opened in accordance with this schedule. The profit on such sales should be carried over to the food schedule as 'Sundry Banquet Income'.

Each function is a separate occasion. It has its own price, menu and staffing. It must be closely controlled, specially when food production takes place in a separate kitchen and a bar. The revenue and the direct costs can be ascertained with accuracy. (Ref fig. 11.50) The main records include :

1. A function agreement, which summarizes the arrangement for each function
2. A function diary, which lists details of all functions in date order
3. A function chart, which provides a visual record of all functions arranged for a period ahead

4. In-house information and restriction lists.

The revenue and the direct costs can be ascertained with accuracy. The volume of identical meals prepared and served together enables the hotel to have high profit managers, as such functions represent the second most profitable hotel product after rooms.

REVENUE

The various sources of revenue and cost of banquet are :

1. Music and entertainment
2. Decorations
3. Mechanical work and equipment
4. Other labour
5. Printing and stationery
6. Souvenirs and favours
7. Rentals of equipment
8. Miscellaneous.

EXPENSES

MUSIC AND ENTERTAINMENT

Music and entertainment hired for banquet purposes.

ABC Hotels Ltd.
Sundry Banquet Income Schedule

NET SALES	Current period
Music and Entertainment	₹ ....
Decorations	....
Mechanical Work and Equipment	....
Other Labour	....
Priming and Stationery	....
Souvenirs and Favours	....
Rental of Equipment	....
Miscellaneous	....
Total Net Revenue	₹ ....
COSTS	
Music and Entertainment	₹ ....
Decorations	....
Mechanical Work and Equipment	....
Other Labour	....
Printing and Stationery	....
Souvenirs and Favours	....
Rental of Equipment	....

Miscellaneous	....
Total Costs	₹ ....
Department Income (Profit)	....
Music And Entertainment	₹ ....
Decorations	....
Mechanical Work and Equipment	....
Other Labour	....
Printing and Stationery	....
Souvenirs and Favours	....
Rental of Equipment	....
Miscellaneous	....
Total Net Revenue	₹ ....

Note: Various arrangements of additional columns for comparisons and percentages could be added.

Fig. : 11.50 : Analysis of Income and Expenses of Sundry Banquet Income

DECORATIONS

Cost of flowers, plants and decorations purchased for banquet purposes and charged to banquet engagers. If, however, the hotel operates a florist department, the sales and cost of flowers, plant and other decorations furnished by the florist should be credited and charged, respectively, to that department.

MECHANICAL WORK AND EQUIPMENT

Setting up and removing stages or scenery, specific electric wiring, spotlights, moving picture projectors, stereophonic and other equipment, material d labour furnished by the mechnical department.

OTHER INCOMES

There are many other sources of hotel income which are not connected directly with the operational activities (Ref. Fig. 11.51). All these incomes are received in small amounts from different heads :

RENTALS

There are many spaces which are used for the operations of a hotel as a part of usual hotel service. Rental received from these are credited to Rental Account. Some of these sub-heads of income are :

OFFICE RENTALS

It includes the rent income from space in the hotel building used as offices by tenants other than concessionaires.

RENT FROM CLUBS

Rent received from rooms allotted to club are included under this head and all expenses related to the club room are also charged to this account.

OTHERS

It includes :

1. Rent from lobby space
2. Rent from show cases
3. Rent from other spaces.

Commission paid to renting agents is charged against the gross income from rentals and after adjustment of expenses net rental income is calculated.

CONCESSIONS

Revenue received from outside for the privilege of operating departments which might be operated by the hotel itself as part of the usual hotel service. Expenses to the hotel in connection with the operation of a concession which would be charged as departmental expenses. If the department were operated by the hotel, should be charged against the income received from the concessionnarie are credited to this account. Some of the sources of revenue of concessions are :

1. Barber shop
2. Cigars and news stand
3. Guest laundry
4. Beauty shop
5. Gift shops
6. Public stenographers
7. Restaurants
8. Transportation
9. Foreign exchange
10. Gaming machine revenue.
11. Swimming pool, cabanas and baths
12. Valet
13. Show case rent.

INTEREST

The hotel earns interest on bank deposits and other investment of sparefunds.

FOREIGN EXCHANGE

Foreign currency and travellers' cheques are normally exchanged by hotels for guests at rates more favourable to the hotel than those offered by banks to safeguard against fluctuations in rates between their encashment by the hotel and their sale to the bank, and sometimes also to include a charge for the service rendered.

COMMISSIONS

The following incomes received as commissions are credited to this account :

1. Commission from telegram
2. Commission from taxi and car hire
3. Commission from garage and parking lot
4. Commission from auto rentals
5. Commission from radio and television
6. Commission from photographers
7. Commission from theatre and travel agencies and other suppliers to guests.

If a telephone company occupies space in the lobby, the income to the hotel from such space should be credited to rentals even though the income is determined on the percentage basis. Similarly, so called "commissions" from concessionaires should be included in the income from concessions.

VENDING MACHINES

The revenue derived from vending machines less the cost of merchandise sold is credited to this head.

CASH DISCOUNT EARNED

All discount earned from creditors due to cash payment within the discount period are credited to this account.

SALVAGE

It includes revenue derived from the sale of waste paper, incidental articles, obsolete material and used cooking oil.

MISCELLANEOUS

Sundry incomes which cannot be grouped under any of the above heads are credited to this account.

ABC Hotels Ltd.
Other Incomes Schedule

	Current period
Rentals Inside Space	₹ ....
Offices	....
Clubs	....
Others	....
Total Rentals	₹ ....
Concession	....
Barber Shop	₹ ....
Beauty Shop	....
Checkrooms and Washrooms	....
Cigar and Gift Shop	....
Public Stenographer	....
Restaurant	....
Swimming Pool, Cabanas and Baths	....
Transportation	....
Valet	....
Total Concessions	₹ ....
Commissions	
Auto Rentals	₹ ....
Flowers	....
Garage and Parking Lot	....
Radio and Television	....
Laundry	....
Valet	....
Games and Vending Machines	....
In-house movies	....

Taxicabs	....
Telegraph	....
Others	....
Total Commissions	....
Electronic Games and Pin Ball Machines	₹ ....
Vending Machines	....
Cash Discounts Earned	....
Foreited Advance Deposits	....
Interest Income	....
Salvage	
Miscellaneous	....
Total Other Incomes	₹ ....

Note : Various arrangements of additional columns for comparisons and percentages could be added.

Fig. 11.51 : Analysis of Income and Expenses of Other Incomes

OTHER OPERATED DEPARTMENTS

A hotel may have operated other departments and provide many other services for the benefit of guests. A separate schedule for all such services could be prepared as given in Fig. 11.52.

ABC HOTELS LTD.
OTHER OPERATED DEPARTMENTS SCHEDULE

	Current Period
Revenue	
Service	....
Sales of Merchandise	....
Total Revenue	₹ ....
Allowances	....
Net Revenue	....
Cost of Merchandise Sold	....
Gross Profit (Loss)	....
Expenses	
Salaries and Wages	....
Employee Benefits	....
Total Payroll and Related Expenses	....
Other Expenses	
China and Glassware	....
Contract Services	....
Laundry	....
Linen	....
Operating Supplies	....
Uniforms	....
Others	....
Total Other Expenses	....
Department Income (Loss)	₹ ....

Note : Various arrangements of additional columns for comparisons and percentages could be added.

Fig. 11.52 : Analysis of Income and Expenses of Other Operated Departments

QUESTIONS AND ASSIGNMENTS

1. Draw an organisational chart of the Banquet Deptt. of a 5-star hotel having six variable banquet halls with a total capacity of 3,000-guests. Also give a three line description of the function of each of these staff.
2. Prepare a Function Prospectus of a wedding party of 350-pax. Booked for 10th February, 2000-from 5 p.m. to 11 p.m., you are required to serve evening tea snacks and dinner. Make your over assumption where ever necessary. ***(IHMs)***
3. (*a*) What is Credit Card ?
   (*b*) How do you accept payment through it and what precaution will you take while dealing with it ? ***(IHMs)***
4. (*a*) What are the traveller cheques ?
   (*b*) What are the procedures involved in making payment through them? ***(IHMs)***
5. (*a*) What is telex ?
   (*b*) What are the procedure for incoming and outgoing message. What is the difference between telex and fax ? ***(IHMs)***
6. Write down the duties and responsibilities of Door man. How does he controls car parking ? ***(IHMs)***
7. (*a*) What is left luggage ?
   (*b*) What kind of records are maintained for it ?
   (*c*) What is the procedure for accepting baggage for store ? ***(IHMs)***
8. What is the paging and how it is done in the hotel ? ***(IHMs)***
9. What is a Fax? How Fax is different from Telex ?
10. What is the Safe Deposit Locker handover process to the guest? ***(IHMs)***
11. What is Travel Agent Voucher and how it is different from Traveller's Cheque ? ***(IHMs)***
12. Why is it necessary for a hotel to provide safe deposit lockers for the valuables of the guests? Explain procedure for allocating a safe deposit locker to a guest. ***(IHMs)***
13. Discuss the main methods of paging for hotel guests with the merits and demerits of each methods. ***(IHMs)***
14. Discuss the various types of telephone calls that can be made from a hotel. ***(IHMs)***
15. Give the step by step procedure for out going telex message with the help of formats wherever necessary ***(IHMs)***
16. List the steps to be followed when planning a laundry. ***(IHMs)***
17. What steps must be followed to organise a linen inventory ? ***(IHMs)***
18. Draw a list of leisure areas in the hotel. Explain briefly how swimming pool is cleaned.
19. (*a*) Draw a flow process chart of the Industrial Laundering with a brief explanation of each stage.
   (*b*) What are the advantages and disadvantages of having a laundry on the premises ?
20. (*a*) What are the various styles of flower arrangement ?
   (*b*) List the various materials and equipment required for flower arrangement. ***(IHMs)***
   (*c*) Discuss possible locations for flower arrangements in a hotel in order to enhance the ambience and provide 'the personal touch'. ***(IHMs)***
21. Design and explain function prospectus form required for the banquet department of a 5-Star hotel. ***(IHMs)***

22. What is the importanace of a banquet service ? Explain. ***(IHMs)***

23. As a Banquet manager of a 5- star hotel you have been approached to make arrangements for the annual dinner of Indian Hotelier and Caterers Association to be served in the month of December, 2000. You are required to make arrangements for cocktail reception followed by a sit down dinner for 250-persons. Hon'ble minister of tourism is the chief guest:-

(*a*) Submit a suitable seating plan assuming the banquet to be formal and 21-guests are to be seated at the top table.

(*b*) Submit a menu consisting of five courses.

(*c*) Name the drinks and savouries you will serve in the cooktail Reception.

(*d*) You are charging ₹ 400 per person; mention how much you will spend towards food cost.

(*e*) Estimate the requirement of furniture and service staff. ***(IHMs)***

24. Prepare a simple Banquet Menu file for evening snacks function, with necessary instructions for the organisers to choose the dishes. ***(IHMs)***

25. What are the different table layouts used for formal Banquet function ? What are the major factors taken into consideration to identify by the suitable layout. ***(IHMs)***

26. List the protocol regulations to be kept in mind while making the seating plan for formal Banquets. ***(IHMs)***

27. Differentiate between Fork Buffet and Finger Buffet. ***(IHMs)***

28. In the form of a report to your Managing Director, draft proposals for marketing and selling banquet and conference business in either an hotel or a residential centre. In your report draw up procedures for handling individual booking arrangements. ***(HCMA, London)***

29. With the help of a flow chart illustrate the restaurant control cycle using the triplicate checking system. ***(IHMs)***

30. Illustrate with the help of a flow chart the Triplicate checking system of a restaurant control. *(IHMs)*

31. An effective control system is necessary for maximising F & B sales. How do KOTS contribute in achieving this end ? ***(IHMs)***

32. Pilferage and wastage reduce profits in F & B sales. How do KOTS help to overcome these problems ? Explain in about 200–250 words. ***(IHMs)***

33. Discuss the view that successful catering today seems to rely increasingly on the use of statistical and financial analysis to the extent that managers can no longer afford the time to develop their personal flair and traditional skills.

34. As a catering manager of a food and beverage unit of your choice, suggest steps you would take to increase and sustain the volume of profitable business. ***(HCIMA, London)***

35. A busy catering operation comprises a restaurant with a full table service, grill bar, a cocktail bar, a public bar with snack counter, and banquet accommodation, Indicate how would you set about establishing a price structure for each of these outlets and show the need for and how would you develop a forward pricing policy. ***(HCIMA, Lodnon)***

36. To what extent do you judge that in order to satisfy profit targets today, the catering industry has misjudged long-term consumer expectations by reducing 'service' so drastically that it could never be reintroduced ? ***(HCIMA, London)***

37. Identify the principal areas of management control required for the successful functioning of food operation. Describe briefly how could you set and maintain standards in these areas. course or at the end of dinner (choose the appropriate one).

38. Prepare a job description of a Banquet Captain. ***(IHMs)***

39. Draw up a carefully designed function prospectus format. ***(IHMs)***

40. As a banquet manager plan the staff required in the Banquet department of a 5-star hotel operating 6-banquet halls with a maximum capacity of 2000-pax in all. ***(IHMs)***

41. Calculate the length of the top and spring table for a formal sit down banquet of 250-pax with 11-persons on the top table. Illustrate with the help of a neat diagram. ***(IHMs)***

42. Prepare a job description of a Banquet Captain. ***(IHMs)***

43. Explain banqueting and draw up a carefully designed 'Function Prospectus' format.

44. The marketing of Banquet Department is by the Banquet Folder which consists of banquet menu file, room layouts, and terms and conditions.

45. Briefly describe the facilities available in a health club of various types of hotels.

46. Define the terms 'banqueting'. Explain in detail the full procedure of banqueting activities in a medium sized hotel. ***(PGDT&HM)***

47. Indicate the operational aspect of catering at a banquet function which a big industrialist is holding in your hotel. ***(PGT&HM)***

48. Draw an organisation chart of the Banquet Department of a five star international hotel having six variable banquet halls with a total capacity of 3,000-guests. Also give a three line development of the function of each of these staff. ***(MTA)***

49. What are the different layouts used for formal banquet function ? What are the major factors taken into consideration to identify the suitable layout? ***(IHMs)***

50. As a Banquet manager plan the staff required in the Banquet Department of a 5-star hotel operating six Banquet Halls with a maximum capacity of 2000-pax in all. ***(IHMs)***

51. Stepwise mention the protocol to be maintained in a formal state banquet. ***(IHMs)***

52. State the formalities to be carried out for setting up a temporary bar for a banquet. ***(IHMs)***

OBJECTIVE TYPE QUESTIONS

53. **Answer the following:**

(*a*) Size of a 4 covers square table is ....

(*b*) Name five banquet tools: (1)............ (2)............ (3)............ (4)........... (5)..........

(*c*) Banquet Memorandum means .... (Function Sheet/Banquet Diary/Function Prospectus).

(*d*) Capacity of margarita (a stemware) is .... $\left(5\text{ OZ}/5\frac{1}{2}\text{OZ}/5\frac{1}{2}\text{OZ}/6\text{OZ}.\right)$.

(*e*) Air space at top of a wine barrel due to evaporation or leakage is called ....

(*f*) In a formal banquet toasting is done at the begining of dinner or at the middle with rest course or at the end of dinner. (Choose the appropriate one).

(*g*) Henry Charpentier accidentally invented flambe dish in the year ....

(*h*) For a buffet service of 300-pax total space required would be .... sq. ft.**(IHMs)**

CHAPTER 12

Finance, Accounting, Audit, Budget & Control

OBJECTIVES

After studying this chapter you should be able to :

1. *Understand the role of accounting and finance*
2. *Explain budgeting, auditing and control*
3. *Understand the organisation of finance, accounting budgeting and control*
4. *Understand the working of a store and*
5. *Appreciate the application of computers.*

ORGANISATION

Behind the scene in a hotel just as in any other business there must be an adequate recording of all business transactions. The accounting and control department of a hotel is of vital importance specially because of the peculiarities of this business. Most functions of this department are of technical nature and they require a good deal of background and training for comprehension. Every manager should have a knowledge of and a sound background in accounting and control techniques and procedures.

The head of this department is styled as Financial Controller/Vice President (Finance)/ Chief Controller/Chief Accounts Officer/Auditor.

DIRECTOR FINANCE/FINANCIAL CONTROLLER

He must have thorough knowledge of general and analytical accountancy and of the organisation of the hotel and its service. He has to organise and direct accounting operations of the hotel. He is also responsible for organising and carrying out inspections and verifications. He advises on accounting and financial matters and informs the manager regarding the result of the business.

DEPUTY FINANCE CONTROLLER

He should have good knowledge of the administrative procedures. A controller should have knowledge about the various services the hotel offers and their operation. He must know the process of price fixation. The main responsibilities of the controller are to supervise the administrative running of services, to check the delivery orders and issue of the stores. He checks the suppliers and equipment and any loss, breakages etc., must be brought to the knowledge of the manager.

Pix. 12.1 : Planning are Financial Management

Pix. 12.2 : Working on a Computer

CONTROLLER (FINANCE & ACCOUNTS)

He is one of the major departmental heads in a large hotel. In small hotel this position is held by Chief Accounts Officers or Accountant. In chain hotel he is responsible to Corporate Controller or Vice President (Finance). Thus he has dual responsibility to the Controller, Corporate Finance and to the General Manager of the hotel. The title clearly suggests that he is the one who controls and not merely records the incomes and expenses of the hotel.

In respect of hotel's incomes he checks the accuracy of the amount reported, thus ensuring that the hotel receives 100% of the money spent by guests. Checking of expenses required more than the verification of the mathematical accuracy of creditors' bill. He is responsible to the checking of the legitimacy of the charges as to both quantity received and proceed charged.

The General Manager or a designated representative approves all the hotel's purchases, the controller in effect checks the General Manager. As such, it is easier and the result is more meaningful to check the work of the person who does not have the sole authority to hire or fire you. However, this does not in any way alter the primary function and responsibilities of the Controller. He fully cooperates with the General Manager and provides all the reports and statistics required to properly evaluate and operate the hotel business activities.

Since the Controller is an active member of the top management team, it adds new responsibilities to his position. The complexities and diversification of finance, accounts, budgeting, control and auditing department's responsibilities are best reflected through the organisational chart of this department. It differs from hotel to hotel and many hotels change it to satisfy their own priorities on the requirements of the hotel. However, in most large hotels the chart reflects two different aspects of the department's responsibilities. The 'first, 'through the deputy controller and such departmental heads under them, is the accounting and audit function. The 'second', those reporting directly to the Controller, a lesser known area of responsibility, the direct participation of the accounting staff in guest relations. To the general public, cashiers, credit personnel and night auditors are restaurant cashiers and checkers are part of food and beverages.

The accounting, finance, control and auditing departments in a hotel require standardization. Each hotel is required to forward forecasts, reports, statistics and operating result to the head office. These are valuable tools to judge the operation of the hotel. These reports should be uniform in contents and in the methods used to assemble the information and comparison. The controller is called upon to draw up new formats to present the desired information and interpret the findings.

All hotels operate on budgets. The Controller is responsible for the budget preparation and budgetary control. The budget is an estimate or forecast of revenues and expenses for a fiscal year in the future. All the primary departmental heads with the aid of their department and sub-departmental heads are best qualified to make these forecasts. The Controller gets these forecasts based on past performance and current price levels and future bookings. Based on these he prepares the budget and presents it to the Corporate Controller and management for final approval. This is done few months before the start of the period concerned. On approval by the board of directors, each member of the management team is responsible for budget implementation. They have to hold their departmental expenses to the allocated amount as per the budget. Any change requires frequent consultation with the departmental heads and meetings with the management both before and after approval. Thus the function of the Controller is an all-round full-time job.

The classification of employees connected with this department is given in Table 12.1.

Table 12.1: Classification of Employees in function, Accounting, Audit, Budget and Control

ACCOUNT OFFICE	
1. Chief Account Officer/Chief Accountant	8. Assistants
2. Chief/head cashier	9. General Cashiers
3. Book-keepers	10. Income Auditor's
4. Controllers	11. Payroll Clerks
5. Statisticians	12. File Clerks
6. Stenographers	13. Typists
7. Clerks	14. Office Boys etc.
DATA PROCESSING	
1. Supervisors	5. Analysists
2. System Personnel	6. Programmers
3. Operators	7. Data processing clerks
4. Key punchers	8. Code clerks
CREDIT OFFICE	
1. Credit Manager	4. Assistants
2. Credit Investigators	5. Stenographers
3. File Clerks	
RECEIVING SECTION	
1. General Receiving Clerks	
2. Food and Beverage Receiving Clerks	
3. Restaurant Suppliers Receiving Clerks	
NIGHT AUDITORS	
1. Chief Night Auditors	
2. Night Auditors	
3. Transcript Clerks.	

ACCOUNTS OFFICER

The accounts officer is responsible for :

1. Writing of all books of accounts and preparation of vouchers/credit notes
2. How the supplier's bills are scrutinised and payment made against the vouchers ?
3. He must acquaint himself with the following :
   (*i*) Trial balance of the sundry debtors ledger
   (*ii*) Sundry creditors ledger
   (*iii*) General ledger

(*iv*) Preparation of payrolls and relevant sheets

(*v*) Preparation of statement pertaining to sales tax and other taxes

(*vi*) How the various monthly statutory returns to appropriate government authorities are submitted e.g. provident funds, family pensions, off-days etc.

(*vii*) Maintaining of fixed assets register as well as statistical records and registers.

4. Preparation of the following statements :

   (*i*) Profit and Loss Account

   (*ii*) Income and Expenditure

   (*iii*) Balance Sheet

   (*iv*) Monthly and Annual Accounts

5. Attend to auditors
6. Hotel insurance matters
7. Monthly stock-taking and spot checking of stock entries
8. Bills and catering records
9. Outstanding bills
10. Statement of travel agents regarding outstanding payments
11. Catering statements like food cost, staff food, complementaries as well as relevant reports to head office
12. Payment of wages and salaries and other dues to the staff member at the end of the each month
13. Drawing of money from the bank as and when required
14. To maintain register for the following :

    (*i*) Cheque deposited in bank

    (*ii*) Unpaid wages and salaries

    (*iii*) Revenue stamps etc.

15. How the accounts are recorded for cash, money, cheques, foreign currency, demand drafts and how the above are deposited daily in the bank
16. Various correspondence on all matters.

COST CONTROLLER

Finance and cost control techniques are inter-related to the accounting cycle and a pre-requisite for any Cost Controller is a sound basic knowledge of the double entry accounting procedures. For purposes of effective directions and controls the establishment may be sub-divided into the major and minor revenue producing departments. The activities of each department may be controlled by organising and imposing a control system network. The head of the department should be responsible that the principles and procedures of finance and cost control system are adhered to by the members of the staff in the department. They should ensure that all information data, reports, statements and statistical data required by the Controller are favoured to the Controller at the correct appointed time. The information must be up- to-date so that corrective action may be taken immediately. The functions of the Cost Controller are :

1. To devise a simple cost control system which may be adapted to the general patterns of business.

2. To ensure the cooperation of all the concerned departments.
3. To ensure that all forms and procedures devised for the system are properly utilised and maintained for an effective control.
4. To ensure that the staff is rightly instructed and assisted in the completion of cost control documents as majority of the personnel may not be familiar with them and do not understand their purposes.

FOOD AND BEVERAGE CONTROLLER

The food and beverage controller keeps a check on all the food and beverage outlets of the hotel. The control is done on two broad spheres, namely:

1. Food
2. Beverage and smokes alcoholic non alcoholic

For food items, all the food checks are collected daily from all the food and beverage outlets and arranged serialwise. These are tallied with the KOTs. The price is checked and total sale is calculated to see whether the amount is justified or is in excess. If any discrepancy is discovered, the concerned employees are informed and necessary action is taken. Thus the main objectives of food and beverage control are :

1. To keep a constant check on costs of food and beverage production and hence maintain a food cost level
2. To ensure that misappropriation of food and beverage does not take place
3. To prevent spoilage, pilferage and wastage of materials
4. To indicate what is going wrong where and to try and remedy the problem with regard to food and beverage
5. To keep a strict check on liquor, as it is a high cost item and small losses can lead to light monetary losses.

The food and beverage cost controller is responsible for activities such as:

1. Actual cost procedures of food and beverage department.
2. How the daily and monthly food and beverage reports are prepared.
3. Preparation of statistics and budget.
4. Records of complementaries, staff meals, check etc.
5. Spot checking on various points and previous day's balance to check food and beverage cost.
6. Costing of store issue and banquet menus.
7. Checking of KOTs and other food and beverage controls, periodical stocks and verification of inventories.
8. Daily inventory of hard liquor and what measures are exercised to control the same.
9. Occasional market surveys and its report.
10. Portion control and control of wastage.
11. Menu planning and standard recipes.

INCOME ACCOUNTANT

He is responsible for ensuring daily that all cash and credit sales and services rendered by the hotel have been correctly charged and accounted for. At the close of each day, a complete summary of the type and business done by each department is prepared after checking the night auditor's report and other revenue data for the previous day. Copies of daily report are sent to the General Manager and concerned departmental heads. At the end of the months, the departmental sales are posted to the ledger which are used for preparing monthly financial statement.

ACCOUNTS CLERK (EXPENSES)

His work involves handling of expenses. Purchases are initiated by individual departmental heads. All purchases must be certified, recorded and paid. On receipt of invoices it must be certified by the departmental head that goods are received, they are in order, and the charge is correct. These invoices are returned to the accounts department for recording and passed to the manager for approval. All invoices for food and beverages are channeled through Food and Beverage Controller for statistical and control analysis. The accounts clerk prepares a list for all outstanding creditors and a summary of all payment made over the period at the end of each accounting period.

PAYROLL

This work is looked after by a payroll clerk. He prepares the payroll and checks the individual time sheets to ensure its correctness. A summary sheet of the payroll for each department will be prepared to draw the amount and make up the individual pay packets for payment.

FRONT OFFICE CASHIER

The Chief Front Office cashier is responsible for all cash transactions at the front office. He is responsible to the Chief Accounts Officer or Income Accountant depending upon the size of the hotel. Close cooperation between the front office and the cashier's section is required to avoid financial loss and ensure prompt payment to guest financial requirements. The various control measures are indicated in Fig. 12.1.

Control Measures and Methods of Payment

Method of payment	Control measures
1. Cash	1. Record amount received in payment of account in Cash
	2. Received book
	3. Total cash received book to tally with amount in bill
	4. Record payment on tab ledger/against cash code on computer
	5. Receipt guests account to denote payment
	6. Allocate an individual till to all cashiers on duty at one time
	7. Sign cash floats in and out
2. Cheques	1. Check cheque completed properlydate, company name; amount; signature
	2. Cheque must be signed in presence of cashier
	3. Check cheque card guarantees payment of cashier
	4. Check cheque card as means of identification

(Contd...)

Method of payment	Control measures
	5. Cheque card guarantees payment of a cheque to a certain amount as per the hotel's rules
	6. Only one cheque should be used for one transaction
	7. If more amount cashier must write cheque card number on back this means transaction is charged as a cash transaction and guest cannot stop it later
3. Travellers' cheques	1. Often proof of identity, e.g., passport is required before travellers' cheques are acceptedto be retained whilst guest signs travellers' cheques
	2. Travellers' cheque must have been signed on issue from bank
	3. Cashier must watch guest make second signatureif not guest must sign on back
	4. Check two signatures, check with passport signature, check date
4. Foreign currency	1. If going to accept foreign currency, have a well organised system.
	2. Know which currencies will and will not be accepted
	3. Foreign currency legally may only be accepted in payment of accounta foreign exchange should not be set up
	4. Check exchange rates daily if not more often
	5. Charge a realistic commission to cover administrative charges and unexpected fluctuations in exchange rate
	6. Monitor it carefully as it is easier to defraud establishment this way than with other methods of payment
5. Credit cards (*i*) Visa/Access	1. Check individual credit limit if account is over a fixed amounteither by phone or computerised terminal
	2. Complete a sales voucher and credit card imprint
	3. Guest must sign
	4. Check validity of credit carddate of expiry, signature against signature on sales voucher
	5. Give copy to guest and retain copiesone to go to credit card company for payment
(*ii*) Travel/ Entertainment Crdit Cards. e.g. American Express	6. As above
	7. Establishment must pay a commission to company for franchise
6. Travel agents vouches	1. Check detailscompany, amount, signature, etc.
	2. Guest must signcheck signature
	3. Retain copy for submission to Travel Agents with commission
7. Transfer to Outstanding	1. Ensure guest checks and signs account

(*Contd.*)

Accounts Ledger	2. Send copy to control/accounts office
	3. Record form of payment appropriately in accounting systemmust be segregated from other forms of payment
	4. Only creditworthy customers with satisfactory references will be offered this facility
	5. Require authorised users and credit limits if companies/business houses allow this facility.

Fig. 12.1 : Control Measures and Methods of Payment

The Front Office Cashier is responsible for posting all guest charges as are received from the various departments. The department charges are posted by night auditors. He balances all guest bills and prepares a recapitulation of day business. The Chief Front Office Cashier is responsible for ensuring that all guest bills are at all times posted up-to-date and are ready for immediate check out. His section is the last contact between the hotel and the guest as such vitally important in the hotel business.

The Front Office Cashier must be an honest and cautious person and should have a wide experience of accounts with a good general education. The main duties of a front office cashier are:

1. He should be responsible for the funds entrusted to him by the manager.
2. He should carry out all the front office cash transactions and prepare the related document.
3. He should analyse and check the guest bills and receive the payment.
4. If authorised by the management he should carry out the foreign exchange transactions and accept the payment in cheque against settlement of bills.
5. On settlement of bills he will issue the official receipt to the customer.
6. He issues the cashier clearance card so that the luggage of the guest could be removed from the hotel on departure.
7. In some of the hotels he is authorised to accept the valuables and other articles from the customers and keeps them in safe deposit.
8. He maintains the record of the foreign exchange transactions in a foreign exchange book/sheet.
9. Each day he deposits the previous day's receipts in the hotel funds.
10. He is responsible for returning all the credit bills after getting them signed by the customers to the concerned establishment. In large hotel this job is assigned to the Accounts Department.

Most of the luxury hotels have complete automation of the front office reservation and accounting functions. Automation is designed to improve guest relations. It provides fast and accurate information to speed up the registration and check out procedure, upto the minute reports and analysis to the management and thus reduces maintenance and operating costs. Introduction of computers eliminates the need for room racks, rack slips, stock card, guest bills and telephone and information rack. For guest with reservation the rate, type of room location etc. is already in the computer and those who are walking in the clerk must input the information and the computer assigns the room to the guests. On registration of the guest, an electronic in-house folio is created and switch board terminal is up-dated to include the guest name and room member, which helps the telephone operators in immediately accepting incoming calls or messages. The electronic folio remains in the computer until the guests checkout. At the time of check out the computer produces, completely itemised guest folios and transfers them to the proper city ledger if they are not paid in full.

Thus an automated system eliminates most of the accounting functions of the night auditors. Room rents and taxes are automatically posted to guest bills each night.

Although cashier and night auditors are not members of the front office staff, they work closely with the room clerk and are directly involved in guest relations. They are in direct contact with the guest during their stay. They give the guest change, convert their foreign currency and cash their travellers' cheques.

The cashier's desk is situated at a place where the guests go to check out and settle their bills. The cashier is the last member to come into direct contact with the guest. Close cooperation between the front office cashier and front office is required in order to avoid financial loss to the hotel and to ensure prompt attention to guest's financial requirements.

AUDITORS

The main duties of the auditors are :

1. To post all charges not posted by bill clerks
2. To verify the accuracy and completeness of all guest accounts
3. To analyse the nature and value of all transactional documentation
4. To be responsible for guest folio entries and departmental record balancing.

RESTAURANT AND BAR CASHIER

These cashiers are attached to different restaurants of the hotel. They must have perfect knowledge of menu of the establishment and its prices. They should be able to operate the cash register. The important duties of the cashiers are :

1. To carry out all the cash operation
2. To be responsible for cash in the register
3. To receive the customer's order voucher from the station waiter and make out the bills
4. To check the cash register everyday and account for existing funds
5. To send to the secretariate the vouchers to be debited to the hotel guests.

Cashiers are essential. No restaurant or food out-let can open without them. In most of the hotels the cashiers report to the controller of the hotel but for all practical purposes, the cashiers work much close with food and beverage department.

He has dual responsibility to the General Manager and to the Vice- President (Finance) in the home office. His job and duties will depend upon the size of the establishment and volume of work to be done. In a small hotel he will keep books of account and do a good part of the general office work. In a large hotel he will, of course, have a number of assistants depending upon the need of the establishment. In still larger hotels the work of this department is sub-divided into two partstreasurers office and credit department. Fig. 12.2, 12.3 and 12.4 indicate the different types of organisational structure of this department.

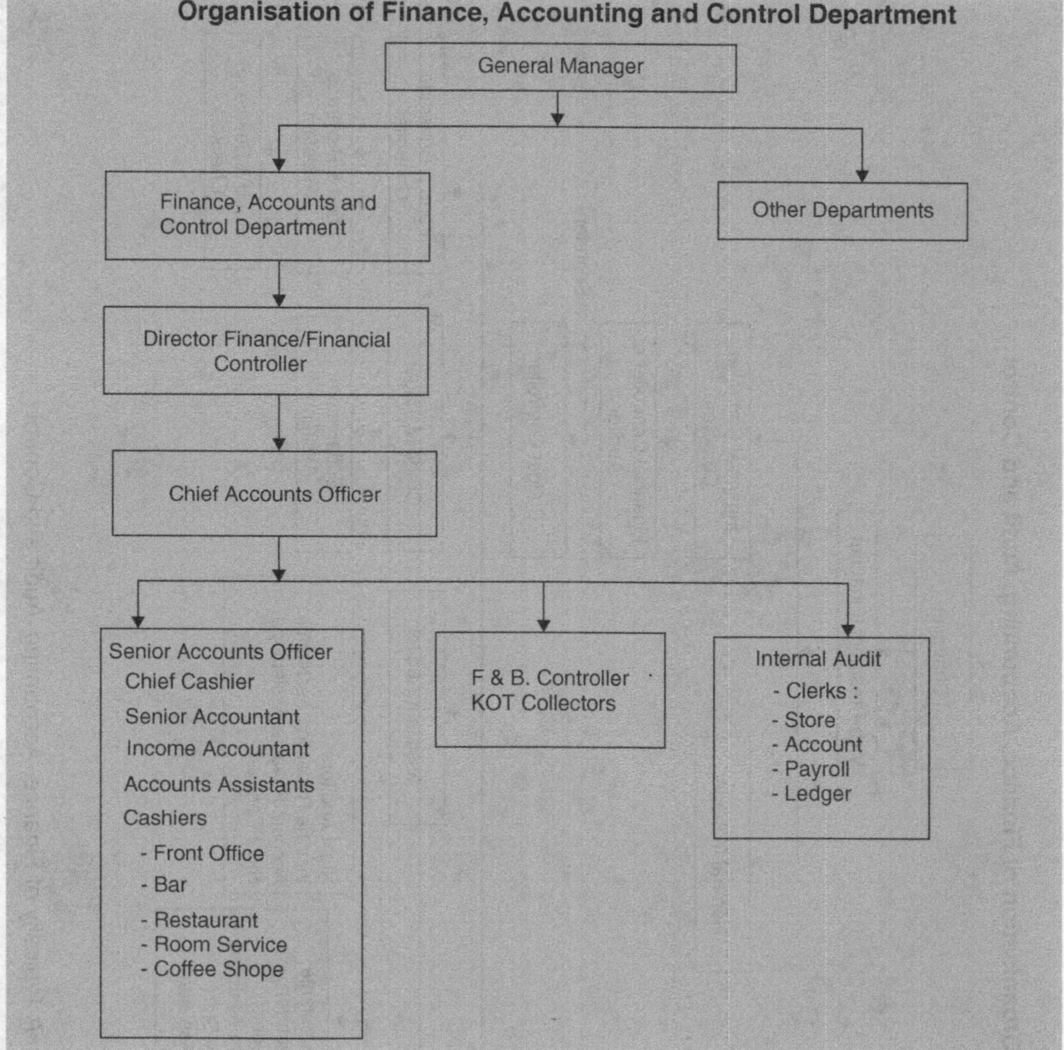

Fig. 12.2 : A Typical Organisation of Finance, Accounting, Audit & Control Department

The accounting department is concerned with the guest's bills, paying wages to the hotel staff, paying bills rendered for the hotel purchases and maintaining books, recording all items of income and expenditure. Many of the accounting records are kept in original outside the accounts office. Accounts with resident guest are kept with the front office.

This department provides records and information of out-goings which provide management at regular intervals with the necessary road to gauge the efficiency and profitability of each department. Final accounts are prepared at the end of the year which depicts the pictures of the hotel business performance for that particular period. After the completion of all the financial statements the next job is to complete the statistical reports. These reports are pertaining to a period regarding comparison of room, food and beverage and incomes and expenses which are necessary for successful hotel operations.

STATUTORY RECORDS

The following records are required to be maintained as per different laws/bye-laws:

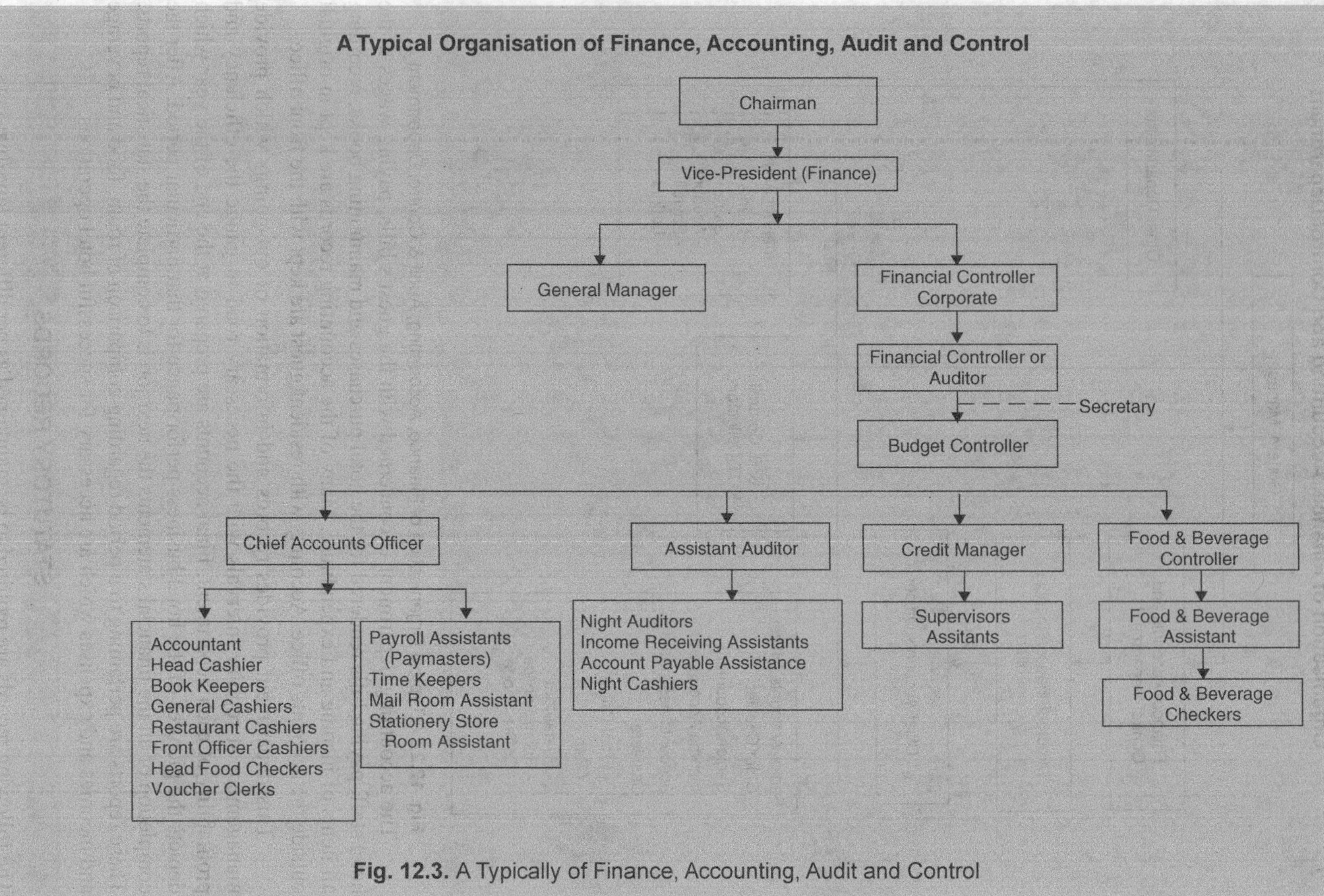

Fig. 12.3. A Typically of Finance, Accounting, Audit and Control

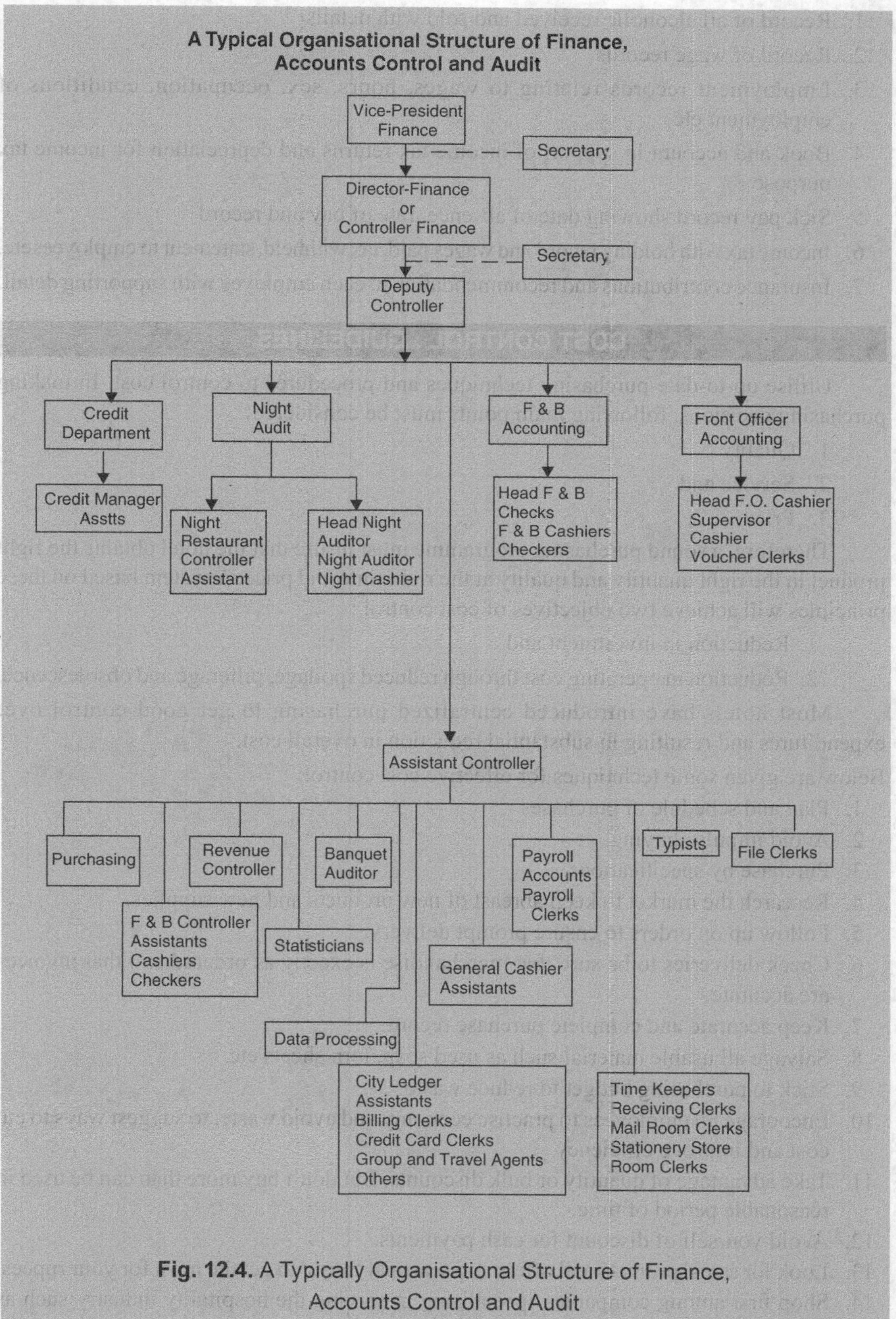

Fig. 12.4. A Typically Organisational Structure of Finance, Accounts Control and Audit

1. Record of all alcoholic received and sold with details
2. Record of wage records
3. Employment records relating to wages, hours, sex, occupation, conditions of employment etc.
4. Book and account in support of income tax returns and depreciation for income tax purpose
5. Sick pay record showing date of absence, rate of pay and record
6. Income tax with holding record and wages paid, tax withheld, statement to employees etc.
7. Insurance contributions and recommendation to each employee with supporting detail.

COST CONTROL : GUIDELINES

Utilise up-to-date purchasing techniques and procedures to control cost. In making purchasing decisions, following main points must be considered:

1. Quality
2. Service and
3. Price.

Therefore, a sound purchasing programme must insure that the hotel obtains the right product in the right quantity and quality at the right time and price. A system based on these principles will achieve two objectives of cost control :

1. Reduction in investment and
2. Reduction in operating cost through reduced spoilage, pilferage and obsolescence.

Most hotels have introduced centralized purchasing to get good control over expenditures and resulting in substantial reduction in overall cost.

Below are given some techniques for effective cost control:

1. Plan and schedule of purchases.
2. Avoid impulse buying.
3. Purchase by specifications.
4. Research the market to keep abreast of new products and new supplies.
5. Follow up on orders to ensure prompt delivery.
6. Check deliveries to be sure that merchandise is exactly as ordered and that invoices are accurate.
7. Keep accurate and complete purchase record.
8. Salvage all usable material such as used soap, torn sheets etc.
9. Stick to purchasing budget to reduce waste
10. Encourage all employees to practise economy and avoid waste, to suggest ways to cut cost and improve efficiency.
11. Take advantage of quantity or bulk discounts. But don't buy more than can be used in reasonable period of time.
12. Avoid yourself of discount for cash payments.
13. Look for sales' promotional offers and seasonal 'buys' to get the most for your rupees.
14. Shop first among companies specialising in serving the hospitality industry such as contract furnishers.

15. In purchasing services such as painting and plumbing etc., don't go bargain hunting. This is one area where it pays to emphasize reliability and competence rather than price alone.

Hotels, catering budget minded travellers, may use the following techniques to reduce costs :

1. Install one piece 'wipe clean' fibre glass shower stalled with rounded covers to reduce bathroom cleaning time.
2. Equip all lavatories with one faucet only.
3. Use styrofoam drinking glasses to avoid regular washing.
4. Visit by 'maintenance staff' to take care of painting and rail repair, emergency.
5. Arrange the visit of a travelling houskeeper to teach maid the latest cleaning techniques and introduce them to new products.
6. Wash all linen in own premises laundry.
7. Buy the best products such as mattresses, hardware and appliances as they are economical on the long-term.
8. Save money by making bulk purchases.
9. Keep a daily record of time taken in cleaning a room by maids. If it takes more than 30 minutes, she is wasting time. On the other hand if she takes less than 30 minutes, she is not cleaning properly.

Employ husband and wife team to manage the hotel such as, retired couple, ex-defence employee etc.

CONTROL OF FOOD SERVICE COSTS

You may consider the following suggestions to control food service costs in your food service outlets :

1. Reduce number of items offered on the menu
2. Feature cooked to order items
3. Concentrate on serving one main category of guest such as business men or young people
4. Limit hours of service
5. Control portions carefully
6. Base sales forecast on past experience
7. Purchase competitively
8. Take advantage of seasonal food bargains
9. Check quantity, quality and billing of food items delivered
10. Avoid spoilage as a result of improper storage
11. Prevent unauthorized use of food supplies.

CONTROL OF BEVERAGE COSTS

The important thing to keep in mind in boosting beverage profit is that you must know how much it costs to pour a drink and whether you are getting the full potential income from each bottle.

Pix. 12.3 : Financial Techniques

Pix. 12.4 : Financial Planning for Future

The control of beverage service cost is quite different due to the requirement of complying with central, state and regulations regarding hours of sale, age of customers. You may use the following control measures and report to be submitted :

1. The beverage cost control begins with an analysis of the potential customer who will offer the best chance for profit for particular hotel and then specializes in securing that type of customer.
2. The quantity discount on liquor purchases can be sizable, therefore, limit the number of brands offered, guided by the taste of regular customers.
3. Liquor is a high profit item, therefore, use portion control techniques such as dispensers or bottled individual servings of liquor and beer rather than service by glass.
4. Have accurate monthly forecasts to avoid tying up money in liquor inventory. The good rule of thumb is that total liquor inventory should not exceed the value of one month's cost of goods sold.
5. Use beverage control system :

   (*i*) Cost of goods sold percentage system

   (*ii*) Daily inventory control system

   (*iii*) Sales potential analyses.

The *first* method depends on the taking of inventory, the result is not known until several weeks after the close of the period. The overall figure is the total of many individual transactions at different mark-ups, it can be skewed by unusual sales mixes.

The *second* method requires taking a bar inventory at the end of each day. It helps in improving profitability and being aware of the operating problems of the beverage function. The main limitation of this method is the time factor which it takes to inventory and calculate usage.

The *third* technique does not require inventory. It provides the current information as regards to actual sales. The whole procedure requires less than half an hour a day and takes very little time of the management. To establish a sales potential analysis for beverage control system, you may require the following :

(*i*) A standard price list and portion specifications for all drinks at the bar or serving unit.

(*ii*) Computation of the potential sales value of each bottle of liquor based on these data.

(*iii*) A supply 'Par Stock' for the serving unit sufficient to prevent running out during the serving period.

(*iv*) A requisition system to ensure that the 'par stock' is maintained, possibly by swapping empty bottles for full ones.

(*v*) An analysis sheet with daily entries showing the sale of all stocks and the running totals of actual sales.

6. Use electronic and mechanical devices and methods on the market designed to reduce liquor waste, discourage theft and improve profit. An electronic liquor dispensing system cuts bar costs by eliminating spillage and over pouring. It also provides a recorded sale for every drinks proved direct from locked inventory.

LABOUR COST CONTROL

The hospitality industry being a service business has a heavy labour content. You may require to control payroll for economies by adopting following approaches :

1. Work constantly at method improvements and try to motivate employees to be more productive.
2. Application of modern technology in hotel operationselectronic data processing and automation.

You may introduce the following labour cost saving devices :

1. Reduction in hours of services: e.g. opening during room for lunch and dinners only, closing down room service after 11.00 p.m.
2. Elimination of luxury type services.
3. Utilization of handicaped, senior or citizens, part-time or temporary people wherever possible.
4. Work simplification : elimination of unnecessry or duplicating procedures.
5. Reduction in overtime paymentbetter scheduling and use of temporary and partime help.
6. Improvement in recruitment, selection, orientation and training to obtain and retain qualified and motivated employees.
7. Supervision which sets clear and attainable objectives, assists in overcoming problems and requires high standard of performance by employees.

A specialist incharge of the cash and accounting within a hotel lessens the possibility of defective accounting procedures. In large hotels a resident auditor is in charge of all accounting transactions taking place in the hotel. The night auditor would report to him. Every cashier in each sales outlet/restaurant reports to him rather than the Restaurants Managers. A restaurant cannot open until the cashier arrives on the scene. All cash and accounting of restaurant sales goes directly to the auditor's office.

The hotel accounting presents some unique problems. The input data are generated almost round the clock and has to be checked and processed almost immediately to up-date guest and house accounts. Depending upon the volume of such accounting activities hotel companies employ several methods. In small hotels with slow guest turnover a manual or hand-written method is the most suitable one. In large hotels where there may be multiple data generating departments a rapid and less error-prone handling of accounting data is required. It may be electronic or mechanical posting machines. The most latest methods for these operations is the computer billing system. With the advent of computers and micro-processors, the hotels have started their use to handle reservations, guests' registration accounting, night audit and management reports. It eliminates redundant typing, sorting, alphabetising and filing from department to department. Communication of information is handled accurately and at electronic speeds, which results in better management control, better guest service and high revenues. Computerised reservation provides fast and accurate information to the customers seeking reservations, allows for immediate response to the guest, enables management to forecast occupancies and revenues in advance, reduce clerical procedures and eliminate paper work. The computerised room management can provide better knowledge of room status and productivity and maximise occupancy through improved guest services at the desk. Introduction of computerised accounting system will have postings at the point of sale by means of electronic input data from the operating departments. The auditing of accounting information becomes an on-going process and the accounting control could be monitored and used by the management at anytime. Thus it will have the following advantages :

1. Direct guest charge postings which reduce communication and posting errors.
2. Automatic night auditing which will reduce unauthorised and erroneous postings.
3. Electronic guest account settlement which will speed up guest check-out.
4. Folio display and printing.

A Case Study 12.1
Finance and Accounting

Situation :

The accounting procedure of a large hotel required that restaurant checks be totalled twice by the dinning room Cashier and again by the Night Revenue Controller.

Results of Analysis :

Accounting procedure was changed so that the restaurant cashier totalled checks, once except in instances where a page of the restaurant control report failed to balance. The position of night revenue control was eliminated by incorporating it in day revenue control. ₹ 75,000/- in salaries were saved per years.

A Case Study 12.2
Payroll

Situation :

Management of a certain hotel was very payroll conscious. It kept the hotel staff at a minimum. However, an analysis of the Kitchen payroll shaved excessive overtime.

Results of Analysis :

It was found that the present employees could not complete all the work required in normal working hours. Two employees were hired to reduce the tremendous pressure on the minimum staff. This eliminated most of the overtime payments with a reduction in aggregate salary expense.

A Case Study 12.3
Payroll Cost

Situation :

A municipal regulation required that a fire watch be maintained at all public functions in hotels at a particular city. The regulation was sprung on the management of a particular hotel in the midst of a public function. Casting about the some one to fill the watch a plumber who had not gone home was pressed into services. The plumber continued the job of fire watch at time - and - a - half wages. No one thought to hire less expensive labour.

Results of Analysis:

Another employee was hired to do the job at a saving of ₹ 60,000/- per year in payroll costs.

A Case Study 12.4
Payroll

Situation :

A certain hotel served an average of 500 - room service break fasts from about 7 : 00 to 11 : 00 AM. However, most of the soiled dishes did not reach the dish washing station until late at 10.00 clock. In the dinning room the bulk of the service took place from 8.30 to 9.30 P.M. The complete dish washing crew reported the work at 7.00 P.M.

At night, after the dinning room closed, only the dance room remained open. It closed about 2.00 a.m. in the morning; a complete dish washing crew remained until 2.00 0'clock.

Results of Analysis :

Employees were not needed on the morning shift until 9.00 AM. On the night shift only one of the two personnel was required between 9.00 PM and 2.00 AM. One-third of the employees were not needed. When these were eliminated ₹ 1,50,000/- of payroll was saved per year.

MANAGEMENT INFORMATION (MIS)

The success of planning, operation and control of hotel depends on accurate, timely and complete management information. The sources of information include :

1. Guest Registration Forms
2. Guest Charge Vouchers
3. Requisitions
4. Purchase Order
5. Bank Checks
6. Records of deposits
7. All original records
8. Summary records, such as
   (*i*) Front Office Cash Sheet
   (*ii*) Guest Ledger Transcript
   (*iii*) Payroll Sheet
   (*iv*) Journal of various kinds
   (*v*) General Ledger
   (*vi*) Other records of transaction.

All these records are used to aid in preparing :

1. The Balance Sheet
2. The Income Statement
3. Room Sales Comparison
4. Cost of certain items
5. Account Receivable, etc.

The information so collected is analysed and helps in decision making regarding :

1. Budgeting and budgetary control
2. Pricing of product and services
3. Capital expenditures
4. Advertising and promotion
5. Financing of property etc.

The uniform system of account for hotels is the best document which sets up a common financial denominator and facilitates comparison of operational and financial results among different hotels. It helps in achieving the following objectives of management information:

1. Provides a complete and permanent record of all business transactions which is understanable, accurate, timely and reliable.
2. Include control which will avoid losses through theft, embezzlement, errors or ineptitude.
3. Furnishes the data needed to optimise profit in useful form at a time when decisions are being made by the management.

Different types of information/reports such as guest account folio, revenue report, city ledger, summary report, department-wise revenue report etc., could be available from the computers. In addition to these reports, specific information related to reservation, room management and front office account could be obtained which can provide management with up-to-date and productive data. The management information could be pertaining to revenue analysis, operating statistics, financial analysis and balance sheet reports. These will be of benefit to management in the following ways :

1. Control over revenue of the hotel
2. Control over receivables and payables
3. Tip to the minimum reports and analysis will enable to take decisive action to influence future business.

BUDGETARY CONTROL

Actual result of the business should always be compared to plans to check progress and identify areas that need attention. Management control in the process of ensuring that resources are obtained and used effectively to achieve the objectives of the hotel business. The control cycle may be as follows :

1. Formulation of the plan
2. Recording of the plan
3. Carrying out the plan
4. Monitoring performance against the plan
5. Evaluation and control.

Thus, there are three fundamental points to run business well, 'first', making plans, 'second', reviewing actual results, and 'third', making corrective actions. The management control means being aware of changes that adversely affect the earnings of the hotel and cash flows and counteracting them, and finally identifying opportunities for greater profitability of the hotel.

BUDGETING, AUDITING AND CONTROL

Budgeting in hotel business is very important. It is an estimate of the income and expenses for a given period in the future. The controller is responsible for the budgeting and directing his staff to make the forecasts. With these figures as guide he prepares the budget and presents it to top management for final approval. Once the budget is approved, each member of the management team is obligated to abide by the budget. Fig. 12.5 indicates the budgetary control system in hotels.

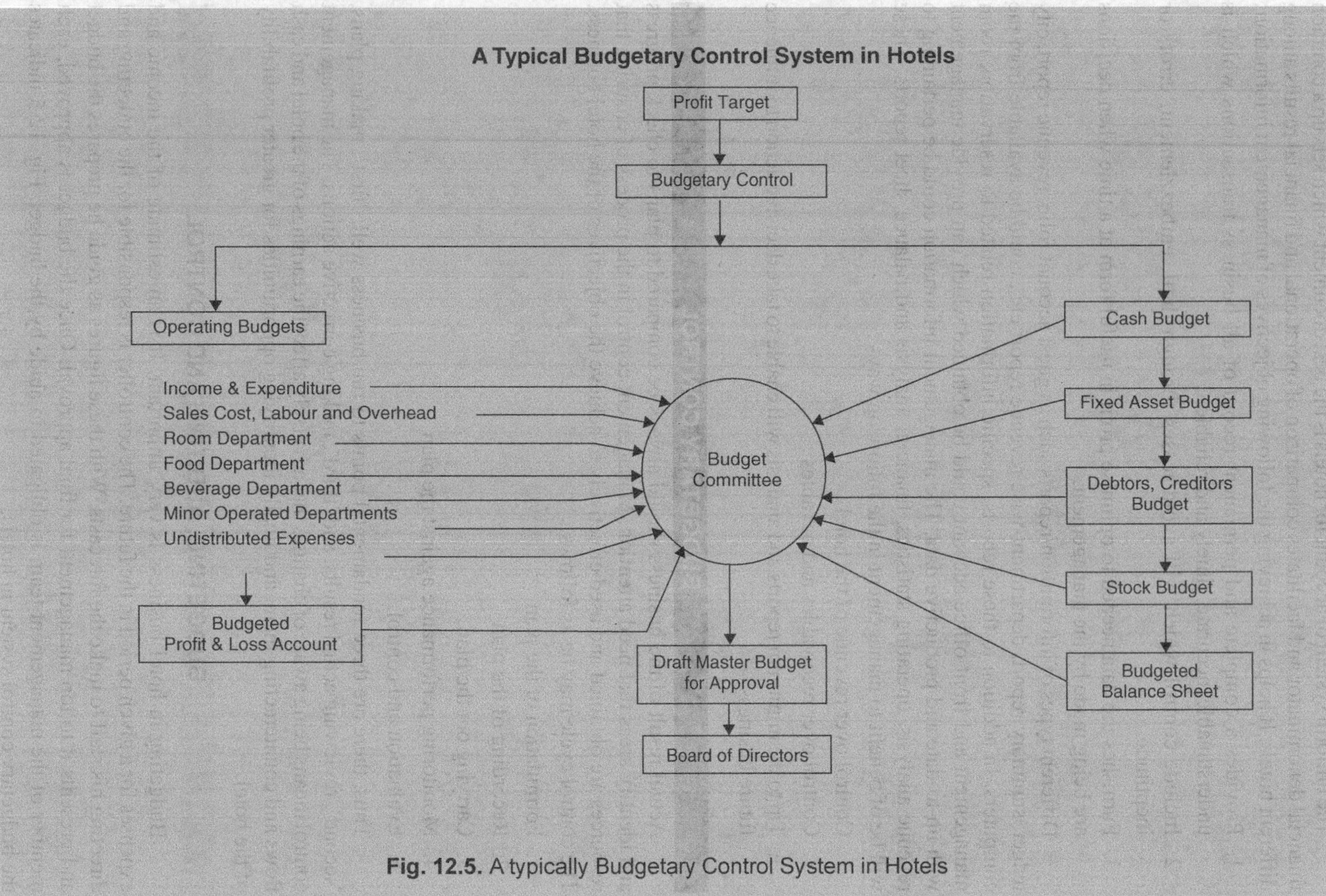

Fig. 12.5. A typically Budgetary Control System in Hotels

The work of this department can be divided into the following parts :

1. Revenue/incomes
2. Expenses/accounts payable
3. Payroll
4. Cash receipts and banking
5. Front office accounting and credit
6. Purchasing method
7. Stores
8. Budgeting
9. MIS-statistical reports : internal reports, audit reports, financial statements.

In respect of revenues the position involves the checking of accuracy of the amount reported, thus ensuring that the hotel receives 100% of the money spent by guests. Checking the expenses requires verification of mathematical accuracy of the creditors bills. The legitimacy of the charges as to both quantity received and price charged must be checked. The controller has to cooperate with the General Manager and provide all reports and statistics required and needed to evaluate and operate the property.

The management requires periodic monthly, quarterly and annual financial statements to indicate whether each department is operating effectively and which will help to pre-determine budget normally agreed to by the departmental heads and senior management. Proper procedure to record sales and expenditure is required to maintain proper control. Most of the large hotels have introduced accounting machines and computers for economic and quick processing and analysis of information.

All expenses need to be analysed and projected. These could be divided into the following categories :

1. Payroll and related expenses
2. Operating supplies
3. Cost of food, beverage and other items of sales
4. Cost of utilities (heat, light and power)
5. Advertising and publicity
6. Repair maintenance
7. Replacement of linens, china, glass and silverware
8. Capital improvement.

ORGANISATION

MANAGER (STORES)

He is incharge of stores. He has a thorough knowledge of the various commodities, foodstuffs and their prices. He must know what foods are perishable and their proper storage and preservation specially of fruits and vegetables.

HEAD STOREKEEPER

He is also incharge of the store and must be an honest man. A head storekeeper must have the knowledge of the various commodities and their prices. He must have the knowledge of perishable foodstuffs, fruits and vegetables and their preservation. The main duties of head storekeeper are:

1. To be responsible for the efficiency of stores
2. To prepare contacts
3. To purchase perishable foodstuffs in consultation with the 'Chef de Cuisine'
4. To supervise the store and preservation of foods
5. To maintain up-to-date inventories of stock .
6. To ensure that all vouchers, records, receipts etc., are collected and checked
7. To be responsible for the store staff and make suggestions concerning their job.

HEAD CELLARMAN

He should have the thorough knowledge of the difficult categories of wines and their characteristics and preservation of wine. He is responsible for :

1. Wines, their preservation and the efficiency of the cellar.
2. Checking and regulations of the temperature in the different wine cells.
3. To be in touch with the 'Maitred'hotel'and inform him about the wines that must be consumed earlier one due to their lesser life.
4. Inform the head storekeeper of the supplies required.
5. Maintain the register of deliveries and withdrawals up-to-date.

STORE CONTROLLER

It is an administrative job. The store-controller must have good knowledge of the function and running of the various departments of the store. He should have adequate administrative experience and knowledge of the commodities and products and their market prices. He assists the head storekeeper in his various duties. He also replaces the head storekeeper in his absence.

STORE ACCOUNTS CLERK

He requires the knowledge of various commodities and must be able to detect the defects of the product purchased. His duties are to supervise the delivery of goods and check weights, quantities, qualities and prices. He has the right to reject goods not supplied according to the order. He enters movement of goods in a register and notifies any accident to the head storekeeper.

STOREKEEPER

Knowledge of various commodities and their storage techniques is essential for a storekeeper. He takes order from the head storekeeper. Arranges goods in stores, issues stores against withdrawal vouchers and keeps the store check list up-to-date. He is responsible for all the stored goods.

CELLARMAN

A cellarman must have the knowledge of the different categories of wines and their preservation. His duties are to take orders from the head cellarman and to be responsible for washing and rinsing all bottles and flasks for the cleanliness of the equipment and premises. He replaces head cellarman in his absence.

ASSISTANT STORE CONTROLLER

He must have the knowledge of functioning and running of the various departments of the hotel. He is also required to have the knowledge of the principal commodities and their prices. He assists the store controller in supervising the deliveries and withdrawals of goods and the checking of stock.

ASSISTANT CELLARMAN

He assists in handling the stores. He washes and rinses all goods and cleans the cellars.

At the end of accounting period, the Accounts Department prepares Financial Statement, Profit and Loss account and Balance Sheet. The accounts office provides the controlling figure as well as carries out accounting function. The control stems from forecasting, which takes into account past performance as well as future plans on the basis of which the management draws up a budget.

There should be a close cooperation and coordination between all the departments. If the departmental manager commands the respect and loyalty from his staff and they in turn are respected by their assistants and juniors, the running of the hotel will be smooth. It is essential for a hotel that every aspect of its organisation should function smoothly.

Fig. 12.6 indicates the organisational structure of a store. Fig. 12.7 shows the Material Control Flow Chart. Fig. 12.8 shows the Purchase Flow Charts and Fig. 12.9 indicates the Store Flow Chart.

PURCHASES AND STORES

This department should be completely independent of the other departments of the hotel. The department can be sub-divided into :

1. Purchasing
2. Storing
3. Receiving
4. Issuing.

PURCHASING

The creation of atmosphere by right choice of furnishings and equipment is a contributing factor to the success of food and beverage service area. Therefore, the choice of furnitures and its placing, linen, tableware, small equipment and glassware is to be carefully determined by considering the following points :

1. The type of customers expected
2. The site or location of the restaurant
3. The total layout of the food and service area
4. The type of the restaurant
5. The type of service offered
6. The funds available.

The following points need to be considered when purchasing equipment for the food and beverage service area :

1. Type of service being offered
2. Flexibility of use

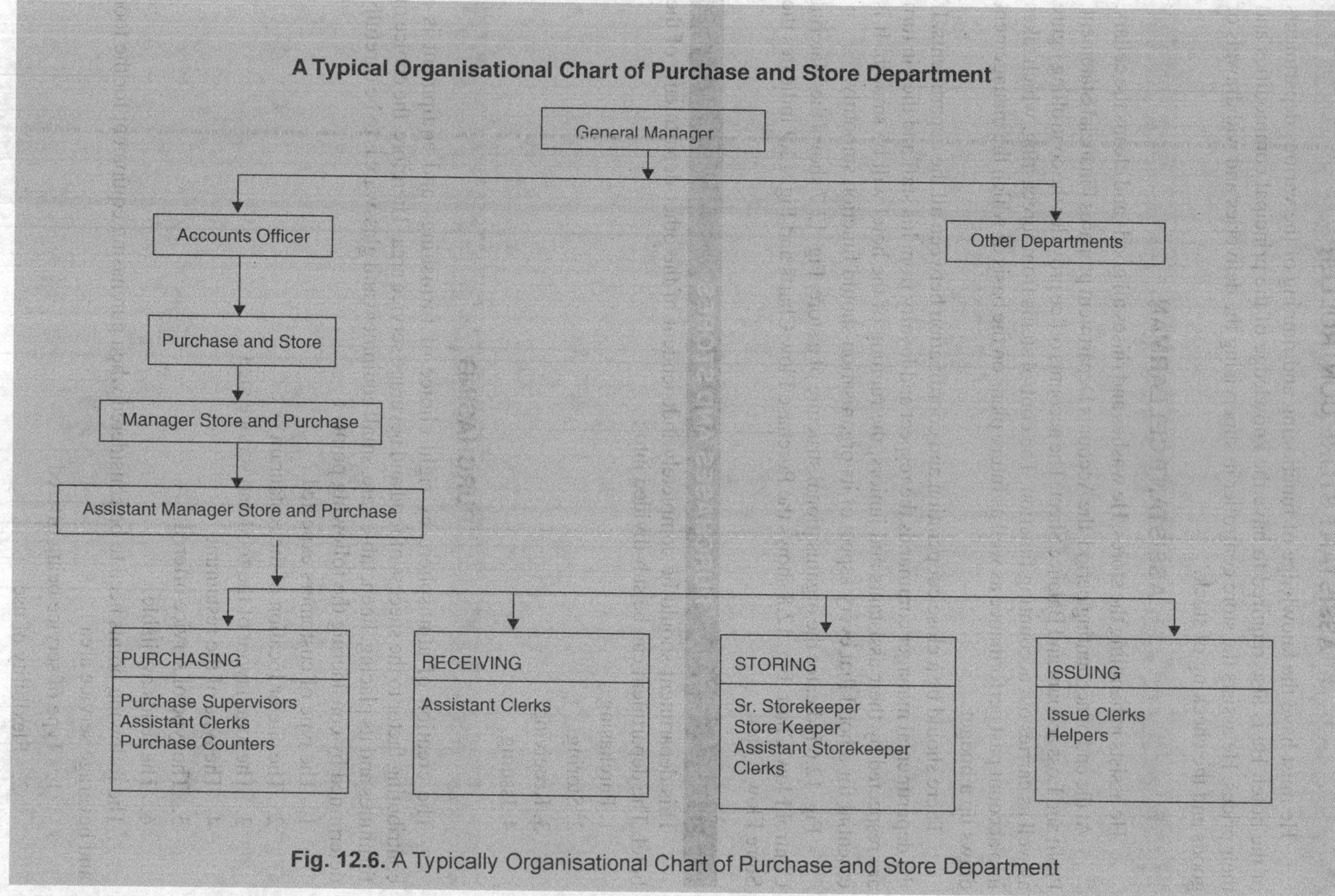

Fig. 12.6. A Typically Organisational Chart of Purchase and Store Department

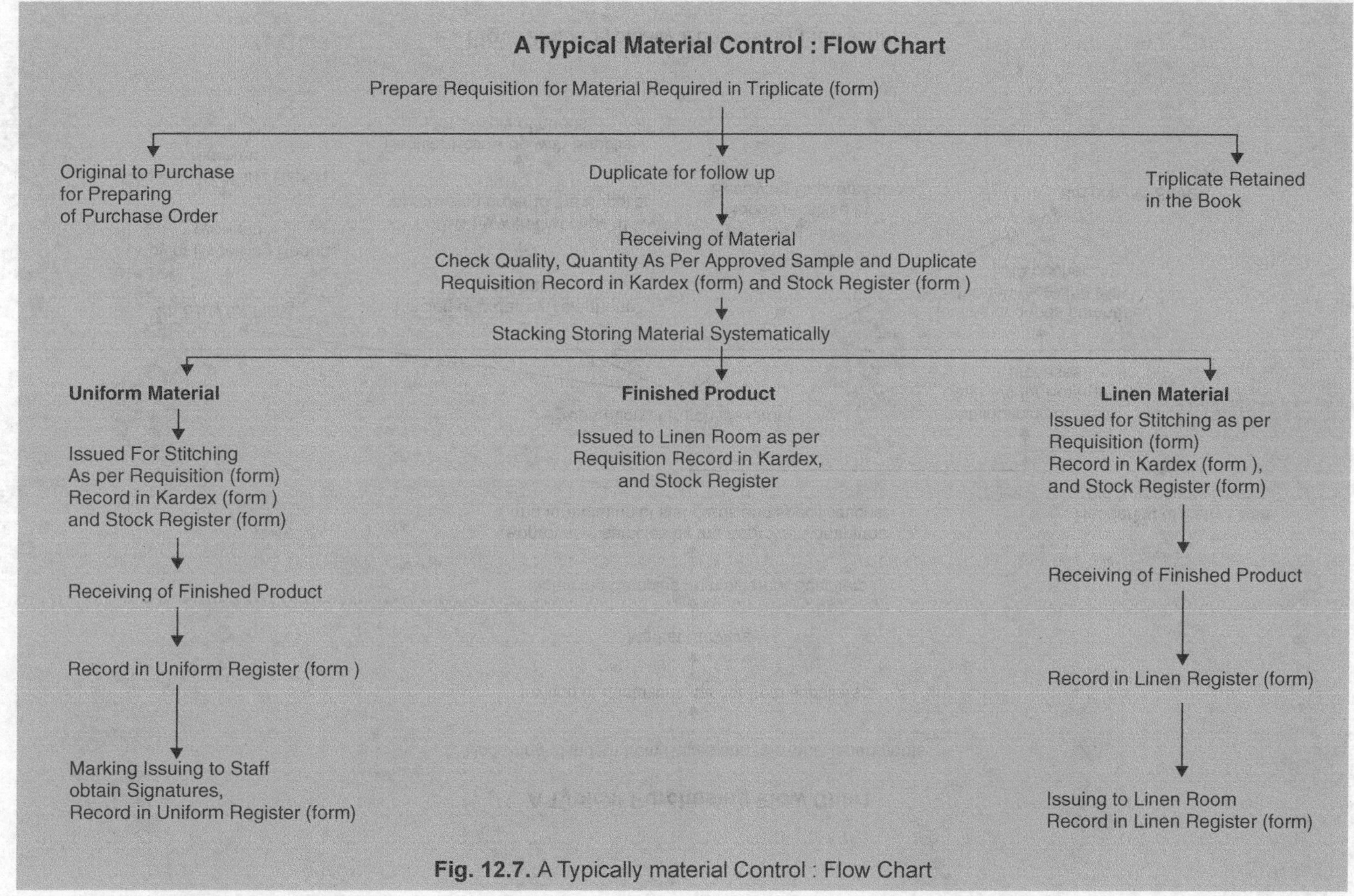

Fig. 12.7. A Typically material Control : Flow Chart

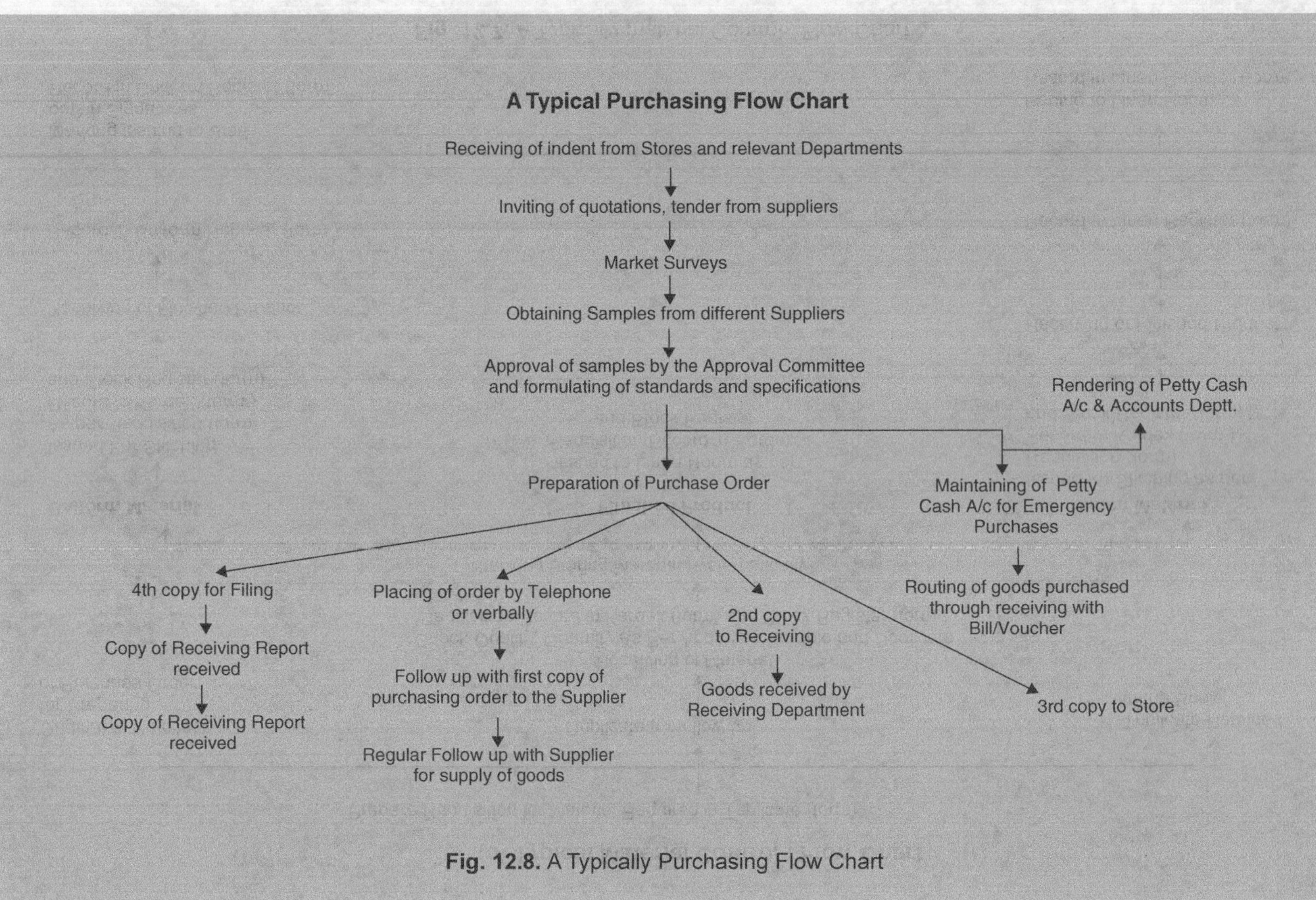

Fig. 12.8. A Typically Purchasing Flow Chart

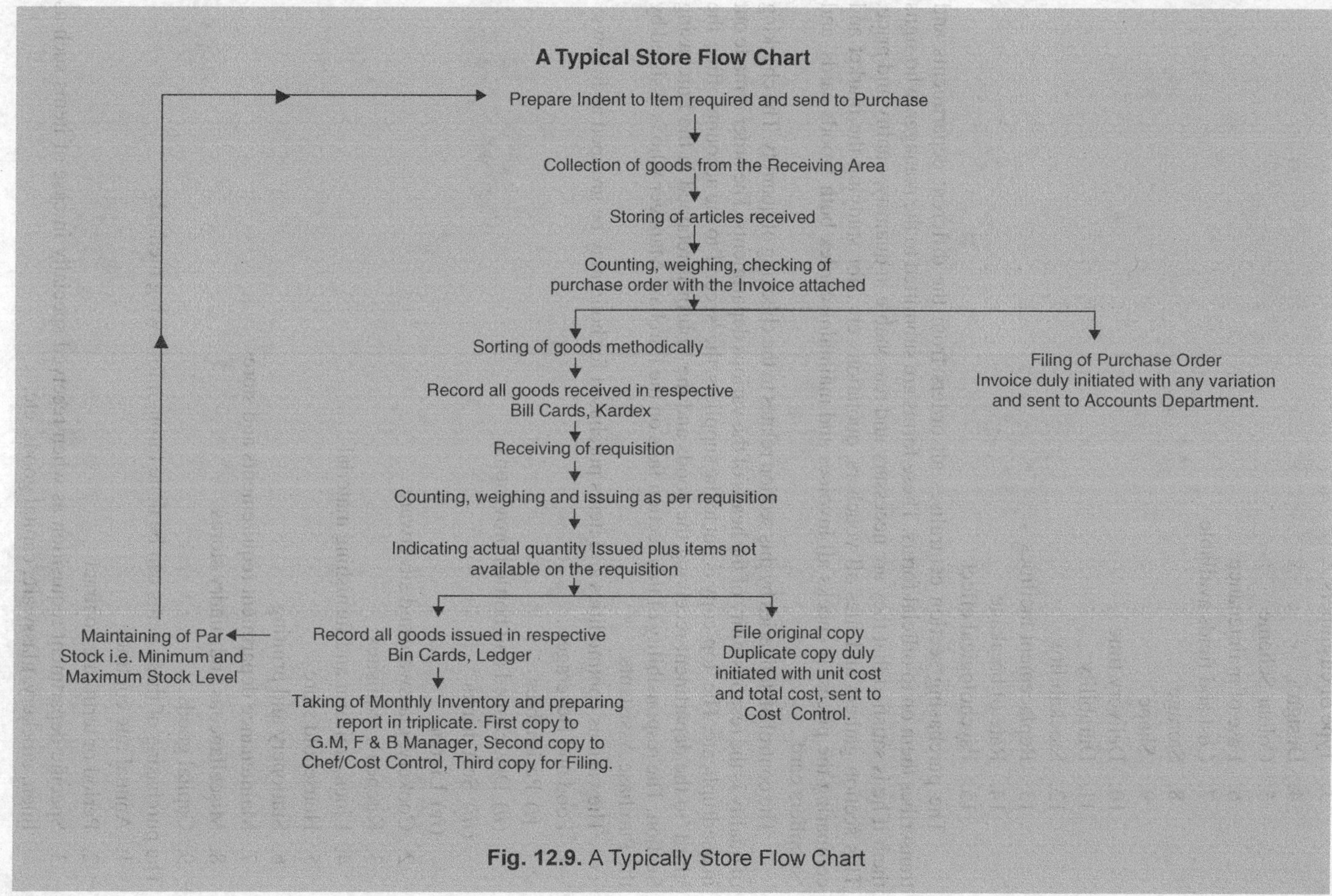

Fig. 12.9. A Typically Store Flow Chart

3. Type of customers
4. Design
5. Colour Scheme
6. Ease of maintenance
7. Cost and funds available
8. Storage
9. Shape
10. Delivery time
11. Durability
12. Stockability
13. Replacement facilities
14. Rate of breakage
15. Psychological effect

The purchasing section centralises all orders from the different departments and transcribes them on to official forms. These forms are submitted to the manager, who signs them if he is satisfied that they are necessary and reasonable in quantity, quality and price. This section gathers and files all vouchers, quotations etc., for studying the market and comparing the prices. It checks all invoices and maintains cardex both 'goods cards' and 'suppliers card'.

The control of deliveries by this section relates to the checking of quantity. The checking of quality is the responsibility of the heads of the various departments. The order is made out in quadruplicate. The 'top' copy is put to the suppliers, the 'second' to the accounts office, the 'third' to the department receiving the goods and the 'fourth' is retained in the Purchasing Section. The responsibility of this section falls on the Purchase Manager who is assisted by the Purchase Assistants.

The various commodities and items purchased for hotel may be grouped as follows:

1. Food and Beverages :
   (*i*) Perishables
   (*ii*) Dry, canned and bottled provisions
   (*iii*) Soft drinks
   (*iv*) Liquor
2. Cookery, glassware and silverware
3. Kitchen's requisites
4. Linen, uniform and furnishing material
5. Household store
6. Stationery and printing
7. Maintenance department requirements and stores
8. Miscellaneous and sundry stores
9. Capital goods.

The purchasing of these items can be done through following methods:

1. Annual rate contract
2. Period or term rate contract
3. Specific department requisition as when received specially in case of items such as linen, crockery, glassware, capital goods, etc.

4. Regular store item as and when necessary
5. Emergency and miscellaneous.

Proper purchase policy requires the coordination between finance, production, F & B Store and Receiving General Manager, and the Purchase Manager as regards to qualities and quantities.

Although the Purchase Department is a non-revenue producing activity, it has to ensure continuity in supply of raw material and spares while at the same time reduce the ultimate cost of goods and service offered by the hotel. The cheapest price does not necessarily corresponds to the best buy, therefore, this department must be seen as a profit centre because it :

1. Accounts for major portion of cash outlets
2. Brings information about new products
3. 60% of sales go in for the purchases of the hotel
4. 5% cut in total cost of good purchased can result 30% increase in turnover or 20% reduction in labour cost
5. This results in a considerable reduction of expenditure.

In brief, the parameters to ensure effective and smooth working of this department and savings on capital are :

1. Right price : Negotiations market surveys and value analysis
2. Right quality : Standardization and specification
3. Right quantity : Demand/supply analysis and economic ordering quantity
4. Right source : Vendor rating and purchase research
5. Right time : Lead time analysis
6. Right plan for deliveries
7. Right contract : Legal aspect and consequence.

All purchases are based on certain specification in order to maintain quality of the products. Figs. 12.10 and 12.11 are analysis tables of some of the commodities used in hotel and restaurant business.

An Analysis of Meat, Poultry and Fish-Specifications

Item	Purveyor	Grade	How Purchased
		Beef :	
Filet (Tender loin)	.....	Choice	Long, 30% max. fat. Average Weight:7-8 1bs. Chilled
Ribs	.....	Prime	Oven-prepared 1/2" 3/4" fat covering 4" eye A.W. 16-18 lbs. Chilled.
Strip Loins (Shell)	.....	Choice	1/2" 3/4" fat covering Oven-prepared A.W. 13-15 lbs. Well marbled 4" eye, Chilled.
Round	.....	Prime	Rump on shank off A.W. : 60 - 65 lbs. frozen or chilled.
Chuck	.....	Choice	Boneless, square cut A.W. 40-60 lbs.

(Cont...)

Item		Grade	Specification
Pickled Tongue	.....	Fancy	A.W. : 4-6 lbs.
Beef Bones	.....		Selected
		Lamb :	
Leg of Lamb	.....	Choice	Single, 7-8 lbs.
Racks of Lamb	.....	Choice	Double 8 ribs, 6-8 lbs.
Shoulder of Lamb	.....	Choice	Round cut, 3½ – 4½ lbs.
		Pork :	
Leg of Pork	.....	US/1	12-15 lbs frozen
Smoked Pork Loin	.....	US/1	Full Loin, 12-14 lbs.frozen.
Pork Loin	.....	US/1	Full loin-Frozen A.W. 10-12 lbs.
Bacon	.....	No. 1 Fancy	Hotel Pack, 18 - 20 slices.
Cured Ham	.....	Premium	5-6 lbs.
Smoked Ham	.....	Premium	12-15 lbs.
Pork Ling			
Sausages	.....	No. 1	5 lbs.
Canadian bacon	.....	Top choice	Lean, 6-8 lbs.
Back fat	.....		
		Veal :	
Leg of Veal lbs.	.....	Prime or Choice	Single, 23-27
Back of Veal	.....	Prime or Choice	6-7 inches 9-12 lbs.
Sweetbreads	.....	No 1 Fancy	3/4-1 lbs.
Veal Kidney	.....	Frozen	1 – 1½ lbs.
Calf's Liver	.....	Frozen	2-3 lbs, frozen
Veal Steak	.....		
Cafeteria, 4 oz. p.c.			
Veal Bones	.....		
		Provisions :	
Frankfurters	.....	Frozen	1 lb. pkg.
Pupu Franks	.....	Frozen	5 lbs. 1 box
Spiced Frankfurter	.....	Frozen	5 lbs. 1 box
Salami	.....	Chilled	6-7 lbs.
Prosciutto Ham	.....	Frozen	6-8 lbs.
Portuguese Sausages	.....	Chilled	8-10 oz. per pkg.
Pastrami	.....	Chilled	2-3 lbs. single.
		Poultry :	
Chicken Liver			Frozen
Fryers	.....	US- A	2-2½ lbs. fresh or frozen
Roasters	.....	US- A	3 – 3½ lbs. Frozen
Cornish Hens	.....	US- A	14 – 18 oz. Norbesi
Duckling	.....	US- A	Frozen 4 1/2 -6 lbs. long island
Turkey Breast	.....	US- A	6-6 1/2 lbs.

(*Cont...*)

Cooked Turkey			
Breast	.....	US- A	Frozen
Whole Turkey	.....	US- A	24-26 lbs. Forzen
		Fish :	
D & D Shrimps	.....	Frozen	50 lbs/ 10 of 5/ count 26.
Panama Baby Shrimps	.....	Frozen	5/ lbs/10 of 5/
Cooked baby Shrimps	.....	Frozen	50 lbs/10 of 5/ Count 16-20.
Breaded shrimps Shrimps	.....	Frozen	25 lbs. 10 of 2 1/2 lbs, count 16.
Crabmeat	.....	Frozen	Alaska King Crab 30 lbs. 6 at 5.
Lobstertails	.....	Frozen	20 lbs. - count 37-38.
Scallops	.....	Frozen	50 lbs. - 10 of 5.
Frog legs	.....	Frozen	30 lbs. - 10 pf 3.
Filet of sole	.....	Frozen	60 lbs. 5 at 12.
Fresh Salmon Okada	.....	Fresh Frozen	7-10 lbs.
Smoked Salmon	.....	Fresh Frozen	5-6 lbs.
Swordfish	.....	Fresh Frozen	Centre Cuts
Oysters	....	Fresh Frozen	
Abalone	.....	Fresh	50 lbs. -10 at 5
Steaks	.....	Frozen	
Rainbow	.....	Fresh	24 counts per case
Trout	.....	Frozen	5 oz. ea.

Fig. 12.10 : An Analysis of Meat, Poultry and Fish-Specifications

Analysis of Food Purveyors Specifications

Category	Specifications	Category	Specifications
Beverage :		Chutney Mango 1 gal.	
Coffee	.....	Kitchen Bouquet	
Instant Coffee	.....	Magg's	
Pos um	.....	Dusseldorf Mustard	
Medgela E' Ora	.....	Dijon Mustard	
Sanka	.....	Coleman's Mustard	
Hilton Tea	.....	Gallon Mustard	
Green Tea	.....	Parmesan Cheese No. 1	
Iced Tea Bags	.....	Parmesan Cheese No. 5	
Instant Cocoa	.....	Shoyu	
Cereal :		Tabasco	
Cream of Wheat	.....	Ketchup (Heinz) 14 oz.	
Quaker Oats	.....	Ketchup (Hunts) 14 p.z.	

(Cont...)

Bran Flakes	.....	Ketchup gal.
Corn	.....	Cider Vineger
Flakes	.....	White Vineger
Rice Krispies	.....	Wine Vinegar
Fruit Loops	.....	Worcestershire 5 oz.
Shreadded Wheat	.....	**Flour Products :**
Special K	.....	Baking Powder
Sugar Flakes	.....	Baking Soda
Sugar Pops	.....	Sweet Chocolate
Kellog's Pep.	.....	Pancake Mix
Grape Nuts	.....	Cornstarch
Ry-Krisp	.....	Minute Tapioca
Melba Snacks	.....	Whiten All
Oyster Crackers	.....	Barley
Ritz Crackers	.....	Mashed Potate
Sumshine Crackers	.....	Macaroni
Cheese Biscuits	.....	Vermicelli
Condiments :	.....	Spaghetti
Sauce 57 Heinz	.....	Egg Noodle
Liquid Smoke	.....	Wild Rice
Fancy Hot Mustard	.....	Softasilk
Escoffier Diable	.....	All Purpose
Escoffier Robert	.....	Blendako
A-1 Sauce 5 ox.		Patna Rice
Chilli Sauce - No. 10 cn	.....	Pearl Rice
Fish and Can Meat :	.....	**Juices :**
Kipper Snacks	.....	Pineapple
Sardines	.....	Prune
Crabmeat	.....	Guava Nectar
Oysters	.....	Papaya Nectar
Snail Shells	.....	Tomato Juice
Tuna 7 oz.	.....	V-8 Juice
Tuna No. 4	.....	Guava Nectar 7 oz.
Corned Beaf	.....	Tomato Juice 5 oz.
Fat and Oil	.....	Grapefruit Juice 6 oz.
Olive Oil		**Nuts :**
Olive Oil Gal		Sliced almonds
Wesson Oil		Macadamia Nuts 1/-/
Fruits :		Macadamia Nuts - Ice Cream
Apple Sauce		
Cranberry Sauce		Macadamia 12 oz.
Figs		Pistachio No. 10 cn.
Mandarin Oranges		Pistachio 7 oz.
Peach Halves		Mixed Nuts

(Cont...)

Sliced Peaches/10 cn.
Sliced Peaches 2 1/2 cn.
Bartlett pears
Sliced Pineapples
Grapes
Seedless Grapes
Lychee
Apricot Preserves
Black Cherries
PapayePineapple
Preserve
Stawberry Preserves
Poha Preserve
Guava Jelly
Red Current Jelly
Orange Marmalade
Preserved Kumquat
No. 10 cn.
Peanut Butter
Honey No. 4

Juices :

Apple
Grape fruit

Pickles and Olives :

Stuffed Queen
Cocktail onion
Pimentos
Pepperoncini
Sweet Relish
Picadilli
Dill Pickle

Salt :

Table Salt
Pepper Midgets
Medium
Granulated

Bread :

Light Rye
Pappadums
Pumperrnickle Triangle
Pumpernickle Sokelands
Pumpernickle Rounds
Poultry Seasoning

Walnuts
Macadamia for Frt,
Bskt.
Bits of Macadamia
Peanuts
Pastry Shop Items :
Cooketts
Primex
Sweetex
Almond Paste
Apricot Candy
Sparkle Glaze
Rasburry Dandy
Foundant Icing
Tragacanth
Gelatine No. 1
Gelatine Imported
Gream of Tartar
Jello
Prepared Cherries
Prepared Lemons

Spices :

Nutmeg
Ginger
Pickling Spice
Cardamom
Whole Black Pepper
Coarse Black Pepper
Cayenne
White Pepper
Thyme
Cinnamoa
Mustard Seed
Whole Clove
Whole Tarrangon
All Speices
Cumin Seed
Dalmatian Sage
Savory
Marjorm

(Contd.)

Brown Rye
Wheat
Sugar :
Powdered Sugar
Sugar Fine
Cocktail Cube
Brown sugar Golden
Sugar Packets
Granulated Sugar
6/10 Sugar
Powdered Sugar
Asstd. Colored Sugar
Sacrinpak
Spices :
Capers
Tarrangon
Curry Powder
Sesame Seed
Whole B k Pepper
Celery Seed
Chilli Powder
Poppy Seed
Syrup :
Cherries Whole
Pi tod Cherries
Sweet Caramel
Fudgerite
Marshmallow
Crushed Pineapple
Hershey's
Maple Syrup 100%
Vanilla Syrup
Strawberry Syrup
Liquid Malt
Stem Cherries
Vegetables :
Sliced Beets
Bamboo Shoots
Whole Carrots
Artichoke Hearts
Olive Oil
Artichoke HeartsVinegar
Artichoke Bottom

Ground Oregano
Mace
Dill Seed
Ground Cloves
Coriander Seed
Caraway Seed
Oregano Leaves
Paprika
Powdered Garlic
Bay Leaves
Saffron
Marjoram Leaves
Celery Salt
Basil Leaves
Soups :
Consomme
Turtle Soup
Syrup :
Coconut Syrup Kukui
Marachino Cherriea Halves
Root Beer

Butter :
Print Butter
Sweet Butter
Butter Patties
Margarine
Yeast
Cheese :
Camembert
Gouda
Cream Cheese, Kraft
Brie
Blue Cheese
Edam
Gerogonzolla
Cheddar
Swiss CheeseDomestic
Monterey Jack
Crown Brand Grueyre
Roquefort
Swiss Knight
Swiss CheeseImported

(*Contd.*)

Whole Chestnut	Mozzarella
Kidney Beans	Sharp Cheese
Button Mushrooms Serco	Am. Cheese
Nami Shitake	Tillamook
Mushroom Pfifferlinge	Mohawk Valley
Hearts of Palm	Kay Natural
Peas	**Eggs and Misc.:**
Tomato Paste	Eggs
Tomato Puree	Prunes
Solid Pack Tomatoes	Anchovies
Sauer Kraut	Pate De Foie De
Crab Apples	Strasbury
Stewed Onions	Horse Radish
Sweat Potatoes	Caviar
Corn-on-Cob	Preserved Cherries
Asparagus-Libbeys	Truffle
Oyster Sauce	Coconut Milk
Potatoes-Salad	Walnut
Patatoes-Baking	Sliced Filberts.
Onion	

Fig. 12.11 : Analysis of Food Purveyors Specifications

Everything a hotel sells or uses has to be purchased. As a manager you should be involved in all purchasing. You must check prices and quality regularly but above all do not be beholden to any supplier. Use the check list of reminders as given in Fig. 12.12:

Check List for Purchasing

Quotations : In a large hotel, get at least three quotations. Try all local suppliers, national companies or a large supplier in the nearest city.

Price Review : Review prices of all items daily or at least three times per week else the price comparison chart.

Guarantees : Make suppliers guarantee prices for at least a week. You will notice that very rarely do meat and vegetable prices vary and fluctuate over the period of one week. Always take advantages of margins and special offers outside the main price list.

Price Lists : You must go for a printed price list from all current and prospective suppliers and compare them. For example, if a supplier is too small to produce a list, they are probably too small firm to be able to buy at the best prices.

Receiving : Receiving must be undertaken by a reliable person who knows the specification and quality required.

Standards : Set standards for suppliers particularly about meat. According to the current menu, write down the type of cut, weight and detail such as term and make sure everybody quotes and delivers to your specification. The less work that has to be done in the kitchen the better so, with reason, get items as far as possible prepared for serving.

Approved Suppliers :	Prepare an approved suppliers list, or master list for every thing you purchase including housekeeping goods, glasses, dry goods and beverage. Remember not more than two or three suppliers for each item.
Approved Item Purchase List :	Make an 'Approved Item Purchase List' for all items you use in the hotel. This list will prevent items being ordered from other sources. If hotel requires special one off purchase, the manager should approve the purchase.
Stocks :	You must keep stocks to the minimum. Over-stocking means, tying up of money, which would cost the equivalent of at least 10% interest.
Orders :	Make an official order for everything except food and beverage items. Ensure there is a record of the order showing number and pieces. A triplicate book will serve the purposes. 'Top'copy should be sent to the supplier, 'second'to the storeman/ person responsible for receiving. Each order should be priced and contain as much detail as possible. Any differences should be queried with the suppliers as soon as possible. Remember that without an order being raised, invoices get paid, without goods being delivered and sometimes paid without anything being ordered.

Fig. 12.12 : Check List for Purchasing

RECEIVING

The receiving section is mainly concerned with the receipts of goods and is managed by a receiving manager, who may be assisted by receiving assistants. All items which are purchased by the hotel have to go through receiving department which ensures that the quantity and quality of the product are up-to-the specification and standard required. Figure 12.13 indicates the Receiving Flow Chart.

STORAGE AND ISSUE

The manager (stores) is responsible for receiving the goods delivered to the hotel. He inevitably spends most of the time in his own department. The storekeepers are responsible for its maintenance and for controlling its issue, withdrawal and exchange. They inform the manager (store) when new equipment is required and keep record of all deliveries, issue, exchanges and withdrawals. These details are summarised periodically and entered in the Stock Books and Bin Card. A specimen Bin Card is given in Figure 12.14.

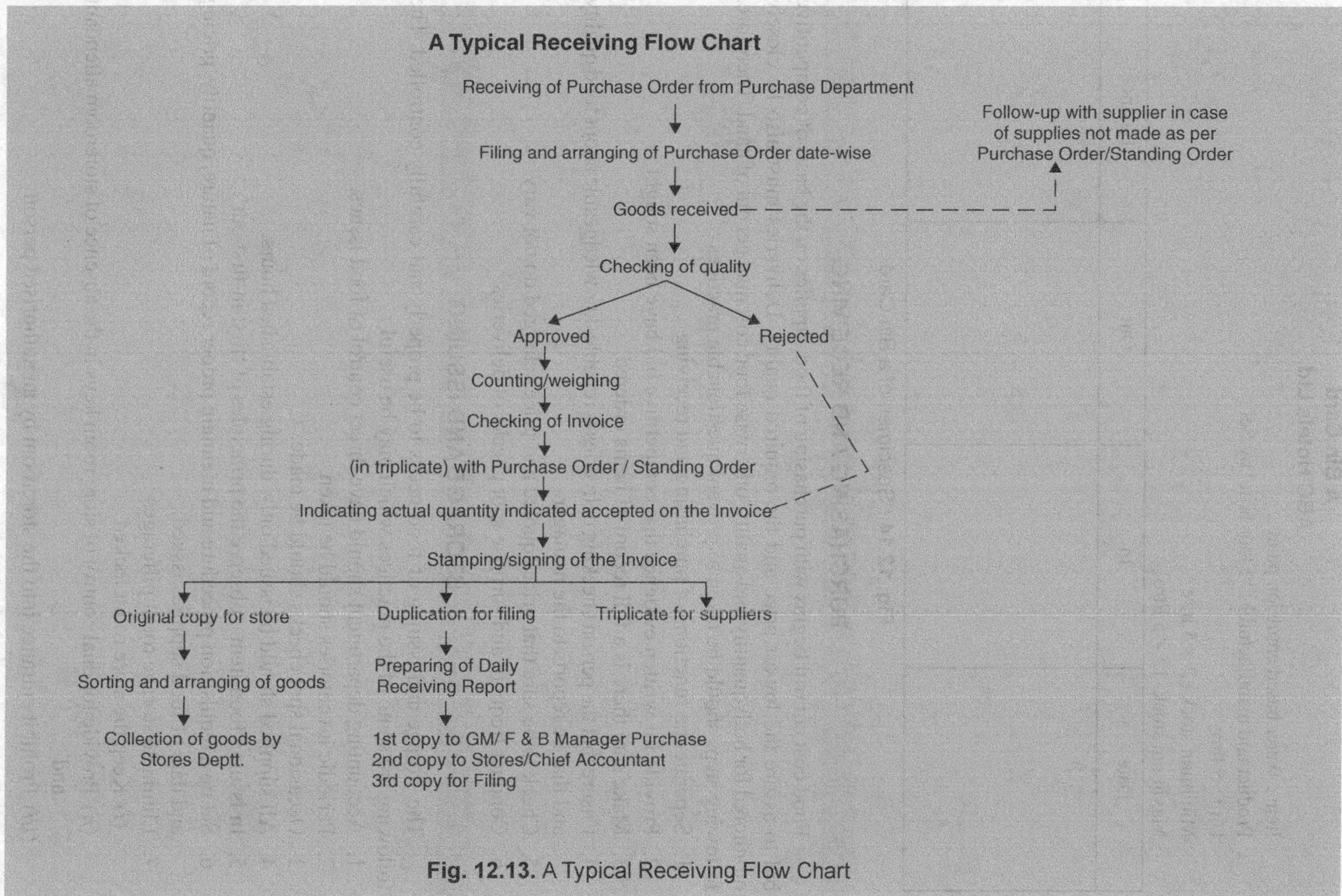

Fig. 12.13. A Typical Receiving Flow Chart

A Bin Card
ABC Hotels Ltd.

Item : Water based emulsion paint
Product and manufacturer : "Floor brite' by Sel
Unit : 5 litre
Minimum stock : 2 × 5 litre
Maximum stock 12 × 5 litre

Date	In	Out	Balance

Fig. 12.14 : Specimen of a Bin Card

PURCHASING AND RECEIVING

Food cost control begins with purchasing of food supplies on the basis of competitive bid to assure the lowest price and the required quality. Deliveries must also be closely monitored for both quantity and quality, otherwise food cost may get out of hand. Therefore, following steps should be taken to prevent questionable practices :

1. Separate the functions of purchasing and receiving
2. Provide for written evidence that competitive bid have been sought.
3. Make sure there is a full record of items ordered
4. Ensure that the person checking deliveries is reliable, knowledgeable about food quality and that he reports to the manager.
5. Check to be sure that prices quoted and prices charged do not vary
6. Conduct frequent and surprise spot checks of deliveries.

STORAGE AND ISSUING

The storage and issuing of food needs to be properly and carefully controlled. The following are some of the practices which may be useful :

1. Accounting department should have direct control of food issues.
2. Periodic inventories should be taken.
3. Occasional spot checks should be made.
4. All supplied should be issued only, during established hours.
5. In issuing food items, observe the principles of 'first in-first out'.
6. Set up a requisition procedure and maintain proper record of nature, quantity, pricing and date of food supplies issued.
7. Eliminate storage room pilferages :
   (*i*) Keep the store room locked
   (*ii*) Provide for dual control of store room keys in the absence of storeroom attendant and
   (*iii*) Prohibit entrance into the storeroom by an authorised person.

FOOD AND BEVERAGE STORE

The food and beverages store is one of the 'backs of the house facility' serving the food and beverage sales. These stores could be divided into :

1. Dry stores/general stores
2. Perishable store
3. Cold rooms
4. Beverage stores or cellar
5. Linen, china, glass and silver stores.

The storage arrangement of hotels may vary. A dry store may include items such as cleaning materials, stationery and guest suppliers. Similarly a cellar may be used for storing minerals, beers, wines and spirits, cigars, cigarettes, tobacco etc. Restaurant linen may be stored in the Housekeeping Department or in the users department with china, glass and silver.

The stores in a hotel may have different rooms for storing different items. There are walk-in refrigerators and walk-in deep freezers for storing perishables. Apart from these there are different storage areas for liquor, soft drinks, flour and oils, smokes, spices, canned food, crockery, cutlery, holloware stationery etc.

INVENTORY MANAGEMENT–ABC ANALYSIS

The accounting system and the paper work operate as internal control in a hospitalitry business. It also serves as a contraint upon irregularities. The internal control system should be periodically reviewed to determine that appropriate procedures are being followed and those procedure are themselves adequate. Stringent control as cash receipts and disbursements are essential by introducing careful supervision and meticulours sale check control at each stage from writing up the order at the customer's table to receiving and recording the cash receipts at the cash register. Similarly, control over inventories must be stringent because food and bevergas establishment are valnerable to pilferage, loss, and spoilage. Periodical accounting reports are an indication of effectiveness of control system. However, for day to day operations, you require a proper inventry reporting system and procedure for controlling dishoursements and kitchen procedures.

ABC ANALYSIS

The determination of inventory policy requires that management make a series of trade offs between the cost of ordering and the cost of holding inventory; and between the cost of holding safety stocks and the possible cost of running out of stock. By grouping foods into several categories some inventory-taking may be reduced from a weekly count to a once a month basis. This first group may be entitled "Group A". In to it should be placed all items that are non-perishable, of low value, and are used constantly. Dry frozen and canned goods items may be ordered on a weekly basis. Meal and poultry several times per week; and produce, dairy and bread products daily. Purchasing agents and food contollers should further modify this practice by breaking down each major food category into '*A*' '*B*', and '*C*' items, and thus take into consideration the value of these items as well as their peristability. Further examination of dry goods and canned products should reveal that 'B' and 'C' items do exit.

'B' items may be classified as those that are non-perishable, are used on a consistent basis, and are moderate in cost. Examples of this might be frozen or canned goods following into price range of ₹ 50 to ₹ 100 per case. Fruit, vegetables, and juices are often in this category.

'C' item may be categorised as those that are non-perishable and used consitantly, but are most costly. Their large amounts, would not be kept on hand. Canned and frozen meats, fish and poultry might be placed into this category.

Lastly, a catagory might be established for those item that are only used occasionally, either for special events or for menus that might occur during a specified period of time. Specially items such as smoked claues or oysters, quails, game & hens, pre-prepared hors 'd' oeuvres, and like items might be listed in this category.

The food and beverage controller or chef could classify these items as being in stock should a special function be planned for the given calander period.

Perishable items must be placed into several categories as well. Here the break-down is dictated by the degree of perishability and the frequency of delivery. If a produce is deliver daily, inventories may be physically checked everyday. If deliveries are made semi-weekly, then the count could be made just prior to ordering.

Inventory verification (the physical count of merchandise) takes time and thus costs money. Whenever it is possible to reduce the member of items that must be counted without adding too much to the cost of inventory on hand, total handling cost may be reduced. Since hundreds of items, or even thousands may be kept is stock (consider the member of paper goods items that are low in cost but not perishable) the ABC Analysis System will give management adequate control while at the same time reducing handling costs.

The ABC system of rest account inventory management is very useful to attain greater efficiency and profit. In any food and beverage operation, you will find a large percentage of annual usage application to a small percentage of the member of items, while on the other hand, there will be large per centage of items contributing relatively little to annual usage. The degree of concentration will vary from establishment to establishment. Although the percentage of inventory investment for low and medium value items can normally be expected to increase, the result is an overall decrease in inventory investment brought through a closer control of high value items, offset only, partially, by the increase in low usage value inventory items. By reducing receipt quantities and safety stock levels of high value items while at the same time increasing receipt frequencies, the turnover can often be almost doubled and the inventory almost halved.

Under the ABC Analysis, inventory control policies can be formulated differently for each class of items by identifying its inventory items under the following three broad categories :

1. Category 'A' items – high usage value
2. Category 'B' items – medium usage value
3. Category 'C' items – low usage value

For each of these categories following inventory control policies could be formulated as given in Table 12.2 and Fig. 12.15.

TABLE 12.2. Category Inventory Control Policies

'A' item	:	1. Frequent deliveries 2. Maintain minimum safety stocks 3. Maintain strong perchasing control 4. Review records frequently
'B' item	:	1. Maintain strong purchasing control 2. Record pre-determined recorder points based on average usage 4. Review records on an 'exception' basis and arbitrarily determine safety stock
'C' items	:	1. Review 3 to 12 months supply (assume staples if food stuffs) at a time. 2. Use physical recorder points. 3. Exercise less control over purchasing.

Example

The Nightangle Restaurant, decided to introduce the ABC Analysis System of inventory control. All items have been categorised as 'A' 'B' and 'C'. It is estimated that 10% of the member of items account for 65% of the annual usage and 65% of the member of items accounts for only 10% of the annual usage and the balance 25% accounts for median value items.

You are required to depict the relationship between these items by using bar diagram.

Solution:

ABC Analysis of Inventory Control

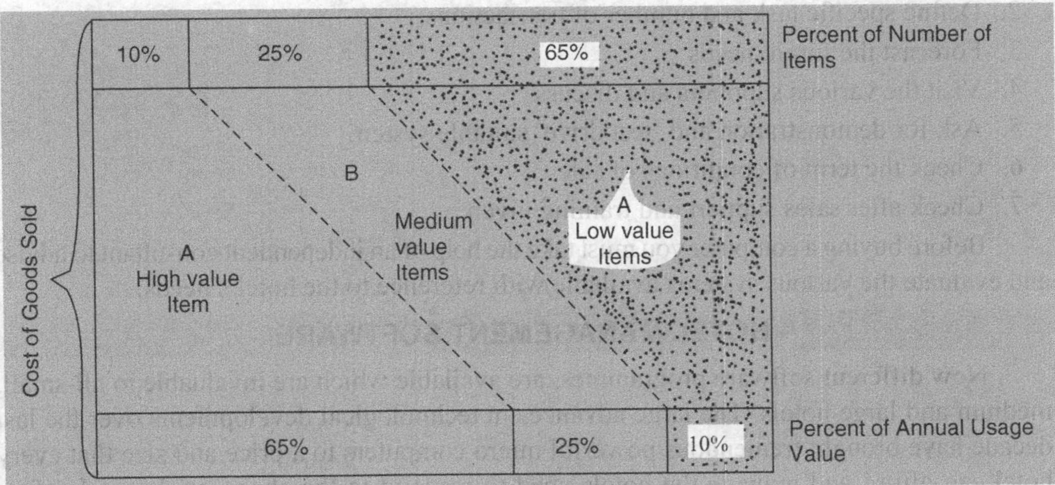

Fig. 12.15. Diagraphate Presentation of ABC Analysis

One of the important advantages of this methods is the reduction in record-keeping costs for the large number of low value items which can be removed from purchasing control records and put under physical contol. The concerned employees are free from the task of keeping records of the money immaterial items in an inventory. They can devote more time and greater attention to purchasing and recorder control system for high value and medium value item of inventory in which the usage is comparatively greater.

COMPUTERS DATA PROCESSING

With the modern generation of computer, called mini or micro computer, all hotels have realised its importance. These computers work with the high speed and can react very quickly if it shows up something going wrong in any department of the hotel. Your demand should be straightforward and relevant and the output will be of enormous value. Most medium and large sized hotels install mini computers for pure accounting functions. The two areas most in need of consideration are,'firstly,'the front office, including advance reservations, room status, arrivals and departures and guest billing. The 'second'is the food and beverage control. Accurate record keeping is essential if a hotel is to make money and reduce expenses.

In a 100-room hotel there is a choice you may install either the desk top computers such as the NCR 250 range or a full-blown 'on-line' real-time system with a VDU at the front desk, two terminals in the f & b outlets. You may require programme that will do :

1. Guest accounting
2. Advance reservation
3. Payroll
4. Sales ledger
5. Purchase ledger and
6. Nominal ledger.

Choosing a suitable computer system is a complicated task. The following guidelines could be of help in this respect:

1. Functions you want computer to carry out
2. Define specific task and number of transactions
3. Forecast the future needs
4. Visit the various suppliers and discuss
5. Ask for demonstration and 'test drive' suitable system
6. Check the term of conditions of sale
7. Check after sales support and training given

Before buying a computer you must take the help of an independent consultant to advise and evaluate the various systems available with reference to the hotel's needs.

HOTEL MANAGEMENT SOFTWARE

Now different software programmes, are available which are invaluable to all-small, medium and large hotels. The large advances in technological developments over the last decade have brought tremendous powerful micro computers to a price and size that every hotel can afford and manage the hotels need to respond to the changing demands of its customers. The speed with which it can change will affect the cost of providing the service and the profitability of the venture. The hotel requires, to acquire, collate, and manupulate information in order to make fast and accurate decisions with in the establishment. A good hotel have to plan for the future and this requires manging information effectivley. The computer could be used to collect information within the organisation. It can make sure it is able to provide any information, in any format when and where it is needed and provide in a systematic way for different manager; eg. chef, executive housekeeper, food and beverage manager. Increasing use of information technology has meant the changes from recording and communicating information on paper to digital recording using computers. Computing and information technology is a complicated subject and may be more difficult because the computing industry has invented new words and created a jargon of its own, without which it is not possible to understand fully how the computer is able to help the hotel and torism Industry.

Record of detailed information can be kept for all advance bookings, so that the hotel knows who to expect, when the guest will arrive or depart, and what kind of room is required. The computer, can also assist by writing the information letters, keeping messages for guests and advising the management about regular guests, so improving the level of service to the hotel offers. When the guest arrives at the hotel the same information can be used to produce a range information for other departments, for example in the telephone department it is helpful to those who answer the telephone to know who is in each room and be able to offer a fast and friendly service.

The Housekeeping department needs to know which rooms are being vacated , so that linen can be changed and the room prepared for the next arrival. If a room is not let for some time the housekeeper can be advised, to ensure that the heating is turned off or that maintenance or repairs are carried out during this period. The professional haousekeeper must know the names of regular guest and their individual preferences. These are the little details but make people feel welcome and will ensure that they return on another occasion. Computer can help my keeping all this information up to date.

Whenever meals are provided in quantity, it is necessary to examine the costs which occur and to ensure that same control exists to monitor payments to suppliers and staff and to ensure that these costs are accounted for. At the end of the day, profit levels can therefore be calculated, costs could be compared against allowences so that over spending does not occur. For example, in an industrial catering house, the addtional expence of ₹ 1 per meal per person, becomes very significant, if to the member of people being fed in 10,000 twice daily, five days a week, at the end of the year this represent the sum of as follows :

10,000 people × 2 meals × 5 days × 52 weeks × ₹ 1 = ₹ 52,000

In most of the hotel, food costs are calculated manually. The main element in calculating food cost is the stock taking. The simple formula for calculating the cost of each item is :

Opening Stock + Receipts of Purchases – Closing Stock = Consumption.

Some stock items had to be counted before the value of the closing stock could be worked out. Many of these items would have been weighted and then valued at a cost per period or kilogram. All these items could have to be counted and multiplied by their price. In some hotels. This needs to be done every week or every month for six hundred or a thousand stock items. It means a lot of paper work. It is very time consuming findings the right price of each item and multiplying it by the quantity which was left. It is likely, therefore, that the opening stock, receipts and closing stock be worked out by measurement of weight, volume or members and only express the consumption in monetary value. It becomes difficult to get a preview result and calculation become for more complicated if you like to know the value of the receipts and closing stock. Other figures might also added to these to make allowances for transfer from one kitchen to another, or to 'write off' food items which have been spoilt or wasted through over production.

All the prices are stored in the programme and every thing can be measured in terms of money, and if neccessary converted to weights and measures. Conversely, if given the weights and measures the computer could express them in monetary value. It does not relieve you from counting every item at the end of the period, but it does reduce the amout of the work. The computer prepares the paper with all the information printed on them and then it only requires you to enter the amounts of the closing stock in figures, decimals or fractions.

Receipts of course are gathered on a daily basis as goods are received. The invoices are entered into the system against each item, so that at the end of each period not only can the value of receipts be calculated that also you are in a position to make exact payments to each supplier the price of each ingradient is collected from each invoice so that the system can value all the items at the correct price.

As new technology has been developed now for collecting information for closing stock. Small hand-held terminals with special light sensitive pens can read the stock members of items and allow the stock taker to enter the quantities on a small key board just like a calculator. This information can be put straight into the system for processing, thus reducing even further the amount of work to be done by the operator. Stock which are manually calculated recuired 10 to 15 days for completion, whereas with the help of the computer the entire process can be completed in an hour for two.

The procedure to arrive the value of stock consumed could be calculated by another method. Divide the quantities of the different ingradient by the number of portions each by each recipe provides and then multiplying that quantity by the number of portions prepared or sold. This will give a 'national' or 'theoratical' stock conxomption figure. To make projections, the computer must have not only the recipes which have been used but also it detils of the number of portions provde by each recipe.

PRODUCTION CONTROL : RECIPE REPORT SHEETS

The breaking down of menus and receipes into ingredients is known as menu expositions or recipe exposition. This need to be gauge more accurately to ensure a reasonable delivery system. These are usually performed manually. Now due to the use of computers, all ingredients are already in the system for stocking purposes. This record would be used as a source of data from which recipe could be made. Of course, ingredients are rarely used in the same measures as they are purchased and it is therefore necessary to have a complete set of conversion tables so that of an ingredient is bought by the pound or kilo it can be used in receipes by the gram or ounce. The units of measure are obbreviated to make the system easy to use.

The operator could build up a group of ingredients into recipes and express each recipe in cost per portion. See the cost of each recipe, should the price of any ingredient change, so too would the cost of all recipes using that ingredient. This application is generally reformed to as 'production control' and presents major advantages such as :

1. You can obtain from the computer comparision of your ahead consumption with your notional consumption and give the variance, or difference, in terms of money and quantity. This will enable you to see clearly not only what you actually used but what you should be using if the recipes are followed correctly. Explanation could be sought for large variables but the computer can indication for the first time which ingrediants should be investigeted.

2. By putting a series of menus for some days ahead you can ask the system what ingrediants are required for the next period.

3. If a list of suppliers were maintained alongside the recipes and ingredients files, then the computer could easily produce a perchase order list exactly to be specification required by you.

4. In airline catering (in flight) it may be necessary to write an invoice for meals supplied to passengers abroad a particular flight. Some times it may be necessary to have more than one selling price for each item, so that a complex marketing policy can be followed.

5. In case of stock system required for managing liquor stocks in bars, it is quite common for the same be or to beer more expensive in one bar than another although the purchase price costs the same.

6. You may also make budgets for the future and keeping figures from the past, compare performance with the objects and your important decisions are based on reliable information.

ELECTRONIC POINT OF SALE (EPOS)

All sales are recorded and cash and credit card payments one recorded in a 'Cash Register'. This provides somewhere safe for the money and provides some control in case mistake are made. The new electronic point of sale works in much the same way on the computer system. Both are electronic and could be linked together (interfaced) to exchange information. There must be a number of registers in different areas, such as restaurant, the bar or the room service, all reporting back to the main computer in order to provide important sale information or to change the cost of a meal to the bill of a hotel guest. This equipment can also pass information rapidly to other departments. The orders taken in the restaurant can be transmitted electronically to the kitchen which receives this on a small printer. EPOS systems can record not only which soup was sold and by whom, but it can also provide the time at which it was sold, in order to enable butter planning or the next day. To study the relationship between profit and popularity it is important to know why certain dishes are popular or why the organisation makes a loss on some. How to make the recipes popular and proftable requires a great deal of information not only for the kitchen but also for the customers.

Thus the computer is a valuable tool in finance, accounting and audit department. A great deal of accurate financial information is required for smooth running of an organisation. Accounting department needs to know who owns money to the hotel and to whom it owes money. Detail of debtors and creditors play an important part in hotel management. The hotel relies on computer to ensure that there is sufficient money in the bank to pay suppliers or to provide wage payment at the end of each month. Computarized payroll system can be linked to computers at the bank and monthly wages or salaries can be translated electronically into employees bank accounts. Fig. 12.16 is a Data Processing Schedule indicating analysis of all data processing expenses.

ABC Hotels Ltd.
Data Processing Schedule

	Current Period
Salaries and Wages	₹..................
Employees' Benefits	....
Total Payroll and Related Expenses	....
Other Expenses :	
Dues and Subscriptions	....
Training	....
Maintenance :	
Hardware	....
Software	....
Operating supplies	....
Service Bureau Fees	....
Others	....
Total Other Expenses	....
Total Data Processing Expenses	....

Note : Various arrangements of additional columns for comparisons and percentages could be added.

Fig. 12.16 : Analysis of Expenses of Data Processing

QUESTIONS AND ASSIGNMENTS

1. What are the various types of budgets prepared in a hotel ? Explain any TWO in detail. *(IHMs)*
2. Define cost accounting. How does cost accounting facilitate managerial decision making in a hotel ? *(IHMs)*
3. What is a Funds Flow Statement? How is it prepared? *(IHMs)*
4. What is a sales budget ? Discuss the principal factors that should be considered in a sales budget. *(IHMs)*
5. Discuss the importance of internal control in the hospitality industry. *(IHMs)*
6. Briefly explain the objectives of internal control in the hotel industry. *(IHMs)*
7. "Budgetary control means worrying before work rather than after. Its key notes are planning, co-ordination and control". Explain this statement. *(IHMs)*
8. (*a*) Write short notes on any four:- *(IHMs)*
   (1) Standards
   (2) Controls
   (3) Budget
   (4) Ratio Analysis
   (5) Trade Union.
9. Distinguish between:-
   (*a*) Private Limited Company and Partnership.
   (*b*) Fixed Budget and Flexible Budget. *(IHMs)*
10. Explain the following in not more than 100-words:-
    (*a*) Pay-back Period
    (*b*) Off-the-Job Training
    (*c*) Internal Control. *(IHMs)*
11. Define the term 'auditing'. Explain the procedure of night audit in a hotel. *(IHMs)*

12. Explain the system of record and control of room sales in a medium-sized hotel. ***(IHMs)***

13. Define 'Daily Report'. Give a suitable proforma of a Daily Report incorporating there in a few imaginary items. ***(IHMs)***

14. Define 'uniform system of accounting'. What are the advantages and limitations of application of uniform system of accounting in a hotel ? ***(IHMs)***

15. Explain the different types of accounting machines and their uses. Suggest the important accounting machines suitable for a large sized hotel. ***(IHMs)***

16. Give specimen ruling and explain the purpose of any *four* of the following :
    - (*i*) Visitors Tabular Ledger
    - (*ii*) Sales Journal
    - (*iii*) Purchase Journal
    - (*iv*) Cash Book
    - (*v*) Hotel Ledger
    - (*vi*) Computer. ***(IHMs)***

17. Explain the credit security measures adopted in a hotel in relation to guest to safeguard the interest of the hotel. ***(IHMs)***

18. Write short notes on any two of the following : ***(IHMs)***
    - (*i*) Night Audit
    - (*ii*) Current Ratio
    - (*iii*) Forfeiture of Shares
    - (*iv*) Garner Vs Murray.

19. Describe the various types of ledgers that can be maintained by a large hotel. Explain city ledger in detail. ***(IHMs)***

20. Write notes on the following : ***(IHMs)***
    - (*a*) Revenue Producing Departments of a Hotel.
    - (*b*) Preference Shares.

21. Explain the use and operation of N.C.R. (class 42) Posting Machine in a big hotel. ***(IHMs)***

22. Describe the following with their advantages:– ***(IHMs)***
    - (*a*) Tabular System of Book-Keeping:
    - (*b*) Guests Weekly Bill.

23. Who is a Night Auditor of a hotel? Describe his main duties. ***(IHMs)***

24. Write shorts on :
    - (*a*) Revenue Producing Department of a Hotel
    - (*b*) Hubbart Formula;
    - (*c*) Uniform Accounting System for Hotels. ***(IHMs)***

25. Explain any Four of the following :–
    - (*a*) Sales Mix in a Hotel;
    - (*b*) Food Cost;
    - (*c*) Kitchen Profit;
    - (*d*) Service Charge;
    - (*e*) Operating Costs;
    - (*f*) Current Assets. ***(IHMs)***

26. Critically examine the role that a computer may play in a large hotel. ***(IHMs)***

27. Write notes on:

(*i*) Apportionment of overheads

(*ii*) Computers in hotel accounting

(*iii*) Sales-mix. ***(IHMs)***

28. Explain any **Four** of the following:

(*a*) Sales-mix in a hotel

(*b*) Daily Report

(*c*) Service Charge

(*d*) City Ledger

(*e*) Current Ratio

(*f*) Inter-hotel Comparison. ***(IHMs)*0**

29. Explain the purposes that can be served by using a computer in a hotel. What information can it provide to hotel's top management ? ***(IHMs)***

30. Describe various credit security measures which can be adopted by a manager to safeguard the interest of the hotel. ***(IHMs)***

31. What are the functions of Night Auditors of a hotel ? What points should be looked in opening and closing of visitors tabulation register ? ***(IHMs)***

32. What is the significance of controlling accounts in a hotel? Describe the procedure for exercising effective control over incoming and outgoing cash. ***(IHMs)***

33. Write short notes on the following :

(*i*) Uniform system of accounting

(*ii*) Hotel ledger. ***(IHMs)***

34. A hotel prepares its daily report. You have been asked to suggest a suitable *proforma* of the daily report. Explain the main points which a daily report usually contains. ***(IHMs)***

35. "The one man control is the best in the world, if that man is big enough to manage everything." Comment on this statement. Do you agree with it ? ***(IHMs)***

36. What is the finance function ? Explain its importance in hotel management. ***(IHMs)***

37. What do you mean by internal check ? Discuss a system for internal check of wages disbursements in a hotel. ***(IHMs)***

38. Define financial management. Explain the functions of a finance executive of a five star hotel. ***(IHMs)***

39. Compare the methods used, and the costs involved, to obtain long-term finance for a large company. Discuss the relative merits of the different methods. ***HCIMA (LONDON)***

40. Explain the process of control. What are the pre-requisites for establishing a control system in an organization? List some control methods used in the key areas of a hotel. ***(IHMs)***

41. What are the public institutions that help in hotel financing ? What role do they play in it and how ? ***(IHMs)***

42. What is control and what is its procedure ? Discuss few control techniques commonly used in hotels. ***(IHMs)***

43. Explain the characteristics of financing and investing in a hotel project. What is the role of Tourism Finance Corporation in advancing loans to tourism related projects ? *(IHMs)*

44. Explain the following:

(*a*) Industrial Finance Corporation of India

(*b*) Investing in Hotels

(*c*) Sources of Hotel Finance. ***(IHMs)***

45. Define the term Control. Explain the full control cycle related to the sale of food and beverage items in a hotel. ***(IHMs)***

46. Explain the following :

(*a*) Star Ranking of Hotel

(*b*)Tourism Finance Corporation of India

(*c*) Foreign Collaboration in Hotel

(*d*)Types of Beds

(*e*) Night Auditing. ***(MTM)***

47. Writes notes on :

(*a*) Menu

(*b*) Hubbart formula

(*c*) Hotel Corporation of India

(*d*) Liquidity Ratio

(*e*) Financial Statement

(*f*) Induction

(*g*) Foreign Exchange Regulations

(*h*) House Count

(*i*) Interior Decoration.

48. Give a brief description about the principles and procedures of store purchasing in a large hotel. ***(PGT&HM)***

49. Define uniform system of accounting. What are the advantage and limitations of applications of uniform system of accounting in hotels ? ***(MTA)***

50. What is 'cycle of control' ? You are appointed manager of a newly started restaurant. Illustrate the application of the 'concept of control' in setting up of control system of the restaurant. ***(MTA)***

51. As far as the accounting process is concerned, what is the role of the night auditor? Explain the duties of a night auditor. ***(IHMs)***

52. Draw an organisation chart for the Finance and Accounting of Control Department of a deluxe hypothetical hotel.

53. Write a job description listing the responsibilities and duties of each staff position of Finance and Control and Audit Department.

54. Discuss the nature and contents of planning in the finance area of hotel business.

55. Discuss the problems of centralised control systems within a large multi-unit organisation, suggesting how management at unit level can prepare for and cope with these problems. ***HCIMA* (*London*)**

56. What is the difference between a capital budget and an operating budget. ***(IHMs)***

57. How can the operating budget be used as a tool to control express ? ***(IHMs)***

58. What steps would be followed to organise a linear inventory ?

59. Give three reasons for discrepancies between actual stock taking and the book stock.

60. What are some of the typical expenses (or line items) an executive housekeeper might encounter when preparing the department's budget ? What are the four basic methods used to control expenses ? ***(IHMs)***

61. What is budget ? What is the difference between a capital budget and an operating budget ? How can the operating budget be used as a tool to control expenses ? ***(IHMs)***

62. Illustrate with the help of a flow chart, the triplicate checking system of restaurant sales control. ***(IHMs)***

63. (*a*) Outline the various basic information and factors necessary for a good standard purchase specification.

(*b*) What method of purchasing you would use for purchase of perishable food?

(*c*) Assume you have been hired as a Purchase Officer of a new restaurant located in an area/city that is completely unfamiliar to you, in such a situation how would you obtain information on sources of supply ? ***(IHMs)***

64. (*a*) List the essential details that must be included in the format or proforma for a purchase order.

(*b*) With the help of a flow chart, elucidate the importance of Purchase Functions and Transactions. ***(IHMs)***

65. (*a*) Describe the various procedure/methods which can be followed for receiving of goods in a store.

(*b*) What do you understand by meat tag ? Explain it's use and advantages.

(*c*) Distinguish between food direct and indirect. ***(IHMs)***

66. Explain the following methods of stock pricing :

(*i*) Actual Purchase Price

(*ii*) Weighted Average Price

(*iii*) Standard Price.

67. List five different major items of equipment that would be required in a storage area.

68. Assuming that beef sent by supplier was not as per specifications and had to be rejected, draw the proforma that you would use for it's return. ***(IHMs)***

69. (*a*) Why is portion control essential in a catering establishment's food and beverage control system ?

(*b*) List at least ten items of equipment which would assist in portion control.

70. Write in detail various objectives of Food Cost Control. ***(IHMs)***

71. While deciding on a selling price of a dish, which two factors would need to be considered by the management of a new establishment ?

72. What is the correct method of dealing with staff meals from costing point of view ? ***(IHMs)***

73. (*a*) What is meant by pricing ?

(*b*) Explain in detail the menu pricing techniques based on the following terms:

(*i*) Mark up on cost

(*ii*) Base cost method.

(*c*) Explain the special pricing considerations used in Food and Beverage pricing with respect to :

(*i*) Happy hours (*ii*) Loss Leader (*iii*) Exclusive clientele. ***(IHMs)***

74. (*a*) What is meant by the term Standard Costing ?

(*b*) How does Standard Costing helps in Variance Analysis ?

(*c*) Explain the importance of Standard Costing in Food Cost Control.

(*d*) Explain the importance of profit reconciliation in Food Cost Control.

75. (*a*) What is meant by the term Breakeven Point ?

(*b*) What is the financial position of a business at Break-even Point ?

(*c*) Explain how breakeven point is calculated using :

(*i*) Graph method

(*ii*) Mathematical Formula

(*iii*) Chart method. ***(IHMs)***

76. (*a*) What is break-even analysis ?

(*b*) Hill Top Ltd. operates three Restaurants in Bombay. The information are as follows:

Restaurant	*Sales-mix*	*F&B Cost %*
(1) Indian Speciality Restaurant.	30%	30%
(2) Chinese Restaurant	40%	25%
(3) Maxican Restaurant	30%	60%

The fixed cost of all the three restaurants totalled ₹ 50 Lakhs. Calculate overall break-even sales. ***(IHMs)***

77. What do you understand by pricing ? Explain briefly different methods of pricing in catering operations. ***(IHMs)***

78. Distinguish between the following (*any two*):

(*a*) Perpetual Inventory System and Physical Inventory System.

(*b*) Standard Recipe and Standard Purchase Specification

(*c*) Operating Budgets and Capital Budgets. ***(IHMs)***

79. What are the determinates of stock levels ? Give graphical representation to illustrate various stock levels. ***(IHMs)***

80. Define :

(*a*) Sales Mix

(*b*) Margin of Safety

(*c*) Budgetary Control

(*d*) Variance Analysis

(*e*) Contribution. ***(IHMs)***

81. Discuss the following (*any two*):

(*a*) Pricing Technique

(*b*) Menu as a Marketing Tool

(*c*) Beverage Control. ***(IHMs)***

82. Explain the various sales concepts and its uses in the Food & Beverage Department. ***(IHMs)***

83. (*a*) Outline the various basic information and factors necessary for a good standard purchase specification.

(*b*) What method of purchasing you would use for purchase of perishable food?

(*c*) Assume you have been hired as a Purchase Officer of a new restaurant located in an area/city that is completely unfamiliar to you, in such a situation how would you obtain information on sources of supply ? ***(IHMs)***

84. (*a*) List the essential details that must be included in the format or proforma for a purchase order.

(*b*) With the help of a flow chart, elucidate the importance of Purchase Functions and Transactions. ***(IHMs)***

85. (*a*) Why is portion control essential in a catering establishment's food and beverage control system ?

(*b*) List at least ten items of equipment which would assist in portion control.

86. List reasons why standard yield, standard portions and standard recipes are important for the success of a restaurant in a five star hotel. ***(IHMs)***

87. How would each of the following adversely affect the average sale in a restaurant:

(*a*) Deterioration in service standards

(*b*) Inadequate sales promotion. ***(IHMs)***

88. State eight practices that help to increase the efficiency of a refrigerated storage. ***(IHMs)***

89. Write in detail various objectives of Food Cost Control. ***(IHMs)***

90. While deciding on a selling price of a dish, which two factors would need to be considered by the management of a new establishment ?

91. From the following Balance Sheets of the Johnson Hotel, you are required to prepare.

(*i*) A Schedule of Charge in Working Capital and

(*ii*) A status of Flow of Funds.

Johnson Hotel

Balance Sheets

Liabilities	*31st Dec. 2000*	*31st Dec. 2000*
Capital	₹ 1,60,000	₹ 170,000
Profit and Loss Approximately	29,000	49,000
Creditors	18,000	10,000
Mortgage	—	10,000
Provision for Daubtful debts	2,000	2,6,00
₹ 2,09,000	₹ 2,41,600	
Assets		
Land and Building	₹ 100,000	₹ 100,000
Plant or Machinery	48,000	68,000
Store	18,000	14,000
Debtor	35,000	41,600
Cash at Bank	8,000	18,000
	₹ 2,09,000	₹ 2,41,600

OBJECTIVE TYPE QUESTIONS

92. Answer the following questions :

(1) What is the formula to calculate average check ?

(2) What is Menu Fatigue ?

(3) What is meant by the term Margin of Safety ?

(4) Volume Forecasting is also known as ....

(5) A cardex card replaces a bin card – State True or False. **(*IHMs*)**

93. What are the important sources of hotel finance ? Explain the role of foreign capital and foreign collaboration in Indian hotel industry. ***(PGDT)***

94. Fill in the blanks with appropriate answers/words :

(*i*) Gross profit or kitchen profit is the difference between the.................of the food and the ....of the food.

(*ii*) Net profit is the difference between ....of the food and the total cost

(*iii*) Increase in liability is.............(debited/credited).

(*iv*) The normal balance of the Owner's Equity Account would be a ....

(*v*) The minimum number of members in a public company is........................ .

(*vi*) The liability of a sole trader is ....(limited/unlimited).

(*vii*) The number of owners in a sole trade organisation is.............................. .

(*viii*) A partner who is not participating in the management of the firm is called..............

(*ix*) ....minus sales return = Net sales.

(*x*) ITDC is established as a...............(public/pvt./govt./special) Company. (*IHMs*)

95. Answer the following questions:

(*a*) Fill in the blanks :

(*i*) The food plan which includes breakfast and lunch or dinner with the room tariff is the...................... .

(*ii*) Before accepting a credit card, the cashier should check for.......................date.

(*iii*) Inventory is also known as........................... .

(*iv*) The Balance Sheet equation is......................... .

(*v*) Entries recorded on both the sides of Cash Book are called .... and ....

(*b*) Choose the correct answer:

(*i*) Depreciation is a:

(*a*) Charge against profit
(*b*) Reduction in capital
(*c*) Appropriation of profit
(*d*) None of above.

(*ii*) What is correct:–

(*a*) Capital = Assets – Liabilities
(*b*) Liabilities = Capital – Liabilities
(*c*) Capital = Net Assets.

(*iii*) Machine repaired at a cost of ₹ 2,000/- is a:

(*a*) Capital Expenditure
(*b*) Revenue Expenditure
(*c*) Deferred Revenue Expenditure.

(*iv*) Depreciation arises from:

(*a*) Fall in the market value of an asset
(*b*) Physical wear and tear
(*c*) Fall in the value of money.

(*v*) Which of the following mistakes would not be revealed in the Trial Balance:

(*a*) Payment of wages entered in the Cash Book but not in the wages account in the ledger.
(*b*) Sale of an old machinery credited to Sales A/c instead of Machinery A/c.
(*c*) Purchase of a typewriter entered in Purchase A/c instead of Office Machinery A/c. (*IHMs*)

96. Indicate the correct answer:

(Answer strictly as per the serial order of the question)

(*i*) The total of purchase book is posted periodically to the:

(*a*) Credit to sales A/c
(*b*) Debit of purchase A/c
(*c*) Credit of individual A/c.

(*ii*) Heavy advertising to launch a new product is:

(*a*) Capital expenditure
(*b*) Revenue expenditure
(*c*) Deferred revenue expenditure.

(*iii*) Certain transactions of miscellaneous nature which do not find a place in the subsidiary books are passed through
(*a*) Trading A/c
(*b*) Profit and Loss A/c
(*c*) Journal Proper.

(*iv*) Capital account is related to:
(*a*) Real Account
(*b*) Nominal Account
(*c*) Personal Account.

(*v*) Trading account is prepared to know:
(*a*) Net Sales
(*b*) Net Profit
(*c*) Cross Profit. **(*IHMs*)**

A CASE STUDY

97. Mr. R. Nath, front office manager of Himland and Hotel, has finished talking with Mr. Jacob, the night author. He has spent the majority of his shift trying to track down five posting errors totalling $343.21. This is not the first time in the past two weeks that this mistry during their duty has taken place. Last Sunday night a charge of $32.68 was posted to the incorrect account, and on Tuesday night a $12.45 room service charge was posted as $12.54. Mr. Jacob told Mr. R. Nath that he has been at the Himaland Hotel for ever 10 years, and in his experience these mistakes are usually the result of improper training of new front-desk clerks. Mr. R. Nath thanked Jacob for the information and told him he would look into the matter.

Mr. R. Nath calls Preeti into her office. Preeti, she is the lead person on the first shift. She trained the new front desk clerk; Johny and Ranjan. Both Johny and Ranjan were good trainees and seem to understand all the tasks involved in operating the system. Mr. R. Nath asks Preeti to relate the procedure she used to train these new recruits.

Preeti says she described the full operating system to them and then let them post some dummy charges an the training module. Then she had them correct each other mistakes. After fifteen minutes of practice the front office become very busy, and they had to turn the training mode off and activate the regular operating mode. Johny posted several paid out charges and vouchers. Ranjan was little more reluctant to touch the machine but after the coffee break, he wanted to try to post guest payments.

Mr. R. Nath realizes that the development of a training programme is his responsibility, and he has let that responsibility slip. How would you help Mr. R. Nath prepare an effective training programme than teaches new front office clerks the following:

(1) Whey to post guest charges ?
(2) Why to post guest payments ?
(3) How to post guest charges ?
(4) How to post guest payments ?

CHAPTER 13

Performance Measurement

OBJECTIVE

After studying this topic you should be able to :

1. *Understand the nature of fixed expenses in a hotel business*
2. *Understand the statement of financial position and statement of income*
3. *Explain various types of assets and liabilities and income and expenses and*
4. *Appreciate the importance of balance sheet, profit and loss accounts and the use of various ratios and percentages analysis.*

HOTEL INFORMATION

Several people are interested in the information of the hotel. These belong to various groups such as :

1. Owners/Shareholders
2. Lenders
3. Managers/Employees

Therefore, the financial position and performance of a hotel are reflected by two separate statements :

1. Balance Sheet, and
2. Profit & Loss account.

The owners/shareholders and long-term lenders are interested in the sustained profitability of the hotel. They would like to know the return on investment, relationship between equity/owners' capital and loans. The trade creditors and short-term lenders would like to be satisfied that the hotel can meet its current obligations. They would like to know the relationship between current assets and current liabilities. The management has responsibilities to both long-term and short-term investors as well as with the planning and day-to-day control of business. Therefore, management requires a detailed and frequented financial statement to enable it to direct control and monitor the progress of the hotel.

For purpose of management information control and decision making the following statements are produced with related ratios and supporting schedules :

1. Daily Statement of Hotel Revenue
2. Weekly Statement of Cost of Sales and Payroll
3. Monthly Operating Statement of Revenue, Cost and Expenses
4. Quarterly Balance Sheet.

A hotel operator should fix certain set of standards to measure its performance. These standards are guidelines. These are in the form of ratios, or expressed as percentages. Performance standards given in Fig. 13.1 are suitable for a hotel of any size or standard. However, these may be considered as variable according to the size of the hotel, management policy, seasonal factors and standard/star category of the hotel.

Standard Performance Percentage Guidelines for Hotels and Restaurants

Departmental Standards	Performance %
Room Department	
Room wages to room revenue	10-18%
Laundry : Weekly cost to total room revenue	4-8%
Cost of Serving Twin-room to net room rate (Including wages and material cost to sale)	20-22%
Rooms Trading Profit	
(Sales less wages and material cost to sales)	70-80%
Food Production	
Food Production Wages	
Restaurants	20-25%
Coffee shops	20-25%
Material Cost :	
Luxury restaurants	33-35%
Steak bars	45-48%
Coffee shop/Medium-sized restaurant	40-45%
Food Trading Profit :	
Sales less cost of materials and wages to sales	25-40%
Food Stock Turn-Over Per Year :	26 times or two weeks' usage at cost
Beverage Department :	
Wages	
Cocktail bars	10-11%
Public bars	12-15%
Material cost percentage	
Cocktail bars	35%
Public bars	55-60%
Trading Frofit	
Cocktail bars	55%
Public bars	30-40%
Stock turn-over per year	12 times or 20-30 days' stock

(Contd..)

Administration and General :	
Wages to total sales	4-6%
Advertising and Sales Promotion :	
Costs to total sales	3%
Repair & Maintenance to Total Sales :	
Depending on age of property	4-6%
Monthly Debts / Total Annual Sales :	less than 6%
Net Profit / Total Sales :	15-25%
Return on Capital Invested :	12-20%
Gross Operating Profit :	35-45%

Fig. 13.1 : Standard Performance Percentage Guidelines for Hotels and Restaurants

RENT PROPERTY TAXES AND INSURANCE

This head includes the following :

RENT

It includes the rent paid for the hotel property whether furnished or unfurnished. If the rent is paid for ground only the amount will be debited to ground rent account.

REAL ESTATE TAXES

1. **Real Estate Taxes :** Taxes imposed by central and state government and local bodies are induced in this head.
2. **Personal Property Tax :** All taxes relating to personal property are included under this head.
3. **Sewer Tax and Utility :** These taxes are charged by the municipality for the use of sewer and utility.

INSURANCE ON BUILDING AND CONTENTS

The building of the hotel and its contents are insured against damage or destruction by fire, tornado, sprinkler, leakage, boiler explosion, plant glass breakage or any other cause. All expenses relating to it should be debited to this account.

DISTRIBUTION OF RENT INSURANCE AND MUNICIPAL TAXES

Rent and real estate taxes could be allocated on the basis of square foot or cubic foot of area. In case any space occupied by stores etc., have a greater value than other space of premises, the allocation may be weighted so that the more valuable space would have a higher ratio of allocation per square foot or cubic foot of area.

Municipal Taxes such as property tax, sewer and utility taxes can be allocated to the departments on the basis of the personal property applicable to each and other taxes on the basis of departments using the services.

Insurance on building and contents may be equitably allocated on the basis of the insurable property applicable to the respective departments.

Figs 13.2 indicates fixed charges analysis in a fixed charges schedule. Fig. 13.3 is an Rent, Property Taxes and Insurance schedule analysing all related expenes.

ABC Hotels Ltd.
Fixed Charges-Schedule

	Current Period
Rent	
Land Processing Building	₹ ....
Data Processing Equipment	....
Telephone Equipment	....
Other Equipments	....
Total	₹ ....
Taxes other than Income and Payroll	
Real Estate Taxes	....
Personal Property Taxes	....
Utility Taxes	....
Business and Occupation Taxes	₹ ....
Others	....
Total	₹ ....
Insurance on Building and Contents	
Total Rent, Property Taxes and Insurances	
Interest Expense	
Mortgages	₹ ....
Notes Payable	....
Interest on Capital Leases	....
Other Long-Term Debts	....
Amortization of Deferred Financing Costs	....
Others	....
Total	₹
Depreciation And Amortization	
Building and Improvements	₹ ....
Leaseholds and Leasehold Improvements	....
Furnishings and Equipment	....
Capital Leases	....
Preopening Expenses	....
Others	....
Total	₹ ....
Gain or Loss on Sale of Property	₹ ....

Fig. 13.2 : Analysis of Fixed Charges

ABC Hotels Ltd.
Rents, Property Taxes and Insurance Schedule

	Current period
Rent	₹ ....
Municipal Taxes	₹ ....
Real Estate	....
Personal Property	....
Sewer	....
Utility	₹ ....
Business	....
Others	....
Total Municipal Taxes	₹ ....
Insurance on Building and Contents	....
Total Rent, Municipal Taxes and Insurance	₹ ....

Fig. : 13.3 : Analysis of Rents, Property Taxes and Insurance

INTEREST

This account is debited with the following accounts :

1. Interest on bonds
2. Interest on mortgages
3. Interest on tax arrears
4. Interest on other indebtedness of the hotel.

DISTRIBUTION OF INTEREST

This item should not be considered over-head to be allocated to operating departments. In case the hotel likes to allocate, it would be on the basis of pro-rata share of the assets covered by the obligation applicable to a particular department. Fig. 13.4 is a interest schedule, analysing interest.

ABC Hotels Ltd.
Interest Schedule

Interest on each class of obligation should be shown separately	
Total Interest	₹

Fig. 13.4 : Analysis of Interest

DEPRECIATION AND AMORTIZATION

DEPRECIATION

It includes the following :

1. **Depreciation of building :** It includes estimated decrease in the value of the building resulting from wear and tear and obsolescence.

2. **Depreciation of furniture and equipment :** The gradual reduction in the value of the furniture and equipment resulting from wear and tear is debited to this account.

AMORTIZATION

The proportionate cost of lease is written off every year in order to extinguish it over its life.

AMORTIZATION OF LEASEHOLD IMPROVEMENTS

Any cost of permanent improvement made to leasehold property originally treated as an asset, should be written off over a certain number of years.

AMORTIZATION OF BOND DISCOUNT AND MORTGAGE EXPENSES

The proportionate part of expenses incurred in floating on issue of bonds or placing a mortgage should be charged to this account including discount on bonds, fees, stamps and other similar items.

DISTRIBUTION OF DEPRECIATION AND AMORTIZATION

The most equitable basis of allocation of depreciation of assets and amortization of least hold improvement would be on the basis of the property value applicable to each department.

The allocation of the cost of lease-hold on the basis of square foot or cubic foot of area similar to the distribution of rent would be the most equitable one. Fig. 13.5 is a schedule for depreciation and expenses Amortization analysing depreciation and expense an amortization.

ABC Hotels Ltd.
Depreciation And Expense Amortization Schedule

Depreciation of Building	₹ ....
Depreciation of Furniture	....
and Equipment	....
Amortization of Leasehold	....
Amortization of Leasehold	....
Improvements	....
Amortization of Bond Discount and	....
Mortgages expenses	....
Total Fepreciation and	....
Expense Amortization	₹ ....

Fig. 13.5 : Analysis of Depreciation and Expense Amortization

CENTRAL AND STATE TAXES

INCOME TAX

Income tax charged by the central government is charged to this head.

FRANCHISE TAX

Taxes charged by the state for the privilege to do business as corporation should be charged to this account.

The schedules for Central and State Taxes and Income Tax are given in Figs 13.6 and 13.7 respectively. All related expenses are anaysed in these schedules.

ABC Hotels Ltd. Central And State Taxes Schedule	
State Franchise Tax	₹............
Central Income Tax	....
Total State and Central Taxes	₹ ....

Note : Various arrangements of additional columns for comparisons and percentages could be added.

Fig. 13.6 Analysis of State and Central Taxes

ABC Hotels Ltd. Income Taxes Schedule	
	Current Period
Central	
Current	....
Deferred	....
Total	₹ ....
State	
Current	....
Deferred	....
Total	₹ ....
Others	
Current	....
Deferred	....
Total	₹ ....
Total Central and State Income Taxes	₹ ....

Fig. 13.7 : Analysis of Income Tax

ENERGY COST : HEAT, LIGHT AND POWER

The credits of this department are divided into following sections :

1. Sales :

(*a*) Electric bulbs
(*b*) Electric current
(*b*) Steam
(*d*) Water
(*e*) Miscellaneous.

2. Charges To Other Departments :

(*a*) Room
(*b*) Gas for refrigeration and cooling
(*c*) Food and Beverages
(*d*) Electricity for cooking

3. Miscellaneous

The expenses included under this head are :

EMPLOYEES' REMUNERATION AND BENEFITS

Salaries, wages and other benefits paid to employees connected with these activities are included under this head :

1. Chief Engineer
2. Assistant Engineer
3. Office and Store Room Employees
4. Stenographers
5. Time Clerks
6. Statistician
7. Inventory Clerks
8. Store-keeper.

1. Engineers :

(*a*) Water Engineers
(*b*) Boiler Room Engineers
(*c*) Oilers
(*d*) Elevator Engineer
(*e*) Air-conditioning Control Men
(*f*) Boilermen.

2. Firemen :

(*a*) Firemen
(*b*) Coal Passers.

3. Refrigeration :

(*a*) Refrigeration Mechanics
(*b*) Ice Putters
(*c*) Ice Makers.

(*iv*) MISCELLANEOUS :

(*a*) Cleaners
(*b*) Yardmen
(*c*) Incinerator Men.

EMPLOYEES' MEALS

The cost of food furnished to the related employees is debited to this account.

CLEANING SUPPLIES

Same basis as in the room department.

ELECTRIC BULBS

The cost of light and power purchased from outside producers including break-down service is debited to this account.

ELECTRIC CURRENT

The cost of electric bulbs put into use should be charged to this account.

ENGINEERING SUPPLIES

It is debited with all the supplies to engineering department like :

(*a*) Alkalies
(*b*) Fuses
(*c*) Oils
(*d*) Shovel
(*e*) Waste
(*f*) Boiler compound
(*g*) Greases
(*h*) Packing
(*i*) Solvents
(*j*) Water purifier and softeners.

FUEL

The cost of fuel consumed like coal, oil, gas, etc., excepting those used in kitchen and restaurant should be charged to this account.

GAS FOR REFRIGERATION

Gas used for individual apartments is debited to this head.

PRINTING AND STATIONERY

It includes the cost of all printed forms, service manuals, stationery and office supplies used in this section.

REFRIGERATION SUPPLIES

The cost of supplies for the refrigeration plant, including ammonia, brine calcium and other refrigerants, are debited to this account.

REMOVAL OF ASHES

The cost of disposal of coal ashes is debited to this account.

STEAM

It includes the cost of steam purchased from outside.

UNIFORMS

Same basis as in the room department.

WATER

The cost of water consumed, water specially treated for circulation, ice- water system and water purchased for drinking purposes.

MISCELLANEOUS

All other charges are debited to this head.

DISTRIBUTION OF HEAT, LIGHT AND POWER

The allocation/distribution of these expenses on the basis of square foot or cubic foot of area might be considered equitable for this overhead. Fig. 13.8 is a schedule for energy cost. Heat, Light and lower analysing energy cost, heat, light and power.

ABC Hotels Ltd.
Energy Cost : Heat, Light And Power Schedule

	Current period
Salaries and Wages	₹ ....
Vacation and Holidays Pay	....
Employees' Meals	....
Payroll Taxes and Employee Benefits	....
Total Payroll and Related Expenses	₹ ....
Other Expenses	....
Cleaning Supplies	₹ ....
Electric Bulbs	....

(Contd..)

Electric Current	₹ ....
Engineering Supplies	....
Fuel	....
Gas for Refrigeration	....
Miscellaneous	....
Printing and Stationery	....
Removal of Ashes	....
Removal of Waste Matter	....
Steam	....
Uniforms	....
Water	....
Total Other Expenses	₹ ....
Total Direct Expenses	₹ ....
Credits	....
Sales	₹ ....
Charges to Other Departments	....
Total Credits	₹ ....
Net Cost Of Heat, Light And Power	₹ ....

Note : Various arrangements of additional columns for comparisons and percentages could be added.

Fig. 13.8 : Analysis of Energy Cost-Heat : Light and Power.

Fig. 13.9 is an analyses of energy cost, is an Energy Schedule

ABC Hotels
Energy Costs Schedule

	Current Period
Electric Current	₹ ....
Fuel	....
Steam	....
Water	₹ ....
Total Energy Costs	₹ ....

Fig. 13.9 : Analysis of Energy Cost

OTHER ADDITIONS AND DEDUCTIONS SCHEDULE

It includes all extraordinary expenses or income not applicable to regular hotel operations reflected by the department and undistributed income and expense schedules entering into the net operating profit or loss shown in the profit and loss schedule. For example,

1. Income received from interest
2. Profit or loss on the sale of securities
3. Profit or loss on the sale of capital or fixed assets
4. Judgment or settlement of claims for damages
5. Pre-opening expenses
6. Organisation and financing expenses.

PAYROLL TAXES AND EMPLOYEES' BENEFITS

As indicated in Fig. 13.10 this head of expenditure includes the following :

GROUP INSURANCE

It is a premium paid to insurance companies representing cost of life, health, accident, hospitalisation and other insurance for employees.

PENSION INSURANCE FUND

It includes the contributions or premiums paid for the pension funds.

EMPLOYEES STATE INSURANCE

Amount paid to employees state insurance for health insurance coverage is charged to this account.

TRADE UNION INSURANCE

Contributions or premiums paid into union employees benefit funds for insurance of life, health, accident, hospitalisaiton and other purposes.

WORKMEN'S COMPENSATION INSURANCE

Workmen's compensation and employee's ability insurance premium is charged to this head.

SALARIES AND WAGES

It includes the salaries and wages paid to personnel director, secretaries and clerks.

VACATION AND HOLIDAYS PAY

Vacation and holidays, festival, bonus, etc., paid to employees of this department is charged to this account.

PAYROLL TAXES AND EMPLOYEES' BENEFITS

As applicable to this department.

MEDICAL EXPENSES

Physician's fees, cost of medicines, drugs and clinic and first aid supplies are charged to this account.

PENSION

Any pension payment to individuals is charged to this account.

SOCIAL AND SPORT ACTIVITIES

It includes the cost of entertainment, dinners, parties, outings or other social functions for the benefit of the employees. In addition it includes cost of promoting, maintaining or financially assessing sports and athletic teams or activities of the employees.

SUGGESTION AWARDS

This account is debited with the awards and prizes for meritorious suggestions advanced by the employees.

MISCELLANEOUS

Under this head will be grouped such items as are not distributable under other options.

DISTRIBUTION OF PAYROLL TAXES AND EMPLOYEES' BENEFITS

These expenses should be pro-rated to all departments on the basis of the payroll applicable to each department. Payroll taxes should be pro-rated on the basis of the taxable payroll applicable to each department. Workmen's compensation insurance should be allocated on the basis of the amount applicable to each department based on the payroll used in computing the amount of contribution. Other major expenses included under this head would be distributed on the basis of the pro-rated share of the base applicable to a particular department. Payroll taxes and Employees Benefits Schedule ii given in Figure 13.10 indicating analysis of payroll taxes and employees benefits.

ABC Hotels Ltd.
Payroll Taxes and Employees' Benefits Schedule

	Current period
Payroll Taxes	
Central Retirement	₹
Central Unemployment	....
State Unemployment	....
Total Payroll Taxes	₹ ....
Social Insurance	
Group Insurance	....
Non-Union Insurance fund	....
Pension Insurance fund	....
State Health Insurance	....
Trade Union Insurance fund	....
Workmen's Compensation Insurance	....
Total Social Insurance	₹ ....
Other Expenses	
Salaries and Wages	₹ ....
Vacation and Holidays Pay	....
Employees' Meals	....
Payroll Taxes and Employee Benefits	....
Total Other Expenses	₹ ....
Credit Union	₹ ....
House Organ	....
Medical Expenses	....
Pension	....
Social and Sport Activities	....
Suggestion Awards	....
Miscellaneous	....
Total Other Expenses	₹
Total Payroll Taxes and	....
Employee Benefits	₹ ....

(Contd..)

Charged To Departments :		
Rooms		₹....................
Food	(Schedule)	
Beverage	(Schedule)	
Telephone	(Schedule)	
Barber Shop	(Schedule)	
Beauty Parlour	(Schedule)	
Check-rooms and Wash-rooms	(Schedule)	
Cigar and News-stand	(Schedule)	
Fountain and Gift Shop	(Schedule)	
Garage, Parking lot	(Schedule)	
Guest Laundry	(Schedule)	
Swimming Pool, Cabanas and Baths	(Schedule)	
Other Operated Department	(Schedule)	
Data Processing	(Schedule)	
Human Resources	(Schedule)	
Transportation	(Schedule)	
Marketing	(Schedule)	
House laundry	(Schedule)	
Valet	(Schedule)	
Administrative and General Expenses	(Schedule)	
Advertising & Sales Promotion	(Schedule)	
Heat, Light and Power	(Schedule)	
Property Operations and Maintenance	(Schedule)	
Total Payroll and Employees' Benefits		₹

Fig. 13.10 : Analysis of Payroll Taxes and Employees' Benefits

SALARIES AND WAGES

The salaries and wages constitute an important head of expenses in the hotel trade. The description of all the employees connected with each department has already been explained. Fig 13.11 indicates the consolidated statement of all the salaries and wages paid to the employees of the hotel the break-up of which is given under respective schedules :

ABC Hotels Ltd.
Salaries and Wages Schedule

	No. of Employees	Regular Amount	Extra Amount
Rooms			
Assistant Manager		₹	₹ ....
Front Office		....	....

(*Contd.*)

House-keeping	....	....
House-keeping & Assistant	....	....
Linen Room	....	....
Maids	....	....
House men	....	....
Night Cleaners	....	....
Window Cleaners	....	....
Service		
Front	....	....
Elevators	....	....
Floors	....	....
Doormen and Footmen	....	....
Package Room and Baggage Porters	....	....
Miscellaneous	....	....
Public Rooms (Non-Banquet)	....	....
House Officers and Watchmen	....	....
TOTAL	₹	₹ ....
Less : Charged to Other Departments	....	....
Assistant Manager	....	....
Linen Room	....	....
Housemen	....	....
Night Cleaners	....	....
Window Cleaners	....	....
Elevator Service	....	....
Public Rooms (Non-Banquet)	....	....
House Officers & Watchmen	....	....
Total Rooms (Schedule)	₹	₹ ....
Food and Beverages	....	....
(Applicable to both F & B)	₹	₹ ....
Maitre d' hotel, Manager and Assistants	....	....
Restaurant Service	....	....
Head waiter, Captain, Scrub Captains	....	....
and Hostesses	₹	₹ ....
Waiters & Waitresses	....	....
Commis	....	....
Bus boys	....	....
Dummy men	....	....
Tea Room, Cafeteria or Coffee Shop	....	....
Manager, Assistants and Hostesses	....	....
Counter men	....	....
Waitresses	....	....
Bus boys	....	....
Dish washers	....	....

(*Contd.*)

Dummy men	....	....
Room Service	....	....
Head Waiters and Captains	....	....
Waiters	....	....
Bus boys	....	....
Order taker	....	....
Dummy men	....	....
Banquet Service	....	....
Captain, Head waiters	....	....
Waiters	....	....
Charges from other departments	....	....
Public Rooms (Banquet)	....	....
General	....	....
Cashier	....	....
Checkers	....	....
Ice men and Yard men	....	....
Charges from other departments	....	....
Miscellaneous	....	....
Total Food & Beverages	₹..............	₹..............
(To be allocated between Food and Beverages)	....	....
Total food and beverage b/f	....	....
(To be allocated between Food and Beverages)	....	....
Food	....	....
Steward And Assistants	....	....
Chef and Assistants	....	....
Preparation	....	....
Cooks	....	....
Potwashers (Cook's Helpers)	....	....
Butchers	....	....
Vegetable Cleaners	....	....
Pastry	....	....
Bakery	....	....
Ice Cream	....	....
Pantry, Oyster, Coffee	....	....
Miscellaneous	....	....
Employees' Dining Rooms	....	....
General	....	....
Food control	....	....
Store-keepers	....	....
Warewashing and cleaning	....	....
Food Purchase	....	....
Charges from other departments	....	....

(Contd.)

Total Food-Direct	₹	₹ ....
Allocated from Food & Beverage		
Total Food (Schedule)	₹	....
Beverages		
Wine Stewards and Assistants	₹	₹ ....
Bartenders	....	....
Bar Porters	....	....
Cellarmen	....	
Beverage Control	....	....
Glasswashers	....	....
Total Beverage Direct	₹	₹ ....
Allocated from food and beverages	₹	₹ ....
Total Beverages	₹	₹ ....
Grand Total : Food And Beverages	₹	₹ ....
Total Rooms Brought Forward	₹	₹ ....
Total Food And Beverages – Brought Forward	₹	₹ ....
Telephone (Schedule)	₹	₹ ....
Barber Shop (Schedule)	₹	₹ ....
Beauty Parlour (Schedule)	₹	₹ ....
Checkrooms And Washrooms (Schedule)	₹	....
Cigar And News Stand (Schedule)	₹	....
Fountain And Gift Lot (Schedule)	₹	₹ ....
Guest Laundry	₹	₹ ....
Swimming Pool, Cabanas, Baths (Schedule)	₹	₹ ....
Valet (Schedule)	₹	₹ ....
Administration and General		
Manager's office	₹	₹ ....
Accounting office		....
Data Processing	....	....
Front office book-keeping	....	....
Night Auditors	....	....
Credit office	....	....
Time-keepers	....	....
Receiving clerks	....	....
Employment office	....	....

(*Contd.*)

Employees' Locker Attendants	....	....
Total Administration and General	₹	₹ ....
Advertising And		
Sales Promotion	₹	₹ ....
Heat, Light And Power :		
Chief Engineer and Assistant	₹	₹ ....
Office and Storeroom Employees	....	....
Engineers	....	....
Firemen	....	....
Oilers	....	....
Refrigeration	....	....
Miscellaneous	....	....
Total Heat, Light and Power	₹	₹ ....
Repairs And Maintenance		
Carpenters and Furniture Repairs	₹	₹ ....
Upholsterers	....	....
Carpet Repairs	....	....
Curtain Repairs	....	....
Painters and Paperhangers	....	....
General Mechanical	....	....
Plumbers and steamfitters	....	....
Radio and Television Man	....	....
Electrician	....	....
Grounds and Landscaping	....	....
Silver-platers and Burnishers	....	....
Total	₹	₹ ....
Deductions :		
Charges to other departments	₹	₹ ....
Charges to improvements and Additions	....	....
Total Deductions	₹	₹ ....
Total Repairs & Maintenance (Schedule)	....	....
Employee Benefits (Schedule)	....	....
House Laundry	....	....
Managers and Assistants	₹	₹
Washing	....	....
Finishing	....	....
Miscellaneous	....	....
Total House Laundry (Schedule)	₹	₹ ....
Total Salaries	....	....
And Wages	₹	₹ ....

Fig. 13.11 : Analysis of Salaries and Wages

Fig. 13.12 is a schedule for salaris and wages analysing are salaries and wages.

ABC Hotels Ltd.
Salaries And Wages Schedule

	Number of Employees	Current Period Amount
Rooms		
Management		₹ ....
Front Office		....
Housekeeping		....
Service		....
Security		....
Total (Schedule Room)		....
Food And Beverage		....
Management		....
Kitchen		....
Service		....
Others		....
Total (Schedule Food and Beverage)		₹ ....
Telephone (Schedule)		....
Gift Shop (Schedule)		....
Garage and Parking (Schedule)		....
Other Operated Departments (Schedule)		....
Administrative and General		....
Manager's Office		....
Accounting Office		....
Credit Office		....
Front Office Keeping		....
Night Auditors		....
Receiving Clerks		....
Timekeepers		....
Total (Schedule)		....
Data Processing (Schedule)		₹ ....
Human Resources (Schedule)		....
Transportation (Schedule)		....
Marketing (Schedule)		....
Property Operation and Maintenance		....
Management		....
Engineers		....

(*Contd.*)

Grounds	....
Office and Storeroom	....
Others	....
Total (Schedule Property Operation and Maintenance)	₹ ....
	....
House Laundry	....
Managers and Assistants	....
Finishing	....
Washing	....
Others	....
Total (Schedule Housekeeping)	....
Total Salaries and Wages	₹ ....

Fig. 13.12 : Analysis of Salaries & Wages

FINANCIAL STATEMENTS

Financial statements are prepared to monitor the performance of the hotel. The information of the accounts books is summarised into financial statement. Statement so prepared can be compared against the budget of the hotel and performance in previous periods. These statements are very useful to formulate budgets for the next period. The three main financial statements prepared by hotels are :

1. Cash Flow Statement
2. Profit and Loss Statement
3. Balance Sheet

CASH FLOW STATEMENT

A cash flow statement summarises all receipts and payments of the hotel for a particular period. The information is drawn from the cash book. It shows how delay in the receipt of payment affects profits before it turns into cash at the bank. This statement could be compared with the forecast for the same period and see where problem may have arisen. It may also point out where problem could ease in future and if there will be a head for further funding of the hotel. An analysis of cash flow statement and variances will ensure the corrective action to improve the cash flow. This may include

1. Better control over credit given to customers
2. Better credit terms from suppliers
3. Use of cash balances
4. Increased revenues
5. Reduced costs
6. Stock levels.

A specimen of Cash Flow Statement is given in Fig. 13.13.

Cash Flow Statement

	April Budger	April Actual	Variance	May Budget	June Budger	July Budger	August Budger	Sept. Budger	Oct. Budger	Nov. Budger	Dec. Budger
Receipts Cash Sales Credit Sales Miscellancous											
Total											
Expenditure Food & Beverage Wages Pay & ESI General Expenses Income Tax Capital Items Re... Light & Heat Telephone & Post Bank Charges BookKeeper Professional Fees Loan Interest & Drawings Drawings											
Total Payments											
Net Cash Flow For Month Balance B/f											
Closing Bank Balance											

Fig. 13.13 : Cash Flow Statement

CASH FLOW

To maintain liquidity and to optimise profitability, you as a hotel manager must assure yourself of an adequate cash flow *i.e.*, the profit after taxes. Below are given some ways to accomplish adequate cash flow:

1. Expense Reduction :
   (*i*) Cutting waste and spoilage
   (*ii*) Better utilization of manpower
   (*iii*) Astute purchasing
2. Sales Improvement :
   (*i*) Tapping new market
   (*ii*) Getting guests to stay longer and come more frequently
   (*iii*) Promoting high profit sales

3. Freezing up cash :
   (*i*) Holding inventories low
   (*ii*) Keeping a close watch on receivables
   (*iii*) Leasing rather than purchasing
4. Financial Management :
   (*i*) Borrowing fund at a rate lower than the return you can make them earn
   (*ii*) Utilizing the principles of leverage
5. Increasing Price :
   (*i*) Rate should reflect increase in costs but needs to be competitive. Because of fixed overhead, a small increase in prices could mean a substantial rise in profits.

STATEMENT OF FINANCIAL POSITION / STATEMENT OF ASSETS AND LIABILITIES / BALANCE SHEET

The balance sheet of a hotel company/hotel may be modified according to its own requirement. The grouping of items is left to the discretion of each hotel, however, items of sufficient importance should be shown separately. A specimen of the statement of assets and liabilities of a hotel company is given in Fig. 13.14.

The balance sheet gives a view of the position of the business at a particular point of time about the ways money has been raised and about the form it takes in the business. Different forms of capital employed are represented by various types of assets. All items of balance sheet are grouped into different sections :

1. Fixed assets
2. Current assets
3. Long-term liabilities
4. Short-term liabilities.

The investment intensity in hotel business is very high since bulk of the investment is in fixed assets. Current assets tend to be small in hotel business, because they are convertible into debtors or cash relatively quickly. Hence, it is estimated that 80-90% of the total investment is in the form of fixed assets which gives an investment intensity of four or more.

The long-term liability is a form of total financing of the hotel and the short-term financing are the amounts owned to suppliers. The difference between the total assets and total liabilities is the equity or the net worth of the hotel business, which represents the owner's/partners'/ shareholders' capital. Capital could be increased by putting in more or by profits not drawn out by owners and yet more can also be borrowed as loans.

ABC Hotels Ltd.
Balance Sheet

	Date	
	20	20
Current Assets	....	....
Cash	....	....
House Banks	₹	₹ ....
Demand Deposits	....	....
Temporary Cash Investments	....	....

(*Contd.*)

Total Cash	....	....
Marketable Securities	....	....
Receivables	....	....
Accounts ReceivableTrade	....	....
Notes Receivable	....	....
Others	....	....
Total Receivables	....	....
Less Allowance for Doubtful Accounts	....	....
Net Receivables	....	....
Inventories	....	....
Prepaid Expenses	....	....
Others	....	....
Total Current Assets	....	....
Investments	....	....
Property And Equipment	....	....
Land		
Buildings		
Leaseholds and Leasehold Improvements	....	....
Construction in Progress		
Furnishings and Equipment		
China, Glassware, Silver, Linen and Uniforms		
Less Accumulated Depreciation	....	....
and Amortization	....	....
Net Property and Equipment	....	....
Other Assets	....	....
Security Deposits	....	....
Pre-opening Expenses	....	....
Deferred Charges	....	....
Others	....	....
Total Other Assets	....	....
Total Assets	₹	₹ ....
Current Liabilities	₹	₹ ....
Notes Payable	....	....
Current Maturities of Long-term Debt	....	....
Accounts Payable	....	....
Central, State and Municipal Income Taxes	....	....
Deferred Income Taxes	....	....
Accrued Expenses	....	....
Advance Deposits	....	....
Others	....	....
Total Current Liabilities	....	....
Long-Term Debt	....	....
Notes and Other Similar Liabilities	....	....

(*Contd.*)

Obligations under Capital Leases	....	
Less Current Maturities	....	
Total Long-Term Debt	₹	₹ ....
Other Long-Term Liabilities	....	....
Deferred Income Taxes	....	....
Commitments And Contingencies	....	....
Owners'	....	....
Preferred stock, Par Values ₹	....	....
Authorised .... Shares		
Issued .... Shares	....	....
Common Stock, Par Values ₹	....	....
Authorized .... Shares	....	....
Issued .... Shares	....	....
	₹	₹ ....
Addition Paid-In Capital	....	....
Retained Earnings	....	
Total Owners' Equity	....	
Total Liabilities and Owners' Equity	₹	₹ ....

Fig. 13.14 : Analysis of Balance Sheet

RATIO ANALYSIS

The relationship between current assets and current liabilities is of significance. The excess of current assets over current liabilities represents the net working capital of the business. This is calculated by dividing current liabilities and current assets and represents a measure of the liquidity of the business. In hotel business due to low stock in relation to total current assets and their rapid turnover, a ratio of 1:1 is normally considered acceptable.

The investors and lenders are interested in the return on total assets irrespective of the source of funds, but capital gearing influences their risks. This is indicated by calculating the relationship between equity and liability and the ratio calculated is known as capital gearing. The net worth is divided by total liabilities or where current liabilities fluctuate, the net worth is divided by the amount of long-term debt. If the proportion of indebtedness is high in relation to owners' capital, small changes in profit may have a significant impact on the return available to owners, as interest on loans and instalments have to be paid when due. Fig. 13.15 is a specimen of a standard Financial Analysis Sheet.

ABC Hotels Ltd.
Financial Analysis Sheet Period Covered From........

	Actual	Budget
Liquidity:		
1. Current Ratio	:	....
2. Quick Ratio	:	....
Leverage :		

(*Contd.*)

1. Debt to Total Assets	:	
2. Debt to Net Worth	:	....
Activity :		
1. Inventory Turnover Food/Beverage	%	....
2. Account Receivable Sales	%	
3. Sales to Total Assets	%	....
Profitability :		
1. Net Profit before Taxes to Sales	%	....
2. Return on Total Assets	%	....
3. Return of Net Worth	%	....
4. Number of times Room Rate was earned	%	....
5. House Profit to Room Sales	%	....
6. House Profit to Total Sales	%	....
Departmental Ratios :		
1. Percentage of Room Occupancy	%	....
2. Percentage of Double Occupancy	%	....
3. (*i*) Average room rate per occupied room:		....
(*ii*) Average bed rate per occupied room:		....
4. Food Sales Ratio to Room Sales	%	....
5. Beverage sales : Ratio to Food Sales	%	....
6. Payroll and related expenses to total Sales	%	....
Ratio of Total and Room Sales of :		
1. Administration and General Expenses to total	:	....
2. Advertising and Promotion to total	:	....
Cost Per Available Room of :		
1. Heat, Light and Power	:	....
2. Repairs and Maintenance	:	....
3. Rent	:	....
4. Property	:	....
5. Rates	:	....
6. Interest	:	....
7. Depreciation :		....
Departmental Wages to Sales :		
1. Room Wages to Room Sales	%	....
2. Food Wages to Food Sales	%	....

(*Contd.*)

3.	Beverage Wages to Beverage Sales	%	....
4.	Administration Wages to Total Sales	%	....

Departmental Trading Profits :

1.	Food Trading Profits	%	....
2.	Beverage Trading Profits	%	....
3.	Food Cost to Food Sales	%	....
4.	Beverage Cost to Beverage Sales	%	....
5.	Turnround Cost to Twin Bedded Room	%	....
6.	Turnround Cost to Single Bed	%	....

Fig. 13.15 : Analysis of Financial Analysis Sheet

STATEMENT OF INCOME OR PROFIT AND LOSS ACCOUNT

The form of this statement should contain the revenue and expenses for the current period but the true significance of the amount of the revenue and expenses can be understood only in their relation to each other and the corresponding amounts of preceding periods. Some hotels prepare monthly and quarterly statements to include the total amount of each item of revenue and expense from the beginning of the current month or quarter. Percentages of all items may be given in separate column of the various schedules or the percentages of only the more important items of cost and expenses may be included at the bottom of schedule or in a separate sheet.

The most convenient form of the statement of income is to have on one sheet the figure for the current period and those for the corresponding period of the preceding year, and on another sheet the figures of the current year to date and those for the preceding year to the corresponding date. Fig. 13.16 is the specimen of statement of income of a hotel company.

ABC Hotels Ltd.
Statement Of Income

		Current Period				
	Schedule	Net Revenue	Cost of Sales	Payroll and Related Expenses	Other Expenses	Income (Loss)
Operated Departments						
Rooms		₹	₹	₹	₹	₹
Food and Beverage		....	....	....	....	....
Telephone		....	....	....	....	....
Gift Shop		....	....	....	....	....
Garage and Parking		....	....	....	....	....
Other Operated Departments		....	....	....	....	....
Rentals and Other Income		....	....	....	....	....
Total Operated Department		....	....	....	....	....
Undistributed Operating Expenses		....	....	....	....	....

(*Contd.*)

Administrative and General	....	....	....	....	....
Data Processing	....	....	....	....	....
Human Resources	....	....	....	....	....
Transportation	....	....	....	....	....
Marketing	....	....	....	....	....
Property Operation and Maintenance	....	....	....	....	....
Energy Costs	....	....	....	....	....
Total Undustributed Operating	....	....	....	....	....
Expenses	....	....	....	....	....
Income before Management	....	....	....	....	....
Fees and Fixed Charges	....	....	....	....	....
Management Fees	....	....	....	....	....
Rent, Property Taxes and Insurance	....	....	....	....	....
Interest Expense	....	....	....	....	....
Depreciation and Amortization	....	....	....	....	....
Income Before Income Taxes	....	....	....	....	....
And Gain or Loss on Sale	....	....	....	....	....
Of Property	....	....	....	....	....
Gain or Loss on Sale of Property	....	....	....	....	....
Income before Income Taxes	....	....	....	....	....
Income Taxes	....	....	....	....	....
Net Income	....	....	....	....	....

Fig. 13.16 : Analysis of Statement of Income

The main profit and loss concepts applied are :

1. Revenue/incomes are classified by department/product showing the revenue mix
2. Cost and expenses are classified by type of cost and expenses into cost of sales payroll, other direct expenses undistributed operating expenses and fixed charges
3. Cost of departmental sales (opening stock + purchase—closing stock) is related to each category of sales (food, beverages, minor operated departments)
4. Departmental payroll is related to each category of sales (room, food, beverage, minor operated departments)
5. Direct departmental expenses incurred in the operation of a department are allocated to that department
6. Operating expenses relating to the whole hotel, which are not distributed to departments, are distinguished from fixed charge related to assets and capital.

Hotel companies prepare a general profit and loss account and a simplified statement of income and expenditure. It shows the revenue and costs and expenses incurred in earning that revenue for a given period. The main basis of preparation is the definite grouping of operated or producing departments. To these accounts are credited the respective sales against which are charged the direct costs and expenses. The summary operating statement enables profit margins to be arrived at various levels. There are several profit levels :

1. Profit from operated Departmental Sales (Cost + Expenses) : It indicates the excess of sales over costs and expenses of the hotel.

2. Gross Operating Income = Profit from operated Department + Other Income : 'Other income' representing income not produced by any department, such as concessions and discounts, is added to 'profit from operated departments'. The total is called as gross operating income.
3. House Profit or Total House Income or Expenses and Profit = Gross Operating Income Undistributable expenses. It represents the gross operating income less the expenses which are general in nature. These are undistributed expenses applicable to the hotel as a whole such as executives' salaries, advertising, fuel, electric current and repairs etc.
4. Gross Operating Profit = House Profit + Store Rental : Profit before Interest and Depreciation = Gross Operating Profit Rent, Taxes and Income :
5. Net Operating Profit (Loss) = Profit before Interest and Depreciation (Interest + depreciation) : It is calculated by deducting interest and depreciation of tangible assets and amortization of bond discount, mortgage expenses and other intangibles.
6. Net Operating Profit (Loss) = Net Operating Profit + Extraordinary expenses Unusual expenses.

After adjusting the extraordinary incomes and expenses not applicable to the hotel operations with net operating profit, the net income is calculated. This amount is transferred to retained earning.

The departmental gross profit is the responsibility of the *chef*, head barmen and telephone supervisor. The departmental operating profit is the responsibility of the Front Hall Manager and Food and Beverage Manager; the hotel operating profit is the responsibility of the Hotel Manager.

The main purpose of ratios is to enable each operating department to control each element of cost and expenses in relation to the sale of that department. The total departmental costs and expenses as well as undistributed operating expenses and fixed charges can be controlled in relation to total hotel revenue.

Ratios assist the management in decision making. Take, for example, the prime cost of food and beverage operation. It covers both the cost of food and beverages and the labour cost including preparation and service. It is very helpful in menu pricing. In any comparison between fresh food and convenience foods, the prime cost and the departmental net margin ratios provide a basis for evaluating alternative means of operation.

A number of ratios may be calculated from the profit and loss account, such as :

1. For each operated department, each element of cost as a percentage of departmental sale :
   (*i*) Cost of sale percentage
   (*ii*) Payroll percentage
   (*iii*) Other departmental expenses percentage.
2. Each profit margin as a percentage of departmental sales departmental gross profit percentage
   (*i*) Net margin percentage.
   (*ii*) Operating profit percentage.

3. For the hotel cost rentals and other income, undistributed operating expenses and fixed charges may be expressed as a percentage of total hotel revenue as given below:
   (*i*) Percentage of rental to sales.
   (*ii*) Percentage of undistributed operating expenses.
   (*iii*) Percentage of fixed charges.
4. Operating income, operating gross profit and net profit as percentage of total hotel revenue :
   (*i*) Operating income percentage
   (*ii*) Operating gross profit percentage
   (*iii*) Operating net profit percentage.

BALANCE SHEET AND PROFIT & LOSS RELATIONSHIP

There are many items of balance sheet and profit and loss statement which are directly related to each other. For example :

1. Assets are used up	:	They become an expense due to depreciation
2. Stocks are used up of sales	:	They become the cost
3. Creation of revenue	:	Creation of assets sales, generate cash/debtors
4. Credit purchases	:	Create liabilities
5. Profit in business	:	Increase in net worth
6. Loss in business	:	Reduces the net worth.

All such income, expenses, assets and liabilities have a relationship which must be taken into account while making financial analysis of a hotel business.

EARNINGS AND ASSETS

It measures the effective of management in employing assets to generate profits.

RATE OF STOCK TURNOVER

It is calculated by dividing the cost of food, beverage and other sales by the average stock. The rate so calculated represents the number of times a particular stock turns over in a year. It is an indicator to avoid over-stocking.

RATE OF DEBT TURNOVER

It shows the speed with which debts are collected from customers. It is measured by dividing credit sales by average debtors.

THE RATE OF CREDIT TURNOVER

It measures the speed with which credit accounts are settled by the hotel. It is arrived at by dividing credit purchases by average trade creditors.

STATISTICAL REPORTS

A financial report of a hotel should contain sufficient information to aid the management in arriving at sound conclusions as to the efficiency of the operation of the various departments. The statistical report in the periodical reports is of even greater importance than the expense ratios, for the latter may be easily determined from the statements by simple calculations. While little of the essential statistical information can thus be obtained.

A hotel may require the following statistical information contained in its financial reports :

ROOMS

1. Number of rooms in the hotel
2. Percentage of occupancy
3. Percentage of double occupancy
4. Average daily rate per guest
5. Number of pieces of room laundry per occupied room per day.

RESTAURANT

Average receipts per cover, classfied by restaurant and meals (break-fast, lunch, dinner etc.)

1. Gas consumption (Cubic feat)
2. Gas consumption to the 100 covers
3. Number of pieces of restaurant laundry per cover.

VALET AND GUEST LAUNDRY

1. Number of orders
2. Number of orders per hundred guests
3. Average receipt per order
4. Average cost per order.

HEAT, LIGHT AND POWER

1. Fuel Consumption (Pounds of coal or gallons of oil)
2. Electric Consumption (khw)
3. Steam Consumption (Pounds)
4. Water Consumption (Gallons or cubic feet)
5. Degree days.

The statistical informaiton may be submitted in the form of a separate Statistical Schedules or alternatively may be added to the respective departmental and expense schedule.

QUESTIONS AND ASSIGNMENTS

1. How are the following ratios calculated and what is their purpose and significance:
   (*i*) Liquidity Ratio *(IHMs)*
   (*ii*) Solvency Ratio
   (*iii*) Current Ratio
   (*iv*) Debt Equity Ratio

2. What do you understand by control of accounts ? Explain the procedure of controlling food and accommodation sales in a hotel. *(IHMs)*

3. Define the following terms : *(IHMs)*
   (*i*) Proprietary Ratio
   (*ii*) Gross Profit Ratio
   (*iii*) Debt Equity Ratio.

4. What are the purposes of financial analysis ? If you are asked to make an analytical study of financial performance of a five star hotel, what steps will you take for this purpose ? ***(IHMs)***

5. Explain the following :
   (*i*) Computers in hotel trade
   (*ii*) Inter-firm comparison
   (*iii*) Acid test ratio
   (*iv*) Control of room sales. ***(IHMs)***

6. On the basis of given information work out total current assets and total current liabilities and also the value of stock:
   (*i*) Working Capital 2,52,000
   (*ii*) Current Ratio 2.5 : 1
   (*iii*) Acid Test Ratio 0.95 : 1 ***(IHMs)***

7. Write an essay explaining four of the problems encountered when interpreting conventionally prepared balance sheets and revenue accounts of hotels, which cover a period during which there has been inflation. (The explanation of each problem should have a numerical illustration to support it). ***HCIMA (LONDON)***

8. Explain why the attitude of the Inspector of Taxes, towards the trading, profit and loss accounts, is different from that of other interested parties. What is the effect of this different attitude ? (Illustrate your answer with numerical examples). ***HCIMA (LONDON)***

9. A hotelier has been very disappointed to find that the net trading results of the year has been substantially lower than that of the immediate proceding years. Discuss how with the application of accounting ratios he can get idea about the possible reasons for such short fall, dealing with at least three such ratios.

10. How is control exercised over finance with the help of ratio analysis ? Explain some significant ratio used in hotel business. ***(MTA)***

11. Write notes on:
   (*i*) Performance appraisal
   (*ii*) Leadership
   (*iii*) Manpower planning
   (*iv*) Joint consultation.

OBJECTIVE TYPE QUESTIONS

12. In each of the following sentences find the missing words or phrases, write the correct word or phrase that belongs in each blank:

(*i*) A ...., also called a balance sheet, lists the.................. and.............. of a business, to determine...................... .

(*ii*) Financial statements are normally prepared................................ .

(*iii*) Equity or......................refers to the theoretical momentary value of a business as determined by subtracting total..................from total................

(*iv*) Assets that change in values, such as accounts receivable , are called....................Assets, like equipment, that have a definite price are called........................

(*v*) Assume that a hotel makes monthly payment of ₹ 35,000 on a business loan for which the agency still owes ₹ 92,300. The account ₹....................must be shown on the financial statement as a current liability. ₹....................must be shown as long term debt.

(*vi*) A...................is an obligation that must be paid in the near future. A..................is an obligation that must be repaid in the more distant future.

(*vii*) Total .... are substracted from total................to compute the networth of the hotel business also called................. . To check the accuracy of the arthimetic, ... is added to.................. . If the calculations are correct, the same will equal ....

(*viii*) An................., sometimes called a profit and loss sheet, or P & L reflects the business's .... and ....

(*ix*) In an operating statement.........................are subtracted from....................to determine...............

(*x*) The percentage allows the management to view the relationship between expenses and sales, and to estimate......................

A CASE STUDY

13. R.B. quit his job as head chef in a provincial hotel and started business in 1968 with a 28-seat cafe in Henwood. Two years later he opened another unit two miles away which seated 63, was considerably up-market from his first venture and included a successful lounge bar. Profits for the first unit fluctuated throughout the year between 9% and 19% according to season and averaged around 17%. These profits were not trading profit before tax. The profits of the second establishment averaged 16% net, before tax, fairly evenly throughout the year.

After four year at the beginning of 20......, R.B. opened a third establishment in Berkhampton, a city 32 miles from Henwood. This was a larger city centre restaurant which specialised in hamburgers, pizzas, waffles and pancakes. After showing an initial expected net profit rate of 18% net before tax in the first year, this unit's profit rate dipped to 12%.

Half-way through 20 ...... the first unit ran into unusually intractable labour problems and R.B. congratulated himself on being able to step into the kitchen and do the shop-floor work himself for the three months that it took to replace the cook/chef.

Midway through after two year sixth year 20 ...... R.B. opened two more unit in spite of experiencing some difficulty in acquiring capital. One unit was a country inn in a small town lying 24-miles from Henwood and 31-miles from Berkhampton. The inn was becoming run-down and thus needed a considerable amount of capital to be spent on the public rooms and the 12-bedrooms in order to create the exclusive atmosphere that R.B. felt was required and to comply with fire regulations R.B. thought the commercial customers could be attracted mid-week and tourist during weekends and holiday periods as the local Tourist Board was just beginning an attempt to promote the area as a tourist attraction.

The second of the two new units was a 120-seats cafe similar to his very first unit R.B. has been able to pick this up for what appeared to be a very modest price.

After seven year during 20...... the average net profit before tax for the units as a whole fell from 16% to 14% and in after eight year 20...... to 11%. R.B. was by this time barely able to service the capital which he had borrowed and his creditors were beginning to pay him a great deal of attention.

R.B. decided to look into the accounts of his city centre restaurant in Berkhampton and found that the food cost had increased out of all proportion to inflation, the occupancy rate having declined only a little. He decided that he would have a blitz on all of his establishments and in order to help him to do this he selected the chef from the inn which was not very busy anyway as his personal assistant.

This freed R.B. to spend much of his time filling-in for missing members of staff as a result of high labour turnover within the organisation which from his own experience he knew to be endemic in the hotel and catering industry.

In order to ensure that a responsible person was in charge of all of his establishments he decided to give the most senior member of staff in each unit overall responsibility except in the case of the inn where a manager was already employed . This would in most cases be the chef and in others the head waiter.

(1) Comment upon the way that R.B. managed his business to date.

(2) Describe the recommendations you would make to R.B. concerning the future operation of his business

***HCIMA* (*London*)**

APPENDICES

Appendix A

A Typical Organisation Chart of a Hotel Having Less Than 300 Rooms

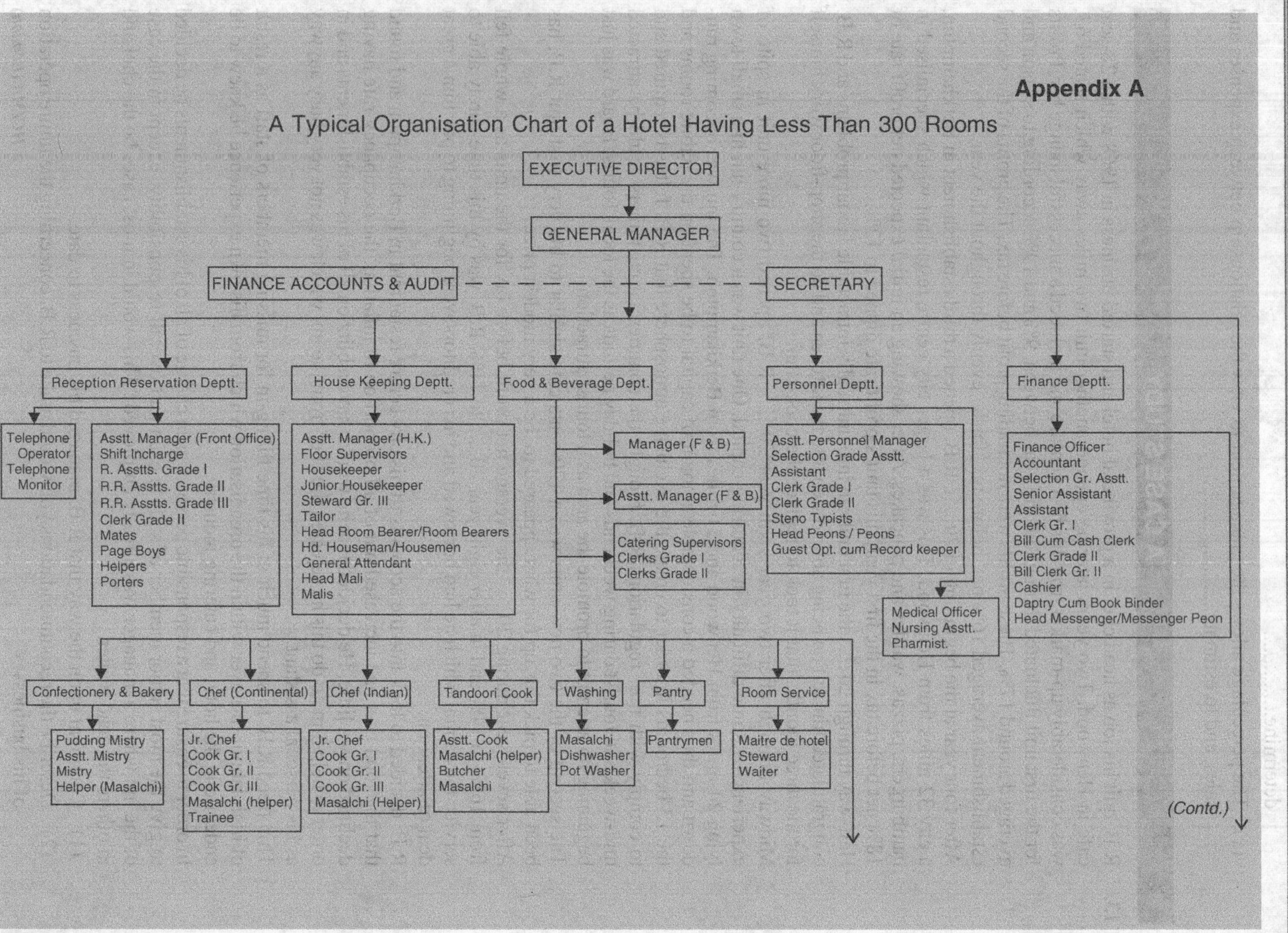

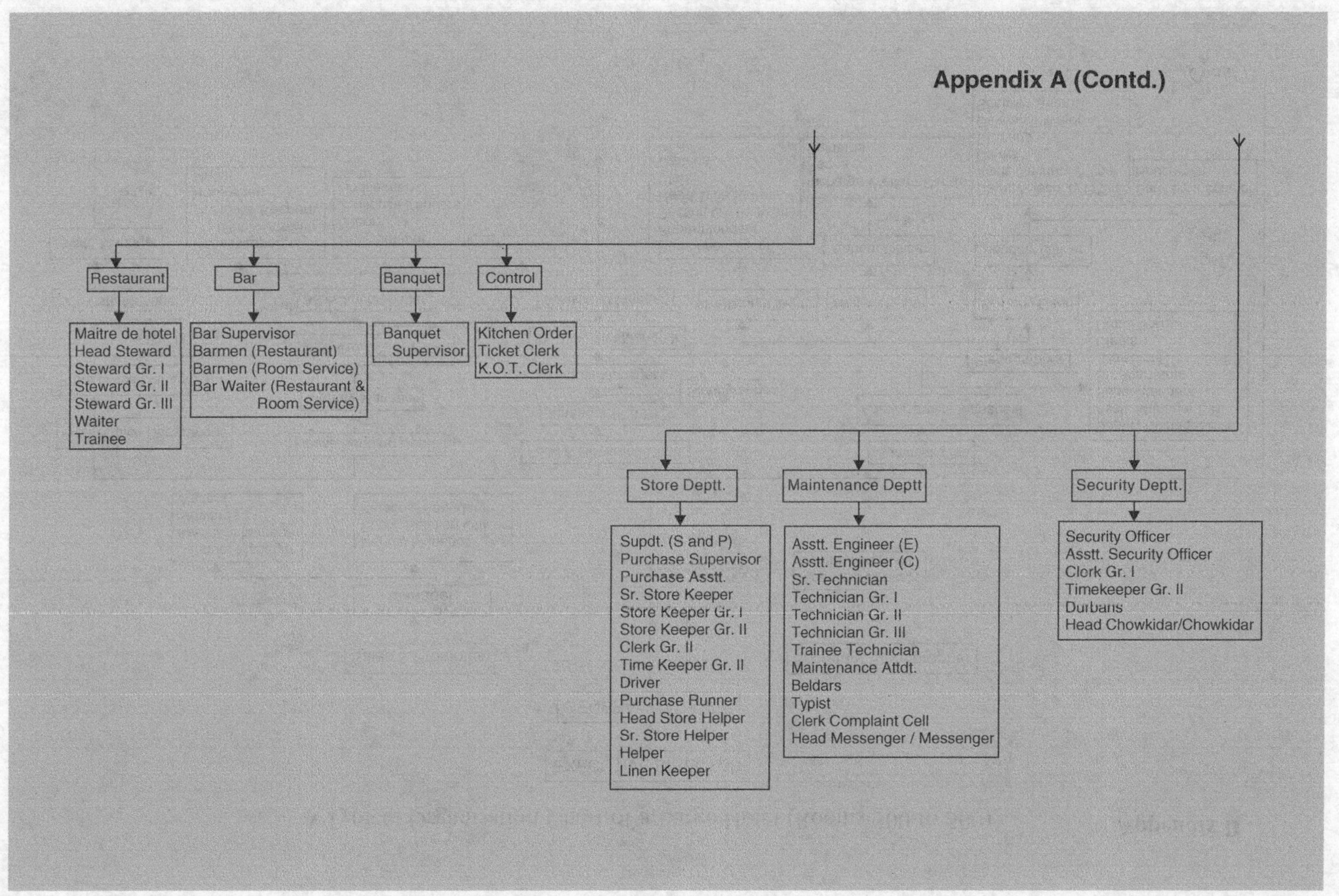
Appendix A (Contd.)
Restaurant
Maitre de hotel
Head Steward
Steward Gr. I
Steward Gr. II
Steward Gr. III
Waiter
Trainee
Bar
Bar Supervisor
Barmen (Restaurant)
Barmen (Room Service)
Bar Waiter (Restaurant & Room Service)
Banquet
Banquet Supervisor
Control
Kitchen Order Ticket Clerk
K.O.T. Clerk
Store Deptt.
Supdt. (S and P)
Purchase Supervisor
Purchase Asstt.
Sr. Store Keeper
Store Keeper Gr. I
Store Keeper Gr. II
Clerk Gr. II
Time Keeper Gr. II
Driver
Purchase Runner
Head Store Helper
Sr. Store Helper
Helper
Linen Keeper
Maintenance Deptt
Asstt. Engineer (E)
Asstt. Engineer (C)
Sr. Technician
Technician Gr. I
Technician Gr. II
Technician Gr. III
Trainee Technician
Maintenance Attdt.
Beldars
Typist
Clerk Complaint Cell
Head Messenger / Messenger
Security Deptt.
Security Officer
Asstt. Security Officer
Clerk Gr. I
Timekeeper Gr. II
Durbans
Head Chowkidar/Chowkidar

Appendix B

A Typical Organisation Chart of a Large Hotel (Rooms 300 to 500)

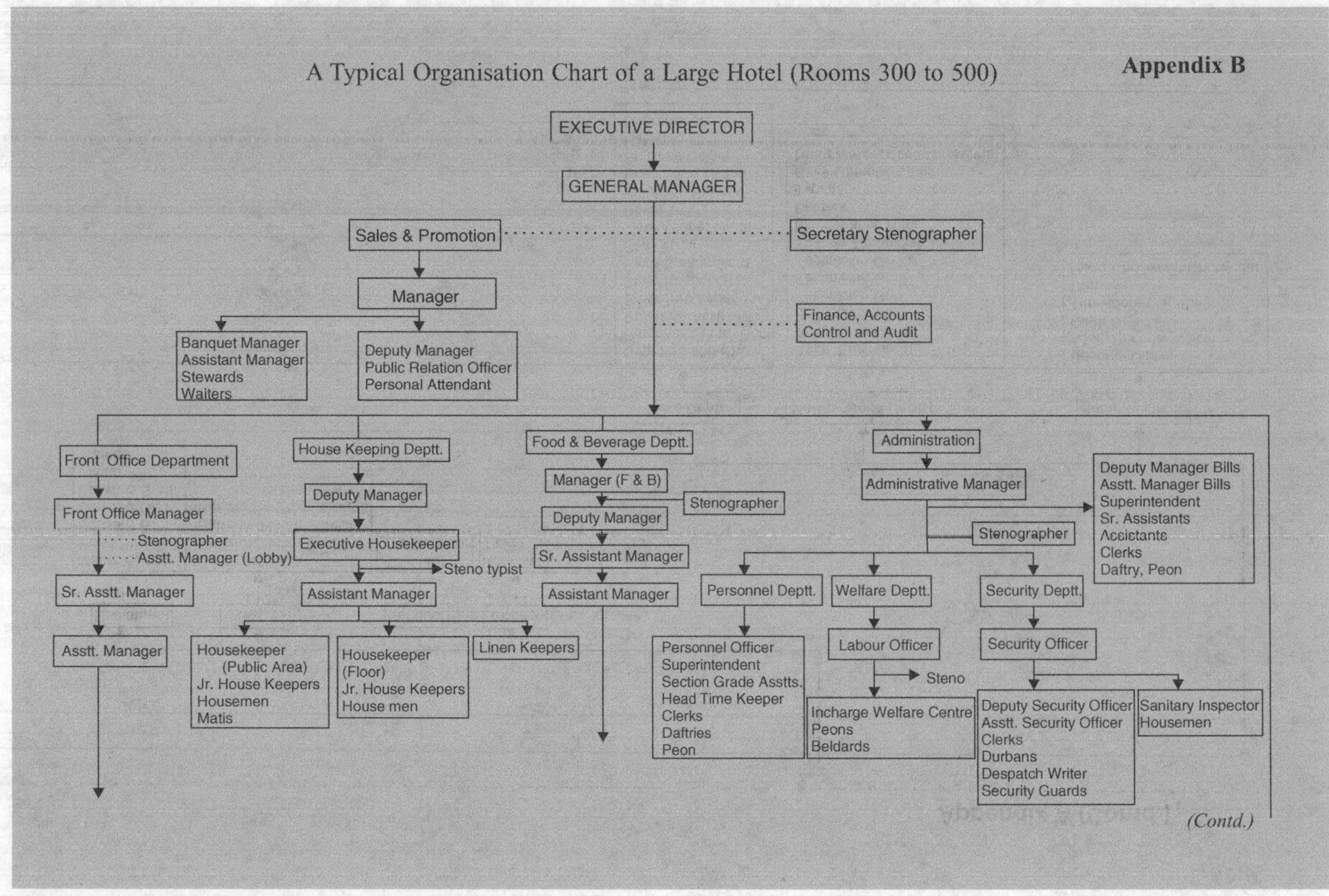

(Contd.)

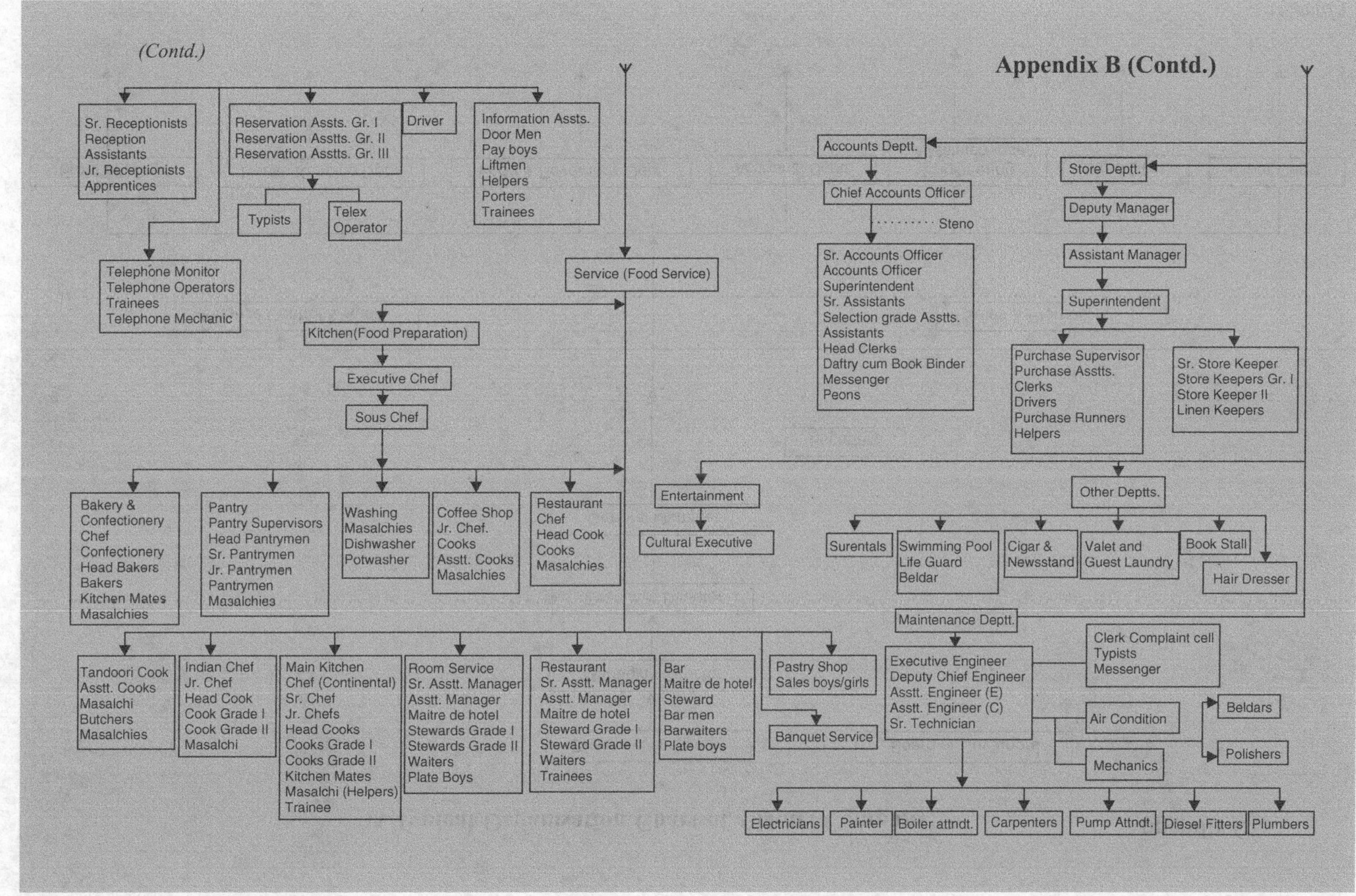

(Contd.)
Appendix B (Contd.)
Sr. Receptionists
Reception Assistants
Jr. Receptionists
Apprentices
Reservation Assts. Gr. I
Reservation Asstts. Gr. II
Reservation Asstts. Gr. III
Driver
Information Assts.
Door Men
Pay boys
Liftmen
Helpers
Porters
Trainees
Typists
Telex Operator
Telephone Monitor
Telephone Operators
Trainees
Telephone Mechanic
Service (Food Service)
Kitchen(Food Preparation)
Executive Chef
Sous Chef
Bakery & Confectionery Chef
Confectionery
Head Bakers
Bakers
Kitchen Mates
Masalchies
Pantry
Pantry Supervisors
Head Pantrymen
Sr. Pantrymen
Jr. Pantrymen
Pantrymen
Masalchies
Washing
Masalchies
Dishwasher
Potwasher
Coffee Shop
Jr. Chef.
Cooks
Asstt. Cooks
Masalchies
Restaurant
Chef
Head Cook
Cooks
Masalchies
Tandoori Cook
Asstt. Cooks
Masalchi
Butchers
Masalchies
Indian Chef
Jr. Chef
Head Cook
Cook Grade I
Cook Grade II
Masalchi
Main Kitchen
Chef (Continental)
Sr. Chef
Jr. Chefs
Head Cooks
Cooks Grade I
Cooks Grade II
Kitchen Mates
Masalchi (Helpers)
Trainee
Room Service
Sr. Asstt. Manager
Asstt. Manager
Maitre de hotel
Stewards Grade I
Stewards Grade II
Waiters
Plate Boys
Restaurant
Sr. Asstt. Manager
Asstt. Manager
Maitre de hotel
Steward Grade I
Steward Grade II
Waiters
Trainees
Bar
Maitre de hotel
Steward
Bar men
Barwaiters
Plate boys
Pastry Shop
Sales boys/girls
Banquet Service
Accounts Deptt.
Chief Accounts Officer
Steno
Sr. Accounts Officer
Accounts Officer
Superintendent
Sr. Assistants
Selection grade Asstts.
Assistants
Head Clerks
Daftry cum Book Binder
Messenger
Peons
Store Deptt.
Deputy Manager
Assistant Manager
Superintendent
Purchase Supervisor
Purchase Asstts.
Clerks
Drivers
Purchase Runners
Helpers
Sr. Store Keeper
Store Keepers Gr. I
Store Keeper II
Linen Keepers
Entertainment
Cultural Executive
Other Deptts.
Surentals
Swimming Pool
Life Guard
Beldar
Cigar & Newsstand
Valet and Guest Laundry
Book Stall
Hair Dresser
Maintenance Deptt.
Executive Engineer
Deputy Chief Engineer
Asstt. Engineer (E)
Asstt. Engineer (C)
Sr. Technician
Clerk Complaint cell
Typists
Messenger
Air Condition
Beldars
Polishers
Mechanics
Electricians
Painter
Boiler attndt.
Carpenters
Pump Attndt.
Diesel Fitters
Plumbers

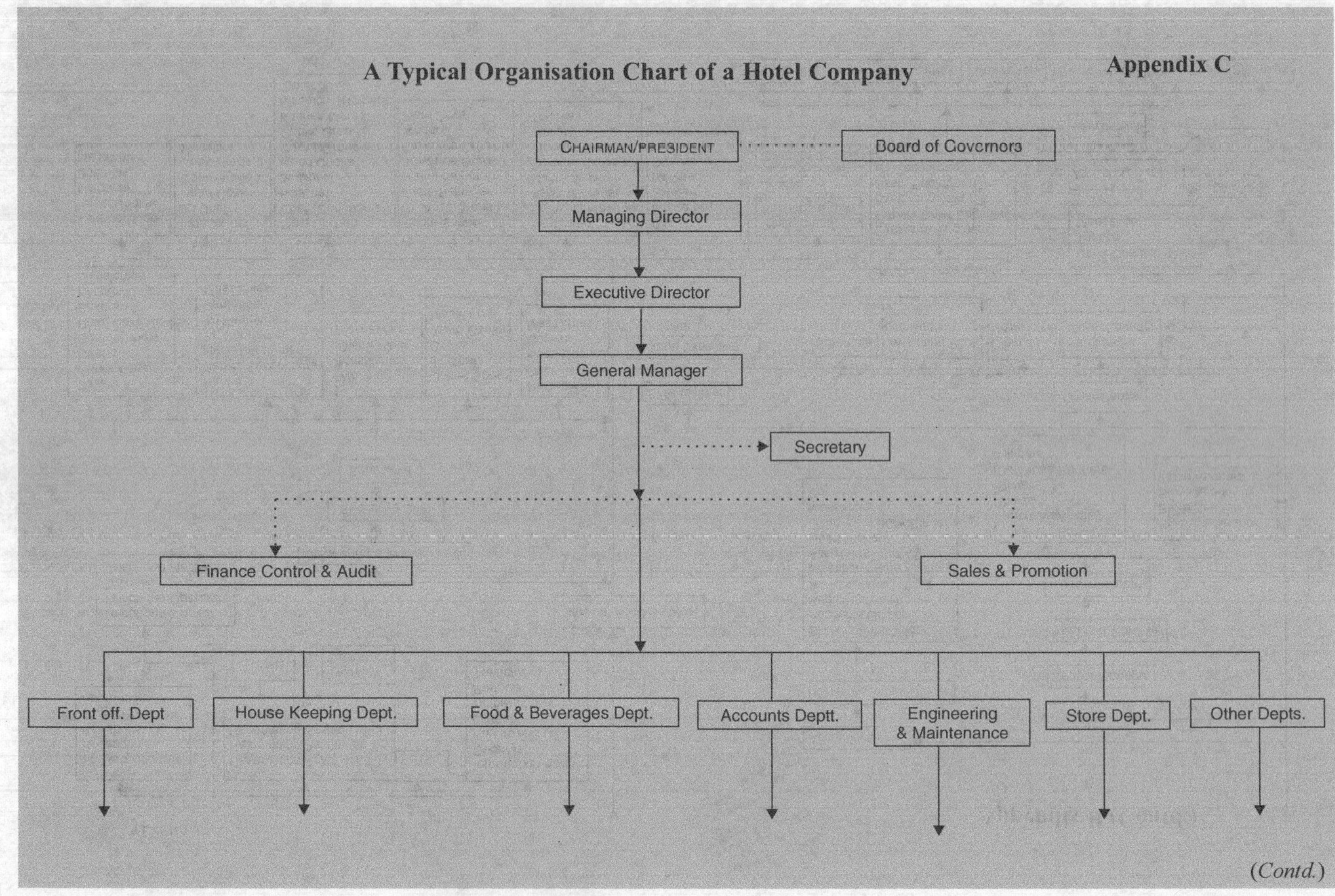
Appendix C
A Typical Organisation Chart of a Hotel Company
CHAIRMAN/PRESIDENT
Board of Governors
Managing Director
Executive Director
General Manager
Secretary
Finance Control & Audit
Sales & Promotion
Front off. Dept
House Keeping Dept.
Food & Beverages Dept.
Accounts Deptt.
Engineering & Maintenance
Store Dept.
Other Depts.
(Contd.)

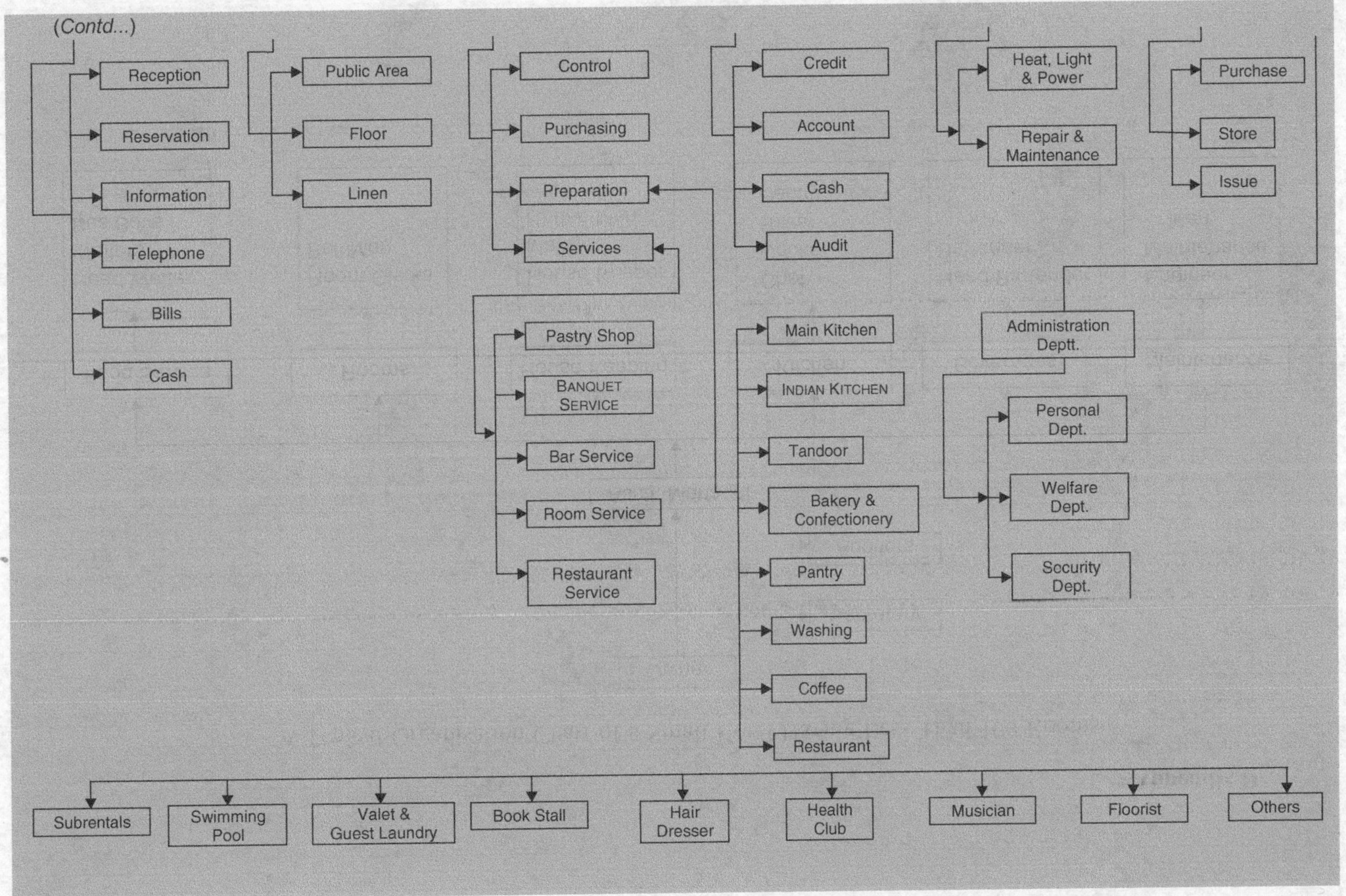
(Contd...)
Reception
Reservation
Information
Telephone
Bills
Cash
Public Area
Floor
Linen
Control
Purchasing
Preparation
Services
Pastry Shop
BANQUET SERVICE
Bar Service
Room Service
Restaurant Service
Credit
Account
Cash
Audit
Main Kitchen
INDIAN KITCHEN
Tandoor
Bakery & Confectionery
Pantry
Washing
Coffee
Restaurant
Heat, Light & Power
Repair & Maintenance
Administration Deptt.
Personal Dept.
Welfare Dept.
Socurity Dept.
Purchase
Store
Issue
Subrentals
Swimming Pool
Valet & Guest Laundry
Book Stall
Hair Dresser
Health Club
Musician
Floorist
Others

Appendix D

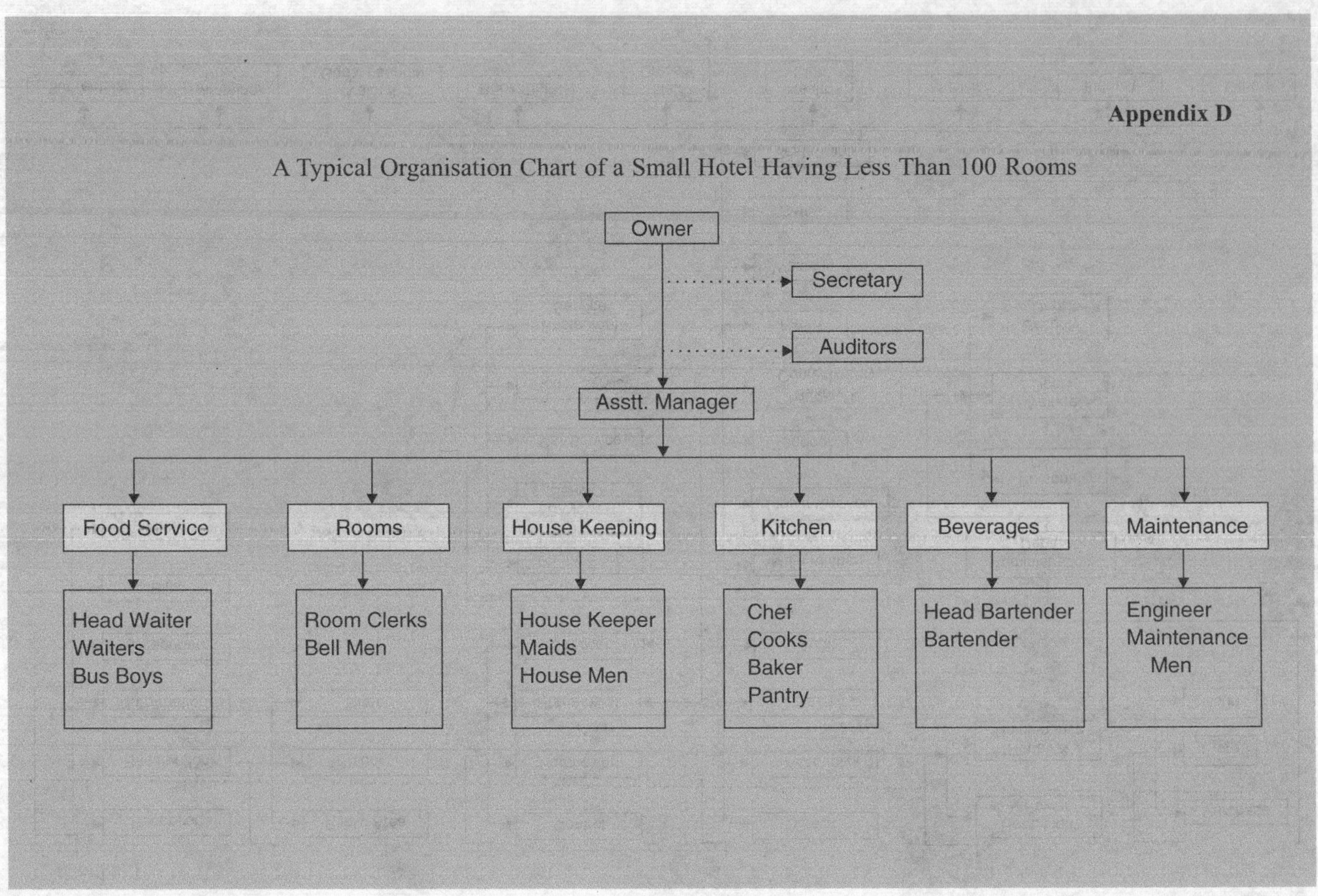

A Typical Organisation Chart of a Small Hotel Having Less Than 100 Rooms

Appendix E

OFFICIAL ABBREVIATIONS USED IN HOTELS

1. Accom.	Accommodate	24. Limo.	Limousine
2. Aircond.	Air condition	25. Mi.	Miles
3. Arpt.	Airport	26. Mtg.	Meeting
4. Aavail	Available	27. Mtn.	Mountain
5. Befrnt	Beach front	28. Nr.	Near
6. Bus	Business	29. Nrby.	Nearby
7. Cntr.	Centre	30. Opp.	Opposite
8. Coff.	Coffee	31. Out Dr.	Out door
9. Cotv.	Colour TV	32. Overlkg.	Over looking
10. Conv.	Convention	**33. Park.**	Parking
11. CrSty.	Courtesy	34. Rest.	Restaurant
12. Disco.	Discotheque	35. Rms.	Room
13. Dntwn.	Down Town	36. Rntl.	Rental
14. Ent.	Entertainment	37. Rr.	Rail Road
15. Fin.	Entertainment	38. Rr.	Rail Road
16. Fin.	Financial	39. Specity.	Speciality
17. HeAt.	Heated	40. Sta.	Station
18. Heth.	Health	41. Subrbn.	Suburban
19. Htl.	Hotel	42. Svce.	Service
20. Hwy.	Highway	43. W/	With
21. Indr.	Indoor	44. Ip-one	Person
22. Kid.	Kiddie	45. 2p-two	Person
23. Loc.	Location		

Appendix F

IMPORTANT ABBREVIATIONS

A

AHMA	:	American Hotel & Motel Association
AP	:	American Plan
ARTA	:	Association of Retail Travel Agents
ATC	:	Air Traffic Conference
AIT	:	Academic International du Tourism
AIEST	:	Association International d'
	:	Experts Scientifiques du Tourism
ASI	:	Archaeological Survey of India
ASTA	:	American Society of Travel Agents
ATC	:	Air Traffic Conference
AI	:	Air India

ABTA	:	Association of British Travel Agent
AFTA	:	Australian Federation of Travel Agents
AMEXCC	:	American Express Corporation
AAUI	:	Automobile Association of Upper India
ADC	:	Affinity Group Travel
ASAE	:	Advice of Duration and Charge
ASTA	:	American Society of Association Executive!
ASAE	:	American Society of Travel Agents.
BIT	:	Bulk Indusine Tour
BTA	:	British Tourist Authority
BHRA	:	British Hotel and Restaurant Association
BTHA	:	British Travel and Hotel Association
BA	:	British Airways

B

CTC	:	Certified Travel Counselor
CIF	:	Cost Insurance and Freight
CBF	:	Cash Book Folio
CRT	:	Cathode Ray Tube

D

DET	:	Domestic Escorted Tours
DATO	:	Discover American Travel Organisation
DC	:	Dinners Club
DGCA	:	Directorate General of Civil Aviation
DGT	:	Directorate General of Tourism
DIT	:	Domestic Individual Tour
DT	:	Deptt. of Tourism

E

EP	:	European Plan
ECSOC	:	Economic and Social Council of the United Nations
ETC	:	European Travel Commision
ECAFE	:	Economic Commission for. Asia and Far East

F

FIT	:	Foreign Independent. Tour/Travel; a prepaid escorted tour package that include, lodging and air transportation at single price.
FRRO	:	Foreign Regional Registration Office
FTT	:	Foreign Travel Tax
FTS	:	Foreign Travel Scheme
FHRAT	:	Federation of Hotels and Restaurant Association of India

G

GIT	:	Group Inclusive Tour
GR	:	Guest Registration Card/Form.

H

HSMA	:	Hotel Sales Management Association
HOT	:	Hotel Organisation Training
HMAA	:	Hotel & MOtel Association of America
HCI	:	Hotel Corporation of India

I

International HORECA	:	International Union of National Association of Hotel.
	:	Restaurant and Cafe Keepers
IATA	:	International Air Transport Association, a self-regulatory body of International Airlines.
ICAO	:	International Civil Aviation Organisation
ICTA	:	Institute of Certified Travel Agents
ILO	:	International Labour Organisation
IHA	:	International Hotel Association
IIT	:	Inclusive Independent Tour
ITC	:	Inclusive Tour Charter
IAAI	:	International Airport Authority of India
IUOTO	:	International Union of Official Travel Organisation
IYHF	:	International Youth Hotel Federation
IT	:	Inclusine Tour
ICIC	:	Industrial Credit and Investment Corporation of India
IAAI	:	International Airport Authority of India
IUNTPO	:	International Union of National Tourist Propaganda Organisation
IFC	:	Industreial Finance Corporation
ICCA	:	International Congress and Convention Association
IDBI	:	Industrial Development Bank of India
ICCTA	:	International Consultation Council of Travel Agents
IAC	:	Indian Airlines Corporation
ITDC	:	Indian Tourism Development Corporation
IA	:	Indian Airlines
ILO	:	International Labour Organisation
INTOURIST	:	Russian Foreign Tourist Organisation
JET	:	Junior Executive Training

M

MAP	:	Modified American Plan : The room rates including breakfast and dinner
MCO	:	Miscellaneous Charges Order : a voucher authorising accommodation to be provided to the person(s) name on the form, proof of payment 'oo' or 'ooo' A room is not availabe for sale due to construction, repair, maintenance refurnishing, etc, and, therefore, is not included in the room inventory

N

NCAER	:	National Council of Applied Economic Research
NDC	:	National Development Council
NTB	:	National Tourism Board
NTO	:	National Tourism Organisation
NCR	:	National Cash Register

O

OAG	:	Official Airlines Guide
OECD	:	Organisation for Economic Cooperation and Development
OEEC	:	Organisation of European Economic Cooperation

P

PBX	:	Private Branch Exchange, the Central Switchboard

PABX	:	Private Automatic Branch Exchange
PATA	:	Pacific Area Travel Association

R

RTPA	:	Rail Travel Promotion Agency
RBI	:	Reserve Bank of India
RTO	:	Regional Tourist office
RTAC	:	Regional Tourist Advisory Committee

S

SATO	:	South American Travel Organisation
SATWA	:	Society of American Travel Writers
SST	:	Super Sonic Transport
SSA	:	Supersonic Aircraft
SARTC	:	South Asia Regional Transport Council
STDC	:	Slate Tourism Development Corporation
S&R	:	Sell and Report
STD	:	Subscriber Trunk Dialling

T

TA	:	Travel Agent
T&E	:	Travel and Entertainment Expenses
TBRE	:	Tourist Baggage Re-export
TDC	:	Tourism Development Corporation
TIB	:	Travel Information Bureau
TWA	:	Trans World Airlines
TAAI	:	Travel Agents Association of India

U

UFTAA	:	Universal Federation of Travel Agent Association
UN	:	United Nations
UNDP	:	United Nations Development Programme
UNCTAD	:	United Nations Conference on Trade and Development
UNESCO	:	United Nations Education, Scientific and Cultural Organisation
USTS	:	United State Travel Service

V

VIP	:	Very Important Person, a guest who receives special attention, accommodations or services
VTL	:	Visitors Tabular Ledger

W

WHO	:	World Health Organisation
WTAO	:	World Transport and Automobile Organisation
WATA	:	World Association of Travel Agents
WATS	:	Wide Area Telephone Service: a toll free telephone service
WTO	:	World Tourism Organisation

X

XO	:	Exchange Order

Y

YMCA	:	Youngmen Christian Association
YWCA	:	Youngwomen Christian Association
YHAI	:	Youth Hostel Association of India

Appendix G

HOTEL AND TOURISM TERMINOLOGY

Account : A document in which all charges and payments of a client are recorded in the guest bill.

Accounts Payable : Movies that are owned by the hotel to vendors.

Accounts Receivable : Movies that are owned to the hotel by clients with established credit.

Advance Deposit : A deposit paid by a guest prior to arrival to guarantee a room reservation.

Affiliate : A property that is related to another property or to a chain by a contract.

Allotment : The number of rooms set aside for a particular purpose, such as group sales or tour wholesale.

Arrival : Estimated check-in date, also a guest scheduled to check-in the current rate.

Audit : The procedure to trace the posting of accounting date in order to verify accuracy.

Average room rate : The average daily room rate, calculated by dividing total revenues from room sales by the number of rooms occupied.

Airway Bill : It is equivalent to the term air consignment note, meaning the document entitled. "Airway bill/Consignment note" made up by or on behalf of the shipper which evidence contract between the shipper and the carrier(s) for carriage of goods over routes for the carriers.

Affinity Group : It is a group bound together by a common interest on affinity. Where charters are concerned, this common bond makes the members eligible for chartered flights. Persons must have been the members of the group for six months or larger. They must travel together, on the departure and return flight, but they can travel independently, where ground arrangements are concerned.

A la carte : When a customer orders *a la carte* he chooses whatever dish he may desire from all those *in a la carte* menu. The charges for the meal will be sum total of the prices of individual dishes served to him. Each dish is priced individually.

American Plan (AP) : The tariff fixed includes boarding and lodging. It is an inclusive full board tariff. Accommodation and the meal, dinner are included in the price of the room. It is also called Full Pension.

Baggage Accompained : The baggage carried on the same aircraft as that on which the passenger is carried.

Baggage Excess : It is that part of the baggage allowance, for which the passenger has to pay extra freight charges.

Baggage Tag : A document issued by the carrier solely for identification of checked baggage, the baggage (strap) tag portion of which is attached by carrier to a particular article of checked baggage and the baggage (claim) tag portion of which is given to the passenger.

Baggage Unaccompained : The oaggage not carried on the same aircraft as that on which the passenger is carried.

Back office : The department of the hotel that is responsible for accounting, data processing and management reports.

Bed and Breakfast plan : A room tariff that includes a full breakfast.

Bermuda Plan : Same as Bed and Break-fast Plan.

Block : A number of rooms set aside for a particular client or purpose, usually a group booking.

Book : To sell a reservation.

Brunch : Combination of break-fast and lunch, often accompained by champagne.

Bucket : A system in which guest records are filed consecutively by room number.

Brochure : It is a pamphlet bound in the form of a booklet.

Bulletin : A brief, periodically issued mailing a promotion piece, painted outdoor display.

Camping Site : A place providing simple and inexpensive shelter to travellers. The site provides way-side amenities for tourists travelling by long distance coach tours and self-driven cars.

Cargo : It is equivalent to the term goods, meaning anything carried, as to be carried in an aircraft, other than mail or baggage.

Cargo Transit : Cargo arriving at a point and departing therefrom by the same through flight.

Carriage Domestic : Carriage in which the place of departure, the place of destination or stopover and the entire transportation are within one nation or its territories.

Carriage : It is equivalent to the term transportation, meaning carriage of passengers and/or baggage by air.

Carriage International : Carriage in which the place of departure and any place of landing are situated in more than one country.

Carrier : It is a term used for a public transport company e.g., airline, steamship, rail, road, truck, bus, etc.

Carriers : A professional travel escort who accompanies carriers.

Chartered Flight : When a flight is booked exclusively for the use of specific group of persons who belong to the same organisation and who are being 'treated' to the flight by a single host, are called as chartered flight. These flights are very cheap as compared to regularly scheduled line services. These flights are not for sale to the general public, some time they are also carried out by regularly sheduled or supplemented carriers.

Concierge : He is the incharge of information and Hall porter and is responsible for informing guests of community services and making external booking such as theatre reservations and guided tours.

Conducted tours : It is also known as Escorted Tour. It is a prepaid and pre-arranged vacation tour by a group. The group travels, under the guidance of a tour leader who stays with them throughout the trip.

Cabana : A room on the beach, or separated from the main building: a structure designed to shade beach patrons from the sun.

Cancellation : The voiding of a confirmed reservation.

Cathode Ray Tjibe (CRT): A computer terminal, technically, the video screen, but commonly used to refer to both the screen and the keyboard.

Check In : The process of greeting and registering a guest, verifying the method of payment and dispending room keys.

Check Out : The process of facilitating the guest's departure and settling the guest account.

City Ledger : An accounts receivable journal for clients that have established credit with the hotel.

Class : A category based on the overall quality and service of a lodging establishment e.g., deluxe, first class, tourist class.

Close : The conclusion of a room sale i.e., reservation, also the end of the shift or business day.

Commercial Hotel : A hotel that emphasizes the sale of rooms to business Travellers.

Commissionable : A reservation made by a travel agent and for which commission is paid.

Complimentary : A service that is furnished without charge.

Confirm : To insure that a reservation will be honoured.

Convention Centre : A hotel that emphasizes room sales to groups, with meeting and banquet facilities.

Credit Authorization : The maximum amount of charges that have been authorized by a credit card company to be made on a guest credit card.

Cut Off : The date on which a group reservation must be fulfilled, and after which any uncommitted rooms are returned to the availability pool. It is the time by which a guaranteed reservation must be cancelled to avoid for forfeiting the deposit.

Continental Breakfast : This generally consists of pastry and beverage (coffee, tea. juice, cocoa or marmalade). In some of the Scandinavian countries (Holland and Norway) cheese, cold cuts of fish are also provided.

Continental Plan (CP) : The guest tariffs includes lodging and breakfast such as pastry, juice and coffee or tea. For other services and things he is separately billed.

Couchettes : It is a sleeping accommodation provided on some European rail road. It consists a day compartment which can be converted into bunk for four passengers. Pillow and blankets are also provided. The charges in this case are slightly more than the ordinary rail-road fare.

Coupons or vouchers : These are the documents issued by tour operation in exchange of which travellers receive prepaid accommodation, meals, sight seeing trips etc.

Courier : This is the name given to a professional travel escort. He is also called as a tour leader, tour escort or tour manager; sometimes he is an employee of the uniform staff to deliver mail and meet the guest at airport.

Day Rate : A reduced rate for occupying a room during the day, with check-out before 5 P.M.

Dead Move : The act of transferring a guest to different room while the guest is absent.

Debit (Dr) : An amount that increased the balance of a guest account.

Deluxe : The highest level of elegance and service.

Density Board : A reservation system using a chalk board or sign on which room occupancy is indicated.

Deposit : A partial payment made by a guest to guarantee a reservation or to be applied towards charges such as telephone service, restaurant charges etc.

Disbursement : Any money paid by the hotel for an operating expenses.

Double : A room occupied by two adults; a bed suitable for two people.

Double Double : A room with two double beds.

Double Occupancy : A rate based on two adults occupying the same room.

Down Bell : The act of summoning a bell attendant to transport guest luggage to the lobby.

Down Grade : Charge a reservation to a lower room class or rate.

Dump : To back up computer data into storage medium, such as a disk or tape.

English Break-fast : It usually includes hot or cold cereal, bacon or ham and eggs toast, butter, jam or marmalade and a beverage (not juice). This type of breakfast is generally served in the British Isles including Ireland.

European Plan (EP) : The guest is booked to pay for lodging only. He is separately charged for all other things or services he enjoys or consumes in the hotel.

Excursion fare : Excursion fare on a round trip at reduced price excursion. It has limitation as to day of departure, time of departure, time of the day, length of stay, etc.

Early Arrival : A guest who arrives prior to the scheduled check on date.

Efficiency : Accommodation with kitchen facilities.

Extra Guest : A charge applied in addition to the normal room rate for adults in excess to the maximum occupancy (usually two).

First Class : Medium priced, near luxurious or luxurious accommodations.

FIT : Free Independent Traveller, Foreign Independent Tour: a prepaid, unescorted tour package that includes lodging and air transportation at a single price.

Floor Limit : The set credit limit established by management for guest account.

Folio : A guest record.

Forecast : A projection of availability, room occupancy or sales reserve in the future.

Forfeit : To give up a deposit. A no show forfeits the guarantee if the reservation is not cancelled prior to cut off.

Full House : A hotel is sold out: 100 per cent occupancy.

Full Service : A lodging establishment that has food and beverage service and a bell staff.

Final Itinerary : It is a schedule prepared by the travel agent. It tells in detail the exact progamme mapped out for a particular tourist or tourists. It includes flight and train numbers, departure times, etc. It is derived shortly before actual departure.

Familiarisation Tour : It is an educational tour programme arranged for travel agents and airline personnel to a destination for inspection of transit facilities, at a reduced rate.

Family Plan : It is a speciality rate provided by the hotel for the family. Usually no charges are levied for children sharing same room with parents.

Facilitation : Promoting any measure which will facilitate international travel with prime emphasis on achieving minimum entry and exit formalities for temporary visitors.

Garni : When it is used to the name of a hotel, it means that the establishment does not have a restaurant or dining rooms.

Group : A reservation for multiple rooms based on reduced tour or negotiated rates.

Group Inclusion Tour : GIT includes group, air and ground arrangement for a minimum of 15 persons. They may or may not stay together as a group for both. the land and air portion of the trip.

Guaranteed Tour : It is tour guaranteed to operate unless cancelled 60 days prior to departure. In the event of cancellation within 60 days of departure date, full commission is paid to Agents of the 3rd clients. i

Guide : Person who is given a licence for authorising him to take guests on local sightseeing excursions.

Guarantee : A method ensuring that a room will be reserved, such as in advance deposit or credit card number.

Guest : Client, any person staying at a hotel.

Guest History : A record of a guest in prior visits at the hotel.

Guest Ledger : An accounting of all the charges and payments for guests of the hotel. J

Guided Tour : A tour conducted only by local city guides.

Hotelier : It is a person, a firm or a corporation which provides hotel accommodation and/or meals, refreshmnts, etc., to visitors.

Hard Copy : A print information that is displayed on a computer screen.

High Balance Report : A report listing guest account that exceeds the credit authorization or house limit.

Hospitality : The industry comprising lodging establishments, restaurants and cocktail j lounge, the friendly reception and treatment of guests and strangers.

Hospitality Suite : Accommodation for entertaining at conventions, trade shows and meetings.

House Call : A telephone call made by a member of the hotel staff.

House Limit : A set credit limit established by the management for guest account.

Inclusive : A service that is provided as part of the normal room rate such as golf course, tennis court fees, car rental, scuba diving etc.

Inseason Rate : The maximum rate during the period of peak occupancy.

Inside Call : A telephone call from the department or room of the hotel to another department or room.

Inclusion tour : A tour which includes all elements of an itinerary, making it unnecessary for a passenger to spend money for anything except personal extras during the course of the tour.

Joint Agent : A person having authority to transact business for two or more transportation lines.

Late Arrival : A guest who arrives after the scheduled arrival date, or after 6.00 p.m. without a guaranteed reservation.

Limited Service : A lodging establishment that does not have a restaurant, cocktail lounge or bell service on the premises.

Live Move : The act of transferring a guest to a different room while the guest is present.

Log : A record of activities, problems, events or complaints.

Land Arrangements/ Ground Arrangements : All services provided for the traveller by his tour operator after the traveller reaches his first foreign destination. It does not apply to overseas travel.

Modified American Plan(MAP) : Hotel accommodation which includes break-fast and either lunch or dinner in the price of the room. It generally includes continental break-fast and either *table d'hole* lunch or dinner in the room rates. This is also called a demi-person.

Machine Balance : A report that reconciles all the charges and payments reported by various departments of the hotel.

Maitre d : Head waiter, host or hostess.

Market : The group of customers for a particular product, any category of customer who purchases room space, such as business or leisure traveller, tour wholesaler, etc.

Master Key : A key that can unlock any door in the hotel or on a particular floor.

Message Light : A light on a guest telephone that flashes when message is waiting at the front desk.

Miscellaneous Charges Order(MCO) : A voucher authorising accommodation to be provided to the person(s) named on the form, proof of prepayment.

Mom & Pop : A small family owned property. A property that is managed by a couple who handle all, or nearly all, of the functions.

Night Auditor : An employee of the front office responsible for book keeping functions and front desk duties during the night shift.

Night Auditor's Report : A report that summarises room occupancy sales and revenues for the previous business day.

No Show : A guest who has confirmed reservation but fails to arrive.

Occupancy : The number or percentage of rooms that are occupied by guests.

Off Season Rate : Reduced room rates offered during a period of low occupancy.

Out of Order : A room that is not available for sale due to construction, repair, maintenance, refurnishings, etc., and, therefore, is not included in the room inventory.

Overstay : A guest who remains in the hotel after the scheduled departure date.

Option : In travel terminology this word means a choice of taking or not taking the service mentioned. If one takes it there will always be an additional charge as it is not included on the basic tour price.

Pension : It is a French word and is mostly in use in Europe. It means a guest house or a boarding house.

Plat du jour : Some of the restaurants or hotels prepare each day on the *a la carte* menu a dish called, *'Plat dujour'*. This is also to a main dish of the *table d'hote* meal. When a dish is the *plat du jour* it is on the *a la carte menu* at a fixed price. Its price is also less than the price normally charged on other days. This is always a ready dish. Potatoes and vegetables as a garnish are generally included in the price of *'plat du jour'*.

Package : Combined travel services, such as air transportation, lodging, car rental etc.

Package Rate : A room rate offered as part of tour packaging; a special promotional rate, such as weekend package.

Pass Key : A master key that unlocks certain rooms.

Plan : A room rate that includes meals.

Pre-assign : Assignment of rooms prior to guest arrival.

Queen : The second largest bedding available, approximately 60 inches by 80 inches.

Quote : To state but not guarantee a rate.

Rack : A board with slots where such slips or cards are kept. It is a system of organising reservations and room occupancy.

Rack Rate : The normal or published rates of the hotel that are offered to general public. These are undiscounted rates.

Rack Slip : A slip/card on which information about a reservation on guest is written.

Rate : The price of a particular room based on its location, size, bedding and occupancy.

Recap : A summary of accounting or sales activity for a particular day.

Referral : A reservation system for independent properties.

Register : Check in i.e., signing of guest folio or registration card, obliging guest to pay all charges that he or she may incur.

Resort : A hotel that emphasizes room sales to leisure travellers, with food and beverage service and creational facilities.

Rooming : The act of assigning, coordinating and monitoring guest rooms.

Room/Inventory : Total number of guest rooms, whether occupied or vacant.

Room Status : The current condition of a guest room; an indication of whether a room is vacant or occupied and dirty or clean.

Run of the House : The best available accommodations at the time of check-in

Service Elevator : An elevator used for bell attendants, kitchen personnel and house-keeping and engineering.

Skip : To depart without paying.

Stay : The period of time for which the room is occupied.

Studio : Accommodations in which a sofa converts into a bed.

Suite : Accommodation made up of multiple, adjoining rooms, usually a sitting room, bedroom and sometimes a kitchen.

Schedule Carrier : It is a name of an airline which publishes a tariff and carries out regular flights between given points. Most of the scheduled carriers belong to the International Air Transport Association and Air Transport Association in international service and domestic service, respectively.

Suggested Itinerary : It is a preliminary itinerary drawn by the tour operator for the consideration of the tourist. It shows the route, approximate time, hotels, sightseeing excursions etc. It also clearly explains the condition under which these services will be provided.

Supplemented Carrier : Some of the airlines are certified by the government to carry out chartered flights. These are not permitted to engage in regularly scheduled services.

Stop Over : A point, between origin and destination of an itinerary, at which a passenger remains for a period of time.

Table d'hote : The customer chooses the dishes from a more restricted list. The list is usually divided into courses. A guest cannot make any deviation without increasing additional charge. In Europe *table d' hole* menus hardly even include coffee or tea after the meal. These are considered extras.

Tariffs : The published fares, rates, charges and/or related condition of carriage of a carrier.

Tour basing fare : It is only for those passengers who purchase pre-planned and pre-paid tour arrangements prior to their departure. In this case a reduced, round trip fare is available on specific dates and between specified times.

Tour Conductor : A professional employee of a tour operator who accompanies a group on tour. Not to be compared with guide.

Tourist Charter : A flight booked exclusively for the use of a specific group of tourists who, generally, belong to the same organisation or who are being 'treated' to the flight by a single host.

Transient : Individual reservation.

Turn Down : A service provided in the evening, involving the replacement of towels and preparation of bedding linens.

Tour Manager : One who controls, directs and manages an enterprise with judicious economy and care.

Tour Operator : A company which specializes in the planning and pre-peration of pre-paid, pre-planned vacation and makes these available to the general public through travel agents.

Tour Organiser : It is a name given to an individual who organises tour for special groups. Usually he is not connected with the travel industry.

Tour Package : It is a travel plan which includes all elements of vacation such as transportation, accommodation and sightseeing etc.

Tourist Visa : A document issued under the authority of the Government to a person visiting a particular country as a tourist. This document is effective for a three-month stay in India.

Transfer : Transfer is a service provided to a tourist or tourists when they arrive or depart a given city. It includes, taking them from the airport, air terminal pier, or railway station to their hotel and vice versa. There is a variation in cost as (i) the transfer may be carried out by private chauffeur-driven car or by taxi or (ii) the transfer is provided between airport and downtown air terminals. The transfer is generally accompanied by the local representative of the American tour operator who planned the tour.

Travel Agent : A person, firm or corporation qualified to provide tours, cruises, transportation, hotel accommodation, meals, transfers, sightseeing and all other elements of travel to the public as a service.

Travel Kit : It is a sort of container which contains necessaries or tools. Travel kit contains various types of tools and necessaries, folders, pamphlets, exhibits, presentation items, give away etc., which helps travel managers in promotional activities. It is an aid which helps in promoting and projecting a product.

Under Stay : A guest who checks out prior to the scheduled departure date.

Upbell : The act of summoning a bell attendant to transport guest luggage to stock room.

Upgrade : Change a reservation to a higher class a rate, usually, without additional charge.

Vacancy : The number of rooms that are not occupied.

Voucher : A document that authorises its holder for accommodations; proof of prepayment.

Wake Up Call : A telphone call made to awaken a guest.

Walk : To escort a guest who has been denied a room due to overbooking to another hotel. To deny room to a guest who has a reservation.

Walk In : A guest who arrives in the hotel without reservation.

Waste : Wide Area Telephone Service: a toll-free telephone number.

SELECTED BIBLIOGRAPHY

Abraben (E): Resort Hotel Planning & Management; Reinhold Pub. Co. New York.

Allen (Elleng): Japanese Flower Arrangement; Japan-C. & G. Juttle Co.

America Hospital Association: Manual of Hospital Housekeeping; American H. Association.

Arthur Neil: Running your Own Hotel; Hotchmann, London.

Barrett (T.j.): Hotels Accounts; Lon-Gee & Co. Ltd.

Batliboi (J.r.): Principles & Practice of Auditing; Bombay-Standard Publications.

Bedi (Yashpal): A Hand Book of Hygiene & Public Health; Delhi-Atma Ram & Sons.

Beharrell (B), Ubbeham (J): Cases in Hospitality Management; Lon-Heinemann

Best (Bessi Brooks): Food Service in Institutions; Lon-John Willey & Sons.

Better Homes & Gardens: Salad Book; N. York-Meridith Press.

Boni (G. De): Hotel Organisation & Management; Lon-Sir Issac Pitman & Sons London.

Boni, Face (Bg) & Cooper (C): The Geography of Travel and Tourism; Butler Worth Heinemann.

Branoson (Joan C): Hotel Housekeeping Principal & Practice; Lon-Adward Arnold Ltd.

Brigham (Grace H): House-Keeping for Hotel, Motels, Hospitals, Clubs and Schools; New York-Ahrens Pub. Co.

Bronder (Joseph): Profitable Food and Beverage Operation; Ahrens Pub. Co. New York.

Bull (Frank J): Hotel & Catering Law; Barrie & Rockliff,

Carling (T.e.): The Complete Book of Drinks; Lon-Practical Press Ltd.

Carter (Yongman): Drinking Champagne and Brandy; Lon-H. Hamilton.

Coe (Stella): The Art of Japanese Flower Arrangement; Lon-H. Jenkino.

Coltman (M.m.): Hospitality Management and Accountancy; INCRBI Pub. Co.

Combs (Steve): Dictionary of Cusine French; Lon-Barric & Rockliff.

Coombs (Jamesh): Bar Service A Non-technical Manual for Male and Female Bar Staff; Lon-Barrie & Rockliff.

Cooms (James H): Bar Service; Lon-Barrie & Rockliff.

Cooper (Cd): Progress in Tourism Reception and Hospitality Management Vol. I, II & III; ND CBS Pub. Distributor

Davidson (G): Ika-bana Simplified Flower Arrangement; Lon-Arthur Barker Ltd.

Dorwell (Roger): Case Studies in Hotel Management; Lon-Berrie & Rockliff

Dosswell (Roger): Approach to Hotel Planning, Lon-New University Education.

Doswell, Roger & Philip: Case Studies in Hotel Management; Barrie & Reckliff London.<%0>

Dr. Negi Jagmohan: Financial and Cost Control Techniques in the Hotel and Catering Industry; Metropolitan, N. Delhi

Dukas (Peter): Hotel Front Office Operation and Management; U.S.A. W.M.C. Brown & Company

Dukas (Peter): How to Operate a Restaurant; N. York-Ahrens Pub. Co.

Embury (David A): Fine Art of Mixing Drinks; Lon-Faber & Faber.

F. Medlik; The Business of Hotel; Heinemann, London.

Forester (A): American Culinary Art; N.Y. Ahrens Pub. Co.

Foster (D.l): Food and Beverage Operational Methods and Control; Glenoc, Macmillan

Foster (D.l.): Sales and Marketing for Hotels, Motels & Resorts; Glencoc Macmillan

Foster (Dl): An Introduction to Travel and Tourism; Glencoc MacMillan;

Fuller (John): Catering Management in Technological Age; Lon-Barrie & Rockliff.

Fuller (John): Chef's Manual of Kitchen Management; Batsford Lon.

Fuller (John): Hotel Keeping & Catering as a Career; Lon-Batsford Ltd.

Fuller (John): The Chef's Compendium of Professional Recipes; Heimemann-Lon.

Fuller (John): The Restaurant's Guide to Gueridon Lamp Cookery; Lon-Barrie & Rockliff.

Gerald W Lattin: Modern Hotel and Motel Management; WH Freeman and Co.

Ghadwell (D.c.): Practical Management & Equipment for Hotelier; Lon-Barrie & Rockliff.

Goring (O.g.): Hotel & Institutional Housekeeping; Barrie & Rockliff London.

Gray (M): How to be Successful in a Restaurant Business; Chicago, Nelso Hall Co.

Green (Melvyn): Marketing of Hotel and Restaurants in 1990's; Lon-Heinemann

Grey Saluatore: Hotel Management and Operation; Beajley Mitchen

Grossman (Harold J): Practical Bar Management; N. York Ahrens Pub. Co.

H.M.S.O: Investment in Hotel & Catering; London - H.M.S.O.

Haines, (Robert G): Food Preparation for Hotels, Restaurants and Cafeterias; Chicaco-American Technicial Society

Hare (R.a.p.): Best Food from India; Arco Pub. Ltd. Lon.

Harris (E.a.): Professional Restaurant Service; Lon-McGraw Hill, (London and New York)

Hatfield (Doris) Writer (C): Housekeeping for Hotels Professional Housekeeping; Lon-Huchinson

Hobb (Betty. C): Hygienic Food Handling; Lon-St. John. Ambulance

Hook Ann: Restaurant Menu Planning; U.S.A. John Willey

Horwath (Earnest): Hotel Accounting; N. York-The Ronald Press Co.

Hume (R) Dawnes: Corden Blue Cook Book; Lon-WCI Andre D.

ILO: Carrier in Hotel and Tourism; ILO, Geneva

Janet Housden: Franchise and other Business Relationship in Hotel and Catering Services; Heinemann, London.

John (Vonne John): Hospitality and Catering Advanced Text Book; Butterworth Heinemann

John Fuller: Hotelkeeping and Caterer as Career; BT Batsford, London.

Jones (P) Upizam (A): International Hospitality Industry; NY John Willey

Kapoor (A.N.): A Handbook of Commercial Correspondence; N. Delhi-Pub. House.

Khote (H.d.): Hygiene & Public Health; Bom-Popular Prakashan.

Kinton (R): The Theory of Catering; Lon-Adward Arnold Pub.Ltd. London.

Kotas (R): An Approach to Food Costing; Lon-Berrie & Rockliff.

Kotas (R): Book-keeping in the Hotel & Catering Industries; Lon-Evan Brothers.

Kotas (Richards): Accounting in the Hotel & Catering Industry; Lon-Inter Text Books.

Koteschevar (Lendal): Standard Principles & Techniques in Quantity Food Production; California M.P.C.

Koteshcherar(Lendal): Standard Principle & Techniques, in Quantity Food Production; Calfornia - M.P.C.

Koteshchervar (Lendal-H): Food Service Planning Layout & Equipment; Lon-John Willey.

Koteshchevar (Lendal H): Food Service Planning Layout & Equipment; John Willey & Sons Inc. New York.

Lancaster (Hylda M): The Principles of Laundry and Practice; lon-Sir Issac Pitman Ltd.

Lattin (Gerald W): Modern Hotel & Motel Management; San Fransisco W.H. Freeman.

Lean John: Tourism and Development in the Third World; Lon-Routledge.

Lesure (J.d.): Planning & Operating Motels and Moter Hotels; N. York - Ahrens Pub. Co.

Lesure (John D) Podd (George D.): Planning Operating Motels & Motor Hotels; Ahrens Book Co. Inc.

Lilicrap (Dr), & Cousins (Ja): Food and Beverage Service; ELBS with Holder Strong-hton

Lundberg (D.e.): The Management of People in Hotel & Restaurant & Clubs; Lon-W.M.C. Brown and Co.

Lundburg, E.donald: The Hotel and Restaurant Business; CBI, Massachusetts

Ma (Nancy Chin): Chinese Cook Book; Japan-Charles E, Tuttle & Co.

Mac Swaney (Ff): Public Relation and Publicity for Hotel and Restaurant; Lon-Barrie, Jenkinsons

Malcelm: Mood and Atmosphere in Restaurant; Lon-Barrie & Rockliff.

Martin (E.r.a.): Practical Food Inspection; Lon-H.K. Lewis & Co.

Medlic (S): The British Hotel & Catering Industry; Lon-Sir Issac Pitman

Morel (J.j.); Scientific Catering & Hotel Operating; Lon-Sir Issac Pitman

Morphy (C): Recipes of all Nations; Herbert Joseph Ltd., Lon.

Morris (Harriett): The Art of Korian Cooking; Japan-Charlest.

National Productivity Council: Report of Hotel Industry in U.S.A. & Japan; New Delhi-N.P.L.

Negi Jagmohan: Tourism & Travel Concepts & Principles; S.Chand & Co. Pvt. Ltd. New Delhi

NEGI JMS; Tourism & Hoteliering; Gitanjali Publication, New Delhi.

Negi, Dr. Jagmohan: Hotels for Tourism Development, Economic Planning & Financial Management; Metropolitan N. Delhi.

Negi, J.M.S.: Principles of Grading and Classification of Hotels, Tourism Resorts and Restaurants; NRI Publications N. Delhi.

Negi, Jagmohan: Tourism Development & Resource Conservation; Metropolitan New Delhi.

Negi, Jagmohan: Travel Agency and Tour Operation, Kanishka Pub. New Delhi.

Newell (Macolm): Mood & Atmosphere in Restaurant; Lon-Barrie & Rockliff.

Page, Boardman R.d: Catering Costs and Control Hotel and Catering and Budgets; Grace Cassel, London. Heinemann London

Pannet (Alan): Principles of Hotel and Catering Law; Cassel, London

Pellapart (Hp): Modern French Culinary Art; Lon-J. Kramer Ltd.

Peter Venison: Managing Hotels; Quiller Press, London.

Modern Cookery for Teaching and Trade; N.Delhi - Oriental Longman.

Prizeman (John): Kitchen a Design, Layout & Equipment; Lon-Macdonald & Co.

Rawat, Gs & Negi, J.: Elements of Hotel Accoutancy; H.K.S. International, Surjit Book Depo. Delhi.

Richard Kotas Bernard Davis: Food and Beverage Control; International Text Book Company, Glasgow.

Richard Kotas Lee M.kureel: Management Accountancy and Restaurants; Hayden Book Co; INC. New Jersey.

Roberts (P.E.): Table Setting Entertaining and Etiquette; Lon-Thamas & Hudson.

Ruth (AH): The Art of Flower & Foliage Arrangement; N.Y.-Macmillan & Co.

Rutherford (Dg): Hotel Management and Operation; Van Nostrand Reinhold NY.

S. Saulinier: Le-Repetoire De La Cusine English Standard Edition; Lon-leon Jaggi & Sons.

Saulinier (L): Le Repetoire De Lo Cusine; Lon-Leon Jaggi & Sons.

School Of Hotel Administration: The Essentials of Good Table Service; N.Y. Ithaca, Cornell University.

Seaton (Dora): Cookery for the Hotel & Catering Industry; Lon-Evan's Brothers Ltd.

Simon (Andre): A Guide to Good Food and Wine; Lon-Collins

Singh (Mrs. Balbir): Indian Cookery; Mills & Boon, Ltd.

Smith (Henry): Classical Recipes of the World; Practical Press Ltd.

T. Lucey: Management Information Systems; ELBI Pub.

Taylor (Drek): Hotel & Catering Sales Promotion; Lon-T. Life Books Ltd.

Tourist Association Hongkong: Hongkong the Great Eating Adventure; Hong Kong Tourist Ass.

Turner (E) Neil (A): A Small Hotel of your Own; Lon-Barrie & Rockliff

Veeraswamy: Indian Cookery; Lon-Arco Publishings House.

Weller (D.e.): Hotel Housekeeping; Lon-Pitman & Sons Ltd.

Winslet (V.g.): Accountancy for Caterers; Lon-Practical Press Ltd.

Witzky (Horbert K): Modern Hotel-Motel Management Method; New York-Ahrens Book Co.

HOTEL MANAGEMENT TERMINOLOGY

Term Definition

A

A la Carte Menu: A food and drink menu in which each item is listed and priced separately.

Adjoining Rooms: Guestrooms that are located next to each other, but without a connecting door between them.

Advance Deposit: Money paid, usually by credit card or cheque, by a guest before they arrive at the hotel to guarantee a reservation. The amount is generally equal to one night's lodging fees. The full amount is applied to the guest's bill upon check-out.

Aesthetic Balance: In meal planning, a pleasing combination obtained by making use of the colours flavours and textures of foods.

Affiliate Reservation System: A hotel chain's reservation systems in which all participating properties are contractually related. Each hotel is represented in the computer database and is required to provide room availability data to the reservation centre in a timely manner.

Affiliated Hotel: A hotel that is a member of a franchise, chain or referral system. Membership usually provides special advantages, such as the use of a national reservation system.

Air Change: Ventilation rate in terms of building or room volume. The figure is typically expressed as air changes per hour.

Air Handling Unit: An all-air HVAC (heating, ventilating, and air conditioning) system that consists of filters, fresh air intakes, coils (through which chilled water or steam/hot water is circulated from central boilers and chillers), exhaust air discharges, and in some cases, humidification equipment.

Airline-Related Guests: Airplane passengers and crew members who need emergency accommodations.

Airport Hotel: Lodging properties located near a public airport (usually within 5 miles), which derive a significant amount of demand from the airport. Although airport hotels vary widely in service levels and size, they are generally full-service and are more likely than other hotels to have in-room films, call accounting systems and computerized property management systems.

Alcoholic Beverage Menu: A menu that lists wines, cocktails, and other alcoholic beverages offered to guests. They may be included on the regular menu or listed on a separate menu. Many beverage menus also include no- or low-alcohol drinks. Restaurants with a large selection of wines may have a separate wine list.

All-Expense Tour: A tour that offers all or most services: meals, lodging, transportation, sightseeing (etc), for a pre-established price. However, the terms 'all-expense' and 'all-inclusive' are normally much misused, as almost no tour rate will cover everything. The terms and conditions of a tour contract should specify exactly what is covered.

All-Suite Hotel: A hotel that features suites, which are larger than the typical hotel room, with a separate living space in addition to the bedroom. A suite may also have a whirlpool or kitchenette.

Alternative Tourism: Smaller scale tourism in terms of the dimensions of tourism development and the number of tourists.

Ambiance: ● Applied to environments, a mood or feeling associated with a particular place, person, or thing, an atmosphere.

● A feeling about or an identity for an establishment created by the combination of lighting, decor, furnishings, and other features.

Ambient Air Temperature: The surrounding inside air temperature, usually considered ideal for human comfort at 18-24°C (65–75°F).

Ambient Lighting: Lighting that holds together varied elements of the decor and provides atmosphere.

Amenity: An item or service placed in guestrooms or offered to guests for their comfort and convenience, and at no extra cost.

Examples include various guest services (such as automatic check-out, in-room entertainment systems, concierge services free parking and multilingual staff) in addition to an array of personal bathroom items offered by most hotels. Amenities are designed to enhance a guest's stay, increase a hotel's appeal, and encourage guests to return.

American Service: A pre-plated restraint service, which means that the food is served into the guest's plate in the kitchen itself and brought to the guest. The kitchen predetermines the portion and the accompaniments served with the dish balance the entire presentation in terms of nutrition and colour.

Apartment Hotel: Accommodation in apartment-style units rather than rooms, with in-suite cooking facilities.

Automatic Form Number Reader (AFNR): A feature of a guest bill (check) printer that helps order entry procedures. A barcode imprinted on the guest bill presents the bill's serial number in a machine-readable format, rather than the server having to manually input the bill serial number to access the account.

Average Daily Rate (ADR): The total room revenue for a given period (day, month, month to date, year to date), divided by the number of rooms occupied for the same period. The ADR is ratio that indicates average room rate, and to what extent rooms are being discounted or up-sold, and is frequently used as a measure of economic performance.

Average Published Rate (APR): The average of single low, single high, double low and double high published room rates.

B

Back: Any beverage a guest orders that is to be served in a separate glass along with their drink.

Back of the House: The functional areas of a hotel in which employees have little or no direct guest contact; for example, the accounting department, engineering and maintenance, or kitchen areas.

Backbar: That part of the back wall of a bar that is used for storage and display, which may consist of photographs, mirrors, or memorabilia.

Backup Drinks: Two drinks purchased at one time by or for one guest.

Banquet: A meal that is prepared for a particular group, for which the menu and the number of guests are predetermined. Most hotel properties offering banquet service have special facilities for banquet food production and service.

Banquet Menu: A table d'hôte menu; a set meal with few, if any, choices, prepared for a large group of people.

Banquette: A benches, usually upholstered, that is built in along a wall in a restaurant, bar or other seating area.

Bar: The area in which drinks are prepared and from which drinks are sold.

Bar and Beverage Operations: A term that includes all possible combinations of establishments serving alcoholic beverages. Typical examples are lounges and bars.

Bar Menu: The primary types of drinks that a beverage operation is prepared to serve, including mixed drinks, bottled and/or draft beers, wine, and specialty drinks. The bar menu usually includes the projected drink preferences of the operation's target markets.

Bar Par: The amount established for each type of beverage to be stored in the backbar. This amount is generally based on expected consumption.

Bay: The principal compartment, typically of a suite, that is the space equivalent of a standard guestroom. A suite may have a multiple-bay or single-bay living room.

Bed and Breakfast (B&B) : ● A small lodge or inn that provides a room and a breakfast. A B&B is often in a residential home setting and/or a historic building.

● A type of room rate that includes the price of the room and breakfast. Also known as Continental Plan.

Bellboy: Also known as Bellhop or Bellman.

A person employed by a hotel to assist guests, by carrying luggage and doing errands.

Billed-To-Room Call: An operator-assisted call that allows guests to have an operator places their calls and then informs the hotel of the charges.

Billing Clerk: The person responsible for charging to hotel guests all vouchers representing room service, beverages, food, and merchandise purchases.

Booking Engine: An online system used by hotels that allows prospective hotel guests to check availability and make reservations at the hotel over the Internet.

Boutique Hotel: Historical, classic buildings, remodelled into hotels with usually less than 30 rooms.

Buffet: An assortment of foods offered on a table for guests to choose in self-service fashion.

Buffet Service: Hot and cold foods attractively arranged on platters are placed on large serving tables and guests walk up and choose in self-service fashion. Service personnel, such as carvers, may be required to assist guests. In some cases, each course may be placed on a separate table.

Business Mix: A hotel's desired blend of business from various segments such as corporate group, business transient, leisure and convention.

C

Cabana: A guestroom that is situated adjacent to the pool area, with or without sleeping facilities.

Cafeteria: A food service operation in which guests pass through serving lines and help themselves to food items or receive food items from service staff.

Call Accounting System: A system that is part of the telephone equipment that prices phone calls made by hotel guests and sends the information to the property management system (PMS) for billing.

Calling Card: A credit card for making telephone calls; issued by either a long-distance company or the local phone company.

Calling Card Call: A call typically billed to a code number on a calling card issued by either a long-distance company or the local phone company, usually with a per-call surcharge.

Cancellation: A reservation voided by a guest.

Cancellation Hour: A specific time after which a hotel may release all unclaimed non-guaranteed room reservations.

Cancellation Number: A number issued to a guest who properly cancels a room reservation, proving that a cancellation was received and acted upon.

Canteen: A type of business and industrial food service that includes mobile or portable on-street catering.

Capsule Hotel: A (primarily Japanese) hotel system of extremely dense occupancy. Guest space is reduced in size to a modular fiberglass or plastic block, approximately 2 × 1 × 1.25 m, providing just enough room to sleep. These capsules are stacked side by side and two units top to bottom, with steps providing access to the second level rooms. A curtain or a fiberglass door at the open end of the capsule ensures privacy.

Most capsules include entertainment facilities such as a television, an electronic console, and wireless Internet connection. Washrooms are communal and most hotels include restaurants, or at least vending machines, pools, and other facilities.

This style of hotel accommodation was developed in Japan, although Western variants with larger accommodations and often-private bathrooms are being developed in Kuala Lumpur, London, New York and Amsterdam.

Card Key: A plastic card, resembling a credit card, which is used to open a guestroom door in place of a metal key. Card keys require electronic locks.

Casino Hotel: A hotel that features gambling, with the hotel operation secondary to the gambling operation.

Catering Manager: A hotel manager who promotes and sells a hotel's banquet facilities and uses their expertise to plan, organizes, and carries out hotel banquets.

Central Reservation System (CRS): An external reservation network, which allows guests to make a reservation for one hotel out of a number by contacting one agency. The hotels acting as a group, to operate a 'central' reservation service, contract the CRS.

Chain Operating Company: A firm that operates several properties, such as Hilton Hotels Corporation or Holiday Inn Worldwide. Such an operator provides both a reservation system and a trademark as an integral part of the management of its managed properties.

Check-In: The procedures for a hotel guest's arrival and registration.

Check-Out: ● A room status term indicating that the guest has returned their room keys, the settled account, and left the property.

● The procedures for a guest's departure and the settling of their account.

Chef de Partie: The chef in charge of a particular food production area in the kitchen.

Chef du Rang: The employee in a restaurant who is responsible for taking orders, serving drinks, preparing food at the table, and collecting sales income.

If the restaurant has no wine steward or sommelier, the chef du rang may also serve wine.

Children's Menu: A menu for children featuring simple, food served in smaller portions. The actual physical menu may also be designed to entertain the child: they may have word games, stories, or mazes printed on them; be shaped like animals; or fold into masks or hats.

Closed Circuit Television (CCTV): Often used as part of a surveillance system on hotel premises, where images captured by cameras are streamed onto monitors and recorded on video or DVD recorders. Along with alarm and access control systems, CCTV cameras are used as a security measure, and provide security staff with a visual aid for monitoring visitors and staff.

Club Manager: The hired professional responsible for guiding all of the elements of a private club's operation.

Coffee Maker: A semi-automatic or automatic machine that makes coffee and dispenses it into individual cups or into a coffee pot.

Commercial Agency: A travel agency that specializes in commercial business and usually has little or no walk-in clientele.

Commercial Hotel: Also known as a Transient Hotel.

A property, usually located in a city centre or business district, which caters primarily to business clients. Commercial hotels tend to be busiest Monday to Thursday.

Commis du Rang: The employee who assists the chef du rang in a restaurant. They may take food orders to the kitchen, pick up the food when it is ready, and take it to the cart at tableside for further preparation.

A commis du rang may also serve food to guests and deliver drink orders.

Commissary: ● A centralized servicing area for mobile food service units.

● A central food production area from which food is transported to individual outlets for final preparation and service.

Complimentary Occupancy Percentage: A ratio that shows the percentage of occupied rooms that are complimentary (and therefore do not generate any revenue). This figure is calculated by dividing complimentary rooms for a period by total available rooms for the same period.

Complimentary Room: Also known as a Comp Room.

An occupied room for which the guest is not charged. This may include a room occupied by a hotel employee.

A hotel may offer complimentary rooms to a group in ratio to the total number of rooms the group occupies. For example, 1 comp room may be offered for every 25 rooms occupied.

Concierge: An employee whose basic task is to serve as the guest's liaison with hotel and non-hotel facilities, attractions, activities and services.

Condominium Hotel: A hotel in which a customer takes title to a specific hotel room. Unit owners may live in the hotel permanently or use it as a second home. Depending on the management company, unit owners have varying degrees of access to their hotel's amenities and services. Unit owners also incur budgeted maintenance and operating expenses.

Depending on the hotel's policy, unit owners may rent their units independently when they are not using the room or through the management company's rental program and derive income through a revenue-sharing arrangement. The unit owner generally expects to receive a gain from the increase in value of the hotel over time, as well as receive ongoing income from the rental of their room.

Conference Centre: A specialized hotel, usually accessible to major market areas but in less busy locations, that almost exclusively books executive meetings, conferences and seminars. A conference centre often also provides extensive leisure facilities.

Confirmed Reservation: A written or oral statement by the hotel that they have received a reservation and will honour it. Confirmed reservations may be either guaranteed or non-guaranteed.

Oral confirmations have virtually no legal worth, and even written or emailed confirmations have implied or specified limitations. For example, unless late arrival is specified, a hotel is not obligated to honour a confirmed reservation if the guest arrives after 6 pm.

Connecting Rooms: Two or more guestrooms with private connecting doors that give guests access between rooms without having to go into the corridor.

Continental Breakfast: A small morning meal that usually includes a drink, rolls, butter, and jam or marmalade. Better hotels may serve brioches and croissants.

There are variations to the Continental Breakfast. Cafe com-plate refers to Continental Breakfast with coffee (or tea) while cafe simple refers to just coffee or tea with nothing to eat.

Cooling Degree-Day (CDD): A measure of the need for air conditioning based upon outdoor temperatures. Cooling degree-days are calculated as follows:

Daily mean temperature – 65°F (18.3°C)

For example, if the average temperature for a given day was 85°F, then that would be a 20 degree day. Cooling degree-days can be added over periods of time to provide a rough estimate of seasonal cooling requirements. For example, the number of cooling degree-days in Florida is likely to be much higher than those in Alaska.

Corporate Hotel Chain: Hotel organization that has its own brand (or brands), which may be managed by a conglomerate or by the corporate chain.

Credit Card Commission: A fee paid to credit card companies based upon a contracted percentage of credit card charges accepted.

Cruise Ship: Passenger ship designed for holidaymakers. Today's cruise ships feature a variety of entertainment and activities and can be thought of as floating resort hotels.

D

Dais: A raised platform on which the head table is placed at a banquet.

Day Rate: A special room rate for less than an overnight stay.

Design Theme: A theme that has been established to ensure overall consistency in the design of interior decor.

Dessert Menu: A separate menu designed to remind guests of the dessert items listed on the regular menu. It may also include dessert specials and list desserts not shown on the regular menu. Some restaurants may include dessert wines, cordials, liqueurs and brandies on the dessert menu.

Destination Club: A niche market that most closely resembles country clubs in ownership structure, and targets the most affluent of travellers. Customers pay high initiation fees and annual dues, and in return, they can stay for weeks at a time in multi-million pound villas and residences in prime resort and urban locations and enjoy a full range of services and amenities.

Developer-Owner: The owner of a managed hotel who either purchased an existing hotel or developed and retained the property.

Digital Video Server (DVS): A system that is designed for the hospitality market as a turnkey entertainment solution, providing guests with pay per view/on demand video, satellite/cable TV, on-screen guest information, games and Internet access. Televisions in hotel guest rooms can usually be linked to the DVS via a set-top box and are controlled by hotel guests using a remote control or wireless keyboard.

Dinner Cost: The standard food cost for items combined to form dinners or other meals that are priced and sold as one menu selection.

Director of Sales (DOS): The manager of a hotel sales department.

Domestic Tourism: Travel within the traveller's country of residence.

Doorknob Menu: A type of room service menu that a housekeeper can leave in the guestroom, which lists the times that breakfast can be served and a limited number of breakfast items. Guests select what they want to eat and the time they want the food delivered, then hang the menu outside the door on the doorknob. The menus are collected and the orders are prepared and sent to the rooms at the specified times.

Double: Double Room - A guestroom assigned to two people.

Double Occupancy Rate: A rate used that bases the per-person charge on two to a room.

Double-Loaded Slab: A guestroom floor configuration in which rooms are laid out on both sides of a central corridor.

Double-Locked Room: An occupied room for which the guest has locked the room from the inside with a dead bolt.

A room attendant using a standard passkey cannot access double-locked rooms.

E

Early Arrival: A guest who arrives at the property before the date or specified time of their reservation.

Ecotourism: Low-impact tourism that avoids harming the normal or natural environment. In this relatively new approach to promoting protection, as well as enjoyment, of the environment, tourists seek out tours or holidays, which, in some way, improve or add to their knowledge of an environment and/or environmentally sensitive travel.

English Breakfast: A more elaborate breakfast style than Continental. A typical English breakfast may include:

- Stewed fruit (prunes, pears, apples, figs)
- Chilled fruit juices (orange, pineapple, tomato, grapefruit)
- Cereals (porridge, cornflakes)
- Eggs (poached, boiled, scrambled, fried, omelettes) - served with grilled tomatoes, sautéed mushrooms, baked beans, and fried potatoes.
- Fish (smoked haddock, kippers)
- Meat (sausages, bacon, kidney)
- Breads (toast, rolls, brioche, croissant)
- Preserves (jam, marmalade, honey)
- Beverage (tea, coffee, hot chocolate)

English Service: A style of restaurant service in which food is brought on platters by the waiter and is shown to the host for approval. The waiter then places the platters on the tables. After initially being assisted by the waiters, the guests then help themselves.

Executive Floor: A floor of a hotel that offers exceptional service to business and other travellers.

Executive Housekeeper: The person in charge of a housekeeping department in a hotel. The executive housekeeper is a member of the management team.

Expected Arrival/Departure Report: A daily report that shows the number and names of guests expected to arrive with reservations, along with the number and names of guests expected to depart.

Expediter: A staff member who acts as a communication link between servers and kitchen personnel. Servers give their orders to the expediter, who calls the orders to the appropriate kitchen stations. The expediter must provide leadership during hectic rush periods. They must also know cooking times and coordinate them to sequentially deliver cooked foods for pickup.

Extended Stay: A hotel category comprised of properties that focus on attracting hotel guest for extended periods of time. These properties quote weekly rates, and their typical guest may stay 4–7 nights.

Extended-Stay Hotels: Hotel that caters mostly to persons who must be in an area for a week or longer. The guestrooms of extended-stay hotels tend to have more living space than standard hotel guestrooms, and may also have kitchen facilities. Guestrooms in these hotels tend to be less expensive than guestrooms in full-service or all-suite hotels.

F

Facilities: Core physical features; for example, restaurants, bars, accommodation and meeting rooms.

Familiarization Tour: A reduced-rate, often complimentary, tour or trip offered to incentive travel planners, travel agents, wholesalers, travel writers, photographers or broadcasters, to promote a destination or a hotel.

Family Life Cycle: A series of stages used to distinguish between types of travellers; variables used to determine family life cycle stages are:

- Age
- Marital status
- Presence and ages of children

Family Rate: A special room rate for parents and children occupying one guestroom.

Family-Style Service: A table service style in which food is placed on large platters or in large bowls before being taken to the tables by servers. Guests serve themselves and pass the food around their table.

Fiber Optics: Pure glass strands that transmit light signals over long distances. Fiber optics are used in the hospitality industry for high-speed Internet access and hotel lighting.

Finish: A liquid applied to floors that enhances the appearance of the floor and dries to a protective coating. Finishes come in wax-based or polymer types.

Flying Food Show: A procedure for delivering cooked menu items to guests as soon as the food is ready. The first server to arrive at the pickup point delivers the menu items that are ready for service.

The flying food show can only be implemented if order tickets show, which guest at which table, is to receive each order.

Folio: The guest's bill that all hotel and incidental charges are posted to.

Food and Beverage (F&B) Division: The division in a hospitality organization that is responsible for preparing and serving food and beverages within the organization or property. The F&B division also includes catering and room service.

Food and Beverage (F&B) Manager: The person who is in charge of planning, directing, organizing, and controlling all phases of the food and beverage departments of an establishment.

Franchise: The right granted by the manufacturer, developer or distributor to market a service and/or product in return for a fee. Franchises are prevalent in the fast food industry but are increasingly being adopted within the hotel community.

French Service: Also known as Tableside Service or Cart Service. A style of table service used by servers for preparing menu items beside the guest's table in the dining room. Menu items are cooked, and sometimes flambéed, in front of the guest.

Frequent Independent Traveller (FIT): A visitor who stays at the hotel on their own (as opposed to being a part of an organized group) on a regular basis.

Front Bar: A place where guests may sit down and order and consume beverages and that also serves as a workspace for the bartender.

The front bar is divided into two functional areas: the underbar (the bartender's main working area) and the backbar (the back wall, for storage and display).

Front Desk Agent: A hotel employee whose responsibilities centre on the registration process, but also typically include room status coordination, pre-registration activities, along with message, mail and information requests.

Front of the House: The functional areas of a hotel in which employees have extensive guest contact, such as the front desk.

Front Office: An office usually situated in the lobby of the hotel, whose primary function is to control the sale of guest rooms, maintain guest accounts, render bills, receive payments as well as providing information to other departments within the hotel.

Full Pension: A type of room rate that includes the price of the room, breakfast, lunch, and dinner.

Full-Menu Restaurant: A restaurant that has more than a dozen or so main-course items on the menu, and cooks them to order.

Full-Service Hotel: A hotel with a full range of amenities and services, which may include meeting facilities, fitness centre, onsite restaurant and lounge, pool, business centre, etc.

G

General Manager: The chief operating officer of a hotel.

Glass Rail: An area on which a bartender can set glasses while pouring drinks.

Global Distribution System (GDS): A network of Internet reservation systems that provide a central place where travel agents and travellers can check availability and reserve travel related products such as hotels, airline and car rentals. These systems are formed and managed by the airline industry and includes system such as Amadeus, Sabre, Apollo and Pegasus.

Group Pick-Up: The guestrooms that are actually rented by a group that are held in a Group Reservation.

Group Reservation: A block of multiple guestrooms that are being held under an individual or business' name at a particular hotel for a specific date or range of dates. Generally used for conferences, conventions, weddings, receptions, meetings, and so on.

Guaranteed Reservation: A reservation of a hotel room that is paid in advance, usually with a cheque or credit card. The payment is normally held until the arrival date or until check-out time the next day. The guest forfeits the payment if the reservation is not cancelled in advance.

Guest Account: Also known as Guest Bill, Guest Folio or Guest Statement.

An itemized record of a guest's credits and charges, which is maintained in the front office until their departure.

Guest History: A record maintained for each guest who has stayed at the hotel with a separate entry for each visit and details of rooms assigned, rates, special needs, credit rating and personal preferences. Guest histories are a valuable reference tool for marketing, reservations and credit departments, and are now more readily available through the increased use of computers and other technology.

Guest History File: A file containing guest history cards maintained for marketing purposes and is referred to for return visits.

Guest House: A personal residence with a small amount of overnight accommodation. Guesthouses typically provide breakfast, which is included within the room rate.

Guest Information Services: Automated information devices in public hotel areas that enable guests to find out about local activities and in-house events.

Guest Ledger: Also known as Front Office Ledger, Transient Ledger or Room Ledger.

A ledger that consists of individual records (known as folios) of the hotel's registered guests, providing the current status on guest charges and payments. The front office is responsible for summarizing these transactions during the guest's stay.

Guest Mix: The variety and percentage distribution of hotel guests (for example, business, leisure, individual or group) who stay at a hotel or patronize a restaurant.

Guest Profile: A list of the characteristics that a hotel's guests have in common. This helps management to identify which market the property appeals to and which segments the property wants to attract.

Guest Relations: The establishment of goodwill and personal rapport with guests through service and attention to individual guest needs.

It can also include the entertainment of VIPs, the promotion of in-house services and products, and the handling of social functions.

Guest Service Directory: A documented listing of all of the features of a hotel together with general and relevant information about the local community. Directories are usually provided within each guest room.

Guest Service Manager (GSM): Manager of the guest services department.

Guest Service Representative (GSR): Employees who provide check-in check-out, keys, mail, messages, and information services for guests.

Guest Survey: A questionnaire completed by guests and used by managers to improve the operation and to define current markets. Managers may leave the questionnaires with guests to fill out or they may talk them through the survey.

Guestroom Control Book: A book used to monitor and control the number of guestrooms committed to groups, by providing the sales office with the maximum number of guestrooms it can sell to groups on a given day. The remaining guestrooms (along with any unsold guestrooms allotted to groups) are available for individual guests.

Guestroom Key: A key that opens a single guestroom door.

Guestroom Maintenance: A form of preventive maintenance that involves the inspection of a number of items in the guestroom, repair of obvious small problems, and, when needed, the initiation of a work order for more substantial problems.

H

Hand Caddy: A portable container for holding, storing, and transporting cleaning supplies. The hand caddy is typically located on the top shelf of the room attendant's cart.

Heating Degree-Day (HDD): A measure of the need for heating based upon outdoor temperatures. Heating degree-days are calculated as follows:

Daily mean temperature - 65°F (18.3°C)

For example, if the average temperature for a given day was 50°F, then that would be a 15 degree day. Heating degree-days can be added over periods of time to provide a rough estimate of seasonal heating requirements. For example, the number of heating degree-days in Florida is likely to be much lower than those in London.

High Season: Also known as Peak Season.

The period of consecutive months during which optimum revenues, room/suite occupancy and average room rates are generated. This is often over the summer months, or school holidays.

Hospitality: Derived from the Latin term 'hospes' - a guest.

A term used in travel and tourism to describe the cordial and generous reception of guests, including welcoming, greeting and food-service.

Hospitality Industry: Lodging and food service businesses that provide food and/or short-term or transitional lodging.

Hospitality Suite: A room used for entertaining; usually a function room.

Hotel: A large lodging facility that also often provides food and beverage services on site. Hotels often provide a number of additional guest services such as a swimming pool, fitness centre or childcare. Some hotels have meeting rooms and conference services and encourage groups to hold conventions and meetings at their location.

Hotel Chain: A group of affiliated hotels.

Hotel Guest Cycle: The sequence of events that begins with pre-sale activities, continues through point-of-sale procedures, and concludes with post-sale transactions. The phases identify the financial exchanges that physical contacts and occur between guests and various revenue centers within a lodging operation.

Hotel Management: The professional management techniques used in the hospitality sector. These can include hotel administration, marketing, accounts, front office or front of house, housekeeping, food and beverage management, maintenance and catering.

Hotel Management Company: A company that is hired to professionally manage a hotel (or hotels) for other owners.

Hotel Representative: An individual or firm who offers hotel reservations to travel agents, wholesalers, and the public. A hotel 'rep' may be paid by the hotels they represent by commission or on a fee basis. Many hotel representatives also offer marketing and other services.

Hotelier: The owner or manager of a hotel.

Housekeeping Department: A department of the rooms division, responsible for cleaning the hotel's public areas and guestrooms.

Hotel/Motel: A standard hotel or motel operation.

I

In-Room Beverage Service System: A computer-based system capable of monitoring sales transactions and determining inventory replenishment quantities. Popular systems include microprocessor-based vending machines and non-automated honour bars.

In-Room Check-Out: A computer-based check-out procedure that allows guests to access and review their bill, and to approve and settle their accounts in their rooms. The technology involves interfacing the guestroom telephone, the television, and an in-room computer with the property management system's guest accounting module.

In-Room Guest Console: A multi-feature phone that may include such functions as:

- Remote control of heating, ventilating, and air-conditioning, television, and room lights
- Jack for portable computer use
- Two-way speakerphone capability
- Radio
- Theft alarm
- Alarm clock
- Energy management

In-Room Movie System: Guestroom entertainment provided through a dedicated television pay channel. Charges for the use of this in-room entertainment are posted to the guest bill.

Incidental Charges: Guest charges on a bill or folio for items other than room and tax such as, phone calls, food, drinks, movies, etc.

Inclusive Tour: A tour in which specific elements (such as air fare, transfers, accommodation) are included for a flat rate. An inclusive tour rate does not necessarily cover all costs.

Independent Food Service Operation: An operation with one or more properties having no chain relationship. Menus, operating procedures, food purchase specifications, etc. May differ among the owned properties.

Independent Hotel: A hotel with no franchise or chain affiliation. An individual proprietor or a group of investors may own it.

Inn: A smaller lodging facility, generally with limited service and 1-3 stories.

Intelligent Hotel: Properties that use state of the art technology systems for their operations. These hotels have replaced the traditional systems to reduce their energy cost and usually have integrated systems, which join analogue, and digital systems to achieve an effective communication in their hotels. The return on investment is reflected in the comfort they provide to their guests and the energy-cost savings.

International Tourism: Travel people make outside their country of residence.

K

Kapok: Natural plant fiber used to stuff solid mattresses.

King Bed: In the UK, a bed 152 × 198 cm (60 × 78 in). In the US, one that measures 193 × 203 cm (76 × 80 in).

L

Lanai: A guestroom with a patio or balcony, overlooking a garden or water.

Late Arrival: A guest who holds a reservation, but who plans to arrive after the hotel's designated cancellation hour and has notified the hotel.

Late Charge: A charged purchase made by a guest that is posted to the guest's folio after the guest has settled their account.

Late Check-Out: A guest who is allowed to check out later than the property's standard check-out time.

Latex Mattress: A mattress made of whipped synthetic rubber.

Limited Service Hotel: A lodging facility that offers no or very few amenities, extra facilities or services such as pools, restaurants or meeting rooms. Inns and motels are normally limited service; these properties are often located near business areas such as cities, industrial parks and airport terminals.

Limited-Menu Restaurant: A restaurant with limited services and a small selection of food. Limited-menu restaurants give emphasis to speed of preparation and delivery, making convenience one of the main reasons for their appeal.

Linen Room: An area in a hotel that is often considered the headquarters of the housekeeping department.

This is where the housekeeping employee normally reports to work, receives room status reports, room assignments, and keys; assembles and organizes cleaning supplies; and checks out at the end of their shift.

Lodge: A hotel that is normally small and often located in a rustic outdoors environment, offering activities such as, skiing, fishing, boating, eco-tours.

Lodging Facility: A business that rents guestrooms to the public on a nightly or short-term range of dates, i.e. weekly, month to month.

Lodging Industry: Lodging and food service businesses that provide transitional or short-term lodging.

Low Season: Also known as Off-Peak Season.

The consecutive months during which the lowest revenues, room/suite occupancy and average room rates are generated.

Luncheon: A light midday meal.

Luxury Hotel: A hotel with high room rates that features exceptional amenities and service.

Luxury Restaurant: A restaurant that features fine dining and employs well-trained, creative chefs and skilled food servers.

Luxury restaurants are generally small and independently operated, with more employees per guest than other types of restaurants.

M

Mass Tourism: Wide-scale travel by a large number of people from all walks of life, brought about by the increase in discretionary income, leisure time, and reliable and inexpensive modes of transportation such as the car and plane.

Master Folio: A bill that all charges for the members of a group are posted to.

Master Key: A key that can open all guestroom doors those are not double-locked.

Menu Board: A keyboard overlay for an ECR (Electronic Cash Register) or POS (Point of Sale) system terminal used in a restaurant that identifies the function performed by each key during a specific meal period.

Mid-Range Service Hotel: A modest but sufficient level of service that appeals to the largest segment of the travelling public. This type of property may offer:

- ❖ Special rates for certain guests
- ❖ Airport limousine service
- ❖ Uniformed service
- ❖ Food and beverage room service
- ❖ Specialty restaurant
- ❖ Coffee shop
- ❖ Lounge

Mini Bar: A specially designed small floor mounted refrigerator located in guest rooms containing a variety of snacks and drinks, with individual guest room key access. This amenity serves as a more profitable substitute for room service.

MOD: Acronym for 'Manager On Duty'.

Motel: A smaller lodging facility originally targeted to car travellers and therefore situated at roadside locations.

A more contemporary definition would be a limited service hotel that provides accommodation only, with no other amenities. The properties then to be one to two stories with exterior entrance rooms that guest can drive up to.

The word 'motel' is a portmanteau of 'motor' and 'hotel' or 'motorists hotel'.

Multiple Guest Splits: Charges that are to be divided among a group of guests.

N

Napery: A term used to describe table linens, such as tablecloths and napkins.

O

Occupancy: The percentage of available rooms occupied for a given period of consecutive time.

The occupancy figure (expressed a s a percentage) is calculated by dividing the number of rooms occupied for a period by the number of rooms available for the same period.

Occupancy Report: A report prepared each night by a front desk agent that lists rooms occupied that night. The occupancy report also lists those guests expected to check out the following day.

Occupied Room: The use and/or booking of a room by a guest for the purpose of accommodation, conference or any other use that means that the hotel staff may not allocate the room to another guest.

Online Reservation System: An Internet based system used by hotels that allows prospective hotel guests to check availability and make reservations at the hotel online.

Out of Order: A room status term that indicates that a room cannot be assigned to a guest. A room may be out-of-order for refurbishing, maintenance, deep cleaning, or other reasons.

Outside Air: Air taken from outside the building and not previously cooled or heated by the building's mechanical systems.

Overbooking: A situation in which a hotel has accepted more room reservations than the property is able to accommodate. Hotels use historic no-show information to determine what percentage they can over-commit rooms. This practice is intended to enable 100% occupancy for the hotel.

Hotels that use overbooking as a policy are increasingly being targeted by tour operators and wholesalers in an attempt to better control and minimize the serious adverse marketing effects which overbooking has for all stakeholders.

Overstay: A guest who remains at the property after their stated departure date.

P

Package: A special offering of services and products created by a hotel to increase sales. In adition to the guestroom, packages may include meals, the use of the property's recreational facilities, entertainment, champagne and chocolates - all in one special price. Examples include honeymoon packages, weekend packages, or New Years packages.

Package Tour: A tour put together by a tour operator, offering several travel elements that a traveller would otherwise purchase separately. These may include any combination of flights, airport transfers, car hire, accommodation, meals, sight-seeing, attractions or entertainment - all for an inclusive price.

Travellers who buy the package make the trips by themselves rather than with a large group. A package tour may include more than one destination.

Paid Occupancy Percentage: A ratio that indicates management's success in selling its product. The paid occupancy percentage is calculated by dividing the number of rooms sold by the number of available rooms.

Plate Service: A basic service style in a restaurant in which fully cooked menu items are individually portioned, plated (put on plates) in the kitchen, and carried to each guest directly.

Platter Service: A table service style in a restaurant in which servers carry platters of fully cooked food to the dining room, present them to the guest for approval, and then serve the food.

Point of Sale System (POS): A computerized system that retail outlets such as gift shops and restaurants enter orders and maintain various accounting information. The POS generally interfaces with the property management system (PMS).

Porcelain: A hard ceramic substance used in the hospitality industry for tableware and kitchen items. Quality hotel porcelain is normally dishwasher friendly and microwave/grill resistant.

Porte Cochere: From the French: porte, door + cochère, for coaches.

A canopy designed to provide greater visibility to the main entrance and protect hotel guests from poor weather.

Porter: A person employed to carry travellers' baggage at a hotel.

Portion: A standard quantity of beverage or food served for one person.

Portion Cost: The food cost for an item that is sold as a single menu selection. This figure indicates the cost incurred by preparing one portion of the menu item according to its standard recipe.

Private Branch Exchange (PBX): A private telephone network used by hotels to manage a certain number of external lines. The system enables guests to use their room telephone to make calls to external numbers, without the hotel having to go to the expense of installing individual lines in each room.

Property Management System (PMS): A computerized front desk system that deals with online reservations, guest bookings, point of sale, telephone and other amenities. Some property management systems also include payroll, back office and guest billing.

Property Types: Hotel classifications driven primarily by building structure and secondarily by service level. Property types include: All-Suite

Properties that offer only suite room accommodations. Suite rooms will be the only type of room offered at properties that fall in this category. Conference

Lodging properties that place major focus on conference operations. Convention

Lodging properties that place major focus on convention operations. These properties offer or are located near convention facilities. Gaming

Lodging properties that place major focus on casino operations.

Proprietary Booking Engine: An Internet reservation system that is owned and operated by an individual hotel (or group of hotels) to enable them to take reservation on their own website without paying a fee to a franchise reservation systems, third party booking engines or Global Distribution System (GDS).

Public Bar: A bar where bartenders prepare soft drinks and alcoholic beverages, either for waiter-service or service by the bartenders themselves.

Puzzle: In menu management, an unpopular menu item that gives a high contribution margin.

Q

Quad Room: A guestroom assigned to four people; this will have two or more beds.

Quality Group: A group of travellers for whom the quality of their holiday is of principal importance. They want and are willing to pay for first-class service and accommodations.

Queen Bed: In the US, a bed that measures 152 × 203 cm (60 × 80 in), this is approximately equivalent to a King Size bed in the UK. (Although it is actually a little longer).

The term 'Queen Size' is not used in the UK or continental Europe.

R

Radio Frequency Identification (RFID): A system used as an alternative to bar coding, in which specialized equipment is used to transmit data to an RFID receiver.

Reception: Also known as Front Desk.

A designated area in the hotel lobby with a counter where guests are received. This is the first point of call for any visitor or guest. Here, guests are registered, assigned rooms, given keys (entry cards) and checked out.

The receptionists are responsible for dealing with customer queries, requests and complaints.

Regional Getaway Guests: Guests who check into a hotel close to home in order to enjoy a night or a few days away.

Registration Card: A form on which guests record their names, addresses, and other details (such as length of stay, method of payment, nationality, purpose of visit and car registration number) when they check-in. A space is also provided for signature, room number and room rate. Additional questions may be included as a part of the hotel's market research platform.

Relocation Guests: Those families or individuals relocating to an area who require lodging until permanent housing can be found.

Reservation: A guestroom that is being held under an individual or business' name for a specific date or range of dates at a particular hotel.

Reservations Agent: An employee, either in the front office or in a separate department, who is responsible for all aspects of reservations processing.

Reservations Department: A department within a hotel's rooms division staffed by skilled telemarketing personnel, who quote prices and available dates, answer questions about facilities, take reservations over the phone, and sell to callers who are shopping around.

Resident Manager: The manager in charge of the rooms division in a mid-size to large hotel. In some cases, the resident manager may also be in charge of security.

Resort Hotel: A hotel, usually located in a desirable holiday spot, which offers exceptional service, fine dining, recreational activities unavailable at most other properties, in a more aesthetically pleasing setting, than other hotels.

These hotels are located in natural and attractive tourism destinations and their attractions vary depending on the region; some might offer tennis, golf, scuba diving and, depending on the natural surroundings, may also arrange other recreational activities.

Retail Travel Agent: An individual qualified to arrange and sell transportation and other travel products and services directly to the public.

Revenue per Available Guest (revpag): The revenue per available guest. Hotels should consider not only the revenue generated by each room (revpar), but also the revenue generated by each guest, from booking to check out. This may include additional revenue generated by dining, recreation (golf, spa services, excursions and so on) and meeting facilities.

A hotel when conducting their revenue management often considers Revpag.

Revenue per Available Room (revpar): A statistic used in the hotel industry used to measure revenue per available room. Revpar is the key indicator of performance for hotels and can be broken down into two parts reflecting occupancy and rates:

Revpar = occupancy (percentage of available rooms occupied) × average room rate per night.

The figure can be used to compare companies but only if they have broadly similar hotels - i.e. similarly priced in similar locations.

Room Attendant's Cart: A lightweight, wheeled vehicle used by room attendants for transporting linen, cleaning supplies, and equipment needed to fulfill a block of cleaning assignments.

Room Block: A predetermined number of rooms reserved in advance for members of a group (for example, tour or conference).

Room Data Card: A card used to record information concerning the major elements and basic characteristics of an individual guestroom.

Room Inspection: A detailed process in which guestrooms are systematically checked for maintenance needs and cleanliness.

Room Night: One guestroom occupied for one night.

Room Occupancy Sensor: A device that uses ultrasonic sound waves or infrared light to sense the physical occupancy of a room. Sensors have the ability to turn on appliances and devices such as air conditioning, heating and lights whenever a guest enters a room, and to turn these appliances and devices off when the guest leaves.

Room Rack: A card index system that is continually updated to reflect vacant and occupied rooms. In the evening, the room rack will only contain forms for registered guests remaining for the night who are to be charged for rooms. A daily room report can be prepared from the room rack.

Room Rate: The price a hotel charges for overnight accommodation.

Room Revenue: Total room revenue generated from the rental of rooms.

Room Service: The department within a food and beverage (F&B) division that is responsible for delivering food or drinks to guests in their rooms. The department may also be responsible for preparing the food and drinks.

Room Service Menu: A menu offered by hotels and other lodging properties that serve food to guests in the room. As it is difficult to maintain food quality while transporting the food to the guest, room service menus usually offer a limited number of items.

Room Status: Information about current and future availability of rooms in a hotel. Information about availability data, which extends several days into the future, is important because it may affect the length of stay of in-house guests.

Current availability is determined through housekeeping data, whilst future availability is determined through reservations data.

Room Status Discrepancy: A situation in which the room status information that guides the front desk employee in assigning rooms to guests differs from the housekeeping department's description of a room's status. Discrepancies can seriously affect a property's ability to satisfy guests and maximize room revenue.

Rooming List: A list of the guests who will occupy reserved accommodations.

Rooms Activity Forecast: Information on anticipated arrivals, stay-overs, departures and vacancies. Managers use this forecast to determine staffing needs in housekeeping areas and at the front desk.

Rooms Allotment Report: A report that summarizes rooms committed (blocked or booked), by future date.

Rooms Availability Report: A report that lists, by room type. the number of available rooms each day (net remaining rooms in each category).

Rooms Checklist: A list of all the items in the guestroom with a brief notation opposite each item of the type of inspection, repair, adjustments, lubrication, or cleaning activity to be performed.

Rooms Discrepancy Report: A report that notes any variances between housekeeping and front desk room status updates. It often alerts management to investigate the possibility of sleepers.

Rooms Division: The largest, and usually most profitable, division in a hotel. The rooms division typically consists of four departments:

- ❖ Reservations
- ❖ Front office
- ❖ Housekeeping
- ❖ Uniformed service

Rooms History Report: A computer-based report that depicts the use and revenue history of each room-by-room type. This report is particularly useful to those properties that use an automatic room assignment function.

Rooms Management Module: A front office application of a computer-based property management system. The module:

- ❖ Assists in the assignment of rooms during registration
- ❖ Maintains up-to-date information on the status of rooms
- ❖ Helps coordinate various guest services

Rooms Productivity Report: A report that ranks room types by percentage of occupancy and/or by percentage of total rooms revenue.

Rooms Sold: The number of rooms sold (excludes complimentary rooms).

Rooms Status Report: A report that indicates the current status of rooms according to housekeeping designations, such as:

- ❖ Out-of-order
- ❖ On-change
- ❖ On-makeup
- ❖ Clean and ready for inspection

Russian Service: An elaborate silver service where the food is portioned and carved by the waiter in full view of the guests. The principle involved is to have whole joints, poultry, game and fish elaborately dressed and garnished, presented to guests and carved and portioned by the waiter. Display and presentation are a major part of this service.

Ryokan: Traditional Japanese lodging facilities (similar to a bed and breakfast) featuring landscaped gardens, communal baths, and tatami mat floors.

S

Safety Deposit Boxes: Individual boxes located either in a central, secure, and supervised location or in individual guest rooms, provided for the safekeeping of guest valuables.

Service Bar: A relatively small bar where bartenders prepare beverages for servers to present to guests. Guests typically do not order or pick up their own beverages.

Service Charge: A percentage of the bill (usually 10–20%) added to the guest charge for distribution to service employees in lieu of direct tipping.

Service Station: A small work island located in a hotel's dining room.

Serving: The control point in which finished menu items are transferred from the production department to guests.

Shift Manager: The manager in charge of a hotel during a period of time, usually a 6-8-hour shift.

Shoulder Season: The period between high (peak) and low (off-peak) season.

Side-By-Side Suite: A suite that consists of two small bays, each with windows to the outside.

Side stand: A service stand that holds supplies of condiments, tableware, ice, dairy products, and some beverages for easy access.

Sidework: Setup and cleanup work that must be done before and after dining rooms are opened. Examples include filling salt and pepper shakers, and restocking server supply stations.

Silence Cloth: Oilcloth or other padded material placed under a tablecloth in a restaurant to absorb noise.

Single Bed: Also known as King Single in the US.

A bed approximately 91 × 191 cm (36 × 75 in).

Skipper: A hotel guest who leaves without paying.

Sleeper: A vacant room that is believed to be occupied because the registration card or room rack slip was not removed from the rack when the previous guest departed.

Solid Mattress: A mattress stuffed with cotton, hair, or some other material.

Sommelier: A trained and knowledgeable wine professional who specializes in all facets of wine service. Their principal work is in the area of wine procurement, storage, and wine cellar rotation. They are also responsible for the development of wine lists and the training for the other restaurant staff.

Working along with the culinary team, sommeliers will often suggest wines that will best complement each particular food menu item. A professional sommelier also works on the floor of the restaurant, with a responsibility to work within the taste preference and budget parameters of the patron.

Sous Chef: The direct assistant of the executive chef and second in command in the kitchen. They may be responsible for scheduling, and filling in for the executive chef when they are off-duty, and will also normally fill in for or assist the chef de partie (line cooks) when needed.

Larger operations may have multiple sous chefs, whilst smaller operations may not have any.

Spa Hotel: A hotel that provides professionally administered spa services, fitness and wellness components and spa cuisine menu choices.

Specialty Menu: A menu that differs from the typical breakfast, lunch, or dinner menu. Specialty menus are usually designed for specific guest groups or for special events. Examples include banquet menus, children's menus and dessert menus.

Specialty Restaurant: A theme restaurant that features certain types of food.

Split Service: A food service method in which servers deliver courses separately. This form of service helps to maintain food safety and quality as each course can be portioned and served when it is ready, eliminating short-term holding in the kitchen.

St Julian the Hospitaller: The patron saint of innkeepers, travellers, and pilgrims.

Star Ratings: The star classification system is a common one for rating hotels. Higher star ratings indicate more luxury.

❖ No Category Hotels

These hotels include motels, cottages, bungalows and others with limited services.

- One Star Hotel

  Low budget hotels; inexpensive; may not have maid service or room service.

- Two Star Hotel

  Budget hotels; slightly more expensive, usually has daily maid service.

- Three Star Hotel

  Middle class hotels; moderately priced; has daily maid service, room service, and may have dry-cleaning, Internet access, and a swimming pool.

- Four Star Hotel

  First class hotels; expensive (by middle-class standards); has all of the previously mentioned services; has many 'luxury' services (for example: massages or a health spa).

- Five Star Hotel

  Luxury hotels; most expensive hotels/resorts; numerous extras to enhance the quality of the client's stay (for example: private golf courses and even a small private airport).

Stayover: A room status term indicating that the guest is not checking out and will remain at least another night.

Steam Tunnel: Laundry equipment that moves clothes on hangers through a tunnel where they are steamed and de-wrinkled as they are moved through.

Studio: A guestroom having one or two sofas that converts into beds.

Suburban Hotel: A hotel that is somewhat smaller than a city centre hotel (typically 250-500 rooms), is usually part of a chain, and has bars, restaurants, and other amenities found at city centre hotels.

Suite: A guestroom with a parlour area in addition to a sleeping room, and perhaps a small kitchen.

Suite Hotel: A hotel whose rooms have separate bedroom and living room or parlour areas, and perhaps a small kitchen.

T

Table d'Hote Menu: French: 'host's table'.

A menu that offers a full-course meal at a fixed price. The menu planner sets meals on table d'hôte menus and guests are given few, if any, choices. In some cases, two or more complete meals are offered on the menu, each with its own price.

Table Service: A type of restaurant service in which guests are seated at a table and waited on by food servers. Four basic styles of table service are:

- American
- English
- French
- Russian

Table Skirt: A piece of linen that covers the sides of the table.

Table Top Display: A portable display that can be placed on top of a table.

Tableware: Eating, drinking and serving utensils used when setting a table for dining. These can include:

- ❖ Cutlery, such as knives, forks, and spoons
- ❖ Glassware
- ❖ Hollowware such as cups, bowls and serving dishes
- ❖ Plates

Theme Restaurant: A restaurant distinguished by its combination of atmosphere, decor, and menu, all of which relate to a particular theme.

Third Party Booking Engine: An Internet site that provides a booking engine where a traveller can search a large number of hotels for availability and reserve a room. The hotels are not affiliated with the site and typically pay a fee for the business that the site generates.

Tour: Any pre-arranged (but not necessarily prepaid) journey to one or more places and back to the point of origin.

Tour Operator: An organization or individual that puts together travel tours and sells them directly to independent travellers or groups, or through travel agencies.

Tourism Development: The long-term process of preparing for the arrival of tourists. This includes all the services and facilities that serve the tourist, such as planning, building, and managing attractions, accommodation and transportation.

Tourism Enclave: A self-contained resort complex that caters to all the needs of tourists who arrive as part of a tour or other type of package.

Tower: A guestroom floor configuration in which rooms are grouped around a central vertical core.

Traditional Lodging: A type of accommodation where guests pay nightly rates for suites single or rooms and have full access to the hotels' range of services and amenities. Rates begin at 'rack,' but vary widely, based on time of season and week and nearby attractions and events.

Transfer: The transportation of visitors between their point of arrival and selected hotel, and back again on departure.

Travel Club : A type of travel agency that charges an annual fee to its members in return for providing packaged holidays at reduced prices.

Turkish Bath: Consists of one or a series of hot, dry rooms, where hotel guests can bathe and perspire freely. The rooms are controlled at different temperatures allowing the guests to move through increasing in temperature possibly followed by a plunge pool, wash and massage and in some cases, a cooling and relaxation room.

Twin: Twin Room - a guestroom with two single beds.

Twin Bed: A bed size used in the US, approximately 75 × 190 cm (30 × 75 in).

U

Underbars: The primary working space for the bartender. The underbar is the area of the bar that is in front of the bartender as they face the guests and mostly (but not entirely) below the level of the bar itself.

Under stay: A guest who checks out before their stated departure date.

Upgrade: To move to a better class of service or accommodation.

V

Vacant: A room status term that indicates that the room has been cleaned and inspected, and is ready for the arriving guest.

Ventilation: The process of removing air from or supplying air to an interior space.

Virtual Private Network (VPN): A system used in the hospitality industry to allow users to send, receive and share private information or encrypted data over a public infrastructure.

Voice Mail: A system that is part of the telephone equipment, which provides for hotel guests to retrieve a messages left by a caller.

Voice over Internet Protocol (voip): The technology used to transmit voice conversations over a data network using the Internet Protocol. Voip is also known as Internet telephony, Broadband Phone and Voice over Broadband.

W

Wake Up Call: A telephone call made by front office to a guest room to waken the guest at a time requested by them.

Walk-In Refrigerator/Freezer: A large fridge or freezer used in high-volume kitchens for storage of perishable items.

Walked Guest: When a guest room is not available for a confirmed guest (i.e. The hotel is overbooked), then the hotel helps the guest find alternative accommodation elsewhere. This is known as 'walking the guest' to another hotel.

Each hotel has its own walk compensation policy that the manager will follow during this process. This usually includes paying for transportation to the hotel and covering any difference in the room rate at the hotel the guest was 'walked in '.

Watermark Hotel: A hotel that offers large recreational water elements such large pools, slides, multiple pools, or other water related amenities.

Y

Yield Management: A strategy or process that hotel operators use to maximize their hotel room revenue by achieving the right balance between occupancy and room rates that generates the most revenue.

Z

Zero Call: A telephone call placed with an operator's assistance. Examples may include credit card and calling card; collect calls, and third-party calls.

Zone Lighting: Lighting designed to facilitate traffic from one space to another.

INDEX

A

D

E

F

N

O

P

Q

R

V

W

Y